Hollywood Character Actors

Books by James Robert Parish

As Author:
The Fox Girls*
The Paramount Pretties*
The Slapstick Queens
The RKO Gals*
Good Dames
Hollywood's Great Love Teams*
The Elvis Presley Scrapbook
The Great Movie Heroes
Great Child Stars
Film Directors Guide: Western Europe
Great Western Stars
The Jeanette MacDonald Story
The Tough Guys*
Film Actors Guide: Western Europe

As Co-Author:
The Emmy Awards: A Pictorial History
The Cinema of Edward G. Robinson
The MGM Stock Company: The Golden Era*
The Great Spy Pictures
The George Raft File
The Glamour Girls*
Vincent Price Unmasked
Liza!
The Debonairs*
The Swashbucklers*
The Great Western Pictures
The Great Gangster Pictures
Film Directors Guide: The U.S.
Hollywood Players: The Forties*
Hollywood Players: The Thirties*
The Great Science Fiction Pictures
The All-Americans*
The Leading Ladies*

As Editor:
The Great Movie Series
Actors Television Credits: 1950-72 & Supplement

As Associate Editor:
The American Movies Reference Book: The Sound Era
TV Movies

*Published by Arlington House

Hollywood Character Actors

JAMES ROBERT PARISH

**with Earl Anderson, Richard E. Braff,
John Robert Cocchi, and Harry Purvis**

Research Associates

ROBERT A. EVANS ☐ WILLIAM T. LEONARD ☐ FLORENCE SOLOMON

ARLINGTON HOUSE·PUBLISHERS
NEW ROCHELLE, NEW YORK

Parish, James Robert.
  Hollywood character actors.

  1. Moving-picture actors and actresses—United States—
Biography.   I.   Title.
PN1998.A2P32177   791.43′028′0922 [B]   78-17553
ISBN O-87000-384-4

Key to Abbreviations

AA	Allied Artists Picture Corporation
AIP	American International Pictures
Associated FN	Associated First National Pictures, Inc. (became part of First National Pictures, Inc.)
Avco Emb	Avco Embassy Pictures Corporation
Br	British
BSAAA	Best Supporting Actor/Actress Academy Award
BV	Buena Vista Distribution Co., Inc.
Cin	Cinerama, Inc.
Col	Columbia Pictures Industries, Inc.
CUE	Commonwealth United Entertainment
DCA	Distributor Corporation of America
EL	Eagle Lion Films, Inc.
Emb	Embassy Pictures Corporation (became part of Avco Embassy Pictures Corporation)
FBO	Film Booking Offices of America
FD	First Division Pictures, Inc.
FN	First National Pictures, Inc. (became part of Warner Bros.)
Fox	Fox Film Corporation (became part of Twentieth Century-Fox Corporation)
Fr	French
G	Goldwyn Pictures Corporation
Ger	German
GN	Grand National Films, Inc.
It	Italian
Lip	Lippert Pictures, Inc.
M	Metro Pictures (became part of Metro-Goldwyn-Mayer, Inc.)
Mex	Mexican
MG	Metro-Goldwyn Corporation (became part of Metro-Goldwyn-Mayer, Inc.)
MGM	Metro-Goldwyn-Mayer, Inc.
Mon	Monogram Pictures Corporation

Par	Paramount Pictures Corporation
Pathé	Pathé Exchange, Inc.
	(became part of RKO Radio Pictures Corporation)
PDC	Producers Distributing Corporation
PRC	Producers Releasing Corporation
Rep	Republic Pictures Corporation
Rus	Russian
Sp	Spanish
Tif	Tiffany Productions, Inc.
Tri	Triangle Film Corporation
20th	Twentieth Century-Fox Corporation
UA	United Artists Corporation
Univ	Universal (-International) Pictures, Inc.
US	United States
Vit	Vitagraph Company of America
WB	Warner Bros., Inc.
WB-7 Arts	Warner Bros.-Seven Arts, Inc.
WW	World Wide Pictures, Inc.

Acknowledgments

Academy of Motion Picture Arts and Sciences Library
Kingsley Canham
Edward Connor
Morris Everett, Jr.
Pierre Guinle
Hollywood Revue of Movie Memorabilia
Charles Hoyt
Ken D. Jones
Lois Kibbee
Doug McClelland
Peter Miglierini
Norman Miller
Michael R. Pitts
Tony Scaramozi
Lucy Smith
Charles K. Stumpf
T. Allan Taylor
Jack Tillmany

Special thanks to Paul Myers, curator of the Theatre Collection at the Lincoln Center Library
for the Performing Arts (New York City), and his staff: Monty Arnold, David Bartholomew,
Rod Bladel, Donald Fowle, Maxwell Silverman, Dorothy Swerdlove, and Betty Wharton, and to
Don Madison of Photo Services.

PUBLISHER'S NOTE: Despite the extensive and thorough research that went into this book, some of the biographical facts regarding the players herein could not be found. We have left a line where the data would have gone, for example: Married Jean _____ . The author would appreciate hearing from readers who are able to supply any of these missing facts. Letters should be addressed to James Robert Parish, c/o Arlington House Publishers, New Rochelle, New York 10801.

AUTHOR'S NOTE: The film listing for each character actor includes all known feature films over 4 reels in length and serials. Short subjects and TV movies are not included.

Hollywood Character Actors

WALTER ABEL
(Walter Charles Abel)

Walter Abel, Donald MacBride, and Lloyd Nolan in Michael Shayne, Private Detective *(1940).*

Born June 6, 1898, St. Paul, Minnesota. Married Marietta Bitters (1926), children: Michael, Jonathan. A well-groomed top farceur, usually portraying the well-bred, but harassed, family friend, executive, or father. Occasionally broke out of the mold as in his D'Artagnan in 1935's *The Three Musketeers*. A frequent stage/radio/TV performer, where his well-modulated voice and capacity for genteel exasperation is ably served.

Walter Abel to Fred Astaire in *Holiday Inn:* "Ted, if I'm not the best manager in the business, I'll eat a garage mechanic's shirt."

Films

Out of a Clear Sky (Par, 1918)
The North Wind's Malice (G, 1920)
Liliom (Fox, 1930)
The Three Musketeers (RKO, 1935)
Two in the Dark (RKO, 1936)
The Lady Consents (RKO, 1936)
The Witness Chair (RKO, 1936)
Second Wife (RKO, 1936)
Fury (MGM, 1936)
We Went to College (MGM, 1936)
Green Light (WB, 1937)
Portia on Trial (Rep, 1937)
Wise Girl (RKO, 1937)
Law of the Underworld (RKO, 1938)

Racket Busters (WB, 1938)
Men with Wings (Par, 1938)
King of the Turf (UA, 1939)
Dance, Girl, Dance (RKO, 1940)
Arise, My Love (Par, 1940)
Who Killed Aunt Maggie? (Rep, 1940)
Michael Shayne, Private Detective (20th, 1940)
Miracle on Main Street (Col, 1940)
Hold Back the Dawn (Par, 1941)
Skylark (Par, 1941)
Glamour Boy (Par, 1941)
Holiday Inn (Par, 1942)
Star Spangled Rhythm (Par, 1942)

Beyond the Blue Horizon (Par, 1942)
Wake Island (Par, 1942)
Fired Wife (Univ, 1943)
So Proudly We Hail (Par, 1943)
An American Romance (MGM, 1944)
Follow the Boys (Univ, 1944)
The Hitler Gang (Par, 1944) [narrator]
Mr. Skeffington (WB, 1944)
The Affairs of Susan (Par, 1945)
Kiss and Tell (Col, 1945)
Duffy's Tavern (Par, 1945)
13 Rue Madeleine (20th, 1946)
The Kid from Brooklyn (RKO, 1946)
Dream Girl (Par, 1948)

That Lady in Ermine (20th, 1948)
So This Is Love (WB, 1953)
Island in the Sky (WB, 1953)
Night People (20th, 1954)
The Indian Fighter (UA, 1955)

The Steel Jungle (WB, 1956)
Raintree County (MGM, 1957)
Bernardine (20th, 1957)
Handle with Care (MGM, 1958)
Mirage (Univ, 1965)

7 Different Ways [a.k.a. *The Confession/ Quick, Let's Get Married!*] (Adrian Weiss, 1971)
Silent Night, Bloody Night (Cannon, 1973)

LUTHER ADLER

Louis Guss and Luther Adler in Crazy Joe *(1974).*

Born May 4, 1903, New York City, New York. Married Sylvia Sidney (1938), child: Jody; divorced (1946). Member of distinguished acting family who gained fame as part of the Group Theatre. Characterized by his stocky build, swarthy looks, and intense acting style. Often seen as an ethnic gangland figure: *Hoodlum Empire* (Nicky Mancani), *The Miami Story* (Tony Brill), *The Brotherhood* (Dominick Bertolo), etc.

Luther Adler to John Wayne in *Wake of the Red Witch:* "I'm not one of those 'eye for an eye' men. No, I always take two eyes."

Films

Lancer Spy (20th, 1937)
Cornered (RKO, 1945)
Saigon (Par, 1948)
The Loves of Carmen (Col, 1948)
Wake of the Red Witch (Rep, 1948)
House of Strangers (20th, 1949)
D.O.A. (UA, 1949)
South Sea Sinner (Univ, 1950)

Under My Skin (20th, 1950)
Kiss Tomorrow Goodbye (WB, 1950)
M (Col, 1951)
The Magic Face (Col, 1951)
The Desert Fox (20th, 1951)
Hoodlum Empire (Rep, 1952)
The Tall Texan (Lip, 1953)
The Miami Story (Col, 1954)

Crashout (Filmakers, 1955)
The Girl in the Red Velvet Swing (20th, 1955)
Hot Blood (Col, 1956)
The Last Angry Man (Col, 1959)
Cast a Giant Shadow (UA, 1966)
The Brotherhood (Par, 1968)
Crazy Joe (Col, 1974)

14

Murph the Surf [a.k.a. *Live a Little, Steal a Lot*] (AIP, 1974) *The Man in the Glass Booth* (American Film Theatre, 1975) *Mean Johnny Barrows* (Atlas Films, 1975) *Voyage of the Damned* (Avco Emb, 1976)

IRIS ADRIAN
(Iris Adrian Hostetter)

In *The Love Bug* *(1968).*

Born May 29, 1913, Los Angeles, California. Married 1) Charles Over (1935); divorced (1936); 2) George Jay; 3) "Fido" Murphy. Along with Veda Ann Borg and Barbara Pepper, perhaps the most famous of the gum-chewing, smart-mouthed cinema blondes. Whether as waitress, B-girl, streetwalker, or noisy neighbor, her character was never at a loss for a sharp retort. Recently cameoed in several Walt Disney movies. TV series: "The Ted Knight Show."

Iris Adrian to George Raft in *Broadway:* "You've got to get a classy name. That 'George Raft' is too ordinary."

Films

Paramount on Parade (Par, 1930)
Rumba (Par, 1935)
The Gay Deception (Fox, 1935)
Stolen Harmony (Par, 1935)
Murder at Glen Athol [a.k.a. The Criminal

Within] (Invincible, 1935)
A Message to Garcia (20th, 1936)
One Rainy Afternoon (UA, 1936)
Stage Struck (WB, 1936)
Our Relations (MGM, 1936)

Mr. Cinderella (MGM, 1936)
Lady Luck (Chesterfield, 1936)
Gold Diggers of 1937 (WB, 1936)
Back Door to Heaven (Par, 1939)
One Third of a Nation (Par, 1939)

Meet the Wildcat (Univ, 1940)
Go West (MGM, 1940)
Road to Zanzibar (Par, 1941)
Horror Island (Univ, 1941)
Meet the Chump (Univ, 1941)
Lady from Cheyenne (Univ, 1941)
Wild Geese Calling (20th, 1941)
Sing Another Chorus (Univ, 1941)
Too Many Blondes (Univ, 1941)
Hard Guy (PRC, 1941)
Swing It Soldier (Univ, 1941)
I Killed That Man (Mon, 1941)
Roxie Hart (20th, 1942)
To the Shores of Tripoli (20th, 1942)
Rings on Her Fingers (20th, 1942)
Juke Box Jenny (Univ, 1942)
Broadway (Univ, 1942)
Highways by Night (RKO, 1942)
Fingers at the Window (MGM, 1942)
Moonlight Masquerade (Rep, 1942)
Orchestra Wives (20th, 1942)
The McGuerins from Brooklyn (UA, 1942)
Thunder Birds (20th, 1942)
The Crystal Ball (UA, 1943)
Taxi, Mister (UA, 1943)
Lady of Burlesque (UA, 1943)
He's My Guy (Univ, 1943)
Spotlight Scandals (Mon, 1943)
Submarine Base (PRC, 1943)
Hers to Hold (Univ, 1943)
Ladies' Day (RKO, 1943)
Action in the North Atlantic (WB, 1943)
Calaboose (UA, 1943)
Shake Hands with Murder (PRC, 1944)
The Million Dollar Kid (Mon, 1944)

Career Girl (PRC, 1944)
Alaska (Mon, 1944)
Bluebeard (PRC, 1944)
Once upon a Time (Col, 1944)
The Singing Sheriff (Univ, 1944)
I'm from Arkansas (PRC, 1944)
Swing Hostess (PRC, 1944)
Woman in the Window (RKO, 1944)
Road to Alcatraz (Rep, 1945)
It's a Pleasure (RKO, 1945)
Steppin' in Society (Rep, 1945)
The Stork Club (Par, 1945)
Boston Blackie's Rendezvous (Col, 1945)
The Bamboo Blonde (RKO, 1946)
Vacation in Reno (RKO, 1946)
Cross My Heart (Par, 1946)
The Fall Guy (Mon, 1947)
Love and Learn (WB, 1947)
Philo Vance Returns (PRC, 1947)
The Trouble with Women (Par, 1947)
The Wistful Widow of Wagon Gap (Univ, 1947)
Smart Woman (AA, 1948)
The Paleface (Par, 1948)
Out of the Storm (Rep, 1948)
The Lovable Cheat (Film Classics, 1949)
Sky Dragon (Mon, 1949)
Miss Mink of 1949 (20th, 1949)
Trail of the Yukon (Mon, 1949)
Always Leave Them Laughing (WB, 1949)
Flamingo Road (WB, 1949)
My Dream Is Yours (WB, 1949)
Mighty Joe Young (RKO, 1949)
There's a Girl in My Heart (AA, 1949)
The Woman on Pier 13 [a.k.a. I Married a Communist] (RKO, 1949)

Tough Assignment (Lip, 1949)
Once a Thief (UA, 1950)
Blondie's Hero (Col, 1950)
Sideshow (Mon, 1950)
Hi-Jacked (Lip, 1950)
Stop That Cab (Lip, 1951)
My Favorite Spy (Par, 1951)
Varieties on Parade (Lip, 1951)
G.I. Jane (Lip, 1951)
The Racket (RKO, 1951)
Joe Palooka in Humphrey Takes a Chance (Mon, 1951)
Carson City (WB, 1952)
Take the High Ground (MGM, 1953)
Crime Wave (WB, 1953)
The Helen Morgan Story (WB, 1953)
Highway Dragnet (AA, 1954)
The Fast and Furious (American Releasing, 1954)
Carnival Rock (Howco International, 1957)
The Buccaneer (Par, 1958)
Blue Hawaii (Par, 1961)
The Errand Boy (Par, 1962)
Fate Is the Hunter (20th, 1964)
That Darn Cat! (BV, 1965)
The Odd Couple (Par, 1968)
The Love Bug (BV, 1968)
The Barefoot Executive (BV, 1971)
Scandalous John (BV, 1971)
The Apple Dumpling Gang (BV, 1975)
No Deposit, No Return (BV, 1976)
Gus (BV, 1976)
The Shaggy D.A. (BV, 1976)
Freaky Friday (BV, 1976)

PHILIP AHN

Humphrey Bogart, Richard Cutting, and Philip Ahn in The Left Hand of God *(1955).*

Born March 29, 1911, Los Angeles, California. Died February 28, 1978, Los Angeles, California. One of the leading exponents of the villainous Japanese types on screen (although of Korean heritage). Became a Hollywood staple as the cunning, cold Oriental. TV series: "Kung Fu."

Philip Ahn to Shirley Temple in *Stowaway:* "May your shadow lengthen always in the sun of happiness."

Films

The General Died at Dawn (Par, 1936)
Stowaway (20th, 1936)
Something to Sing About (GN, 1937)
China Passage (RKO, 1937)
Roaring Timber (Col, 1937)
Thank You, Mr. Moto (20th, 1937)
Daughter of Shanghai (Par, 1937)
Hawaii Calls (RKO, 1938)
Red Barry (Univ serial, 1938)
Charlie Chan in Honolulu (20th, 1938)
Disputed Passage (Par, 1939)
Barricade (20th, 1939)
King of Chinatown (Par, 1939)
Passage from Hong Kong (WB, 1941)
They Met in Bombay (MGM, 1941)
We Were Dancing (MGM, 1942)
China Girl (20th, 1942)
A Yank on the Burma Road (MGM, 1942)
Across the Pacific (WB, 1942)
Let's Get Tough (Mon, 1942)
They Got Me Covered (RKO, 1943)
The Amazing Mrs. Holliday (Univ, 1943)
Adventures of Smilin' Jack (Univ serial, 1943)
Dragon Seed (MGM, 1944)
The Story of Dr. Wassell (Par, 1944)
The Purple Heart (20th, 1944)
Forever Yours [a.k.a. *They Shall Have Faith*] (Mon, 1944)

The Keys of the Kingdom (20th, 1944)
Back to Bataan (RKO, 1945)
God Is My Co-Pilot (WB, 1945)
Blood on the Sun (UA, 1945)
China's Little Devils (Mon, 1945)
Betrayal from the East (RKO, 1945)
China Sky (RKO, 1945)
Intrigue (UA, 1947)
The Chinese Ring (Mon, 1947)
Singapore (Univ, 1947)
Women in the Night (Film Classics, 1948)
The Miracle of the Bells (RKO, 1948)
The Cobra Strikes (EL, 1948)
Rogues' Regiment (Univ, 1948)
The Creeper (20th, 1948)
Impact (UA, 1949)
Boston Blackie's Chinese Venture (Col, 1949)
State Department—File 649 (Film Classics, 1949)
The Big Hangover (MGM, 1950)
Halls of Montezuma (20th, 1951)
China Corsair (Col, 1951)
The Sickle or the Cross (Astor, 1951)
I Was an American Spy (AA, 1951)
Japanese War Bride (20th, 1952)
Red Snow (Col, 1952)
Macao (RKO, 1952)

Target: Hong Kong (Col, 1952)
Battle Zone (AA, 1952)
Battle Circus (MGM, 1953)
Fair Wind to Java (Rep, 1953)
China Venture (Col, 1953)
His Majesty O'Keefe (WB, 1953)
Hell's Half Acre (Rep, 1954)
The Shanghai Story (Rep, 1954)
The Left Hand of God (20th, 1955)
Love Is a Many-Splendored Thing (20th, 1955)
Around the World in 80 Days (UA, 1956)
Battle Hymn (Univ, 1957)
The Way to the Gold (20th, 1957)
Hong Kong Confidential (UA, 1958)
Never So Few (MGM, 1959)
The Great Impostor (Univ, 1960)
Yesterday's Enemy (Col, 1960)
Confessions of an Opium Eater (AA, 1962)
A Girl Named Tamiko (Par, 1962)
Diamond Head (Col, 1962)
Shock Corridor (AA, 1963)
Paradise—Hawaiian Style (Par, 1966)
Thoroughly Modern Millie (Univ, 1967)
Voodoo Heartbeat (Two National, 1972)
The World's Greatest Athlete (BV, 1973)
Jonathan Livingston Seagull (Par, 1973) [voice only]

CLAUDE AKINS

With Joan Blondell in Waterhole No. 3 *(1967).*

Born May 25, 1936, Nelson, Georgia. Married Theresa Fairchild, children: Claude, Wendy, Michelle. Stocky, surly, self-sufficient. Frequently cast as a Western bad guy; was the detective (*Porgy and Bess*), Sergeant Ben Puzo (*Skyjacked*), Aldo (*Battle for the Planet of the Apes*). TV series: "Movin' On."

Claude Akins to Colleen Miller in *Hot Summer Night:*
"Nobody gets tricky with me. You understand that, lady?
Nobody ever gets tricky with me."

Films

From Here to Eternity (Col, 1953)
Bitter Creek (AA, 1954)
The Caine Mutiny (Col, 1954)
The Raid (20th, 1954)
The Human Jungle (AA, 1954)
Down Three Dark Streets (UA, 1954)
Shield for Murder (UA, 1954)
The Sea Chase (WB, 1955)
Battle Stations (Col, 1956)
The Proud and Profane (Par, 1956)
Johnny Concho (UA, 1956)
The Burning Hills (WB, 1956)
The Sharkfighters (UA, 1956)
Hot Summer Night (MGM, 1957)
The Kettles on Old MacDonald's Farm (Univ, 1957)

The Lonely Man (Par, 1957)
Joe Dakota (Univ, 1957)
The Defiant Ones (UA, 1958)
Onionhead (WB, 1958)
Rio Bravo (WB, 1959)
Don't Give Up the Ship (Par, 1959)
Porgy and Bess (Col, 1959)
Yellowstone Kelly (WB, 1959)
Hound Dog Man (20th, 1959)
Comanche Station (Col, 1960)
Inherit the Wind (UA, 1960)
Claudelle Inglish (WB, 1961)
Merrill's Marauders (WB, 1962)
How the West Was Won (MGM, 1962)
Black Gold (WB, 1963)
A Distant Trumpet (WB, 1964)

The Killers (Univ, 1964)
Ride Beyond Vengeance (Col, 1966)
Return of the Seven (UA, 1966)
Incident at Phantom Hill (Univ, 1966)
First to Fight (WB, 1967)
Waterhole No. 3 (Par, 1967)
The Devil's Brigade (UA, 1968)
The Great Bank Robbery (WB, 1969)
Flap (WB, 1970)
A Man Called Sledge (Col, 1971)
Skyjacked (MGM, 1972)
Battle for the Planet of the Apes (20th, 1973)
Tentacles (It, 1977)

FRANK ALBERTSON

Charles Williams, Frank Albertson (with application), and Frankie Thomas (leaning on desk) in Flying Cadets *(1941).*

Born February 2, 1909, Fergus Falls, Minnesota. Married (1) Virginia Shelley, child: one; divorced; (2) Grace _____ , child: daughter. Died February 29, 1964, Santa Monica, California. Soft-acting leading man who turned to character roles: Katharine Hepburn's annoyed brother (*Alice Adams*), the confused hayseed playwright (*Room Service*), etc.

Frank Albertson to Joan Crawford in *The Shining Hour:* "If I ever get a decent horn, I'll have a band of my own in a year."

Films

Prep and Pep (Fox, 1928)
The Farmer's Daughter (Fox, 1928)
Salute (Fox, 1929)
Words and Music (Fox, 1929)
Blue Skies (Fox, 1929)
Son of the Gods (FN, 1930)
The Big Party (Fox, 1930)
Happy Days (Fox, 1930)
Born Reckless (Fox, 1930)
Men Without Women (Fox, 1930)
So This Is London (Fox, 1930)
Wild Company (Fox, 1930)
Just Imagine (Fox, 1930)
Spring Is Here (FN, 1930)
A Connecticut Yankee (Fox, 1931)
The Brat (Fox, 1931)
Big Business Girl (FN, 1931)
Traveling Husbands (RKO, 1931)
Way Back Home (RKO, 1931)

The Cohens and Kellys in Hollywood (Univ, 1932)
Huddle (MGM, 1932)
Dangerous Crossroads (Col, 1932)
Air Mail (Univ, 1932)
Racing Youth (Univ, 1932)
Ever in My Heart (WB, 1933)
Ann Carver's Profession (Col, 1933)
Midshipman Jack (RKO, 1933)
Billion Dollar Scandal (Par, 1933)
The Cohens and Kellys in Trouble (Univ, 1933)
Rainbow over Broadway (Chesterfield, 1933)
The Last Gentleman (UA, 1934)
Hollywood Hoodlum (Regal, 1934)
The Life of Vergie Winters (RKO, 1934)
Enter Madame! (Par, 1934)
Bachelor of Arts (Fox, 1934)

Doubting Thomas (Fox, 1935)
Alice Adams (RKO, 1935)
Waterfront Lady (Mascot, 1935)
Ah, Wilderness! (MGM, 1935)
Personal Maid's Secretary (WB, 1935)
Kind Lady (MGM, 1935)
East of Java (Univ, 1935)
The Farmer in the Dell (RKO, 1936)
Fury (MGM, 1936)
The Plainsman (Par, 1936)
Navy Blue and Gold (MGM, 1937)
Hold That Kiss (MGM, 1938)
Spring Madness (MGM, 1938)
The Shining Hour (MGM, 1938)
Mother Carey's Chickens (RKO, 1938)
Fugitives for a Night (RKO, 1938)
Room Service (RKO, 1938)
Bachelor Mother (RKO, 1939)
The Ghost Comes Home (MGM, 1940)

Framed (Univ, 1940)
Dr. Christian Meets the Women (RKO, 1940)
When the Daltons Rode (Univ, 1940)
Behind the News (Rep, 1940)
Ellery Queen's Penthouse Mystery (Col, 1941)
Man-Made Monster (Univ, 1941)
Father Steps Out (Mon, 1941)
Flying Cadets (Univ, 1941)
Citadel of Crime (Rep, 1941)
City Limits (Mon, 1941)
Burma Convoy (Univ, 1941)
Louisiana Purchase (Par, 1941)
Wake Island (Par, 1942)

Underground Agent (Col, 1942)
Junior G-Men of the Air (Univ serial, 1942)
The Man from Headquarters (Mon, 1942)
Shepherd of the Ozarks (Rep, 1942)
City of Silent Men (PRC, 1942)
Keep 'em Slugging (Univ, 1943)
Here Comes Elmer (Rep, 1943)
Mystery Broadcast (Rep, 1943)
O, My Darling Clementine (Rep, 1943)
And the Angels Sing (Par, 1944)
Rosie the Riveter (Rep, 1944)
I Love a Soldier (Par, 1945)
Arson Squad (PRC, 1945)
How Do You Do? (PRC, 1945)

Gay Blades (Rep, 1946)
It's a Wonderful Life (RKO, 1946)
They Made Me a Killer (Par, 1946)
Ginger (Mon, 1946)
The Hucksters (MGM, 1947)
Killer Dill (Screen Guild, 1947)
Shed No Tears (EL, 1948)
Nightfall (Col, 1956)
The Enemy Below (20th, 1957)
The Last Hurrah (Col, 1958)
Psycho (Par, 1960)
Don't Knock the Twist (Col, 1962)
Bye, Bye Birdie (Col, 1963)
Johnny Cool (UA, 1963)

BEN ALEXANDER
(Nicholas Benton Alexander)

Ben Alexander and William Hall in The Spy Ring *(1938).*

Born May 26, 1911, Goldfield, Nevada. Married Lesley Spurgeon (1950), children: daughter, son. Died June 1969, Westchester, California. Sympathetic child actor in silents: Douglas Fairbanks' brother *(Hearts of the World)*, Penrod Schofield *(Penrod and Sam)*, etc. Graduated to supporting leads in talkies: Kemmerich *(All Quiet on the Western Front)*, Captain Don Mayhew *(The Spy Ring)*; some bits: Evans the bandleader *(Shall We Dance?)*. Best remembered as Jack Webb's heavy-set partner (Officer Frank Smith) in the "Dragnet" teleseries (1952–1959) and feature film. Other TV series: "Felony Squad."

Ben Alexander to Russell Gleason in *All Quiet on the Western Front:* "Why, it's an *honor* to have those boots in your face. They're the best pair in the Army."

Films

The Little Americans (Par, 1917)
Each Pearl a Tear (Par, 1918)
The Heart of Rachael (Hodkinson, 1918)
Macbeth (Tri, 1918)
Little Orphan Annie (Pioneer, 1918)

Hearts of the World (World, 1918)
The Turn in the Road (Mutual, 1919)
The White Heather (Par, 1919)
Josselyn's Wife (Exhibitors Mutual, 1919)

Tangled Threads (Robertson-Cole, 1919)
The Better Wife (Select, 1919)
Through the Eyes of Men (Radin–States Rights, 1920)

Family Honor (Associated FN, 1920)
The Hushed Hour (Garson, 1920)
The Heart Line (Pathé, 1921)
In the Name of the Law (FBO, 1922)
Boy of Mine (Associated FN, 1923)
Penrod and Sam (Associated FN, 1923)
Jealous Husbands (Associated FN, 1923)
A Self-Made Failure (Associated FN, 1924)
Frivolous Sal [a.k.a. Flaming Love] (FN, 1925)
Pampered Youth (Vit, 1925)
The Shining Adventure (Astor, 1925)
The Highbinders (Associated Exhibitors, 1926)
Scotty of the Scouts (Rayart serial, 1926)
Fighting for Fame (Rayart serial, 1927)
All Quiet on the Western Front (Univ, 1930)

Suicide Fleet (RKO, 1931)
Many a Slip (Univ, 1931)
It's a Wise Child (MGM, 1931)
Are These Our Children? (RKO, 1931)
The Strange Love of Molly Louvain (FN, 1932)
High Pressure (WB, 1932)
Tom Brown of Culver (Univ, 1932)
The Vanishing Frontier (Par, 1932)
What Price Innocence? (Col, 1933)
Stage Mother (MGM, 1933)
This Day and Age (Par, 1933)
The Life of Vergie Winters (RKO, 1934)
The Most Precious Thing in Life (Col, 1934)
Flirtation (FD, 1934)
Once to Every Woman (Col, 1934)
Annapolis Farewell (Par, 1935)
Grand Old Girl (RKO, 1935)

Reckless Roads (Majestic, 1935)
Born to Gamble (Liberty, 1935)
The Fire Trap (Empire, 1935)
Splendor (UA, 1935)
Hearts in Bondage (Rep, 1936)
Red Lights Ahead (Chesterfield, 1937)
The Life of the Party (RKO, 1937)
The Outer Gate (Mon, 1937)
Shall We Dance? (RKO, 1937)
Behind Prison Bars (Mon, 1937)
Western Gold (20th, 1937)
Mr. Doodle Kicks Off (RKO, 1938)
The Spy Ring (Univ, 1938)
Convicts' Code (Mon, 1939)
Buried Alive (PRC, 1939)
The Leather Pushers (Univ, 1940)
Criminals Within (PRC, 1941)
Dragnet (WB, 1954)
Man in the Shadow (Univ, 1957)

SARA ALLGOOD

With Ginger Rogers in Roxie Hart *(1942).*

Born October 31, 1883, Dublin, Ireland. Married George Hanson (1917); widowed. Died September 13, 1950, Woodland Hills, California. Versatile stage (Dublin's Abbey Players) and cinema player who made an indelible impression in her American film debut: Donald Crisp's wife and Roddy McDowall's mother in *How Green Was My Valley* (Oscar-nominated but lost BSAAA to Mary Astor of *The Great Lie*). At her best as the motherly type, albeit to family, tenants, or employers.

Sara Allgood to Roddy McDowall in *How Green Was My Valley:* "Fight again, and when you come home not a look shall you have from me . . . not a word."

21

Films

Just Peggy (Australian, 1918)
To What Red Hell (Br, 1929)
Blackmail (Br, 1929)
Juno and the Paycock (Br, 1930)
The World, the Flesh and the Devil (Br, 1932)
The Fortunate Fool (Br, 1933)
Lily of Killarney [a.k.a. The Bride of the Lake] (Br, 1934)
Irish Hearts [a.k.a. Norah O'Neale] (Br, 1934)
Peg of Old Drury (Br, 1935)
The Passing of the Third Floor Back (Br, 1935)
Riders to the Sea (Irish, 1935)
Lazy Bones (Br, 1935)
It's Love Again (Br, 1936)
Pot Luck (Br, 1936)
Southern Roses (Br, 1936)
Storm in a Teacup (UA Br, 1937)

The Sky's the Limit (Br, 1937)
Kathleen Mavourneen [a.k.a. Kathleen] (Irish, 1938)
The Londonderry Air (Br, 1938)
On the Night of the Fire [a.k.a. The Fugitive] (Br, 1939)
That Hamilton Woman (UA Br, 1941)
How Green Was My Valley (20th, 1941)
Dr. Jekyll and Mr. Hyde (MGM, 1941)
Lydia (UA, 1941)
It Happened in Flatbush (20th, 1942)
The War Against Mrs. Hadley (MGM, 1942)
Roxie Hart (20th, 1942)
This Above All (20th, 1942)
Life Begins at 8:30 (20th, 1942)
Forever and a Day (RKO, 1943)
City Without Men (Col, 1943)
The Lodger (20th, 1944)
Between Two Worlds (WB, 1944)

Jane Eyre (20th, 1944)
The Keys of the Kingdom (20th, 1944)
The Strange Affair of Uncle Harry (Univ, 1945)
Kitty (Par, 1945)
The Spiral Staircase (RKO, 1946)
Cluny Brown (20th, 1946)
The Fabulous Dorseys (UA, 1947)
Ivy (Univ, 1947)
Mother Wore Tights (20th, 1947)
Mourning Becomes Electra (RKO, 1947)
My Wild Irish Rose (WB, 1947)
The Man from Texas (EL, 1948)
The Girl from Manhattan (UA, 1948)
The Accused (Par, 1948)
One Touch of Venus (Univ, 1948)
Challenge to Lassie (MGM, 1949)
Cheaper by the Dozen (20th, 1950)
Sierra (Univ, 1950)

LEON AMES
(Leon Waycoff)

In *No Greater Sin* (1941).

Born January 20, 1903, Portland, Indiana. Married Christine Gossett (1938), children: Shelley, Leon. Occasional hero (*Murders in the Rue Morgue*), sometimes leading man of quickies (*Cipher Bureau, Panama Patrol*, etc.). Best known for character leads at MGM during the 1940s: *Meet Me in St. Louis* (sympathetic father of Judy Garland, et al.), *The Postman Always Rings Twice* (District Attorney Kyle Sackett), *A Date with Judy* (Elizabeth Taylor's dad), etc. TV series: "Life with Father," "Father of the Bride," and "Mister Ed."

Leon Ames in *Meet Me in St. Louis:* "Either I've lost some soup or I've found a spoon."

Films

As Leon Waycoff:
Murders in the Rue Morgue (Univ, 1932)
13 Women (RKO, 1932)
The Famous Ferguson Case (FN, 1932)
State's Attorney (RKO, 1932)
A Successful Calamity (WB, 1932)
Silver Dollar (FN, 1932)
Cannonball Express (WW, 1932)
Uptown New York (WW, 1932)
Parachute Jumper (WB, 1933)
Alimony Madness (Mayfair, 1933)
The Man Who Dared (Fox, 1933)
Forgotten (Invincible, 1933)
Ship of Wanted Men (Showmen's Pictures, 1933)
The Count of Monte Cristo (UA, 1934)
I'll Tell the World (Univ, 1934)
Now I'll Tell (Fox, 1934)
Reckless (MGM, 1935)
Strangers All (RKO, 1935)
Mutiny Ahead (Majestic, 1935)
Get That Man (Empire, 1935)

As Leon Ames:
Stowaway (20th, 1936)
Dangerously Yours (20th, 1937)
Death in the Air (Puritan, 1937)
Murder in Greenwich Village (Col, 1937)
Charlie Chan on Broadway (20th, 1937)
45 Fathers (20th, 1937)
International Settlement (20th, 1938)
Bluebeard's Eighth Wife (Par, 1938)
Walking Down Broadway (20th, 1938)
The Spy Ring (Univ, 1938)
Island in the Sky (20th, 1938)
Come on Leathernecks (Rep, 1938)
Mysterious Mr. Moto (20th, 1938)
Strange Faces (Univ, 1938)
Cipher Bureau (GN, 1938)
Suez (20th, 1938)

Secrets of a Nurse (Univ, 1938)
Mr. Moto in Danger Island (20th, 1938)
Risky Business (Univ, 1939)
I Was a Convict (Rep, 1939)
Pack Up Your Troubles (20th, 1939)
Panama Patrol (GN, 1939)
Man of Conquest (Rep, 1939)
Fugitive at Large (Col, 1939)
Code of the Streets (Univ, 1939)
Legion of Lost Flyers (Univ, 1939)
Calling All Marines (Rep, 1939)
Thunder Afloat (MGM, 1939)
Marshal of Mesa City (RKO, 1939)
East Side Kids (Mon, 1940)
No Greater Sin (University Film Products, 1941)
Ellery Queen and the Murder Ring (Col, 1941)
Crime Doctor (Col, 1943)
The Iron Major (RKO, 1943)
Meet Me in St. Louis (MGM, 1944)
Thirty Seconds over Tokyo (MGM, 1944)
The Thin Man Goes Home (MGM, 1944)
Son of Lassie (MGM, 1945)
Week-End at the Waldorf (MGM, 1945)
They Were Expendable (MGM, 1945)
Yolanda and the Thief (MGM, 1945)
The Postman Always Rings Twice (MGM, 1946)
Lady in the Lake (MGM, 1946)
No Leave, No Love (MGM, 1946)
The Show-Off (MGM, 1946)
The Cockeyed Miracle (MGM, 1946)
Undercover Maisie (MGM, 1947)
Song of the Thin Man (MGM, 1947)
Merton of the Movies (MGM, 1947)
Alias a Gentleman (MGM, 1948)
On an Island with You (MGM, 1948)
A Date with Judy (MGM, 1948)
The Velvet Touch (RKO, 1948)

Little Women (MGM, 1949)
Any Number Can Play (MGM, 1949)
Scene of the Crime (MGM, 1949)
Battleground (MGM, 1949)
Ambush (MGM, 1949)
The Big Hangover (MGM, 1950)
Dial 1119 (MGM, 1950)
Watch the Birdie (MGM, 1950)
The Skipper Surprised His Wife (MGM, 1950)
The Happy Years (MGM, 1950)
Crisis (MGM, 1950)
Cattle Drive (Univ, 1951)
On Moonlight Bay (WB, 1951)
It's a Big Country (MGM, 1951)
Angel Face (RKO, 1952)
By the Light of the Silvery Moon (WB, 1953)
Let's Do It Again (Col, 1953)
Sabre Jet (UA, 1953)
Peyton Place (20th, 1957)
From the Terrace (20th, 1960)
The Absent-Minded Professor (BV, 1961)
Son of Flubber (BV, 1963)
The Misadventures of Merlin Jones (BV, 1964)
The Monkey's Uncle (BV, 1965)
On a Clear Day You Can See Forever (Par, 1970)
Tora! Tora! Tora! (20th, 1970)
Toklat (Sun International, 1971)
Cool Breeze (MGM, 1972)
Hammersmith Is Out (Cin, 1972)
The Timber Tramp (Alaska Pictures, 1973)
Brother of the Wind (Sun International, 1973) [narrator]
The Meal (Ambassador Releasing, 1975)

DAME JUDITH ANDERSON
(Frances Margaret Anderson)

Frank McHugh, Judith Anderson, Humphrey Bogart, and Kaaren Verne in All Through the Night *(1942).*

Born February 10, 1898, Adelaide, South Australia. Married 1) Benjamin Lehman; divorced; 2) Luther Greene; divorced. Diminutive actress who towers on stage and film. Caught the public's fancy as viperish Mrs. Danvers in *Rebecca*. (Oscar-nominated; lost BSAAA to Jane Darwell of *The Grapes of Wrath*.) Demonic as *Lady Scarface*; stylish as the amorous admirer of Vincent Price in *Laura*. Displayed a rarely seen sympathetic side as the wife-victim of Big Daddy (Burl Ives) in *Cat on a Hot Tin Roof*.

> **Judith Anderson** to Joan Fontaine in *Rebecca:* "I watched you go down, just as I watched *her* a year ago. Even in the same dress, you couldn't *compare*."

Films

Blood Money (UA, 1933)
Rebecca (UA, 1940)
Forty Little Mothers (MGM, 1940)
Kings Row (WB, 1941)
Free and Easy (MGM, 1941)
Lady Scarface (RKO, 1941)
All Through the Night (WB, 1942)
Edge of Darkness (WB, 1943)
Stage Door Canteen (UA, 1943)
Laura (20th, 1944)

And Then There Were None (20th, 1945)
The Diary of a Chambermaid (UA, 1946)
The Strange Love of Martha Ivers (Par, 1946)
Specter of the Rose (Rep, 1946)
Tycoon (RKO, 1947)
The Red House (UA, 1947)
Pursued (WB, 1947)
The Furies (Par, 1950)
Salome (Col, 1953)

The Ten Commandments (Par, 1956)
Cat on a Hot Tin Roof (MGM, 1958)
Cinderfella (Par, 1960)
Why Bother to Knock? (Seven Arts, 1961)
A Man Called Horse (National General, 1970)
Inn of the Damned (Australian, 1974)

WARNER ANDERSON

Erin O'Brien-Moore and Warner Anderson in Destination Moon *(1950).*

Born March 10, 1911, Brooklyn, New York. Married Leeta _____ , child: Michael. Died August 26, 1976, Santa Monica, California. Clear eyes and a well-modulated voice. Supporting parts in many MGM pictures of the 1940s: Dr. Campbell (*Weekend-End at the Waldorf*), Dr. Monolaw (*Song of the Thin Man*), etc. More engaging roles thereafter: Cargraves (*Destination Moon*), Sims (*Detective Story*). TV series: "The Doctors," "The Line-Up" (as Lieutenant Ben Guthrie), and "Peyton Place" (as Matthew Swain, the newspaper editor).

Warner Anderson to Marshall Reed in *The Line-Up:* "I don't know what to think. The whole case doesn't add up."

Films

Sunbeam (M, 1916)
This Is the Army (WB, 1943)
Destination Tokyo (WB, 1943)
Objective Burma (WB, 1945)
Bud Abbott and Lou Costello in Hollywood (MGM, 1945)
Dangerous Partners (MGM, 1945)
Her Highness and the Bellboy (MGM, 1945)
Week-End at the Waldorf (MGM, 1945)
My Reputation (WB, 1946)
Three Wise Fools (MGM, 1946)
Bad Bascomb (MGM, 1946)
Faithful in My Fashion (MGM, 1946)
The Arnelo Affair (MGM, 1947)

Dark Delusion (MGM, 1947)
High Wall (MGM, 1947)
The Beginning or the End (MGM, 1947)
Song of the Thin Man (MGM, 1947)
Tenth Avenue Angel (MGM, 1948)
Alias a Gentleman (MGM, 1948)
Command Decision (MGM, 1948)
The Lucky Stiff (UA, 1949)
The Doctor and the Girl (MGM, 1949)
Destination Moon (EL, 1950)
Bannerline (MGM, 1951)
The Blue Veil (RKO, 1951)
Detective Story (Par, 1951)
Go for Broke (MGM, 1951)
Santa Fe (Col, 1951)

Only the Valiant (WB, 1951)
The Star (20th, 1952)
The Last Posse (Col, 1953)
A Lion Is in the Streets (WB, 1953)
The Caine Mutiny (Col, 1954)
Yellow Tomahawk (UA, 1954)
Drum Beat (WB, 1954)
The Violent Men (Col, 1955)
The Blackboard Jungle (MGM, 1955)
A Lawless Street (Col, 1955)
The Line-Up (Col, 1958)
Armored Command (AA, 1961)
Rio Conchos (20th, 1964)

EDWARD ANDREWS
(Edward Bryan Andrews, Jr.)

In The Thrill of It All *(1963).*

Born October 9, 1914, Griffin, Georgia. Married Emily Barnes (1955), children: Edward III, Abigail, Tabatha. Many-faceted performer, equally at ease as a vicious skunk (crime boss Rhett Tanner of *The Phenix City Story*), a harassed military officer (defense secretary of *The Absent-Minded Professor),* or a farceur (husband of expectant Arlene Francis in *The Thrill of It All).* Extremely expressive (bespectacled) eyes, smile, and varied vocal range. TV series: "Broadside."

Edward Andrews to Doris Day in *The Thrill of It All:* "Call your baby! My wife's having a husband!"

Films

The Phenix City Story (AA, 1955)
The Harder They Fall (Col, 1956)
Tea and Sympathy (MGM, 1956)
These Wilder Years (MGM, 1956)
The Unguarded Moment (Univ, 1956)
Tension at Table Rock (RKO, 1956)
Three Brave Men (20th, 1957)
Hot Summer Night (MGM, 1957)
The Tattered Dress (Univ, 1957)
Trooper Hook (UA, 1957)
The Fiend That Walked the West (20th, 1958)
Night of the Quarter Moon (MGM, 1959)
Elmer Gantry (UA, 1960)

The Absent-Minded Professor (BV, 1961)
The Young Savages (UA, 1961)
Love in a Goldfish Bowl (Par, 1961)
Advise and Consent (Col, 1962)
Forty Pounds of Trouble (Univ, 1962)
Son of Flubber (BV, 1963)
The Thrill of It All (Univ, 1963)
A Tiger Walks (BV, 1964)
The Brass Bottle (Univ, 1964)
Good Neighbor Sam (Col, 1964)
Kisses for My President (WB, 1964)
Youngblood Hawke (WB, 1964)
Send Me No Flowers (Univ, 1964)
The Man from Galveston (WB, 1964)

Fluffy (Univ, 1965)
The Glass Bottom Boat (MGM, 1966)
Birds Do It (Col, 1966)
Tora! Tora! Tora! (20th, 1970)
The Trouble with Girls (MGM, 1970)
$1,000,000 Duck (BV, 1971)
How to Frame a Figg (Univ, 1971)
Now You See Him, Now You Don't (BV, 1972)
Avanti! (UA, 1972)
Charley and the Angel (BV, 1973)
The Photographer (Avco Emb, 1975)

STANLEY ANDREWS

Stanley Andrews and Randolph Scott in Colt .45 *(1950).*

Born 1892. Died June 23, 1969, Los Angeles, California. Tall, angular, moustached figure of many movies. TV series: "Death Valley Days" (as the Old Ranger host).

Stanley Andrews to Victor Mature in *My Gal Sal:* "You're going to theological school tomorrow—and you're going in *that suit!*"

Films

Evelyn Prentice (MGM, 1934)
All the King's Horses (Par, 1935)
Private Worlds (Par, 1935)
The Crusades (Par, 1935)
The Big Broadcast of 1936 (Par, 1935)
Mississippi (Par, 1935)
People Will Talk (Par, 1935)
It's in the Air (MGM, 1935)
Hold 'em Yale (Par, 1935)
College Scandal (Par, 1935)
Wanderer of the Wasteland (Par, 1935)
Murder Man (MGM, 1935)
Escape from Devil's Island (Col, 1935)
Nevada (Par, 1935)
After Office Hours (MGM, 1935)
She Couldn't Take It (Col, 1935)
The Texas Rangers (Par, 1936)
Pennies from Heaven (Col, 1936)
Drift Fence (Par, 1936)
Alibi for Murder (Col, 1936)
Dangerous Intrigue (Col, 1936)
Desire (Par, 1936)
In His Steps (GN, 1936)

Florida Special (Par, 1936)
Wild Brian Kent (RKO, 1936)
Happy Go Lucky (Rep, 1936)
Madame X (MGM, 1937)
John Meade's Woman (Par, 1937)
The Devil's Playground (Col, 1937)
Easy Living (Par, 1937)
The Man Who Found Himself (RKO, 1937)
Big City (MGM, 1937)
Nancy Steele Is Missing (20th, 1937)
She's Dangerous (Univ, 1937)
High, Wide and Handsome (Par, 1937)
Hold that Co-ed (20th, 1938)
The Buccaneer (Par, 1938)
Juvenile Court (Col, 1938)
When G-Men Step In (Col, 1938)
Forbidden Valley (Univ, 1938)
Cocoanut Grove (Par, 1938)
Alexander's Ragtime Band (20th, 1938)
I'll Give a Million (20th, 1938)
Spawn of the North (Par, 1938)
Adventure in Sahara (Col, 1938)

Shine on Harvest Moon (Rep, 1938)
Kentucky (20th, 1938)
Blondie (Col, 1938)
The Mysterious Rider (Par, 1938)
Prairie Moon (Rep, 1938)
The Lone Ranger (Rep serial, 1938) [feature version: Hi Yo Silver, Rep, 1940]
The Lady Objects (Col, 1938)
Homicide Bureau (Col, 1939)
The Lady's from Kentucky (Par, 1939)
Mr. Smith Goes to Washington (Col, 1939)
Beau Geste (Par, 1939)
Coast Guard (Col, 1939)
Golden Boy (Col, 1939)
Geronimo (Par, 1939)
Union Pacific (Par, 1939)
The Blue Bird (20th, 1940)
The Man Who Wouldn't Talk (20th, 1940)
Little Old New York (20th, 1940)
Maryland (20th, 1940)

Brigham Young—Frontiersman (20th, 1940)

King of the Royal Mounted (Rep serial, 1940) [feature version: *Yukon Patrol*, Rep, 1942]

Kit Carson (UA, 1940)

Play Girl (RKO, 1940)

Dead Men Tell (20th, 1941)

Meet John Doe (WB, 1941)

Strange Alibi (WB, 1941)

Time Out for Rhythm (Col, 1941)

Wild Geese Calling (20th, 1941)

Mr. and Mrs. North (MGM, 1941)

Borrowed Hero (Mon, 1941)

North to the Klondike (Univ, 1942)

Canal Zone (Col, 1942)

The Major and the Minor (Par, 1942)

To the Shores of Tripoli (20th, 1942)

My Gal Sal (20th, 1942)

Ten Gentlemen from West Point (20th, 1942)

The Postman Didn't Ring (20th, 1942)

Crash Dive (20th, 1943)

Flight for Freedom (RKO, 1943)

In Old Oklahoma [a.k.a. *War of the Wildcats*] (Rep, 1943)

Daredevils of the West (Rep serial, 1943)

Murder, My Sweet (RKO, 1944)

The Man from Frisco (Rep, 1944)

Follow the Boys (Univ, 1944)

Tucson Raiders (Rep, 1944)

Sensations of 1945 (UA, 1944)

The Princess and the Pirate (RKO, 1944)

Wing and a Prayer (20th, 1944)

Practically Yours (Par, 1944)

Road to Utopia (Par, 1945)

Adventure (MGM, 1945)

The Daltons Ride Again (Univ, 1945)

Atlantic City (Rep, 1945)

The Virginian (Par, 1946)

Smoky (20th, 1946)

It's a Wonderful Life (RKO, 1946)

Till the Clouds Roll By (MGM, 1946)

The Michigan Kid (Univ, 1947)

Killer Dill (Screen Guild, 1947)

Millie's Daughter (Col, 1947)

Desire Me (MGM, 1947)

Robin Hood of Texas (Rep, 1947)

Adventures of Frank and Jesse James (Rep serial, 1948)

Mr. Blandings Builds His Dream House (Selznick Releasing Organization, 1948)

Docks of New Orleans (Mon, 1948)

The Fuller Brush Man (Col, 1948)

Best Man Wins (Col, 1948)

The Return of Wildfire (Screen Guild, 1948)

Jinx Money (Mon, 1948)

The Dead Don't Dream (UA, 1948)

Perilous Waters (Mon, 1948)

Northwest Stampede (EL, 1948)

The Paleface (Par, 1948)

The Valiant Hombre (UA, 1948)

Last of the Wild Horses (Screen Guild, 1948)

Leather Gloves (Col, 1948)

Sinister Journey (UA, 1948)

The Man from Colorado (Col, 1948)

Brothers in the Saddle (RKO, 1949)

The Last Bandit (Rep, 1949)

Fighting Fools (Mon, 1949)

Blondie's Big Deal (Col, 1949)

Trail of the Yukon (Mon, 1949)

Brimstone (Rep, 1949)

Tough Assignment (Lip, 1949)

The Nevadan (Col, 1950)

Arizona Cowboy (Rep, 1950)

Blonde Dynamite (Mon, 1950)

Two Flags West (20th, 1950)

Tyrant of the Sea (Col, 1950)

Outcasts of Black Mesa (Col, 1950)

Salt Lake Raiders (Rep, 1950)

Trigger, Jr. (Rep, 1950)

Mule Train (Col, 1950)

Streets of Ghost Town (Col, 1950)

West of Wyoming (Mon, 1950)

Across the Badlands (Col, 1950)

Short Grass (AA, 1950)

Where Danger Lives (RKO, 1950)

Colt .45 (WB, 1950)

Under Mexicali Skies (Rep, 1950)

Vengeance Valley (MGM, 1951)

Saddle Legion (RKO, 1951)

Al Jennings of Oklahoma (Col, 1951)

The Texas Rangers (Col, 1951)

Silver Canyon (Col, 1951)

Hot Lead (RKO, 1951)

Utah Wagon Train (Rep, 1951)

And Now Tomorrow (Westminster, 1952)

Woman of the North Country (Rep, 1952)

Thundering Caravans (Rep, 1952)

Fargo (Mon, 1952)

Montana Belle (RKO, 1952)

Talk About a Stranger (MGM, 1952)

Waco (Mon, 1952)

Kansas Territory (Mon, 1952)

The Man from the Black Hills (Mon, 1952)

The Bad and the Beautiful (MGM, 1952)

Lone Star (MGM, 1952)

Ride, Vaquero! (MGM, 1953)

Canadian Mounties vs. Atomic Invaders (Rep serial, 1953) [feature version: *Missile Base at Taniak*]

Dangerous Crossing (20th, 1953)

El Paso Stampede (Rep, 1953)

Appointment in Honduras (RKO, 1953)

Dawn at Socorro (Univ, 1954)

Southwest Passage (UA, 1954)

The Steel Cage (UA, 1954)

The Treasure of Ruby Hills (AA, 1955)

Frontier Gambler (Associated Films, 1956)

Cry Terror! (MGM, 1958)

MORRIS ANKRUM

John Larch, Morris Ankrum, and Rory Calhoun in The Saga of Hemp Brown *(1958).*

Born August 29, 1897, Danville, Illinois. Died September 2, 1964, Pasadena, California. Former associate professor of economics and little-theater director at the University of Southern California. Made screen debut in a rash of *Hopalong Cassidy* series films. Generally cast as a low-life sagebrush villain, well-attired attorney, or judge; later in several science fiction entries.

> **Morris Ankrum** to Jeff Morrow, Mara Corday, and Robert Shayne in *The Giant Claw:* "Hundreds of planes from every command are combing the skies—searching for this overgrown buzzard."

Films

As Stephen Morris:
Hopalong Cassidy Returns (Par, 1936)
Trail Dust (Par, 1936)
Borderland (Par, 1937)
Hills of Old Wyoming (Par, 1937)
North of the Rio Grande (Par, 1937)
Rustler's Valley (Par, 1937)

As Morris Ankrum:
Knights of the Range (Par, 1940)
The Showdown (Par, 1940)
Buck Benny Rides Again (Par, 1940)
Three Men from Texas (Par, 1940)
The Light of Western Stars (Par, 1940)
Cherokee Strip (Par, 1940)
The Roundup (Par, 1941)
This Woman Is Mine (Univ, 1941)
Doomed Caravan (Par, 1941)
In Old Colorado (Par, 1941)
Pirates on Horseback (Par, 1941)

Border Vigilantes (Par, 1941)
Wide Open Town (Par, 1941)
The Bandit Trail (RKO, 1941)
I Wake Up Screaming [a.k.a. *Hot Spot*] (20th, 1941)
Road Agent (Univ, 1941)
Ride 'em Cowboy (Univ, 1942)
Roxie Hart (20th, 1942)
Ten Gentlemen from West Point (20th, 1942)
The Loves of Edgar Allan Poe (20th, 1942)
Tales of Manhattan (20th, 1942)
The Omaha Trail (MGM, 1942)
Reunion in France (MGM, 1942)
Tennessee Johnson (MGM, 1942)
Time to Kill (20th, 1942)
Let's Face It (Par, 1943)
Dixie Dugan (20th, 1943)
Swing Fever (MGM, 1943)
The Human Comedy (MGM, 1943)

The Heavenly Body (MGM, 1943)
Rationing (MGM, 1944)
Meet the People (MGM, 1944)
The Thin Man Goes Home (MGM, 1944)
Barbary Coast Gent (MGM, 1944)
Marriage Is a Private Affair (MGM, 1944)
Gentle Annie (MGM, 1944)
Adventure (MGM, 1945)
The Hidden Eye (MGM, 1945)
The Harvey Girls (MGM, 1946)
Courage of Lassie (MGM, 1946)
Little Mr. Jim (MGM, 1946)
The Cockeyed Miracle (MGM, 1946)
Lady in the Lake (MGM, 1946)
The Mighty McGurk (MGM, 1946)
Undercover Maisie (MGM, 1947)
Cynthia (MGM, 1947)
The Sea of Grass (MGM, 1947)
Desire Me (MGM, 1947)

Good News (MGM, 1947)
The High Wall (MGM, 1947)
For the Love of Mary (Univ, 1948)
Joan of Arc (RKO, 1948)
Badmen of Tombstone (AA, 1948)
Fighting Back (20th, 1948)
We Were Strangers (Col, 1949)
Colorado Territory (WB, 1949)
Slattery's Hurricane (20th, 1949)
The Damned Don't Cry (WB, 1950)
Chain Lightning (WB, 1950)
Borderline (Univ, 1950)
In a Lonely Place (Col, 1950)
Rocketship X-M (Lip, 1950)
Southside 1-1000 (AA, 1950)
Short Grass (AA, 1950)
The Redhead and the Cowboy (Par, 1950)
Fighting Coast Guard (Rep, 1951)
Along the Great Divide (WB, 1951)
The Lion Hunters (Mon, 1951)
Tomorrow Is Another Day (WB, 1951)
My Favorite Spy (Par, 1951)
Flight to Mars (Mon, 1951)
Mutiny (UA, 1952)
Red Planet Mars (UA, 1952)
And Now Tomorrow (Westminster, 1952)
The Son of Ali Baba (Univ, 1952)

The Raiders (Univ, 1952)
Hiawatha (AA, 1952)
Fort Osage (Mon, 1952)
The Man Behind the Gun (WB, 1952)
Invaders from Mars (20th, 1953)
Arena (MGM, 1953)
Devil's Canyon (RKO, 1953)
Fort Vengeance (AA, 1953)
Sky Commando (Col, 1953)
Mexican Manhunt (AA, 1953)
The Moonlighter (WB, 1953)
Three Young Texans (20th, 1954)
Taza, Son of Cochise (Univ, 1954)
Apache (UA, 1954)
Silver Lode (RKO, 1954)
Two Guns and a Badge (AA, 1954)
Southwest Passage (UA, 1954)
Drums Across the River (Univ, 1954)
Vera Cruz (Univ, 1954)
The Saracen Blade (Col, 1954)
The Outlaw Stallion (Col, 1954)
Cattle Queen of Montana (RKO, 1954)
The Steel Cage (UA, 1954)
Chief Crazy Horse (Univ, 1955)
Jupiter's Darling (MGM, 1955)
The Silver Star (Lip, 1955)
Abbott and Costello Meet the Mummy (Univ, 1955)

The Eternal Sea (Rep, 1955)
Tennessee's Partner (RKO, 1955)
Crashout (Filmakers, 1955)
No Man's Woman (Rep, 1955)
Fury at Gunsight Pass (Col, 1956)
Quincannon, Frontier Scout (UA, 1956)
Earth vs. the Flying Saucers (Col, 1956)
Walk the Proud Land (Univ, 1956)
When Gangland Strikes (Rep, 1956)
Death of a Scoundrel (RKO, 1956)
Drango (UA, 1957)
Half Human (DCA, 1957)
Zombies of Mora-Tau (Col, 1957)
Kronos (20th, 1957)
The Giant Claw (Col, 1957)
Hell's Crossroads (Rep, 1957)
Beginning of the End (Rep, 1957)
Omar Khayyam (Par, 1957)
Badman's Country (WB, 1958)
Young and Wild (Rep, 1958)
Twilight for the Gods (Univ, 1958)
The Saga of Hemp Brown (Univ, 1958)
From the Earth to the Moon (WB, 1958)
Frontier Gun (20th, 1958)
How to Make a Monster (AIP, 1958)
Giant from the Unknown (Astor, 1958)
The Most Dangerous Man Alive (Col, 1961)

PEDRO ARMENDARIZ

With Heidi Bruhl in Captain Sinbad *(1963).*

Born May 9, 1912, Mexico City, Mexico. Married Carmen Bohn (1939), children: Pedro, two daughters. Died June 18, 1963, Los Angeles, California. Popular, virile Mexican performer who made his Hollywood screen bow as the police lieutenant in John Ford's *The Fugitive.* Later for Ford in *Three Godfathers* (as one of title figures, along with John Wayne and Harry Carey, Jr.) and *Fort Apache* (Sergeant Beaufort). Final film: *From Russia with Love* (Kerim Bey).

Pedro Armendariz to Yvonne De Carlo in *Border River:* "So you prefer the gringo. Well, I'll tell you one thing—you'll never have him."

Films

Maria Elena (Mex, 1935)
Rosario (Mex, 1935)
Con los Dorados de Pancho Villa (Mex, 1937)
Jalisco Nunca Pierde (Mex, 1937)
Los Olvidados de Dios (Mex, 1937)
Canto a Mi Tierra (Mex, 1938)
Mi Candidato (Mex, 1938)
El Indio (Mex, 1939)
La China Hilaria (Mex, 1939)
La Reina del Rio (Mex, 1940)
Mala Hierra (Mex, 1940)
El Torro de Falisco (Mex, 1940)
El Secreto del Sacer Dote (Mex, 1941)
La E Ropeya del Camino (Mex, 1941)
Del Ranco a la Capital (Mex, 1941)
La Isla de la Pasion (Mex, 1941)
Soy Puro Mexicano (Mex, 1942)
Las Calaveras del Terror (Mex, 1943)

Guadalajara (Mex, 1943)
Flor Silvestre (Mex, 1943)
Konga Roja (Mex, 1943)
The Life of Simon Bolivar (Mex, 1943)
Distinto Amanecer (Mex, 1943)
Maria Candelaria (Mex, 1943)
El Corsario Negro (Mex, 1944)
Tierra de Pasiones (Mex, 1944)
Alma de Bronce (Mex, 1944)
La Campana de Mi Pueblo (Mex, 1944)
Las Abandonadas (Mex, 1944)
El Capitan Malacara (Mex, 1944)
Entre Hermanos (Mex, 1944)
Bugambilia (Mex, 1944)
Rayando el Sol (Mex, 1945)
La Perla (Mex, 1945)
Enamorada (Mex, 1946)
La Casa Colorada (Mex, 1947)
Juan Charrasqueado (Mex, 1947)

The Fugitive (RKO, 1947)
Maclovia (Mex, 1948)
En la Hacienda de la Flor (Mex, 1948)
Al Caer de la Tarde (Mex, 1948)
Three Godfathers (MGM, 1948)
Fort Apache (RKO, 1948)
La Lalquerida (Mex, 1949)
Villa Vuelve (Mex, 1949)
La Masquerada (Mex, 1949)
El Abandonado (Mex, 1949)
We Were Strangers (Col, 1949)
Tulsa (EL, 1949)
The Torch (EL, 1950)
Rosauro Castro (Mex, 1950)
Tierra Baja (Mex, 1950)
La Loga de la Casa (Mex, 1950)
Puerta Falsa (Mex, 1950)
Nos Veremos en el Cielo (Mex, 1950)
Elly y Yo (Mex, 1951)

El Rebozo de Soledad (Mex, 1952)
Lucretia Borgia [a.k.a. Sins of the Borgias 1956] (It, 1952)
Gli Amanti di Toledo [a.k.a. The Lovers of Toledo 1954] (It, 1953)
El Bruto (Mex, 1954)
Border River (Univ, 1954)
The Littlest Outlaw (BV, 1955)
Diane (MGM, 1955)

The Conqueror (RKO, 1956)
Viva Revolution (Mex, 1956)
The Big Boodle (UA, 1957)
Stowaway Girl [a.k.a. Manuela] (Par, 1957)
Conqueror of the Desert (It, 1958)
The Little Savage (20th, 1959)
Flor de Mayo [a.k.a. Beyond All Limits] (Mex, 1959)

The Wonderful Country (UA, 1959)
Soldiers of Pancho Villa (Mex, 1960)
La Cucaracha (Mex, 1961)
Francis of Assisi (20th, 1961)
La Bandida (Mex, 1962)
Captain Sinbad (MGM, 1963)
My Son, the Hero (UA, 1963)
From Russia with Love (UA, 1964)

HENRY ARMETTA

Douglass Dumbrille, Marian Marsh, Robert Middlemass, Henry Armetta, and Arthur Vinton in The Unknown Woman *(1935).*

Born July 4, 1888, Palermo, Italy. Married _____ , children: John, Louis, Rosalie. Died October 21, 1945, San Diego, California. Tubby Italian-born stage actor who found a Hollywood haven. In sound era had opportunity to demonstrate a beguiling array of excitable portly individuals. He could be as comically amusing with wild gesticulations as Billy Gilbert was with his sneeze or Edgar Kennedy with his slow burn. Played Papa Gambini, the volatile family man in 20th Century-Fox's series of sport actioners—*Road Demon, Winner Take All,* etc.

Henry Armetta to Harpo Marx in *The Big Store:* "Hey, pressa' the grapes—no pressa' my wife."

Films

The Nigger (Fox, 1915)
The Silent Command (Fox, 1923)
The Desert's Price (Fox, 1925)
Seventh Heaven (Fox, 1927)

Street Angel (Fox, 1928)
Homesick (Fox, 1929)
The Trespasser (UA, 1929)
In Old Arizona (Fox, 1929)

Lady of the Pavements (UA, 1929)
Love, Live and Laugh (Fox, 1929)
Jazz Heaven (RKO, 1929)
Ladies Love Brutes (Par, 1930)

A Lady to Love (MGM, 1930)
Die Sehnsuht Jeder Frau [German version of *A Lady to Love*] (MGM, 1930)
The Climax (Univ, 1930)
The Little Accident (Univ, 1930)
Lovin' the Ladies (RKO, 1930)
Romance (MGM, 1930)
Sins of the Children (MGM, 1930)
Laughing Sinners (MGM, 1931)
Strangers May Kiss (MGM, 1931)
A Tailor-Made Man (MGM, 1931)
Five and Ten (MGM, 1931)
Hush Money (Fox, 1931)
The Unholy Garden (UA, 1931)
Speak Easily (MGM, 1932)
Hat Check Girl (Fox, 1932)
Scarface: The Shame of a Nation (UA, 1932)
Arsene Lupin (MGM, 1932)
The Passionate Plumber (MGM, 1932)
The Doomed Battalion (Univ, 1932)
Tiger Shark (FN, 1932)
Weekends Only (Fox, 1932)
Central Park (FN, 1932)
Steady Company (Univ, 1932)
Huddle (MGM, 1932)
Prosperity (MGM, 1932)
A Farewell to Arms (Par, 1932)
Uptown New York (WW, 1932)
Okay, America (Univ, 1932)
Men of America (RKO, 1932)
Deception (Col, 1932)
The Devil's Brother (MGM, 1933)
The Cohens and the Kellys in Trouble (Univ, 1933)
They Just Had to Get Married (Univ, 1933)

Her First Mate (Univ, 1933)
Too Much Harmony (Par, 1933)
Laughing at Life (Mascot, 1933)
What! No Beer? (MGM, 1933)
So This Is Africa (Col, 1933)
Don't Bet on Love (Univ, 1933)
The Cat and the Fiddle (MGM, 1934)
Half a Sinner (Univ, 1934)
Let's Talk It Over (Univ, 1934)
One Night of Love (Col, 1934)
The Black Cat (Univ, 1934)
Cross Country Cruise (Univ, 1934)
Viva Villa! (MGM, 1934)
Poor Rich (Univ, 1934)
Hide-Out (Univ, 1934)
Embarrassing Moments (Univ, 1934)
Gift of Gab (Univ, 1934)
Two Heads on a Pillow (Liberty, 1934)
Wake Up and Dream (Univ, 1934)
Imitation of Life (Univ, 1934)
The Merry Widow (MGM, 1934)
Kiss and Make Up (Par, 1934)
Cheating Cheaters (Univ, 1934)
Romance in the Rain (Univ, 1934)
The Man Who Reclaimed His Head (Univ, 1934)
Straight from the Heart (Univ, 1935)
Vanessa—Her Love Story (MGM, 1935)
Manhattan Moon (Univ, 1935)
Night Life of the Gods (Univ, 1935)
After Office Hours (MGM, 1935)
I've Been Around (Univ, 1935)
Dinky (WB, 1935)
Princess O'Hara (Univ, 1935)
The Unknown Woman (Col, 1935)
Three Kids and a Queen (Univ, 1935)
Magnificent Obsession (Univ, 1935)

Let's Sing Again (Par, 1936)
The Crime of Doctor Forbes (20th, 1936)
Poor Little Rich Girl (20th, 1936)
The Magnificent Brute (Univ, 1936)
Two in a Crowd (Univ, 1936)
Top of the Town (Univ, 1937)
Make a Wish (RKO, 1937)
Manhattan Merry-Go-Round (Rep, 1937)
Everybody Sing (MGM, 1938)
Speed to Burn (20th, 1938)
Road Demon (20th, 1938)
Submarine Patrol (20th, 1938)
Fisherman's Wharf (RKO, 1939)
The Lady and the Mob (Col, 1939)
Winner Take All (20th, 1939)
I Stole a Million (Univ, 1939)
Dust Be My Destiny (WB, 1939)
The Escape (20th, 1939)
Three Cheers for the Irish (WB, 1940)
We Who Are Young (MGM, 1940)
You're Not So Tough (Univ, 1940)
The Man Who Talked Too Much (WB, 1940)
Caught in the Act (PRC, 1941)
The Big Store (MGM, 1941)
Thank Your Lucky Stars (WB, 1943)
Stage Door Canteen (UA, 1943)
Good Luck, Mr. Yates (Col, 1943)
Once upon a Time (Col, 1944)
Allergic to Love (Univ, 1944)
The Ghost Catchers (Univ, 1944)
Penthouse Rhythm (Univ, 1945)
A Bell for Adano (20th, 1945)
Colonel Effingham's Raid (20th, 1945)
Anchors Aweigh (MGM, 1945)

SIG ARNO
(Siegfried Aron)

Sig Arno and Desi Arnaz in Holiday in Havana *(1949).*

Born December 27, 1895, Hamburg, Germany. Married 1) _____ ; 2) _____ ; 3) Kitty Mattern; 4) Lia Dahms, child: Peter. Died August 17, 1975, Woodland Hills, California. Ever-busy German stage and film performer; cast in the U.S. as comedy-relief foreigner: *Two Latins from Manhattan* (Felipe Rudolfo MacIntyre), *The Crystal Ball* (waiter at Stukov's), *The Great Lover* (attendant), etc. Was a well-regarded portrait painter. TV series: "My Friend Irma."

Sig Arno to Warren William in *Passport to Suez:* "I can bring you much information, for which you will pay me many shillings."

Films

As Siegfried Arno:
Schicksal (Ger, 1923)
Frau Von 40 Jahren (Ger, 1924)
Der Sohn der Hannibal (Ger, 1925)
Manon Lescaut (Ger, 1926)
Schatz mach' Kasse (Ger, 1926)
Der Panzergewolbe (Ger, 1926)
Bigoudis (Ger, 1927)
Moral (Ger, 1927)
Die Liebe der Jeanne Ney (Ger, 1927)
Beef and Steak (Ger, 1927)
Leise Flehen Meine Leider (Ger, 1928)
Sigi, der Matrose (Ger, 1928)
Der Schoenste Mann in Staate (Ger, 1928)
Un Eine Nasenlaenge (Ger, 1928)
Trgodie im Zirkus Royal (Ger, 1928)
G'schicten aus dem Wienerwald (Ger, 1928)
Rutschbahn (Ger, 1928)
Moderne Piraten (Ger, 1928)
Aufruhr im Junggesellenheim (Ger, 1929)

Die Buchse der Pandora (Ger, 1929)
Ihr Dunkler Punkt (Ger, 1929)
Das Tagebuch einer Verlorenen (Ger, 1929)
Wir Halten Fest und Treu Zusamen (Ger, 1929)
Wien Du Stadt der Lieder (Ger, 1930)
Die vom Rummelplatz (Ger, 1930)
Im Kampf mit der Unterwelt (Ger, 1930)
Heute Nacht-Eventuell (Ger, 1930)
Schritzenfest im Schilda (Ger, 1931)
Eine Freundin so Goldig Wie Due (Ger, 1931)
Der Schoenste Mann im Staate (Ger, 1931)
Das Geheimmer der Roten Katze (Ger, 1931)
Schactmatt (Ger, 1931)
Die Nacht ohne Pause (Ger, 1931)
Um Eine Nasenlange (Ger, 1931)
Der Storch Streikt (Ger, 1931)
Ein Ausgekochter Junge (Ger, 1931)
Schubert's Freuhlingstraum (Ger, 1931)
Keine Feier Ohne Meyer (Ger, 1931)

Moritz Macht Sein Glueck (Ger, 1931)
Die Grosse Attraktion (Ger, 1931)
Zapfenstreich am Rhein (Ger, 1933)

As Sig Arno:
The Star Maker (Par, 1939)
Bridal Suite (MGM, 1939)
The Great Dictator (UA, 1940)
The Mummy's Hand (Univ, 1940)
Diamond Frontier (Univ, 1940)
Dark Streets of Cairo (Univ, 1940)
A Little Bit of Heaven (Univ, 1940)
This Thing Called Love (Col, 1941)
New Wine [a.k.a. *Melody Master*] (UA, 1941)
It Started with Eve (Univ, 1941)
Two Latins from Manhattan (Col, 1941)
Gambling Daughters (PRC, 1941)
Two Yanks in Trinidad (Col, 1942)
Pardon My Sarong (Univ, 1942)
Tales of Manhattan (20th, 1942)
Juke Box Jenny (Univ, 1942)

The Palm Beach Story (Par, 1942)
The Devil with Hitler (UA, 1942)
The Crystal Ball (UA, 1943)
Larceny with Music (Univ, 1943)
Taxi, Mister (UA, 1943)
Passport to Suez (Col, 1943)
Let's Have Fun (Col, 1943)
His Butler's Sister (Univ, 1943)
Up in Arms (RKO, 1944)

Once upon a Time (Col, 1944)
Song of the Open Road (UA, 1944)
Standing Room Only (Par, 1944)
Bring on the Girls (Par, 1945)
Roughly Speaking (WB, 1945)
A Song to Remember (Col, 1945)
One More Tomorrow (WB, 1946)
The Great Lover (Par, 1949)
Holiday in Havana (Col, 1949)

Nancy Goes to Rio (MGM, 1950)
The Duchess of Idaho (MGM, 1950)
The Toast of New Orleans (MGM, 1950)
On Moonlight Bay (WB, 1951)
Diplomatic Courier (20th, 1952)
Fast Company (MGM, 1953)
The Great Diamond Robbery (MGM, 1953)

EDWARD ARNOLD
(Guenther Schneider)

With Frances Rafferty in The Hidden Eye *(1945).*

Born February 18, 1890, New York City, New York. Married 1) Harriet Marshall (1917), children: Elizabeth, Jane, William; divorced (1927); 2) Olive Emerson (1929); divorced (1948); 3) Cleo McClain (1951). Died April 26, 1956, Encino, California. Characterized by a conspiratorial twinkle in his eye, a portly frame often shaking with laughter, and a convivial lilt to his voice. Generally (type)cast as a grasping tycoon, a sinister businessman, or a crooked politician. Could give credence to a wide variety of roles, often adding sympathetic overtones to a stock assignment. Frequently played historical roles in the Thirties (King Louis XIII in *Cardinal Richelieu*). Could be earnest as a celluloid sleuth (*Meet Nero Wolfe*) or very hammy (*Roman Scandals*) or the devious manipulator (*Annie Get Your Gun*). Perfected his doubletake and eyeroll for put-upon-father roles (*Janie*). TV series: "Edward Arnold Theatre" and "Strange Stories."

Edward Arnold to George Bancroft in *John Meade's Woman*:
"I'm an expert at getting even with people."

Films

The Slacker's Heart (Emerald, 1917)
Phil-for-Short (World, 1919)
A Broadway Saint (World, 1919)

The Cost (Par, 1920)
Three on a Match (WB, 1932)
Rasputin and the Empress (MGM, 1932)

Afraid to Talk (Univ, 1932)
Okay, America (Univ, 1932)
Whistling in the Dark (MGM, 1933)

The White Sister (MGM, 1933)
Jennie Gerhardt (Par, 1933)
Her Bodyguard (Par, 1933)
I'm No Angel (Par, 1933)
The Barbarian (MGM, 1933)
Secret of the Blue Room (Univ, 1933)
Roman Scandals (UA, 1933)
Madame Spy (Univ, 1934)
Million Dollar Ransom (Univ, 1934)
Thirty-Day Princess (Par, 1934)
The President Vanishes (Par, 1934)
Unknown Blonde (Majestic, 1934)
Wednesday's Child (RKO, 1934)
Sadie McKee (MGM, 1934)
Hide-Out (MGM, 1934)
Biography of a Bachelor Girl (MGM, 1935)
Diamond Jim (Univ, 1935)
Cardinal Richelieu (UA, 1935)
The Glass Key (Par, 1935)
Remember Last Night? (Univ, 1935)
Crime and Punishment (Col, 1935)
Sutter's Gold (Univ, 1936)
Meet Nero Wolfe (Col, 1936)
Come and Get It (UA, 1936)
John Meade's Woman (Par, 1937)
Easy Living (Par, 1937)
Blossoms on Broadway (Par, 1937)
The Toast of New York (RKO, 1937)
The Crowd Roars (MGM, 1938)
You Can't Take It with You (Col, 1938)

Idiot's Delight (MGM, 1939)
Man About Town (Par, 1939)
Mr. Smith Goes to Washington (Col, 1939)
Let Freedom Ring (MGM, 1939)
Slightly Honorable (UA, 1939)
The Earl of Chicago (MGM, 1940)
Johnny Apollo (20th, 1940)
Lillian Russell (20th, 1940)
Meet John Doe (WB, 1941)
The Penalty (MGM, 1941)
The Lady from Cheyenne (Univ, 1941)
Nothing but the Truth (Par, 1941)
Unholy Partners (MGM, 1941)
Design for Scandal (MGM, 1941)
Johnny Eager (MGM, 1941)
All That Money Can Buy [a.k.a. *The Devil and Daniel Webster*] (RKO, 1941)
The War Against Mrs. Hadley (MGM, 1942)
Eyes in the Night (MGM, 1942)
The Youngest Profession (MGM, 1943)
Kismet [TV title: *Oriental Dream*] (MGM, 1944)
Janie (WB, 1944)
Standing Room Only (Par, 1944)
Mrs. Parkington (MGM, 1944)
Main Street After Dark (MGM, 1945)
Weekend at the Waldorf (MGM, 1945)
The Hidden Eye (MGM, 1945)
Three Wise Fools (MGM, 1946)

Janie Gets Married (WB, 1946)
The Mighty McGurk (MGM, 1946)
No Leave, No Love (MGM, 1946)
Ziegfeld Follies (MGM, 1946)
My Brother Talks to Horses (MGM, 1946)
Dear Ruth (Par, 1947)
The Hucksters (MGM, 1947)
Big City (MGM, 1948)
Three Daring Daughters (MGM, 1948)
Wallflower (WB, 1948)
John Loves Mary (WB, 1949)
Command Decision (MGM, 1948)
Take Me out to the Ball Game (MGM, 1949)
Dear Wife (Par, 1949)
Big Jack (MGM, 1949)
The Yellow Cab Man (MGM, 1950)
The Skipper Surprised His Wife (MGM, 1950)
Annie Get Your Gun (MGM, 1950)
Dear Brat (Par, 1951)
Belles on Their Toes (20th, 1952)
City That Never Sleeps (Rep, 1953)
Man of Conflict (Atlas, 1953)
Living It Up (Par, 1954)
The Ambassador's Daughter (UA, 1956)
The Houston Story (Col, 1956)
Miami Exposé (Col, 1956)

ROSCOE ATES

Roscoe Ates (left) and Preston Foster (right) in The People's Enemy *(1935).*

Born January 20, 1895, Grange, Missouri. Married 1) Clara Callahan; 2) Lenore Belle Jumps (1949); widowed (1955); 3) Beatrice Heisser (1960). Died March 1, 1962, Hollywood, California. Remarkable scene-stealer, whose stutter, pop-eyes, bobbing Adam's apple, and facial contortions won him long-lasting audience recognition. Cast as Soapy, the sidekick of Eddie Dean, in PRC and Eagle Lion Westerns.

Roscoe Ates to Polly Moran in *Politics:* "What's my p-pants doing wrapped around your b–b–bird cage?"

Films

South Sea Rose (Fox, 1929)
Reducing (MGM, 1930)
Caught Short (MGM, 1930)
The Big House (MGM, 1930)
The Lone Star Ranger (Fox, 1930)
City Girl (Fox, 1930)
Billy the Kid [TV title: *The Highwayman Rides*] (MGM, 1930)
Love in the Rough (MGM, 1930)
The Great Lover (MGM, 1931)
Cracked Nuts (RKO, 1931)
The Champ (MGM, 1931)
A Free Soul (MGM, 1931)
Cimarron (RKO, 1931)
Politics (MGM, 1931)
Too Many Cooks (RKO, 1931)
The Big Shot (RKO, 1931)
Freaks (MGM, 1932)
Ladies of the Jury (RKO, 1932)
The Rainbow Trail (Fox, 1932)
Young Bride [a.k.a. *Love Starved*] (RKO, 1932)

Roadhouse Murder (RKO, 1932)
Hold 'em, Jail! (RKO, 1932)
Come On, Danger (RKO, 1932)
Renegades of the West (RKO, 1933)
The Past of Mary Holmes (RKO, 1933)
Cheyenne Kid (RKO, 1933)
Golden Harvest (Par, 1933)
Alice in Wonderland (Par, 1933)
What! No Beer? (MGM, 1933)
Lucky Devils (RKO, 1933)
The Scarlet River (RKO, 1933)
She Made Her Bed (Par, 1934)
Merry Wives of Reno (WB, 1934)
Woman in the Dark (RKO, 1934)
The People's Enemy (RKO, 1935)
God's Country and the Woman (FN, 1936)
Riders of the Black Hills (Rep, 1938)
The Great Adventures of Wild Bill Hickok (Col serial, 1938)
Gone with the Wind (MGM, 1939)
Three Texas Steers (Rep, 1939)
Rancho Grande (Rep, 1940)

Cowboy from Sundown (Mon, 1940)
Untamed (Par, 1940)
Captain Caution (UA, 1940)
I Want a Divorce (Par, 1940)
Chad Hanna (20th, 1940)
Mountain Moonlight (Rep, 1941)
Birth of the Blues (Par, 1941)
She Knew All the Answers (Col, 1941)
Sullivan's Travels (Par, 1941)
I'll Sell My Life (Select, 1941)
Robin Hood of the Pecos (Rep, 1941)
Bad Men of Missouri (WB, 1941)
Reg'lar Fellers (PRC, 1941)
One Foot in Heaven (WB, 1941)
The Affairs of Jimmy Valentine (Rep, 1942)
The Palm Beach Story (Par, 1942)
Can't Help Singing (Univ, 1944)
Colorado Serenade (PRC, 1946)
Down Missouri Way (PRC, 1946)
Driftin' River (PRC, 1946)
Stars over Texas (PRC, 1946)

Tumbleweed Trail (PRC, 1946)
Wild West (PRC, 1946)
Wild Country (PRC, 1947)
West to Glory (PRC, 1947)
Range Beyond the Blue (PRC, 1947)
Shadow Valley (EL, 1947)
Inner Sanctum (Film Classics, 1948)
Black Hills (EL, 1948)
The Westward Trail, (EL, 1948)
The Hawk of Powder River (EL, 1948)
The Tioga Kid (EL, 1948)
Tornado Range (EL, 1948)

Thunder in the Pines (Screen Guild, 1948)
Check Your Guns (EL, 1948)
Prairie Outlaws (EL, 1948)
The Hills of Oklahoma (Rep, 1950)
Father's Wild Game (Mon, 1950)
Honeychile (Rep, 1951)
The Blazing Forest (Par, 1952)
Those Redheads from Seattle (Par, 1953)
The Stranger Wore a Gun (Col, 1953)
Abbott and Costello Meet the Keystone Kops (Univ, 1955)

Lucy Gallant (Par, 1955)
Come Next Spring (Rep, 1956)
The Birds and the Bees (Par, 1956)
The Kettles in the Ozarks (Univ, 1956)
Meet Me in Las Vegas (MGM, 1956)
Run of the Arrow (Univ, 1957)
The Big Caper (UA, 1957)
Short Cut to Hell (Par, 1957)
The Sheepman (MGM, 1958)
The Silent Call (20th, 1961)
The Errand Boy (Par, 1961)

LIONEL ATWILL

George J. Lewis and Lionel Atwill in the serial Captain America *(1944).*

Born March 1, 1885, Croydon, England. Married 1) Phyllis Ralph (1917); divorced (1919); 2) Elsie Mackay (1919), child: John; divorced (1928); 3) Louise Stoltesbury (1930); divorced (1943); 4) Mary Shelstone (1944), child: Lionel. Died April 22, 1946, Pacific Palisades, California. One of the most efficient Hollywood Hissables. His solid (some insisted stolid) villains became a staple of 1930s films: *Doctor X* (berserk scientist), *The Mystery of the Wax Museum* (Ivan Igor), etc. Bewitched by femme fatale Marlene Dietrich (*The Song of Songs, The Devil Is a Woman*). Made an appropriate De Rochefort in the Ritz Brothers' *The Three Musketeers*. Was efficient as assorted Germanic types in Universal's later *Frankenstein* series. Ended his career performing overzealous Third Reich fanatics in action serials: *Junior G-Men of the Air* (the Baron), *Lost City of the Jungle* (Sir Eric Hazarias), etc.

Lionel Atwill to Basil Rathbone in *Son of Frankenstein:* "One doesn't easily forget, Herr Baron, an arm torn out by the roots."

Films

Eve's Daughter (Par, 1918)
For Sale (Pathé, 1918)
The Marriage Price (Par, 1919)
The Highest Bidder (G, 1921)
Indiscretion (Pioneer, 1921)
Silent Witness (Fox, 1932)
Doctor X (FN, 1932)
The Vampire Bat (Majestic, 1933)
Secret of Madame Blanche (MGM, 1933)
The Mystery of the Wax Museum (WB, 1933)
Murders in the Zoo (Par, 1933)
The Sphinx (Mon, 1933)
The Song of Songs (Par, 1933)
Solitaire Man (MGM, 1933)
The Secret of the Blue Room (Univ, 1933)
Beggars in Ermine (Mon, 1934)
Nana (UA, 1934)
Stamboul Quest (MGM, 1934)
One More River (Univ, 1934)
Age of Innocence (RKO, 1934)
The Firebird (WB, 1934)
The Man Who Reclaimed His Head (Univ, 1934)
Mark of the Vampire (MGM, 1935)
The Devil Is a Woman (Par, 1935)
Murder Man (MGM, 1935)
Rendezvous (MGM, 1935)

Captain Blood (FN, 1935)
Lady of Secrets (Col, 1936)
Absolute Quiet (MGM, 1936)
Till We Meet Again (Par, 1936)
The High Command (Br, 1937)
The Road Back (Univ, 1937)
The Last Train from Madrid (Par, 1937)
Lancer Spy (20th, 1937)
The Wrong Road (Rep, 1937)
The Great Garrick (WB, 1937)
Three Comrades (MGM, 1938)
The Great Waltz (MGM, 1938)
Son of Frankenstein (Univ, 1939)
The Three Musketeers (20th, 1939)
The Hound of the Baskervilles (20th, 1939)
The Mad Empress (WB, 1939)
The Gorilla (20th, 1939)
The Sun Never Sets (Univ, 1939)
Mr. Moto Takes a Vacation (20th, 1939)
The Secret of Dr. Kildare (MGM, 1939)
Balalaika (MGM, 1939)
Charlie Chan in Panama (20th, 1940)
Johnny Apollo (20th, 1940)
Charlie Chan's Murder Cruise (20th, 1940)
The Girl in 313 (20th, 1940)
Boom Town (MGM, 1940)
The Great Profile (20th, 1940)

Man-Made Monster (Univ, 1941)
Junior G-Men of the Air (Univ serial, 1942)
The Ghost of Frankenstein (Univ, 1942)
To Be or Not to Be (UA, 1942)
The Strange Case of Doctor Rx (Univ, 1942)
Pardon My Sarong (Univ, 1942)
Cairo (MGM, 1942)
Night Monster (Univ, 1942)
Sherlock Holmes and the Secret Weapon (Univ, 1942)
The Mad Doctor of Market Street (Univ, 1942)
Frankenstein Meets the Wolf Man (Univ, 1943)
Captain America (Rep serial, 1944)
Lady in the Death House (PRC, 1944)
Raiders of Ghost City (Univ serial, 1944)
Secrets of Scotland Yard (Rep, 1944)
House of Frankenstein (Univ, 1945)
Fog Island (PRC, 1945)
Crime, Inc. (PRC, 1945)
House of Dracula (Univ, 1945)
Genius at Work (RKO, 1946)
Lost City of the Jungle (Univ serial, 1946)

MISCHA AUER
(Mischa Ounskowsky)

With Martha Mattox in The Monster Walks *(1932).*

Born November 17, 1905, St. Petersburg, Russia. Married 1) Norma Tillman (1931), children: Anthony, Zoe; divorced (1940); 2) Joyce Hunter (1941); divorced (1950); 3) Susanne Kalish (1950), child: daughter; divorced; 4) Elise Souls (1965). Died March 5, 1967, Rome, Italy. Beanpole thin Soviet who migrated to the Broadway stage and then to the West Coast. Interpretation of parasitic, frenetic Carlo in *My Man Godfrey* won him Oscar nomination. (Lost BSAAA to Walter Brennan of *Come and Get It.*)Established as leading interpreter of English-mangling, self-indulgent eccentric *(You Can't Take It with You, Destry Rides Again)*. Virtuoso madcaps wore thin in the 1940s. Found professional refuge in European-made features: Orson Welles' *Mr. Arkadin*, etc.

Mischa Auer in *My Man Godfrey:* "Oh, money—money—money! It's the Frankenstein monster that destroys souls."

Films

Something Always Happens (Par, 1928)
Marquis Preferred (Par, 1929)
The Studio Murder Mystery (Par, 1929)
The Mighty (Par, 1929)
The Benson Murder Case (Par, 1930)
Paramount on Parade (Par, 1930)
Inside the Lines (RKO, 1930)
Just Imagine (Fox, 1930)
No Limit (Par, 1931)
The Unholy Garden (UA, 1931)
Delicious (Fox, 1931)
The Yellow Ticket (Fox, 1931)
Command Performance (Tif, 1931)
Drums of Jeopardy (Tif, 1931)
Women Love Once (Par, 1931)

The Lady from Nowhere (Chesterfield, 1931)
The Midnight Patrol (Mon, 1932)
Arsene Lupin (MGM, 1932)
Call Her Savage (Fox, 1932)
Rasputin and the Empress (MGM, 1932)
Sinister Hands (Willis Kent, 1932)
Drifting Souls (Tower, 1932)
The Monster Walks (Mayfair, 1932)
Beauty Parlor (Chesterfield, 1932)
Murder at Dawn (Big Four, 1932)
No Greater Love (Col, 1932)
Scarlet Dawn (WB, 1932)
The Unwritten Law (Majestic, 1932)
Western Code (Col, 1932)

The Intruder (Allied, 1932)
The Infernal Machine (Fox, 1933)
Sucker Money (Hollywood, 1933)
Corruption (Imperial, 1933)
Tarzan the Fearless (Principal serial, 1933)
After Tonight (RKO, 1933)
The Cradle Song (Par, 1933)
Girl Without a Room (Par, 1933)
Dangerously Yours (Fox, 1933)
The Flaming Signal (Invincible, 1933)
The Crosby Case (Univ, 1934)
Student Tour (MGM, 1934)
Viva Villa! (MGM, 1934)
Change of Heart (Fox, 1934)

Wharf Angel (Par, 1934)

Bulldog Drummond Strikes Back (UA, 1934)

Stamboul Quest (MGM, 1934)

Woman Condemned (Marcy Pictures, 1934)

Condemned to Live (Chesterfield, 1935)

Biography of a Bachelor Girl (MGM, 1935)

The Adventures of Rex and Rinty (Mascot serial, 1935)

The Lives of a Bengal Lancer (Par, 1935)

The Crusades (Par, 1935)

Clive of India (UA, 1935)

Mystery Woman (Fox, 1935)

Murder in the Fleet (MGM, 1935)

I Dream Too Much (RKO, 1935)

We're Only Human (RKO, 1936)

Here Comes Trouble (20th, 1936)

Tough Guy (MGM, 1936)

The House of a Thousand Candles (Rep, 1936)

One Rainy Afternoon (UA, 1936)

The Gay Desperado (UA, 1936)

Sons O' Guns (WB, 1936)

The Princess Comes Across (Par, 1936)

My Man Godfrey (Univ, 1936)

Winterset (RKO, 1936)

That Girl from Paris (RKO, 1936)

Three Smart Girls (Univ, 1937)

We Have Our Moments (Univ, 1937)

One Hundred Men and a Girl (Univ, 1937)

Top of the Town (Univ, 1937)

Merry-Go-Round of 1938 (Univ, 1937)

Prescription for Romance (Univ, 1937)

Pick a Star (MGM, 1937)

Marry the Girl (WB, 1937)

Vogues of 1938 (UA, 1937)

It's All Yours (Col, 1938)

The Rage of Paris (Univ, 1938)

Service de Luxe (Univ, 1938)

Little Tough Guys in Society (Univ, 1938)

Sweethearts (MGM, 1938)

You Can't Take It with You (Col, 1938)

East Side of Heaven (Univ, 1939)

Destry Rides Again (Univ, 1939)

Unexpected Father (Univ, 1939)

Alias the Deacon (Univ, 1940)

Sandy Is a Lady (Univ, 1940)

Margie (20th, 1940)

Spring Parade (Univ, 1940)

Seven Sinners (Univ, 1940)

Trail of the Vigilantes (Univ, 1940)

Public Deb No. 1 (20th, 1940)

Flame of New Orleans (Univ, 1941)

Cracked Nuts (Univ, 1941)

Hold That Ghost (Univ, 1941)

Sing Another Chorus (Univ, 1941)

Moonlight in Hawaii (Univ, 1941)

Hellzapoppin (Univ, 1941)

Don't Get Personal (Univ, 1942)

Twin Beds (UA, 1942)

Around the World (RKO, 1943)

Lady in the Dark (Par, 1944)

Up in Mabel's Room (UA, 1944)

A Royal Scandal (20th, 1945)

Brewster's Millions (UA, 1945)

And Then There Were None (20th, 1945)

Sentimental Journey (20th, 1946)

She Wrote the Book (Univ, 1946)

For You I Die (Film Classics, 1947)

Sofia (Film Classics, 1948)

Fame and the Devil (Fr, 1950)

The Sky Is Red (Fr, 1952)

Song of Paris [a.k.a. *Bachelor in Paris*] (Br, 1952)

Frou-Frou (Fr, 1955)

The Monte Carlo Story (UA, 1957)

Mam'zelle Pigalle [a.k.a. *Cette Sacree Gamine/That Naughty Girl*] (Fr, 1958)

The Foxiest Girl in Paris (Times Films, 1958)

Future Vedettes [a.k.a. *School for Love*] (Fr, 1959)

A Pied, a Cheval et un Sputnik [a.k.a. *A Dog, a Mouse and a Sputnik*] (Films Around the World, 1960)

Mr. Arkadin [a.k.a. *Confidential Report*] (Filmorsa, 1962)

We Joined the Navy (Br, 1962)

Ladies First (Fr, 1963)

Dynamite Girl (Fr, 1963)

The Christmas That Almost Wasn't (Childhood Productions, 1966)

Arrivederci, Baby (Par, 1966)

IRVING BACON

Sara Haden, Irving Bacon, Peggy Ann Garner, Lon McCallister, Dabbs Greer, Gene Reynolds, and Skip Homeier in The Big Cat (1949).

Born September 6, 1893, St. Joseph, Missouri. Married _____ , children: two sons, one daughter. Died February 5, 1965, Hollywood, California. Stage, screen, and TV performer employed by Mack Sennett in the 1910s before making feature film bow in 1927. Tall somber-faced type often seen as a bemused, rural dweller and/or an official who hid wisdom behind dour looks. Later cavorted as the Dagwood-plagued mailman in the *Blondie* series.

Irving Bacon to Charlie Ruggles in *Six of a Kind:* "I can give you a nice room with a bath."

Films

Anna Christie (Associated FN, 1923)
California or Bust (FBO, 1927)
The Goodbye Kiss (FN, 1928)
The Head Man (FN, 1928)
Three Sinners (Par, 1928)
Half Way to Heaven (Par, 1929)
Side Street (FBO, 1929)
The Saturday Night Kid (Par, 1929)
Two Sisters (Rayart, 1929)
Street of Chance (Par, 1930)
Alias the Bad Man (Tif, 1931)
Branded Men (Tif, 1931)
File No. 113 (Allied, 1932)
This Is the Night (Par, 1932)
Million Dollar Legs (Par, 1932)
No One Man (Par, 1932)
Union Depot (FN, 1932)
Central Park (FN, 1932)
The Match King (FN, 1932)
He Learned About Women (Par, 1933)
Hello, Everybody! (Par, 1933)
Private Detective 62 (WB, 1933)

Big Executive (Par, 1933)
Lone Cowboy (Par, 1933)
Miss Fane's Baby Is Stolen (Par, 1934)
Six of a Kind (Par, 1934)
It Happened One Night (Col, 1934)
The Hell Cat (Col, 1934)
No Ransom (Liberty, 1934)
Shadows of Sing Sing (Col, 1934)
You Belong to Me (Par, 1934)
Hat, Coat and Glove (RKO, 1934)
The Pursuit of Happiness (Par, 1934)
Ready for Love (Par, 1934)
Here Comes Cookie (Par, 1935)
Millions in the Air (Par, 1935)
West of the Pecos (RKO, 1935)
Powder Smoke Range (RKO, 1935)
Private Worlds (Par, 1935)
Goin' to Town (Par, 1935)
The Glass Key (Par, 1935)
The Virginia Judge (Par, 1935)
Ship Cafe (Par, 1935)
Two-Fisted (Par, 1935)

It's a Small World (Fox, 1935)
Diamond Jim (Univ, 1935)
Manhattan Moon (Univ, 1935)
Bright Lights (FN, 1935)
It's a Great Life (Par, 1935)
Love on a Bet (RKO, 1936)
Three Cheers for Love (Par, 1936)
Murder with Pictures (Par, 1936)
The Texas Rangers (Par, 1936)
Petticoat Fever (MGM, 1936)
Earthworm Tractors (FM, 1936)
Drift Fence (Par, 1936)
Hollywood Boulevard (Par, 1936)
Lady, Be Careful (Par, 1936)
Wives Never Know (Par, 1936)
Valiant Is the Word for Carrie (Par, 1936)
The Big Broadcast of 1937 (Par, 1936)
Hopalong Cassidy Returns (Par, 1936)
Let's Make a Million (Par, 1936)
Arizona Mahoney (Par, 1936)
It's Love I'm After (WB, 1937)
Internes Can't Take Money (Par, 1937)

Exclusive (Par, 1937)
Seventh Heaven (20th, 1937)
Big Town Girl (20th, 1937)
The Big City (MGM, 1937)
Marry the Girl (WB, 1937)
Midnight Intruder (Univ, 1938)
The Cowboy and the Lady (UA, 1938)
Professor Beware (Par, 1938)
You Can't Take It with You (Col, 1938)
Exposed (Univ, 1938)
The Big Broadcast of 1938 (Par, 1938)
The First Hundred Years (MGM, 1938)
The Texans (Par, 1938)
The Chaser (MGM, 1938)
Tip-Off Girls (Par, 1938)
The Arizona Wildcat (20th, 1938)
Sing, You Sinners (Par, 1938)
Spawn of the North (Par, 1938)
Kentucky Moonshine (20th, 1938)
There Goes My Heart (UA, 1938)
The Amazing Dr. Clitterhouse (WB,1938)
The Sisters (WB, 1938)
Too Busy to Work (20th, 1939)
The Adventures of Huckleberry Finn (MGM, 1939)
Tail Spin (20th, 1939)
The Gracie Allen Murder Case (Par, 1939)
Lucky Night (MGM, 1939)
Second Fiddle (20th, 1939)
Hollywood Cavalcade (20th, 1939)
Gone with the Wind (MGM, 1939)
I Stole a Million (Univ, 1939)
Blondie Takes a Vacation (Col, 1939)
Rio (Univ, 1939)
Blondie Brings Up Baby (Col, 1939)
The Oklahoma Kid (WB, 1939)
Torchy Runs for Mayor (WB, 1939)
Indianapolis Speedway (WB, 1939)
Heaven with a Barbed Wire Fence (20th, 1939)
The Man Who Wouldn't Talk (20th, 1940)
The Grapes of Wrath (20th, 1940)
Star Dust (20th, 1940)
You Can't Fool Your Wife (RKO, 1940)
The Story of Dr. Ehrlich's Magic Bullet (WB, 1940)
Young People (20th, 1940)
Blondie on a Budget (Col, 1940)
Manhattan Heartbeat (20th, 1940)
The Return of Frank James (20th, 1940)
Gold Rush Maisie (MGM, 1940)
The Howards of Virginia (Col, 1940)
Dreaming Out Load (RKO, 1940)
Blondie Has Servant Trouble (Col, 1940)

Michael Shayne, Private Detective (20th, 1940)
Blondie Plays Cupid (Col, 1940)
Meet John Doe (WB, 1941)
Great Guns (20th, 1941)
Henry Aldrich for President (Par, 1941)
Cadet Girl (20th, 1941)
A Girl, a Guy and a Gob (RKO, 1941)
Tobacco Road (20th, 1941)
Blondie Goes Latin (Col, 1941)
She Couldn't Say No (WB, 1941)
Western Union (20th, 1941)
Ride On, Vaquero (20th, 1941)
Caught in the Draft (Par, 1941)
Accent on Love (20th, 1941)
Too Many Blondes (Univ, 1941)
Moon over Her Shoulder (20th, 1941)
It Started with Eve (Univ, 1941)
Never Give a Sucker an Even Break (Univ, 1941)
Blondie in Society (Col, 1941)
Remember the Day (20th, 1941)
The Bashful Bachelor (RKO, 1942)
Through Different Eyes (20th, 1942)
Juke Girl (WB, 1942)
Young America (20th, 1942)
Pardon My Sarong (Univ, 1942)
Holiday Inn (Par, 1942)
Footlight Serenade (20th, 1942)
Give Out, Sisters (Univ, 1942)
Between Us Girls (Univ, 1942)
Get Hep to Love (Univ, 1942)
Blondie for Victory (Col, 1942)
The Amazing Mrs. Holliday (Univ, 1943)
The Desperados (Col, 1943)
A Stranger in Town (MGM, 1943)
Shadow of a Doubt (Univ, 1943)
Dixie Dugan (20th, 1943)
Johnny Come Lately (UA, 1943)
Hers to Hold (Univ, 1943)
Follow the Band (Univ, 1943)
King of the Cowboys (Rep, 1943)
Two Weeks to Live (RKO, 1943)
Happy Go Lucky (Par, 1943)
So's Your Uncle (Univ, 1943)
The Good Fellows (Par, 1943)
In Old Oklahoma (Rep, 1943)
Action in the North Atlantic (WB, 1943)
Weekend Pass (Univ, 1944)
Pin-Up Girl (20th, 1944)
Wing and a Prayer (20th, 1944)
Chip off the Old Block (Univ, 1944)
Her Primitive Man (Univ, 1944)
Since You Went Away (UA, 1944)
Heavenly Days (RKO, 1944)
Roughly Speaking (WB, 1945)

Patrick the Great (Univ, 1945)
Out of This World (Par, 1945)
Guest Wife (UA, 1945)
Under Western Skies (Univ, 1945)
Hitchhike to Happiness (Rep, 1945)
One Way to Love (Col, 1945)
Night Train to Memphis (Rep, 1946)
Wake Up and Dream (20th, 1946)
My Brother Talks to Horses (MGM, 1946)
Monsieur Verdoux (UA, 1947)
The Bachelor and the Bobby-Soxer (RKO, 1947)
Saddle Pals (Rep, 1947)
State of the Union (MGM, 1948)
Albuquerque (Par, 1948)
Moonrise (Rep, 1948)
The Velvet Touch (RKO, 1948)
Adventures in Silverado (Col, 1948)
Good Sam (RKO, 1948)
Rocky (Mon, 1948)
Family Honeymoon (Univ, 1948)
John Loves Mary (WB, 1949)
Dear Wife (Par, 1949)
The Green Promise (RKO, 1949)
Night unto Night (WB, 1949)
The Big Cat (EL, 1949)
Dynamite (Par, 1949)
It's a Great Feeling (WB, 1949)
Woman in Hiding (Univ, 1949)
Manhandled (Par, 1949)
Wabash Avenue (20th, 1950)
Born to Be Bad (RKO, 1950)
Emergency Wedding (Col, 1950)
Sons of New Mexico (Col, 1950)
Honeychile (Rep, 1951)
Cause for Alarm (MGM, 1951)
Katie Did It (Univ, 1951)
Desert of Lost Men (Rep, 1951)
Room for One More (WB, 1952)
O'Henry's Full House (20th, 1952)
Devil's Canyon (RKO, 1953)
Kansas Pacific (UA, 1953)
Sweethearts on Parade (Rep, 1953)
Fort Ti (Col, 1953)
Ma and Pa Kettle at Home (Univ, 1954)
Black Horse Canyon (Univ, 1954)
The Glenn Miller Story (Univ, 1954)
Duffy of San Quentin (WB, 1954)
A Star Is Born (WB, 1954)
Run for Cover (Par, 1955)
At Gunpoint (AA, 1955)
Hidden Guns (Rep, 1956)
Dakota Incident (Rep, 1956)
Ambush at Cimarron Pass (20th, 1958)
Fort Massacre (UA, 1958)

FAY BAINTER

With Lionel Barrymore in This Side of Heaven *(1934).*

Born December 7, 1892, Los Angeles, California. Married Reginald Venable (1922), child: Reginald. Died April 16, 1968, Los Angeles, California. Popular Broadway star who enhanced her every film. Won a BSAAA for Aunt Belle in Bette Davis' *Jezebel*. (Same year was nominated as Best Actress for the housekeeper of *White Banners*, but lost Oscar to Miss Davis.) An intelligent interpreter of motherly types, bolstered by her sensitive, darting eyes and ingratiating husky voice. Oscar-nominated again for her final screen role: the troublemaker's grandmother in *The Children's Hour* (lost BSAAA to Patty Duke of *The Miracle Worker*).

> **Fay Bainter** to Donald Crisp (regarding Bette Davis) in *Jezebel:* "I love her most when she's the meanest, 'cause that's when I know she's lovin' the most."

Films

This Side of Heaven (MGM, 1934)
Quality Street (RKO, 1937)
The Soldier and the Lady [a.k.a. Michael Strogoff] (RKO, 1937)
Make Way for Tomorrow (Par, 1937)
Jezebel (WB, 1938)
White Banners (WB, 1938)
Mother Carey's Chickens (RKO, 1938)
The Arkansas Traveler (Par, 1938)
The Shining Hour (MGM, 1938)
Yes, My Darling Daughter (WB, 1939)
The Lady and the Mob (Col, 1939)
Daughters Courageous (WB, 1939)
Our Neighbors the Carters (Par, 1939)
Young Tom Edison (MGM, 1940)

A Bill of Divorcement (RKO, 1940)
Our Town (UA, 1940)
Maryland (20th, 1940)
Babes on Broadway (MGM, 1941)
Woman of the Year (MGM, 1942)
The War Against Mrs. Hadley (MGM, 1942)
Mrs. Wiggs of the Cabbage Patch (Par, 1942)
Journey for Margaret (MGM, 1942)
The Human Comedy (MGM, 1943)
Presenting Lily Mars (MGM, 1943)
Salute to the Marines (MGM, 1943)
Cry Havoc (MGM, 1943)
The Heavenly Body (MGM, 1943)

Dark Waters (UA, 1944)
Three Is a Family (UA, 1944)
State Fair (20th, 1945)
The Kid from Brooklyn (RKO, 1946)
The Virginian (Par, 1946)
Deep Valley (WB, 1947)
The Secret Life of Walter Mitty (RKO, 1947)
Give My Regards to Broadway (20th, 1948)
June Bride (WB, 1948)
Close to My Heart (WB, 1951)
The President's Lady (20th, 1953)
The Children's Hour (UA, 1961)

MARTIN BALSAM

Martin Balsam and Victor Mature in After the Fox *(1966).*

Born November 4, 1919, New York City, New York. Married 1) Pearl Somner (1952); divorced (1954); 2) Joyce Van Patten (1959), child: Talia; divorced (1962); 3) Irene Miller (1963), children: son, daughter. Respected stage/screen/TV player. Early features found him the plodding **do-gooder**: reporter Mack Kelley *(Al Capone)*, political underling *(Ada)*, etc. Audiences jumped when he was stabbed on the staircase in *Psycho*. Won a BSAAA as the establishment-bound brother of unconventional Jason Robards in *A Thousand Clowns*. Eschewed typecasting in the 1970s: *The Anderson Tapes* (the homosexual robbery accomplice), *The Stone Killer* (Vescari, the vengeful Mafia boss), *Summer Wishes, Winter Dreams* (Joanne Woodward's fulfillment-seeking spouse), *All the President's Men* (the hard-hitting newspaper executive).

Martin Balsam to Carroll Baker in *Harlow*: "Try to stay the same unspoiled movie star you always were."

Films

On the Waterfront (Col, 1954)
Twelve Angry Men (UA, 1957)
Time Limit (UA, 1957)
Marjorie Morningstar (WB, 1958)
Middle of the Night (Col, 1959)
Al Capone (AA, 1959)
Psycho (Par, 1960)
Ada (MGM, 1961)
Breakfast at Tiffany's (Par, 1961)
Cape Fear (Univ, 1962)
Everybody Go Home! (Davis-Royal, 1962)
Who's Been Sleeping in My Bed? (Par, 1963)

Seven Days in May (Par, 1964)
The Carpetbaggers (Par, 1964)
Harlow (Par, 1965)
The Bedford Incident (Col, 1965)
Conquered City (It, 1965)
A Thousand Clowns (UA, 1965)
After the Fox (UA, 1966)
Hombre (20th, 1967)
Me, Natalie (National General, 1969)
The Good Guys and the Bad Guys (WB-7 Arts, 1969)
Tora! Tora! Tora! (20th, 1970)
The Anderson Tapes (Col, 1971)
The Man (Par, 1972)

The Stone Killer (Col, 1973)
Summer Wishes, Winter Dreams (Col, 1973)
Counselor at Crime (It, 1973)
The Taking of Pelham One Two Three (UA, 1974)
Murder on the Orient Express (Par, 1974)
Confessions of a Police Captain (It, 1974)
Mitchell (AA, 1975)
All the President's Men (WB, 1976)
Shadow of a Killer (It, 1977)
The Sentinel (Univ, 1977)
Death Rage (It, 1977)
Silver Bears (Col, 1977)

GEORGE BANCROFT

George Bancroft and Harry Allen in Rich Man's Folly *(1931).*

Born September 30, 1882, Philadelphia, Pennsylvania. Married 1) Edna Brothers; divorced; 2) Octavia Brooke, child: one. Died October 2, 1956, Santa Monica, California. Rugged Broadway performer who gained top screen recognition in a quartet of Josef von Sternberg gangster melodramas in late 1920s: *Underworld, The Docks of New York, The Dragnet*, and *Thunderbolt* (for which he was Oscar-nominated; lost to Warner Baxter of *In Old Arizona*). As major Paramount star played determined roughnecks: Joe Froziati in *Ladies Love Brutes*, Bolshevik sailor Kylenko in *The World and the Flesh*, etc. When new breed of tough stars came along in early 1930s, popularity waned; free-lanced mostly in crime melodramas, usually in modified second-string Wallace Beery manner. Was Curley Wilcox, guarding the passengers in John Ford's *Stagecoach*; Mickey Rooney's dad in *Young Tom Edison*, etc.

> **George Bancroft** to Jack Oakie in *Little Men:* "I won't lose his love and respect, not even if I have to *steal* the money to prove that I'm honest."

Films

Journey's End (Hodkinson, 1921)
The Prodigal Judge (Vit, 1922)
Driven (Univ, 1923)
The Deadwood Coach (Fox, 1924)
Teeth (Fox, 1924)
Code of the West (Par, 1925)
The Rainbow Trail (Fox, 1925)
The Pony Express (Par, 1925)
The Splendid Road (FN, 1925)
The Enchanted Hill (Par, 1926)
Sea Horses (Par, 1926)
Old Ironsides (Par, 1926)
The Runaway (Par, 1926)
White Gold (PDC, 1927)
The Rough Riders (Par, 1927)
Too Many Crooks (Par, 1927)
Underworld (Par, 1927)
Tell It to Sweeney (Par, 1927)

The Docks of New York (Par, 1928)
Showdown (Par, 1928)
The Dragnet (Par, 1928)
The Wolf of Wall Street (Par, 1929)
Thunderbolt (Par, 1929)
The Mighty (Par, 1929)
Ladies Love Brutes (Par, 1930)
Derelict (Par, 1930)
Paramount on Parade (Par, 1930)
Scandal Sheet (Par, 1931)
Rich Man's Folly (Par, 1931)
The World and the Flesh (Par, 1932)
Lady and Gent (Par, 1932)
Blood Money (UA, 1933)
Elmer and Elsie (Par, 1934)
Hell-Ship Morgan (Col, 1936)
Mr. Deeds Goes to Town (Col, 1936)
Wedding Present (Par, 1936)

John Meade's Woman (Par, 1937)
Racketeers in Exile (Col, 1937)
A Doctor's Diary (Par, 1937)
Submarine Patrol (20th, 1938)
Angels with Dirty Faces (WB, 1938)
Each Dawn I Die (WB, 1939)
Espionage Agent (WB, 1939)
Rulers of the Sea (Par, 1939)
Stagecoach (UA, 1939)
Green Hell (Univ, 1940)
Young Tom Edison (MGM, 1940)
When the Daltons Rode (Univ, 1940)
North West Mounted Police (Par, 1940)
Little Men (RKO, 1940)
Texas (Col, 1941)
The Bugle Sounds (MGM, 1941)
Syncopation (RKO, 1942)
Whistling in Dixie (MGM, 1942)

GEORGE BARBIER

In News Is Made at Night *(1939).*

Born February 27, 1862, Philadelphia, Pennsylvania. Died July 19, 1945, Hollywood, California. Portly, well-settled individual competent in boastful, cranky, but basically good-hearted parts.

George Barbier to Eleanor Holm in *Tarzan's Revenge:* "Yes, sir, I'm going to take back to Evansville a bunch of rare animals that'll make the New York zoo look like a hicksville proposition."

Films

Monsieur Beaucaire (Par, 1924)
The Big Pond (Par, 1930)
The Sap from Syracuse (Par, 1930)
The Smiling Lieutenant (Par, 1931)
24 Hours (Par, 1931)
Girls About Town (Par, 1931)
Touchdown (Par, 1931)
One Hour with You (Par, 1932)
No One Man (Par, 1932)
Strangers in Love (Par, 1932)
The Broken Wing (Par, 1932)
The Strange Case of Clara Deane (Par, 1932)
Million Dollar Legs (Par, 1932)
Skyscraper Souls (Par, 1932)
The Big Broadcast (Par, 1932)
The Phantom President (Par, 1932)
Evenings for Sale (Par, 1932)

No Man of Her Own (Par, 1932)
Madame Racketeer (Par, 1932)
Hello, Everybody! (Par, 1933)
Mama Loves Papa (Par, 1933)
Sunset Pass (Par, 1933)
Under the Tonto Rim (Par, 1933)
This Day and Age (Par, 1933)
Turn Back the Clock (MGM, 1933)
A Lady's Profession (Par, 1933)
Love, Honor and Oh, Baby! (Univ, 1933)
Tillie and Gus (Par, 1933)
Miss Fane's Baby Is Stolen (Par, 1934)
The Notorious Sophie Lang (Par, 1934)
Journal of a Crime (FN, 1934)
The Merry Widow (MGM, 1934)
Elmer and Elsie (Par, 1934)
She Loves Me Not (Par, 1934)
The Cat's Paw (Fox, 1934)

Ladies Should Listen (Par, 1934)
College Rhythm (Par, 1934)
Many Happy Returns (Par, 1934)
Life Begins at Forty (Fox, 1935)
McFadden's Flats (Par, 1935)
Hold 'em, Yale! (Par, 1935)
Broadway Gondolier (WB, 1935)
Old Man Rhythm (RKO, 1935)
The Crusades (Par, 1935)
Here Comes Cookie (Par, 1935)
Millions in the Air (Par, 1935)
Wife vs. Secretary (MGM, 1936)
The Milky Way (Par, 1936)
The Preview Murder Mystery (Par, 1936)
The Princess Comes Across (Par, 1936)
Early to Bed (Par, 1936)
Three Married Men (Par, 1936)
Spendthrift (Par, 1936)

On the Avenue (20th, 1937)
Waikiki Wedding (Par, 1937)
Hotel Haywire (Par, 1937)
It's Love I'm After (FN, 1937)
A Girl with Ideas (Univ, 1937)
The Adventures of Marco Polo (UA, 1938)
Tarzan's Revenge (20th, 1938)
Hold That Kiss (MGM, 1938)
Little Miss Broadway (20th, 1938)
My Lucky Star (20th, 1938)
Sweethearts (MGM, 1938)
Thanks for Everything (20th, 1938)

Hold that Co-ed (20th, 1938)
Straight, Place, and Show (20th, 1938)
Wife, Husband, and Friend (20th, 1939)
S.O.S. Tidal Wave (Rep, 1939)
News Is Made at Night (20th, 1939)
Smuggled Cargo (Rep, 1939)
Remember? (MGM, 1939)
Village Barn Dance (Rep, 1940)
The Return of Frank James (20th, 1940)
Weekend in Havana (20th, 1941)
Marry the Boss's Daughter (20th, 1941)
Million Dollar Baby (WB, 1941)

Repent at Leisure (RKO, 1941)
The Man Who Came to Dinner (WB, 1941)
Song of the Islands (20th, 1942)
Yankee Doodle Dandy (WB, 1942)
The Magnificent Dope (Fox, 1942)
Thunder Birds (20th, 1942)
Hello, Frisco, Hello (20th, 1943)
Weekend Pass (Univ, 1944)
Blonde Ransom (Univ, 1945)
Her Lucky Night (Univ, 1945)

ROY BARCROFT
(Howard Clifford Kavenscroft)

Robert Livingston, Roy Rogers, and Roy Barcroft in Grand Canyon Trail (1948).

Born September 7, 1902, Weeping Water, Texas. Married 1) _____, children: one son, one daughter; divorced (1930); 2) Vera Thompson (1932), child: Michael. Died November 28, 1969. Undoubtedly the king of Western villains. The beefy actor spent some two decades harassing Western leads and serial heroes at Republic Pictures. Whether playing the title role in the cliff-hanger *The Purple Monster Strikes* or menacing law enforcers on the range, he brought tremendous enthusiasm to his array of heavies.

Roy Barcroft to Eugene Roth in *Ghost of Zorro*: "The jobs being handled by some eastern dude named Ken Mason. He'll be easy pickin's."

Films

Mata Hari (MGM, 1931)

A Woman Commands (RKO, 1932)

Join the Marines (Rep, 1937)

Dick Tracy (Rep serial, 1937)

Night Key (Univ, 1937)

S.O.S. Coast Guard (Rep serial, 1937)

Rosalie (MGM, 1937)

Heroes of the Hills (Rep, 1938)

The Crowd Roars (MGM, 1938)

Blondes at Work (WB, 1938)

Stranger from Arizona (Col, 1938)

The Frontiersman (Par, 1938)

Flaming Frontiers (Univ serial, 1938)

Silver on the Sage (Par, 1939)

Mexicali Rose (Rep, 1939)

Renegade Trail (Par, 1939)

Yukon Flight (Mon, 1939)

Crashing Thru (Mon, 1939)

They All Come Out (MGM, 1939)

The Phantom Creeps (Univ serial, 1939)

Daredevils of the Red Circle (Rep serial, 1939)

Another Thin Man (MGM, 1939)

The Oregon Trail (Univ serial, 1939)

Rancho Grande (Rep, 1940)

Hidden Gold (Par, 1940)

Bad Man from Red Butte (Univ, 1940)

Stage to Chino (RKO, 1940)

Ragtime Cowboy Joe (Univ, 1940)

Winners of the West (Univ serial, 1940)

Santa Fe Trail (WB, 1940)

East of the River (WB, 1940)

Flash Gordon Conquers the Universe (Univ serial, 1940) [feature version: Purple Death from Outer Space]

Deadwood Dick (Col serial, 1940)

The Green Hornet Strikes Again (Univ serial, 1940)

White Eagle (Col serial, 1941)

Pals of the Pecos (Rep, 1941)

The Bandit Trail (RKO, 1941)

Wide Open Town (Par, 1941)

Jesse James at Bay (Rep, 1941)

Outlaws of the Cherokee Trail (Rep, 1941)

The Masked Rider (Univ, 1941)

West of Cimarron (Rep, 1941)

King of the Texas Rangers (Rep serial, 1941)

Riders of Death Valley (Univ serial, 1941)

Riders of the Badlands (Col, 1941)

They Died with Their Boots On (WB, 1941)

Sky Raiders (Univ serial, 1941)

Sunset on the Desert (Rep, 1942)

Romance on the Range (Rep, 1942)

Stardust on the Sage (Rep, 1942)

West of the Law (Mon, 1942)

Pirates of the Prairie (RKO, 1942)

Land of the Open Range (RKO, 1942)

The Lone Rider in Cheyenne (PRC, 1942)

The Valley of Vanishing Men (Col serial, 1942)

Dawn on the Great Divide (Mon, 1942)

Nazi Agent (MGM, 1942)

Northwest Rangers (MGM, 1942)

Sunset Serenade (Rep, 1942)

Tennessee Johnson (MGM, 1942)

Below the Border (Mon, 1942)

The Old Chisholm Trail (Univ, 1943)

Hoppy Serves a Writ (UA, 1943)

Cheyenne Roundup (Univ, 1943)

Calling Wild Bill Elliott (Rep, 1943)

Carson City Cyclone (Rep, 1943)

The Stranger from Pecos (Mon, 1943)

Bordertown Gun Fights (Rep, 1943)

False Colors (UA, 1943)

Wagon Tracks West (Rep, 1943)

Riders of the Rio Grande (Rep, 1943)

The Masked Marvel (Rep serial, 1943)

Chatterbox (Rep, 1943)

Dr. Gillespie's Criminal Case (MGM, 1943)

Hands Across the Border (Rep, 1943)

Idaho (Rep, 1943)

In Old Oklahoma [a.k.a. War of the Wildcats] (Rep, 1943)

Man from Music Mountain (Rep, 1943)

Overland Mail Robbery (Rep, 1943)

Raiders of Sunset Pass (Rep, 1943)

Sagebrush Law (RKO, 1943)

Six-Gun Gospel (Mon, 1943)

Call of the South Seas (Rep, 1944)

The Girl Who Dared (Rep, 1944)

The Laramie Trail (Rep, 1944)

Hidden Valley Outlaws (Rep, 1944)

Code of the Prairie (Rep, 1944)

Lights of Old Santa Fe (Rep, 1944)

Stagecoach to Monterey (Rep, 1944)

Firebrands of Arizona (Rep, 1944)

Sheriff of Sundown (Rep, 1944)

Cheyenne Wildcat (Rep, 1944)

The Big Bonanza (Rep, 1944)

The Fighting Seabees (Rep, 1944)

Haunted Harbor (Rep serial, 1944)

Man from Frisco (Rep, 1944)

Rosie the Riveter (Rep, 1944)

Storm over Lisbon (Rep, 1944)

Tuscon Raiders (Rep, 1944)

The Vampire's Ghost (Rep, 1945)

Bells of Rosarita (Rep, 1945)

Sunset in El Dorado (Rep, 1945)

Dakota (Rep, 1945)

Along the Navajo Trail (Rep, 1945)

Marshal of Laredo (Rep, 1945)

Manhunt of Mystery Island (Rep serial, 1945)

The Purple Monster Strikes (Rep serial, 1945) [feature version: D-Day on Mars]

Wagon Wheels Westward (Rep, 1945)

Santa Fe Saddlemates (Rep, 1945)

Colorado Pioneers (Rep, 1945)

Trail of Kit Carson (Rep, 1945)

Topeka Terror (Rep, 1945)

Corpus Christi Bandits (Rep, 1945)

Home on the Range (Rep, 1946)

Alias Billy the Kid (Rep, 1946)

Sun Valley Cyclone (Rep, 1946)

My Pal Trigger (Rep, 1946)

Night Train to Memphis (Rep, 1946)

Traffic in Crime (Rep, 1946)

The Phantom Rider (Rep serial, 1946)

Stagecoach to Denver (Rep, 1946)

Daughter of Don Q (Rep serial, 1946)

Plainsman and the Lady (Rep, 1946)

Crime of the Century (Rep, 1946)

Last Frontier Uprising (Rep, 1946)

Oregon Trail Scouts (Rep, 1947)

The Web of Danger (Rep, 1947)

Vigilantes of Boomtown (Rep, 1947)

Spoilers of the North (Rep, 1947)

Rustlers of Devil's Canyon (Rep, 1947)

Springtime in the Sierras (Rep, 1947)

Wyoming (Rep, 1947)

Marshal of Cripple Creek (Rep, 1947)

Blackmail (Rep, 1947)

Along the Oregon Trail (Rep, 1947)

The Wild Frontier (Rep, 1947)

Bandits of Dark Canyon (Rep, 1947)

Son of Zorro (Rep serial, 1947)

G-Men Never Forget (Rep serial, 1948) [feature version: Code 645]

The Bold Frontiersman (Rep, 1948)

Old Los Angeles (Rep, 1948)

The Main Street Kid (Rep, 1948)

Madonna of the Desert (Rep, 1948)

Lightnin' in the Forest (Rep, 1948)

Oklahoma Badlands (Rep, 1948)

Secret Service Investigator (Rep, 1948)

The Timber Trail (Rep, 1948)

Train to Alcatraz (Rep, 1948)

Out of the Storm (Rep, 1948)

Eyes of Texas (Rep, 1948)

Sons of Adventure (Rep, 1948)

Grand Canyon Trail (Rep, 1948)

Renegades of Sonora (Rep, 1948)

Desperadoes of Dodge City (Rep, 1948)

Marshal of Amarillo (Rep, 1948)

Sundown in Santa Fe (Rep, 1948)

The Far Frontier (Rep, 1948)

Duke of Chicago (Rep, 1949)

Federal Agents vs. Underworld Inc. (Rep serial, 1949) [feature version: Golden Hands of Kurigal]

Ghost of Zorro (Rep serial, 1949)

Sheriff of Wichita (Rep, 1949)

Prince of the Plains (Rep, 1949)

Frontier Investigator (Rep, 1949)

Law of the Golden West (Rep, 1949)

South of Rio (Rep, 1949)
Down Dakota Way (Rep, 1949)
San Antone Ambush (Rep, 1949)
Ranger of Cherokee Strip (Rep, 1949)
Outcasts of the Trail (Rep, 1949)
Powder River Rustlers (Rep, 1949)
Pioneer Marshal (Rep, 1949)
The James Brothers of Missouri (Rep serial, 1950)
Desperadoes of the West (Rep serial, 1950)
Vigilante Hideout (Rep, 1950)
The Vanishing Westerner (Rep, 1950)
The Savage Horde (Rep, 1950)
Federal Agent at Large (Rep, 1950)
Under Mexicali Stars (Rep, 1950)
Surrender (Rep, 1950)
Salt Lake Raiders (Rep, 1950)
Rustlers on Horseback (Rep, 1950)
Gunmen of Abilene (Rep, 1950)
Rock Island Trail (Rep, 1950)
Radar Patrol vs. Spy King (Rep serial, 1950)
Women from Headquarters (Rep, 1950)
Don Daredevil Rides Again (Rep serial, 1951)
Wells Fargo Gunmaster (Rep, 1951)
In Old Amarillo (Rep, 1951)
Insurance Investigator (Rep, 1951)
Night Riders of Montana (Rep, 1951)
The Dakota Kid (Rep, 1951)
The Rodeo King and the Senorita (Rep, 1951)
Fort Dodge Stampede (Rep, 1951)
Arizona Manhunt (Rep, 1951)

Utah Wagon Train (Rep, 1951)
Street Bandits (Rep, 1951)
Honeychile (Rep, 1951)
Pals of the Golden West (Rep, 1951)
Government Agents vs. Phantom Legion (Rep serial, 1951) [voice only]
Desert of Lost Men (Rep, 1951)
Leadville Gunslinger (Rep, 1952)
Radar Men from the Moon (Rep serial, 1952) [feature version: Retik, the Moon Menace]
Oklahoma Annie (Rep, 1952)
Hoodlum Empire (Rep, 1952)
Border Saddlemates (Rep, 1952)
Wild Horse Ambush (Rep, 1952)
Black Hills Ambush (Rep, 1952)
Thundering Caravans (Rep, 1952)
Old Oklahoma Plains (Rep, 1952)
Desperadoes' Outpost (Rep, 1952)
Ride the Man Down (Rep, 1952)
The WAC from Walla Walla (Rep, 1952)
South Pacific Trail (Rep, 1952)
Captive of Billy the Kid (Rep, 1952)
Montana Belle (RKO, 1952)
Tropical Heat Wave (Rep, 1952)
Marshal of Cedar Rock (Rep, 1953)
Down Laredo Way (Rep, 1953)
Iron Mountain Trail (Rep, 1953)
Bandits of the West (Rep, 1953)
Savage Frontier (Rep, 1953)
Old Overland Trail (Rep, 1953)
El Paso Stampede (Rep, 1953)
Shadows of Tombstone (Rep, 1953)
Rogue Cop (MGM, 1954)

Man with the Steel Whip (Rep serial, 1954)
The Desperado (AA, 1954)
Two Guns and a Badge (AA, 1954)
Man Without a Star (Univ, 1955)
Oklahoma! (Magna, 1955)
The Cobweb (MGM, 1955)
The Spoilers (Univ, 1955)
Gun Brothers (UA, 1956)
The Last Hunt (MGM, 1956)
Gun Duel in Durango (UA, 1957)
The Kettles on Old MacDonald's Farm (Univ, 1957)
Domino Kid (Col, 1957)
Last Stagecoach West (Rep, 1957)
Band of Angels (WB, 1957)
Escort West (UA, 1959)
Freckles (20th, 1960)
Ten Who Dared (BV, 1960)
When the Clock Strikes (UA, 1961)
Six Black Horses (Univ, 1962)
He Rides Tall (Univ, 1964)
Billy the Kid vs. Dracula (Emb, 1966)
Destination Inner Space (Magna, 1966)
Gunpoint (Univ, 1966)
Texas Across the River (Univ, 1966)
The Way West (UA, 1967)
Rosemary's Baby (Par, 1968)
Bandolero! (20th, 1968)
The Reivers (National General, 1969)
Gaily, Gaily (UA, 1969)
Monte Walsh (National General, 1970)

ROBERT BARRAT

Nolan Leary and Robert Barrat in Strangler of the Swamp *(1945).*

Born July 10, 1891, New York City, New York. Married Mary _____. Died January 7, 1970, Los Angeles, California. Imposing figure with prominent nose. Hard-working member of the Warner Bros. troupe: *I Loved a Woman* (Charles Lane), *Dark Hazard* (Tex), *Hi, Nellie!* (Beau Brownell), etc. Equally at ease playing on either side of the law, or adopting a dialect for an ethnic character role. In subsequent years, mostly in Westerns.

Robert Barrat to Donald O'Connor in *Double Crossbones:*
"We have our own ways of testing a man's mettle."

Films

The Mayor of Hell (WB, 1933)
King of the Jungle (Par, 1933)
Picture Snatcher (WB, 1933)
The Silk Express (WB, 1933)
Baby Face (WB, 1933)
Lilly Turner (FN, 1933)
Heroes for Sale (FN, 1933)
Captured (WB, 1933)
Wild Boys of the Road (FN, 1933)
The Kennel Murder Case (WB, 1933)
I Loved a Woman (FN, 1933)
From Headquarters (WB, 1933)
Ann Carver's Profession (Col, 1933)
The Secret of the Blue Room (Univ, 1933)
I Sell Anything (FN, 1934)
Dark Hazard (FN, 1934)
Massacre (FN, 1934)
Wonder Bar (FN, 1934)
A Very Honorable Guy (FN, 1934)
Midnight Alibi (FN, 1934)
Hi, Nellie! (WB, 1934)
Gambling Lady (WB, 1934)

Upper World (WB, 1934)
The Dragon Murder Case (FN, 1934)
Friends of Mr. Sweeney (WB, 1934)
Fog over Frisco (FN, 1934)
Here Comes the Navy (WB, 1934)
Housewife (WB, 1934)
Return of the Terror (FN, 1934)
Big-Hearted Herbert (FN, 1934)
The St. Louis Kid (WB, 1934)
The Firebird (WB, 1934)
I Am a Thief (WB, 1934)
While the Patient Slept (FN, 1935)
Dressed to Thrill (Fox, 1935)
Captain Blood (FN, 1935)
Bordertown (WB, 1935)
Devil Dogs of the Air (WB, 1935)
The Florentine Dagger (WB, 1935)
Stranded (WB, 1935)
Special Agent (WB, 1935)
Dr. Socrates (WB, 1935)
Moonlight on the Prairie (WB, 1935)
Village Tale (RKO, 1935)

The Murder Man (MGM, 1935)
Exclusive Story (MGM, 1936)
Trail of the Lonesome Pine (Par, 1936)
The Country Doctor (20th, 1936)
I Married a Doctor (FN, 1936)
Sons o' Guns (WB, 1936)
Draegerman Courage (WB, 1936)
The Charge of the Light Brigade (WB, 1936)
God's Country and the Woman (WB, 1936)
Trailin' West (FN, 1936)
The Black Legion (WB, 1936)
Mary of Scotland (RKO, 1936)
The Last of the Mohicans (UA, 1936)
The Life of Emile Zola (WB, 1937)
Souls at Sea (Par, 1937)
Confession (WB, 1937)
Love Is on the Air (FN, 1937)
The Barrier (Par, 1937)
Mountain Justice (WB, 1937)
Bad Man of Brimstone (MGM, 1937)

Forbidden Valley (Univ, 1938)
Marie Antoinette (MGM, 1938)
The Buccaneer (Par, 1938)
Penitentiary (Col, 1938)
The Texans (Par, 1938)
Charlie Chan in Honolulu (20th, 1938)
Breaking the Ice (RKO, 1938)
Shadows over Shanghai (GN, 1938)
Colorado Sunset (Rep, 1939)
Union Pacific (Par, 1939)
Bad Lands (RKO, 1939)
Conspiracy (RKO, 1939)
Allegheny Uprising (RKO, 1939)
The Cisco Kid and the Lady (20th, 1939)
Man of Conquest (Rep, 1939)
Heritage of the Desert (Par, 1939)
Return of the Cisco Kid (20th, 1939)
Northwest Passage (MGM, 1940)
The Man from Dakota (MGM, 1940)
Go West (MGM, 1940)
Captain Caution (UA, 1940)
Fugitive from a Prison Camp (Col, 1940)
Laddie (RKO, 1940)
They Met in Argentina (RKO, 1941)
Parachute Battalion (RKO, 1941)
Riders of the Purple Sage (20th, 1941)

Fall In (UA, 1942)
The Girl from Alaska (Rep, 1942)
American Empire (UA, 1942)
Bomber's Moon (20th, 1943)
Johnny Come Lately (UA, 1943)
They Came to Blow Up America (20th, 1943)
A Stranger in Town (MGM, 1943)
Enemy of Women (Mon, 1944)
The Adventures of Mark Twain (WB, 1944)
The Road to Utopia (Par, 1945)
Grissly's Millions (Rep, 1945)
Dakota (Rep, 1945)
The Great John L (UA, 1945)
Strangler of the Swamp (PRC, 1945)
San Antonio (WB, 1945)
Wanderer of the Wasteland (RKO, 1945)
They Were Expendable (MGM, 1945)
Dangerous Millions (20th, 1946)
Just Before Dawn (Col, 1946)
The Time of Their Lives (Univ, 1946)
Sunset Pass (RKO, 1946)
The Magnificent Doll (Univ, 1946)
The Road to Rio (Par, 1947)
The Sea of Grass (MGM, 1947)

The Fabulous Texan (MGM, 1947)
I Love Trouble (Col, 1948)
Joan of Arc (RKO, 1948)
Relentless (Col, 1948)
Bad Men of Tombstone (AA, 1948)
Canadian Pacific (20th, 1949)
The Doolins of Oklahoma (Col, 1949)
Song of India (Col, 1949)
The Lone Wolf and His Lady (Col, 1949)
Riders of the Range (RKO, 1949)
The Baron of Arizona (Lip, 1950)
The Kid from Texas (Univ, 1950)
Davy Crockett—Indian Scout (UA, 1950)
An American Guerrilla in the Philippines (20th, 1950)
Pride of Maryland (Rep, 1951)
Flight to Mars (Mon, 1951)
Double Crossbones (Univ, 1951)
Darling, How Could You? (Par, 1951)
Distant Drums (WB, 1951)
The Denver and the Rio Grande (Par, 1952)
Son of Ali Baba (Univ, 1952)
Cow Country (AA, 1953)
Tall Man Riding (WB, 1955)

ALBERT BASSERMAN

With Joan Crawford in A Woman's Face *(1941).*

Born September 7, 1867, Mannheim, Germany. Married Else Schiff, child: one. Died May 15, 1952, Zurich, Switzerland. Among the talented German-born refugees who fled to Hollywood in the late 1930s. Specialized in kindly roles: elderly Dutch diplomat kidnapped in *Foreign Correspondent* (Oscar-nominated; lost BSAAA to Walter Brennan of *The Westerner*); the gentle doctor (*The Moon and Sixpence*). Very impressive as the cobbler without necessary identification papers in *Passport to Heaven*.

Albert Basserman to Herbert Marshall in *Foreign Correspondent:* "You cried *peace,* Fisher—*peace*—and there was no peace—only war—and death."

Films

Alraune (Ger, 1931)
Voruntersuchung (Ger, 1931)
1914: The Last Days Before the War (Ger, 1932)
Kadetten (Ger, 1933)
Ein Gewisser Herr Gran (Ger, 1934)
Letzte Liebe (Ger, 1938)
Le Famille Lefrançois [a.k.a. Heroes of the Marne] (Fr, 1939)
The Story of Dr. Ehrlich's Magic Bullet (WB, 1940)
Knute Rockne—All American (WB, 1940)

Moon over Burma (Par, 1940)
A Dispatch from Reuter's (WB, 1940)
Foreign Correspondent (UA, 1940)
Escape (MGM, 1940)
New Wine (UA, 1941)
A Woman's Face (MGM, 1941)
The Shanghai Gesture (UA, 1941)
Fly by Night (Par, 1942)
Desperate Journey (WB, 1942)
The Invisible Agent (Univ, 1942)
The Moon and Sixpence (UA, 1942)
Once upon a Honeymoon (RKO, 1942)

Reunion (MGM, 1942)
Good Luck Mr. Yates (Col, 1943)
Passport to Heaven [a.k.a. I Was a Criminal] (Film Classics, 1943)
Madame Curie (MGM, 1943)
Since You Went Away (UA, 1944)
Rhapsody in Blue (WB, 1945)
The Searching Wind (Par, 1946)
Strange Holiday (PRC, 1946)
The Private Affairs of Bel Ami (UA, 1947)
Escape Me Never (WB, 1947)
The Red Shoes (Br, 1948)

FLORENCE BATES
(Florence Rabe)

With S. Z. Sakall in Lullaby of Broadway *(1951).*

Born April 15, 1888, San Antonio, Texas. Married 1) _____ (1909), child: Ann; divorced; 2) Will Jacoby (1929); widowed (1951). Died January 31, 1954, Burbank, California. A former attorney. In 1940, appeared as the domineering, selfish matron Mrs. Van Hopper in Alfred Hitchcock's *Rebecca*. At ease playing a freewheeling native hotelkeeper (*The Moon and Sixpence*), the officious dowager (*Since You Went Away*), the all-knowing theatre owner (*Tonight and Every Night*), the zesty Oriental Karsha (*Kismet*), many others.

Florence Bates to Joan Fontaine in *Rebecca:* "The trouble is, with me laid up like this, you haven't had enough to do."

Films

The Man in Blue (Univ, 1937)
Rebecca (UA, 1940)
Calling All Husbands (WB, 1940)
The Son of Monte Cristo (UA, 1940)
Hudson's Bay (20th, 1940)
Kitty Foyle (RKO, 1940)
Road Show (UA, 1941)
Strange Alibi (WB, 1941)
The Devil and Miss Jones (RKO, 1941)
Love Crazy (MGM, 1941)
The Chocolate Soldier (MGM, 1941)
Mexican Spitfire at Sea (RKO, 1942)
We Were Dancing (MGM, 1942)
The Tuttles of Tahiti (RKO, 1942)
The Moon and Sixpence (UA, 1942)
My Heart Belongs to Daddy (Par, 1942)
They Got Me Covered (RKO, 1943)
Slightly Dangerous (MGM, 1943)
Mister Big (Univ, 1943)
Mr. Lucky (RKO, 1943)
Heaven Can Wait (20th, 1943)
His Butler's Sister (Univ, 1943)
The Mask of Dimitrios (WB, 1944)

The Racket Man (Col, 1944)
Since You Went Away (UA, 1944)
Kismet [TV title: Oriental Dream]
  (MGM, 1944)
The Belle of the Yukon (RKO, 1944)
Tahiti Nights (Col, 1944)
Saratoga Trunk (WB, 1945)
Tonight and Every Night (Col, 1945)
Out of This World (Par, 1945)
San Antonio (WB, 1945)
Whistle Stop (UA, 1946)
The Diary of a Chambermaid (UA, 1946)
Cluny Brown (20th, 1946)
Claudia and David (20th, 1946)
The Time, the Place and the Girl (WB,
  1946)
The Brasher Doubloon (20th, 1947)
Love and Learn (WB, 1947)
The Secret Life of Walter Mitty (RKO,
  1947)
Desire Me (MGM, 1947)
The Inside Story (Rep, 1948)

I Remember Mama (RKO, 1948)
Winter Meeting (WB, 1948)
River Lady (Univ, 1948)
Texas, Brooklyn and Heaven (UA, 1948)
My Dear Secretary (UA, 1948)
A Letter to Three Wives (20th, 1948)
Portrait of Jennie (Selznick Releasing
  Organization, 1948)
The Judge Steps Out (RKO, 1949)
The Girl from Jones Beach (WB, 1949)
On the Town (MGM, 1949)
Belle of Old Mexico (Rep, 1950)
County Fair (Mon, 1950)
The Second Woman (UA, 1951)
The Lullaby of Broadway (WB, 1951)
Father Takes the Air (Mon, 1951)
The Tall Target (MGM, 1951)
Havana Rose (Rep, 1951)
The San Francisco Story (WB, 1952)
Les Miserables (20th, 1952)
Main Street to Broadway (MGM, 1953)
Paris Model (Col, 1953)

GRANVILLE BATES

Jack Oakie and Granville Bates (center) in The Sap from Syracuse *(1930).*

Born January 7, 1882, Chicago, Illinois. Died July 9, 1940, Hollywood, California. Resilient character performer: *Jealousy* (lawyer), *Chatterbox* (Phillips Holmes' father), *Green Light* (sheriff), *My Favorite Wife* (judge), etc.

Granville Bates to Dick Foran in *The Cowboy from Brooklyn:*
"When I was your age I didn't let any city slicker steal *my* gal from under my nose."

54

Films

Jealousy (Par, 1929)
The Sap from Syracuse (Par, 1930)
The Smiling Lieutenant (Par, 1931)
The Wiser Sex (Par, 1932)
Midnight (Univ, 1934)
Woman in the Dark (RKO, 1934)
Woman Wanted (MGM, 1935)
O'Shaughnessy's Boy (MGM, 1935)
Pursuit (MGM, 1935)
Here Comes Trouble (20th, 1936)
Chatterbox (RKO, 1936)
The Plainsman (Par, 1936)
Thirteen Hours by Air (Par, 1936)
Times Square Playboy (WB, 1936)
Poppy (Par, 1936)
Beloved Enemy (UA, 1936)
Sing Me a Love Song (FN, 1936)
The Captain's Kid (WB, 1936)
Green Light (WB, 1937)
Nancy Steele Is Missing (20th, 1937)
Larceny on the Air (Rep, 1937)

When's Your Birthday? (RKO, 1937)
Waikiki Wedding (Par, 1937)
Let's Get Married (Col, 1937)
Mountain Justice (WB, 1937)
They Won't Forget (WB, 1937)
Back in Circulation (WB, 1937)
The Perfect Specimen (FN, 1937)
It Happened in Hollywood (Col, 1937)
Wells Fargo (Par, 1937)
Under Suspicion (Col, 1937)
The Jury's Secret (Univ, 1938)
Gold Is Where You Find It (WB, 1938)
Go Chase Yourself (RKO, 1938)
Romance on the Run (Rep, 1938)
The Cowboy from Brooklyn (WB, 1938)
The Affairs of Annabel (RKO, 1938)
Mr. Chump (WB, 1938)
Youth Takes a Fling (Univ, 1938)
Garden of the Moon (WB, 1938)
Hard to Get (WB, 1938)
A Man to Remember (RKO, 1938)

The Next Time I Marry (RKO, 1938)
The Great Man Votes (RKO, 1939)
Jesse James (20th, 1939)
Blackwell's Island (WB, 1939)
Twelve Crowded Hours (RKO, 1939)
Pride of the Blue Grass (WB, 1939)
Fast and Furious (MGM, 1939)
Naughty but Nice (WB, 1939)
Our Neighbors, the Carters (Par, 1939)
Sweepstakes Winner (WB, 1939)
Indianapolis Speedway (WB, 1939)
Of Mice and Men (UA, 1939)
Thou Shalt Not Kill (Rep, 1939)
Charlie McCarthy, Detective (Univ, 1939)
Millionaire Playboy (RKO, 1940)
My Favorite Wife (RKO, 1940)
Brother Orchid (WB, 1940)
The Mortal Storm (MGM, 1940)
Private Affairs (Univ, 1940)
Men Against the Sky (RKO, 1940)
Flowing Gold (WB, 1940)

DON BEDDOE
(Donald T. Beddoe)

Michael Whalen and Don Beddoe in Outside These Walls *(1939).*

Born July 1, 1888, Pittsburgh, Pennsylvania. Married Joyce Mathews (1974). College journalism major who played in stock and on Broadway. Populated scores of features, frequently as law enforcer or newspaperman: *Blondie Meets the Boss* and *Blondie on a Budget* (both as Marvin Williams), *The Lone Wolf Takes a Chance* (Sheriff Haggerty), *Francis Goes to the Races* (Dr. Quimby), *The Enforcer* (Thomas O'Hara), etc.

Don Beddoe in *Midnight Manhunt:* "Everybody knows everything around here, but me. I'm just a detective."

Films

There's That Woman Again (Col, 1938)
The Lone Wolf Spy Hunt (Col, 1939)
Flying G-Men (Col serial, 1939)
Good Girls Go to Paris (Col, 1939)
Outside These Walls (Col, 1939)
Mandrake the Magician (Col serial, 1939)
Romance of the Redwoods (Col, 1939)
Missing Daughters (Col, 1939)
Golden Boy (Col, 1939)
Taming of the West (Col, 1939)
The Man They Could Not Hang (Col, 1939)
Beware Spooks! (Col, 1939)
Blondie Meets the Boss (Col, 1939)
Those High Gray Walls (Col, 1939)
The Amazing Mr. Williams (Col, 1939)
My Son Is Guilty (Col, 1939)
Scandal Sheet (Col, 1940)
The Lone Wolf Strikes (Col, 1940)
Konga—The Wild Stallion (Col, 1940)
Blondie on a Budget (Col, 1940)
Charlie Chan's Murder Cruise (20th, 1940)
Men Without Souls (Col, 1940)
Island of Doomed Men (Col, 1940)
The Man from Tumbleweeds (Col, 1940)
Manhattan Heartbeat (20th, 1940)
West of Abilene (Col, 1940)
Girls of the Road (Col, 1940)
The Secret Seven (Col, 1940)
Beyond the Sacramento (Col, 1940)
Military Academy (Col, 1940)
Before I Hang (Col, 1940)
Glamour for Sale (Col, 1940)
The Lone Wolf Keeps a Date (Col, 1941)
This Thing Called Love (Col, 1941)
Submarine Zone [a.k.a. Escape to Glory] (Col, 1941)
The Lone Wolf Takes a Chance (Col, 1941)
The Face Behind the Mask (Col, 1941)
Sing for Your Supper (Col, 1941)
Under Age (Col, 1941)
The Big Boss (Col, 1941)
Sweetheart of the Campus (Col, 1941)
The Blonde from Singapore (Col, 1941)
Texas (Col, 1941)
Unholy Partners (MGM, 1941)
Two Latins from Manhattan (Col, 1941)

Harvard, Here I Come (Col, 1942)
Shut My Big Mouth (Col, 1942)
Meet the Stewarts (Col, 1942)
The Talk of the Town (Col, 1942)
Sabotage Squad (Col, 1942)
Honolulu Lu (Col, 1942)
Lucky Legs (Col, 1942)
Junior Army (Col, 1942)
Not a Ladies' Man (Col, 1942)
Smith of Minnesota (Col, 1942)
The Boogie Man Will Get You (Col, 1942)
Power of the Press (Col, 1943)
Crime, Inc. (PRC, 1945)
Midnight Manhunt [a.k.a. One Exciting Night] (Par, 1945)
Getting Gertie's Garter (UA, 1945)
Behind Green Lights (20th, 1946)
O.S.S. (Par, 1946)
The Well-Groomed Bride (Par, 1946)
The Notorious Lone Wolf (Col, 1946)
The Best Years of Our Lives (RKO, 1946)
The Farmer's Daughter (RKO, 1947)
Buck Privates Come Home (Univ, 1947)
Welcome Stranger (Par, 1947)
They Won't Believe Me (RKO, 1947)
The Bachelor and the Bobby-Soxer (RKO, 1947)
Black Bart (Univ, 1948)
Another Part of the Forest (Univ, 1948)
An Act of Murder [a.k.a. Live Today for Tomorrow] (Univ, 1948)
Hideout (Rep, 1949)
The Lady Gambles (Univ, 1949)
Once More, My Darling (Univ, 1949)
Easy Living (RKO, 1949)
Flame of Youth (Rep, 1949)
Dancing in the Dark (20th, 1949)
Dear Wife (Par, 1949)
Deadly as the Female [a.k.a. Gun Crazy] (UA, 1949)
Woman in Hiding (Univ, 1949)
The Crime Doctor's Diary (Univ, 1949)
The Great Rupert (EL, 1950)
Young Daniel Boone (Mon, 1950)
Tarnished (Rep, 1950)
Beyond the Purple Hills (Col, 1950)
Emergency Wedding (Col, 1950)
Cyrano de Bergerac (UA, 1950)
The Company She Keeps (RKO, 1950)

Gasoline Alley (Col, 1951)
As Young As You Feel (20th, 1951)
The Racket (RKO, 1951)
Starlift (WB, 1951)
Three Guys Named Mike (MGM, 1951)
Francis Goes to the Races (Univ, 1951)
The Enforcer (WB, 1951)
Million Dollar Pursuit (Rep, 1951)
The Rodeo King and the Senorita (Rep, 1951)
Corky of Gasoline Alley (Col, 1951)
The Unknown Man (MGM, 1951)
Man in the Saddle (Col, 1951)
The Narrow Margin (RKO, 1952)
Washington Story (MGM, 1952)
Hoodlum Empire (Rep, 1952)
Carrie (Par, 1952)
Scandal Sheet (Col, 1952)
Don't Bother to Knock (20th, 1952)
The Iron Mistress (WB, 1952)
Blue Canadian Rockies (Col, 1952)
Stop, You're Killing Me (WB, 1952)
The Clown (MGM, 1953)
The System (WB, 1953)
Cow Country (AA, 1953)
Loophole (AA, 1954)
A Star Is Born (WB, 1954)
River of No Return (20th, 1954)
The Steel Cage (UA, 1954)
Wyoming Renegades (Col, 1955)
Tarzan's Hidden Jungle (RKO, 1955)
The Night of the Hunter (UA, 1955)
Behind the High Wall (Univ, 1956)
Shootout at Medicine Bend (WB, 1957)
Toughest Gun in Tombstone (UA, 1958)
Bullwhip (AA, 1958)
Warlock (20th, 1959)
Pillow Talk (Univ, 1959)
The Wizard of Baghdad (20th, 1960)
The Boy Who Caught a Crook (UA, 1961)
Jack, the Giant Killer (UA, 1962)
Saintly Sinners (UA, 1962)
Papa's Delicate Condition (Par, 1963)
A Very Special Favor (Univ, 1965)
The Impossible Years (MGM, 1968)
Generation (Emb, 1969)
How Do I Love Thee? (Cin, 1970)

JANET BEECHER
(Janet Meysenburg)

Janet Beecher, Cecil Cunningham, Marjorie Rambeau, and Hedda Hopper in a pose for Laugh It Off *(1939).*

Born October 21, 1884, Jefferson City, Missouri. Married 1) Harry R. Guggenheimer; divorced (1919); 2) Dr. Richard H. Hoffmann, child: Wyndham; divorced (1935). Died August 6, 1955, Washington, Connecticut. From 1933 to 1943 the silver-haired actress played genteel ladies with appropriate grace: *The Dark Angel* (Mrs. Shannon—Herbert Marshall's mother), *Yellow Jack* (Miss MacDade), *The Mark of Zorro* (Senora Isabella Vega—Tyrone Power's mother), *Reap the Wild Wind* (Mrs. Mottram), etc. Shone as the staunch matriarch in *So Red the Rose* (Margaret Sullivan's mother).

Janet Beecher to Phillip Terry in *The Parson of Panamint:* "It was a fine sermon, Parson. I hope a few of the people in Panamint will take it to heart."

Films

Gallant Lady (UA, 1933)
The Last Gentleman (UA, 1934)
The President Vanishes (Par, 1934)
The Mighty Barnum (UA, 1934)
Let's Live Tonight (Col, 1935)
Village Tale (RKO, 1935)
The Dark Angel (UA, 1935)
So Red the Rose (Par, 1935)
Love Before Breakfast (Univ, 1936)
I'd Give My Life (Par, 1936)
The Longest Night (MGM, 1936)
The Good Old Soak (MGM, 1937)
The Thirteenth Chair (MGM, 1937)
Between Two Women (MGM, 1937)
The Big City (MGM, 1937)
My Dear Miss Aldrich (MGM, 1937)

Beg, Borrow or Steal (MGM, 1937)
Rosalie (MGM, 1937)
Judge Hardy's Children (MGM, 1938)
Yellow Jack (MGM, 1938)
Woman Against Woman (MGM, 1938)
Say It in French (Par, 1938)
The Story of Vernon and Irene Castle (RKO, 1939)
I Was a Convict (Rep, 1939)
Man of Conquest (Rep, 1939)
Career (RKO, 1939)
Laugh It Off (Univ, 1939)
Slightly Honorable (UA, 1939)
The Gay Caballero (20th, 1940)
The Mark of Zorro (20th, 1940)
All This, and Heaven Too (WB, 1940)

Bitter Sweet (MGM, 1940)
The Man Who Lost Himself (Univ, 1941)
The Lady Eve (Par, 1941)
A Very Young Lady (20th, 1941)
West Point Widow (Par, 1941)
The Parson of Panamint (Par, 1941)
For Beauty's Sake (20th, 1941)
Hi, Neighbor (Rep, 1942)
Men of Texas (Univ, 1942)
Silver Queen (UA, 1942)
Reap the Wild Wind (Par, 1942)
Mrs. Wiggs of the Cabbage Patch (Par, 1942)
Henry Aldrich Gets Glamour (Par, 1943)

NOAH BEERY, JR.

Frank Fenton, John Ireland, Noah Beery, Jr., Charles Kemper, and Randolph Scott in
The Doolins of Oklahoma (1949).

Born August 10, 1913, New York City, New York. Married 1) Maxine Jones (1940), children: Muffett, Buck, Melissa; divorced (1966); 2) Lisa _____ . A contrast to his well-known father and celebrated uncle. Gained repute in early years as the well-meaning co-lead of such serials as *Tailspin Tommy*. Gravitated to playing ruminating country types in later years: *The Cockeyed Cowboys of Calico County* (Eddie), *Little Fauss and Big Halsy* (Scally Fauss), *Walking Tall* (Grandpa Pusser), etc. TV series: "Circus Boy," "Riverboat," "Hondo," "Doc Elliott," and "The Rockford Files" (as Rocky—James Garner's father).

Noah Beery, Jr. to Clark Williams in *The Great Air Mystery*:
"Oh, boy, some landing, Tailspin—and in the dark too!"

Films

The Mark of Zorro (UA, 1920)
Father and Son (Col, 1929)
Heroes of the West (Univ serial, 1932)
The Jungle Mystery (Univ serial, 1932)
Rustler's Roundup (Univ, 1933)
The Three Musketeers (Mascot serial, 1933)
Fighting with Kit Carson (Mascot serial, 1933)
The Trail Beyond (Mon, 1934)
Tailspin Tommy (Univ serial, 1934)
Tailspin Tommy in the Great Air Mystery (Univ serial, 1935)
Call of the Savage (Univ serial, 1935)
Stormy (Univ, 1935)
Parole (Univ, 1936)
Ace Drummond (Univ serial, 1936)
The Road Back (Univ, 1937)
The Mighty Treve (Univ, 1937)
Some Blondes Are Dangerous (Univ, 1937)

Trouble at Midnight (Univ, 1938)
Girls' School (Col, 1938)
Forbidden Valley (Univ, 1938)
Outside the Law (Univ, 1938)
Only Angels Have Wings (Col, 1939)
Flight at Midnight (Rep, 1939)
Of Mice and Men (UA, 1939)
Bad Lands (RKO, 1939)
Parents on Trial (Col, 1939)
The Light of Western Stars (Par, 1940)
Twenty-Mule Team (MGM, 1940)
The Carson City Kid (Rep, 1940)
Passport to Alcatraz (Col, 1940)
Sergeant York (WB, 1941)
Tanks a Million (UA, 1941)
All-American Co-ed (UA, 1941)
Riders of Death Valley (Univ serial, 1941)
Two in a Taxi (Col, 1941)
Overland Mail (Univ serial, 1942)

Dudes Are Pretty People (UA, 1942)
'Neath Brooklyn Bridge (Mon, 1942)
Hay Foot (UA, 1942)
Pardon My Gun (Col, 1943)
Calaboose (UA, 1943)
Gung Ho! (Univ, 1943)
We've Never Been Licked (Univ, 1943)
Corvette K-225 (Univ, 1943)
Top Man (Univ, 1943)
Frontier Badmen (Univ, 1943)
What a Woman! (Col, 1943)
Prairie Chickens (UA, 1943)
See My Lawyer (Univ, 1944)
Weekend Pass (Univ, 1944)
Follow the Boys (Univ, 1944)
Allergic to Love (Univ, 1944)
Hi, Beautiful (Univ, 1945)
Under Western Skies (Univ, 1945)
Her Lucky Night (Univ, 1945)
The Beautiful Cheat (Univ, 1945)

The Daltons Ride Again (Univ, 1945)
Crimson Canary (Univ, 1945)
The Cat Creeps (Univ, 1946)
Red River (UA, 1948)
Indian Agent (RKO, 1948)
The Doolins of Oklahoma (Col, 1949)
Two Flags West (20th, 1950)
Davy Crockett—Indian Scout (UA, 1950)
Rocket Ship X-M (Lip, 1950)
The Savage Horde (Rep, 1950)
The Last Outpost (Par, 1951)
The Cimarron Kid (Univ, 1951)
The Texas Rangers (Col, 1951)

The Story of Will Rogers (WB, 1952)
Wagons West (Mon, 1952)
Wings of the Hawk (Univ, 1953)
War Arrow (Univ, 1953)
The Black Dakotas (Col, 1954)
Yellow Tomahawk (UA, 1954)
White Feather (20th, 1955)
Jubal (Col, 1956)
The Fastest Gun Alive (MGM, 1956)
Decisions at Sundown (Col, 1957)
Escort West (UA, 1959)
Guns of the Timberland (WB, 1960)
Inherit the Wind (UA, 1960)

The Seven Faces of Dr. Lao (MGM 1964)
Incident at Phantom Hill (Univ, 1966)
Heaven with a Gun (MGM, 1969)
Little Fauss and Big Halsy (Par, 1969)
The Cockeyed Cowboys of Calico County (Univ, 1970)
43—The Petty Story [a.k.a. Smash-Up Alley] (Rowland-Lasko—Countrywide Distributing, 1972)
Walking Tall (Cin, 1973)
The Spikes Gang (UA, 1974)
Part II, Walking Tall (AIP, 1975)

NOAH BEERY, SR.

In Pioneers of the West (1940).

Born January 1, 1883, Kansas City, Missouri. Married Marguerite Abbott, child: Noah, Jr. Died April 1, 1946, Los Angeles, California. Burly villain of countless silents: *The Mark of Zorro* (Sergeant Pedro), *The Thundering Herd* (evil Indian agent Booker), *Beau Geste* (sadistic Sergeant Lejaune), etc. Leather-faced moustached player with bushy eyebrows. Bolstered many low-budget talkie features—often as the (over)enthusiastic bad guy. In last years, often given supporting roles at MGM in brother Wallace's starring vehicles: *Bad Man of Brimstone, Salute to the Marines, Barbary Coast Gent*, and *This Man's Navy*.

Noah Beery, Sr. to Cary Grant in *She Done Him Wrong:* "I'm the boss of this district."

Films

The Mormon Maid (Hiller & Wilk, 1917)
Believe Me, Xantippe (Par, 1918)
Less Than Kin (Par, 1918)
The Source (Par, 1918)
The Squaw Man (Par, 1918)
The Whispering Chorus (Par, 1918)
Louisiana (Par, 1919)
The Red Lantern (M, 1919)
The Woman Next Door (Par, 1919)
In Mizzoura (Par, 1919)
The Fighting Shepherdess (Associated FN, 1920)
Go Get It (Associated FN, 1920)
Dinty (Associated FN, 1920)
The Mark of Zorro (UA, 1920)
The Sea Wolf (Par, 1920)
Bob Hampton of Placer (Associated FN, 1921)
Beach of Dreams (Robertson-Cole, 1921)
Bits of Life (Associated FN, 1921)
Lotus Blossom (Associated FN, 1921)
The Call of the North (Par, 1921)
Tillie (Par, 1922)
Belle of Alaska (American Releasing, 1922)
Wild Honey (Univ, 1922)
The Lying Truth (American Releasing, 1922)
Good Men and True (FBO, 1922)
I Am the Law (Affiliated, 1922)
The Crossroads of New York (Associated FN, 1922)
The Heart Specialist (Par, 1922)
Flesh and Blood (Cummings, 1922)
The Power of Love (Perfect, 1922)
Youth to Youth (M, 1922)
Ebb Tide (Par, 1922)
Omar, the Tentmaker (Associated FN, 1922)
Stormswept (FBO, 1923)
The Spider and the Rose (Principal, 1923)
Dangerous Trails (Ambassador, 1923)
Soul of the Beast (M, 1923)
Quicksands (Selznick, 1923)
Main Street (WB, 1923)
Wandering Daughters (Associated FN, 1923)
The Spoilers (G, 1923)
Forbidden Lover (Selznick-Sierra, 1923)
Hollywood (Par, 1923)
Tipped Off (Play Goers, 1923)
When Law Comes to Hades (Sanford, 1923)
To the Last Man (Par, 1923)

The Destroying Angel (Associated Exhibitors, 1923)
His Last Race (G, 1923)
Stephen Steps Out (Par, 1923)
The Call of the Canyon (Par, 1923)
The Heritage of the Desert (Par, 1924)
The Fighting Coward (Par, 1924)
Wanderer of the Wasteland (Par, 1924)
Lily of the Dust (Par, 1924)
Female (Par, 1924)
Welcome Stranger (PDC, 1924)
North of '36 (Par, 1924)
East of Suez (Par, 1925)
The Thundering Herd (Par, 1925)
Contraband (Par, 1925)
Old Shoes (Peerless, 1925)
The Spaniard (Par, 1925)
The Light of Western Stars (Par, 1925)
Wild Horse Mesa (Par, 1925)
The Vanishing American (Par, 1925)
The Coming of Amos (PDC, 1925)
Lord Jim (Par, 1925)
The Enchanted Hill (Par, 1926)
The Crown of Lies (Par, 1926)
Padlocked (Par, 1926)
Beau Geste (Par, 1926)
Paradise (FN, 1926)
The Love Mart (FN, 1927)
The Rough Riders (Par, 1927)
Evening Clothes (Par, 1927)
The Dove (UA, 1927)
Two Lovers (UA, 1928)
Noah's Ark (WB, 1928)
Beau Sabreur (Par, 1928)
Hellship Bronson (Gotham, 1928)
The Four Feathers (Par, 1929)
Passion Song (Excellent Pictures, 1929)
Linda (FD, 1929)
Careers (FN, 1929)
The Isle of Lost Ships (FN, 1929)
Noah's Ark (WB, 1929)
Love in the Desert (RKO, 1929)
The Godless Girl (Pathé, 1929)
False Feathers (El Dorado Productions, 1929)
The Show of Shows (WB, 1929)
Glorifying the American Girl (Par, 1929)
Two O'Clock in the Morning (Bell Pictures, 1929)
Murder Will Out (FN, 1930)
Song of the Flame (FN, 1930)
The Way of All Men [a.k.a. *The Sin Flood*] (FN, 1930)
Under a Texas Moon (WB, 1930)
Golden Dawn (WB, 1930)
Big Boy (WB, 1930)

Isle of Escape (WB, 1930)
Feet First (Par, 1930)
The Love Trader (Tif, 1930)
Renegades (Fox, 1930)
Mammy (WB, 1930)
Tol'able David (Col, 1930)
Bright Lights (FN, 1930)
Oh Sailor, Behave (WB, 1930)
Honeymoon Lane (Par, 1931)
The Millionaire (WB, 1931)
In Line of Duty (Mon, 1931)
A Soldier's Plaything (WB, 1931)
Homicide Squad (Univ, 1931)
Shanghaied Love (Col, 1931)
Riders of the Purple Sage (Fox, 1931)
The Devil Horse (Mascot serial, 1932)
The Drifter (Willis Kent, 1932)
The Kid from Spain (UA, 1932)
Out of Singapore (Steiner, 1932)
Stranger in Town (WB, 1932)
The Stoker (Allied Pictures, 1932)
No Living Witness (Mayfair, 1932)
The Big Stampede (WB, 1932)
Cornered (Col, 1932)
The Flaming Signal (Invincible, 1933)
Fighting with Kit Carson (Mascot serial, 1933)
Sunset Pass (Par, 1933)
To the Last Man (Par, 1933)
She Done Him Wrong (Par, 1933)
Laughing at Life (Mascot, 1933)
The Woman I Stole (Col, 1933)
Man of the Forest (Par, 1933)
Easy Millions (Freuler Films, 1933)
The Thundering Herd (Par, 1933)
David Harum (Fox, 1934)
Kentucky Kernels (RKO, 1934)
Cockeyed Cavaliers (RKO, 1934)
Mystery Liner (Mon, 1934)
Madame Spy (Univ, 1934)
Happy Landing (Mon, 1934)
The Trail Beyond (Mon, 1934)
Caravan (Fox, 1934)
Sweet Adeline (WB, 1935)
King of the Damned (Br, 1935)
The Crimson Circle (Br, 1936)
The Avenging Hand (Br, 1936)
The Marriage of Corbal [a.k.a. *The Prisoner of Corbal*] (Br, 1936)
Strangers on a Honeymoon (Br, 1937)
Our Fighting Navy [a.k.a. *Torpedoed*] (Br, 1937)
The Frog (Br, 1937)
Zorro Rides Again (Rep serial, 1937)
Someone at the Door (Br, 1937)
Bad Man of Brimstone (MGM, 1937)

The Girl of the Golden West (MGM, 1938)
Panamint's Bad Man (20th, 1938)
Mexicali Rose (Rep, 1939)
Mutiny on the Blackhawk (Univ, 1939)
Pioneers of the West (Rep, 1940)
Grandpa Goes to Town (Rep, 1940)
Adventures of Red Ryder (Rep serial, 1940)

A Little Bit of Heaven (Univ, 1940)
The Tulsa Kid (Rep, 1940)
A Missouri Outlaw (Rep, 1941)
Overland Mail (Univ serial, 1942)
The Devil's Trail (Col, 1942)
Outlaws of Pine Ridge (Rep, 1942)
The Isle of Missing Men (Mon, 1942)
Tennessee Johnson (MGM, 1942)
Mr. Muggs Steps Out (Mon, 1943)

Clancy Street Boys (Mon, 1943)
Carson City Cyclone (Rep, 1943)
Salute to the Marines (MGM, 1943)
Block Busters (Mon, 1944)
The Million Dollar Kid (Mon, 1944)
Gentle Annie (MGM, 1944)
Barbary Coast Gent (MGM, 1944)
This Man's Navy (MGM, 1945)
Sing Me a Song of Texas (Col, 1945)

ED BEGLEY
(Edward James Begley)

Ed Begley and Robert Walker in The Road to Salina (1971).

Born March 25, 1901, Hartford, Connecticut. Married 1) Amanda Huff (1922), children: Allene, Edward; widowed (1957); 2) Dorothy Reeves (1961); divorced (1963); 3) Helen Jordan (1963), child: Maureen. Died April 28, 1970, Hollywood, California. Feisty, stocky man—best known for gruff, wheedling characters. Was greedy bigot Dave Burke in Odds Against Tomorrow. Won BSAAA for "Boss" Finley, the Dixie political figure of Sweet Bird of Youth. Had been a circus/carnival/stock company/radio participant in his youth. Was General Midwinter, the right-wing Texas millionaire with his own private army in Billion Dollar Brain. Son Ed, Jr. became an actor too. TV series: "Leave It to Larry."

> **Ed Begley** to Stephen McNally in Wyoming Mail: "I expect you to realize I'm pretty much the law around here. I can make things easier for you, or I can break you. It's up to you."

Films

Boomerang (20th, 1947)
The Roosevelt Story (UA, 1947) [narrator]
The Web (Univ, 1947)
Sitting Pretty (20th, 1948)
Deep Waters (20th, 1948)
The Street with No Name (20th, 1948)
Sorry, Wrong Number (Par, 1948)
It Happens Every Spring (20th, 1949)
The Great Gatsby (Par, 1949)
Tulsa (EL, 1949)
Saddle Tramp (Univ, 1950)
Dark City (Par, 1950)
Stars in My Crown (MGM, 1950)
Wyoming Mail (Univ, 1950)

Backfire (WB, 1950)
Convicted (Col, 1950)
You're in the Navy Now [a.k.a. USS Teakettle] (20th, 1951)
The Lady from Texas (Univ, 1951)
On Dangerous Ground (RKO, 1951)
Boots Malone (Col, 1952)
Deadline U.S.A. (20th, 1952)
Lone Star (MGM, 1952)
The Turning Point (Par, 1952)
Patterns (UA, 1956)
Twelve Angry Men (UA, 1957)
Odds Against Tomorrow (UA, 1959)
The Green Helmet (MGM, 1961)
Sweet Bird of Youth (MGM, 1962)

The Unsinkable Molly Brown (MGM, 1964)
The Oscar (Emb, 1966)
Warning Shot (Par, 1967)
Billion Dollar Brain (UA, 1967)
Hang 'em High (UA, 1968)
Wild in the Streets (AIP, 1968)
Firecreek (WB-7 Arts, 1968)
A Time to Sing (MGM, 1968)
The Monitors (CUE, 1969)
The Violent Enemy (Br, 1969)
The Dunwich Horror (AIP, 1970)
The Road to Salina (Avco Emb, 1971)

BILLY BENEDICT
(William Benedict)

In Melody Ranch (1940).

Born 1917, Haskell, Oklahoma. Perennial happy-go-lucky youth, endlessly cast as the Western Union messenger or office boy. Later was Whitey, one of the followers in the Bowery Boys series. Most recently a seedy type. TV series: "The Blue Knight" (as Toby, the informant).

Billy Benedict to J. Farrell MacDonald in *The Clancy Street Boys:* "It's okay, Flannagan, there ain't gonna' be no rough stuff—not until we find Muggs anyway."

Films

$10 Raise (Fox, 1935)
Doubting Thomas (Fox, 1935)
Ladies Love Danger (Fox, 1935)
College Scandal (Par, 1935)
Silk Hat Kid (Fox, 1935)
Way Down East (Fox, 1935)
Show Them No Mercy (Fox, 1935)
Your Uncle Dudley (Fox, 1935)
Three Kids and a Queen (Univ, 1935)
The Country Doctor (20th, 1936)
Meet Nero Wolf (Col, 1936)
Ramona (20th, 1936)
Adventure in Manhattan (Col, 1936)
The Witness Chair (RKO, 1936)
M'Liss (RKO, 1936)
They Wanted to Marry (RKO, 1936)
Libeled Lady (MGM, 1936)
Tim Tyler's Luck (Univ serial, 1937)
That I May Live (20th, 1937)
The Last Gangster (MGM, 1937)
Laughing at Trouble (20th, 1937)
Walking Down Broadway (20th, 1938)
Hold That Co-ed (20th, 1938)
King of the Newsboys (Rep, 1938)
Young Fugitives (Univ, 1938)
Little Tough Guys in Society (Univ, 1938)
Newsboys' Home (Univ, 1939)
Code of the Streets (Univ, 1939)
Man of Conquest (Rep, 1939)
Call a Messenger (Univ, 1939)
Legion of the Lawless (RKO, 1940)
The Bowery Boy (Rep, 1940)
Melody Ranch (Rep, 1940)
My Little Chickadee (Univ, 1940)
Give Us Wings (Univ, 1940)
Citadel of Crime (Rep, 1941)
The Man Who Lost Himself (Univ, 1941)
Adventures of Captain Marvel (Rep serial, 1941)

The Mad Doctor (Par, 1941)
The Great Mr. Nobody (WB, 1941)
Time Out for Rhythm (Col, 1941)
Tuxedo Junction (Rep, 1941)
Confessions of Boston Blackie (Col, 1941)
Home in Wyomin' (Rep, 1942)
Talk of the Town (Col, 1942)
On the Sunny Side (20th, 1942)
Get Hep to Love (Univ, 1942)
Perils of Nyoka (Rep serial, 1942)
Lady in a Jam (Univ, 1942)
Rings on Her Fingers (20th, 1942)
Mrs. Wiggs of the Cabbage Patch (Par, 1942)
Wildcat (Par, 1942)
Aerial Gunner (Par, 1943)
The Clancy Street Boys (Mon, 1943)
Whispering Footsteps (Rep, 1943)
Adventures of the Flying Cadets (Univ serial, 1943)
Ghosts on the Loose (Mon, 1943)
The Ox-Bow Incident (20th, 1943)
Moonlight in Vermont (Univ, 1943)
Million Dollar Kid (Mon, 1944)
Follow the Leader (Mon, 1944)
Goodnight, Sweetheart (Rep, 1944)
Block Busters (Mon, 1944)
The Merry Monohans (Univ, 1944)
They Live in Fear (Col, 1944)
That's My Baby (Rep, 1944)
Follow the Boys (Univ, 1944)
Bowery Champs (Mon, 1944)
Docks of New York (Mon, 1945)
Brenda Starr, Reporter (Col serial, 1945)
Mr. Muggs Rides Again (Mon, 1945)
Come Out Fighting (Mon, 1945)
Hollywood and Vine (PRC, 1945)
Road to Utopia (Par, 1945)
One More Tomorrow (WB, 1946)

Live Wires (Mon, 1946)
In Fast Company (Mon, 1946)
Spook Busters (Mon, 1946)
Bowery Bombshell (Mon, 1946)
Do You Love Me? (20th, 1946)
Mr. Hex (Mon, 1946)
Never Say Goodbye (WB, 1946)
The Kid from Brooklyn (RKO, 1946)
The Hucksters (MGM, 1947)
Hard-Boiled Mahoney (Mon, 1947)
Bowery Buckaroos (Mon, 1947)
Fun on a Week-End (UA, 1947)
The Pilgrim Lady (Rep, 1947)
News Hounds (Mon, 1947)
Angels' Alley (Mon, 1948)
Jinx Money (Mon, 1948)
Trouble Makers (Mon, 1948)
Secret Service Investigator (Rep, 1948)
Master Minds (Mon, 1949)
Hold That Baby (Mon, 1949)
Fighting Fools (Mon, 1949)
Angels in Disguise (Mon, 1949)
Blonde Dynamite (Mon, 1950)
Blues Busters (Mon, 1950)
Triple Trouble (Mon, 1950)
Bowery Battalion (Mon, 1951)
Ghost Chasers (Mon, 1951)
Let's Go, Navy (Mon, 1951)
Last Train from Gun Hill (Par, 1959)
Lover Come Back (Univ, 1961)
Zebra in the Kitchen (MGM, 1965)
The Hallelujah Trail (UA, 1965)
What Am I Bid? (Emerson, 1967)
Hello, Dolly (20th, 1969)
The Sting (Univ, 1973)
Homebodies (Avco Emb, 1974)
Farewell, My Lovely (Avco Emb, 1975)
Won Ton Ton, the Dog Who Saved Hollywood (Par, 1976)

WILLIE BEST

In David Harum (1934).

Born 1913, Sunflower, Mississippi. Died February 27, 1962, Hollywood, California. First billed in pictures as Sleep 'n' Eat. Developed into one of the screen's most enduring ethnic types: the pop-eyed, shuffling, black servant, usually stuck saying "Yes, sir" or "No, sir." In later *Charlie Chan* pictures he played Chattanooga Brown, alternating with Mantan Moreland (Birmingham) as chauffeur to the Oriental sleuth. TV series: "The Stuart Erwin Show" and "My Little Margie."

Willie Best to Paulette Goddard in *The Ghost Breakers:* "I'm Alex—the old family detainer."

Films

As Sleep 'n' Eat:
Feet First (Par, 1930)
Up Pops the Devil (Par, 1931)
The Monster Walks (Mayfair, 1932)
David Harum (Fox, 1934)
Kentucky Kernels (RKO, 1934)
Little Miss Marker (Par, 1934)
West of the Pecos (RKO, 1934)
Murder on a Honeymoon (RKO, 1935)

As Willie Best:
The Nitwits (RKO, 1935)
Jalna (RKO, 1935)
The Arizonian (RKO, 1935)
Hot Tip (RKO, 1935)
The Littlest Rebel (Fox, 1935)
Murder on a Bridle Path (RKO, 1936)
The Bride Walks Out (RKO, 1936)
Mummy's Boys (RKO, 1936)
Racing Lady (RKO, 1936)
Make Way for a Lady (RKO, 1936)

Thank You, Jeeves (20th, 1936)
General Spanky (MGM, 1936)
Two in Revolt (RKO, 1936)
Down the Stretch (FN, 1936)
Breezing Home (Univ, 1937)
The Lady Fights Back (Univ, 1937)
Super Sleuth (RKO, 1937)
Saturday's Heroes (RKO, 1937)
Meet the Missus (RKO, 1937)
Gold Is Where You Find It (WB, 1938)
Blondie (Col, 1938)
Merrily We Live (MGM, 1938)
Youth Takes a Fling (Univ, 1938)
Spring Madness (MGM, 1938)
Everybody's Doing It (RKO, 1938)
I'm from the City (RKO, 1938)
Goodbye Broadway (Univ, 1938)
Vivacious Lady (RKO, 1938)1(RKO, 1938)
Nancy Drew, Trouble Shooter (WB, 1939)
At the Circus (MGM, 1939)

The Covered Trailer (Rep, 1939)
I Take This Woman (MGM, 1940)
The Ghost Breakers (Par, 1940)
Money and the Woman (WB, 1940)
Who Killed Aunt Maggie? (Rep, 1940)
Road Show (UA, 1941)
Kisses for Breakfast (WB, 1941)
The Lady from Cheyenne (Univ, 1941)
High Sierra (WB, 1941)
Flight from Destiny (WB, 1941)
Scattergood Baines (RKO, 1941)
The Body Disappears (WB, 1941)
Nothing but the Truth (Par, 1941)
Highway West (WB, 1941)
The Smiling Ghost (WB, 1941)
Juke Girl (WB, 1942)
Whispering Ghosts (20th, 1942)
A-Haunting We Will Go (20th, 1942)
Busses Roar (WB, 1942)
Maisie Gets Her Man (MGM, 1942)
The Hidden Hand (WB, 1942)

Scattergood Survives a Murder (RKO, 1942)
Cabin in the Sky (MGM, 1943)
The Kansan (UA, 1943)
Thank Your Lucky Stars (WB, 1943)
Cinderella Swings It (RKO, 1943)
The Adventures of Mark Twain (WB, 1944)
Home in Indiana (20th, 1944)

The Girl Who Dared (Rep, 1944)
The Monster and the Ape (Col serial, 1945)
Hold That Blonde (Par, 1945)
Pillow to Post (WB, 1945)
Red Dragon (Mon, 1945)
The Bride Wore Boots (Par, 1946)
Dangerous Money (Mon, 1946)
She Wouldn't Say Yes (Col, 1946)

The Face of Marble (Mon, 1946)
Suddenly It's Spring (Par, 1947)
The Red Stallion (EL, 1947)
Smart Woman (AA, 1948)
Half Past Midnight (20th, 1948)
The Shanghai Chest (Mon, 1948)
Jiggs and Maggie in Jackpot Jitters (Mon, 1949)
South of Caliente (Rep, 1951)

CLEM BEVANS

Albert Dekker, Claire Trevor, Herbert Rawlinson, and Clem Bevans in The Woman of the Town (1943).

Born October 16, 1879, Cozaddale, Ohio. Married 1) _____ , child: Edith; 2) Lillian Luppee (1930), children: Clemene, Luppee, Clark. Died August 11, 1963, Woodland Hills, California. Veteran of vaudeville, stock, burlesque, and Broadway. Screen debut as Doc Wiggins (1935's *Way Down East*). Lanky frame, long face, and (later) white hair. A natural to portray grizzly old prospectors and cantankerous senior citizens: *Sergeant York* (Zeke), *Saboteur* (Neilson), *The Yearling* (Pa Forrester), *The Kentuckian* (Pilot), etc.

Clem Bevans to Mabel Paige in *Happy Go Lucky:* "I remember legs like other people remember faces. I can't help it."

Films

Way Down East (Fox, 1935)
Come and Get It (UA, 1936)
Rhythm on the Range (Par, 1936)
Idol of the Crowds (Univ, 1937)
Riding on Air (RKO, 1937)
The Big City (MGM, 1937)
Mr. Chump (WB, 1938)
Valley of the Giants (WB, 1938)

Of Human Hearts (MGM, 1938)
Young Fugitives (Univ, 1938)
Comet over Broadway (FN, 1938)
Tom Sawyer, Detective (Par, 1938)
Hold That Co-ed (20th, 1938)
Ambush (Par, 1939)
Maisie (MGM, 1939)
Hell's Kitchen (WB, 1939)

Idiot's Delight (MGM, 1939)
Night Work (Par, 1939)
Outside These Walls (Col, 1939)
Thunder Afloat (MGM, 1939)
Main Street Lawyer (Rep, 1939)
Undercover Doctor (Par, 1939)
Zenobia (UA, 1939)
They Made Me a Criminal (WB, 1939)

Dodge City (WB, 1939)
Stand Up and Fight (MGM, 1939)
The Cowboy Quarterback (WB, 1939)
Abe Lincoln in Illinois (RKO, 1940)
Young Tom Edison (MGM, 1940)
Go West (MGM, 1940)
Twenty-Mule Team (MGM, 1940)
The Captain Is a Lady (MGM, 1940)
Untamed (Par, 1940)
The Girl from God's Country (Rep, 1940)
Calling All Husbands (WB, 1940)
Granny Get Your Gun (WB, 1940)
Half a Sinner (Univ, 1940)
She Couldn't Say No (WB, 1941)
Sergeant York (WB, 1941)
Pacific Blackout [a.k.a. *Midnight Angel*] (Par, 1941)
The Parson of Panamint (Par, 1941)
The Smiling Ghost (WB, 1941)
Tombstone, the Town Too Tough to Die (Par, 1942)
Saboteur (Univ, 1942)
The Forest Rangers (Par, 1942)

Captains of the Clouds (WB, 1942)
Mrs. Wiggs of the Cabbage Patch (Par, 1942)
The Human Comedy (MGM, 1943)
The Kansan (UA, 1943)
Lady Bodyguard (Par, 1943)
Happy Go Lucky (Par, 1943)
The Woman of the Town (UA, 1943)
Night Club Girl (Univ, 1944)
Grissly's Millions (Rep, 1945)
Captain Eddie (20th, 1945)
Gallant Bess (MGM, 1946)
Wake Up and Dream (20th, 1946)
The Yearling (MGM, 1946)
The Millerson Case (Col, 1947)
The Yankee Fakir (Rep, 1947)
Mourning Becomes Electra (RKO, 1947)
Relentless (Col, 1948)
Texas, Brooklyn and Heaven (UA, 1948)
The Paleface (Par, 1948)
Moonrise (Rep, 1948)
Portrait of Jennie (Selznick Releasing Corp, 1948)

Highway 13 (Screen Guild, 1948)
Loaded Pistols (Col, 1949)
Big Jack (MGM, 1949)
Streets of Laredo (Par, 1949)
Rim of the Canyon (Col, 1949)
Deputy Marshal (Screen Guild, 1949)
The Gal Who Took the West (Univ, 1949)
Tell It to the Judge (Col, 1949)
Joe Palooka Meets Humphrey (Mon, 1950)
Harvey (Univ, 1950)
Gold Raiders (UA, 1951)
Silver City Bonanza (Rep, 1951)
Man in the Saddle (Col, 1951)
Captive of Billy the Kid (Rep, 1952)
Hangman's Knot (Col, 1952)
The Stranger Wore a Gun (Col, 1953)
The Boy from Oklahoma (WB, 1954)
Ten Wanted Men (Col, 1955)
The Kentuckian (UA, 1955)
Davy Crockett and the River Pirates (BV, 1956)

ABNER BIBERMAN

Sammy Stein, Abner Biberman, and Nestor Paiva in Broadway *(1942).*

Born April 1, 1909, Milwaukee, Wisconsin. Married Sibil Kamban (1954), children: Thor, Toby, Tony. Died June 20, 1977, San Diego, California. Although he was from the Midwest, most of his earlier screen parts were as natives—from India *(Gunga Din)*, Polynesia *(South of Pago-Pago, South of Tahiti, Beyond the Blue Horizon)*—or Italian gangster types *(Broadway)*. Later became director of TV shows and feature films: *Price of Fear* (1954), *Behind the High Wall* (1956), *Gun for a Coward* (1957), etc. TV series: "Kodiak."

Abner Biberman to Brian Donlevy in *South of Tahiti:* "You have broken tribal law. Native girl, daughter of chief, not for white man."

Films

Soak the Rich (Par, 1936)
The Rains Came (20th, 1939)
Panama Patrol (GN, 1939)
Each Dawn I Die (WB, 1939)
Balalaika (MGM, 1939)
Gunga Din (RKO, 1939)
Panama Lady (RKO, 1939)
Another Thin Man (MGM, 1939)
South of Pago-Pago (UA, 1940)
His Girl Friday (Col, 1940)
The Girl from Havana (Rep, 1940)
Zanzibar (Univ, 1940)
Enemy Agent (Univ, 1940)
South to Karanga (Univ, 1940)

The Monster and the Girl (Par, 1941)
Singapore Woman (WB, 1941)
This Woman Is Mine (Univ, 1941)
The Gay Vagabond (Rep, 1941)
South of Tahiti (Univ, 1941)
The Devil Pays Off (Rep, 1941)
Whispering Ghosts (20th, 1942)
Beyond the Blue Horizon (Par, 1942)
Broadway (Univ, 1942)
Little Tokyo, U.S.A. (20th, 1942)
The Leopard Man (RKO, 1943)
Submarine Alert (Par, 1943)
The Bridge of San Luis Rey (UA, 1944)
The Keys of the Kingdom (20th, 1944)

Two-Man Submarine (Col, 1944)
Back to Bataan (RKO, 1945)
Captain Kidd (UA, 1945)
Betrayal from the East (RKO, 1945)
Salome, Where She Danced (Univ, 1945)
Strange Conquest (Univ, 1946)
Winchester 73 (Univ, 1950)
Roaring City (Lip, 1951)
Viva Zapata (20th, 1952)
Elephant Walk (Par, 1954)
Knock on Wood (Par, 1954)
The Golden Mistress (UA, 1954)

THEODORE BIKEL

In Darker Than Amber (1970).

Born May 2, 1924, Vienna, Austria. Married 1) Ofra Ichilov (1942); divorced (1943); 2) Rita Weinberg (1967), children: Robert, another son. Versatile, stocky Continental who smoothly played characters of diverse nationalities: *The African Queen* (First Officer of the *Louisa*), *Melba* (Paul Brotha), *The Vintage* (Eduardo Urburri), *Fraulein* (Dmitri), etc. Oscar-nominated for BSAAA for playing the sheriff in *The Defiant Ones* (lost to Burl Ives of *The Big Country*).

Theodore Bikel to John Wengraf in *The Pride and the Passion:* "How these Spaniards love their moment of truth—to drench the ground with their blood—to die. Why?"

Films

The African Queen (UA, 1951)
Moulin Rouge (UA, 1952)
Never Let Me Go (MGM, 1953)
Melba (UA, 1953)
Desperate Moment (Br, 1953)
A Day to Remember (Br, 1953)
The Love Lottery (Br, 1954)
The Little Kidnappers (UA, 1954)
Chance Meeting (Br, 1955)
The Divided Heart (Br, 1955)
Forbidden Cargo (Br, 1956)
The Vintage (MGM, 1957)
The Pride and the Passion (UA, 1957)

The Enemy Below (20th, 1957)
Fraulein (20th, 1958)
I Want to Live! (UA, 1958)
I Bury the Living (UA, 1958)
The Defiant Ones (UA, 1958)
The Blue Angel (20th, 1959)
Woman Obsessed (20th, 1959)
The Angry Hills (MGM, 1959)
A Dog of Flanders (20th, 1960)
My Fair Lady (WB, 1964)
Sands of the Kalahari (Par, 1965)
The Russians Are Coming! The Russians Are Coming! (UA, 1966)

The Last Chapter (Ben-Lar, 1966) [narrator]
My Side of the Mountain (Par, 1967)
Festival (Peppercorn-Wormser, 1967)
Sweet November (WB–7 Arts, 1968)
The Desperate Ones (AIP, 1968)
Flap (WB, 1970)
Darker Than Amber (National General, 1970)
200 Motels (UA, 1971)
The Little Ark (National General, 1972)

HERMAN BING

In Maytime *(1937).*

Born March 30, 1889, Frankfurt, Germany. Married _____ , child: Ellen; widowed. Died January 9, 1947, Los Angeles, California. Pudgy comedy-relief performer who made a habit of the heavy-accented flustered Teutonic: 1934's *The Merry Widow* (manager of Maxime's), *20th Century* (First Beard), *Rose-Marie* (Mr. Daniels), *Bitter Sweet* (market keeper), etc. Committed suicide when his speciality had run its course and screen work was difficult to obtain.

> **Herman Bing** to Nelson Eddy in *Maytime:* "I have known people to have died to be shouted at when sleeping, ain't it?"

Films

Sunrise—A Song of Two Humans (Fox, 1927)
A Song of Kentucky (Fox, 1929)
Married in Hollywood (Fox, 1930)
Show Girl in Hollywood (FN, 1930)

Menschen Hinter Gettern (MGM, 1930—German version of Men of the North)
The Three Sisters (Fox, 1930)
The Great Lover (MGM, 1931)

The Guardsman (MGM, 1931)
Women Love Once (Par, 1931)
The Tenderfoot (FN, 1932)
Jewel Robbery (WB, 1932)
Silver Dollar (FN, 1932)

Hypnotized (Sono-Art-World Wide, 1932)
Flesh (MGM, 1932)
The Nuisance (MGM, 1933)
After Tonight (RKO, 1933)
Dinner at Eight (MGM, 1933)
The Bowery (MGM, 1933)
My Lips Betray (Fox, 1933)
The Great Jasper (RKO, 1933)
Footlight Parade (WB, 1933)
The College Coach (WB, 1933)
Hide-Out (MGM, 1934)
Mandalay (FN, 1934)
Melody in Spring (Par, 1934)
The Merry Widow (MGM, 1934)
Manhattan Love Song (Mon, 1934)
I'll Tell the World (Univ, 1934)
The Black Cat (Univ, 1934)
20th Century (Col, 1934)
Embarrassing Moments (Univ, 1934)
Love Time (Fox, 1934)
Crimson Romance (Mascot, 1934)
When Strangers Meet (Liberty, 1934)

The Mighty Barnum (UA, 1934)
It Happened in New York (Univ, 1935)
The Great Hotel Murder (Fox, 1935)
Redheads on Parade (Fox, 1935)
Call of the Wild (UA, 1935)
The Florentine Dagger (WB, 1935)
Don't Bet on Blondes (WB, 1935)
Calm Yourself (MGM, 1935)
In Caliente (FN, 1935)
Every Night at Eight (Par, 1935)
His Family Tree (RKO, 1935)
Three Kids and a Queen (Univ, 1935)
Fighting Youth (Univ, 1935)
$1,000 a Minute (Rep, 1935)
The Night Is Young (MGM, 1935)
Thunder in the Night (Fox, 1935)
Hands Across the Table (Par, 1935)
Rose-Marie (MGM, 1936)
The Great Ziegfeld (MGM, 1936)
Three Wise Guys (MGM, 1936)
Human Cargo (20th, 1936)
Dimples (20th, 1936)
The King Steps Out (Col, 1936)

Adventure in Manhattan (Col, 1936)
That Girl from Paris (RKO, 1936)
Laughing Irish Eyes (Rep, 1936)
The Music Goes Round (Col, 1936)
Tango (Invincible, 1936)
Come Closer, Folks (Col, 1936)
The Champagne Waltz (Par, 1937)
Maytime (MGM, 1937)
Beg, Borrow or Steal (MGM, 1937)
Every Day's a Holiday (Par, 1937)
Paradise for Three (MGM, 1938)
Vacation from Love (MGM, 1938)
Sweethearts (MGM, 1938)
The Great Waltz (MGM, 1938)
Bluebeard's Eighth Wife (Par, 1938)
Four's a Crowd (WB, 1938)
Bitter Sweet (MGM, 1940)
The Devil with Hitler (UA, 1942)
Where Do We Go from Here? (20th, 1945)
Rendezvous 24 (20th, 1946)
Night and Day (WB, 1946)

SIDNEY BLACKMER

J. Scott Smart (far left), Sidney Blackmer (center), and Charlotte Wynters in
Girl Overboard *(1937).*

Born July 13, 1894, Salisbury, North Carolina. Married 1) Lenore Ulric (1928); divorced (1939); 2) Suzanne Kaaren (1942), children: two sons. Died October 5, 1973, New York City, New York. Extremely competent stage and screen personality who bowed on camera in Pearl White's serial *The Perils of Pauline*. A specialist at the oily gangster and the suave, drawing room villain. Played Teddy Roosevelt frequently on stage and on screen (*This Is My Affair, Buffalo Bill*, etc.). Last on camera in *Rosemary's Baby* as Ruth Gordon's satanic spouse.

Sidney Blackmer to Carole Lombard in *From Hell to Heaven:*
"I never *could* be sensible where you're concerned."

Films

The Perils of Pauline (Eclectic serial, 1914)
A Most Immoral Lady (FN, 1929)
The Love Racket (FN, 1930)
Strictly Modern (FN, 1930)
The Bad Man (FN, 1930)
Kismet (FN, 1930)
Little Caesar (FN, 1930)
Mothers Cry (FN, 1930)
Sweethearts and Wives (FN, 1930)
Woman Hungry (FN, 1931)
The Lady Who Dared (FN, 1931)
It's a Wise Child (MGM, 1931)
One Heavenly Night (UA, 1931)
From Hell to Heaven (Par, 1933)
The Cocktail Hour (Col, 1933)
The Wrecker (Col, 1933)
The Deluge (RKO, 1933)
Goodbye Love (RKO, 1934)
This Man Is Mine (RKO, 1934)
Transatlantic Merry-Go-Round (UA, 1934)
The President Vanishes (Par, 1934)
Down to Their Last Yacht (RKO, 1934)
The Count of Monte Cristo (UA, 1934)
The Great God Gold (Mon, 1935)
A Notorious Gentleman (Univ, 1935)
The Little Colonel (Fox, 1935)
Behind the Green Lights (Mascot, 1935)
Streamline Express (Mascot, 1935)
Smart Girl (Par, 1935)
The Girl Who Came Back (Chesterfield, 1935)
False Pretenses (Chesterfield, 1935)
Fire Trap (Empire, 1935)
Forced Landing (Rep, 1935)
Woman Trap (Par, 1936)
Early to Bed (Par, 1936)
The President's Mystery (Rep, 1936)
Missing Girls (Chesterfield, 1936)
The Florida Special (Par, 1936)
Heart of the West (Par, 1936)
Shadows of the Orient (Mon, 1937)

House of Secrets (Chesterfield, 1937)
A Doctor's Diary (Par, 1937)
John Meade's Woman (Par, 1937)
This Is My Affair (20th, 1937)
Heidi (20th, 1937)
Wife, Doctor and Nurse (20th, 1937)
Charlie Chan at Monte Carlo (20th, 1937)
Thank You, Mr. Moto (20th, 1937)
Girl Overboard (Univ, 1937)
Women Men Marry (MGM, 1937)
The Last Gangster (MGM, 1937)
Michael O'Halloran (Rep, 1937)
In Old Chicago (20th, 1938)
Speed to Burn (20th, 1938)
Sharpshooters (20th, 1938)
Straight, Place and Show (20th, 1938)
Suez (20th, 1938)
Orphans of the Street (Rep, 1938)
Trade Winds (UA, 1938)
While New York Sleeps (Rep, 1938)
Convict's Code (Mon, 1939)
Fast and Loose (MGM, 1939)
It's a Wonderful World (MGM, 1939)
Unmarried (Par, 1939)
Law of the Pampas (Par, 1939)
Elsa Maxwell's Hotel for Women (20th, 1939)
Trapped in the Sky (Col, 1939)
Within the Law (MGM, 1939)
Maryland (20th, 1940)
Framed (Univ, 1940)
Third Finger, Left Hand (MGM, 1940)
Dance, Girl, Dance (RKO, 1940)
I Want a Divorce (Par, 1940)
Murder Among Friends (20th, 1941)
Cheers for Miss Bishop (UA, 1941)
Rookies on Parade (Rep, 1941)
The Great Swindle (Col, 1941)
Love Crazy (MGM, 1941)
Angels with Broken Wings (Rep, 1941)
Obliging Young Lady (RKO, 1941)
Ellery Queen and the Perfect Crime (Col, 1941)

Down Mexico Way (Rep, 1941)
The Feminine Touch (MGM, 1941)
The Officer and the Lady (Col, 1941)
Always in My Heart (WB, 1942)
Nazi Agent (MGM, 1942)
Gallant Lady [a.k.a. *Prison Girls*] (PRC, 1942)
Quiet Please, Murder (20th, 1942)
The Panther's Claw (PRC, 1942)
Sabotage Squad (Col, 1942)
Murder in Times Square (Col, 1943)
I Escaped from the Gestapo [a.k.a. *No Escape*] (Mon, 1943)
In Old Oklahoma [a.k.a. *War of the Wildcats*] (Rep, 1943)
Buffalo Bill (20th, 1944)
Broadway Rhythm (MGM, 1944)
The Lady and the Monster (Rep, 1944)
Wilson (20th, 1944)
Duel in the Sun (Selznick Releasing Organization, 1946)
My Girl Tisa (WB, 1948)
A Song Is Born (RKO, 1948)
Farewell to Yesterday (20th, 1950) [narrator]
People Will Talk (20th, 1951)
Saturday's Hero (Col, 1951)
The San Francisco Story (WB, 1952)
The Washington Story (MGM, 1952)
Johnny Dark (Univ, 1954)
The High and the Mighty (WB, 1954)
The View from Pompey's Head (20th, 1955)
High Society (MGM, 1956)
Beyond a Reasonable Doubt (RKO, 1956)
Accused of Murder (Rep, 1956)
Tammy and the Bachelor (Univ, 1957)
Joy in the Morning (MGM, 1965)
How to Murder Your Wife (UA, 1965)
A Covenant with Death (WB, 1967)
Rosemary's Baby (Par, 1968)

ERIC BLORE

With Glenda Farrell in Breakfast for Two *(1937).*

Born December 23, 1887, London, England. Married 1) Violet Winter; widowed; 2) Clara Mackin, child: one, divorced. Died March 1, 1959, Hollywood, California. The archetypal gentleman's gentleman who could administer scorn with a raised eyebrow or a sniveling smile, and deliver an acid comment in a stinging, lisping way. Had a range of unctuous worker guises in Fred Astaire–Ginger Rogers pictures: *Flying Down to Rio* (assistant hotel manager), *The Gay Divorcee* (waiter), *Top Hat* (Bates, the manservant), *Swing Time* (Gordon, the huffy dance school manager), *Shall We Dance* (Cecil Flintridge, the hotel floor manager). In the 1940s emerged as Jamison, the bumptious butler/man Friday supporting Warren William in *The Lone Wolf* detective series. Could be exceedingly fatuous and asinine when cast in roles like the (hammy) genie in the Bowery Boys' *Bowery to Bagdad*, his final film.

Eric Blore to Fred Astaire in *Top Hat:* "Allow us to introduce ourselves, sir. We are Bates."

Films

A Night Out and a Day In (Br, 1920)
The Great Gatsby (Par, 1926)
Laughter (Par, 1930)
My Sin (Par, 1931)
Tarnished Lady (Par, 1931)
Flying Down to Rio (RKO, 1933)
The Gay Divorcee (RKO, 1934)
Limehouse Blues (Par, 1934)
Behold My Wife (Par, 1934)
Folies Bergere (UA, 1935)
To Beat the Band (RKO, 1935)
The Good Fairy (Univ, 1935)
Diamond Jim (Univ, 1935)
The Casino Murder Case (MGM, 1935)
I Live My Life (MGM, 1935)
Top Hat (RKO, 1935)
I Dream Too Much (RKO, 1935)
Seven Keys to Baldpate (RKO, 1935)

Two in the Dark (RKO, 1936)
The Ex-Mrs. Bradford (RKO, 1936)
Swing Time (RKO, 1936)
The Smartest Girl in Town (RKO, 1936)
Sons o' Guns (WB, 1936)
Piccadilly Jim (MGM, 1936)
The Soldier and the Lady [a.k.a. *Michael Strogoff*] (RKO, 1937)
Quality Street (RKO, 1937)
Shall We Dance (RKO, 1937)
Breakfast for Two (RKO, 1937)
Hitting a New High (RKO, 1937)
It's Love I'm After (WB, 1937)
Joy of Living (RKO, 1938)
Swiss Miss (MGM, 1938)
A Desperate Adventure (Rep, 1938)
Island of Lost Men (Par, 1939)
$1,000 a Touchdown (Par, 1939)

A Gentleman's Gentleman (Br, 1939)
Music in My Heart (Col, 1940)
The Man Who Wouldn't Talk (20th, 1940)
The Lone Wolf Strikes (Col, 1940)
The Lone Wolf Meets a Lady (Col, 1940)
The Lone Wolf Keeps a Date (Col, 1940)
Till We Meet Again (WB, 1940)
South of Suez (WB, 1940)
The Boys from Syracuse (Univ, 1940)
The Earl of Puddlestone (Rep, 1940)
Secrets of the Lone Wolf (Col, 1941)
The Lady Eve (Par, 1941)
The Lone Wolf Takes a Chance (Col, 1941)
Road to Zanzibar (Par, 1941)
Red Head (Mon, 1941)
Lady Scarface (RKO, 1941)
New York Town (Par, 1941)

The Shanghai Gesture (UA, 1941)
Sullivan's Travels (Par, 1941)
Three Girls About Town (Col, 1941)
The Moon and Sixpence (UA, 1942)
Counter Espionage (Col, 1942)
Confirm or Deny (20th, 1942)
Happy Go Lucky (Par, 1943)
The Sky's the Limit (RKO, 1943)
Forever and a Day (RKO, 1943)
Holy Matrimony (20th, 1943)

Submarine Base (PRC, 1943)
Passport to Suez (Col, 1943)
One Dangerous Night (Col, 1943)
San Diego, I Love You (Univ, 1944)
Penthouse Rhythm (Univ, 1945)
Men in Her Diary (Univ, 1945)
Easy to Look At (Univ, 1945)
Kitty (Par, 1945)
The Notorious Lone Wolf (Col, 1946)
Two Sisters from Boston (MGM, 1946)

Abie's Irish Rose (UA, 1946)
Winter Wonderland (Rep, 1947)
The Lone Wolf in London (Col, 1947)
The Lone Wolf in Mexico (Col, 1947)
Romance on the High Seas (WB, 1948)
Love Happy (UA, 1949)
Adventures of Ichabod and Mr. Toad (RKO, 1949) [voice only]
Fancy Pants (Par, 1950)
Bowery to Bagdad (AA, 1954)

FORTUNIO BONANOVA

Fortunio Bonanova, Bob Burns, and Martha Raye in Tropic Holiday *(1938).*

Born January 13, 1896, Palma de Mallorca, Spain. Married 1) _____, child: Marie; 2) _____, child: Joanne. Died April 2, 1969, Woodland Hills, California. Moved to the United States (where he managed a repertory company) after an extensive career as a South American opera impresario and singer. Was much in demand during period of Good Neighbor–Latin American policy as the overbearing (in size, style, and projection) South American. Sometimes serious, as in *For Whom the Bell Tolls* (Fernando).

Fortunio Bonanova (during an air raid) in *Five Graves to Cairo:* "I wish I was in Milano. . . . No, Milano is not good either."

Films

Don Juan (Sp, 1924)
A Successful Calamity (WB, 1932)
Careless Lady (Fox, 1932)
El Desaparicido (Sp, 1936)
Podoroso Caballero (Sp, 1936)

Romance in the Dark (Par, 1938)
Tropic Holiday (Par, 1938)
Bulldog Drummond in Africa (Par, 1938)
La Inmaculada (Sp, 1939)
I Was an Adventuress (20th, 1940)

Down Argentine Way (20th, 1940)
That Night in Rio (20th, 1941)
Mr. and Mrs. North (MGM, 1941)
Obliging Young Lady (RKO, 1941)
They Met in Argentina (RKO, 1941)

Citizen Kane (RKO, 1941)
Blood and Sand (20th, 1941)
Moon over Miami (20th, 1941)
A Yank in the R.A.F. (20th, 1941)
Two Latins from Manhattan (Col, 1941)
Sing Your Worries Away (RKO, 1942)
Larceny, Inc. (WB, 1942)
Girl Trouble (20th, 1942)
The Black Swan (20th, 1942)
Call Out the Marines (RKO, 1942)
Five Graves to Cairo (Par, 1943)
The Sultan's Daughter (Mon, 1943)
For Whom the Bell Tolls (Par, 1943)
Going My Way (Par, 1944)
Ali Baba and the Forty Thieves (Univ, 1944)
The Falcon in Mexico (RKO, 1944)
My Best Gal (Rep, 1944)

Double Indemnity (Par, 1944)
Mrs. Parkington (MGM, 1944)
Brazil (Rep, 1944)
Where Do We Go from Here? (20th, 1945)
A Bell for Adano (20th, 1945)
The Red Dragon (Mon, 1945)
Hit the Hay (Col, 1945)
Man Alive (RKO, 1945)
Monsieur Beaucaire (Par, 1946)
Fiesta (MGM, 1947)
The Fugitive (RKO, 1947)
Rose of Santa Rosa (Col, 1947)
Romance on the High Seas (WB, 1948)
Bad Men of Tombstone (AA, 1948)
Angel on the Amazon (Rep, 1948)
Adventures of Don Juan (WB, 1948)
Whirlpool (20th, 1949)
Nancy Goes to Rio (MGM, 1950)

September Affair (Par, 1950)
Havana Rose (Rep, 1951)
Second Chance (RKO, 1953)
Conquest of Cochise (Col, 1953)
The Moon Is Blue (UA, 1953)
Thunder Bay (Univ, 1953)
So This Is Love (WB, 1953)
New York Confidential (WB, 1955)
Kiss Me Deadly (UA, 1955)
Jaquar (Rep, 1956)
An Affair to Remember (20th, 1957)
The Saga of Hemp Brown (Univ, 1958)
Thunder in the Sun (Par, 1959)
The Running Man (Col Br, 1963)
The Million Dollar Collar (Independent, 1967)

WARD BOND

With John Wayne in Operation Pacific *(1951).*

Born April 9, 1905, Denver, Colorado. Married 1) Doris Sellers (1936); divorced (1944); 2) Mary Lou May (1954). Died November 5, 1960, Dallas, Texas. One of filmdom's most reliable supporting players. A long-time favorite of director John Ford and star John Wayne. Often cast as a rugged, gruff guy who sometimes was a soft touch: *It Happened One Night* (bus driver), *Devil Dogs of the Air* (senior instructor), *You Only Live Once* (guard), *Gone with the Wind* (Tom, the Yankee captain), Humphrey Bogart's *The Maltese Falcon* (Detective Tom Polhaus), *They Came to Blow Up America* (Mr. Craig). Frequently employed by director Ford: *Salute* (football player—along with John Wayne), *Submarine Patrol* (Olaf Swanson), *Young Mr. Lincoln* (John Palmer Cass), *The Grapes of Wrath* (cop), *The Long Voyage Home* (Yank), *The Quiet Man* (Father Peter Lonergan), etc. TV series: "Wagon Train" (Wagonmaster Seth Adams).

Ward Bond to Richard Greene in *Little Old New York:* "Why, you dribblin' young pup—I'll break you in two!"

73

Films

Salute (Fox, 1929)
Words and Music (Fox, 1929)
Born Reckless (Fox, 1930)
The Big Trail (Fox, 1930)
High Speed (Col, 1932)
White Eagle (Col, 1932)
Rackety Rax (Fox, 1932)
Hello, Trouble (Col, 1932)
Virtue (Col, 1932)
When Strangers Marry (Col, 1933)
Heroes for Sale (FN, 1933)
Wild Boys of the Road (FN, 1933)
The Wrecker (Col, 1933)
Unknown Valley (Col, 1933)
Police Car No. 17 (Col, 1933)
Obey the Law (Col, 1933)
The Sundown Rider (Col, 1933)
Whirlpool (Col, 1933)
Most Precious Thing in Life (Col, 1934)
Straightaway (Col, 1934)
The Poor Rich (Univ, 1934)
Frontier Marshal (Fox, 1934)
Broadway Bill (Col, 1934)
It Happened One Night (Col, 1934)
The Defense Rests (Col, 1934)
Fighting Ranger (Col, 1934)
Here Comes the Groom (Par, 1934)
The Fighting Code (Col, 1934)
The Voice in the Night (Col, 1934)
A Man's Game (Col, 1934)
The Crime of Helen Stanley (Col, 1934)
Girl in Danger (Col, 1934)
The Human Side (Univ, 1934)
Kid Millions (UA, 1934)
Against the Law (Col, 1934)
Devil Dogs of the Air (WB, 1935)
Little Big Shot (WB, 1935)
The Informer (RKO, 1935)
The Crimson Trail (Univ, 1935)
She Gets Her Man (Univ, 1935)
His Night Out (Univ, 1935)
Black Fury (FN, 1935)
Western Courage (Col, 1935)
Fighting Shadows (Col, 1935)
Guard That Girl (Col, 1935)
Murder in the Fleet (MGM, 1935)
The Headline Woman (Mascot, 1935)
Waterfront Lady (Rep, 1935)
Men of the Night (Col, 1935)
Justice of the Range (Col, 1935)
Too Tough to Kill (Col, 1935)
Cattle Thief (Col, 1936)
Muss 'em Up (RKO, 1936)
The Bride Walks Out (RKO, 1936)
Second Wife (RKO, 1936)
Without Orders (RKO, 1936)
Crash Donovan (Univ, 1936)
Conflict (Univ, 1936)
They Met in a Taxi (Col, 1936)

The Man Who Lived Twice (Col, 1936)
The Legion of Terror (Col, 1936)
The Leathernecks Have Landed (Rep, 1936)
Pride of the Marines (Col, 1936)
Avenging Waters (Col, 1936)
You Only Live Once (UA, 1937)
Dead End (UA, 1937)
Park Avenue Logger [a.k.a. Tall Timber] (RKO, 1937)
The Devil's Playground (Col, 1937)
23½ Hours Leave (GN, 1937)
Night Key (Univ, 1937)
Escape by Night (Rep, 1937)
The Wildcatter (Univ, 1937)
A Fight to the Finish (Col, 1937)
Born to Be Wild (Rep, 1938)
Flight into Nowhere (Col, 1938)
Hawaii Calls (RKO, 1938)
Reformatory (Col, 1938)
Gun Law (RKO, 1938)
The Law West of Tombstone (RKO, 1938)
Professor Beware (Par, 1938)
Mr. Moto's Gamble (20th, 1938)
Submarine Patrol (20th, 1938)
Prison Break (Univ, 1938)
Numbered Woman (Mon, 1938)
Over the Wall (WB, 1938)
The Amazing Dr. Clitterhouse (WB, 1938)
They Made Me a Criminal (WB, 1939)
Made for Each Other (UA, 1939)
Dodge City (WB, 1939)
Waterfront (WB, 1939)
Gone with the Wind (MGM, 1939)
Trouble in Sundown (RKO, 1939)
The Return of the Cisco Kid (20th, 1939)
Young Mr. Lincoln (20th, 1939)
Frontier Marshal (20th, 1939)
The Girl from Mexico (RKO, 1939)
The Kid from Kokomo (WB, 1939)
Drums Along the Mohawk (20th, 1939)
Dust Be My Destiny (WB, 1939)
The Oklahoma Kid (WB, 1939)
Heaven with a Barbed Wire Fence (20th, 1939)
Virginia City (WB, 1940)
The Cisco Kid and the Lady (20th, 1940)
The Grapes of Wrath (20th, 1940)
Little Old New York (20th, 1940)
Santa Fe Trail (WB, 1940)
Buck Benny Rides Again (Par, 1940)
The Mortal Storm (MGM, 1940)
Kit Carson (UA, 1940)
The Long Voyage Home (UA, 1940)
Tobacco Road (20th, 1941)
A Man Betrayed (Rep, 1941)
The Shepherd of the Hills (Par, 1941)
Swamp Water (20th, 1941)
Sergeant York (WB, 1941)

Manpower (WB, 1941)
Doctors Don't Tell (Rep, 1941)
Wild Bill Hickok Rides (WB, 1941)
The Maltese Falcon (WB, 1941)
The Falcon Takes Over (RKO, 1942)
In This Our Life (WB, 1942)
Ten Gentlemen from West Point (20th, 1942)
Gentleman Jim (WB, 1942)
Sin Town (Univ, 1942)
Hello, Frisco, Hello (20th, 1943)
A Guy Named Joe (MGM, 1943)
Hitler—Dead or Alive (Ben Judell, 1943)
Slightly Dangerous (MGM, 1943)
They Came to Blow Up America (20th, 1943)
Home in Indiana (20th, 1944)
The Sullivans (20th, 1944)
Tall in the Saddle (RKO, 1944)
Dakota (Rep, 1945)
They Were Expendable (MGM, 1945)
Canyon Passage (Univ, 1946)
It's a Wonderful Life (RKO, 1946)
My Darling Clementine (20th, 1946)
The Fugitive (RKO, 1947)
Unconquered (Par, 1947)
Fort Apache (RKO, 1948)
The Time of Your Life (UA, 1948)
Tap Roots (Univ, 1948)
Joan of Arc (RKO, 1948)
Three Godfathers (MGM, 1948)
Riding High (Par, 1950)
Wagonmaster (RKO, 1950)
Singing Guns (Rep, 1950)
The Great Missouri Raid (Par, 1950)
Kiss Tomorrow Goodbye (WB, 1950)
Operation Pacific (WB, 1951)
Only the Valiant (WB, 1951)
On Dangerous Ground (RKO, 1951)
The Quiet Man (Rep, 1952)
Hellgate (Lip, 1952)
Thunderbirds (Rep, 1952)
Blowing Wild (WB, 1953)
The Moonlighter (WB, 1953)
Hondo (WB, 1953)
Gypsy Colt (MGM, 1954)
Johnny Guitar (Rep, 1954)
The Bob Mathias Story (AA, 1954)
The Long Gray Line (Col, 1955)
Mr. Roberts (WB, 1955)
A Man Alone (Rep, 1955)
The Searchers (WB, 1956)
Dakota Incident (Rep, 1956)
Pillars of the Sky (Univ, 1956)
The Wings of Eagles (MGM, 1957)
The Halliday Brand (UA, 1957)
China Doll (UA, 1958)
Rio Bravo (WB, 1959)
Alias Jesse James (UA, 1959)

BEULAH BONDI
(Beulah Bondy)

Beulah Bondi, Barbara Read, and Thomas Mitchell in Make Way for Tomorrow *(1937).*

Born May 3, 1892, Chicago, Illinois. Perhaps the most consummate of all character players. Twice Oscar-nominated for BSAAA: as Rachel Jackson in *The Gorgeous Hussy* (lost to Gale Sondergaard of *Anthony Adverse*); as Mary Wilkins, James Stewart's mother in *Of Human Hearts* (beaten by Fay Bainter of *Jezebel*). Won her laurels recreating her stage role of Emma Jones, the crotchety tenement dweller in *Street Scene*. Often seen as a mature rural type: *The Trail of the Lonesome Pine* (Melissa), *The Shepherd of the Hills* (Aunt Mollie Matthews). Extremely touching as the aging city dweller in *Make Way for Tomorrow* who, along with husband Victor Moore, discovers her children no longer want her presence. Could be staunch: the patriotic schoolteacher of *Back to Bataan*, sentimental *(So Dear to My Heart)*, or persnickety *(A Summer Place)*.

> **Beulah Bondi** to Ralph Remley in *Ready for Love:* "Chester . . . stay away from that cider. Remember the strawberry festival when you were flirting about telling everyone you were a butterfly."

Films

Street Scene (UA, 1931)
Arrowsmith (UA, 1931)
Rain (UA, 1932)
The Stranger's Return (MGM, 1933)
Christopher Bean (MGM, 1933)
Two Alone (RKO, 1934)
Finishing School (RKO, 1934)
Registered Nurse (WB, 1934)
The Painted Veil (MGM, 1934)
Ready for Love (Par, 1934)
Bad Boy (Fox, 1935)
The Good Fairy (Univ, 1935)
The Trail of the Lonesome Pine (Par, 1936)

The Moon's Our Home (Par, 1936)
The Case Against Mrs. Ames (Par, 1936)
The Invisible Ray (Univ, 1936)
Hearts Divided (WB, 1936)
The Gorgeous Hussy (MGM, 1936)
Maid of Salem (Par, 1937)
Make Way for Tomorrow (Par, 1937)
The Buccaneer (Par, 1938)
Of Human Hearts (MGM, 1938)
Vivacious Lady (RKO, 1938)
The Sisters (WB, 1938)
On Borrowed Time (MGM, 1939)
The Under-Pup (Univ, 1939)

Mr. Smith Goes to Washington (Col, 1939)
Remember the Night (Par, 1940)
Our Town (UA, 1940)
The Captain Is a Lady (MGM, 1940)
The Shepherd of the Hills (Par, 1941)
Penny Serenade (Col, 1941)
One Foot in Heaven (WB, 1941)
Tonight We Raid Calais (20th, 1943)
Watch on the Rhine (WB, 1943)
And Now Tomorrow (Par, 1944)
I Love a Soldier (Par, 1944)
Our Hearts Were Young and Gay (Par, 1944)

She's a Soldier Too (Col, 1944)
The Very Thought of You (WB, 1944)
Back to Bataan (RKO, 1945)
The Southerner (UA, 1945)
Breakfast in Hollywood (UA, 1946)
Sister Kenny (RKO, 1946)
It's a Wonderful Life (RKO, 1946)
High Conquest (Mon, 1947)
So Dear to My Heart (RKO, 1948)
The Sainted Sisters (Par, 1948)

The Snake Pit (20th, 1948)
Reign of Terror [a.k.a. The Black Book] (EL, 1949)
Mr. Soft Touch (Col, 1949)
The Life of Riley (Univ, 1949)
The Baron of Arizona (Lip, 1950)
The Furies (Par, 1950)
Lone Star (MGM, 1952)
Latin Lovers (MGM. 1953)
Track of the Cat (WB, 1954)

Back from Eternity (RKO, 1956)
The Unholy Wife (Univ, 1957)
The Big Fisherman (BV, 1959)
A Summer Place (WB, 1959)
Tammy Tell Me True (Univ, 1961)
The Wonderful World of the Brothers Grimm (MGM, 1962)
Tammy and the Doctor (Univ, 1963)

VEDA ANN BORG

In Arkansas Judge *(1941)*.

Born January 11, 1915, Boston, Massachusetts. Married 1) Paul Herrick (1942); divorced; 2) Andrew McLaglen (1946), child: Andrew; divorced (1958). Died August 16, 1973, Hollywood, California. A dark-haired lass at Warner Bros. *(Variety Show,* etc.); a tawdry blonde type in the 1940s (underwent plastic surgery in 1939 after a car accident). Exuded delicious cheapness as the wisecracking tramp, waitress, moll, etc. Occasionally revealed her heart of gold. Was sympathetic at the end of her career as Blind Nell, a pioneer type in John Wayne's *The Alamo.*

Veda Ann Borg to June Haver in *Irish Eyes Are Smiling:* "What are you doing in my $85 feathered robe? Take it off!"

Films

Three Cheers for Love (Par, 1936)
Marry the Girl (WB, 1937)
Varsity Show (WB, 1937)

Men in Exile (WB, 1937)
Kid Galahad (WB, 1937)
The Case of the Stuttering Bishop (WB,

1937)
Public Wedding (WB, 1937)
The Singing Marine (WB, 1937)

Confession (WB, 1937)
San Quentin (WB, 1937)
It's Love I'm After (WB, 1937)
Submarine D-1 (WB, 1937)
Missing Witnesses (WB, 1937)
Alcatraz Island (WB, 1938)
She Loved a Fireman (WB, 1938)
Over the Wall (WB, 1938)
Cafe Hostess (Col, 1939)
The Law Comes to Texas (Col, 1939)
The Shadow (Col serial, 1940)
A Miracle on Main Street (Col, 1940)
I Take This Oath (PRC, 1940)
Dr. Christian Meets the Women (RKO, 1940)
Melody Ranch (Rep, 1940)
Laughing at Danger (Mon, 1940)
Glamour for Sale (Col, 1940)
Bitter Sweet (MGM, 1940)
Behind the News (Rep, 1940)
Down in San Diego (MGM, 1941)
The Getaway (MGM, 1941)
Arkansas Judge (Rep, 1941)
The Penalty (MGM, 1941)
I'll Wait for You (MGM, 1941)
The Pittsburgh Kid (Rep, 1941)
Honky Tonk (MGM, 1941)
The Corsican Brothers (UA, 1941)
Duke of the Navy (PRC, 1942)
I Married an Angel (MGM, 1942)
About Face (UA, 1942)
She's in the Army Now (Mon, 1942)
Two Yanks in Trinidad (Col, 1942)

Lady in a Jam (Univ, 1942)
Murder in Times Square (Col, 1943)
The Isle of Forgotten Sins (PRC, 1943)
Revenge of the Zombies (Mon, 1943)
The Girl from Monterey (PRC, 1943)
The Unknown Guest (Mon, 1943)
False Faces (Rep, 1943)
Something to Shout About (Col, 1943)
Smart Guy (Mon, 1943)
Standing Room Only (Par, 1944)
Irish Eyes Are Smiling (20th, 1944)
Detective Kitty O'Day (Mon, 1944)
Marked Trails (Mon, 1944)
The Girl Who Dared (Rep, 1944)
The Big Noise (20th, 1944)
The Falcon in Hollywood (RKO, 1944)
What a Blonde (RKO, 1945)
Fog Island (PRC, 1945)
Rough, Tough and Ready (Col, 1945)
Bring on the Girls (Par, 1945)
Don Juan Quilligan (20th, 1945)
Scared Stiff [TV title: *Treasure of Fear*] (Par, 1945)
Nob Hill (20th, 1945)
Dangerous Intruder (PRC, 1945)
Love, Honor and Goodbye (Rep, 1945)
Mildred Pierce (WB, 1945)
Jungle Raiders (Col serial, 1945)
Life with Blondie (Col, 1946)
Avalanche (PRC, 1946)
Accomplice (PRC, 1946)
Wife Wanted (Mon, 1946)
The Fabulous Suzanne (Rep, 1946)

The Pilgrim Lady (Rep, 1947)
Big Town (Par, 1947)
The Bachelor and the Bobby-Soxer (RKO, 1947)
Mother Wore Tights (20th, 1947)
Blonde Savage (EL, 1947)
Julia Misbehaves (MGM, 1948)
Chicken Every Sunday (20th, 1948)
Mississippi Rhythm (Mon, 1949)
One Last Fling (WB, 1949)
Forgotten Women (Mon, 1949)
Rider from Tucson (RKO, 1950)
The Kangaroo Kid (EL, 1950)
Hold That Line (Mon, 1952)
Aaron Slick from Punkin Crick (Par, 1952)
Big Jim McLain (WB, 1952)
A Perilous Journey (Rep, 1953)
Mister Scoutmaster (20th, 1953)
Hot News (AA, 1953)
Three Sailors and a Girl (WB, 1953)
Bitter Creek (AA, 1954)
You're Never Too Young (Par, 1955)
Guys and Dolls (MGM, 1955)
I'll Cry Tomorrow (MGM, 1955)
Love Me or Leave Me (MGM, 1955)
Frontier Gambler (Associated Film, 1956)
The Wings of Eagles (MGM, 1957)
The Fearmakers (UA, 1958)
Thunder in the Sun (Par, 1959)
The Alamo (UA, 1960)

ALICE BRADY

In When Ladies Meet *(1933)*.

Born November 2, 1892, New York City, New York. Married James L. Crane (1919), child: Donald; divorced (1922). Died October 28, 1939, New York City, New York. A Broadway star. Became the captivating leading lady of scores of silent features. Entries for World made by her (Broadway) producer father, William A. Brady—some adaptations of her stage hits: *Sinners, Anna Ascends,* etc. *His Bridal Night* was first screen comedy. Later wed the leading man (James Crane). Returned as a leading featured player after being away from the screen for a decade. Role in *When Ladies Meet* as the daffy society hostess led to a succession of such parts, each radiating her artistry. Was a deft combination of Mary Boland, Fay Bainter, and Margaret Dumont, exuding a zaniness that made screwball comedies possible and so popular. Oscar-nominated for a BSAAA for playing Carole Lombard's addled blue-blood mama in *My Man Godfrey* (lost to Gale Sondergaard of *Anthony Adverse*). Won in the same category in 1938 for her dramatic interpretation of Mrs. O'Leary (whose cow did you-know-what) in *In Old Chicago*. Final film was memorable interpretation of Mrs. Clay, mother of accused murderer in *Young Mr. Lincoln*.

> **Alice Brady** to Ginger Rogers in *The Gay Divorcee:* "I do adore Paris. It's so much like Chicago. . . . It's such a relief when you travel to feel that you've never left home at all."

Films

As Ye Sow (World, 1914)
The Boss (World, 1915)
The Cup of Chance (Knickerbocker, 1915)
The Lure of Woman (World, 1915)

The Rack (World, 1916)
The Ballet Girl (World, 1916)
The Woman in 47 (World, 1916)
Then I'll Come Back to You (World, 1916)
Tangled Fates (World, 1916)

La Boheme (World, 1916)
Miss Petticoats (World, 1916)
The Gilded Cage (World, 1916)
Bought and Paid For (World, 1916)
A Woman Alone (World, 1917)

A Hungry Heart (World, 1917)
The Dancer's Peril (World, 1917)
Darkest Russia (World, 1917)
Maternity (World, 1917)
The Divorce Game (World, 1917)
A Self-Made Widow (World, 1917)
Betsy Ross (World, 1917)
A Maid of Belgium (World, 1917)
Her Silent Sacrifice (Select, 1918)
Woman and Wife (Select, 1918)
The Knife (Select, 1918)
The Spurs of Sybil (World, 1918)
At the Mercy of Men (Select, 1918)
The Trap (World, 1918)
The Whirlpool (Select, 1918)
The Death Dance (Select, 1918)
The Ordeal of Rosetta (Select, 1918)
The Better Half (Select, 1918)
In the Hollow of Her Hand (Select, 1918)
Her Great Chance (Select, 1918)
The Indestructible Wife (Select, 1919)
The World to Live In (Select, 1919)

Marie, Ltd. (Select, 1919)
The Redhead (Select, 1919)
His Bridal Night (Select, 1919)
The Fear Market (Realart, 1920)
Sinners (Realart, 1920)
A Dark Lantern (Realart, 1920)
The New York Idea (Realart, 1920)
Out of the Chorus (Realart, 1921)
The Land of Hope (Realart, 1921)
Little Italy (Realart, 1921)
Dawn of the East (Realart, 1921)
Hush Money (Realart, 1921)
Missing Millions (Par, 1922)
Anna Ascends (Par, 1922)
The Leopardess (Par, 1923)
The Snow Bride (Par, 1923)
When Ladies Meet (MGM, 1933)
Broadway to Hollywood (MGM, 1933)
Beauty for Sale (MGM, 1933)
Stage Mother (MGM, 1933)
Should Ladies Behave? (MGM, 1933)
Miss Fane's Baby Is Stolen (Par, 1934)

The Gay Divorcee (RKO, 1934)
Let 'em Have It (UA, 1935)
Gold Diggers of 1935 (WB, 1935)
Lady Tubbs (Univ, 1935)
Metropolitan (20th, 1935)
The Harvester (Rep, 1936)
My Man Godfrey (Univ, 1936)
Go West, Young Man (Par, 1936)
Mind Your Own Business (Par, 1936)
Three Smart Girls (Univ, 1937)
Call It a Day (WB, 1937)
Mama Steps Out (MGM, 1937)
Mr. Dodd Takes the Air (WB, 1937)
100 Men and a Girl (Univ, 1937)
Merry-Go-Round of 1938 (Univ, 1937)
In Old Chicago (20th, 1938)
Joy of Living (RKO, 1938)
Goodbye Broadway (Univ, 1938)
Zenobia (UA, 1939)
Young Mr. Lincoln (20th, 1939)

HENRY BRANDON
(Henry Kleinbach)

Walter Klavun and Henry Brandon in Okefenokee *(1959).*

Born June 8, 1912, Berlin, Germany. Striking-looking villain of five decades of movies: *Babes in Toyland* (Barnaby), *Jungle Jim* serial (the Cobra), *Drums of Fu Manchu* serial (the sinister Oriental lead), etc.

Henry Brandon in *Buck Rogers*: "Wait! We'll take them alive and force the secret of the Hidden City from them."

Films

As Henry Kleinbach:
Babes in Toyland (MGM, 1934)
The Preview Murder Mystery (Par, 1936)
Big Brown Eyes (Par, 1936)

As Henry Brandon:
Killer at Large (Col, 1936)
The Garden of Allah (UA, 1936)
Black Legion (WB, 1936)
I Promise to Pay (Col, 1937)
Island Captives (Principal, 1937)
Jungle Jim (Univ serial, 1937)
Conquest (MGM, 1937)
Last Train from Madrid (Par, 1937)
Wells Fargo (Par, 1937)
West Bound Limited (Univ, 1937)
Secret Agent X-9 (Univ serial, 1937)
If I Were King (Par, 1938)
Three Comrades (MGM, 1938)
The Last Warning (Univ, 1938)
Spawn of the North (Par, 1938)
Conspiracy (RKO, 1939)
Buck Rogers (Univ serial, 1939)
Pirates of the Skies (Univ, 1939)
Nurse Edith Cavell (RKO, 1939)

Beau Geste (Par, 1939)
Marshal of Mesa City (RKO, 1939)
Ski Patrol (Univ, 1940)
Half a Sinner (Univ, 1940)
The Ranger and the Lady (Rep, 1940)
Under Texas Skies (Rep, 1940)
The Son of Monte Cristo (UA, 1940)
Dark Streets of Cairo (Univ, 1940)
Drums of Fu Manchu (Rep serial, 1940)
The Shepherd of the Hills (Par, 1941)
Underground (WB, 1941)
Hurricane Smith (Rep, 1941)
Bad Man of Deadwood (Rep, 1941)
Two in a Taxi (Col, 1941)
Edge of Darkness (WB, 1943)
Northwest Outpost (Rep, 1947)
Old Los Angeles (Rep, 1948)
Canon City (EL, 1948)
The Paleface (Par, 1948)
Hollow Triumph [a.k.a. *The Scar*] (EL, 1948)
Joan of Arc (RKO, 1948)
The Fighting O'Flynn (Univ, 1949)
Cattle Drive (Univ, 1951)
The Golden Horde (Univ, 1951)

The Flame of Araby (Univ, 1951)
Harem Girl (Col, 1952)
Scarlet Angel (Univ, 1952)
Hurricane Smith (Par, 1952)
Tarzan and the She-Devil (RKO, 1953)
War Arrow (Univ, 1953)
The War of the Worlds (Par, 1953)
Pony Express (Par, 1953)
Scared Stiff (Par, 1953)
Raiders of the Seven Seas (UA, 1953)
The Caddy (Par, 1953)
Vera Cruz (UA, 1954)
Silent Fear (Gibraltar, 1955)
The Ten Commandments (Par, 1956)
The Searchers (WB, 1956)
Omar Khayyam (Par, 1957)
Auntie Mame (WB, 1958)
The Buccaneer (Par, 1958)
The Big Fisherman (BV, 1959)
Okefenokee (Filmservice Corp, 1959)
Two Rode Together (Col, 1961)
The Manhandlers (Premiere Releasing, 1973)
When the North Wind Blows (Sunn Classic, 1975)

WALTER BRENNAN

With Loretta Young in Kentucky *(1938).*

Born July 25, 1894, Swampscott, Massachusetts. Married Ruth Wells (1920), children: Arthur, Walter, Ruth. Died September 21, 1974, Oxnard, California. Three-time BSAAA winner: *Come and Get It* (Swan Bostrom), *Kentucky* (Peter Goodwin), *The Westerner* (Judge Roy Bean). Made a career of playing assorted old men, claiming that his only acting technique was whether or not he used his false teeth for an assignment. As good with dialects as with cackles, limps, and pensiveness. Oscar-nominated for his Pastor Rosier Pile in Gary Cooper's *Sergeant York* (but lost BSAAA to Donald Crisp of *How Green Was My Valley*). TV series: "The Real McCoys," "Tycoon," "Guns of Will Sonnett," and "To Rome, With Love."

Walter Brennan to Jack Lambert in *Brimstone:* "A man that ain't no good at gun slingin' ain't no good to me—even if he is my son."

Films

The Ridin' Rowdy (Pathé, 1927)
Tearin' into Trouble (Pathé, 1928)
The Ballyhoo Buster (Pathé, 1928)
Smilin' Guns (Univ, 1929)
The Lariat Kid (Univ, 1929)
The Long, Long Trail (Univ, 1929)
One Hysterical Night (Univ, 1929)
The Shannons of Broadway (Univ, 1929)
King of Jazz (Univ, 1930)
Dancing Dynamite (Capitol Films, 1931)
Neck and Neck (Sono-Art-World Wide, 1931)
Law and Order (Univ, 1932)
The Texas Cyclone (Col, 1932)
Two-Fisted Law (Col, 1932)
The All-American (Univ, 1932)

Man of Action (Col, 1933)
Fighting for Justice (Col, 1933)
The Keyhole (WB, 1933)
Lilly Turner (FN, 1933)
Baby Face (WB, 1933)
Female (FN, 1933)
From Headquarters (WB, 1933)
Sing, Sinner, Sing (Majestic, 1933)
One Year Later (Alliance, 1933)
Strange People (Chesterfield, 1933)
Parachute Jumper (WB, 1933)
Housewife (WB, 1934)
Desirable (WB, 1934)
Half a Sinner (Univ, 1934)
Riptide (MGM, 1934)
Stamboul Quest (MGM, 1934)

The Painted Veil (MGM, 1934)
Good Dame (Par, 1934)
The Man on the Flying Trapeze (Par, 1935)
Seven Keys to Baldpate (RKO, 1935)
Barbary Coast (UA, 1935)
The Bride of Frankenstein (Univ, 1935)
Lady Tubbs (Univ, 1935)
Northern Frontier (Ambassador, 1935)
The Wedding Night (UA, 1935)
Law Beyond the Range (Col, 1935)
Three Godfathers (MGM, 1936)
Fury (MGM, 1936)
Come and Get It (UA, 1936)
Banjo on My Knee (20th, 1936)
These Three (UA, 1936)

The Moon's Our Home (Par, 1936)
The Prescott Kid (Col, 1936)
When Love Is Young (Univ, 1937)
Wild and Woolly (20th, 1937)
She's Dangerous (Univ, 1937)
The Affairs of Cappy Ricks (Rep, 1937)
The Buccaneer (Par, 1938)
The Texans (Par, 1938)
Adventures of Tom Sawyer (UA, 1938)
Kentucky (20th, 1938)
Mother Carey's Chickens (RKO, 1938)
The Cowboy and the Lady (UA, 1938)
Stanley and Livingstone (20th, 1939)
The Story of Vernon and Irene Castle (RKO, 1939)
They Shall Have Music (UA, 1939)
Joe and Ethel Turp Call on the President (MGM, 1939)
Maryland (20th, 1940)
Northwest Passage (MGM, 1940)
The Westerner (UA, 1940)
Meet John Doe (WB, 1941)
Sergeant York (WB, 1941)
Rise and Shine (20th, 1941)
Nice Girl? (Univ, 1941)
Swamp Water (20th, 1941)
This Woman Is Mine (Univ, 1941)

The Pride of the Yankees (RKO, 1942)
Stand By for Action (MGM, 1942)
Slightly Dangerous (MGM, 1943)
Hangmen Also Die (UA, 1943)
The North Star [a.k.a. *Armored Attack*] (RKO, 1943)
The Princess and the Pirate (RKO, 1944)
Home in Indiana (20th, 1944)
To Have and Have Not (WB, 1944)
Dakota (Rep, 1945)
Nobody Lives Forever (WB, 1946)
A Stolen Life (WB, 1946)
Centennial Summer (20th, 1946)
My Darling Clementine (20th, 1946)
Driftwood (Rep, 1947)
Scudda Hoo! Scudda Hay! (20th, 1948)
Red River (UA, 1948)
Blood on the Moon (RKO, 1948)
The Green Promise (RKO, 1949)
Brimstone (Rep, 1949)
Task Force (WB, 1949)
Curtain Call at Cactus Creek (Univ, 1950)
A Ticket to Tomahawk (20th, 1950)
Singing Guns (Rep, 1950)
Surrender (Rep, 1950)
The Showdown (Rep, 1950)
The Wild Blue Yonder (Rep, 1951)

Along the Great Divide (WB, 1951)
Best of the Bad Men (RKO, 1951)
Lure of the Wilderness (20th, 1952)
Return of the Texan (20th, 1952)
Sea of Lost Ships (Rep, 1953)
Drums Across the River (Univ, 1954)
Four Guns to the Border (Univ, 1954)
Bad Day at Black Rock (MGM, 1954)
The Far Country (Univ, 1955)
At Gunpoint (AA, 1955)
The Proud Ones (20th, 1956)
Glory (RKO, 1956)
Come Next Spring (Rep, 1956)
Goodbye, My Lady (WB, 1956)
Tammy and the Bachelor (Univ, 1957)
God Is My Partner (20th, 1957)
The Way to the Gold (20th, 1957)
Rio Bravo (WB, 1959)
How the West Was Won (MGM, 1962)
Those Calloways (BV, 1964)
The Oscar (Emb, 1966)
Who's Minding the Mint? (Col, 1967)
The Gnome-Mobile (BV, 1967)
The One and Only Genuine Original Family Band (BV, 1968)
Support Your Local Sheriff (UA, 1969)

FELIX BRESSART

Felix Bressart, Philip Dorn, and Hedy Lamarr in Ziegfeld Girl *(1941).*

Born March 2, 1880, Eydtkuhnen, Germany. Married Frieda Lehner. Died March 17, 1949, Los Angeles, California. Unique contributor to Hollywood filmmaking. This German emigré was under MGM contract for most of his American film years. With floppy hair, soulful eyes, and a big nose, the lean figure was often seen in downcast, philosophical roles: Buljanoff (one of the trio of converted Soviet emissaries in *Ninotchka*), Vanya (*Comrade X*), Mischa (*Ziegfeld Girl*), Poldi Schlamm (*The Seventh Cross*), Professor Gerkikoff (one of the seven dour musical scholars who take up jazz in *A Song Is Born*). Remarkably effective as Greenberg, a Jewish member of the Jack Benny–Carole Lombard acting troupe in *To Be or Not to Be*.

Felix Bressart to Philip Dorn in *Ziegfeld Girl:* "It's a disgrace
to your violin to make *jazz* music."

Films

Drei von ver Tankstele (Ger, 1931)
Der Wahre Jakob (Ger, 1931)
Das Alte Lied (Ger, 1931)
Nie Wieder Liebe (Ger, 1931)
Eine Freundin so Goldig wie Du (Ger, 1931)
Der Schrecken der Garnison (Ger, 1932)
Hirsekorn Greift Ein (Ger, 1932)
Der Herr Buerovorsteher (Ger, 1932)
Holzapfel Weiss Alles (Ger, 1933)
Drei Tage Mittelarrest (Ger, 1933)
Der Sohn der Weissen Berge (Ger, 1933)
Der Glueckszylinger (Ger, 1934)
Und Wer Kuesst Mich? (Ger, 1935)
Three Smart Girls Grow Up (Univ, 1939)
Bridal Suite (MGM, 1939)
Swanee River (20th, 1939)

Ninotchka (MGM, 1939)
The Shop Around the Corner (MGM, 1940)
It All Came True (WB, 1940)
Edison the Man (MGM, 1940)
Third Finger, Left Hand (MGM, 1940)
Bitter Sweet (MGM, 1940)
Comrade X (MGM, 1940)
Escape (MGM, 1940)
Ziegfeld Girl (MGM, 1941)
Blossoms in the Dust (MGM, 1941)
Married Bachelor (MGM, 1941)
Kathleen (MGM, 1941)
Mr. and Mrs. North (MGM, 1941)
To Be or Not to Be (UA, 1942)
Crossroads (MGM, 1942)
Iceland (20th, 1942)

Three Hearts for Julia (MGM, 1943)
Song of Russia (MGM, 1943)
Above Suspicion (MGM, 1943)
Greenwich Village (20th, 1944)
The Seventh Cross (MGM, 1944)
Blonde Fever (MGM, 1944)
Dangerous Partners (MGM, 1945)
Without Love (MGM, 1945)
Ding Dong Williams (RKO, 1946)
I've Always Loved You (Rep, 1946)
The Thrill of Brazil (Col, 1946)
Her Sister's Secret (PRC, 1946)
A Song Is Born (RKO, 1948)
Portrait of Jenny (Selznick Releasing Organization, 1948)
Take One False Step (Univ, 1949)

HELEN BRODERICK

Wendy Barrie, Helen Broderick, and Gene Raymond in Love on a Bet *(1936).*

Born August 11, 1891, Philadelphia, Pennsylvania. Married Lester Crawford, child: Broderick. Died September 25, 1959, Beverly Hills, California. Unconventional, striking looks (once a Ziegfeld Follies performer). Bolstered many pictures with her sparkling arch delivery. Especially remembered for her deadpan-comedy moments in *Top Hat* (as Madge Hardwick, the matchmaking wife of Edward Everett Horton) and in *Swing Time* (Mabel Anderson, the flippant dance studio receptionist). Mother of actor Broderick Crawford.

Helen Broderick to Danielle Darrieux in *The Rage of Paris:* "I married a hoofer. All he had was a time step and a 'shuffle off to Buffalo.' Later in life he became ambitious . . . and got 20 years."

Films

50 Million Frenchmen (WB, 1931)
Top Hat (RKO, 1935)
To Beat the Band (RKO, 1935)
Love on a Bet (RKO, 1936)
Murder on the Bridle Path (RKO, 1936)
Swing Time (RKO, 1936)
The Bride Walks Out (RKO, 1936)
Smartest Girl in Town (RKO, 1936)
We're on the Jury (RKO, 1937)
Meet the Missus (RKO, 1937)
Life of the Party (RKO, 1937)

Radio City Revels (RKO, 1938)
She's Got Everything (RKO, 1938)
The Rage of Paris (Univ, 1938)
The Road to Reno (Univ, 1938)
Service de Luxe (Univ, 1938)
Stand Up and Fight (MGM, 1939)
Naughty but Nice (WB, 1939)
Honeymoon in Bali (Par, 1939)
The Captain Is a Lady (MGM, 1940)
No, No, Nanette (RKO, 1940)
Virginia (Par, 1941)

Nice Girl? (Univ, 1941)
Father Takes a Wife (RKO, 1941)
Are Husbands Necessary? (Par, 1942)
Stage Door Canteen (UA, 1943)
Chip off the Old Block (Univ, 1944)
Her Primitive Man (Univ, 1944)
Three Is a Family (UA, 1944)
Love, Honor and Goodbye (Rep, 1945)
Because of Him (Univ, 1946)

J. EDWARD BROMBERG

Robert Kent, Rochelle Hudson, and J. Edward Bromberg in That I May Live *(1937)*.

Born December 25, 1903, Temesvar, Hungary. Married Goldie Doberman (1927), children: three. Died December 6, 1951, London, England. European who abandoned jobs as laundry worker, cloth salesman, etc., to become stage actor. Later theatrical jobs in New York led to 20th Century–Fox contract in 1936. His stocky figure turned up in an assortment of parts: *Stowaway* (Judge Booth), *Charlie Chan on Broadway* (Murdock, the newspaper editor), *Suez* (Said), *Rebecca of Sunnybrook Farm* (Dr. Hill), *The Mark of Zorro* (Don Luis Quintero), etc. In the 1940s, mostly at Universal: *Invisible Agent* (Heiser), Claude Rains' *The Phantom of the Opera* (Amoit), *Salome, Where She Danced* (Professor Max), etc.

> **J. Edward Bromberg** to Alice Faye in *Hollywood Cavalcade:* It'll be chiseled on my tombstone—Dave Spingold—Schlemiel."

Films

Under Two Flags (20th, 1936)
Sins of Man (20th, 1936)
The Crime of Dr. Forbes (20th, 1936)
Girls' Dormitory (20th, 1936)
Star for a Night (20th, 1936)
Ladies in Love (20th, 1936)
Reunion (20th, 1936)
Stowaway (20th, 1936)
Fair Warning (20th, 1937)
That I May Live (20th, 1937)
Seventh Heaven (20th, 1937)
Charlie Chan on Broadway (20th, 1937)
Second Honeymoon (20th, 1937)
Mr. Moto Takes a Chance (20th, 1938)

The Baroness and the Butler (20th, 1938)
One Wild Night (20th, 1938)
Four Men and a Prayer (20th, 1938)
Sally, Irene and Mary (20th, 1938)
Rebecca of Sunnybrook Farm (20th, 1938)
I'll Give a Million (20th, 1938)
Suez (20th, 1938)
Jesse James (20th, 1939)
Wife, Husband and Friend (20th, 1939)
Hollywood Cavalcade (20th, 1939)
Three Sons (20th, 1939)
Strange Cargo (MGM, 1940)
The Return of Frank James (20th, 1940)
The Mark of Zorro (20th, 1940)

Hurricane Smith (Rep, 1941)
Dance Hall (20th, 1941)
The Devil Pays Off (Rep, 1941)
Pacific Blackout [a.k.a. Midnight Angel] (Par, 1942)
Invisible Agent (Univ, 1942)
Life Begins at 8:30 (20th, 1942)
Tennessee Johnson (MGM, 1942)
Reunion (MGM, 1942)
Half Way to Shanghai (Univ, 1942)
Lady of Burlesque (UA, 1943)
The Phantom of the Opera (Univ, 1943)
Son of Dracula (Univ, 1943)
Chip off the Old Block (Univ, 1944)

Voice in the Wind (UA, 1944)
Easy to Look At (Univ, 1945)
The Missing Corpse (PRC, 1945)
Pillow of Death (Univ, 1945)
Salome, Where She Danced (Univ, 1945)

The Walls Came Tumbling Down (Col, 1946)
Tangier (Univ, 1946)
Cloak and Dagger (WB, 1946)
Queen of the Amazons (Screen Guild, 1947)

1947)
Arch of Triumph (UA, 1948)
A Song Is Born (RKO, 1948)
I Shot Jesse James (Screen Guild, 1949)
Guilty Bystander (Film Classics, 1950)

ED BROPHY
(Edward S. Brophy)

Ed Brophy, Lloyd Corrigan, Gloria De Haven, William Powell, Ed Gargan, and Donald Meek (seated) in The Thin Man Goes Home (1944).

Born February 27, 1895, New York City, New York. Married Ann _____. Died May 27, 1960, Pacific Palisades, California. Cigar-chewing rotund player who simulated toughness (e.g., Morelli of The Thin Man) but who usually emerged comical and gentle. Was the pop-eyed valet Bates in The Gay Falcon; returned to the detective series occasionally in the role of Goldie Locke.

Ed Brophy to Andy Devine in A Dangerous Game: "Y' know, you ain't a bad guy, if you wasn't batty."

Films

Yes or No (Associated FN, 1920)
West Point (MGM, 1927)
The Cameraman (MGM, 1928)
Doughboys (MGM, 1930)
Our Blushing Brides (MGM, 1930)
Remote Control (MGM, 1930)
Those Three French Girls (MGM, 1930)
Free and Easy (MGM, 1930)

Paid (MGM, 1930)
Parlor, Bedroom and Bath (MGM, 1931)
A Free Soul (MGM, 1931)
The Champ (MGM, 1931)
A Dangerous Affair (Col, 1931)
The Big Shot (RKO, 1931)
Flesh (MGM, 1932)
Freaks (MGM, 1932)

Speak Easily (MGM, 1932)
What, No Beer? (MGM, 1933)
Broadway to Hollywood (MGM, 1933)
The Thin Man (MGM, 1934)
Paris Interlude (MGM, 1934)
Hide-Out (MGM, 1934)
Death on the Diamond (MGM, 1934)
Evelyn Prentice (MGM, 1934)

I'll Fix It (Col, 1934)
Naughty Marietta (MGM, 1935)
The Whole Town's Talking (Col, 1935)
Shadow of Doubt (MGM, 1935)
Mad Love (MGM, 1935)
China Seas (MGM, 1935)
People Will Talk (Par, 1935)
She Gets Her Man (Univ, 1935)
Remember Last Night? (Univ, 1935)
I Live My Life (MGM, 1935)
Show Them No Mercy (Fox, 1935)
$1,000 a Minute (Rep, 1935)
Strike Me Pink (UA, 1936)
Woman Trap (Par, 1936)
The Case Against Mrs. Ames (Par, 1936)
Spendthrift (Par, 1936)
Wedding Present (Par, 1936)
All-American Chump (MGM, 1936)
Kelly the Second (MGM, 1936)
Here Comes Trouble (20th, 1936)
Career Woman (20th, 1936)
Great Guy (GN, 1936)
Mr. Cinderella (MGM, 1936)
Hideaway Girl (Par, 1937)
The Soldier and the Lady [a.k.a. Michael Strogoff] (RKO, 1937)
The Great Gambini (Par, 1937)
Blossoms on Broadway (Par, 1937)
Varsity Show (WB, 1937)
Jim Hanvey, Detective (Rep, 1937)
The Hit Parade (Rep, 1937)
Oh, Doctor! (Univ, 1937)
The Last Gangster (MGM, 1937)

The Girl Said No (GN, 1937)
Trapped by G-Men [a.k.a. The River of Missing Men] (Col, 1937)
A Slight Case of Murder (WB, 1938)
Romance on the Run (Rep, 1938)
Come On, Leathernecks (Rep, 1938)
Gambling Ship (Univ, 1938)
Hold That Kiss (MGM, 1938)
Vacation from Love (MGM, 1938)
Passport Husband (20th, 1938)
Pardon Our Nerve (20th, 1938)
Gold Diggers in Paris (WB, 1938)
You Can't Cheat an Honest Man (Univ, 1939)
For Love or Money (Univ, 1939)
Society Lawyer (MGM, 1939)
The Kid from Kokomo (WB, 1939)
Golden Boy (Col, 1939)
The Amazing Mr. Williams (Col, 1939)
Kid Nightingale (WB, 1939)
The Big Guy (Univ, 1940)
Calling Philo Vance (WB, 1940)
Alias the Deacon (Univ, 1940)
Golden Gloves (Par, 1940)
The Great Profile (20th, 1940)
Dance, Girl, Dance (RKO, 1940)
Sandy Gets Her Man (Univ, 1940)
A Dangerous Game (Univ, 1940)
Sleepers West (20th, 1941)
The Invisible Woman (Univ, 1941)
Dumbo (RKO, 1941) [voice only]
Thieves Fall Out (WB, 1941)
The Bride Came C.O.D. (WB. 1941)

Buy Me That Town (Par, 1941)
Nine Lives Are Not Enough (WB, 1941)
The Gay Falcon (RKO, 1941)
Steel Against the Sky (WB, 1941)
Larceny, Inc. (WB, 1942)
Broadway (Univ, 1942)
Madame Spy (Univ, 1942)
All Through the Night (WB, 1942)
Destroyer (Col, 1943)
Lady Bodyguard (Par, 1943)
Air Force (WB, 1943)
It Happened Tomorrow (UA, 1944)
Cover Girl (Col, 1944)
A Night of Adventure (RKO, 1944)
The Thin Man Goes Home (MGM, 1944)
Wonder Man (RKO, 1945)
I'll Remember April (Univ, 1945)
See My Lawyer (Univ, 1945)
Penthouse Rhythm (Univ, 1945)
The Falcon in San Francisco (RKO, 1945)
Girl on the Spot (Univ, 1946)
Swing Parade of 1946 (Mon, 1946)
Sweethearts of Sigma Chi (Mon, 1946)
Renegade Girl (Screen Guild, 1946)
The Falcon's Adventure (RKO, 1946)
It Happened on 5th Avenue (AA, 1947)
Arson, Inc. (Lip, 1949)
Pier 23 (Lip, 1951)
Danger Zone (Lip, 1951)
Roaring City (Lip, 1951)
Bundle of Joy (RKO, 1956)
The Last Hurrah (Col, 1958)

NIGEL BRUCE

Nigel Bruce, Victor McLaglen, Claudette Colbert, and Ronald Colman in Under Two Flags *(1936).*

Born February 4, 1895, Ensenada, Mexico. Married Violet Campbell, children: Jennifer, Pauline. Died October 8, 1953, Santa Monica, California. Well-bred thick-set Britisher who mumbled, tweaked his own moustache and shuffled his feet in a convincing measure of amiable incompetence: Leslie Howard's *The Scarlet Pimpernel* (Prince Regent), *The Charge of the Light Brigade* (Sir Benjamin Warrenton), *Rebecca* (Major Giles Lacy), *Suspicion* (Beaky), *The Corn Is Green* (the Squire), etc. Most heralded as the jocular, slightly foggy Dr. Watson to Basil Rathbone's perspicacious Sherlock Holmes in the film series. Decided asset during heyday of Hollywood's anglomania.

Nigel Bruce, regarding rabbit's foot, to Basil Rathbone in *The Adventures of Sherlock Holmes:* "I've always thought those things in very poor taste. Fancy going about with a dead animal's foot dangling from your pocket."

Films

Red Aces (Br, 1929)
The Squeaker (Br, 1931)
Escape (Br, 1931)
Birds of Prey (Br, 1931)
The Calendar (Br, 1931)
Lord Camber's Ladies (Br, 1932)
The Midshipmaid (Br, 1932)
Channel Crossing (Br, 1933)
I Was a Spy (Br, 1934)
Springtime for Henry (Fox, 1934)
Coming Out Party (Fox, 1934)
Stand Up and Cheer (Fox, 1934)

Murder in Trinidad (Fox, 1934)
The Lady Is Willing (Col, 1934)
Treasure Island (MGM, 1934)
The Scarlet Pimpernel (UA, 1935)
She (RKO, 1935)
Becky Sharp (RKO, 1935)
Jalna (RKO, 1935)
The Man Who Broke the Bank at Monte Carlo (Fox, 1935)
The Trail of the Lonesome Pine (Par, 1936)
Under Two Flags (20th, 1936)
The White Angel (WB, 1936)

The Charge of the Light Brigade (WB, 1936)
Follow Your Heart (Rep, 1936)
The Man I Marry (Univ, 1936)
Make Way for a Lady (RKO, 1936)
Thunder in the City (Col Br, 1937)
The Last of Mrs. Cheyney (MGM, 1937)
Kidnapped (20th, 1938)
Suez (20th, 1938)
The Baroness and the Butler (20th, 1938)
The Hound of the Baskervilles (20th, 1939)
The Adventures of Sherlock Holmes (20th, 1939)

The Rains Came (20th, 1939)
Adventure in Diamonds (Par, 1940)
The Blue Bird (20th, 1940)
Lillian Russell (20th, 1940)
Hudson's Bay (20th, 1940)
Rebecca (UA, 1940)
Susan and God (MGM, 1940)
A Dispatch from Reuter's (WB, 1940)
Play Girl (RKO, 1940)
This Woman Is Mine (Univ, 1941)
Free and Easy (MGM, 1941)
The Chocolate Soldier (MGM, 1941)
Suspicion (RKO, 1941)
This Above All (20th, 1942)
Journey for Margaret (MGM, 1942)
Roxie Hart (RKO, 1942)
Eagle Squadron (Univ, 1942)

Sherlock Holmes and the Voice of Terror (Univ, 1942)
Sherlock Holmes and the Secret Weapon (Univ, 1942)
Crazy House (Univ, 1943)
Sherlock Holmes in Washington (Univ, 1943)
Forever and a Day (RKO, 1943)
Lassie Come Home (MGM, 1943)
Sherlock Holmes Faces Death (Univ, 1943)
The Pearl of Death (Univ, 1944)
Follow the Boys (Univ, 1944)
Gypsy Wildcat (Univ, 1944)
The Spider Woman (Univ, 1944)
The Scarlet Claw (Univ, 1944)
Frenchman's Creek (Par, 1944)
Son of Lassie (MGM, 1945)

House of Fear (Univ, 1945)
The Corn Is Green (WB, 1945)
Pursuit to Algiers (Univ, 1945)
The Woman in Green (Univ, 1945)
Terror by Night (Univ, 1946)
Dressed to Kill (Univ, 1946)
Dragonwyck (20th, 1946)
The Two Mrs. Carrolls (WB, 1947)
The Exile (Univ, 1947)
Julia Misbehaves (MGM, 1948)
Vendetta (RKO, 1950)
Hong Kong (Par, 1951)
Limelight (UA, 1952)
Bwana Devil (UA, 1952)
World for Ransom (AA, 1954)

EDGAR BUCHANAN

In The Sheepman *(1958).*

Born March 20, 1903, Humansville, Missouri. Married Mildred Spence (1928), child: Bucky. Former dentist who could convey a wide range of dramatic meanings by the squint of an eye or a contraction of his lips. Equally at ease as a rustic sidekick, a sagebrush villain, or an urban philosopher. Memorable as printing-press worker Applejack *(Penny Serenade)* and as the irascible judge *(Move Over, Darling).* TV series: "Hopalong Cassidy," "Judge Roy Bean," "The Rifleman," "Petticoat Junction" (as Joe Carson), and "Cade's County."

Edgar Buchanan to Richard Dix in *Tombstone, the Town Too Tough to Die:* "Seems like every time I get a town organized, *you* show up."

Films

My Son Is Guilty (Col, 1939)
When the Daltons Rode (Univ, 1940)
Three Cheers for the Irish (WB, 1940)
The Doctor Takes a Wife (Col, 1940)
The Sea Hawk (WB, 1940)
Submarine Zone [a.k.a. *Escape to Glory*] (Col, 1940)
Too Many Husbands (Col, 1940)
Tear Gas Squad (WB, 1940)
Arizona (Col, 1940)
The Richest Man in Town (Col, 1941)
Penny Serenade (Col, 1941)
Texas (Col, 1941)
You Belong to Me (Col, 1941)
Her First Beau (Col, 1941)
The Talk of the Town (Col, 1942)
Tombstone, the Town Too Tough to Die (Par, 1942)
City Without Men (Col, 1943)
The Desperadoes (Col, 1943)
Destroyer (Col, 1943)
Good Luck, Mr. Yates (Col, 1943)
The Impatient Years (Col, 1944)
Buffalo Bill (20th, 1944)
Bride by Mistake (RKO, 1944)
The Strange Affair (Col, 1944)
The Fighting Guardsman (Col, 1945)
The Bandit of Sherwood Forest (Col, 1946)
If I'm Lucky (20th, 1946)
Renegades (Col, 1946)
Perilous Holiday (Col, 1946)
The Walls Came Tumbling Down (Col, 1946)

Abilene Town (UA, 1946)
Framed (Col, 1947)
The Sea of Grass (MGM, 1947)
The Swordsman (Col, 1947)
Adventures in Silverado (Col, 1948)
The Best Man Wins (Col, 1948)
The Black Arrow (Col, 1948)
The Wreck of the Hesperus (Col, 1948)
Coroner Creek (Col, 1948)
The Untamed Breed (Col, 1948)
The Man from Colorado (Col, 1948)
Red Canyon (Univ, 1949)
Any Number Can Play (MGM, 1949)
Lust for Gold (Col, 1949)
The Walking Hills (Col, 1949)
The Devil's Doorway (MGM, 1950)
Cheaper by the Dozen (20th, 1950)
The Big Hangover (MGM, 1950)
Cargo to Capetown (Col, 1950)
The Great Missouri Raid (Par, 1950)
Flaming Feather (Par, 1951)
Silver City (Par, 1951)
Rawhide (20th, 1951)
Cave of Outlaws (Univ, 1951)
Wild Stallion (Mon, 1952)
The Big Trees (WB, 1952)
Toughest Man in Arizona (Rep, 1952)
It Happens Every Thursday (Par, 1953)
Shane (Par, 1953)
She Couldn't Say No (RKO, 1954)
Make Haste to Live (Rep, 1954)
Human Desire (Col, 1954)
Dawn at Socorro (Univ, 1954)

Destry (Univ, 1954)
Rage at Dawn (RKO, 1955)
Wichita (AA, 1955)
The Silver Star (Lip, 1955)
The Lonesome Trail (Lip, 1955)
Come Next Spring (Rep, 1956)
Spoilers of the Forest (Rep, 1957)
The Sheepman (MGM, 1958)
The Devil's Partner (Filmgroup, 1958)
Day of the Bad Man (Univ, 1958)
King of the Wild Stallions (AA, 1959)
It Started with a Kiss (MGM, 1959)
Hound Dog Man (20th, 1959)
Edge of Eternity (Col, 1959)
Four Fast Guns (Univ, 1959)
Cimarron (MGM, 1960)
Stump Run (Aschroft, 1960)
The Chartroose Caboose (Univ, 1960)
The Comancheros (20th, 1961)
Tammy Tell Me True (Univ, 1961)
Ride the High Country (MGM, 1962)
A Ticklish Affair (MGM, 1963)
Move Over, Darling (20th, 1963)
McLintock! (UA, 1963)
The Rounders (MGM, 1965)
The Man from Button Willow (United Screen Art, 1965) [voice only]
Gunpoint (Univ, 1966)
Welcome to Hard Times (MGM, 1967)
Angel in My Pocket (Univ, 1969)
Benji (Mulberry Square, 1975)

VICTOR BUONO

Victor Buono, Stella Stevens, and Dean Martin in The Silencers *(1966).*

Born February 3, 1938, San Diego, California. Massive actor. Latter-day aspirant to the mammoth acting mantle worn by Sydney Greenstreet and Laird Cregar. Won a following as the effete, mother-dominated Edward Flagg in *What Ever Happened to Baby Jane?* (Won nomination for BSAAA but lost to Ed Begley of *Sweet Bird of Youth.*) Since then has been a performer in search of decent roles. Quite good in *The Strangler* as the mad killer on the prowl in Boston.

> **Victor Buono** to Dean Martin in *The Silencers:* "The explosion will raise a cloud of radioactive dust that will settle over vast areas of the Southwest. . . . *Beautiful!*"

Films

What Ever Happened to Baby Jane? (WB, 1962)
Four for Texas (WB, 1963)
My Six Loves (Par, 1963)
The Strangler (AA, 1964)
Robin and the Seven Hoods (WB, 1964)

Hush . . . Hush, Sweet Charlotte (20th, 1965)
The Greatest Story Ever Told (UA, 1965)
Young Dillinger (AA, 1965)
The Silencers (Col, 1966)
Who's Minding the Mint? (Col, 1967)

Beneath the Planet of the Apes (20th, 1970)
The Wrath of God (MGM, 1972)
Arnold (Cin, 1973)
Moon Child (Filmakers Ltd., 1974)
The Mad Butcher (Ellman Pictures, 1974)
The Evil (New World, 1978)

RAYMOND BURR

John Lund (third from left) and Raymond Burr in Bride of Vengeance *(1949).*

Born May 21, 1917, New Westminster, British Columbia, Canada. Married 1) Annette Sutherland, child: Michael; widowed (1943); 2) Isabella Ward; divorced; 3) Laura Andrena Morgan; widowed (1955). Earned a steady living as a burly screen heavy long before he won TV fame: *His Kind of Woman* (deported gangster Nick Ferraro), *Meet Danny Wilson* (racketeer club owner Nick Driscoll), etc. Especially forceful as white-haired wife-killer Lars Thorwald in *Rear Window*. Often cast in low-budget quickies: *Thunder Pass, Godzilla, King of the Monsters*, etc. TV series: "Perry Mason," "Ironside," and "Kingston: Confidential."

> **Raymond Burr** to Marjorie Rambeau in *Abandoned:* "I was just thinking how nice life used to be when I stuck to blackmail and petty larceny."

Films

Without Reservations (RKO, 1946)
San Quentin (RKO, 1946)
Code of the West (RKO, 1947)
Desperate (RKO, 1947)
Pitfall (UA, 1948)
Raw Deal (EL, 1948)
Fighting Father Dunne (RKO, 1948)
Ruthless (EL, 1948)
Sleep My Love (UA, 1948)
Adventures of Don Juan (WB, 1948)
Walk a Crooked Mile (Col, 1948)
Station West (RKO, 1948)
I Love Trouble (Col, 1948)
Criss Cross (Univ, 1949)
Bride of Vengeance (Par, 1949)
Black Magic (UA, 1949)
Abandoned (Univ, 1949)
Red Light (UA, 1949)
Love Happy (UA, 1949)
Unmasked (Rep, 1950)

Borderline (Univ, 1950)
Key to the City (MGM, 1950)
A Place in the Sun (Par, 1951)
His Kind of Woman (RKO, 1951)
Bride of the Gorilla (Realart, 1951)
New Mexico (UA, 1951)
M (Col, 1951)
FBI Girl (Lip, 1951)
The Whip Hand (RKO, 1951)
Meet Danny Wilson (Univ, 1952)
Mara Maru (WB, 1952)
Horizons West (Univ, 1952)
The Blue Gardenia (WB, 1953)
Fort Algiers (UA, 1953)
Bandits of Corsica (UA, 1953)
Tarzan and the She-Devil (RKO, 1953)
Serpent of the Nile (Col, 1953)
Casanova's Big Night (Par, 1954)
Gorilla at Large (20th, 1954)
Khyber Patrol (UA, 1954)

Rear Window (Par, 1954)
Passion (RKO, 1954)
Thunder Pass (Lip, 1954)
They Were So Young (Lip, 1955)
You're Never Too Young (Par, 1955)
Count Three and Pray (Col, 1955)
A Man Alone (Rep, 1955)
The Brass Legend (UA, 1956)
Please Murder Me (DCA, 1956)
Godzilla, King of the Monsters (Emb-Jewel, 1956)
Great Day in the Morning (RKO, 1956)
Secret of Treasure Mountain (Col, 1956)
A Cry in the Night (WB, 1956)
Ride the High Iron (Col, 1956)
Crime of Passion (UA, 1957)
Affair in Havana (AA, 1957)
Desire in the Dust (20th, 1960)
P.J. (Univ, 1968)
Tomorrow Never Comes (Br, 1978)

CHARLES BUTTERWORTH

With Una Merkel in Baby Face Harrington *(1935).*

Born July 26, 1896, South Bend, Indiana. Married Ethel Kenyon Sutherland (1932); divorced (1939). Died June 13, 1946, Los Angeles, California. Onetime reporter who turned to stage and screen acting. Could double-talk in the Roland Young manner, but had his own style of portraying the vacillating upper-crust gentleman, the perennially indecisive millionaire bachelor: *Love Me Tonight* (Count de Savignac), *Ruggles of Red Gap* (George Vane Bassingwell). Could be a proletarian too: *Baby Face Harrington* (as Willis, the timid clerk mistaken for Public Enemy No. 2), *Every Day's a Holiday* (Charles Winninger's butler Graves, who becomes involved with Mae West), etc.

Charles Butterworth to Paulette Goddard in *Second Chorus:*
"I said *music* and Father said *bottlecaps*. Father won."

Films

The Life of the Party (WB, 1930)
Illicit (WB, 1930)
The Bargain (FN, 1931)
Side Show (WB, 1931)
The Mad Genius (WB, 1931)
Beauty and the Boss (WB, 1932)
Love Me Tonight (Par, 1932)
Manhattan Parade (WB, 1932)
The Nuisance (MGM, 1933)
Penthouse (MGM, 1933)
My Weakness (Fox, 1933)
The Cat and the Fiddle (MGM, 1934)
Student Tour (MGM, 1934)
Forsaking All Others (MGM, 1934)

Bulldog Drummond Strikes Back (UA, 1934)
Hollywood Party (MGM, 1934)
Ruggles of Red Gap (Par, 1935)
The Night Is Young (MGM, 1935)
Baby Face Harrington (MGM, 1935)
Orchids to You (Fox, 1935)
The Magnificent Obsession (Univ, 1935)
The Moon's Our Home (Par, 1936)
Half Angel (20th, 1936)
We Went to College (MGM, 1936)
Rainbow on the River (RKO, 1936)
Swing High, Swing Low (Par, 1937)
Every Day's a Holiday (Par, 1937)
Thanks for the Memory (Par, 1938)

Let Freedom Ring (MGM, 1939)
The Boys from Syracuse (Univ, 1940)
Second Chorus (Par, 1940)
Road Show (UA, 1941)
Blonde Inspiration (MGM, 1941)
Sis Hopkins (Rep, 1941)
What's Cookin'? (Univ, 1942)
Night in New Orleans (Par, 1942)
Give Out, Sisters (Univ, 1942)
Always a Bridesmaid (Univ, 1943)
The Sultan's Daughter (Mon, 1943)
This Is the Army (WB, 1943)
Bermuda Mystery (20th, 1944)
Dixie Jamboree (PRC, 1944)
Follow the Boys (Univ, 1944)

SPRING BYINGTON

With Joseph Cotten in Walk Softly, Stranger *(1950).*

Born October 17, 1886, Colorado Springs, Colorado. Married Roy Chandler, children: Lois, Phyllis; divorced. Died September 7, 1971, Hollywood, California. A polished stage actress, who won popularity in her initial feature, *Little Women* (as Marmee, the mother of Katharine Hepburn, et al.). Could be addled, snooty, and gossipy as in *Dodsworth* and *Theodore Goes Wild*. Played in 20th Century-Fox's long-running *Jones Family* series as Mrs. Jones, was Andy Hardy's mother in the initial MGM entry (*A Family Affair*). Enjoyed most success and an Oscar-nomination for her role as Penny Sycamore, the lady with the creative urge in *You Can't Take It with You* (lost BSAAA to Fay Bainter of *Jezebel*). TV series: "December Bride" and "Laramie."

> **Spring Byington** to Fay Bainter in *The War Against Mrs. Hadley:* "I just wanted to know what stand I should take about the cherry trees. They're so decorative—but they *are* Japanese."

Films

Little Women (RKO, 1933)
Werewolf of London (Univ, 1935)
The Great Impersonation (Univ, 1935)
Love Me Forever (Col, 1935)
Orchids to You (Fox, 1935)
Way Down East (Fox, 1935)
Mutiny on the Bounty (MGM, 1935)
Ah, Wilderness! (MGM, 1935)
Broadway Hostess (WB, 1935)
Every Saturday Night (20th, 1936)
Educating Father (20th, 1936)
Back to Nature (20th, 1936)
The Voice of Bugle Ann (MGM, 1936)
Palm Springs (Par, 1936)
Stage Struck (WB, 1936)
The Charge of the Light Brigade (WB, 1936)

The Girl on the Front Page (Univ, 1936)
Dodsworth (UA, 1936)
Theodora Goes Wild (Col, 1936)
The Green Light (WB, 1937)
Penrod and Sam (WB, 1937)
Off to the Races (20th, 1937)
Big Business (20th, 1937)
Hot Water (20th, 1937)
Borrowing Trouble (20th, 1937)
Hotel Haywire (Par, 1937)
The Road Back (Univ, 1937)
It's Love I'm After (WB, 1937)
Clarence (Par, 1937)
A Family Affair (MGM, 1937)
Love on a Budget (20th, 1938)
A Trip to Paris (20th, 1938)
Safety in Numbers (20th, 1938)

The Buccaneer (Par, 1938)
Penrod and His Twin Brother (WB, 1938)
Jezebel (WB, 1938)
You Can't Take It with You (Col, 1938)
The Adventures of Tom Sawyer (UA,1938)
Down on the Farm (20th, 1938)
The Story of Alexander Graham Bell (20th, 1939)
The Jones Family in Hollywood (20th, 1939)
Everybody's Baby (20th, 1939)
Quick Millions (20th, 1939)
Chicken Wagon Family (20th, 1939)
Too Busy to Work (20th, 1939)
A Child Is Born (WB, 1940)
The Blue Bird (20th, 1940)
On Their Own (20th, 1940)

The Ghost Comes Home (MGM, 1940)
My Love Came Back (WB, 1940)
Lucky Partners (RKO, 1940)
Laddie (RKO, 1940)
Young As You Feel (20th, 1940)
Arkansas Judge (Rep, 1941)
Meet John Doe (WB, 1941)
The Devil and Miss Jones (RKO, 1941)
When Ladies Meet (MGM, 1941)
Ellery Queen and the Perfect Crime (Col, 1941)
The Vanishing Virginian (MGM, 1941)
Roxie Hart (20th, 1942)
The Affairs of Martha (MGM, 1942)
The War Against Mrs. Hadley (MGM, 1942)
Rings on Her Fingers (20th, 1942)
Presenting Lily Mars (MGM, 1943)
Heaven Can Wait (20th, 1943)

The Heavenly Body (MGM, 1943)
I'll Be Seeing You (UA, 1944)
Thrill of a Romance (MGM, 1945)
Captain Eddie (20th, 1945)
Salty O'Rourke (Par, 1945)
The Enchanted Cottage (RKO, 1945)
A Letter for Evie (MGM, 1945)
Dragonwyck (20th, 1946)
Meet Me on Broadway (Col, 1946)
Little Mr. Jim (MGM, 1946)
Faithful in My Fashion (MGM, 1946)
My Brother Talks to Horses (MGM, 1946)
Singapore (Univ, 1947)
Living in a Big Way (MGM, 1947)
It Had to Be You (Col, 1947)
Cynthia (MGM, 1947)
B. F.'s Daughter (MGM, 1948)

In the Good Old Summertime (MGM, 1949)
The Big Wheel (UA, 1949)
Please Believe Me (MGM, 1950)
The Devil's Doorway (MGM, 1950)
Louisa (Univ, 1950)
Walk Softly, Stranger (RKO, 1950)
The Reformer and the Redhead (MGM, 1950) [voice only]
The Skipper Surprised His Wife (MGM, 1950)
Angels in the Outfield (MGM, 1951)
Bannerline (MGM, 1951)
According to Mrs. Hoyle (Mon, 1951)
No Room for the Groom (Univ, 1952)
Because You're Mine (MGM, 1952)
The Rocket Man (20th, 1954)
Please Don't Eat the Daisies (MGM, 1960)

ARTHUR BYRON

With Janet Beecher in The President Vanishes *(1934).*

Born April 3, 1872, Brooklyn, New York. Married 1) _____; 2) Kathryn Keys, children: Eileen, Arthur, another daughter. Died July 17, 1943, Hollywood, California. Offered an imposing series of vignettes in 1930s films: *20,000 Years in Sing Sing* (the warden), *The Mayor of Hell* (Judge Gilbert), *The Man with Two Faces* (Dr. Kendall), *The Whole Town's Talking* (District Attorney Spencer), etc.

> **Arthur Byron** to Claudette Colbert in *Tonight Is Ours:* "You must summon together all that splendid courage I've seen you display in the past."

Films

Fast Life (MGM, 1932)
The Mummy (Univ, 1932)
20,000 Years in Sing Sing (FN, 1933)
Tonight Is Ours (Par, 1933)
Gabriel over the White House (MGM, 1933)
Silk Express (WB, 1933)
The Mayor of Hell (WB, 1933)
Private Detective 62 (WB, 1933)

College Coach (WB, 1933)
The House of Rothschild (UA, 1934)
Stand Up and Cheer (Fox, 1934)
Two Alone (RKO, 1934)
Fog over Frisco (FN, 1934)
The Man with Two Faces (FN, 1934)
The Notorious Sophie Lang (Par, 1934)
That's Gratitude (Col, 1934)
Marie Galante (Fox, 1934)

The President Vanishes (Par, 1934)
The Secret Bride (WB, 1935)
The Casino Murder Case (MGM, 1935)
Shadow of Doubt (MGM, 1935)
The Whole Town's Talking (Col, 1935)
Oil for the Lamps of China (WB, 1935)
Murder in the Fleet (MGM, 1935)
The Prisoner of Shark Island (20th, 1936)

LOUIS CALHERN

At MGM in 1952.

Born February 19, 1895, New York City, New York. Married 1) Ilka Chase; divorced; 2) Julia Hoyt; divorced; 3) Natalie Schafer; divorced; 4) Marianne Stewart; divorced. Died May 12, 1956, Tokyo, Japan. Patrician performer (with Roman nose) who moved back and forth from stage to screen throughout his career. Could be a suave con artist (Dapper Dan Barker of *Blonde Crazy*), or an unscrupulous sort (Major Dort of *The Life of Emile Zola*). Later joined MGM as the imposing elder type. Oscar-nominated for his Judge Oliver Wendell Holmes in *The Magnificent Yankee* (but lost Best Actor award to Jose Ferrer of *Cyrano de Bergerac*). Esteemed for his Alonzo D. Emmerich—the corrupt lawyer with Marilyn Monroe as his mistress—of *The Asphalt Jungle*. Gave dimension to the role of *Julius Casear*, but was rightly embarrassed as Nahreeb the high priest in Lana Turner's *The Prodigal*. Died during the filming of *The Teahouse of the August Moon* (was replaced by Paul Ford as Colonel Purdy).

Louis Calhern to Richard Anderson in *The Magnificent Yankee*: "It's a free country. Everybody's entitled to his opinion—even the President of the United States."

Films

The Blot (F. B. Warren Corp, 1921)
Too Wise Wives (Par, 1921)
What's Worth While? (Par, 1921)
Woman, Wake Up (Associated Exhibitors, 1922)
The Last Moment (G, 1923)
Blonde Crazy [a.k.a. *Larceny Lane*] (WB, 1931)
Stolen Heaven (Par, 1931)
Road to Singapore (WB, 1931)
Okay, America (Univ, 1932)
They Call It Sin (FN, 1932)
Night After Night (Par, 1932)
Afraid to Talk (Univ, 1932)
20,000 Years in Sing Sing (WB, 1933)
The Woman Accused (Par, 1933)
Duck Soup (Par, 1933)
Frisco Jenny (WB, 1933)
Strictly Personal (Par, 1933)
The World Gone Mad (Majestic, 1933)
Diplomaniacs (RKO, 1933)
The Count of Monte Cristo (UA, 1934)
The Affairs of Cellini (UA, 1934)
The Man with Two Faces (FN, 1934)
The Arizonian (RKO, 1935)
The Last Days of Pompeii (RKO, 1935)

Sweet Adeline (WB, 1935)
Woman Wanted (MGM, 1935)
The Gorgeous Hussy (MGM, 1936)
The Life of Emile Zola (WB, 1937)
Her Husband Lies (Par, 1937)
Fast Company (MGM, 1938)
Juarez (WB, 1939)
Fifth Avenue Girl (RKO, 1939)
Charlie McCarthy, Detective (Univ, 1939)
The Story of Dr. Ehrlich's Magic Bullet (WB, 1940)
I Take This Woman (MGM, 1940)
Heaven Can Wait (20th, 1943)
Nobody's Darling (Rep, 1943)
The Bridge of San Luis Rey (UA, 1944)
Up in Arms (RKO, 1944)
Notorious (RKO, 1946)
Arch of Triumph (UA, 1948)
The Red Danube (MGM, 1949)
The Red Pony (Rep, 1949)
Nancy Goes to Rio (MGM, 1950)
Two Weeks with Love (MGM, 1950)
The Magnificent Yankee (MGM, 1950)
The Devil's Doorway (MGM, 1950)
A Life of Her Own (MGM, 1950)
The Asphalt Jungle (MGM, 1950)

Annie Get Your Gun (MGM, 1950)
The Man with a Cloak (MGM, 1951)
It's a Big Country (MGM, 1951) [narrator]
Invitation (MGM, 1952)
The Bad and the Beautiful (MGM, 1952) [voice only]
We're Not Married (20th, 1952)
The Prisoner of Zenda (MGM, 1952)
The Washington Story (MGM, 1952)
Confidentially Connie (MGM, 1953)
Julius Caesar (MGM, 1953)
Remains to Be Seen (MGM, 1953)
Main Street to Broadway (MGM, 1953)
Latin Lovers (MGM, 1953)
Rhapsody (MGM, 1954)
Executive Suite (MGM, 1954)
The Student Prince (MGM, 1954)
Men of the Fighting Lady (MGM, 1954)
Betrayed (MGM, 1954)
Athena (MGM, 1954)
The Blackboard Jungle (MGM, 1955)
The Prodigal (MGM, 1955)
High Society (MGM, 1956)
Forever, Darling (MGM, 1956)

JOSEPH CALLEIA

(Joseph Spurin-Calleia)

Victor Kilian and Joseph Calleia in Riffraff *(1935).*

Born August 4, 1897, Malta. Married Eleonore Vassallo (1929); widowed (1968). Died October 31, 1975. Abandoned a Continental/Broadway singing career for picture-making. Proficient as celluloid gangster: Dancer, the nefarious club owner of *After the Thin Man*; the political murderer Vasquez of *Five Came Back*, etc. Could be on the right side of the law: the inspector *(Algiers)*. Displayed a sense of humor as the saloon owner/masked bandit of Mae West–W. C. Field's *My Little Chickadee*. Sometimes employed his swarthy looks to play ethnic types (Papa Theodore of *Hot Blood)*, etc.

Joseph Calleia to Wade Boteler in *Exclusive Story*: "I'll cut your ears off for that, copper."

Films

His Woman (Par, 1931)
Public Hero No. 1 (MGM, 1935)
Riffraff (MGM, 1935)
Tough Guy (MGM, 1936)
Exclusive Story (MGM, 1936)
Sworn Enemy (MGM, 1936)
His Brother's Wife (MGM, 1936)
Sinner Take All (MGM, 1936)
After the Thin Man (MGM, 1936)
Man of the People (MGM, 1937)
Bad Man of Brimstone (MGM, 1937)
Algiers (UA, 1938)
Four's a Crowd (WB, 1938)
Marie Antoinette (MGM, 1938)
Juarez (WB, 1939)
The Gorilla (20th, 1939)
Five Came Back (RKO, 1939)
Golden Boy (Col, 1939)

Full Confession (RKO, 1939)
My Little Chickadee (Univ, 1940)
Wyoming (MGM, 1940)
The Monster and the Girl (Par, 1941)
Sundown (UA, 1941)
Jungle Book (UA, 1942)
The Glass Key (Par, 1942)
For Whom the Bell Tolls (Par, 1943)
The Cross of Lorraine (MGM, 1943)
The Conspirators (WB, 1944)
Gilda (Col, 1946)
Deadline at Dawn (RKO, 1946)
The Beginning or the End (MGM, 1947)
Lured (UA, 1947)
The Noose Hangs High (EL, 1948)
Four Faces West (UA, 1948)
Captain Carey, U.S.A. (Par, 1950)
Vendetta (RKO, 1950)

Branded (Par, 1950)
Valentino (Col, 1951)
The Light Touch (MGM, 1952)
When in Rome (MGM, 1952)
Yankee Buccaneer (Univ, 1952)
The Iron Mistress (WB, 1952)
The Caddy (Par, 1953)
Underwater! (RKO, 1955)
The Treasure of Pancho Villa (RKO, 1955)
The Littlest Outlaw (BV, 1955)
Hot Blood (Col, 1956)
Serenade (WB, 1956)
Wild Is the Wind (Par, 1957)
Touch of Evil (Univ, 1958)
The Light in the Forest (BV, 1958)
Cry Tough (UA, 1959)
The Alamo (UA, 1960)

HARRY CAREY

Harry Carey and Randolph Scott in Sunset Pass *(1933).*

Born January 16, 1880, New York City, New York. Married 1) Alma Fern; divorced; 2) Olive Fuller Golden, children: Harry, Jr., Ellen. Died September 21, 1947, Brentwood, California. Favored Western star of the 1910–1920s. After a three-year hiatus, returned to the screen—wired for sound—as a co-lead in *Trader Horn*. Offered sterling performances in a wide range of Westerns: *Law and Order* (Ed Brandt), *Powdersmoke Range* (Tucson Smith), Marlene Dietrich's *The Spoilers* (Dextry), *Duel in the Sun* (Lem Smoot), etc. Continued his Americana roles with Frank Capra's *Mr. Smith Goes to Washington* (Senate president). Oscar-nominated for that part (but lost BSAAA to Thomas Mitchell of *Stagecoach*). Final roles: *So Dear to My Heart* (the judge) and *Red River* (Melville); in latter, actor son Harry, Jr. played Dan Latimer.

Harry Carey to Lloyd Nolan and Robert Preston in *King of Alcatraz:* "Man and boy, I've sailed the sea for thirty years . . . and I've never lost a ship."

Films

Judith of Bethulia (Biograph, 1913)
McVeagh of the South Seas [a.k.a. Brute Island] (Progressive Motion Picture Company, 1914)
Graft (Univ serial, 1916)
Beloved Jim (Univ, 1917)
The Fighting Gringo (Red Feather–Univ, 1917)
Straight Shooting (Univ, 1917)
The Secret Man (Univ, 1917)
A Marked Man (Univ, 1917)
Bucking Broadway (Univ, 1917)
Wild Women (Univ, 1918)
Three Mounted Men (Univ, 1918)
Thieves' Gold (Univ, 1918)

The Scarlet Drop (Univ, 1918)
The Phantom Riders (Univ, 1918)
Hell Bent (Univ, 1918)
Roped (Univ, 1919)
Blind Husbands (Univ, 1919)
A Fight for Love (Univ, 1919)
Bare Fists (Univ, 1919)
Riders of Vengeance (Univ, 1919)
Outcasts of Poker Flats (Univ, 1919)
Ace of the Saddle (Univ, 1919)
A Gun Fightin' Gentleman (Univ, 1919)
Rider of the Law (Univ, 1919)
Marked Men (Univ, 1919)
Sure Shot Morgan (Univ, 1919)
Overland Red (Univ, 1920)

West Is West (Univ, 1920)
Sundown Slim (Univ, 1920)
Human Stuff (Univ, 1920)
Bullet Proof (Univ, 1920)
Blue Streak McCoy (Univ, 1920)
"If Only" Jim (Univ, 1921)
The Freeze Out (Univ, 1921)
Hearts Up (Univ, 1921)
The Wallop (Univ, 1921)
Desperate Trails (Univ, 1921)
The Fox (Univ, 1921)
Man to Man (Univ, 1922)
The Kickback (FBO, 1922)
Good Men and True (FBO, 1922)
Canyon of the Fools (FBO, 1923)

Crashin' Thru (FBO, 1923)
Desert Driven (FBO, 1923)
The Miracle Baby (FBO, 1923)
The Night Hawk (Hodkinson, 1923)
The Man from Texas (PDC, 1924)
Tiger Thompson (Hodkinson, 1924)
The Lightning Rider (Hodkinson, 1924)
Roaring Rails (PDC, 1924)
The Flaming Frontiers (PDC, 1924)
Soft Shoes (PDC, 1925)
Beyond the Border (PDC, 1925)
Silent Sanderson (PDC, 1925)
The Texas Trail (PDC, 1925)
Wanderer (Par, 1925)
The Bad Lands (PDC, 1925)
The Prairie Pirate (PDC, 1925)
The Man from Red Gulch (PDC, 1925)
Driftin' Thru (Pathé, 1926)
The Seventh Bandit (Pathé, 1926)
The Frontier Trail (Pathé, 1926)
Satan Town (Pathé, 1926)
A Little Journey (MGM, 1927)
Slide, Kelly, Slide (MGM, 1927)
The Trail of '98 (MGM, 1928)
The Border Patrol (Pathé, 1928)
Burning Bridges (Pathé, 1928)
Trader Horn (MGM, 1931)
Bad Company (Pathé, 1931)
The Vanishing Legion (Mascot serial, 1931)
Border Devils (Artclass, 1932)
Cavalier of the West (Artclass, 1932)

Without Honor (Artclass, 1932)
Law and Order (Univ, 1932)
Last of the Mohicans (Mascot serial, 1932)
The Devil Horse (Mascot serial, 1932)
Night Rider (Artclass, 1932)
Man of the Forest (Par, 1933)
Sunset Pass (Par, 1933)
The Thundering Herd (Par, 1934)
Last of the Clintons (Ajax, 1935)
Rustler's Paradise (Ajax, 1935)
Powdersmoke Range (RKO, 1935)
Barbary Coast (UA, 1935)
Wagon Trail (Ajax, 1935)
Wild Mustang (Ajax, 1935)
The Prisoner of Shark Island (20th, 1936)
Little Miss Nobody (20th, 1936)
The Last Outlaw (RKO, 1936)
Sutter's Gold (Univ, 1936)
Valiant Is the Word for Carrie (Par, 1936)
The Accusing Finger (20th, 1936)
Racing Lady (RKO, 1937)
Born Reckless (20th, 1937)
Kid Galahad (WB, 1937)
Souls at Sea (Par, 1937)
Ghost Town (Commodore, 1937)
Border Cafe (RKO, 1937)
Annapolis Salute (RKO, 1937)
Aces Wild (Commodore, 1937)
Danger Patrol (RKO, 1937)
You and Me (Par, 1938)
Sky Giant (RKO, 1938)

The Law West of Tombstone (RKO, 1938)
Gateway (20th, 1938)
Port of Missing Girls (Mon, 1938)
King of Alcatraz (Par, 1938)
Burn 'em Up O'Connor (MGM, 1939)
Code of the Streets (Univ, 1939)
Inside Information (Univ, 1939)
Mr. Smith Goes to Washington (Col, 1939)
Street of Missing Men (Rep, 1939)
My Son Is Guilty (Col, 1939)
Outside the Three-Mile Limit (Col, 1940)
Beyond Tomorrow (RKO, 1940)
They Knew What They Wanted (RKO, 1940)
Among the Living (Par, 1941)
The Shepherd of the Hills (Par, 1941)
Parachute Battalion (RKO, 1941)
Sundown (UA, 1941)
The Spoilers (Univ, 1942)
Air Force (WB, 1943)
Happy Land (20th, 1943)
The Great Moment (Par, 1944)
China's Little Devils (Mon, 1945)
Duel in the Sun (Selznick Releasing Organization, 1946)
The Angel and the Badman (Rep, 1947)
The Sea of Grass (MGM, 1947)
Red River (UA, 1948)
So Dear to My Heart (RKO, 1948)

RICHARD CARLE

Monte Blue, Richard Carle, Raymond Hatton, Larry "Buster" Crabbe, and Sid Saylor in Nevada *(1935).*

Born July 7, 1871, Somerville, Massachusetts. Died June 28, 1941, North Hollywood, California. Baldheaded man. Effective sporting a pince-nez and bestowing a benign smile. Specialized in bankers and wealthy-men roles.

> **Richard Carle** to Roland Young in *One Hour with You:* "Professor, speaking detectively, you're as good as divorced right now."

Films

The Coming of Amos (PDC, 1925)
The Mad Marriage (Rosemary Films, 1925)
Zander the Great (MG, 1925)
Eve's Leaves (PDC, 1926)
Soft Cushions (Par, 1927)
The Understanding Heart (MGM, 1927)
While the City Sleeps (MGM, 1928)
The Fleet's In (Par, 1928)
It Can Be Done (Univ, 1929)
Madame X (MGM, 1929)
His Glorious Night (MGM, 1929)
Brothers (Col, 1930)
A Lady to Love (MGM, 1930)
Free and Easy (MGM, 1930)
Grand Parade (Pathé, 1930)
Flying High (MGM, 1931)
One Hour with You (Par, 1932)
Fireman, Save My Child (FN, 1932)
The Night of June 13th (Par, 1932)
Private Jones (Univ, 1933)
Man Hunt (RKO, 1933)

Diplomaniacs (RKO, 1933)
Morning Glory (RKO, 1933)
Golden Harvest (Par, 1933)
Ladies Must Love (Univ, 1933)
Harold Teen (WB, 1934)
Hollywood Party (MGM, 1934)
The Last Round-Up (Par, 1934)
Beloved (Univ, 1934)
Sing and Like It (RKO, 1934)
George White's Scandals (Fox, 1934)
The Old-Fashioned Way (Par, 1934)
The Witching Hour (Par, 1934)
Such Women Are Dangerous (Fox, 1934)
The Ghost Walks (Chesterfield, 1934)
Affairs of a Gentleman (Univ, 1934)
Caravan (Fox, 1934)
Wake Up and Dream (Univ, 1934)
Night Life of the Gods (Univ, 1935)
Life Returns (Univ, 1935)
Home on the Range (Par, 1935)
Baby Face Harrington (MGM, 1935)
Love in Bloom (Par, 1935)

Moonlight on the Prairie (WB, 1935)
The Gay Deception (Col, 1935)
Nevada (Par, 1935)
Here Comes Cookie (Par, 1935)
Dangerous (WB, 1935)
When a Man's a Man [TV title: Saga of the West] (Fox, 1935)
The Bride Comes Home (Par, 1935)
The Texas Rangers (Par, 1936)
Love Before Breakfast (Univ, 1936)
The Trail of the Lonesome Pine (Par, 1936)
Anything Goes [TV title: Tops Is the Limit] (Par, 1936)
Drift Fence (Par, 1936)
Let's Sing Again (RKO, 1936)
Little Red Schoolhouse (Chesterfield, 1936)
One Rainy Afternoon (UA, 1936)
The Case Against Mrs. Ames (Par, 1936)
Arizona Mahoney (Par, 1936)
Three of a Kind (Invincible, 1936)
The Arizona Raiders (Par, 1936)
Spendthrift (Par, 1936)

Easy to Take (Par, 1936)
The Man I Marry (Univ, 1936)
College Holiday (Par, 1936)
True Confession (Par, 1937)
She's Dangerous (Univ, 1937)
Outcast (Par, 1937)
Top of the Town (Univ, 1937)
Racketeers in Exile (Col, 1937)
Rhythm in the Clouds (Rep, 1937)
It's All Yours (Col, 1937)
She Asked for It (Par, 1937)
Love in a Bungalow (Univ, 1937)
The Man in Blue (Univ, 1937)
Forty-Five Fathers (20th, 1937)

I'll Take Romance (Col, 1937)
Persons in Hiding (Par, 1939)
It's a Wonderful World (MGM, 1939)
Undercover Doctor (Par, 1939)
Maisie (MGM, 1939)
Ninotchka (MGM, 1939)
Remember? (MGM, 1939)
Ma, He's Making Eyes at Me (Univ, 1940)
Parole Fixer (Par, 1940)
Lillian Russell (20th, 1940)
The Great McGinty (Par, 1940)
Comin' Round the Mountain (Par, 1940)
One Night in the Tropics (Univ, 1940)

Seven Sinners (Univ, 1940)
The Golden Fleecing (MGM, 1940)
The Ghost Comes Home (MGM, 1940)
That Uncertain Feeling (UA, 1941)
A Dangerous Game (Univ, 1941)
The Devil and Miss Jones (RKO, 1941)
Million Dollar Baby (WB, 1941)
Buy Me That Town (Par, 1941)
New Wine [TV title: *Melody Master*] (UA, 1941)
Moonlight in Hawaii (Univ, 1941)
My Life with Caroline (RKO, 1941)

MORRIS CARNOVSKY

With Betsy Drake in The Second Woman *(1951).*

Born September 5, 1897, St. Louis, Missouri. Married 1) _____ (1922); divorced (1933); 2) Phoebe Brand (1941), child: son. Respected stage performer who makes occasional films. Proficient in dialectal roles: *The Life of Emile Zola* (Anatole France), *Edge of Darkness* (Sixtus Andresen), *Our Vines Have Tender Grapes* (Bjorn Bjornson), etc. Could be kindly (Papa Gershwin, father of George and Ira, in *Rhapsody in Blue*) but was as effective as a disreputable figure in *Dead Reckoning* (Martinelli), *Saigon* (Alex Maris), etc.

Morris Carnovsky to Humphrey Bogart in *Dead Reckoning:* "You place me in an extremely distasteful position, Mr. Murdock. Brutality has always revolted me."

Films

The Life of Emile Zola (WB, 1937)
Tovarich (WB, 1937)
Edge of Darkness (WB, 1943)
Address Unknown (Col, 1944)
The Master Race (RKO, 1944)
Our Vines Have Tender Grapes (MGM, 1945)
Rhapsody in Blue (WB, 1945)
Cornered (RKO, 1945)

Miss Susie Slagle's (Par, 1945)
Dead Reckoning (Col, 1947)
Dishonored Lady (UA, 1947)
Joe Palooka in the Knockout (Mon, 1947)
Saigon (Par, 1948)
Man-Eater of Kumaon (UA, 1948)
The Siren of Atlantis (UA, 1948)
Gun Crazy [a.k.a. Deadly Is the Female] (UA, 1949)

Thieves' Highway (20th, 1949)
Western Pacific Agent (Lip, 1950)
Cyrano de Bergerac (UA, 1950)
The Second Woman (UA, 1951)
A View from the Bridge (Continental, 1962)
The Gambler (Par, 1974)

JOHN CARRADINE
(Richmond Reed Carradine)

Lloyd Corrigan, Evelyn Ankers, and John Carradine in Captive Wild Woman (1943).

Born February 5, 1906, New York City, New York. Married 1) Ardanelle Cosner (1935), children: Bruce, David; divorced (1944); 2) Sonia Sorel (1945), children: Christopher, John, Keith; divorced (1955); 3) Doris Rich (1957); widowed (1971); 4) Emily Cisneros (1975). Indefatigable performer whose lanky, gaunt figure, and stentorian tones have graced scores of films. Rose from bit player (a Roman in Claudette Colbert's Cleopatra) to 20th Century-Fox contractee where he was effective as a snarling, sinister figure (Sergeant Rankin of The Prisoner of Shark Island), full-dimensional blackguard (Bob Ford in both Jesse James and The Return of Jesse James) and sterling player (the baffled Casey of The Grapes of Wrath). In the 1940s and thereafter he free-lanced, mostly in program fodder (I Escaped from the Gestapo), often in horror junk (Revenge of the Zombies), but occasionally in some fascinating low-budget items (title role of Bluebeard). Has become a staple of low-quality science fiction (The Cosmic Man) and horror trash (Half Human) in recent years. Well known as the still-working father of an actor brood (including David and Keith). TV series: "Trapped" (as the host), "My Friend Irma," and "The Munsters" (as Mr. Gateman—Fred Gwynne's employer).

John Carradine to Jon Hall in *The Invisible Man's Revenge:*
"Pioneers have always had to contend with fools."

Films

As John Peter Richmond:

Tol'able David (Col, 1930)
Heaven on Earth (Univ, 1931)
The Sign of the Cross (Par, 1932)
Forgotten Commandments (Par, 1932)
The Invisible Man (Univ, 1933)
This Day and Age (Par, 1933)

As John Carradine:

The Black Cat (Univ, 1934)
Of Human Bondage (RKO, 1934)
Cleopatra (Par, 1934)
The Man Who Broke the Bank at Monte Carlo (Fox, 1935)
Alias Mary Dow (Univ, 1935)
Les Miserables (UA, 1935)
The Crusades (Par, 1935)
Bride of Frankenstein (Univ, 1935)
Clive of India (UA, 1935)
She Gets Her Man (Univ, 1935)
Cardinal Richelieu (UA, 1935)
Anything Goes (Par, 1936)
Transient Lady (Univ, 1936)
Captain January (20th, 1936)
The Prisoner of Shark Island (20th, 1936)
Under Two Flags (20th, 1936)
White Fang (20th, 1936)
Ramona (20th, 1936)
Dimples (20th, 1936)
Mary of Scotland (RKO, 1936)
Daniel Boone (RKO, 1936)
Winterset (RKO, 1936)
The Garden of Allah (UA, 1936)
A Message to Garcia (20th, 1936)
Nancy Steele Is Missing (20th, 1937)
Danger—Love at Work (20th, 1937)
This Is My Affair (20th, 1937)
Love Under Fire (20th, 1937)
Thank You, Mr. Moto (20th, 1937)
Captains Courageous (MGM, 1937)
The Last Gangster (MGM, 1937)
The Hurricane (UA, 1937)
Laughing at Trouble (20th, 1937)
Ali Baba Goes to Town (20th, 1937)
International Settlement (20th, 1938)
Four Men and a Prayer (20th, 1938)
I'll Give a Million (20th, 1938)
Kentucky Moonshine (20th, 1938)
Kidnapped (20th, 1938)
Alexander's Ragtime Band (20th, 1938)
Gateway (20th, 1938)
Submarine Patrol (20th, 1938)
Of Human Hearts (MGM, 1938)
Jesse James (20th, 1939)
The Hound of the Baskervilles (20th, 1939)
Frontier Marshal (20th, 1939)
Drums Along the Mohawk (20th, 1939)

The Three Musketeers (20th, 1939)
Stagecoach (UA, 1939)
Captain Fury (UA, 1939)
Five Came Back (RKO, 1939)
Mr. Moto's Last Warning (20th, 1939)
The Grapes of Wrath (20th, 1940)
The Return of Frank James (20th, 1940)
Brigham Young—Frontiersman (20th, 1940)
Chad Hanna (20th, 1940)
Western Union (20th, 1941)
King of the Zombies (Mon, 1941)
Blood and Sand (20th, 1941)
Man Hunt (20th, 1941)
Swamp Water (20th, 1941)
Whispering Ghosts (20th, 1942)
Son of Fury (20th, 1942)
Northwest Rangers (MGM, 1942)
Reunion (MGM, 1942)
Silver Spurs (Rep, 1943)
Gangway for Tomorrow (MGM, 1943)
Captive Wild Woman (Univ, 1943)
Hitler's Madman (MGM, 1943)
I Escaped from the Gestapo [a.k.a. *No Escape*] (Mon, 1943)
The Isle of Forgotten Sins (PRC, 1943)
Revenge of the Zombies (Mon, 1943)
Bluebeard (PRC, 1944)
The Mummy's Ghost (Univ, 1944)
Barbary Coast Gent (MGM, 1944)
The Adventures of Mark Twain (WB, 1944)
Black Parachute (Col, 1944)
The Invisible Man's Revenge (Univ, 1944)
The Return of the Ape Man (Mon, 1944)
Voodoo Man (Mon, 1944)
Alaska (Mon, 1944)
House of Frankenstein (Univ, 1944)
House of Dracula (Univ, 1945)
Fallen Angel (20th, 1945)
Captain Kidd (UA, 1945)
It's in the Bag (UA, 1945)
Down Missouri Way (PRC, 1946)
The Face of Marble (Mon, 1946)
The Private Affairs of Bel Ami (UA, 1947)
C-Man (Film Classics, 1949)
Thunder Pass (Lip, 1954)
Casanova's Big Night (Par, 1954)
Johnny Guitar (Rep, 1954)
The Egyptian (20th, 1954)
Stranger on Horseback (UA, 1955)
Desert Sands (UA, 1955)
The Kentuckian (UA, 1955)
Dark Venture (First National Releasing, 1955)
Female Jungle (AIP, 1956)
The Black Sleep (UA, 1956)

The Ten Commandments (Par, 1956)
Around the World in 80 Days (UA, 1956)
Hidden Guns (Rep, 1956)
The Court Jester (Par, 1956)
The Unearthly (Rep, 1957)
Half Human (DCA, 1957)
Hellship Mutiny (Rep, 1957)
The True Story of Jesse James (20th, 1957)
The Story of Mankind (WB, 1957)
The Proud Rebel (BV, 1958)
The Last Hurrah (Col, 1958)
Showdown at Boot Hill (20th, 1958)
The Oregon Trail (20th, 1959)
The Cosmic Man (AA, 1959)
Invisible Invaders (UA, 1959)
The Adventures of Huckleberry Finn (MGM, 1960)
Tarzan the Magnificent (Par, 1960)
Sex Kittens Go to College (AA, 1960)
The Incredible Petrified World (Governor, 1960)
Invasion of the Animal People (Warren, 1962)
The Man Who Shot Liberty Valance (Par, 1962)
The Patsy (Par, 1964)
Cheyenne Autumn (WB, 1964)
The Wizard of Mars (American Releasing Corp, 1964)
Billy the Kid vs. Dracula (Emb, 1966)
Night Train to Mundo Fine (Hollywood Star, 1966)
Dr. Terror's Gallery of Horrors (Independent, 1966)
The Hostage (Crown International, 1966)
Munster, Go Home (Univ, 1966)
Hillbillies in the Haunted House (Woolner Bros, 1967)
Creatures of the Red Planet (American Releasing Corp, 1967)
The Astro-Zombies (Gemeni, 1967)
Blood of Dracula's Castle (Crown International, 1969)
The Good Guys and the Bad Guys (WB-7 Arts, 1969)
The Trouble with Girls (MGM, 1969)
The McMasters (Chevron, 1970)
Myra Breckinridge (20th, 1970)
Hell's Bloody Devils [a.k.a. *The Fakers*] (Independent International, 1970)
Cain's Way (Colby Productions, 1971)
Shinbone Alley (AA, 1971) [voice only]
Five Bloody Graves (Independent International, 1971)
Blood of the Iron Maiden (Hollywood Star, 1971)

Horror of the Blood Monsters (Independent International, 1971)
The Seven Minutes (20th, 1971)
Bigfoot (Ellman Enterprises, 1971)
Richard (Aurora, 1972)
Boxcar Bertha (AIP, 1972)
Everything You Always Wanted to Know About Sex but Were Afraid to Ask (UA, 1972)
The Gatling Gun (Ellman Enterprises, 1972)
Blood of Ghostly Horror (Independent International, 1972)
Silent Night, Bloody Night (Cannon, 1973)
Terror in the Wax Museum (Cin, 1973)
Bad Charleston Charlie (International Cinema, 1973)
Hex (20th, 1973)
Superchick (Crown International, 1973)
The House of Seven Corpses (Internationa Amusement Corp, 1974)
Moonchild (American Films, 1974)
Mary, Mary, Bloody Mary (Black Lion Productions, 1975)
Won Ton Ton, the Dog Who Saved Hollywood (Par, 1976)
Crash (Group One, 1976)
The Killer Inside Me (WB, 1976)
The Shootist (Par, 1976)
The Last Tycoon (Par, 1976)
The Sentinel (Univ, 1977)
Shock Waves (Cinema Shares, 1977)
The White Buffalo (UA, 1977)
Golden Rendezvous (Br, 1977)

LEO CARRILLO

Peggy Moran, Robert Cummings, and Leo Carrillo in One Night in the Tropics *(1940).*

Born August 6, 1881, Los Angeles, California. Married Edith Haeselbarth (1940), child: Antoinette; widowed (1953). Died September 10, 1961, Santa Monica, California. High-grade background as a Spanish-American aristocrat, but was usually on camera as a grubby eccentric (of many nationalities) who mangled the English language more than Desi Arnaz. Extremely effective as the punk gangster who would sacrifice all for Grace Moore in *Love Me Forever;* could hold his own with such prime scene-stealers as Bobby Breen (*Fisherman's Wharf*), Wallace Beery (*Twenty-Mule Team*), or Maria Montez (*Gypsy Wildcat*). TV series: "The Cisco Kid" (as the flavorful sidekick of Duncan Renaldo).

Leo Carrillo to Buddy Ebsen in *Girl of the Golden West:* "Hey, who *say* the West she don't be wild some more?"

Films

The Dove (UA, 1928)
Mr. Antonio (Tif, 1929)
Hell Bound (Tif, 1931)
Lasca of the Rio Grande (Univ, 1931)
Guilty Generation (Col, 1931)
Homicide Squad (Univ, 1931)
The Broken Wing (Par, 1932)
Girl of the Rio (RKO, 1932)
Deception (Col, 1932)
Men Are Such Fools (RKO, 1932)
Obey the Law (Col, 1933)
Before Morning (Arthur Greenblatt, 1933)
Moonlight and Pretzels (Univ, 1933)
Race Track (WW, 1933)
Parachute Jumper (WB, 1933)
Viva Villa! (MGM, 1934)
Manhattan Melodrama (MGM, 1934)
The Gay Bride (MGM, 1934)
Four Frightened People (Par, 1934)
The Band Plays On (MGM, 1934)
The Winning Ticket (MGM, 1935)
Love Me Forever (Col, 1935)
In Caliente (WB, 1935)
If You Could Only Cook (Col, 1935)
It Had to Happen (20th, 1936)
Moonlight Murder (MGM, 1936)
The Gay Desperado (UA, 1936)
I Promise to Pay (Col, 1937)
History Is Made at Night (UA, 1937)

52nd Street (UA, 1937)
Hotel Haywire (Par, 1937)
The Barrier (Par, 1937)
Manhattan Merry-Go-Round (Rep, 1937)
Girl of the Golden West (MGM, 1938)
Too Hot to Handle (MGM, 1938)
Arizona Wildcat (20th, 1938)
City Streets (Col, 1938)
Little Miss Roughneck (Col, 1938)
Flirting with Fate (MGM, 1938)
Blockade (UA, 1938)
Fisherman's Wharf (RKO, 1939)
The Girl and the Gambler (RKO, 1939)
Society Lawyer (MGM, 1939)
Chicken Wagon Family (20th, 1939)
Rio (Univ, 1939)
Twenty-Mule Team (MGM, 1940)
Wyoming (MGM, 1940)
Lillian Russell (20th, 1940)
Captain Caution (UA, 1940)
One Night in the Tropics (Univ, 1940)
Horror Island (Univ, 1941)
Barnacle Bill (MGM, 1941)
Riders of Death Valley (Univ serial, 1941)
Tight Shoes (Univ, 1941)
The Kid from Kansas (Univ, 1941)
Road Agent (Univ, 1941)
What's Cookin'? (Univ, 1942)

Unseen Enemy (Univ, 1942)
Escape from Hong Kong (Univ, 1942)
Men of Texas (Univ, 1942)
Top Sergeant (Univ, 1942)
Sin Town (Univ, 1942)
Timber (Univ, 1942)
American Empire (UA, 1942)
Danger in the Pacific (Univ, 1942)
Crazy House (Univ, 1943)
Frontier Bad Men (Univ, 1943)
Larceny with Music (Univ, 1943)
The Phantom of the Opera (Univ, 1943)
Follow the Band (Univ, 1943)
Babes on Swing Street (Univ, 1944)
Bowery to Broadway (Univ, 1944)
The Ghost Catchers (Univ, 1944)
Gypsy Wildcat (Univ, 1944)
Moonlight and Cactus (Univ, 1944)
Under Western Skies (Univ, 1945)
Crime, Inc. (PRC, 1945)
Mexicana (Rep, 1945)
The Fugitive (RKO, 1947)
Valiant Hombre (UA, 1948)
The Gay Amigo (UA, 1949)
Satan's Cradle (UA, 1949)
The Daring Caballero (UA, 1949)
The Girl from San Lorenzo (UA, 1950)
Pancho Villa Returns (Mex, 1952)

LEO G. CARROLL

In the late 1950s.

Born October 25, 1892, Weedon, Northants, England. Married Edith _____, child: William. Died October 16, 1972, Hollywood, California. One of the hardest-working of the British colony in Hollywood, frequently employed by Alfred Hitchcock: *Rebecca* (Dr. Baker), *Suspicion* (Captain Melbeck), *Spellbound* (as the homicidal Dr. Murchison), *The Paradine Case* (Sir Joseph Farrell), *Strangers on a Train* (Senator Morton), and *North by Northwest* (the professor). TV series: "Topper" (as the quizzical banker husband of Lee Patrick), "The Man from U.N.C.L.E." and "The Girl from U.N.C.L.E." (in both as Alexander Waverly, the head of the organization), and "Going My Way" (with Gene Kelly).

> **Leo G. Carroll** to Sidney Toler in *Charlie Chan in City of Darkness:* "You know a lot about this acid. Did you ever have a taste of it?"

Films

What Every Woman Knows (MGM, 1934)
Sadie McKee (MGM, 1934)
Outcast Lady (MGM, 1934)
Stamboul Quest (MGM, 1934)
The Barretts of Wimpole Street (MGM, 1934)
Murder on a Honeymoon (RKO, 1935)
The Right to Live (WB, 1935)
Clive of India (UA, 1935)
The Casino Murder Case (MGM, 1935)

London by Night (MGM, 1937)
A Christmas Carol (MGM, 1938)
The Private Lives of Elizabeth and Essex (WB, 1939)
Wuthering Heights (UA, 1939)
Bulldog Drummond's Secret Police (Par, 1939)
Charlie Chan in City in Darkness (20th, 1939)
Tower of London (Univ, 1939)
Rebecca (UA, 1940)

Charlie Chan's Murder Cruise (20th, 1940)
Waterloo Bridge (MGM, 1940)
Scotland Yard (20th, 1941)
Bahama Passage (Par, 1941)
This Woman Is Mine (Univ, 1941)
Suspicion (RKO, 1941)
The House on 92nd Street (20th, 1945)
Spellbound (UA, 1945)
Forever Amber (20th, 1947)
Time out of Mind (Univ, 1947)

Song of Love (MGM, 1947)
The Paradine Case (Selznick Releasing Organization, 1948)
So Evil My Love (Par, 1948)
Enchantment (RKO, 1948)
The Happy Years (MGM, 1950)
Father of the Bride (MGM, 1950)
The First Legion (UA, 1951)
Strangers on a Train (WB, 1951)
The Desert Fox (20th, 1951)

The Snows of Kilimanjaro (20th, 1952)
The Bad and the Beautiful (MGM, 1952)
Rogues' March (MGM, 1952)
Treasure of the Golden Condor (20th, 1953)
Young Bess (MGM, 1953)
We're No Angels (Par, 1955)
Tarantula (Univ, 1955)
The Swan (MGM, 1956)
North by Northwest (MGM, 1959)

The Parent Trap (BV, 1961)
One Plus One (Selected Pictures Distributors, 1961)
The Prize (MGM, 1963)
That Funny Feeling (Univ, 1965)
The Spy with My Face (MGM, 1966)
One of Our Spies Is Missing (MGM, 1966)
One Spy Too Many (MGM, 1966)

WALTER CATLETT

Charles Butterworth, William Frawley, and Walter Catlett in Give Out, Sisters *(1942).*

Born February 4, 1889, San Francisco, California. Married 1) Zanetta Watrous; widowed; 2) Ruth Verney, child: one; divorced; 3) Kathlene Martyn. Died November 14, 1960, Woodland Hills, California. The wide-eyed, fidgety, imperious sort (with big ears) who indulged in low-voiced comic tantrums when pressured by on screen opposition: Pat O'Brien's *The Front Page* (Murphy), Irene Dunne's *Back Street* (Bakeless), *Mr. Deeds Goes to Town* (Morrow), *Bringing Up Baby* (Constable Slocum), etc. Usually had the soul of a con artist beneath his braggard spiels (Colonel Truckee of *My Gal Sal*). Could be dramatic: Ronald Colman's *A Tale of Two Cities* (Barsad). In late 1940s joined with Raymond Walburn in low-budget Monogram series starting with *Henry the Rainmaker*. Final role as politician Al Smith in Bob Hope's *Beau James*.

Walter Catlett to Deanna Durbin in *His Butler's Sister:* "You know, the minute I laid my eyes on you I says to myself— Mort, there's a little lady that ain't gonna be wrestlin' with that broom much longer."

Films

Second Youth (MGM, 1924)
Summer Bachelors (Fox, 1926)
Why Leave Home? (Fox, 1929)
Married in Hollywood (Fox, 1929)
Happy Days (Fox, 1930)
Let's Go Places (Fox, 1930)
The Golden Calf (Fox, 1930)
The Big Party (Fox, 1930)
The Floradora Girl (MGM, 1930)
The Front Page (UA, 1931)
Platinum Blonde (Col, 1931)
Palmy Days (UA, 1931)
The Maker of Men (Col, 1931)
The Expert (WB, 1932)
Cock of the Air (UA, 1932)
Big City Blues (WB, 1932)
Sky Devils (UA, 1932)
It's Tough to Be Famous (FN, 1932)
Back Street (Univ, 1932)
Rain (UA, 1932)
Rockabye (RKO, 1932)
Okay, America (Univ, 1932)
Sport Parade (RKO, 1932)
Private Jones (Univ, 1933)
Only Yesterday (Univ, 1933)
Mama Loves Papa (Par, 1933)
Arizona to Broadway (Fox, 1933)
Olsen's Big Moment (Fox, 1934)
Lightning Strikes Twice (RKO, 1934)
The Captain Hates the Sea (Col, 1934)
Unknown Blonde (Majestic, 1934)
Every Night at Eight (Par, 1935)
A Tale of Two Cities (MGM, 1935)
Affair of Susan (Univ, 1935)
Mr. Deeds Goes to Town (Col, 1936)
We Went to College (MGM, 1936)
Follow Your Heart (Rep, 1936)
Sing Me a Love Song (FN, 1936)
Cain and Mabel (WB, 1936)
Banjo on My Knee (20th, 1936)
Four Days' Wonder (Univ, 1937)

On the Avenue (20th, 1937)
Love Is News (20th, 1937)
Wake Up and Live (20th, 1937)
Love Under Fire (20th, 1937)
Danger—Love at Work (20th, 1937)
Varsity Show (WB, 1937)
Every Day's a Holiday (Par, 1937)
Bringing Up Baby (RKO, 1938)
Going Places (WB, 1938)
Zaza (Par, 1939)
Exile Express (GN, 1939)
Kid Nightingale (WB, 1939)
Pop Always Pays (RKO, 1940)
Li'l Abner (RKO, 1940)
Remedy for Riches (RKO, 1940)
Comin' Round the Mountain (Par, 1940)
The Quarterback (Par, 1940)
Spring Parade (Univ, 1940)
Half a Sinner (Univ, 1940)
Pinocchio (RKO, 1940) [voice only]
You're the One (Par, 1941)
Honeymoon for Three (WB, 1941)
Horror Island (Univ, 1941)
Wild Bill Hickok Rides (WB, 1941)
It Started with Eve (Univ, 1941)
Wild Man of Borneo (MGM, 1941)
Million Dollar Baby (WB, 1941)
Hello, Sucker (Univ, 1941)
Manpower (WB, 1941)
Bad Men of Missouri (WB, 1941)
Unfinished Business (Univ, 1941)
Steel Against the Sky (WB, 1941)
My Gal Sal (20th, 1942)
Between Us Girls (Univ, 1942)
Maisie Gets Her Man (MGM, 1942)
Yankee Doodle Dandy (WB, 1942)
Give Out, Sisters, (Univ, 1942)
Heart of the Golden West (Rep, 1942)
Star Spangled Rhythm (Par, 1942)
The Hit Parade of 1943 (Rep, 1943)
West Side Kid (Rep, 1943)

They Got Me Covered (RKO, 1943)
Fired Wife (Univ, 1943)
His Butler's Sister (Univ, 1943)
How's About It? (Univ, 1943)
Cowboy in Manhattan (Univ, 1943)
Get Going (Univ, 1943)
Pardon My Rhythm (Univ, 1944)
I Love a Soldier (Par, 1944)
The Ghost Catchers (Univ, 1944)
Hat Check Honey (Univ, 1944)
Up in Arms (RKO, 1944)
Lady, Let's Dance! (Mon, 1944)
Hi, Beautiful (Univ, 1944)
My Gal Loves Music (Univ, 1944)
Three Is a Family (UA, 1944)
Lake Placid Serenade (Rep, 1944)
Her Primitive Man (Univ, 1944)
I Love a Bandleader (Col, 1945)
The Man Who Walked Alone (PRC, 1945)
Riverboat Rhythm (RKO, 1946)
Slightly Scandalous (Univ, 1946)
I'll Be Yours (Univ, 1947)
Mr. Reckless (Par, 1948)
Are You with It? (Univ, 1948)
The Boy with Green Hair (RKO, 1948)
Henry the Rainmaker (Mon, 1949)
Look for the Silver Lining (WB, 1949)
Dancing in the Dark (20th, 1949)
The Inspector General (WB, 1949)
Leave It to Henry (Mon, 1949)
Father's Wild Game (Mon, 1950)
Father Makes Good (Mon, 1950)
Honeychile (Rep, 1951)
Father Takes the Air (Mon, 1951)
Here Comes the Groom (Par, 1951)
Davy Crockett and the River Pirates (BV, 1956)
Friendly Persuasion (AA, 1956)
Beau James (Par, 1957)

PAUL CAVANAGH

James Burke, Rita Johnson, Ruth Hussey, Paul Cavanagh, and Paul Kelly in Within the Law *(1939).*

Born December 8, 1895, Chislehurst, Kent, England. Married Katherine Layfield Luhn (1946), child: one. Died March 15, 1964. Thin-faced, moustached Britisher who brought professionalism to his roles, whether as the honest or the (usually) shifty bad guy: Katharine Hepburn's *A Bill of Divorcement* (Gray Meredith), *Tarzan and His Mate* (Martin Arlington), *Goin' to Town* (Edward Carrington, the geological engineer pursued by Mae West), *Maisie Was a Lady* (Cap Bigelow), etc. Played Joan Crawford's aging, tolerant husband in *Humoresque*.

> **Paul Cavanagh** to Basil Rathbone in *The Scarlet Claw:*
> "Several of our most responsible citizens have actually
> seen the strange apparition on the moors at night."

Films

Woman in the Night (Sono-Art-World Wide, 1929)
The Runaway Princess (Br, 1929)
Two Drummer Boys (Br, 1929)
Tesha (Br, 1929)
Grumpy (Par, 1930)
The Devil to Pay (UA, 1930)
The Storm (Univ, 1930)
Strictly Unconventional (MGM, 1930)
The Virtuous Sin (Par, 1930)
Born to Love (Pathé, 1931)
Unfaithful (Par, 1931)
Transgression (RKO, 1931)
Always Goodbye (Fox, 1931)
Heartbreak (Fox, 1931)
The Squaw Man (MGM, 1931)
The Devil's Lottery (Fox, 1932)
The Crash (FN, 1932)

A Bill of Divorcement (RKO, 1932)
Tonight Is Ours (Par, 1933)
In the Money (Chesterfield, 1933)
The Sin of Nora Moran (Majestic, 1933)
The Kennel Murder Case (WB, 1933)
Curtain at Eight (Majestic, 1934)
The Notorious Sophie Lang (Par, 1934)
Menace (Par, 1934)
Shoot the Works (Par, 1934)
Tarzan and His Mate (MGM, 1934)
Uncertain Lady (Univ, 1934)
Escapade (MGM, 1934)
One Exciting Adventure (Univ, 1934)
Goin' to Town (Par, 1935)
Without Regret (Par, 1935)
Thunder in the Night (Fox, 1935)
Splendor (UA, 1935)
Crime over London (UA Br, 1936)

Champagne Charlie (20th, 1936)
Romance in Flanders [a.k.a. *Lost on the Western Front*] (Br, 1937)
Cafe Collette [a.k.a. *Danger in Paris*] (Br, 1937)
Within the Law (MGM, 1939)
The Under-Pup (Univ, 1939)
Reno (RKO, 1939)
I Take This Woman (MGM, 1940)
Maisie Was a Lady (MGM, 1941)
The Case of the Black Parrot (WB, 1941)
Shadows on the Stairs (WB, 1941)
Passage from Hong Kong (WB, 1941)
The Strange Case of Dr. X (Univ, 1942)
Captains of the Clouds (WB, 1942)
Pacific Rendezvous (MGM, 1942)
Eagle Squadron (Univ, 1942)
The Hard Way (WB, 1942)

The Gorilla Man (WB, 1942)
Adventure in Iraq (WB, 1943)
Maisie Goes to Reno (MGM, 1944)
Marriage Is a Private Affair (MGM, 1944)
The Scarlet Claw (Univ, 1944)
The Man in Half Moon Street (Par, 1944)
The Woman in Green (Univ, 1945)
Club Havana (PRC, 1945)
House of Fear (Univ, 1945)
This Man's Navy (MGM, 1945)
Night and Day (WB, 1946)
A Night in Paradise (Univ, 1946)
The Verdict (WB, 1946)
Wife Wanted (Mon, 1946)
Humoresque (WB, 1946)
Dishonored Lady (UA, 1947)
Ivy (Univ, 1947)
The Black Arrow (Col, 1948)
Secret Beyond the Door (Univ, 1948)

The Babe Ruth Story (AA, 1948)
You Gotta Stay Happy (Univ, 1948)
Madame Bovary (MGM, 1949)
The Iroquois Trail (UA, 1950)
Rogues of Sherwood Forest (Col, 1950)
Hi-Jacked (Lip, 1950)
Hit Parade of 1951 (Rep, 1950)
Hollywood Story (Par, 1951)
The Strange Door (Univ, 1951)
Son of Dr. Jekyll (Col, 1951)
Bride of the Gorilla (Realart, 1951)
All That I Have (Family Films, 1951)
Tales of Robin Hood (Lip, 1951)
The Golden Hawk (Col, 1952)
Port Sinister (RKO, 1953)
Mississippi Gambler (Univ, 1953)
House of Wax (WB, 1953)
Bandits of Corsica (UA, 1953)
Flame of Calcutta (Col, 1953)
The All-American (Univ, 1953)

Magnificent Obsession (Univ, 1954)
The Law vs. Billy the Kid (Col, 1954)
The Raid (20th, 1954)
Khyber Patrol (UA, 1954)
The Iron Glove (Col, 1954)
Casanova's Big Night (Par, 1954)
The Prodigal (MGM, 1955)
The Purple Mask (Univ, 1955)
The Scarlet Coat (MGM, 1955)
The King's Thief (MGM, 1955)
Diane (MGM, 1955)
Francis in the Haunted House (Univ, 1956)
The Man Who Turned to Stone (Col, 1957)
She Devil (20th, 1957)
God Is My Partner (20th, 1957)
In the Money (AA, 1958)
The Four Skulls of Jonathan Drake (UA, 1959)

HOBART CAVANAUGH

Hobart Cavanaugh and Charles Winninger in The Inside Story *(1948).*

Born September 22, 1896, Virginia City, Nevada. Married Florence _____, child: Patricia. Died April 26, 1950, Woodland Hills, California. Migrated into the film industry after studying engineering at college, and a stage career. Constantly assigned to be the Casper Milquetoast office type or the henpecked family man.

Hobart Cavanaugh to Richard Dix in *The Kansan:* "Marshal, I'm the mayor here. Aren't you overstepping your authority?"

Films

San Francisco Nights (Gotham, 1928)
Goodbye Again (FN, 1933)
Mary Stevens, M.D. (WB, 1933)
Private Detective 62 (WB, 1933)
The Kennel Murder Case (WB, 1933)
The Mayor of Hell (WB, 1933)
From Headquarters (WB, 1933)
I Cover the Waterfront (UA, 1933)
Broadway Through a Keyhole (UA, 1933)
Lilly Turner (FN, 1933)
Havana Widows (FN, 1933)
Convention City (FN, 1933)
Headline Shooter (RKO, 1933)
No Marriage Ties (RKO, 1933)
The Devil's Mate (Mon, 1933)
My Woman (Col, 1933)
Footlight Parade (WB, 1933)
Picture Snatcher (WB, 1933)
Study in Scarlet (WW, 1933)
Gold Diggers of 1933 (WB, 1933)
Moulin Rouge (UA, 1934)
Dark Hazard (FN, 1934)
Wonder Bar (FN, 1934)
Mandalay (FN, 1934)
Hi, Nellie! (WB, 1934)
Easy to Love (WB, 1934)
I've Got Your Number (WB, 1934)
Harold Teen (WB, 1934)
Jimmy the Gent (WB, 1934)
Merry Wives of Reno (WB, 1934)
The Key (WB, 1934)
A Very Honorable Guy (FN, 1934)
A Modern Hero (WB, 1934)
Now I'll Tell (Fox, 1934)
The Firebird (WB, 1934)
I Sell Anything (FN, 1934)
I Am a Thief (WB, 1934)
St. Louis Kid (WB, 1934)
Housewife (WB, 1934)
Fashions of 1934 (FN, 1934)
Madame Du Barry (WB, 1934)
A Lost Lady (FN, 1934)
Kansas City Princess (WB, 1934)
Bordertown (WB, 1935)
Wings in the Dark (Par, 1935)
While the Patient Slept (FN, 1935)
Captain Blood (FN, 1935)
Don't Bet on Blondes (WB, 1935)
We're in the Money (WB, 1935)
Broadway Gondolier (WB, 1935)
Page Miss Glory (WB, 1935)
Dr. Socrates (WB, 1935)

A Midsummer Night's Dream (WB, 1935)
I Live for Love (WB, 1935)
The Lady Consents (RKO, 1936)
Love Letters of a Star (Univ, 1936)
Colleen (WB, 1936)
Love Begins at Twenty (FN, 1936)
Two Against the World (FN, 1936)
Hearts Divided (FN, 1936)
Sing Me a Love Song (FN, 1936)
Cain and Mabel (WB, 1936)
Here Comes Carter (FN, 1936)
The Golden Arrow (FN, 1936)
Stage Struck (FN, 1936)
Wife vs. Secretary (MGM, 1936)
Mysterious Crossing (Univ, 1937)
The Great O'Malley (WB, 1937)
Three Smart Girls (Univ, 1937)
The Mighty Treve (Univ, 1937)
Night Key (Univ, 1937)
Girl Overboard (Univ, 1937)
Love in a Bungalow (Univ, 1937)
Reported Missing (Univ, 1937)
That's My Story (Univ, 1938)
Cowboy from Brooklyn (WB, 1938)
Orphans of the Street (Rep, 1938)
Career (RKO, 1939)
Idiot's Delight (MGM, 1939)
Zenobia (UA, 1939)
Rose of Washington Square (20th, 1939)
Tell No Tales (MGM, 1939)
Chicken Wagon Family (20th, 1939)
Reno (RKO, 1939)
That's Right, You're Wrong (RKO, 1939)
The Covered Trailer (Rep, 1939)
The Honeymoon's Over (20th, 1939)
Adventures of Jane Arden (WB, 1939)
I Stole a Million (Univ, 1939)
Naughty but Nice (WB, 1939)
A Child Is Born (WB, 1940)
You Can't Fool Your Wife (RKO, 1940)
Shooting High (20th, 1940)
An Angel from Texas (WB, 1940)
Street of Memories (20th, 1940)
Stage to Chino (RKO, 1940)
Hired Wife (Univ, 1940)
Public Deb No. 1 (20th, 1940)
The Great Plane Robbery (Col, 1940)
Santa Fe Trail (WB, 1940)
Charter Pilot (20th, 1940)
Love, Honor and Oh, Baby! (Univ, 1940)
The Ghost Comes Home (MGM, 1940)
Playmates (RKO, 1941)

Horror Island (Univ, 1941)
I Wanted Wings (Par, 1941)
Thieves Fall Out (WB, 1941)
Meet the Chump (Univ, 1941)
Our Wife (Col, 1941)
Land of the Open Range (RKO, 1941)
Skylark (Par, 1941)
My Favorite Spy (RKO, 1942)
Tarzan's New York Adventure (MGM, 1942)
A Tragedy at Midnight (Rep, 1942)
The Magnificent Dope (20th, 1942)
Jackass Mail (MGM, 1942)
Whistling in Dixie (MGM, 1942)
Stand By for Action (MGM, 1942)
The Meanest Man in the World (20th, 1943)
The Kansan (UA, 1943)
Dangerous Blondes (Col, 1943)
The Man from Down Under (MGM, 1943)
Gildersleeve on Broadway (RKO, 1943)
Sweet Rosie O'Grady (20th, 1943)
Jack London (UA, 1943)
What a Woman (Col, 1943)
The Human Comedy (MGM, 1943)
San Diego, I Love You (Univ, 1944)
Kismet [TV title: *Oriental Dream*] (MGM, 1944)
Louisiana Hayride (Col, 1944)
Roughly Speaking (WB, 1945)
House of Fear (Univ, 1945)
I'll Remember April (Univ, 1945)
Don Juan Quilligan (20th, 1945)
Lady on a Train (Univ, 1945)
Cinderella Jones (WB, 1946)
The Spider Woman Strikes Back (Univ, 1946)
Faithful in My Fashion (MGM, 1946)
The Black Angel (Univ, 1946)
Night and Day (WB, 1946)
Little Iodine (UA, 1946)
Margie (20th, 1946)
Driftwood (Rep, 1947)
Up in Central Park (Univ, 1948)
Best Man Wins (Col, 1948)
You Gotta Stay Happy (Univ, 1948)
The Inside Story (Rep, 1948)
A Letter to Three Wives (20th, 1948)
Stella (20th, 1950)

GEORGE CHANDLER

With Roy Rogers in Man from Oklahoma *(1945).*

Born June 30, 1902, Waukegan, Illinois. Married Catherine Ward (1935), children: Gary, Ward, Mike. One of the most familiar screen faces, often seen as a newsman or a hyperactive comic figure: in the Mack Sennett short *The Fatal Glass of Beer* (1933) played W. C. Fields' repentant son; in *Roxie Hart* cast as Ginger Rogers' cuckolded husband, etc. TV series: "Lassie" (as Uncle Petrie) and "Ichabod and Me."

George Chandler to Kay Medford (regarding a messed-up Jean Rogers) in *Swing Shift Maisie:* "A genuine 4-F would waste his time on *her*. Phooey!"

Films

The Kid's Clever (Univ, 1929)
Black Hills (Big Three, 1929)
The Cloud Dodger (Univ, 1929)
In Gay Madrid (MGM, 1930)
The Florodora Girl (MGM, 1930)
The Last Dance (Audible Pictures, 1930)
The Light of Western Stars (Par, 1930)
Only Saps Work (Par, 1930)
Man of the World (Par, 1931)
Doctors' Wives (Fox, 1931)
Too Many Cooks (RKO, 1931)
The Tenderfoot (FN, 1932)
The Strange Love of Molly Louvain (FN, 1932)
Blessed Event (FN, 1932)
The Famous Ferguson Case (FN, 1932)
Me and My Gal (Fox, 1932)
Afraid to Talk (Univ, 1932)
Bureau of Missing Persons (FN, 1933)
Parachute Jumper (WB, 1933)
Lady Killer (WB, 1933)

The Keyhole (WB, 1933)
Hi, Nellie! (WB, 1934)
He Was Her Man (WB, 1934)
Fog over Frisco (FN, 1934)
The Murder Man (MGM, 1935)
Stars over Broadway (WB, 1935)
The Woman in Red (FN, 1935)
Speed (MGM, 1936)
The Princess Comes Across (Par, 1936)
Sworn Enemy (MGM, 1936)
Here Comes Trouble (20th, 1936)
Pennies from Heaven (Col, 1936)
Reunion (20th, 1936)
Neighborhood House (MGM, 1936)
Fury (MGM, 1936)
Libeled Lady (MGM, 1936)
Old Hutch (MGM, 1936)
Three Men on a Horse (FN, 1936)
The Country Doctor (20th, 1936)
Time Out for Romance (20th, 1937)
Nancy Steele Is Missing (20th, 1937)
Wake Up and Live (20th, 1937)

Danger! Love at Work (20th, 1937)
Big Town Girl (20th, 1937)
They Gave Him a Gun (MGM, 1937)
Woman Chases Man (UA, 1937)
Nothing Sacred (UA, 1937)
Small Town Boy (GN, 1937)
Saratoga (MGM, 1937)
The Singing Marine (WB, 1937)
The Shining Hour (MGM, 1938)
Three Comrades (MGM, 1938)
Men with Wings (Par, 1938)
In Old Chicago (20th, 1938)
Secrets of a Nurse (Univ, 1938)
Man-Proof (MGM, 1938)
Mannequin (MGM, 1938)
Shopworn Angel (MGM, 1938)
Gateway (20th, 1938)
Valley of the Giants (WB, 1938)
St. Louis Blues (Par, 1939)
Young Mr. Lincoln (20th, 1939)
The Light That Failed (Par, 1939)
Beau Geste (Par, 1939)

The Jones Family in Hollywood (20th, 1939)
Jesse James (20th, 1939)
Exile Express (GN, 1939)
King of the Turf (UA, 1939)
Everything's on Ice (RKO, 1939)
Second Fiddle (20th, 1939)
Calling All Marines (Rep, 1939)
I Stole a Million (Univ, 1939)
Edison the Man (MGM, 1940)
Shooting High (20th, 1940)
Thou Shalt Not Kill (Rep, 1940)
The Man Who Wouldn't Talk (20th, 1940)
Manhattan Heartbeat (20th, 1940)
The Return of Frank James (20th, 1940)
Arizona (Col, 1940)
Model Wife (Univ, 1941)
Buy Me That Town (Par, 1941)
Western Union (20th, 1941)
The Mad Doctor (Par, 1941)
Tobacco Road (20th, 1941)
Reaching for the Sun (Par, 1941)
Mountain Moonlight (Rep, 1941)
Private Nurse (20th, 1941)
Night in New Orleans (Par, 1942)
Roxie Hart (20th, 1942)
Isle of Missing Men (Mon, 1942)
The Great Man's Lady (Par, 1942)
Scattergood Survives a Murder (RKO, 1942)
Call Out the Marines (RKO, 1942)
Here We Go Again (RKO, 1942)
Swing Fever (MGM, 1943)
The Ox-Bow Incident (20th, 1943)
Sweet Rosie O'Grady (20th, 1943)
Never a Dull Moment (Univ, 1943)
It Happened Tomorrow (UA, 1944)

Wing and a Prayer (20th, 1944)
Three Men in White (MGM, 1944)
Buffalo Bill (20th, 1944)
Allergic to Love (Univ, 1944)
Since You Went Away (UA, 1944)
Goin' to Town (RKO, 1944)
Man from Oklahoma (Rep, 1945)
Without Love (MGM, 1945)
Captain Eddie (20th, 1945)
This Man's Navy (MGM, 1945)
Tell It to a Star (Rep, 1945)
Strange Confession [a.k.a. *The Missing Head*] (Univ, 1945)
Pardon My Past (Col, 1946)
Lover Come Back (Univ, 1946)
Suspense (Mon, 1946)
Little Giant (Univ, 1946)
Strange Impersonation (Rep, 1946)
A Guy Could Change (Rep, 1946)
The Glass Alibi (Rep, 1946)
Strange Conquest (Univ, 1946)
Black Angel (Univ, 1946)
Behind the Mask (Mon, 1946)
The Missing Lady (Mon, 1946)
The Kid from Brooklyn (RKO, 1946)
Helldorado (Rep, 1946)
Suddenly It's Spring (Par, 1947)
Nightmare Alley (20th, 1947)
Night Song (RKO, 1947)
It Had to Be You (Col, 1947)
The Secret Life of Walter Mitty (RKO, 1947)
Road to Rio (Par, 1947)
Dead Reckoning (Col, 1947)
The Vigilantes Return (Univ, 1947)
Saddle Pals (Rep, 1947)
Michigan Kid (Univ, 1947)
Magic Town (RKO, 1947)

Silver River (WB, 1948)
Lightnin' in the Forest (Rep, 1948)
The Girl from Manhattan (UA, 1948)
The Miracle of the Bells (RKO, 1948)
Hollow Triumph (EL, 1948)
Hazard (Par, 1948)
Sons of Adventure (Rep, 1948)
Perfect Strangers (WB, 1950)
Singing Guns (Rep, 1950)
The Happy Years (MGM, 1950)
Kansas Raiders (Univ, 1950)
Triple Trouble (Mon, 1950)
Pretty Baby (WB, 1950)
Across the Wide Missouri (MGM, 1951)
This Woman Is Dangerous (WB, 1952)
And Now Tomorrow (Westminster Productions, 1952)
My Man and I (MGM, 1952)
The WAC from Walla Walla (Rep, 1952)
Hans Christian Andersen (RKO, 1952)
Island in the Sky (WB, 1953)
Rails into Laramie (Univ, 1954)
The Steel Cage (UA, 1954)
The High and the Mighty (WB, 1954)
Apache Ambush (Col, 1955)
The Girl Rush (Par, 1955)
Spring Reunion (UA, 1957)
Gunsight Ridge (UA, 1957)
Dead Ringer (WB, 1964)
Law of the Lawless (Par, 1964)
Apache Uprising (Par, 1966)
The Ghost and Mr. Chicken (Univ, 1966)
Buckskin (Par, 1968)
One More Train to Rob (Univ, 1971)
One More Time (UA, 1971)
Pickup on 101 (AIP, 1972)
Capone (20th, 1975)
Escape to Witch Mountain (BV, 1975)

SPENCER CHARTERS

Porter Hall, Spencer Charters, Bob Burns, Dennis O'Keefe, and Peggy Moran in Alias the Deacon *(1940).*

Born 1875, Duncannon, Pennsylvania. Married Irene Myers, child: Irene; widowed (1941). Died January 25, 1943, Hollywood, California. Generally the country fellow who managed to outfox the crafty city slicker.

Spencer Charters as the judge in *Young Mr. Lincoln:* "Come, come, gentlemen. You've got to give the boys a fair trial—a jury trial, before you hang 'em."

Films

Little Old New York (G, 1923)
Janice Meredith (MG, 1924)
Dancing Mothers (Par, 1926)
Whoopee (UA, 1930)
The Bat Whispers (UA, 1930)
Lonely Wives (Pathé, 1931)
The Front Page (UA, 1931)
Traveling Husbands (RKO, 1931)
Palmy Days (UA, 1931)
The Tenderfoot (FN, 1932)
Hold 'em Jail (RKO, 1932)
Movie Crazy (Par, 1932)
Jewel Robbery (WB, 1932)
The Crooked Circle (WW, 1932)
The Match King (FN, 1932)
Central Park (FN, 1932)
20,000 Years in Sing Sing (FN, 1933)
So This Is Africa (Col, 1933)
Broadway Bad (Fox, 1933)
Gambling Ship (Par, 1933)
Female (FN, 1933)
The Kennel Murder Case (WB, 1933)
Fashions of 1934 (WB, 1934)

The Circus Clown (FN, 1934)
Hips, Hips, Hooray (RKO, 1934)
Half a Sinner (Univ, 1934)
The Loudspeaker (Mon, 1934)
The Firebird (WB, 1934)
Success at Any Price (RKO, 1934)
Wake Up and Dream (Univ, 1934)
The St. Louis Kid (WB, 1934)
It's a Gift (Par, 1934)
Million Dollar Ransom (Univ, 1934)
Wonder Bar (FN, 1934)
Blind Date (Col, 1934)
Pursuit of Happiness (Par, 1934)
The Ghost Walks (Chesterfield, 1934)
Murder on a Honeymoon (RKO, 1935)
Stranded (WB, 1935)
In Person (RKO, 1935)
The Nut Farm (Mon, 1935)
Eight Bells (Col, 1935)
The Raven (Univ, 1935)
Welcome Home (Fox, 1935)
Don't Bet on Blondes (WB, 1935)
The Goose and the Gander (WB, 1935)

Whispering Smith Speaks (Fox, 1935)
Alibi Ike (WB, 1935)
$1,000 a Minute (Rep, 1935)
The Secret Bride (WB, 1935)
The Texas Rangers (Par, 1936)
Love on a Bet (RKO, 1936)
Murder on the Bridle Path (RKO, 1936)
Career Woman (20th, 1936)
Banjo on My Knee (20th, 1936)
The Preview Murder Mystery (Par, 1936)
The Moon's Our Home (Par, 1936)
Till We Meet Again (Par, 1936)
Spendthrift (Par, 1936)
Don't Get Personal (Univ, 1936)
The Mine with the Iron Door (Col, 1936)
Mr. Deeds Goes to Town (Col, 1936)
The Harvester (Rep, 1936)
All American Chump (MGM, 1936)
The Farmer in the Dell (RKO, 1936)
F-Man (Par, 1936)
Colleen (WB, 1936)
Postal Inspector (Univ, 1936)
The Lady from Nowhere (Col, 1936)

Libeled Lady (MGM, 1936)
Fugitive in the Sky (WB, 1937)
Four Days' Wonder (Univ, 1937)
Back in Circulation (WB, 1937)
Fifty Roads to Town (20th, 1937)
Wife, Doctor and Nurse (20th, 1937)
Danger—Love at Work (20th, 1937)
Big Town Girl (20th, 1937)
They Wanted to Marry (RKO, 1937)
Checkers (20th, 1937)
Pick a Star (MGM, 1937)
Mountain Music (Par, 1937)
Dangerous Number (MGM, 1937)
Girl Loves Boy (GN, 1937)
Wells Fargo (Par, 1937)
The Mighty Treve (Univ, 1937)
Venus Makes Trouble (Col, 1937)
The Prisoner of Zenda (UA, 1937)
The Hurricane (UA, 1937)
Behind the Mike (Univ, 1937)
Mr. Boggs Steps Out (GN, 1937)
Married Before Breakfast (MGM, 1937)
The Perfect Specimen (FN, 1937)
Spring Madness (MGM, 1938)
Stablemates (MGM, 1938)
Lady Behave (Rep, 1938)
In Old Chicago (20th, 1938)
Joy of Living (RKO, 1938)
Valley of the Giants (WB, 1938)
One Wild Night (20th, 1938)
Forbidden Valley (Univ, 1938)
Three Blind Mice (20th, 1938)
Crime School (WB, 1938)

Inside Story (20th, 1938)
Breaking the Ice (RKO, 1938)
Professor Beware (Par, 1938)
The Road to Reno (Univ, 1938)
The Texans (Par, 1938)
Mr. Chump (WB, 1938)
Five of a Kind (20th, 1938)
Woman Doctor (Rep, 1939)
I'm from Missouri (Par, 1939)
Women in the Wind (WB, 1939)
Jesse James (20th, 1939)
Young Mr. Lincoln (20th, 1939)
Second Fiddle (20th, 1939)
Drums Along the Mohawk (20th, 1939)
Yes, My Darling Daughter (WB, 1939)
Topper Takes a Trip (UA, 1939)
The Covered Trailer (Rep, 1939)
The Flying Irishman (RKO, 1939)
They Made Her a Spy (RKO, 1939)
In Name Only (RKO, 1939)
Two Thoroughbreds (RKO, 1939)
The Hunchback of Notre Dame (RKO, 1939)
Unexpected Father (Univ, 1939)
They Asked for It (Univ, 1939)
The Under-Pup (Univ, 1939)
Exile Express (GN, 1939)
Dodge City (WB, 1939)
Lucky Cisco Kid (20th, 1940)
Remember the Night (Par, 1940)
Kitty Foyle (RKO, 1940)
He Married His Wife (20th, 1940)
Our Town (UA, 1940)

Alias the Deacon (Univ, 1940)
Three Faces West (Rep, 1940)
Maryland (20th, 1940)
The Girl from God's Country (Rep, 1940)
Friendly Neighbors (Rep, 1940)
The Golden Fleecing (MGM, 1940)
Meet the Missus (Rep, 1940)
Blondie Plays Cupid (Col, 1940)
Santa Fe Trail (WB, 1940)
The Lady from Cheyenne (Univ, 1941)
So Ends Our Night (UA, 1941)
She Couldn't Say No (WB, 1941)
High Sierra (WB, 1941)
Petticoat Politics (Rep, 1941)
Tobacco Road (20th, 1941)
The Singing Hill (Rep, 1941)
Moon over Miami (20th, 1941)
Man at Large (20th, 1941)
Mr. District Attorney in the Carter Case (Rep, 1941)
Look Who's Laughing (RKO, 1941)
Pacific Blackout [a.k.a. *Midnight Angel*] (Par, 1942)
The Remarkable Andrew (Par, 1942)
Right to the Heart (20th, 1942)
The Night Before the Divorce (20th, 1942)
The Postman Didn't Ring (20th, 1942)
The Affairs of Jimmy Valentine (Rep, 1942)
Scattergood Survives a Murder (RKO, 1942)
Juke Girl (WB, 1942)
Slightly Dangerous (MGM, 1943)

BERTON CHURCHILL

James Millican, John Arledge, Arthur Rankin, Berton Churchill, and Robert Middlemass in Panic on the Air *(1936)*.

Born December 9, 1876, Toronto, Ontario, Canada. Married Harriet Gardner. Died October 10, 1940, New York City, New York. White-haired, serious-faced, gruff, and always working in pictures. Could be the hale and hearty capitalist or the victim-prone small-towner. Often the heroine's unbending father.

Berton Churchill to Helen Westley in *Dimples:* "It's common gossip that Alan has become involved with an actress . . . that he spends most of his time with these low people of the theater."

Films

Six Cylinder Love (Fox, 1923)
Tongues of Flame (Univ, 1924)
Nothing but the Truth (Par, 1929)
Secrets of a Secretary (Par, 1931)
Air Eagles (Continental Pictures, 1931)
Husband's Holiday (Par, 1931)
The Rich Are Always with Us (FN, 1932)
Cabin in the Cotton (FN, 1932)
This Reckless Age (Par, 1932)
The Dark Horse (FN, 1932)
Taxi! (WB, 1932)
Impatient Maiden (Univ, 1932)
Scandal for Sale (Univ, 1932)
Two Seconds (FN, 1932)
Week-Ends Only (Fox, 1932)
American Madness (Col, 1932)
Crooked Circle (WW, 1932)

I Am a Fugitive from a Chain Gang (WB, 1932)
False Faces (WW, 1932)
Big Stampede (WB, 1932)
Okay, America (Univ, 1932)
Laughter in Hell (Univ, 1932)
Washington Parade (MGM, 1932)
Fast Companions (Univ, 1932)
Afraid to Talk (Univ, 1932)
Madame Butterfly (Par, 1932)
It's Tough to Be Famous (FN, 1932)
The Mouthpiece (WB, 1932)
The Wet Parade (MGM, 1932)
The Information Kid (Univ, 1932)
If I Had a Million (Par, 1932)
Forgotten Commandments (Par, 1932)
So This Is Africa (Col, 1933)
Elmer the Great (FN, 1933)

Private Jones (Univ, 1933)
Hard to Handle (WB, 1933)
Her First Mate (Univ, 1933)
Only Yesterday (Univ, 1933)
The Little Giant (FN, 1933)
The Big Brain (RKO, 1933)
Heroes for Sale (FN, 1933)
Golden Harvest (Par, 1933)
Master of Men (Col, 1933)
Ladies Must Love (Univ, 1933)
The Avenger (Mon, 1933)
Dr. Bull (Fox, 1933)
College Coach (WB, 1933)
From Hell to Heaven (Par, 1933)
Employees' Entrance (FN, 1933)
The Mysterious Rider (Par, 1933)
Billion Dollar Scandal (Par, 1933)
Judge Priest (Fox, 1934)

Hi, Nellie! (WB, 1934)
Babbitt (FN, 1934)
Menace (Par, 1934)
Half a Sinner (Univ, 1934)
Let's Be Ritzy (Univ, 1934)
Frontier Marshal (Fox, 1934)
Helldorado (Fox, 1934)
Sing Sing Nights (Mon, 1934)
Red Head (Mon, 1934)
Strictly Dynamite (RKO, 1934)
Bachelor Bait (RKO, 1934)
Murder in the Private Car (MGM, 1934)
Men in White (MGM, 1934)
Bachelor of Arts (Fox, 1934)
Dames (WB, 1934)
Friends of Mr. Sweeney (WB, 1934)
Take the Stand (Liberty, 1934)
Kid Millions (UA, 1934)
The County Chairman (Fox, 1935)
$10 Raise (Fox, 1935)
Steamboat 'Round the Bend (Fox, 1935)
A Night at the Ritz (WB, 1935)
Page Miss Glory (WB, 1935)
I Live for Love (WB, 1935)
Vagabond Lady (MGM, 1935)

The Rainmakers (RKO, 1935)
Speed Devils (Hoffberg, 1935)
The Spanish Cape Mystery (Rep, 1935)
Coronado (Par, 1935)
Dizzy Dames (Liberty, 1936)
Colleen (WB, 1936)
You May Be Next (Col, 1936)
Three of a Kind (Invincible, 1936)
Panic on the Air (Col, 1936)
Parole (Univ, 1936)
Dimples (20th, 1936)
Under Your Spell (20th, 1936)
Bunker Bean (RKO, 1936)
The Dark Hour (Chesterfield, 1936)
Racing Lady (RKO, 1937)
You Can't Beat Love (RKO, 1937)
Parnell (MGM, 1937)
The Singing Marine (WB, 1937)
Wild and Woolly (Fox, 1937)
Public Wedding (WB, 1937)
Sing and Be Happy (20th, 1937)
Quick Money (RKO, 1938)
He Couldn't Say No (WB, 1938)
In Old Chicago (20th, 1938)
Four Men and a Prayer (20th, 1938)

Wide Open Faces (Col, 1938)
Kentucky Moonshine (20th, 1938)
Meet the Mayor (Times Pictures, 1938)
The Cowboy and the Lady (UA, 1938)
Sweethearts (MGM, 1938)
Ladies in Distress (Rep, 1938)
Down in Arkansas (Rep, 1938)
Danger on the Air (Univ, 1938)
Stagecoach (UA, 1939)
Daughters Courageous (WB, 1939)
Should Husbands Work? (Rep, 1939)
Angels Wash Their Faces (WB, 1939)
Hero for a Day (Univ, 1939)
On Your Toes (WB, 1939)
Brother Rat and a Baby (WB, 1940)
Saturday's Children (WB, 1940)
Twenty-Mule Team (MGM, 1940)
Turnabout (UA, 1940)
Way of All Flesh (Par, 1940)
Cross-Country Romance (RKO, 1940)
I'm Nobody's Sweetheart Now (Univ, 1940)
Public Deb No. 1 (20th, 1940)
Alias the Deacon (Univ, 1940)

EDUARDO CIANNELLI

(a.k.a. Edward Ciannelli)

Werner Klemperer, Eduardo Ciannelli, and Sophia Loren in Houseboat *(1958).*

Born August 30, 1888, Naples, Italy. Married Alma Wolfe (1918), children: Eduardo, Lewis; widowed (1968). Died October 8, 1969, Rome, Italy. Former opera singer and Broadway performer who made his cinema niche re-creating his stage role of Trock Estrella in *Winterset*. Later was the well-dictioned, smart-dressed racketeer Johnny Manning who made Bette Davis a *Marked Woman*. Played the maniacal Gura of *Gunga Din*, the deranged title character of the serial *Mysterious Dr. Satan*, and the Indian Prairie Dog (*MacKenna's Gold*). An avid scene-stealer. Occasionally performed an upbeat role—the thoughtful bartender of *Kitty Foyle*. TV series: "Johnny Staccato."

> **Eduardo Ciannelli** to John Litel in *Marked Woman:* "Me, I don't make deals with nobody . . . they make deals with me. All the time I've been that way—ever since I was 'that' big."

Films

Reunion in Vienna (MGM, 1933)
The Scoundrel (Par, 1935)
Winterset (RKO, 1936)
Hitting a New High (RKO, 1937)
On Such a Night (Par, 1937)
Super Sleuth (RKO, 1937)
The Girl from Scotland Yard (Par, 1937)
Criminal Lawyer (RKO, 1937)
The League of Frightened Men (Col, 1937)
Marked Woman (WB, 1937)
Law of the Underworld (RKO, 1938)
Blind Alibi (RKO, 1938)
Angels Wash Their Faces (WB, 1939)
Gunga Din (RKO, 1939)
Society Lawyer (MGM, 1939)

Risky Business (Univ, 1939)
Bulldog Drummond's Bride (Par, 1939)
Strange Cargo (MGM, 1940)
Zanzibar (Univ, 1940)
Foreign Correspondent (UA, 1940)
Forgotten Girls (Rep, 1940)
Outside the Three-Mile Limit (Col, 1940)
Mysterious Dr. Satan [feature version: Dr. Satan's Robots] (Rep serial, 1940)
The Mummy's Hand (Univ, 1940)
Kitty Foyle (RKO, 1940)
Ellery Queen's Penthouse Mystery (Col, 1941)
They Met in Bombay (MGM, 1941)
I Was a Prisoner on Devil's Island (Col,

1941)
Sky Raiders (Univ serial, 1941)
Paris Calling (Univ, 1941)
Cairo (MGM, 1942)
You Can't Escape Forever (WB, 1942)
Dr. Broadway (Par, 1942)
For Whom the Bell Tolls (Par, 1943)
They Got Me Covered (RKO, 1943)
Flight for Freedom (RKO, 1943)
The Constant Nymph (WB, 1943)
The Conspirators (WB, 1944)
Passage to Marseille (WB, 1944)
The Mask of Dimitrios (WB, 1944)
Storm over Lisbon (Rep, 1944)
A Bell for Adano (20th, 1945)

Dillinger (Mon, 1945)
Incendiary Blonde (Par, 1945)
The Crime Doctor's Warning (Col, 1946)
The Wife of Monte Cristo (PRC, 1946)
Joe Palooka—Champ (Mon, 1946)
Heartbeat (RKO, 1946)
Perilous Holiday (Col, 1946)
California (Par, 1946)
Rose of Santa Rosa (Col, 1947)
Seven Keys to Baldpate (RKO, 1947)
The Lost Moment (Univ, 1947)
The Crime Doctor's Gamble (Col, 1947)
I Love Trouble (Col, 1948)
The Creeper (20th, 1948)

On Our Merry Way [a.k.a. *A Miracle Can Happen*] (UA, 1948)
To the Victor (WB, 1948)
Rapture (Four Continents, 1950)
The People Against O'Hara (MGM, 1951)
Fugitive Lady (Rep, 1951)
Volcano (UA, 1953)
The City Stands Trial (It, 1954)
Voice of Silence (It, 1954)
The Stranger's Hand (DCA, 1955)
Mambo (Par, 1955)
Helen of Troy (WB, 1955)
Love Slaves of the Amazon (Univ, 1957)

The Monster from Green Hell (DCA, 1957)
Houseboat (Par, 1958)
Attila (Lux, 1958)
Forty Pounds of Trouble (Univ, 1962)
The Visit (20th, 1964)
The Brotherhood (Par, 1968)
MacKenna's Gold (Col, 1969)
The Secret of Santa Vittoria (UA, 1969)
Stiletto (Avco Emb, 1969)
Boot Hill (It, 1969)
The Syndicate: A Death in the Family (It, 1969)

FRED CLARK
(Frederic Leonard Clark)

In Sergeant Deadhead *(1965).*

Born March 9, 1914, Lincoln, California. Married 1) Benay Venuta (1952); divorced (1963); 2) Gloria Glaser (1966). Died December 5, 1968, Santa Monica, California. From unassuming roles like the detective in *The Unsuspected* to that of the underworld figure Trader in *White Heat*, he switched to tense executives, officers, and fathers who vented their frustration on the nearest target: *Here Come the Girls* (Harry Fraser, nemesis of stage actor Bob Hope), *The Solid Gold Cadillac* (crafty Clifford Snell, one of the board coping with "naive" Judy Holliday), *Visit to a Small Planet* ("protecting" his daughter from alien Jerry Lewis), etc. TV series: "George Burns–Gracie Allen Show" (as neighbor Harry Morton), "The Double Life of Henry Phyfe," and "The Beverly Hillbillies" (as Dr. Roy Clyburn).

Fred Clark to Janet Leigh in *Living It Up:* "I am sitting here, Miss Cook, toying with the idea of removing your heart and stuffing it like an olive."

Films

Ride the Pink Horse (Univ, 1947)
The Unsuspected (WB, 1947)
Hazard (Par, 1948)
Fury at Furnace Creek (20th, 1948)
Mr. Peabody and the Mermaid (Univ, 1948)
Two Guys from Texas (WB, 1948)
Cry of the City (20th, 1948)
Flamingo Road (WB, 1949)
The Younger Brothers (WB, 1949)
Task Force (WB, 1949)
Alias Nick Beal (Par, 1949)
The Lady Takes a Sailor (WB, 1949)
White Heat (WB, 1949)
Sunset Boulevard (Par, 1950)
The Eagle and the Hawk (Par, 1950)
Return of the Frontiersman (WB, 1950)
The Jackpot (20th, 1950)
Mrs. O'Malley and Mr. Malone (MGM, 1950)
A Place in the Sun (Par, 1951)
The Lemon Drop Kid (Par, 1951)
The Hollywood Story (Univ, 1951)
Meet Me After the Show (20th, 1951)

Dreamboat (20th, 1952)
Three for Bedroom C (WB, 1952)
The Caddy (Par, 1953)
Here Come the Girls (Par, 1953)
How to Marry a Millionaire (20th, 1953)
The Stars Are Singing (Par, 1953)
Living It Up (Par, 1954)
How to Be Very Very Popular (20th, 1955)
Abbott and Costello Meet the Keystone Kops (Univ, 1955)
Daddy Long Legs (20th, 1955)
The Court-Martial of Billy Mitchell (WB, 1955)
The Solid Gold Cadillac (Col, 1956)
Miracle in the Rain (WB, 1956)
Back from Eternity (RKO, 1956)
The Birds and the Bees (Par, 1956)
Joe Butterfly (Univ, 1957)
Don't Go Near the Water (MGM, 1957)
The Fuzzy Pink Nightgown (UA, 1957)
Mardi Gras (20th, 1958)
Auntie Mame (WB, 1958)
The Mating Game (MGM, 1959)
It Started with a Kiss (MGM, 1959)

The Passionate Thief (Emb, 1959)
Visit to a Small Planet (Par, 1960)
Bells Are Ringing (MGM, 1960)
Hemingway's Adventures of a Young Man (20th, 1962)
Boys' Night Out (MGM, 1962)
Zotz! (Col, 1962)
Move Over, Darling (20th, 1963)
John Goldfarb, Please Come Home (20th, 1964)
The Curse of the Mummy's Tomb (Col Br, 1964)
Sergeant Deadhead (AIP, 1965)
When the Boys Meet the Girls (MGM, 1965)
Dr. Goldfoot and the Bikini Machine (AIP, 1965)
War—Italian Style (AIP, 1966)
The Horse in the Gray Flannel Suit (BV, 1968)
Skidoo (Par, 1968)
Eve (CUE, 1969)

GEORGE CLEVELAND

Fuzzy Knight, George Cleveland, Bonita Granville, Oscar O'Shea, and Bob Merrill in Senorita from the West (1945).

Born 1883, Sydney, Nova Scotia, Canada. Married Dorothy Melick. Died July 15, 1957, Burbank, California. Round-faced veteran of every available acting medium. Consistently used in motion pictures to portray small-timers, kindly (grand) fathers, and bedraggled prospectors: *The Lone Ranger* serial (Blanchard), *Drums of Fu Manchu* serial (Professor Parker, author of the Dalai Plaque), Marlene Dietrich's *The Spoilers* (Banty), *Johnny Come Lately* (Willie Ferguson), *Mother Wore Tights* (Grandfather McKinley), *A Date with Judy* (Gramps), *Untamed Heiress* (Cactus Clayton), etc. TV series: "Lassie" (as Gramps).

George Cleveland to Karin Booth in *Cripple Creek:* "It won't be long before we have that big house in Denver like we both wanted, honey."

Films

Girl o' My Dreams (Mon, 1934)
Monte Carlo Nights (Mon, 1934)
The Man from Utah (Mon, 1934)
Star Packer (Mon, 1934)
School for Girls (Liberty, 1934)
Mystery Liner (Mon, 1934)
Blue Steel (Mon, 1934)
City Limits (Mon, 1934)
Keeper of the Bees (Mon, 1935)
Make a Million (Mon, 1935)
His Night Out (Univ, 1935)
The Spanish Cape Mystery (Rep, 1935)
Forced Landing (Rep, 1935)
I Conquer the Sea (Academy Pictures, 1936)
Revolt of the Zombies (Academy Pictures, 1936)

Flash Gordon (Univ serial, 1936) [feature versions: *Perils from the Planet Mongo; Spaceship to the Unknown*]
Robinson Crusoe of Clipper Island (Rep serial, 1936)
North of Nome (Col, 1936)
Don't Get Personal (Univ, 1936)
Rio Grande Romance (Victory, 1936)
Brilliant Marriage (Invincible, 1936)
Put on the Spot (Principal, 1936)
The Man in Blue (Univ, 1937)
Paradise Express (Rep, 1937)
Trapped by G-Men [a.k.a. *The River of Missing Men*] (Col, 1937)
Swing It Professor! (Conn Pictures, 1937)
Boy of the Streets (Mon, 1937)

The Adventure's End (Univ, 1937)
The Lone Ranger (Rep serial, 1938) [feature version: *Hi-Yo Silver!*, 1940]
Valley of the Giants (WB, 1938)
Port of Missing Girls (Mon, 1938)
Rose of the Rio Grande (Mon, 1938)
Romance of the Limberlost (Mon, 1938)
Under the Big Top (Mon, 1938)
Ghost Town Riders (Univ, 1938)
Home on the Prairie (Rep, 1939)
The Phantom Stage (Univ, 1939)
Streets of New York (Mon, 1939)
Wolf Call (Mon, 1939)
Stunt Pilot (Mon, 1939)
Mutiny in the Big House (Mon, 1939)
Overland Mail (Mon, 1939)
Midnight Limited (Mon, 1940)

Tomboy (Mon, 1940)
The Haunted House (Mon, 1940)
Queen of the Yukon (Mon, 1940)
The Old Swimmin' Hole (Mon, 1940)
Pioneers of the West (Rep, 1940)
Drums of Fu Manchu (Rep serial, 1940)
One Man's Law (Rep, 1940)
Blazing Six Shooters (Col, 1940)
West of Abilene (Col, 1940)
Chasing Trouble (Mon, 1940)
Konga—The Wild Stallion (Col, 1940)
The Ape (Mon, 1940)
A Girl, a Guy and a Gob (RKO, 1941)
All That Money Can Buy [a.k.a. *The Devil and Daniel Webster*] (RKO, 1941)
Nevada City (Rep, 1941)
Sunset in Wyoming (Rep, 1941)
Two in a Taxi (Col, 1941)
Obliging Young Lady (RKO, 1941)
Man at Large (20th, 1941)
Riders of the Purple Sage (20th, 1941)
Look Who's Laughing (RKO, 1941)
Playmates (RKO, 1941)
The Spoilers (Univ, 1942)
My Favorite Spy (RKO, 1942)
The Falcon Takes Over (RKO, 1942)
The Mexican Spitfire's Elephant (RKO, 1942)
The Big Street (RKO, 1942)
Army Surgeon (RKO, 1942)
Seven Miles from Alcatraz (RKO, 1942)
The Traitor Within (Rep, 1942)
Powder Town (RKO, 1942)
Highways by Night (RKO, 1942)
Call Out the Marines (RKO, 1942)
Valley of the Sun (RKO, 1942)

Here We Go Again (RKO, 1942)
Klondike Kate (Col, 1943)
Cowboy in Manhattan (Univ, 1943)
The Woman of the Town (UA, 1943)
Johnny Come Lately (UA, 1943)
Ladies' Day (RKO, 1943)
The Man from Music Mountain (Rep, 1943)
It Happened Tomorrow (UA, 1944)
Man from Frisco (Rep, 1944)
Abroad with Two Yanks (UA, 1944)
Alaska (Mon, 1944)
Yellow Rose of Texas (Rep, 1944)
My Best Gal (Rep, 1944)
When the Lights Go on Again (PRC, 1944)
Home in Indiana (20th, 1944)
Can't Help Singing (Univ, 1944)
My Pal Wolf (RKO, 1944)
Song of the Sarong (Univ, 1945)
It's in the Bag (UA, 1945)
Dakota (Rep, 1945)
Senorita from the West (Univ, 1945)
Pillow of Death (Univ, 1945)
Sunbonnet Sue (Mon, 1945)
Her Highness and the Bellboy (MGM, 1945)
She Wouldn't Say Yes (Col, 1946)
Little Giant (Univ, 1946)
Wake Up and Dream (20th, 1946)
The Runaround [a.k.a. *Deadly Enemies*] (Univ, 1946)
Angel on My Shoulder (UA, 1946)
Step by Step (RKO, 1946)
Wild Beauty (Univ, 1946)
Courage of Lassie (MGM, 1946)

The Show-Off (MGM, 1946)
Mother Wore Tights (20th, 1947)
I Wonder Who's Kissing Her Now (20th, 1947)
The Wistful Widow of Wagon Gap (Univ, 1947)
Easy Come, Easy Go (Par, 1947)
My Wild Irish Rose (WB, 1947)
Albuquerque (Par, 1948)
Fury at Furnace Creek (20th, 1948)
Miraculous Journey (Film Classics, 1948)
The Plunderers (Rep, 1948)
A Date with Judy (MGM, 1948)
Kazan (Col, 1949)
Miss Grant Takes Richmond (Col, 1949)
Rimfire (Lip, 1949)
Home in San Antone (Col, 1949)
The Boy from Indiana (EL, 1950)
Please Believe Me (MGM, 1950)
Frenchie (Univ, 1950)
Trigger, Jr. (Rep, 1950)
Flaming Feather (Par, 1951)
Fort Defiance (Univ, 1951)
Carson City (WB, 1952)
The WAC from Walla Walla (Rep, 1952)
Cripple Creek (Col, 1952)
San Antone (Rep, 1953)
Affair with a Stranger (RKO, 1953)
Walking My Baby Back Home (Univ, 1953)
Fireman, Save My Child (Univ, 1954)
Untamed Heiress (Rep, 1954)
The Outlaw's Daughter (20th, 1954)
Racing Blood (20th, 1954)

E. E. CLIVE

E. E. Clive and Robert Taylor in Personal Property *(1937).*

Born 1880, Blaennavon, Monmouthshire, Wales. Married Eleanor Ellis (1925), child: David John. Died June 6, 1940, North Hollywood, California. The dyspeptic-looking Britisher who was repeatedly assigned to be a butler, manservant, etc. Played Tenny in Paramount's *Bulldog Drummond* detective series. Other roles: *Bride of Frankenstein* (burgomaster), *A Tale of Two Cities* (judge at Old Bailey), *The Charge of the Light Brigade* (Sir Humphrey Harcourt), *The Adventures of Sherlock Holmes* (Inspector Bristol), etc.

E. E. Clive in *Night Must Fall:* "And now, ladies and gentlemen, if you will draw a little closer, you will see the exact spot where the body was recovered."

Films

The Invisible Man (Univ, 1933)
The Poor Rich (Univ, 1934)
The Gay Divorcee (RKO, 1934)
The Long Lost Father (RKO, 1934)
One More River (Univ, 1934)
Riptide (MGM, 1934)
Bulldog Drummond Strikes Back (UA, 1934)
Charlie Chan in London (Fox, 1934)
Mystery of Edwin Drood (Univ, 1935)
Bride of Frankenstein (Univ, 1935)
Remember Last Night? (Univ, 1935)
We're in the Money (WB, 1935)
Gold Diggers of 1935 (FN, 1935)
Stars over Broadway (WB, 1935)
A Tale of Two Cities (MGM, 1935)
Captain Blood (WB, 1935)
Atlantic Adventure (Col, 1935)

Father Brown, Detective (Par, 1935)
Sylvia Scarlett (RKO, 1935)
The Widow from Monte Carlo (WB, 1935)
The King Steps Out (Col, 1936)
Little Lord Fauntleroy (UA, 1936)
Love Before Breakfast (Univ, 1936)
Dracula's Daughter (Univ, 1936)
The Unguarded Hour (MGM, 1936)
Trouble for Two (MGM, 1936)
Piccadilly Jim (MGM, 1936)
All American Chump (MGM, 1936)
Libeled Lady (MGM, 1936)
Tarzan Escapes (MGM, 1936)
Camille (MGM, 1936)
The Golden Arrow (FN, 1936)
Isle of Fury (WB, 1936)
The Charge of the Light Brigade (WB, 1936)

Cain and Mabel (WB, 1936)
Palm Springs (Par, 1936)
Ticket to Paradise (Rep, 1936)
Lloyds of London (20th, 1936)
The Dark Hour (Chesterfield, 1936)
Live, Love and Learn (MGM, 1937)
They Wanted to Marry (RKO, 1937)
Maid of Salem (Par, 1937)
Bulldog Drummond Escapes (Par, 1937)
Bulldog Drummond's Revenge (Par, 1937)
Ready, Willing and Able (WB, 1937)
It's Love I'm After (FN, 1937)
On the Avenue (20th, 1937)
Love Under Fire (20th, 1937)
Danger—Love at Work (20th, 1937)
Personal Property (MGM, 1937)
Night Must Fall (MGM, 1937)
The Emperor's Candlesticks (MGM, 1937)

Beg, Borrow or Steal (MGM, 1937)
Arsene Lupin Returns (MGM, 1938)
The First 100 Years (MGM, 1938)
The Last Warning (Univ, 1938)
Kidnapped (20th, 1938)
Gateway (20th, 1938)
Submarine Patrol (20th, 1938)
Bulldog Drummond's Peril (Par, 1938)
Bulldog Drummond in Africa (Par, 1938)

Arrest Bulldog Drummond! (Par, 1939)
I'm from Missouri (Par, 1939)
The Little Princess (20th, 1939)
Bulldog Drummond's Secret Police (Par, 1939)
Man About Town (Par, 1939)
Bulldog Drummond's Bride (Par, 1939)
The Hound of the Baskervilles (20th, 1939)
Rose of Washington Square (20th, 1939)

The Adventures of Sherlock Holmes (20th, 1939)
The Honeymoon's Over (20th, 1939)
Raffles (UA, 1939)
Bachelor Mother (RKO, 1939)
The Earl of Chicago (MGM, 1940)
Congo Maisie (MGM, 1940)
Pride and Prejudice (MGM, 1940)
Foreign Correspondent (UA, 1940)

ANDY CLYDE

Whip Wilson, Virginia Herrick, and Andy Clyde in Silver Raiders *(1950).*

Born March 25, 1892, Blairgowrie, Scotland. Married Elsie Tarron (1933), child: John. Died May 18, 1967, Los Angeles, California. Though a Scot, he rarely played one on screen. Instead, played an American rube—whether in two-reelers or features. For a time was William Boyd's sidekick, California Carlson, in the *Hopalong Cassidy* Westerns. Could offer a salty characterization without benefit of dentures, like Walter Brennan. TV series: "Lassie" (as Cully) and "Circus Boy."

Andy Clyde to Richard Dix in *Cherokee Strip:* "You're gonna need a deputy, ain't cha?"

Films

Should a Girl Marry? (Rayart, 1928)
Branded Men (Rayart, 1928)
The Good-Bye Kiss (FN, 1928)
Ships of the Night (Rayart, 1928)
Blindfold (Fox, 1929)
Midnight Daddies (WW, 1930)
The Million Dollar Legs (Par, 1932)

Romance in Manhattan (RKO, 1934)
The Little Minister (RKO, 1934)
McFadden's Flats (Par, 1935)
Village Tale (RKO, 1935)
Annie Oakley (RKO, 1935)
Yellow Dust (RKO, 1936)
Straight from the Shoulder (Par, 1936)

Two in a Crowd (Univ, 1936)
Red Lights Ahead (Chesterfield, 1937)
The Barrier (Par, 1937)
It's a Wonderful World (MGM, 1939)
Bad Lands (RKO, 1939)
Abe Lincoln in Illinois (RKO, 1940)
Three Men from Texas (Par, 1940)

Cherokee Strip (Par, 1940)	*False Colors* (UA, 1943)	*The Dead Don't Dream* (UA, 1948)
Border Vigilantes (Par, 1941)	*Riders of the Deadline* (UA, 1943)	*Sinister Journey* (UA, 1948)
Doomed Caravan (Par, 1941)	*Texas Masquerade* (UA, 1944)	*False Paradise* (UA, 1948)
In Old Colorado (Par, 1941)	*Lumberjack* (UA, 1944)	*Strange Gamble* (UA, 1948)
Pirates on Horseback (Par, 1941)	*Forty Thieves* (UA, 1944)	*Borrowed Trouble* (UA, 1948)
Wide Open Town (Par, 1941)	*Mystery Man* (UA, 1944)	*Range Land* (Mon, 1949)
Riders of the Timberline (Par, 1941)	*Roughly Speaking* (WB, 1945)	*Crashing Through* (Mon, 1949)
Twilight on the Trail (Par, 1941)	*Song of the Prairie* (Col, 1945)	*Riders of the Dusk* (Mon, 1949)
Stick to Your Guns (Par, 1941)	*The Green Years* (MGM, 1946)	*Shadows of the West* (Mon, 1949)
Secrets of the Wasteland (Par, 1941)	*That Texas Jamboree* (Col, 1946)	*Haunted Trail* (Mon, 1949)
Outlaws of the Desert (Par, 1941)	*Throw a Saddle on a Star* (Col, 1946)	*Arizona Territory* (Mon, 1950)
This Above All (20th, 1942)	*The Devil's Playground* (UA, 1946)	*Gunslingers* (Mon, 1950)
Undercover Man (UA, 1942)	*Fool's Gold* (UA, 1946)	*Fence Riders* (Mon, 1950)
Lost Canyon (UA, 1943)	*The Plainsman and the Lady* (Rep, 1946)	*Outlaws of Texas* (Mon, 1950)
Border Patrol (UA, 1943)	*The Unexpected Guest* (UA, 1946)	*Silver Raiders* (Mon, 1950)
The Leather Burners (UA, 1943)	*Hoppy's Holiday* (UA, 1947)	*Cherokee Uprising* (Mon, 1950)
Hoppy Serves a Writ (UA, 1943)	*Dangerous Venture* (UA, 1947)	*Abilene Trail* (Mon, 1951)
Colt Comrades (UA, 1943)	*The Marauders* (UA, 1947)	*Carolina Cannonball* (Rep, 1955)
Bar 20 (UA, 1943)	*Silent Conflict* (UA, 1948)	*The Road to Denver* (Rep, 1955)

LEE J. COBB
(Leo Jacoby)

Rex Harrison and Lee J. Cobb in Anna and the King of Siam *(1946).*

Born December 9, 1911, New York City, New York. Married 1) Helen Beverly (1940), children: Vincent, Julie; divorced (1952); 2) Mary Hirsch (1957), children: two sons, Tony, Jerry. Died February 12, 1976, Woodland Hills, California. A henchman in *Hopalong Cassidy* entries; gravitated to strong, meaty, mature roles: William Holden's father in *Golden Boy*, Dr. Dozous in *The Song of Bernadette*, Kralahome in *Anna and the King of Siam*, Chief Robinson in *Boomerang*, and the psychiatrist (to escaped murderer William Holden) in *The Dark Past*. Oscar-nominated for playing the union racketeer Johnny Friendly in *On the Waterfront* (but lost BSAAA to Edmond O'Brien of *The Barefoot Contessa*). Physically and emotionally too strong an actor to be successful in featherweight comedy (*Come Blow Your Horn*), but enjoyed success in the tongue-in-cheek espionage entries *Our Man Flint* and *In Like Flint*—played Z.O.W.I.E. chief Cramden, who capers "in drag" in a segment of latter entry. TV series: "The Virginian" (as Judge Henry Garth) and "The Young Lawyers."

Lee J. Cobb to Dana Andrews in *Boomerang:* "I never *did* like politicians."

Films

North of the Rio Grande (Par, 1937)
Rustler's Valley (Par, 1937)
Ali Baba Goes to Town (20th, 1937)
Danger on the Air (Univ, 1938)
Golden Boy (Col, 1939)
The Phantom Creeps (Univ serial, 1939) [stock footage from earlier film]
This Thing Called Love (Col, 1941)
Men of Boys Town (MGM, 1941)
Paris Calling (Univ, 1941)
The Moon Is Down (20th, 1943)
Tonight We Raid Calais (20th, 1943)
The Song of Bernadette (20th, 1943)
Buckskin Frontier (UA, 1943)
Anna and the King of Siam (20th, 1946)
Boomerang (20th, 1947)
Captain from Castile (20th, 1947)
Johnny O'Clock (Col, 1947)
Carnival in Costa Rica (20th, 1947)
Miracle of the Bells (RKO, 1948)
Call Northside 777 (20th, 1948)
The Luck of the Irish (20th, 1948)
The Dark Past (Col, 1949)
Thieves' Highway (20th, 1949)
The Man Who Cheated Himself (20th, 1950)

Sirocco (Col, 1951)
The Family Secret (Col, 1951)
The Fighter (UA, 1952)
The Tall Texan (Lip, 1953)
Yankee Pasha (Univ, 1954)
Gorilla at Large (20th, 1954)
On the Waterfront (Col, 1954)
Day of Triumph (George J. Schaefer, 1954)
The Racers (20th, 1955)
The Road to Denver (Rep, 1955)
The Left Hand of God (20th, 1955)
The Man in the Gray Flannel Suit (20th, 1956)
Miami Expose (Col, 1956)
Twelve Angry Men (UA, 1957)
The Three Faces of Eve (20th, 1957)
The Garment Jungle (Col, 1957)
The Brothers Karamazov (MGM, 1958)
Man of the West (UA, 1958)
Party Girl (MGM, 1958)
The Trap (Par, 1959)
Green Mansions (MGM, 1959)
But Not for Me (Par, 1959)
Exodus (UA, 1960)
How the West Was Won (MGM, 1962)

The Four Horsemen of the Apocalypse (MGM, 1962)
Come Blow Your Horn (Par, 1963)
Our Man Flint (20th, 1965)
In Like Flint (20th, 1967)
They Came to Rob Las Vegas [a.k.a. *Our Man from Las Vegas*] (WB-7 Arts, 1968)
Il giorno della civetta [a.k.a. *Mafia*] (It, 1968)
MacKenna's Gold (Col, 1968)
Coogan's Bluff (Univ, 1968)
The Liberation of L. B. Jones (Col, 1970)
Macho Callahan (Avco Emb, 1970)
Lawman (UA, 1971)
The Man Who Loved Cat Dancing (MGM, 1973)
La polizia sta a guardare (It, 1973)
The Exorcist (WB, 1973)
Venditore di palloncini (It, 1974)
Mark il poliziotto [a.k.a. *Blood, Sweat and Fear*] (It, 1975)
Ultimatum alla citta (It, 1975)
That Lucky Touch (Br, 1975)
Nick the Sting (It, 1976)
Cross Shot (It, 1976)

CHARLES COBURN
(Charles Douville Coburn)

Joel McCrea, Jean Arthur, Charles Coburn, and Richard Gaines in The More the Merrier *(1943).*

Born June 19, 1877, Savannah, Georgia. Married 1) Ivah Wills (1906); widowed (1937); 2) Winifred Natzka (1939). Died August 30, 1961, New York City, New York. Energetic stage actor who evolved into famed elder statesman of the screen. Monocled, flabby face which could register hate, amusement, or tenderness with facility. In such dramas as *Yellow Jack* (Dr. Finlay), *The Story of Alexander Graham Bell* (Gardner Hubbard), *In Name Only* (Mr. Walker, Cary Grant's father), *Kings Row* (the sadistic Dr. Henry Gordon), *In This Our Life* (William Fitzroy, the lecherous rich uncle of Bette Davis and Olivia de Havilland), *Lured* (Scotland Yard Inspector Temple). Comedies included: *Vivacious Lady* (father of Jimmy Stewart), *The Devil and Miss Jones* (the millionaire who masquerades as a clerk in his own department store—Oscar-nominated but lost BSAAA to Donald Crisp of *How Green Was My Valley*), *The Lady Eve* ("Colonel" Harrington, the cardsharp dad of Barbara Stanwyck), *Over 21* (grumpy newspaper publisher Robert Gow), *Louisa* (competing with Edmund Gwenn for Spring Byington's affections), *Gentlemen Prefer Blondes* (Sir Francis Beekman, the elderly roué who lusts for Marilyn Monroe). Won a BSAAA for his Benjamin Dingle, one of those in wartime Washington, D.C., sharing a crowded apartment with Jean Arthur and Joel McCrea in *The More the Merrier*. Third Oscar nomination for Alexander "Dandy" Gow in *The Green Years* (lost BSAAA to Harold Russell of *The Best Years of Our Lives*).

Charles Coburn to Jean Arthur in *The More the Merrier:* "I missed two Sundays of 'Superman' once, and I've never felt the same since."

Films

Say It with Flowers (Br, 1934)
The People's Enemy (RKO, 1935)
Of Human Hearts (MGM, 1938)
Yellow Jack (MGM, 1938)

Lord Jeff (MGM, 1938)
Vivacious Lady (RKO, 1938)
Idiot's Delight (MGM, 1939)
Made for Each Other (UA, 1939)

The Story of Alexander Graham Bell (20th, 1939)
Stanley and Livingstone (20th, 1939)
Bachelor Mother (RKO, 1939)

In Name Only (RKO, 1939)
The Road to Singapore (Par, 1940)
Three Faces West [a.k.a. The Refugee] (Rep, 1940)
Florian (MGM, 1940)
Edison the Man (MGM, 1940)
The Captain Is a Lady (MGM, 1940)
The Devil and Miss Jones (RKO, 1941)
The Lady Eve (Par, 1941)
H. M. Pulham, Esq. (MGM, 1941)
Kings Row (WB, 1941)
Our Wife (Col, 1941)
Unexpected Uncle (RKO, 1941)
In This Our Life (WB, 1942)
George Washington Slept Here (WB, 1942)
The Constant Nymph (WB, 1943)
The More the Merrier (Col, 1943)
Heaven Can Wait (20th, 1943)
Princess O'Rourke (WB, 1943)
My Kingdom for a Cook (Col, 1943)
Knickerbocker Holiday (UA, 1944)

Wilson (20th, 1944)
The Impatient Years (Col, 1944)
Together Again (Col, 1944)
A Royal Scandal (20th, 1945)
Colonel Effingham's Raid (20th, 1945)
Shady Lady (Univ, 1945)
Over 21 (Col, 1945)
Rhapsody in Blue (WB, 1945)
The Green Years (MGM, 1946)
Lured [a.k.a. Personal Column] (UA, 1947)
The Paradine Case (Selznick Releasing Organization, 1947)
B. F.'s Daughter (MGM, 1948)
Green Grass of Wyoming (20th, 1948)
Everybody Does It (20th, 1949)
The Doctor and the Girl (MGM, 1949)
Yes Sir, That's My Baby (Univ, 1949)
The Gal Who Took the West (Univ, 1949)
Impact (UA, 1949)
Peggy (Univ, 1949)

Mr. Music (Par, 1950)
Louisa (Univ, 1950)
The Highwayman (AA, 1951)
Has Anybody Seen My Gal? (Univ, 1952)
Monkey Business (20th, 1952)
Trouble Along the Way (WB, 1953)
Gentlemen Prefer Blondes (20th, 1953)
The Rocket Man (20th, 1954)
The Long Wait (UA, 1954)
How to Be Very, Very Popular (20th, 1955)
Around the World in 80 Days (UA, 1956)
The Power and the Prize (MGM, 1956)
Town on Trial (Col, 1957)
The Story of Mankind (WB, 1957)
How to Murder a Rich Uncle (Col, 1958)
Stranger in My Arms (Univ, 1959)
The Remarkable Mr. Pennypacker (20th, 1959)
John Paul Jones (WB, 1959)
Pepe (Col, 1960)

CHARLES COLEMAN

Charles Coleman and Edward Everett Horton in Her Master's Voice *(1936).*

Born December 22, 1885, Sydney, Australia. Died March 8, 1951, Woodland Hills, California. Most often on tap as a well-mannered butler who despite his portliness could bow properly to his superiors.

Charles Coleman to Charlie Ruggles in *One Hour with You:*
"M'sieur, I did so want to see you in tights."

Films

Big Dan (Fox, 1923)
Second Hand Love (Fox, 1923)
That French Lady (Fox, 1924)
The Vagabond Trail (Fox, 1924)
Sandy (Fox, 1926)
Good Morning, Judge (Univ, 1928)
That's My Daddy (Univ, 1928)
Lawful Larceny (RKO, 1930)
Once a Gentleman (WW, 1930)
What a Man (WW, 1930)
Bachelor Apartment (RKO, 1931)
Beyond Victory (Pathe, 1931)
High Stakes (RKO, 1931)
One Hour with You (Par, 1932)
The Heart of New York (WB, 1932)
Play Girl (WB, 1932)
Winner Take All (WB, 1932)
Silver Dollar (FN, 1932)
As the Devil Commands (Col, 1932)
Merrily We Go to Hell (Par, 1932)
Jewel Robbery (FN, 1932)
Sailor Be Good (RKO, 1933)
Midnight Club (Par, 1933)
Gallant Lady (UA, 1933)
Diplomaniacs (RKO, 1933)
Born to Be Bad (UA, 1934)
Shock (Mon, 1934)
Housewife (WB, 1934)
The Merry Frinks (FN, 1934)
Embarrassing Moments (Univ, 1934)
Down to Their Last Yacht (RKO, 1934)
Million Dollar Ransom (Univ, 1934)
Girl from Missouri (MGM, 1934)
Rendezvous (MGM, 1935)
Becky Sharp (RKO, 1935)
Murder Man (MGM, 1935)
His Family Tree (RKO, 1935)
The Goose and the Gander (WB, 1935)
The Man Who Broke the Bank at Monte Carlo (Fox, 1935)
Lloyds of London (20th, 1936)
The King Steps Out (Col, 1936)
Born to Dance (MGM, 1936)
Don't Get Personal (Univ, 1936)

Colleen (WB, 1936)
Everybody's Old Man (20th, 1936)
Her Master's Voice (Par, 1936)
Poor Little Rich Girl (20th, 1936)
Walking on Air (RKO, 1936)
Mummy's Boys (RKO, 1936)
Three Smart Girls (Univ, 1937)
Love Is News (20th, 1937)
Too Many Wives (RKO, 1937)
There Goes My Girl (RKO, 1937)
Danger—Love at Work (20th, 1937)
The Last Gangster (MGM, 1937)
Fight for Your Lady (RKO, 1937)
The Rage of Paris (Univ, 1938)
The Affairs of Annabel (RKO, 1938)
Alexander's Ragtime Band (20th, 1938)
Gateway (20th, 1938)
Little Orphan Annie (Par, 1938)
Little Miss Broadway (20th, 1938)
That Certain Age (Univ, 1938)
Always Goodbye (20th, 1938)
The Shining Hour (MGM, 1938)
Bridal Suite (MGM, 1939)
The Under-Pup (Univ, 1939)
First Love (Univ, 1939)
Mexican Spitfire (RKO, 1939)
Everything's on Ice (RKO, 1939)
You Can't Cheat an Honest Man (Univ, 1939)
Mexican Spitfire Out West (RKO, 1940)
Michael Shayne, Private Detective (20th, 1940)
Raffles (UA, 1940)
The Westerner (UA, 1940)
Buck Privates (Univ, 1941)
Free and Easy (MGM, 1941)
It Started with Eve (Univ, 1941)
Melody Lane (Univ, 1941)
Design for Scandal (MGM, 1941)
Twin Beds (UA, 1942)
Pittsburgh (Univ, 1942)
Miss Annie Rooney (UA, 1942)
Almost Married (Univ, 1942)
The Great Impersonation (Univ, 1942)

Arabian Nights (Univ, 1942)
He Hired the Boss (20th, 1942)
Lady in a Jam (Univ, 1942)
What's Cookin'? (Univ, 1942)
Jail House Blues (Univ, 1942)
Between Us Girls (Univ, 1942)
Highways by Night (RKO, 1942)
Air Raid Wardens (MGM, 1943)
It Ain't Hay (Univ, 1943)
DuBarry Was a Lady (MGM, 1943)
Mexican Spitfire's Blessed Event (RKO, 1943)
It Comes Up Love (Univ, 1943)
Petticoat Larceny (RKO, 1943)
Lady in the Dark (Par, 1944)
In Society (Univ, 1944)
The Whistler (Col, 1944)
Frenchman's Creek (Par, 1944)
The White Cliffs of Dover (MGM, 1944)
Jane Eyre (20th, 1944)
Roughly Speaking (WB, 1945)
The Picture of Dorian Gray (MGM, 1945)
Billy Rose's Diamond Horseshoe (20th, 1945)
The Missing Corpse (PRC, 1945)
The Stork Club (Par, 1945)
Anchors Aweigh (MGM, 1945)
Kitty (Par, 1945)
Cluny Brown (20th, 1946)
Ziegfeld Follies (MGM, 1946)
In Fast Company (Mon, 1946)
The Magnificent Rogue (Rep, 1946)
The Runaround [a.k.a. *Deadly Enemies*] (Univ, 1946)
Never Say Goodbye (WB, 1946)
The Pilgrim Lady (Rep, 1947)
Variety Girl (Par, 1947)
The Imperfect Lady (Par, 1947)
Trouble Makers (Mon, 1948)
Grand Canyon Trail (Rep, 1948)
Marshal of Amarillo (Rep, 1948)
My Friend Irma (Par, 1949)

CONSTANCE COLLIER

(Laura Constance Hardie)

With Ricardo Cortez in Shadow of Doubt *(1935).*

Born January 22, 1875, Windsor, England. Married Julian L'Estrange (1912); widowed (1918). Died April 25, 1955, New York City, New York. Former elite star (who acted/directed/produced/scripted) of the British stage. Skirmished in silent films, starring with Sir Herbert Tree in *Macbeth*. Gained a foothold in 1930s' Hollywood as a drama coach and returned to the screen as the oft sharp-tongued peculiar matron: Greta Garbo's *Anna Karenina* (Countess Lidia), *Wee Willie Winkie* (Mrs. Allardyce), *Stage Door* (superannuated actress Catherine Luther), *Week-End at the Waldorf* (Mme. Jaleska), *Kitty* (Lady Susan Dowitt), Betty Hutton's *The Perils of Pauline* (Julia Gibbs, the old trouper), etc.

Constance Collier to Katharine Hepburn in *Stage Door:*
"You're an *actress* now. *You belong to these people!"*

Films

Macbeth (Reliance, 1916)
The Code of Marcia Gray (Par, 1916)
Tongues of Men (Morosco, 1916)
The Impossible Woman (Br, 1919)
Bleak House (Br, 1920)
The Bohemian Girl (Br, 1922)
Shadow of Doubt (MGM, 1935)
Anna Karenina (MGM, 1935)
Peter Ibbetson (Par, 1935)
Professional Soldier (Fox, 1935)

Girls' Dormitory (20th, 1936)
Little Lord Fauntleroy (UA, 1936)
Wee Willie Winkie (20th, 1937)
Thunder in the City (Col Br, 1937)
Stage Door (RKO, 1937)
A Damsel in Distress (RKO, 1937)
Zaza (Par, 1939)
Susan and God (MGM, 1940)
Half a Sinner (Univ, 1940)
Kitty (Par, 1945)

Week-End at the Waldorf (MGM, 1945)
The Dark Corner (20th, 1946)
Monsieur Beaucaire (Par, 1946)
The Perils of Pauline (Par, 1947)
Rope (WB, 1948)
The Girl from Manhattan (UA, 1948)
An Ideal Husband (20th Br, 1948)
Whirlpool (20th, 1949)

PATRICIA COLLINGE

In The Little Foxes *(1941).*

Born September 20, 1892, Dublin, Ireland. Married James Nichols Smith. Died April 10, 1974. Dependable London and Broadway actress. Oscar-nominated for re-creating her stage role of frightened Aunt Birdie Hubbard in *The Little Foxes* (lost BSAAA to Mary Astor of *The Great Lie*). Twice more teamed with her niece of *The Little Foxes* (Teresa Wright): *Shadow of a Doubt* (Aunt Emma Newton wed to Henry Travers) and *Casanova Brown* (Mrs. Drury, the mother of Gary Cooper's first wife). Final film appearance as Sister William (*The Nun's Story*).

Patricia Collinge to John Ericson in *Teresa:* "You'll never be a salesman, sonny."

Films

The Little Foxes (RKO, 1941)
Shadow of a Doubt (Univ, 1943)
Tender Comrade (RKO, 1943)

Casanova Brown (RKO, 1944)
Cluny Brown (20th, 1946)
Teresa (MGM, 1951)

The Washington Story (MGM, 1952)
The Nun's Story (WB, 1959)

RAY COLLINS

In The Solid Gold Cadillac *(1956).*

Born December 10, 1889, Sacramento, California. Married 1) Margaret Marriott; divorced (1924); 2) Joan Uron (1926), child: Junius. Died July 11, 1965, Santa Monica, California. One of Orson Welles' Mercury Players who participated in *Citizen Kane* (Boss Jim Gladys) and *The Magnificent Ambersons* (Jack Amberson). Later played Adair to Orson Welles' Hank Quinlan in *Touch of Evil.* Gravitated to an assortment of assignments from loving uncles to corrupt political bosses, and onward to stern business executives. Turned up in the *Ma and Pa Kettle* comedy series as the snooty in-law to Marjorie Main and Percy Kilbride. TV series: "Perry Mason" (as Lieutenant Tragg).

Ray Collins to Turhan Bey in *A Night in Paradise:* "In my youth I had to choose between being a career man and a *carouse* man."

Films

The Grapes of Wrath (20th, 1940)
Citizen Kane (RKO, 1941)
The Big Street (RKO, 1942)
Highways by Night (RKO, 1942)
The Navy Comes Through (RKO, 1942)
Commandos Strike at Dawn (Col, 1942)
The Magnificent Ambersons (RKO, 1942)
The Human Comedy (MGM, 1943)
Madame Curie (MGM, 1943) [voice only]
Slightly Dangerous (MGM, 1943)

Crime Doctor (Col, 1943)
Salute to the Marines (MGM, 1943)
Whistling in Brooklyn (MGM, 1943)
See Here, Private Hargrove (MGM, 1944)
The Hitler Gang (Par, 1944)
The Eve of St. Mark (20th, 1944)
The Seventh Cross (MGM, 1944)
Barbary Coast Gent (MGM, 1944)
Can't Help Singing (Univ, 1944)
Roughly Speaking (WB, 1945)
The Hidden Eye (MGM, 1945)

Miss Susie Slagle's (Par, 1945)
Leave Her to Heaven (20th, 1945)
Up Goes Maisie (MGM, 1946)
A Night in Paradise (Univ, 1946)
Badman's Territory (RKO, 1946)
Boys' Ranch (MGM, 1946)
Crack-Up (RKO, 1946)
Three Wise Fools (MGM, 1946)
Two Years Before the Mast (Par, 1946)
The Return of Monte Cristo (Col, 1946)
The Best Years of Our Lives (RKO, 1946)

133

The Bachelor and the Bobby-Soxer (RKO, 1947)
The Red Stallion (EL, 1947)
The Swordsman (Col, 1947)
The Senator Was Indiscreet (Univ, 1947)
Homecoming (MGM, 1948)
A Double Life (Univ, 1948)
Good Sam (RKO, 1948)
For the Love of Mary (Univ, 1948)
The Man from Colorado (Col, 1948)
Command Decision (MGM, 1948)
Red Stallion in the Rockies (EL, 1949)
Hideout (Rep, 1949)
It Happens Every Spring (20th, 1949)
The Fountainhead (WB, 1949)
The Heiress (Par, 1949)
Free for All (Univ, 1949)

Francis (Univ, 1949)
Paid in Full (Par, 1950)
Kill the Umpire (Col, 1950)
The Reformer and the Redhead (MGM, 1950)
Summer Stock (MGM, 1950)
You're in the Navy Now [a.k.a. *U.S.S. Tea-kettle*] (20th, 1951)
Ma and Pa Kettle Back on the Farm (Univ, 1951)
Vengeance Valley (MGM, 1951)
Reunion in Reno (Univ, 1951)
I Want You (RKO, 1951)
The Racket (RKO, 1951)
Invitation (MGM, 1952)
Dreamboat (20th, 1952)
Young Man with Ideas (MGM, 1952)

The Desert Song (WB, 1953)
Ma and Pa Kettle at the Fair (Univ, 1953)
Column South (Univ, 1953)
Ma and Pa Kettle on Vacation (Univ, 1953)
The Kid from Left Field (20th, 1953)
Bad for Each Other (Col, 1953)
Rose-Marie (MGM, 1954)
Athena (MGM, 1954)
The Desperate Hours (Par, 1955)
Texas Lady (RKO, 1955)
Never Say Goodbye (Univ, 1956)
The Solid Gold Cadillac (Col, 1956)
Spoilers of the Forest (Rep, 1957)
Touch of Evil (Univ, 1958)
I'll Give My Life (Howco, 1961)

WALTER CONNOLLY

With Mary Martin in The Great Victor Herbert *(1939).*

Born April 8, 1887, Cincinnati, Ohio. Married Nedda Harrigan (1923), child: Ann. Died May 28, 1940, Beverly Hills, California. Talented Broadway actor who succumbed to Hollywood late in his career, signing a pact with Columbia Pictures. Heavyset and flabby. Could fly into a rage (Claudette Colbert's confounded dad in *It Happened One Night*), shake his large frame in anger as the newspaper publisher of *Nothing Sacred*, or well interpret the theatrical backer in the screwball classic *Twentieth Century*. Could be very believable in drama: *The Bitter Tea of General Yen* (as the American Mr. Jones, buying and advising General Nils Asther), *Whom the Gods Destroy* (theatrical producer John Forrester thought dead), *The Good Earth* (Uncle, the rascally gambler), etc. Last assignments included title role of composer in musical *The Great Victor Herbert*.

Walter Connolly to Francis Compton in *Soak the Rich:* "I'm a firm believer in democracy; provided that it lets *me* alone."

Films

Man Against Woman (Col, 1932)
Washington Merry-Go-Round (Col, 1932)
No More Orchids (Col, 1932)
The Bitter Tea of General Yen (Col, 1933)
Lady for a Day (Col, 1933)
Master of Men (Col, 1933)
East of 5th Avenue (Col, 1933)
A Man's Castle (Col, 1933)
Paddy, the Next Best Thing (Fox, 1933)
Eight Girls in a Boat (Par, 1934)
It Happened One Night (Col, 1934)
20th Century (Col, 1934)
Once to Every Woman (Col, 1934)
Whom the Gods Destroy (Col, 1934)
Servants' Entrance (Fox, 1934)

Lady by Choice (Col, 1934)
Broadway Bill (Col, 1934)
The Captain Hates the Sea (Col, 1934)
White Lies (Col, 1934)
Father Brown, Detective (Par, 1935)
She Couldn't Take It (Col, 1935)
So Red the Rose (Par, 1935)
One Way Ticket (Col, 1935)
The Music Goes 'Round (Col, 1936)
Soak the Rich (Par, 1936)
The King Steps Out (Col, 1936)
Libeled Lady (MGM, 1936)
The Good Earth (MGM, 1937)
Nancy Steele Is Missing (20th, 1937)
Let's Get Married (Col, 1937)
The League of Frightened Men (Col, 1937)

First Lady (WB, 1937)
Nothing Sacred (UA, 1937)
Penitentiary (Col, 1938)
Start Cheering (Col, 1938)
Four's a Crowd (WB, 1938)
Too Hot to Handle (MGM, 1938)
Girl Downstairs (MGM, 1939)
Bridal Suite (MGM, 1939)
Good Girls Go to Paris (Col, 1939)
Coast Guard (Col, 1939)
Those High Gray Walls (Col, 1939)
5th Avenue Girl (RKO, 1939)
The Great Victor Herbert (Par, 1939)
The Adventures of Huckleberry Finn (MGM, 1939)

WILLIAM CONRAD

Barry Sullivan and William Conrad in Tension *(1949).*

Born September 27, 1920, Louisville, Kentucky. Married 1) June Nelson (1943); 2) Susan Randell, child: Christopher. Earned his cinema reputation as the stocky menace of many crime films (like the slightly less bulky Raymond Burr): *The Killers* (Max, the hired assassin), *Body and Soul* (Quinn), *The Racket* (Turck), etc. Occasionally in a comedy: *The Milkman* with Jimmy Durante; some Westerns: *Four Faces West, Johnny Concho* (as Tallman, the gunslinger), etc.; and costumed drama: *The Sword of Monte Cristo.* Supplied radio voice of "Gunsmoke's" Matt Dillon. Produced and directed such films as *My Blood Runs Cold* and *Brainstorm,* both 1965 releases. TV series: "The Fugitive" (narrator), "Cannon," "Wild, Wild World of Animals" (narrator), and "Tales of the Unexpected" (narrator).

William Conrad to Audrey Totter in *Tension:* "Makes a bad impression—you running away like that."

Films

The Killers (Univ, 1946)	*East Side, West Side* (MGM, 1949)	*The Desert Song* (WB, 1953)
Body and Soul (UA, 1947)	*One Way Street* (Univ, 1950)	*The Naked Jungle* (Par, 1954)
Arch of Triumph (UA, 1948)	*Dial 1119* (MGM, 1950)	*The Naked Sea* (RKO, 1955) [narrator]
Four Faces West (UA, 1948)	*The Milkman* (Univ, 1950)	*Five Against the House* (Col, 1955)
To the Victor (WB, 1948)	*Cry Danger* (RKO, 1951)	*The Conqueror* (RKO, 1956)
Sorry, Wrong Number (Par, 1948)	*The Sword of Monte Cristo* (20th, 1951)	*Johnny Concho* (UA, 1956)
Joan of Arc (RKO, 1948)	*The Racket* (RKO, 1951)	*The Ride Back* (UA, 1957)
Any Number Can Play (MGM, 1949)	*Lone Star* (MGM, 1952)	*-30-* (WB, 1959)
Tension (MGM, 1949)	*Cry of the Hunted* (MGM, 1953)	*Moonshine County* (New World, 1977)

HANS CONRIED

In the 1970s.

Born April 15, 1917, Baltimore, Maryland. Married Margaret Grant (1942), children: Trilby, Hans, Alex, Edith. Lanky and angular. Added zest to many walk-on parts with a sharp bit of pantomime, a peculiarly accented dialect, or a wild burst of bizarre energy. Frequently seen as a waiter, desk clerk, journalist, or photographer. TV series: "Make Room for Daddy" and "Make Room for Granddaddy" (as Uncle Tonoose), "Hoppity Hooper" (as the voice of Uncle Waldo), "Rocky and His Friends" (as the voice of Snively Whiplash), and "The Tony Randall Show" (as the star's father).

Hans Conried to guard in *Siren of Bagdad:* "I beg your pardon. I realize they haven't been invented yet, but do you have a match?"

Films

Dramatic School (MGM, 1938)
It's a Wonderful World (MGM, 1939)
Never Say Die (Par, 1939)
On Borrowed Time (MGM, 1939)
Dulcy (MGM, 1940)
Bitter Sweet (MGM, 1940)
Maisie Was a Lady (MGM, 1941)
Underground (WB, 1941)
The Gay Falcon (RKO, 1941)
Unexpected Uncle (RKO, 1941)
Weekend for Three (RKO, 1941)
A Date with the Falcon (RKO, 1941)
Joan of Paris (RKO, 1942)
Saboteur (Univ, 1942)
The Wife Takes a Flyer (Col, 1942)
The Falcon Takes Over (RKO, 1942)
Pacific Rendezvous (MGM, 1942)
Blondie's Blessed Event (Col, 1942)
Journey into Fear (RKO, 1942)
Underground Agent (Col, 1942)
The Big Street (RKO, 1942)
Nightmare (Univ, 1942)
Once upon a Honeymoon (RKO, 1942)
Hitler's Children (RKO, 1942)
Hostages (Par, 1943)

A Lady Takes a Chance (RKO, 1943)
Crazy House (Univ, 1943)
His Butler's Sister (Univ, 1943)
Passage to Marseille (WB, 1944)
Mrs. Parkington (MGM, 1944)
The Senator Was Indiscreet (Univ, 1947)
Design of Death (RKO, 1948) [narrator]
The Barkleys of Broadway (MGM, 1949)
My Friend Irma (Par, 1949)
Bride for Sale (RKO, 1949)
On the Town (MGM, 1949)
Nancy Goes to Rio (MGM, 1950)
Summer Stock (MGM, 1950)
The Light Touch (MGM, 1951)
Rich, Young and Pretty (MGM, 1951)
Behave Yourself! (RKO, 1951)
Texas Carnival (MGM, 1951)
Too Young to Kiss (MGM, 1951)
Three for Bedroom C (WB, 1952)
The World in His Arms (Univ, 1952)
Big Jim McLain (WB, 1952)
Peter Pan (RKO, 1952) [voice only]
Siren of Bagdad (Col, 1953)
The Twonky (UA, 1953)
The Affairs of Dobie Gillis (MGM, 1953)

The 5,000 Fingers of Dr. T (Col, 1953)
Davy Crockett, King of the Wild Frontier (BV, 1955)
You're Never Too Young (Par, 1955)
The Birds and the Bees (Par, 1956)
Bus Stop (20th, 1956)
The Monster That Challenged the World (UA, 1957)
Jet Pilot (Univ, 1957)
The Big Beat (Univ, 1958)
Rock-a-Bye Baby (Par, 1958)
Juke Box Rhythm (Col, 1959)
1001 Arabian Nights (Col, 1959) [voice only]
My Six Loves (Par, 1963)
The Patsy (Par, 1964)
Robin and the Seven Hoods (WB, 1964)
The Jay Ward Intergalactic Film Festival (Joseph Brenner Associates, 1968) [voice only]
The Brothers O'Toole (American National Enterprises, 1973)
The Shaggy D.A. (BV, 1977)

FRANK CONROY

Charles McGraw and Frank Conroy in The Threat *(1949).*

Born October 14, 1890, Derby, England. Married Helen Robbins, child: one. Died February 24, 1964, Paramus, New Jersey. Best suited to imperious roles, whether as the hotel manager of *Grand Hotel* or the loudmouthed ex-Confederate Major Tetley leading the lynch mob of *The Ox-Bow Incident*. Final role: Dr. Kelsey, *The Bramble Bush*.

Frank Conroy to Richard Dix in *Ace of Aces:* "Don't let this first kill lull you into a false sense of security."

Films

The Royal Family of Broadway (Par, 1930)
Bad Company (Pathé, 1931)
Hell Divers (MGM, 1931)
Possessed (MGM, 1931)
Manhattan Parade (WB, 1932)
West of Broadway (MGM, 1932)
Disorderly Conduct (Fox, 1932)
Grand Hotel (MGM, 1932)
Midnight Mary [a.k.a. *Lady of the Night*] (MGM, 1933)
Ann Carver's Profession (Col, 1933)
Night Flight (MGM, 1933)
The Kennel Murder Case (WB, 1933)
Ace of Aces (RKO, 1933)
The Cat and the Fiddle (MGM, 1934)
The Crime Doctor (RKO, 1934)
Frontier Marshal (Fox, 1934)
Keep 'em Rolling (RKO, 1934)
Little Miss Marker (Par, 1934)
The White Parade (Fox, 1934)
Manhattan Melodrama (MGM, 1934)
Such Women Are Dangerous (Fox, 1934)
Return of the Terror (FN, 1934)
I'll Fix It (Col, 1934)

Wednesday's Child (RKO, 1934)
Evelyn Prentice (MGM, 1934)
The Little Minister (RKO, 1934)
Sadie McKee (MGM, 1934)
She Couldn't Take It (Col, 1935)
West Point of the Air (MGM, 1935)
Charlie Chan in Egypt (Fox, 1935)
Call of the Wild (UA, 1935)
I Live My Life (MGM, 1935)
The Last Days of Pompeii (RKO, 1935)
Show Them No Mercy (Fox, 1935)
The White Angel (FN, 1936)
Meet Nero Wolfe (Col, 1936)
The Gorgeous Hussy (MGM, 1936)
Charlie Chan at the Opera (20th, 1936)
Nobody's Fool (Univ, 1936)
Stolen Holiday (WB, 1936)
Nancy Steele Is Missing (20th, 1937)
Love Is News (20th, 1937)
This Is My Affair (20th, 1937)
Big Business (20th, 1937)
That I May Live (20th, 1937)
The Emperor's Candlesticks (MGM, 1937)
Music for Madame (RKO, 1937)

The Last Gangster (MGM, 1937)
Wells Fargo (Par, 1937)
This Woman Is Mine (Univ, 1941)
The Adventures of Martin Eden (Col, 1942)
Crossroads (MGM, 1942)
The Loves of Edgar Allan Poe (20th, 1942)
Crash Dive (20th, 1943)
Lady of Burlesque (UA, 1943)
The Ox-Bow Incident (20th, 1943)
That Hagen Girl (WB, 1947)
Rogues' Regiment (Univ, 1948)
The Naked City (Univ, 1948)
All My Sons (Univ, 1948)
Sealed Verdict (Par, 1948)
For the Love of Mary (Univ, 1948)
The Snake Pit (20th, 1948)
The Threat (RKO, 1949)
Lightning Strikes Twice (WB, 1951)
The Day the Earth Stood Still (20th, 1951)
The Last Mile (UA, 1959)
Compulsion (20th, 1959)
The Young Philadelphians (WB, 1959)
The Bramble Bush (WB, 1960)

ELISHA COOK, JR.

In The Black Bird *(1975).*

Born December 26, 1902, San Francisco, California. Married Mary _____ (1929); divorced (1942). Pint-sized actor. Immortalized by role of Wilmer the gunsel in Humphrey Bogart's *The Maltese Falcon*. Played happy-go-lucky collegiates in his earlier films. Then specialized in an array of celluloid neurotics and cowardly characters: *The Big Sleep* (as Harry Jones, the stoolpigeon murdered by Tom Steele), *The Falcon's Alibi* (the weasel disc jockey Nick secretly wed to Jane Greer), *The Killing* (George Peatty, the racetrack cashier married to grasping Marie Windsor), etc. Reprised the part of Wilmer in *The Black Bird*, the misfire comedy follow-up to *The Maltese Falcon*.

Elisha Cook, Jr. to Humphrey Bogart in *The Maltese Falcon:*
"Keep on ridin' me, they're gonna be pickin' iron out of your liver."

Films

Her Unborn Child (Windsor, 1930)
Two in a Crowd (Univ, 1936)
Pigskin Parade (20th, 1936)
Love Is News (20th, 1937)
Breezing Home (Univ, 1937)
Wife, Doctor and Nurse (20th, 1937)
Danger—Love at Work (20th, 1937)
Life Begins in College (20th, 1937)
They Won't Forget (WB, 1937)
The Devil Is Driving (Col, 1937)
My Lucky Star (20th, 1938)
Submarine Patrol (20th, 1938)

Three Blind Mice (20th, 1938)
Grand Jury Secrets (Par, 1939)
Newsboys' Home (Univ, 1939)
He Married His Wife (20th, 1940)
Stranger on the Third Floor (RKO, 1940)
Public Deb No. 1 (20th, 1940)
Tin Pan Alley (20th, 1940)
Man at Large (20th, 1941)
Love Crazy (MGM, 1941)
Sergeant York (WB, 1941)
Ball of Fire (RKO, 1941)
The Maltese Falcon (WB, 1941)

I Wake Up Screaming [a.k.a. *Hot Spot*] (20th, 1941)
A Gentleman at Heart (20th, 1942)
In This Our Life (WB, 1942)
Sleepytime Gal (Rep, 1942)
A-Haunting We Will Go (20th, 1942)
Manila Calling (20th, 1942)
Wildcat (Par, 1942)
Casanova Brown (RKO, 1944)
Phantom Lady (Univ, 1944)
Up in Arms (RKO, 1944)

Dark Mountain (Par, 1944)
Dark Waters (UA, 1944)
Dillinger (Mon, 1945)
Why Girls Leave Home (PRC, 1945)
The Big Sleep (WB, 1946)
Blonde Alibi (Univ, 1946)
Cinderella Jones (WB, 1946)
The Falcon's Alibi (RKO, 1946)
Joe Palooka—Champ (Mon, 1946)
Two Smart People (MGM, 1946)
Born to Kill (RKO, 1947)
The Fall Guy (Mon, 1947)
The Long Night (RKO, 1947)
The Gangster (AA, 1947)
Flaxy Martin (WB, 1949)
The Great Gatsby (Par, 1949)
Behave Yourself! (RKO, 1951)
Don't Bother to Knock (20th, 1952)
I, the Jury (UA, 1953)
Thunder over the Plains (WB, 1953)
Shane (Par, 1953)

The Outlaw's Daughter (20th, 1954)
Drum Beat (WB, 1954)
Timberjack (Rep, 1955)
The Indian Fighter (UA, 1955)
Trial (MGM, 1955)
The Killing (UA, 1956)
Accused of Murder (Rep, 1956)
The Lonely Man (Par, 1957)
Voodoo Island (UA, 1957)
Baby Face Nelson (UA, 1957)
Plunder Road (20th, 1957)
Chicago Confidential (UA, 1957)
The House on Haunted Hill (AA, 1958)
Day of the Outlaw (UA, 1959)
Platinum High School (MGM, 1960)
College Confidential (Univ, 1960)
One-Eyed Jacks (Par, 1961)
Papa's Delicate Condition (Par, 1963)
The Haunted Palace (AIP, 1963)
Black Zoo (AA, 1963)
Johnny Cool (UA, 1963)

Blood on the Arrow (AA, 1964)
The Glass Cage (Futuramic Releasing, 1964)
Welcome to Hard Times (MGM, 1967)
Rosemary's Baby (Par, 1968)
The Great Bank Robbery (WB—7 Arts, 1969)
El Condor (National General, 1970)
The Great Northfield, Minnesota Raid (Univ, 1972)
Blacula (AIP, 1972)
Emperor of the North Pole (20th, 1973)
Electra Glide in Blue (UA, 1973)
The Outfit (MGM, 1973)
The Black Bird (Col, 1975)
Messiah of Evil (International Cine Film Corp, 1975)
Winterhawk (Howco International, 1975)
St. Ives (WB, 1976)

MELVILLE COOPER

David Niven and Melville Cooper in Enchantment *(1948).*

Born October 15, 1896, Birmingham, England. Married 1) Gladys Grice; divorced; 2) Rita Page; widowed; 3) Elizabeth Sutherland. Died March 29, 1973, Woodland Hills, California. An alumnus of the British stage and screen. Emerged as one of Hollywood's ablest portrayers of the pompous buffoon (aided not a little by his basset-hound eyes): *The Adventures of Robin Hood* (the high sheriff), *Four's a Crowd* (Bingham, the butler at Walter Connolly's manse), *The Lady Eve* (Gerald the cardsharp), etc. At his droll, uncompromising, snooty best as Mr. Collins, Greer Garson's erstwhile suitor in *Pride and Prejudice* who is cowed by his patroness, Edna May Oliver.

Melville Cooper to Joan Fontaine in *This Above All:* "For generations the Cathaways have been leaders, Prudence—not followers."

Films

The Calendar [a.k.a. *Bachelor's Folly*] (Br, 1931)
Two White Arms (Br, 1932)
Forging Ahead (Fox Br, 1933)
Leave It to Me (Br, 1933)
The Private Life of Don Juan (UA Br, 1934)
The Scarlet Pimpernel (UA Br, 1934)
The Bishop Misbehaves (MGM, 1935)
The Gorgeous Hussy (MGM, 1936)
The Last of Mrs. Cheyney (MGM, 1937)
Thin Ice (20th, 1937)
The Great Garrick (WB, 1937)
Tovarich (WB, 1937)
Women Are Like That (WB, 1938)
The Adventures of Robin Hood (WB, 1938)
Gold Diggers in Paris (WB, 1938)
Four's a Crowd (WB, 1938)
Hard to Get (WB, 1938)
The Dawn Patrol (WB, 1938)
Comet over Broadway (WB, 1938)
Dramatic School (MGM, 1938)

The Garden of the Moon (WB, 1938)
I'm from Missouri (Par, 1939)
Blind Alley (Col, 1939)
The Sun Never Sets (Univ, 1939)
Two Bright Boys (Univ, 1939)
Rebecca (UA, 1940)
Too Many Husbands (Col, 1940)
Pride and Prejudice (MGM, 1940)
Murder over New York (20th, 1940)
Submarine Zone [a.k.a. *Escape to Glory*] (Col, 1941)
The Flame of New Orleans (Univ, 1941)
The Lady Eve (Par, 1941)
Scotland Yard (20th, 1941)
You Belong to Me (Col, 1941)
This Above All (20th, 1942)
The Affairs of Martha [a.k.a. *Once upon a Thursday*] (MGM, 1942)
Random Harvest (MGM, 1942)
Life Begins at 8:30 (20th, 1942)
The Immortal Sergeant (20th, 1943)
Hit Parade of 1943 (Rep, 1943)

Holy Matrimony (20th, 1943)
My Kingdom for a Cook (Col, 1943)
Heartbeat (RKO, 1946)
13 Rue Madeleine (20th, 1946)
The Imperfect Lady (Par, 1947)
Enchantment (RKO, 1948)
The Red Danube (MGM, 1949)
Love Happy (UA, 1949)
And Baby Makes Three (Col, 1949)
The Underworld Story (UA, 1950)
Father of the Bride (MGM, 1950)
Let's Dance (Par, 1950)
The Petty Girl (Col, 1950)
It Should Happen to You (Col, 1953)
Moonfleet (MGM, 1955)
The King's Thief (MGM, 1955)
Diane (MGM, 1955)
Bundle of Joy (RKO, 1956)
Around the World in 80 Days (UA, 1956)
The Story of Mankind (WB, 1957)
From the Earth to the Moon (WB, 1958)

ELLEN CORBY
(Ellen Hansen)

In The Glass Bottom Boat *(1966).*

Born June 13, 1914, Racine, Wisconsin. Married Francis Corby; divorced (1944). Began as a movie script girl and eventually played one on camera: *The Legend of Lylah Clare.* Oscar-nominated for her appearance as Aunt Trina in *I Remember Mama* (but lost BSAAA to Claire Trevor of *Key Largo*). Frequently seen as the gossiping neighbor or starched spinster. Offbeat part as Victor Buono's neurotic mama in *The Strangler.* TV series: "Please Don't Eat the Daisies" and "The Waltons" (as Grandma Esther Walton).

Ellen Corby to Gail Russell in *Captain China:* "A man! I need a man with a hammer!"

Films

Twisted Rails (Independent, 1933)
Cornered (RKO, 1945)
The Dark Corner (20th, 1946)
From This Day Forward (RKO, 1946)
It's a Wonderful Life (RKO, 1946)
Till the End of Time (RKO, 1946)
Bedlam (RKO, 1946)
The Scarlet Horseman (Univ serial, 1946)
In Old Sacramento (Rep, 1946)
Cuban Pete (Univ, 1946)
Crack-Up (RKO, 1946)
The Spiral Staircase (RKO, 1946)

Sister Kenny (RKO, 1946)
Lover Come Back (Univ, 1946)
The Truth About Murder (RKO, 1946)
Hal Roach Comedy Carnival (UA, 1947)
Railroaded (EL, 1947)
Beat the Band (RKO, 1947)
Born to Kill (RKO, 1947)
Forever Amber (20th, 1947)
They Won't Believe Me (RKO, 1947)
Driftwood (Rep, 1947)
Fighting Father Dunne (RKO, 1948)
The Dark Past (Col, 1948)

Strike It Rich (AA, 1948)
I Remember Mama (RKO, 1948)
The Noose Hangs High (EL, 1948)
If You Knew Susie (RKO, 1948)
Mighty Joe Young (RKO, 1949)
Little Women (MGM, 1949)
Rusty Saves a Life (Col, 1949)
The Judge Steps Out (RKO, 1949)
A Woman's Secret (RKO, 1949)
Madame Bovary (MGM, 1949)
Captain China (Par, 1949)
The Gunfighter (20th, 1950)

142

Caged (WB, 1950)
Peggy (Univ, 1950)
Edge of Doom (RKO, 1950)
Harriet Craig (Col, 1950)
On Moonlight Bay (WB, 1951)
Goodbye, My Fancy (WB, 1951)
The Mating Season (Par, 1951)
Angels in the Outfield (MGM, 1951)
The Sea Hornet (Rep, 1951)
The Barefoot Mailman (Col, 1951)
The Big Trees (WB, 1952)
Fearless Fagan (MGM, 1952)
Monsoon (UA, 1953)
Shane (Par, 1953)
The Woman They Almost Lynched (Rep, 1953)
The Vanquished (Par, 1953)

A Lion Is in the Streets (WB, 1953)
Untamed Heiress (Rep, 1954)
Susan Slept Here (RKO, 1954)
About Mrs. Leslie (Par, 1954)
The Bowery Boys Meet the Monsters (AA, 1954)
Sabrina (Par, 1954)
Illegal (WB, 1955)
Slightly Scarlet (RKO, 1956)
Stagecoach to Fury (20th, 1956)
Night Passage (Univ, 1957)
The Seventh Sin (MGM, 1957)
God Is My Partner (20th, 1957)
Rockabilly Baby (20th, 1957)
All Mine to Give (Univ, 1957)
Macabre (AA, 1958)
Vertigo (Par, 1958)

Visit to a Small Planet (Par, 1960)
A Pocketful of Miracles (UA, 1961)
Saintly Sinners (UA, 1962)
The Caretakers (UA, 1963)
The Strangler (AA, 1964)
The Family Jewels (Par, 1965)
Hush . . . Hush, Sweet Charlotte (20th, 1965)
The Night of the Grizzly (Par, 1966)
The Glass Bottom Boat (MGM, 1966)
The Gnome-Mobile (BV, 1966)
The Legend of Lylah Clare (MGM, 1968)
A Quiet Couple (National General, 1969)
Support Your Local Gunfighter (UA, 1971)
Napoleon and Samantha (BV, 1972)

JEROME COWAN
(Jerome Palmer Cowan)

In 1942.

Born October 6, 1897, New York City, New York. Married 1) _____, child: William; divorced; 2) Helen Dodge (1938), child: Suzanne. Died January 24, 1972, Hollywood, California. Famed for his easygoing dapper manner. Began in motion pictures as the bellicose Irish patriot O'Rourke in *Beloved Enemy*. Soon became popular for his smiling "other-man" roles: *The Old Maid* (Joe Ralston, Miriam Hopkins' second-choice husband), *Torrid Zone* (Bob Anderson, wed to fun-chasing Helen Vinson), *The Maltese Falcon* (Miles Archer, cuckolded spouse of Gladys George and short-living partner of Humphrey Bogart), *Mr. Skeffington* (one of Bette Davis' rejected but faithful suitors). An excellent farceur. Could attack comedy broadly and did so in several of the later *Blondie* series as George Radcliffe, Dagwood's boss. TV series: "Valiant Lady" (as Mr. Emerson), "The Tab Hunter Show," "Tycoon," and "Many Happy Returns."

143

Jerome Cowan to Edward Everett Horton in *Shall We Dance:* "Well, to tell you the truth, I don't know you well enough to tell you the truth."

Films

Beloved Enemy (UA, 1936)
You Only Live Once (UA, 1937)
Shall We Dance (RKO, 1937)
New Faces of 1937 (RKO, 1937)
The Hurricane (UA, 1937)
Vogues of 1938 (UA, 1937)
The Goldwyn Follies (UA, 1938)
There's Always a Woman (Col, 1938)
St. Louis Blues (Par, 1939)
The Gracie Allen Murder Case (Par, 1939)
The Great Victor Herbert (Par, 1939)
The Saint Strikes Back (RKO, 1939)
East Side of Heaven (Univ, 1939)
She Married a Cop (Rep, 1939)
The Old Maid (WB, 1939)
Exile Express (GN, 1939)
Framed (Univ, 1940)
The Wolf of New York (Rep, 1940)
Ma, He's Making Eyes at Me (Univ, 1940)
Meet the Wildcat (Univ, 1940)
Torrid Zone (WB, 1940)
City for Conquest (WB, 1940)
Castle on the Hudson (WB, 1940)
Street of Memories (20th, 1940)
The Quarterback (Par, 1940)
Victory (Par, 1940)
Melody Ranch (Rep, 1940)
High Sierra (WB, 1941)
The Roundup (Par, 1941)
Affectionately Yours (WB, 1941)
One Foot in Heaven (WB, 1941)
Kisses for Breakfast (WB, 1941)
Kiss the Boys Goodbye (Par, 1941)
Rags to Riches (Rep, 1941)
Too Many Blondes (Univ, 1941)
Mr. and Mrs. North (MGM, 1941)
The Great Lie (WB, 1941)
Singapore Woman (WB, 1941)
Out of the Fog (WB, 1941)
The Maltese Falcon (WB, 1941)
The Bugle Sounds (MGM, 1941)
Street of Chance (Par, 1942)
Frisco Lil (Univ, 1942)
Moontide (20th, 1942)

Through Different Eyes (20th, 1942)
The Girl from Alaska (Rep, 1942)
Joan of Ozark (Rep, 1942)
Who Done It? (Univ, 1942)
A Gentleman at Heart (20th, 1942)
The Song of Bernadette (20th, 1943)
No Place for a Lady (Col, 1943)
Ladies' Day (RKO, 1943)
Mission to Moscow (WB, 1943)
Silver Spurs (Rep, 1943)
Hi Ya, Sailor (Univ, 1943)
Find the Blackmailer (WB, 1943)
The Crime Doctor's Strangest Case (Col, 1943)
Sing a Jingle (Univ, 1944)
Guest in the House (UA, 1944)
Crime by Night (WB, 1944)
Mr. Skeffington (WB, 1944)
South of Dixie (Univ, 1944)
The Minstrel Man (PRC, 1944)
Fog Island (PRC, 1945)
Divorce (Mon, 1945)
Getting Gertie's Garter (UA, 1945)
The Crime Doctor's Courage (Col, 1945)
Behind City Lights (Rep, 1945)
Jungle Captive (Univ, 1945)
G.I. Honeymoon (Mon, 1945)
Hitchhike to Happiness (Rep, 1945)
Blonde Ransom (Univ, 1945)
One Way to Love (Col, 1945)
My Reputation (WB, 1946)
Murder in the Music Hall (Rep, 1946)
Claudia and David (20th, 1946)
The Kid from Brooklyn (RKO, 1946)
Flight to Nowhere (Screen Guild, 1946)
One Exciting Week (Rep, 1946)
Blondie Knows Best (Col, 1946)
Mr. Ace (UA, 1946)
Deadline at Dawn (RKO, 1946)
Deadline for Murder (20th, 1946)
A Night in Paradise (Univ, 1946)
Blondie's Holiday (Col, 1947)
Driftwood (Rep, 1947)
The Perfect Marriage (Par, 1947)
Riffraff (RKO, 1947)
Miracle on 34th Street (20th, 1947)

The Unfaithful (WB, 1947)
Cry Wolf (WB, 1947)
Dangerous Years (20th, 1947)
Blondie's Anniversary (Col, 1947)
Blondie's Big Moment (Col, 1947)
Blondie in the Dough (Col, 1947)
So This Is New York (UA, 1948)
Wallflower (WB, 1948)
Night Has a Thousand Eyes (Par, 1948)
Blondie's Reward (Col, 1948)
Arthur Takes Over (20th, 1948)
June Bride (WB, 1948)
Scene of the Crime (MGM, 1949)
Blondie's Secret (Col, 1949)
Blondie Hits the Jackpot (Col, 1949)
Blondie's Big Deal (Col, 1949)
The Girl from Jones Beach (WB, 1949)
The Fountainhead (WB, 1949)
Always Leave Them Laughing (WB, 1949)
Young Man with a Horn (WB, 1950)
Joe Palooka Meets Humphrey (Mon, 1950)
The Fuller Brush Girl (Col, 1950)
Peggy (Univ, 1950)
When You're Smiling (Col, 1950)
The West Point Story (WB, 1950)
Dallas (WB, 1950)
The Fat Man (Univ, 1951)
Criminal Lawyer (Col, 1951)
Disc Jockey (AA, 1951)
The System (WB, 1953)
Have Rocket Will Travel (Col, 1959)
Visit to a Small Planet (Par, 1960)
Private Property (Citation, 1960)
All in a Night's Work (Par, 1961)
Pocketful of Miracles (UA, 1961)
Critic's Choice (WB, 1963)
Black Zoo (AA, 1963)
The Patsy (Par, 1964)
John Goldfarb, Please Come Home (20th, 1964)
Frankie and Johnny (UA, 1965)
Penelope (MGM, 1966)
The Gnome-Mobile (BV, 1967)
The Comic (Col, 1969)

ALEC CRAIG

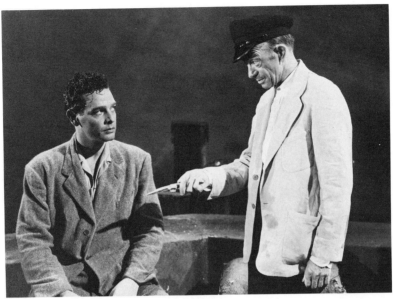

Robert Lowery and Alec Craig in Dangerous Passage *(1944).*

Born 1885, Scotland. Married _____ . Died July 25, 1945, Glendale, California. Prune-faced Scotsman who specialized in excessively thrifty and pessimistic souls.

Alec Craig to Raymond Massey in *Action in the North Atlantic:* "I'll give you all the steam you need in half an hour, sir—and maybe before that!"

Films

The Little Minister (RKO, 1934)
The Old Homestead (Liberty, 1935)
Mutiny on the Bounty (MGM, 1935)
Vanessa, Her Love Story (MGM, 1935)
Sweepstakes Annie (Liberty, 1935)
That Girl from Paris (RKO, 1936)
Mary of Scotland (RKO, 1936)
Winterset (RKO, 1936)
China Passage (RKO, 1937)
The Woman I Love (RKO, 1937)
Meet the Missus (Rep, 1937)
There Goes My Girl (RKO, 1937)
Hideaway (RKO, 1937)
Super Sleuth (RKO, 1937)
Wise Girl (RKO, 1937)
The Man Who Found Himself (RKO, 1937)
She's Got Everything (RKO, 1938)
Double Danger (RKO, 1938)
The Arkansas Traveler (Par, 1938)
Crashing Hollywood (RKO, 1938)
If I Were King (Par, 1938)
Vivacious Lady (RKO, 1938)
They Made Her a Spy (RKO, 1939)
Night Work (Par, 1939)
Let Us Live (Col, 1939)
Lone Wolf Spy Hunt (Col, 1939)

Confessions of a Nazi Spy (WB, 1939)
Rulers of the Sea (Par, 1939)
Charlie McCarthy, Detective (Univ, 1939)
Three Cheers for the Irish (WB, 1940)
Zanzibar (Univ, 1940)
Abe Lincoln in Illinois (RKO, 1940)
Phantom Raiders (MGM, 1940)
Tom Brown's School Days (RKO, 1940)
The Sea Hawk (WB, 1940)
Golden Gloves (Par, 1940)
Stranger on the Third Floor (RKO, 1940)
Shining Victory (WB, 1941)
Dr. Jekyll and Mr. Hyde (MGM, 1941)
Barnacle Bill (MGM, 1941)
Three Girls About Town (Col, 1941)
Footlight Fever (RKO, 1941)
Out of the Fog (WB, 1941)
A Date with the Falcon (RKO, 1941)
To Be or Not to Be (UA, 1942)
Her Cardboard Lover (MGM, 1942)
The Night Before the Divorce (20th, 1942)
Mrs. Miniver (MGM, 1942)
Orchestra Wives (20th, 1942)
Wildcat (Par, 1942)
The Undying Monster (20th, 1942)
Life Begins at 8:30 (20th, 1942)
Random Harvest (MGM, 1942)

Cat People (RKO, 1942)
Wrecking Crew (Par, 1942)
Tennessee Johnson (MGM, 1942)
Forever and a Day (RKO, 1943)
Appointment in Berlin (Col, 1943)
Action in the North Atlantic (WB, 1943)
The Ghost Ship (RKO, 1943)
Calling Dr. Death (Univ, 1943)
Holy Matrimony (20th, 1943)
Lassie Come Home (MGM, 1943)
Northern Pursuit (WB, 1943)
Career Girl (PRC, 1943)
Ghost Catchers (Univ, 1944)
Jane Eyre (20th, 1944)
The White Cliffs of Dover (MGM, 1944)
The Spider Woman (Univ, 1944)
And Now Tomorrow (Par, 1944)
Jungle Woman (Univ, 1944)
Dangerous Passage (Par, 1944)
A Tree Grows in Brooklyn (20th, 1945)
Love Letters (Par, 1945)
Kitty (Par, 1945)
Tonight and Every Night (Col, 1945)
Girl on the Spot (Univ, 1946)
Three Strangers (WB, 1946)

FRANK CRAVEN

With Fay Bainter in Our Neighbors—The Carters *(1939).*

Born August 24, 1875, Boston, Massachusetts. Married Mazie B. Daly, child: John. Died September 1, 1945, Beverly Hills, California. Turned to scenario work at Fox Films after some late 1920s screen assignments, but returned to pictures in Will Rogers' *State Fair*. Most noted for his stage and film interpretation of the cracker-barrel-philosophizing stage manager in *Our Town*. (Played an urban counterpart, the Old Timer, in *City for Conquest*.) Later was the repressed father of Bette Davis and Olivia de Havilland in *In This Our Life*.

Frank Craven to Henry Hull in *Miracles for Sale*: "New York is the only town I've ever been in that you could learn to hate in a day."

Films

We Americans (Univ, 1928)
The Very Idea (RKO, 1929)
State Fair (Fox, 1933)
City Limits (Mon, 1934)
He Was Her Man (WB, 1934)
Let's Talk It Over (Univ, 1934)
That's Gratitude (Col, 1934)
Car 99 (Par, 1935)
Vagabond Lady (MGM, 1935)
Barbary Coast (UA, 1935)
Small Town Girl (MGM, 1936)
The Harvester (Rep, 1936)
Penrod and Sam (WB, 1937)

Blossoms on Broadway (Par, 1937)
You're Only Young Once (MGM, 1938)
Penrod and His Twin Brother (WB, 1938)
Miracles for Sale (MGM, 1939)
Our Neighbors—The Carters (Par, 1939)
Our Town (UA, 1940)
City for Conquest (WB, 1940)
Dreaming Out Loud (RKO, 1940)
The Lady from Cheyenne (Univ, 1941)
The Richest Man in Town (Col, 1941)
In This Our Life (WB, 1942)
Pittsburgh (Univ, 1942)
Through Different Eyes (20th, 1942)

Girl Trouble (20th, 1942)
Keeper of the Flame (MGM, 1942)
Son of Dracula (Univ, 1943)
Harrigan's Kid (MGM, 1943)
Jack London (UA, 1943)
The Human Comedy (MGM, 1943)
Destiny (Univ, 1944)
My Best Gal (Rep, 1944)
They Shall Have Faith [a.k.a. *Forever Yours*] (Mon, 1944)
Colonel Effingham's Raid (20th, 1945)

LAURA HOPE CREWS

Laura Hope Crews and Olivia de Havilland in Gone with the Wind *(1939).*

Born December 12, 1879, San Francisco, California. Died November 13, 1942, New York City, New York. Came to the West Coast as drama coach to stars making the transition to talkies. Gained screen fame re-creating her stage role of Mrs. Phelps, the dominating mother in Irene Dunne's *The Silver Cord*. Role of flighty stout Prudence in Greta Garbo's *Camille* seemed but a warm-up for her part as flibbertigibbet Aunt Pitty-Pat of *Gone with the Wind*.

Laura Hope Crews to Eric Linden in *The Silver Cord:* "I always suspected there was insanity in her family. She had a brother who was an aviator in the war. Everybody knows that aviators are lunatics."

Films

Charming Sinners (Par, 1929)
New Morals for Old (MGM, 1932)
Rockabye (RKO, 1932)
The Silver Cord (RKO, 1933)
I Loved You Wednesday (Fox, 1933)
Blind Adventure (RKO, 1933)
If I Were Free (RKO, 1933)
Female (FN, 1933)
Ever in My Heart (WB, 1933)
Out All Night (Univ, 1933)
Rafter Romance (RKO, 1934)
Age of Innocence (RKO, 1934)
Behold My Wife! (Par, 1934)

Lightning Strikes Twice (RKO, 1934)
The Flame Within (MGM, 1935)
Escapade (MGM, 1935)
The Melody Lingers On (UA, 1935)
Her Master's Voice (Par, 1936)
Camille (MGM, 1936)
The Road Back (Univ, 1937)
Confession (WB, 1937)
Angel (Par, 1937)
Dr. Rhythm (Par, 1938)
Thanks for the Memory (Par, 1938)
The Sisters (WB, 1938)
Idiot's Delight (MGM, 1939)

Remember? (MGM, 1939)
Gone with the Wind (MGM, 1939)
The Star Maker (Par, 1939)
The Rains Came (20th, 1939)
Reno (RKO, 1939)
The Blue Bird (20th, 1940)
Lady with Red Hair (WB, 1940)
The Flame of New Orleans (Univ, 1941)
One Foot in Heaven (WB, 1941)
The Man Who Came to Dinner (WB, 1941) [cut from release print]

DONALD CRISP

Edmund Gwenn and Donald Crisp in Challenge to Lassie *(1949)*.

Born July 27, 1880, Abefeddy, Scotland. Married 1) Marie Stark; divorced (1919); 2) Jane Murfin (1932); divorced (1944). Died May 25, 1974, Van Nuys, California. Frequently part of D. W. Griffith's stock company during the 1910s: *The Escape* (Bull McGee), *The Birth of a Nation* (General U. S. Grant), *Broken Blossoms* (Battling Burrows, the sadistic boxer-father of Lillian Gish), etc. From *Ramona* onward, Crisp was a very active director, especially at Paramount; occasionally appeared in his own productions: *Don Q, Son of Zorro* (as Don Sebastian, interacting with swashbuckling hero Douglas Fairbanks). Stocky, short filmmaker (who never lost his Scottish accent). By the 1930s had turned exclusively to acting, often as the stern father, commanding officer, or executive: *Mutiny on the Bounty* (Burkitt), *The Charge of the Light Brigade* (Colonel Campbell), Errol Flynn's *The Dawn Patrol* (Phills), *The Private Lives of Elizabeth and Essex* (Francis Bacon), *Wuthering Heights* (Dr. Kenneth), *National Velvet* (Mr. Brown), *Spencer's Mountain* (Grandpa), etc. Won BSAAA for his Welsh miner-familyman in *How Green Was My Valley*.

Donald Crisp to Errol Flynn in *The Charge of the Light Brigade*:
"When you've been soldiering as long as I have, you'll find it's best to follow orders regardless."

Films

The Battle of the Sexes (Reliance, 1914)
The Great Leap (Reliance, 1914)
The Escape (Reliance, 1914)
Home Sweet Home (Mutual, 1914)
The Avenging Conscience (Mutual, 1914)
The Birth of a Nation (Epoch-Mutual, 1915)
The Love Route (Par, 1915)
The Blue or the Gray (Par, 1915)
The Girl of Yesterday (Par, 1915)
The Foundling (Par, 1915)
Ramona (Clune, 1916)

Joan, the Woman (Par, 1917)
Broken Blossoms (UA, 1919)
The Bonnie Brier Bush (Par Br, 1921)
Don Q, Son of Zorro (UA, 1925)
The Black Pirate (UA, 1926)
The River Pirate (Fox, 1928)
Trent's Last Case (Fox, 1929)
The Pagan (MGM, 1929)
The Return of Sherlock Holmes (Par, 1929)
Scotland Yard (Fox, 1930)
Svengali (WB, 1931)
Kick-In (Par, 1931)

A Passport to Hell (Fox, 1932)
Red Dust (MGM, 1932)
Broadway Bad (Fox, 1933)
The Crime Doctor (RKO, 1934)
The Little Minister (RKO, 1934)
The Life of Vergie Winters (RKO, 1934)
What Every Woman Knows (MGM, 1934)
The Key (WB, 1934)
Vanessa: Her Love Story (MGM, 1935)
Laddie (RKO, 1935)
Mutiny on the Bounty (MGM, 1935)

148

Oil for the Lamps of China (WB, 1935)
The White Angel (WB, 1936)
The Charge of the Light Brigade (WB, 1936)
Mary of Scotland (RKO, 1936)
A Woman Rebels (UA, 1936)
Beloved Enemy (UA, 1936)
The Great O'Malley (WB, 1937)
Parnell (MGM, 1937)
The Life of Emile Zola (WB, 1937)
Confession (WB, 1937)
That Certain Woman (WB, 1937)
Sergeant Murphy (WB, 1938)
The Beloved Brat (WB, 1938)
Jezebel (WB, 1938)
The Amazing Dr. Clitterhouse (WB, 1938)
Valley of the Giants (WB, 1938)
The Sisters (WB, 1938)
Dawn Patrol (WB, 1938)
Comet over Broadway (WB, 1938)
Wuthering Heights (UA, 1939)

Juarez (WB, 1939)
Daughters Courageous (WB, 1939)
The Old Maid (WB, 1939)
The Private Lives of Elizabeth and Essex (WB, 1939)
The Oklahoma Kid (WB, 1939)
The Story of Dr. Ehrlich's Magic Bullet (WB, 1940)
Brother Orchid (WB, 1940)
The Sea Hawk (WB, 1940)
City for Conquest (WB, 1940)
Knute Rockne—All-American (WB, 1940)
Dr. Jekyll and Mr. Hyde (MGM, 1941)
How Green Was My Valley (20th, 1941)
Shining Victory (WB, 1941)
The Gay Sisters (WB, 1942)
Battle of Midway (1942) [narrator]
Forever and a Day (RKO, 1943)
Lassie Come Home (MGM, 1943)
The Adventures of Mark Twain (WB, 1944)

The Uninvited (Par, 1944)
National Velvet (MGM, 1944)
Son of Lassie (MGM, 1945)
Valley of Decision (MGM, 1945)
Ramrod (UA, 1947)
Hills of Home (MGM, 1948)
Whispering Smith (Par, 1948)
Challenge to Lassie (MGM, 1949)
Bright Leaf (WB, 1950)
Home Town Story (MGM, 1951)
Prince Valiant (20th, 1954)
The Long Gray Line (Col, 1955)
The Man from Laramie (Col, 1955)
Drango (UA, 1957)
Saddle the Wind (MGM, 1958)
The Last Hurrah (Col, 1958)
A Dog of Flanders (20th, 1959)
Pollyanna (BV, 1960)
Greyfriars' Bobby (BV, 1961)
Spencer's Mountain (WB, 1963)

HENRIETTA CROSMAN

In Personal Property (1937).

Born September 2, 1861, Wheeling, West Virginia. Married Maurice Campbell, children: Maurice, another child; widowed (1942). Died October 31, 1944, Pelham Manor, New York. Onetime adored leading stage actress. Returned to the screen in 1930 to play to the hilt the matriarch (who dies with greasepaint on) in *The Royal Family of Broadway*. Could be somber (*Pilgrimage*) or effervescent (*The Moon's Our Home*), but was always grand and very effective.

Henrietta Crosman to Arnold Korff in *The Royal Family of Broadway:* "Ring down the curtain? Are you *mad,* Wolfe? Ring down the curtain? Cavendishes *never* ring down the curtain! We always finish the play!"

Films

The Unwelcome Mrs. Hatch (Par, 1914)
How Molly Made Good (Sterling, 1915)
Broadway Broke (Selznick, 1923)
Wandering Fires (Arrow, 1925)
The Royal Family of Broadway (Par, 1930)
Pilgrimage (Fox, 1933)
Three on a Honeymoon (Fox, 1934)

Carolina (Fox, 1934)
Such Women Are Dangerous (Fox, 1934)
Among the Missing (Col, 1934)
The Curtain Falls (Chesterfield, 1934)
Menace (Par, 1934)
Elinor Norton (Fox, 1935)
The Right to Live (WB, 1935)

The Dark Angel (UA, 1935)
Hitch Hike to Heaven (Invincible, 1936)
Charlie Chan's Secret (20th, 1936)
The Moon's Our Home (Par, 1936)
Girl of the Ozarks (Par, 1936)
Follow Your Heart (Rep, 1936)
Personal Property (MGM, 1937)

CECIL CUNNINGHAM

In the early 1940s.

Born August 2, 1888, St. Louis, Missouri. Married Jean Havez (1915); divorced (1917). Died April 17, 1959, Los Angeles, California. Cut a striking figure with her close-cropped grayish hair. Often appeared as the all-knowing confidante, the smirking bachelor girl, or the wisecracking secretary. Stage-trained.

Cecil Cunningham to Greer Garson in *Blossoms in the Dust:* "My husband and I have decided to give the advantage of our home to one of your foundlings, Mrs. Gladney. . . . Of course, we wouldn't want one that cries."

Films

Their Own Desire (MGM, 1929)
Anybody's Woman (Par, 1930)
Paramount on Parade (Par, 1930)
Playboy of Paris (Par, 1930)
Monkey Business (Par, 1931)
Age for Love (UA, 1931)
Mata Hari (MGM, 1931)
Safe in Hell (WB, 1931)
Susan Lenox, Her Fall and Rise (MGM, 1931)
The Impatient Maiden (Univ, 1932)
Love Is a Racket (FN, 1932)
It's Tough to Be Famous (FN, 1932)
The Rich Are Always with Us (FN, 1932)
Blonde Venus (Par, 1932)
Those We Love (WW, 1932)
If I Had a Million (Par, 1932)
Love Me Tonight (Par, 1932)
Ladies They Talk About (WB, 1933)
From Hell to Heaven (Par, 1933)
Baby Face (WB, 1933)
We Live Again (UA, 1934)
Bottoms Up (Fox, 1934) [cut from release print]
Manhattan Love Song (Mon, 1934)
The Life of Vergie Winters (RKO, 1934)

Return of the Terror (FN, 1934)
People Will Talk (Par, 1935)
Mr. Deeds Goes to Town (Col, 1936)
Come and Get It (UA, 1936)
Swing High—Swing Low (Par, 1937)
King of Gamblers (Par, 1937)
Artists and Models (Par, 1937)
This Way Please (Par, 1937)
The Awful Truth (Col, 1937)
Night Club Scandal (Par, 1937)
Daughter of Shanghai (Par, 1937)
Scandal Street (Par, 1938)
College Swing (Par, 1938)
Kentucky Moonshine (20th, 1938)
Blond Cheat (RKO, 1938)
Marie Antoinette (MGM, 1938)
Four Men and a Prayer (20th, 1938)
You and Me (Par, 1938)
Wives Under Suspicion (Univ, 1938)
Girls' School (Col, 1938)
The Family Next Door (Univ, 1939)
It's a Wonderful World (MGM, 1939)
Winter Carnival (UA, 1939)
Lady of the Tropics (MGM, 1939)
Laugh It Off (Univ, 1939)
Lillian Russell (20th, 1940)

The Captain Is a Lady (MGM, 1940)
New Moon (MGM, 1940)
Play Girl (RKO, 1940)
The Great Profile (20th, 1940)
Kitty Foyle (RKO, 1940)
Back Street (Univ, 1941)
Blossoms in the Dust (MGM, 1941)
Repent at Leisure (RKO, 1941)
Hurry, Charlie, Hurry (RKO, 1941)
Cowboy Serenade (Rep, 1942)
The Wife Takes a Flyer (Col, 1942)
Are Husbands Necessary? (Par, 1942)
I Married an Angel (MGM, 1942)
Twin Beds (UA, 1942)
Cairo (MGM, 1942)
The Hidden Hand (WB, 1942)
In Old Oklahoma [a.k.a. *War of the Wildcats*] (Rep, 1943)
Du Barry Was a Lady (MGM, 1943)
Above Suspicion (MGM, 1943)
Wonder Man (RKO, 1945)
Saratoga Trunk (WB, 1945)
The Horn Blows at Midnight (WB, 1945)
My Reputation (WB, 1946)
The Bride Goes Wild (MGM, 1948)

ESTHER DALE

With Chester Morris and Richard Arlen in Wrecking Crew *(1942).*

Born November 10, 1885, Beaufort, South Carolina. Married Arthur J. Beckhard; widowed (1961). Died July 23, 1961, Hollywood, California. A superior interpreter of no-nonsense domestics, commanding mothers, stern nurses, and prissy matrons. Sometimes an aggravating busybody as in her continuing role of Mrs. Hicks in the *Ma and Pa Kettle* series.

Esther Dale to Claudette Colbert in *Private Worlds*: "In the old days we fed our patients well and dosed them on castor oil."

Films

Crime Without Passion (Par, 1934)
The Wedding Night (UA, 1935)
I Live My Life (MGM, 1935)
I Dream Too Much (RKO, 1935)
Private Worlds (Par, 1935)
Curly Top (Fox, 1935)
In Old Kentucky (Fox, 1935)
The Great Impersonation (Univ, 1935)
The Farmer in the Dell (RKO, 1936)
Lady of Secrets (Col, 1936)
Timothy's Quest (Par, 1936)
Fury (MGM, 1936)
The Case Against Mrs. Ames (Par, 1936)
Hollywood Boulevard (Par, 1936)
The Magnificent Brute (Univ, 1936)
Outcast (Par, 1937)
Wild Money (Par, 1937)
Damaged Goods (GN, 1937)
Easy Living (Par, 1937)
Dead End (UA, 1937)
On Such a Night (Par, 1937)
The Awful Truth (Col, 1937)
Of Human Hearts (MGM, 1938)
Stolen Heaven (Par, 1938)
Condemned Woman (RKO, 1938)
Prison Farm (Par, 1938)
Girls on Probation (WB, 1938)
Made for Each Other (UA, 1939)
Broadway Serenade (MGM, 1939)
Big Town Czar (Univ, 1939)

Sergeant Madden (MGM, 1939)
Tell No Tales (MGM, 1939)
The Women (MGM, 1939)
6,000 Enemies (MGM, 1939)
Blackmail (MGM, 1939)
Swanee River (20th, 1939)
Convicted Woman (Col, 1940)
A Child Is Born (WB, 1940)
Women Without Names (Par, 1940)
Village Barn Dance (Rep, 1940)
And One Was Beautiful (MGM, 1940)
Opened by Mistake (Par, 1940)
The Mortal Storm (MGM, 1940)
Untamed (Par, 1940)
Laddie (RKO, 1940)
Blondie Has Servant Trouble (Col, 1940)
Love Thy Neighbor (Par, 1940)
Arise, My Love (Par, 1940)
Back Street (Univ, 1941)
Mr. and Mrs. Smith (RKO, 1941)
There's Magic in Music (Par, 1941)
Aloma of the South Seas (Par, 1941)
Unfinished Business (Univ, 1941)
All-American Co-ed (UA, 1941)
Dangerously They Live (WB, 1941)
Blondie Goes to College (Col, 1942)
I Married an Angel (MGM, 1942)
Ten Gentlemen from West Point (20th, 1942)
What's Cookin'? (Univ, 1942)

Maisie Gets Her Man (MGM, 1942)
Wrecking Crew (Par, 1942)
The Amazing Mrs. Holliday (Univ, 1943)
Swing Your Partner (Rep, 1943)
Murder in Times Square (Col, 1943)
The North Star (RKO, 1943)
Old Acquaintance (WB, 1943)
Bedside Manner (UA, 1945)
On Stage, Everybody (Univ, 1945)
Out of This World (Par, 1945)
Behind City Lights (Rep, 1945)
My Reputation (WB, 1946)
A Stolen Life (WB, 1946)
Smoky (20th, 1946)
Margie (20th, 1946)
The Egg and I (Univ, 1947)
The Unfinished Dance (MGM, 1947)
A Song Is Born (RKO, 1948)
Ma and Pa Kettle (Univ, 1949)
Anna Lucasta (Col, 1949)
Holiday Affair (RKO, 1949)
No Man of Her Own (Par, 1950)
Walk Softly, Stranger (RKO, 1950)
Surrender (Rep, 1950)
Too Young to Kiss (MGM, 1951)
Ma and Pa Kettle at the Fair (Univ, 1952)
Monkey Business (20th, 1952)
Ma and Pa Kettle at Waikiki (Univ, 1955)
Betrayed Woman (AA, 1955)
The Oklahoman (AA, 1957)

HENRY DANIELL

Efrem Zimbalist, Jr. and Henry Daniell in The Chapman Report *(1962).*

Born May 5, 1894, London, England. Married Ann Knox. Died October 31, 1963, Santa Monica, California. Calculating, austere villain who could appreciate the wiliness of his way. Very angular features and thin build accentuated his portrayals. Well suited to costumed adventure yarns, playing the devious manipulator: *Marie Antoinette* (La Motte), *The Private Lives of Elizabeth and Essex* (Sir Robert Cecil), *The Sea Hawk* (Lord Wolfingham), *The Bandit of Sherwood Forest* (the Regent), *The Story of Mankind* (the Bishop of Beauvais), etc. Could play comedy (the minister of propaganda in *The Great Dictator*), or display a sense of sinister poetic justice, as when dealing with his unfaithful mistress (Greta Garbo) in *Camille*. Son Henry, Jr. became an actor.

Henry Daniell to Cornel Wilde in *The Bandit of Sherwood Forest:* "Yes, Lady Catherine will have the pleasure of watching me kill you."

Films

Jealousy (Par, 1929)
The Awful Truth (Pathé, 1929)
The Last of the Lone Wolf (Col, 1930)
Path of Glory (Br, 1934)
Unguarded Hour (MGM, 1936)
Camille (MGM, 1936)
Under Cover of Night (MGM, 1937)
The Thirteenth Chair (MGM, 1937)
The Firefly (MGM, 1937)
Madame X (MGM, 1937)
Holiday (Col, 1938)
Marie Antoinette (MGM, 1938)
The Private Lives of Elizabeth and Essex (WB, 1939)
We Are Not Alone (WB, 1939)
All This and Heaven Too (WB, 1940)
The Sea Hawk (WB, 1940)

The Great Dictator (UA, 1940)
The Philadelphia Story (MGM, 1940)
A Woman's Face (MGM, 1941)
Dressed to Kill (20th, 1941)
Four Jacks and a Jill (RKO, 1941)
The Feminine Touch (MGM, 1941)
Castle in the Desert (20th, 1942)
Random Harvest (MGM, 1942)
Sherlock Holmes and the Voice of Terror (Univ, 1942)
Reunion in France (MGM, 1942)
The Great Impersonation (Univ, 1942)
Nightmare (Univ, 1942)
Mission to Moscow (WB, 1943)
Sherlock Holmes in Washington (Univ, 1943)
Watch on the Rhine (WB, 1943)

Jane Eyre (20th, 1944)
The Suspect (Univ, 1944)
The Chicago Kid (Rep, 1945)
Hotel Berlin (WB, 1945)
The Woman in Green (Univ, 1945)
The Body Snatcher (RKO, 1945)
Captain Kidd (UA, 1945)
The Bandit of Sherwood Forest (Col, 1946)
Song of Love (MGM, 1947)
The Exile (Univ, 1947)
Siren of Atlantis (UA, 1948)
Wake of the Red Witch (Rep, 1948)
The Secret of St. Ives (Col, 1949)
Buccaneer's Girl (Univ, 1950)
The Egyptian (20th, 1954)
The Prodigal (MGM, 1955)
Diane (MGM, 1955)

The Man in the Gray Flannel Suit (20th, 1956)
Lust for Life (MGM, 1956)
Les Girls (MGM, 1957)
The Story of Mankind (WB, 1957)
The Sun Also Rises (20th, 1957)
Witness for the Prosecution (UA, 1957)

Mr. Cory (Univ, 1957)
From the Earth to the Moon (WB, 1958)
The Four Skulls of Jonathan Drake (UA, 1959)
Voyage to the Bottom of the Sea (20th, 1961)
The Comancheros (20th, 1961)

Madison Avenue (20th, 1962)
The Notorious Landlady (Col, 1962)
Five Weeks in a Balloon (20th, 1962)
The Chapman Report (WB, 1962)
My Fair Lady (WB, 1964)

ROYAL DANO

In The Wild Party (1975).

Born November 16, 1922. A solid supporting player: *The Red Badge of Courage* (the tattered man), Gregory Peck's *Moby Dick* (Elijah), *The Adventures of Huckleberry Finn* (sheriff), *The King of Kings* (Peter), etc.

Royal Dano to Sterling Hayden in *Johnny Guitar:* "Bart ain't gonna be happy to see you, mister."

Films

Undercover Girl (Univ, 1950)
Under the Gun (Univ, 1950)
The Red Badge of Courage (MGM, 1951)
Flame of Araby (Univ, 1951)
Bend of the River (Univ, 1952)
Johnny Guitar (Rep, 1954)
The Far Country (Univ, 1955)
The Trouble with Harry (Par, 1955)
Tribute to a Bad Man (MGM, 1956)
Santiago (WB, 1956)
Moby Dick (WB, 1956)

Tension at Table Rock (RKO, 1956)
Crime of Passion (UA, 1957)
Trooper Hook (UA, 1957)
All Mine to Give (Univ, 1957)
Man in the Shadow (Univ, 1957)
Saddle the Wind (MGM, 1958)
Handle with Care (MGM, 1958)
Man of the West (UA, 1958)
Never Steal Anything Small (Univ, 1959)
These Thousand Hills (20th, 1959)
Hound-Dog Man (20th, 1959)

Face of Fire (AA, 1959)
The Adventures of Huckleberry Finn (MGM, 1960)
Cimarron (MGM, 1960)
Posse from Hell (Univ, 1961)
The King of Kings (MGM, 1961)
Savage Sam (BV, 1963)
The Seven Faces of Dr. Lao (MGM, 1964)
Gunpoint (Univ, 1966)
Welcome to Hard Times (MGM, 1967)
The Last Challenge (MGM, 1967)

154

Day of the Evil Gun (MGM, 1968)
If He Hollers, Let Him Go (Cin, 1968)
The Undefeated (20th, 1969)
Backtrack (Univ, 1969)
The Great Northfield, Minnesota Raid (Univ, 1972)
The Culpepper Cattle Company (20th, 1972)

Howzer (URI, 1972)
Ace Eli and Rodgers of the Skies (20th, 1973)
Cahill, United States Marshal (WB, 1973)
Electric Glide in Blue (UA, 1973)
Big Bad Mama (New World, 1974)
The Wild Party (AIP, 1975)

Messiah of Evil (International Cine Film Corp, 1975)
Capone (20th, 1975)
Drum (UA, 1976)
The Outlaw Josey Wales (WB, 1976)
The Killer Inside Me (WB, 1976)

JANE DARWELL
(Patti Woodward)

In the mid-1930s.

Born October 15, 1879, Palmyra, Missouri. Died August 14, 1967, Woodland Hills, California. Easily the most famous of the (grand)motherly types on screen. Graduated from playing bit film roles as neighborhood gossips to contract-player status with (20th Century-) Fox. Brightened several Shirley Temple vehicles as housekeepers, villagers, et al. (*Curly Top, Bright Eyes, Captain January, Poor Little Rich Girl,* etc.). On loan from Fox, played Atlanta matron Dolly Merriwether in *Gone with the Wind.* Frequently used to provide Americana: *Jesse James* (Mrs. Samuels), *Brigham Young—Frontiersman* (Eliza), *The Loves of Edgar Allan Poe* (Mrs. Clemm), *Captain Tugboat Annie* (title role), etc. For director John Ford, played Ma Joad in *The Grapes of Wrath* and won BSAAA; also for Ford such entries as *My Darling Clementine* (Kate Nelson), *Three Godfathers* (Miss Florie), *Wagonmaster* (Sister Ledeyard), *The Sun Shines Bright* (Amora Ratchitt), and *The Last Hurrah* (Delia Boylan). Finale to her screen and stage career was the pathetic "Bird Woman" of *Mary Poppins.*

155

Jane Darwell to Don Ameche and Loretta Young in *Ramona:* "As far as I'm concerned, a Christian's a Christian, no matter what the color of his skin."

Films

Rose of the Rancho (Par, 1914)
The Only Son (Par, 1914)
Brewster's Millions (Par, 1914)
The Master Mind (Par, 1914)
Tom Sawyer (Par, 1930)
Huckleberry Finn (Par, 1931)
Fighting Caravans (Par, 1931)
Ladies of the Big House (Par, 1931)
Hot Saturday (Par, 1932)
Back Street (Univ, 1932)
No One Man (Par, 1932)
Murders in the Zoo (Par, 1932)
Bondage (Fox, 1933)
Jennie Gerhardt (Par, 1933)
Bed of Roses (RKO, 1933)
One Sunday Afternoon (Par, 1933)
Before Dawn (RKO, 1933)
Only Yesterday (Univ, 1933)
Air Hostess (Col, 1933)
Child of Manhattan (Col, 1933)
Women Won't Tell (Chesterfield, 1933)
Emergency Call (RKO, 1933)
Roman Scandals (UA, 1933)
He Couldn't Take It (Mon, 1933)
Design for Living (Par, 1933)
Finishing School (RKO, 1934)
Once to Every Woman (Col, 1934)
Happiness Ahead (WB, 1934)
Wonder Bar (WB, 1934)
Fashions of 1934 (WB, 1934)
Desirable (WB, 1934)
Wake Up and Dream (Univ, 1934)
The Firebird (WB, 1934)
Let's Talk It Over (Univ, 1934)
David Harum (Fox, 1934)
Heat Lightning (WB, 1934)
Change of Heart (Fox, 1934)
Most Precious Thing in Life (Col, 1934)
The Scarlet Empress (Par, 1934)
Blind Date (Col, 1934)
Embarrassing Moments (Univ, 1934)
Gentlemen Are Born (WB, 1934)
Journal of a Crime (WB, 1934)
Jimmy the Gent (WB, 1934)
The White Parade (Fox, 1934)
Million Dollar Ransom (Univ, 1934)
One Night of Love (Col, 1934)
Bright Eyes (Fox, 1934)
One More Spring (Fox, 1935)
McFadden's Flats (Par, 1935)
Life Begins at 40 (Fox, 1935)
Curly Top (Fox, 1935)
Metropolitan (Fox, 1935)

Navy Wife [a.k.a. *Beauty's Daughter*] (Fox, 1935)
Paddy O'Day (Fox, 1935)
Tomorrow's Youth (Mon, 1935)
We're Only Human (RKO, 1936)
Country Doctor (20th, 1936)
Little Miss Nobody (20th, 1936)
Captain January (20th, 1936)
The First Baby (20th, 1936)
Poor Little Rich Girl (20th, 1936)
Private Number (20th, 1936)
Star for a Night (20th, 1936)
White Fang (20th, 1936)
Ramona (20th, 1936)
Craig's Wife (Col, 1936)
Love Is News (20th, 1937)
Laughing at Trouble (20th, 1937)
Nancy Steele Is Missing (20th, 1937)
Fifty Roads to Town (20th, 1937)
Slave Ship (20th, 1937)
The Singing Marine (WB, 1937)
The Great Hospital Mystery (20th, 1937)
Dangerously Yours (20th, 1937)
Wife, Doctor and Nurse (20th, 1937)
The Jury's Secret (Univ, 1938)
Change of Heart (20th, 1938)
Battle of Broadway (20th, 1938)
Three Blind Mice (20th, 1938)
Five of a Kind (20th, 1938)
Time Out for Murder (20th, 1938)
Little Miss Broadway (20th, 1938)
Inside Story (20th, 1938)
Up the River (20th, 1938)
Jesse James (20th, 1939)
Unexpected Father (Univ, 1939)
The Zero Hour (Rep, 1939)
Grand Jury Secrets (Par, 1939)
The Rains Came (20th, 1939)
Gone with the Wind (MGM, 1939)
20,000 Men a Year (20th, 1939)
The Grapes of Wrath (20th, 1940)
Brigham Young—Frontiersman (20th, 1940)
A Miracle on Main Street (Col, 1940)
Youth Will Be Served (20th, 1940)
Chad Hanna (20th, 1940)
Untamed (Par, 1940)
All That Money Can Buy [a.k.a. *The Devil and Daniel Webster*] (RKO, 1941)
Private Nurse (20th, 1941)
Small Town Deb (20th, 1941)
Thieves Fall Out (WB, 1941)
Young America (20th, 1942)

It Happened in Flatbush (20th, 1942)
Men of Texas (Univ, 1942)
On the Sunny Side (20th, 1942)
Highways by Night (RKO, 1942)
The Great Gildersleeve (RKO, 1942)
All Through the Night (WB, 1942)
The Loves of Edgar Allan Poe (20th, 1942)
Government Girl (RKO, 1943)
Stage Door Canteen (UA, 1943)
The Ox-Bow Incident (20th, 1943)
Tender Comrade (RKO, 1943)
Gildersleeve's Bad Day (RKO, 1943)
The Impatient Years (Col, 1944)
Reckless Age (Univ, 1944)
Sunday Dinner for a Soldier (20th, 1944)
She's a Sweetheart (Col, 1944)
Music in Manhattan (RKO, 1944)
Double Indemnity (Par, 1944)
Captain Tugboat Annie (Rep, 1945)
Three Wise Fools (MGM, 1946)
My Darling Clementine (20th, 1946)
Dark Horse (Univ, 1946)
A Yank in London (Br, 1946)
Red Stallion (EL, 1947)
Keeper of the Bees (Col, 1947)
Three Godfathers (MGM, 1948)
Train to Alcatraz (Rep, 1948)
Red Canyon (Univ, 1949)
Wagonmaster (RKO, 1950)
The Daughter of Rosie O'Grady (WB, 1950)
Caged (WB, 1950)
Redwood Forest Trail (Rep, 1950)
Surrender (Rep, 1950)
Three Husbands (UA, 1950)
The Second Face (EL, 1950)
Father's Wild Game (Mon, 1950)
Excuse My Dust (MGM, 1951)
The Lemon Drop Kid (Par, 1951)
Journey into Light (20th, 1951)
Fourteen Hours (20th, 1951)
We're Not Married (20th, 1952)
It Happens Every Thursday (Univ, 1953)
The Sun Shines Bright (Rep, 1953)
Affair with a Stranger (RKO, 1953)
The Bigamist (Filmakers, 1953)
A Life at Stake (Filmakers, 1955)
Hit the Deck (MGM, 1955)
There's Always Tomorrow (Univ, 1956)
Girls in Prison (AIP, 1956)
The Last Hurrah (Col, 1958)
Hound-Dog Man (20th, 1959)
Mary Poppins (BV, 1964)

HARRY DAVENPORT

Eve Arden, Harry Davenport, and Melvyn Douglas in That Uncertain Feeling
(1941).

Born January 19, 1866, New York City, New York. Married Phyllis Rankin, children: Dorothy, three others; widowed. Died August 9, 1949, Los Angeles, California. Distinguished descendant of a long line of actors. Tall, thin, and resourceful. Esteemed for interpreting his roles simply and gracefully. Some silent features. Returned to the screen in *Her Unborn Child* (starring Elisha Cook, Jr.) as Dr. Remington. Later came: *They Won't Forget* (veteran), *The Life of Emile Zola* (chief of staff), *Maytime* (opera director), *Marie Antoinette* (Monsieur de Cosse), etc. As Grandpa, he joined with James, Lucille, and Russell Gleason in *The Higgins Family* domestic comedy series at Republic. Made his mark as Dr. Meade the kindly old Atlanta physician in *Gone with the Wind*. Much in demand in the 1940s portraying an array of senior citizens: Colonel Skeffington *(Kings Row)*, Grandpa *(Meet Me in St. Louis)*, Old John *(The Enchanted Forest)*, Old Jolyn Forsyte *(That Forsyte Woman)*, etc. Daughter Dorothy or a silent screen actress, married to actor/co-star Wallace Reid from 1913 until his death in 1923.

Harry Davenport to Judy Garland in *Meet Me in St. Louis*:
"You know, suits are like men. They like to step out once in
a while with a pretty girl."

Films

Father and the Boy (Univ, 1915)
One Night (Vit, 1916)
Sowers and Reapers (M, 1917)
The False Friend (Artcraft, 1917)
The Planter (Mutual, 1917)
A Man's Law (Overland-Mammoth, 1917)
A Girl at Bay (Vit, 1919)
The Unknown Quantity (Vit, 1919)
Her Unborn Child (Windsor, 1930)
My Sin (Par, 1931)
His Woman (Par, 1931)
Get That Venus (Regent, 1933)
The Scoundrel (Par, 1935)
The Case of the Black Cat (FN, 1936)

Three Cheers for Love (Par, 1936)
Legion of Terror (Col, 1936)
King of Hockey (WB, 1936)
Three Men on a Horse (WB, 1936)
Fly-Away Baby (WB, 1937)
Under Cover of Night (MGM, 1937)
Her Husband's Secretary (WB, 1937)
White Bondage (WB, 1937)
They Won't Forget (WB, 1937)
The Life of Emile Zola (WB, 1937)
Four Days' Wonder (Univ, 1937)
Maytime (MGM, 1937)
The Great Garrick (WB, 1937)
Radio Patrol (Univ serial, 1937)
Mountain Justice (WB, 1937)

Mr. Dodd Takes the Air (WB, 1937)
First Lady (WB, 1937)
The Perfect Specimen (WB, 1937)
Paradise Express (Rep, 1937)
As Good as Married (Univ, 1937)
Wells Fargo (Par, 1937)
Armored Car (Univ, 1937)
Fit for a King (RKO, 1937)
The Sisters (WB, 1938)
Gold Is Where You Find It (WB, 1938)
Saleslady (Mon, 1938)
The First Hundred Years (MGM, 1938)
Long Shot (GN, 1938)
Young Fugitives (Univ, 1938)
Marie Antoinette (MGM, 1938)

The Cowboy and the Lady (UA, 1938)
Reckless Living (Univ, 1938)
Rage of Paris (Univ, 1938)
You Can't Take It with You (Col, 1938)
The Higgins Family (Rep, 1938)
Orphans of the Street (Rep, 1938)
Juarez (WB, 1939)
Made for Each Other (UA, 1939)
My Wife's Relatives (Rep, 1939)
Should Husbands Work? (Rep, 1939)
The Covered Trailer (Rep, 1939)
Tail Spin (20th, 1939)
Money to Burn (Rep, 1939)
The Story of Alexander Graham Bell (20th, 1939)
Gone with the Wind (MGM, 1939)
Exile Express (GN, 1939)
Death of a Champion (Par, 1939)
The Hunchback of Notre Dame (RKO, 1939)
The Story of Dr. Ehrlich's Magic Bullet (WB, 1940)
Granny Get Your Gun (WB, 1940)
All This and Heaven Too (WB, 1940)
Too Many Husbands (Col, 1940)
Grandpa Goes to Town (Rep, 1940)
Earl of Puddlestone (Rep, 1940)
Lucky Partners (RKO, 1940)
Foreign Correspondent (UA, 1940)
I Want a Divorce (Par, 1940)
That Uncertain Feeling (UA, 1941)

I Wanted Wings (Par, 1941)
Meet John Doe (WB, 1941) [cut from release print]
Hurricane Smith (Rep, 1941)
One Foot in Heaven (WB, 1941)
The Bride Came C.O.D. (WB, 1941)
Kings Row (WB, 1941)
Tales of Manhattan (20th, 1942)
Larceny, Inc. (WB, 1942)
Son of Fury (20th, 1942)
Ten Gentlemen from West Point (20th, 1942)
Shantytown (Rep, 1943)
Headin' for God's Country (Rep, 1943)
We've Never Been Licked (Univ, 1943)
Gangway for Tomorrow (RKO, 1943)
The Amazing Mrs. Holliday (Univ, 1943)
Government Girl (RKO, 1943)
Jack London (UA, 1943)
The Ox-Bow Incident (20th, 1943)
Princess O'Rourke (WB, 1943)
Meet Me in St. Louis (MGM, 1944)
The Impatient Years (Col, 1944)
The Thin Man Goes Home (MGM, 1944)
Kismet [TV title: *Oriental Dreams*] (MGM, 1944)
Music for Millions (MGM, 1944)
The Enchanted Forest (PRC, 1945)
Too Young to Know (WB, 1945)
This Love of Ours (Univ, 1945)
Adventure (MGM, 1945)

She Wouldn't Say Yes (Col, 1946)
A Boy, a Girl and a Dog (Film Classics, 1946)
Pardon My Past (Col, 1946)
Courage of Lassie (MGM, 1946)
Blue Skies (Par, 1946)
Faithful in My Fashion (MGM, 1946)
Three Wise Fools (MGM, 1946)
G.I. War Brides (Rep, 1946)
Claudia and David (20th, 1946)
Lady Luck (RKO, 1946)
Stallion Road (WB, 1947)
The Farmer's Daughter (RKO, 1947)
That Hagen Girl (WB, 1947)
The Bachelor and the Bobby-Soxer (RKO, 1947)
Keeper of the Bees (Col, 1947)
Sport of Kings (Col, 1947)
The Fabulous Texan (Rep, 1947)
Three Daring Daughters (MGM, 1948)
The Man from Texas (EL, 1948)
For the Love of Mary (Univ, 1948)
That Lady in Ermine (20th, 1948)
The Decision of Christopher Blake (WB, 1948)
Down to the Sea in Ships (20th, 1949)
Little Women (MGM, 1949)
That Forsyte Woman (MGM, 1949)
Tell It to the Judge (Col, 1949)
Riding High (Par, 1950)

JOHN DAVIDSON

In the 1930s.

Born December 25, 1886, New York City, New York. Died January 15, 1969. A favorite villain of features and serials. Brought a coolness to his interpretation of the lean bad guy.

John Davidson to Robert Strange in *The Adventures of Captain Marvel:* "The men of the hills are gathering. The symbol says that the white men are to be driven from the Valley of Tombs."

Films

Danger Signal (Edison-Kleine, 1915)
The Green Cloak (Edison-Kleine, 1915)
Sentimental Lady (Edison-Kleine, 1915)
The Wall Between (M, 1916)
A Million a Minute (M, 1916)
Pawn of Fate (World, 1916)
Romeo and Juliet (M, 1916)
The Spurs of Sybil (Peerless-World, 1918)
Through the Toils (World, 1919)
Black Circle (World, 1919)
Forest Rivals (World, 1919)
The Genius Pierre (World, 1919)
Cheated Love (Univ, 1921)
The Bronze Bell (Par, 1921)
No Woman Knows (Univ, 1921)
The Idle Rich (M, 1921)
Fool's Paradise (Par, 1921)
Saturday Night (Par, 1922)
The Woman Who Walked Alone (Par, 1922)
Under Two Flags (Univ, 1922)
His Children's Children (Par, 1923)

Monsieur Beaucaire (Par, 1924)
Ramshackle House (PDC, 1924)
The Rescue (UA, 1929)
Queen of the Night Clubs (WB, 1929)
Kid Gloves (Pathé, 1929)
The Time, the Place, the Girl (WB, 1929)
The Thirteenth Chair (MGM, 1929)
Skin Deep (WB, 1929)
Life of the Party (WB, 1930)
Arsene Lupin (MGM, 1932)
Docks of San Francisco (Mayfair, 1932)
Six Hours to Live (Fox, 1932)
Behind Jury Doors (Mayfair, 1932)
The Mad Game (Fox, 1933)
Dinner at Eight (MGM, 1933)
Murder in Trinidad (Fox, 1934)
Hollywood Hoodlum (Regal, 1934)
Bombay Mail (Univ, 1934)
Hold That Girl (Fox, 1934)
The Scarlet Empress (Par, 1934)
Lightning Strikes Twice (RKO, 1934)
Burn 'em Up Barnes (Mascot serial, 1934)

Stand Up and Cheer (Fox, 1934)
Perils of Pauline (Univ serial, 1934)
Tailspin Tommy (Univ serial, 1934)
Call of the Savage (Univ serial, 1935)
Behind Green Lights (Mascot, 1935)
A Shot in the Dark (Chesterfield, 1935)
The Last Days of Pompeii (RKO, 1935)
A Tale of Two Cities (MGM, 1935)
The Fighting Devil Dogs (Rep serial, 1938)
Live, Love and Learn (MGM, 1937)
Mr. Moto Takes a Vacation (20th, 1938)
Arrest Bulldog Drummond! (Par, 1939)
Mr. Moto's Last Warning (20th, 1939)
Devil Bat (PRC, 1940)
Miracles for Sale (MGM, 1939)
King of the Royal Mounted (Rep serial, 1940) [feature version: *The Yukon Patrol*]
The Adventures of Captain Marvel (Rep serial, 1941)
Dick Tracy vs. Crime, Inc. (Rep serial, 1941)

Perils of Nyoka (Rep serial, 1942) [feature version: *Nyoka and the Lost Secrets of Hippocrates*]
Secret Service in Darkest Africa (Rep serial, 1943) [feature version: *The Baron's African War*]
Captain America (Rep serial, 1944)
Call of the Jungle (Mon, 1944)

Charlie Chan in the Chinese Cat (Mon, 1944)
Where Do We Go from Here? (20th, 1945)
The Purple Monster Strikes (Rep serial, 1945)
Sentimental Journey (20th, 1946)
Shock (20th, 1946)
Daisy Kenyon (20th, 1947)

Bungalow 13 (20th, 1948)
The Luck of the Irish (20th, 1948)
A Letter to Three Wives (20th, 1948)
That Wonderful Urge (20th, 1948)
Slattery's Hurricane (20th, 1949)
Oh, You Beautiful Doll! (20th, 1949)
A Gathering of Eagles (Univ, 1963)

WILLIAM B. DAVIDSON

Robert Wilcox, John Howard, and William B. Davidson in Let Them Live! *(1937).*

Born June 16, 1888, Dobbs Ferry, New York. Died September 28, 1947, Santa Monica, California. Whether acting with Ethel Barrymore (*A Modern Cinderella*), Texas Guinan (*Queen of the Night Clubs*), or still later as a frequent Warner Bros. player (of newsmen, judges), offered a crispness of performance. Was Ernest Brown, the Chump, in Mae West's *I'm No Angel*.

William B. Davidson to Lupe Velez in *Laughing Boy:* "There are *lots* of girls who would like to be nice to me."

Films

The White Raven (M, 1917)
A Modern Cinderella (Fox, 1917)
The Call of Her People (M, 1917)
Persuasive Peggy (Mayfair, 1917)
Greatest Power (M, 1917)
Our Little Wife (G, 1918)
Why I Would Not Marry (Fox, 1918)
Friend Husband (G, 1918)
The Capitol (Pathé, 1919)

A Woman There Was (Fox, 1919)
The Lure of Ambition (Fox, 1919)
La Belle Russe (Fox, 1919)
Impossible Catherine (Pathe, 1919)
Partners of the Night (G, 1920)
The Girl from Nowhere (Selznick, 1921)
Conceit (Selznick, 1921)
Destiny's Isle (American Releasing Company, 1922)

Nobody (Associated FN, 1922)
Adam and Eva (Par, 1923)
Salomy Jane (Par, 1923)
The Storm Daughter (Univ, 1924)
Hearts and Spurs (Fox, 1925)
Recompense (WB, 1925)
Ports of Call (Fox, 1925)
Women and Gold (Gotham, 1925)
The Cradle Snatchers (Fox, 1927)

The Last Trail (Fox, 1927)
A Gentleman of Paris (Par, 1927)
Love Makes 'em Wild (Fox, 1927)
The Gaucho (UA, 1928)
Good Morning Judge (Univ, 1928)
The Carnation Kid (Par, 1929)
Woman Trap (Par, 1929)
Painted Faces (Tif, 1929)
Blaze o' Glory (WW, 1929)
Queen of the Night Clubs (WB, 1929)
Men Are Like That (Par, 1930)
For the Defense (Par, 1930)
Hell's Angels (UA, 1930)
A Man from Wyoming (Par, 1930)
Playboy of Paris (Par, 1930)
The Silver Horde (RKO, 1930)
Hook, Line and Sinker (RKO, 1930)
Oh, for a Man! (Fox, 1930)
The Costello Case (WW, 1930)
Scarlet Pages (FN, 1930)
Sunny (FN, 1930)
Captain Applejack (WB, 1931)
The Secret Call (Par, 1931)
Vice Squad (Par, 1931)
Graft (Univ, 1931)
No Limit (Par, 1931)
The Animal Kingdom (RKO, 1932)
Scarface: The Shame of a Nation (UA, 1932)
The Menace (Col, 1932)
Sky Devils (UA, 1932)
Guilty as Hell (Par, 1932)
The Thirteenth Guest (Mon, 1932)
Her Mad Night [a.k.a. *Held for Murder*] (Mayfair, 1932)
Guilty or Not Guilty (Mon, 1932)
The Intruder (Allied, 1932)
I'm No Angel (Par, 1933)
Sitting Pretty (Par, 1933)
Meet the Baron (MGM, 1933)
Lady Killer (WB, 1933)
Torch Singer (Par, 1933)
Billion Dollar Scandal (Par, 1933)
Dangerously Yours (Fox, 1933)
Hello, Everybody! (Par, 1933)
Massacre (FN, 1934)
Fog over Frisco (FN, 1934)
Laughing Boy (MGM, 1934)
The Big Shakedown (FN, 1934)
Housewife (WB, 1934)
Circus Clown (FN, 1934)
Friends of Mr. Sweeney (WB, 1934)
The Dragon Murder Case (WB, 1934)
The Lemon Drop Kid (Par, 1934)
St. Louis Kid (WB, 1934)
The Secret Bride (WB, 1935)
Sweet Music (WB, 1935)
Bordertown (WB, 1935)
Devil Dogs of the Air (WB, 1935)
A Night at the Ritz (WB, 1935)
Oil for the Lamps of China (WB, 1935)
Special Agent (WB, 1935)
Dangerous (WB, 1935)

Go into Your Dance (WB, 1935)
The Crusades (Par, 1935)
In Caliente (WB, 1935)
Woman Wanted (MGM, 1935)
Show Them No Mercy (Fox, 1935)
Bright Lights (FN, 1935)
The Man Who Reclaimed His Head (Univ, 1935)
Satan Met a Lady (WB, 1936)
Road Gang (WB, 1936)
Fatal Lady (Par, 1936)
The Singing Kid (FN, 1936)
Murder by an Aristocrat (FN, 1936)
The Big Noise (WB, 1936)
Earthworm Tractors (WB, 1936)
Gold Diggers of 1937 (WB, 1936)
Mind Your Own Business (Par, 1936)
It Happened in Hollywood (Col, 1937)
Marked Woman (WB, 1937)
Midnight Court (WB, 1937)
Ever Since Eve (WB, 1937)
The Hurricane (UA, 1937)
Marry the Girl (WB, 1937)
Melody for Two (WB, 1937)
Hollywood Hotel (WB, 1937)
Let Them Live! (Univ, 1937)
The Road Back (Univ, 1937)
The Affairs of Cappy Ricks (Rep, 1937)
Paradise Isle (Mon, 1937)
Something to Sing About (GN, 1937)
Easy Living (Par, 1937)
Behind the Mike (Univ, 1937)
Sergeant Murphy (WB, 1938)
Love on Toast (Par, 1938)
The Jury's Secret (Univ, 1938)
Cocoanut Grove (Par, 1938)
Mr. Doodle Kicks Off (RKO, 1938)
Illegal Traffic (Univ, 1938)
Blockade (UA, 1938)
The Cowboy from Brooklyn (WB, 1938)
Letter of Introduction (Univ, 1938)
Wings of the Navy (WB, 1939)
They Made Me a Criminal (WB, 1939)
On Trial (WB, 1939)
Off the Record (WB, 1939)
Indianapolis Speedway (WB, 1939)
Dust Be My Destiny (WB, 1939)
Private Detective (WB, 1939)
Hidden Power (Col, 1939)
Each Dawn I Die (WB, 1939)
Smashing the Money Ring (WB, 1939)
Honeymoon in Bali (Par, 1939)
The Honeymoon's Over (20th, 1939)
Tin Pan Alley (20th, 1940)
Three Cheers for the Irish (WB, 1940)
Florian (MGM, 1940)
Lillian Russell (20th, 1940)
Half a Sinner (Univ, 1940)
My Love Came Back (WB, 1940)
The Girl in 313 (20th, 1940)
Sailor's Lady (20th, 1940)
Maryland (20th, 1940)
Hired Wife (Univ, 1940)

Seven Sinners (Univ, 1940)
A Night at Earl Carroll's (Par, 1940)
Sandy Gets Her Man (Univ, 1940)
My Little Chickadee (Univ, 1940)
San Francisco Docks (Univ, 1940)
The Lady with Red Hair (WB, 1940)
Three Girls About Town (Col, 1941)
Man-Made Monster (Univ, 1941)
In the Navy (Univ, 1941)
The Lady from Cheyenne (Univ, 1941)
Thieves Fall Out (WB, 1941)
Sun Valley Serenade (20th, 1941)
Hold That Ghost (Univ, 1941)
Highway West (WB, 1941)
Three Sons o' Guns (WB, 1941)
Keep 'em Flying (Univ, 1941)
The Male Animal (WB, 1942)
Tennessee Johnson (MGM, 1942)
In This Our Life (WB, 1942)
Juke Girl (WB, 1942)
The Affairs of Jimmy Valentine [a.k.a. *Unforgotten Crime*] (Rep, 1942)
Larceny, Inc. (WB, 1942)
The Magnificent Dope (20th, 1942)
Careful, Soft Shoulders (20th, 1942)
Over My Dead Body (20th, 1942)
Truck Busters (WB, 1943)
Mission to Moscow (WB, 1943)
Murder on the Waterfront (WB, 1943)
Calaboose (UA, 1943)
The Good Fellows (Par, 1943)
Hers to Hold (Univ, 1943)
In Old Oklahoma [a.k.a. *War of the Wildcats*] (Rep, 1943)
Up in Arms (RKO, 1944)
San Diego, I Love You (Univ, 1944)
Make Your Own Bed (WB, 1944)
Greenwich Village (20th, 1944)
The Imposter [a.k.a. *Bayonet Charge*] (Univ, 1944)
In Society (Univ, 1944)
Shine On Harvest Moon (WB, 1944)
Allergic to Love (Univ, 1944)
Song of Nevada (Rep, 1944)
Since You Went Away (UA, 1944)
Blonde Ransom (Univ, 1945)
Circumstantial Evidence (20th, 1945)
The Man Who Walked Alone (PRC, 1945)
See My Lawyer (Univ, 1945)
Tell It to a Star (Rep, 1945)
They Were Expendable (MGM, 1945)
Lover Come Back (Univ, 1946)
My Darling Clementine (20th, 1946)
The Cat Creeps (Univ, 1946)
Ding Dong Williams (RKO, 1946)
The Notorious Lone Wolf (Col, 1946)
The Plainsman and the Lady (Rep, 1946)
Dick Tracy's Dilemma (RKO, 1947)
The Farmer's Daughter (RKO, 1947)
That's My Man (Rep, 1947)
My Wild Irish Rose (WB, 1947)
That Hagen Girl (WB, 1947)

NIGEL DE BRULIER

Nazimova and Nigel de Brulier in A Doll's House *(1922).*

Born 1878, England. Died January 30, 1948. British actor. Impressive career in silents: *The Four Horsemen of the Apocalypse* (Tchernoff), *The Three Musketeers* (Richelieu), *The Hunchback of Notre Dame* (Dom Claude), *Ben-Hur* (Simonides). Career diminished to bits as talkies emerged. Played Shazam, the Giver of Power to Billy Batson in the serial *The Adventures of Captain Marvel*.

Nigel De Brulier to Warner Oland in *Charlie Chan in Egypt:*
"The gods of Egypt are powerful gods. Their vengeance
has taken Professor Arnold, and now his son."

Films

Ghosts (Mutual, 1915)
Intolerance (Wark, 1916)
The Kaiser—The Beast of Berlin (Univ, 1918)
Sahara (Hodkinson, 1919)
Boomerang (National Pioneer, 1919)
Flames of the Flesh (Fox, 1919)
The Dwelling Place of Light (Hodkinson, 1920)
The Mystery of 13 (Burston Films serial, 1920)
The Virgin of Stamboul (Univ, 1920)
The Mother of His Children (Fox, 1920)
Without Benefit of Clergy (Pathé, 1921)

The Four Horsemen of the Apocalypse (M, 1921)
That Something (Celebrated Players Film Corp, 1921)
His Pajama Girl (C. B. Price, 1921)
Cold Steel (Robertson-Cole, 1921)
The Three Musketeers (UA, 1921)
The Devil Within (Fox, 1921)
A Doll's House (UA, 1922)
Omar, the Tentmaker (Associated FN, 1922)
Salome (Allied, 1922)
Rupert of Hentzau (Selznick, 1923)
The Eleventh Hour (Fox, 1923)

The Hunchback of Notre Dame (Univ, 1923)
St. Elmo (Fox, 1923)
Wild Oranges (G, 1924)
Three Weeks (G, 1924)
A Boy of Flanders (MG, 1924)
Mademoiselle Midnight (MG, 1924)
The Ancient Mariner (Fox, 1925)
Ben-Hur (MGM, 1925)
A Regular Fellow (Par, 1925)
Yellow Fingers (Fox, 1926)
The Greater Glory (FN, 1926)
Don Juan (WB, 1926)
Wings (Par, 1927)

The Beloved Rogue (UA, 1927)
The Patent Leather Kid (FN, 1927)
Soft Cushions (Par, 1927)
Surrender (Univ, 1927)
Two Lovers (UA, 1928)
Loves of an Actress (Par, 1928)
Divine Sinner (Rayart, 1928)
Me, Gangster (Fox, 1928)
The Gaucho (UA, 1928)
Noah's Ark (WB, 1929)
The Iron Mask (UA, 1929)
Thru Different Eyes (Fox, 1929)
The Wheel of Life (Par, 1929)
The Green Goddess (WB, 1929)
Redemption (MGM, 1930)
Golden Dawn (WB, 1930)

Moby Dick (WB, 1930)
Son of India (MGM, 1931)
Miss Pinkerton (FN, 1932)
Rasputin and the Empress (MGM, 1932)
I'm No Angel (Par, 1933)
Life in the Raw (Fox, 1933)
Charlie Chan in Egypt (Fox, 1935)
The Three Musketeers (RKO, 1935)
The Garden of Allah (UA, 1936)
Half Angel (20th, 1936)
Down to the Sea (Rep, 1936)
Mary of Scotland (RKO, 1936)
The White Legion (GN, 1936)
The Californian (20th, 1937)
Zorro Rides Again (Rep serial, 1937)
Marie Antoinette (MGM, 1938)

The Man in the Iron Mask (UA, 1939)
The Mad Empress (WB, 1939)
Heaven with a Barbed Wire Fence (20th, 1939)
The Hound of the Baskervilles (20th, 1939)
Juarez (WB, 1939)
Mutiny in the Big House (Mon, 1939)
Viva Cisco Kid! (20th, 1940)
One Million B.C. (UA, 1940)
For Beauty's Sake (20th, 1941)
The Adventures of Captain Marvel (Rep serial, 1941)
Tonight We Raid Calais (20th, 1943)
Adventures of Smilin' Jack (Univ serial, 1943)

ROSEMARY DE CAMP

Helen Brown, Bruce Bennett, Wanda Hendrix, Rosemary De Camp, Robert Arthur, and Kent Smith in Nora Prentiss (1947).

Born November 14, 1914, Prescott, Arizona. Married John Shidler (1941), children: Margaret, Martha, Valerie, Nita. Specialized in drab mother types from a still youthful age, giving warmth and integrity to her impersonations: Robert Alda and Herbert Rudley's mother (Rhapsody in Blue), Doris Day's mother (Look for the Silver Lining and By the Light of the Silvery Moon), Kathryn Grayson's mother (So This Is Love). Long-suffering wife of Chester A. Riley (William Bendix) in feature version of The Life of Riley. TV series: "The Life of Riley" (married to title figure Jackie Gleason), "Love That Bob" (Bob Cummings' widowed sister), "That Girl" (Marlo Thomas' mother), and "The Partridge Family" (Shirley Jones' mother). Video spokeswoman for 20 Mule Team Borax on "Death Valley Days."

Rosemary De Camp to Walter Huston in *Yankee Doodle Dandy:* "Not on the hand. He has to play the violin."

Films

Cheers for Miss Bishop (UA, 1941)
The Wagons Roll at Night (WB, 1941)
Hold Back the Dawn (Par, 1941)
Commandos Strike at Dawn (Col, 1942)
Jungle Book (UA, 1942)
Yankee Doodle Dandy (WB, 1942)
Eyes in the Night (MGM, 1942)
Smith of Minnesota (Col, 1942)
This Is the Army (WB, 1943)
The Merry Monahans (Univ, 1944)
Bowery to Broadway (Univ, 1944)
Practically Yours (Par, 1944)
Pride of the Marines (WB, 1945)

Rhapsody in Blue (WB, 1945)
Danger Signal (WB, 1945)
Too Young to Know (WB, 1945)
Blood on the Sun (UA, 1945)
Week-End at the Waldorf (MGM, 1945)
From This Day Forward (RKO, 1946)
Two Guys from Milwaukee (WB, 1946)
Nora Prentiss (WB, 1947)
Night unto Night (WB, 1949)
The Life of Riley (Univ, 1949)
Look for the Silver Lining (WB, 1949)
The Story of Seabiscuit (WB, 1949)
The Big Hangover (MGM, 1950)

On Moonlight Bay (WB, 1951)
Night into Morning (MGM, 1951)
Scandal Sheet (Col, 1952)
Treasure of Lost Canyon (Univ, 1952)
By the Light of the Silvery Moon (WB, 1953)
Main Street to Broadway (MGM, 1953)
So This Is Love (WB, 1953)
Many Rivers to Cross (MGM, 1955)
Strategic Air Command (Par, 1955)
Thirteen Ghosts (Col, 1960)

TED DE CORSIA

In Gun Battle at Monterey *(1957).*

Born September 29, 1903, Brooklyn, New York. Married 1) Mary Robertson; divorced (1935); 2) Rachel Thurber (1939), children: two daughters; widowed. Died April 12, 1973, Encino, California. Thickly built interpreter of criminal roles, whether as wrongdoer Sidney Broome *(The Lady from Shanghai)*, corrupt cop Randy Kennan *(The Killing)*, the vicious Kumlek *(The Conqueror)*, or assorted other brutish thugs.

Ted de Corsia to Merry Anders in *The Quick Gun:* "In case anyone starts dealin' from the bottom of the deck, my men here ain't got no religion about killin' a woman."

164

Films

The Lady from Shanghai (Col, 1948)
The Naked City (Univ, 1948)
It Happens Every Spring (20th, 1949)
Neptune's Daughter (MGM, 1949)
Mr. Soft Touch (Col, 1949)
The Life of Riley (Univ, 1949)
The Outriders (MGM, 1950)
Cargo to Capetown (Col, 1950)
Three Secrets (WB, 1950)
The Enforcer (WB, 1951)
Vengeance Valley (MGM, 1951)
New Mexico (UA, 1951)
Inside the Walls of Folsom Prison (WB, 1951)
A Place in the Sun (Par, 1951)
Captain Pirate (Col, 1952)
The Turning Point (Par, 1952)
The Savage (Par, 1952)
Man in the Dark (Col, 1953)

Ride, Vaquero! (MGM, 1953)
Hot News (AA, 1953)
Crime Wave (WB, 1954)
20,000 Leagues Under the Sea (BV, 1954)
The Big Combo (AA, 1955)
Man with the Gun (UA, 1955)
Kismet (MGM, 1955)
The Conqueror (RKO, 1956)
The Kettles in the Ozarks (Univ, 1956)
The Steel Jungle (WB, 1956)
Slightly Scarlet (RKO, 1956)
Mohawk (20th, 1956)
The Killing (UA, 1956)
Showdown at Abilene (Univ, 1956)
Dance with Me, Henry (UA, 1956)
Gunfight at the OK Corral (Par, 1957)
The Midnight Story (Univ, 1957)
The Lawless Eighties (Rep, 1957)
The Joker Is Wild (Par, 1957)

Gun Battle at Monterey (AA, 1957)
Baby Face Nelson (UA, 1957)
Man on the Prowl (UA, 1957)
Handle with Care (MGM, 1958)
Enchanted Island (WB, 1958)
The Buccaneer (Par, 1958)
Inside the Mafia (UA, 1959)
Oklahoma Territory (UA, 1960)
Noose for a Gunman (UA, 1960)
From the Terrace (20th, 1960)
Spartacus (Univ, 1960)
Blood on the Arrow (AA, 1964)
The Quick Gun (Col, 1964)
Nevada Smith (Par, 1966)
The King's Pirate (Univ, 1967)
Five Card Stud (Par, 1968)
The Outside Man (UA, 1973)

JOHN DEHNER
(John Forkum)

Randolph Scott and John Dehner (center) in Tall Man Riding *(1955).*

Born February 10, 1915, New York City, New York. Married _____, children: two. Sharply handsome features and well-modulated voice made his heavy roles a standout, whether in low-budget Westerns or inexpensive costumed films. Played Pat Garrett to Paul Newman's Billy the Kid in *The Left-Handed Gun*; later seen in such well-mounted claptraps as *The Chapman Report* (Glynis Johns' unique husband), *Youngblood Hawke* (James Franciscus' dishonest uncle), etc. TV series: "The Roaring 20s," "The Doris Day Show" (her editor-boss Cyril Bennett), "The Virginian" (Starr, a ranch hand), and "Temperatures Rising."

John Dehner to Rory Calhoun in *Apache Territory*: "A good commander never leaves his post under fire."

Films

Captain Eddie (20th, 1945)
Club Havana (PRC, 1945)
State Fair (20th, 1945)
The Corn Is Green (WB, 1945)
Christmas in Connecticut (WB, 1945)
She Went to the Races (MGM, 1945)
The Searching Wind (Par, 1946)
The Undercover Woman (Rep, 1946)
Catman of Paris (Rep, 1946)
The Last Crooked Mile (Rep, 1946)
Out California Way (Rep, 1946)
Vigilantes of Boomtown (Rep, 1947)
Blonde Savage (EL, 1947)
Prejudice (New World, 1949)
Secret of St. Ives (Col, 1949)
Kazan (Col, 1949)
Bandits of El Dorado (Col, 1949)
Horsemen of the Sierras (Col, 1949)
Feudin' Rhythm (Col, 1949)
Barbary Pirate (Col, 1949)
Captive Girl (Col, 1950)
Backfire (WB, 1950)
Dynamite Pass (RKO, 1950)
David Harding—Counterspy (Col, 1950)
Destination Murder (RKO, 1950)
Texas Dynamo (Col, 1950)
Rogues of Sherwood Forest (Col, 1950)
Bodyhold (Col, 1950)
Mary Ryan, Detective (Col, 1950)
Counterspy Meets Scotland Yard (Col, 1950)
Last of the Buccaneers (Col, 1950)
Al Jennings of Oklahoma (Col, 1951)

China Corsair (Col, 1951)
When the Redskins Rode (Col, 1951)
Lorna Doone (Col, 1951)
The Texas Rangers (Col, 1951)
Fort Savage Raiders (Col, 1951)
Corky of Gasoline Alley (Col, 1951)
Ten Tall Men (Col, 1951)
Hot Lead (Col, 1951)
Scaramouche (MGM, 1952)
Aladdin and His Lamp (Mon, 1952)
Harem Girl (Col, 1952)
Desert Passage (RKO, 1952)
California Conquest (Col, 1952)
Junction City (Col, 1952)
Cripple Creek (Col, 1952)
Plymouth Adventure (MGM, 1952)
The Steel Lady (UA, 1953)
Man on a Tightrope (20th, 1953)
Powder River (20th, 1953)
Fort Algiers (UA, 1953)
Gun Belt (UA, 1953)
The Cowboy (Lip, 1954) [narrator]
Apache (UA, 1954)
The Bowery Boys Meet the Monsters (AA, 1954)
Southwest Passage (UA, 1954)
The Man from Bitter Ridge (Univ, 1955)
The Prodigal (MGM, 1955)
Tall Man Riding (WB, 1955)
The Scarlet Coat (MGM, 1955)
The King's Thief (MGM, 1955)
Duel on the Mississippi (Col, 1955)
Top Gun (UA, 1955)

Carousel (20th, 1956)
Please Murder Me (DCA, 1956)
A Day of Fury (Univ, 1956)
Terror at Midnight (Rep, 1956)
The Fastest Gun Alive (MGM, 1956)
Tension at Table Rock (RKO, 1956)
Revolt at Fort Laramie (UA, 1957)
The Iron Sheriff (UA, 1957)
Trooper Hook (UA, 1957)
The Girl in Black Stockings (UA, 1957)
The Left-Handed Gun (WB, 1958)
Apache Territory (Col, 1958)
Man of the West (UA, 1958)
Cast a Long Shadow (UA, 1959)
Timbuktu (UA, 1959)
The Sign of Zorro (BV, 1960)
The Canadians (20th, 1961)
The Chapman Report (WB, 1962)
Critic's Choice (WB, 1963)
Youngblood Hawke (WB, 1964)
The Hallelujah Trail (UA, 1965) [narrator]
Support Your Local Gunfighter (UA, 1971)
Slaughterhouse-Five (Univ, 1972)
The Day of the Dolphin (Avco Emb, 1973)
The Killer Inside Me (WB, 1976)
Guardian of the Wilderness (Sunn Classic Pictures, 1976)
Fun with Dick and Jane (Col, 1977)
The Lincoln Conspiracy (Sunn Classic Pictures, 1977)

ALBERT DEKKER

With Constance Bennett in As Young As You Feel *(1951).*

Born December 20, 1905, Brooklyn, New York. Married Esther Guerini (1929), children: Jan, John, Benjamin; divorced. Died May 5, 1968, Hollywood, California. Consummate performer who was a bad guy on camera from almost the start: Provence *(Marie Antoinette)*. Established his forte for malfeasance playing the bespectacled *Dr. Cyclops,* the demented scientist who reduces his victims to doll size. Always up to no good, squinting his eyes, smirking beneath his moustache, and twisting any situation to his advantage, whether in Westerns *(Honky Tonk, In Old Oklahoma, The Kansan),* comedies *(Hold That Blonde),* or adventure yarns *(Two Years Before the Mast).*

Albert Dekker to Paul Fix in *Dr. Cyclops:* "Are you forgetting who is master and who is pupil?"

Films

The Great Garrick (WB, 1937)
Marie Antoinette (MGM, 1938)
The Last Warning (Univ, 1938)
She Married an Artist (Col, 1938)
The Lone Wolf in Paris (Col, 1938)
Extortion (Col, 1938)
Paris Honeymoon (Par, 1939)
Never Say Die (Par, 1939)
Hotel Imperial (Par, 1939)
Beau Geste (Par, 1939)
The Man in the Iron Mask (UA, 1939)
The Great Commandment (20th, 1939)
Dr. Cyclops (Par, 1940)
Strange Cargo (MGM, 1940)
Rangers of Fortune (Par, 1940)
Seven Sinners ((Univ, 1940)
You're the One (Par, 1941)
Blonde Inspiration (MGM, 1941)
Reaching for the Sun (Par, 1941)
Buy Me That Town (Par, 1941)
Honky Tonk (MGM, 1941)

Among the Living (Par, 1941)
Night in New Orleans (Par, 1942)
Wake Island (Par, 1942)
Once upon a Honeymoon (RKO, 1942)
Star Spangled Rhythm (Par, 1942)
The Lady Has Plans (Par, 1942)
In Old California (Rep, 1942)
Yokel Boy (Par, 1942)
The Forest Rangers (Par, 1942)
The Woman of the Town (UA, 1943)
In Old Oklahoma [a.k.a. *War of the Wild-cats*] (Rep, 1943)
Buckskin Frontier (UA, 1943)
The Kansan (UA, 1943)
Experiment Perilous (RKO, 1944)
The Hitler Gang (Par, 1944) [narrator]
Incendiary Blonde (Par, 1945)
Hold That Blonde (Par, 1945)
Salome, Where She Danced (Univ, 1945)
Two Years Before the Mast (Par, 1946)
The French Key (Rep, 1946)

The Killers (Univ, 1946)
California (Par, 1946)
Suspense (Mon, 1946)
The Pretender (Rep, 1947)
Gentleman's Agreement (20th, 1947)
Wyoming (Rep, 1947)
Cass Timberlane (MGM, 1947)
Slave Girl (Univ, 1947)
The Fabulous Texan (Rep, 1947)
Fury at Furnace Creek (20th, 1948)
Lulu Belle (Col, 1948)
Search for Danger (Film Classics, 1949)
Bride of Vengeance (Par, 1949)
Tarzan's Magic Fountain (RKO, 1949)
The Kid from Texas (Univ, 1950)
Destination Murder (RKO, 1950)
The Furies (Par, 1950)
As Young As You Feel (20th, 1951)
Wait Till the Sun Shines, Nellie (20th, 1952)
The Silver Chalice (WB, 1954)

ANDY DEVINE

With Phyllis Fraser in Fighting Youth *(1935).*

Born October 7, 1905, Flagstaff, Arizona. Married Dorothy House (1933), children: Denny, Ted. Died February 20, 1977, Orange, California. Heavyset jovial individual whose gravelly voice made him a distinctive player in talkies. Donned tights to play Peter in Norma Shearer's *Romeo and Juliet*, was Buck the driver in *Stagecoach*, and joined with Richard Arlen in some low-budget actioners at Universal (*Hot Steel*, *Men of the Timberland*, etc.). Supplied comedy relief for many a picture, including Maria Montez's *Ali Baba and the Forty Thieves*. TV series: "Wild Bill Hickok" (as the oversized Jingles forever screaming, "Bill, wait for me"), "Andy's Gang" (as the host), and "Flipper."

> **Andy Devine** to Fay Holden in *Double or Nothing:* "I don't like radium—all you get is a lot of static and too much advertising."

Films

We Americans (Univ, 1928)
Red Lips (Univ, 1928)
Lonesome (Univ, 1928)
Naughty Baby (FN, 1929)
Hot Stuff (FN, 1929)
The Criminal Code (Col, 1930)
Spirit of Notre Dame (Univ, 1931)
Danger Island (Univ serial, 1931)
Law and Order (Univ, 1932)
Impatient Maiden (Univ, 1932)
Man Wanted (WB, 1932)
Man from Yesterday (Par, 1932)
Radio Patrol (Univ, 1932)
Tom Brown of Culver (Univ, 1932)
Three Wise Girls (Col, 1932)
Fast Companions (Univ, 1932)

The All-American (Univ, 1932)
Destry Rides Again (Univ, 1932)
The Information Kid (Univ, 1932)
The Cohens and Kellys in Trouble (Univ, 1933)
Saturday's Children (Univ, 1933)
Song of the Eagle (Par, 1933)
Midnight Mary (MGM, 1933)
Chance at Heaven (RKO, 1933)
Dr. Bull (Fox, 1933)
The Big Cage (Univ, 1933)
The Poor Rich (Univ, 1934)
Let's Talk It Over (Univ, 1934)
Upper World (WB, 1934)
Wake Up and Dream (Univ, 1934)
Stingaree (RKO, 1934)

Hell in the Heavens (Fox, 1934)
Gift of Gab (Univ, 1934)
Million Dollar Ransom (Univ, 1934)
The President Vanishes (Par, 1934)
Hold 'em Yale (Par, 1935)
Straight from the Heart (Univ, 1935)
Chinatown Squad (Univ, 1935)
Fighting Youth (Univ, 1935)
The Farmer Takes a Wife (Fox, 1935)
Way Down East (Fox, 1935)
Coronado (Par, 1935)
Small Town Girl (MGM, 1936)
Romeo and Juliet (MGM, 1936)
Yellowstone (Univ, 1936)
Flying Hostess (Univ, 1936)
The Big Game (RKO, 1936)

Mysterious Crossing (Univ, 1937)
The Road Back (Univ, 1937)
You're a Sweetheart (Univ, 1937)
A Star Is Born (UA, 1937)
Double or Nothing (Par, 1937)
In Old Chicago (20th, 1938)
The Storm (Univ, 1938)
Strange Faces (Univ, 1938)
Swing That Cheer (Univ, 1938)
Dr. Rhythm (Par, 1938)
Men with Wings (Par, 1938)
Yellow Jack (MGM, 1938)
Personal Secretary (Univ, 1938)
Never Say Die (Par, 1939)
Stagecoach (UA, 1939)
Mutiny on the Blackhawk (Univ, 1939)
The Spirit of Culver (Univ, 1939)
Tropic Fury (Univ, 1939)
Legion of Lost Flyers (Univ, 1939)
Geronimo (Par, 1939)
Trail of the Vigilantes (Univ, 1940)
Little Old New York (20th, 1940)
Buck Benny Rides Again (Par, 1940)
Torrid Zone (WB, 1940)
Hot Steel (Univ, 1940)
Black Diamonds (Univ, 1940)
The Man from Montreal (Univ, 1940)
Danger on Wheels (Univ, 1940)
When the Daltons Rode (Univ, 1940)
The Leather Pushers (Univ, 1940)
The Devil's Pipeline (Univ, 1940)
Flame of New Orleans (Univ, 1941)
Mutiny in the Arctic (Univ, 1941)
Lucky Devils (Univ, 1941)
Raiders of the Desert (Univ, 1941)
Badlands of Dakota (Univ, 1941)
A Dangerous Game (Univ, 1941)

South of Tahiti (Univ, 1941)
Road Agent (Univ, 1941)
The Kid from Kansas (Univ, 1941)
Men of the Timberland (Univ, 1941)
Top Sergeant (Univ, 1942)
Timber (Univ, 1942)
North to the Klondike (Univ, 1942)
Unseen Enemy (Univ, 1942)
Escape from Hong Kong (Univ, 1942)
Between Us Girls (Univ, 1942)
Danger in the Pacific (Univ, 1942)
Sin Town (Univ, 1942)
Rhythm of the Islands (Univ, 1943)
Corvette K-225 (Univ, 1943)
Crazy House (Univ, 1943)
Frontier Badmen (Univ, 1943)
Ali Baba and the Forty Thieves (Univ, 1944)
The Ghost Catchers (Univ, 1944)
Follow the Boys (Univ, 1944)
Babes on Swing Street (Univ, 1944)
Bowery to Broadway (Univ, 1944)
Sudan (Univ, 1945)
Frontier Gal (Univ, 1945)
That's the Spirit (Univ, 1945)
Frisco Sal (Univ, 1945)
Canyon Passage (Univ, 1946)
The Michigan Kid (Univ, 1947)
The Vigilantes Return (Univ, 1947)
Bells of San Angelo (Rep, 1947)
Springtime in the Sierras (Rep, 1947)
The Fabulous Texan (Rep, 1947)
The Marauders (UA, 1947)
Slave Girl (Univ, 1947)
On the Old Spanish Trail (Rep, 1947)
The Gallant Legion (Rep, 1948)
The Gay Ranchero (Rep, 1948)

Old Los Angeles (Rep, 1948)
Under California Stars (Rep, 1948)
Eyes of Texas (Rep, 1948)
Grand Canyon Trail (Rep, 1948)
Night-Time in Nevada (Rep, 1948)
The Far Frontier (Rep, 1948)
The Last Bandit (Rep, 1949)
The Traveling Saleswoman (Col, 1950)
Never a Dull Moment (RKO, 1950)
Slaughter Trail (RKO, 1951)
New Mexico (UA, 1951)
The Red Badge of Courage (MGM, 1951)
Montana Belle (RKO, 1952)
Island in the Sky (WB, 1953)
Thunder Pass (Lip, 1954)
Pete Kelly's Blues (WB, 1955)
Around the World in 80 Days (UA, 1956)
The Adventures of Huckleberry Finn (MGM, 1960)
Two Rode Together (Col, 1961)
The Man Who Shot Liberty Valance (Par, 1962)
How the West Was Won (MGM, 1962)
It's a Mad, Mad, Mad, Mad World (UA, 1963)
Zebra in the Kitchen (MGM, 1965)
Ballad of Josie (Univ, 1967)
The Road Hustlers (AIP, 1968)
Myra Breckinridge (20th, 1970)
The Phynx (WB, 1970)
Robin Hood (BV, 1973) [voice only]
Won Ton Ton, the Dog Who Saved Hollywood (Par, 1976)
The Mouse and His Child (Sanrio Films, 1977) [voice only]

East of Eden (WB, 1955)	Suddenly, Last Summer (Col, 1959)	Come Spy with Me (20th, 1967)
Kiss Me Deadly (UA, 1955)	The Sound and the Fury (20th, 1959)	Gammera, the Invincible (World Enter-
Illegal (WB, 1955)	These Thousand Hills (20th, 1959)	tainment Corp, 1968)
She Devil (20th, 1957)	Middle of the Night (Col, 1959)	The Wild Bunch (WB-7 Arts, 1969)
Machete (UA, 1958)	The Wonderful Country (UA, 1959)	

WILLIAM DEMAREST

In The Blazing Forest *(1952).*

Born February 27, 1894, St. Paul, Minnesota. Married 1) Estelle Collette; 2) Lucille Thayer (1939). Long-time stage performer who excelled at the deadpan look of suspicion and exasperation. Made an enduring contribution as a member of Preston Sturges' comedy stock company at Paramount: especially remembered as Officer Kockenlocker, father of Betty Hutton and Diana Lynn in the zany *The Miracle of Morgan's Creek*. Nominated for BSAAA for *The Jolson Story* as the star's old burlesque pal, but lost to Harold Russell of *The Best Years of Our Lives*. Most recently the hip clergyman in *The Wild McCullochs*. TV series: "Wells Fargo," "Love and Marriage," and "My Three Sons" (as Uncle Charley).

William Demarest to Cliff Clark in *Miracles for Sale:* "Even dead guys disappear on us. I don't like this magic stuff."

Films

When the Wife's Away (Col, 1926)
Finger Prints (WB, 1927)
Don't Tell the Wife (WB, 1927)
The Gay Old Bird (WB, 1927)
Matinee Ladies (WB, 1927)
A Million Bid (WB, 1927)
Simple Sis (WB, 1927)
What Happened to Father (WB, 1927)
The Black Diamond Express (WB, 1927)
The First Auto (WB, 1927)
The Bush Leaguer (WB, 1927)
A Sailor's Sweetheart (WB, 1927)
The Jazz Singer (WB, 1927)
A Reno Divorce (WB, 1927)
Sharp Shooters (Fox, 1928)
The Escape (Fox, 1928)
Pay As You Enter (WB, 1928)
The Butter and Egg Man (FN, 1928)
The Crash (FN, 1928)
5 and 10 Cent Annie (WB, 1928)
A Girl in Every Port (Fox, 1928) [cut
  from release print]
Many Happy Returns (Par, 1934)
Fog over Frisco (FN, 1934)
White Lies (Col, 1934)
Circus Clown (FN, 1934)
Fugitive Lady (Col, 1934)
Diamond Jim (Univ, 1935)
Murder Man (MGM, 1935)
Bright Lights (FN, 1935)
Hands Across the Table (Par, 1935)
Wedding Present (Par, 1936)
Mind Your Own Business (Par, 1936)
Love on the Run (MGM, 1936)
Charlie Chan at the Opera (20th, 1936)
Time Out for Romance (20th, 1937)
Don't Tell the Wife (RKO, 1937)
The Great Hospital Mystery (20th, 1937)
Wake Up and Live (20th, 1937)
The Hit Parade (Rep, 1937)
Oh, Doctor! (Univ, 1937)
Easy Living (Par, 1937)
The Great Gambini (Par, 1937)
Blonde Trouble (Par, 1937)
The Big City (MGM, 1937)
Rosalie (MGM, 1937)
Rebecca of Sunnybrook Farm (20th, 1938)
One Wild Night (20th, 1938)
Josette (20th, 1938)
While New York Sleeps (20th, 1938)

Peck's Bad Boy with the Circus (RKO,
  1938)
Romance on the Run (Rep, 1938)
King of the Turf (UA, 1939)
The Gracie Allen Murder Case (Par,
  1939)
The Great Man Votes (RKO, 1939)
The Cowboy Quarterback (WB, 1939)
Miracles for Sale (MGM, 1939)
Mr. Smith Goes to Washington (Col,
  1939)
Laugh It Off (Univ, 1939)
Wolf of New York (Rep, 1940)
Tin Pan Alley (20th, 1940)
Little Men (RKO, 1940)
The Farmer's Daughter (Par, 1940)
The Great McGinty (Par, 1940)
Comin' 'Round the Mountain (Par, 1940)
Christmas in July (Par, 1940)
The Golden Fleecing (MGM, 1940)
The Lady Eve (Par, 1941)
Ride On, Vaquero (20th, 1941)
Glamour Boy (Par, 1941)
Dressed to Kill (20th, 1941)
Rookies on Parade (Rep, 1941)
Country Fair (Rep, 1941)
The Devil and Miss Jones (RKO, 1941)
Sullivan's Travels (Par, 1941)
Pardon My Sarong (Univ, 1942)
The Palm Beach Story (Par, 1942)
All Through the Night (WB, 1942)
True to the Army (Par, 1942)
My Favorite Spy (RKO, 1942)
Behind the Eight Ball (Univ, 1942)
Life Begins at 8:30 (20th, 1942)
Johnny Doughboy (Rep, 1942)
True to Life (Par, 1943)
Dangerous Blondes (Col, 1943)
Stage Door Canteen (UA, 1943)
The Great Moment (Par, 1944)
Hail the Conquering Hero (Par, 1944)
The Miracle of Morgan's Creek (Par,
  1944)
Nine Girls (Col, 1944)
Once upon a Time (Col, 1944)
Salty O'Rourke (Par, 1945)
Duffy's Tavern (Par, 1945)
Along Came Jones (RKO, 1945)
Pardon My Past (Col, 1946)
The Jolson Story (Col, 1946)

Our Hearts Were Growing Up (Par,
  1946)
Perils of Pauline (Par, 1947)
Variety Girl (Par, 1947)
On Our Merry Way [a.k.a. A Miracle
  Can Happen] (UA, 1948)
The Sainted Sisters (Par, 1948)
Night Has a Thousand Eyes (Par, 1948)
Whispering Smith (Par, 1948)
Jolson Sings Again (Col, 1949)
Sorrowful Jones (Par, 1949)
Red, Hot and Blue (Par, 1949)
When Willie Comes Marching Home
  (20th, 1950)
Riding High (Par, 1950)
He's a Cockeyed Wonder (Col, 1950)
Never a Dull Moment (RKO, 1950)
The First Legion (UA, 1951)
Excuse My Dust (MGM, 1951)
Behave Yourself! (RKO, 1951)
The Strip (MGM, 1951)
The Blazing Forest (Par, 1952)
What Price Glory? (20th, 1952)
The Lady Wants Mink (Rep, 1953)
Dangerous When Wet (MGM, 1953)
Escape from Fort Bravo (MGM, 1953)
Here Come the Girls (Par, 1953)
Yellow Mountain (Univ, 1954)
The Far Horizons (Par, 1955)
Jupiter's Darling (MGM, 1955)
The Private War of Major Benson (Univ,
  1955)
Sincerely Yours (WB, 1955)
Hell on Frisco Bay (WB, 1955)
Lucy Gallant (Par, 1955)
The Rawhide Years (Univ, 1956)
The Mountain (Par, 1956)
Pepe (Col, 1960)
King of the Roaring '20s: The Story of
  Arnold Rothstein (AA, 1961)
Twenty Plus Two (AA, 1961)
Son of Flubber (BV, 1963)
It's a Mad, Mad, Mad, Mad World (UA,
  1963)
Viva Las Vegas (MGM, 1964)
That Darn Cat! (BV, 1965)
The Wild McCullochs (AIP, 1975)
Won Ton Ton, the Dog Who Saved Hol-
  lywood (Par, 1976)

REGINALD DENNY
(Reginald Leigh Daymore)

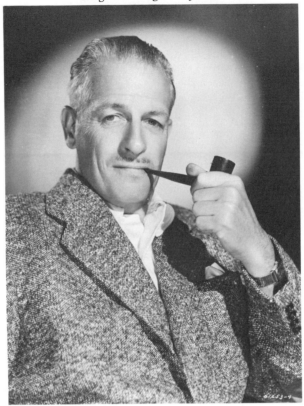

In Eyes in the Night *(1942).*

Born November 20, 1891, Richmond, Surrey, England. Married 1) Irene Haisman (1913), child: Barbara; divorced (1927); 2) Isobel Steiffel (1928), children: Reginald, Joan. Died June 16, 1967, Surrey, England. Genteelly handsome Britisher with excellent physique who plowed through many athletic roles in silent features and shorts: was Prince Alex in John Barrymore's *Sherlock Holmes*, and made a series of popular features at Universal including *Skinner's Dress Suit* with Laura La Plante. MGM's *Private Lives* sets tone for sound career: played Victor Paynne, Norma Shearer's rather pompous groom, stiff-lipped and slightly baffled. Played Algy in Paramount's late 1930s' *Bulldog Drummond* detective series. Was Frank Crawley in *Rebecca*: Mr. Simms in *Mr. Blandings Builds His Dream House*. Last few roles included the off-kilter Commodore Schmidlapp in 1966's *Batman*.

Reginald Denny to Norma Shearer in *Private Lives:* "Well, here we are, you and I, on our honeymoon."

Films

Bringing Up Betty (World, 1919)
The Oakdale Affair (World, 1919)
Experience (Par, 1920)
A Dark Lantern (Realart, 1920)
39 East (Realart, 1920)
Disraeli (UA, 1921)
Footlights (Par, 1921)
Paying the Piper (Par, 1921)

The Iron Trail (UA, 1921)
The Price of Possession (Par, 1921)
Tropical Love (Associated Exhibitors, 1921)
The Kentucky Derby (Univ, 1922)
Sherlock Holmes (G, 1922)
The Abysmal Brute (Univ, 1923)
The Thrill Chaser (Univ, 1923)

Sporting Youth (Univ, 1924)
The Fast Workers (Univ, 1924)
The Reckless Age (Univ, 1924)
California Straight Ahead (Univ, 1925)
Oh, Doctor! (Univ, 1925)
I'll Show You the Town (Univ, 1925)
Where Was I? (Univ, 1925)
Skinner's Dress Suit (Univ, 1925)

What Happened to Jones? (Univ, 1925)
Rolling Home (Univ, 1926)
Take It from Me (Univ, 1926)
The Cheerful Fraud (Univ, 1927)
On Your Toes (Univ, 1927)
Fast and Furious (Univ, 1927)
Out All Night (Univ, 1927)
The Night Bird (Univ, 1928)
Good Morning, Judge (Univ, 1928)
That's My Daddy (Univ, 1928)
Clear the Decks (Univ, 1929)
His Lucky Day (Univ, 1929)
Red Hot Speed (Univ, 1929)
One Hysterical Night (Univ, 1929)
Madam Satan (MGM, 1930)
What a Man! (WW, 1930)
Embarrassing Moments (Univ, 1930)
Those Three French Girls (MGM, 1930)
A Lady's Morals (MGM, 1930)
Oh, For a Man (Fox, 1930)
Kiki (UA, 1931)
Parlor, Bedroom and Bath (MGM, 1931)
Private Lives (MGM, 1931)
Stepping Out (MGM, 1931)
The Iron Master (Allied Pictures, 1932)
Strange Justice (RKO, 1932)
The Barbarian (MGM, 1933)
Only Yesterday (Univ, 1933)
The Big Bluff (Tower, 1933)
Fog (Col, 1934)
One More River (Univ, 1934)
The Lost Patrol (RKO, 1934)
Of Human Bondage (RKO, 1934)
The Richest Girl in the World (RKO, 1934)
We're Rich Again (RKO, 1934)
The Little Minister (RKO, 1934)
The World Moves On (Fox, 1934)
Dancing Man (Pyramid, 1934)
Lottery Lover (Fox, 1935)

No More Ladies (MGM, 1935)
Vagabond Lady (MGM, 1935)
Anna Karenina (MGM, 1935)
Here's to Romance (Fox, 1935)
Remember Last Night? (Univ, 1935)
Midnight Phantom (Reliable, 1935)
The Lady in Scarlet (Chesterfield, 1935)
The Preview Murder Mystery (Par, 1936)
It Couldn't Have Happened (Invincible, 1936)
We're in the Legion Now [a.k.a. *The Rest Cure*] (GN, 1936)
Two in a Crowd (Univ, 1936)
More Than a Secretary (Col, 1936)
Penthouse Party (Liberty, 1936)
Romeo and Juliet (MGM, 1936)
Join the Marines (Rep, 1937)
Bulldog Drummond Comes Back (Par, 1937)
The Great Gambini (Par, 1937)
Bulldog Drummond Escapes (Par, 1937)
Bulldog Drummond's Revenge (Par, 1937)
Beg, Borrow or Steal (MGM, 1937)
Women of Glamour (Col, 1937)
Let's Get Married (Par, 1937)
Jungle Menace (Col serial, 1937)
Bulldog Drummond's Peril (Par, 1938)
Bulldog Drummond in Africa (Par, 1938)
Everybody's Baby (20th, 1938)
Four Men and a Prayer (20th, 1938)
Blockade (20th, 1938)
Bulldog Drummond's Bride (Par, 1939)
Arrest Bulldog Drummond! (Par, 1939)
Bulldog Drummond's Secret Police (Par, 1939)
Rebecca (UA, 1940)
Spring Parade (Univ, 1940)
Seven Sinners (Univ, 1940)
International Squadron (WB, 1941)
One Night in Lisbon (Par, 1941)

Appointment for Love (Univ, 1941)
Thunder Birds (20th, 1942)
Captains of the Clouds (WB, 1942)
Over My Dead Body (20th, 1942)
Eyes in the Night (MGM, 1942)
Sherlock Holmes and the Voice of Terror (Univ, 1942)
The Ghost Ship (RKO, 1943)
The Crime Doctor's Strangest Case (Col, 1943)
Song of the Open Road (UA, 1944)
Love Letters (Par, 1945)
Tangier (Univ, 1946)
The Locket (RKO, 1946)
My Favorite Brunette (Par, 1947)
The Macomber Affair (UA, 1947)
Escape Me Never (WB, 1947)
Christmas Eve [a.k.a. *Sinners' Holiday*] (UA, 1947)
The Secret Life of Walter Mitty (RKO, 1947)
Mr. Blandings Builds His Dream House (Selznick Releasing Organization, 1948)
The Iroquois Trail (UA, 1950)
Abbott and Costello Meet Dr. Jekyll and Mr. Hyde (Univ, 1953)
Fort Vengeance (AA, 1953)
The Hindu [a.k.a. *Sabaka*] (Ferrin, 1953)
World for Ransom (AA, 1954)
Bengal Brigade (Univ, 1954)
The Snow Creature (UA, 1954)
Escape to Burma (RKO, 1955)
Around the World in 80 Days (UA, 1956)
Street of Sinners (UA, 1957)
Advance to the Rear (MGM, 1964)
Cat Ballou (Col, 1965)
Assault on a Queen (Par, 1966)
Batman (20th, 1966)

DUDLEY DIGGES

With David Niven in Raffles *(1940).*

Born June 9, 1879, Dublin, Ireland. Married Mary Roden Quinn; widowed (1947). Died October 24, 1947, New York City, New York. Versatile Irish actor who lent strength to many American-made films. Was the evil Gutman in the Ricardo Cortez version of *The Maltese Falcon.* Joined with Paul Robeson in *The Emperor Jones.* Was Dr. Bachus in Clark Gable's *Mutiny on the Bounty,* the helpful London lawyer Bartholomew Pratt in *Son of Fury,* etc.

Dudley Digges to Ian Wolfe in *The Searching Wind:* "I hate the opera. There's something insane about people opening their mouths very wide."

Films

Condemned (UA, 1929)
Outward Bound (WB, 1930)
The Maltese Falcon (WB, 1931)
Alexander Hamilton (WB, 1931)
Devotion (Pathé, 1931)
The Ruling Voice (FN, 1931)
The Hatchet Man (FN, 1932)
The Strange Case of Clara Deane (Par, 1932)
Roar of the Dragon (RKO, 1932)
The First Year (Fox, 1932)
Tess of the Storm Country (Fox, 1932)
The King's Vacation (WB, 1933)
The Narrow Corner (WB, 1933)

Mayor of Hell (WB, 1933)
The Emperor Jones (UA, 1933)
Before Dawn (RKO, 1933)
The Invisible Man (Univ, 1933)
Silk Express (WB, 1933)
Massacre (FN, 1934)
Fury of the Jungle (Col, 1934)
The World Moves On (Fox, 1934)
I Am a Thief (WB, 1934)
Caravan (Fox, 1934)
What Every Woman Knows (MGM, 1934)
A Notorious Gentleman (Univ, 1935)
China Seas (MGM, 1935)

Mutiny on the Bounty (MGM, 1935)
The Bishop Misbehaves (MGM, 1935)
Kind Lady (MGM, 1935)
Three Live Ghosts (MGM, 1935)
The Voice of Bugle Ann (MGM, 1936)
The Unguarded Hour (MGM, 1936)
The General Died at Dawn (Par, 1936)
Valiant Is the Word for Carrie (Par, 1936)
Love Is News (20th, 1937)
The Light That Failed (Par, 1939)
Raffles (UA, 1940)
The Fight for Life (Col, 1940)
Son of Fury (20th, 1942)
The Searching Wind (Par, 1946)

ALAN DINEHART

Eddie Cantor and Alan Dinehart (second from right) in Ali Baba Goes to Town *(1937).*

Born October 3, 1889, Missoula, Montana. Married 1) Louise Dyer, child: one; divorced; 2) Mozelle Britonee, children: two. Died July 17, 1944, Hollywood, California. One of the more overworked supporting players, especially in demand at 20th Century-Fox in the mid-30s. Frequently cast as the hypertense businessman.

Alan Dinehart to Virginia Bruce in *Born to Dance:* "Famous Actress in Love with Gob. What an angle! Why, the public'll eat it up."

Films

The Brat (Fox, 1931)
Wicked (Fox, 1931)
Sob Sister (Fox, 1931)
Girls About Town (Par, 1931)
Good Sport (Fox, 1931)
Disorderly Conduct (Fox, 1932)
The Trial of Vivienne Ware (Fox, 1932)
Street of Women (WB, 1932)
Bachelor's Affairs (Fox, 1932)
Almost Married (Fox, 1932)
Washington Merry-Go-Round (Col, 1932)
Rackety Rax (Fox, 1932)
The Devil Is Driving (Par, 1932)
Lawyer Man (WB, 1932)
As the Devil Commands (Col, 1932)
Okay, America (Univ, 1932)
Sweepings (RKO, 1933)
Supernatural (Par, 1933)
Study in Scarlet (WW, 1933)
I Have Lived (Chesterfield, 1933)
No Marriage Ties (RKO, 1933)

Her Bodyguard (Par, 1933)
Bureau of Missing Persons (FN, 1933)
Dance, Girl, Dance (Invincible, 1933)
The World Changes (FN, 1933)
The Sin of Nora Moran (Majestic, 1933)
Cross Country Cruise (Univ, 1934)
Fury of the Jungle (Col, 1934)
Jimmy the Gent (WB, 1934)
The Crosby Case (Univ, 1934)
A Very Honorable Guy (FN, 1934)
Love Captive (Univ, 1934)
The Cat's Paw (Fox, 1934)
Baby Take a Bow (Fox, 1934)
Lottery Lover (Fox, 1935)
$10 Raise (Fox, 1935)
Dante's Inferno (Fox, 1935)
In Old Kentucky (Fox, 1935)
The Pay-Off (WB, 1935)
Redheads on Parade (Fox, 1935)
Your Uncle Dudley (Fox, 1935)
Thanks a Million (Fox, 1935)
It Had to Happen (20th, 1936)

Everybody's Old Man (20th, 1936)
Human Cargo (20th, 1936)
The Country Beyond (20th, 1936)
Parole! (Univ, 1936)
The Crime of Dr. Forbes (20th, 1936)
Charlie Chan at the Race Track (20th, 1936)
Born to Dance (MGM, 1936)
King of the Royal Mounted (20th, 1936)
Reunion (20th, 1936)
Woman Wise (20th, 1937)
Step Lively, Jeeves (20th, 1937)
Midnight Taxi (20th, 1937)
Fifty Roads to Town (20th, 1937)
This Is My Affair (20th, 1937)
Dangerously Yours (20th, 1937)
Danger—Love at Work (20th, 1937)
Big Town Girl (20th, 1937)
Ali Baba Goes to Town (20th, 1937)
Love on a Budget (20th, 1938)
The First Hundred Years (MGM, 1938)
Rebecca of Sunnybrook Farm (20th, 1938)

Up the River (20th, 1938)
Fast and Loose (MGM, 1939)
King of the Turf (UA, 1939)
The House of Fear (Univ, 1939)
Second Fiddle (20th, 1939)
Two Bright Boys (Univ, 1939)
Elsa Maxwell's Hotel for Women (20th, 1939)

Everything Happens at Night (20th, 1939)
Slightly Honorable (UA, 1939)
Girl Trouble (20th, 1942)
Sweet Rosie O'Grady (20th, 1943)
Fired Wife (Univ, 1943)
The Heat's On (Col, 1943)
What a Woman! (Col, 1943)
Moon over Las Vegas (Univ, 1944)

Seven Days Ashore (RKO, 1944)
Johnny Doesn't Live Here Any More (Mon, 1944)
The Whistler (Col, 1944)
Minstrel Man (PRC, 1944)
A Wave, a Wac and a Marine (Mon, 1944)
Oh, What a Night (Mon, 1944)

CHARLES DINGLE

Jim Davis, Charles Dingle, O. Z. Whitehead (rear), Gail Davis, Van Johnson, Kermit Maynard, and Russell Simpson in The Romance of Rosy Ridge *(1947).*

Born December 28, 1887, Wabash, Indiana. Married Dorothy White (1916), children: Charles, John. Died January 19, 1956, Worcester, Massachusetts. Short, stocky, avaricious sort who created an indelible impression as Bette Davis' greedy brother Oscar Hubbard in *The Little Foxes* (the vaudeville/stage veteran was repeating his Broadway role). Played Andrew Holmes, the factory owner who creates chaos for Cary Grant in *The Talk of the Town*. Remained in form to the end of his career—persecuting Senator Fullerton in Gary Cooper's *The Court-Martial of Billy Mitchell*. Frequent radio and TV performer. TV series: "Road of Life" (as Conrad Overton).

Charles Dingle to Ray Milland in *Are Husbands Necessary?*
"It is my privilege to lose control when I *want* to—and I'm losing it *right now!*"

Films

One Third of a Nation (Par, 1939)
The Little Foxes (RKO, 1941)
Unholy Partners (MGM, 1941)
Johnny Eager (MGM, 1941)
Calling Dr. Gillespie (MGM, 1942)
Are Husbands Necessary? (Par, 1942)
The Talk of the Town (Col, 1942)
George Washington Slept Here (WB, 1942)
Tennessee Johnson (MGM, 1942)
Somewhere I'll Find You (MGM, 1942)
Edge of Darkness (WB, 1943)
Lady of Burlesque (UA, 1943)
Someone to Remember (Rep, 1943)
She's for Me (Univ, 1943)
The Song of Bernadette (20th, 1943)

Home in Indiana (20th, 1944)
The National Barn Dance (Par, 1944)
Together Again (Col, 1944)
A Medal for Benny (Par, 1945)
Here Come the Co-eds (Univ, 1945)
Guest Wife (UA, 1945)
Cinderella Jones (WB, 1946)
The Wife of Monte Cristo (PRC, 1946)
Centennial Summer (20th, 1946)
Three Wise Fools (MGM, 1946)
Sister Kenny (RKO, 1946)
The Beast with Five Fingers (WB, 1946)
Duel in the Sun (Selznick Releasing Organization, 1946)
My Favorite Brunette (Par, 1947)

Welcome Stranger (Par, 1947)
The Romance of Rosy Ridge (MGM, 1947)
State of the Union (MGM, 1948)
If You Knew Susie (RKO, 1948)
A Southern Yankee (MGM, 1948)
Big Jack (MGM, 1949)
Never Wave at a WAC (RKO, 1952)
Call Me Madam (20th, 1953)
The President's Lady (20th, 1953)
Half a Hero (MGM, 1953)
The Court-Martial of Billy Mitchell (WB, 1955)

RUTH DONNELLY

In the mid-1930s.

Born May 17, 1896, Trenton, New Jersey. Married Basil de Guichard (1932); widowed (1958). One of the most proficient of the Warner Bros. stock company in the 1930s—earned her keep as the sharp-mouthed, self-sufficient gal a la Glenda Farrell, or sometimes as the vain dame supporting a gigolo lover. Had a marvelous way of flirting with would-be protégés (e.g., as Guy Kibbee's wife Mrs. Simpson in *Wonder Bar*). Still up to her suspicious-eyed nonsense as Joan Crawford's landlord-friend Liz in *Autumn Leaves*. Quite effective as Ruth, the asylum inmate in *The Snake Pit*. Song-writing and religion have recently become her major interests.

Ruth Donnelly to Mary Brian in *Hard to Handle:* "We're going back to New York if we have to ride in the conductor's whiskers."

Films

Rubber Heels (Par, 1927)
Transatlantic (Fox, 1931)
The Spider (Fox, 1931)
Wicked (Fox, 1931)
The Rainbow Trail (Fox, 1932)
Blessed Event (WB, 1932)
Jewel Robbery (WB, 1932)
Make Me a Star (Par, 1932)
Female (WB, 1933)
Convention City (WB, 1933)
42nd Street (WB, 1933)
Private Detective 62 (WB, 1933)
Bureau of Missing Persons (WB, 1933)
Ever in My Heart (WB, 1933)
Hard to Handle (WB, 1933)
Goodbye Again (WB, 1933)
Footlight Parade (WB, 1933)
Employees' Entrance (WB, 1933)
Ladies They Talk About (WB, 1933)
Lilly Turner (WB, 1933)
Havana Widows (FN, 1933)
Sing, Sinner, Sing (Majestic, 1933)
Romance in the Rain (Univ, 1934)
You Belong to Me (Par, 1934)
Wonder Bar (WB, 1934)
Heat Lightning (WB, 1934)
Mandalay (WB, 1934)
Merry Wives of Reno (WB, 1934)
Housewife (WB, 1934)
Happiness Ahead (WB, 1934)
Maybe It's Love (WB, 1935)

Hands Across the Table (Par, 1935)
White Cockatoo (WB, 1935)
Traveling Saleslady (WB, 1935)
Alibi Ike (WB, 1935)
Red Salute [a.k.a. *Her Enlisted Man*] (UA, 1935)
Metropolitan (Fox, 1935)
Personal Maid's Secret (WB, 1935)
Song and Dance Man (20th, 1936)
Mr. Deeds Goes to Town (Col, 1936)
13 Hours by Air (Par, 1936)
Fatal Lady (Par, 1936)
Cain and Mabel (WB, 1936)
More Than a Secretary (Col, 1936)
Roaring Timber (Col, 1937)
Portia on Trial (Rep, 1937)
Holiday (Col, 1938)
A Slight Case of Murder (WB, 1938)
Army Girl (Rep, 1938)
Annabel Takes a Tour (RKO, 1938)
Affairs of Annabel (RKO, 1938)
Meet the Girls (20th, 1938)
Personal Secretary (Univ, 1938)
Mr. Smith Goes to Washington (Col, 1939)
The Family Next Door (Univ, 1939)
The Amazing Mr. Williams (Col, 1939)
My Little Chickadee (Univ, 1940)
Scatterbrain (Rep, 1940)
Meet the Missus (Rep, 1940)
Sailors on Leave (Rep, 1941)

Model Wife (Univ, 1941)
Petticoat Politics (Rep, 1941)
The Roundup (Par, 1941)
The Gay Vagabond (Rep, 1941)
Rise and Shine (20th, 1941)
You Belong to Me (Col, 1941)
Johnny Doughboy (Rep, 1942)
This Is the Army (WB, 1943)
Thank Your Lucky Stars (WB, 1943)
Sleepy Lagoon (Rep, 1943)
Pillow to Post (WB, 1945)
The Bells of St. Mary's (RKO, 1945)
Cross My Heart (Par, 1946)
Cinderella Jones (WB, 1946)
In Old Sacramento (Rep, 1946)
Little Miss Broadway (Col, 1947)
The Fabulous Texan (Rep, 1947)
The Ghost Goes Wild (Rep, 1947)
Millie's Daughter (Col, 1947)
Fighting Father Dunne (RKO, 1948)
The Snake Pit (20th, 1948)
Where the Sidewalk Ends (20th, 1950)
I'd Climb the Highest Mountain (20th, 1951)
The Secret of Convict Lake (20th, 1951)
The Wild Blue Yonder (Rep, 1951)
A Lawless Street (Col, 1955)
The Spoilers (Univ, 1955)
Autumn Leaves (Col, 1956)
The Way to the Gold (20th, 1957)

DOUGLASS DUMBRILLE

Tom Seidel, Pedro de Cordoba, and Douglass Drumbrille in Charlie Chan in City in Darkness *(1939).*

Born October 13, 1888, Hamilton, Ontario, Canada. Married 1) _____; 2) Patricia Mowbray (1960), children: two sons. Died April 2, 1974, Woodland Hills, California. Stern-faced, moustached, with a sharply etched speech pattern. Exuded nastiness and made it a paying commodity. Bothered Jeanette MacDonald in *Naughty Marietta, The Firefly,* and *I Married an Angel;* was a foil for the zany Marx Brothers in *A Day at the Races* and *The Big Store;* annoyed Abbott and Costello in *Ride 'em Cowboy, Lost in a Harem,* and *Abbott and Costello in the Foreign Legion;* traded insults with Bob Hope in *Road to Utopia, Monsieur Beaucaire,* and *Son of Paleface.* Equally at ease in period adventures (*The Buccaneer*—both versions), detective stories (*Mr. Moto in Danger Island, Ellery Queen and the Perfect Crime,* etc.), or horror tales (*The Frozen Ghost, The Cat Creeps,* etc.). TV series: "The Life of Riley" and "The Grand Jury."

> **Douglass Dumbrille** to Gary Cooper and Franchot Tone
> in *Lives of a Bengal Lancer:* "Little bamboo slivers ... but when
> they're driven under the fingernails and *lighted,* we find
> them very effective.

Films

His Woman (Par, 1931)
The Wiser Sex (Par, 1932)
Blondie of the Follies (MGM, 1932)
That's My Boy (Col, 1932)
Laughter in Hell (Univ, 1932)
I Am a Fugitive from a Chain Gang (WB, 1932)
The Working Man (WB, 1933)
Elmer the Great (WB, 1933)
Heroes for Sale (FN, 1933)
Female (FN, 1933)
The World Changes (FN, 1933)

Silk Express (WB, 1933)
Voltaire (WB, 1933)
Lady Killer (WB, 1933)
Convention City (FN, 1933)
King of the Jungle (Par, 1933)
Smoke Lightning (Fox, 1933)
Baby Face (WB, 1933)
Rustlers' Roundup (Univ, 1933)
The Big Brain (RKO, 1933)
The Man Who Dared (Fox, 1933)
The Way to Love (Par, 1933)
Massacre (FN, 1934)

Hi, Nellie! (WB, 1934)
Fog over Frisco (FN, 1934)
Harold Teen (WB, 1934)
Journal of a Crime (FN, 1934)
Operator 13 (MGM, 1934)
Treasure Island (MGM, 1934)
The Secret Bride (WB, 1935)
Lives of a Bengal Lancer (Par, 1935)
Naughty Marietta (MGM, 1935)
Love Me Forever (Col, 1935)
Crime and Punishment (Col, 1935)
Cardinal Richelieu (UA, 1935)

Peter Ibbetson (Par, 1935)
The Public Menace (Col, 1935)
Air Hawks (Col, 1935)
Unknown Woman (Col, 1935)
The Calling of Dan Matthews (Col, 1936)
The Lone Wolf Returns (Col, 1936)
The Music Goes 'Round (Col, 1936)
You May Be Next (Col, 1936)
Mr. Deeds Goes to Town (Col, 1936)
End of the Trail (Col, 1936)
The Witness Chair (RKO, 1936)
M'Liss (RKO, 1936)
The Princess Comes Across (Par, 1936)
A Day at the Races (MGM, 1937)
The Emperor's Candlesticks (MGM, 1937)
The Firefly (MGM, 1937)
Ali Baba Goes to Town (20th, 1937)
Counterfeit Lady (Col, 1937)
Woman in Distress (Col, 1937)
The Buccaneer (Par, 1938)
Stolen Heaven (Par, 38)
The Mysterious Rider (Par, 1938)
Storm over Bengal (Rep, 1938)
Crime Takes a Holiday (Col, 1938)
Fast Company (MGM, 1938)
Sharpshooters (20th, 1938)
Kentucky (20th, 1938)
The Three Musketeers (20th, 1939)
Charlie Chan at Treasure Island (20th, 1939)
Charlie Chan in City in Darkness (20th, 1939)
Captain Fury (UA, 1939)
Tell No Tales (MGM, 1939)
Thunder Afloat (MGM, 1939)
Rovin' Tumbleweeds (Rep, 1939)
Mr. Moto in Danger Island (20th, 1939)
Slightly Honorable (UA, 1940)
Virginia City (WB, 1940)

South of Pago Pago (UA, 1940)
Michael Shayne, Private Detective (20th, 1940)
Murder Among Friends (20th, 1941)
Washington Melodrama (MGM, 1941)
Ellery Queen and the Perfect Crime (Col, 1941)
The Roundup (Par, 1941)
The Big Store (MGM, 1941)
I Married an Angel (MGM, 1942)
Ten Gentlemen from West Point (20th, 1942)
Stand By for Action (MGM, 1942)
Castle in the Desert (20th, 1942)
Ride 'em Cowboy (Univ, 1942)
A Gentleman After Dark (UA, 1942)
Du Barry Was a Lady (MGM, 1943)
False Colors (UA, 1943)
Lost in a Harem (MGM, 1944)
Lumberjack (UA, 1944)
Uncertain Glory (WB, 1944)
Jungle Woman (Univ, 1944)
Forty Thieves (UA, 1944)
Gypsy Wildcat (Univ, 1944)
A Medal for Benny (Par, 1945)
The Frozen Ghost (Univ, 1945)
Jungle Queen (Univ serial, 1945)
Road to Utopia (Par, 1945)
The Daltons Ride Again (Mon, 1945)
Flame of the West (Mon, 1945)
Pardon My Past (Col, 1946)
A Night in Paradise (Univ, 1946)
The Catman of Paris (Rep, 1946)
Spook Busters (Mon, 1946)
The Cat Creeps (Univ, 1946)
Monsieur Beaucaire (Par, 1946)
Under Nevada Skies (Rep, 1946)
The Fabulous Texan (Rep, 1947)

Christmas Eve [a.k.a. *Sinners' Holiday*] (UA, 1947)
It's A Joke, Son! (EL, 1947)
Dragnet (Screen Guild, 1947)
Dishonored Lady (UA, 1947)
Blonde Savage (EL, 1948)
Last of the Wild Horses (Screen Guild, 1948)
Dynamite (Par, 1949)
Alimony (EL, 1949)
Tell It to the Judge (Col, 1949)
Joe Palooka in the Counterpunch (Mon, 1949)
Riders of the Whistling Pines (Col, 1949)
The Lone Wolf and His Lady (Col, 1949)
Buccaneer's Girl (Univ, 1950)
Riding High (Par, 1950)
Rapture (Film Classics, 1950)
The Savage Horde (Rep, 1950)
Abbott and Costello in the Foreign Legion (Univ, 1950)
A Millionaire for Christy (20th, 1951)
Son of Paleface (Par, 1952)
Apache War Smoke (MGM, 1952)
Sky Full of Moon (MGM, 1952)
Julius Caesar (MGM, 1953)
Plunder of the Sun (WB, 1953)
Captain John Smith and Pocahontas (UA, 1953)
The World for Ransom (AA, 1954)
Lawless Rider (UA, 1954)
Jupiter's Darling (MGM, 1955)
The Ten Commandments (Par, 1956)
The Buccaneer (Par, 1958)
High Time (20th, 1960)
Air Patrol (20th, 1962)
Shock Treatment (20th, 1964)
What a Way to Go! (20th, 1964)

EMMA DUNN

Emma Dunn, Jane Bryan, and James Cagney in Each Dawn I Die *(1939).*

Born February 26, 1875, Cheshire, England. Married John Stokes; divorced. Died December 14, 1966, Los Angeles, California. Began excelling in matronly roles on stage even while still a relatively young woman. Best recalled for portraying the kindly mother of Lew Ayres and the wife of Samuel S. Hinds in the *Dr. Kildare* series.

Emma Dunn to Samuel S. Hinds in *Young Dr. Kildare:* "Our boy's going to go to the finest hospital in New York—and he's going to be the greatest doctor in the country."

Films

Old Lady 31 (Br, 1920)
Pied Piper Malone (Par, 1924)
Side Street (RKO, 1929)
Manslaughter (Par, 1930)
The Texan (Par, 1930)
Too Young to Marry (WB, 1931)
The Prodigal [a.k.a. *The Southerner*] (MGM, 1931)
Bad Company (Pathé, 1931)
Morals for Women (Tif, 1931)
Bad Sister (Univ, 1931)
This Modern Age (MGM, 1931)
The Guilty Generation (Col, 1931)
Big Business Girl (FN, 1931)
Wet Parade (MGM, 1932)
The Man I Killed [a.k.a. *Broken Lullaby*] (Par, 1932)
The Cohens and Kellys in Hollywood (Univ, 1932)
Hell's House (Capital, 1932)
Letty Lynton (MGM, 1932)
It's Tough to Be Famous (FN, 1932)
Blessed Event (WB, 1932)

Under Eighteen (WB, 1932)
Elmer the Great (FN, 1933)
Private Jones (Univ, 1933)
It's Great to Be Alive (Fox, 1933)
Walls of Gold (Fox, 1933)
Hard to Handle (WB, 1933)
Grand Slam (WB, 1933)
Man of Sentiment (Chesterfield, 1933)
Dark Hazard (FN, 1934)
The Quitter (Chesterfield, 1934)
Dr. Monica (WB, 1934)
George White's 1935 Scandals (Fox, 1935)
The Glass Key (Par, 1935)
The Crusades (Par, 1935)
Keeper of the Bees (Mon, 1935)
Ladies Crave Excitement (Mascot, 1935)
The Little Big Shot (WB, 1935)
Another Face (RKO, 1935)
Seven Keys to Baldpate (RKO, 1935)
This Is the Life (Fox, 1935)
Mr. Deeds Goes to Town (Col, 1936)
The Harvester (Rep, 1936)

Second Wife (RKO, 1936)
When You're in Love (Col, 1937)
Hideaway (RKO, 1937)
Varsity Show (WB, 1937)
Circus Girl (Rep, 1937)
The Emperor's Candlesticks (MGM, 1937)
Madame X (MGM, 1937)
The Cowboy from Brooklyn (WB, 1938)
Thanks for the Memory (Par, 1938)
Lord Jeff (MGM, 1938)
Three Loves Has Nancy (MGM, 1938)
The Duke of West Point (UA, 1938)
Young Dr. Kildare (MGM, 1938)
The Cowboy and the Lady (UA, 1938)
Son of Frankenstein (Univ, 1939)
Calling Dr. Kildare (MGM, 1939)
The Secret of Dr. Kildare (MGM, 1939)
Hero for a Day (Univ, 1939)
Each Dawn I Die (WB, 1939)
The Llano Kid (Par, 1939)
High School (20th, 1940)
Little Orvie (RKO, 1940)
Dr. Kildare's Strange Case (MGM, 1940)

You Can't Fool Your Wife (RKO, 1940)
Half a Sinner (Univ, 1940)
One Crowded Night (RKO, 1940)
Dance, Girl, Dance (RKO, 1940)
Dr. Kildare Goes Home (MGM, 1940)
The Great Dictator (UA, 1940)
Yesterday's Heroes (20th, 1940)
The Monster and the Girl (Par, 1941)
Scattergood Baines (RKO, 1941)
The Penalty (MGM, 1941)
Scattergood Pulls the Strings (RKO, 1941)
Mr. and Mrs. Smith (RKO, 1941)
Dr. Kildare's Wedding Day (MGM, 1941)

Scattergood Meets Broadway (RKO, 1941)
Ladies in Retirement (Col, 1941)
Rise and Shine (20th, 1941)
Babes on Broadway (MGM, 1942)
The Postman Didn't Ring (20th, 1942)
The Talk of the Town (Col, 1942)
I Married a Witch (UA, 1942)
When Johnny Comes Marching Home (Univ, 1942)
Hoosier Holiday (Rep, 1943)
North Star [TV title: Armored Attack] (RKO, 1943)
Minesweeper (Par, 1943)

The Cross of Lorraine (MGM, 1943)
It Happened Tomorrow (Par, 1944)
Are These Our Parents? (Mon, 1944)
The Bridge of San Luis Rey (UA, 1944)
My Buddy (Rep, 1944)
The Horn Blows at Midnight (WB, 1945)
The Hoodlum Saint (MGM, 1946)
Night Train from Memphis (Rep, 1946)
Life with Father (WB, 1947)
Mourning Becomes Electra (RKO, 1947)
The Woman in White (WB, 1948)

MILDRED DUNNOCK

In Seven Women (1965).

Born January 25, 1900, Baltimore, Maryland. Married Keith Urmy (1933), children: Linda, Mary. Despite her birdlike petite frame, a powerful if mannered stage, film, and TV actress. Oscar-nominated for re-creating her role of Linda, Willy Loman's ultrapatient wife in *Death of a Salesman* (but lost BSAAA to Kim Hunter of *A Streetcar Named Desire*). Nominated for another BSAAA, for her Aunt Rose Comfort in *Baby Doll* (but lost to Dorothy Malone of *Written in the Wind*). Repeated her stage role of understanding Aunt Nonnie in *Sweet Bird of Youth* and was one of Geraldine Page's victims in *Whatever Happened to Aunt Alice?*

Mildred Dunnock to June Allyson in *The Girl in White:*
"Don't wait and turn into a spinster like me."

Films

The Corn Is Green (WB, 1945)
Kiss of Death (20th, 1947)
I Want You (RKO, 1951)
Death of a Salesman (Col, 1951)
Viva Zapata! (20th, 1952)
The Girl in White (MGM, 1952)
The Jazz Singer (WB, 1953)
Bad for Each Other (Col, 1953)
Hansel and Gretel (RKO, 1954) [voice only]

The Trouble with Harry (Par, 1955)
Love Me Tender (20th, 1956)
Baby Doll (WB, 1956)
Peyton Place (20th, 1957)
The Story on Page One (20th, 1959)
The Nun's Story (WB, 1959)
Butterfield 8 (MGM, 1960)
Something Wild (UA, 1961)
Sweet Bird of Youth (MGM, 1962)
Behold a Pale Horse (Col, 1964)

Youngblood Hawke (WB, 1964)
Seven Women (MGM, 1965)
Whatever Happened to Aunt Alice? (Cin, 1969)
One Summer Love (AIP, 1976)

MAUDE EBURNE

George "Gabby" Hayes, Roy Rogers, Dale Evans, Maude Eburne, and Roger Pryor in
Man from Oklahoma *(1945).*

Born 1875. Died October 15, 1960, Hollywood, California. With a "puss" in the Marie Dressler tradition, she played variations of the housekeeper: a screaming one in *Vampire Bat*, the sharp-tongued Mrs. Hastings in the six Jean Hersholt *Dr. Christian* entries, and earlier the down-to-earth Ma Pettingill who has a run-in with Charles Laughton in *Ruggles of Red Gap.*

Maude Eburne to crowd outside a restaurant in *Ruggles of
Red Gap:* "Make way for a lady, you laughin' hyenas."

Films

The Bat Whispers (UA, 1931)
Lonely Wives (Pathé, 1931)
Indiscreet (UA, 1931)
Bought (WB, 1931)
The Man in Possession (MGM, 1931)
The Guardsman (MGM, 1931)
Her Majesty Love (FN, 1931)
Blonde Crazy (WB, 1931)
Under Eighteen (WB, 1932)
Panama Flo (RKO, 1932)
Polly of the Circus (MGM, 1932)
The Passionate Plumber (MGM, 1932)
This Reckless Age (Par, 1932)
The Woman from Monte Carlo (FN, 1932)
The Trial of Vivienne Ware (Fox, 1932)
The First Year (Fox, 1932)
Stranger in Town (WB, 1932)
Vampire Bat (Majestic, 1933)
Robbers' Roost (Fox, 1933)
Ladies They Talk About (WB, 1933)
The Warrior's Husband (Fox, 1933)
Shanghai Madness (Fox, 1933)
Big Executive (Par, 1933)
My Lips Betray (Fox, 1933)
Ladies Must Love (Univ, 1933)
Havana Widows (FN, 1933)
East of Fifth Avenue (Col, 1933)
Fog (Col, 1934)
Lazy River (MGM, 1934)
Love Birds (Univ, 1934)
Here Comes the Navy (WB, 1934)
Girl from Missouri (MGM, 1934)
Return of the Terror (FN, 1934)

When Strangers Meet (Liberty, 1934)
Ruggles of Red Gap (Par, 1935)
Maybe It's Love (FN, 1935)
Party Wire (Col, 1935)
Don't Bet on Blondes (WB, 1935)
Happiness C.O.D. (Chesterfield, 1935)
Man Hunt (WB, 1936)
The Leavenworth Case (Rep, 1936)
Doughnuts and Society (Mascot, 1936)
Poppy (Par, 1936)
Valiant Is the Word for Carrie (Par, 1936)
Reunion (20th, 1936)
When's Your Birthday? (RKO, 1937)
Champagne Waltz (Par, 1937)
Paradise Express (Rep, 1937)
Fight for Your Lady (RKO, 1937)
Hollywood Cowboy [a.k.a. Wings over Wyoming] (RKO, 1937)
Live, Love and Learn (MGM, 1937)
Riders of the Black Hill (Rep, 1938)
Exile Express (GN, 1939)
My Wife's Relatives (Rep, 1939)
Mountain Rhythm (Rep, 1939)
Meet Dr. Christian (RKO, 1939)
Sabotage (Rep, 1939)
The Covered Trailer (Rep, 1939)
The Courageous Dr. Christian (RKO, 1940)
Dr. Christian Meets the Women (RKO, 1940)
Remedy for Riches (RKO, 1940)
The Border Legion (Rep, 1940)
Melody for Three (RKO, 1941)

West Point Widow (Par, 1941)
Among the Living (Par, 1941)
You Belong to Me (Col, 1941)
They Meet Again (RKO, 1941)
There's One Born Every Minute (Univ, 1942)
The Boogie Man Will Get You (Col, 1942)
Henry and Dizzy (Par, 1942)
To Be or Not to Be (UA, 1942)
Almost Married (Univ, 1942)
Henry Aldrich, Editor (Par, 1942)
Reveille with Beverly (Col, 1943)
Lady Bodyguard (Par, 1943)
Bowery to Broadway (Univ, 1944)
Up in Arms (RKO, 1944)
Goodnight Sweetheart (Rep, 1944)
I'm from Arkansas (PRC, 1944)
Henry Aldrich Plays Cupid (Rep, 1944)
The Princess and the Pirate (RKO, 1944)
Rosie the Riveter (Rep, 1944)
The Suspect (Univ, 1944)
The Town Went Wild (PRC, 1944)
Man from Oklahoma (Rep, 1945)
Hitchhike to Happiness (Rep, 1945)
Leave It to Blondie (Col, 1945)
Mother Wore Tights (20th, 1947)
The Secret Life of Walter Mitty (RKO, 1947)
Slippy McGee (Rep, 1948)
The Plunderers (Rep, 1948)
Arson, Inc. (Lip, 1949)
The Prince of Peace (Hallmark, 1951)

HELEN JEROME EDDY

In A Man's Castle *(1933)*.

Born February 25, 1897, New York City, New York. Stately actress whose presence helped to showcase the stars: Norma Talmadge in *Camille* (the maid), Corinne Griffith in *The Divine Lady* (Lady Nelson), Greta Garbo in *Mata Hari* (Sister Genevieve), Mae West in *Klondike Annie* (Sister Annie Alden, the missionary lady), etc.

Helen Jerome Eddy in *The Great Meadow:* "There's queer death in the wilderness."

Films

Pasquale (Par, 1916)
Rebecca of Sunnybrook Farm (Par, 1917)
The Trembling Hour (Univ, 1920)
Pollyanna (UA, 1920)
One Man in a Million (Robertson-Cole, 1921)
The First Born (Robertson-Cole, 1921)
The Other Woman (Hodkinson, 1921)
The Ten Dollar Raise (Associated Producers, 1921)
The March Hare (Realart, 1921)
The Flirt (Univ, 1922)
When Love Comes (FBO, 1922)
An Old Fashioned Sweetheart of Mine (Metro, 1923)
The Country Kid (WB, 1923)
To the Ladies (Par, 1923)

The Fire Patrol (Chadwick, 1924)
Marry Me (Par, 1925)
The Dark Angel (FN, 1925)
Padlocked (Par, 1926)
Camille (FN, 1927)
Quality Street (MGM, 1927)
13 Washington Square (Univ, 1928)
Two Lovers (UA, 1928)
Chicago After Midnight (FBO, 1928)
The Speed Classic (Excellent, 1928)
The Divine Lady (FN, 1929)
Blue Skies (Fox, 1929)
Midstream (Tif, 1929)
War Nurse (MGM, 1930)
The Great Meadow (MGM, 1931)
Girls Demand Excitement (Fox, 1931)
Skippy (Par, 1931)

Reaching for the Moon (UA, 1931)
Sooky (Par, 1931)
Mata Hari (MGM, 1931)
No Greater Love (Col, 1932)
Impatient Maiden (Univ, 1932)
Make Me a Star (Par, 1932)
The Night of June 13th (Par, 1932)
Madame Butterfly (Par, 1932)
A Parisian Romance (Allied Pictures, 1932)
The Bitter Tea of General Yen (Col, 1933)
Frisco Jenny (FN, 1933)
A Man's Castle (Col, 1933)
The Masquerader (UA, 1933)
Torch Singer (Par, 1933)
Broadway Thru a Keyhole (UA, 1933)
Riptide (MGM, 1934)

Unknown Blonde (Majestic, 1934)	*Girl from 10th Avenue* (FN, 1935)	*The Garden of Allah* (UA, 1936)
Girl of the Limberlost (Mon, 1934)	*A Shot in the Dark* (Chesterfield, 1935)	*Jim Hanvey—Detective* (Rep, 1937)
Strictly Personal (Par, 1934)	*Stowaway* (20th, 1936)	*City Streets* (Col, 1938)
Helldorado (Fox, 1935)	*The Country Doctor* (20th, 1936)	*Outside the Law* (Univ, 1938)
Rendezvous at Midnight (Univ, 1935)	*Klondike Annie* (Par, 1936)	*Blondie Brings Up Baby* (Col, 1938)
Keeper of the Bees (Mon, 1935)	*Winterset* (RKO, 1936)	*Strike Up the Band* (MGM, 1940)

JACK ELAM

In Support Your Local Sheriff *(1969).*

Born November 15, 1916, Miami, Arizona. Married 1) _____ (1937), children: Jeri, Scott; widowed (1960); 2) Margaret Jennison (1961), child: Jacqueline. Gained a sizable following from his interpretations of vicious heavies. Has a scraggy face and sightless left eye. Displayed an intriguing presence, whether as town drunk Chris Boldt out to kill Jimmy Stewart for a buck in *The Man from Laramie* or as Fatso in Don Siegel's *Baby Face Nelson*. Most regularly in Westerns: could be brutal as in Sergio Leone's *Once upon a Time in the West* or a near buffoon in *Support Your Local Sheriff, The Cockeyed Cowboys of Calico County, Support Your Local Gunfighter*, etc. TV series: "The Dakotas," "Temple Houston," and "The Texas Wheelers."

Jack Elam to Raymond Barnes in *Wichita:* "Get Wyatt Earp . . . never mind the others. . . . They're no good without him."

186

Films

The Sundowners (EL, 1950)
One Way Street (Univ, 1950)
High Lonesome (EL, 1950)
An American Guerrilla in the Philippines
 (20th, 1950)
A Ticket to Tomahawk (20th, 1950)
Bird of Paradise (20th, 1951)
Rawhide (20th, 1951)
Kansas City Confidential (UA, 1952)
The Bushwackers (Realart, 1952)
The Battle at Apache Pass (Univ, 1952)
Rancho Notorious (RKO, 1952)
High Noon (UA, 1952)
Montana Territory (Col, 1952)
My Man and I (MGM, 1952)
The Ring (UA, 1952)
Lure of the Wilderness (20th, 1952)
Gun Belt (UA, 1953)
Count the Hours (RKO, 1953)
Ride, Vaquero! (MGM, 1953)
The Moonlighter (WB, 1953)
Appointment in Honduras (RKO, 1953)
Ride Clear of Diablo (Univ, 1954)
Jubilee Trail (Rep, 1954)
Cattle Queen of Montana (RKO, 1954)

Vera Cruz (UA, 1954)
Princess of the Nile (20th, 1954)
Tarzan's Hidden Jungle (RKO, 1955)
Moonfleet (MGM, 1955)
The Far Country (Univ, 1955)
Kiss Me Deadly (UA, 1955)
The Man from Laramie (Col, 1955)
Artists and Models (Par, 1955)
Kismet (MGM, 1955)
Man Without a Star (Univ, 1955)
Wichita (AA, 1955)
Jubal (Col, 1956)
Pardners (Par, 1956)
Thunder over Arizona (Rep, 1956)
Dragoon Wells Massacre (AA, 1957)
Gunfight at the O. K. Corral (Par, 1957)
Night Passage (Univ, 1957)
Lure of the Swamp (20th, 1957)
Baby Face Nelson (UA, 1957)
The Gun Runners (UA, 1958)
Edge of Eternity (Col, 1959)
The Last Sunset (Univ, 1961)
The Comancheros (20th, 1961)
Pocketful of Miracles (UA, 1961)
Four for Texas (WB, 1963)

The Rare Breed (Univ, 1966)
Night of the Grizzly (Par, 1966)
The Way West (UA, 1967)
The Last Challenge (MGM, 1967)
Firecreek (WB-7 Arts, 1968)
Never a Dull Moment (BV, 1968)
Once upon a Time in the West (Par, 1968)
Support Your Local Sheriff (UA, 1969)
The Cockeyed Cowboys of Calico County
 (Univ, 1970)
Dirty Dingus Magee (MGM, 1970)
Rio Lobo (National General, 1970)
Support Your Local Gunfighter (UA,
 1971)
The Wild Country (BV, 1971)
The Last Rebel (Col, 1971)
Hannie Caulder (Par, 1972)
Pat Garrett & Billy the Kid (MGM, 1973)
A Knife for the Ladies (Bryanston, 1974)
Hawmps! (Mulberry Productions,
 1976)
Creature from Black Lake (Howco Inter-
 national, 1976)
Grayeagle (AIP, 1977)

ROBERT ELLIOTT

Robert Elliott, Bud Wolfe, Chester Morris, Florence Eldridge, Norma Shearer, and
Jack Trent in The Divorcee (1930).

Born 1879, Ireland. Died November 15, 1951. A frequent leading man in silent films (e.g., with
Theda Bara in *A Woman There Was* and Pearl White in *A Virgin Paradise*). Gravitated to talkies in
supporting roles in minor pictures. Occasionally in a major production: *Gone with the Wind* (as the
Yankee major guarding Rhett Butler in the Atlanta jail).

Robert Elliott to Jean Hersholt in *Crime of the Century:* "Tell me, where were *you* when the lights went out?"

Films

Mary Moreland (Powell-Mutual, 1917)
Spirit of Lafayette (Powell-Mutual, 1917)
Unknown Love (Powell-Mutual, 1917)
Resurrection (Par, 1918)
Checkers (Fox, 1919)
A Woman There Was (Fox, 1919)
L'Apache (Pathé, 1919)
The Empire of Diamonds (Pathé, 1920)
Lonely Heart (Affiliated, 1921)
The Money Maniac (Pathé, 1921)
A Virgin Paradise (Fox, 1921)
A Pasteboard Crown (Associated Exhibitors, 1922)
Fair Lady (UA, 1922)
Without Fear (Fox, 1922)
The Broken Silence (Arrow, 1922)
Man and Wife (Arrow, 1923)
Romance of the Underworld (Fox, 1928)
Lights of New York (WB, 1928)
Happiness Ahead (FN, 1928)
Obey Your Husband (Anchor, 1928)
The Lone Wolf's Daughter (Col, 1929)

Protection (Fox, 1929)
Thunderbolt (Par, 1929)
Hide-Out (Univ, 1930)
Captain Thunder (WB, 1930)
The Divorcee (MGM, 1930)
Kathleen Mavourneen (Tif, 1930)
The Doorway to Hell (WB, 1930)
Sweet Mama (FN, 1930)
Men of the North (MGM, 1930)
Finger Points (FN, 1931)
The Maltese Falcon (WB, 1931)
Five Star Final (FN, 1931)
Star Witness (WB, 1931)
Murder at Midnight (Tif, 1931)
Madison Square Garden (Par, 1932)
Behind Stone Walls (Mayfair, 1932)
Midnight Patrol (Mon, 1932)
White Eagle (Col, 1932)
Phantom of Crestwood (RKO, 1932)
Self-Defense (Mon, 1933)
Lady Killer (WB, 1933)
Crime of the Century (Par, 1933)
Return of Casey Jones (Mon, 1933)

Gambling Lady (WB, 1934)
Twin Husbands (Chesterfield, 1934)
Woman Who Dared (Imperial, 1934)
Transatlantic Merry-Go-Round (UA, 1934)
Girl of the Limberlost (Mon, 1934)
Port of Lost Dreams (Chesterfield, 1934)
Times Square Lady (MGM, 1935)
The World Accuses (Chesterfield, 1935)
Black Sheep (Fox, 1935)
Circumstantial Evidence (Chesterfield, 1935)
I'd Give My Life (Par, 1936)
Trade Winds (UA, 1938)
Gone with the Wind (MGM, 1939)
The Roaring Twenties (WB, 1939)
I Stole a Million (Univ, 1939)
Mickey the Kid (Rep, 1939)
The Saint Strikes Back (RKO, 1939)
Half a Sinner (Univ, 1940)
Captain Tugboat Annie (Rep, 1945)
The Devil's Playground (UA, 1946)

ISOBEL ELSOM
(Isabel Reed)

In the 1950s.

Born March 16, 1893, Chesterton, Cambridge, England. Married Maurice Elvey; divorced. Spent lengthy span as a very attractive star of the British stage and screen. Migrated to Hollywood where she established herself as a consummate purveyor of the class-conscious matron. Typically told others their moral duties (e.g., Jennifer Jones in *Love Is a Many-Splendored Thing*). A favorite straight lady in the Margaret Dumont tradition for Jerry Lewis: *Rock-a-Bye Baby, The Bellboy,* etc. Played Mrs. Eynsford-Hill in *My Fair Lady.* TV series: "A Date with the Angels."

Isobel Elsom to Jennifer Jones in *Love Is a Many-Splendored Thing*: "There are certain conventions here that must be observed."

Films

A Prehistoric Love Story (Br, 1915)
Milestones (Br, 1916)
The Way of an Eagle (Br, 1918)
Tinker, Tailor, Soldier, Sailor (Br, 1918)
The Elder Miss Blossom [a.k.a. *Wanted: A Wife*] (Br, 1918)
God Bless Our Red, White and Blue (Br, 1918)
Onward Christian Soldiers (Br, 1918)
The Man Who Won (Br, 1918)
Quinneys (Br, 1919)
Hope (Br, 1919)
Linked by Fate (Br, 1919)
A Member of Tattersall's (Br, 1919)
Edge o' Beyond (Br, 1919)
Mrs. Thompson (Br, 1919)
Nance (Br, 1920)
Aunt Rachel (Br, 1920)
For Her Father's Sake (Br, 1921)
The Game of Life (Br, 1922)
Dick Turpin's Ride to York (Br, 1922)
A Debt of Honour (Br, 1922)
Broken Shadows (Br, 1922)
The Harbour Lights (Br, 1923)
The Sign of the Four (Br, 1923)
Just a Mother (Br, 1923)
The Wandering Jew (Br, 1923)
The Love Story of Aliette Brunton (Br, 1924)

Who Is This Man? (Br, 1924)
The Last Witness (Br, 1925)
The Tower of London (Br, 1926)
Human Law (Br, 1926)
Dance Magic (Br, 1927)
Stranglehold (Br, 1930)
The Other Woman (Br, 1931)
The Crooked Lady (Br, 1931)
Illegal (WB Br, 1932)
The Thirteenth Candle (WB Br, 1933)
The Primrose Path (Par Br, 1934)
Ladies in Retirement (Col, 1941)
Eagle Squadron (Univ, 1942)
The War Against Mrs. Hadley (MGM, 1942)
Seven Sweethearts (MGM, 1942)
You Were Never Lovelier (Col, 1942)
First Comes Courage (Col, 1943)
Forever and a Day (RKO, 1943)
My Kingdom for a Cook (Col, 1943)
Between Two Worlds (WB, 1944)
Casanova Brown (RKO, 1944)
The White Cliffs of Dover (MGM, 1944)
The Unseen (Par, 1945)
Of Human Bondage (WB, 1946)
Two Sisters from Boston (MGM, 1946)
Escape Me Never (WB, 1947)
The Ghost and Mrs. Muir (20th, 1947)
The Two Mrs. Carrolls (WB, 1947)

Ivy (Univ, 1947)
Love from a Stranger (EL, 1947)
Smart Woman (AA, 1948)
The Secret Garden (MGM, 1949)
Her Wonderful Lie (Col, 1950)
Desiree (20th, 1954)
Deep in My Heart (MGM, 1954)
The King's Thief (MGM, 1955)
Love Is a Many-Splendored Thing (20th, 1955)
Over-Exposed (Col, 1956)
Twenty-Three Paces to Baker Street (20th, 1956)
Lust for Life (MGM, 1956)
Guns of Fort Petticoat (Col, 1957)
Rock-a-Bye Baby (Par, 1958)
The Young Philadelphians (WB, 1959)
The Miracle (WB, 1959)
The Bellboy (Par, 1960)
The Second Time Around (20th, 1961)
The Errand Boy (Par, 1962)
Who's Minding the Store? (Par, 1963)
My Fair Lady (WB, 1964)
The Pleasure Seekers (20th, 1964)

HOPE EMERSON

Alvin Hammer, Hope Emerson, William Powell, and Fred Kelsey in Dancing in the Dark *(1949).*

Born April 29, 1897, Hawarden, Iowa. Died April 25, 1960, Hollywood, California. Boasted a man-sized frame and a face that harbored no beauty or compromise. Riveted in a variety of genres: Olympia La Pere, the circus strongwoman who hoists Spencer Tracy into midair in the comedy *Adam's Rib;* the cruel prison matron Evelyn Harper in *Caged* (Oscar-nominated but lost BSAAA to Josephine Hull of *Harvey*); the pioneer type of *Westward the Women* (Patience Hawley) and *Guns of Fort Petticoat* (Hannah Lacey). TV series: "Doc Corkle," "Peter Gunn" (as Mother—the nightclub owner), and "The Dennis O'Keefe Show."

> **Hope Emerson** to other pirates regarding Donald O'Connor in *Double Crossbones:* "By Judas, you weak-livered cowards, here stands a man!"

Films

Cry of the City (20th, 1948)
That Wonderful Urge (20th, 1948)
House of Strangers (20th, 1949)
Adam's Rib (MGM, 1949)
Dancing in the Dark (20th, 1949)
Roseanna McCoy (RKO, 1949)
Thieves' Highway (20th, 1949)

Caged (WB, 1950)
Copper Canyon (Par, 1950)
Double Crossbones (Univ, 1951)
Westward the Women (MGM, 1951)
Belle le Grande (Rep, 1951)
The Lady Wants Mink (Rep, 1953)
Champ for a Day (Rep, 1953)

A Perilous Journey (Rep, 1953)
Casanova's Big Night (Par, 1954)
Untamed (20th, 1955)
Guns of Fort Petticoat (Col, 1957)
All Mine to Give (Univ, 1957)
Rock-a-Bye Baby (Par, 1958)

GILBERT EMERY
(Gilbert Emery Pottle)

In the 1930s.

Born June 11, 1875, Naples, New York. Died October 27, 1945. Utilized his cultivated bearing to play aristocratic men of high official duty: Helen Hayes' *A Farewell to Arms* (British major), *The House of Rothschild* (prime minister), *Goin' to Town* (Winslow, the business manager), *The Life of Emile Zola* (war minister), *That Hamilton Woman* (Lord Spencer), *Sundown* (Ashburten), etc.

Gilbert Emery to Gary Cooper in *Now and Forever:* "Your mode of life is not one that fits you to bring up a child—my sister's child."

Films

The Sentimental Bloke (Australian, 1918)
Cousin Kate (Vit, 1921)
Any Wife (Fox, 1922)
Behind That Curtain (Fox, 1929)
The Sky Hawk (Fox, 1929)
Sarah and Son (Par, 1930)
The Prince of Diamonds (Col, 1930)
Let Us Be Gay (MGM, 1930)
A Lady's Morals (MGM, 1930)
A Royal Bed (RKO, 1931)
Scandal Sheet (Par, 1931)
The Lady Refuses (RKO, 1931)
Ladies' Man (Par, 1931)
Party Husband (FN, 1931)
Rich Man's Folly (Par, 1931)
The Ruling Voice (FN, 1931)

A Man Called Back (Tif, 1932)
A Farewell to Arms (Par, 1932)
Gallant Lady (UA, 1934)
Coming-Out Party (Fox, 1934)
All of Me (Par, 1934)
The House of Rothschild (UA, 1934)
Where Sinners Meet (RKO, 1934)
I Believed in You (Fox, 1934)
One More River (Univ, 1934)
Now and Forever (Par, 1934)
Grand Canary (Fox, 1934)
Whom the Gods Destroy (Col, 1934)
The Man Who Reclaimed His Head (Univ, 1934)
Clive of India (UA, 1935)
Night Life of the Gods (Univ, 1935)

Cardinal Richelieu (UA, 1935)
Goin' to Town (Par, 1935)
Reckless Roads (Majestic, 1935)
Let's Live Tonight (Col, 1935)
Ladies Crave Excitement (Mascot, 1935)
Harmony Lane (Mascot, 1935)
Without Regret (Par, 1935)
Peter Ibbetson (Par, 1935)
Magnificent Obsession (Univ, 1935)
Little Lord Fauntleroy (UA, 1936)
Wife vs. Secretary (MGM, 1936)
Dracula's Daughter (Univ, 1936)
Bullets or Ballots (WB, 1936)
Girl on the Front Page (Univ, 1936)
The Great Barrier (Br, 1937)
The Life of Emile Zola (WB, 1937)

Double or Nothing (Par, 1937)
Souls at Sea (Par, 1937)
Making the Headlines (Col, 1938)
The House of Mystery (Col, 1938)
The Buccaneer (Par, 1938)
Always Goodbye (20th, 1938)
Lord Jeff (MGM, 1938)
A Man to Remember (RKO, 1938)
Storm over Bengal (Rep, 1938)
The Saint Strikes Back (RKO, 1939)
Juarez (WB, 1939)
The Lady's from Kentucky (Par, 1939)

Nurse Edith Cavell (RKO, 1939)
Raffles (UA, 1940)
The House of the Seven Gables (Univ, 1940)
Anne of Windy Poplars (RKO, 1940)
The River's End (WB, 1940)
South of Suez (WB, 1940)
That Hamilton Woman (UA, 1941)
Rage in Heaven (MGM, 1941)
Adam Had Four Sons (Col, 1941)
Scotland Yard (20th, 1941)
A Woman's Face (MGM, 1941)

Singapore Woman (WB, 1941)
New Wine [TV title: *Melody Master*] (UA, 1941)
Sundown (UA, 1941)
The Remarkable Andrew (Par, 1942)
Escape from Hong Kong (Univ, 1942)
The Loves of Edgar Allan Poe (20th, 1942)
The Return of the Vampire (Col, 1943)
Between Two Worlds (WB, 1944)
The Brighton Strangler (RKO, 1945)

ROBERT EMHARDT

Shirley Knight, Robert Emhardt, and James Broderick in The Group *(1966).*

Born July 16, 1916, Indianapolis, Indiana. Married Silvia Sideli, children: four. Midwesterner who learned acting in London, understudied Sydney Greenstreet on an American tour, and was later frequently on Broadway. Rotund, of drawling diction, and suspicious squinting eyes. Played syndicate director Earl Connors in *Underworld U.S.A.;* equally effective as Shirley Knight's insane but gracious gourmet father, Mr. Andrews, in *The Group.* Can make much of a cameo (e.g., the fussy man in *The Stone Killer).* TV series: "Another World" (as MacKenzie Corey).

Robert Emhardt to George Montgomery in *Hostile Guns:*
"This is a disgrace . . . a railroad commissioner shackled to a goat stealer. Someone will pay for this!"

192

Films

The Iron Mistress (WB, 1952)
The Big Knife (UA, 1955)
3:10 to Yuma (Col, 1957)
The Badlanders (MGM, 1958)
Wake Me When It's Over (20th, 1960)
Underworld U.S.A. (Col, 1961)
I Hate Your Guts [a.k.a. *The Intruder*] (Cinema Distributors of America, 1962)

Kid Galahad (UA, 1962)
The Group (UA, 1966)
Hostile Guns (Par, 1967)
Where Were You When the Lights Went Out? (MGM, 1968)
Rascal (BV, 1969)
Change of Habit (Univ, 1969)
Suppose They Gave a War and Nobody Came (Cin, 1971)

Lawman (UA, 1972)
The Stone Killer (Col, 1973)
Scorpio (UA, 1973)
It's Alive (WB, 1974)
Alex and the Gypsy (20th, 1976)
Fraternity Row (Par, 1977)

STUART ERWIN

Franchot Tone and Stuart Erwin in Exclusive Story *(1936).*

Born February 14, 1902, Squaw Valley, California. Married June Collyer (1931), children: Stuart, Judy. Died December 21, 1967, Beverly Hills, California. Blessed with a kind but befuddled, youthful look. Turned the characteristic into a full-time acting career. Was the bumbling movie-crazy Merton Gill of *Make Me a Star,* and interpreted the comic-strip boxer Joe in *Palooka.* Oscar-nominated for *Pigskin Parade,* as Judy Garland's hick brother who could pass a football (but lost the BSAAA to Walter Brennan of *Come and Get It*). Typified Americana. Played Howie Newsome the milkman in *Our Town,* and continued with an assortment of well-meaning boobs thereafter (e.g., the father of triplets in *Pillow to Post*). TV series: "The Trouble with Father" (with his real-life wife, actress June Collyer), "The Greatest Show on Earth," and "The Bing Crosby Show."

Stuart Erwin to Leo Carrillo in *Viva Villa!:* "If you're looking for money, you're going to be disappointed. I'm a newspaper man."

Films

Mother Knows Best (Fox, 1928)
Happy Days (Fox, 1929)
Speakeasy (MGM, 1929)
New Year's Eve (Fox, 1929)
Thru Different Eyes (Fox, 1929)
Dangerous Curves (Par, 1929)
The Cock-Eyed World (Fox, 1929)
The Trespasser (UA, 1929)
The Exalted Flapper (Fox, 1929)
Sweetie (Par, 1929)
This Thing Called Love (Pathé, 1929)
Along Came Youth (Par, 1930)
Men Without Women (Fox, 1930)
Young Eagles (Par, 1930)
Paramount on Parade (Par, 1930)
Dangerous Nan McGrew (Par, 1930)
Love Among the Millionaires (Par, 1930)
Maybe It's Love (WB, 1930)
Playboy of Paris (Par, 1930)
Only Saps Work (Par, 1930)
No Limit (Par, 1931)
Up Pops the Devil (Par, 1931)
Dude Ranch (Par, 1931)
Working Girls (Par, 1931)
The Magnificent Lie (Par, 1931)
Two Kinds of Women (Par, 1932)
The Misleading Lady (Par, 1932)
Strangers in Love (Par, 1932)
The Big Broadcast (Par, 1932)
Make Me a Star (Par, 1933)

He Learned About Women (Par, 1933)
Face in the Sky (Fox, 1933)
Crime of the Century (Par, 1933)
International House (Par, 1933)
Under the Tonto Rim (Par, 1933)
Hold Your Man (MGM, 1933)
The Stranger's Return (MGM, 1933)
Day of Reckoning (MGM, 1933)
Going Hollywood (MGM, 1933)
Before Dawn (RKO, 1933)
Palooka (UA, 1934)
Viva Villa! (MGM, 1934)
Chained (MGM, 1934)
Have a Heart (MGM, 1934)
Bachelor Bait (RKO, 1934)
The Band Plays On (MGM, 1934)
The Party's Over (Col, 1934)
After Office Hours (MGM, 1935)
Ceiling Zero (WB, 1935)
Exclusive Story (MGM, 1936)
Absolute Quiet (MGM, 1936)
Women Are Trouble (MGM, 1936)
All American Chump (MGM, 1936)
Pigskin Parade (20th, 1936)
Dance Charlie Dance (WB, 1937)
Second Honeymoon (20th, 1937)
Checkers (20th, 1937)
Small Town Boy (GN, 1937)
I'll Take Romance (Col, 1937)
Mr. Boggs Steps Out (GN, 1937)

Three Blind Mice (20th, 1938)
Passport Husband (20th, 1938)
It Could Happen to You (20th, 1939)
Hollywood Cavalcade (20th, 1939)
Back Door to Heaven (Par, 1939)
The Honeymoon's Over (20th, 1939)
Our Town (UA, 1940)
When the Daltons Rode (Univ, 1940)
A Little Bit of Heaven (Univ, 1940)
Sandy Gets Her Man (Univ, 1940)
The Bride Came C.O.D. (WB, 1941)
Cracked Nuts (Univ, 1941)
The Adventures of Martin Eden (Col, 1942)
Drums of the Congo (Univ, 1942)
Blondie for Victory (Col, 1942)
Through Different Eyes (20th, 1942)
He Hired the Boss (20th, 1943)
The Great Mike (PRC, 1944)
Pillow to Post (WB, 1945)
Killer Dill (Screen Guild, 1947)
Heaven Only Knows (UA, 1947)
Headin' for Heaven (EL, 1947)
Strike It Rich (AA, 1948)
Father Is a Bachelor (Col, 1950)
For the Love of Mike (20th, 1960)
Son of Flubber (BV, 1963)
The Misadventures of Merlin Jones (BV, 1964)

FRANK FAYLEN
(Frank Ruf)

Nat Pendleton, Frank Faylen, Guy Kibbee (seated), Edgar Kennedy, and Grady Sutton in It's a Wonderful World *(1939).*

Born December 8, 1909, St. Louis, Missouri. Married Carol Hughes (1936), children: Catherine, Carol. Had a man-of-the-street mien. A natural to play cabdrivers, bartenders, factory workers, etc. Contracted by Paramount in 1943 after several years at other studios, including Warner Brothers. Notable as the jitterbugger in *And the Angels Sing* and as Bim, the unyielding male nurse in *The Lost Weekend*. On target as Mandel, a co-social worker with Brian Keith in *Dino*. TV series: "The Many Loves of Dobie Gillis" (as Herbert T. Gillis) and "That Girl" (as Bert Hollinger, Ted Bessell's father).

> Cabbie **Frank Faylen** to James Stewart in *No Time for Comedy:* "I ain't givin' no information on subways. We're competitors."

Films

Thanks a Million (Fox, 1935)
Bullets or Ballots (WB, 1936)
Border Flight (Par, 1936)
Down the Stretch (FN, 1936)
King of Hockey (WB, 1936)
The Cherokee Strip (WB, 1937)
Wine, Women and Horses (WB, 1937)
Kid Galahad (WB, 1937)
That Certain Woman (WB, 1937)
Marked Woman (WB, 1937)
They Won't Forget (WB, 1937)
Talent Scout (WB, 1937)
The Case of the Stuttering Bishop (WB, 1937)
Dance, Charlie, Dance (WB, 1937)
Headin' East (Col, 1937)

Invisible Menace (WB, 1938)
Reno (RKO, 1939)
Waterfront (WB, 1939)
The Star Maker (Par, 1939)
No Place to Go (WB, 1939)
It's a Wonderful World (MGM, 1939)
Nick Carter—Master Detective (MGM, 1939)
Married and in Love (RKO, 1940)
The Grapes of Wrath (20th, 1940)
Curtain Call (RKO, 1940)
No Time for Comedy (WB, 1940)
Margie (Univ, 1940)
Come Live with Me (MGM, 1941)
Thieves Fall Out (WB, 1941)
Father Steps Out (Mon, 1941)

Let's Go Collegiate (Mon, 1941)
City Limits (Mon, 1941)
Top Sergeant Mulligan (Mon, 1941)
No Hands on the Clock (Par, 1941)
Dudes Are Pretty People (UA, 1942)
Across the Pacific (WB, 1942)
Fall In (UA, 1942)
Silver Skates (Mon, 1943)
She's for Me (Univ, 1943)
Taxi, Mister (UA, 1943)
Good Morning, Judge (Univ, 1943)
Mission to Moscow (WB, 1943)
That Nazty Nuisance (UA, 1943)
Yanks Ahoy (UA, 1943)
Prairie Chickens (UA, 1943)
Get Going (Univ, 1943)

The Mystery of the 13th Guest (Mon, 1943)
Address Unknown (Col, 1944)
And the Angels Sing (Par, 1944)
The Canterville Ghost (MGM, 1944)
The Affairs of Susan (Par, 1945)
The Lost Weekend (Par, 1945)
You Came Along (Par, 1945)
Bring on the Girls (Par, 1945)
The Blue Dahlia (Par, 1946)
Blue Skies (Par, 1946)
The Well-Groomed Bride (Par, 1946)
Our Hearts Were Growing Up (Par, 1946)
It's a Wonderful Life (RKO, 1946)
Two Years Before the Mast (Par, 1946)
To Each His Own (Par, 1946)
California (Par, 1946)
Variety Girl (Par, 1947)
Welcome Stranger (Par, 1947)

Easy Come, Easy Go (Par, 1947)
The Perils of Pauline (Par, 1947)
Suddenly It's Spring (Par, 1947)
The Trouble with Women (Par, 1947)
Road to Rio (Par, 1947)
Hazard (Par, 1948)
Race Street (RKO, 1948)
Whispering Smith (Par, 1948)
Blood on the Moon (RKO, 1948)
Francis (Univ, 1949)
Copper Canyon (Par, 1950)
The Nevadan (Col, 1950)
The Eagle and the Hawk (Par, 1950)
Convicted (Col, 1950)
Detective Story (Par, 1951)
Fourteen Hours (20th, 1951)
Passage West (Par, 1951)
The Sniper (Col, 1952)
The Lusty Men (RKO, 1952)
Hangman's Knot (Col, 1952)

99 River Street (UA, 1953)
Red Garters (Par, 1954)
Riot in Cell Block 11 (AA, 1954)
The Looters (Univ, 1955)
The McConnell Story (WB, 1955)
Away All Boats (Univ, 1956)
Terror at Midnight (Rep, 1956)
The Seventh Cavalry (Col, 1956)
Everything but the Truth (Univ, 1956)
The Gunfight at the O.K. Corral (Par, 1957)
Three Brave Men (20th, 1957)
Dino (AA, 1957)
North to Alaska (20th, 1960)
Fluffy (Univ, 1965)
When the Boys Meet the Girls (MGM, 1965)
The Monkey's Uncle (BV, 1965)
Funny Girl (Col, 1968)

FRITZ FELD

In Idiot's Delight *(1939).*

Born October 5, 1900, Berlin, Germany. Married Virginia Christine (1940), children: Steven, Daniel. Co-founder of the Hollywood Playhouse. A personification of the enthusiastic character actor. Exceedingly effective as pompous maitre d', snide waiter, temperamental film director, and egocentric psychiatrist. Characterized by his prominent nose, accented and lisping speech, and haughty bearing—one of filmdom's most recognized personalities. Makes a loud cork-popping sound which has become his trademark.

Fritz Feld to Margaret Hamilton in *George White's Scandals:*
"There's a limit to how much of your type of beauty a man
can stand, and I'm rapidly reaching the limit."

Films

The Golem (Ger, 1917)
The Last Command (Par, 1928)
A Ship Comes In (Pathe, 1928)
Blindfold (Fox, 1928)
One Hysterical Night (Univ, 1929)
Broadway (Univ, 1929)
Black Magic (Fox, 1929)
The Charlatan (Univ, 1929)
I Met Him in Paris (Par, 1937)
Expensive Husbands (WB, 1937)
True Confession (Par, 1937)
Tovarich (WB, 1937)
Hollywood Hotel (WB, 1937)
Lancer Spy (20th, 1937)
Bringing Up Baby (RKO, 1938)
Go Chase Yourself (RKO, 1938)
Romance in the Dark (Par, 1938)
Affairs of Annabel (RKO, 1938)
Campus Confessions (Par, 1938)
Artists and Models Abroad (Par, 1938)
Gold Diggers in Paris (WB, 1938)
I'll Give a Million (20th, 1938)
Idiot's Delight (MGM, 1939)
At the Circus (MGM, 1939)
When Tomorrow Comes (Univ, 1939)
Little Accident (Univ, 1939)
Everything Happens at Night (20th, 1939)
Little Old New York (20th, 1940)
It's a Date (Univ, 1940)
Millionaire Playboy (RKO, 1940)
Ma, He's Making Eyes at Me (Univ, 1940)
I Was an Adventuress (20th, 1940)
Sandy Is a Lady (Univ, 1940)
Victory (Par, 1940)
World Premiere (Par, 1941)
Mexican Spitfire's Baby (RKO, 1941)
Three Sons o' Guns (WB, 1941)
You Belong to Me (Col, 1941)
Shut My Big Mouth (Col, 1942)

Sleepytime Gal (Rep, 1942)
Maisie Gets Her Man (MGM, 1942)
Iceland (20th, 1942)
Henry Aldrich Swings It (Par, 1943)
Phantom of the Opera (Univ, 1943)
Holy Matrimony (20th, 1943)
Four Jills in a Jeep (20th, 1944)
Knickerbocker Holiday (UA, 1944)
Passport to Adventure (RKO, 1944)
Take It Big (Par, 1944)
Ever Since Venus (Col, 1944)
The Great John L. (UA, 1945)
George White's Scandals (RKO, 1945)
Captain Tugboat Annie (Rep, 1945)
Wife of Monte Cristo (PRC, 1946)
Catman of Paris (Rep, 1946)
Her Sister's Secret (PRC, 1946)
I've Always Loved You (Rep, 1946)
Gentleman Joe Palooka (Mon, 1946)
Carnival in Costa Rica (20th, 1947)
The Secret Life of Walter Mitty (RKO, 1947)
Fun on a Weekend (UA, 1947)
If You Knew Susie (RKO, 1948)
The Noose Hangs High (EL, 1948)
My Girl Tisa (WB, 1948)
Julia Misbehaves (MGM, 1948)
Mexican Hayride (Univ, 1948)
Trouble Makers (Mon, 1948)
You Gotta Stay Happy (Univ, 1948)
Lovable Cheat (Film Classics, 1949)
The Jackpot (20th, 1950)
Belle of Old Mexico (Rep, 1950)
Missing Women (Rep, 1951)
Appointment with Danger (Par, 1951)
Rhythm Inn (Mon, 1951)
Kentucky Jubilee (Lip, 1951)
Little Egypt (Univ, 1951)
Sky High (Lip, 1951)
O. Henry's Full House (20th, 1952)

Aaron Slick from Punkin' Crick (Par, 1952)
Has Anybody Seen My Gal? (Univ, 1952)
Call Me Madam (20th, 1953)
Riding Shotgun (WB, 1954)
Living It Up (Par, 1954)
Jail Busters (AA, 1955)
Up in Smoke (AA, 1957)
Juke Box Rhythm (Col, 1959)
Don't Give Up the Ship (Par, 1959)
Pocketful of Miracles (UA, 1961)
Ladies' Man (Par, 1961)
The Errand Boy (Par, 1962)
Wives and Lovers (Par, 1963)
Who's Minding the Store? (Par, 1963)
Four for Texas (WB, 1963)
The Patsy (Par, 1964)
Harlow (Par, 1965)
The Miracle of Santa's White Reindeer (Gernos Productions, 1965)
Three on a Couch (Col, 1966)
Caprice (20th, 1967)
Barefoot in the Park (Par, 1967)
The Wicked Dreams of Paula Schultz (UA, 1968)
The Comic (Col, 1969)
Hello, Dolly! (20th, 1969)
Which Way to the Front? (WB, 1970)
The Computer Wore Tennis Shoes (BV, 1970)
The Phynx (WB, 1970)
Herbie Rides Again (BV, 1974)
The Strongest Man in the World (BV, 1975)
The Sunshine Boys (MGM-UA, 1975)
Won Ton Ton, the Dog Who Saved Hollywood (Par, 1976)
Silent Movie (20th, 1976)
Freaky Friday (BV, 1976)
The World's Greatest Lover (20th, 1977)

STANLEY FIELDS

Edward G. Robinson, George E. Stone, and Stanley Fields in Little Caesar *(1930).*

Born May 20, 1883, Allegheny, Pennsylvania. Married Alta Travis. Died April 23, 1941, Los Angeles, California. Onetime prizefighter and vaudevillian (blackface comic). Made a strong impression as hoodlum Sam Vettori in *Little Caesar*. Thereafter played many variations of the serious and comic underworld figure. Also displayed a sense for the country type: in Irene Dunne's *Cimarron* (Lon Yountis) and her *Showboat* (Jeb). Played Muspratt in Clark Gable's *Mutiny on the Bounty* and Carlos in *Algiers*. Was set for a role in *Lady Scarface* (1941) when he died.

> **Stanley Fields** to Laurel and Hardy in *Way Out West:* "And there's one thing we *don't* allow. And that's messin' with our women!"

Films

Street of Chance (Par, 1930)
Mammy (WB, 1930)
Ladies Love Brutes (Par, 1930)
The Border Legion (Par, 1930)
Manslaughter (Par, 1930)
Her Man (Par, 1930)
Little Caesar (FN, 1930)
See America Thirst (Univ, 1930)
Hook, Line and Sinker (RKO, 1930)
Cimarron (RKO, 1931)
Cracked Nuts (RKO, 1931)
City Streets (Par, 1931)
Traveling Husbands (RKO, 1931)
Holy Terror (Fox, 1931)
Skyline (Fox, 1931)
Riders of the Purple Sage (Fox, 1931)
Way Back Home (RKO, 1931)
The Mouthpiece (WB, 1932)
Two Kinds of Women (Par, 1932)
Destry Rides Again (Univ, 1932)

Girl of the Rio (RKO, 1932)
Girl Crazy (RKO, 1932)
Painted Woman (Fox, 1932)
Hell's Highway (RKO, 1932)
Rackety Rax (Fox, 1932)
Sherlock Holmes (Fox, 1932)
The Kid from Spain (UA, 1932)
Island of Lost Souls (Par, 1933)
The Constant Woman [a.k.a. Hell in a Circus] (WW, 1933)
Destination Unknown (Univ, 1933)
He Couldn't Take It (Mon, 1933)
Palooka (UA, 1934)
Sing and Like It (RKO, 1934)
Many Happy Returns (Par, 1934)
Strictly Dynamite (RKO, 1934)
Name the Woman (Col, 1934)
Rocky Rhodes (Univ, 1934)
Kid Millions (UA, 1934)
Helldorado (Fox, 1935)

Baby Face Harrington (MGM, 1935)
The Daring Young Man (Fox, 1935)
Mutiny on the Bounty (MGM, 1935)
Life Returns (Univ, 1935)
Showboat (Univ, 1936)
It Had to Happen (20th, 1936)
The King Steps Out (Col, 1936)
O'Malley of the Mounted (20th, 1936)
The Mine with the Iron Door (Col, 1936)
Ticket to Paradise (Rep, 1936)
The Gay Desperado (UA, 1936)
Way Out West (MGM, 1936)
The Devil Is a Sissy (MGM, 1936)
Maid of Salem (Par, 1937)
Midnight Court (WB, 1937)
The Three Legionnaires (General Films, 1937)
All over Town (Rep, 1937)
The Sheik Steps Out (Rep, 1937)
The Toast of New York (RKO, 1937)

Souls at Sea (Par, 1937)
Wife, Doctor and Nurse (20th, 1937)
Danger! Love at Work (20th, 1937)
Counsel for Crime (Col, 1937)
Ali Baba Goes to Town (20th, 1937)
Wells Fargo (Par, 1937)
The Adventures of Marco Polo (UA, 1938)
Wide Open Faces (Col, 1938)
Algiers (UA, 1938)
Panamint's Bad Man (20th, 1938)

Flirting with Fate (MGM, 1938)
Painted Desert (RKO, 1938)
Straight, Place and Show (20th, 1938)
Crashing Through Danger (Excelsior, 1938)
The Kid from Kokomo (WB, 1939)
Hell's Kitchen (WB, 1939)
Fugitive at Large (Col, 1939)
Pack Up Your Troubles (MGM, 1939)
Blackwell's Island (WB, 1939)

Exile Express (GN, 1939)
Viva Cisco Kid (20th, 1940)
King of the Lumberjacks (WB, 1940)
Ski Patrol (Univ, 1940)
New Moon (MGM, 1940)
The Great Plane Robbery (Col, 1940)
Where Did You Get That Girl? (Univ, 1941)
I'll Sell My Life (Select, 1941)
The Lady from Cheyenne (Univ, 1941)

BARRY FITZGERALD
(William Joseph Shields)

Sonny Tufts and Barry Fitzgerald in Easy Come, Easy Go *(1947).*

Born March 10, 1888, Dublin, Ireland. Died January 4, 1961, Dublin, Ireland. Middle-aged when he abandoned his civil-service post to try acting. Soon became a member of Dublin's Abbey Players. Diminutive (5'3") performer with a strong Irish accent. Became a regular interpreter of blarney—Hollywood-style—although not always as a good guy. Played a safecracker in *The Saint Strikes Back*, the unpleasant steward Cocky in *The Long Voyage Home*. Won BSAAA for the role of Father Fitzgibbon who enjoys a teary reunion with his aged mother (Adeline DeWalt Reynolds) in Bing Crosby's *Going My Way*. Kept in type thereafter by Paramount, save when he escaped occasionally: Twite *(None but the Lonely Heart)*, Judge Quincannon *(And Then There Were None)*, Lieutenant Dan Muldoon *(The Naked City)*. Later played Bette Davis' brother Jack in *The Catered Affair*. In real life was the brother of actor Arthur Shields.

Barry Fitzgerald to Bing Crosby in *Going My Way:* "The joy of giving is indeed a pleasure—especially when you get rid of something you don't want."

Films

Juno and the Paycock (Br, 1930)
When Knights Were Bold (Br, 1936)
The Plough and the Stars (RKO, 1936)
Ebb Tide (Par, 1937)
Bringing Up Baby (RKO, 1938)
Pacific Liner (RKO, 1938)
The Dawn Patrol (WB, 1938)
Four Men and a Prayer (20th, 1938)
The Saint Strikes Back (RKO, 1939)
Full Confession (RKO, 1939)
The Long Voyage Home (UA, 1940)
San Francisco Docks (Univ, 1941)
The Sea Wolf (WB, 1941)
How Green Was My Valley (20th, 1941)
Tarzan's Secret Treasure (MGM, 1941)

Two Tickets to London (Univ, 1943)
The Amazing Mrs. Holliday (Univ, 1943)
Corvette K-225 (Univ, 1943)
I Love a Soldier (Par, 1944)
Going My Way (Par, 1944)
None but the Lonely Heart (RKO, 1944)
Incendiary Blonde (Par, 1945)
And Then There Were None (20th, 1945)
Duffy's Tavern (Par, 1945)
The Stork Club (Par, 1945)
Two Years Before the Mast (Par, 1946)
California (Par, 1946)
Welcome Stranger (Par, 1947)
Easy Come, Easy Go (Par, 1947)
Variety Girl (Par, 1947)

The Sainted Sisters (Par, 1948)
The Naked City (Univ, 1948)
Miss Tatlock's Millions (Par, 1948)
The Story of Seabiscuit (WB, 1949)
Top o' the Morning (Par, 1949)
Union Station (Par, 1950)
Silver City (Par, 1951)
The Quiet Man (Rep, 1952)
Tonight's the Night (AA, 1954)
The Catered Affair (MGM, 1956)
Rooney (Br, 1958)
Broth of a Boy (Kingsley International, 1959)

PAUL FIX
(Paul Fix Morrison)

Stuart Whitman, DeForrest Kelley, and Paul Fix (second from right) in Night of the Lepus (1972).

Born March 13, 1902, Dobbs Ferry, New York. Married 1) _____, child: daughter; divorced (1945); 2) Beverly _____ (1949). One of the more imposing performers in American films. Demonstrated authority from the start: Ezra Talbot, Gary Cooper's brother in *The First Kiss*. Whether as a convict (Eddie Werner of *The Last Mile*), a participant in a *Hopalong Cassidy* Western (Gil of *Bar-20 Rides Again*), or a participant in a detective entry (Phil Byrnes of *After the Thin Man*), demonstrated a resiliency that has kept him active in pictures for six decades. Often cast as a rancher or sheriff (the latter role in one of his most recent features, *Night of the Lepus*).

Paul Fix to Gavin Muir in *Charlie Chan at the Race Track:*
"That Chinese dick is wise to the whole thing."

Films

The First Kiss (Par, 1928)
Lucky Star (Fox, 1929)
Man Trouble (Fox, 1930)
Ladies Love Brutes (Par, 1930)
Bad Girl (Fox, 1931)
Three Girls Lost (Fox, 1931)
Good Bad Girl (Col, 1931)
The Fighting Sheriff (Col, 1931)
The Last Mile (WW, 1932)
Dancers in the Dark (Par, 1932)
South of the Rio Grande (Col, 1932)
Fargo Express (WW, 1932)
Back Street (Univ, 1932)
Sky Devils (UA, 1932)
The Racing Strain (Maxim Productions, 1932)
The Avenger (Mon, 1933)
Zoo in Budapest (Fox, 1933)
The Mad Game (Fox, 1933)
The Sphinx (Mon, 1933)
The Devil's Mate (Mon, 1933)
Emergency Call (RKO, 1933)
Somewhere in Sonora (WB, 1933)
Gun Law (Majestic, 1933)
Little Man, What Now? (Univ, 1934)
The Woman Who Dared (Imperial, 1934)
Rocky Rhodes (Univ, 1934)
The Crimson Trail (Univ, 1935)
The World Accuses (Chesterfield, 1935)
Let 'em Have It (UA, 1935)
Men Without Names (Par, 1935)
The Desert Trail (Mon, 1935)
The Eagle's Brood (Par, 1935)
His Fighting Blood (Ambassador, 1935)
Bar-20 Rides Again (Par, 1935)
Miss Pacific Fleet (WB, 1935)
Mutiny Ahead (Majestic, 1935)
The Throwback (Univ, 1935)
Bulldog Courage (Puritan, 1935)
Valley of Wanted Men (Conn Pictures, 1935)
The Prisoner of Shark Island (20th, 1936)
The Road to Glory (20th, 1936)
The Bridge of Sighs (Invincible, 1936)
The Ex-Mrs. Bradford (RKO, 1936)
Winterset (RKO, 1936)
Two in a Crowd (Univ, 1936)
The Plot Thickens (RKO, 1936)
Straight from the Shoulder (Par, 1936)
Yellowstone (Univ, 1936)
After the Thin Man (MGM, 1936)
Daughter of Shanghai (Par, 1937)
Woman in Distress (Col, 1937)
King of Gamblers (Par, 1937)
Souls at Sea (Par, 1937)
Border Cafe (RKO, 1937)
Armored Car (Univ, 1937)
On Such a Night (Par, 1937)

The Game That Kills (Col, 1937)
Paid to Dance (Col, 1937)
The Buccaneer (Par, 1938)
King of Alcatraz (Par, 1938)
Mannequin (MGM, 1938)
Penitentiary (Col, 1938)
When G-Men Step In (Col, 1938)
Crime Takes a Holiday (Col, 1938)
The Night Hawk (Rep, 1938)
Crime Ring (RKO, 1938)
Smashing the Rackets (RKO, 1938)
Code of the Streets (Univ, 1939)
Mutiny on the Blackhawk (Univ, 1939)
Star Reporter (Mon, 1939)
The Girl and the Gambler (RKO, 1939)
News Is Made at Night (20th, 1939)
Behind Prison Gates (Col, 1939)
Those High Grey Walls (Col, 1939)
Heritage of the Desert (Par, 1939)
Undercover Doctor (Par, 1939)
Outside the Three-Mile Limit (Col, 1940)
Dr. Cyclops (Par, 1940)
Black Friday (Univ, 1940)
The Crooked Road (Rep, 1940)
The Ghost Breakers (Par, 1940)
Triple Justice (RKO, 1940)
Black Diamonds (Univ, 1940)
Virginia City (WB, 1940)
The Great Plane Robbery (Col, 1940)
Trail of the Vigilantes (Univ, 1940)
Glamour for Sale (Col, 1940)
The Roar of the Press (Mon, 1941)
Citadel of Crime (Rep, 1941)
Down Mexico Way (Rep, 1941)
A Missouri Outlaw (Rep, 1941)
Public Enemies (Rep, 1941)
Jail House Blues (Univ, 1942)
South of Santa Fe (Rep, 1942)
Escape from Crime (WB, 1942)
Highways by Night (RKO, 1942)
That Other Woman (20th, 1942)
Pittsburgh (Univ, 1942)
Sherlock Holmes and the Secret Weapon (Univ, 1942)
Hitler—Dead or Alive (Ben Judell, 1943)
In Old Oklahoma [a.k.a. *War of the Wildcats*] (Rep, 1943)
Mug Town (Univ, 1943)
Tall in the Saddle (RKO, 1944)
The Fighting Seabees (Rep, 1944)
Grissly's Millions (Rep, 1945)
Back to Bataan (RKO, 1945)
Flame of Barbary Coast (Rep, 1945)
Dakota (Rep, 1945)
Tycoon (RKO, 1947)
Wake of the Red Witch (Rep, 1948)
Angel in Exile (Rep, 1948)
The Plunderers (Rep, 1948)

Force of Evil (MGM, 1948)
Red River (UA, 1948)
Hellfire (Rep, 1949)
The Fighting Kentuckian (Rep, 1949)
Fighting Man of the Plains (20th, 1949)
Surrender (Rep, 1950)
The Great Missouri Raid (Par, 1950)
California Passage (Rep, 1950)
Warpath (Par, 1951)
Denver and the Rio Grande (Par, 1952)
Ride the Man Down (Rep, 1952)
What Price Glory? (20th, 1952)
Fair Wind to Java (Rep, 1953)
Island in the Sky (WB, 1953)
Star of Texas (AA, 1953)
Hondo (WB, 1953)
Johnny Guitar (Rep, 1954)
The High and the Mighty (WB, 1954)
Ring of Fear (WB, 1954)
Top of the World (UA, 1955)
The Sea Chase (WB, 1955)
Blood Alley (WB, 1955)
Giant (WB, 1956)
Santiago (WB, 1956)
Toward the Unknown (WB, 1956)
Man in the Vault (RKO, 1956)
The Bad Seed (WB, 1956)
Stagecoach to Fury (20th, 1956)
Night Passage (Univ, 1957)
Jet Pilot (Univ, 1957)
The Devil's Hairpin (Par, 1957)
Man in the Shadow (Univ, 1957)
Lafayette Escadrille (WB, 1958)
The Notorious Mr. Monks (Rep, 1958)
Guns, Girls and Gangsters (UA, 1958)
To Kill a Mockingbird (Univ, 1962)
The Outrage (MGM, 1964)
Mail Order Bride (MGM, 1964)
Baby, the Rain Must Fall (Col, 1965)
The Sons of Katie Elder (Par, 1965)
Shenandoah (Univ, 1965)
Nevada Smith (Par, 1966)
Ride Beyond Vengeance (Col, 1966)
An Eye for an Eye (Emb, 1966)
Incident at Phantom Hill (Univ, 1966)
El Dorado (Par, 1967)
Welcome to Hard Times (MGM, 1967)
The Ballad of Josie (Univ, 1967)
Day of the Evil Gun (MGM, 1968)
Dirty Dingus Magee (MGM, 1970)
Something Big (National General, 1971)
Shoot Out (Univ, 1971)
Night of the Lepus (MGM, 1972)
Pat Garrett & Billy the Kid (MGM, 1973)
Cahill, United States Marshal (WB, 1973)

JAY C. FLIPPEN

Jim Hutton, Barbara Nichols, Jay C. Flippen, and Connie Francis in Where the Boys Are *(1960).*

Born 1898, Little Rock, Arkansas. Married Ruth Brooks (1946). Died February 3, 1971, Los Angeles, California. Seasoned performer in vaudeville, minstrel shows, Broadway, etc. Made two films in the 1930s, abandoned the medium, returned in *Brute Force* as the prison warden. Characterized by his pudgy, leathery face and thickset figure. Destined to play toughs, but also displayed a facility for fractured farce: Red Skelton's *The Yellow Cab Man* and Bob Hope's *The Lemon Drop Kid*. Frequently cast in Jimmy Stewart Westerns: *Winchester 73* (Sergeant Wilkes), *Bend of the River* (Jeremy Baile), *The Far Country* (Rube). Popped up in *Oklahoma!* (Skidmore) and Howard Keel's *Kismet* (Jawan), and was Father Gilhooey in *Studs Lonigan*. Played his final film job (Luther in *The Seven Minutes)* from a wheelchair. TV series: "Ensign O'Toole" (as Captain Homer Nelson).

Jay C. Flippen to James Stewart in *Bend of the River:* "When an apple's rotten, there's nothing you can do but throw it away, or else it'll spoil the whole barrel."

Films

Marie Galante (Fox, 1934)
Million Dollar Ransom (Univ, 1934)
Brute Force (Univ, 1947)
Intrigue (UA, 1947)
They Live by Night [a.k.a. The Twisted Road] (RKO, 1948)
A Woman's Secret (RKO, 1949)
Down to the Sea in Ships (20th, 1949)
Oh, You Beautiful Doll (20th, 1949)
Buccaneer's Girl (Univ, 1950)
The Yellow Cab Man (MGM, 1950)
Love That Brute (20th, 1950)

Winchester 73 (Univ, 1950)
Two Flags West (20th, 1950)
The Lemon Drop Kid (Par, 1951)
Flying Leathernecks (RKO, 1951)
The People Against O'Hara (MGM, 1951)
The Lady from Texas (Univ, 1951)
The Model and the Marriage Broker (20th, 1951)
The Las Vegas Story (RKO, 1952)
Bend of the River (Univ, 1952)
Woman of the North Country (Rep, 1952)

Thunder Bay (Univ, 1953)
Devil's Canyon (RKO, 1953)
East of Sumatra (Univ, 1953)
The Wild One (Col, 1954)
Carnival Story (RKO, 1954)
Six Bridges to Cross (Univ, 1955)
The Far Country (Univ, 1955)
Man Without a Star (Univ, 1955)
It's Always Fair Weather (MGM, 1955)
Kismet (MGM, 1955)
Oklahoma! (Magna Pictures Corp., 1955)

Strategic Air Command (Par, 1955)
The Killing (UA, 1956)
The Seventh Cavalry (Col, 1956)
The King and Four Queens (UA, 1956)
The Restless Breed (20th, 1957)
The Halliday Brand (UA, 1957)
Hot Summer Night (MGM, 1957)
Public Pigeon No. 1 (Univ, 1957)
Night Passage (Univ, 1957)

Run of the Arrow (Univ, 1957)
The Midnight Story (Univ, 1957)
Jet Pilot (Univ, 1957)
The Deerslayer (20th, 1957)
Lure of the Swamp (20th, 1957)
Escape from Red Rock (20th, 1958)
From Hell to Texas (20th, 1958)
Wild River (20th, 1960)
Studs Lonigan (UA, 1960)

Where the Boys Are (MGM, 1960)
The Plunderers (AA, 1960)
How the West Was Won (MGM, 1962)
Looking for Love (MGM, 1964)
Cat Ballou (Col, 1965)
The Spirit Is Willing (Par, 1967)
Firecreek (WB–7 Arts, 1968)
The Hellfighters (Univ, 1969)
The Seven Minutes (20th, 1971)

FRANCIS FORD
(Francis O'Feeney)

In Young Mr. Lincoln *(1939).*

Born September 15, 1882, Portland, Maine. Married Mary Armstrong (1935), children: Phil, Robert, William. Died September 5, 1953, Los Angeles, California. Slender leading man of 1910s serials. Often in tandem with Grace Cunard: *Lucille Love, Girl of Mystery; The Mystery of 13; The Purple Mask;* etc. Also made features with athletic Miss Cunard: *The Campbells Are Coming,* etc. Turned his hand to directing features and serials, many of which starred him (directed all the entries above). Last directorial assignment was *Call of the Heart* in 1928. Appeared in very subordinate roles throughout the 1920s, in Fox features directed by his brother Jack [John] Ford: *The Village Blacksmith* (Asa Martin), *Hearts of Oak* (Bit), *The Black Watch* (Major MacGregor), etc. Continued at Fox throughout the 1930s, usually performing small jobs in his brother's projects, alternating with varying-sized parts in *Charlie Chan* entries and others. Final assignment: Feenly in John Ford's *The Sun Shines Bright.*

Francis Ford to Willard Parker in *Renegades:* "Prairie Dog's sure gonna miss you, Doc."

Films

Lucille Love, Girl of Mystery (Univ serial, 1914)
The Mysterious Rose (Univ, 1914)
Three Bad Men and a Girl (Univ, 1915)
The Hidden City (Univ, 1915)
The Doorway of Destruction (Univ, 1915)
The Broken Coin (Univ serial, 1915)
The Campbells Are Coming (Univ, 1915)
The Adventures of Peg o' the Ring (Univ, 1916)
The Purple Mask (Univ, 1916)
The Lumber Yard Gang (Univ, 1916)
Chicken-Hearted Jim (Univ, 1916)
The Bandit's Wager (Univ, 1916)
Who Was the Other Man? (Univ, 1917)
John Ermine of Yellowstone (Univ, 1917)
Silent Mystery (Burston serial, 1918)
The Craving (Univ, 1918)
The Mystery of 13 (Burston serial, 1919)
Riders of Vengeance (Univ, 1919)
Thunderbolt Jack (Arrow serial, 1920)
The Crimson Shoals (Monopol, 1920)
Cyclone Bliss (Arrow, 1921)
Action (Univ, 1921)
The Lady from Longacre (Fox, 1921)
The Stampede (Krelbar, 1921)
The Man from Nowhere (Arrow, 1921)
I Am the Woman (Kremer, 1921)
The Great Reward (Burston serial, 1921)
So This Is Arizona? (Merit, 1922)
Trail's End (Merit, 1922)
Angel Citizens (Merit, 1922)
Thundering Hoofs (Anchor, 1922)
Another Man's Boots (Anchor, 1922)
They're Off (Anchor, 1922)
The Heart of Lincoln (Anchor, 1922)
Storm Girl (Anchor, 1922)
The Village Blacksmith (Fox, 1922)
Gold Grabbers (Merit, 1922)
The Boss of Camp 4 (Fox, 1922)
Cross Roads (Merit, 1922)
Three Jumps Ahead (Fox, 1923)
The Fighting Skipper (Arrow serial, 1923)
Mine to Keep (Grand-Asher, 1923)
Western Feuds (Arrow, 1924)
A Rodeo Mixup (Arrow, 1924)
Western Yesterdays (Arrow, 1924)
Lash of the Whip (Arrow, 1924)
Range Blood (Arrow, 1924)
In the Days of the Covered Wagon (Merit, 1924)
Cupid's Rustler (Arrow, 1924)
Midnight Shadows (Arrow, 1924)

The Cowboy Prince (Arrow, 1924)
The Diamond Bandit (Arrow, 1924)
Hearts of Oak (Fox, 1924)
The Lash of Pinto Pete (Arrow, 1924)
The Measure of a Man (Univ, 1924)
Soft Shoes (PDC, 1925)
The Sign of the Cactus (Univ, 1925)
A Roaring Adventure (Univ, 1925)
The Taming of the West (Univ, 1925)
Scar Hanan (FBO, 1925)
Ridin' Thunder (Univ, 1925)
The Red Rider (Univ, 1925)
The Fighting Heart (Fox, 1925)
The Four from Nowhere (Goodwill, 1925)
Perils of the Wild (Univ serial, 1925)
The Winking Idol (Univ serial, 1926)
Her Own Story (Goodwill, 1926)
The Ghetto Shamrock (Goodwill, 1926)
Speed Cop (Rayart, 1926)
Melodies (Goodwill, 1926)
False Friends (Goodwill, 1926)
Upstream (Fox, 1927)
Wolves of the Air (Sterling, 1927)
Men of Daring (Univ, 1927)
The Heart of Maryland (WB, 1927)
The Devil's Saddle (FN, 1927)
The Cruise of the Hellion (Rayart, 1927)
Wolf's Trail (Univ, 1927)
The Wreck of the Hesperus (Pathe, 1927)
Uncle Tom's Cabin (Univ, 1927)
One Glorious Scrap (Univ, 1927)
The Branded Sombrero (Fox, 1928)
Call of the Heart (Univ, 1928)
The Four-Footed Ranger (Univ, 1928)
Sisters of Eve (Rayart, 1928)
The Lariat Kid (Univ, 1929)
The Black Watch (Fox, 1929)
The Drake Case (Univ, 1929)
The Mounted Stranger (Univ, 1930)
Kathleen Mavourneen (Tif, 1930)
Song of the Caballero (Univ, 1930)
Sons of the Saddle (Univ, 1930)
The Seas Beneath (Fox, 1931)
The Last Ride (Univ, 1932)
Tangled Fortunes (Big Four, 1932)
Airmail (Univ, 1932)
Pilgrimage (Fox, 1933)
Charlie Chan's Greatest Case (Fox, 1933)
Life in the Raw (Fox, 1933)
The Man from Monterey (WB, 1933)
Gun Justice (Univ, 1934)
Murder in Trinidad (Fox, 1934)
Cheaters (Bert Lubin, 1934)
Pirate Treasure (Univ serial, 1934)
Judge Priest (Fox, 1934)
The Informer (RKO, 1935)

The Arizonian (RKO, 1935)
Steamboat 'Round the Bend (Fox, 1935)
Charlie Chan's Secret (Fox, 1935)
Paddy O'Day (Fox, 1935)
The Whole Town's Talking (Col, 1935)
Goin' to Town (Par, 1935)
This Is the Life (Fox, 1935)
The Prisoner of Shark Island (20th, 1936)
Gentle Julia (20th, 1936)
Charlie Chan at the Circus (20th, 1936)
Sins of Man (20th, 1936)
Educating Father (20th, 1936)
Slave Ship (20th, 1937)
Checkers (20th, 1937)
In Old Chicago (20th, 1938)
Kentucky Moonshine (20th, 1938)
Girl of the Golden West (MGM, 1938)
The Texans (Par, 1938)
Stagecoach (UA, 1939)
Young Mr. Lincoln (20th, 1939)
Drums Along the Mohawk (20th, 1939)
Geronimo (Par, 1939)
Bad Lands (RKO, 1939)
Viva Cisco Kid (20th, 1940)
South of Pago Pago (Univ, 1940)
Diamond Frontier (Univ, 1940)
Lucky Cisco Kid (20th, 1940)
Tobacco Road (20th, 1941)
Last of the Duanes (20th, 1941)
Riders of the Purple Sage (20th, 1941)
Western Union (20th, 1941)
The Man Who Wouldn't Die (20th, 1942)
The Loves of Edgar Allan Poe (20th, 1942)
Outlaws of Pine Ridge (Rep, 1942)
The Ox-Bow Incident (20th, 1943)
Girls in Chains (PRC, 1943)
The Climax (Univ, 1944)
The Big Noise (20th, 1944)
Bowery Champs (Mon, 1944)
The Princess and the Pirate (RKO, 1944)
State Fair (20th, 1945)
Hangover Square (20th, 1945)
My Darling Clementine (20th, 1946)
Gilda (Col, 1946)
A Stolen Life (WB, 1946)
Sister Kenny (RKO, 1946)
Renegades (Col, 1946)
Gallant Journey (Col, 1946)
High Tide (Mon, 1947)
Three Godfathers (MGM, 1948)
The Plunderers (Rep, 1948)
Wagon Masters (RKO, 1950)
The Quiet Man (Rep, 1952)
The Sun Shines Bright (Rep, 1953)

WALLACE FORD
(Samuel Jones Grundy)

In Back Door to Heaven *(1939).*

Born February 12, 1898, Bolton, England. Married Martha Harworth (1922), child: Patricia; widowed (1966). Died June 11, 1966, Woodland Hills, California. Good-natured, sometimes pugnacious, Irish-style mug who began in vaudeville at age 11. Enjoyed some leading roles in the early 1930s: the hero of *Freaks,* Walter Huston's dishonest brother in *Beast of the City.* Later settled into mostly character roles. A standout as Frankie McPhillip, one of those tattled on by Victor McLaglen in *The Informer.* Usually cast as the seedy prospector, bum, or derelict relative in later years after his hair whitened. Rejoined director John Ford for *The Last Hurrah* (Charles J. Hennessey) and ended his filmmaking as Ole Pa in *A Patch of Blue.* TV series: "The Deputy."

Wallace Ford to Joan Blondell in *Two Girls on Broadway:*
"You've been *big time* all your life, Molly."

Films

Possessed (MGM, 1931)
Freaks (MGM, 1932)
The Wet Parade (MGM, 1932)
Are You Listening? (MGM, 1932)
Skyscraper Souls (MGM, 1932)
Prosperity (MGM, 1932)
Hypnotized (WW, 1932)
Central Park (FN, 1932)
Beast of the City (MGM, 1932)
Goodbye Again (FN, 1933)
Headline Shooter (RKO, 1933)

Night of Terror (Col, 1933)
My Woman (Col, 1933)
East of 5th Avenue (Par, 1933)
Three-Cornered Moon (Par, 1933)
Employees' Entrance (FN, 1933)
The Big Cage (Univ, 1933)
She Had to Say Yes (FN, 1933)
A Woman's Man (Mon, 1934)
Money Means Nothing (Mon, 1934)
The Lost Patrol (RKO, 1934)
Men in White (MGM, 1934)

I Hate Women (Goldsmith, 1934)
The Man Who Reclaimed His Head (Univ, 1934)
The Nut Farm (Mon, 1935)
The Informer (RKO, 1935)
Another Face (RKO, 1935)
Swell Head (Col, 1935)
The Whole Town's Talking (Col, 1935)
In Spite of Danger (Col, 1935)
Men of the Hour (Col, 1935)
She Couldn't Take It (Col, 1935)

Mysterious Mr. Wong (Mon, 1935)
One Frightened Night (Mascot, 1935)
Mary Burns—Fugitive (Par, 1935)
Get That Man (Empire, 1935)
Sanders of the River (UA Br, 1935)
Two in the Dark (RKO, 1936)
Absolute Quiet (MGM, 1936)
A Son Comes Home (Par, 1936)
Rogues' Tavern (Puritan, 1936)
He Loved an Actress [a.k.a. *Mad About Money*] (Br, 1937)
O.H.M.S. [a.k.a. *You're in the Army Now*] (Br, 1937)
Swing It Sailor (GN, 1937)
Exiled to Shanghai (Rep, 1937)
Dark Sands (Br, 1938)
Back Door to Heaven (Par, 1939)
Isle of Destiny (RKO, 1940)
Two Girls on Broadway (MGM, 1940)
Love, Honor and Oh, Baby! (Univ, 1940)
The Mummy's Hand (Univ, 1940)
Give Us Wings (Univ, 1940)
Scatterbrain (Rep, 1940)
A Man Betrayed (Rep, 1941)
The Roar of the Press (Mon, 1941)
Murder by Invitation (Mon, 1941)
Blues in the Night (WB, 1941)
You're in the Army Now (WB, 1941)
Inside the Law (PRC, 1942)
Scattergood Survives a Murder (RKO, 1942)
All Through the Night (WB, 1942)
X Marks the Spot (Rep, 1942)

Seven Days' Leave (RKO, 1942)
The Mummy's Tomb (Univ, 1942)
The Marines Come Through (Astor, 1943)
The Ape Man (Mon, 1943)
The Cross of Lorraine (MGM, 1943)
Shadow of a Doubt (Univ, 1943)
Machine Gun Mama (PRC, 1944)
Secret Command (Col, 1944)
The Woman Who Came Back (Rep, 1945)
The Great John L. (UA, 1945)
On Stage, Everybody (Univ, 1945)
Spellbound (UA, 1945)
They Were Expendable (MGM, 1945) [cut from release print]
Blood on the Sun (UA, 1945)
The Green Years (MGM, 1946)
A Guy Could Change (Rep, 1946)
The Black Angel (Univ, 1946)
Crack-Up (RKO, 1946)
Lover Come Back (Univ, 1946)
Rendezvous with Annie (Rep, 1946)
Dead Reckoning (Col, 1947)
Magic Town (RKO, 1947)
T-Men (EL, 1947)
Shed No Tears (EL, 1948)
Embraceable You (WB, 1948)
Belle Starr's Daughter (20th, 1948)
The Man from Texas (EL, 1948)
Coroner Creek (Col, 1948)
The Set-Up (RKO, 1949)
Red Stallion in the Rockies (EL, 1949)
The Breaking Point (WB, 1950)

Harvey (Univ, 1950)
Dakota Lil (20th, 1950)
The Furies (Par, 1950)
Warpath (Par, 1951)
He Ran All the Way (UA, 1951)
Painting the Clouds with Sunshine (WB, 1951)
Flesh and Fury (Univ, 1952)
Rodeo (Mon, 1952)
The Nebraskan (Col, 1953)
She Couldn't Say No (RKO, 1954)
The Boy from Oklahoma (WB, 1954)
Three Ring Circus (Par, 1954)
Destry (Univ, 1954)
The Man from Laramie (Col, 1955)
The Spoilers (Univ, 1955)
Lucy Gallant (Par, 1955)
A Lawless Street (Col, 1955)
Wichita (AA, 1955)
The Maverick Queen (Rep, 1956)
Thunder over Arizona (Rep, 1956)
Stagecoach to Fury (20th, 1956)
Johnny Concho (UA, 1956)
The Rainmaker (Par, 1956)
The First Texan (AA, 1956)
The Last Hurrah (Col, 1958)
Twilight for the Gods (Univ, 1958)
The Matchmaker (Par, 1958)
Warlock (20th, 1959)
Tess of the Storm Country (20th, 1961)
A Patch of Blue (MGM, 1965)

BYRON FOULGER

Henry Fonda, Maureen O'Sullivan, Alan Baxter, and Byron Foulger in Let Us Live! *(1939).*

Born 1900, Ogden, Utah. Married Dorothy Adams, children: Amanda, Rachel. Died April 4, 1970, Hollywood, California. The usually bespectacled, mealymouthed whiner, often seen as the overly concerned clerk or bank teller. TV series: "Dennis the Menace" (as Mr. Timberlake of the National Birdwatchers Society) and "Captain Nice."

> **Byron Foulger** (on phone) to Robert Middlemass in *I Am the Law:* "Mr. Kitchell, they're going to grab the books of those witnesses."

Films

Larceny on the Air (Rep, 1937)
The Duke Comes Back (Rep, 1937)
The Awful Truth (Col, 1937)
A Day at the Races (MGM, 1937)
Dick Tracy (Rep serial, 1937)
The Prisoner of Zenda (UA, 1937)
Born to Be Wild (Rep, 1938)
Lady in the Morgue (Univ, 1938)
Delinquent Parents (Progressive, 1938)
It's All in Your Mind [a.k.a. *Fools of Desire*] (B. B. Ray, 1938)
10th Avenue Kid (Rep, 1938)
Tarnished Angel (RKO, 1938)
I Am the Law (Col, 1938)
I Am a Criminal (Mon, 1938)
At the Circus (MGM, 1939)
In Name Only (RKO, 1939)
Union Pacific (Par, 1939)
Let Us Live! (Col, 1939)
Mutiny on the Blackhawk (Univ, 1939)
Exile Express (GN, 1939)
The Girl from Rio (Mon, 1939)

The Man They Could Not Hang (Col, 1939)
Television Spy (Par, 1939)
The Great McGinty (Par, 1940)
Heroes of the Saddle (Rep, 1940)
The Man with Nine Lives (Col, 1940)
Edison the Man (MGM, 1940)
Ellery Queen, Master Detective (Col, 1940)
Sky Murder (MGM, 1940)
Arizona (Col, 1940)
Man-Made Monster (Univ, 1941)
Ridin' on a Rainbow (Rep, 1941)
The Gay Vagabond (Rep, 1941)
Sweetheart of the Campus (Col, 1941)
Mystery Ship (Col, 1941)
Dude Cowboy (RKO, 1941)
Sullivan's Travels (Par, 1941)
The Panther's Claw (PRC, 1942)
The Tuttles of Tahiti (RKO, 1942)
Man from Headquarters (Mon, 1942)
Reap the Wild Wind (Par, 1942)
Harvard, Here I Come (Col, 1942)

Quiet Please, Murder (20th, 1942)
Stand by for Action (MGM, 1942)
The Human Comedy (MGM, 1943)
So Proudly We Hail (Par, 1943)
Sweet Rosie O'Grady (20th, 1943)
The Adventures of a Rookie (RKO, 1943)
In Old Oklahoma [a.k.a. *War of the Wildcats*] (Rep, 1943)
Hi Diddle Diddle (UA, 1943)
Hoppy Serves a Writ (UA, 1943)
Hangmen Also Die (UA, 1943)
Dixie Dugan (20th, 1943)
Coney Island (20th, 1943)
Silver Spurs (Rep, 1943)
The Black Raven (PRC, 1943)
Enemy of Women (Mon, 1944)
Summer Storm (UA, 1944)
Roger Touhy—Gangster (20th, 1944)
The Whistler (Col, 1944)
Henry Aldrich's Little Secret (Par, 1944)
Since You Went Away (UA, 1944)
Dark Mountain (Par, 1944)

Beautiful but Broke (Col, 1944)
Swing in the Saddle (Col, 1944)
Marriage Is a Private Affair (MGM, 1944)
Ministry of Fear (Par, 1944)
Let's Go Steady (Col, 1945)
Brewster's Millions (UA, 1945)
It's in the Bag (UA, 1945)
The Master Key (Univ serial, 1945)
Grissly's Millions (Rep, 1945)
Circumstantial Evidence (20th, 1945)
The Hidden Eye (MGM, 1945)
The Adventures of Kitty O'Day (Mon, 1945)
Arson Squad (PRC, 1945)
The Blonde from Brooklyn (Col, 1945)
Snafu (Col, 1945)
Sensation Hunters (Mon, 1945)
Sentimental Journey (20th, 1946)
Just Before Dawn (Col, 1946)
The Postman Always Rings Twice (MGM, 1946)
The Mysterious Mr. M (Univ serial, 1946)
Till the Clouds Roll By (MGM, 1946)
The French Key (Rep, 1946)
Dick Tracy vs. Cueball (RKO, 1946)
The Plainsman and the Lady (Rep, 1946)
The Michigan Kid (Univ, 1947)
Hard-Boiled Mahoney (Mon, 1947)
The Bells of San Fernando (Screen Guild, 1947)

The Adventures of Don Coyote (UA, 1947)
Too Many Winners (PRC, 1947)
Stallion Road (WB, 1947)
The Red Hornet (Mon, 1947)
The Chinese Ring (Mon, 1947)
The Hunted (AA, 1948)
Arch of Triumph (EL, 1948)
Out of the Storm (Rep, 1948)
The Return of October (Col, 1948)
I Surrender Dear (Col, 1948)
Samson and Delilah (Par, 1949)
I Shot Jesse James (Screen Guild, 1949)
Arson, Inc. (Lip, 1949)
The Inspector General (WB, 1949)
The Dalton Gang (Screen Guild, 1949)
Satan's Cradle (UA, 1949)
Dancing in the Dark (20th, 1949)
Red Desert (Lip, 1949)
The Girl from San Lorenzo (UA, 1950)
Champagne for Caesar (UA, 1950)
Salt Lake Raiders (Rep, 1950)
The Return of Jesse James (Lip, 1950)
Experiment Alcatraz (RKO, 1950)
FBI Girl (Lip, 1951)
Lightning Strikes Twice (WB, 1951)
Footlight Varieties (RKO, 1951)
Gasoline Alley (Col, 1951)
Home Town Story (MGM, 1951)
A Millionaire for Christy (20th, 1951)
The Sea Hornet (Rep, 1951)
My Six Convicts (Col, 1952)
Apache Country (Col, 1952)

Cripple Creek (Col, 1952)
The Steel Fist (Mon, 1952)
Confidentially Connie (MGM, 1953)
Paris Model (Col, 1953)
The Magnetic Monster (UA, 1953)
Cruisin' Down the River (Col, 1953)
Bandits of the West (Rep, 1953)
You Can't Run Away from It (Col, 1956)
The River's Edge (20th, 1957)
Sierra Stranger (Col, 1957)
Dino (AA, 1957)
The Buckskin Lady (UA, 1957)
Gun Battle at Monterey (AA, 1957)
Up in Smoke (AA, 1957)
Man from God's Country (AA, 1958)
Going Steady (Col, 1958)
The Long, Hot Summer (20th, 1958)
King of the Wild Stallions (AA, 1959)
Ma Barker's Killer Brood (Film Service, 1960)
Twelve Hours to Kill (20th, 1960)
The Devil's Partner (Filmgroup, 1961)
Ride the High Country (MGM, 1962)
Marriage on the Rocks (WB, 1965)
The Gnome-Mobile (BV, 1967)
The Spirit Is Willing (Par, 1967)
The Cockeyed Cowboys of Calico Country (Univ, 1970)
There Was a Crooked Man (WB, 1970)

DOUGLAS FOWLEY

Ralf Harolde and Douglas Fowley in One Mile from Heaven *(1937).*

Born May 30, 1911, New York City, New York. Married 1) _____, child: Kim; 2) _____; 3) Mary Hunter (1944), child: Gretchen; 4) Vivian Chamber (1947), child: daughter; 5) Joy Torstup (1950), child: son; 6) Mary Ann Walsh (1954); divorced (1955); 7) Maria _____. One-time club and stage singer/dancer/comedian who proved an able film player. Often at 20th Century–Fox in the late 1930s. Frequently cast as a bemused underworld figure. Later the weathered individual in many Westerns. Played Roscoe Dexter, the shouting film director in *Singin' in the Rain.* TV series: "The Life and Legend of Wyatt Earp" and "Pistols 'n' Petticoats."

Douglas Fowley to George Lloyd in *The Denver Kid:* "One of these days that Denver Kid is gonna make a slip, and I'm gonna be around to trip him."

Films

The Mad Game (Fox, 1933)
The Gift of Gab (Univ, 1934)
The Thin Man (MGM, 1934)
The Woman Who Dared (Imperial, 1934)
Student Tour (MGM, 1934)
I Hate Women (Goldsmith, 1934)
Let's Talk It Over (Univ, 1934)
Girl from Missouri (MGM, 1934)
Miss Pacific Fleet (WB, 1935)
Straight from the Heart (Univ, 1935)
Transient Lady (Univ, 1935)
Night Life of the Gods (Univ, 1935)
Two for Tonight (Par, 1935)
Old Man Rhythm (RKO, 1935)
Ring Around the Moon (Chesterfield, 1936)
Small Town Girl (MGM, 1936)
Big Brown Eyes (Par, 1936)
Navy Born (Rep, 1936)

Crash Donovan (Univ, 1936)
Sing, Baby, Sing (20th, 1936)
Thirty-Six Hours to Kill (20th, 1936)
15 Maiden Lane (20th, 1936)
Woman Wise (20th, 1937)
On the Avenue (20th, 1937)
Time Out for Romance (20th, 1937)
Fifty Roads to Town (20th, 1937)
Wake Up and Live (20th, 1937)
This Is My Affair (20th, 1937)
Wild and Woolly (20th, 1937)
One Mile from Heaven (20th, 1937)
Charlie Chan on Broadway (20th, 1937)
She Had to Eat (20th, 1937)
Love and Kisses (20th, 1937)
City Girl (20th, 1937)
Walking Down Broadway (20th, 1938)
Mr. Moto's Gamble (20th, 1938)
Alexander's Ragtime Band (20th, 1938)

Keep Smiling (20th, 1938)
Passport Husband (20th, 1938)
Time Out for Murder (20th, 1938)
Inside Story (20th, 1938)
Submarine Patrol (20th, 1938)
Arizona Wildcat (20th, 1938)
Lucky Night (MGM, 1939)
Dodge City (WB, 1939)
The Boy Friend (20th, 1939)
It Could Happen to You (20th, 1939)
Charlie Chan at Treasure Island (20th, 1939)
Slightly Honorable (UA, 1939)
Cafe Hostess (Col, 1940)
Twenty-Mule Team (MGM, 1940)
Wagons Westward (Rep, 1940)
Pier 13 (20th, 1940)
The Leather Pushers (Univ, 1940)
Cherokee Strip (Par, 1940)

East of the River (WB, 1940)

Ellery Queen, Master Detective (Col, 1940)

The Great Swindle (Col, 1941)

Henry Goes Arizona (MGM, 1941)

The Parson of Panamint (Par, 1941)

Tanks a Million (UA, 1941)

Doctors Don't Tell (Rep, 1941)

Dangerous Lady (PRC, 1941)

Secrets of the Wasteland (Par, 1941)

Mr. District Attorney in the Carter Case (Rep, 1941)

Mississippi Gambler (Univ, 1942)

The Devil with Hitler (UA, 1942)

Sunset on the Desert (Rep, 1942)

Mr. Wise Guy (Mon, 1942)

Hay Foot (UA, 1942)

So's Your Aunt Emma [a.k.a. Meet the Mob] (Mon, 1942)

I Live on Danger (Par, 1942)

The Man in the Trunk (20th, 1942)

Stand By for Action (MGM, 1942)

Jitterbugs (20th, 1943)

Gildersleeve's Bad Day (RKO, 1943)

Bar-20 (UA, 1943)

Minesweeper (Par, 1943)

Colt Comrades (UA, 1943)

The Kansan (UA, 1943)

Sleepy Lagoon (Rep, 1943)

Riding High (Par, 1943)

Lost Canyon (UA, 1943)

Racket Man (Col, 1944)

Rationing (MGM, 1944)

One Body Too Many (Par, 1944)

See Here, Private Hargrove (MGM, 1944)

Shake Hands with Murder (PRC, 1944)

Detective Kitty O'Day (Mon, 1944)

Lady in the Death House (PRC, 1944)

Don't Fence Me In (Rep, 1945)

Life with Blondie (Col, 1945)

Along the Navajo Trail (Rep, 1945)

Chick Carter, Detective (Col serial, 1946)

'Neath Canadian Skies (Screen Guild, 1946)

Her Sister's Secret (PRC, 1946)

Drifting Along (Mon, 1946)

In Fast Company (Mon, 1946)

The Glass Alibi (Rep, 1946)

Rendezvous 24 (20th, 1946)

Larceny in Her Heart (PRC, 1946)

Freddie Steps Out (Mon, 1946)

High School Hero (Mon, 1946)

Wild Country (PRC, 1947)

Undercover Maisie (MGM, 1947)

Backlash (20th, 1947)

Three on a Ticket (PRC, 1947)

Yankee Fakir (Rep, 1947)

Jungle Flight (Par, 1947)

Desperate (RKO, 1947)

The Hucksters (MGM, 1947)

The Trespasser (Rep, 1947)

Gas House Kids in Hollywood (EL, 1947)

Scared to Death (Screen Guild, 1947)

Ridin' Down the Trail (Mon, 1947)

Roses Are Red (20th, 1947)

Merton of the Movies (MGM, 1947)

Rose of Santa Rosa (Col, 1947)

Docks of New Orleans (Mon, 1948)

Waterfront at Midnight (Par, 1948)

If You Knew Susie (RKO, 1948)

The Dude Goes West (AA, 1948)

Coroner Creek (Col, 1948)

Joe Palooka in Winner Take All (Mon, 1948)

Behind Locked Doors (EL, 1948)

Gun Smugglers (RKO, 1948)

The Denver Kid (Rep, 1948)

Badmen of Tombstone (AA, 1948)

Flaxy Martin (WB, 1949)

Massacre River (AA, 1949)

Battleground (MGM, 1949)

Susanna Pass (Rep, 1949)

Arson, Inc. (Screen Guild, 1949)

Search for Danger (Film Classics, 1949)

Mighty Joe Young (RKO, 1949)

Satan's Cradle (UA, 1949)

Renegades of the Sage (Col, 1949)

Joe Palooka in the Counterpunch (Mon, 1949)

Bunco Squad (RKO, 1950)

Rider from Tucson (RKO, 1950)

Armored Car Robbery (RKO, 1950)

Hoedown (Col, 1950)

Edge of Doom (RKO, 1950)

Killer Shark (Mon, 1950)

He's a Cockeyed Wonder (Col, 1950)

Mrs. O'Malley and Mr. Malone (MGM, 1950)

Rio Grande Patrol (RKO, 1950)

Stage to Tucson (Col, 1950)

Beware of Blondie (Col, 1950)

Chain of Circumstance (Col, 1951)

Tarzan's Peril (RKO, 1951)

Callaway Went Thataway (MGM, 1951)

Across the Wide Missouri (MGM, 1951)

Criminal Lawyer (Col, 1951)

South of Caliente (Rep, 1951)

Just This Once (MGM, 1952)

Singin' in the Rain (MGM, 1952)

This Woman Is Dangerous (WB, 1952)

A Slight Case of Larceny (MGM, 1953)

The Band Wagon (MGM, 1953)

Cruisin' Down the River (Col, 1953)

Kansas Pacific (AA, 1953)

Deep in My Heart (MGM, 1954)

The Naked Jungle (Par, 1954)

Cat-Women of the Moon (Astor, 1954)

Casanova's Big Night (Par, 1954)

Lone Gun (UA, 1954)

The High and the Mighty (WB, 1954)

Three-Ring Circus (Par, 1954)

Untamed Heiress (Rep, 1954)

The Girl Rush (Par, 1955)

Texas Lady (RKO, 1955)

Broken Star (UA, 1956)

Bandido (UA, 1956)

The Man from Del Rio (UA, 1956)

Rock Pretty Baby (Univ, 1956)

Bayou (UA, 1957)

Kelly and Me (Univ, 1957)

The Badge of Marshal Brennan (UA, 1957)

Raiders of Old California (Rep, 1957)

These Thousand Hills (20th, 1959)

Desire in the Dust (20th, 1960)

Barabbas (Col, 1962)

Miracle of the White Stallions (BV, 1963)

Who's Been Sleeping in My Bed? (Par, 1963)

The Seven Faces of Dr. Lao (MGM, 1964)

The Good Guys and the Bad Guys (WB-7 Arts, 1969)

Walking Tall (Cin, 1973)

Homebodies (Avco Emb, 1974)

From Noon till Three (UA, 1977)

Black Oak Conspiracy (New World, 1977)

The White Buffalo (UA, 1977)

VICTOR FRANCEN

Art Foster, Victor Francen, Lauren Bacall, and George Coulouris in Confidential
Agent *(1945).*

Born August 6, 1888, Tirlemont, Belgium. Married Eleanor Kreutzer (1938). Died December
1977, Aix-En-Provence, France. Transferred to Hollywood during World War II after a career
on the European stage and screen. Occasionally at MGM (university president in *Madame Curie*)
and 20th Century-Fox (Arturo in the Charles Laughton episode of *Tales of Manhattan*). Most
often at his home lot, Warner Bros. An intense actor with haunting eyes and serious demeanor;
displayed a believable cunningness in musicals (*The Desert Song*), patriotic yarns (*Passage to
Marseille*), melodrama (*The Mask of Dimitrios*), and fantasy (*The Beast with Five Fingers*). A prime
scene stealer. Made a few additional pictures after returning to Europe, including *Top-Crack* in
Italy with Terry-Thomas.

> **Victor Francen** to Hedy Lamarr in *The Conspirators:* "I've
> seen many men attracted to you, my dear, and I've always
> admired the way you handled their infatuation."

Films

Crepuscule d'espouvante (Fr, 1921)
La Neige sur les pas (Fr, 1923)
La Doute (Fr, 1924)
Apres L'Amour (Fr, 1931)
L'Aiglon (Fr, 1931)
La Fin du Monde (Fr, 1932)
Les Ailes Brisees (Fr, 1933)
Melo (Fr, 1933)
Le Voleur (Fr, 1933)
L'Aventurier (Fr, 1934)
Ariane jeune fille Russe (Fr, 1934)
Le Chemineau (Fr, 1935)
Veille d'Armes (Fr, 1935)
La Porte du Large (Fr, 1936)

L'Appel de la Vie (Fr, 1936)
Nuits de Feu (Fr, 1936)
Tamara la Complaisante (Fr, 1937)
Feu! (Fr, 1937)
Forfaiture (Fr, 1937)
Double Crime sur la Ligne Maginot (Fr, 1937)
Le Roi (Fr, 1938)
J'Accuse (Fr, 1938)
La Vierge Falle (Fr, 1938)
Sacrifice d'Honneur (Fr, 1938)
La Fin du Jour (Fr, 1939)
L'Homme du Niger (Fr, 1939)
Entente Cordiale (Fr, 1939)

Hold Back the Dawn (Par, 1941)
The Tuttles of Tahiti (RKO, 1942)
Ten Gentlemen from West Point (20th, 1942)
Tales of Manhattan (20th, 1942)
Mission to Moscow (WB, 1943)
Madame Curie (MGM, 1943)
The Desert Song (WB, 1943)
Hollywood Canteen (WB, 1944)
Follow the Boys (Univ, 1944)
Passage to Marseille (WB, 1944)
The Mask of Dimitrios (WB, 1944)
The Conspirators (WB, 1944)
In Our Time (WB, 1944)

San Antonio (WB, 1945)
Confidential Agent (WB, 1945)
Devotion (WB, 1946)
Night and Day (WB, 1946)
The Beast with Five Fingers (WB, 1946)

The Beginning or the End? (MGM, 1947)
To the Victor (WB, 1948)
Le Nuit s'Acheve (Fr, 1949)
The Adventures of Captain Fabian (Rep, 1951)

Hell and High Water (20th, 1954)
Bedevilled (MGM, 1955)
A Farewell to Arms (20th, 1957)
Fanny (WB, 1961)
Top-Crack (It, 1966)

WILLIAM FRAWLEY

In the early 1960s.

Born February 26, 1887, Burlington, Iowa. Married Edna Louise Broedt (1914), divorced (1927). Died March 3, 1966, Los Angeles, California. Thickset, bald performer who excelled at snarling, cigar-chewing types or the fast-talking but usually confounded cop or detective. A former vaudevillian. Spent most of the 1930s at Paramount doing variations of "the mug." Drinking had nearly ended his professional work in the early 1950s when he was hired by Desi Arnaz for a TV series. Tremendously fond of baseball; was thrilled to partake in such sports films as *The Babe Ruth Story, Rhubarb,* and *Safe at Home,* the last featuring his revered New York Yankees. TV series: "I Love Lucy" (as cantankerous Fred Mertz), "My Three Sons" (as grandfather "Bub").

Football coach **William Frawley** to Wayne Morris in *The Quarterback:* "You've got to pass those midterm exams this week or they won't let you play."

Films

Moonlight and Pretzels (Univ, 1933)
Hell and High Water (Par, 1933)
Miss Fane's Baby Is Stolen (Par, 1934)
Bolero (Par, 1934)
The Witching Hour (Par, 1934)
Shoot the Works (Par, 1934)
Here Is My Heart (Par, 1934)
The Lemon Drop Kid (Par, 1934)
The Crime Doctor (RKO, 1934)
Car 99 (Par, 1935)
Hold 'em, Yale (Par, 1935)
College Scandal (Par, 1935)
Ship Cafe (Par, 1935)
Alibi Ike (WB, 1935)
Welcome Home (Fox, 1935)
Harmony Lane (Mascot, 1935)
Strike Me Pink (UA, 1936)
Desire (Par, 1936)
The Princess Comes Across (Par, 1936)
F-Man (Par, 1936)
Three Cheers for Love (Par, 1936)
Three Married Men (Par, 1936)
The General Died at Dawn (Par, 1936)
Rose Bowl (Par, 1936)
High, Wide and Handsome (Par, 1937)
Double or Nothing (Par, 1937)
Blossoms on Broadway (Par, 1937)
Something to Sing About (GN, 1937)
Mad About Music (Univ, 1938)
Professor Beware (Par, 1938)
Sons of the Legion (Par, 1938)
Touchdown, Army! (Par, 1938)
Crime Takes a Holiday (Col, 1938)
Persons in Hiding (Par, 1939)
St. Louis Blues (Par, 1939)
Ambush (Par, 1939)
Grand Jury Secrets (Par, 1939)
Night Work (Par, 1939)

The Adventures of Huckleberry Finn (MGM, 1939)
Rose of Washington Square (20th, 1939)
Stop, Look and Love (20th, 1939)
Ex-Champ (Univ, 1939)
The Farmer's Daughter (Par, 1940)
Opened by Mistake (Par, 1940)
Untamed (Par, 1940)
Golden Gloves (Par, 1940)
Rhythm on the River (Par, 1940)
The Quarterback (Par, 1940)
One Night in the Tropics (Univ, 1940)
Sandy Gets Her Man (Univ, 1940)
Those Were the Days (Par, 1940)
Blondie in Society (Col, 1940)
The Bride Came C.O.D. (WB, 1941)
Public Enemies (Rep, 1941)
Cracked Nuts (Univ, 1941)
Footsteps in the Dark (WB, 1941)
Six Lessons from Madame La Zonga (Univ, 1941)
Treat 'em Rough (Univ, 1942)
Roxie Hart (20th, 1942)
It Happened in Flatbush (20th, 1942)
Give Out, Sisters (Univ, 1942)
Moonlight in Havana (Univ, 1942)
Wildcat (Par, 1942)
Gentleman Jim (WB, 1942)
Larceny with Music (Univ, 1943)
We've Never Been Licked (Univ, 1943)
Whistling in Brooklyn (MGM, 1943)
Minstrel Man (PRC, 1944)
Going My Way (Par, 1944)
Lake Placid Serenade (Rep, 1944)
The Fighting Seabees (Rep, 1944)
Flame of Barbary Coast (Rep, 1945)
Lady on a Train (Univ, 1945)
Hitchhike to Happiness (Rep, 1945)

The Virginian (Par, 1946)
Rendezvous with Annie (Rep, 1946)
Ziegfeld Follies (MGM, 1946)
The Inner Circle (Rep, 1946)
The Crime Doctor's Man Hunt (Col, 1946)
Mother Wore Tights (20th, 1947)
Miracle on 34th Street (20th, 1947)
My Wild Irish Rose (WB, 1947)
I Wonder Who's Kissing Her Now (20th, 1947)
Monsieur Verdoux (UA, 1947)
Blondie's Anniversary (Col, 1947)
Down to Earth (Col, 1947)
The Hit Parade of 1947 (Rep, 1947)
The Babe Ruth Story (AA, 1948)
Good Sam (RKO, 1948)
Joe Palooka in Winner Take All (Mon, 1948)
Texas, Brooklyn and Heaven (UA, 1948)
Chicken Every Sunday (20th, 1948)
The Girl from Manhattan (UA, 1948)
Home in San Antone (Col, 1949)
The Lady Takes a Sailor (WB, 1949)
East Side, West Side (MGM, 1949)
The Lone Wolf and His Lady (Col, 1949)
Kiss Tomorrow Goodbye (WB, 1950)
Pretty Baby (WB, 1950)
Kill the Umpire (Col, 1950)
Blondie's Hero (Col, 1950)
The Lemon Drop Kid (Par, 1951)
Rhubarb (Par, 1951)
Abbott and Costello Meet the Invisible Man (Univ, 1951)
Rancho Notorious (RKO, 1952)
Safe at Home (Col, 1962)

ROBERT FRAZER

With Barbara Bedford in Women Who Give *(1924).*

Born June 29, 1891, Worcester, Massachusetts. Married Mildred Bright. Died August 17, 1944, Los Angeles, California. Sharp-featured handsome leading man of the silent era who ran the gamut from athletic roles to drawing-room love stories: Captain Valmar (Mae Murray's *Jazzmania*), Jim Owens/Eiphan Owens (father and son in Elaine Hammerstein's *The Foolish Virgin*), Bob Stanton (vying with Walter Long for Renee Adoree's affections in *Back to God's Country*), etc. With the arrival of talkies, switched to playing heavies, mostly in low-budget Westerns and contemporary programmers. Played Chief Black Wing, head of the Ravenhead tribe in Tom Mix's serial *The Miracle Rider*, and the high priest in *The Tiger Woman* cliffhanger.

> **Robert Frazer** to Madge Bellamy in *White Zombie:* "You can raise me up to paradise—or you can blast me into nothingness."

Films

The Lone Star Rush (Eclair-Alliance, 1915)
The Ballet Girl (Brady-World, 1916)
The Feast of Life (World, 1916)
The Decoy (World, 1916)
The Light at Dusk (Lubin, 1916)
The Dawn of Love (M, 1916)
Her Code of Honor (World, 1919)
Bolshevism on Trial (Select, 1919)
Without Limit (M, 1921)
Love, Hate and a Woman (Arrow, 1921)
Partners of the Sunset (Lubin, 1922)
Fascination (M, 1922)
The Faithless Sex (Signet, 1922)
How Women Love (B. B. Features, 1922)
When the Desert Calls (American, 1922)
My Friend, the Devil (Fox, 1922)

As a Man Lives (American, 1923)
Jazzmania (M, 1923)
The Love Piker (G, 1923)
A Chapter in Her Life (Univ, 1923)
After the Ball (FBO, 1924)
When a Man's a Man (Associated FN, 1924)
Women Who Give (MG, 1924)
Men (Par, 1924)
Traffic in Hearts (Col, 1924)
The Foolish Virgin (Col, 1924)
Broken Barriers (MG, 1924)
Bread (MGM, 1924)
The Mine with the Iron Door (Principle, 1924)
Miss Bluebeard (Par, 1925)
The White Desert (MG, 1925)

The Charmer (Par, 1925)
The Scarlet West (FN, 1925)
The Love Gamble (Banner, 1925)
The Keeper of the Bees (FBO, 1925)
Why Women Love (FN, 1925)
The Other Woman's Story (B. P. Shulberg, 1925)
The Golden Strain (Fox, 1925)
The Splendid Road (FN, 1925)
Secret Orders (FBO, 1926)
Desert Gold (Par, 1926)
The Isle of Retribution (FBO, 1926)
The Speeding Venus (PDC, 1926)
Dame Chance (American Cinema Associates, 1926)
The City (Fox, 1926)
Sin Cargo (Tif, 1926)

One Hour of Love (Tif, 1927)
Wanted—A Coward (Banner, 1927)
The Silent Hero (Rayart, 1927)
Back to God's Country (Univ, 1927)
Out of the Past (Peerless, 1927)
Burning Up Broadway (Sterling, 1928)
The Scarlet Dove (Tif, 1928)
Out of the Ruins (FN, 1928)
City of Purple Dreams (Rayart, 1928)
Black Butterflies (Quality, 1928)
Sioux Blood (MGM, 1929)
The Woman I Love (FBO, 1929)
Careers (FN, 1929)
The Drake Case (Univ, 1929)
Frozen Justice (Fox, 1929)
Beyond the Law (Syndicated Pictures, 1930)
Ten Nights in a Barroom (Roadshow Productions, 1931)
Two-Gun Caballero (Imperial, 1931)
The Rainbow Trail (Fox, 1932)
Discarded Lovers (Tower, 1932)
Arm of the Law (Mon, 1932)
Saddle Buster (RKO, 1932)
The King Murder (Chesterfield, 1932)
White Zombie (UA, 1932)
The Crooked Circle (WW, 1932)
Vampire Bat (Majestic, 1933)
Justice Takes a Holiday (Majestic, 1933)
Notorious but Nice (Chesterfield, 1933)
Whispering Shadows (Mascot serial, 1933)
The Fighting Parson (Allied Pictures, 1933)
Found Alive (Ideal, 1933)
Men in White (MGM, 1934)

Love Past Thirty (Freuler Film Associates, 1934)
Guilty Parents (Syndicate, 1934)
Monte Carlo Nights (Mon, 1934)
Fifteen Wives (Invincible, 1934)
The Trail Beyond (Mon, 1934)
Fighting Trooper (Ambassador, 1934)
One in a Million (Invincible, 1934)
The World Accuses (Chesterfield, 1935)
Circumstantial Evidence (Chesterfield, 1935)
Public Opinion (Chesterfield, 1935)
Murder Man (MGM, 1935)
The Fighting Pilot (Ajax, 1935)
The Miracle Rider (Mascot serial, 1935)
Ladies Crave Excitement (Mascot, 1935)
Death from a Distance (Invincible, 1935)
Never Too Late (Reliable, 1935)
Murder at Glen Athol (Invincible, 1935)
The Rest Cure (Hirliman Enterprises, 1936)
It Couldn't Have Happened (Invincible, 1936)
Easy Money (Invincible, 1936)
The Clutching Hand (Stage & Screen serial, 1936)
The Black Coin (Weiss-Mintz serial, 1936)
The Garden of Allah (UA, 1936)
Below the Deadline (Chesterfield, 1936)
Gambling with Souls (Jay Dee Kay Productions, 1936)
Black Aces (Univ, 1937)
Renfrew on the Great White Trail (GN, 1938)
Cipher Bureau (GN, 1938)

Religious Racketeers (Fanchon Royer, 1938)
Delinquent Parents (Progressive Pictures, 1938)
Navy Secrets (Mon, 1939)
Six-Gun Rhythm (GN, 1939)
Juarez (WB, 1939)
Mystic Circle Murder (Merit, 1939)
Daughter of the Tong (Times Pictures, 1939)
Crashing Through (Mon, 1939)
One Man's Law (Rep, 1940)
Pals of the Pecos (RKO, 1941)
Law of the Wild (Zeihm, Inc., 1941)
Roar of the Press (Mon, 1941)
Gangs of Sonora (Rep, 1941)
Gunman from Bodie (Mon, 1941)
Dick Tracy vs. Crime, Inc. (Rep serial, 1941)
Black Dragons (Mon, 1942)
Riders of the West (Mon, 1942)
A Night for Crime (PRC, 1942)
Dawn on the Great Divide (Mon, 1942)
The Stranger from Pecos (Mon, 1943)
Wagon Tracks West (Rep, 1943)
Daredevils of the West (Rep serial, 1943)
Captain America (Rep serial, 1944)
The Tiger Woman (Rep serial, 1944)
Forty Thieves (UA, 1944)
Lawmen (Mon, 1944)
Partners of the Trail (Mon, 1944)

KATHLEEN FREEMAN

In the mid-1960s.

Born February 17, ca. 1919. Pug-nosed, stocky comedienne with very expressive eyes who enjoyed several lively encounters on screen with Jerry Lewis: *Artists and Models, The Ladies' Man, The Errand Boy,* etc. Played the articulate diction coach in *Singin' in the Rain* and Bobby Dean Loner, wife of John Huston in *Myra Breckinridge.* TV series: "Topper" (as Katie, the maid), "Mayor of the Town," "It's About Time," "Funny Face," and "Lotsa Luck."

Kathleen Freeman to Dean Martin in *Marriage on the Rocks:*
"My shorthand is 150 and my typing is 100."

Films

Behind Locked Doors (EL, 1948)
Casbah (Univ, 1948)
The Saxon Charm (Univ, 1948)
The Naked City (Univ, 1948)
Mr. Belvedere Goes to College (20th, 1949)
The Reformer and the Redhead (MGM, 1950)
A Life of Her Own (MGM, 1950)
The House by the River (Rep, 1950)
Once a Thief (UA, 1950)
Lonely Hearts Bandits (Rep, 1950)
Appointment with Danger (Par, 1951)
A Place in the Sun (Par, 1951)
The Company She Keeps (RKO, 1951)
The Wild Blue Yonder (Rep, 1951)
Singin' in the Rain (MGM, 1952)
Kid Monk Baroni (Realart, 1952)
O. Henry's Full House (20th, 1952)
Talk About a Stranger (MGM, 1952)
Love Is Better Than Ever (MGM, 1952)

The Glass Wall (Col, 1953)
She's Back on Broadway (WB, 1953)
The Affairs of Dobie Gillis (MGM, 1953)
Half a Hero (MGM, 1953)
Athena (MGM, 1954)
The Far Country (Univ, 1955)
Artists and Models (Par, 1955)
The Midnight Story (Univ, 1957)
Kiss Them for Me (20th, 1957)
Pawnee (Rep, 1957)
The Fly (20th, 1958)
The Missouri Traveler (BV, 1958)
Houseboat (Par, 1958)
The Buccaneer (Par, 1958)
North to Alaska (20th, 1960)
The Ladies' Man (Par, 1961)
The Errand Boy (Par, 1961)
Madison Avenue (20th, 1962)
The Nutty Professor (Par, 1963)
The Disorderly Orderly (Par, 1964)

Mail Order Bride (MGM, 1964)
The Rounders (MGM, 1965)
Marriage on the Rocks (WB, 1965)
Three on a Coach (Col, 1966)
Point Blank (MGM, 1967)
Hook, Line and Sinker (Col, 1968)
The Good Guys and the Bad Guys (WB-7 Arts, 1969)
Myra Breckinridge (20th, 1970)
The Ballad of Cable Hogue (WB, 1971)
Which Way to the Front? (WB, 1971)
Support Your Local Gunfighter (UA, 1972)
Head On (Leon, 1971)
Stand Up and Be Counted (Col, 1973)
Where Does It Hurt? (Cin, 1973)
Unholy Rollers (AIP, 1973)
Your Three Minutes Are Up (Cin, 1973)
The Strongest Man in the World (BV, 1975)

BLANCHE FRIDERICI

May Robson and Blanche Friderici in If I Had a Million *(1932).*

Born 1878, New York City, New York. Died December 23, 1933, Los Angeles, California. Severe-looking actress who made her dour presence known to filmgoers through the quality of her work and the starkness of her presence. Wed to tyrannical reformer Lionel Barrymore in *Sadie Thompson*, the wife of cattleman Russell Simpson in Johnny Mack Brown's *Billy the Kid*, interpreted Madame Si-Si in *The Hatchet Man*, played Dona Elena in *Flying Down to Rio*. Fourteen-year screen career ended with *It Happened One Night*, in which she played Zeke's (Arthur Hoyt) spouse.

Blanche Friderici to Claudette Colbert in *It Happened One Night:* "And listen, next time you'd better not come back here. I run a *respectable place.*"

Films

Trespassing (Hodkinson, 1922)
Sadie Thompson (UA, 1928)
Gentlemen Prefer Blondes (Par, 1928)
Fleetwing (Fox, 1928)
Stolen Love (FBO, 1928)
The Awful Truth (PDC, 1929)
Wonder of Women (MGM, 1929)
The Trespasser (UA, 1929)
Jazz Heaven (RKO, 1929)
Personality (Col, 1930)
The Bad One (UA, 1930)
Courage (WB, 1930)
Numbered Men (FN, 1930)
Soldiers and Women (Col, 1930)
Last of the Duanes (Fox, 1930)
The Office Wife (WB, 1930)
Billy the Kid [TV title: *The Highwayman Rides*] (MGM, 1930)

Kismet (FN, 1930)
The Cat Creeps (Univ, 1930)
Woman Hungry (FN, 1931)
10¢ a Dance (Col, 1931)
Woman Between (RKO, 1931)
Night Nurse (WB, 1931)
Murder by the Clock (Par, 1931)
Wicked (Fox, 1931)
Honor of the Family (FN, 1931)
Friends and Lovers (RKO, 1931)
A Dangerous Affair (Col, 1931)
Mata Hari (MGM, 1931)
The Hatchet Man (FN, 1932)
Lady with a Past (RKO, 1932)
Young Bride (RKO, 1932)
So Big (WB, 1932)
Night Club Lady (Col, 1932)
Love Me Tonight (Par, 1932)

Miss Pinkerton (FN, 1932)
Thirteen Women (RKO, 1932)
If I Had a Million (Par, 1932)
A Farewell to Arms (Par, 1932)
Behind Jury Doors (Mayfair, 1932)
Secrets (UA, 1933)
The Barbarian (MGM, 1933)
Alimony Madness (Mayfair, 1933)
Adorable (Fox, 1933)
Hold Your Man (MGM, 1933)
Man of the Forest (Par, 1933)
Aggie Appleby, Maker of Men (RKO, 1933)
The Way to Love (Par, 1933)
The Thundering Herd (Par, 1933)
Flying Down to Rio (RKO, 1933)
All of Me (Par, 1934)
It Happened One Night (Col, 1934)

DWIGHT FRYE

Bela Lugosi and Dwight Frye in Dracula *(1931).*

Born February 22, 1899, Salina, Kansas. Married Laurette Bullwant (1928). Died November 7, 1943, Los Angeles, California. Appeared in dozens of features, but it was his horror-film assignments that stick in the memory: the insect-eating Renfield traveling to Transylvania in *Dracula;* Fritz, the hunchbacked mad dwarf in *Frankenstein* who is strangled by the monster (Boris Karloff); Dr. Praetorius' weird assistant in *Bride of Frankenstein.* Also showed up in *The Ghost of Frankenstein* and *Frankenstein Meets the Wolfman,* but was only an extra in *Son of Frankenstein.* On a more conventional note: played Wilmer in the first *Maltese Falcon,* joined in James Cagney's musical *Something to Sing About,* and was jury foreman in *The People vs. Dr. Kildare.*

Dwight Frye to Bela Lugosi in *Dracula:* "You *will* keep your promise when we get to London, won't you, master? You *will* see that I get lives—not human lives—but small ones with blood in them?"

Films

The Doorway to Hell (WB, 1930)
Man to Man (WB, 1930)
Dracula (Univ, 1931)
The Maltese Falcon (WB, 1931)
The Black Camel (Fox, 1931)
Frankenstein (Univ, 1931)
Attorney for the Defense (Col, 1932)
By Whose Hand? (Col, 1932)
The Western Code (Col, 1932)
A Strange Adventure (Mon, 1932)
The Vampire Bat (Majestic, 1933)
The Circus Queen Murder (Col, 1933)
The Invisible Man (Univ, 1933)
Bride of Frankenstein (Univ, 1935)

Atlantic Adventure (Col, 1935)
The Great Impersonation (Univ, 1935)
The Crime of Dr. Crespi (Rep, 1935)
Florida Special (Par, 1936)
Alibi for Murder (Col, 1936)
Beware of Ladies (Rep, 1936)
Great Guy (GN, 1936)
Sea Devils (RKO, 1937)
The Man Who Found Himself (RKO, 1937)
The Road Back (Univ, 1937)
Something to Sing About (GN, 1937)
Renfrew of the Royal Mounted (GN, 1937)
The Shadow (Col, 1937)

Who Killed Gail Preston? (Col, 1938)
The Invisible Enemy (Rep, 1938)
Sinners in Paradise (Univ, 1938)
Fast Company (MGM, 1938)
The Night Hawk (Rep, 1938)
Adventure in Sahara (Col, 1938)
Son of Frankenstein (Univ, 1939)
The Man in the Iron Mask (UA, 1939)
Conspiracy (RKO, 1939)
I Take This Woman (MGM, 1939)
Drums of Fu Manchu (Rep serial, 1940)
Gangs of Chicago (Rep, 1940)
The Son of Monte Cristo (UA, 1940)
Phantom Raiders (MGM, 1940)

Sky Bandits (Criterion-Mon, 1940)
Mystery Ship (Col, 1941)
The People vs. Dr. Kildare (MGM, 1941)
The Blonde from Singapore (Col, 1941)
The Devil Pays Off (Rep, 1941)
Sleepytime Gal (Rep, 1942)

The Ghost of Frankenstein (Univ, 1942)
Danger in the Pacific (Univ, 1942)
Prisoner of Japan (PRC, 1942)
Frankenstein Meets the Wolfman (Univ, 1943)
Dead Men Walk (PRC, 1943)

Hangmen Also Die (UA, 1943)
Submarine Alert (Par, 1943)
Dangerous Blondes (Col, 1943)

ED GARGAN

Charlie Ruggles, Ed Gargan, and Mary Boland in Night Work *(1939).*

Born ca. 1902, Brooklyn, New York. Married Catherine Conlan (1938). Died February 19, 1964, New York City, New York. Congenial but dumb-looking tousled-haired brother of William Gargan. Portrayed unintelligent (funny) cops and battered fight managers. Replaced Edward Brophy as the misguided Bates in the George Sanders/Tom Conway *The Falcon* series. On radio in "This Is Your F.B.I." series.

Ed Gargan to Carole Lombard in *Hands Across the Table:*
"You'll sperl your dinner if you keep on eatin' them nuts."

Films

The Girl in 419 (Par, 1933)
Gambling Ship (Par, 1933)
Three-Cornered Moon (Par, 1933)
Registered Nurse (FN, 1934)
David Harum (Fox, 1934)
Twentieth Century (Col, 1934)
Wild Gold (Fox, 1934)
Belle of the Nineties (Par, 1934)
The Lemon Drop Kid (Par, 1934)
Port of Lost Dreams (Chesterfield, 1934)

Behold My Wife! (Par, 1934)
The Band Plays On (MGM, 1934)
Two for Tonight (Par, 1935)
Miss Pacific Fleet (WB, 1935)
The Gilded Lily (Par, 1935)
Behind Green Lights (Mascot, 1935)
The Bride Comes Home (Par, 1935)
Ceiling Zero (WB, 1935)
Hold 'em Yale (Par, 1935)
We're in the Money (WB, 1935)

Here Comes Cookie (Par, 1935)
Hands Across the Table (Par, 1935)
False Pretenses (Chesterfield, 1935)
Anything Goes (Par, 1936)
Dangerous Waters (Univ, 1936)
Roaming Lady (Col, 1936)
Hearts in Bondage (Rep, 1936)
My Man Godfrey (Univ, 1936)
Wives Never Know (Par, 1936)
Nobody's Fool (Univ, 1936)

Two in a Crowd (Univ, 1936)
Stage Struck (FN, 1936)
Grand Jury (RKO, 1936)
Great Guy (GN, 1936)
We're on the Jury (RKO, 1937)
Wake Up and Live (20th, 1937)
The Go-Getter (WB, 1937)
You Can't Buy Luck (RKO, 1937)
Jim Hanvey—Detective (Rep, 1937)
High, Wide and Handsome (Par, 1937)
Big City (MGM, 1937)
Danger Patrol (RKO, 1937)
A Girl with Ideas (Univ, 1937)
Spring Madness (MGM, 1938)
That's My Story (Univ, 1938)
The Devil's Party (Univ, 1938)
The Texans (Par, 1938)
While New York Sleeps (20th, 1938)
Up the River (20th, 1938)
Crime School (WB, 1938)
The Rage of Paris (Univ, 1938)
Gateway (20th, 1938)
Straight, Place and Show (20th, 1938)
Thanks for the Memory (Par, 1938)
Annabel Takes a Tour (RKO, 1938)
Honolulu (MGM, 1939)
The Saint Strikes Back (RKO, 1939)
$1,000 a Touchdown (Par, 1939)
Another Thin Man (MGM, 1939)
Yes, My Darling Daughter (WB, 1939)
Lucky Night (MGM, 1939)
For Love or Money (Univ, 1939)
Fixer Dugan (RKO, 1939)
They All Come Out (MGM, 1939)
Pack Up Your Troubles (20th, 1939)
Night Work (Par, 1939)
20,000 Men a Year (20th, 1939)
Road to Singapore (Par, 1940)
Three Cheers for the Irish (WB, 1940)
Spring Parade (Univ, 1940)
Go West (MGM, 1940)
Wolf of New York (Rep, 1940)
Brother Rat and a Baby (WB, 1940)
Street of Memories (20th, 1940)
Queen of the Mob (Par, 1940)

The Girl from God's Country (Rep, 1940)
The Bowery Boy (Rep, 1940)
San Francisco Docks (Univ, 1940)
Northwest Passage (MGM, 1940)
Tugboat Annie Sails Again (WB, 1940)
An Angel from Texas (WB, 1940)
Navy Blues (WB, 1941)
The Lone Wolf Keeps a Date (Col, 1941)
Meet the Chump (Univ, 1941)
Flight from Destiny (WB, 1941)
Here Comes Happiness (WB, 1941)
Thieves Fall Out (WB, 1941)
Tight Shoes (Univ, 1941)
Tillie the Toiler (Col, 1941)
Niagara Falls (UA, 1941)
A Date with the Falcon (RKO, 1941)
Dr. Kildare's Victory (MGM, 1941)
Fly-by-Night (Par, 1942)
The Falcon Takes Over (RKO, 1942)
Meet the Stewarts (Col, 1942)
They All Kissed the Bride (Col, 1942)
Miss Annie Rooney (UA, 1942)
Between Us Girls (Univ, 1942)
Lady in a Jam (Univ, 1942)
A-Haunting We Will Go (20th, 1942)
The Falcon's Brother (RKO, 1942)
Over My Dead Body (20th, 1942)
The Falcon Strikes Back (RKO, 1943)
Prairie Chickens (UA, 1943)
The Falcon in Danger (RKO, 1943)
Taxi, Mister (UA, 1943)
Hit the Ice (Univ, 1943)
Princess O'Rourke (WB, 1943)
My Kingdom for a Cook (Col, 1943)
The Falcon and the Coeds (RKO, 1943)
In Old Oklahoma [a.k.a. *War of the Wildcats*] (Rep, 1943)
Detective Kitty O'Day (Mon, 1944)
The Falcon Out West (RKO, 1944)
San Diego, I Love You (Univ, 1944)
San Fernando Valley (Rep, 1944)
The Thin Man Goes Home (MGM, 1944)
The Beautiful Cheat (Univ, 1945)
Billy Rose's Diamond Horseshoe (20th, 1945)

The Bullfighters (20th, 1945)
Earl Carroll Vanities (Rep, 1945)
Follow That Woman (Par, 1945)
Her Highness and the Bellboy (MGM, 1945)
See My Lawyer (Univ, 1945)
The Naughty Nineties (Univ, 1945)
High Powered (Par, 1945)
Life with Blondie (Col, 1945)
Sing Your Way Home (RKO, 1945)
A Sporting Chance (Rep, 1945)
Wonder Man (RKO, 1945)
Behind the Mask (Mon, 1946)
She Wouldn't Say Yes (Col, 1946)
Cinderella Jones (WB, 1946)
Little Giant (Univ, 1946)
Gallant Bess (MGM, 1946)
The Dark Horse (Univ, 1946)
Gay Blades [a.k.a. *Tournament Tempo*] (Rep, 1946)
The Inner Circle (Rep, 1946)
That's My Gal (Rep, 1947)
Saddle Pals (Rep, 1947)
Web of Danger (Rep, 1947)
Exposed (Rep, 1947)
Linda, Be Good (EL, 1947)
Little Miss Broadway (Col, 1947)
The Dude Goes West (AA, 1948)
Campus Honeymoon (Rep, 1948)
The Argyle Secrets (Film Classics, 1948)
Waterfront at Midnight (Par, 1948)
You Gotta Stay Happy (Univ, 1948)
Scudda Hoo! Scudda Hay! (20th, 1948)
Strike It Rich (AA, 1948)
Hold That Baby (Mon, 1949)
Red Light (UA, 1949)
Dynamite (Par, 1949)
Love Happy (UA, 1949)
Belle of Old Mexico (Rep, 1950)
Square Dance Katy (Mon, 1950)
Hit Parade of 1951 (Rep, 1950)
Triple Trouble (Mon, 1950)
Cuban Fireball (Rep, 1951)
Bedtime for Bonzo (Univ, 1951)
Abbott and Costello Meet the Invisible Man (Univ, 1951)

MARJORIE GATESON

Craig Reynolds, Dorothy Appleby, Beverly Roberts, Marjorie Gateson, Jack Holt, Tom Kennedy, and Corbet Morris in Making the Headlines *(1938).*

Born January 17, 1891, Brooklyn, New York. Died April 17, 1977, New York City, New York. The quintessence of the aristocratic blue blood, generally the mercenary wife who deserved to be wronged, as in *Chained* where her husband (Otto Kruger) loved Joan Crawford. TV series: "One Man's Family" (as Fanny Barbour) and "Search for Tomorrow" (as Grace Tyrell).

Marjorie Gateson to Morgan Wallace in *Goin' to Town:* "I'll spare no cost to disgrace that woman and chase her out of Southampton."

Films

The Beloved Bachelor (Par, 1931)
The False Madonna (Par, 1931)
Husband's Holiday (Par, 1932)
Street of Women (WB, 1932)
Society Girl (Fox, 1932)
Silver Dollar (FN, 1932)
Okay, America (Univ, 1932)
The World Changes (FN, 1933)
The King's Vacation (WB, 1933)
Employees' Entrance (FN, 1933)
Cocktail Hour (Col, 1933)
Lilly Turner (FN, 1933)
Melody Cruise (RKO, 1933)
Bureau of Missing Persons (FN, 1933)
Walls of Gold (Fox, 1933)
Blind Adventure (RKO, 1933)
Lady Killer (WB, 1933)
Operator 13 (MGM, 1934)
Hi, Nellie! (WB, 1934)
Coming-Out Party (Fox, 1934)

Fog (Col, 1934)
Let's Fall in Love (Col, 1934)
Side Streets (FN, 1934)
Chained (MGM, 1934)
Happiness Ahead (FN, 1934)
Big-Hearted Herbert (WB, 1934)
Million Dollar Ransom (Univ, 1934)
Down to Their Last Yacht (RKO, 1934)
Gentlemen Are Born (FN, 1934)
Goin' to Town (Par, 1935)
His Family Tree (RKO, 1935)
Your Uncle Dudley (Fox, 1935)
The Milky Way (Par, 1936)
Big Brown Eyes (Par, 1936)
The First Baby (20th, 1936)
Private Number (20th, 1936)
Three Married Men (Par, 1936)
Wife vs. Secretary (MGM, 1936)
The Gentleman from Louisiana (Rep, 1936)

The Man I Marry (Univ, 1936)
Arizona Mahoney (Par, 1936)
We Have Our Moments (Univ, 1937)
Turn Off the Moon (Par, 1937)
Vogues of 1938 (UA, 1937)
First Lady (WB, 1937)
The House of Mystery (Col, 1938)
No Time to Marry (Col, 1938)
Making the Headlines (Col, 1938)
Gateway (20th, 1938)
The Duke of West Point (UA, 1938)
Spring Madness (MGM, 1938)
Stablemates (MGM, 1938)
My Wife's Relatives (Rep, 1939)
Geronimo (Par, 1939)
Too Busy to Work (20th, 1939)
Till We Meet Again (WB, 1940)
Parole Fixer (Par, 1940)
In Old Missouri (Rep, 1940)
Pop Always Pays (RKO, 1940)

I'm Nobody's Sweetheart Now (Univ, 1940)
Back Street (Univ, 1941)
Submarine Zone (Col, 1941)
Here Comes Happiness (WB, 1941)
Passage from Hong Kong (WB, 1941)
International Lady (UA, 1941)
Moonlight in Hawaii (Univ, 1941)
Obliging Young Lady (RKO, 1941)

You'll Never Get Rich (Col, 1941)
Rings on Her Fingers (20th, 1942)
Juke Box Jenny (Univ, 1942)
Dudes Are Pretty People (UA, 1942)
Meet the Stewarts (Col, 1942)
Rhythm of the Islands (Univ, 1943)
The Youngest Profession (MGM, 1943)
The Sky's the Limit (RKO, 1943)
I Dood It (MGM, 1943)

No Time for Love (Par, 1943)
Casanova in Burlesque (Rep, 1944)
Ever Since Venus (Col, 1944)
Hi, Good Lookin' (Univ, 1944)
Seven Days Ashore (RKO, 1944)
One More Tomorrow (WB, 1946)
Passage West (Par, 1951)
The Caddy (Par, 1953)

GLADYS GEORGE
(Gladys Anna Clare)

Gladys George and Joan Bennett in The House Across the Bay *(1940).*

Born September 13, 1900, Hatton, Maine. Married 1) Arthur Erway; divorced (1930); 2) Edward Fowler (1933); divorced (1935); 3) Leonard Penn (1935); divorced (1944); 4) Kenneth Bradley (1946); divorced (1950). Died December 8, 1954, Los Angeles, California. A great performer who was too often overlooked by Hollywood. Elevated the dame-with-a-heart-of-gold role to an art. After a quintet of silent features, made her place in cinema history with the Oscar-nominated role of self-sacrificing Carrie Snyder in the tearjerker *Valiant Is the Word for Carrie.* (Luise Rainer won the Best Actress Academy Award that year for *The Great Ziegfeld.*) All-suffering and superb in the 1937 remake of *Madame X;* displayed loyalty and pathos as the discarded moll of James Cagney in *The Roaring Twenties;* sported a a wry sense of lechery as Jerome Cowan's widow Iva hungering for Humphrey Bogart in *The Maltese Falcon.* Final roles included Doris Day's has-been chanteuse mother in *The Lullaby of Broadway.*

Gladys George to James Cagney in *The Roaring Twenties:*
"You're battin' out of your league, buster. You're used to travelin' around with—dames like me."

Films

Red Hot Dollars (Par, 1920)
Woman in the Suitcase (Par, 1920)
Chickens (Par, 1921)
The Easy Road (Par, 1921)
The House That Jazz Built (Realart, 1921)
Straight Is the Way (MGM, 1934)
Valiant Is the Word for Carrie (Par, 1936)
They Gave Him a Gun (MGM, 1937)
Madame X (MGM, 1937)
Love Is a Headache (MGM, 1938)
Marie Antoinette (MGM, 1938)

I'm from Missouri (Par, 1939)
Here I Am a Stranger (20th, 1939)
The Roaring Twenties (WB, 1939)
A Child Is Born (WB, 1940)
The House Across the Bay (UA, 1940)
The Way of All Flesh (Par, 1940)
The Lady from Cheyenne (Univ, 1941)
The Maltese Falcon (WB, 1941)
Hit the Road (Univ, 1941)
The Hard Way (WB, 1942)
The Crystal Ball (UA, 1943)
Nobody's Darling (Rep, 1943)
Minstrel Man (PRC, 1944)

Christmas Holiday (Univ, 1944)
Steppin' in Society (Rep, 1945)
The Best Years of Our Lives (RKO, 1946)
Millie's Daughter (Col, 1947)
Alias a Gentleman (MGM, 1948)
Flamingo Road (WB, 1949)
Bright Leaf (WB, 1950)
The Undercover Girl (Univ, 1950)
The Lullaby of Broadway (WB, 1951)
He Ran All the Way (UA, 1951)
Detective Story (Par, 1951)
Silver City (Par, 1951)
It Happens Every Thursday (Univ, 1953)

CONNIE GILCHRIST

Donna Reed and Connie Gilchrist in Apache Trail *(1942).*

Born July 29, 1901, Brooklyn, New York. Married Edwin O'Hanlon (1928), child, Dorothy. Plump, vivacious, and capable. Scored in an array of brief but well-handled MGM assignments. Proved a strong adversary for Marjorie Main in Wallace Beery's *Barnacle Bill* (the "romantic" triangle was repeated in *Rationing* and *Bad Bascomb*). Beneath toothy smile lay gutsiness: e.g., Joan Crawford's opinioned underling, Christina Lalvik, in *A Woman's Face.* Also played a Mexican dancing with Spencer Tracy in *Tortilla Flat* and a squaw in *Apache Trail.* Dueted "Every Little Movement" with Judy Garland in *Presenting Lily Mars.* Often seen as a housekeeper or cleaning lady. Had some sparkling screen moments as Mrs. Finney, Linda Darnell's crude mother who has Thelma Ritter for a drinking partner in *A Letter to Three Wives.* TV series: "Long John Silver" (as Purity Pinker) and "The Real McCoys" (as Mrs. Jensen).

Connie Gilchrist to James Craig in *Swing Shift Maisie:* "I'll look after her like she was my own daughter—wherever she is."

Films

Hullabaloo (MGM, 1940)
Down in San Diego (MGM, 1941)
Dr. Kildare's Wedding Day (MGM, 1941)
H. M. Pulham, Esq. (MGM, 1941)
Two-Faced Woman (MGM, 1941)
Billy the Kid (MGM, 1941)
The Wild Man of Borneo (MGM, 1941)
A Woman's Face (MGM, 1941)
Johnny Eager (MGM, 1941)
Barnacle Bill (MGM, 1941)
We Were Dancing (MGM, 1942)
This Time for Keeps (MGM, 1942)

Born to Sing (MGM, 1942)
Tortilla Flat (MGM, 1942)
Sunday Punch (MGM, 1942)
Grand Central Murder (MGM, 1942)
The War Against Mrs. Hadley (MGM, 1942)
Apache Trail (MGM, 1942)
Presenting Lily Mars (MGM, 1943)
Swing Shift Maisie (MGM, 1943)
Cry Havoc (MGM, 1943)
The Heavenly Body (MGM, 1943)
Thousands Cheer (MGM, 1943)
The Human Comedy (MGM, 1943)

Rationing (MGM, 1944)
Nothing but Trouble (MGM, 1944)
Music for Millions (MGM, 1944)
See Here, Private Hargrove (MGM, 1944)
The Seventh Cross (MGM, 1944)
The Thin Man Goes Home (MGM, 1944)
Valley of Decision (MGM, 1945)
Junior Miss (20th, 1945)
Bad Bascomb (MGM, 1946)
Faithful in My Fashion (MGM, 1946)
Young Widow (UA, 1946)
Merton of the Movies (MGM, 1946)
Cloak and Dagger (WB, 1946)

Song of the Thin Man (MGM, 1947)
Good News (MGM, 1947)
The Hucksters (MGM, 1947)
Big City (MGM, 1948)
10th Avenue Angel (MGM, 1948)
Luxury Liner (MGM, 1948)
Chicken Every Sunday (20th, 1948)
An Act of Violence (MGM, 1948)
A Letter to Three Wives (20th, 1948)
The Bride Goes Wild (MGM, 1948)
Little Women (MGM, 1949)
The Story of Molly X (Univ, 1949)
Louisa (Univ, 1950)
A Ticket to Tomahawk (20th, 1950)
Stars in My Crown (MGM, 1950)
Buccaneer's Girl (Univ, 1950)
Peggy (Univ, 1950)
Undercover Girl (Univ, 1950)

Tripoli (Par, 1950)
The Killer That Stalked New York (Col, 1950)
Here Comes the Groom (Par, 1951)
Thunder on the Hill (Univ, 1951)
Chain of Circumstance (Col, 1951)
Flesh and Fury (Univ, 1952)
One Big Affair (UA, 1952)
The Half-Breed (RKO, 1952)
Houdini (Par, 1953)
The Great Diamond Robbery (MGM, 1953)
It Should Happen to You (Col, 1954)
Long John Silver (DCA, 1955)
The Far Country (Univ, 1955)
The Man in the Gray Flannel Suit (20th, 1956)
Auntie Mame (WB, 1958)

Some Came Running (MGM, 1958)
Say One for Me (20th, 1959)
Machine Gun Kelly (AIP, 1959)
The Interns (Col, 1962)
Swingin' Along (20th, 1962)
The Misadventures of Merlin Jones (BV, 1964)
A Tiger Walks (BV, 1964)
A House Is Not a Home (Emb, 1964)
Two on a Guillotine (WB, 1965)
Sylvia (Par, 1965)
Fluffy (Univ, 1965)
Tickle Me (AA, 1965)
The Monkey's Uncle (BV, 1965)
Some Kind of a Nut (UA, 1969)

CLAUDE GILLINGWATER

With Shirley Temple in Poor Little Rich Girl (1936).

Born August 2, 1870, Lauseanna, Missouri. Married Carolyn Stellith, child: one. Died November 1, 1939, Beverly Hills, California. Tall, bald, and crotchety. Hit his cinema stride in 1921's *Little Lord Fauntleroy* as the chill-hearted earl who learns tenderness from his grandson. Frequently played in domestic comedies in the 1920s: *Wages for Wives*, etc. With Shirley Temple in several 1930s films: *Poor Little Rich Girl* (Simon Peck), *Just Around the Corner* (Samuel G. Henshaw), and *Little Miss Broadway* (Judge). Played Jarvis Lorry in Ronald Colman's *A Tale of Two Cities* and uplifted many other pictures.

Claude Gillingwater to Shirley Temple in *Poor Little Rich Girl:* "So they sent you in here to soften me up, did they? Well, young lady, you're wasting your time."

Films

Little Lord Fauntleroy (UA, 1921)
My Boy (Associated FN, 1921)
Fools First (Associated FN, 1922)
The Dust Flower (G, 1922)
Remembrance (G, 1922)
The Stranger's Banquet (G, 1922)
The Christian (G, 1923)
Souls for Sale (G, 1923)
Crinoline and Romance (M, 1923)
Alice Adams (Associated Exhibitors, 1923)
Dulcy (Associated FN, 1923)
Three Wise Fools (G, 1923)
A Chapter in Her Life (Univ, 1923)
Tiger Rose (WB, 1923)
Daddies (WB, 1924)
How to Educate a Wife (WB, 1924)
Madonna of the Streets (Associated FN, 1924)
Idle Tongues (Associated FN, 1924)
A Thief in Paradise (FN, 1925)
Cheaper to Marry (MG, 1925)
Winds of Chance (FN, 1925)
Seven Sinners (WB, 1925)
We Moderns (FN, 1925)
Wages for Wives (Fox, 1925)
For Wives Only (PDC, 1926)
That's My Baby (Par, 1926)
Into Her Kingdom (FN, 1926)

Fast and Furious (Univ, 1927)
Naughty but Nice (FN, 1927)
The Gorilla (FN, 1927)
Barbed Wire (Par, 1927)
Husbands for Rent (WB, 1927)
The Little Shepherd of Kingdom Come (FBO, 1928)
Oh, Kay! (FN, 1928)
Women They Talk About (WB, 1928)
Stark Mad (WB, 1929)
The Great Divide (FN, 1929)
So Long, Letty (WB, 1929)
Stolen Kisses (WB, 1929)
The Glad Rag Doll (WB, 1929)
Smiling Irish Eyes (FN, 1929)
Dumbbells in Ermine (WB, 1930)
The Flirting Widow (FN, 1930)
Illicit (WB, 1931)
The Conquering Horde (Par, 1931)
Kiss Me Again (FN, 1931)
Gold Dust Gertie (WB, 1931)
Daddy Long Legs (Fox, 1931)
Compromised (FN, 1931)
Tess of the Storm Country (Fox, 1932)
Ann Carver's Profession (Col, 1933)
The Avenger (Mon, 1933)
Skyway (Mon, 1933)
Ace of Aces (RKO, 1933)
Before Midnight (Col, 1933)

Broadway Bill (Col, 1934)
The Show-Off (MGM, 1934)
You Can't Buy Everything (MGM, 1934)
City Limits (Mon, 1934)
The Unknown Blonde (Majestic, 1934)
In Love with Life (Chesterfield, 1934)
Back Page (General Pictures, 1934)
Green Eyes (Chesterfield, 1934)
The Captain Hates the Sea (Col, 1934)
Baby Face Harrington (MGM, 1935)
Mississippi (Par, 1935)
Woman in Red (FN, 1935)
Calm Yourself (MGM, 1935)
A Tale of Two Cities (MGM, 1935)
The Prisoner of Shark Island (20th, 1936)
Florida Special (Par, 1936)
Ticket to Paradise (Rep, 1936)
Counterfeit (Col, 1936)
Poor Little Rich Girl (20th, 1936)
Wives Never Know (Par, 1936)
Can This Be Dixie? (20th, 1936)
Conquest (MGM, 1937)
Top of the Town (Univ, 1937)
A Yank at Oxford (MGM, 1938)
Just Around the Corner (20th, 1938)
Little Miss Broadway (20th, 1938)
There Goes My Heart (UA, 1938)
Cafe Society (Par, 1939)

ETIENNE GIRARDOT

Etienne Girardot, Jack Haley, Ann Sothern, Benny Bartlett (the boy), Walter Catlett, John Carradine, and Mary Boland in Danger—Love at Work *(1937).*

Born 1856, London, England. Died November 10, 1939, Hollywood, California. Debonair Frenchman. Had some silent film credits (including Vitagraph shorts, 1912-1914), but it was in talkies that he rose to prominence. In dramas: *Little Man, What Now?* (Spannfuss); whodunits: *The Kennel Murder Case, The Dragon Murder Case, The Garden Murder Case* (the antiseptic coroner Dr. Doremus of the Philo Vance series); and comedies: *20th Century* (religious zealot Matthew J. Clark), Mae West's *Go West, Young Man* (Professor Rigby), etc. Also played the king's physician in Charles Laughton's *The Hunchback of Notre Dame.*

Etienne Girardot to Eugene Pallette in *The Dragon Murder Case:* "Heath, don't you call me out here again unless you've got a corpse! I'm a coroner, not a doctor!"

Films

The Violin of Monsieur (Vit, 1912)
The Belle of New York (Selznick, 1919)
The Kennel Murder Case (WB, 1933)
Blood Money (UA, 1933)
Advice to the Lovelorn (UA, 1933)
Fashions of 1934 (FN, 1934)
Mandalay (FN, 1934)
20th Century (Col, 1934)
Little Man, What Now? (Univ, 1934)
The Dragon Murder Case (FN, 1934)
Return of the Terror (FN, 1934)
The Firebird (WB, 1934)
Grand Old Girl (RKO, 1935)
The Whole Town's Talking (Col, 1935)
Clive of India (UA, 1935)
Hooray for Love (RKO, 1935)
Curly Top (Fox, 1935)

In Old Kentucky (Fox, 1935)
The Bishop Misbehaves (MGM, 1935)
I Live My Life (MGM, 1935)
Metropolitan (Fox, 1935)
Chasing Yesterday (RKO, 1935)
The Garden Murder Case (MGM, 1936)
The Music Goes 'Round (Col, 1936)
Hearts Divided (FN, 1936)
Half Angel (20th, 1936)
The Devil Is a Sissy (MGM, 1936)
The Longest Night (MGM, 1936)
College Holiday (Par, 1936)
Go West, Young Man (Par, 1936)
Wake Up and Live (20th, 1937)
The Road Back (Univ, 1937)
The Great Garrick (WB, 1937)
Breakfast for Two (RKO, 1937)

Danger—Love at Work (20th, 1937)
Professor Beware (Par, 1938)
Port of Seven Seas (MGM, 1938)
The Arizona Wildcat (20th, 1938)
There Goes My Heat (UA, 1938)
The Story of Vernon and Irene Castle (RKO, 1939)
Fast and Loose (MGM, 1939)
Exile Express (GN, 1939)
For Love or Money (Univ, 1939)
Little Accident (Univ, 1939)
Hawaiian Nights (Univ, 1939)
The Hunchback of Notre Dame (RKO, 1939)
Isle of Destiny (RKO, 1940)

JAMES GLEASON

Sheldon Leonard and James Gleason in Take One False Step *(1949).*

Born May 23, 1886, New York City, New York. Married Lucille Webster (1905), child: Russell; widowed (1947). Died April 12, 1959, Woodland Hills, California. Stage actor/playwright who came into demand in the late 1920s as a dialoguer and performer. Characterized by his flintiness and unique Brooklynese or Irish brogue, delivered out of the side of his mouth. Charged through a horde of features—acidy, pugnacious, and exasperated—often as army officers or politicians. Was Inspector Oscar Piper to Edna May Oliver's Hildegarde Withers in *Murder on the Blackboard, Murder on a Honeymoon,* etc. (Had a similar role as Inspector Mike O'Hara in some *Falcon* films.) Was in the *Higgins Family* series at Republic, a cozy affair with Gleason's real-life wife (Lucille) and son (Russell) joining in the low-budget entries. Could be touching, e.g., McDonnell in *Crash Dive,* Tyrone Power's service buddy with the serious heart condition.

James Gleason to John Alexander in *Arsenic and Old Lace:*
"Well, Colonel, you've blown your last bugle."

Films

Polly of the Follies (Associated FN, 1922)
The Count of Ten (Univ, 1928)
His First Command (Pathé, 1929)
The Broadway Melody (MGM, 1929)
High Voltage (Pathé, 1929)
The Flying Fool (Pathé, 1929)
The Shannons of Broadway (Univ, 1929)
Oh, Yeah (Pathé, 1930)
Puttin' on the Ritz (UA, 1930)
The Swellhead (Tif, 1930)
Dumbbells in Ermine (WB, 1930)
The Matrimonial Bed (WB, 1930)
Her Man (Pathé, 1930)
What a Widow! (UA, 1930)
Big Money (Par, 1930)
It's a Wise Child (MGM, 1931)
A Free Soul (MGM, 1931)
Sweepstakes (RKO, 1931)

The Big Gamble (Pathé, 1931)
Suicide Fleet (Pathé, 1931)
Beyond Victory (Pathé, 1931)
Fast Companions (Univ, 1932)
Lady and Gent (Par, 1932)
The Crooked Circle (WW, 1932)
Blondie of the Follies (MGM, 1932)
The All-American (Univ, 1932)
The Penguin Pool Murder (RKO, 1932)
The Information Kid (Univ, 1932)
The Devil Is Driving (Par, 1932)
Hoopla (Fox, 1933)
Orders Is Orders (Br, 1933)
Billion Dollar Scandal (Par, 1933)
Clear All Wires (MGM, 1933)
Search for Beauty (Par, 1934)
Change of Heart (Fox, 1934)
Murder on the Blackboard (RKO, 1934)

The Meanest Gal in Town (RKO, 1934)
Helldorado (Fox, 1935)
Murder on a Honeymoon (RKO, 1935)
Hot Tip (RKO, 1935)
West Point of the Air (MGM, 1935)
We're Only Human (RKO, 1936)
Murder on a Bridle Path (RKO, 1936)
The Ex-Mrs. Bradford (RKO, 1936)
Don't Turn 'em Loose (RKO, 1936)
The Big Game (RKO, 1936)
The Plot Thickens (RKO, 1936)
Yours for the Asking (Par, 1936)
Forty Naughty Girls (RKO, 1937)
Manhattan Merry-Go-Round (Rep, 1937)
Army Girl (Rep, 1938)
The Higgins Family (Rep, 1938)
My Wife's Relatives (Rep, 1939)
Should Husbands Work? (Rep, 1939)

The Covered Trailer (Rep, 1939)
On Your Toes (WB, 1939)
Money to Burn (Rep, 1940)
Grandpa Goes to Town (Rep, 1940)
Earl of Puddlestone (Rep, 1940)
Meet John Doe (WB, 1941)
Affectionately Yours (WB, 1941)
Here Comes Mr. Jordan (Col, 1941)
Nine Lives Are Not Enough (WB, 1941)
Tanks a Million (UA, 1941)
A Date with the Falcon (RKO, 1941)
Babes on Broadway (MGM, 1941)
Hayfoot (UA, 1942)
My Gal Sal (20th, 1942)
Footlight Serenade (20th, 1942)
Tales of Manhattan (20th, 1942)
Manila Calling (20th, 1942)
All Through the Night (WB, 1942)
The Falcon Takes Over (RKO, 1942)
Tramp, Tramp, Tramp (Col, 1942)
Crash Dive (20th, 1943)
A Guy Named Joe (MGM, 1943)
Once upon a Time (Col, 1944)

Arsenic and Old Lace (WB, 1944)
Keys of the Kingdom (20th, 1944)
This Man's Navy (MGM, 1945)
A Tree Grows in Brooklyn (20th, 1945)
The Clock (MGM, 1945)
Captain Eddie (20th, 1945)
Home Sweet Homicide (20th, 1946)
The Hoodlum Saint (MGM, 1946)
Lady Luck (RKO, 1946)
The Well-Groomed Bride (Par, 1946)
Down to Earth (Col, 1947)
The Homestretch (20th, 1947)
The Bishop's Wife (RKO, 1947)
The Tycoon (RKO, 1947)
The Dude Goes West (AA, 1948)
When My Baby Smiles at Me (20th, 1948)
Smart Woman (AA, 1948)
Return of October (Col, 1948)
The Life of Riley (Univ, 1949)
Bad Boy (AA, 1949)
Miss Grant Takes Richmond (Col, 1949)
Take One False Step (Univ, 1949)
Riding High (Par, 1950)

The Yellow Cab Man (MGM, 1950)
Key to the City (MGM, 1950)
The Jackpot (20th, 1950)
Joe Palooka in the Triple Cross (Mon, 1951)
Come Fill the Cup (WB, 1951)
I'll See You in My Dreams (WB, 1951)
Two Gals and a Guy (UA, 1951)
We're Not Married (20th, 1952)
What Price Glory (20th, 1952)
The Will Rogers Story (WB, 1952)
Forever Female (Par, 1953)
Suddenly (UA, 1954)
Night of the Hunter (UA, 1955)
Girl Rush (Par, 1955)
A Star in the Dust (Univ, 1956)
Spring Reunion (UA, 1957)
Loving You (Par, 1957)
Man in the Shadow (Univ, 1957)
The Female Animal (Univ, 1958)
Once upon a Horse (Univ, 1958)
Man or Gun (Rep, 1958)
The Last Hurrah (Col, 1958)
Rockabye Baby (Par, 1958)

MINNA GOMBELL

Adrian Booth and Minna Gombell in The Last Bandit *(1949).*

Born May 28, 1893, Baltimore, Maryland. Married 1) Howard Rumsey; divorced; 2) Joseph Sefton; 3) Myron Fagan; widowed. Died April 14, 1973, Santa Monica, California. Generally played the smart-mouthed babe who has seen it all. Added vibrancy to films as: the divorced wife of the title figure (Edward Ellis) in *The Thin Man;* a tough burlesque performer, Tim Adams, in *Comet over Broadway;* Spanish Eva in *Boom Town;* a hardened asylum nurse, Miss Hart, in *The Snake Pit,* etc. Also known as Nancy Garter and Winifred Lee.

Minna Gombell to William Frawley in *Stop, Look and Love:*
"Joe, you've got to cultivate taste, now that you're coming
up in the world."

Films

The Great Power (Exhibitors Film Exchange, 1929)
Bad Girl (Fox, 1931)
Sob Sister (Fox, 1931)
The Good Sport (Fox, 1931)
Doctors' Wives (Fox, 1931)
The Rainbow Trail (Fox, 1932)
Dance Team (Fox, 1932)
Stepping Sisters (Fox, 1932)
After Tomorrow (Fox, 1932)
Careless Lady (Fox, 1932)
Bachelor's Affairs (Fox, 1932)
The First Year (Fox, 1932)
Wild Girl (Fox, 1932)
Pleasure Cruise (Fox, 1933)
Hello, Sister! [a.k.a. *Walking Down Broadway*] (Fox, 1933)
What Price Innocence? (Col, 1933)
The Big Brain (RKO, 1933)
The Way to Love (Par, 1933)
Wild Boys of the Road (FN, 1933)
Hoopla (Fox, 1933)
Cross-Country Cruise (Univ, 1934)
Keep 'em Rolling (RKO, 1934)
No More Women (Par, 1934)
Marrying Widows (Tower, 1934)
The Thin Man (MGM, 1934)

Registered Nurse (FN, 1934)
Strictly Dynamite (RKO, 1934)
Hell Cat (Col, 1934)
The Merry Widow (MGM, 1934)
The Lemon Drop Kid (Par, 1934)
Babbitt (WB, 1934)
Cheating Cheaters (Univ, 1934)
Women Must Dress (Mon, 1935)
The White Cockatoo (WB, 1935)
Two Sinners (Rep, 1935)
Miss Pacific Fleet (WB, 1935)
Champagne Charlie (20th, 1936)
Banjo on My Knee (20th, 1936)
Make Way for Tomorrow (Par, 1937)
Slave Ship (20th, 1937)
Wife, Doctor and Nurse (20th, 1937)
Blockheads (MGM, 1938)
Going Places (WB, 1938)
The Great Waltz (MGM, 1938)
Comet over Broadway (WB, 1938)
Second Fiddle (20th, 1939)
Stop, Look and Love (20th, 1939)
The Hunchback of Notre Dame (RKO, 1939)
Boom Town (MGM, 1940)
High Sierra (WB, 1941)
Doomed Caravan (Par, 1941)

Thieves Fall Out (WB, 1941)
Mexican Spitfire Sees a Ghost (RKO, 1942)
Cadets on Parade (Col, 1942)
Salute for Three (Par, 1943)
Chip off the Old Block (Univ, 1944)
Destiny (Univ, 1944)
Johnny Doesn't Live Here Anymore (Mon, 1944)
The Town Went Wild (PRC, 1944)
Night Club Girl (Univ, 1945)
Swingin' on a Rainbow (Rep, 1945)
Man Alive (RKO, 1945)
Penthouse Rhythm (Univ, 1945)
Sunbonnet Sue (Mon, 1945)
Swingin' on Broadway (Rep, 1945)
The Best Years of Our Lives (RKO, 1946)
Perilous Holiday (Col, 1946)
Wyoming (Rep, 1947)
Mr. Reckless (Par, 1948)
Return of the Bad Men (RKO, 1948)
The Snake Pit (20th, 1948)
The Last Bandit (Rep, 1949)
Pagan Love Song (MGM, 1950)
I'll See You in My Dreams (WB, 1951)
Here Comes the Groom (Par, 1951)

THOMAS GOMEZ

Thomas Gomez, Laraine Day, and William Talman in The Woman on Pier 13 *(1949).*

Born July 10, 1905, Long Island, New York. Died June 18, 1971, Santa Monica, California. Characterized by his swinish, swarthy look, and his capacity to display viciousness. A marvelous villain. Challenged the array of studio contractees during his 1940s tenure at Universal: Abbott and Costello in *Who Done It?* and *In Society;* Maria Montez in *Arabian Nights* and *White Savage;* Basil Rathbone–Nigel Bruce in *Sherlock Holmes and the Voice of Terror,* etc. Oscar-nominated for his role of Pancho, the carousel operator in Robert Montgomery's *Ride the Pink Horse* (but lost BSAAA to Edmund Gwenn of *Miracle on 34th Street*). Perhaps best remembered as the oily Curley Hoff, one of Edward G. Robinson's gangland associates in *Key Largo.* TV series: "Life with Luigi" (as Pasquale).

Thomas Gomez to Basil Rathbone in *Sherlock Holmes and the Voice of Terror:* "Maybe the next time you see me I'll be in a position of authority—of power—no longer hiding in the dark—*giving* the orders, not *taking* them. What do you say to that?"

Films

Sherlock Holmes and the Voice of Terror (Univ, 1942)
Arabian Nights (Univ, 1942)
Pittsburgh (Univ, 1942)
Who Done It? (Univ, 1942)
White Savage (Univ, 1943)
Corvette K-225 (Univ, 1943)
Frontier Badmen (Univ, 1943)
The Climax (Univ, 1944)
Crazy House (Univ, 1943)
Phantom Lady (Univ, 1944)
Dead Man's Eyes (Univ, 1944)
Follow the Boys (Univ, 1944)
In Society (Univ, 1944)

Bowery to Broadway (Univ, 1944)
Can't Help Singing (Univ, 1944)
Patrick the Great (Univ, 1945)
I'll Tell the World (Univ, 1945)
The Daltons Ride Again (Univ, 1945)
Frisco Sal (Univ, 1945)
A Night in Paradise (Univ, 1946)
Swell Guy (Univ, 1946)
Dark Mirror (Univ, 1946)
Singapore (Univ, 1947)
Ride the Pink Horse (Univ, 1947)
Captain from Castile (20th, 1947)
Johnny O'Clock (Col, 1947)
Casbah (Univ, 1948)

Angel in Exile (Rep, 1948)
Key Largo (WB, 1948)
Force of Evil (MGM, 1948)
Come to the Stable (20th, 1949)
Sorrowful Jones (Par, 1949)
That Midnight Kiss (MGM, 1949)
The Woman on Pier 13 [a.k.a. *I Married a Communist*] (RKO, 1949)
Kim (MGM, 1950)
The Toast of New Orleans (MGM, 1950)
The Eagle and the Hawk (Par, 1950)
The Furies (Par, 1950)
Anne of the Indies (20th, 1951)
The Harlem Globetrotters (Col, 1951)

The Sellout (MGM, 1951)
The Merry Widow (MGM, 1952)
Macao (RKO, 1952)
Pony Soldier (20th, 1952)
Sombrero (MGM, 1953)
The Gambler from Natchez (20th, 1954)
The Adventures of Haji Baba (20th, 1954)

1954)
The Looters (Univ, 1955)
The Magnificent Matador (20th, 1955)
Las Vegas Shakedown (AA, 1955)
Night Freight (AA, 1955)
Trapeze (UA, 1956)
The Conqueror (RKO, 1956)

John Paul Jones (WB, 1959)
But Not for Me (Par, 1959)
Summer and Smoke (Par, 1961)
Stay Away, Joe (MGM, 1968)
Beneath the Planet of the Apes (20th, 1970)

LEO GORDON

Ted De Corsia, Perry Lopez, and Leo Gordon in The Steel Jungle *(1956).*

Born December 2, 1922, New York City, New York. Married Lynn Cartwright, child: Tara. Muscularly built with leathery countenance and deep-set eyes. Well cast as Carnie, one of the convicts in *Riot in Cell Block 11*. Used again by director Don Siegel to play John Dillinger in *Baby Face Nelson*. Equally efficient as the rabble-rouser in Westerns and costume pictures. Sometimes scripted films in which he appeared: *Black Patch, Escort West,* and *Tobruk*.

Leo Gordon to Myron Healey in *Apache Territory*: "I'm not waitin' around here for an Apache arrow in my belly."

Films

China Venture (Col, 1953)
Gun Fury (Col, 1953)
Hondo (WB, 1953)
All the Brothers Were Valiant (MGM, 1953)
Riot in Cell Block 11 (AA, 1954)
Sign of the Pagan (Univ, 1954)
The Yellow Mountain (Univ, 1954)
The Bamboo Prison (Col, 1954)

Seven Angry Men (AA, 1955)
Ten Wanted Men (Col, 1955)
Santa Fe Passage (Rep, 1955)
Robber's Roost (UA, 1955)
Soldier of Fortune (20th, 1955)
Tennessee's Partner (RKO, 1955)
Man with the Gun (UA, 1955)
The Conqueror (RKO, 1956)
The Steel Jungle (WB, 1956)

Red Sundown (Univ, 1956)
The Man Who Knew Too Much (Par, 1956)
Great Day in the Morning (RKO, 1956)
Johnny Concho (UA, 1956)
7th Cavalry (Col, 1956)
The Restless Breed (20th, 1957)
Black Patch (WB, 1957)
The Tall Stranger (AA, 1957)

Baby Face Nelson (UA, 1957)
Man in the Shadow (Univ, 1957)
The Notorious Mr. Monks (Rep, 1958)
Quantrill's Raiders (AA, 1958)
Ride a Crooked Trail (Univ, 1958)
Apache Territory (Col, 1958)
Escort West (UA, 1959)
The Big Operator (MGM, 1959)
The Jayhawkers (Par, 1959)
Noose for a Gunman (UA, 1960)

I Hate Your Guts [a.k.a. The Intruder] (Cinema Distributors of America, 1962)
The Nun and the Sergeant (UA, 1962)
Tarzan Goes to India (MGM, 1962)
The Haunted Palace (AIP, 1963)
McLintock! (UA, 1963)
Kings of the Sun (UA, 1963)
L'Arme a Gauche (Fr, 1964)
The Night of the Grizzly (Par, 1966)

Beau Geste (Univ, 1966)
Tobruk (Univ, 1967)
Devil's Angels (AIP, 1967)
Hostile Guns (Par, 1967)
Buckskin (Par, 1968)
You Can't Win 'em All (Col, 1971)
Bonnie's Kids (General Film, 1972)
My Name Is Nobody (Univ, 1974)

MARY GORDON

Brenda Joyce and Mary Gordon in Pillow of Death (1945).

Born 1882, Glasgow, Scotland. Married _____, child: daughter; widowed (1917). Died August 23, 1963, Pasadena, California. Short, stocky, with a beaming countenance and her hair often in a bun. Played scrubwomen and crowd extras in scores of films. With her Irish looks (actually was Scottish) was sometimes cast in celluloid blarney: *The Irish in Us* (James Cagney, Pat O'Brien, and Frank McHugh's ma), *Laughing Irish Eyes*, *The Plough and the Stars* (first woman), etc. In several of the Basil Rathbone–Nigel Bruce *Sherlock Holmes* features (played Mrs. Hudson, the Baker Street housekeeper). Later in the 1940s turned up as Mrs. Mahoney, Leo Gorcey's mother in the *Bowery Boy* series (*Angels' Alley*, etc.).

Mary Gordon to Pat O'Brien in *The Irish in Us*: "Pat, did you ever see your father, drunk or sober, go out of that door without kissin' me goodbye?"

Films

The Home Maker (Univ, 1925)
The People vs. Nancy Preston (PDC, 1925)
Tessie (Arrow, 1925)
Black Paradise (Fox, 1926)
Clancy's Kosher Wedding (FBO, 1927)
Naughty Nanette (FBO, 1927)
The Old Code (Arrow, 1928)
Dynamite (Pathé, 1929)
The Saturday Night Kid (Par, 1929)
One of the Bravest (Lumas, 1929)
Oh, For a Man! (Fox, 1930)
Subway Express (Col, 1931)
The Black Camel (Fox, 1931)
The Texas Cyclone (Col, 1932)
Dancers in the Dark (Par, 1932)
Almost Married (Fox, 1932)
My Woman (Col, 1933)
Beloved (Univ, 1934)
The Little Minister (RKO, 1934)
Vanessa—Her Love Story (MGM, 1935)
Bonnie Scotland (MGM, 1935)
Bride of Frankenstein (Univ, 1935)
The Irish in Us (WB, 1935)
The Whole Town's Talking (Col, 1935)
Waterfront Lady (Rep, 1935)
Mutiny on the Bounty (MGM, 1935)
Laughing Irish Eyes (Rep, 1936)
Forgotten Faces (Par, 1936)
Mary of Scotland (RKO, 1936)
Stage Struck (FN, 1936)
Yellowstone (Univ, 1936)
Way Out West (MGM, 1936)
Great Guy (GN, 1936)
The Plough and the Stars (RKO, 1936)
The Man in Blue (Univ, 1937)
Meet the Boy Friend (Rep, 1937)
Pick a Star (MGM, 1937)
Double Wedding (MGM, 1937)
The Great O'Malley (WB, 1937)
A Damsel in Distress (RKO, 1937)
Lady Behave (Rep, 1938)
Gateway (20th, 1938)
Kidnapped (20th, 1938)
City Streets (Col, 1938)
Angels with Dirty Faces (WB, 1938)
The Cowboy from Brooklyn (WB, 1938)
Wings of the Navy (WB, 1939)
Day Time Wife (20th, 1939)

Tail Spin (20th, 1939)
The Jones Family in Hollywood (20th, 1939)
Parents on Trial (Col, 1939)
My Son Is Guilty (Col, 1939)
The Hound of the Baskervilles (20th, 1939)
The Adventures of Sherlock Holmes (20th, 1939)
Captain Fury (UA, 1939)
She Married a Cop (Rep, 1939)
Rulers of the Sea (Par, 1939)
Joe and Ethel Turp Call on the President (MGM, 1939)
Marshal of Mesa City (RKO, 1939)
My Son, My Son (UA, 1940)
Kitty Foyle (RKO, 1940)
Tear Gas Squad (WB, 1940)
The Last Alarm (Mon, 1940)
I Take This Oath (PRC, 1940)
When the Daltons Rode (Univ, 1940)
No, No, Nanette (RKO, 1940)
Queen of the Mob (Par, 1940)
Nobody's Children (Col, 1940)
Flight from Destiny (WB, 1941)
Pot o' Gold (UA, 1941)
How Green Was My Valley (20th, 1941)
The Invisible Woman (Univ, 1941)
Borrowed Hero (Mon, 1941)
It Started with Eve (Univ, 1941)
Appointment for Love (Univ, 1941)
Riot Squad (Mon, 1941)
Sherlock Holmes and the Voice of Terror (Univ, 1942)
Sherlock Holmes and the Secret Weapon (Univ, 1942)
Bombay Clipper (Univ, 1942)
Fly by Night (Par, 1942)
Dr. Broadway (Par, 1942)
Gentleman Jim (WB, 1942)
Powder Town (RKO, 1942)
Meet the Stewarts (Col, 1942)
It Happened in Flatbush (20th, 1942)
The Mummy's Tomb (Univ, 1942)
Boss of Big Town (PRC, 1942)
Half Way to Shanghai (Univ, 1942)
Two Tickets to London (Univ, 1943)
Sweet Rosie O'Grady (20th, 1943)
Forever and a Day (RKO, 1943)

Here Comes Kelly (Mon, 1943)
Keep 'em Slugging (Univ, 1943)
Sarong Girl (Mon, 1943)
Sherlock Holmes Faces Death (Univ, 1943)
Smart Guy (Mon, 1943)
Whispering Footsteps (Rep, 1943)
Ever Since Venus (Col, 1944)
Million Dollar Kid (Mon, 1944)
The Hour Before the Dawn (Par, 1944)
Pearl of Death (Univ, 1944)
The Last Ride (WB, 1944)
Follow the Leader (Mon, 1944)
Hat Check Honey (Univ, 1944)
Hollywood Canteen (WB, 1944)
The Racket Man (Col, 1944)
Sherlock Holmes and the Spider Woman (Univ, 1944)
Divorce (Mon, 1945)
See My Lawyer (Univ, 1945)
Captain Eddie (20th, 1945)
Kitty (Par, 1945)
The Woman in Green (Univ, 1945)
Strange Confession [a.k.a. The Missing Head] (Univ, 1945)
Pillow of Death (Univ, 1945)
Little Giant (Univ, 1946)
Sentimental Journey (20th, 1946)
The Dark Horse (Univ, 1946)
The Hoodlum Saint (MGM, 1946)
In Fast Company (Mon, 1946)
Sing While You Dance (Col, 1946)
Shadows over Chinatown (Mon, 1946)
Sister Kenny (RKO, 1946)
The Secret Life of Walter Mitty (RKO, 1947)
Exposed (Rep, 1947)
Stallion Road (WB, 1947)
The Invisible Wall (20th, 1947)
Angels' Alley (Mon, 1948)
The Strange Mrs. Crane (EL, 1948)
Highway 13 (Screen Guild, 1948)
Haunted Trails (Mon, 1949)
Mighty Joe Young, (RKO, 1949)
Deputy Marshal (Screen Guild, 1949)
Shamrock Hill (Screen Guild, 1949)
West of Wyoming (Mon, 1950)

LAWRENCE GRANT

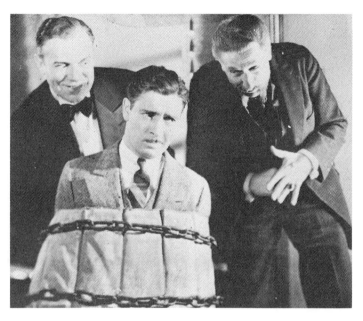

Montagu Love, Ronald Colman, and Lawrence Grant in Bulldog Drummond
(1929).

Born October 31, 1869, Bournemouth, England. Married Iphigenia Hay. Died February 19, 1952, Santa Barbara, California. Imposing British performer who for a time made a practice of playing the bellicose ruler of World War I Germany: *To Hell with the Kaiser, The Great Impersonation,* etc. Later displayed his versatility in such silents as: *A Gentleman of Paris* (General Baron de Latour), *Red Hair* (Judge Rufus Lennon, one of Clara Bow's suitors), and *The Case of Lena Smith* (commissioner). In talkies was Dr. Lakington, the sadistic adversary of Ronald Colman's *Bulldog Drummond;* the austere Reverend Mr. Carmichael in Marlene Dietrich's *Shanghai Express;* the prosecuting attorney at Old Bailey in *A Tale of Two Cities;* the baron in *The Son of Monte Cristo;* and Lord Fetting in *Confidential Agent,* his final film.

Lawrence Grant to Boris Karloff in *The Mask of Fu Manchu:*
"Fu Manchu, I'm not for sale!"

Films

To Hell with the Kaiser (M, 1918)
Extravagance (M, 1921)
The Great Impersonation (Par, 1921)
Abraham Lincoln (Associated FN, 1924)
Happiness (MG, 1924)
His Hour (MG, 1924)
The Grand Duchess and the Waiter (Par, 1926)
The Duchess of Buffalo (FN, 1926)
Service for Ladies (Par, 1927)
A Gentleman of Paris (Par, 1927)
Serenade (Par, 1927)
Red Hair (Par, 1928)
Doomsday (Par, 1928)
Something Always Happens (Par, 1928)
The Woman from Moscow (Par, 1928)
Hold 'em Yale (Pathé, 1928)

The Rainbow (Tif, 1929)
The Case of Lena Smith (Par, 1929)
The Canary Murder Case (Par, 1929)
Bulldog Drummond (UA, 1929)
The Exalted Flapper (Fox, 1929)
Is Everybody Happy? (WB, 1929)
Oh! Sailor, Behave (WB, 1930)
Safety in Numbers (Par, 1930)
The Cat Creeps (Univ, 1930)
The Boudoir Diplomat (Univ, 1930)
Command Performance (Tif, 1931)
The Squaw Man (MGM, 1931)
Their Mad Moment (Fox, 1931)
The Unholy Garden (UA, 1931)
Daughter of the Dragon (Par, 1931)
Shanghai Express (Par, 1932)
Man About Town (Par, 1932)

Speak Easily (MGM, 1932)
Divorce in the Family (MGM, 1932)
Faithless (MGM, 1932)
Jewel Robbery (FN, 1932)
The Mask of Fu Manchu (MGM, 1932)
Clear All Wires (MGM, 1933)
Looking Forward (MGM, 1933)
Queen Christina (MGM, 1933)
By Candlelight (Univ, 1934)
Nana (UA, 1934)
The Count of Monte Cristo (UA, 1934)
I'll Tell the World (Univ, 1934)
The Man Who Reclaimed His Head (Univ, 1934)
Vanessa—Her Love Story (MGM, 1935)
The Devil Is a Woman (Par, 1935)
Werewolf of London (Univ, 1935)

The Dark Angel (UA, 1935)
Three Kids and a Queen (Univ, 1935)
A Feather in Her Hat (Col, 1935)
A Tale of Two Cities (MGM, 1935)
The House of a Thousand Candles (Rep, 1936)
Mary of Scotland (RKO, 1936)

Under the Red Robe (20th, 1937)
S.O.S. Coast Guard (Rep serial, 1937)
The Prisoner of Zenda (UA, 1937)
Service de Luxe (Univ, 1938)
Bluebeard's Eighth Wife (Par, 1938)
The Young in Heart (UA, 1938)
Wife, Husband and Friend (20th, 1939)

Rulers of the Sea (Par, 1939)
Women in War (Rep, 1940)
The Son of Monte Cristo (UA, 1940)
Dr. Jekyll and Mr. Hyde (MGM, 1941)
The Living Ghost (Mon, 1942)
Confidential Agent (WB, 1945)

CHARLEY GRAPEWIN

With Jean Arthur in Party Wire *(1935).*

Born December 20, 1869, Xenia, Ohio. Married Anna Chance. Died February 2, 1956, Corona, California. The embodiment of the wheezing, lanky, elderly man for three decades of film-making. After many serviceable roles, very effective as Gramps Maple, the old codger relative of Bette Davis in *The Petrified Forest*. Most famous as Grandpa (*The Grapes of Wrath*) and Jeeter Lester (*Tobacco Road*). Later the clean-cut Inspector Queen to sleuthing son Ellery (Ralph Bellamy and then William Gargan) in the *Ellery Queen* series. In the classic *The Wizard of Oz*, was Judy Garland's Uncle Henry, married to Clara Blandick (Auntie Em).

Charley Grapewin to Errol Flynn in *They Died with Their Boots On:* "My business is shootin'—not salutin'."

Films

Only Saps Work (Par, 1930)
The Shannons of Broadway (Univ, 1930)
The Millionaire (WB, 1931)
Gold Dust Gertie (WB, 1931)
Hell's House (Capitol, 1932)
Big Timer (Fox, 1932)

Disorderly Conduct (Fox, 1932)
The Woman in Room 13 (Fox, 1932)
Lady and Gent (Par, 1932)
No Man of Her Own (Par, 1932)
Wild Horse Mesa (Par, 1932)
The Night of June 13th (Par, 1932)

Heroes for Sale (FN, 1933)
Wild Boys of the Road (FN, 1933)
Midnight Mary (MGM, 1933)
Beauty for Sale (MGM, 1933)
Pilgrimage (Fox, 1933)
Don't Bet on Love (Univ, 1933)

Torch Singer (Par, 1933)
Hell and High Water (Par, 1933)
Hello, Everybody! (Par, 1933)
The Kiss Before the Mirror (Univ, 1933)
Two Alone (RKO, 1934)
Anne of Green Gables (RKO, 1934)
Judge Priest (Fox, 1934)
She Made Her Bed (Par, 1934)
The President Vanishes (Par, 1934)
The Quitter (Chesterfield, 1934)
The Loud Speaker (Mon, 1934)
Return of the Terror (FN, 1934)
Caravan (Fox, 1934)
One Frightened Night (Mon, 1935)
In Spite of Danger (Col, 1935)
Party Wire (Col, 1935)
Shanghai (Par, 1935)
Alice Adams (RKO, 1935)
King Solomon of Broadway (Univ, 1935)
Rendezvous (MGM, 1935)
Ah, Wilderness! (MGM, 1935)
Eight Bells (Col, 1935)
Superspeed (Col, 1935)
The Petrified Forest (WB, 1936)
The Voice of Bugle Ann (MGM, 1936)
Small Town Girl (MGM, 1936)
Libeled Lady (MGM, 1936)

Sinner Take All (MGM, 1936)
Without Orders (RKO, 1936)
The Good Earth (MGM, 1937)
A Family Affair (MGM, 1937)
Captains Courageous (MGM, 1937)
Between Two Women (MGM, 1937)
Broadway Melody of 1938 (MGM, 1937)
Bad Guy (MGM, 1937)
The Big City (MGM, 1937)
Bad Man of Brimstone (MGM, 1937)
Of Human Hearts (MGM, 1938)
Girl of the Golden West (MGM, 1938)
Three Comrades (MGM, 1938)
Three Loves Has Nancy (MGM, 1938)
Listen, Darling (MGM, 1938)
Artists and Models Abroad (Par, 1938)
Stand Up and Fight (MGM, 1939)
Burn 'em Up O'Connor (MGM, 1939)
The Wizard of Oz (MGM, 1939)
Sudden Money (Par, 1939)
The Man Who Dared (WB, 1939)
Hero for a Day (Univ, 1939)
Dust Be My Destiny (WB, 1939)
Sabotage (Rep, 1939)
The Grapes of Wrath (20th, 1940)
Johnny Apollo (20th, 1940)
Earthbound (20th, 1940)

Rhythm on the River (Par, 1940)
Texas Rangers Ride Again (Par, 1940)
Ellery Queen, Master Detective (Col, 1940)
Tobacco Road (20th, 1941)
Ellery Queen's Penthouse Mystery (Col, 1941)
Ellery Queen and the Perfect Crime (Col, 1941)
Ellery Queen and the Murder Ring (Col, 1941)
They Died with Their Boots On (WB, 1941)
Enemy Agents Meet Ellery Queen (Col, 1942)
A Close Call for Ellery Queen (Col, 1942)
A Desperate Chance for Ellery Queen (Col, 1942)
Crash Dive (20th, 1943)
Follow the Boys (Univ, 1944)
Atlantic City (Rep, 1944)
The Impatient Years (Col, 1944)
Gunfighters (Col, 1947)
The Enchanted Valley (EL, 1948)
Sand (20th, 1949)
When I Grow Old (UA, 1951)

SYDNEY GREENSTREET

James Flavin, Peter Lorre, and Sydney Greenstreet in Hollywood Canteen *(1944).*

Born December 27, 1879, Sandwich, Kent, England. Married Dorothy Marie Ogden (1918), child: one son. Died January 18, 1954, Los Angeles, California. Distinguished stage actor who made a delayed screen bow at age 61, displaying consummate artistry beneath an imposing girth. Riveting performance as avaricious Casper Gutman in *The Maltese Falcon* (Oscar-nominated but lost BSAAA to Donald Crisp of *How Green Was My Valley*). Reteamed with pop-eyed Peter Lorre in several other Warner Bros. ventures, including *Three Strangers* and *The Verdict*. Played a law enforcer in *Conflict, The Velvet Touch,* etc.—contrary to belief that his frame, chuckle, and impressive mien qualified him only for villainous roles. Occasionally allowed to play comedy (*Pillow to Post*) or romantic fiction (*Christmas in Connecticut*)—was quite good. Strongest screen opponents include Joan Crawford in *Flamingo Road.*

Sydney Greenstreet to Paul Henreid in *The Conspirators:* "It's pleasant to believe that one has found a man of integrity in this day of depravity and ruin."

Films

They Died with Their Boots On (WB, 1941)
The Maltese Falcon (WB, 1941)
Across the Pacific (WB, 1942)
Casablanca (WB, 1942)
Background to Danger (WB, 1943)
Hollywood Canteen (WB, 1944)
Passage to Marseille (WB, 1944)
Between Two Worlds (WB, 1944)

The Conspirators (WB, 1944)
The Mask of Dimitrios (WB, 1945)
Conflict (WB, 1945)
Christmas in Connecticut (WB, 1945)
Pillow to Post (WB, 1945)
Devotion (WB, 1946)
Three Strangers (WB, 1946)
The Verdict (WB, 1946)
That Way with Women (WB, 1947)

The Hucksters (MGM, 1947)
The Velvet Touch (RKO, 1948)
Ruthless (EL, 1948)
The Woman in White (WB, 1948)
Flamingo Road (WB, 1949)
Malaya (MGM, 1949)
It's a Great Feeling (WB, 1949)
Mandalay (MGM, 1949)

ROBERT GREIG

Robert Greig, Luise Rainer, and William Powell in The Great Ziegfeld *(1936).*

Born December 27, 1880, Melbourne, Australia. Died June 27, 1958, Hollywood, California. The pear-shaped interpreter of snooty butlers in many pictures.

Robert Greig to Onslow Stevens in *Peg o' My Heart:* "I beg your pardon, Sir Gerald. There's an unkempt sort of an individual outside to see you."

Films

Animal Crackers (Par, 1930)
Tonight or Never (UA, 1931)
Stepping Sisters (Fox, 1932)
Beauty and the Boss (WB, 1932)
The Cohens and Kellys in Hollywood (Univ, 1932)
Merrily We Go to Hell (Par, 1932)
Horse Feathers (Par, 1932)
Jewel Robbery (FN, 1932)
Trouble in Paradise (Par, 1932)
Man Wanted (WB, 1932)
The Tenderfoot (FN, 1932)
Love Me Tonight (Par, 1932)
They Just Had to Get Married (Univ, 1933)
Dangerously Yours (Fox, 1933)
Robbers' Roost (Fox, 1933)
Men Must Fight (MGM, 1933)
Pleasure Cruise (Fox, 1933)
Mind Reader (FN, 1933)
It's Great to Be Alive (Fox, 1933)
Easy to Love (WB, 1934)
Love Captive (Univ, 1934)
Upper World (WB, 1934)

One More River (Univ, 1934)
Cockeyed Cavaliers (RKO, 1934)
Folies Bergere (UA, 1935)
Clive of India (UA, 1935)
Woman Wanted (MGM, 1935)
The Bishop Misbehaves (MGM, 1935)
The Gay Deception (Col, 1935)
I Live for Love (WB, 1935)
Tough Guy (MGM, 1936)
Small Town Girl (MGM, 1936)
Rose-Marie (MGM, 1936)
The Unguarded Hour (MGM, 1936)
Trouble for Two (MGM, 1936)
The Devil Doll (MGM, 1936)
The Great Ziegfeld (MGM, 1936)
Easy to Take (Par, 1936)
Lloyds of London (20th, 1936)
Theodora Goes Wild (Col, 1936)
Michael O'Halloran (Rep, 1937)
Easy Living (Par, 1937)
My Dear Miss Aldrich (MGM, 1937)
Midnight Intruder (Univ, 1938)
The Adventures of Marco Polo (UA, 1938)
Ambush (Par, 1939)

It Could Happen to You (20th, 1939)
Way Down South (RKO, 1939)
Drums Along the Mohawk (20th, 1939)
No Time for Comedy (WB, 1940)
The Thief of Bagdad (UA, 1940)
Hudson's Bay (20th, 1940)
The Lady Eve (Par, 1941)
Moon over Miami (20th, 1941)
Sullivan's Travels (Par, 1941)
I Married a Witch (UA, 1942)
Tales of Manhattan (20th, 1942)
The Palm Beach Story (Par, 1942)
Son of Fury (20th, 1942)
The Moon and Sixpence (UA, 1942)
Summer Storm (UA, 1944)
The Great Moment (Par, 1944)
Million Dollar Kid (Mon, 1944)
The Picture of Dorian Gray (MGM, 1945)
Earl Carroll Vanities (Rep, 1945)
Nob Hill (20th, 1945)
Love, Honor and Goodbye (Rep, 1945)
The Cheaters (Rep, 1945)
Forever Amber (20th, 1947)
Unfaithfully Yours (20th, 1948)

PAUL GUILFOYLE

Eduardo Ciannelli, Paul Guilfoyle, and Margo in Winterset *(1936).*

Born July 14, 1902, Jersey City, New Jersey. Married Kathleen Mulqueen, child: son. Died June 27, 1961. Rarely allowed a sympathetic role (one exception, Garth, the remorseful violinist in *Winterset*), he gravitated to playing gangsters of the weak-willed or punk variety. Left a strong impression as Roy Parker, the hood shoved into the car trunk by James Cagney in *White Heat*. Late in career, turned to film directing: *Captain Scarface* (1953), *A Life at Stake* (1954), and *Tess of the Storm Country* (1960).

Paul Guilfoyle to Charles Arnt in *Remember the Night:* "First offender at Christmas time is tougher than tiger meat."

Films

Special Agent (WB, 1935)
The Crime of Dr. Crespi (Rep, 1935)
Roaming Lady (Col, 1936)
Two-Fisted Gentleman (Col, 1936)
Winterset (RKO, 1936)
Wanted: Jane Turner (RKO, 1936)
The Soldier and the Lady [a.k.a. *Michael Strogoff*] (RKO, 1937)
The Woman I Love (RKO, 1937)
You Can't Buy Luck (RKO, 1937)
Behind the Headlines (RKO, 1937)
You Can't Beat Love (RKO, 1937)
Hideaway (RKO, 1937)
Super-Sleuth (RKO, 1937)
Fight for Your Lady (RKO, 1937)
Flight from Glory (RKO, 1937)

Danger Patrol (RKO, 1937)
Double Danger (RKO, 1938)
Crashing Hollywood (RKO, 1938)
Quick Money (RKO, 1938)
Law of the Underworld (RKO, 1938)
The Saint in New York (RKO, 1938)
This Marriage Business (RKO, 1938)
I'm from the City (RKO, 1938)
Sky Giant (RKO, 1938)
Blind Alibi (RKO, 1938)
Fugitives for a Night (RKO, 1938)
Tarnished Angel (RKO, 1938)
Law West of Tombstone (RKO, 1938)
The Mad Miss Manton (RKO, 1938)
Pacific Liner (RKO, 1939)
Society Lawyer (MGM, 1939)

Heritage of the Desert (Par, 1939)
Unexpected Father (Univ, 1939)
News Is Made at Night (20th, 1939)
Our Leading Citizen (Par, 1939)
Sabotage (Rep, 1939)
One Hour to Live (Univ, 1939)
The Grapes of Wrath (20th, 1940)
Remember the Night (Par, 1940)
Thou Shalt Not Kill (Rep, 1940)
The Saint Takes Over (RKO, 1940)
Brother Orchid (WB, 1940)
Millionaires in Prison (RKO, 1940)
One Crowded Night (RKO, 1940)
East of the River (WB, 1940)
Wildcat Bus (RKO, 1940)
The Saint in Palm Springs (RKO, 1941)

Who Is Hope Schuyler? (20th, 1942)
The Man Who Returned to Life (Col, 1942)
Time to Kill (20th, 1942)
White Savage (Univ, 1943)
Petticoat Larceny (RKO, 1943)
The North Star [a.k.a. *Armored Attack*] (RKO, 1943)
Three Russian Girls (UA, 1943)
It Happened Tomorrow (UA, 1944)
The Seventh Cross (MGM, 1944)
The Mark of the Whistler (Col, 1944)
The Master Race (RKO, 1944)
The Missing Corpse (PRC, 1945)

Why Girls Leave Home (PRC, 1945)
Sweetheart of Sigma Chi (Mon, 1946)
The Virginian (Par, 1946)
The Millerson Case (Col, 1947)
Second Chance (20th, 1947)
Roses Are Red (20th, 1947)
Follow Me Quietly (RKO, 1949)
Mighty Joe Young (RKO, 1949)
The Woman on Pier 13 [a.k.a. *I Married a Communist*] (RKO, 1949)
The Judge (Film Classics, 1949)
Miss Mink of 1949 (20th, 1949)
There's a Girl in My Heart (AA, 1949)
Trouble Preferred (20th, 1949)

White Heat (WB, 1949)
Messenger of Peace (Astor, 1950)
Davy Crockett—Indian Scout (UA, 1950)
Bomba and the Hidden City (Mon, 1950)
When I Grow Up (UA, 1951)
Actors and Sin (UA, 1952)
Confidence Girl (UA, 1952)
Julius Caesar (MGM, 1953)
Torch Song (MGM, 1953)
Apache (UA, 1954)
The Golden Idol (AA, 1954)
Chief Crazy Horse (Univ, 1955)
The Boy and the Pirates (UA, 1960)

EDMUND GWENN

Tom Drake, Edmund Gwenn, Lassie, and Janet Leigh in Hills of Home *(1948).*

Born February 26, 1875, Glamorgan, Wales. Married Minnie Terry (1901), divorced. Died September 6, 1959, Woodland Hills, California. Appeared for years on the British stage (frequently in George Bernard Shaw plays) and in English films. Became a Hollywood fixture in the late 1930s. Soft-spoken with a benign countenance and sparkling eyes. Well employed as the long-suffering Mr. Bennett in *Pride and Prejudice*, Rowlie in *Lassie Come Home* (and others of the canine series), and the Reverend Dr. Lloyd in *Life with Father*. Won a BSAAA for his Kris Kringle role, the Macy's Santa Claus who believed he was St. Nick in *Miracle on 34th Street*. Earned another Oscar bid for his Skipper Miller, the elderly, unorthodox counterfeiter in *Mister 880* (but lost BSAAA to George Sanders of *All About Eve*).

Edmund Gwenn to Mickey Rooney in *A Yank at Eton:* "Eton is too big to worry about where a boy comes from."

Films

The Real Thing at Last (Br, 1916)
How He Lied to Her Husband (Br, 1931)
The Skin Game (Br, 1931)
Money for Nothing (Br, 1931)
Hindle Wakes (Br, 1931)
Condemned to Death (Br, 1932)
Frail Woman (Br, 1932)
Love on Wheels (Br, 1932)
The Admiral's Secret (Br, 1932)
Tell Me Tonight (Ger, 1932)
Early to Bed (Br, 1932)
Smithy (FN Br, 1933)

The Good Companions (Br, 1933)
Cash [a.k.a. For Love] (Par Br, 1933)
Marooned (Fox, Br, 1933)
Channel Crossing (Br, 1934)
Friday the Thirteenth (Br, 1934)
I Was a Spy (Br, 1934)
Waltzes from Vienna [a.k.a. Strauss's Great Waltz] (Br, 1934)
Be Mine Tonight (Br, 1934)
Wakefield, the City Man (Br, 1934)
Warn London (Br, 1934)
Spring in the Air (Br, 1934)

Penny Paradise (Br, 1934)
Passing Shadows (Fox Br, 1934)
Father and Son (Fox Br, 1934)
Java Head (FN Br, 1934)
Sylvia Scarlett (RKO, 1935)
Country Bumpkin (Br, 1935)
Anthony Adverse (WB, 1936)
The Walking Dead (WB, 1936)
Mad Holiday (MGM, 1936)
Laburnum Grove (Br, 1936)
All American Chump (MGM, 1936)
Parnell (MGM, 1937)

A Yank at Oxford (MGM, 1938)
An Englishman's Home [a.k.a. Mad Men of Europe] (Br, 1939)
South Riding (UA Br, 1939)
Cheer, Boys, Cheer (UA Br, 1939)
The Earl of Chicago (MGM, 1940)
The Doctor Takes a Wife (Col, 1940)
Pride and Prejudice (MGM, 1940)
Foreign Correspondent (UA, 1940)
Cheers for Miss Bishop (UA, 1941)
One Night in Lisbon (Par, 1941)
The Devil and Miss Jones (RKO, 1941)
Scotland Yard (20th, 1941)
Charley's Aunt (20th, 1941)
A Yank at Eton (MGM, 1942)
The Meanest Man in the World (20th, 1943)

Forever and a Day (RKO, 1943)
Lassie Come Home (MGM, 1943)
Between Two Worlds (WB, 1944)
The Keys of the Kingdom (20th, 1944)
Dangerous Partners (MGM, 1945)
Bewitched (MGM, 1945)
She Went to the Races (MGM, 1945)
Of Human Bondage (WB, 1946)
Undercurrent (MGM, 1946)
Miracle on 34th Street (20th, 1947)
Life with Father (WB, 1947)
Thunder in the Valley (MGM, 1947)
Green Dolphin Street (MGM, 1947)
Hills of Home (MGM, 1948)
Apartment for Peggy (20th, 1948)
Challenge to Lassie (MGM, 1949)
Pretty Baby (WB, 1950)

Louisa (Univ, 1950)
Mister 880 (20th, 1950)
For Heaven's Sake (20th, 1950)
A Woman of Distinction (Col, 1950)
Peking Express (Par, 1951)
Sally and St. Anne (Univ, 1952)
Les Miserables (20th, 1952)
Bonzo Goes to College (Univ, 1952)
Something for the Birds (20th, 1952)
Mr. Scoutmaster (20th, 1953)
The Bigamist (Filmakers, 1953)
The Student Prince (MGM, 1954)
Them (WB, 1954)
It's a Dog's Life (MGM, 1955)
The Trouble with Harry (Par, 1955)
Rocket from Calabuch (Trans-Lux, 1958)

HUGO HAAS

John Wengraf, Evelyn Keyes, Allyn Joslyn, Hugo Haas, Tonio Selwart, Marguerite Chapman, Edgar Buchanan, Nina Foch (back to camera), and Frank Jenks in Strange Affair *(1944).*

Born February 19, 1902, Brno, Czechoslovakia. Married Marie de Bibkov (1938), child: Ivan; divorced (1953). Died December 1, 1968, Vienna, Austria. Stocky, thick-accented Czechoslovakian: Vera Ralston's *Dakota* (Marko Poli) and *The Fighting Kentuckian* (General Paul De Marchand); *The Private Affairs of Bel Ami* (Monsieur Walter); *Casbah* (Omar); *King Solomon's Mines* (Van Brun); etc. Starred in a series of low-budget, poorly received pictures which he wrote and directed, frequently with Cleo Moore as his leading lady: *Strange Fascination, One Girl's Confession,* etc. Directed and appeared in *Lizzie*, which showcased Eleanor Parker; superior account of woman with split personality.

> **Hugo Haas** to Cleo Moore in *The Other Woman:* "Your whole story's a cheap trick. I never even touched you. I couldn't have been that drunk that I wouldn't have remembered."

243

Films

Skeleton on Horseback (Michael Mindlin, 1940)
Days of Glory (RKO, 1944)
The Princess and the Pirate (RKO, 1944)
Strange Affair (Col, 1944)
Summer Storm (UA, 1944)
A Bell for Adano (20th, 1945)
Dakota (Rep, 1945)
Jealousy (Rep, 1945)
What Next, Corporal Hargrove? (MGM, 1945)
Holiday in Mexico (MGM, 1946)

Two Smart People (MGM, 1946)
Northwest Outpost (Rep, 1947)
The Private Affairs of Bel Ami (UA, 1947)
Fiesta (MGM, 1947)
Merton of the Movies (MGM, 1947)
The Foxes of Harrow (20th, 1947)
Casbah (Univ, 1948)
My Girl Tisa (WB, 1948)
For the Love of Mary (Univ, 1948)
The Fighting Kentuckian (Rep, 1949)
King Solomon's Mines (MGM, 1950)
Vendetta (RKO, 1950)

Girl on the Bridge (20th, 1951)
Pickup (Col, 1951)
Strange Fascination (Col, 1952)
Thy Neighbor's Wife (20th, 1953)
One Girl's Confession (Col, 1953)
Bait (Col, 1954)
The Other Woman (20th, 1954)
Edge of Hell (Univ, 1956)
Hit and Run (UA, 1957)
Lizzie (MGM, 1957)
Born to Be Loved (Univ, 1959)
Paradise Alley (Sutton, 1962)

SARA HADEN

Sara Haden, Jane Withers, Helen Wood, and Donald Cook in Can This Be Dixie? *(1936).*

Born November 17, 1897, Galveston, Texas. Married Richard Abbott (1921); divorced (1948). Brought to Hollywood to play Etta Dawson in Katharine Hepburn's *Spitfire*, repeating her Broadway assignment. Best as movie spinster, reaching her peak as stiff but sweet Aunt Milly in the MGM *Andy Hardy* series; generally pioneer women in Westerns after she left Metro.

Sara Haden to Lewis Stone in *The Hardys Ride High:* "You may as well know—Mr. Archer's interest in me was the sale of a gilt-edged piece of property."

Films

Spitfire (RKO, 1934)
The Fountain (RKO, 1934)
Finishing School (RKO, 1934)
Anne of Green Gables (RKO, 1934)
The Life of Vergie Winters (RKO, 1934)
Hat, Coat and Glove (RKO, 1934)
Affairs of a Gentleman (Univ, 1934)
The White Parade (Fox, 1934)
Music in the Air (Fox, 1934)
Black Fury (FN, 1935)
Mad Love (MGM, 1935)
O'Shaughnessy's Boy (MGM, 1935)
Way Down East (Fox, 1935)
Magnificent Obsession (Univ, 1935)
Everybody's Old Man (20th, 1936)
Little Miss Nobody (20th, 1936)
Captain January (20th, 1936)
Half Angel (20th, 1936)
Poor Little Rich Girl (20th, 1936)
The Crime of Dr. Forbes (20th, 1936)
Can This Be Dixie? (20th, 1936)
Reunion (20th, 1936)
Under Cover of Night (MGM, 1937)
A Family Affair (MGM, 1937)
Laughing at Trouble (20th, 1937)
The Last of Mrs. Cheyney (MGM, 1937)
First Lady (WB, 1937)
The Barrier (Par, 1937)
You're Only Young Once (MGM, 1938)
Judge Hardy's Children (MGM, 1938)

Out West with the Hardys (MGM, 1938)
Four Girls in White (MGM, 1939)
The Hardys Ride High (MGM, 1939)
Tell No Tales (MGM, 1939)
Andy Hardy Gets Spring Fever (MGM, 1939)
Remember? (MGM, 1939)
The Secret of Dr. Kildare (MGM, 1939)
Judge Hardy and Son (GM, 1939)
The Shop Around the Corner (MGM, 1940)
Andy Hardy Meets Debutante (MGM, 1940)
Boom Town (MGM, 1940)
Hullabaloo (MGM, 1940)
The Trial of Mary Dugan (MGM, 1941)
Andy Hardy's Private Secretary (MGM, 1941)
Washington Melodrama (MGM, 1941)
Love Crazy (MGM, 1941)
Barnacle Bill (MGM, 1941)
Life Begins for Andy Hardy (MGM, 1941)
H. M. Pulham, Esq. (MGM, 1941)
Keeping Company (MGM, 1941)
The Courtship of Andy Hardy (MGM, 1942
The Affairs of Martha [a.k.a. *Once upon a Thursday*] (MGM, 1942)
Woman of the Year (MGM, 1942)
Andy Hardy's Double Life (MGM, 1942)

The Youngest Profession (MGM, 1943)
Above Suspicion (MGM, 1943)
Best Foot Forward (MGM, 1943)
Thousands Cheer (MGM, 1943)
Lost Angel (MGM, 1943)
Andy Hardy's Blonde Trouble (MGM, 1944)
Bathing Beauty (MGM, 1944)
Our Vines Have Tender Grapes (MGM, 1945)
She Wouldn't Say Yes (Col, 1945)
Bad Bascomb (MGM, 1946)
Our Hearts Were Growing Up (Par, 1946)
She-Wolf of London (Univ, 1946)
Mr. Ace (UA, 1946)
Love Laughs at Andy Hardy (MGM, 1946)
So Goes My Love (Univ, 1946)
The Bishop's Wife (RKO, 1947)
Rachel and the Stranger (RKO, 1948)
The Big Cat (EL, 1949)
Roughshod (RKO, 1949)
The Great Rupert (EL, 1950)
A Life of Her Own (MGM, 1950)
Rodeo (Mon, 1952)
A Lion Is in the Streets (WB, 1953)
The Outlaw's Daughter (20th, 1954)
Betrayed Women (AA, 1955)
Andy Hardy Comes Home (MGM, 1958)

ALAN HALE
(Rufus Alan MacKahn)

Alan Hale, David Bruce (rear), and Errol Flynn in The Sea Hawk *(1940).*

Born February 10, 1892, Washington, D.C. Married Gretchen Hartman (1914), children: Alan, Karen, Jeanne. Died January 22, 1950, Hollywood, California. A giant personality in the character-actor field. Bluff and hearty big-boned screen figure who found his ideal part in Douglas Fairbanks' silent *Robin Hood,* playing oafish Little John. Repeated the role in Errol Flynn's 1938 version and in John Derek's 1950 *Rogues of Sherwood Forest,* his final film assignment. A long-time member of the Warner Bros. stock company; usually the hero's garrulous, back-slapping pal, especially as comic relief in Errol Flynn vehicles: *Dodge City* (Rusty Hart), *The Private Lives of Elizabeth and Essex* (very serious Earl of Tyrone), *The Sea Hawk* (Carl Pitt), *Desperate Journey* (Flight Sergeant Kirk Edwards), *Gentleman Jim* (Pat Corbett), etc. Rejected by Barbara Stanwyck in *Stella Dallas,* murdered by Ida Lupino in *They Drive by Night,* battled with Marjorie Rambeau in *Tugboat Annie Sails Again,* and confounded by Danny Kaye in *The Inspector General,* but as Emil in 1934's *Of Human Bondage* he abandoned Bette Davis. Son Alan, Jr. became an actor.

> **Alan Hale** toasting Ida Lupino and George Raft in *They Drive by Night:* "Early to rise and early to bed, makes a man healthy but socially dead."

Films

The Power of the Press (Biograph, 1914)
Dora Thorne (Biograph, 1915)
East Lynne (Biograph, 1915)
The Purple Lady (M, 1916)
Love Thief (Fox, 1916)
Rolling Stones (Par, 1916)
The Scarlet Oath (World, 1916)
Pudd'n Head Wilson (Mark Twain Company, 1916)

The Woman in the Case (Univ, 1917)
The Price She Paid (Selznick, 1917)
Life's Whirlpool (Rolfe-Metro, 1917)
The Eternal Temptress (Par, 1917)
One Hour (Hoffman, 1917)
Masks and Faces (World, 1918)
Moral Suicide (Graphic, 1918)
The Whirlpool (Select, 1918)
Love Hunger (Hodkinson, 1919)

The Trap (Univ, 1919)
The Blue Bonnet (Hodkinson, 1919)
The Four Horsemen of the Apocalypse (M, 1921)
A Voice in the Dark (G, 1921)
The Barbarian (Pioneer, 1921)
A Wise Fool (Par, 1921)
Over the Wire (M, 1921)
The Great Impersonation (Par, 1921)

The Fox (Univ, 1921)
One Glorious Day (Par, 1922)
A Doll's House (UA, 1922)
The Trap (Univ, 1922)
The Dictator (Par, 1922)
Robin Hood (UA, 1922)
Shirley of the Circus (Fox, 1922)
The Covered Wagon (Fox, 1922)
Quicksands (Selznick, 1923)
Main Street (WB, 1923)
The Eleventh Hour (Fox, 1923)
Hollywood (Par, 1923)
Cameo Kirby (Fox, 1923)
Long Live the King (M, 1923)
The Cricket (Selznick, 1923)
Black Oxen (Associated FN, 1923)
Code of the Wilderness (Vit, 1924)
Girls Men Forget (Principle, 1924)
One Night in Rome (MG, 1924)
For Another Woman (Rayart, 1924)
Troubles of a Bride (Fox, 1924)
Braveheart (PDC, 1925)
Dick Turpin (Fox, 1925)
The Scarlet Honeymoon (Fox, 1925)
The Crimson Runner (PDC, 1925)
Flattery (Chadwick, 1925)
The Wedding Song (PDC, 1925)
Ranger of the Big Pines (Vit, 1925)
Heart and Fists (Associated Exhibitors, 1926)
Forbidden Waters (PDC, 1926)
The Sporting Lover (FN, 1926)
Risky Business (PDC, 1926)
Redheads Preferred (Tif, 1926)
Rubber Tires (PDC, 1927)
Vanity (PDC, 1927)
The Wreck of the Hesperus (Pathé, 1927)
The Spieler (Pathé, 1928)
The Leopard Lady (Pathé, 1928)
Skyscraper (Pathé, 1928)
Oh, Kay! (FN, 1928)
The Cop (Pathé, 1928)
Power (Pathé, 1928)
Sal of Singapore (Pathé, 1928)
The Leatherneck (Pathé, 1929)
Sailor's Holiday (Pathé, 1929)
Red Hot Rhythm (Pathé, 1929)
The Sap (WB, 1929)
She Got What She Wanted (Tif, 1930)
Night Angel (Par, 1931)
Rebound (Pathé, 1931)
Aloha (Tif, 1931)
Susan Lennox, Her Fall and Rise (MGM, 1931)

The Sin of Madelon Claudet (MGM, 1931)
The Sea Ghost (Peerless, 1931)
So Big (WB, 1932)
Union Depot (WB, 1932)
Rebecca of Sunnybrook Farm (Fox, 1932)
The Match King (WB, 1932)
What Price Decency (Majestic, 1933)
The Eleventh Commandment (Allied, 1933)
Destination Unknown (Univ, 1933)
Picture Brides (Allied, 1933)
Miss Fane's Baby Is Stolen (Par, 1934)
Little Man, What Now? (Univ, 1934)
Great Expectations (Univ, 1934)
Imitation of Life (Univ, 1934)
Of Human Bondage (RKO, 1934)
The Little Minister (RKO, 1934)
The Lost Patrol (RKO, 1934)
It Happened One Night (Col, 1934)
Fog over Frisco (WB, 1934)
The Scarlet Letter (Majestic, 1934)
There's Always Tomorrow (Univ, 1934)
Babbitt (WB, 1934)
Grand Old Girl (RKO, 1935)
The Last Days of Pompeii (RKO, 1935)
Another Face (RKO, 1935)
The Good Fairy (Univ, 1935)
The Crusades (Par, 1935)
Two in the Dark (RKO, 1936)
The Country Beyond (20th, 1936)
A Message to Garcia (20th, 1936)
Parole (Univ, 1936)
Yellowstone (Univ, 1936)
Our Relations (MGM, 1936)
God's Country and the Woman (WB, 1936)
The Prince and the Pauper (WB, 1937)
Stella Dallas (UA, 1937)
When Thief Meets Thief (UA, 1937)
High, Wide and Handsome (Par, 1937)
Thin Ice (20th, 1937)
Music for Madame (RKO, 1937)
The Adventures of Marco Polo (UA, 1938)
The Adventures of Robin Hood (WB, 1938)
Algiers (UA, 1938)
Four Men and a Prayer (20th, 1938)
Listen, Darling (MGM, 1938)
Valley of the Giants (WB, 1938)
The Sisters (WB, 1938)
Dodge City (WB, 1939)
The Man in the Iron Mask (UA, 1939)
Dust Be My Destiny (WB, 1939)
On Your Toes (WB, 1939)

The Private Lives of Elizabeth and Essex (WB, 1939)
The Fighting 69th (WB, 1940)
Virginia City (WB, 1940)
Three Cheers for the Irish (WB, 1940)
They Drive by Night (WB, 1940)
The Sea Hawk (WB, 1940)
Tugboat Annie Sails Again (WB, 1940)
Santa Fe Trail (WB, 1940)
Green Hell (Univ, 1940)
Strawberry Blonde (WB, 1941)
Footsteps in the Dark (WB, 1941)
Thieves Fall Out (WB, 1941)
Manpower (WB, 1941)
The Great Mr. Nobody (WB, 1941)
The Smiling Ghost (WB, 1941)
Captains of the Clouds (WB, 1942)
Juke Girl (WB, 1942)
Desperate Journey (WB, 1942)
Gentleman Jim (WB, 1942)
Action in the North Atlantic (WB, 1943)
Thank Your Lucky Stars (WB, 1943)
This Is the Army (WB, 1943)
Destination Tokyo (WB, 1943)
The Adventures of Mark Twain (WB, 1944)
Hollywood Canteen (WB, 1944)
Make Your Own Bed (WB, 1944)
Janie (WB, 1944)
Roughly Speaking (WB, 1945)
Hotel Berlin (WB, 1945)
God Is My Co-Pilot (WB, 1945)
Escape in the Desert (WB, 1945)
The Man I Love (WB, 1946)
Night and Day (WB, 1946)
Perilous Holiday (Col, 1946)
The Time, the Place and the Girl (WB, 1946)
Pursued (WB, 1947)
That Way with Women (WB, 1947)
My Wild Irish Rose (WB, 1947)
Cheyenne (WB, 1947)
Whiplash (WB, 1948)
My Girl Tisa (WB, 1948)
Adventures of Don Juan (WB, 1948)
South of St. Louis (WB, 1949)
The Younger Brothers (WB, 1949)
The House Across the Street (WB, 1949)
Always Leave Them Laughing (WB, 1949)
The Inspector General (WB, 1949)
Stars in My Crown (MGM, 1950)
Colt .45 (WB, 1950)
Rogues of Sherwood Forest (Col, 1950)

JONATHAN HALE
(Jonathan Hatley)

In the 1930s.

Born 1891, Ontario, Canada. Married _____, children: two sons; widowed. Died February 28, 1966, Woodland Hills, California. A onetime consular general. Thrived on filmmaking for three decades, frequently playing the annoyed executive who must supervise the hero at the office: the nettled J. C. Dithers in many of the *Blondie* series and Inspector Fernack in *The Saint* films with Louis Hayward and George Sanders. Sandwiched in scores of other parts: *Boys Town* (Hargraves), *Her Jungle Love* (J. C. Martin), *In Name Only* (Dr. Gateson), *Calling Dr. Gillespie* (Frank Marshall Todwell), *Since You Went Away* (conductor), *Johnny Belinda* (Dr. Gray), etc.

Jonathan Hale to the others in *The Cat Creeps:* "Undoubtedly Miss Palmer held the secret of this entire affair. That's why the killer disposed of her."

Films

Lightning Strikes Twice (RKO, 1934)
Alice Adams (RKO, 1935)
Three Live Ghosts (MGM, 1935)
Charlie Chan's Secret (20th, 1936)
Fury (MGM, 1936)
Charlie Chan at the Race Track (20th, 1936)
36 Hours to Kill (20th, 1936)
The Singing Kid (FN, 1936)
Flying Hostess (Univ, 1936)
Happy Go Lucky (Rep, 1936)
The Devil Is a Sissy (MGM, 1936)
Too Many Parents (Par, 1936)
The Case Against Mrs. Ames (Par, 1936)
Educating Father (20th, 1936)
The Voice of Bugle Ann (MGM, 1936)
You Only Live Once (UA, 1937)
Man of the People (MGM, 1937)
Saratoga (MGM, 1937)

Madame X (MGM, 1937)
Outcast (Par, 1937)
John Meade's Woman (Par, 1937)
Midnight Madonna (Par, 1937)
Mysterious Crossing (Univ, 1937)
Racketeers in Exile (Col, 1937)
This Is My Affair (20th, 1937)
Danger—Love at Work (20th, 1937)
Exiled to Shanghai (Rep, 1937)
She's Dangerous (Univ, 1937)
Charlie Chan at the Olympics (20th, 1937)
League of Frightened Men (Col, 1937)
Big Town Girl (20th, 1937)
Men with Wings (Par, 1938)
Arsene Lupin Returns (MGM, 1938)
Judge Hardy's Children (MGM, 1938)
Blondie (Col, 1938)
There's That Woman Again (Col, 1938)

Yellow Jack (MGM, 1938)
Boys Town (MGM, 1938)
Road Demon (20th, 1938)
Her Jungle Love (Par, 1938)
Duke of West Point (UA, 1938)
Wives Under Suspicion (Univ, 1938)
Letter of Introduction (Univ, 1938)
Over the Wall (WB, 1938)
The Saint in New York (RKO, 1938)
Fugitives for a Night (RKO, 1938)
Breaking the Ice (RKO, 1938)
Tarnished Angel (RKO, 1938)
Gangs of New York (Rep, 1938)
The First Hundred Years (MGM, 1938)
Stand Up and Fight (MGM, 1939)
Thunder Afloat (MGM, 1939)
Wings of the Navy (WB, 1939)
The Saint Strikes Back (RKO, 1939)
In Name Only (RKO, 1939)

Blondie Meets the Boss (Col, 1939)
Fugitive at Large (Col, 1939)
Blondie Brings Up Baby (Col, 1939)
The Amazing Mr. Williams (Col, 1939)
Tail Spin (20th, 1939)
The Story of Alexander Graham Bell (20th, 1939)
Barricade (20th, 1939)
In Old Monterey (Rep, 1939)
The Big Guy (Univ, 1940)
The Saint's Double Trouble (RKO, 1940)
Johnny Apollo (20th, 1940)
The Saint Takes Over (RKO, 1940)
Private Affairs (Univ, 1940)
We Who Are Young (MGM, 1940)
Blondie Has Servant Trouble (Col, 1940)
Dulcy (MGM, 1940)
Melody and Moonlight (Rep, 1940)
Blondie Plays Cupid (Col, 1940)
Blondie Goes Latin (Col, 1941)
Flight from Destiny (WB, 1941)
Strange Alibi (WB, 1941)
The Great Swindle (Col, 1941)
Her First Beau (Col, 1941)
Ringside Maisie (MGM, 1941)
The Pittsburgh Kid (Rep, 1941)
Blondie in Society (Col, 1941)
The Saint in Palm Springs (RKO, 1941)
The Bugle Sounds (MGM, 1942)
The Lone Star Ranger (20th, 1942)
Joe Smith, American (MGM, 1942)
Blondie Goes to College (Col, 1942)
Miss Annie Rooney (UA, 1942)
Flight Lieutenant (Col, 1942)
Calling Dr. Gillespie (MGM, 1942)
The Amazing Mrs. Holliday (Univ, 1943)
Nobody's Darling (Rep, 1943)

Sweet Rosie O'Grady (20th, 1943)
Blondie's Blessed Event (Col, 1943)
Blondie for Victory (Col, 1943)
Hangmen Also Die (UA, 1943)
Jack London (UA, 1943)
This Is the Life (Univ, 1944)
The Black Parachute (Col, 1944)
Since You Went Away (UA, 1944)
Hollywood Canteen (WB, 1944)
Dead Man's Eyes (Univ, 1944)
My Buddy (Rep, 1944)
And Now Tomorrow (Par, 1944)
The End of the Road (Rep, 1944)
Allotment Wives (Mon, 1945)
Dakota (Rep, 1945)
G. I. Honeymoon (Mon, 1945)
Leave It to Blondie (Col, 1945)
Man Alive (RKO, 1945)
The Phantom Speaks (Rep, 1945)
Life with Blondie (Col, 1946)
Angel on My Shoulder (UA, 1946)
Blondie Knows Best (Col, 1946)
Blondie's Lucky Day (Col, 1946)
The Cat Creeps (Univ, 1946)
Easy to Wed (MGM, 1946)
Gay Blades [a.k.a. *Tournament Tempo*] (Rep, 1946)
Riverboat Rhythm (RKO, 1946)
The Strange Mr. Gregory (Mon, 1946)
The Walls Came Tumbling Down (Col, 1946)
Wife Wanted (Mon, 1946)
The Beginning or the End? (MGM, 1947)
The Ghost Goes Wild (Rep, 1947)
Rolling Home (Screen Guild, 1947)
The Vigilantes Return (Univ, 1947)
Her Husband's Affairs (Col, 1947)

High Wall (MGM, 1947)
Michael O'Halloran (Mon, 1948)
King of the Gamblers (Rep, 1948)
Silver River (WB, 1948)
Johnny Belinda (WB, 1948)
Rocky (Mon, 1948)
Call Northside 777 (20th, 1948)
A Dangerous Profession (RKO, 1949)
Rose of the Yukon (Rep, 1949)
Stampede (AA, 1949)
The Judge (Film Classics, 1949)
State Department File 649 (Film Classics, 1949)
Federal Agent at Large (Rep, 1950)
Three Husbands (UA, 1950)
Short Grass (AA, 1950)
Triple Trouble (Mon, 1950)
The Rodeo King and the Senorita (Rep, 1951)
On the Sunny Side of the Street (Col, 1951)
Let's Go, Navy (Mon, 1951)
Strangers on a Train (WB, 1951)
Insurance Investigator (Rep, 1951)
Scandal Sheet (Col, 1952)
The Steel Trap (20th, 1952)
My Pal Gus (20th, 1952)
Taxi! (20th, 1953)
A Blueprint for Murder (20th, 1953)
Kansas Pacific (AA, 1953)
Duffy of San Quentin (WB, 1954)
She Couldn't Say No (RKO, 1954)
Riot in Cell Block 11 (AA, 1954)
The Night Holds Terror (Col, 1955)
Jaguar (Rep, 1956)

PORTER HALL
(Clifford Porter Hall)

In the late 1940s.

Born September 19, 1888, Cincinnati, Ohio. Married Geraldine Brown (1927), children: David, Sarah Jane. Died October 6, 1953, Los Angeles, California. Compactly built, grim-faced, dishonest guy of assorted films; e.g., as Jack McCall in *The Plainsman* he shot Gary Cooper in the back. A frequent member of the Preston Sturges comedy unit at Paramount in the 1940s. Appropriate as the mealy mouthed husband of Marjorie Main in the wacky black comedy *Murder, He Says*.

Porter Hall to Charley Grapewin in *The Petrified Forest:* "If he heads this way, we Black Horse Vigilantes will handle *that* gent."

Films

The Thin Man (MGM, 1934)
Murder in the Private Car (MGM, 1934)
The Case of the Lucky Legs (WB, 1935)
The Story of Louis Pasteur (WB, 1935)
The Petrified Forest (WB, 1936)
Too Many Parents (Par, 1936)
The Princess Comes Across (Par, 1936)
And Sudden Death (Par, 1936)
The General Died at Dawn (Par, 1936)
Satan Met a Lady (WB, 1936)
The Plainsman (Par, 1936)
Snowed Under (FN, 1936)

Let's Make a Million (Par, 1937)
Bulldog Drummond Escapes (Par, 1937)
Souls at Sea (Par, 1937)
Make Way for Tomorrow (Par, 1937)
King of the Gamblers (Par, 1937)
Hotel Haywire (Par, 1937)
This Way, Please (Par, 1937)
True Confession (Par, 1937)
Wild Money (Par, 1937)
Wells Fargo (Par, 1937)
Scandal Street (Par, 1938)
Stolen Heaven (Par, 1938)

Dangerous to Know (Par, 1938)
Bulldog Drummond's Peril (Par, 1938)
Prison Farm (Par, 1938)
King of Alcatraz (Par, 1938)
The Arkansas Traveler (Par, 1938)
Men with Wings (Par, 1938)
Tom Sawyer—Detective (Par, 1938)
Mr. Smith Goes to Washington (Col, 1939)
Grand Jury Secrets (Par, 1939)
They Shall Have Music (UA, 1939)
His Girl Friday (Col, 1940)

Dark Command (Rep, 1940)
Arizona (Col, 1940)
Trail of the Vigilantes (Univ, 1940)
Sullivan's Travels (Par, 1941)
The Parson of Panamint (Par, 1941)
Mr. and Mrs. North (MGM, 1941)
The Remarkable Andrew (Par, 1942)
Butch Minds the Baby (Univ, 1942)
A Stranger in Town (MGM, 1943)
The Desperadoes (Col, 1943)
The Woman of the Town (UA, 1943)
Standing Room Only (Par, 1944)
The Miracle of Morgan's Creek (Par, 1944)

Going My Way (Par, 1944)
Double Indemnity (Par, 1944)
The Great Moment (Par, 1944)
The Mark of the Whistler (Col, 1944)
Blood on the Sun (UA, 1945)
Bring on the Girls (Par, 1945)
Kiss and Tell (Col, 1945)
Murder, He Says (Par, 1945)
Week-End at the Waldorf (MGM, 1945)
Unconquered (Par, 1947)
Miracle on 34th Street (20th, 1947)
Singapore (Univ, 1947)
You Gotta Stay Happy (Univ, 1948)
That Wonderful Urge (20th, 1948)

The Beautiful Blonde from Bashful Bend (20th, 1949)
Intruder in the Dust (MGM, 1949)
Chicken Every Sunday (20th, 1949)
The Big Carnival [a.k.a. Ace in the Hole] (Par, 1951)
The Half-Breed (RKO, 1952)
Carbine Williams (MGM, 1952)
Holiday for Sinners (MGM, 1952)
Pony Express (Par, 1953)
Vice Squad (UA, 1953)
Return to Treasure Island (UA, 1954)

THURSTON HALL

Roy Rogers, Dale Evans, and Thurston Hall in Song of Nevada (1944).

Born May 10, 1882, Boston, Massachusetts. Married Quenda _____ . Died February 20, 1958, Beverly Hills, California. Veteran stage performer and touring-company operator. Turned to silents as Marc Antony to Theda Bara's Cleopatra, was the Alaskan railroad magnate in The Iron Trail, etc. After a lengthy film hiatus returned to the medium in the mid-1930s, typecast as the fleshy, silver-haired, dyspeptic businessman who was forever clearing his throat as he thought of some crooked scheme. Played Inspector Crane in several of the Warren William The Lone Wolf whodunit entries. TV series: "Topper" (as Mr. Schuyler, the bank president).

Thurston Hall to Brian Donlevy in The Great McGinty: "I will not pay graft. Millions for defense but not one cent for tribute."

Films

Idle Hands (Pioneer, 1921)

The Iron Trail (UA, 1921)

Mother Eternal (Graphic Film Corp, 1921)

Fair Lady (UA, 1922)

Wilderness of Youth (Graphic Film Corp, 1922)

The Royal Oak (Br, 1923)

The Girl Friend (Col, 1935)

Too Tough to Kill (Col, 1935)

The Black Room (Col, 1935)

Love Me Forever (Col, 1935)

Public Menace (Col, 1935)

One Way Ticket (Col, 1935)

Case of the Missing Man (Col, 1935)

A Feather in Her Hat (Col, 1935)

Hooray for Love (RKO, 1935)

Metropolitan (Fox, 1935)

Guard That Girl (Col, 1935)

Crime and Punishment (Col, 1935)

The Lone Wolf Returns (Col, 1936)

Don't Gamble with Love (Col, 1936)

The Man Who Lived Twice (Col, 1936)

Killer at Large (Col, 1936)

Theodora Goes Wild (Col, 1936)

The Devil's Squadron (Col, 1936)

The King Steps Out (Col, 1936)

Trapped by Television (Col, 1936)

Shakedown (Col, 1936)

Three Wise Guys (MGM, 1936)

Pride of the Marines (Col, 1936)

Roaming Lady (Col, 1936)

Two-Fisted Gentleman (Col, 1936)

Lady from Nowhere (Col, 1936)

I Promise to Pay (Col, 1937)

All American Sweetheart (Col, 1937)

Women of Glamour (Col, 1937)

Don't Tell the Wife (RKO, 1937)

Parole Racket (Col, 1937)

It Can't Last Forever (Col, 1937)

Venus Makes Trouble (Col, 1937)

Counsel for Crime (Col, 1937)

Murder in Greenwich Village (Col, 1937)

We Have Our Moments (Univ, 1937)

Oh, Doctor (Univ, 1937)

No Time to Marry (Col, 1938)

Women in Prison (Col, 1938)

The Main Event (Col, 1938)

There's Always a Woman (Col, 1938)

Little Miss Roughneck (Col, 1938)

Campus Confessions (Par, 1938)

Extortion (Col, 1938)

The Affairs of Annabel (RKO, 1938)

Professor Beware (Par, 1938)

Women Are Like That (WB, 1938)

Squadron of Honor (Col, 1938)

The Amazing Dr. Clitterhouse (WB, 1938)

Hard to Get (WB, 1938)

Fast Company (MGM, 1938)

Going Places (WB, 1938)

You Can't Cheat an Honest Man (Univ, 1939)

Dodge City (WB, 1939)

First Love (Univ, 1939)

Stagecoach (UA, 1939)

Ex-Champ (Univ, 1939)

Our Neighbors—The Carters (Par, 1939)

Mutiny on the Blackhawk (Univ, 1939)

Hawaiian Nights (Univ, 1939)

Million Dollar Legs (Par, 1939)

Each Dawn I Die (WB, 1939)

The Star Maker (Par, 1939)

Jeepers Creepers (Rep, 1939)

Money to Burn (Rep, 1939)

The Day the Bookies Wept (RKO, 1939)

Dancing Co-ed (MGM, 1939)

Sued for Libel (RKO, 1940)

The Blue Bird (20th, 1940)

Blondie on a Budget (Col, 1940)

In Old Missouri (Rep, 1940)

Alias the Deacon (Univ, 1940)

Millionaires in Prison (RKO, 1940)

The Lone Wolf Meets a Lady (Col, 1940)

The Great McGinty (Par, 1940)

City for Conquest (WB, 1940)

Friendly Neighbors (Rep, 1940)

The Golden Fleecing (MGM, 1940)

Virginia City (WB, 1940)

The Lone Wolf Takes a Chance (Col, 1941)

The Invisible Woman (Univ, 1941)

Flight from Destiny (WB, 1941)

The Lone Wolf Keeps a Date (Col, 1941)

The Great Lie (WB, 1941)

Where Did You Get That Girl? (Univ, 1941)

Washington Melodrama (MGM, 1941)

She Knew All the Answers (Col, 1941)

Repent at Leisure (RKO, 1941)

Accent on Love (20th, 1941)

Secrets of the Lone Wolf (Col, 1941)

Design for Scandal (MGM, 1941)

Tuxedo Junction (Rep, 1941)

Pacific Blackout [a.k.a. Midnight Angel] (Par, 1941)

Remember the Day (20th, 1941)

Sleepytime Gal (Rep, 1942)

Counter Espionage (Col, 1942)

Night Before the Divorce (20th, 1942)

Rings on Her Fingers (20th, 1942)

Shepherd of the Ozarks (Rep, 1942)

The Great Man's Lady (Par, 1942)

Hello, Annapolis (Col, 1942)

Call of the Canyon (Rep, 1942)

The Hard Way (WB, 1942)

The Great Gildersleeve (RKO, 1942)

We Were Dancing (MGM, 1942)

Crash Dive (20th, 1943)

One Dangerous Night (Col, 1943)

The Youngest Profession (MGM, 1943)

This Land Is Mine (RKO, 1943)

I Dood It (MGM, 1943)

Sherlock Holmes in Washington (Univ, 1943)

Hoosier Holiday (Rep, 1943)

Here Comes Elmer (Rep, 1943)

He Hired the Boss (20th, 1943)

The Adventures of Mark Twain (WB, 1944)

Wilson (20th, 1944)

Goodnight, Sweetheart (Rep, 1944)

Something for the Boys (20th, 1944)

Cover Girl (Col, 1944)

The Great Moment (Par, 1944)

In Society (Univ, 1944)

Ever Since Eve (Col, 1944)

Song of Nevada (Rep, 1944)

Bring On the Girls (Par, 1945)

The Blonde from Brooklyn (Col, 1945)

Brewster's Millions (UA, 1945)

Colonel Effingham's Raid (20th, 1945)

Don Juan Quilligan (20th, 1945)

The Gay Senorita (Col, 1945)

Lady on a Train (Univ, 1945)

West of the Pecos (RKO, 1945)

Dangerous Business (Col, 1946)

One More Tomorrow (WB, 1946)

She Wrote the Book (Univ, 1946)

Three Little Girls in Blue (20th, 1946)

Two Sisters from Boston (MGM, 1946)

Without Reservations (RKO, 1946)

Swing the Western Way (Col, 1947)

The Farmer's Daughter (RKO, 1947)

Welcome Stranger (Par, 1947)

Black Gold (AA, 1947)

The Secret Life of Walter Mitty (RKO, 1947)

Unfinished Dance (MGM, 1947)

It Had to Be You (Col, 1947)

Mourning Becomes Electra (RKO, 1947)

Son of Rusty (Col, 1947)

King of Gamblers (Rep, 1948)

Up in Central Park (Univ, 1948)

Miraculous Journey (Film Classics, 1948)

Blondie's Reward (Col, 1949)

Manhattan Angel (Col, 1949)

Stagecoach Kid (RKO, 1949)

Blondie's Secret (Col, 1949)

Rim of the Canyon (Col, 1949)

Square Dance Jubilee (Lip, 1949)

Bride for Sale (RKO, 1949)

Rusty Saves a Life (Col, 1949)

Girl's School (Col, 1949)

Tell It to the Judge (Col, 1949)

Belle of Old Mexico (Rep, 1950)

Federal Agent at Large (Rep, 1950)

Bright Leaf (WB, 1950)

Chain Gang (Col, 1950)

Bandit Queen (Lip, 1950)

One Too Many (Hallmark, 1950)

Whirlwind (Col, 1951)

Belle Le Grande (Rep, 1951)   *Night Stage to Galveston* (Col, 1952)   *Carson City* (WB, 1952)
Texas Carnival (MGM, 1951)   *Woman of the North Country* (Rep, 1952)   *The WAC from Walla Walla* (Rep, 1952)
One Big Affair (UA, 1952)   *Skirts Ahoy* (MGM, 1952)   *Affair in Reno* (Rep, 1957)

JOHN HALLIDAY

In the 1930s.

Born September 14, 1880, Brooklyn, New York. Married 1) Camille Personi; divorced; 2) Eva Lang; divorced; 3) Eleanor Griffith. Died October 17, 1947, Honolulu, Hawaii. First with the British Army in the Boer War, then a mining engineer in Nevada, later a performer of Gilbert and Sullivan operettas and a stage actor, then a screen actor. Debonair. Cast repeatedly in films as the tolerant husband or friend, but sometimes went asunder—the jealous spouse accidentally killed by Gary Cooper in *Peter Ibbetson*. Seen as Carlos Margoli, Marlene Dietrich's wily, dapper co-thief in *Desire*; the same year played John Blakeford, the has-been actor caught in scandal in *Hollywood Boulevard*; later was Katharine Hepburn's well-meaning but errant dad in *The Philadelphia Story*.

John Halliday to Marlene Dietrich in *Desire*: "Before I tell you what I plan to do with you before I'm through, allow me to compliment you. You're looking more beautiful than ever."

Films

The Woman Gives (FN, 1920)
East Side Sadie (Worldart, 1929)
Recaptured Love (WB, 1930)
Scarlet Pages (FN, 1930)
Captain Applejack (WB, 1930)
Father's Son (FN, 1930)
The Ruling Voice (FN, 1931)
Fifty Million Frenchmen (WB, 1931)
Smart Woman (RKO, 1931)
Transatlantic (Fox, 1931)
Consolation Marriage (RKO, 1931)
Millie (RKO, 1931)
The Spy (Fox, 1931)
Once a Sinner (Fox, 1931)
Bird of Paradise (RKO, 1932)
Men of Chance (RKO, 1932)
The Impatient Maiden (Univ, 1932)

Week-Ends Only (Fox, 1932)
The Age of Consent (RKO, 1932)
The Man Called Back (Tif, 1932)
The Woman Accused (Par, 1933)
Perfect Understanding (UA, 1933)
Terror Aboard (Par, 1933)
Bed of Roses (RKO, 1933)
The House on 56th Street (WB, 1933)
A Woman's Man (Mon, 1934)
Happiness Ahead (FN, 1934)
Registered Nurse (FN, 1934)
Desirable (WB, 1934)
Return of the Terror (FN, 1934)
Finishing School (RKO, 1934)
The Witching Hour (Par, 1934)
Housewife (WB, 1934)
Mystery Woman (Fox, 1935)

The Dark Angel (UA, 1935)
The Melody Lingers On (UA, 1935)
Peter Ibbetson (Par, 1935)
Desire (Par, 1936)
Fatal Lady (Par, 1936)
Three Cheers for Love (Par, 1936)
Hollywood Boulevard (Par, 1936)
Blockade (UA, 1938)
Arsene Lupin Returns (MGM, 1938)
That Certain Age (Univ, 1938)
Elsa Maxwell's Hotel for Women (20th, 1939)
Intermezzo—A Love Story (UA, 1939)
The Philadelphia Story (MGM, 1940)
Submarine Zone [a.k.a. *Escape to Glory*] (Col, 1941)
Lydia (UA, 1941)

CHARLES HALTON

Charles Halton, Randolph Scott, and Forrest Tucker in The Nevadan *(1950).*

Born March 16, 1876, Washington, D.C. Died April 16, 1959, Los Angeles, California. The caustic, bespectacled little man who dealt with any opposition, whether as the passport officer in 1937's *The Prisoner of Zenda*, the suspicious physician coping with the Marx Brothers in *Room Service*, or as Dobosh, the harried stage producer in *To Be or Not to Be*.

Charles Halton to John McGuire in *Stranger on the Third Floor:* "This is a respectable house, I want you to know."

Films

Sing Me a Love Song (FN, 1936)
Gold Diggers of 1937 (WB, 1936)
Stolen Holiday (WB, 1936)
Come and Get It (UA, 1936)
More Than a Secretary (Col, 1936)
The Black Legion (WB, 1936)
Penrod and Sam (WB, 1937)
Ready, Willing and Able (WB, 1937)
Talent Scout (WB, 1937)
Pick a Star (MGM, 1937)
Woman Chases Man (UA, 1937)
Dead End (UA, 1937)
Blossoms on Broadway (Par, 1937)
Partners in Crime (Par, 1937)
The Prisoner of Zenda (UA, 1937)
Trouble at Midnight (Univ, 1938)
Penrod's Double Trouble (WB, 1938)
Penrod and His Twin Brother (WB, 1938)
Penitentiary (Col, 1938)
A Man to Remember (RKO, 1938)
Stolen Heaven (Par, 1938)
The Saint in New York (RKO, 1938)

Room Service (RKO, 1938)
I'll Give a Million (20th, 1938)
I Am the Law (Col, 1938)
Bluebeard's Eighth Wife (Par, 1938)
Jesse James (20th, 1939)
Young Mr. Lincoln (20th, 1939)
News Is Made at Night (20th, 1939)
Swanee River (20th, 1939)
Federal Manhunt (Rep, 1939)
They Made Her a Spy (RKO, 1939)
Reno (RKO, 1939)
Dodge City (WB, 1939)
Indianapolis Speedway (WB, 1939)
Charlie Chan at Treasure Island (20th, 1939)
I'm from Missouri (Par, 1939)
Juarez (WB, 1939)
They Asked for It (Univ, 1939)
The Shop Around the Corner (MGM, 1940)
The Story of Dr. Ehrlich's Magic Bullet (WB, 1940)

Dr. Cyclops (Par, 1940)
They Drive by Night (WB, 1940)
Twenty-Mule Team (MGM, 1940)
Lillian Russell (20th, 1940)
Foreign Correspondent (UA, 1940)
Gangs of Chicago (Rep, 1940)
Behind the News (Rep, 1940)
Young People (20th, 1940)
Stranger on the Third Floor (RKO, 1940)
The Westerner (UA, 1940)
The Doctor Takes a Wife (Col, 1940)
Tugboat Annie Sails Again (WB, 1940)
Calling All Husbands (WB, 1940)
Behind the News (Rep, 1940)
Brigham Young—Frontiersman (20th, 1940)
Three Girls About Town (Col, 1941)
Footlight Fever (RKO, 1941)
Tobacco Road (20th, 1941)
Mr. District Attorney (Rep, 1941)
Mr. and Mrs. Smith (RKO, 1941)
Meet the Chump (Univ, 1941)

A Very Young Lady (20th, 1941)
Million Dollar Baby (WB, 1941)
I Was a Prisoner on Devil's Island (Col, 1941)
Dance Hall (20th, 1941)
The Smiling Ghost (WB, 1941)
Three Sons o' Guns (WB, 1941)
Look Who's Laughing (RKO, 1941)
Unholy Partners (MGM, 1941)
H. M. Pulham, Esq. (MGM, 1941)
To Be or Not to Be (UA, 1942)
Juke Box Jenny (Univ, 1942)
Whispering Ghosts (20th, 1942)
The Spoilers (Univ, 1942)
In Old California (Rep, 1942)
Priorities on Parade (Par, 1942)
Across the Pacific (WB, 1942)
You Can't Escape Forever (WB, 1942)
Henry Aldrich, Editor (Par, 1942)
That Other Woman (20th, 1942)

My Kingdom for a Cook (Col, 1943)
Lady Bodyguard (Par, 1943)
Jitterbugs (20th, 1943)
Government Girl (RKO, 1943)
Flesh and Fantasy (Univ, 1943)
Whispering Footsteps (Rep, 1943)
Wilson (20th, 1944)
Rationing (MGM, 1944)
The Town Went Wild (PRC, 1944)
Address Unknown (Col, 1944)
Shadows in the Night (Col, 1944)
The Thin Man Goes Home (MGM, 1944)
A Tree Grows in Brooklyn (20th, 1945)
Rhapsody in Blue (WB, 1945)
Mama Loves Papa (RKO, 1945)
She Went to the Races (MGM, 1945)
The Fighting Guardsman (Col, 1945)
Midnight Manhunt (Par, 1945)
Because of Him (Univ, 1946)
Three Little Girls in Blue (20th, 1946)

Singin' in the Corn (Col, 1946)
Sister Kenny (RKO, 1946)
The Best Years of Our Lives (RKO, 1946)
The Ghost Goes West (Rep, 1947)
Three Godfathers (MGM, 1948)
Hideout (Rep, 1949)
The Daring Caballero (UA, 1949)
The Sickle or the Cross (Astor, 1949)
The Nevadan (Col, 1950)
When Willie Comes Marching Home (20th, 1950)
Stella (20th, 1950)
The Traveling Saleswoman (Col, 1950)
Stella (20th, 1950)
Here Comes the Groom (Par, 1951)
Gasoline Alley (Col, 1951)
Carrie (Par, 1952)
A Slight Case of Larceny (MGM, 1953)
The Moonlighter (WB, 1953)
Friendly Persuasion (AA, 1956)

MARGARET HAMILTON

Frances Dee and Margaret Hamilton in Meet the Stewarts *(1942).*

Born September 12, 1902, Cleveland, Ohio. Married Paul Meserve (1931), child: Hamilton; divorced (1938). The unforgettable Wicked Witch of the West in *The Wizard of Oz*. Has enlivened many films with her sharp-featured looks, usually as the pushy town gossip or disgruntled spinster. Played dour Myrtle Ferguson, the newspaper office worker in *Johnny Come Lately*; was Harold Lloyd's unwed sister Flora Diddlebock in *Mad Wednesday*. Familiar to TV viewers as Cora of the coffee commercials. TV series: "Ethel and Albert," "The Patty Duke Show," "The Addams Family" (as Esther Frump), "Search for Tomorrow," and "Sigmund and the Sea Monsters."

Margaret Hamilton to Wallace Beery in *Stablemates*: "I look the same . . . wet or dry."

256

Films

Another Language (MGM, 1933)
Hat, Coat and Glove (RKO, 1934)
There's Always Tomorrow (Univ, 1934)
Broadway Bill (Col, 1934)
By Your Leave (RKO, 1934)
The Farmer Takes a Wife (Fox, 1935)
Way Down East (Fox, 1935)
People Will Talk (Par, 1935)
Chatterbox (RKO, 1936)
The Witness Chair (RKO, 1936)
These Three (UA, 1936)
The Trail of the Lonesome Pine (Par, 1936)
The Moon's Our Home (Par, 1936)
Good Old Soak (MGM, 1937)
You Only Live Once (UA, 1937)
Nothing Sacred (UA, 1937)
When's Your Birthday? (RKO, 1937)
Mountain Justice (WB, 1937)
Saratoga (MGM, 1937)
I'll Take Romance (Col, 1937)
Laughing at Trouble (20th, 1937)
A Slight Case of Murder (WB, 1938)
The Adventures of Tom Sawyer (UA, 1938)
Stablemates (MGM, 1938)
Four's a Crowd (WB, 1938)
Mother Carey's Chickens (RKO, 1938)

Breaking the Ice (RKO, 1938)
The Wizard of Oz (MGM, 1939)
Babes in Arms (MGM, 1939)
Angels Wash Their Faces (WB, 1939)
Main Street Lawyer (Rep, 1939)
My Little Chickadee (Univ, 1940)
I'm Nobody's Sweetheart Now (Univ, 1940)
The Villain Still Pursued Her (RKO, 1940)
Play Girl (RKO, 1941)
The Shepherd of the Hills (Par, 1941)
The Invisible Woman (Univ, 1941)
The Gay Vagabond (Rep, 1941)
Babes on Broadway (MGM, 1941)
Twin Beds (UA, 1942)
The Affairs of Martha [a.k.a. *Once upon a Thursday*] (MGM, 1942)
Meet the Stewarts (Col, 1942)
Journey for Margaret (MGM, 1942)
City Without Men (Col, 1943)
The Ox-Bow Incident (20th, 1943)
Johnny Come Lately (UA, 1943)
Guest in the House (20th, 1944)
George White's Scandals (RKO, 1945)
Faithful in My Fashion (MGM, 1946)
Janie Gets Married (WB, 1946)

Driftwood (Rep, 1947)
Dishonored Lady (UA, 1947)
Mad Wednesday [a.k.a. *The Sin of Harold Diddlebock*] (UA, 1947)
Bungalow 13 (20th, 1948)
State of the Union (MGM, 1948)
Texas, Brooklyn and Heaven (UA, 1948)
The Sun Comes Up (MGM, 1949)
The Red Pony (Rep, 1949)
The Beautiful Blonde from Bashful Bend (20th, 1949)
Riding High (Par, 1950)
Wabash Avenue (20th, 1950)
The Great Plane Robbery (UA, 1950)
Comin' Round the Mountain (Univ, 1951)
People Will Talk (20th, 1951)
Thirteen Ghosts (Col, 1960)
Paradise Alley (Astor, 1962)
The Daydreamer (Emb, 1966) [voice only]
Rosie! (Univ, 1967)
Angel in My Pocket (Univ, 1969)
Brewster McCloud (MGM, 1970)
The Anderson Tapes (Col, 1971)
Journey Back to Oz (Filmation, 1974) [voice only]

WALTER HAMPDEN
(Walter Hampden Dougherty)

Charles Boyer, Leo G. Carroll, and Walter Hampden in The First Legion *(1951).*

Born June 30, 1879, Brooklyn, New York. Married Mabel Moore, children: Mabel, Paul. Died June 11, 1955, Hollywood, California. Distinguished veteran thespian with an imposing beaked nose. Made one silent feature, returning to the screen 22 years later to play Claude in *The Hunchback of Notre Dame.* Brought aristocratic dignity to all roles: Big Bear *(North West Mounted Police),* Senator Sharp *(They Died with Their Boots On),* Commodore Devereaux *(Reap the Wild Wind),* etc. Presented Anne Baxter with the Sarah Siddons Award in *All About Eve.*

Walter Hampden to Bette Davis in *All This and Heaven Too:*
"Admit the sinful passion that led to this murder. Denounce this man who betrayed you."

Films

Warfare of the Flesh (F.B. Warren, 1917)
The Hunchback of Notre Dame (RKO, 1939)
All This and Heaven Too (WB, 1940)
North West Mounted Police (Par, 1940)
They Died with Their Boots On (WB, 1941)

Reap the Wild Wind (Par, 1942)
The Adventures of Mark Twain (WB, 1944)
All About Eve (20th, 1950)
The First Legion (UA, 1951)
Five Fingers (20th, 1952)
Sombrero (MGM, 1953)

Treasure of the Golden Condor (20th, 1953)
The Silver Chalice (WB, 1954)
Sabrina (Par, 1954)
Strange Lady in Town (WB, 1955)
The Prodigal (MGM, 1955)
The Vagabond King (Par, 1956)

SIR CEDRIC HARDWICKE

In Things to Come *(1936).*

Born February 19, 1893, Stourbridge, England. Married 1) Helena Pickard (1928), son: Edward; divorced (1948); 2) Mary Scott (1950); divorced (1961). Died August 6, 1964, New York City, New York. The elegantly professional British stage and film performer who was too frequently ill-used by Hollywood. Played the missing doctor found by determined reporter Spencer Tracy in *Stanley and Livingstone* and death's emissary in *On Borrowed Time.* Guided Jimmy Lydon through Rugby in *Tom Brown's School Days* as headmaster Dr. Thomas Arnold; the same year was Richard Cobb, the villain of *The Invisible Man Returns.* Was Ludwig Frankenstein, an unhappy heir of the family problems in *The Ghost of Frankenstein.* During World War II he made a minor career of playing heinous Axis officials *(Invisible Agent, The Moon Is Down).* Wasted in the 1950s in a series of minor roles in costume epics (e.g., the high judge of *The Story of Mankind*); an exception: his King Edward IV in Laurence Olivier's *Richard III.* TV series: "Mrs. G. Goes to College" (with his *A Majority of One* Broadway co-star Gertrude Berg).

> **Sir Cedric Hardwicke** to Jimmy Lydon in *Tom Brown's School Days:* "I believe you, Brown, because you are your father's son—and because a liar would have told a more plausible story."

Films

Riches and Rogues (Br, 1913)
Nelson (Br, 1926)
Dreyfus [a.k.a. *The Dreyfus Case*] (Br, 1931)
Rome Express (Univ Br, 1933)
The Ghoul (Br, 1933)
Orders Is Orders (Br, 1934)
The Lady Is Willing (Col Br, 1934)
Nell Gwynn (UA Br, 1934)
Jew Suss [a.k.a. *Power*] (Br, 1934)
King of Paris (UA Br, 1934)
Becky Sharp (RKO, 1935)
Les Miserables (Fox, 1935)

Peg of Old Drury (UA Br, 1935)
Bella Donna (Br, 1935)
Tudor Rose [a.k.a. *Nine Days a Queen*] (Br, 1936)
Things to Come (UA Br, 1936)
Calling the Tune (Br, 1936)
Laburnum Grove (Br, 1936)
Green Light (WB, 1937)
King Solomon's Mines (Br, 1937)
On Borrowed Time (MGM, 1939)
Stanley and Livingstone (20th, 1939)
The Hunchback of Notre Dame (RKO, 1939)

The Invisible Man Returns (Univ, 1940)
Tom Brown's School Days (RKO, 1940)
The Howards of Virginia (Col, 1940)
Victory (Par, 1940)
Suspicion (RKO, 1941)
Sundown (UA, 1941)
Valley of the Sun (RKO, 1942)
The Ghost of Frankenstein (Univ, 1942)
Invisible Agent (Univ, 1942)
Commandos Strike at Dawn (Col, 1942)
The Moon Is Down (20th, 1943)
Forever and a Day (RKO, 1943)
The Cross of Lorraine (MGM, 1943)

A Wing and a Prayer (20th, 1944)
The Lodger (20th, 1944)
Wilson (20th, 1944)
The Keys of the Kingdom (20th, 1944)
The Picture of Dorian Gray (MGM, 1945)
[narrator]
Sentimental Journey (20th, 1946)
Tycoon (RKO, 1947)
A Woman's Vengeance (Univ, 1947)
Beware of Pity (Br, 1947)
The Imperfect Lady (Par, 1947)
Lured (UA, 1947)
Ivy (Univ, 1947)
Song of My Heart (AA, 1947)
Nicholas Nickleby (Br, 1947)

I Remember Mama (RKO, 1948)
Rope (WB, 1948)
A Connecticut Yankee in King Arthur's Court (Par, 1949)
Now Barabbas Was a Robber (WB, Br, 1949)
The Winslow Boy (EL, 1950)
The White Tower (RKO, 1950)
Mr. Imperium (MGM, 1951)
The Desert Fox (20th, 1951)
The Green Glove (UA, 1952)
Caribbean (Par, 1952)
Botany Bay (Par, 1953)
War of the Worlds (Par, 1953)
[narrator]

Salome (Col, 1953)
Bait (Col, 1954)
Helen of Troy (WB, 1955)
Diane (MGM, 1955)
Gaby (MGM, 1956)
Richard III (Br, 1956)
The Vagabond King (Par, 1956)
The Power and the Prize (MGM, 1956)
The Ten Commandments (Par, 1956)
Around the World in 80 Days (UA, 1956)
The Story of Mankind (WB, 1957)
Baby Face Nelson (UA, 1957)
Five Weeks in a Balloon (20th, 1962)
The Pumpkin Eater (Br, 1964)

LUMSDEN HARE

Douglas Fairbanks, Jr., Joan Fontaine, Montagu Love, and Lumsden Hare in Gunga Din (1939).

Born October 2, 1875, Cashel, Ireland. Married Selene Johnson, child: Norah. Died August 28, 1964, Hollywood, California. The Irish player who frequently interpreted English roles: John Barrymore's *Sherlock Holmes* (Dr. Leighton), Will Rogers' *So This Is London* (Lord Percy Worthing). Played Publius in 1953's *Julius Caesar*.

Lumsden Hare to Fritz Leiber in *Under Two Flags*: "You understand, of course, that I'm here merely as an observer for the British government."

Films

Avalanche (ArtClass, 1919)
The Education of Elizabeth (Par, 1921)
Sherlock Holmes (G, 1922)
On the Banks of the Wabash (Vit, 1923)
Second Youth (MG, 1924)

One Way Street (FN, 1925)
Fugitives (Fox, 1929)
The Black Watch (Fox, 1929)
Masquerade (Fox, 1929)
Girls Gone Wild (Fox, 1929)

Salute (Fox, 1929)
The Sky Hawk (Fox, 1929)
Under Suspicion (Fox, 1930)
Crazy That Way (Fox, 1930)
So This Is London (Fox, 1930)

Scotland Yard (Fox, 1930)
Svengali (WB, 1931)
Road to Singapore (WB, 1931)
Arrowsmith (UA, 1931)
Charlie Chan Carries On (Fox, 1931)
Always Goodbye (Fox, 1931)
The Silent Witness (Fox, 1932)
The Crusader (Majestic, 1932)
International House (Par, 1933)
College Humor (Par, 1933)
His Double Life (Par, 1933)
The Little Minister (RKO, 1934)
The House of Rothschild (UA, 1934)
Man of Two Worlds (RKO, 1934)
Black Moon (Col, 1934)
The World Moves On (Fox, 1934)
Outcast Lady (MGM, 1934)
Clive of India (UA, 1935)
Lives of a Bengal Lancer (Par, 1935)
The Crusades (Par, 1935)
Cardinal Richelieu (UA, 1935)
The Three Musketeers (RKO, 1935)
The Bishop Misbehaves (MGM, 1935)
Freckles (RKO, 1935)
Folies Bergere (UA, 1935)
She (RKO, 1935)
Lady Tubbs (Univ, 1935)
The Great Impersonation (Univ, 1935)
Professional Soldier (Fox, 1935)
Under Two Flags (20th, 1936)

Lloyds of London (20th, 1936)
The Princess Comes Across (Par, 1936)
The Charge of the Light Brigade (WB, 1936)
The Life of Emile Zola (WB, 1937)
The Last of Mrs. Cheyney (MGM, 1937)
Gunga Din (RKO, 1939)
Captain Fury (UA, 1939)
Northwest Passage (MGM, 1940)
Rebecca (UA, 1940)
A Dispatch from Reuter's (WB, 1940)
Hudson's Bay (20th, 1940)
Shadows on the Stairs (WB, 1941)
Dr. Jekyll and Mr. Hyde (MGM, 1941)
The Blonde from Singapore (Col, 1941)
Suspicion (RKO, 1941)
Passage from Hong Kong (WB, 1941)
London Blackout Murders (Rep, 1942)
The Gorilla Man (WB, 1942)
Forever and a Day (RKO, 1943)
Mission to Moscow (WB, 1943)
Holy Matrimony (20th, 1943)
Jack London (UA, 1943)
The Lodger (20th, 1944)
Passport to Destiny (RKO, 1944)
The Canterville Ghost (MGM, 1944)
The Keys of the Kingdom (20th, 1944)
The White Cliffs of Dover (MGM, 1944)
The Picture of Dorian Gray (MGM, 1945)
Love Letters (Par, 1945)

Three Strangers (WB, 1946)
Sister Kenny (RKO, 1946)
The Secret Life of Walter Mitty (RKO, 1947)
Private Affairs of Bel Ami (UA, 1947)
The Swordsman (Col, 1947)
The Exile (Univ, 1947)
Mr. Peabody and the Mermaid (Univ, 1948)
Hills of Home (MGM, 1948)
The Fighting O'Flynn (Univ, 1949)
That Forsyte Woman (MGM, 1949)
Challenge to Lassie (MGM, 1949)
Fortunes of Captain Blood (Col, 1950)
Rogues of Sherwood Forest (Col, 1950)
David and Bathsheba (20th, 1951)
The Lady and the Bandit (Col, 1951)
My Cousin Rachel (20th, 1952)
And Now Tomorrow (Westminster, 1952)
Young Bess (MGM, 1953)
Julius Caesar (MGM, 1953)
Johnny Tremain (BV, 1957)
King Richard and the Crusaders (WB, 1954)
Count Your Blessings (MGM, 1959)
The Four Skulls of Jonathan Drake (UA, 1959)
The Oregon Trail (20th, 1959)

FORRESTER HARVEY

Hugh Williams and Forrester Harvey in Outcast Lady *(1934).*

Born 1890, County Cork, Ireland. Died December 14, 1945, Laguna Beach, California. Flinty character actor well utilized in motion pictures: *Red Dust* (Limey), *Captain Blood* (Honesty Nuthall), *Rebecca* (Chalcroft), etc.

Forrester Harvey to himself in *The Mystery of Edwin Drood*: "Why they want to go down among the dead 'uns at night beats Derdles."

Films

The Lilac Sunbonnet (Br, 1922)
Somebody's Darling (Br, 1925)
Nell Gwynn (Br, 1926)
If Youth But Knew (BR, 1926)
The Flag Lieutenant (Br, 1926)
Cash on Delivery (Br, 1926)
The Ring (Br, 1927)
That Brute Simmons (Br, 1928)
The White Sheik (Br, 1928)
A Tailor-Made Man (MGM, 1931)
Man in Possession (MGM, 1931)
Guilty Hands (MGM, 1931)
Devotion (Pathé, 1931)
Sky Devils (UA, 1932)
Tarzan the Ape Man (MGM, 1932)
But the Flesh Is Weak (MGM, 1932)
The Wet Parade (MGM, 1932)
Mystery Ranch (Fox, 1932)
Kongo (MGM, 1932)
Those We Love (Sono Art–World Wide, 1932)
Smilin' Through (MGM, 1932)
Red Dust (MGM, 1932)
Destination Unknown (Univ, 1933)
The Eagle and the Hawk (Par, 1933)
Midnight Club (Par, 1933)

The Invisible Man (Univ, 1933)
Man of Two Worlds (RKO, 1934)
Mystery of Mr. X (MGM, 1934)
Tarzan and His Mate (MGM, 1934)
Menace (Par, 1934)
Outcast Lady (MGM, 1934)
Limehouse Blues (Par, 1934)
The Painted Veil (MGM, 1934)
Great Expectations (Univ, 1934)
The Best Man Wins (Univ, 1935)
The Mystery of Edwin Drood (Univ, 1935)
The Woman in Red (FN, 1935)
Vagabond Lady (MGM, 1935)
Jalna (RKO, 1935)
The Gilded Lily (Par, 1935)
The Perfect Gentleman (MGM, 1935)
Captain Blood (WB, 1935)
Love Before Breakfast (Univ, 1936)
Petticoat Fever (MGM, 1936)
Lloyds of London (20th, 1936)
White Hunter (20th, 1936)
Suzy (MGM, 1936)
Bulldog Drummond Comes Back (Par, 1937)
Personal Property (MGM, 1937)
The Prince and the Pauper (WB, 1937)

The Man Who Cried Wolf (Univ, 1937)
Thoroughbreds Don't Cry (MGM, 1937)
Kidnapped (20th, 1938)
The Mysterious Mr. Moto (20th, 1938)
Bulldog Drummond's Secret Police (Par, 1939)
The Lady's from Kentucky (Par, 1939)
The Witness Vanishes (Univ, 1939)
Let Us Live! (Col, 1939)
The Invisible Man Returns (Univ, 1940)
Rebecca (RKO, 1940)
A Chump at Oxford (UA, 1940)
Tom Brown's School Days (RKO, 1940)
On Their Own (20th, 1940)
The Earl of Puddlestone (Rep, 1940)
Little Nellie Kelly (MGM, 1940)
The Wolf Man (Univ, 1941)
Free and Easy (MGM, 1941)
Dr. Jekyll and Mr. Hyde (MGM, 1941)
Mercy Island (Rep, 1941)
Random Harvest (MGM, 1942)
Mrs. Miniver (MGM, 1942)
The Mysterious Doctor (WB, 1943)
Scotland Yard Investigator (Rep, 1945)
Devotion (WB, 1946)

PAUL HARVEY

Paul Harvey, Regina Wallace, and Russell Wade in The Bamboo Blonde *(1946).*

Born September 10, 1883, Illinois. Married Ottye _____ . Died December 14, 1953, Hollywood, California. Assigned on various occasions to be the overwrought executive; just as easily could play thoughtful relatives. Made the rounds of most of the studios. Recalled for his appearances as Reverend Mr. Galsworthy in *Father of the Bride* and *Father's Little Dividend*.

Paul Harvey to Don Briggs in *Forgotten Woman:* "Get some kind of a conviction on that mob, and you're on your way up."

Films

The Awful Truth (Pathé, 1929)
The Wiser Sex (Par, 1932)
Advice to the Lovelorn (UA, 1933)
Looking for Trouble (UA, 1934)
The House of Rothschild (UA, 1934)
Charlie Chan's Courage (Fox, 1934)
The Affairs of Cellini (UA, 1934)
Broadway Bill (Col, 1934)
Born to Be Bad (UA, 1934)
Hat, Coat and Glove (RKO, 1934)
Handy Andy (Fox, 1934)
Kid Millions (UA, 1934)
She Was a Lady (Fox, 1934)
A Wicked Woman (MGM, 1934)
The President Vanishes (Par, 1934)
The Whole Town's Talking (Col, 1935)
I'll Love You Always (Col, 1935)
Four Hours to Kill (Par, 1935)
Goin' to Town (Par, 1935)
Alibi Ike (WB, 1935)
Broadway Melody of 1936 (MGM, 1935)
Thanks a Million (Fox, 1935)
Rose of the Rancho (Par, 1936)
The Return of Sophie Lang (Par, 1936)
Mind Your Own Business (Par, 1936)
The Plainsman (Par, 1936)
The Petrified Forest (WB, 1936)
The Walking Dead (WB, 1936)
Three Men on a Horse (WB, 1936)
The Witness Chair (RKO, 1936)
Private Number (20th, 1936)
Yellowstone (Univ, 1936)
August Week-End (Chesterfield, 1936)
Postal Inspector (Univ, 1936)
The Black Legion (WB, 1937)
On Again, Off Again (RKO, 1937)
High Flyers (RKO, 1937)
The Devil Is Driving (Col, 1937)
23½ Hours Leave (GN, 1937)
Big City (MGM, 1937)
My Dear Miss Aldrich (MGM, 1937)
The Soldier and the Lady [a.k.a. *Michael Strogoff*] (RKO, 1937)
Love on a Budget (20th, 1938)
Rebecca of Sunnybrook Farm (20th, 1938)
I'll Give a Million (20th, 1938)
Charlie Chan in Honolulu (20th, 1938)
There's That Woman Again (Col, 1938)
Algiers (UA, 1938)
The Higgins Family (Rep, 1938)
The Sisters (WB, 1938)
If I Were King (Par, 1938)
A Slight Case of Murder (WB, 1938)
Never Say Die (Par, 1939)
The Gorilla (20th, 1939)
News Is Made at Night (20th, 1939)

Stanley and Livingstone (20th, 1939)
Mr. Moto in Danger Island (20th, 1939)
They Shall Have Music (UA, 1939)
Forgotten Woman (Univ, 1939)
Meet Dr. Christian (RKO, 1939)
High School (20th, 1940)
Brother Rat and a Baby (WB, 1940)
The Marines Fly High (RKO, 1940)
Remember the Night (Par, 1940)
Typhoon (Par, 1940)
Manhattan Heartbeat (20th, 1940)
Maryland (20th, 1940)
Arizona (Col, 1940)
Behind the News (Rep, 1940)
High Sierra (WB, 1941)
Ride On, Vaquero (20th, 1941)
Out of the Fog (WB, 1941)
Puddin'head (Rep, 1941)
Law of the Tropics (WB, 1941)
Great Guns (20th, 1941)
Three Girls About Town (Col, 1941)
Mr. District Attorney in the Carter Case (Rep, 1941)
A Tragedy at Midnight (Rep, 1942)
The Man Who Wouldn't Die (20th, 1942)
Moonlight Masquerade (Rep, 1942)
You Can't Escape Forever (WB, 1942)
Heart of the Golden West (Rep, 1942)
We Were Dancing (MGM, 1942)
Larceny, Inc. (WB, 1942)
The Man from Music Mountain (Rep, 1943)
Mystery Broadcast (Rep, 1943)
Four Jills in a Jeep (20th, 1944)
Henry Aldrich Plays Cupid (Par, 1944)
Two Thoroughbreds (Rep, 1944)
Jamboree (Rep, 1944)
In the Meantime, Darling (20th, 1944)
Don't Fence Me In (Rep, 1945)
Spellbound (UA, 1945)
Mama Loves Papa (RKO, 1945)
The Chicago Kid (Rep, 1945)
State Fair (20th, 1945)
The Horn Blows at Midnight (WB, 1945)
Swingin' on a Rainbow (Rep, 1945)
Pillow to Post (WB, 1945)
The Southerner (UA, 1945)
Gay Blades [a.k.a. *Tournament Tempo*] (Rep, 1946)
They Made Me a Killer (Par, 1946)
Up Goes Maisie (MGM, 1946)
Easy to Wed (MGM, 1946)
In Fast Company (Mon, 1946)
Blondie's Lucky Day (Col, 1946)
I've Always Loved You (Rep, 1946)
The Bamboo Blonde (RKO, 1946)

Helldorado (Rep, 1946)
The Beginning or the End? (MGM, 1947)
Out of the Blue (EL, 1947)
The Late George Apley (20th, 1947)
High Barbaree (MGM, 1947)
Danger Street (Par, 1947)
Perils of Pauline (Par, 1947)
Wyoming (Rep, 1947)
When a Girl's Beautiful (Col, 1947)
Waterfront at Midnight (Par, 1948)
Call Northside 777 (20th, 1948)
Lightnin' in the Forest (Rep, 1948)
Give My Regards to Broadway (20th, 1948)
Blondie's Reward (Col, 1948)
Family Honeymoon (Univ, 1948)
Smuggler's Cove (Mon, 1948)
Speed to Spare (Par, 1948)
John Loves Mary (WB, 1949)
Down to the Sea in Ships (20th, 1949)
Mr. Belvedere Goes to College (20th, 1949)
Duke of Chicago (Rep, 1949)
Take One False Step (Univ, 1949)
The Fountainhead (WB, 1949)
The Girl from Jones Beach (WB, 1949)
Side Street (MGM, 1949)
Make-Believe Ballroom (Col, 1949)
The Yellow Cab Man (MGM, 1950)
Riding High (Par, 1950)
Father of the Bride (MGM, 1950)
The Lawless (Par, 1950)
The Skipper Surprised His Wife (MGM, 1950)
Three Little Words (MGM, 1950)
The Flying Missile (Col, 1950)
The Milkman (Univ, 1950)
Stella (20th, 1950)
Thunder in God's Country (Rep, 1951)
Father's Little Dividend (MGM, 1951)
The Tall Target (MGM, 1951)
Up Front (Univ, 1951)
Excuse My Dust (MGM, 1951)
Let's Go, Navy (Mon, 1951)
The First Time (Col, 1952)
Here Come the Nelsons [a.k.a. *Meet the Nelsons*] (Univ, 1952)
Has Anybody Seen My Gal? (Univ, 1952)
Dreamboat (20th, 1952)
April in Paris (WB, 1952)
Remains to Be Seen (MGM, 1953)
The Girl Who Had Everything (MGM, 1953)
Calamity Jane (WB, 1953)
Sabrina (Par, 1954)
High Society (MGM, 1955)
Three for the Show (Col, 1955)

RAYMOND HATTON

Raymond Hatton, Loretta Young, and George Barraud in The Road to Paradise *(1930).*

Born July 7, 1887, Red Oak, Iowa. Married Florence Roberts. Died October 21, 1971, Palmdale, California. Onetime vaudeville and touring-show performer. Appeared in many shorts before his feature film debut at Paramount where he remained for a long spree. Acted with comic Victor Moore in the *Chimmie Fadden* pictures, played King Charles VIII in Geraldine Farrar's *Joan the Woman*, was Count Jules de Destin in Mary Pickford's *The Little American*, was Gringoire in Lon Chaney's *The Hunchback of Notre Dame*, and was Shorty in Kenneth Harlan's *The Virginian*. Inspired teaming of him with hulking Wallace Beery began with *We're in the Navy Now* and led to a string of service comedies. Started his tenure as the scruffy tobacco-chewing sidekick of Westerns in early 1930s. Joined *The Three Mesquiteers* entries as Rusty Joslin, replacing Max Terhune by 1939 (with *Wyoming Outlaw*). Frequently co-starred with Robert Livingston and Duncan Renaldo. Next was with Tim McCoy and Buck Jones in *The Rough Riders* installments, and later supported Johnny Mack Brown in many sagebrush films. Made his final movie appearance as an old hitchhiker in *In Cold Blood*.

Raymond Hatton to Jon Hall in *Kit Carson:* "Mighty spirited gal that—beautiful hair. . . . I can just see it dryin' outside of some Shoshone tepee."

Films

The Circus Man (Par, 1914)
The Girl of the Golden West (Par, 1915)
The Arab (Par, 1915)
The Golden Chance (Par, 1915)
The Unafraid (Par, 1915)
Chimmie Fadden (Par, 1915)
The Unknown (Par, 1915)
Chimmie Fadden Out West (Par, 1915)
The Immigrant (Par, 1915)
Kindling (Par, 1915)

Public Opinion (Par, 1916)
Tennessee's Partner (Par, 1916)
To Have and to Hold (Par, 1916)
The Lash (Par, 1916)
The Love Mask (Par, 1916)
The Sowers (Par, 1916)
Temptation (Par, 1916)
Oliver Twist (Par, 1916)
The Honorable Friend (Par, 1916)
Joan the Woman (Par, 1917)

The American Consul (Par, 1917)
Hashimura Togo (Par, 1917)
What Money Can't Buy (Par, 1917)
The Little American (Par, 1917)
The Devil Stone (Par, 1917)
Nan of Music Mountain (Par, 1917)
The Woman God Forgot (Par, 1917)
Crystal Gazer (Par, 1917)
Sandy (Par, 1917)
Romance of the Redwoods (Par, 1917)

The Goat (Par, 1918)
Arizona (Par, 1918)
The Source (Par, 1918)
The Firefly of France (Par, 1918)
Cruise of the Makebelieve (Par, 1918)
Less Than Kin (Par, 1918)
Jules of the Strongheart (Par, 1918)
The Whispering Chorus (Par, 1918)
We Can't Have Everything (Par, 1918)
The Love Burglar (Par, 1919)
For Better, For Worse (Par, 1919)
The Dub (Par, 1919)
The Squaw Man (Par, 1919)
The Wild Goose Chase (Tri, 1919)
You're Fired! (Par, 1919)
Everywoman (Par, 1919)
Maggie Pepper (Par, 1919)
Male and Female (Par, 1919)
Secret Service (Par, 1919)
Experimental Marriage (Select, 1919)
Poor Boob (Par, 1919)
The Dancing Fool (Par, 1919)
Officer 666 (G, 1920)
Stop Thief (G, 1920)
Jes' Call Me Jim (G, 1920)
The Concert (G, 1921)
Doubling for Romeo (G, 1921)
The Ace of Hearts (G, 1921)
The Affairs of Anatol (Par, 1921)
Bunty Pulls the Strings (G, 1921)
All's Fair in Love (G, 1921)
Peck's Bad Boy (Associated FN, 1921)
Pilgrims of the Night (Associated FN, 1921)
Salvage (Robertson-Cole, 1921)
His Back Against the Wall (G, 1922)
Ebb Tide (Par, 1922)
Head over Heels (G, 1922)
Manslaughter (Par, 1922)
Pink Gods (Par, 1922)
The Hottentot (Associated FN, 1922)
To Have and to Hold (Associated FN, 1922)
The Hunchback of Notre Dame (Univ, 1923)
The Virginian (Par, 1923)
Three Wise Fools (G, 1923)
The Barefoot Boy (Col, 1923)
Java Head (Par, 1923)
Big Brother (Par, 1923)
Enemies of Children (Mammoth, 1923)
A Man of Action (Associated FN, 1923)
The Tie That Binds (WB, 1923)
Trimmed in Scarlet (Univ, 1923)
Triumph (Par, 1924)
Cornered (WB, 1924)
The Fighting American (Univ, 1924)
Half-a-Dollar Bill (M, 1924)
True as Steel (MG, 1924)
The Mine with the Iron Door (Principle, 1924)
Adventure (Par, 1925)

The Thundering Herd (Par, 1925)
Contraband (Par, 1925)
A Son of His Father (Par, 1925)
The Devil's Cargo (Par, 1925)
The Top of the World (Par, 1925)
The Lucky Devil (Par, 1925)
In the Name of Love (Par, 1925)
Tomorrow's Love (Mon, 1925)
We're in the Navy Now (Par, 1926)
Behind the Front (Par, 1926)
Silence (PDC, 1926)
Forlorn River (Par, 1926)
Born to the West (Par, 1926)
Fashions for Women (Par, 1927)
Fireman, Save My Child (Par, 1927)
Now We're in the Air (Par, 1927)
Partners in Crime (Par, 1927)
The Big Killing (Par, 1928)
The Wife Savers (Par, 1928)
The Office Scandal (Pathe, 1929)
Dear Vivian (Par, 1929)
Trent's Last Case (Fox, 1929)
Hell's Heroes (Univ, 1929)
The Mighty (Par, 1929)
Murder on the Roof (Col, 1930)
Midnight Mystery (RKO, 1930)
The Road to Paradise (FN, 1930)
The Silver Horde (RKO, 1930)
Her Unborn Child (Windsor, 1930)
Rogue of the Rio Grande (WW, 1930)
The Squaw Man (MGM, 1931)
Woman Hungry (FN, 1931)
The Lion and the Lamb (Col, 1931)
Honeymoon Lane (Par, 1931)
Polly of the Circus (MGM, 1932)
Law and Order (Univ, 1932)
Drifting Souls (Tower, 1932)
The Fourth Horseman (Univ, 1932)
Uptown New York (WW, 1932)
Exposed (Eagle, 1932)
The Crooked Circle (WW, 1932)
Vanity Street (Col, 1932)
Malay Nights (Mayfair, 1932)
Stranger in Town (WB, 1932)
Vanishing Frontier (Par, 1932)
Alias Mary Smith (Mayfair, 1932)
Cornered (Col. 1932)
Alice in Wonderland (Par, 1933)
Terror Trail (Univ, 1933)
Under the Tonto Rim (Par, 1933)
Hidden Gold (Univ, 1933)
The Big Cage (Univ, 1933)
Penthouse (MGM, 1933)
Day of Reckoning (MGM, 1933)
The Women in His Life (MGM, 1933)
Lady Killer (WB, 1933)
State Trooper (Col, 1933)
The Thundering Herd (Par, 1933)
Lazy River (MGM, 1934)
The Defense Rests (Col, 1934)
Fifteen Wives (Invincible, 1934)
Straight Is the Way (MGM, 1934)

Once to Every Bachelor (Liberty, 1934)
Wagon Wheels (Par, 1934)
Red Morning (RKO, 1934)
Times Square Lady (MGM, 1935)
The Daring Young Man (Fox, 1935)
G-Men (WB, 1935)
Murder in the Fleet (MGM, 1935)
Calm Yourself (MGM, 1935)
Steamboat 'Round the Bend (Fox, 1935)
Wanderer of the Wasteland (Par, 1935)
Stormy (Univ, 1935)
Nevada (Par, 1935)
Rustlers of Red Gap (Univ serial, 1935)
Exclusive Story (MGM, 1936)
Women Are Trouble (MGM, 1936)
Mad Holiday (MGM, 1936)
Laughing Irish Eyes (Rep, 1936)
Desert Gold (Par, 1936)
Arizona Raiders (Par, 1936)
Timothy's Quest (Par, 1936)
Yellowstone (Univ, 1936)
The Vigilantes Are Coming (Rep serial, 1936)
Jungle Jim (Univ serial, 1937)
Marked Woman (WB, 1937)
Fly Away Baby (WB, 1937)
Public Wedding (WB, 1937)
Roaring Timber (Col, 1937)
The Adventurous Blonde (WB, 1937)
Over the Goal (WB, 1937)
Love Is on the Air (FN, 1937)
The Missing Witness (WB, 1937)
Come On, Rangers (Rep, 1938)
He Couldn't Say No (WB, 1938)
Over the Wall (WB, 1938)
Love Finds Andy Hardy (MGM, 1938)
The Texans (Par, 1938)
Touchdown, Army! (Par, 1938)
Tom Sawyer, Detective (Par, 1938)
Rough Riders' Roundup (Rep, 1939)
Frontier Pony Express (Rep, 1939)
Wyoming Outlaw (Rep, 1939)
New Frontier (Rep, 1939)
Kansas Terror (Rep, 1939)
Cowboys from Texas (Rep, 1939)
Wall Street Cowboy (Rep, 1939)
I'm from Missouri (Par, 1939)
Paris Honeymoon (Par, 1939)
Ambush (Par, 1939)
Undercover Doctor (Par, 1939)
6,000 Enemies (MGM, 1939)
Career (RKO, 1939)
Covered Wagon Days (Rep, 1940)
Oklahoma Renegades (Rep, 1940)
Rocky Mountain Rangers (Rep, 1940)
Pioneers of the West (Rep, 1940)
Heroes of the Saddle (Rep, 1940)
Kit Carson (UA, 1940)
Queen of the Mob (Par, 1940)
Arizona Bound (Mon, 1941)
Gunman from Bodie (Mon, 1941)
White Eagle (Col serial, 1941)

Reap the Wild Wind (Par, 1942)
West of the Law (Mon, 1942)
The Girl from Alaska (Rep, 1942)
Below the Border (Mon, 1942)
Ghost Town Law (Mon, 1942)
Down Texas Way (Mon, 1942)
Forbidden Trails (Mon, 1942)
Riders of the West (Mon, 1942)
Dawn on the Great Divide (Mon, 1942)
Cadets on Parade (Col, 1942)
The Ghost Rider (Mon, 1943)
Six-Gun Gospel (Mon, 1943)
The Stranger from Pecos (Mon, 1943)
Prairie Chickens (UA, 1943)
The Texas Kid (Mon, 1943)
Outlaws of Stampede Pass (Mon, 1943)
Ghost Guns (Mon, 1944)
Land of the Outlaws (Mon, 1944)
Raiders of the Border (Mon, 1944)
Range Law (Mon, 1944)
West of the Rio Grande (Mon, 1944)
Law of the Valley (Mon, 1944)
Law Men (Mon, 1944)
Partners of the Trail (Mon, 1944)
Tall in the Saddle (RKO, 1944)
Flame of the West (Mon, 1945)
Frontier Flame (Mon, 1945)
Gun Smoke (Mon, 1945)
Navajo Trail (Mon, 1945)
Rhythm Roundup (Mon, 1945)

Sunbonnet Sue (Mon, 1945)
Frontier Feud (Mon, 1945)
The Lost Trail (Mon, 1945)
Northwest Trail (Screen Guild, 1945)
Stranger from Santa Fe (Mon, 1945)
Border Bandits (Mon, 1946)
The Gentleman from Texas (Mon, 1946)
Shadows on the Range (Mon, 1946)
Under Arizona Skies (Mon, 1946)
The Haunted Mine (Mon, 1946)
Drifting Along (Mon, 1946)
Raiders of the South (Mon, 1946)
Silver Range (Mon, 1946)
Trigger Fingers (Mon, 1946)
Fool's Gold (UA, 1946)
Rolling Home (Screen Guild, 1946)
Land of the Lawless (Mon, 1947)
Valley of Fear (Mon, 1947)
Black Gold (AA, 1947)
The Law Comes to Gunsight (Mon, 1947)
Unconquered (Par, 1947)
Trailing Danger (Mon, 1947)
Flashing Guns (Mon, 1947)
Gun Talk (Mon, 1947)
Code of the Saddle (Mon, 1947)
Prairie Express (Mon, 1947)
Triggerman (Mon, 1948)
Crossed Trail (Mon, 1948)
Overland Trails (Mon, 1948)
Frontier Agent (Mon, 1948)

Back Trail (Mon, 1948)
Gunning for Justice [a.k.a. *Gunning for Trouble*] (Mon, 1949)
The Sheriff of Medicine Bow (Mon, 1948)
The Fighting Ranger (Mon, 1948)
Silver Range (Mon, 1948)
Hidden Danger (Mon, 1949)
County Fair (Mon, 1950)
Operation Haylift (Lip, 1950)
West of Brazos (Lip, 1950)
Marshal of Heldorado (Lip, 1950)
Colorado Ranger (Lip, 1950)
Crooked River (Lip, 1950)
Fast on the Draw (Lip, 1950)
Hostile Country (Lip, 1950)
Skipalong Rosenbloom (UA, 1951)
Kentucky Jubilee (Lip, 1951)
The Golden Hawk (Col, 1952)
Cow Country (Col, 1953)
The Treasure of Ruby Hills (AA, 1955)
Twinkle in God's Eye (Rep, 1955)
Dig That Uranium (AA, 1956)
Shake, Rattle and Rock (AIP, 1956)
Pawnee (Rep, 1957)
Invasion of the Saucer Men (AIP, 1957)
Motorcycle Gang (AIP, 1957)
Alaska Passage (20th, 1959)
The Quick Gun (Col, 1964)
Requiem for a Gunfighter (Emb, 1965)
In Cold Blood (Col, 1967)

HARRY HAYDEN

Herbert Ashley, Harry Hayden, and Richard Dix in Here I Am a Stranger
(1939).

Born 1884, Indian Territory, Oklahoma. Married Lela Bliss (1923), children: Don, Richard. Died July 24, 1955, West Los Angeles, California. Minute roles as the chubby, bespectacled clerk, secretary, or bank teller whose expression ranged from querulous to exasperated. In the 1940s was with Preston Sturges' Paramount stock company: *The Palm Beach Story* (Prospect), *Hail the Conquering Hero* (Doc Bissell), etc. Played Mr. Mallison, Claude Jarman, Jr.'s father in *Intruder in the Dust*. TV series: "Trouble with Father."

Harry Hayden to Humphrey Bogart in *Two Against the World:* "This woman of sin, this murderess . . . is marrying her daughter to an unsuspecting boy. This is something that will revolt the entire world. I was shocked, Mr. Scott—*shocked.*"

Films

I Married a Doctor (FN, 1936)
Public Enemy's Wife (WB, 1936)
Two Against the World (WB, 1936)
The Man I Marry (Univ, 1936)
Killer at Large (Col, 1936)
God's Country and the Woman (WB, 1936)
Black Legion (WB, 1936)
The Case of the Black Cat (FN, 1936)
Three Men on a Horse (FN, 1936)
Love Is News (20th, 1937)
Love Is on the Air (FN, 1937)
John Meade's Woman (Par, 1937)
Melody for Two (WB, 1937)
Ever Since Eve (WB, 1937)

Artists and Models (Par, 1937)
Double Danger (RKO, 1938)
Delinquent Parents (Progressive Pictures, 1938)
Saleslady (Mon, 1938)
Straight, Place and Show (20th, 1938)
Four Men and a Prayer (20th, 1938)
I'll Give a Million (20th, 1938)
Hold That Co-ed (20th, 1938)
Kentucky (20th, 1938)
Angels with Dirty Faces (WB, 1938)
The Under-Pup (Univ, 1939)
Wife, Husband and Friend (20th, 1939)
Society Smugglers (Univ, 1939)
Hidden Power (Col, 1939)

The Rains Came (20th, 1939)
Flight at Midnight (Rep, 1939)
Frontier Marshal (20th, 1939)
Barricade (20th, 1939)
Swanee River (20th, 1939)
Here I Am a Stranger (20th, 1939)
The Cisco Kid and the Lady (20th, 1940)
The Great McGinty (Par, 1940)
He Married His Wife (20th, 1940)
I Love You Again (MGM, 1940)
I Want a Divorce (Par, 1940)
Lillian Russell (20th, 1940)
Christmas in July (Par, 1940)
Yesterday's Heroes (20th, 1940)
Manhattan Heartbeat (20th, 1940)

The Man Who Wouldn't Talk (20th, 1940)

Knute Rockne—All American (WB, 1940)

The Stork Pays Off (Col, 1941)

A Man Betrayed [a.k.a. *Wheel of Fortune*] (Rep, 1941)

Sleepers West (20th, 1941)

The Parson of Panamint (Par, 1941)

Mountain Moonlight (Rep, 1941)

The Night of January 16th (Par, 1941)

Remember the Day (20th, 1941)

High Sierra (WB, 1941)

The Getaway (MGM, 1941)

You're Telling Me (Univ, 1942)

The Lone Star Ranger (20th, 1942)

Rings on Her Fingers (20th, 1942)

Yokel Boy (Rep, 1942)

Whispering Ghosts (20th, 1942)

Get Hep to Love (Univ, 1942)

The Magnificent Dope (20th, 1942)

Joan of Ozark (Rep, 1942)

Tales of Manhattan (20th, 1942)

Springtime in the Rockies (20th, 1942)

The Palm Beach Story (Par, 1942)

Hello, Frisco, Hello (20th, 1943)

How's About It? (Univ, 1943)

The Meanest Man in the World (20th, 1943)

The Unknown Guest (Mon, 1943)

True to Life (Par, 1943)

She Has What It Takes (Col, 1943)

Up in Mabel's Room (UA, 1944)

The Great Moment (Par, 1944)

Hail the Conquering Hero (Par, 1944)

Since You Went Away (UA, 1944)

Barbary Coast Gent (MGM, 1944)

Up in Arms (RKO, 1944)

Weird Woman (Univ, 1944)

The Big Noise (20th, 1944)

The Thin Man Goes Home (MGM, 1944)

Colonel Effingham's Raid (20th, 1945)

Two Sisters from Boston (MGM, 1946)

If I'm Lucky (20th, 1946)

Till the Clouds Roll By (MGM, 1946)

The Killers (Univ, 1946)

My Brother Talks to Horses (MGM, 1946)

Without Reservations (RKO, 1946)

The Secret Heart (MGM, 1946)

Till the End of Time (RKO, 1946)

The Bride Wore Boots (Par, 1946)

Out of the Past (RKO, 1947)

Variety Girl (Par, 1947)

Millie's Daughter (Col, 1947)

The Unfinished Dance (MGM, 1947)

Key Witness (Col, 1947)

Merton of the Movies (MGM, 1947)

For the Love of Rusty (Col, 1947)

The Dude Goes West (AA, 1948)

Silver River (WB, 1948)

Docks of New Orleans (Mon, 1948)

Good Sam (RKO, 1948)

One Touch of Venus (Univ, 1948)

Out of the Storm (Rep, 1948)

Every Girl Should Be Married (RKO, 1948)

Smart Girls Don't Talk (WB, 1948)

Adventure in Baltimore (RKO, 1949)

Joe Palooka in the Big Fight (Mon 1949)

The Beautiful Blonde from Bashful Bend (20th, 1949)

The Judge Steps Out (RKO, 1949)

Abbott and Costello Meet the Killer, Boris Karloff (Univ, 1949)

Intruder in the Dust (MGM, 1949)

Deadly as the Female [a.k.a. *Gun Crazy*] (UA, 1949)

The Lone Wolf and His Lady (Col, 1949)

Prison Warden (Col, 1949)

Union Station (Par, 1950)

Traveling Saleswoman (Col, 1950)

Pier 13 (Lip, 1951)

Street Bandits (Rep, 1951)

Double Dynamite [a.k.a. *It's Only Money*] (Rep, 1951)

Carrie (Par, 1952)

And Now Tomorrow (Westminster, 1952)

Army Bound (Mon, 1952)

GEORGE "GABBY" HAYES

George "Gabby" Hayes, Elisabeth Risdon, and Francis McDonald in Roll On, Texas Moon *(1946).*

Born May 7, 1885, Wellsville, New York. Married 1) Olive Ireland (1914); divorced; 2) Dorothy Earle; widowed (1957). Died February 9, 1969, Burbank, California. A bewhiskered, toothless ranch cook in later films. Noted for the phrase "You're durn tootin'." Earlier a clean-shaven young man in vaudeville who entered films in the 1920s. Made his talkie debut in 1929: *Smiling Irish Eyes* (taxi driver), etc. Sometimes played a villain in early 1930s Westerns. In 1933 teamed with John Wayne for the *Lone Star* Westerns at Monogram. Popped up in contemporary dramas infrequently: e.g., the ranchers' spokesman in *Mr. Deeds Goes to Town*. With the William Boyd *Hopalong Cassidy* series from the start, although it was not until *Bar 20 Rides Again* that he assumed the character of Windy Holliday, which he rehashed for 19 entries. Under contract to Republic in the 1940s where the garrulous comedy-relief artist was nicknamed "Gabby." Supported Roy Rogers, Don Barry, and others in their Westerns, occasionally returning to John Wayne's side (*In Old Oklahoma, Tall in the Saddle*). TV series: "The Gabby Hayes Show."

George "Gabby" Hayes in *Trail Street*: "Larkin, you're gonna get thirty days for that killin'. Then we're gonna hang yuh."

Films

The Rainbow Man (Par, 1929)
Smiling Irish Eyes (FN, 1929)
Big News (Pathé, 1929)
Rose of the Rio Grande (Syndicate, 1931)
God's Country and the Man (Syndicate, 1931)
Nevada Buckaroo (Tif, 1931)
Cavalier of the West (Artclass, 1931)
Dragnet Patrol (Mayfair, 1932)
Love Me Tonight (Par, 1932)
Border Devils (Artclass, 1932)

Riders of the Desert (WW, 1932)
Night Rider (Artclass, 1932)
The Man from Hell's Edges (WW, 1932)
Without Honor (Artclass, 1932)
From Broadway to Cheyenne (Mon, 1932)
Klondike (Mon, 1932)
Texas Buddies (WW, 1932)
The Boiling Point (Allied Pictures, 1932)
The Fighting Champ (Mon, 1932)
Wild Horse Mesa (Par, 1932)
Self Defense (Mon, 1933)

Sagebrush Trail (Mon, 1933)
Trailing North (Mon, 1933)
The Return of Casey Jones (Mon, 1933)
The Gallant Fool (Mon, 1933)
Skyway (Mon, 1933)
The Ranger's Code (Mon, 1933)
Galloping Romeo (Mon, 1933)
The Fugitive (Mon, 1933)
The Sphinx (Mon, 1933)
Phantom Broadcast (Mon, 1933)
Riders of Destiny (Mon, 1933)

The Devil's Mate (Mon, 1933)
Breed of the Border (Mon, 1933)
The Fighting Texans (Mon, 1933)
Monte Carlo Nights (Mon, 1934)
The Star Packer (Par, 1934)
The Man from Utah (Mon, 1934)
Brand of Hate (Steiner, 1934)
In Old Santa Fe (Mon, 1934)
'Neath Arizona Skies (Mon, 1934)
West of the Divide (Mon, 1934)
The Lucky Texan (Mon, 1934)
Beggars in Ermine (Mon, 1934)
Mystery Liner (Mon, 1934)
Blue Steel (Mon, 1934)
Randy Rides Alone (Mon, 1934)
The Lost Jungle (Mascot serial, 1934)
House of Mystery (Mon, 1934)
City Limits (Mon, 1934)
Justice of the Range (Col, 1935)
Smokey Smith (Steiner, 1935)
Texas Terrors (Rep, 1935)
Tumbling Tumbleweeds (Rep, 1935)
$1,000 a Minute (Rep, 1935)
The Throwback (Univ, 1935)
Lawless Frontier (Mon, 1935)
Death Flies East (Col, 1935)
The Lost City (Krellberg serial, 1935)
Rainbow Valley (Mon, 1935)
The Hoosier Schoolmaster (Mon, 1935)
Honeymoon Limited (Mon, 1935)
Headline Woman (Mon, 1935)
Ladies Crave Excitement (Mon, 1935)
Hopalong Cassidy (Par, 1935)
Thunder Mountain (Fox, 1935)
The Eagle's Brood (Par, 1935)
Bar 20 Rides Again (Par, 1935)
Welcome Home (Fox, 1935)
The Outlaw Tamer (Empire, 1935)
Hitchhike Lady (Rep, 1935)
Call of the Prairie (Par, 1936)
The Plainsman (Par, 1936)
Swifty (FD, 1936)
Three on the Trail (Par, 1936)
The Lawless Nineties (Rep, 1936)
Hearts in Bondage (Rep, 1936)
I Married a Doctor (FN, 1936)
Valley of the Lawless (Supreme, 1936)

Mr. Deeds Goes to Town (Col, 1936)
Hearts of the West (Par, 1936)
The Texas Rangers (Par, 1936)
Valint Is the Word for Carrie (Par, 1936)
Hopalong Cassidy Returns (Par, 1936)
The Plainsman (Par, 1936)
Trail Dust (Par, 1936)
Borderland (Par, 1937)
Hills of Old Wyoming (Par, 1937)
Mountain Music (Par, 1937)
North of the Rio Grande (Par, 1937)
Rustler's Valley (Par, 1937)
Hopalong Rides Again (Par, 1937)
Texas Trail (Par, 1937)
Gold Is Where You Find It (WB, 1938)
Heart of Arizona (Par, 1938)
Bar 20 Justice (Par, 1938)
Pride of the West (Par, 1938)
In Old Mexico (Par, 1938)
Sunset Trail (Par, 1938)
The Frontiersman (Par, 1938)
Fighting Thoroughbreds (Rep, 1939)
Man of Conquest (Rep, 1939)
Let Freedom Ring (MGM, 1939)
Southward Ho (Rep, 1939)
In Old Caliente (Rep, 1939)
In Old Monterey (Rep, 1939)
Wall Street Cowboy (Rep, 1939)
The Arizona Kid (Rep, 1939)
Saga of Death Valley (Rep, 1939)
Days of Jesse James (Rep, 1939)
Silver on the Sage (Par, 1939)
Renegade Trail (Par, 1939)
Wagons Westward (Rep, 1940)
Dark Command (Rep, 1940)
Young Buffalo Bill (Rep, 1940)
The Carson City Kid (Rep, 1940)
The Ranger and the Lady (Rep, 1940)
Colorado (Rep, 1940)
Young Bill Hickok (Rep, 1940)
Melody Ranch (Rep, 1940)
The Border Legion (Rep, 1940)
Robin Hood of the Pecos (Rep, 1941)
In Old Cheyenne (Rep, 1941)
Sheriff of Tombstone (Rep, 1941)
Nevada City (Rep, 1941)
Jesse James at Bay (Rep, 1941)

Bad Men of Deadwood (Rep, 1941)
Red River Valley (Rep, 1941)
South of Santa Fe (Rep, 1942)
Sunset on the Desert (Rep, 1942)
Man from Cheyenne (Rep, 1942)
Romance on the Range (Rep, 1942)
Sons of the Pioneers (Rep, 1942)
Sunset Serenade (Rep, 1942)
Heart of the Golden West (Rep, 1942)
Ridin' Down the Canyon (Rep, 1942)
Calling Wild Bill Elliott (Rep, 1943)
Bordertown Gun Fighters (Rep, 1943)
Wagon Tracks West (Rep, 1943)
Death Valley Manhunt (Rep, 1943)
In Old Oklahoma [a.k.a. War of the Wildcats] (Rep, 1943)
Tucson Raiders (Rep, 1944)
Hidden Valley Outlaws (Rep, 1944)
Marshal of Reno (Rep, 1944)
Mojave Firebrand (Rep, 1944)
Tall in the Saddle (RKO, 1944)
Lights of Old Santa Fe (Rep, 1944)
The Big Bonanza (Rep, 1944)
Utah (Rep, 1945)
Bells of Rosarita (Rep, 1945)
The Man from Oklahoma (Rep, 1945)
Sunset in Eldorado (Rep, 1945)
Don't Fence Me In (Rep, 1945)
Along the Navajo Trail (Rep, 1945)
Home in Oklahoma (Rep, 1946)
Song of Arizona (Rep, 1946)
Badman's Territory (RKO, 1946)
Rainbow over Texas (Rep, 1946)
My Pal Trigger (Rep, 1946)
Roll On, Texas Moon (Rep, 1946)
Under Nevada Skies (Rep, 1946)
Helldorado (Rep, 1946)
Trail Street (RKO, 1947)
Wyoming (Rep, 1947)
Albuquerque (Par, 1948)
The Untamed Breed (Col, 1948)
Return of the Bad Men (RKO, 1948)
El Paso (Par, 1949)
Bells of Coronado (Rep, 1950)
The Cariboo Trail (20th, 1950)

MYRON HEALEY

Frank Richards, Louise Franklin, and Myron Healey in Thunder over Sangoland *(1956).*

Born June 8, 1922, Petaluma, California. Married: 1) Ann Sumney (1940), children: Christine, Ann; divorced (1949); 2) Elizabeth _____ , child: Mikel; 3) Adair Jameson (1971). Began in films with MGM's *Crime Does Not Pay* short subjects. Largely in Westerns, occasionally scripted boot-and-saddle features in which he appeared: *Outlaw Gold* and *Colorado Ambush*.

Myron Healey in *Apache Territory:* "Come out, you heathens! Come out where I can see you!"

Films

I Dood It (MGM, 1943)
Salute to the Marines (MGM, 1943)
Thousands Cheer (MGM, 1943)
The Iron Major (RKO, 1943)
Meet the People (MGM, 1944)
Crime Doctor's Man Hunt (Col, 1946)
The Man from Colorado (Col, 1948)
Blondie's Reward (Col, 1948)
Hidden Danger (Mon, 1948)
South of Rio (Rep, 1949)
Trail's End (Mon, 1949)
Gun Law Justice (Mon, 1949)
Across the Rio Grande (Mon, 1949)
Western Renegades (Mon, 1949)
Haunted Trails (Mon, 1949)
Riders of the Dusk (Mon, 1949)
Brand of Fear (Mon, 1949)
Laramie (Col, 1949)
Rusty's Birthday (Col, 1949)
Slightly French (Col, 1949)
Pioneer Marshal (Rep, 1949)
Salt Lake Raiders (Rep, 1950)
Trail of the Rustlers (Col, 1950)
Over the Border (Mon, 1950)
West of Wyoming (Mon, 1950)

Fence Riders (Mon, 1950)
Hot Rod (Mon, 1950)
Short Grass (AA, 1950)
Law of the Panhandle (Mon, 1950)
Outlaw Gold (Mon, 1950)
Night Riders of Montana (Rep, 1951)
Texas Rangers (Col, 1951)
Colorado Ambush (Mon, 1951)
Montana Desperado (Mon, 1951)
Bonanza Town (Col, 1951)
Slaughter Trail (RKO, 1951)
Roar of the Iron Horse (Col serial, 1951)
Bomba and the Elephant Stampede (Mon, 1951)
Rodeo (Mon, 1952)
Fort Osage (Mon, 1952)
The Maverick (Mon, 1952)
Storm over Tibet (Col, 1952)
Montana Territory (Col, 1952)
The Kid from Broken Gun (Col, 1952)
Desperadoes' Outpost (Rep, 1952)
Apache War Smoke (MGM, 1952)
The Longhorn (Mon, 1952)
Fargo (Mon, 1952)
Monsoon (UA, 1953)

White Lightning (AA, 1953)
Kansas Pacific (AA, 1953)
Saginaw Trail (Col, 1953)
Combat Squad (Col, 1953)
Hot News (AA, 1953)
Cattle Queen of Montana (RKO, 1954)
Rage at Dawn (RKO, 1955)
Panther Girl of the Kongo (Rep serial, 1955)
Gang Busters (Visual Drama Inc., 1955)
Man Without a Star (Univ, 1955)
African Manhunt (Rep, 1955)
Jungle Moon Men (Col, 1955)
The Man from Bitter Ridge (Univ, 1955)
Count Three and Pray (Col, 1955)
The Magnificent Roughnecks (AA, 1956)
Dig That Uranium (AA, 1956)
The Young Guns (AA, 1956)
Thunder over Sangoland (Lip, 1956)
The White Squaw (Col, 1956)
Running Target (UA, 1956)
Calling Homicide (AA, 1956)
Shoot-Out at Medicine Bend (WB, 1957)
The Restless Breed (20th, 1957)
Hell's Crossroads (Rep, 1957)

The Unearthly (Rep, 1957)
Undersea Girl (AA, 1957)
The Hard Man (Col, 1957)
Escape from Red Rock (20th, 1958)
Cole Younger, Gunfighter (AA, 1958)
Quantrill's Raiders (AA, 1958)

Apache Territory (Col, 1958)
Gunfight at Dodge City (UA, 1959)
Rio Bravo (WB, 1959)
The George Raft Story (AA, 1961)
Convicts Four (AA, 1962)
Harlow (Par, 1965)

Mirage (Univ, 1965)
Journey to Shiloh (Univ, 1968)
True Grit (Par, 1969)
Which Way to the Front? (WB, 1970)

O. P. HEGGIE

In Midnight *(1934).*

Born September 17, 1879, Angaston, South Australia. Died February 7, 1936, Los Angeles, California. Thought of becoming a singer or lawyer but tried the theater instead; was later employed on stage in London and New York. Well into middle age before entering films. Played Inspector Nayland Smith to Warner Oland's Oriental menace in *The Mysterious Dr. Fu Manchu* and *The Return of Dr. Fu Manchu;* Abbe Faria in 1934's *The Count of Monte Cristo;* and the blind hermit befriending the monster (Boris Karloff) in *Bride of Frankenstein.*

O. P. Heggie to Robert Donat in *The Count of Monte Cristo:*
"Together we will dig our way to freedom, and one half the treasure shall be yours."

Films

The Actress (MGM, 1928)
The Letter (Par, 1928)
The Mysterious Dr. Fu Manchu (Par, 1929)
The Mighty (Par, 1929)
The Wheel of Life (Par, 1929)
The Return of Dr. Fu Manchu (Par, 1930)
The Vagabond King (Par, 1930)
One Romantic Night (UA, 1930)
The Bad Man (FN, 1930)

Playboy of Paris (Par, 1930)
Sunny (FN, 1930)
East Lynne (Fox, 1931)
The Woman Between (RKO, 1931)
Too Young to Marry (WB, 1931)
Devotion (Pathé, 1931)
Smilin' Through (MGM, 1932)
The King's Vacation (WB, 1933)
Zoo in Budapest (Fox, 1933)
Midnight (Univ, 1934)

Peck's Bad Boy (Fox, 1934)
The Count of Monte Cristo (UA, 1934)
Anne of Green Gables (RKO, 1934)
Bride of Frankenstein (Univ, 1935)
Ginger (Fox, 1935)
A Dog of Flanders (RKO, 1935)
Chasing Yesterday (RKO, 1935)
The Prisoner of Shark Island (20th, 1936)

HOLMES HERBERT

With Alma Rubens in Week-End Husbands *(1924).*

Born July 30, 1882, Mansfield, England. Married 1) Elinor Ince; divorced; 2) Beryl Mercer, child: Joan. Died December 26, 1956, Hollywood, California. Reliable leading player of silent cinema: was Henry Spoffard, the wealthiest U.S. bachelor in the 1920s' *Gentlemen Prefer Blondes.* Became a featured player in many talkies: *The Count of Monte Cristo* (judge), *Captain Blood* (Captain Gardiner); assorted contrasting roles in some of Basil Rathbone's *Sherlock Holmes* pictures.

Holmes Herbert to Warner Baxter in *Kidnapped:* "Prisoner,
have you naught to say as to why this sentence should not
be executed?"

Films

A Doll's House (Univ, 1917)
The Whirlpool (Select, 1918)
White Heather (Hiller & Wilk, 1919)
His House in Order (Par, 1920)
Black Is White (Par, 1920)
My Lady's Garter (Par, 1920)
Lady Rose's Daughter (Par, 1920)
The Right to Love (Par, 1920)
The Wild Goose (Par, 1921)
Her Lord and Master (Vit, 1921)
Heedless Moths (Equity, 1921)
The Family Closet (Associated Exhibitors, 1921)
The Inner Chamber (Vit, 1921)
Any Wife (Fox, 1922)
Divorce Coupons (Vit, 1922)
A Woman's Woman (UA, 1922)
Evidence (Selznick, 1922)
Moonshine Valley (Fox, 1922)
A Stage Romance (Fox, 1922)

Toilers of the Sea (Selznick, 1923)
I Will Repay (FBO, 1923)
Another Scandal (PDC, 1924)
Her Own Free Will (PDC, 1924)
Sinners in Heaven (Par, 1924)
Week-End Husbands (Equity, 1924)
The Enchanted Cottage (FN, 1924)
Love's Wilderness (FN, 1924)
Up the Ladder (Univ, 1925)
Wildfire (Univ, 1925)
Daddy's Gone a-Hunting (MG, 1925)
Wreckage (Banner, 1925)
A Woman of the World (Par, 1925)
The Fire Brigade (MGM, 1926)
The Honeymoon Express (WB, 1926)
The Wanderer (Par, 1926)
The Passionate Quest (WB, 1926)
Josselyn's Wife (Tif, 1926)
One Increasing Purpose (Fox, 1927)
When a Man Loves (WB, 1927)

The Heart of Salome (Fox, 1927)
Mr. Wu (MGM, 1927)
Lovers? (MGM, 1927)
Slaves of Beauty (Fox, 1927)
The Gay Retreat (Fox, 1927)
East Side, West Side (Fox, 1927)
The Nest (Excellent, 1927)
The Silver Slave (WB, 1927)
Gentlemen Prefer Blondes (Par, 1928)
Their Hour (Tif, 1928)
The Sporting Age (Col, 1928)
The Terror (WB, 1928)
Through the Breakers (Gotham, 1928)
On Trial (WB, 1928)
Her Private Life (FN, 1929)
The Charlatan (Univ, 1929)
Madame X (MGM, 1929)
Careers (FN, 1929)
The Thirteenth Chair (MGM, 1929)
Say It with Songs (WB, 1929)

The Careless Age (FN, 1929)
Untamed (MGM, 1929)
The Kiss (MGM, 1929)
The Ship from Shanghai (MGM, 1930)
The Hot Heiress (FN, 1931)
The Single Sin (Tif, 1931)
Chances (FN, 1931)
Broadminded (FN, 1931)
Daughter of the Dragon (Par, 1931)
Shop Angel (Tower, 1932)
Dr. Jekyll and Mr. Hyde (Par, 1932)
Miss Pinkerton (FN, 1932)
Central Park (FN, 1932)
Mystery of the Wax Museum (WB, 1933)
Sister to Judas (Mayfair, 1933)
The Invisible Man (Univ, 1933)
Beloved (Univ, 1934)
The House of Rothschild (UA, 1934)
The Count of Monte Cristo (UA, 1934)
The Pursuit of Happiness (Par, 1934)
The Curtain Falls (Chesterfield, 1934)
One in a Million (Invincible, 1934)
Cardinal Richelieu (UA, 1935)
Mark of the Vampire (MGM, 1935)
Sons of Steel (Chesterfield, 1935)
Accent on Youth (Par, 1935)
Captain Blood (WB, 1935)
The Country Beyond (20th, 1936)
15 Maiden Lane (20th, 1936)
Brilliant Marriage (Invincible, 1936)
Lloyds of London (20th, 1936)
The Gentleman from Louisiana (Rep, 1936)
The Charge of the Light Brigade (WB, 1936)

Wife Versus Secretary (MGM, 1936)
The Prince and the Pauper (WB, 1937)
The Girl Said No (GN, 1937)
Here's Flash Casey (GN, 1937)
Slave Ship (20th, 1937)
Love Under Fire (20th, 1937)
House of Secrets (Chesterfield, 1937)
Lancer Spy (20th, 1937)
The Buccaneer (Par, 1938)
Marie Antoinette (MGM, 1938)
Mystery of Mr. Wong (Mon, 1938)
Say It in French (Par, 1938)
The Black Doll (Univ, 1938)
The Adventures of Robin Hood (WB, 1938)
Mystery of the White Room (Univ, 1939)
The Sun Never Sets (Univ, 1939)
Trapped in the Sky (Col, 1939)
Hidden Power (Col, 1939)
The Little Princess (20th, 1939)
Stanley and Livingstone (20th, 1939)
The Adventures of Sherlock Holmes (20th, 1939)
Everything Happens at Night (20th, 1939)
We Are Not Alone (WB, 1939)
Juarez (WB, 1939)
Wolf Call (Mon, 1939)
Bad Boy (Gateway Productions, 1939)
British Intelligence (WB, 1940)
An Angel from Texas (WB, 1940)
Foreign Correspondent (UA, 1940)
Man Hunt (20th, 1941)
International Squadron (WB, 1941)
This Above All (20th, 1942)
Invisible Agent (Univ, 1942)
Lady in a Jam (Univ, 1942)

The Undying Monster (20th, 1942)
Two Tickets to London (Univ, 1943)
Sherlock Holmes and the Secret Weapon (Univ, 1943)
Corvette K-225 (Univ, 1943)
Sherlock Holmes in Washington (Univ, 1943)
The Bermuda Mystery (20th, 1944)
Pearl of Death (Univ, 1944)
Our Hearts Were Young and Gay (Par, 1944)
Enter Arsene Lupin (Univ, 1944)
The House of Fear (Univ, 1945)
The Mummy's Curse (Univ, 1945)
Confidential Agent (WB, 1945)
Three Strangers (WB, 1946)
The Verdict (WB, 1946)
Over the Santa Fe Trail (Col, 1947)
Singapore (Univ, 1947)
Bulldog Drummond Strikes Back (Col, 1947)
Bulldog Drummond at Bay (Col, 1947)
This Time for Keeps (MGM, 1947)
The Swordsman (Col, 1947)
Johnny Belinda (WB, 1948)
The Wreck of the Hesperus (Col, 1948)
Jungle Jim (Col, 1948)
The Stratton Story (MGM, 1949)
Barbary Pirate (Col, 1949)
Post Office Investigator (Rep, 1949)
David and Bathsheba (20th, 1951)
Anne of the Indies (20th, 1951)
The Unknown Man (MGM, 1951)
At Sword's Point (RKO, 1952)
The Brigand (Col, 1952)

HUGH HERBERT

In The Perfect Specimen *(1937).*

Born August 10, 1887, Binghamton, New York. Married 1) Rose Epstein (1932); divorced (1949); 2) Anita Pam. Died March 12, 1952, North Hollywood, California. Stage comedian who had written many vaudeville sketches before joining Fox in 1927, where he wrote the dialogue for Air Circus (1928). Co-author of story/dialogue for first all-talking feature. Warner Bros.' *Lights of New York* (1928); and wrote dialogue for Sono Art's *The Great Gabbo* (1929). Co-directed/co-scripted Lowell Sherman's *He Knew Women* (1930) and same year was dialogue director/actor in *Danger Lights*. Best known as a prime comedy-relief man on camera. Characterized by fluttering fingers, darting eyes, and a trademarked "woo woo." A giddy scene-stealer. Among his roles: *Footlight Parade* (Charlie Bowers), *Fashions of 1934* (Joe Ward), *Fog over Frisco* (Izzy Wright), *A Midsummer Night's Dream* (Snout), *The Perfect Specimen* (Killigrew Shaw), *The Beautiful Blonde from Bashful Bend* (the doctor), etc. On screen he was everyone's favorite sheepish philanderer.

Hugh Herbert to Glenda Farrell in *Gold Diggers of 1935:*
"Snuff is not to be sneezed at."

Films

Husbands for Rent (WB, 1927)
Caught in the Fog (WB, 1928)
Danger Lights (RKO, 1930)
Hook, Line and Sinker (RKO, 1930)
Second Wife (RKO, 1930)
The Sin Ship (RKO, 1931)
Laugh and Get Rich (RKO, 1931)
Traveling Husbands (RKO, 1931)

Friends and Lovers (RKO, 1931)
Cracked Nuts (RKO, 1931)
Faithless (MGM, 1932)
The Lost Squadron (RKO, 1932)
Million Dollar Legs (Par, 1932)
Goldie Gets Along (RKO, 1933)
Goodbye Again (FN, 1933)
Bureau of Missing Persons (FN, 1933)

Footlight Parade (WB, 1933)
College Coach (WB, 1933)
From Headquarters (WB, 1933)
She Had to Say Yes (FN, 1933)
Convention City (FN, 1933)
Strictly Personal (Par, 1933)
Diplomaniacs (RKO, 1933)
Fashions of 1934 (FN, 1934)

Easy to Love (WB, 1934)
Dames (WB, 1934)
Kansas City Princess (WB, 1934)
Wonder Bar (FN, 1934)
Harold Teen (WB, 1934)
Merry Wives of Reno (WB, 1934)
Sweet Adeline (WB, 1934)
Fog over Frisco (FN, 1934)
The Merry Frinks (FN, 1934)
The Traveling Saleslady (WB, 1935)
Gold Diggers of 1935 (FN, 1935)
A Midsummer Night's Dream (WB, 1935)
We're in the Money (WB, 1935)
Miss Pacific Fleet (WB, 1935)
To Beat the Band (RKO, 1935)
Mind Your Own Business (Par, 1936)
Colleen (WB, 1936)
Love Begins at Twenty (FN, 1936)
Sing Me a Love Song (FN, 1936)
One Rainy Afternoon (UA, 1936)
We Went to College (MGM, 1936)
That Man's Here Again (WB, 1937)
The Singing Marine (WB, 1937)
Marry the Girl (WB, 1937)

The Pefect Specimen (WB, 1937)
Sh! The Octopus (WB, 1937)
Hollywood Hotel (WB, 1937)
Top of the Town (Univ, 1937)
Men Are Such Fools (WB, 1938)
Gold Diggers in Paris (WB, 1938)
Four's a Crowd (WB, 1938)
The Great Waltz (MGM, 1938)
Eternally Yours (UA, 1939)
The Little Accident (Univ, 1939)
The Family Next Door (Univ, 1939)
The Lady's from Kentucky (Par, 1939)
La Conga Nights (Univ, 1940)
Private Affairs (Univ, 1940)
Slightly Tempted (Univ, 1940)
A Little Bit of Heaven (Univ, 1940)
The Villain Still Pursued Her (RKO, 1940)
Hit Parade of 1941 (Rep, 1940)
Meet the Chump (Univ, 1941)
The Black Cat (Univ, 1941)
Hello, Sucker (Univ, 1941)
Badlands of Dakota (Univ, 1941)
Hellzapoppin (Univ, 1941)

There's One Born Every Minute (Univ, 1942)
Don't Get Personal (Univ, 1942)
You're Telling Me (Univ, 1942)
Mrs. Wiggs of the Cabbage Patch (Par, 1942)
Stage Door Canteen (UA, 1943)
Ever Since Venus (Col, 1944)
Kismet [TV title: *Oriental Dreams*] (MGM, 1944)
Music for Millions (MGM, 1944)
One Way to Love (Col, 1945)
Blondie in the Dough (Col, 1947)
On Our Merry Way [a.k.a. *A Miracle Can Happen*] (UA, 1948)
One Touch of Venus (Univ, 1948)
So This Is New York (UA, 1948)
A Song Is Born (RKO, 1948)
The Girl from Manhattan (UA, 1948)
The Beautiful Blonde from Bashful Bend (20th, 1949)
Havana Rose (Rep, 1951)

JEAN HERSHOLT

Jean Hersholt and Lewis Stone in Unashamed *(1932).*

Born July 12, 1886, Copenhagen, Denmark. Married Via Andersen (1914), child: Allan. Died June 2, 1956, Beverly Hills, California. Portrayed kindly Dr. Christian in films (and on radio; once on TV) and Dr. DaFoe in the Dionne quintuplet series (*The Country Doctor, Reunion*, etc.). A most versatile character lead in silents and talkies. Role of Marcus Schouler in Erich von Stroheim's *Greed*, as ZaSu Pitts' revengeful suitor, highlighted his pre-talkie career. Gave quality performances as MGM character lead in the 1930s: *Grand Hotel* (the porter), *The Mask of Fu Manchu* (Professor Von Berg), *Dinner at Eight* (the Broadway producer Jo Stengel), etc. Founder of the Motion Picture Relief Fund; onetime president of the Academy of Motion Picture Arts and Sciences. An honorary Oscar was named for him—the Jean Hersholt Humanitarian Award.

Jean Hersholt in *The Country Doctor:* "I want a hospital more than anything else in the world!"

Films

The Disciple (Tri, 1915)
The Aryan (Tri, 1916)
Hell's Hinges (Tri, 1916)
The Desert (Tri, 1916)
Kinkaid-Gambler (Univ, 1916)
Bullets and Brown Eyes (Tri, 1916)
Fighting for Love (Univ, 1917)
Love Aflame (Univ, 1917)
The Terror (Univ, 1917)
The Soul Herder (Univ, 1917)
The Saintly Sinner (Univ, 1917)

The Show-Down (Univ, 1917)
Southern Justice (Univ, 1917)
The Greater Law (Univ, 1917)
Stormy Knights (Univ, 1917)
49-17 (Univ, 1917)
Princess Virtue (Univ, 1918)
Madame Spy (Univ, 1918)
In the Land of the Setting Sun (Multnomah Films, 1919)
The Servant in the House (FBO, 1920)
The Red Lane (Univ, 1920)

Merely Mary Ann (Fox, 1920)
The Four Horsemen of the Apocalypse (M, 1921)
A Certain Rich Man (G, 1921)
The Deceiver (Arrow, 1921)
Golden Trail (Arrow, 1921)
Man of the Forest (Hodkinson, 1921)
Golden Dreams (G, 1922)
The Gray Dawn (Hodkinson, 1922)
Tess of the Storm Country (UA, 1922)
When Romance Rides (G, 1922)

277

Heart's Haven (Hodkinson, 1922)
The Stranger's Banquet (G, 1922)
Jazzmania (Tif, 1923)
Quicksand (Selznick, 1923)
Red Lights (G, 1923)
Torment (Associated FN, 1924)
The Goldfish (Associated FN, 1924)
The Woman on the Jury (Associated FN, 1924)
Sinners in Silk (MG, 1924)
Her Night of Romance (Associated FN, 1924)
Cheap Kisses (FBO, 1924)
So Big (Associated FN, 1924)
Greed (MGM, 1924)
Fifth Avenue Model (Univ, 1925)
Dangerous Innocence (Univ, 1925)
A Woman's Faith (Univ, 1925)
If Marriage Fails (Univ, 1925)
Don Q, Son of Zorro (UA, 1925)
Stella Dallas (UA, 1925)
My Old Dutch (Univ, 1926)
The Greater Glory (FN, 1926)
It Must Be Love (FN, 1926)
Flames (Associate Exchange, 1926)
The Wrong Mr. Wright (Univ, 1927)
The Student Prince in Old Heidelberg (MGM, 1927)
Alias the Deacon (Univ, 1928)
13 Washington Square (Univ, 1928)
The Secret Hour (Par, 1928)
The Battle of the Sexes (Univ, 1928)
Jazz Mad (Univ, 1928)
Give and Take (Univ, 1928)

Abie's Irish Rose (Par, 1928)
The Younger Generation (Col, 1929)
Modern Love (Univ, 1929)
The Girl on the Barge (Univ, 1929)
Hell Harbor (UA, 1930)
Climax (Univ, 1930)
The Case of Sergeant Grischa (RKO, 1930)
Mamba (Tif, 1930)
Viennese Nights (WB, 1930)
The Cat Creeps (Univ, 1930)
East Is West (Univ, 1930)
The Third Alarm (Tif, 1930)
Daybreak (MGM, 1931)
A Soldier's Plaything (WB, 1931)
Susan Lennox, Her Fall and Rise (MGM, 1931)
The Phantom of Paris (MGM, 1931)
Transatlantic (Fox, 1931)
The Sin of Madelon Claudet (MGM, 1931)
Private Lives (MGM, 1931)
Beast of the City (MGM, 1932)
Emma (MGM, 1932)
Are You Listening? (MGM, 1932)
Grand Hotel (MGM, 1932)
Night Court (MGM, 1932)
New Morals for Old (MGM, 1932)
Skyscraper Souls (MGM, 1932)
Unashamed (MGM, 1932)
Hearts of Humanity (Majestic, 1932)
Flesh (MGM, 1932)
The Mask of Fu Manchu (MGM, 1932)
The Crime of the Century (Par, 1933)

Dinner at Eight (MGM, 1933)
Song of the Eagle (Par, 1933)
The Late Christopher Bean (MGM, 1933)
The Cat and the Fiddle (MGM, 1934)
Men in White (MGM, 1934)
The Fountain (RKO, 1934)
The Painted Veil (MGM, 1934)
Mark of the Vampire (MGM, 1935)
Murder in the Fleet (MGM, 1935)
Break of Hearts (RKO, 1935)
Tough Guy (MGM, 1936)
The Country Doctor (20th, 1936)
Sins of Man (20th, 1936)
His Brother's Wife (MGM, 1936)
Reunion (20th, 1936)
One in a Million (20th, 1936)
Seventh Heaven (20th, 1937)
Heidi (20th, 1937)
Happy Landing (20th, 1938)
Alexander's Ragtime Band (20th, 1938)
I'll Give a Million (20th, 1938)
Five of a Kind (20th, 1938)
Mr. Moto in Danger Island (20th, 1939)
Meet Dr. Christian (RKO, 1939)
Courageous Dr. Christian (RKO, 1940)
Dr. Christian Meets the Women (RKO, 1940)
Remedy for Riches (RKO, 1940)
Melody for Three (RKO, 1941)
They Meet Again (RKO, 1941)
Stage Door Canteen (UA, 1943)
Dancing in the Dark (20th, 1949)
Run for Cover (Par, 1955)

RUSSELL HICKS

Rose Hobart, Ken Murray, and Russell Hicks in A Night at Earl Carroll's *(1940).*

Born June 4, 1895, Baltimore, Maryland. Married Virginia _____ , children: five daughters. Died June 1, 1957, Hollywood, California. One of the busiest performers in Hollywood, interpreting the hearty senior citizen; sometimes a congenial businessman, military officer, or upper-crust father: *The Toast of New York* (lawyer), *Maytime* (voice coach), *The Story of Alexander Graham Bell* (Barrows), *The Bank Dick* (J. Frothingham Waterbury), *The Little Foxes* (William Marshall), *The Sea of Grass* (Major Harney), etc. TV series: "The Secret Storm" (as Mr. Tyrell) and "A Date with the Angels."

> **Russell Hicks** to John Payne in *To the Shores of Tripoli:* "You realize, Winters, that this may mean prison and dishonorable discharge?"

Films

Before Morning (Greenblatt, 1933)
Enlighten Thy Daughter (Exploitation, 1933)
Happiness Ahead (FN, 1934)
Gentlemen Are Born (FN, 1934)
The Case of the Howling Dog (WB, 1934)
The Firebird (WB, 1934)
The St. Louis Kid (WB, 1934)
Babbit (FN, 1934)
Murder in the Clouds (FN, 1934)
Sweet Music (WB, 1935)
While the Patient Slept (FN, 1935)
Living on Velvet (FN, 1935)
Devil Dogs of the Air (WB, 1935)
The Woman in Red (FN, 1935)
Cardinal Richelieu (UA, 1935)
Honeymoon Limited (Mon, 1935)
Lady Tubbs (Univ, 1935)

Thunder in the Night (Fox, 1935)
Charlie Chan in Shanghai (Fox, 1935)
Ladies Love Danger (Fox, 1935)
Grand Exit (Col, 1935)
$1,000 a Minute (Rep, 1935)
Ladies Crave Excitement (Mascot, 1935)
Two in the Dark (RKO, 1936)
Fatal Lady (Par, 1936)
Follow the Fleet (RKO, 1936)
Special Investigator (RKO, 1936)
Grand Jury (RKO, 1936)
We Who Are About to Die (RKO, 1936)
Woman Trap (Par, 1936)
Laughing Irish Eyes (Rep, 1936)
Hearts in Bondage (Rep, 1936)
15 Maiden Lane (20th, 1936)
The Sea Spoilers (Univ, 1936)
Ticket to Paradise (Rep, 1936)

Trapped by Television (Col, 1936)
Bunker Bean (RKO, 1936)
Secret Valley (20th, 1936)
Maytime (MGM, 1937)
Midnight Taxi (20th, 1937)
Espionage (MGM, 1937)
Pick a Star (MGM, 1937)
23½ Hours Leave (GN, 1937)
Girl Overboard (Univ, 1937)
The Westland Case (Univ, 1937)
On Again, Off Again (RKO, 1937)
The Big Shot (RKO, 1937)
The Toast of New York (RKO, 1937)
Fit for a King (RKO, 1937)
Criminals of the Air (Col, 1937)
Laughing at Trouble (20th, 1937)
The Wildcatter (Univ, 1937)
Fifty Roads to Town (20th, 1937)

Partners in Crime (Par, 1937)
Let Them Live! (Univ, 1937)
Kidnapped (20th, 1938)
Men with Wings (Par, 1938)
In Old Chicago (20th, 1938)
Little Miss Broadway (20th, 1938)
Gateway (20th, 1938)
Hold That Co-ed (20th, 1938)
Kentucky (20th, 1938)
Fugitives for a Night (RKO, 1938)
The Big Broadcast of 1938 (Par, 1938)
Boy Trouble (Par, 1939)
The Three Musketeers (20th, 1939)
The Story of Alexander Graham Bell (20th, 1939)
Hollywood Cavalcade (20th, 1939)
The Honeymoon's Over (20th, 1939)
Swanee River (20th, 1939)
Stanley and Livingstone (20th, 1939)
I Was a Convict (Rep, 1939)
The Real Glory (UA, 1939)
Joe and Ethel Turp Call on the President (MGM, 1939)
East Side of Heaven (Univ, 1939)
The Big Guy [a.k.a. Warden of the Big House] (Univ, 1939)
Union Pacific (Par, 1939)
The Lady with Red Hair (WB, 1940)
The Blue Bird (20th, 1940)
Virginia City (WB, 1940)
Johnny Apollo (20th, 1940)
Enemy Agent (Univ, 1940)
The Mortal Storm (MGM, 1940)
Earthbound (20th, 1940)
Sporting Blood (MGM, 1940)
The Return of Frank James (20th, 1940)
East of the River (WB, 1940)
Seven Sinners (Univ, 1940)
A Night at Earl Carroll's (Par, 1940)
The Bank Dick (Univ, 1940)
No, No, Nanette (RKO, 1940)
Love Thy Neighbor (Par, 1940)
The Great Lie (WB, 1941)
Western Union (20th, 1941)
The Arkansas Judge (Rep, 1941)
A Man Betrayed (Rep, 1941)
Man-Made Monster (Univ, 1941)
Strawberry Blonde (WB, 1941)
Ellery Queen's Penthouse Mystery (Col, 1941)

Here Comes Happiness (WB, 1941)
They Died with Their Boots On (WB, 1941)
Blood and Sand (20th, 1941)
The Big Store (MGM, 1941)
The Parson of Panamint (Par, 1941)
Buy Me That Town (Par, 1941)
Hold That Ghost (Univ, 1941)
The Little Foxes (RKO, 1941)
Great Guns (20th, 1941)
Doctors Don't Tell (Rep, 1941)
The Man Who Lost Himself (Univ, 1941)
Public Enemies (Rep, 1941)
Pacific Blackout [a.k.a. Midnight Angel] (Par, 1941)
Joe Smith, American (MGM, 1942)
To the Shores of Tripoli (20th, 1942)
Fingers at the Window (MGM, 1942)
Butch Minds the Baby (Univ, 1942)
Tarzan's New York Adventure (MGM, 1942)
We Were Dancing (MGM, 1942)
Tennessee Johnson (MGM, 1942)
Pacific Rendezvous (MGM, 1942)
Lady in a Jam (Univ, 1942)
Strictly in the Groove (Univ, 1942)
We Were Dancing (MGM, 1942)
What a Woman! (Col, 1943)
Northern Pursuit (WB, 1943)
Hitler—Dead or Alive (Ben Judell, 1943)
Someone to Remember (Rep, 1943)
Follow the Band (Univ, 1943)
Harrigan's Kid (MGM, 1943)
King of the Cowboys (Rep, 1943)
Air Raid Wardens (MGM, 1943)
The Woman of the Town (UA, 1943)
Hat Check Honey (Univ, 1944)
Janie (WB, 1944)
Louisiana Hayride (Col, 1944)
Port of Forty Thieves (Rep, 1944)
Flame of Barbary Coast (Rep, 1945)
A Game of Death (RKO, 1945)
A Guy, a Gal and a Pal (Col, 1945)
The Hidden Eye (MGM, 1945)
Scarlet Street (Univ, 1945)
She Gets Her Man (Univ, 1945)
The Valley of Decision (MGM, 1945)
The Bachelor's Daughters (UA, 1946)
Till the Clouds Roll By (MGM, 1946)
The Bandit of Sherwood Forest (Col, 1946)

A Close Call for Boston Blackie (Col, 1946)
Dark Alibi (Mon, 1946)
Gay Blades [a.k.a. Tournament Tempo] (Rep, 1946)
G.I. War Brides (Rep, 1946)
The Plainsman and the Lady (Rep, 1946)
Swing Parade of 1946 (Mon, 1946)
She Wouldn't Say Yes (Col, 1946)
Smoky River Serenade (Col, 1947)
Fun on a Weekend (UA, 1947)
The Pilgrim Lady (Rep, 1947)
The Sea of Grass (MGM, 1947)
Louisiana (Mon, 1947)
Web of Danger (Rep, 1947)
Variety Girl (Par, 1947)
Exposed (Rep, 1947)
One Sunday Afternoon (WB, 1948)
The Hunted (AA, 1948)
Silver River (WB, 1948)
Assigned to Danger (EL, 1948)
The Gallant Legion (Rep, 1948)
The Black Arrow (Col, 1948)
Race Street (RKO, 1948)
My Dear Secretary (UA, 1948)
The Velvet Touch (RKO, 1948)
The Shanghai Chest (Mon, 1948)
The Plunderers (Rep, 1948)
The Return of October (Col, 1948)
Jiggs and Maggie in Court (Mon, 1948)
Manhattan Angel (Col, 1949)
I Cheated the Law (20th, 1949)
Samson and Delilah (Par, 1949)
Barbary Pirate (Col, 1949)
Blue Grass of Kentucky (Mon, 1950)
The Flying Saucer (Film Classics, 1950)
Unmasked (Rep, 1950)
The Big Hangover (MGM, 1950)
Square Dance Katy (Mon, 1950)
Halls of Montezuma (20th, 1950)
Kentucky Jubilee (Lip, 1951)
Bowery Battalion (Mon, 1951)
All That I Have (Family Films, 1951)
Fourteen Hours (20th, 1951)
Overland Telegraph (RKO, 1951)
As You Were (Lip, 1951)
Old Oklahoma Plains (Rep, 1952)
Rodeo (Mon, 1952)
The Maverick (Mon, 1952)
Man of Conflict (Atlas, 1953)
The Seventh Cavalry (Col, 1956)

SAMUEL S. HINDS

Shaking hands with Wendy Barrie in A Girl with Ideas *(1937).*

Born April 4, 1875, Brooklyn, New York. Married _____ , children: Florence, Mary. Died October 13, 1948, Pasadena, California. Abandoned his law career after the Depression hit; concentrated on acting. Co-founder of the Pasadena Playhouse. Often seen as the wise physician, dishonest attorney, or thoughtful father. Lew Ayres' dad in the *Dr. Kildare* series.

Samuel S. Hinds to Lionel Atwill in *Man-Made Monster:*
"This theory of yours isn't science. It's . . . it's black magic."

Films

If I Had a Million (Par, 1932)
The World Changes (FN, 1933)
The Crime of the Century (Par, 1933)
Gabriel over the White House (MGM, 1933)
The Nuisance (MGM, 1933)
Day of Reckoning (MGM, 1933)
Lady for a Day (Col, 1933)
Bed of Roses (RKO, 1933)
Berkeley Square (Fox, 1933)
The Deluge (RKO, 1933)
Little Women (RKO, 1933)
One Man's Journey (RKO, 1933)
Penthouse (MGM, 1933)
Hold the Press (Col, 1933)
This Day and Age (Par, 1933)
Son of a Sailor (FN, 1933)
Female (FN, 1933)
The House on 56th Street (WB, 1933)
Convention City (FN, 1933)
Women in His Life (MGM, 1933)
Fog (Col, 1934)
The Big Shakedown (FN, 1934)
Manhattan Melodrama (MGM, 1934)
Operator 13 (MGM, 1934)

Sadie McKee (MGM, 1934)
The Cat's Paw (Fox, 1934)
A Wicked Woman (MGM, 1934)
Most Precious Thing in Life (Col, 1934)
Evelyn Prentice (MGM, 1934)
He Was Her Man (WB, 1934)
The Ninth Guest (Col, 1934)
No Greater Glory (Col, 1934)
Sisters Under the Skin (Col, 1934)
Massacre (FN, 1934)
Men in White (MGM, 1934)
The Crime Doctor (RKO, 1934)
Straightaway (Col, 1934)
The Defense Rests (Col, 1934)
Have a Heart (MGM, 1934)
A Lost Lady (FN, 1934)
Hat, Coat and Glove (RKO, 1934)
Sequoia (MGM, 1934)
Bordertown (WB, 1935)
Devil Dogs of the Air (WB, 1935)
Black Fury (FN, 1935)
Wings in the Dark (Par, 1935)
West of the Pecos (RKO, 1935)
Strangers All (RKO, 1935)
She (RKO, 1935)

In Person (RKO, 1935)
Mills of the Gods (Col, 1935)
Behind the Evidence (Col, 1935)
Dr. Socrates (WB, 1935)
Rumba (Par, 1935)
Private Worlds (Par, 1935)
College Scandal (Par, 1935)
Accent on Youth (Par, 1935)
Annapolis Farewell (Par, 1935)
Big Broadcast of 1936 (Par, 1935)
Two-Fisted (Par, 1935)
Millions in the Air (Par, 1935)
Shadow of Doubt (Univ, 1935)
Rendezvous (MGM, 1935)
The Raven (Univ, 1935)
Living on Velvet (FN, 1935)
Timothy's Quest (Par, 1936)
Woman Trap (Par, 1936)
Trail of the Lonesome Pine (Par, 1936)
Border Flight (Par, 1936)
Fatal Lady (Par, 1936)
Rhythm on the Range (Par, 1936)
Sworn Enemy (MGM, 1936)
His Brother's Wife (MGM, 1936)
Love Letters of a Star (Univ, 1936)

The Longest Night (MGM, 1936)
Black Legion (WB, 1936)
The Lady Fights Back (Univ, 1937)
Top of the Town (Univ, 1937)
The Mighty Treve (Univ, 1937)
Night Key (Univ, 1937)
Wings over Honolulu (Univ, 1937)
The Road Back (Univ, 1937)
A Girl with Ideas (Univ, 1937)
Prescription for Romance (Univ, 1937)
Double or Nothing (Par, 1937)
She's Dangerous (Univ, 1937)
Navy Blue and Gold (MGM, 1937)
Stage Door (RKO, 1937)
The Jury's Secret (Univ, 1938)
The Devil's Party (Univ, 1938)
Wives Under Suspicion (Univ, 1938)
Rage of Paris (Univ, 1938)
The Road to Reno (Univ, 1938)
The Storm (Univ, 1938)
Swing That Cheer (Univ, 1938)
Secrets of a Nurse (Univ, 1938)
Test Pilot (MGM, 1938)
You Can't Take It with You (Col, 1938)
Double Danger (RKO, 1938)
Forbidden Valley (Univ, 1938)
Young Dr. Kildare (MGM, 1938)
Personal Secretary (Univ, 1938)
Calling Dr. Kildare (MGM, 1939)
Ex-Champ (Univ, 1939)
Hawaiian Nights (Univ, 1939)
The Under-Pup (Univ, 1939)
One Hour to Live (Univ, 1939)
Destry Rides Again (Univ, 1939)
Newsboys' Home (Univ, 1939)
Within the Law (MGM, 1939)
Charlie McCarthy, Detective (Univ, 1939)
Career (RKO, 1939)
Tropic Fury (Univ, 1939)
Rio (Univ, 1939)
First Love (Univ, 1939)
Hero for a Day (Univ, 1939)

The Secret of Dr. Kildare (MGM, 1939)
It's a Date (Univ, 1940)
Zanzibar (Univ, 1940)
Dr. Kildare's Strange Case (MGM, 1940)
Ski Patrol (Univ, 1940)
The Boys from Syracuse (Univ, 1940)
I'm Nobody's Sweetheart Now (Univ, 1940)
Dr. Kildare Goes Home (MGM, 1940)
Spring Parade (Univ, 1940)
Seven Sinners (Univ, 1940)
Trail of the Vigilantes (Univ, 1940)
Man-Made Monster (Univ, 1941)
Back Street (Univ, 1941)
Buck Privates (Univ, 1941)
The Lady from Cheyenne (Univ, 1941)
Adventure in Washington (Col, 1941)
Tight Shoes (Univ, 1941)
Blossoms in the Dust (MGM, 1941)
The Shepherd of the Hills (Par, 1941)
Dr. Kildare's Wedding Day (MGM, 1941)
Unfinished Business (Univ, 1941)
Badlands of Dakota (Univ, 1941)
Mob Town (Univ, 1941)
Road Agent (Univ, 1941)
Keep 'em Flying (Univ, 1941)
Ride 'em Cowboy (Univ, 1941)
Frisco Lil (Univ, 1942)
Jail House Blues (Univ, 1942)
The Strange Case of Dr. Rx (Univ, 1942)
Kid Glove Killer (MGM, 1942)
The Spoilers (Univ, 1942)
Grand Central Murder (MGM, 1942)
Lady in a Jam (Univ, 1942)
Pardon My Sarong (Univ, 1942)
Pittsburgh (Univ, 1942)
He's My Guy (Univ, 1943)
Mr. Big (Univ, 1943)
Top Man (Univ, 1943)
Fired Wife (Univ, 1943)
Larceny with Music (Univ, 1943)

Son of Dracula (Univ, 1943)
It Ain't Hay (Univ, 1943)
Good Morning, Judge (Univ, 1943)
Follow the Band (Univ, 1943)
Hers to Hold (Univ, 1943)
We've Never Been Licked (Univ, 1943)
Sing a Jingle (Univ, 1944)
Chip off the Old Block (Univ, 1944)
Follow the Boys (Univ, 1944)
Ladies Courageous (Univ, 1944)
Jungle Woman (Univ, 1944)
South of Dixie (Univ, 1944)
Cobra Woman (Univ, 1944)
The Singing Sheriff (Univ, 1944)
Swing Out, Sister (Univ, 1945)
Frisco Sal (Univ, 1945)
I'll Remember April (Univ, 1945)
Escape in the Desert (WB, 1945)
Week-End at the Waldorf (MGM, 1945)
The Strange Affair of Uncle Harry (Univ, 1945)
Lady on a Train (Univ, 1945)
Men in Her Diary (Univ, 1945)
Scarlet Street (Univ, 1945)
Secret Agent X-9 (Univ serial, 1945)
It's a Wonderful Life (RKO, 1946)
White Tie and Tails (Univ, 1946)
Inside Job (Univ, 1946)
Blonde Alibi (Univ, 1946)
Strange Conquest (Univ, 1946)
The Runaround [a.k.a. *Deadly Enemies*] (Univ, 1946)
Little Miss Big (Univ, 1946)
Danger Woman (Univ, 1946)
The Egg and I (Univ, 1947)
Time Out of Mind (Univ, 1947)
Call Northside 777 (20th, 1948)
Perilous Water [a.k.a. *In Self-Defense*] (Mon, 1948)
The Return of October (Col, 1948)
The Boy with Green Hair (RKO, 1948)
The Bribe (MGM, 1949)

HALLIWELL HOBBES
(Herbert Halliwell Hobbes)

Paul Cavanagh, Olaf Hytten, Cyril Maude, and Halliwell Hobbes in Grumpy (1930).

Born November 16, 1877, Stratford-on-Avon, England. Married Nancie B. Marsland. Died February 20, 1962, Santa Monica, California. Baldpated Britisher who was repeatedly on camera as a butler, a bobby, or a low-keyed familyman; occasionally a police chief (*Charlie Chan in Shanghai*) or a physician (Dr. Lister in *The Story of Louis Pasteur*).

Halliwell Hobbes to Nigel Bruce in *Sherlock Holmes Faces Death:* "Oh, no, Dr. Watson, Lady Clarinda only walks in the *west* wing. No one ever met a ghost in *this* part of the 'ouse."

Films

Jealousy (Par, 1929)
Lucky in Love (Pathé, 1929)
Charley's Aunt (Col, 1930)
Grumpy (Par, 1930)
Scotland Yard (Fox, 1930)
Bachelor Father (MGM, 1931)
Platinum Blonde (Col, 1931)
The Right of Way (FN, 1931)
The Woman Between (RKO, 1931)
Five and Ten (MGM, 1931)
The Sin of Madelon Claudet (MGM, 1931)
Dr. Jekyll and Mr. Hyde (Par, 1932)
Lovers Courageous (MGM, 1932)
The Menace (Col, 1932)
Forbidden (Univ, 1932)
The Devil's Lottery (Fox, 1932)
Man About Town (Fox, 1932)
Week-Ends Only (Fox, 1932)
Six Hours to Live (Fox, 1932)

Love Affair (Col, 1932)
Payment Deferred (MGM, 1932)
Looking Forward (MGM, 1933)
Midnight Mary (MGM, 1933)
Should Ladies Behave? (MGM, 1933)
A Study in Scarlet (WW, 1933)
Captured (WB, 1933)
Lady for a Day (Col, 1933)
The Masquerader (UA, 1933)
I Am Suzanne! (Fox, 1934)
All Men Are Enemies (Fox, 1934)
Mandalay (FN, 1934)
British Agent (FN, 1934)
The Key (WB, 1934)
Riptide (MGM, 1934)
Double Door (Par, 1934)
Menace (Par, 1934)
Bulldog Drummond Strikes Back (UA, 1934)
Madame Du Barry (WB, 1934)

Folies Bergere (UA, 1935)
The Story of Louis Pasteur (WB, 1935)
Whipsaw (MGM, 1935)
Cardinal Richelieu (UA, 1935)
Right to Live (WB, 1935)
Millions in the Air (Par, 1935)
Jalna (RKO, 1935)
Charlie Chan in Shanghai (Fox, 1935)
Father Brown, Detective (Par, 1935)
Here Comes Trouble (20th, 1936)
Dracula's Daughter (Univ, 1936)
Love Letters of a Star (Univ, 1936)
The White Angel (FN, 1936)
Hearts Divided (FN, 1936)
Give Me Your Heart (WB, 1936)
Spendthrift (Par, 1936)
Maid of Salem (Par, 1937)
The Prince and the Pauper (WB, 1937)
Varsity Show (WB, 1937)
Fit for a King (RKO, 1937)

The Jury's Secret (Univ, 1938)
Service de Luxe (Univ, 1938)
Bulldog Drummond's Peril (Par, 1938)
Storm over Bengal (Rep, 1938)
Kidnapped (20th, 1938)
You Can't Take It with You (Col, 1938)
Pacific Liner (RKO, 1939)
The Hardys Ride High (MGM, 1939)
Naughty but Nice (WB, 1939)
Nurse Edith Cavell (RKO, 1939)
Tell No Tales (MGM, 1939)
Remember? (MGM, 1939)

The Light That Failed (Par, 1939)
The Earl of Chicago (MGM, 1940)
Third Finger, Left Hand (MGM, 1940)
The Sea Hawk (WB, 1940)
That Hamilton Woman (UA, 1941)
Here Comes Mr. Jordan (Col, 1941)
To Be or Not to Be (UA, 1942)
The War Against Mrs. Hadley (MGM, 1942)
Journey for Margaret (MGM, 1942)
The Undying Monster (20th, 1942)
Son of Fury (20th, 1942)

Forever and a Day (RKO, 1943)
Sherlock Holmes Faces Death (Univ, 1943)
The Invisible Man's Revenge (Univ, 1944)
Gaslight (MGM, 1944)
Mr. Skeffington (WB, 1944)
Casanova Brown (RKO, 1944)
Canyon Passage (Univ, 1946)
If Winter Comes (MGM, 1947)
You Gotta Stay Happy (Univ, 1948)
The Black Arrow (Col, 1948)
That Forsyte Woman (MGM, 1949)
Miracle in the Rain (WB, 1956)

ARTHUR HOHL

In Idaho (1943).

Born May 21, 1889, Pittsburgh, Pennsylvania. Serious-looking performer who undertook a wide scope of roles: Claudette Colbert's *Cleopatra* (Brutus), *The Whole Town's Talking* (Detective Sergeant Mike Boyle), *Show Boat* (Pete), *Sherlock Holmes and the Spider Woman* (Gilflower), *Monsieur Verdoux* (real estate agent), etc.

Arthur Hohl to Loretta Young in *A Man's Castle:* "With Bill in the jug, you're gonna need a man around."

284

Films

It Is the Law (Fox, 1929)
The Cheat (Par, 1931)
The Night of June 13th (Par, 1932)
The Sign of the Cross (Par, 1932)
Infernal Machine (Fox, 1933)
Man's Castle (Col, 1933)
Island of Lost Souls (Par, 1933)
The Life of Jimmy Dolan (WB, 1933)
Narrow Corner (WB, 1933)
The Silk Express (FN, 1933)
Private Detective 62 (FN, 1933)
The World Changes (FN, 1933)
Captured (WB, 1933)
Baby Face (WB, 1933)
Brief Moment (Col, 1933)
Footlight Parade (WB, 1933)
The Kennel Murder Case (WB, 1933)
College Coach (WB, 1933)
Wild Boys of the Road (FN, 1933)
Massacre (FN, 1934)
A Modern Hero (WB, 1934)
Jimmy the Gent (WB, 1934)
Bulldog Drummond Strikes Back (Par, 1934)
Among the Missing (Col, 1934)
Cleopatra (Par, 1934)
The Defense Rests (Col, 1934)
Lady by Choice (Col, 1934)
Romance in Manhattan (RKO, 1934)
Against the Law (Col, 1934)
Jealousy (Col, 1934)
The Whole Town's Talking (Col, 1935)

I'll Love You Always (Col, 1935)
In Spite of Danger (Col, 1935)
Eight Bells (Col, 1935)
One Frightened Night (Mascot, 1935)
Village Tale (RKO, 1935)
After the Dance (Col, 1935)
Unknown Woman (Col, 1935)
Atlantic Adventure (Col, 1935)
The Case of the Missing Man (Col, 1935)
Guard That Girl (Col, 1935)
Superspeed (Col, 1935)
It Had to Happen (20th, 1936)
The Lone Wolf Returns (Col, 1936)
We're Only Human (RKO, 1936)
Forgotten Faces (Par, 1936)
Show Boat (Univ, 1936)
The Devil Doll (MGM, 1936)
Lloyds of London (20th, 1936)
Slave Ship (20th, 1937)
Mountain Music (Par, 1937)
The Road Back (Univ, 1937)
Trapped by G-Men [a.k.a. River of Missing Men] (Col, 1937)
Hot Water (20th, 1937)
Bad Man of Brimstone (MGM, 1937)
Penitentiary (Col, 1938)
Kidnapped (20th, 1938)
Crime Takes a Holiday (Col, 1938)
Stablemates (MGM, 1938)
Boy Slaves (RKO, 1939)
You Can't Cheat an Honest Man (Univ, 1939)

They Shall Have Music (UA, 1939)
Blackmail (MGM, 1939)
Fugitive at Large (Col, 1939)
The Adventures of Sherlock Holmes (20th, 1939)
The Hunchback of Notre Dame (RKO, 1939)
Twenty-Mule Team (MGM, 1940)
Blondie Has Servant Trouble (Col, 1940)
Men of Boys Town (MGM, 1941)
Ride On, Vaquero (20th, 1941)
We Go Fast (20th, 1941)
Son of Fury (20th, 1942)
Whispering Ghosts (20th, 1942)
Moontide (20th, 1942)
Idaho (Rep, 1943)
The Woman of the Town (UA, 1943)
The Scarlet Claw (Univ, 1944)
Sherlock Holmes and the Spider Woman (Univ, 1944)
The Eve of St. Mark (20th, 1944)
Salome, Where She Danced (Univ, 1945)
The Frozen Ghost (Univ, 1945)
Love Letters (Par, 1945)
Our Vines Have Tender Grapes (MGM, 1945)
The Yearling (MGM, 1946)
It Happened on Fifth Avenue (AA, 1947)
Monsieur Verdoux (UA, 1947)
The Vigilantes Return (Univ, 1947)
You Gotta Stay Happy (Univ, 1948)
Down to the Sea in Ships (20th, 1949)

FAY HOLDEN
(Fay Hammerton)

Fay Holden, Mickey Rooney, Sara Haden, Lewis Stone, and Cecilia Parker in Andy Hardy's Double Life *(1942)*.

Born September 26, 1893, Birmingham, England. Married David Clyde (1914); widowed (1945). Died June 23, 1973, Los Angeles, California. Although a Britisher, she became symbolic of American domesticity as Mother Hardy in the long-running *Andy Hardy* series.

Fay Holden to Lewis Stone in *Judge Hardy's Children*: "Nobody ever paid anybody $200 a day for anything honest."

Films

Polo Joe (WB, 1936)
White Angel (FN, 1936)
I Married a Doctor (FN, 1936)
Wives Never Know (Par, 1936)
Bulldog Drummond Escapes (Par, 1937)
Double or Nothing (Par, 1937)
King of Gamblers (Par, 1937)
Souls at Sea (Par, 1937)
Exclusive (Par, 1937)
You're Only Young Once (MGM, 1938)
Sweethearts (MGM, 1938)
Judge Hardy's Children (MGM, 1938)
Test Pilot (MGM, 1938)
Love Is a Headache (MGM, 1938)
The Battle of Broadway (20th, 1938)
Love Finds Andy Hardy (MGM, 1938)

Hold That Kiss (MGM, 1938)
Out West with the Hardys (MGM, 1938)
Sergeant Madden (MGM, 1939)
The Hardys Ride High (MGM, 1939)
Andy Hardy Gets Spring Fever (MGM, 1939)
Judge Hardy and Son (MGM, 1939)
Andy Hardy Meets Debutante (MGM, 1940)
Bitter Sweet (MGM, 1940)
Ziegfeld Girl (MGM, 1941)
Blossoms in the Dust (MGM, 1941)
H. M. Pulham, Esq. (MGM, 1941)
Andy Hardy's Private Secretary (MGM, 1941)
Washington Melodrama (MGM, 1941)

I'll Wait for You (MGM, 1941)
Life Begins for Andy Hardy (MGM, 1941)
The Courtship of Andy Hardy (MGM, 1942)
Andy Hardy's Double Life (MGM, 1942)
Andy Hardy's Blonde Trouble (MGM, 1944)
Love Laughs at Andy Hardy (MGM, 1946)
Little Miss Big (Univ, 1946)
Canyon Passage (Univ, 1946)
Whispering Smith (Par, 1948)
Samson and Delilah (Par, 1949)
The Big Hangover (MGM, 1949)
Andy Hardy Comes Home (MGM, 1958)

GLORIA HOLDEN

Deborah Kerr, Clark Gable, and Gloria Holden in The Hucksters *(1947).*

Born September 5, 1908, London, England. Married 1) _____ ; 2) _____ , child: son. Strangely haunting in the title role of *Dracula's Daughter*. Thereafter in: *The Life of Emile Zola* (Alexandrine, wife of Paul Muni), *Dodge City* (Mrs. Cole, married to John Litel), etc. Subordinate roles followed.

> **Gloria Holden** to Otto Kruger in *Dracula's Daughter:*
> "You're the one person who stands between me and utter destruction."

Films

Wife Versus Secretary (MGM, 1936)
Dracula's Daughter (Univ, 1936)
Hawaii Calls (RKO, 1938)
Test Pilot (MGM, 1938)
Girls' School (Col, 1938)
Dodge City (WB, 1939)
Miracles for Sale (MGM, 1939)
A Child Is Born (WB, 1940)
This Thing Called Love (Col, 1941)
Passage from Hong Kong (WB, 1941)
The Corsican Brothers (UA, 1941)

A Gentleman After Dark (UA, 1942)
Miss Annie Rooney (UA, 1942)
Apache Trail (MGM, 1942)
Behind the Rising Sun (RKO, 1943)
Having Wonderful Crime (RKO, 1945)
The Adventures of Rusty (Col, 1945)
Strange Holiday (PRC, 1946)
Hit the Hay (Col, 1946)
Sister Kenny (RKO, 1946)
Girl of the Limberlost (Col, 1946)
The Hucksters (MGM, 1947)

Undercover Maisie (MGM, 1947)
Killer McCoy (MGM, 1947)
Perilous Waters (Mon, 1948)
A Kiss for Corliss [a.k.a. *Almost a Bride*] (UA, 1949)
The Sickle and the Cross (Astor, 1951)
Dream Wife (MGM, 1953)
The Eddy Duchin Story (Col, 1956)
This Happy Feeling (Univ, 1958)

STERLING HOLLOWAY

In It's a Mad, Mad, Mad, Mad World *(1963).*

Born January 4, 1905, Cedartown, Georgia. Characterized by drawling speech and a batter-whipped hairstyle. Played the constant bumpkin youth in a long string of features; some offbeat roles: 1933's *Alice in Wonderland* (the frog), Shirley Temple's *The Blue Bird* (the wild plum tree). Was a dramatic standout in *A Walk in the Sun* (McWilliams). In demand as an offscreen voice for Walt Disney cartoon features because of his unique speech pattern: *Alice in Wonderland* (cheshire cat), *The Jungle Book* (Kaa, the snake), etc. Often does radio and TV commercials. TV series: "The Life of Riley" (as Waldo Benny), "Willy," and "The Baileys of Balboa."

Sterling Holloway, regarding Barbara Stanwyck, to Fred MacMurray in *Remember the Night:* "Ain't she a *peachoreno.* All I can say is *hot dog.*"

Films

Casey at the Bat (Par, 1927)
Blonde Venus (Par, 1932)
Lawyer Man (WB, 1932)
American Madness (Col, 1932)
Elmer the Great (FN, 1933)
Hell Below (MGM, 1933)
International House (Par, 1933)
Alice in Wonderland (Par, 1933)
Gold Diggers of 1933 (WB, 1933)
Professional Sweetheart (RKO, 1933)
Wild Boys of the Road (FN, 1933)
Advice to the Lovelorn (UA, 1933)
Dancing Lady (MGM, 1933)
Blondie Johnson (FN, 1933)
Fast Workers (MGM, 1933)
Female (FN, 1933)
Adorable (Fox, 1934)
The Merry Widow (MGM, 1934)
Gift of Gab (Univ, 1934)

Down to Their Last Yacht (RKO, 1934)
Strictly Dynamite (RKO, 1934)
A Wicked Woman (MGM, 1934)
Tomorrow's Youth (Mascot, 1934)
Back Page (General Pictures, 1934)
Girl o' My Dreams (Mon, 1934)
Lottery Lover (Fox, 1935)
Life Begins at Forty (Fox, 1935)
Doubting Thomas (Fox, 1935)
$1,000 a Minute (Rep, 1935)
Rendezvous (MGM, 1935)
I Live My Life (MGM, 1935)
Palm Springs (Par, 1936)
Career Woman (20th, 1936)
Maid of Salem (Par, 1937)
Join the Marines (Par, 1937)
Behind the Mike (Univ, 1937)
The Woman I Love (RKO, 1937)
When Love Is Young (Univ, 1937)

Varsity Show (WB, 1937)
Of Human Hearts (MGM, 1938)
Spring Madness (MGM, 1938)
Dr. Rhythm (Par, 1938)
Professor Beware (Par, 1938)
Nick Carter, Master Detective (MGM, 1939)
Remember the Night (Par, 1940)
The Blue Bird (20th, 1940)
Street of Memories (20th, 1940)
Hit Parade of 1941 (Rep, 1940)
Little Men (RKO, 1940)
Cheers for Miss Bishop (UA, 1941)
Top Sergeant Mulligan (Mon, 1941)
New Wine [TV title: *Melody Master*] (UA, 1941)
Meet John Doe (WB, 1941)
Look Who's Laughing (RKO, 1941)
Dumbo (RKO, 1941) [voice only]

Iceland (20th, 1942)
Bambi (RKO, 1942) [voice only]
Star Spangled Rhythm (Par, 1942)
The Lady Is Willing (Col, 1942)
The Three Caballeros (RKO, 1944) [voice only]
Wildfire (Screen Guild, 1945)
A Walk in the Sun (20th, 1945)
Sioux City Sue (Rep, 1946)
Make Mine Music (RKO, 1946) [voice only]
Death Valley (Screen Guild, 1946)
Robin Hood of Texas (Rep, 1947)
Twilight on the Rio Grande (Rep, 1947)

Saddle Pals (Rep, 1947)
Trail to San Antone (Rep, 1947)
The Beautiful Blonde from Bashful Bend (20th, 1949)
Her Wonderful Lie (Col, 1950)
Alice in Wonderland (RKO, 1951) [voice only]
The Adventures of Huckleberry Finn (MGM, 1960)
Alakazam the Great (AIP, 1961) [voice only]
It's a Mad, Mad, Mad, Mad World (UA, 1963)
Winnie the Pooh (BV, 1964) [voice only]

The Jungle Book (BV, 1967) [voice only]
Live a Little, Love a Little (MGM, 1968)
The Aristocats (BV, 1970) [voice only]
Won Ton Ton, the Dog Who Saved Hollywood (Par, 1976)
Super Seal (Key International, 1976)
Thunder on the Highway (20th, 1977)

ROBERT E. HOMANS

Humphrey Bogart, Robert E. Homans, Eddy Chandler, and Billy Wayne in Black Legion (1936).

Born November 8, 1874, Malden, Massachusetts. Died July 28, 1947, Los Angeles, California. Had a string of guises in silents: *Pals in Peril* (sheriff), *The Masked Angel* (detective), *Smiling Irish Eyes* (Colleen Moore's dad). Was white-haired and sour-faced in talkies; mostly played a cop.

Robert E. Homans to Eddy Waller in *Night Monster*: "Now where are we going to find a man who'd leave bare footprints the size of these?"

Films

Legally Dead (Univ, 1923)
The Breathless Moment (Univ, 1924)
Dark Stairways (Univ, 1924)
Border Justice (Independent, 1925)
The Bandit Buster (Pathé, 1926)
College Days (Tif, 1926)

The Silent Power (Lumas, 1926)
Heroes of the Night (Lumas, 1927)
The Galloping Gobs (Pathé, 1927)
Pals in Peril (Pathé, 1927)
The Fightin' Come Back (Pathé, 1927)
The Princess from Hoboken (Tif, 1927)

Mountains of Manhattan (Lumas, 1927)
Range Courage (Univ, 1927)
The Silent Avenger (Hollywood Pictures, 1927)
Ride 'em High (Pathé, 1927)
Fast and Furious (MGM, 1927)

The Masked Angel (Chadwick Pictures, 1928)
Burning the Wind (Univ, 1928)
Obey Your Husband (Anchor, 1928)
Blindford (Fox, 1928)
Fury of the Wild (RKO, 1929)
Smiling Irish Eyes (FN, 1929)
The Isle of Lost Ships (FN, 1929)
Check and Double Check (RKO, 1930)
Son of the Gods (FN, 1930)
The Lottery Bride (UA, 1930)
Spurs (Univ, 1930)
The Thoroughbred (Tif, 1930)
The Concentratin' Kid (Univ, 1930)
Trigger Tricks (Univ, 1930)
Lightning Flyer (Col, 1931)
Clearing the Range (Capital Films, 1931)
The Drums of Jeopardy (Tif, 1931)
The Black Camel (Fox, 1931)
Silence (Par, 1931)
Alias the Bad Man (Tif, 1931)
Under-Cover Man (Par, 1932)
Madame Racketeer (Par, 1932)
Young America (Fox, 1932)
Son of Oklahoma (WW, 1932)
She Done Him Wrong (Par, 1933)
Have a Heart (MGM, 1934)
The Silver Streak (RKO, 1934)
The Woman in Red (FN, 1935)
The Whole Town's Talking (Col, 1935)
Ship Cafe (Par, 1935)
Suicide Squad (Puritan, 1935)
Here Comes Trouble (20th, 1936)
Laughing Irish Eyes (Rep, 1936)
The Bridge of Sighs (Invincible, 1936)
Easy Money (Invincible, 1936)
It Couldn't Have Happened (Invincible, 1936)
The President's Mystery (Rep, 1936)
Women Are Trouble (MGM, 1936)
Below the Deadline (Chesterfield, 1936)
Sworn Enemy (MGM, 1936)
Black Legion (WB, 1936)
The Singing Marine (WB, 1937)
The Plough and the Stars (RKO, 1936)
Girl Overboard (Univ, 1937)
Penrod and Sam (WB, 1937)
Easy Living (Par, 1937)

Jim Hanvey—Detective (Rep, 1937)
The Thirteenth Man (Mon, 1937)
Dance, Charlie, Dance (WB, 1937)
Forlorn River (Par, 1937)
Gold Is Where You Find It (WB, 1938)
The Devil's Party (Univ, 1938)
Hollywood Stadium Mystery (Rep, 1938)
Over the Wall (WB, 1938)
The Kid Comes Back (WB, 1938)
Gold Mine in the Sky (Rep, 1938)
The Amazing Dr. Clitterhouse (WB, 1938)
Little Miss Thoroughbred (WB, 1938)
Night Hawk (Rep, 1938)
Heart of the North (WB, 1938)
Crashin' Through Danger (Excelsior, 1938)
Slander House (Progressive Pictures, 1938)
Angels with Dirty Faces (WB, 1938)
Letter of Introduction (Univ, 1938)
Young Mr. Lincoln (20th, 1939)
Dodge City (WB, 1939)
Yes, My Darling Daughter (WB, 1939)
Hell's Kitchen (WB, 1939)
Smuggled Cargo (Rep, 1939)
Let Us Live! (Col, 1939)
Here I Am a Stranger (20th, 1939)
The Grapes of Wrath (20th, 1940)
Virginia City (WB, 1940)
West of Carson City (Univ, 1940)
A Dispatch from Reuters (WB, 1940)
Lillian Russell (20th, 1940)
I Take This Oath (PRC, 1940)
Son of Roaring Dan (Univ, 1940)
Beyond Tomorrow (RKO, 1940)
East of the River (WB, 1940)
Barnyard Follies (Rep, 1940)
The Bowery Boy (Rep, 1940)
The Lady with Red Hair (WB, 1940)
Back Street (Univ, 1941)
Whistling in the Dark (MGM, 1941)
Honky Tonk (MGM, 1941)
Blues in the Night (WB, 1941)
It Started with Eve (Univ, 1941)
Mr. Dynamite (Univ, 1941)
You'll Never Get Rich (Col, 1941)
The Gang's All Here (Mon, 1941)

Flight from Destiny (WB, 1941)
Out of the Fog (WB, 1941)
The Getaway (MGM, 1941)
Sierra Sue (Rep, 1941)
Red River Valley (Rep, 1941)
Holiday Inn (Par, 1942)
North to the Klondike (Univ, 1942)
Joe Smith, American (MGM, 1942)
Fingers at the Window (MGM, 1942)
It Happened in Flatbush (20th, 1942)
Night Monster (Univ, 1942)
The Sombrero Kid (Rep, 1942)
Lady in a Jam (Univ, 1942)
X Marks the Spot (Rep, 1942)
I Married a Witch (UA, 1942)
Sweet Rosie O'Grady (20th, 1943)
No Time for Love (Par, 1943)
After Midnight with Boston Blackie (Col, 1943)
You Can't Beat the Law (Mon, 1943)
It Ain't Hay (Univ, 1943)
Shanty Town (Rep, 1943)
Murder in Times Square (Col, 1943)
Jack London (UA, 1943)
Frontier Badmen (Univ, 1943)
It Happened Tomorrow (UA, 1944)
The Adventures of Mark Twain (WB, 1944)
Make Your Own Bed (WB, 1944)
Pin-Up Girl (20th, 1944)
The Whistler (Col, 1944)
The Merry Monahans (Univ, 1944)
Louisiana Hayride (Col, 1944)
Can't Help Singing (Univ, 1944)
Music in Manhattan (RKO, 1944)
The Thin Man Goes Home (MGM, 1944)
The Impatient Years (Col, 1944)
Rogues Gallery (PRC, 1945)
Scarlet Clue (Mon, 1945)
A Medal for Benny (Par, 1945)
Captain Eddie (20th, 1945)
River Gang (Univ, 1945)
Earl Carroll Sketchbook (Rep, 1946)
The Strange Love of Martha Ivers (Par, 1946)
Girl on the Spot (Univ, 1946)

OSCAR HOMOLKA

In I Remember Mama *(1948).*

Born August 12, 1898, Vienna, Austria. Married 1) Grete Mosheim; divorced; 2) Baroness Vally Hatvany; widowed; 3) Florence Meyer, children: Vincent, Laurence; divorced; 4) Joan Tetzel (1949); widowed (1977). Died January 27, 1978, Sussex, England. Thickset, heavy-accented player. A veteran of Max Reinhardt's Viennese stage company and of many New York and London stage productions. Oscar-nominated for his Uncle Chris in *I Remember Mama* (but lost BSAAA to Walter Huston of *The Treasure of the Sierra Madre*). Gave vigor to Audrey Hepburn's *War and Peace* (General Kutuzov). Played Harry Palmer's (Michael Caine's) cunning adversary, Colonel Stok, the Russian intelligence officer in *Funeral in Berlin* and *The Billion Dollar Brain*. Has sometimes acted with his fourth wife, Joan Tetzel, on screen (*Joy in the Morning*) and on TV ("The Legendary Curse of the Hope Diamond").

> **Oscar Homolka** to Ray Milland and Barry Fitzgerald in *Ebb Tide:* "I ain't afraid of the devil himself; once I get a guard-deck under my feet again!"

Films

Dreyfus (Ger, 1930)
Hokuspokus (Ger, 1930)
Der weg nach Rio (Ger, 1931)
Im Geheimdienst (Ger, 1931)
Nachtkolonne (Ger, 1931)
1914, Die Letzten Tage vor dem Weltbrand (Ger, 1931)
Zwischen nacht und Morgen (Ger, 1931)
Die Nachte von Port Said (Par Ger, 1932)
Moral und Liebe (Ger, 1933)
Spione am Werk (Ger, 1933)

Unsichtbare Gegner (Austrian, 1933)
Rhodes (Br, 1935)
Sabotage [a.k.a. *The Woman Alone*] (Br, 1936)
Everything Is Thunder (Br, 1936)
Ebb Tide (Par, 1937)
Hidden Power (Col, 1937)
Seven Sinners (Univ, 1940)
Comrade X (MGM, 1940)
The Invisible Woman (Univ, 1941)
Rage in Heaven (MGM, 1941)

Ball of Fire (RKO, 1941)
Mission to Moscow (WB, 1943)
Hostages (Par, 1943)
The Code of Scotland Yard (Rep, 1947)
The Shop at Sly Corner (Br, 1947)
I Remember Mama (RKO, 1948)
Anna Lucasta (Col, 1949)
The White Flower (RKO, 1950)
Top Secret [a.k.a. *Mr. Potts Goes to Moscow*] (Br, 1952)
The House of the Arrow (Br, 1953)

Prisoner of War (MGM, 1954)	*Boys' Night Out* (MGM, 1962)	*The Billion Dollar Brain* (UA, 1967)
The Seven-Year Itch (20th, 1955)	*The Wonderful World of the Brothers Grimm* (MGM, 1962)	*The Madwoman of Chaillot* (WB–7 Arts, 1969)
War and Peace (Par, 1956)	*The Long Ships* (Col, 1964)	*Assignment to Kill* (WB–7 Arts, 1969)
A Farewell to Arms (20th, 1957)	*Joy in the Morning* (MGM, 1965)	*The Executioner* (Col, 1970)
The Key (Col, 1958)	*Funeral in Berlin* (Par, 1966)	*Song of Norway* (Cin, 1970)
Tempest (Par, 1958)	*The Happening* (Col, 1967)	*The Tamarind Seed* (Avco Emb, 1974)
Mr. Sardonicus (Col, 1961)		

ARTHUR HOYT

With Glenda Farrell in Kansas City Princess *(1934).*

Born March 19, 1873, Georgetown, Colorado. Died January 5, 1953, Woodland Hills, California. Hard-working actor in dozens of silents and talkies: Professor Summerlee in Wallace Beery's *The Lost World*, Mr. Planet in *The Devil and the Deep*, Dr. Meeker in *20,000 Years in Sing Sing*, Ward in Janet Gaynor's *A Star Is Born*, etc. In the 1940s, was a member of Preston Sturges' funster stock company at Paramount.

Arthur Hoyt to Blanche Friderici in *It Happened One Night*:
"But he *looked* like a nice upright young fella', Ma."

Films

Love Never Dies (Univ, 1916)	*Unto the End* (Tri, 1919)	*Don't Neglect Your Wife* (G, 1921)
A Stranger from Somewhere (Univ, 1916)	*Cowardice Court* (Fox, 1919)	*Camille* (M, 1921)
The Devil's Bondwoman (Univ, 1916)	*The Grim Game* (Par, 1919)	*Red Courage* (Univ, 1921)
Little Partner (Univ, 1916)	*The Triflers* (Univ, 1920)	*The Four Horsemen of the Apocalypse* (M, 1921)
The Man Who Took a Chance (Univ, 1917)	*The Girl in No. 29* (Univ, 1920)	*The Foolish Age* (FBO, 1921)
Bringing Home Father (Univ, 1917)	*Nurse Marjorie* (Par, 1920)	*The Understudy* (FBO, 1922)
The Show Down (Univ, 1917)	*The Desperate Hero* (Selznick, 1920)	*Is Matrimony a Failure?* (Par, 1922)
Mr. Opp (Univ, 1917)	*Trumpet Island* (Vit, 1920)	*Little Wildcat* (Vit, 1922)
The Yellow Dog (Univ, 1918)	*A Slave of Vanity* (Robertson-Cole, 1920)	*Kissed* (Univ, 1922)

The Stranger's Banquet (G, 1922)
Love Is an Awful Thing (Selznick, 1922)
Too Much Wife (Par, 1922)
Restless Souls (Vit, 1922)
The Top of New York (Par, 1922)
Souls for Sale (G, 1923)
The Love Piker (G, 1923)
An Old Sweetheart of Mine (M, 1923)
To the Ladies (Par, 1923)
The White Flower (Par, 1923)
Daring Youth (Principle, 1923)
Her Marriage Vow (WB, 1923)
Bluff (Par, 1924)
The Dangerous Blonde (Univ, 1924)
Do It Now (G, 1924)
Sundown (Associated FN, 1924)
When a Man's a Man (Associated FN, 1924)
Any Woman (Par, 1925)
The Sporting Venus (MG, 1925)
Eve's Lover (WB, 1925)
The Coming of Amos (PDC, 1925)
Head Winds (Univ, 1925)
The Lost World (FN, 1925)
Private Affairs (PDC, 1925)
The Midnight Sun (Univ, 1926)
Footloose Widows (WB, 1926)
Dangerous Friends (Sterling, 1926)
The Gilded Butterfly (Fox, 1926)
For Wives Only (PDC, 1926)
The Crown of Lies (Par, 1926)
Monte Carlo (MGM, 1926)
The Danger Girl (PDC, 1926)
Eve's Leaves (PDC, 1926)
Up in Mabel's Room (PDC, 1926)
The Love Thrill (Univ, 1927)
The Rejuvenation of Aunt Mary (PDC, 1927)
An Affair of the Follies (FN, 1927)
The Mysterious Rider (Par, 1927)
Shanghai Bound (Par, 1927)
Husbands for Rent (WB, 1927)
Tillie the Toiler (MGM, 1927)
Ten Modern Commandments (Par, 1927)
A Texas Steer (FN, 1927)
Just Married (Par, 1928)
My Man (WB, 1928)
Home James (Univ, 1928)
The Wheel of Life (Par, 1929)
Her Private Affair (Pathe, 1929)
Stolen Kisses (WB, 1929)
Protection (Fox, 1929)

Along Came Youth (Par, 1930)
Extravagance (Tif, 1930)
Seven Days' Leave (Par, 1930)
Dumbbells in Ermine (WB, 1930)
Going Wild (WB, 1930)
The Life of the Party (WB, 1930)
Night Work (Pathe, 1930)
The Criminal Code (Col, 1931)
The Flood (Col, 1931)
Inspiration (MGM, 1931)
Gold Dust Gertie (WB, 1931)
Peach o' Reno (RKO, 1931)
Impatient Maiden (Univ, 1932)
Love in High Gear (Mayfair, 1932)
Washington Masquerade (MGM, 1932)
American Madness (Col, 1932)
The Devil and the Deep (Par, 1932)
Dynamite Ranch (WW, 1932)
Madame Racketeer (Par, 1932)
Make Me a Star (Par, 1932)
The Crusader (Majestic, 1932)
Washington Merry-Go-Round (Col, 1932)
Red-Haired Alibi (Tower, 1932)
Vanity Street (Col, 1932)
Call Her Savage (Fox, 1932)
The All-American (Univ, 1932)
20,000 Years in Sing Sing (FN, 1933)
Dangerously Yours (Fox, 1933)
Daring Daughters (Capitol, 1933)
The Eleventh Commandment (Alliance, 1933)
Pleasure Cruise (Fox, 1933)
Goldie Gets Along (RKO, 1933)
His Private Secretary (Showman's Pictures, 1933)
A Shriek in the Night (Allied Pictures, 1933)
Shanghai Madness (Fox, 1933)
Sing, Sinner, Sing (Majestic, 1933)
Only Yesterday (Univ, 1933)
In the Money (Chesterfield, 1933)
The Meanest Gal in Town (RKO, 1934)
Million Dollar Ransom (Univ, 1934)
Springtime for Henry (Fox, 1934)
Uncertain Lady (Univ, 1934)
Unknown Blonde (Majestic, 1934)
Let's Try Again (RKO, 1934)
The Notorious Sophie Lang (Par, 1934)
Kansas City Princess (WB, 1934)
College Rhythm (Par, 1934)
Wake Up and Dream (Univ, 1934)

When Strangers Meet (Liberty, 1934)
Babbitt (FN, 1934)
One Hour Late (Par, 1934)
No Ransom (Liberty, 1934)
A Night at the Ritz (WB, 1935)
Murder on a Honeymoon (RKO, 1935)
Chinatown Squad (Univ, 1935)
The Raven (Univ, 1935)
Men of Action (Conn Pictures, 1935)
Welcome Home (Fox, 1935)
$1,000 a Minute (Rep, 1935)
Magnificent Obsession (Univ, 1935)
Mr. Deeds Goes to Town (Col, 1936)
Early to Bed (Par, 1936)
Pennies from Heaven (Col, 1936)
Poor Little Rich Girl (20th, 1936)
Walking on Air (RKO, 1936)
M'liss (RKO, 1936)
Lady Luck (Chesterfield, 1936)
Paradise Express (Rep, 1937)
Easy Living (Par, 1937)
Join the Marines (Rep, 1937)
A Star Is Born (UA, 1937)
Ever Since Eve (WB, 1937)
It's All Yours (Col, 1937)
The Westland Case (Univ, 1937)
The Wrong Road (Rep, 1937)
She's No Lady (Par, 1937)
Love Takes Flight (GN, 1937)
The Cowboy and the Lady (UA, 1938)
The Rage of Paris (Univ, 1938)
Start Cheering (Col, 1938)
Hard to Get (WB, 1938)
The Black Doll (Univ, 1938)
You and Me (Par, 1938)
The Devil's Party (Univ, 1938)
The Sisters (WB, 1938)
Girls on Probation (WB, 1938)
East Side of Heaven (Univ, 1939)
Should Husbands Work? (Rep, 1939)
I Love You Again (MGM, 1940)
The Great McGinty (Par, 1940)
The Lady Eve (Par, 1941)
The Palm Beach Story (Par, 1942)
The Miracle of Morgan's Creek (Par, 1944)
Hail the Conquering Hero (Par, 1944)
Mad Wednesday [a.k.a. *The Sin of Harold Diddlebock*] (UA, 1947)
My Favorite Brunette (Par, 1947)
Brute Force (Univ, 1947)

HAROLD HUBER

Harold Huber, Frances Dee, and Edward Ellis in A Man Betrayed *(1941).*

Born 1910, New York City, New York. Married Ethel _____, child: Margaret. Died September 29, 1959, New York City, New York. Swarthy-complexioned, sinister-appearing man who was recurringly a screen nasty: *20,000 Years in Sing Sing* (Tony), *The Thin Man* (Nunheim), *The Defense Rests* (Castro), *G-Men* (Venke), *Klondike Annie* (Chan Lo), etc. Was on the right side of the law in several *Charlie Chan* entries: *Charlie Chan at Monte Carlo* (French police inspector), *Charlie Chan In Rio* (Chief Souto), etc. Also in some of the *Mr. Moto* series: *Mr. Moto's Gamble* (Lieutenant Riggs), etc. Was Toctai *(The Adventures of Marco Polo)*, Cousin *(The Good Earth)*, Voisin *(Beau Geste)*, etc.

> **Harold Huber** to Warner Oland in *Charlie Chan at Monte Carlo:* "The eyes all night long they have not shut up. I am very depressing."

Films

The Match King (FN, 1932)
Central Park (FN, 1932)
Lawyer Man (WB, 1932)
Parachute Jumper (WB, 1933)
20,000 Years in Sing Sing (FN, 1933)
Frisco Jenny (FN, 1933)
Ladies They Talk About (WB, 1933)
Girl Missing (WB, 1933)
Central Airport (WB, 1933)
Midnight Mary (MGM, 1933)
The Life of Jimmy Dolan (WB, 1933)
The Mayor of Hell (WB, 1933)
The Silk Express (WB, 1933)
Mary Stevens, M.D. (WB, 1933)
Police Car 17 (Col, 1933)
The Bowery (UA, 1933)
Hi, Nellie! (WB, 1934)
Fury of the Jungle (Col, 1934)
No More Women (Par, 1934)
The Line-Up (Col, 1934)
The Crosby Case (Univ, 1934)

A Very Honorable Guy (FN, 1934)
He Was Her Man (WB, 1934)
The Thin Man (MGM, 1934)
The Defense Rests (Col, 1934)
Hide-Out (MGM, 1934)
Cheating Cheaters (Univ, 1934)
Port of Lost Dreams (Chesterfield, 1934)
Naughty Marietta (MGM, 1935)
One New York Night (MGM, 1935)
Mad Love (MGM, 1935)
Pursuit (MGM, 1935)
G-Men (FN, 1935)
Klondike Annie (Par, 1936)
We're Only Human (RKO, 1936)
Muss 'em Up (RKO, 1936)
Kelly the Second (MGM, 1936)
San Francisco (MGM, 1936)
Women Are Trouble (MGM, 1936)
The Devil Is a Sissy (MGM, 1936)
The Gay Desperado (UA, 1936)
The Good Earth (MGM, 1937)

Trouble in Morocco (Col, 1937)
Midnight Taxi (20th, 1937)
Angel's Holiday (20th, 1937)
You Can't Beat Love (RKO, 1937)
Outlaws of the Orient (Col, 1937)
Charlie Chan at Monte Carlo (20th, 1937)
Charlie Chan on Broadway (20th, 1937)
Mr. Moto's Gamble (20th, 1938)
A Slight Case of Murder (WB, 1938)
The Adventures of Marco Polo (UA, 1938)
International Settlement (20th, 1938)
Gangs of New York (Rep, 1938)
Passport Husband (20th, 1938)
A Trip to Paris (20th, 1938)
Going Places (WB, 1938)
Little Tough Guys in Society (Univ, 1938)
Mysterious Mr. Moto in Danger Island (20th, 1938)
While New York Sleeps (20th, 1939)
You Can't Get Away with Murder (WB, 1939)

King of the Turf (UA, 1939)
The Lady and the Mob (Col, 1939)
Chasing Danger (20th, 1939)
6,000 Enemies (MGM, 1939)
Main Street Lawyer (Rep, 1939)
Beau Geste (Par, 1939)
Charlie Chan in City in Darkness (20th, 1939)
Charlie McCarthy, Detective (Univ, 1939)

Dance, Girl, Dance (RKO, 1940)
Kit Carson (UA, 1940)
The Ghost Comes Home (MGM, 1940)
A Man Betrayed [a.k.a. Wheel of Fortune] (Rep, 1941)
Country Fair (Rep, 1941)
Charlie Chan in Rio (20th, 1941)
Down Mexico Way (Rep, 1941)
A Gentleman After Dark (UA, 1942)

Sleepytime Gal (Rep, 1942)
Little Tokyo, USA (20th, 1942)
Manila Calling (20th, 1942)
The Lady from Chungking (PRC, 1942)
Ice-Capades Revue ((Rep, 1942)
Crime Doctor (Col, 1943)
My Friend Irma Goes West (Par, 1950)
Let's Dance (Par, 1950)

HENRY HULL

With Rosalind Russell in Mourning Becomes Electra *(1947).*

Born October 3, 1890, Louisville, Kentucky. Married Juliet van Wyck Fremont (1913), children: Henry, another son, daughter. Died March 8, 1977, Cornwall, England. Respected stage player who starred in silent films: *The Hoosier School Master* (title role), *The Wrongdoers* (ward of Lionel Barrymore). Gaunt, sometimes grizzly character lead—in the John Carradine tradition—in sound era: *The Werewolf of London* (as the mad scientist), *Three Comrades* (Dr. Heinrich Becker), *Jesse James* and *The Return of Frank James* (Major Rufus Todd), *Portrait of Jennie* (Eke), *The Chase* (Briggs), etc.

Henry Hull dictating an editorial to George Chandler in *Jesse James:* "If we are ever to have law and order in the West, the first thing we've got to do is to take out all the lawyers and shoot 'em down like dogs!"

Films

The Volunteer (World, 1918)
One Exciting Night (UA, 1922)
The Last Moment (G, 1923)
A Bride for a Knight (Renown Pictures, 1923)

For Woman's Favor (Art-Lee, 1924)
The Hoosier School Master (PDC, 1924)
Roulette (Selznick, 1924)
Wasted Lives (Second National, 1925)
The Wrongdoers (Astor, 1925)

The Man Who Came Back (Fox, 1931)
Midnight (Univ, 1934)
Great Expectations (Univ, 1934)
The Werewolf of London (Univ, 1935)
Transient Lady (Univ, 1935)

Paradise for Three (MGM, 1938)
Yellow Jack (MGM, 1938)
Three Comrades (MGM, 1938)
Boys Town (MGM, 1938)
The Great Waltz (MGM, 1938)
Jesse James (20th, 1939)
The Return of the Cisco Kid (20th, 1939)
Stanley and Livingstone (20th, 1939)
Spirit of Culver (Univ, 1939)
Miracles for Sale (MGM, 1939)
Babes in Arms (MGM, 1939)
Bad Little Angel (MGM, 1939)
Nick Carter, Master Detective (MGM, 1939)
Judge Hardy and Son (MGM, 1939)
My Son, My Son (UA, 1940)
The Return of Frank James (20th, 1940)
The Ape (Mon, 1940)
High Sierra (WB, 1941)
Queen of Broadway (PRC, 1942)

What a Man (Mon, 1943)
The Woman of the Town (UA, 1943)
The West Side Kid (Rep, 1943)
Lifeboat (20th, 1944)
Goodnight, Sweetheart (Rep, 1944)
Voodoo Man (Mon, 1944)
Objective, Burma! (WB, 1945)
Deep Valley (WB, 1947)
High Barbaree (MGM, 1947)
Mourning Becomes Electra (RKO, 1947)
Scudda Hoo! Scudda Hay! (20th, 1948)
The Walls of Jericho (20th, 1948)
Belle Starr's Daughter (20th, 1948)
Portrait of Jenny (Selznick Releasing Organization, 1948)
Fighter Squadron (WB, 1948)
The Fountainhead (WB, 1949)
Song of Surrender (Par, 1949)
Colorado Territory (WB, 1949)
El Paso (Par, 1949)

Rimfire (Screen Guild, 1949)
The Great Dan Patch (UA, 1949)
The Great Gatsby (Par, 1949)
The Return of Jesse James (Lip, 1950)
The Hollywood Story (Col, 1951)
Treasure of Lost Canyon (Univ, 1952)
The Last Posse (Col, 1953)
Inferno (20th, 1953)
Thunder over the Plains (WB, 1953)
Man with the Gun (UA, 1955)
Buckskin Lady (UA, 1957)
The Sheriff of Fractured Jaw (20th, 1958)
The Buccaneer (Par, 1958)
The Proud Rebel (BV, 1958)
The Oregon Trail (20th, 1959)
Master of the World (AIP, 1961)
The Fool Killer [a.k.a. Violent Journey] (Landau, 1965)
The Chase (Col, 1966)
Covenant with Death (WB, 1967)

BRANDON HURST

Brandon Hurst and Victor McLaglen in The Lost Patrol *(1934).*

Born November 30, 1866, London, England. Died July 15, 1947, Hollywood, California. Made a strong impact as Jehan, the evil master/betrayer of Quasimodo (Lon Chaney) in *The Hunchback of Notre Dame*; was the caliph in *The Thief of Bagdad*; the unyielding but wronged husband Karenin in Greta Garbo's *Love*, etc. Smaller roles in talkies: *The Greene Murder Case* (Sproot), *Murders in the Rue Morgue* (prefect of police), *White Zombie* (Silvers), *The Lost Patrol* (Bell), *Mary of Scotland* (Arian), *The Corn Is Green* (Lewellyn Powell), etc.

> **Brandon Hurst** in *The House of Frankenstein:* "The jugular vein is severed, not cut, but torn apart as though by powerful teeth."

296

Films

Via Wireless (Pathé, 1915)

Legally Dead (Univ, 1923)

The Hunchback of Notre Dame (Univ, 1923)

The World's Applause (Par, 1923)

Cytherea (Associated FN, 1924)

The Lover of Camille (WB, 1924)

He Who Gets Slapped (MG, 1924)

One Night in Rome (MG, 1924)

The Thief of Bagdad (UA, 1924)

The Silent Watcher (Associated FN, 1924)

Lightnin' (Fox, 1925)

The Lady (FN, 1925)

The Enchanted Hill (Par, 1926)

The Lady of the Harem (Par, 1926)

The Amateur Gentleman (FN, 1926)

The Grand Duchess and the Waiter (Par, 1926)

Paris at Midnight (PDC, 1926)

Made for Love (PDC, 1926)

Secret Orders (FBO, 1926)

The Rainmaker (Par, 1926)

The Shamrock Handicap (Fox, 1926)

Volcano (Par, 1926)

High School Hero (Fox, 1927)

Annie Laurie (MGM, 1927)

Love (MGM, 1927)

The King of Kings (Par, 1927)

Seventh Heaven (Fox, 1927)

The Man Who Laughs (Univ, 1928)

The News Parade (Fox, 1928)

Her Private Life (FN, 1929)

The Greene Murder Case (Par, 1929)

Interference (Par, 1929)

The Wolf of Wall Street (Par, 1929)

The Voice of the Storm (RKO, 1929)

High Society Blues (Fox, 1930)

The Eyes of the World (UA, 1930)

A Connecticut Yankee (Fox, 1931)

Right of Way (FN, 1931)

Young as You Feel (Fox, 1931)

Murder at Midnight (Tif, 1931)

Murders in the Rue Morgue (Univ, 1932)

Midnight Lady (Chesterfield, 1932)

Down to Earth (Fox, 1932)

White Zombie (UA, 1932)

Sherlock Holmes (Fox, 1932)

The Lost Patrol (RKO, 1934)

Bombay Mail (Univ, 1934)

Bright Eyes (Fox, 1934)

Crimson Romance (Mascot, 1934)

Sequoia (MGM, 1934)

Red Morning (RKO, 1934)

While the Patient Slept (WB, 1935)

Woman in Red (FN, 1935)

The Great Impersonation (Univ, 1935)

The Moon's Our Home (Par, 1936)

The Charge of the Light Brigade (WB, 1936)

Mary of Scotland (RKO, 1936)

The Plough and the Stars (RKO, 1936)

Maid of Salem (Par, 1937)

Wee Willie Winkie (20th, 1937)

Four Men and a Prayer (20th, 1938)

If I Were King (Par, 1938)

Suez (20th, 1938)

Professor Beware (Par, 1938)

The Adventures of Sherlock Holmes (20th, 1939)

Stanley and Livingstone (20th, 1939)

The Sun Never Sets (Univ, 1939)

The Blue Bird (20th, 1940)

If I Had My Way (Univ, 1940)

Rhythm on the River (Par, 1940)

The Road to Happiness (Mon, 1942)

The Remarkable Andrew (Par, 1942)

Dixie (Par, 1943)

The Adventures of Mark Twain (WB, 1944)

Barbary Coast Gent (MGM, 1944)

The Man in Half Moon Street (Par, 1944)

The Princess and the Pirate (RKO, 1944)

Jane Eyre (20th, 1944)

The House of Frankenstein (Univ, 1944)

The Corn Is Green (WB, 1945)

Devotion (WB, 1946)

Sister Kenny (RKO, 1946)

Road to Rio (Par, 1947)

PAUL HURST

In Island in the Sky *(1938).*

Born 1888, Tulare County, California. Died February 27, 1953, Hollywood, California. First a script-writer, director, and actor in 1910s Westerns; wrote the scenarios for some of his 1920s films (*Table Top Ranch* and *Rangeland*). Among the serials he directed or co-directed were *Lass of the Lumberlands, Lightning Bryce,* and *The Tiger's Trail.* Alternated between bad and (comedy) good-guy roles; distinctive speaking voice a marked asset in talkies. Played Dr. Meadowlark in the Monte Hale Westerns at Republic. Vividly recalled as the marauding Yankee soldier shot by Vivien Leigh on the stairs of Tara in *Gone with the Wind.* Last role was as Sergeant Jimmy Bagby in John Ford's *The Sun Shines Bright.*

> **Paul Hurst** to Warren William in *The Case of the Curious Bride:*
> "That girl had a great future—one of the best in the badger game."

Films

The Tragedy of Bear Mountain (Kalem, 1915)
The Girl Detective (Kalem, 1915)
The Figure in Black (Kalem, 1915)
When Thieves Fall Out (Kalem, 1915)
Stingaree (Kalem, 1915)
The Corsican Sisters (Kalem, 1915)
The Parasite (Kalem, 1915)
Social Pirates (Kalem, 1915)
Whispering Smith (Mustang, 1915)
Judith of the Cumberlands (Mutual, 1916)
The Manager of the B & A (Mutual, 1916)
Medicine Bend (American, 1916)
Lass of the Lumberland (Mutual serial, 1916)

The Railroad Raiders (Mutual serial, 1917)
Play Straight or Fight (Univ, 1918)
Smashing Through (Univ, 1918)
Lightning Bryce (Arrow serial, 1919)
Shadows of the West (Cinema Craft, 1920)
Black Sheep (Pinnacle Pictures, 1921)
The Crow's Nest (Aywon, 1922)
The King Fischer's Roost (Pinnacle, 1922)
The Heart of a Texan (Steiner, 1922)
Rangeland (Steiner, 1922)
Table Top Ranch (Steiner, 1922)
Golden Silence (Sylvanite Productions, 1922)
The Courageous Coward (Sable, 1924)

Branded a Bandit (Arrow, 1924)
The Passing of Wolf MacLean (Ermine, 1924)
Battling Bunyan (Associated Exhibitors, 1924)
The Fighting Cub (Truart, 1925)
The High Hand (Pathé, 1926)
The Outlaw Express (Pathé, 1926)
Buttons (MGM, 1927)
The Devil's Saddle (FN, 1927)
The Man from Hard Pan (Rayart, 1927)
The Range Riders (Rayart, 1927)
The Overland Stage (FN, 1927)
The Red Raiders (FN, 1927)
The Valley of the Giants (FN, 1927)
The Cossacks (MGM, 1928)

The California Mail (FN, 1929)
Oh, Yeah! (Pathé, 1929)
The Lawless Legion (FN, 1929)
The Rainbow (Tif, 1929)
The Racketeer (Pathé, 1929)
Tide of Empire (MGM, 1929)
Sailor's Holiday (Pathé, 1929)
Borrowed Wives (Tif, 1930)
Lucky Larkin (Univ, 1930)
Hot Curves (Tif, 1930)
Officer O'Brien (Pathé, 1930)
Mountain Justice (Univ, 1930)
Runaway Bride (RKO, 1930)
Paradise Island (Tif, 1930)
Shadow of the Law (Par, 1930)
The Swellhead (Tif, 1930)
His First Command (Pathé, 1930)
The Third Alarm (Tif, 1930)
The Single Sin (Tif, 1931)
The Secret Six (MGM, 1931)
Kick In (Par, 1931)
Sweepstakes (RKO, 1931)
The Public Defender (RKO, 1931)
Bad Company (Pathé, 1931)
Secret Witness [a.k.a. Terror by Night]
  (Col, 1931)
Panama Flo (RKO, 1932)
The Phantom President (Par, 1932)
The Thirteenth Guest (Mon, 1932)
Dancers in the Dark (Par, 1932)
Hold 'em Jail (RKO, 1932)
The Big Stampede (WB, 1932)
My Pal, the King (Univ, 1932)
Island of Lost Souls (Par, 1933)
Terror Aboard (Par, 1933)
Men Are Such Fools (RKO, 1933)
Hold Your Man (MGM, 1933)
Tugboat Annie (MGM, 1933)
The Sphinx (Mon, 1933)
Day of Reckoning (MGM, 1933)
Saturday's Millions (Univ, 1933)
Women in His Life (MGM, 1933)
Scarlet River (RKO, 1933)
The Big Race (Showmen's Pictures,
  1933)
Line-Up (Univ, 1934)
Midnight Alibi (FN, 1934)
Among the Missing (Col, 1934)
Take the Stand (Liberty, 1934)
Sequoia (MGM, 1934)
Tomorrow's Youth (Mon, 1935)
Wilderness Mail (Ambassador, 1935)
Shadow of Doubt (MGM, 1935)
Mississippi (Par, 1935)
Public Hero No. 1 (MGM, 1935)
Star of Midnight (RKO, 1935)
Calm Yourself (MGM, 1935)
The Gay Deception (Col, 1935)
Riffraff (MGM, 1935)
The Case of the Curious Bride (FN, 1935)
Robin Hood of Eldorado (MGM, 1936)
The Blackmailer (Col, 1936)

I'd Give My Life (Par, 1936)
To Mary—With Love (20th, 1936)
The Gay Desperado (UA, 1936)
It Had to Happen (20th, 1936)
We Who Are About to Die (RKO, 1936)
North of Nome (Col, 1936)
The Lady Fights Back (Univ, 1937)
Trouble in Morocco (Col, 1937)
Wake Up and Live (20th, 1937)
You Can't Beat Love (RKO, 1937)
Fifty Roads to Town (20th, 1937)
Angel's Holiday (20th, 1937)
This Is My Affair (20th, 1937)
Super-Sleuth (RKO, 1937)
Slave Ship (20th, 1937)
She's No Lady (Par, 1937)
Wife, Doctor and Nurse (20th, 1937)
Small Town Boy (GN, 1937)
Danger—Love at Work (20th, 1937)
Ali Baba Goes to Town (20th, 1937)
Second Honeymoon (20th, 1937)
In Old Chicago (20th, 1938)
No Time to Marry (Col, 1938)
Rebecca of Sunnybrook Farm (20th, 1938)
Josette (20th, 1938)
Alexander's Ragtime Band (20th, 1938)
Island in the Sky (20th, 1938)
Prison Break (Univ, 1938)
My Lucky Star (20th, 1938)
The Last Express (Univ, 1938)
Hold That Co-ed (20th, 1938)
Thanks for Everything (20th, 1939)
Secrets of a Nurse (Univ, 1938)
Topper Takes a Trip (UA, 1938)
Cafe Society (Par, 1939)
Broadway Serenade (MGM, 1939)
It Could Happen to You (Rep, 1939)
Each Dawn I Die (WB, 1939)
Remember? (MGM, 1939)
The Kid from Kokomo (WB, 1939)
Quick Millions (20th, 1939)
Bad Lands (RKO, 1939)
Gone with the Wind (MGM, 1939)
On Your Toes (WB, 1939)
Heaven with a Barbed Wire Fence (20th,
  1939)
Edison the Man (MGM, 1940)
Torrid Zone (WB, 1940)
They Drive by Night (WB, 1940)
South to Karanga (Univ, 1940)
The Westerner (UA, 1940)
Tugboat Annie Sails Again (WB, 1940)
Star Dust (20th, 1940)
Men Against the Sky (RKO, 1940)
Petticoat Politics (Rep, 1941)
Tall, Dark and Handsome (20th, 1941)
Virginia (Par, 1941)
Bowery Boy (Rep, 1941)
Caught in the Draft (Par, 1941)
The Parson of Panamint (Par, 1941)
Ellery Queen and the Murder Ring (Col,
  1941)

This Woman Is Mine (Univ, 1941)
The Great Mr. Nobody (WB, 1941)
Sundown Jim (20th, 1942)
A Night in New Orleans (Par, 1942)
Pardon My Stripes (Rep, 1942)
Dudes Are Pretty People (UA, 1942)
The Ox-Bow Incident (20th, 1943)
Hi Ya, Chum (Univ, 1943)
Young and Willing (UA, 1943)
Coney Island (20th, 1943)
Jack London (UA, 1943)
Calaboose (UA, 1943)
The Sky's the Limit (RKO, 1943)
Barbary Coast Gent (MGM, 1944)
The Ghost That Walks Alone (Col, 1944)
Girl Rush (RKO, 1944)
Summer Storm (UA, 1944)
Greenwich Village (20th, 1944)
Something for the Boys (20th, 1944)
The Big Showoff (Rep, 1945)
Dakota (Rep, 1945)
The Dolly Sisters (20th, 1945)
Penthouse Rhythm (Univ, 1945)
Nob Hill (20th, 1945)
Midnight Manhunt (Par, 1945)
Scared Stiff [a.k.a. Treasure of Fear] (Par,
  1945)
Steppin' in Society (Rep, 1945)
In Old Sacramento (Rep, 1946)
Murder in the Music Hall (Rep, 1946)
The Virginian (Par, 1946)
The Plainsman and the Lady (Rep, 1946)
Death Valley (Screen Guild, 1946)
Angel and the Badman (Rep, 1947)
Under Colorado Skies (Rep, 1947)
The Arizona Ranger (RKO, 1948)
California Firebrand (Rep, 1948)
Pride of Virginia (Rep, 1948)
Son of God's Country (Rep, 1948)
Gun Smugglers (RKO, 1948)
Yellow Sky (20th, 1948)
On Our Merry Way [a.k.a. A Miracle
  Can Happen] (UA, 1948)
Old Los Angeles (Rep, 1948)
Madonna of the Desert (Rep, 1948)
Law of the Golden West (Rep, 1949)
Prince of the Plains (Rep, 1949)
South of Rio (Rep, 1949)
Outcasts of the Trail (Rep, 1949)
Ranger of Cherokee Strip (Rep, 1949)
San Antone Ambush (Rep, 1949)
Pioneer Marshal (Rep, 1950)
The Vanishing Westerner (Rep, 1950)
The Old Frontier (Rep, 1950)
The Missourians (Rep, 1950)
Million Dollar Pursuit (Rep, 1951)
Big Jim McLain (WB, 1952)
The Toughest Man in Arizona (Rep,
  1952)
The Sun Shines Bright (Rep, 1953)

WARREN HYMER

Mae Clarke, Paul Kelly, and Warren Hymer in Silk Hat Kid *(1935).*

Born February 25, 1906, New York City, New York. Married 1) Beau Vasanta; divorced; 2) Virginia Meyer. Died March 25, 1948, Los Angeles, California. Dumb-looking, but astute enough to vary between comedy and heavy parts. Stereotyped as the dim witted, but soft-hearted cop (Steve Burke of *One Way Passage);* sometimes a vicious punk (Muggsy in *You Only Live Once*). Was St. Louis fighter (Mae West's *Belle of the Nineties*), and turned up in several Gary Cooper films: *Mr. Deeds Goes to Town* (bodyguard), *Bluebeard's Eighth Wife* (Kid Mulligan), and *Meet John Doe* (Angelface).

Warren Hymer to Henry Fonda in *You Only Live Once:* "Gee, Eddie, the old cell won't seem the same without you."

Films

Fox Movietone Follies of 1929 (Fox, 1929)
The Far Call (Fox, 1929)
The Girl from Havana (Fox, 1929)
Frozen Justice (Fox, 1929)
Speakeasy (Fox, 1929)
Born Reckless (WB, 1930)
The Lone Star Ranger (Fox, 1930)
Men Without Women (Fox, 1930)
Oh, For a Man! (Fox, 1930)
Up the River (Fox, 1930)
Sinners' Holiday (WB, 1930)
Charlie Chan Carries On (Fox, 1931)
Seas Beneath (Fox, 1931)
Men on Call (Fox, 1931)
Goldie (Fox, 1931)
The Spider (Fox, 1931)
The Unholy Garden (UA, 1931)
The Cockeyed World (Fox, 1931)
Love Is a Racket (FN, 1932)
Hold 'em Jail (RKO, 1932)
One Way Passage (WB, 1932)

The Night Mayor (Col, 1932)
Madison Square Garden (Par, 1932)
I Love That Man (Par, 1933)
Midnight Mary (MGM, 1933)
My Woman (Col, 1933)
Her First Mate (Univ, 1933)
20,000 Years in Sing Sing (FN, 1933)
The Billion Dollar Scandal (Par, 1933)
The Mysterious Rider (Par, 1933)
A Lady's Profession (Par, 1933)
In the Money (Chesterfield, 1933)
Woman Unafraid (Goldsmith Productions, 1934)
The Cat's Paw (Fox, 1934)
She Loves Me Not (Par, 1934)
Young and Beautiful (Mascot, 1934)
Kid Millions (UA, 1934)
King for a Night (Univ, 1934)
George White's Scandals (Fox, 1934)
The Crosby Case (Univ, 1934)
Belle of the Nineties (Par, 1934)

One Is Guilty (Col, 1934)
Little Miss Marker (Par, 1934)
Straight from the Heart (Univ, 1935)
Our Little Girl (Fox, 1935)
The Daring Young Man (Fox, 1935)
Silk Hat Kid (Fox, 1935)
Navy Wife [a.k.a. Beauty's Daughter] (Fox, 1935)
Hong Kong Nights (FN, 1935)
Hold 'em Yale (Par, 1935)
The Gilded Lily (Par, 1935)
The Case of the Curious Bride (FN, 1935)
She Gets Her Man (Univ, 1935)
Confidential (Mascot, 1935)
Show Them No Mercy (Fox, 1935)
Hitchhike Lady (Rep, 1935)
Tango (Invincible, 1936)
Desert Justice (Atlantic, 1936)
The Widow from Monte Carlo (WB, 1936)
The Leavenworth Case (Rep, 1936)
Laughing Irish Eyes (Rep, 1936)

Everybody's Old Man (20th, 1936)
Thirty-Six Hours to Kill (20th, 1936)
Mr. Deeds Goes to Town (Col, 1936)
San Francisco (MGM, 1936)
Rhythm on the Range (Par, 1936)
Nobody's Fool (Univ, 1936)
Love Letters of a Star (Univ, 1936)
You Only Live Once (UA, 1937)
Join the Marines (Rep, 1937)
We Have Our Moments (Univ, 1937)
Navy Blues (Rep, 1937)
Meet the Boy Friend (Rep, 1937)
Sea Racketeers (Rep, 1937)
Wake Up and Live (20th, 1937)
Ali Baba Goes to Town (20th, 1937)
Married Before Breakfast (MGM, 1937)
Bad Guy (MGM, 1937)
She's Dangerous (Univ, 1937)
Lady Behave (Rep, 1938)
Arson Gang Busters (Rep, 1938)

Joy of Living (RKO, 1938)
Gateway (20th, 1938)
Submarine Patrol (20th, 1938)
Telephone Operator (Mon, 1938)
Thanks for Everything (20th, 1938)
Bluebeard's Eighth Wife (Par, 1938)
You and Me (Par, 1938)
The Lady and the Mob (Col, 1939)
Coast Guard (Col, 1939)
The Boy Friend (20th, 1939)
Calling All Marines (Rep, 1939)
Destry Rides Again (Univ, 1939)
Charlie McCarthy, Detective (Univ, 1939)
Mr. Moto in Danger Island (20th, 1939)
I Can't Give You Anything but Love, Baby (Univ, 1940)
Love, Honor and Oh, Baby! (Univ, 1940)
Meet John Doe (WB, 1941)
Buy Me That Town (Par, 1941)
Birth of the Blues (Par, 1941)

Mr. Wise Guy (Mon, 1942)
Girls' Town (PRC, 1942)
Henry and Dizzy (Par, 1942)
Jail House Blues (Univ, 1942)
Dr. Broadway (Par, 1942)
So's Your Aunt Emma [a.k.a. *Meet the Mob*] (Mon, 1942)
One Thrilling Night (Mon, 1942)
Baby Face Morgan (PRC, 1942)
Lure of the Islands (Mon, 1942)
Phantom Killer (Mon, 1942)
Police Bullets (Mon, 1942)
Hitler—Dead or Alive (Ben Judells, 1943)
Danger—Women at Work (PRC, 1943)
Gangway for Tomorrow (RKO, 1943)
Since You Went Away (UA, 1944)
Three Is a Family (UA, 1944)
Joe Palooka—Champ (Mon, 1946)
Gentleman Joe Palooka (Mon, 1946)

RALPH INCE

With Vera Reynolds in Gorilla Ship *(1932).*

Born January 16, 1882, Boston, Massachusetts. Married 1) Lucille Lee Stewart; divorced; 2) Lucilla Mendez (1926). Died April 11, 1937, London, England. Brother of Thomas and John Ince who began directing pictures in 1905. Played Abraham Lincoln in a historical series in 1906 for Vitagraph. Prolific director throughout the 1920s, sometimes starring in his own features: *Wet Gold, Yellow Fingers, Chicago After Midnight,* etc. Supporting player in the 1930s. Between 1934 and 1937 directed many British quota quickies, occasionally appearing in one (*The Perfect Crime*).

> **Ralph Ince** to Edward G. Robinson in *Little Caesar:* "Any guy that can muscle in on Sam Vettori and Little Arnie is on the up and up with me."

Films

Virtuous Men (S-L Films, 1919)
The Bringers (Selznick, 1920)
The Land of Opportunity (Selznick, 1920)
Wet Gold (G, 1921)
After Midnight (Selznick, 1921)
The Highest Law (Selznick, 1921)
A Man's Home (Selznick, 1921)
The Last Door (Selznick, 1921)
Tropical Love (Associated Exhibitors, 1921)
Remorseless Love (Selznick, 1921)
The Referee (Selznick, 1922)
Channing of the Northwest (Selznick, 1922)

Reckless Youth (Selznick, 1922)
A Wide Open Town (Selznick, 1922)
Homeward Bound (Par, 1923)
Counterfeit Love (Selznick, 1923)
Success (M, 1923)
The Chorus Lady (PDC, 1924)
The House of Youth (PDC, 1924)
Dynamite Smith (Pathé, 1924)
The Moral Sinner (Par, 1924)
The Uninvited Guest (MG, 1924)
Alias Mary Flynn (FBO, 1925)
Playing with Souls (FN, 1925)
Lady Robin Hood (FBO, 1925)
Smooth as Satin (FBO, 1925)

The Better Way (Col, 1926)
The Lone Wolf Returns (Col, 1926)
Bigger Than Barnum's (FBO, 1926)
Yellow Fingers (Fox, 1926)
Breed of the Sea (FBO, 1926)
Sea Wolf (Ince-Tri, 1926)
Moulders of Men (FBO, 1927)
Home Struck (FBO, 1927)
Not for Publication (FBO, 1927)
South Sea Love (FBO, 1927)
Shanghaied (FBO, 1927)
Wandering Girls (Col, 1927)
Coney Island (FBO, 1928)
Chicago After Midnight (FBO, 1928)

Hit of the Show (FBO, 1928)
Danger Street (FBO, 1928)
The Singapore Mutiny (FBO, 1928)
Hardboiled (Fox, 1929)
Wall Street (Col, 1929)
The Big Fight (WW, 1930)
Numbered Men (FN, 1930)
Little Caesar (FN, 1930)
A Gentleman's Fate (MGM, 1931)
Hell Bound (Tif, 1931)
The Star Witness (WB, 1931)
The Big Gamble (Pathé, 1931)

Law and Order (Univ, 1932)
The Lost Squadron (RKO, 1932)
The Hatchet Man (FN, 1932)
Men of Chance (RKO, 1932)
Girl of the Rio (RKO, 1932)
The Mouthpiece (WB, 1932)
County Fair (Mon, 1932)
Law of the Sea (Mon, 1932)
State's Attorney (RKO, 1932)
The Tenderfoot (FN, 1932)
Gorilla Ship (Mayfair, 1932)
Guilty as Hell (Par, 1932)

The Pride of the Legion (Mascot, 1932)
Malay Nights (Mayfair, 1932)
The Big Pay-Off (Mascot, 1933)
Men of America (RKO, 1933)
Lucky Devils (RKO, 1933)
Havana Widows (FN, 1933)
No Escape (WB, Br, 1934)
So You Won't Talk (WB Br, 1935)
Rolling Home (Fox Br, 1935)
Blue Smoke (Br, 1935)
Gaol Break (Br, 1936)
The Perfect Crime (Br, 1937)

FRIEDA INESCORT
(Frieda Wightman)

With Ian Hunter in Call It a Day *(1937).*

Born June 29, 1900, Edinburgh, Scotland. Married Ben Ray Redman (1926); widowed (1961). Died February 26, 1976, Woodland Hills, California. Sophisticated stage and screen actress. Often played the wronged woman (Rosamond Melford of *Give Me Your Heart*), the well-bred bitch (Miss Bingley of *Pride and Prejudice*), or the aristocratic, nice relative (Grace Roark of *Another Dawn*). TV series: "Meet Corliss Archer."

Frieda Inescort to Claire Trevor in *Street of Chance:* "You're a clever girl, Ruth. I've always suspected as much."

Films

The Dark Angel (UA, 1935)
If You Could Only Cook (Col, 1935)
The Garden Murder Case (MGM, 1936)

Give Me Your Heart (WB, 1936)
The King Steps Out (Col, 1936)
Mary of Scotland (RKO, 1936)

Hollywood Boulevard (Par, 1936)
Another Dawn (WB, 1937)
Portia on Trial (Rep, 1937)

Call It a Day (WB, 1937)
The Great O'Malley (WB, 1937)
Beauty for the Asking (RKO, 1939)
Woman Doctor (Rep, 1939)
The Zero Hour (Rep, 1939)
Tarzan Finds a Son! (MGM, 1939)
A Woman Is the Judge (Col, 1939)
Convicted Woman (Col, 1940)
The Letter (WB, 1940)
Pride and Prejudice (MGM, 1940)
Father's Son (WB, 1941)
The Trial of Mary Dugan (MGM, 1941)
Shadows on the Stairs (WB, 1941)

Sunny (RKO, 1941)
You'll Never Get Rich (Col, 1941)
Remember the Day (20th, 1941)
The Courtship of Andy Hardy (MGM, 1942)
Street of Chance (Par, 1942)
Sweater Girl (Par, 1942)
The Amazing Mrs. Holliday (Univ, 1943)
It Comes Up Love (Univ, 1943)
Mission to Moscow (WB, 1943)
The Return of the Vampire (Col, 1943)
Heavenly Days (RKO, 1944)
The Judge Steps Out (RKO, 1949)

The Underworld Story (UA, 1950)
A Place in the Sun (Par, 1951)
Never Wave at a WAC (RKO, 1952)
Casanova's Big Night (Par, 1954)
Foxfire (Univ, 1955)
Flame of the Islands (Rep, 1955)
The Eddy Duchin Story (Col, 1956)
Darby's Rangers (WB, 1958)
Senior Prom (Col, 1958)
Juke Box Rhythm (Col, 1959)
The Alligator People (20th, 1959)
The Crowded Sky (WB, 1960)

REX INGRAM

In Your Cheatin' Heart (1964).

Born October 20, 1895, Cairo, Illinois. Died September 19, 1969, Los Angeles, California. Impressive black actor of stage and screen who was De Lawd in The Green Pastures. Was riveting as the genie in tandem with Sabu in The Thief of Bagdad.

Rex Ingram to Mickey Rooney in The Adventures of Huckleberry Finn: "I'm savin' up enuf money to buy myself."

Films

Hearts in Dixie (Fox, 1929)
The Sign of the Cross (Par, 1932)
King Kong (RKO, 1933)
The Emperor Jones (UA, 1933)

Harlem After Midnight (Micheaux Films, 1934)
Captain Blood (WB, 1935)
The Green Pastures (WB, 1936)

The Adventures of Huckleberry Finn (MGM, 1939)
The Thief of Bagdad (UA Br, 1940)
The Talk of the Town (Col, 1942)

Sahara (Col, 1943)
Cabin in the Sky (MGM, 1943)
Fired Wife (Univ, 1943)
Dark Waters (UA, 1944)
A Thousand and One Nights (Col, 1945)
Moonrise (Rep, 1948)
King Solomon's Mines (MGM, 1950)

Tarzan's Hidden Jungle (RKO, 1955)
The Ten Commandments (Par, 1956)
Congo Crossing (Univ, 1956)
Hell on Devil's Island (20th, 1957)
God's Little Acre (UA, 1958)
Anna Lucasta (UA, 1958)
Escort West (UA, 1959)

Watusi (MGM, 1959)
Desire in the Dust (20th, 1960)
Elmer Gantry (UA, 1960)
Your Cheatin' Heart (MGM, 1964)
Hurry Sundown (Par, 1967)
Journey to Shiloh (Univ, 1967)

SELMER JACKSON

With Maris Wrixon in The Glass Alibi *(1946).*

Born May 7, 1888. Died March 30, 1971. One of the ablest and most overworked interpreters of white-haired fathers, executives, and doctors. In: *My Man Godfrey* (Blake, the guest), *A Family Affair* (Hoyt Wells), *Alexander's Ragtime Band* (radio station manager), *The Grapes of Wrath* (inspector), *Dakota* (Dr. Jackson), *Her Husband's Affairs* (judge), *Autumn Leaves* (Mr. Wetherby), etc.

Selmer Jackson to George Montgomery in *Jack Mc-Call—Desperado:* "Get this through to Major Thompson. I don't have to tell you how important those reinforcements *are* to us."

Films

The Supreme Passion (Associated Exhibitors, 1921)
Thru Different Eyes (Fox, 1929)
Why Bring That Up? (Par, 1929)
Lovin' the Ladies (RKO, 1930)
Subway Express (Col, 1931)
Dirigible (Col, 1931)
The Secret Call (Par, 1931)
Leftover Ladies (Tif, 1931)
You Said a Mouthful (FN, 1932)

Doctor X (FN, 1932)
Forgotten (Invincible, 1933)
Hell and High Water (Par, 1933)
I've Got Your Number (WB, 1934)
Let's Fall in Love (Col, 1934)
Sisters Under the Skin (Col, 1934)
The Witching Hour (Par, 1934)
The Defense Rests (Col, 1934)
I'll Fix It (Col, 1934)
Murder in the Clouds (WB, 1934)

Sadie McKee (MGM, 1934)
Fog over Frisco (FN, 1934)
Stand Up and Cheer (Fox, 1934)
The Secret Bride (WB, 1935)
Traveling Saleslady (FN, 1935)
Public Hero No. 1 (MGM, 1935)
Front Page Woman (WB, 1935)
This Is the Life (Fox, 1935)
Grand Exit (Col, 1935)
Libeled Lady (MGM, 1936)

Bridge of Sighs (Invincible, 1936)
Public Enemy's Wife (WB, 1936)
Parole (Univ, 1936)
My Man Godfrey (Univ, 1936)
Next Time We Love (Univ, 1936)
It Had to Happen (20th, 1936)
Gold Diggers of 1937 (WB, 1936)
Easy Money (Invincible, 1936)
The Golden Arrow (FN, 1936)
The Magnificent Brute (Univ, 1936)
Two Wise Maids (Rep, 1937)
A Family Affair (MGM, 1937)
Girl Overboard (Univ, 1937)
The Case of the Stuttering Bishop (WB, 1937)
My Dear Miss Aldrich (MGM, 1937)
The Man in Blue (Univ, 1937)
Reported Missing (Univ, 1937)
The Thirteenth Man (Mon, 1937)
Meet the Boy Friend (Rep, 1937)
The Westland Case (Univ, 1937)
The Wrong Road (Rep, 1937)
Federal Bullets (Mon, 1937)
Manhattan Merry-Go-Round (Rep, 1937)
Hot Water (20th, 1937)
The Duke Comes Back (Rep, 1937)
West of Shanghai (WB, 1937)
You're Only Young Once (MGM, 1937)
Prison Nurse (Rep, 1938)
Too Hot to Handle (MGM, 1938)
Midnight Intruder (Univ, 1938)
Gateway (20th, 1938)
Arson Gang Busters (Rep, 1938)
Alexander's Ragtime Band (20th, 1938)
The Missing Guest (Univ, 1938)
Gambling Ship (Univ, 1938)
Flight into Fame (Col, 1938)
The Gangster's Boy (Mon, 1938)
Personal Secretary (Univ, 1938)
Secrets of an Actress (WB, 1938)
Down in Arkansaw (Rep, 1938)
Off the Record (WB, 1939)
Society Lawyer (MGM, 1939)
Stand Up and Fight (MGM, 1939)
Espionage Agent (WB, 1939)
Wings of the Navy (WB, 1939)
Naughty but Nice (WB, 1939)
Inside Information (Univ, 1939)
The Under-Pup (Univ, 1939)
The Star Maker (Par, 1939)
On Dress Parade (WB, 1939)
Calling All Marines (Rep, 1939)
South of the Border (Rep, 1939)
Florian (MGM, 1940)
Scandal Sheet (Col, 1940)
No Time for Comedy (WB, 1940)
The Grapes of Wrath (20th, 1940)

Hired Wife (Univ, 1940)
Son of the Navy (Mon, 1940)
Johnny Apollo (20th, 1940)
Wagons Westward (Rep, 1940)
Millionaires in Prison (RKO, 1940)
Babies for Sale (Col, 1940)
Sailor's Lady (20th, 1940)
Men Against the Sky (RKO, 1940)
City for Conquest (WB, 1940)
Brigham Young—Frontiersman (20th, 1940)
Public Deb No. 1 (20th, 1940)
The Ape (Mon, 1940)
The Lady with Red Hair (WB, 1940)
Bowery Boy (Rep, 1940)
Military Academy (Col, 1940)
The Man Who Wouldn't Talk (20th, 1940)
Play Girl (RKO, 1941)
The Man Who Lost Himself (Univ, 1941)
It Started with Eve (Univ, 1941)
Tight Shoes (Univ, 1941)
Paper Bullets [a.k.a. *Gangs, Inc.*] (PRC, 1941)
They Died with Their Boots On (WB, 1941)
Parachute Battalion (RKO, 1941)
Navy Blues (WB, 1941)
International Squadron (WB, 1941)
Remember the Day (20th, 1941)
Back Street (Univ, 1941)
Buck Privates (Univ, 1941)
Here Comes Mr. Jordan (Col, 1941)
Cairo (MGM, 1942)
My Favorite Spy (RKO, 1942)
Powder Town (RKO, 1942)
Road to Happiness (Mon, 1942)
The Falcon Takes Over (RKO, 1942)
Secret Agent of Japan (20th, 1942)
Joe Smith, American (MGM, 1942)
Ten Gentlemen from West Point (20th, 1942)
Miss Annie Rooney (UA, 1942)
Through Different Eyes (20th, 1942)
It Ain't Hay (Univ, 1943)
You Can't Beat the Law (Mon, 1943)
Honeymoon Lodge (Univ, 1943)
Harrigan's Kid (MGM, 1943)
Margin for Error (20th, 1943)
Guadalcanal Diary (20th, 1943)
Someone to Remember (Rep, 1943)
What a Woman! (Col, 1943)
Wing and a Prayer (20th, 1944)
The Big Noise (20th, 1944)
Roger Touhy, Gangster (20th, 1944)
Hey Rookie (Col, 1944)
Sheriff of Las Vegas (Rep, 1944)
The Sullivans (20th, 1944)

Marine Raiders (RKO, 1944)
Stars on Parade (Col, 1944)
They Shall Have Faith [a.k.a. *Forever Yours*] (Mon, 1944)
Allotment Wives (Mon, 1945)
Black Market Babies (Mon, 1945)
The Caribbean Mystery (20th, 1945)
Circumstantial Evidence (20th, 1945)
Dakota (Rep, 1945)
A Sporting Chance (Rep, 1945)
This Love of Ours (Univ, 1945)
Boston Blackie and the Law (Col, 1946)
Child of Divorce (RKO, 1946)
Girl on the Spot (Univ, 1946)
The Time of Their Lives (Univ, 1946)
Dangerous Money (Mon, 1946)
The French Key (Rep, 1946)
The Glass Alibi (Rep, 1946)
Johnny Comes Flying Home (20th, 1946)
Shock (20th, 1946)
Wife Wanted (Mon, 1946)
Key Witness (Col, 1947)
Magic Town (RKO, 1947)
The Pretender (Rep, 1947)
Headin' for Heaven (EL, 1947)
Sarge Goes to College (Mon, 1947)
Her Husband's Affairs (Col, 1947)
Stepchild (PRC, 1947)
The Fuller Brush Man (Col, 1948)
King of Gamblers (Rep, 1948)
Pitfall (UA, 1948)
The Girl from Manhattan (UA, 1948)
Stage Struck (Mon, 1948)
The Gentleman from Nowhere (Col, 1948)
Forgotten Women (Mon, 1949)
Mighty Joe Young (RKO, 1949)
The Crime Doctor's Diary (Col, 1949)
Alaska Patrol (Film Classics, 1949)
Renegades of the Sage (Col, 1949)
The Magnificent Yankee (MGM, 1950)
Gunmen of Abilene (Rep, 1950)
Mark of the Gorilla (Col, 1950)
Buckaroo Sheriff of Texas (Rep, 1951)
That's My Boy (Par, 1951)
Bowery Battalion (Mon, 1951)
Purple Heart Diary (Col, 1951)
Elopement (20th, 1951)
Deadline U.S.A. (20th, 1952)
We're Not Married (20th, 1952)
Sky Commando (Col, 1953)
Rebel City (AA, 1953)
Jack McCall—Desperado (Col, 1953)
Devil Goddess (Col, 1955)
Autumn Leaves (Col, 1956)
Hellcats of the Navy (Col, 1957)
The Lost Missile (UA, 1958)
The Atomic Submarine (AA, 1959)
The Gallant Hours (UA, 1960)

SAM JAFFE

Dan Dailey, Sam Jaffe, Susan Hayward, and Tamara Shayne in I Can Get It for You Wholesale *(1951).*

Born March 8, 1893, New York City, New York. Married 1) Lillian Taiz; 2) Bettye Ackerman (1955). Versatile stage and screen performer who specialized in unusual roles: *The Scarlet Empress* (mad Grand Duke Peter), *Lost Horizon* (the high lama), *Gunga Din* (the title role), *The Asphalt Jungle* (Oscar-nominated for his ex-convict Dr. Riedenschneider, but lost BSAAA to George Sanders of *All About Eve*), etc. One of the founders of Manhattan's Equity Library Theatre. TV series: "Ben Casey" (as Dr. Zorba).

Sam Jaffe to Victor McLaglen in *Gunga Din:* "Could be first-class soldier, sir."

Films

We Live Again (UA, 1934)
The Scarlet Empress (Par, 1934)
Lost Horizon (Col, 1937)
Gunga Din (RKO, 1939)
Stage Door Canteen (UA, 1943)
13 Rue Madeleine (20th, 1946)
Gentleman's Agreement (20th, 1947)
The Accused (Par, 1948)
Rope of Sand (Par, 1949)

The Asphalt Jungle (MGM, 1950)
Under the Gun (Univ, 1950)
I Can Get It for You Wholesale (20th, 1951)
The Day the Earth Stood Still (20th, 1951)
All Mine to Give (Univ, 1957)
The Barbarian and the Geisha (20th, 1958)
Ben-Hur (MGM, 1959)

A Guide for the Married Man (20th, 1967)
Guns for San Sebastian (MGM, 1968)
The Great Bank Robbery (WB-7 Arts, 1969)
The Kremlin Letter (20th, 1970)
The Dunwich Horror (AIP, 1970)
Bedknobs and Broomsticks (BV, 1971)

DEAN JAGGER
(Dean Jeffries)

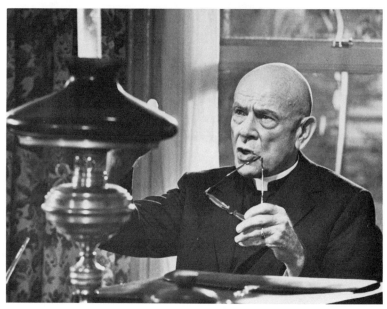

In The Kremlin Letter *(1970).*

Born November 7, 1903, Lima, Ohio. Married 1) Antoinette Lawrence (1935); divorced (1945); 2) Gloria Ling (1947), child: Diane; divorced (1967); 3) Etta Winger (1968). Conventional-looking 6'3" actor who continually made new starts on screen. Was reintroduced to movie audiences in the title role of *Brigham Young—Frontiersman.* Often in sympathetic roles as fathers, doctors, and colonels. Won BSAAA as Major Stovall in *12 O'Clock High;* was General Waverly, the retired World War II officer who opened a winter resort hotel in *White Christmas.* TV series: "Mr. Novak" (as Principal Albert Vane).

Dean Jagger in *Brigham Young—Frontiersman:* "There's good stock here, Lord. About as fine a bunch of men and women as ever lived."

Films

Handcuffed (Rayart, 1928)
The Woman from Hell (Fox, 1929)
College Rhythm (Par, 1934)
Behold My Wife (Par, 1934)
You Belong to Me (Par, 1934)
Home on the Range (Par, 1935)
Wings in the Dark (Par, 1935)
Car 99 (Par, 1935)
People Will Talk (Par, 1935)
Men Without Names (Par, 1935)
Wanderer of the Wasteland (Par, 1935)
Woman Trap (Par, 1936)
Thirteen Hours by Air (Par, 1936)
Revolt of the Zombies (Academy Pictures, 1936)
Pepper (20th, 1936)
Star for a Night (20th, 1936)

Woman in Distress (Col, 1937)
Song of the City (MGM, 1937)
Escape by Night (Rep, 1937)
Dangerous Number (MGM, 1937)
Under Cover of Night (MGM, 1937)
Exiled to Shanghai (Rep, 1937)
Having Wonderful Time (RKO, 1938)
Brigham Young—Frontiersman (20th, 1940)
Western Union (20th, 1941)
The Men in Her Life (Col, 1941)
Valley of the Sun (RKO, 1942)
The Omaha Trail (MGM, 1942)
I Escaped from the Gestapo [a.k.a. No Escape] (Mon, 1943)
The North Star [a.k.a. Armored Attack] (RKO, 1943)

Alaska (Mon, 1944)
When Strangers Marry [a.k.a. Betrayed] (Mon, 1944)
I Lived in Grosvenor Square [a.k.a. A Yank in London] (Br, 1945)
Sister Kenny (RKO, 1946)
Pursued (WB, 1947)
Driftwood (Rep, 1947)
12 O'Clock High (20th, 1949)
C-Man (Film Classics, 1949)
Sierra (Univ, 1950)
Dark City (Par, 1950)
Rawhide (20th, 1951)
Warpath (Par, 1951)
The Denver and Rio Grande (Par, 1952)
My Son John (Par, 1952)
It Grows on Trees (Univ, 1952)

The Robe (20th, 1953)
Executive Suite (MGM, 1954)
Private Hell 36 (Filmakers, 1954)
White Christmas (Par, 1954)
Bad Day at Black Rock (MGM, 1954)
The Eternal Sea (Rep, 1955)
It's a Dog's Life (MGM, 1955)
On the Threshold of Space (20th, 1956)
Red Sundown (Univ, 1956)
The Great Man (Univ, 1956)
Three Brave Men (20th, 1957)
X—The Unknown (WB, 1957)

Forty Guns (20th, 1957)
Bernardine (20th, 1957)
The Proud Rebel (BV, 1958)
King Creole (Par, 1958)
The Nun's Story (WB, 1959)
Cash McCall (WB, 1959)
Elmer Gantry (UA, 1960)
Parrish (WB, 1961)
The Honeymoon Machine (MGM, 1961)
Billy Rose's Jumbo (MGM, 1962)
First to Fight (WB, 1967)
Firecreek (WB-7 Arts, 1968)

Day of the Evil Gun (MGM, 1968)
Smith (BV, 1970)
The Kremlin Letter (20th, 1970)
Vanishing Point (20th, 1971)
The Great Lester Buggs (Starmaster Releasing, 1974)
God Damn Dr. Shagetz (L-T Films, 1975)
Bruce Lee's Game of Death (Golden Harvest, 1977)

ALLEN JENKINS
(Alfred McGonegal)

Allen Jenkins, Ralph Sanford, Shelley Winters, Farley Granger, and Margalo Gillmore in Behave Yourself! *(1951).*

Born April 9, 1900, New York City, New York. Married 1) Mary Landes, child: son; 2) Lillian Kinsella (1948). Died July 20, 1974, Santa Monica, California. Horse-faced Damon Runyon-esque mug who peppered scores of Warner Bros. features: *Three on a Match* (Dick), *The Mayor of Hell* (Mike), *Jimmy the Gent* (Louie), *Marked Woman* (Louis), *Dead End* (Hunk), *Brother Orchid* (Willie the Knife Corson), etc. In Warners' Warren William's *Perry Mason* series: played Sergeant Holcomb in *The Case of the Howling Dog,* but magically transformed into assistant Spudsy for *The Case of the Curious Bride* and *The Case of the Lucky Legs.* At his foolhardy best sharing the lead with Hugh Herbert in the farce *Sh! The Octopus*—as dumb detectives. In the initial three *Falcon* segments starring George Sanders: played the sleuth's chauffeur/stooge. Cameoed as the telegrapher in his final picture, Jack Lemmon's *The Front Page.* TV series: "Hey Jeannie," "The Duke," and "Top Cat" (voice of Officer Dibble).

> **Allen Jenkins** to Bette Davis and the girls in *Marked Woman:* "I positively guarantee you it was stolen from the best shop in town."

Films

The Girl Habit (Par, 1931)
Three on a Match (FN, 1932)
I Am a Fugitive from a Chain Gang (WB, 1932)
Blessed Event (WB, 1932)
Lawyer Man (WB, 1932)
Rackety Rax (Fox, 1932)
42nd Street (WB, 1933)
Employees' Entrance (FN, 1933)
Hard to Handle (WB, 1933)
The Silk Express (WB, 1933)
Ladies They Talk About (WB, 1933)
The Keyhole (WB, 1933)
The Mayor of Hell (WB, 1933)
Bureau of Missing Persons (FN, 1933)
Tomorrow at Seven (RKO, 1933)
Professional Sweetheart (RKO, 1933)
Blondie Johnson (FN, 1933)
The Mind Reader (FN, 1933)
Havana Widows (FN, 1933)
I've Got Your Number (WB, 1934)
Jimmy the Gent (WB, 1934)
The Merry Frinks (FN, 1934)
Twenty Million Sweethearts (FN, 1934)
Happiness Ahead (FN, 1934)
The Big Shakedown (FN, 1934)
The St. Louis Kid (WB, 1934)
Bedside (FN, 1934)
The Case of the Howling Dog (WB, 1934)
Whirlpool (Col, 1934)
Sweet Music (WB, 1935)
While the Patient Slept (FN, 1935)
A Night at the Ritz (WB, 1935)
I Live for Love (WB, 1935)
Miss Pacific Fleet (WB, 1955)
The Case of the Curious Bride (FN, 1935)
Page Miss Glory (WB, 1935)
The Irish in Us (WB, 1935)
The Case of the Lucky Legs (WB, 1935)
Broadway Hostess (FN, 1935)

The Singing Kid (FN, 1936)
Sins of Man (20th, 1936)
Sing Me a Love Song (FN, 1936)
Cain and Mabel (WB, 1936)
Three Men on a Horse (WB, 1936)
Ready, Willing and Able (WB, 1937)
Marked Woman (WB, 1937)
There Goes My Girl (FN, 1937)
Dance, Charlie, Dance (WB, 1937)
Ever Since Eve (WB, 1937)
The Singing Marine (WB, 1937)
The Perfect Specimen (FN, 1937)
Marry the Girl (WB, 1937)
Sh! The Octopus (WB, 1937)
Dead End (UA, 1937)
Talent Scout (WB, 1937)
A Slight Case of Murder (WB, 1938)
Gold Diggers in Paris (WB, 1938)
Swing Your Lady (WB, 1938)
The Amazing Dr. Clitterhouse (WB, 1938)
Racket Busters (WB, 1938)
Hard to Get (WB, 1938)
Heart of the North (WB, 1938)
Fools for Scandal (WB, 1938)
Going Places (WB, 1938)
Five Came Back (RKO, 1939)
Torchy Plays with Dynamite (WB, 1939)
Naughty but Nice (WB, 1939)
Sweepstakes Winner (WB, 1939)
Destry Rides Again (Univ, 1939)
Brother Orchid (WB, 1940)
Oh, Johnny, How You Can Love (Univ, 1940)
Margie (Univ, 1940)
Meet the Wildcat (Univ, 1940)
Tin Pan Alley (20th, 1940)
Footsteps in the Dark (WB, 1941)
Time Out for Rhythm (Col, 1941)
Dive Bomber (WB, 1941)

The Gay Falcon (RKO, 1941)
A Date with the Falcon (RKO, 1941)
Go West, Young Lady (Col, 1941)
Ball of Fire (RKO, 1941)
Eyes in the Night (MGM, 1942)
Tortilla Flat (MGM, 1942)
The Falcon Takes Over (RKO, 1942)
Maisie Gets Her Man (MGM, 1942)
They All Kissed the Bride (Col, 1942)
Stage Door Canteen (UA, 1943)
Wonder Man (RKO, 1945)
Lady on a Train (Univ, 1945)
Meet Me on Broadway (Col, 1946)
Singin' in the Corn (Col, 1946)
The Dark House (Univ, 1946)
The Hat Box Mystery (Screen Guild, 1947)
Wild Harvest (Par, 1947)
The Senator Was Indiscreet (Univ, 1947)
Easy Come, Easy Go (Par, 1947)
Fun on a Weekend (UA, 1947)
The Case of the Baby-Sitter (Screen Guild, 1947)
Inside Story (Rep, 1948)
The Big Wheel (UA, 1949)
Bodyhold (Col, 1950)
Crazy over Horses (Mon, 1951)
Behave Yourself! (RKO, 1951)
Let's Go, Navy (Mon, 1951)
Oklahoma Annie (Rep, 1952)
The WAC from Walla Walla (Rep, 1952)
Pillow Talk (Univ, 1959)
I'd Rather Be Rich (Univ, 1964)
Robin and the Seven Hoods (WB, 1964)
For Those Who Think Young (UA, 1964)
Doctor, You've Got to Be Kidding! (MGM, 1967)
The Front Page (Univ, 1974)

DeWITT JENNINGS

Charles Bickford, Warner Baxter, and DeWitt Jennings in The Squaw Man *(1931).*

Born June 21, 1879, Cameron, Missouri. Married Ethel Conroy, children: three. Died March 1, 1937, Hollywood, California. Authoritarian-looking. Played figures of consequence: Police Lieutenant Ambrose in Bert Lytell's *Alias Ladyfingers,* the American consul in William Boyd and Louis Wolheim's *Two Arabian Knights;* in talkies: *The Bat Whispers* (police captain), *Outside the Law* (police chief), *The Secret Six* (Chief Donlin), etc.

DeWitt Jennings to Warner Baxter in *The Squaw Man:* "No use bluffing, Carson—we know your squaw's inside."

Films

The Warrens of Virginia (Par, 1915)
The Hillcrest Mystery (Pathé, 1918)
Alias Ladyfingers (M, 1921)
From the Ground Up (G, 1921)
The Golden Snare (Associated FN, 1921)
Beating the Game (G, 1921)
The Invisible Power (G, 1921)
The Greater Claim (M, 1921)
The Poverty of Riches (G, 1921)
Three Sevens (Vit, 1921)
There Are No Villains (M, 1921)
The Face Between (M, 1922)
Mixed Faces (Fox, 1922)
Flesh and Blood (Cummings, 1922)
The Right That Failed (M, 1922)
Sherlock Brown (M, 1922)
Blinky (Univ, 1923)
Out of Luck (Univ, 1923)
Circus Days (Associated FN, 1923)
Within the Law (Associated FN, 1923)
Along Came Ruth (MG, 1924)
The Deadwood Coach (Fox, 1924)

By Divine Right (FBO, 1924)
The Desert Outlaw (Fox, 1924)
The Gaiety Girl (Univ, 1924)
The Enemy Sex (Par, 1924)
The Heart Bandit (MG, 1924)
Hit and Run (Univ, 1924)
Merton of the Movies (Par, 1924)
Name the Man (MG, 1924)
The Silent Watcher (Associated FN, 1924)
The Mystic (MG, 1925)
Don't (MGM, 1925)
Go Straight (B. P. Schulberg, 1925)
The Re-Creation of Brian Kent (Principle, 1925)
The Splendid Road (FN, 1925)
Chip of the Flying U (Univ, 1926)
The Fire Brigade (MGM, 1926)
Exit Smiling (MGM, 1926)
The Ice Flood (Univ, 1926)
The Passionate Quest (WB, 1926)
While London Sleeps (WB, 1926)

The Great Mail Robbery (FBO, 1927)
McFadden's Flats (FN, 1927)
Home Made (FN, 1927)
Two Arabian Knights (UA, 1927)
The Air Mail Pilot (Hi-Mark, 1928)
Marry the Girl (Sterling, 1928)
The Crash (FN, 1928)
The Night Flyer (Pathé, 1928)
Alibi (UA, 1929)
Fox Movietone Follies of 1929 (Fox, 1929)
Seven Footprints to Satan (FN, 1929)
Red Hot Speed (Univ, 1929)
Seven Keys to Baldpate (RKO, 1929)
The Trial of Mary Dugan (MGM, 1929)
Thru Different Eyes (Fox, 1929)
The Valiant (Fox, 1929)
The Big House (MGM, 1930)
The Bat Whispers (UA, 1930)
The Big Trail (Fox, 1930)
Captain of the Guard (Univ, 1930)
Min and Bill (MGM, 1930)
Night Ride (Univ, 1930)

311

Scarlet Pages (FN, 1930)
Outside the Law (Univ, 1930)
Those Who Dance (WB, 1930)
In the Next Room (FN, 1930)
The Criminal Code (Col, 1931)
Primrose Path (Hollywood Films, 1931)
The Secret Six (MGM, 1931)
The Squaw Man (MGM, 1931)
Salvation Nell (Tif, 1931)
Caught Plastered (RKO, 1931)
A Dangerous Affair (Col, 1931)
The Deceiver (Col, 1931)
Arrowsmith (UA, 1931)
Silver Dollar (FN, 1932)
Dancers in the Dark (Par, 1932)
Midnight Morals (Mayfair, 1932)
Movie Crazy (Par, 1932)
Tess of the Storm Country (Fox, 1932)

Central Park (FN, 1932)
The Match King (FN, 1932)
The Mystery of the Wax Museum (WB, 1933)
Strictly Personal (Par, 1933)
Ladies They Talk About (WB, 1933)
A Lady's Profession (Par, 1933)
Reform Girl (Tower, 1933)
Police Car 17 (Col, 1933)
One Year Later (Allied, 1933)
Little Man, What Now? (Univ, 1934)
Death on the Diamond (MGM, 1934)
The Fighting Rookie (Mayfair, 1934)
Massacre (FN, 1934)
A Man's Game (Col, 1934)
Take the Stand (Liberty, 1934)
A Wicked Woman (MGM, 1934)
The President Vanishes (Par, 1934)

Secret of the Chateau (Univ, 1934)
Murder on a Honeymoon (RKO, 1935)
Mary Jane's Pa (FN, 1935)
The Daring Young Man (Fox, 1935)
Village Tale (RKO, 1935)
A Dog of Flanders (RKO, 1935)
Mutiny on the Bounty (MGM, 1935)
We Who Are About to Die (RKO, 1936)
Kelly the Second (MGM, 1936)
Sins of Man (20th, 1936)
The Crime of Dr. Forbes (20th, 1936)
Nancy Steele Is Missing (20th, 1937)
Fifty Roads to Town (20th, 1937)
This Is My Affair (20th, 1937)
That I May Live (20th, 1937)
Slave Ship (20th, 1937)

BEN JOHNSON

In Will Penny (1968).

Born June 13, 1919, Pawhuska, Oklahoma. Married Carol Jones (1941). Former cowboy who was the optimistic-looking young player of many John Ford Westerns. Had the top role in Ford's *Wagonmaster*, but never reached star status. Played the romantic lead opposite Terry Moore in *Mighty Joe Young*. In later years became toughened character actor of sterling competence. Won BSAAA for *The Last Picture Show* as Sam the Lion, the cinema and poolhall owner. Played G-man Melvin Purvis after public enemy Warren Oates in *Dillinger* and was Police Captain Tanner hunting lawbreakers Goldie Hawn and William Atherton in *The Sugarland Express*.

Ben Johnson to John Wayne in *She Wore a Yellow Ribbon:*
"That arrow came from the bow of a Southern Cheyenne dog soldier."

Films

Three Godfathers (MGM, 1948)
Fort Apache (RKO, 1948) [stunt work]
She Wore a Yellow Ribbon (RKO, 1949)
Mighty Joe Young (RKO, 1949)
Wagonmaster (RKO, 1950)
Rio Grande (Rep, 1950)
Fort Defiance (UA, 1951)
Wild Stallion (Mon, 1952)
Shane (Par, 1953)
Simba (Lip, 1955)
Rebel in Town (UA, 1956)
War Drums (UA, 1957)
Slim Carter (Univ, 1957)
Fort Bowie (UA, 1958)

Ten Who Dared (BV, 1960)
The Tomboy and the Champ (Univ, 1961)
One-Eyed Jacks (Par, 1961)
Major Dundee (Col, 1965)
The Rare Breed (Univ, 1966)
Will Penny (Par, 1968)
Hang 'em High (UA, 1968)
The Wild Bunch (WB–7 Arts, 1969)
The Undefeated (20th, 1969)
Chisum (WB, 1970)
The Last Picture Show (Col, 1971)
Something Big (National General, 1971)
Junior Bonner (Cin, 1972)

The Getaway (National General, 1972)
Corky (MGM, 1972)
The Train Robbers (WB, 1973)
Kid Blue (20th, 1973)
Dillinger (AIP, 1973)
The Sugarland Express (Univ, 1974)
Bite the Bullet (Col, 1975)
Hustle (Par, 1975)
Breakheart Pass (UA, 1976)
The Town That Dreaded Sundown (AIP, 1977)
The Greatest (Col, 1977)
Grayeagle (AIP, 1977)

GUY KIBBEE

In the early 1940s.

Born March 6, 1882, El Paso, Texas. Married 1) Helen Shea (1918), children: John Patrick, Robert Joseph; divorced (1923); 2) Esther Reed (1925), children: Guy, Shirley Ann. Died May 24, 1956, East Islip, New York. Baldheaded, tubby, pop-eyed smiling character with a deceptively benign appearance. Played the unremorseful cigar-smoking killer Pop Cooley in *City Streets*. Often was the victim of his own lusty arrangements: Abner Dillon, cuckolded by Bebe Daniels in *42nd Street;* Fanueil Hall Peabody, cornered by money-hungry Aline MacMahon in *Gold Diggers of 1933;* Hugh Herbert's cousin Horace P. Hemingway, blackmailed by Joan Blondell in *Dames*, etc. Had the title role of the prejudiced small-towner in *Babbitt,* but generally was the country doctor, lawyer, etc. Starred in the *Scattergood Baines* series. Last two features were for John Ford: *Fort Apache* (Dr. Wilkens) and *Three Godfathers* (the judge). Brother to screen character player Milton Kibbee; the latter's daughter, Lois, is a TV soap-opera villainess and a noted authoress.

Guy Kibbee to Alice Brady in *Joy of Living:* "I've been drinking over 40 years, and I haven't acquired the habit yet."

Films

Stolen Heaven (Par, 1931)
Man of the World (Par, 1931)
City Streets (Par, 1931)
Laughing Sinners (MGM, 1931)
Side Show (WB, 1931)
New Adventures of Get-Rich-Quick Wallingford (MGM, 1931)
Flying High (MGM, 1931)
Blonde Crazy (WB, 1931)
Taxi! (WB, 1932)
Fireman, Save My Child (FN, 1932)
High Pressure (WB, 1932)
Union Depot (FN, 1932)
Play Girl (WB, 1932)
The Crowd Roars (WB, 1932)
Two Seconds (FN, 1932)
Man Wanted (WB, 1932)
The Strange Love of Molly Louvain (FN, 1932)
So Big (WB, 1932)
Winner Take All (WB, 1932)
The Dark Horse (FN, 1932)
Crooner (FN, 1932)
Big City Blues (WB, 1932)
Rain (UA, 1932)
Scarlet Dawn (WB, 1932)
The Conquerors (RKO, 1932)
Central Park (FN, 1932)
The Mouthpiece (WB, 1932)
Weekend Marriage (FN, 1932)
They Just Had to Get Married (Univ, 1933)
42nd Street (WB, 1933)
Girl Missing (WB, 1933)
Gold Diggers of 1933 (WB, 1933)
Lilly Turner (FN, 1933)
The Life of Jimmy Dolan (WB, 1933)
The Silk Express (WB, 1933)

Lady for a Day (Col, 1933)
Footlight Parade (WB, 1933)
The World Changes (FN, 1933)
Havana Widows (FN, 1933)
Convention City (FN, 1933)
Easy to Love (WB, 1934)
Dames (WB, 1934)
Big-Hearted Herbert (WB, 1934)
Harold Teen (WB, 1934)
Merry Wives of Reno (WB, 1934)
Wonder Bar (FN, 1934)
Babbitt (WB, 1934)
The Merry Frinks (FN, 1934)
While the Patient Slept (FN, 1935)
Mary Jane's Pa (FN, 1935)
Don't Bet on Blondes (WB, 1935)
Going Highbrow (WB, 1935)
I Live for Love (WB, 1935)
Captain Blood (WB, 1935)
Little Lord Fauntleroy (UA, 1936)
I Married a Doctor (FN, 1936)
The Big Noise (WB, 1936)
Earthworm Tractors (FN, 1936)
Captain January (20th, 1936)
Three Men on a Horse (FN, 1936)
M'liss (RKO, 1936)
The Captain's Kid (FN, 1937)
Mama Steps Out (MGM, 1937)
Don't Tell the Wife (WB, 1937)
Riding on Air (RKO, 1937)
The Big Shot (RKO, 1937)
Jim Hanvey, Detective (Rep, 1937)
Mountain Justice (WB, 1937)
Bad Man from Brimstone (MGM, 1937)
Of Human Hearts (MGM, 1938)
Three Comrades (MGM, 1938)
Rich Man, Poor Girl (MGM, 1938)
Three Loves Has Nancy (MGM, 1938)

Joy of Living (RKO, 1938)
Let Freedom Ring (MGM, 1939)
It's a Wonderful World (MGM, 1939)
Babes in Arms (MGM, 1939)
Bad Little Angel (MGM, 1939)
Mr. Smith Goes to Washington (Col, 1939)
Our Town (UA, 1940)
Street of Memories (20th, 1940)
Chad Hanna (20th, 1940)
Henry Goes to Arizona (MGM, 1940)
Scattergood Baines (RKO, 1941)
It Started with Eve (Univ, 1941)
Design for Scandal (MGM, 1941)
Scattergood Meets Broadway (RKO, 1941)
Scattergood Pulls the Strings (RKO, 1941)
This Time for Keeps (MGM, 1942)
Sunday Punch (MGM, 1942)
Tish (MGM, 1942)
Miss Annie Rooney (UA, 1942)
Whistling in Dixie (MGM, 1942)
Scattergood Rides High (RKO, 1942)
Scattergood Survives a Murder (RKO, 1942)
Cinderella Swings It (RKO, 1943)
Power of the Press (Col, 1943)
White Savage (Univ, 1943)
Girl Crazy (MGM, 1943)
The Horn Blows at Midnight (WB, 1945)
Singing on the Trail (Col, 1946)
Cowboy Blues (Col, 1946)
Lone Star Moonlight (Col, 1946)
Gentleman Joe Palooka (Mon, 1946)
The Romance of Rosy Ridge (MGM, 1947)
Over the Santa Fe Trail (Col, 1947)
Red Stallion (EL, 1947)
Fort Apache (RKO, 1948)
Three Godfathers (MGM, 1948)

VICTOR KILIAN

Victor Kilian, Nick Dennis, Burt Lancaster, Aline MacMahon, and Francis Pierlot in The Flame and the Arrow (1950).

Born March 6, 1891, Jersey City, New Jersey. Married Daisy Johnson (1915), child; Victor; widowed (1961). Had professional experience with many touring stage companies and made two features at Paramount's Astoria (Long Island) studio before coming to Hollywood in the mid-1930s. Cast as a sheriff (The Adventures of Tom Sawyer, Boys Town, Spellbound), cop (Tovarich), "Pap" Finn (The Adventures of Huckleberry Finn), Abraham Lincoln (Virginia City), preacher (The Return of Frank James), Olsen (Gentleman's Agreement), etc. TV series: "Mary Hartman, Mary Hartman" (the "Fernwood Flasher").

Victor Kilian to Tully Marshall in *This Gun for Hire:*
"Fifteen years! Fifteen years of nursin' you, you old witch!
Wipin' your mouth, listenin' to your raw deals. . . . [to Alan
Ladd] Go ahead—wipe him out."

Films

Gentlemen of the Press (Par, 1929)
The Wiser Sex (Par, 1932)
After the Dance (Col, 1935)
Bad Boy (Fox, 1935)
Air Hawks (Col, 1935)
Public Menace (Col, 1935)
The Girl Friend (Col, 1935)
Riffraff (MGM, 1935)
The Music Goes 'Round (Col, 1936)
Shakedown (Col, 1936)
Adventure in Manhattan (Col, 1936)
Lady from Nowhere (Col, 1936)
The Road to Glory (20th, 1936)
Ramona (20th, 1936)
Banjo on My Knee (20th, 1936)
Fair Warning (20th, 1937)
It Happened in Hollywood (Col, 1937)
Seventh Heaven (20th, 1937)
The League of Frightened Men (Col, 1937
It's All Yours (Col, 1937)

Tovarch (WB, 1937)
The Adventures of Tom Sawyer (UA, 1938)
Marie Antoinette (MGM, 1938)
Orphans of the Street (Rep, 1938)
Gold Diggers in Paris (WB, 1938)
Prison Break (Univ, 1938)
Boys Town (MGM, 1938)
Fighting Thoroughbreds (Rep, 1939)
Paris Honeymoon (Par, 1939)
St. Louis Blues (Par, 1939)
The Adventures of Huckleberry Finn (MGM, 1939)
The Return of the Cisco Kid (20th, 1939)
Only Angels Have Wings (Col, 1939)
Dust Be My Destiny (WB, 1939)
Never Say Die (Par, 1939)
My Favorite Wife (RKO, 1940)
Virginia City (WB, 1940)
Florian (MGM, 1940)

Dr. Cyclops (Par, 1940)
The Mark of Zorro (20th, 1940)
Little Old New York (20th, 1940)
Young Tom Edison (MGM, 1940)
Till We Meet Again (WB, 1940)
King of the Lumberjacks (WB, 1940)
Gold Rush Maisie (MGM, 1940)
Torrid Zone (WB, 1940)
All This, and Heaven Too (WB, 1940)
The Return of Frank James (20th, 1940)
Out West with the Peppers (Col, 1940)
They Knew What They Wanted (RKO, 1940)
Tugboat Annie Sails Again (WB, 1940)
Barnyard Follies (Rep, 1940)
Chad Hanna (20th, 1940)
Western Union (20th, 1941)
Blood and Sand (20th, 1941)
I Was a Prisoner on Devil's Island (Col, 1941)

Mob Town (Univ, 1941)
Secrets of the Lone Wolf (Col, 1941)
A Date with the Falcon (RKO, 1941)
Reap the Wild Wind (Par, 1942)
Atlantic Convoy (Col, 1942)
This Gun for Hire (Par, 1942)
The Ox-Bow Incident (20th, 1943)
Bomber's Moon (20th, 1943)
Hitler's Madman (MGM, 1943)
Johnny Come Lately (UA, 1943)
Belle of the Yukon (RKO, 1944)
Uncertain Glory (WB, 1944)
The Adventures of Mark Twain (WB, 1944)

Barbary Coast Gent (MGM, 1944)
Kismet [TV title: *Oriental Dreams*] (MGM, 1944)
Dangerous Passage (Par, 1944)
The Spanish Main (RKO, 1945)
Behind City Lights (Rep, 1945)
Spellbound (UA, 1945)
The Fighting Guardsman (Col, 1945)
Little Giant (Univ, 1946)
The Yearling (MGM, 1946)
Smoky (20th, 1946)
Gentleman's Agreement (20th, 1947)
Northwest Stampede (EL, 1948)
Yellow Sky (20th, 1948)

I Shot Jesse James (Screen Guild, 1949)
Madame Bovary (MGM, 1949)
Rimfire (Screen Guild, 1949)
Colorado Territory (WB, 1949)
Wyoming Bandit (Rep, 1949)
The Flame and the Arrow (WB, 1950)
Old Frontier (Rep, 1950)
The Return of Jesse James (Lip, 1950)
The Showdown (Rep, 1950)
The Bandit Queen (Lip, 1950)
One Too Many (Hallmark, 1950)
The Tall Target (MGM, 1951)

WALTER KINGSFORD

Barton Hepburn, Martha Scott, Walter Kingsford, and Billie Burke in Hi Diddle Diddle *(1943).*

Born September 20, 1881, Redhill, England. Died February 7, 1958, North Hollywood, California. Impeccably dressed English actor recalled as Dr. Carew of the *Dr. Kildare* series. Was Napoleon III *(The Story of Louis Pasteur)*, Colonel Sandherr *(The Life of Emile Zola)*, Prince Metternich *(Juarez)*, etc.

Walter Kingsford to Lew Ayres in *Calling Dr. Kildare:* "That you're not actually behind bars is due to the prestige of this institution."

Films

Pursuit of Happiness (Par, 1934)
The President Vanishes (Par, 1934)
Frankie and Johnny (RKO, 1935)
The Mystery of Edwin Drood (Univ, 1935)
The White Cockatoo (WB, 1935)
Naughty Marietta (MGM, 1935)

Shanghai (Par, 1935)
I Found Stella Parish (FN, 1935)
The Melody Lingers On (UA, 1935)
Professional Soldier (Fox, 1935)
The Story of Louis Pasteur (WB, 1935)
Hearts Divided (FN, 1936)

Stolen Holiday (WB, 1936)
Little Lord Fauntleroy (UA, 1936)
Trouble for Two (MGM, 1936)
The Music Goes 'Round (Col, 1936)
Mad Holiday (MGM, 1936)
Meet Nero Wolfe (Col, 1936)

Speed (MGM, 1936)
Maytime (MGM, 1937)
Captains Courageous (MGM, 1937)
My Dear Miss Aldrich (MGM, 1937)
Bulldog Drummond Escapes (Par, 1937)
Double or Nothing (Par, 1937)
The Life of Emile Zola (WB, 1937)
The Devil Is Driving (Col, 1937)
The League of Frightened Men (Col, 1937)
I'll Take Romance (Col, 1937)
It Could Happen to You (Rep, 1937)
Paradise for Three (MGM, 1938)
A Yank at Oxford (MGM, 1938)
The Toy Wife (MGM, 1938)
The Lone Wolf in Paris (Col, 1938)
Lord Jeff (MGM, 1938)
There's Always a Woman (Col, 1938)
Algiers (UA, 1938)
The Young in Heart (UA, 1938)
Carefree (RKO, 1938)
If I Were King (Par, 1938)
Say It in French (Par, 1938)
Young Dr. Kildare (MGM, 1938)
Juarez (WB, 1939)
The Man in the Iron Mask (UA, 1939)
Miracles for Sale (MGM, 1939)
Dancing Co-ed (MGM, 1939)
The Secret of Dr. Kildare (MGM, 1939)
The Witness Vanishes (Univ, 1939)
Smashing the Spy Ring (Col, 1939)

Calling Dr. Kildare (MGM, 1939)
Adventure in Diamonds (Par, 1940)
Dr. Kildare's Strange Case (MGM, 1940)
Star Dust (20th, 1940)
Lucky Partners (RKO, 1940)
A Dispatch from Reuters (WB, 1940)
Dr. Kildare Goes Home (MGM, 1940)
Dr. Kildare's Crisis (MGM, 1940)
Kitty Foyle (RKO, 1940)
The Devil and Miss Jones (RKO, 1941)
The Lone Wolf Takes a Chance (Col, 1941)
The People vs. Dr. Kildare (MGM, 1941)
Hit the Road (Univ, 1941)
Ellery Queen and the Perfect Crime (Col, 1941)
Dr. Kildare's Wedding Day (MGM, 1941)
Unholy Partners (MGM, 1941)
Dr. Kildare's Victory (MGM, 1941)
The Corsican Brothers (UA, 1941)
My Favorite Blonde (Par, 1942)
H. M. Pulhman, Esq. (MGM, 1941)
Fly by Night (Par, 1942)
Fingers at the Window (MGM, 1942)
Calling Dr. Gillespie (MGM, 1942)
The Loves of Edgar Allan Poe (20th, 1942)
Dr. Gillespie's New Assistant (MGM, 1942)
Flight for Freedom (RKO, 1943)
Forever and a Day (RKO, 1943)

Mr. Lucky (RKO, 1943)
Bomber's Moon (20th, 1943)
Dr. Gillespie's Criminal Case (MGM, 1943)
Hi Diddle Diddle [a.k.a. *Diamonds and Crime*] (UA, 1943)
Three Men in White (MGM, 1944)
The Hitler Gang (Par, 1944)
Mr. Skeffington (WB, 1944)
Ghost Catchers (Univ, 1944)
Secrets of Scotland Yard (Rep, 1944)
Between Two Women (MGM, 1944)
The Black Arrow (Col, 1948)
The Velvet Touch (RKO, 1948)
Slattery's Hurricane (20th, 1949)
Experiment Alcatraz (RKO, 1950)
My Forbidden Past (RKO, 1951)
Tarzan's Peril (RKO, 1951)
The Desert Fox (20th, 1951)
Two Dollar Bettor (Realart, 1951)
Confidence Girl (UA, 1952)
The Brigand (Col, 1952)
The Pathfinder (Col, 1952)
Loose in London (AA, 1953)
Walking My Baby Back Home (Univ, 1953)
Around the World in 80 Days (UA, 1956)
The Search for Bridey Murphy (Par, 1956)
Merry Andrew (MGM, 1958)

FRED KOHLER

Fred Kohler and Richard Arlen in The Light of Western Stars *(1930).*

Born April 20, 1888, Kansas City, Missouri. Married _____ , child: Fred. Died October 28, 1938, Los Angeles, California. Deemed by many the supreme sagebrush ugly bad guy who would kill his opponent at the slightest provocation. Occasionally in historical melodrama: 1924's *Abraham Lincoln* (New Orleans slave market auctioneer), *Old Ironsides* (second mate); contemporary melodrama: *Little Man, What Now?* (communist); and comedy: Mae West's *Goin' to Town* (Buck Gonzales). Son Fred, Jr. followed in his father's professional tradition.

Fred Kohler to Bing Crosby in *Mississippi:* "You moanin' hyena! Every breath that you take from now on will be a personal present from me!"

Films

Soldiers of Fortune (Hodkinson, 1919)
The Tiger's Trail (Pathé serial, 1919)
A Thousand to One (Associated Producers, 1920)
A Daughter of the Law (Univ, 1921)
That Girl Montana (Pathé, 1921)
Cyclone Bliss (Arrow, 1921)
Partners of the Tide (Hodkinson, 1921)
Thunder Island (Univ, 1921)
The Stampede (Kramer, 1921)
The Son of the Wolf (FBO, 1922)
His Back Against the Wall (G, 1922)
The Scrapper (Univ, 1922)
Without Compromise (Fox, 1922)
Trimmed (Univ, 1922)
Yellow Men and Gold (Univ, 1922)
Anna Christie (Associated FN, 1923)
The Flame of Life (Univ, 1923)
The Eleventh Hour (Fox, 1923)
North of Hudson Bay (Fox, 1923)
Hell's Hole (Fox, 1923)
The Red Warning (Univ, 1923)

Three Who Paid (Fox, 1923)
Shadows of the North (Univ, 1923)
Through the Flames (G, 1923)
The Iron Horse (Fox, 1924)
Abraham Lincoln (Associated FN, 1924)
Fighting Fury (Univ, 1924)
Dick Turpin (Fox, 1925)
Riders of the Purple Sage (Fox, 1925)
The Prairie Pirate (PDC, 1925)
Winds of Chance (FN, 1925)
The Thundering Herd (Par, 1925)
Danger Quest (Rayart, 1926)
The Country Beyond (Fox, 1926)
The Ice Flood (Univ, 1926)
Old Ironsides (Par, 1926)
The Blood Ship (Col, 1927)
The Devil's Masterpiece (Sanford F. Arnold, 1927)
The City Gone Wild (Par, 1927)
The Gay Defender (Par, 1927)
The Rough Riders (Par, 1927)
The Way of All Flesh (Par, 1927)

Shootin' Irons (Par, 1927)
Underworld (Par, 1927)
Open Range (Par, 1927)
Loves of Carmen (Fox, 1927)
Chinatown Charlie (FN, 1928)
Forgotten Faces (Par, 1928)
The Dragnet (Par, 1928)
The Spieler (Pathé, 1928)
The Vanishing Pioneer (Par, 1928)
The Showdown (Par, 1928)
The Case of Lena Smith (Par, 1929)
The Dummy (Par, 1929)
Broadway Babies (FN, 1929)
The Quitter (Col, 1929)
The Leatherneck (Pathé, 1929)
Sal of Singapore (Pathé, 1929)
River of Romance (Par, 1929)
Stairs of Sand (Par, 1929)
Tide of Empire (MGM, 1929)
Thunderbolt (Par, 1929)
Say It with Songs (WB, 1929)
Hell's Heroes (Univ, 1929)

The Light of Western Stars (Par, 1930)
Roadhouse Nights (Par, 1930)
Under a Texas Moon (WB, 1930)
The Lash (FN, 1931)
Fighting Caravans (Par, 1931)
The Right of Way (FN, 1931)
Woman Hungry (FN, 1931)
Other Men's Women (WB, 1931)
A Soldier's Plaything (WB, 1931)
Corsair (UA, 1931)
X Marks the Spot (Tif, 1931)
Carnival Boat (RKO, 1932)
Call Her Savage (Fox, 1932)
Rider of Death Valley (Univ, 1932)
The Texas Bad Man (Univ, 1932)
Wild Horse Mesa (Par, 1932)
The Fourth Horseman (Univ, 1932)
Under the Tonto Rim (Par, 1933)
The Constant Woman [a.k.a. Hell in a Circus] (WW, 1933)

Ship of Wanted Men (Showmen's Pictures, 1933)
The Deluge (RKO, 1933)
Fiddlin' Buckaroo (Univ, 1933)
The Wolf Dog (Mascot serial, 1933)
The Last Round Up (Par, 1934)
Kid Millions (UA, 1934)
Little Man, What Now? (Univ, 1934)
The Man from Hell (Willis Kent, 1934)
West of the Pecos (RKO, 1934)
Times Square Lady (MGM, 1935)
Mississippi (Par, 1935)
Goin' to Town (Par, 1935)
Border Brigand (Univ, 1935)
Hard Rock Harrigan (FN, 1935)
Men of Action (Conn Pictures, 1935)
The Trail's End (Beaumont, 1935)
Storm (Univ, 1935)
The Frisco Kid (WB, 1935)
Dangerous Intrigue (Col, 1936)

For the Service (Univ, 1936)
Heart of the West (Par, 1936)
The Plainsman (Par, 1936)
The Accusing Finger (Par, 1936)
Arizona Mahoney (Par, 1936)
The Vigilantes Are Coming (Rep serial, 1936)
Daughter of Shanghai (Par, 1937)
The Buccaneer (Par, 1938)
Marie Antoinette (MGM, 1938)
Forbidden Valley (Univ, 1938)
Blockade (UA, 1938)
Gangs of New York (Rep, 1938)
Billy the Kid Returns (Rep, 1938)
Painted Desert (RKO, 1938)

HENRY KOLKER

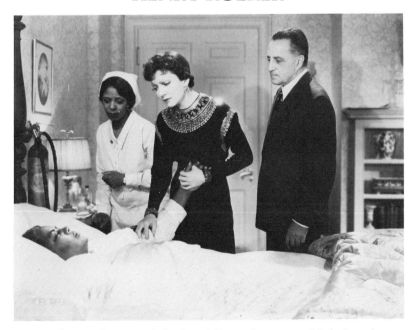

With Louise Beavers and Claudette Colbert in Imitation of Life (1934).

Born November 13, 1874, Berlin, Germany. Married 1) Margaret Bruenn; widowed; 2) Lilian Carroll. Died July 15, 1947, Los Angeles, California. Stern-faced and mustachioed. Could play a roué (Constance Bennett's *Sally, Irene and Mary*) or interpret farce (Bebe Daniels' *A Kiss in a Taxi*), but generally in talkies was a judge (*Maid of Salem, A Woman's Face*), a distrusting husband (Kay Francis' in *Jewel Robbery, The Keyhole, Wonder Bar*), a sophisticated father (Melvyn Douglas' in *Theodora Goes Wild*, Katharine Hepburn's in *Holiday*, Gary Cooper's in *The Adventures of Marco Polo*), etc. Played Friar Laurence in Norma Shearer's *Romeo and Juliet*.

Henry Kolker to Merle Oberon in *The Cowboy and the Lady:* "MARY SMITH IN A RUNAWAY MARRIAGE WITH A COWHAND. That's going to look fine in print!"

Films

The Bigger Man (M, 1915)
How Molly Malone Made Good (Kulee Features, 1915)
The Warning (World, 1915)
Gloria's Romance (Kleine serial, 1916)
The Shell Game (M, 1918)
Social Hypocrites (M, 1918)
The House of Mirth (M, 1918)
Blackie's Redemption (M, 1919)
Red Lantern (M, 1919)
Her Purchase Price (Robertson-Cole, 1919)
Third Generation (Robertson-Cole, 1920)
Bright Skies (Robertson-Cole, 1920)
The Greatest Love (Selznick, 1920)
Man of Stone (Selznick, 1920)
Disraeli (UA, 1921)
The Fighter (Selznick, 1921)
Bucking the Tiger (Selznick, 1921)
Who Am I? (Selznick, 1921)
The Purple Highway (Par, 1923)
The Leopardess (Par, 1923)
The Snow Bride (Par, 1923)
Sally, Irene and Mary (MG, 1925)
Any Woman (Par, 1925)
The Palace of Pleasure (Fox, 1926)
Hell's 400 (Fox, 1926)
West Point (Par, 1926)
Winning the Futurity (Chadwick Pictures, 1926)
A Kiss in a Taxi (Par, 1927)
Rough House Rosie (Par, 1927)
Don't Marry (Fox, 1928)
The Charge of the Gauchos (FBO, 1928)
Midnight Rose (Univ, 1928)
Soft Living (Fox, 1928)
Coquette (UA, 1929)
Pleasure Crazed (Fox, 1929)
Love, Live and Laugh (Fox, 1929)
The Valiant (Fox, 1929)
Du Barry, Woman of Passion (UA, 1930)
The Bad One (UA, 1930)
Good Intentions (Fox, 1930)
East Is West (Univ, 1930)
The Way of All Men (FN, 1930)
Don't Bet on Women (Fox, 1931)
The Spy (Fox, 1931)
Indiscreet (UA, 1931)
I Like Your Nerve (FN, 1931)
Washington Masquerade (MGM, 1931)
The Devil and the Deep (Par, 1932)

The First Year (Fox, 1932)
The Crash (FN, 1932)
Faithless (MGM, 1932)
Jewel Robbery (WB, 1932)
The Keyhole (WB, 1933)
A Bedtime Story (Par, 1933)
Narrow Corner (WB, 1933)
Baby Face (WB, 1933)
Gigolettes of Paris (Equitable, 1933)
The Power and the Glory (Fox, 1933)
Notorious but Nice (Chesterfield, 1933)
Bureau of Missing Persons (FN, 1933)
I Loved a Woman (FN, 1933)
Love, Honor and Oh, Baby! (Univ, 1933)
Golden Harvest (Par, 1933)
Blood Money (UA, 1933)
Meet the Baron (MGM, 1933)
Massacre (FN, 1934)
Wonder Bar (FN, 1934)
Sisters Under the Skin (Col, 1934)
The Hell Cat (Col, 1934)
Whom the Gods Destroy (Col, 1934)
Journal of a Crime (FN, 1934)
Success at Any Price (RKO, 1934)
The Girl from Missouri (MGM, 1934)
Name the Woman (Col, 1934)
Madame Du Barry (WB, 1934)
Now and Forever (Par, 1934)
Blind Date (Col, 1934)
Imitation of Life (Univ, 1934)
One Exciting Adventure (Univ, 1934)
The Band Plays On (MGM, 1934)
A Lost Lady (FN, 1934)
Million Dollar Ransom (Univ, 1934)
Lady by Choice (Col, 1934)
Sing Sing Nights (Mon, 1934)
She Loves Me Not (Par, 1934)
The Ghost Walks (Chesterfield, 1934)
Times Square Lady (MGM, 1935)
Red Hot Tires (FN, 1935)
Shipmates Forever (FN, 1935)
The Case of the Curious Bride (FN, 1935)
Charlie Chan in Paris (Fox, 1935)
Diamond Jim (Univ, 1935)
Three Kids and a Queen (Univ, 1935)
Society Doctor (MGM, 1935)
Mad Love (MGM, 1935)
Red Salute (UA, 1935)
Here Comes the Band (MGM, 1935)
The Mystery Man (Mon, 1935)
Honeymoon Limited (Mon, 1935)
My Marriage (Fox, 1935)

The Florentine Dagger (WB, 1935)
The Last Days of Pompeii (RKO, 1935)
One New York Night (MGM, 1935)
Frisco Waterfront (Rep, 1935)
The Black Room (Col, 1935)
Ladies Love Danger (Fox, 1935)
Collegiate (Par, 1935)
Bullets or Ballots (FN, 1936)
Romeo and Juliet (MGM, 1936)
Sitting on the Moon (Rep, 1936)
In His Steps (GN, 1936)
Great Guy (GN, 1936)
The Man Who Lived Twice (Col, 1936)
Theodora Goes Wild (Col, 1936)
They Wanted to Marry (RKO, 1937)
Under Cover of Night (MGM, 1937)
Conquest (MGM, 1937)
Thoroughbreds Don't Cry (MGM, 1937)
Green Light (WB, 1937)
Once a Doctor (FN, 1937)
Maid of Salem (Par, 1937)
Let Them Live (Univ, 1937)
The Devil Is Driving (Col, 1937)
The Adventures of Marco Polo (UA, 1938)
The Cowboy and the Lady (UA, 1938)
The Invisible Menace (WB, 1938)
Holiday (Col, 1938)
Safety in Numbers (20th, 1938)
Too Hot to Handle (MGM, 1938)
Let Us Live (Col, 1939)
Hidden Power (Col, 1939)
Parents on Trial (Col, 1939)
Union Pacific (Par, 1939)
Should Husbands Work? (Rep, 1939)
Main Street Lawyer (Rep, 1939)
The Real Glory (UA, 1939)
Here I Am a Stranger (20th, 1939)
Grand Old Opry (Rep, 1940)
Money and the Woman (WB, 1940)
The Man Who Lost Himself (Univ, 1941)
Las Vegas Nights (Par, 1941)
Sing for Your Supper (Col, 1941)
A Woman's Face (MGM, 1941)
The Great Swindle (Col, 1941)
The Parson of Panamint (Par, 1941)
Reunion (MGM, 1942)
Sarong Girl (Mon, 1943)
Bluebeard (PRC, 1944)
The Secret Life of Walter Mitty (RKO, 1947)

MARTIN KOSLECK

With Ilona Massey in International Lady *(1941).*

Born March 24, 1907, Barketzen, Germany. Married Eleanora von Mendelssohn (1947); widowed. Characterized by strongly Teutonic looks and an ability to convey an evil demeanor. Quickly cast for Nazi roles during World War II and thereafter. Began portraying Minister of Propaganda Dr. Goebbels in *Confessions of a Nazi Spy;* repeated the role frequently, as recently as 1961's *Hitler.* One of films' more hissable villains.

> **Martin Kosleck** to Basil Rathbone in *The Mad Doctor:* "You're like all the other clever ones. Clever until they meet a *woman,* and then they suddenly become fools—and the *law* gets them, standing with a faraway look in their eyes."

Films

Altrune (Ger–Br, 1930)
Die Singende Stadt (Ger–Br, 1930)
Fashions of 1934 (FN, 1934)
Confessions of a Nazi Spy (WB, 1939)
Nick Carter, Master Detective (MGM, 1939)
Nurse Edith Cavell (RKO, 1939)
Espionage Agent (WB, 1939)
Calling Philo Vance (WB, 1940)
Foreign Correspondent (UA, 1940)
The Mad Doctor (Par, 1941)
International Lady (UA, 1941)
Underground (WB, 1941)
The Devil Pays Off (Rep, 1941)
All Through the Night (WB, 1942)
Fly by Night (Par, 1942)
Nazi Agent (MGM, 1942)

Berlin Correspondent (20th, 1942)
Manila Calling (20th, 1942)
The Chetniks! (20th, 1943)
Bomber's Moon (20th, 1943)
The North Star (a.k.a. *Armored Attack]* (RKO, 1943)
The Hitler Gang (Par, 1944)
Secrets of Scotland Yard (Rep, 1944)
The Mummy's Curse (Univ, 1944)
The Frozen Ghost (Univ, 1945)
Gangs of the Waterfront (Rep, 1945)
Pursuit to Algiers (Univ, 1945)
The Spider (20th, 1945)
Crime of the Century (Rep, 1946)
House of Horrors (Univ, 1946)
Just Before Dawn (Col, 1946)
Strange Holiday (PRC, 1946)

The Wife of Monte Cristo (PRC, 1946)
She-Wolf of London (Univ, 1946)
The Beginning or the End? (MGM, 1947)
Assigned to Danger (EL, 1948)
Half Past Midnight (20th, 1948)
Smuggler's Cove (Mon, 1948)
Hitler (AA, 1961)
Something Wild (UA, 1961)
36 Hours (MGM, 1965)
The Saboteur: Code Name Mortiuri (20th, 1965)
The Agent for H.A.R.M. (Univ, 1966)
The Flesh Eaters (Cinema, 1967)
Which Way to the Front? (WB, 1970)
A Day at the White House (Harnell Productions, 1973)

OTTO KRUGER

With Jacqueline Wells [Julie Bishop] in Counsel for Crime *(1937).*

Born September 6, 1885, Toledo, Ohio. Married Sue MacManamy (1919), child: Ottilie. Died September 6, 1974, Woodland Hills, California. Respected stage and screen star who made one silent feature—*Under the Red Robe* (as rebellious Henri de Cochefort). Returned to the cinema a decade later, sometimes playing against his well-bred, genteel type: e.g., corrupt civic leader Eugene Ferguson in *I Am the Law*, Axis agent Charles Tobin in *Saboteur*. Was Dr. Livesey in Wallace Beery's *Treasure Island*, Joan Crawford's mature lover Richard Field in *Chained;* inherited but messed up Edward Everett Horton's stage classic comedy part in *Springtime for Henry*. Later, a silver-haired elitist, with a deep speaking voice, who bolstered many programmers: Kay Francis' *Allotment Wives*, Constance Bennett's *Smart Woman*, and Dorothy Lamour's *Lulu Belle*. Played Dr. Anderson in *Sex and the Single Girl*, his final feature. TV series: one-time host of "Lux Video Theatre."

Otto Kruger to Robert Cummings in *Saboteur:* "You have the makings of an outstanding boor."

Films

Under the Red Robe (G, 1923)
Turn Back the Clock (MGM, 1933)
Beauty for Sale (MGM, 1933)
Ever in My Heart (WB, 1933)
The Prizefighter and the Lady (MGM, 1933)
Gallant Lady (UA, 1933)
The Women in His Life (MGM, 1933)
Treasure Island (MGM, 1934)
Chained (MGM, 1934)
Men in White (MGM, 1934)
Paris Interlude (MGM, 1934)
The Crime Doctor (RKO, 1934)
Springtime for Henry (Fox, 1934)

Vanessa: Her Love Story (MGM, 1935)
Two Sinners (Rep, 1935)
Living Dangerously (Br, 1936)
Dracula's Daughter (Univ, 1936)
Lady of Secrets (Col, 1936)
Glamorous Nights (Br, 1937)
They Won't Forget (WB, 1937)
Counsel for Crime (Col, 1937)
The Barrier (Par, 1937)
Housemaster (Br, 1938)
Star of the Circus [a.k.a. Hidden Menace] (Br, 1938)
Thanks for the Memory (Par, 1938)
I Am the Law (Col, 1938)

Exposed (Univ, 1938)
Disbarred (Par, 1939)
The Amazing Mr. Forrest [a.k.a. The Gang's All Here] (Br, 1939)
Black Eyes (Br, 1939)
Zero Hour (Rep, 1939)
A Woman Is the Judge (Col, 1939)
Another Thin Man (MGM, 1939)
The Story of Dr. Ehrlich's Magic Bullet (WB, 1940)
A Dispatch from Reuters (WB, 1940)
Scandal Sheet (Col, 1940)
Seventeen (Par, 1940)
The Man I Married (20th, 1940)

The Big Boss (Col, 1941)
The Men in Her Life (Col, 1941)
Mercy Island (Rep, 1941)
Saboteur (Univ, 1942)
Friendly Enemies (UA, 1942)
Secrets of a Co-ed (PRC, 1942)
Hitler's Children (RKO, 1942)
Corregidor (PRC, 1943)
Night Plane from Chungking (Par, 1943)
Stage Door Canteen (UA, 1943)
Tarzan's Desert Mystery (RKO, 1943)
Knickerbocker Holiday (UA, 1944)
Cover Girl (Col, 1944)
Storm over Lisbon (Rep, 1944)
Murder, My Sweet (RKO, 1944)

They Live in Fear (Col, 1944)
The Woman Who Came Back (Rep, 1945)
On Stage, Everybody! (Univ, 1945)
Jungle Captive (Univ, 1945)
The Chicago Kid (Rep, 1945)
The Wonder Man (RKO, 1945)
The Great John L. (UA, 1945)
Allotment Wives (Mon, 1945)
Escape in the Fog (Col, 1945)
Earl Carroll's Vanities (Rep, 1945)
The Fabulous Suzanne (Rep, 1946)
Duel in the Sun (Selznick Releasing
    Organization, 1946)
Love and Learn (WB, 1947)
Smart Woman (AA, 1948)

Lulu Belle (Col, 1948)
711 Ocean Drive (Col, 1950)
Valentino (Col, 1951)
Payment on Demand (RKO, 1951)
High Noon (UA, 1952)
Magnificent Obsession (Univ, 1954)
Black Widow (20th, 1954)
The Last Command (Rep, 1955)
The Colossus of New York (Par, 1958)
The Young Philadelphians (WB, 1959)
Cash McCall (WB, 1959)
The Wonderful World of the Brothers
    Grimm (MGM, 1962)
Sex and the Single Girl (WB, 1964)

FRANK LACKTEEN

In Desert Gold (1926).

Born August 29, 1894, Kubber-Ilias, Asia Minor. Died July 8, 1968, Woodland Hills, California. Gangling, angular-faced. Remarkably adept at portraying villains of many different ethnic backgrounds: an Indian in the *Hawk of the Hills* (title role) and *Heroes of the West* (Buckskin Joe) serials, an Arab in the *Tarzan the Fearless* serial (Abdul), and a sinister Oriental in the *Red Barry* (Quong Lee) and *Don Winslow of the Navy* (Koloki) chapterplays.

Frank Lackteen to Ed Hinton in *Devil Goddess:* "This land taboo. You go."

Films

Less Than the Dust (Par, 1916)

The Yellow Menace (Steiner serial, 1916)

Woman (Heller & Wilke, 1918)

The Veiled Mystery (Vit serial, 1920)

The Avenging Arrow (Pathe serial, 1921)

White Eagle (Pathe serial, 1921)

The Timber Queen (Pathe serial, 1922)

The Fortieth Door (Pathe serial, 1924)

The Virgin (G, 1924)

The Pony Express (Par, 1925)

Sunken Silver (Pathe serial, 1925)

House Without a Key (Pathe serial, 1926)

Desert Gold (Par, 1926)

The Last Frontier (PDC, 1926)

The Unknown Cavalier (FN, 1926)

The Warning (Col, 1927)

Hawk of the Hills (Pathe serial, 1927)

Court-Martial (Col, 1928)

Prowlers of the Sea (Tif, 1928)

Men of the North (MGM, 1930—Sp, Fr, Ger, It versions)

Hell's Valley (National, 1931)

Law of the Tong (Syndicate, 1931)

Land of Wanted Men (Mon, 1932)

Heroes of the West (Univ serial, 1932)

Texas Pioneer (Mon, 1932)

Nagana (Univ, 1933)

Treason (Col, 1933)

Tarzan the Fearless (Principal serial, 1933)

Rustlers Round-Up (Univ, 1933)

Perils of Pauline (Univ serial, 1934)

Escape from Devil's Island (Col, 1935)

Rendezvous (MGM, 1935)

Under Two Flags (20th, 1936)

Women Are Trouble (MGM, 1936)

Mummy's Boys (RKO, 1936)

Anthony Adverse (WB, 1936)

The Charge of the Light Brigade (WB, 1936)

Radio Patrol (Univ serial, 1937)

Isle of Fury (WB, 1936)

I Cover the War (Univ, 1937)

Radio Patrol (Univ serial, 1937)

The Mysterious Pilot (Col serial, 1937)

Red Barry (Univ serial, 1938)

Suez (20th, 1938)

The Girl and the Gambler (RKO, 1939)

The Kansas Terrors (Rep, 1939)

6,000 Enemies (MGM, 1939)

Juarez (WB, 1939)

The Rains Came (20th, 1939)

Union Pacific (Par, 1939)

Lucky Cisco Kid (20th, 1940)

Meet the Wildcat (Univ, 1940)

Stagecoach War (Par, 1940)

Girl from Havana (Rep, 1940)

Moon over Burma (Par, 1940)

The Sea Wolf (WB, 1941)

Passage from Hong Kong (WB, 1941)

Jungle Girl (Rep serial, 1941)

South of Tahiti (Univ, 1941)

Bombs over Burma (PRC, 1942)

Don Winslow of the Navy (Univ serial, 1942)

The Chetniks! (20th, 1943)

Passport to Suez (Col, 1943)

Frontier Badmen (Univ, 1943)

Moonlight and Cactus (Univ, 1944)

Can't Help Singing (Univ, 1944)

The Desert Hawk (Col serial, 1944)

A Thousand and One Nights (Col, 1945)

Frontier Gal (Univ, 1945)

Singin' in the Corn (Col, 1946)

Oregon Trail Scouts (Rep, 1947)

Man-Eater of Kumaon (Univ, 1948)

Daughter of the Jungle (Rep, 1949)

The Mysterious Desperado (RKO, 1949)

Amazon Quest (Film Classics, 1949)

Flaming Feather (Par, 1951)

King of the Khyber Rifles (20th, 1953)

Northern Patrol (AA, 1953)

Bengal Brigade (Univ, 1954)

Devil Goddess (Col, 1955)

Three Came to Kill (UA, 1960)

Requiem for a Gunfighter (Emb, 1965)

ELSA LANCHESTER
(Elizabeth Sullivan)

In Ladies in Retirement *(1941).*

Born October 28, 1902, London, England. Married Charles Laughton (1929); widowed (1962). The irrepressible star of stage (especially one-woman shows), screen, radio, and TV on both sides of the Atlantic. Gained special prominence in dual role of Mary Shelley and the title figure in *Bride of Frankenstein*. Often on camera in support of her husband Charles Laughton: *The Private Life of Henry VIII* (Ann of Cleves), *Rembrandt* (Hendrickje Stoffels), *The Vessel of Wrath* (Martha Jones), *The Big Clock* (Louise Patterson), etc. Played Maria, the mayor's (Gene Lockhart's) wife in Danny Kaye's *The Inspector General*—one of her best assignments. More recently played the blowsy eccentric in Walt Disney films *(That Darn Cat!)* and horror entries *(Willard)*. Was the Miss Marple-like sleuth in the comedy *Murder by Death*. Oscar-nominated for BSAAA as Miss Potts in *Come to the Stable* (lost to Mercedes McCambridge of *All the King's Men*) and for Nurse Plimsoll in *Witness for the Prosecution* (lost to Miyoshi Umeki of *Sayonara*). TV series: "The [New] John Forsythe Show" (as Miss Culver, the principal) and "Nanny and the Professor."

> **Elsa Lanchester** to Charles Laughton in *Witness for the Prosecution:* "Sir Wilfrid, I have never known such insubordination. No, not even when I was a nurse in the front lines during the war."

Films

One of the Best (Br, 1927)
The Constant Nymph (Br, 1927)
Comets (Br, 1930)
The Love Habit (Br, 1931)
The Stronger Sex (Br, 1931)

Potiphar's Wife [a.k.a. *Her Strange Desire*] (Br, 1931)
The Officer's Mess (FN Br, 1931)
The Private Life of Henry VIII (UA Br, 1933)

The Private Life of Don Juan (UA Br, 1934)
David Copperfield (MGM, 1935)
Naughty Marietta (MGM, 1935)
Bride of Frankenstein (Univ, 1935)

The Ghost Goes West (UA Br, 1936)
Rembrandt (UA Br, 1936)
The Vessel of Wrath [a.k.a. The Beach-
    comber] (UA Br, 1938)
Ladies in Retirement (Col, 1941)
Son of Fury (20th, 1942)
Tales of Manhattan (20th, 1942)
Forever and a Day (RKO, 1943)
Thumbs Up (Rep, 1943)
Lassie Come Home (MGM, 1943)
Passport to Adventure (RKO, 1944)
Follow the Boys (Univ, 1944)
Son of Lassie (MGM, 1945)
The Spiral Staircase (RKO, 1946)
The Razor's Edge (20th, 1946)
Northwest Outpost (Rep, 1947)

The Bishop's Wife (RKO, 1947)
The Big Clock (Par, 1948)
Come to the Stable (20th, 1949)
The Secret Garden (MGM, 1949)
The Inspector General (WB, 1949)
The Petty Girl (Col, 1950)
Buccaneer's Girl (Univ, 1950)
Mystery Street (MGM, 1950)
Frenchie (Univ, 1950)
Young Man with Ideas (MGM, 1952)
Androcles and the Lion (RKO, 1952)
Dreamboat (20th, 1952)
Les Miserables (20th, 1952)
The Girls of Pleasure Island (Par, 1953)
Hell's Half Acre (Rep, 1954)
Three-Ring Circus (Par, 1954)

The Glass Slipper (MGM, 1955)
Witness for the Prosecution (UA, 1957)
Bell, Book and Candle (Col, 1958)
Mary Poppins (BV, 1964)
Honeymoon Hotel (MGM, 1964)
Pajama Party (AIP, 1964)
That Darn Cat! (BV, 1965)
Easy Come, Easy Go (Par, 1967)
Blackbeard's Ghost (BV, 1968)
Rascal (BV, 1969)
Me, Natalie (National General, 1969)
Willard (Cin, 1971)
Arnold (Cin, 1973)
Terror in the Wax Museum (Cin, 1973)
Murder by Death (Col, 1976)

DAVID LANDAU

David Landau and James Bell in I Am a Fugitive from a Chain Gang *(1932).*

Born ca. 1878, Philadelphia, Pennsylvania. Married _____. Died September 20, 1935, Hollywood, California. Came late in his acting career to the cinema but had a sizable output of features in a four-year period: *Arrowsmith* (veterinarian), *I Am a Fugitive from a Chain Gang* (warden), *Judge Priest* (defendant), etc.

David Landau to Mae West in *She Done Him Wrong:* "There's
a new dick in town called 'The Hawk.' . . . He's been tipped
off to Gus and he's got the goods on him."

Films

I Take This Woman (Par, 1931)
Street Scene (UA, 1931)
Arrowsmith (UA, 1931)
It's Tough to Be Famous (FN, 1932)
This Reckless Age (Par, 1932)
Taxi (WB, 1932)
Union Depot (FN, 1932)

Polly of the Circus (MGM, 1932)
Amateur Daddy (Fox, 1932)
Roadhouse Murder (RKO, 1932)
The Purchase Price (WB, 1932)
Horse Feathers (Par, 1932)
70,000 Witnesses (Par, 1932)
Lawyer Man (WB, 1932)

I Am a Fugitive from a Chain Gang (WB,
    1932)
False Faces (WW, 1932)
Undercover Man (Par, 1932)
Air Mail (Univ, 1932)
They Just Had to Get Married (Univ,
    1933)

The Crime of the Century (Par, 1933)
She Done Him Wrong (Par, 1933)
Gabriel over the White House (MGM, 1933)
Heritage of the Desert (Par, 1933)

The Nuisance (MGM, 1933)
No Marriage Ties (RKO, 1933)
One Man's Journey (RKO, 1933)
Bedside (FN, 1934)
Death on the Diamond (MGM, 1934)

As the Earth Turns (WB, 1934)
Wharf Angel (Par, 1934)
Man with Two Faces (FN, 1934)
Judge Priest (Fox, 1934)

JESSIE ROYCE LANDIS
(Jessie Royce Medbury)

With Ingrid Bergman (right) in Goodbye Again *(1961).*

Born November 25, 1900, Chicago, Illinois. Married 1) Rex Smith (1937); divorced (1942); 2) Major General J.F.R. Seitz (1956). Died February 2, 1972, Danbury, Connecticut. Played Alice Brady's role of the dizzy society matron in the remake of *My Man Godfrey*. Seemed destined to inherit that actress' mantle as the mature definitive interpreter of screwball comedy but the age for the genre had long since past. Was Grace Kelly's high-toned mother in *To Catch a Thief* and *The Swan* and Cary Grant's eccentric mater in *North by Northwest*. Final film appearance as Mrs. Harriet DuBarry Mossman, the customs smuggler in *Airport*.

> **Jessie Royce Landis** to Cary Grant in *To Catch a Thief:* "Bourbon's the only drink. You can take all that champagne and pour it down the English Channel. Why wait 80 years before you can drink the stuff?"

Films

Derelict (Par, 1930)
Mr. Belvedere Goes to College (20th, 1949)
It Happens Every Spring (20th, 1949)
My Foolish Heart (RKO, 1949)
Mother Didn't Tell Me (20th, 1950)
Tonight at 8:30 [a.k.a. Meet Me Tonight] (Continental, 1953)

She Couldn't Say No (RKO, 1953)
To Catch a Thief (Par, 1955)
The Swan (MGM, 1956)
The Girl He Left Behind (WB, 1956)
My Man Godfrey (Univ, 1957)
I Married a Woman (Univ, 1958)
A Private's Affair (20th, 1959)

North by Northwest (MGM, 1959)
Goodbye Again (UA, 1961)
Bon Voyage! (BV, 1962)
Boys' Night Out (MGM, 1962)
Critic's Choice (WB, 1963)
Gidget Goes to Rome (Col, 1963)
Airport (Univ, 1970)

JOI LANSING
(Joyce Wassmansdoff)

In the late 1950s.

Born April 6, 1928, Salt Lake City, Utah. Married 1) Lance Fuller (1951); divorced (1953); 2) Jerry Safron; 3) Stan Todd (1960). Died August 7, 1972, Santa Monica, California. Shapely blonde interpreter of languorous dolls with tart mouths: e.g., Dorine, Keenan Wynn's moll in *A Hole in the Head*. Worked well with Barbara Nichols, portraying the Coogle sisters in *Who Was That Lady?* TV series: "Love That Bob" and "Klondike."

Joi Lansing in *It Started with a Kiss:* "I like a man who knows what he wants."

Films

The Counterfeiters (20th, 1948)
The Girl from Jones Beach (WB, 1949)
Hot Cars (UA, 1956)
The Brave One (RKO, 1956)

Hot Shots (AA, 1956)
A Hole in the Head (UA, 1959)
It Started with a Kiss (MGM, 1959)
The Atomic Submarine (AA, 1959)

Who Was That Lady? (Col, 1959)
Marriage on the Rocks (WB, 1965)
Bigfoot (Ellman Enterprises, 1971)

JACK LaRUE
(Gaspare Biondolillo)

Jack LaRue, Barton MacLane, and Frank Jenks in Big Town Czar *(1939).*

Born May 4, 1900, New York City, New York. Married 1) Constance Deighton-Simpson (1938); divorced (1946); 2) Edith von Rosenberg (1948); annulled (1955); 3) Mrs. Anne J. Giordano (1952); annulled (1957). A priest in one of his first features—Helen Hayes' *A Farewell to Arms*—but found his forte in the contemptuous Trigger of *The Story of Temple Drake* (derived from William Faulkner's *Sanctuary*) who rapes blue-blooded Miriam Hopkins. Would later play in *No Orchids for Miss Blandish,* based on James Hadley Chase's novel, which also borrowed heavily from the storyline of *Sanctuary.* Usually cast as a grim hood thereafter. On stage played opposite Mae West in a revival of *Diamond Lil.*

> **Jack LaRue** to Jean Rogers in *Charlie Chan in Panama:* "You are very independent for a girl without a passport . . . . Go back to work."

Films

While Paris Sleeps (Fox, 1932)
Radio Patrol (Univ, 1932)
Virtue (Col, 1932)
I Am a Fugitive from a Chain Gang (WB, 1932)
A Farewell to Arms (Par, 1932)
Man Against Woman (Col, 1932)
The All-American (Univ, 1932)
The Mouthpiece (WB, 1932)
Blessed Event (WB, 1932)
Lawyer Man (WB, 1932)
Three on a Match (FN, 1932)
The Woman Accused (Par, 1933)
Christopher Strong (RKO, 1933)
Terror Aboard (Par, 1933)
The Story of Temple Drake (Par, 1933)
Girl in 419 (Par, 1933)
Gambling Ship (Par, 1933)

To the Last Man (Par, 1933)
Headline Shooters (RKO, 1933)
The Kennel Murder Case (WB, 1933)
The Fighting Rookie (Mayfair, 1934)
Good Dame (Par, 1934)
Straight Is the Way (MGM, 1934)
Miss Fane's Baby Is Stolen (Par, 1934)
Take the Stand (Liberty, 1934)
No Ransom (Liberty, 1934)
Secret of the Chateau (Univ, 1934)
Times Square Lady (MGM, 1935)
Calling All Cars (Empire, 1935)
The Daring Young Man (Fox, 1935)
Under the Pampas Moon (Fox, 1935)
Men of the Hour (Col, 1935)
The Headline Woman (Mascot, 1935)
Waterfront Lady (Rep, 1935)
Little Big Shot (WB, 1935)

Special Agent (WB, 1935)
Remember Last Night? (Univ, 1935)
His Night Out (Univ, 1935)
After the Dance (Col, 1935)
Hot off the Press (Victory, 1935)
Strike Me Pink (UA, 1936)
Dancing Pirate (RKO, 1936)
It Couldn't Have Happened (Invincible, 1936)
Yellow Cargo (Pacific, 1936)
Go West, Young Man (Par, 1936)
Mind Your Own Business (Par, 1936)
Born to Fight (Conn Pictures, 1936)
Bridge of Sighs (Invincible, 1936)
That I May Live (20th, 1937)
Her Husband Lies (Par, 1937)
Captains Courageous (MGM, 1937)
Dangerous Holiday (Rep, 1937)

Trapped by G-Men [a.k.a. *River of Missing Men*] (Col, 1937)
Arson Gang Busters (Rep, 1938)
Under the Big Top (Mon, 1938)
Valley of the Giants (WB, 1938)
I Demand Payment (Imperial Distributors, 1938)
Murder in Soho [a.k.a. *Murder in the Night*] (Br, 1939)
The Amazing Mr. Forrest [a.k.a. *The Gang's All Here*] (Br, 1939)
Big Town Czar (Univ, 1939)
In Old Caliente (Rep, 1939)
Forgotten Girls (Rep, 1940)
Charlie Chan in Panama (20th, 1940)
Enemy Agent (Univ, 1940)
Fugitive from a Prison Camp (Col, 1940)
The Sea Hawk (WB, 1940)
East of the River (WB, 1940)
Paper Bullets [a.k.a. *Gangs, Inc.*] (PRC, 1941)

The Hard Guy (PRC, 1941)
Ringside Maisie (MGM, 1941)
The Gentleman from Dixie (Mon, 1941)
Footsteps in the Dark (WB, 1941)
Swamp Woman (PRC, 1941)
Highways by Night (RKO, 1942)
X Marks the Spot (Rep, 1942)
American Empire (UA, 1942)
The Pay-Off (PRC, 1942)
You Can't Beat the Law (Mon, 1943)
The Girl from Monterey (PRC, 1943)
The Desert Song (WB, 1943)
The Law Rides Again (Mon, 1943)
Pistol Packin' Mama (Rep, 1943)
The Sultan's Daughter (Mon, 1943)
Never a Dull Moment (Univ, 1943)
Smart Guy (Mon, 1943)
Leave It to the Irish (Mon, 1944)
The Last Ride (WB, 1944)
Machine Gun Mama (PRC, 1944)
Follow the Leader (Mon, 1944)

Dangerous Passage (Par, 1944)
Steppin' in Society (Rep, 1945)
Dakota (Rep, 1945)
The Spanish Main (RKO, 1945)
Road to Utopia (Par, 1945)
Cornered (RKO, 1945)
Murder in the Music Hall (Rep, 1946)
In Old Sacramento (Rep, 1946)
Bush Pilot (Screen Guild, 1947)
Santa Fe Uprising (Rep, 1947)
Robin Hood of Monterey (Mon, 1947)
My Favorite Brunette (Par, 1947)
No Orchids for Miss Blandish (Br, 1948)
For Heaven's Sake (20th, 1950)
Ride the Man Down (Rep, 1952)
Slaughter on Tenth Avenue (Univ, 1957)
Robin and the Seven Hoods (WB, 1964)
For Those Who Think Young (UA, 1964)

HARRY LAUTER

Lee J. Cobb, Eleanore Tanin, Barry L. Connors, and Harry Lauter in *Miami Expose (1956).*

Born June 19, 1925, New York City, New York. Married _____ , child: daughter. Capable, athletic supporting player of features and serials. More recently has turned to painting; for a time ran a Los Angeles art gallery. TV series: "Tales of the Texas Rangers" and "The Roy Rogers Show" (as Mayor Ralph Cotton).

Harry Lauter to George Montgomery in *The Toughest Gun in Tombstone:* "Terry's the only one who knows what the killer looks like. He's certainly in real danger."

330

Films

A Foreign Affair (Par, 1948)
White Heat (WB, 1949)
Zamba (EL, 1949)
The Great Dan Patch (UA, 1949)
Blue Grass of Kentucky (Mon, 1950)
Experiment Alcatraz (RKO, 1950)
Silver City Bonanza (Rep, 1951)
Thunder in God's Country (Rep, 1951)
Flying Disc Man from Mars (Rep serial, 1951)
Whirlwind (Col, 1951)
According to Mrs. Hoyle (Mon, 1951)
The Kid from Amarillo (Col, 1951)
Valley of Fire (Col, 1951)
Night Stage to Galveston (Col, 1952)
Apache Country (Col, 1952)
The Sea Tiger (Mon, 1952)
The Steel Fist (Mon, 1952)
Yukon Gold (Mon, 1952)
Canadian Mounties vs. Atomic Invaders (Rep serial, 1953)
The Marshal's Daughter (UA, 1953)
Prince of Pirates (Col, 1953)
Topeka (AA, 1953)

Fighter Attack (AA, 1953)
Pack Train (Col, 1953)
Dragonfly Squadron (AA, 1954)
Trader Tom of the China Seas (Rep serial, 1954)
Yankee Pasha (Univ, 1954)
Return to Treasure Island (UA, 1954)
The Forty-Niners (AA, 1954)
King of the Carnival (Rep serial, 1955)
It Came from Beneath the Sea (Col, 1955)
The Creature with the Atom Brain (Col, 1955)
The Crooked Web (Col, 1955)
At Gunpoint (AA, 1955)
Earth vs. the Flying Saucers (Col, 1956)
The Werewolf (Col, 1956)
Miami Expose (Col, 1956)
Dig That Uranium (AA, 1956)
The Women of Pitcairn Island (20th, 1957)
Hellcats of the Navy (Col, 1957)
The Badge of Marshal Brennan (AA, 1957)
Death in Small Doses (AA, 1957)

Raiders of Old California (Rep, 1957)
Return to Warbow (Col, 1958)
The Toughest Gun in Tombstone (UA, 1958)
The Cry Baby Killer (AA, 1958)
Missile Monsters (Rep, 1958)
Tarzan's Fight for Life (MGM, 1958)
Good Day for a Hanging (Col, 1958)
The Gunfight at Dodge City (UA, 1959)
Louisiana Hussy (Howco International, 1960)
Posse from Hell (Univ, 1961)
The Wild Westerners (Col, 1962)
Fort Courageous (20th, 1965)
Convict Stage (20th, 1965)
Ambush Bay (UA, 1966)
Fort Utah (Par, 1967)
Barquero (UA, 1970)
Escape from the Planet of the Apes (20th, 1971)
The Todd Killings (National General, 1971)
Superbeast (UA, 1972)

LUCILLE LaVERNE

In the 1930s.

Born November 8, 1872, Nashville, Tennessee. Died March 4, 1945, Culver City, California. In several D. W. Griffith features: *Orphans of the Storm* (Mother Frochard), *America* (refugee mother), *Abraham Lincoln* (midwife). Cast to type as the crone Ma Magdalena in *Little Caesar* and was less offensive as one of the mothers in John Ford's *Pilgrimage*. On target as the vicious harridan La Vengeance in 1935's *A Tale of Two Cities*.

Lucille LaVerne to Edward G. Robinson in *Little Caesar:* "It's gonna cost you big, because I'm takin' big chances."

Films

Polly of the Circus (G, 1917)
The Life Mask (FN, 1918)
The Praise Agent (World, 1919)
Orphans of the Storm (UA, 1921)
The White Rose (UA, 1923)
Zaza (Par, 1923)
America (UA, 1924)
His Darker Self (PDC, 1924)
Sun-Up (MGM, 1925)
The Last Moment (G, 1928)
Abraham Lincoln (UA, 1930)
Sinner's Holiday (WB, 1930)

Little Caesar (FN, 1930)
An American Tragedy (Par, 1931)
The Great Meadow (MGM, 1931)
Union Depot (FN, 1931)
The Unholy Garden (UA, 1931)
24 Hours (Par, 1931)
She Wanted a Millionaire (Fox, 1932)
Alias the Doctor (FN, 1932)
While Paris Sleeps (Fox, 1932)
Hearts of Humanity (Majestic, 1932)
Breach of Promise (WW, 1932)
Wild Horse Mesa (Par, 1932)

A Strange Adventure [a.k.a. *The Wayne Murder Case*] (Mon, 1932)
Pilgrimage (Fox, 1933)
Last Trail (Fox, 1933)
The Beloved (Univ, 1934)
School for Girls (Liberty, 1934)
The Mighty Barnum (UA, 1934)
School for Girls (Liberty, 1934)
Kentucky Kernels (RKO, 1934)
A Tale of Two Cities (MGM, 1935)
Snow White and the Seven Dwarfs (RKO, 1937) [voice only]

MARC LAWRENCE

In the 1940s.

Born 1910, New York City, New York. Originally a New York stage performer. Swarthy, pock-marked complexion. Well-suited to gangster roles: *San Quentin* (Veneti), *I Am the Law* (Eddie Girard), *Invisible Stripes* (Lefty), *Lady Scarface* (Lefty Landers), etc. Especially effective as Ziggy in *Key Largo* and as the bookmaker Cobby in *The Asphalt Jungle*. Worked mostly abroad in the 1960s and 1970s.

Marc Lawrence to Wendy Barrie in *I Am the Law:* "You know, I think we're workin' this thing all wrong. Instead of takin' the places away from Cronin, we ought to take Cronin away from the places."

Films

White Woman (Par, 1933)
Gambling Ship (Par, 1933)
Death on the Diamond (MGM, 1934)
Man of the Hour (Col, 1935)
Little Big Shot (WB, 1935)
Dr. Socrates (FN, 1935)
Road Gang (WB, 1936)
Desire (Par, 1936)
Trapped by Television (Col, 1936)
Love on a Bet (RKO, 1936)
Counterfeit (Col, 1936)
The Final Hour (Col, 1936)
Night Waitress (RKO, 1936)
I Promise to Pay (Col, 1937)
What Price Vengeance? (Rialto, 1937)
Racketeers in Exile (Col, 1937)
Motor Madness (Col, 1937)
San Quentin (FN, 1937)
Criminals of the Air (Col, 1937)
Counsel for Crime (Col, 1937)
Charlie Chan on Broadway (20th, 1937)
Murder in Greenwich Village (Col, 1937)
The Shadow (Col, 1937)
Penitentiary (Col, 1938)
Who Killed Gail Preston? (Col, 1938)
Convicted (Col, 1938)
I Am the Law (Col, 1938)
Squadron of Honor (Col, 1938)
Adventure in Sahara (Col, 1938)
While New York Sleeps (20th, 1938)
Charlie Chan in Honolulu (20th, 1938)
The Spider's Web (Col serial, 1938)
Sergeant Madden (MGM, 1939)
Homicide Bureau (Col, 1939)
Romance of the Redwoods (Col, 1939)
Ex-Champ (Univ, 1939)
Blind Alley (Col, 1939)
S.O.S. Tidal Wave (Rep, 1939)
The Housekeeper's Daughter (UA, 1939)
Dust Be My Destiny (WB, 1939)
Beware, Spooks! (Col, 1939)
Invisible Stripes (WB, 1940)

Johnny Apollo (20th, 1940)
The Man Who Talked Too Much (WB, 1940)
Charlie Chan at the Wax Museum (20th, 1940)
The Great Profile (20th, 1940)
Brigham Young—Frontiersman (20th, 1940)
The Golden Fleecing (MGM, 1940)
Love, Honor and Oh, Baby! (Univ, 1940)
Tall, Dark and Handsome (20th, 1941)
A Dangerous Game (Univ, 1941)
The Monster and the Girl (Par, 1941)
The Man Who Lost Himself (Univ, 1941)
Blossoms in the Dust (MGM, 1941)
The Shepherd of the Hills (Par, 1941)
Hold That Ghost (Univ, 1941)
Lady Scarface (RKO, 1941)
Sundown (UA, 1941)
Public Enemies (Rep, 1941)
Nazi Agent (MGM, 1942)
This Gun for Hire (Par, 1942)
Yokel Boy (Rep, 1942)
Call of the Canyon (Rep, 1942)
'Neath Brooklyn Bridge (Mon, 1942)
The Ox-Bow Incident (20th, 1943)
Eyes of the Underworld (Univ, 1943)
Calaboose (UA, 1943)
Hit the Ice (Univ, 1943)
The Princess and the Pirate (RKO, 1944)
Rainbow Island (Par, 1944)
Tampico (20th, 1944)
Club Havana (PRC, 1945)
Dillinger (Mon, 1945)
Don't Fence Me In (Rep, 1945)
Flame of Barbary Coast (Rep, 1945)
Life with Blondie (Col, 1945)
Blonde Alibi (Univ, 1946)
Cloak and Dagger (WB, 1946)
The Virginian (Par, 1946)
Yankee Fakir (Rep, 1947)
Captain from Castile (20th, 1947)

I Walk Alone (Par, 1947)
Joe Palooka in the Knock-Out (Mon, 1947)
Unconquered (Par, 1947)
Key Largo (WB, 1948)
Out of the Storm (Rep, 1948)
Jigsaw [a.k.a. Gun Moll] (UA, 1949)
Calamity Jane and Sam Bass (Univ, 1949)
Tough Assignment (Lip, 1949)
The Black Hand (MGM, 1950)
The Asphalt Jungle (MGM, 1950)
Abbott and Costello in the Foreign Legion (Univ, 1950)
The Desert Hawk (Univ, 1950)
Vacanze Col Ganster [a.k.a. Gun Moll] (It, 1951)
Hurricane Island (Col, 1951)
My Favorite Spy (Par, 1951)
I Tre Corsari (It, 1952)
Jolanda, la Figlia del Corsaro Nero (It, 1953)
Helen of Troy (WB, 1956)
Kill Her Gently (Col, 1958)
Johnny Cool (UA, 1963)
Nightmare in the Sun (Zodiac, 1965)
Pampa Selvaje [a.k.a. Savage Pampas] (Sp-US, 1965)
Johnny Tiger (Univ, 1966)
Du mou dans la Gachette [a.k.a. Duex Tueurs/Due Killers in Fuga] (Fr-It, 1966)
Due Mafiosi Control Al Capone [a.k.a. Dos Contro Al Capone] (It-Sp, 1966)
Custer of the West (Cin, 1968)
Un Escercito de 5 Uomini [a.k.a. The Five-Man Army] (It, 1969)
Krakatoa—East of Java (Cin, 1969)
The Kremlin Letter (20th, 1971)
Frasier, the Sensuous Lion (LCS, 1973)
The Man with the Golden Gun (UA, 1974)
Marathon Man (Par, 1976)
A Piece of the Action (WB, 1977)

FRITZ LEIBER

Fritz Leiber and Jean Hersholt in Sins of Man *(1936).*

Born January 31, 1883, Chicago, Illinois. Married Virginia Bronson. Died October 10, 1966, Pacific Palisades, California. Well-regarded Shakespearean actor—with the noble profile—who played Julius Caesar to Theda Bara's *Cleopatra* and King Solomon to Betty Blythe's *Queen of Sheba* in silents. Fourteen years later returned to the screen typed as the white-haired ascetic: *A Tale of Two Cities* (Gaspard), *The Story of Louis Pasteur* (Dr. Charbonnet), *The Hunchback of Notre Dame* (nobleman), *Monsieur Verdoux* (priest), etc.

Fritz Leiber in *The Story of Louis Pasteur*: "I stand here to defend the honor of French medicine against the tricks of a charlatan."

Films

Romeo and Juliet (M, 1916)
Cleopatra (Fox, 1917)
If I Were King (Fox, 1920)
Queen of Sheba (Fox, 1921)
A Tale of Two Cities (MGM, 1935)
The Story of Louis Pasteur (WB, 1935)
Sins of Man (20th, 1936)
Hearts in Bondage (Rep, 1936)
Under Two Flags (20th, 1936)
Anthony Adverse (WB, 1936)
Down to the Sea (Rep, 1936)
Camille (MGM, 1936)
Champagne Waltz (Par, 1937)
The Prince and the Pauper (WB, 1937)
The Great Garrick (WB, 1937)
The Jury's Secret (Univ, 1938)
Flight into Nowhere (Col, 1938)
Gateway (20th, 1938)
Nurse Edith Cavell (RKO, 1939)
They Made Her a Spy (RKO, 1939)

The Hunchback of Notre Dame (RKO, 1939)
Pack Up Your Troubles (20th, 1939)
The Way of All Flesh (Par, 1940)
All This, and Heaven Too (WB, 1940)
The Sea Hawk (WB, 1940)
The Lady with Red Hair (WB, 1940)
The Mortal Storm (MGM, 1940)
Aloma of the South Seas (Par, 1941)
Crossroads (MGM, 1942)
The Desert Song (WB, 1943)
First Comes Courage (Col, 1943)
The Phantom of the Opera (Univ, 1943)
Are These Our Parents? (Mon, 1944)
The Imposter (Univ, 1944)
Cry of the Werewolf (Col, 1944)
The Cisco Kid Returns (Mon, 1945)
This Love of Ours (Univ, 1945)
The Spanish Main (RKO, 1945)
Son of Lassie (MGM, 1945)

Humoresque (WB, 1946)
A Scandal in Paris [a.k.a. Thieves' Holiday] (UA, 1946)
Strange Journey (20th, 1946)
Angel on My Shoulder (UA, 1946)
High Conquest (Mon, 1947)
Bells of San Angelo (Rep, 1947)
The Web (Univ, 1947)
Dangerous Venture (UA, 1947)
Monsieur Verdoux (UA, 1947)
Another Part of the Forest (Univ, 1948)
Adventures of Casanova (EL, 1948)
To the Ends of the Earth (Col, 1948)
Inner Sanctum (Film Classics, 1948)
Bride of Vengeance (Par, 1949)
Song of India (Col, 1949)
Samson and Delilah (Par, 1949)
Bagdad (Univ, 1949)
Devil's Doorway (MGM, 1950)

SHELDON LEONARD
(Sheldon Barshad)

Barbara Hale, Sheldon Leonard, and Tom Conway in The Falcon in Hollywood *(1944).*

Born February 22, 1907, New York City, New York. Married 1) Frances Babor (1935); children: two; 2) Mary Louise _____ , child: Graham. Pug-faced, stocky actor. Best typified by his Harry the Horse in the film *Guys and Dolls*. Spoke fractured English from the side of his mouth, and sported a cigar. Could grand-slam his fist into any opponent's face. Played an admirable underworld figure: *Lucky Jordan* (Slip Morgan), *The Falcon in Hollywood* (Louie), *Jinx Money* (Lippy Harris), *Stop, You're Killing Me* (Lefty), *Money from Home* (Jumbo Schneider), etc. Very successful producer (and sometimes director and actor) of such hit TV series as "Make Room for Daddy" and "I Spy." Co-starred with Sheree North in the short-lived "Big Eddie" teleseries.

Sheldon Leonard to Alan Ladd in *Lucky Jordan:* "I'm going to do you one favor, just for old time's sake. Where do you want it—in the front or in the back?"

Films

Another Thin Man (MGM, 1939)
Tall, Dark and Handsome (20th, 1941)
Week-End in Havana (20th, 1941)
Buy Me That Town (Par, 1941)
Private Nurse (20th, 1941)
Married Bachelor (MGM, 1941)
Rise and Shine (20th, 1941)
Tortilla Flat (MGM, 1942)
Born to Sing (MGM, 1942)
Lucky Jordan (Par, 1942)
Pierre of the Plains (MGM, 1942)
Street of Chance (Par, 1942)
Taxi, Mister (UA, 1943)
Klondike Kate (Col, 1943)
Hit the Ice (Univ, 1943)
The Falcon in Hollywood (RKO, 1944)
Uncertain Glory (WB, 1944)
Gambler's Choice (Par, 1944)
Timber Queen (Par, 1944)
To Have and Have Not (WB, 1944)
Trocadero (Rep, 1944)
Why Girls Leave Home (PRC, 1945)

Zombies on Broadway (RKO, 1945)
Shadow of Terror (PRC, 1945)
River Gang (Univ, 1945)
Frontier Gal (Univ, 1945)
Captain Kidd (UA, 1945)
Radio Stars on Parade (RKO, 1945)
Crime, Inc. (PRC, 1945)
The Last Crooked Mile (Rep, 1946)
The Gentleman Misbehaves (Col, 1946)
Somewhere in the Night (20th, 1946)
Her Kind of Man (WB, 1946)
It's a Wonderful Life (RKO, 1946)
Bowery Bombshell (Mon, 1946)
Decoy (Mon, 1946)
Rainbow over Texas (Rep, 1946)
The Gangster (AA, 1947)
Sinbad the Sailor (RKO, 1947)
Violence (Mon, 1947)
If You Knew Susie (RKO, 1948)
Open Secret (EL, 1948)
Alias a Gentleman (MGM, 1948)
Jinx Money (Mon, 1948)

Madonna of the Desert (Rep, 1948)
Shep Comes Home (Screen Guild, 1948)
My Dream Is Yours (WB, 1949)
Take One False Step (Univ, 1949)
Daughter of the Jungle (Rep, 1949)
The Iroquois Trail (UA, 1950)
Abbott and Costello Meet the Invisible Man (Univ, 1951)
Behave Yourself! (RKO, 1951)
Come Fill the Cup (WB, 1951)
Breakdown (Jack Broder Productions, 1952)
Here Come the Nelsons [a.k.a. *Meet the Nelsons*] (Univ, 1952)
Young Man with Ideas (MGM, 1952)
Stop, You're Killing Me (WB, 1952)
The Diamond Queen (WB, 1953)
Money from Home (Par, 1953)
Guys and Dolls (MGM, 1955)
Pocketful of Miracles (UA, 1961)

JOHN LITEL

George Raft, Ann Sheridan, Humphrey Bogart, Pedro Regas, and John Litel in
They Drive by Night (1940).

Born December 30, 1892. Married 1) Ruth Pichens (1920); widowed (1955); 2) Mrs. Beatrice West (1955). Died February 3, 1972, Woodland Hills, California. Stalwart featured player at Warner Bros. who specialized in well-meaning souls turned distraught: e.g., Kay Francis' jealous spouse in *Comet over Broadway*. Played Bonita Granville's dad in the *Nancy Drew* series and Jimmy Lydon's patient attorney/father in the *Henry Aldrich* entries; later was Ted Donaldson's dad in the *Rusty* (the dog) films.

John Litel to Olivia de Havilland in *They Died with Their Boots On:* "Come, my dear, your soldier won his last fight after all."

Films

On the Border (WB, 1930)
Wayward (Par, 1932)
The Black Legion (WB, 1936)
Fugitive in the Sky (WB, 1937)
Marked Woman (WB, 1937)
Midnight Court (WB, 1937)
Slim (WB, 1937)
The Life of Emile Zola (WB, 1937)
Missing Witness (WB, 1937)
Back in Circulation (WB, 1937)
Alcatraz Island (WB, 1938)
Gold Is Where You Find It (WB, 1938)
A Slight Case of Murder (WB, 1938)
My Bill (WB, 1938)
Broadway Musketeers (WB, 1938)
Love, Honor and Behave (WB, 1938)
Jezebel (WB, 1938)
Over the Wall (WB, 1938)

Little Miss Thoroughbred (WB, 1938)
The Amazing Dr. Clitterhouse (WB, 1938)
Nancy Drew, Detective (WB, 1938)
Valley of the Giants (WB, 1938)
Comet over Broadway (WB, 1938)
Wings of the Navy (WB, 1939)
You Can't Get Away with Murder (WB, 1939)
Secret Service of the Air (WB, 1939)
On Trial (WB, 1939)
Dodge City (WB, 1939)
Dust Be My Destiny (WB, 1939)
Dead End Kids on Dress Parade (WB, 1939)
The Return of Dr. X (WB, 1939)
A Child Is Born (WB, 1939)
One Hour to Live (Univ, 1939)
Nancy Drew, Trouble Shooter (WB, 1939)

Nancy Drew and the Hidden Staircase (WB, 1939)
The Fighting 69th (WB, 1940)
Castle on the Hudson (WB, 1940)
Virginia City (WB, 1940)
An Angel from Texas (WB, 1940)
The Man Who Talked Too Much (WB, 1940)
It All Came True (WB, 1940)
Santa Fe Trail (WB, 1940)
They Drive by Night (WB, 1940)
Murder in the Air (WB, 1940)
Money and the Woman (WB, 1940)
Knute Rockne—All-American (WB, 1940)
The Lady with Red Hair (WB, 1940)
Men Without Souls (Col, 1940)
Flight Angels (WB, 1940)

Gambling on the High Seas (WB, 1940)
Father Is a Prince (WB, 1940)
The Trial of Mary Dugan (MGM, 1941)
Father's Son (WB, 1941)
Thieves Fall Out (WB, 1941)
The Big Boss (Col, 1941)
Henry Aldrich for President (Par, 1941)
The Great Mr. Nobody (WB, 1941)
Don Winslow of the Navy (Univ serial, 1941)
Sealed Lips (Univ, 1941)
They Died with Their Boots On (WB, 1941)
Kid Glove Killer (MGM, 1942)
Henry and Dizzy (Par, 1942)
The Mystery of Marie Roget (Univ, 1942)
Mississippi Gambler (Univ, 1942)
Men of Texas (Univ, 1942)
Invisible Agent (Univ, 1942)
A Desperate Chance for Ellery Queen (Col, 1942)
Henry Aldrich, Editor (Par, 1942)
Boss of Big Town (PRC, 1942)
Madame Spy (Univ, 1942)
Henry Aldrich Gets Glamour (Par, 1943)
Submarine Base (PRC, 1943)
Crime Doctor (Col, 1943)
Murder in Times Square (Col, 1943)
Henry Aldrich Swings It (Par, 1943)
Where Are Your Children? (Mon, 1943)
Henry Aldrich Haunts a House (Par, 1943)
Murder in the Blue Room (Univ, 1944)
Henry Aldrich Plays Cupid (Par, 1944)
Henry Aldrich's Little Secret (Par, 1944)

Faces in the Fog (Rep, 1944)
My Buddy (Rep, 1944)
Lake Placid Serenade (Rep, 1944)
Brewster's Millions (UA, 1945)
The Enchanted Forest (PRC, 1945)
Salome, Where She Danced (Univ, 1945)
San Antonio (WB, 1945)
The Crimson Canary (Univ, 1945)
The Daltons Ride Again (Univ, 1945)
Northwest Trail (Screen Guild, 1945)
The Crime Doctor's Warning (Col, 1946)
The Madonna's Secret (Rep, 1946)
A Night in Paradise (Univ, 1946)
The Return of Rusty (Col, 1946)
She Wrote the Book (Univ, 1946)
Sister Kenny (RKO, 1946)
Swell Guy (Univ, 1946)
Lighthouse (PRC, 1946)
Smooth as Silk (Univ, 1946)
Cass Timberlane (MGM, 1947)
The Beginning or the End? (MGM, 1947)
Easy Come, Easy Go (Par, 1947)
The Guilty (Mon, 1947)
Heaven Only Knows (UA, 1947)
Christmas Eve [a.k.a. Sinners' Holiday] (UA, 1947)
Smart Woman (AA, 1948)
My Dog Rusty (Col, 1948)
Rusty Leads the Way (Col, 1948)
Pitfall (UA, 1948)
The Valiant Hombre (UA, 1948)
Triple Threat (Col, 1948)
I, Jane Doe (Rep, 1948)
The Gal Who Took the West (Univ, 1949)
Outpost in Morocco (UA, 1949)

Shamrock Hill (EL, 1949)
Rusty Saves a Life (Col, 1949)
Rusty's Birthday (Col, 1949)
Woman in Hiding (Univ, 1949)
Mary Ryan, Detective (Col, 1950)
The Fuller Brush Girl (Col, 1950)
Kiss Tomorrow Goodbye (WB, 1950)
The Sundowners (EL, 1950)
Take Care of My Little Girl (20th, 1951)
The Cuban Fireball (Rep, 1951)
The Groom Wore Spurs (Univ, 1951)
Texas Rangers (Col, 1951)
Little Egypt (Univ, 1951)
Two Dollar Bettor (Realart, 1951)
Flight to Mars (Mon, 1951)
Jet Job (Mon, 1952)
Montana Belle (RKO, 1952)
Scaramouche (MGM, 1952)
Jack Slade (AA, 1953)
Sitting Bull (UA, 1954)
Texas Lady (RKO, 1955)
Double Jeopardy (Rep, 1955)
The Kentuckian (UA, 1955)
Comanche (UA, 1956)
The Hired Gun (MGM, 1957)
Decision at Sundown (Col, 1957)
Houseboat (Par, 1958)
Lover Come Back (Univ, 1961)
Voyage to the Bottom of the Sea (20th, 1961)
Pocketful of Miracles (UA, 1961)
The Gun Hawk (AA, 1963)
The Sons of Katie Elder (Par, 1965)
Nevada Smith (Par, 1966)

LUCIEN LITTLEFIELD

Lucien Littlefield, J. Gordon Russell, Barbara Bedford, William S. Hart, and Jack Murphy in Tumbleweeds *(1925).*

Born August 16, 1895, San Antonio, Texas. Married Constance Palmer, child: daughter. Died June 4, 1960, Hollywood, California. The balding codger—with plastered-down wisps of hair—who was as frequently petulant as meek. Played the exasperated Mr. Crosley of the Centerville High School faculty in some of the *Henry Aldrich* series. A stalwart back-up player for five decades of filmmaking. TV series: "Blondie" (as Mr. Beasley, the postman).

Lucien Littlefield to Guy Kibbee in *Whistling in Dixie:* "I'll either have to get new glasses or longer arms."

Films

The Ghost Breaker (Par, 1914)
The Warrens of Virginia (Par, 1915)
A Gentleman of Leisure (Par, 1915)
The Marriage of Kitty (Par, 1915)
The Wild Goose Chase (Par, 1915)
Mr. Grex of Monte Carlo (Par, 1915)
The Unknown (Par, 1915)
The Blacklist (Par, 1916)
Temptation (Par, 1916)
To Have and to Hold (Par, 1916)
The Love Mask (Par, 1916)
A Gutter Magdalene (Par, 1916)
The Golden Fetter (Par, 1917)
On Record (Par, 1917)
Joan the Woman (Par, 1917)
The Cost of Hatred (Par, 1917)
The Squaw Man's Son (Par, 1917)
The Hostage (Par, 1917)
The Wild Goose Chase (Tri, 1919)
Everywoman (Par, 1920)

Jackstraw (Par, 1920)
Double Speed (Par, 1920)
Why Change Your Wife? (Par, 1920)
The 14th Man (Par, 1920)
Sick-a-Bed (Par, 1920)
The Sins of St. Anthony (Par, 1920)
The Round-Up (Par, 1920)
Eyes of the Heart (Par, 1920)
Crazy to Marry (Par, 1921)
The Hell Diggers (Par, 1921)
The Little Clown (Realart, 1921)
The Sheik (Par, 1921)
Too Much Speed (Par, 1921)
Across the Continent (Par, 1922)
Her Husband's Trademark (Par, 1922)
Manslaughter (Par, 1922)
Our Leading Citizen (Par, 1922)
Rent Free (Par, 1922)
The Siren Call (Par, 1922)
Tillie (Par, 1922)

To Have and to Hold (Par, 1922)
Mr. Billings Spends His Dime (Par, 1923)
The Rendezvous (G, 1923)
Three Wise Fools (G, 1923)
The Tiger's Claw (Par, 1923)
The French Doll (M, 1923)
In the Palace of the King (G, 1923)
Name the Man (MG, 1924)
True as Steel (MG, 1924)
Babbitt (WB, 1924)
Gerald Cranston's Lady (Fox, 1924)
Gold Heels (Fox, 1924)
The Painted Lady (Fox, 1924)
Never Say Die (Associated Exhibitors, 1924)
Teeth (Fox, 1924)
A Woman Who Sinned (FBO, 1924)
Gold and the Girl (Fox, 1925)
Tumbleweeds (UA, 1925)
The Deadwood Coach (Fox, 1925)

The Rainbow Trail (Fox, 1925)
Charley's Aunt (PDC, 1925)
Twinkletoes (FN, 1926)
Soul Mates (MGM, 1926)
Take It from Me (Univ, 1926)
The Torrent (MGM, 1926)
Tony Runs Wild (Fox, 1926)
Brooding Eyes (Sterling, 1926)
Bachelor Brides (PDC, 1926)
The Small Bachelor (Univ, 1927)
Taxi, Taxi (Univ, 1927)
Cheating Cheaters (Univ, 1927)
The Cat and the Canary (Univ, 1927)
My Best Girl (UA, 1927)
Uncle Tom's Cabin (Univ, 1927)
A Texas Steer (FN, 1927)
A Blonde for a Night (Pathé, 1928)
Harold Teen (FN, 1928)
The Head Man (FN, 1928)
Heart to Heart (FN, 1928)
A Ship Comes In (Pathé, 1928)
The Man in Hobbles (Tif, 1928)
Do Your Duty (FN, 1928)
Mother Knows Best (Fox, 1928)
Seven Keys to Baldpate (RKO, 1929)
Drag (FN, 1929)
Girl in the Glass Cage (FN, 1929)
Saturday's Children (FN, 1929)
Making the Grade (Fox, 1929)
This Is Heaven (UA, 1929)
Clear the Decks (Univ, 1929)
Dark Streets (FN, 1929)
Captain of the Guard (Univ, 1930)
The Great Divide (FN, 1930)
No, No, Nanette (RKO, 1930)
High Society Blues (Fox, 1930)
Big Money (Pathé, 1930)
Tom Sawyer (Par, 1930)
Clancy in Wall Street (Aristocrat, 1930)
She's My Weakness (RKO, 1930)
It Pays to Advertise (Par, 1931)
Reducing (MGM, 1931)
Misbehaving Ladies (FN, 1931)
Scandal Sheet (Par, 1931)
Young as You Feel (Fox, 1931)
High Pressure (WB, 1932)
Broken Lullaby [a.k.a. *The Man I Killed*] (Par, 1932)
Strangers in Love (Par, 1932)
Shopworn (Col, 1932)
Strangers of the Evening (Tif, 1932)
Miss Pinkerton (FN, 1932)

Downstairs (MGM, 1932)
Speed Madness (Mercury Pictures, 1932)
That's My Baby (Col, 1932)
If I Had a Million (Par, 1932)
Evenings for Sale (Par, 1932)
Pride of the Legion [a.k.a. *The Big Pay-Off*] (Mascot, 1932)
The Big Brain (RKO, 1933)
Professional Sweetheart (RKO, 1933)
Chance at Heaven (RKO, 1933)
Alice in Wonderland (Par, 1933)
East of Fifth Avenue (Col, 1933)
The Bitter Tea of General Yen (Col, 1933)
Sailor's Luck (Fox, 1933)
Sweepings (RKO, 1933)
Skyway (Mon, 1933)
Rainbow over Broadway (Chesterfield, 1933)
Sons of the Desert (MGM, 1933)
Thirty Day Princess (Par, 1934)
Stand Up and Cheer (Fox, 1934)
Kiss and Make Up (Par, 1934)
Mandalay (FN, 1934)
Gridiron Flash (RKO, 1934)
Marrying Widows (Tower, 1934)
Love Time (Fox, 1934)
When Strangers Meet (Liberty, 1934)
Sweepstakes Annie (Liberty, 1935)
Ruggles of Red Gap (Par, 1935)
Man on the Flying Trapeze (Par, 1935)
One Frightened Night (Mascot, 1935)
The Murder Man (MGM, 1935)
She Gets Her Man (Univ, 1935)
The Return of Peter Grimm (RKO, 1935)
I Dream Too Much (RKO, 1935)
Cappy Ricks Returns (Rep, 1935)
Magnificent Obsession (Univ, 1935)
Rose-Marie (MGM, 1936)
Early to Bed (Par, 1936)
The Moon's Our Home (Par, 1936)
Let's Sing Again (RKO, 1936)
High, Wide and Handsome (Par, 1937)
Souls at Sea (Par, 1937)
Hotel Haywire (Par, 1937)
Wild Money (Par, 1937)
Wells Fargo (Par, 1937)
Partners in Crime (Par, 1937)
Bulldog Drummond's Revenge (Par, 1937)
Born to the West (Par, 1937)
Hollywood Stadium Mystery (Rep, 1938)
Scandal Street (Par, 1938)

Wide Open Faces (Col, 1938)
The Night Hawk (Rep, 1939)
The Gladiator (Col, 1938)
Mystery Plane (Mon, 1939)
Unmarried (Par, 1939)
What a Life (Par, 1939)
Sabotage (Rep, 1939)
Jeepers Creepers (Rep, 1939)
Money to Burn (Rep, 1939)
Those Were the Days (Par, 1940)
Murder Among Friends (20th, 1941)
The Great American Broadcast (20th, 1941)
Henry Aldrich for President (Par, 1941)
Man at Large (20th, 1941)
The Little Foxes (RKO, 1941)
Mr. and Mrs. North (MGM, 1941)
The Great Man's Lady (Par, 1942)
Castle in the Desert (20th, 1942)
Hillbilly Blitzkrieg (Mon, 1942)
Bells of Capistrano (Rep, 1942)
Whistling in Dixie (MGM, 1942)
Johnny Come Lately (UA, 1943)
Henry Aldrich Haunts a House (Par, 1943)
Casanova in Burlesque (Rep, 1944)
Goodnight, Sweetheart (Rep, 1944)
The Cowboy and the Senorita (Rep, 1944)
One Body Too Many (Par, 1944)
Lady, Let's Dance (Mon, 1944)
When the Lights Go On Again (PRC, 1944)
When the Lights Go on Again (RC, 1944)
Lights of Old Santa Fe (Rep, 1944)
Scared Stiff [a.k.a. *Treasure of Fear*] (Par, 1945)
The Caribbean Mystery (20th, 1945)
Detour (PRC, 1945)
Rendezvous with Annie (Rep, 1946)
That Brennan Girl (Rep, 1946)
Sweet Genevieve (Col, 1947)
Lightnin' in the Forest (Rep, 1948)
Jinx Money (Mon, 1948)
Bad Men of Tombstone (AA, 1948)
Susanna Pass (Rep, 1949)
At Sword's Point (RKO, 1952)
Roar of the Crowd (AA, 1953)
Casanova's Big Night (Par, 1954)
Sudden Danger (AA, 1955)
Bop Girl Goes Calypso (UA, 1957)
Wink of an Eye (UA, 1958)
The High Cost of Loving (MGM, 1958)

DORIS LLOYD

With Louis Hayward in The Son of Dr. Jekyll *(1951).*

Born July 3, 1896, Liverpool, England. Died May 21, 1968, Santa Barbara, California. Played the Brazilian title figure in the Charles Ruggles' version of *Charley's Aunt*. Same year, 1930, in *Sarah and Son* she and screen husband Gilbert Emery connive to keep Ruth Chatterton's son for their own. In *Reno* joined with Montagu Love to frame his divorce-seeking wife, Ruth Roland. Often cast as a landlady or scrubwoman in later years.

Doris Lloyd to the other villagers in *The Wolf Man:* "Very strange there were no murders here before Larry Talbot arrived."

Films

The Shadow Between (Br, 1920)
Love's Influence (Br, 1922)
The Lady (FN, 1925)
The Man from Red Gulch (PDC, 1925)
The Black Bird (MGM, 1926)
Black Paradise (Fox, 1926)
Exit Smiling (MGM, 1926)
The Midnight Kiss (Fox, 1926)
The Auctioneer (Fox, 1927)
The Broncho Twister (Fox, 1927)
Come to My House (Fox, 1927)
Is Zat So? (Fox, 1927)
Lonesome Ladies (FN, 1927)
Rich but Honest (Fox, 1927)
Two Girls Wanted (Fox, 1927)
The Careless Age (FN, 1929)
The Drake Case (Univ, 1929)
Disraeli (UA, 1929)
The Trail of '98 (MGM, 1929)
Old English (WB, 1930)
Charley's Aunt (Col, 1930)

Reno (WW, 1930)
Way for a Sailor (MGM, 1930)
Sarah and Son (Par, 1930)
Bachelor Father (MGM, 1931)
Transgression (RKO, 1931)
Waterloo Bridge (Univ, 1931)
Bought (WB, 1931)
Once a Lady (Par, 1931)
Devotion (Pathe, 1931)
Tarzan and the Ape Man (MGM, 1932)
Back Street (Univ, 1932)
Washington Masquerade (MGM, 1932)
Robber's Roost (Fox, 1933)
Oliver Twist (Mon, 1933)
Secrets (UA, 1933)
Peg o' My Heart (MGM, 1933)
Looking Forward (MGM, 1933)
A Study in Scarlet (WW, 1933)
Voltaire (WB, 1933)
Tarzan and His Mate (MGM, 1934)
Dangerous Corner (RKO, 1934)

Kiss and Make Up (Par, 1934)
Glamour (Univ, 1934)
British Agent (FN, 1934)
Sisters Under the Skin (Col, 1934)
She Was a Lady (Fox, 1934)
One Exciting Adventure (Univ, 1934)
Madame Du Barry (WB, 1934)
Clive of India (UA, 1935)
Straight from the Heart (Univ, 1935)
Kind Lady (MGM, 1935)
The Perfect Gentleman (MGM, 1935)
The Woman in Red (FN, 1935)
Motive for Revenge (Majestic, 1935)
Chasing Yesterday (RKO, 1935)
Becky Sharp (RKO, 1935)
A Shot in the Dark (Chesterfield, 1935)
A Feather in Her Hat (Col, 1935)
Two for Tonight (Par, 1935)
Peter Ibbetson (Par, 1935)
Brilliant Marriage (Invincible, 1936)
Don't Get Personal (Univ, 1936)

Too Many Parents (Par, 1936)
Mary of Scotland (RKO, 1936)
The Plough and the Stars (RKO, 1936)
Tovarich (WB, 1937)
The Soldier and the Lady [a.k.a. Michael Strogoff] (RKO, 1937)
Alcatraz Island (WB, 1938)
The Black Doll (Univ, 1938)
I'm from Missouri (Par, 1939)
The Under-Pup (Univ, 1939)
Barricade (20th, 1939)
First Love (Univ, 1939)
The Private Lives of Elizabeth and Essex (WB, 1939)
They Made Me a Criminal (WB, 1939)
Vigil in the Night (RKO, 1940)
The Great Plane Robbery (Col, 1940)
'Til We Meet Again (WB, 1940)
The Letter (WB, 1940)
The Great Lie (WB, 1941)
Shining Victory (WB, 1941)

Night Monster (Univ, 1942)
Journey for Margaret (MGM, 1942)
The Ghost of Frankenstein (Univ, 1942)
Mission to Moscow (WB, 1943)
The Constant Nymph (WB, 1943)
Forever and a Day (RKO, 1943)
The Lodger (20th, 1944)
The Invisible Man's Revenge (Univ, 1944)
The Conspirators (WB, 1944)
The White Cliffs of Dover (MGM, 1944)
Frenchman's Creek (Par, 1944)
Phantom Lady (Univ, 1944)
Follow the Boys (Univ, 1944)
Allotment Wives (Mon, 1945)
Molly and Me (20th, 1945)
My Name Is Julia Ross (Col, 1945)
Scotland Yard Investigator (Rep, 1945)
Devotion (WB, 1946)
G.I. War Brides (Rep, 1946)
Holiday in Mexico (MGM, 1946)
Of Human Bondage (WB, 1946)

Tarzan and the Leopard Woman (RKO, 1946)
Three Strangers (WB, 1946)
To Each His Own (Par, 1946)
Sister Kenny (RKO, 1946)
Escape Me Never (WB, 1947)
The Secret Life of Walter Mitty (RKO, 1947)
The Sign of the Ram (Col, 1948)
Tyrant of the Sea (Col, 1950)
Kind Lady (MGM, 1951)
The Son of Dr. Jekyll (Col, 1951)
Young Bess (MGM, 1953)
A Man Called Peter (20th, 1955)
The Swan (MGM, 1956)
Jeanne Eagels (Col, 1957)
The Time Machine (MGM, 1960)
Midnight Lace (Univ, 1960)
The Notorious Landlady (Col, 1962)
The Sound of Music (20th, 1965)
Rosie! (Univ, 1967)

GENE LOCKHART
(Eugene Lockhart)

Jack Holt and Gene Lockhart in Storm over the Andes *(1935).*

Born July 18, 1891, London, Ontario, Canada. Married Kathleen Arthur (1924), child: June. Died March 31, 1957, Santa Monica, California. Professionally active from the age of six when he performed Scottish dances; later a concert singer, a Gilbert and Sullivan performer, and a Broadway participant. Jowly faced, short, and portly. Quite creditable at sympathetic roles: Uncle Sid in stage and film version of *Ah, Wilderness!* and Bob Crachit in *A Christmas Carol.* Excelled at slimy crooks: Gillespie, the gunrunner of *Geronimo* who meets a gory end. Oscar-nominated for his disloyal Regis in *Algiers* (but lost BSAAA to Walter Brennan of *Kentucky*). In Edward G. Robinson's *The Sea Wolf,* played role of alcoholic Dr. Louie Prescott who climbs to the ship's crow's nest and jumps to his death. Occasionally acted with wife Kathleen and daughter June. Also a writer. TV series: "His Honor, Homer Bell."

Gene Lockhart on telephone in *Meet John Doe:* "What about me? It's *my* building he's jumping off of—and I'm up for reelection too."

Films

Smilin' Through (Associated FN, 1922)
The Gay Bride (MGM, 1934)
Ah, Wilderness! (MGM, 1935)
I've Been Around (Univ, 1935)
Captain Hurricane (RKO, 1935)
Star of Midnight (RKO, 1935)
Thunder in the Night (Fox, 1935)
Storm over the Andes (Univ, 1935)
Crime and Punishment (Col, 1935)
Brides Are Like That (FN, 1936)
Times Square Playboy (WB, 1936)
Earthworm Tractors (FN, 1936)
The First Baby (20th, 1936)
Career Woman (20th, 1936)
The Garden Murder Case (MGM, 1936)
The Gorgeous Hussy (MGM, 1936)
The Devil Is a Sissy (MGM, 1936)
Wedding Present (Par, 1936)
Mind Your Own Business (Par, 1936)
Come Closer, Folks (Col, 1936)
Mama Steps Out (MGM, 1937)
Too Many Wives (RKO, 1937)
Make Way for Tomorrow (Par, 1937)
The Sheik Steps Out (Rep, 1937)
Something to Sing About (GN, 1937)
Of Human Hearts (MGM, 1938)
Listen, Darling (MGM, 1938)
A Christmas Carol (MGM, 1938)
Sweethearts (MGM, 1938)
Penrod's Double Trouble (WB, 1938)
Men Are Such Fools (WB, 1938)
Blondie (Col, 1938)
Algiers (UA, 1938)
Sinners in Paradise (Univ, 1938)
Meet the Girls (20th, 1938)
I'm from Missouri (Par, 1939)
Hotel Imperial (Par, 1939)
Our Leading Citizen (Par, 1939)
Geronimo (Par, 1939)
Tell No Tales (MGM, 1939)
Bridal Suite (MGM, 1939)

Blackmail (MGM, 1939)
The Story of Alexander Graham Bell (20th, 1939)
Edison the Man (MGM, 1940)
Dr. Kildare Goes Home (MGM, 1940)
We Who Are Young (MGM, 1940)
South of Pago Pago (UA, 1940)
A Dispatch from Reuters (WB, 1940)
His Girl Friday (Col, 1940)
Abe Lincoln in Illinois (RKO, 1940)
Billy the Kid (MGM, 1941)
Keeping Company (MGM, 1941)
Meet John Doe (WB, 1941)
The Sea Wolf (WB, 1941)
All That Money Can Buy [a.k.a. *The Devil and Daniel Webster*] (RKO, 1941)
One Foot in Heaven (WB, 1941)
Steel Against the Sky (WB, 1941)
International Lady (UA, 1941)
They Died with Their Boots On (WB, 1941)
Juke Girl (WB, 1942)
The Gay Sisters (WB, 1942)
You Can't Escape Forever (WB, 1942)
Forever and a Day (RKO, 1943)
Hangmen Also Die (UA, 1943)
Mission to Moscow (WB, 1943)
Find the Blackmailer (WB, 1943)
The Desert Song (WB, 1943)
Madame Curie (MGM, 1943)
Northern Pursuit (WB, 1943)
The White Cliffs of Dover (MGM, 1944)
Going My Way (Par, 1944)
Action in Arabia (RKO, 1944)
The Man from Frisco (Rep, 1944)
The House on 92nd Street (20th, 1945)
Leave Her to Heaven (20th, 1945)
That's the Spirit (Univ, 1945)
Meet Me on Broadway (Col, 1946)
A Scandal in Paris [a.k.a. *Thieves' Holiday*] (UA, 1946)

She-Wolf of London (Univ, 1946)
The Strange Woman (UA, 1946)
The Shocking Miss Pilgrim (20th, 1947)
Miracle on 34th Street (20th, 1947)
The Foxes of Harrow (20th, 1947)
Cynthia (MGM, 1947)
Honeymoon (RKO, 1947)
Her Husband's Affairs (Col, 1947)
Joan of Arc (RKO, 1948)
The Inside Story (Rep, 1948)
That Wonderful Urge (20th, 1948)
Apartment for Peggy (20th, 1948)
I, Jane Doe (Rep, 1948)
Down to the Sea in Ships (20th, 1949)
Madame Bovary (MGM, 1949)
The Red Light (UA, 1949)
The Inspector General (WB, 1949)
Riding High (Par, 1950)
The Big Hangover (MGM, 1950)
The Sickle and the Cross (Astor, 1951)
I'd Climb the Highest Mountain (20th, 1951)
Rhubarb (Par, 1951)
The Lady from Texas (Univ, 1951)
Hoodlum Empire (Rep, 1952)
A Girl in Every Port (RKO, 1952)
Face to Face (RKO, 1952)
Bonzo Goes to College (Univ, 1952)
Androcles and the Lion (RKO, 1952)
Apache War Smoke (MGM, 1952)
Francis Covers the Big Town (Univ, 1953)
Down Among the Sheltering Palms (20th, 1953)
Confidentially Connie (MGM, 1953)
The Lady Wants Mink (Rep, 1953)
World for Ransom (AA, 1954)
The Vanishing American (Rep, 1955)
Carousel (20th, 1956)
The Man in the Gray Flannel Suit (20th, 1956)
Jeanne Eagels (Col, 1957)

RICHARD LOO

In China Sky *(1945).*

Born 1903, Hawaii. Married: Bessie Sue, children: Beverly Jane, Angeles Marie. Gained screen reputation playing merciless Japanese assailants in the World War II period: e.g., the heinous Colonel Masamoto in *I Was an American Spy* who obliges prisoner Ann Dvorak's request for a drink of water by ordering a water hose pushed down her throat. TV series: "Kung Fu."

Richard Loo to Dana Andrews in *The Purple Heart:* "You see, Captain Ross, you are not my only prisoner. Must I remind you that a chain is no stronger than its weakest link?"

Films

Dirigible (Col, 1931)
War Correspondent (Col, 1932)
Secrets of Wu Sin (Chesterfield, 1932)
The Bitter Tea of General Yen (Col, 1933)
Stranded (WB, 1935)
Shadow of Chinatown (Victory serial, 1936)
The Singing Marine (WB, 1937)
That Certain Woman (WB, 1937)
Thank You, Mr. Moto (20th, 1937)
The Good Earth (MGM, 1937)
West of Shanghai (WB, 1937)
Too Hot to Handle (MGM, 1938)
Blondes at Work (WB, 1938)
Shadows over Shanghai (GN, 1938)
Mr. Wong in Chinatown (Mon, 1939)
Island of Lost Men (Par, 1939)
Daughter of the Tong (Times Pictures, 1939)
Miracles for Sale (MGM, 1939)
The Fatal Hour (Mon, 1940)
Secrets of the Wasteland (Par, 1941)
They Met in Bombay (MGM, 1941)
Star Spangled Rhythm (Par, 1942)
Little Tokyo, USA (20th, 1942)
Bombs over Burma (PRC, 1942)

Across the Pacific (WB, 1942)
The Falcon Strikes Back (RKO, 1943)
Flight for Freedom (RKO, 1943)
China (Par, 1943)
Yanks Ahoy (UA, 1943)
Jack London (UA, 1943)
The Purple Heart (20th, 1944)
The Keys of the Kingdom (20th, 1944)
The Story of Dr. Wassell (Par, 1944)
God Is My Co-Pilot (WB, 1945)
Betrayal from the East (RKO, 1945)
China Sky (RKO, 1945)
Back to Bataan (RKO, 1945)
First Yank into Tokyo (RKO, 1945)
Tokyo Rose (Par, 1945)
Prison Ship (Col, 1945)
Seven Were Saved (Par, 1947)
The Web of Danger (Rep, 1947)
Women in the Night (Film Classics, 1947)
The Cobra Strikes (EL, 1948)
Half Past Midnight (20th, 1948)
Rogues' Regiment (Univ, 1948)
The Clay Pigeon (RKO, 1949)
State Department—File 649 (Film Classics, 1949)

Malaya (MGM, 1949)
The Steel Helmet (Lip, 1951)
I Was an American Spy (AA, 1951)
Five Fingers (20th, 1952)
China Venture (Col, 1953)
Hell and High Water (20th, 1954)
The Shanghai Story (Rep, 1954)
Living It Up (Par, 1954)
The Bamboo Prison (Col, 1954)
Soldier of Fortune (20th, 1955)
Love Is a Many-Splendored Thing (20th, 1955)
Around the World in 80 Days (UA, 1956)
The Conqueror (RKO, 1956)
Battle Hymn (Univ, 1956)
The Quiet American (UA, 1958)
Hong Kong Affair (AA, 1958)
Seven Women from Hell (20th, 1961)
Confessions of an Opium Eater (AA, 1962)
A Girl Named Tamiko (Par, 1962)
The Sand Pebbles (20th, 1966)
One More Train to Rob (Univ, 1971)
Chandler (MGM, 1971)
The Man with the Golden Gun (UA, 1974)

MONTAGU LOVE

In the mid-1940s.

Born March 15, 1877, Portsmouth, England. Died May 17, 1943, Beverly Hills, California. Left his post as a roving newspaper illustrator to act on the London stage. Later signed a leading player's contract with World Films in Fort Lee, New Jersey, where he played such resolute types as *The Grouch, The Steel King,* and *Rasputin, the Black Monk.* In the 1930s cast as severe fathers, British officers (Colonel Weed of *Gunga Din*), or imposing personages (Bishop of Black Canon in *The Adventures of Robin Hood*).

Montagu Love to the others in *Outward Bound:* "You can't touch me. I turned myself into a company years ago."

Films

The Suicide Club (Br, 1914)
Hearts in Exile (World, 1915)
The Face in the Moonlight (World, 1915)
Sunday (World, 1915)
A Royal Family (M, 1915)
The Antique Dealer (Primo, 1915)
The Greater Will (Primo, 1915)
A Woman's Way (World, 1916)
Friday the 13th (World, 1916)
Husband and Wife (World, 1916)
The Gilded Cage (World, 1916)
The Scarlet Oath (World, 1916)
The Hidden Scar (World, 1916)
Bought and Paid For (World, 1916)
The Man She Married (World, 1916)
The Challenge (Pathe, 1916)
Rasputin, the Black Monk (World, 1917)

The Awakening (Peerless-World, 1918)
The Good for Nothing (Peerless-World, 1918)
The Cross Bearer (Peerless-World, 1918)
Vengeance (World, 1918)
Stolen Orders (Brady-World, 1918)
Three Green Eyes (World, 1919)
Hand Invisible (World, 1919)
Through the Toils (World, 1919)
To Him That Hath (World, 1919)
Roughnecks (World, 1919)
The Grouch (World, 1919)
Broadway Saint (World, 1919)
Quickening Flame (World, 1919)
The Steel King ((World, 1920)
Place of Honeymoons (Pioneer, 1920)

The World and His Wife (Par, 1920)
The Wrong Woman (Graphic Film Corp, 1921)
The Case of Becky (Par, 1921)
Shams of Society (Robertson-Cole, 1921)
Forever (Par, 1921)
Love's Redemption (Associated FN, 1922)
The Darling of the Rich (Selznick, 1922)
What's Wrong with Women? (Equity, 1922)
The Secrets of Paris (Master, 1922)
The Beauty Shop (Par, 1922)
The Eternal City (Associated FN, 1923)
The Leopardess (Par, 1923)
Roulette (Selznick, 1924)

Sinners in Heaven (Par, 1924)

A Son of the Sahara (Associated FN, 1924)

Love of Women (Selznick, 1924)

Restless Wives (C. C. Burr, 1924)

Week-End Husbands (Equity, 1924)

Who's Cheating? (Lee-Bradford Corp., 1924)

The Ancient Highway (Par, 1925)

The Desert's Price (Fox, 1925)

The Mad Marriage (Rosemary Films, 1925)

Hands Up! (Par, 1926)

The Son of the Sheik (UA, 1926)

The Social Highwayman (World, 1926)

Out of the Storm (Tif, 1926)

Don Juan (WB, 1926)

The Silent Lover (FN, 1926)

Brooding Eyes (Sterling, 1926)

Good Time Charley (WB, 1927)

The Haunted Ship (Tif, 1927)

Jesse James (Par, 1927)

The King of Kings (Par, 1927)

One Hour of Love (Tif, 1927)

The Night of Love (UA, 1927)

Rose of the Golden West (FN, 1927)

The Tender Hour (FN, 1927)

The Devil's Skipper (Tif, 1928)

The Noose (FN, 1928)

The Hawk's Nest (FN, 1928)

The Haunted House (FN, 1928)

The Wind (MGM, 1928)

The Divine Lady (FN, 1929)

The Last Warning (Univ, 1929)

Synthetic Sin (FN, 1929)

Her Private Life (FN, 1929)

Bulldog Drummond (UA, 1929)

Charming Sinners (Par, 1929)

A Most Immoral Lady (FN, 1929)

Midstream (Tif, 1929)

Silks and Saddles (Univ, 1929)

The Mysterious Island (MGM, 1929)

The Voice Within (Tif, 1929)

Double Cross Roads (Fox, 1930)

Back Pay (FN, 1930)

The Cat Creeps (Univ, 1930)

Kismet (FN, 1930)

Inside the Lines (RKO, 1930)

Love Comes Along (RKO, 1930)

Outward Bound (WB, 1930)

A Notorious Affair (FN, 1930)

Reno (WW, 1930)

Lion and the Lamb (Col, 1931)

Alexander Hamilton (WB, 1931)

Silver Lining (UA, 1932)

Vanity Fair (Hollywood Films, 1932)

Stowaway (Univ, 1932)

Love Bound (Peerless, 1932)

The Midnight Lady (Chesterfield, 1932)

Riding Tornado (Col, 1932)

Out of Singapore (Steiner, 1932)

His Double Life (Par, 1933)

Menace (Par, 1934)

Limehouse Blues (Par, 1934)

Clive of India (UA, 1935)

Hi Gaucho (RKO, 1935)

The Crusades (Par, 1935)

The Man Who Broke the Bank at Monte Carlo (Fox, 1935)

Country Doctor (20th, 1936)

Sing, Baby, Sing (20th, 1936)

Reunion (20th, 1936)

Lloyds of London (20th, 1936)

One in a Million (20th, 1936)

Sutter's Gold (Univ, 1936)

The White Angel (FN, 1936)

Champagne Charlie (20th, 1936)

The Prince and the Pauper (WB, 1937)

The Life of Emile Zola (WB, 1937)

Tovarich (WB, 1937)

Parnell (MGM, 1937)

The Prisoner of Zenda (UA, 1937)

London by Night (MGM, 1937)

A Damsel in Distress (RKO, 1937)

Adventure's End (Univ, 1937)

The Buccaneer (Par, 1938)

The Adventures of Robin Hood (WB, 1938)

Professor Beware (Par, 1938)

Kidnapped (20th, 1938)

If I Were King (Par, 1938)

Gunga Din (RKO, 1939)

Juarez (WB, 1939)

The Man in the Iron Mask (UA, 1939)

Rulers of the Sea (Par, 1939)

We Are Not Alone (WB, 1939)

Northwest Passage (MGM, 1940)

The Son of Monte Cristo (UA, 1940)

The Story of Dr. Ehrlich's Magic Bullet (WB, 1940)

All This, and Heaven Too (WB, 1940)

The Sea Hawk (WB, 1940)

A Dispatch from Reuters (WB, 1940)

The Lone Wolf Strikes (Col, 1940)

Private Affairs (Univ, 1940)

North West Mounted Police (Par, 1940)

The Mark of Zorro (20th, 1940)

Hudson's Bay (20th, 1940)

The Devil and Miss Jones (RKO, 1941)

Shining Victory (WB, 1941)

Lady for a Night (Rep, 1941)

The Remarkable Andrew (Par, 1942)

Sherlock Holmes and the Voice of Terror (Univ, 1942)

Tennessee Johnson (MGM, 1942)

Forever and a Day (RKO, 1943)

The Constant Nymph (WB, 1943)

Holy Matrimony (20th, 1943)

Devotion (WB, 1946)

A Scandal in Paris [a.k.a. *Thieves' Holiday*] (UA, 1946)

WILFRED LUCAS

With Ragsika Dally in The Lily and the Rose *(1915).*

Born January 30, 1871, Ontario, Canada. Died December 5, 1940, Los Angeles, California. Tough, mug type who worked for D. W. Griffith in early silents, including the short *Man's Genesis* (as Brute-Force). By the 1920s usually played a supporting role: *Daughters of Pleasure* (as errant husband who has an affair with Clara Bow); did have a lead in *The Barnstormer*. Played small featured roles in talkies: *Modern Times* (juvenile officer), *Mary of Scotland* (Lexington), *Brother Orchid* (Brother MacDonald), etc.

Wilfred Lucas to Laurel and Hardy in *Pardon Us:* "If you are good prisoners, everything will be okay. If you are not—if you break the rules—then it will be just plain hell on earth!"

Films

The Spanish Jade (Par, 1915)
The Wood Nymph (Tri, 1915)
The Lily and the Rose (Tri, 1915)
Acquitted (Tri, 1916)
A Wild Girl of the Sierras (Tri, 1916)
Intolerance (Wark, 1916)
Macbeth (Tri, 1916)
Hell to Pay Austin (Tri, 1916)
The Rummy (Tri, 1916)
The Microscope Mystery (Tri, 1916)
Jim Bludso (Tri, 1917)
A Love Sublime (Tri, 1917)
Hands Up (Tri, 1917)
Souls Triumphant (Tri, 1917)
Her Excellency, the Governor (Tri, 1917)
The Food Gamblers (Tri, 1917)
The Co-respondent (Univ, 1917)
The Sins of Ambition (Ivan, 1917)

The Judgment House (Par, 1917)
Girl from Nowhere (Selznick, 1919)
The Westerners (Hodkinson, 1919)
The Beautiful Liar (Associated FN, 1921)
The Better Man (Aywon, 1921)
The Fighting Breed (Aywon, 1921)
The Breaking Point (Hodkinson, 1921)
Through the Back Door (UA, 1921)
The Shadow of Lightning Ridge (Aywon, 1921)
Across the Dead-Line (Univ, 1922)
Barriers of Folly (Russell, 1922)
The Barnstormer (Associated FN, 1922)
Heroes of the Street (WB, 1922)
Flesh and Blood (Cummings, 1922)
The Kentucky Derby (Univ, 1922)
Paid Back (Univ, 1922)

The Girl of the Golden West (Associated FN, 1923)
Can a Woman Love Twice? (FBO, 1923)
Innocence (CBC-Col, 1923)
The Greatest Menace (Mayer & Quinn, 1923)
Jazzmania (M, 1923)
Why Women Remarry (Associated Photoplays, 1923)
Trilby (Associated FN, 1923)
Cornered (WB, 1924)
The Beautiful Sinner (Perfection, 1924)
Daughters of Pleasure (Principal, 1924)
The Fatal Mistake (Perfection, 1924)
Dorothy Vernon of Haddon Hall (UA, 1924)
A Fight for Honor (Perfection, 1924)
The Fighting Sap (FBO, 1924)

Lightning Romance (Rayart, 1924)
Girls Men Forget (Principal, 1924)
The Mask of Lopez (FBO, 1924)
On Probation (Sterling, 1924)
North of Nevada (FBO, 1924)
Racing for Life (CBC, 1924)
Passion's Pathway (Art-Lee, 1924)
The Price She Paid (Col, 1924)
Women First (Col, 1924)
The Valley of Hate (Russell, 1924)
A Broadway Butterfly (WB, 1925)
Cyclone Cavalier (Rayart, 1925)
The Bad Lands (PDC, 1925)
How Baxter Butted In (WB, 1925)
Easy Money (Rayart, 1925)
Riders of the Purple Sage (Fox, 1925)
The Man Without a Country (Fox, 1925)
The Snob Buster (Rayart, 1925)
Youth's Gamble (Rayart, 1925)
Was It Bigamy? (Steiner, 1925)
The Wife Who Wasn't Wanted (WB, 1925)

Her Sacrifice (Sanford, 1926)
Burnt Fingers (Pathe, 1927)
The Nest (Excellent Pictures, 1927)
The Arizona Kid (Fox, 1930)
Cock o' the Walk (WW, 1930)
Just Imagine (Fox, 1930)
Hello Sister (WW, 1930)
Madam Satan (MGM, 1930)
Those Who Dance (WB, 1930)
Dishonored (Par, 1931)
Young Donovan's Kid (RKO, 1931)
Pardon Us (MGM, 1931)
Convicted (Artclass Pictures, 1931)
Cross Examination (Artclass Pictures, 1931)
Midnight Patrol (Mon, 1932)
The Unwritten Law (Majestic, 1932)
The Tenderfoot (FN, 1932)
The Intruder (Allied, 1932)
Sister to Judas (Mayfair, 1933)
Racetrack (WW, 1933)
Lucky Larrigan (Mon, 1933)

The Devil's Brother (MGM, 1933)
Phantom Thunderbolt (WW, 1933)
I Cover the Waterfront (UA, 1933)
The Big Cage (Univ, 1933)
Breed of the Border (Mon, 1933)
Strange People (Chesterfield, 1933)
The Sphinx (Mon, 1933)
Notorious but Nice (Chesterfield, 1933)
Day of Reckoning (MGM, 1933)
The Moth (Marcy Exchange, 1934)
The Count of Monte Cristo (UA, 1934)
Chatterbox (RKO, 1936)
Modern Times (UA, 1936)
Mary of Scotland (RKO, 1936)
Criminal Lawyer (RKO, 1937)
Mile a Minute Love (Ace Pictures, 1937)
The Baroness and the Butler (20th, 1938)
A Chump at Oxford (UA, 1940)
Brother Orchid (WB, 1940)
Ragtime Cowboy Joe (Univ, 1940)
Triple Justice (RKO, 1940)
The Sea Wolf (WB, 1941)

KEYE LUKE

Keye Luke and Leo Gorcey (center) in Bowery Blitzkrieg *(1941).*

Born June 18, 1904, Canton, China. Married Ethel Blaney (1942). Onetime architectural student and commercial artist who switched to filmmaking. Perhaps most famous as the always boyish Lee Chan #1 son ("Gee, Pop") in the *Charlie Chan* series (with Warner Oland and later Roland Winters). Also Dr. Lee Wong How, competing with Van Johnson et al. for the post of Dr. Gillespie's new assistant in that Lionel Barrymore series. On Broadway in musical *Flower Drum Song.* TV series: "Kentucky Jones," "Kung Fu," "Anna and the King [of Siam]," and "The Amazing Chan and the Chan Clan" (cartoon voice of Charlie Chan).

Keye Luke to Warner Oland in *Charlie Chan at the Race Track:*
"Aw gee, Pop. When are we gonna arrest somebody?"

Films

The Painted Veil (MGM, 1934)
The Casino Murder Case (MGM, 1935)
Eight Bells (Col, 1935)
Here's to Romance (Fox, 1935)
Mad Love (MGM, 1935)
Charlie Chan in Shanghai (Fox, 1935)
Oil for the Lamps of China (WB, 1935)
Charlie Chan in Paris (Fox, 1935)
Charlie Chan in Egypt (Fox, 1935)
Shanghai (Par, 1935)
Charlie Chan at the Race Track (20th, 1936)
Charlie Chan at the Circus (20th, 1936)
King of Burlesque (20th, 1936)
Anything Goes [TV title: *Tops Is the Limit*] (Par, 1936)
Charlie Chan at the Opera (20th, 1936)
The Good Earth (MGM, 1937)
Charlie Chan at Monte Carlo (20th, 1937)
Charlie Chan on Broadway (20th, 1937)
Charlie Chan at the Olympics (20th, 1937)
International Settlement (20th, 1938)
Mr. Moto's Gamble (20th, 1938)
Disputed Passage (Par, 1939)
Barricade (20th, 1939)
North of Shanghai (Col, 1939)
Sued for Libel (RKO, 1940)
The Green Hornet (Univ serial, 1940)
The Gang's All Here (Mon, 1941)

Let's Go Collegiate (Mon, 1941)
Bowery Blitzkrieg (Mon, 1941)
Burma Convoy (Univ, 1941)
Passage from Hong Kong (WB, 1941)
No Hands on the Clock (Par, 1941)
Mr. and Mrs. North (MGM, 1941)
They Met in Bombay (MGM, 1941)
Journey for Margaret (MGM, 1942)
Invisible Agent (Univ, 1942)
Across the Pacific (WB, 1942)
A Yank on the Burma Road (MGM, 1942)
A Tragedy at Midnight (Rep, 1942)
North to the Klondike (Univ, 1942)
Somewhere I'll Find You (MGM, 1942)
Spy Ship (WB, 1942)
The Falcon's Brother (RKO, 1942)
Destination Unknown (Univ, 1942)
Mexican Spitfire's Elephant (RKO, 1942)
Dr. Gillespie's New Assistant (MGM, 1942)
Dr. Gillespie's Criminal Case (MGM, 1943)
Salute to the Marines (MGM, 1943)
The Adventures of Smilin' Jack (Univ serial, 1943)
Dragon Seed (MGM, 1944)
Three Men in White (MGM, 1944)
Andy Hardy's Blonde Trouble (MGM, 1944)
Between Two Women (MGM, 1944)

First Yank in Tokyo (RKO, 1945)
Tokyo Rose (Par, 1945)
How Do You Do? (PDC, 1945)
Lost City of the Jungle (Univ serial, 1946)
Dark Delusion (MGM, 1947)
Sleep, My Love (UA, 1948)
Waterfront at Midnight (Par, 1948)
The Feathered Serpent (Mon, 1949)
Sky Dragon (Mon, 1949)
Young Man with a Horn (WB, 1950)
Fair Wind to Java (Rep, 1953)
South Sea Woman (WB, 1953)
Hell's Half Acre (Rep, 1954)
The World for Ransom (AA, 1954)
Bamboo Prison (Col, 1954)
Love Is a Many-Splendored Thing (20th, 1955)
Around the World in 80 Days (UA, 1956)
Battle Hell [a.k.a. *The Yangtse Incident*] (Br, 1957)
Nobody's Perfect (Univ, 1968)
Project X (Par, 1969)
The Chairman (20th, 1969)
The Hawaiians (UA, 1970)
Noon Sunday (Crown International, 1971)
Won Ton Ton, the Dog Who Saved Hollywood (Par, 1976)
The Amsterdam Kill (Golden Harvest, 1977)

J. FARRELL MacDONALD

J. Farrell MacDonald and George Arliss in The Working Man *(1933).*

Born June 6, 1875, Waterbury, Connecticut. Married _____ . Died August 2, 1952, Hollywood, California. Former stage performer who made short films in the 1910s with his wife for the IMP studio. By 1919 was a member of John Ford's acting troupe: *Roped* (butler), *A Fight for Love* (the priest), *Riders of Vengeance* (Buell), etc. Demonstrated repeatedly in the 1920s what a fine subordinate player he was: *Over the Border* (moonshiner), *Riding with Death* (sheriff), *The Scarlet Honeymoon* (Shirley Mason's dad), etc. Continued working with Ford: as railroad worker Corporal Casey in *The Iron Horse;* as Mike Costigan, one of the outlaw trio in *Three Bad Men,* etc. In talkies the bald player was, among others, a detective (1931's *The Maltese Falcon*), a warden (*The Whole Town's Talking*), a ship's captain (*Maid of Salem*), a cop (*Topper*), a sheriff (*The Miracle of Morgan's Creek*), etc. Returned to Ford for *Submarine Patrol* (Quincannon), *My Darling Clementine* (Mac, the barman), etc.

> **J. Farrell MacDonald** to Warner Baxter in *The Squaw Man:*
> "Men don't have slaves around here, especially pretty little brown ones. You don't want them saying you're a squaw man, do you?"

Films

The Heart of Maryland (Tif, 1915)
Rags (Par, 1915)
The Price of Power (Tri, 1918)
$5,000 Reward (Univ, 1918)
Fair Enough (Pathé, 1918)
Roped (Univ, 1919)
Molly of the Follies (Pathé, 1919)
A Fight for Love (Univ, 1919)
Riders of Vengeance (Univ, 1919)
Charge It to Me (Pathé, 1919)
Trixie from Broadway (Pathé, 1919)
A Sporting Chance (American, 1919)
This Hero Stuff (American, 1919)
The Outcasts of Poker Flats (Univ, 1919)
Marked Men (Univ, 1919)

Bullet Proof (Univ, 1920)
The Path She Chose (Univ, 1920)
Under Sentence (Univ, 1920)
Hitchin' Posts (Univ, 1920)
Action (Univ, 1921)
The Wallop (Univ, 1921)
Desperate Youth (Univ, 1921)
Bucking the Line (Fox, 1921)
The Freeze Out (Univ, 1921)
Trailin' (Fox, 1921)
Little Miss Hawkshaw (Fox, 1921)
Sky High (Fox, 1921)
Riding with Death (Fox, 1921)
The Bachelor Daddy (Par, 1922)
The Young Rajah (Par, 1922)

The Bonded Woman (Par, 1922)
Tracks (Associated Exhibitors, 1922)
Come On Over (G, 1922)
The Ghost Breaker (Par, 1922)
Over the Border (Par, 1922)
Manslaughter (Par, 1922)
The Age of Desire (FN, 1923)
While Paris Sleeps (Hodkinson, 1923)
Drifting (Univ, 1923)
Racing Hearts (Par, 1923)
Fashionable Fakers (FBO, 1923)
Quicksands (Par, 1923)
Western Luck (Fox, 1924)
The Brass Bowl (Fox, 1924)
The Storm Daughter (Univ, 1924)

Fair Week (Par, 1924)
The Signal Tower (Univ, 1924)
General Cranston's Lady (Fox, 1924)
Mademoiselle Midnight (MG, 1924)
The Iron Horse (Fox, 1924)
Thank You (Fox, 1925)
The Fighting Heart (Fox, 1925)
The Scarlet Honeymoon (Fox, 1925)
Kentucky Pride (Fox, 1925)
Let Women Alone (PDC, 1925)
The Lucky Horseshoe (Fox, 1925)
Lightnin' (Fox, 1925)
Bertha, the Sewing Machine Girl (Fox, 1926)
A Trip to Chinatown (Fox, 1926)
The Country Beyond (Fox, 1926)
Three Bad Men (Fox, 1926)
The Dixie Merchant (Fox, 1926)
The Shamrock Handicap (Fox, 1926)
The Family Upstairs (Fox, 1926)
The First Year (Fox, 1926)
Ankles Preferred (Fox, 1927)
The Cradle Snatchers (Fox, 1927)
East Side, West Side (Fox, 1927)
Colleen (Fox, 1927)
Rich but Honest (Fox, 1927)
Love Makes 'em Wild (Fox, 1927)
Paid to Love (Fox, 1927)
Sunrise—A Song of Two Humans (Fox, 1927)
Bringing Up Father (MGM, 1928)
The Cohens and the Kellys in Paris (Univ, 1928)
Riley the Cop (Fox, 1928)
None but the Brave (Fox, 1928)
Phantom City (FN, 1928)
Masquerade (Fox, 1929)
Masked Emotions (Fox, 1929)
In Old Arizona (Fox, 1929)
The Four Devils (Fox, 1929)
South Sea Rose (Fox, 1929)
Strong Boy (Fox, 1929)
Abie's Irish Rose (Par, 1929)
Happy Days (Fox, 1929)
Girl of the Golden West (FN, 1930)
Painted Angel (FN, 1930)
Truth About Youth (FN, 1930)
Men Without Women (Fox, 1930)
Song o' My Heart (Fox, 1930)
Born Reckless (Fox, 1930)
The Painted Desert (Pathé, 1931)
River's End (WB, 1931)
The Easiest Way (MGM, 1931)
The Millionaire (WB, 1931)
Woman Hungry (FN, 1931)
The Maltese Falcon (FN, 1931)
Other Men's Women (WB, 1931)
The Squaw Man (MGM, 1931)
Too Young to Marry (WB, 1931)
The Brat (Fox, 1931)
Sporting Blood (MGM, 1931)
Spirit of Notre Dame (Univ, 1931)

Touchdown (Par, 1931)
Under Eighteen (WB, 1932)
Discarded Lovers (Tower, 1932)
Hotel Continental (Tif, 1932)
Scandal for Sale (Univ, 1932)
Probation (Chesterfield, 1932)
The Phantom Express (Majestic, 1932)
Week-End Marriage (FN, 1932)
The Thirteenth Guest (Mon, 1932)
70,000 Witnesses (Par, 1932)
The Vanishing Frontier (Par, 1932)
Hearts of Humanity (Majestic, 1932)
This Sporting Age (Col, 1932)
The Pride of the Legion [a.k.a. The Big Pay-Off] (Mascot, 1932)
No Man of Her Own (Par, 1932)
Me and My Gal (Fox, 1932)
Steady Company (Univ, 1932)
The Racing Strain (Maxim Productions, 1932)
The Working Man (WB, 1933)
Peg o' My Heart (MGM, 1933)
Laughing at Life (Mascot, 1933)
The Power and the Glory (Fox, 1933)
Myrt and Marge (Univ, 1933)
I Loved a Woman (FN, 1933)
The Iron Master (Allied Pictures, 1933)
Heritage of the Desert (Par, 1933)
Under Secret Orders (Progressive Pictures, 1933)
Man of Two Worlds (RKO, 1934)
The Crime Doctor (RKO, 1934)
Romance in Manhattan (RKO, 1934)
Once to Every Woman (Col, 1934)
The Cat's Paw (Fox, 1934)
The Crosby Case (Univ, 1934)
Beggar's Holiday (Tower, 1934)
The Square Shooter (Col, 1935)
The Whole Town's Talking (Col, 1935)
Northern Frontier (Ambassador, 1935)
Star of Midnight (RKO, 1935)
The Best Man Wins (Col, 1935)
The Healer (Mon, 1935)
Swell Head (Col, 1935)
Maybe It's Love (FN, 1935)
Let 'em Have It! (UA, 1935)
Our Little Girl (Fox, 1935)
The Irish in Us (WB, 1935)
Front Page Woman (WB, 1935)
Danger Ahead (Victory, 1935)
Stormy (Univ, 1935)
Fighting Youth (Univ, 1935)
Waterfront Lady (Rep, 1935)
Riffraff (MGM, 1935)
Hitchhike Lady (Rep, 1935)
Florida Special (Par, 1936)
Exclusive Story (MGM, 1936)
Showboat (Univ, 1936)
Shadows of the Orient (Mon, 1937)
Maid of Salem (Par, 1937)
Mysterious Crossing (Univ, 1937)
The Silent Barrier (Br, 1937)

Roaring Timber (Col, 1937)
The Hit Parade (Rep, 1937)
Slave Ship (20th, 1937)
County Fair (Mon, 1937)
Slim (WB, 1937)
Topper (MGM, 1937)
My Dear Miss Aldrich (MGM, 1937)
The Game That Kills (Col, 1937)
Courage of the West (Univ, 1937)
My Old Kentucky Home (Mon, 1938)
Numbered Woman (Mon, 1938)
Gang Bullets (Mon, 1938)
State Police (Univ, 1938)
Flying Fists (Treo Productions, 1938)
There Goes My Heart (UA, 1938)
Extortion (Col, 1938)
Little Orphan Annie (Par, 1938)
White Banners (WB, 1938)
Come On, Rangers (Rep, 1938)
The Crowd Roars (MGM, 1938)
Submarine Patrol (20th, 1938)
Susannah of the Mounties (20th, 1939)
Mickey the Kid (Rep, 1939)
East Side of Heaven (Univ, 1939)
Conspiracy (RKO, 1939)
East Side of Heaven (Univ, 1939)
The Gentleman from Arizona (Mon, 1939)
Zenobia (UA, 1939)
Knights of the Range (Par, 1940)
Dark Command (Rep, 1940)
The Light of Western Stars (Par, 1940)
Prairie Law (RKO, 1940)
I Take This Oath (PRC, 1940)
The Last Alarm (Mon, 1940)
Untamed (Par, 1940)
Stagecoach War (Par, 1940)
Friendly Neighbors (Rep, 1940)
Broadway Limited (UA, 1941)
In Old Cheyenne (Rep, 1941)
Meet John Doe (WB, 1941)
The Great Lie (WB, 1941)
Riders of the Timberline (Par, 1941)
Snuffy Smith—Yardbird (Mon, 1942)
Little Tokyo, U.S.A. (20th, 1942)
One Thrilling Night (Mon, 1942)
Phantom Killer (Mon, 1942)
The Living Ghost (Mon, 1942)
The Palm Beach Story (Par, 1942)
Bowery at Midnight (Mon, 1942)
The Ape Man (Mon, 1943)
Clancy Street Boys (Mon, 1943)
True to Life (Par, 1943)
Tiger Fangs (PRC, 1943)
The Miracle of Morgan's Creek (Par, 1944)
Greenwich Village (20th, 1944)
Texas Masquerade (UA, 1944)
The Great Moment (Par, 1944)
Follow the Boys (Univ, 1944)
Shadow of Suspicion (Mon, 1944)
A Tree Grows in Brooklyn (20th, 1945)

Nob Hill (20th, 1945)
Johnny Angel (RKO, 1945)
Fallen Angel (20th, 1945)
Pillow of Death (Univ, 1945)
The Woman Who Came Back (Rep, 1945)
Pardon My Past (Col, 1945)
It's a Wonderful Life (RKO, 1946)
Joe Palooka—Champ (Mon, 1946)
Behind Green Lights (20th, 1946)
Smoky (20th, 1946)
My Darling Clementine (20th, 1946)
Web of Danger (Rep, 1947)

Keeper of the Bees (Col, 1947)
Thunder in the Valley (20th, 1947)
Fury at Furnace Creek (20th, 1948)
Walls of Jericho (20th, 1948)
Sitting Pretty (20th, 1948)
The Luck of the Irish (20th, 1948)
Whispering Smith (Par, 1948)
Belle Starr's Daughter (20th, 1948)
Panhandle (AA, 1948)
Shep Comes Home (Screen Guild, 1948)
Streets of San Francisco (Rep, 1949)
Fighting Man of the Plains (20th, 1949)

Law of the Barbary Coast (Col, 1949)
You're My Everything (20th, 1949)
The Beautiful Blonde from Bashful Bend (20th, 1949)
The Dalton Gang (Screen Guild, 1949)
Dakota Lil (20th, 1950)
Woman on the Run (Univ, 1950)
Hostile Country (Lip, 1950)
Elopement (20th, 1951)
Mr. Belvedere Rings the Bell (20th, 1951)
Here Comes the Groom (Par, 1951)

FRANK McHUGH

Franklin Pangborn, Frank McHugh, Gregory Ratoff, and Frank Darien in Professional Sweetheart (1933).

Born May 23, 1898, Homestead, Pennsylvania. Married Dorothy Spencer (1933), children: Susan, Peter, another son. The jovial ("hee-hee"), pudgy Irish-American pal of the hero with the constant "double-take" look of surprise. One of the busiest members of the Warner Bros. stock company. He would even repeat his *One Way Passage* role of the hero-crook's con-artist associate in the remake *Till We Meet Again*. Played Banks, the perplexed father-to-be in *Life Begins*; Francis, the nervous stage manager in Busby Berkeley's *Footlight Parade*. Often James Cagney's loyal friend: *The Crowd Roars* (Spud Connors), *Here Comes the Navy* (Droopy), *The Roaring Twenties* (Danny Green), etc. Played Ben Crosley, the money saver who weds Lola Lane in the *Four Daughters* series. Appropriately titled character name in *Mighty Joe Young*—Windy. TV series: "The Bing Crosby Show."

> **Frank McHugh** to Rosemary De Camp in *Bowery to Broadway*: "Bessie, those verbal contracts aren't worth the paper they're written on."

351

Films

Top Speed (FN, 1930)
Bright Lights (FN, 1930)
The Dawn Patrol (FN, 1930)
College Lovers (FN, 1930)
The Widow from Chicago (FN, 1930)
Little Caesar (FN, 1930)
Going Wild (WB, 1931)
Millie (RKO, 1931)
Corsair (UA, 1931)
Traveling Husbands (RKO, 1931)
Men of the Sky (FN, 1931)
Bad Company (Pathé, 1931)
The Front Page (UA, 1931)
Up for Murder (Univ, 1931)
Kiss Me Again (FN, 1931)
High Pressure (WB, 1932)
The Strange Love of Molly Louvain (FN, 1932)
One Way Passage (WB, 1932)
Life Begins (FN, 1932)
Blessed Event (WB, 1932)
The Dark Horse (FN, 1932)
Union Depot (FN, 1932)
The Crowd Roars (WB, 1932)
The Mystery of the Wax Museum (WB, 1933)
42nd Street (WB, 1933)
Parachute Jumper (WB, 1933)
Elmer the Great (FN, 1933)
Convention City (FN, 1933)
Son of a Sailor (FN, 1933)
Lilly Turner (FN, 1933)
Havana Widows (FN, 1933)
Footlight Parade (WB, 1933)
Private Jones (Univ, 1933)
Professional Sweetheart (RKO, 1933)
Tomorrow at Seven (RKO, 1933)
Hold Me Tight (Fox, 1933)
The Mad Game (Fox, 1933)
The House on 56th Street (WB, 1933)
Ex-Lady (WB, 1933)

Grand Slam (WB, 1933)
Telegraph Trail (WB, 1933)
Fashions of 1934 (FN, 1934)
Happiness Ahead (FN, 1934)
Maybe It's Love (FN, 1934)
Merry Wives of Reno (WB, 1934)
Heat Lightning (WB, 1934)
Smarty (WB, 1934)
Here Comes the Navy (WB, 1934)
Let's Be Ritzy (Univ, 1934)
Return of the Terror (FN, 1934)
Six Day Bike Rider (FN, 1934)
Devil Dogs of the Air (WB, 1935)
A Midsummer Night's Dream (WB, 1935)
Page Miss Glory (WB, 1935)
Stars over Broadway (WB, 1935)
Gold Diggers of 1935 (FN, 1935)
The Irish in Us (WB, 1935)
Three Kids and a Queen (Univ, 1935)
Freshman Love (WB, 1936)
Snowed Under (FN, 1936)
Bullets or Ballots (FN, 1936)
Stage Struck (FN, 1936)
Three Men on a Horse (FN, 1936)
Moonlight Murder (MGM, 1936)
Ever Since Eve (WB, 1937)
Mr. Dodd Takes the Air (WB, 1937)
Marry the Girl (WB, 1937)
Submarine D-1 (WB, 1937)
Swing Your Lady (WB, 1938)
He Couldn't Say No (WB, 1938)
Little Miss Thoroughbred (WB, 1938)
Boy Meets Girl (WB, 1938)
Four Daughters (WB, 1938)
Valley of the Giants (WB, 1938)
Wings of the Navy (WB, 1939)
Daughters Courageous (WB, 1939)
Indianapolis Speedway (WB, 1939)
Dodge City (WB, 1939)
Dust Be My Destiny (WB, 1939)
The Roaring Twenties (WB, 1939)

Four Wives (WB, 1939)
On Your Toes (WB, 1939)
The Fighting 69th (WB, 1940)
Virginia City (WB, 1940)
Saturday's Children (WB, 1940)
'Til We Meet Again (WB, 1940)
City for Conquest (WB, 1940)
Four Mothers (WB, 1941)
I Love You Again (MGM, 1941)
Back Street (Univ, 1941)
Manpower (WB, 1941)
All Through the Night (WB, 1942)
Her Cardboard Lover (MGM, 1942)
Marine Raiders (RKO, 1944)
Going My Way (Par, 1944)
Bowery to Broadway (Univ, 1944)
A Medal for Benny (Par, 1945)
State Fair (20th, 1945)
Deadline for Murder (20th, 1946)
The Hoodlum Saint (MGM, 1946)
Little Miss Big (Univ, 1946)
The Runaround (Univ, 1946)
Carnegie Hall (UA, 1947)
Easy Come, Easy Go (Par, 1947)
The Velvet Touch (RKO, 1948)
Miss Grant Takes Richmond (Col, 1949)
Mighty Joe Young (RKO, 1949)
Paid in Full (Par, 1950)
The Tougher They Come (Col, 1950)
The Pace That Thrills (RKO, 1952)
My Son John (Par, 1952)
It Happens Every Spring (Univ, 1953)
A Lion Is in the Streets (WB, 1953)
There's No Business Like Show Business (20th, 1954)
The Last Hurrah (Col, 1958)
Say One for Me (20th, 1959)
Career (Par, 1959)
A Tiger Walks (BV, 1964)
Easy Come, Easy Go (Par, 1967)

BARTON MacLANE

Barton MacLane and Charles Bickford in The Storm *(1938).*

Born December 25, 1902, Columbia, South Carolina. Married 1) Martha Stewart, children: two; divorced; 2) Charlotte Wynters (1939). Died January 1, 1969, Santa Monica, California. Gruff–voiced, squinty–eyed, with pursed lips. A nasty-guy staple of Warner Bros. films. Occasionally broke away from the mold, as Detective Lieutenant Steve McBride in the *Torchy Blane* series. Also on the right side of the law as Lieutenant Lundy in 1941's *The Maltese Falcon*, but was back battling Humphrey Bogart for gambling stakes in *The Treasure of the Sierra Madre*. TV series: "The Outlaws" (as Marshal Frank Caine) and "I Dream of Jeannie" (as General Martin Peterson).

> **Barton MacLane** to prison chaplain John Litel in *Men Without Souls:* "This is our rest period, and we don't want any psalm-singin' rats hangin' around. Go peddle your prayers."

Films

The Quarterback (Par, 1926)
The Cocoanuts (Par, 1929)
Man of the Forest (Par, 1933)
Big Executive (Par, 1933)
The Torch Singer (Par, 1933)
To the Last Man [a.k.a. Law of Vengeance]
   (Par, 1933)
Tillie and Gus (Par, 1933)
The Thundering Herd (Par, 1933)
Hell and High Water (Par, 1933)
Lone Cowboy (Par, 1934)
The Last Round-Up (Par, 1934)
Black Fury (FN, 1935)
Go into Your Dance (FN, 1935)
Case of the Curious Bride (FN, 1935)
Stranded (FN, 1935)
Page Miss Glory (WB, 1935)

Dr. Socrates (FN, 1935)
I Found Stella Parish (FN, 1935)
Ceiling Zero (FN, 1935)
G-Men (WB, 1935)
The Case of the Lucky Legs (FN, 1935)
Man of Iron (WB, 1935)
Frisco Kid (WB, 1935)
The Walking Dead (WB, 1936)
Times Square Playboy (WB, 1936)
Jail Break (WB, 1936)
Bullets or Ballots (WB, 1936)
Bengal Tiger (WB, 1936)
Smart Blonde (WB, 1936)
God's Country and the Woman (WB, 1936)
Draegerman Courage (WB, 1937)
You Only Live Once (UA, 1937)

Wine, Women and Horses (WB, 1937)
San Quentin (FN, 1937)
The Prince and the Pauper (WB, 1937)
Born Reckless (20th, 1937)
Ever Since Eve (WB, 1937)
Fly-Away Baby (WB, 1937)
The Adventurous Blonde (WB, 1937)
Tke Kid Comes Back (WB, 1938)
Blondes at Work (WB, 1938)
Torchy Gets Her Man (WB, 1938)
The Storm (Univ, 1938)
Gold Is Where You Find It (WB, 1938)
You and Me (Par, 1938)
Prison Break (Univ, 1938)
Stand Up and Fight (MGM, 1939)
Big Town Czar (Univ, 1939)
Torchy Blane in Chinatown (WB, 1939)

I Was a Convict (Rep, 1939)
Mutiny in the Big House (Mon, 1939)
Men Without Souls (Col, 1940)
Torchy Runs for Mayor (WB, 1940)
The Secret Seven (Col, 1940)
Gangs of Chicago (Rep, 1940)
Melody Ranch (Rep, 1940)
Come Live with Me (MGM, 1941)
High Sierra (WB, 1941)
Western Union (20th, 1941)
Manpower (WB, 1941)
Barnacle Bill (MGM, 1941)
Dr. Jekyll and Mr. Hyde (MGM, 1941)
The Maltese Falcon (WB, 1941)
Wild Geese Calling (20th, 1941)
Hit the Road (Univ, 1941)
Highways by Night (RKO, 1942)
All Through the Night (WB, 1942)
The Big Street (RKO, 1942)
Man of Courage (PRC, 1943)
Bombardier (RKO, 1943)
Song of Texas (Rep, 1943)
The Underdog (PRC, 1943)
The Crime Doctor's Strangest Case (Col, 1943)
Cry of the Werewolf (Col, 1944)
The Mummy's Ghost (Univ, 1944)
Marine Raiders (RKO, 1944)
Secret Command (Col, 1944)
Gentle Annie (MGM, 1944)
Nabonga (PRC, 1944)
The Spanish Main (RKO, 1945)

Scared Stiff [a.k.a. *Treasure of Fear*] (Par, 1945)
Tarzan and the Amazons (RKO, 1945)
Santa Fe Uprising (Rep, 1946)
The Mysterious Intruder (Col, 1946)
Jungle Flight (Par, 1947)
Cheyenne (WB, 1947)
Tarzan and the Huntress (RKO, 1947)
The Treasure of the Sierra Madre (WB, 1948)
Relentless (Col, 1948)
Unknown Island (Film Classics, 1948)
The Dude Goes West (AA, 1948)
Silver River (WB, 1948)
The Walls of Jericho (20th, 1948)
Angel in Exile (Rep, 1948)
Red Light (UA, 1949)
Kiss Tomorrow Goodbye (WB, 1950)
Rookie Fireman (Col, 1950)
The Bandit Queen (Lip, 1950)
Let's Dance (Par, 1950)
Best of the Badmen (RKO, 1951)
Drums in the Deep South (RKO, 1951)
Bugles in the Afternoon (WB, 1952)
The Half-Breed (RKO, 1952)
Thunderbirds (Rep, 1952)
Sea of Lost Ships (Rep, 1953)
Jack Slade (AA, 1953)
Captain Scarface (Astor, 1953)
Kansas Pacific (AA, 1953)
Cow Country (AA, 1953)
Rails into Laramie (Univ, 1954)

The Glenn Miller Story (Univ, 1954)
Jubilee Trail (Rep, 1954)
Hell's Outpost (Rep, 1955)
Last of the Desperadoes (Associated Film, 1955)
The Silver Star (Lip, 1955)
The Treasure of Ruby Hills (AA, 1955)
Foxfire (Univ, 1955)
Jail Busters (AA, 1955)
Backlash (Univ, 1956)
Wetbacks (Banner, 1956)
Jaguar (Rep, 1956)
The Man Is Armed (Rep, 1956)
Three Violent People (Par, 1956)
The Naked Gun (Associated Film, 1956)
Sierra Stranger (Col, 1957)
Naked in the Sun (AA, 1957)
The Storm Rider (20th, 1957)
Hell's Crossroads (Rep, 1957)
The Girl in the Woods (Rep, 1958)
The Geisha Boy (Par, 1958)
Frontier Gun (20th, 1958)
Gunfighters of Abilene (UA, 1960)
Noose for a Gunman (UA, 1960)
Pocketful of Miracles (UA, 1961)
Law of the Lawless (Par, 1964)
The Rounders (MGM, 1965)
Town Tamer (Par, 1965)
Arizona Bushwackers (Par, 1968)
Buckskin (Par, 1968)

ALINE MacMAHON

Walter Huston, Hurd Hatfield, and Aline MacMahon in Dragon Seed *(1944).*

Born May 3, 1899, McKeesport, Pennsylvania. Married Clarence Stein (1928); widowed (1974). Accomplished stage actress whom Warner Bros. originally intended for stardom, but then shunted to top featured leads. Big-boned woman who could outwisecrack Glenda Farrell or Joan Blondell (as Trixie in *Gold Diggers of 1933*). Could be extremely sympathetic with those soulful eyes (Miss Bowers, the head nurse of *Life Begins*). Put on the ritz as the fake countess (a.k.a. Barrelhouse Betty) in *One Way Passage*. Post–Warner Bros.—and as she grew stoutish—turned to playing secretaries, confidantes *(The Lady Is Willing, I Could Go On Singing)*, and matriarchs *(Dragon Seed, The Eddie Cantor Story, All the Way Home)*.

> **Aline MacMahon** to Onslow Stevens in *Once in a Lifetime*: "Miss Walker is a young woman who has a chance of becoming the world's worst actress."

Films

Five Star Final (WB, 1931)
Heart of New York (WB, 1932)
The Mouthpiece (WB, 1932)
Week End Marriage (FN, 1932)
One Way Passage (WB, 1932)
Life Begins (FN, 1932)
Silver Dollar (FN, 1932)
Once in a Lifetime (Univ, 1932)
Gold Diggers of 1933 (WB, 1933)
The Life of Jimmy Dolan (WB, 1933)
Heroes for Sale (WB, 1933)
The World Changes (WB, 1933)
Heat Lightning (WB, 1934)
Side Streets (FN, 1934)
Big-Hearted Herbert (WB, 1934)

Babbitt (FN, 1934)
The Merry Frinks (FN, 1934)
While the Patient Slept (FN, 1935)
Mary Jane's Pa (FN, 1935)
I Live My Life (MGM, 1935)
Kind Lady (MGM, 1935)
Ah, Wilderness! (MGM, 1935)
When You're in Love (Col, 1937)
Back Door to Heaven (Par, 1939)
Out of the Fog (WB, 1941)
The Lady Is Willing (Col, 1942)
Tish (MGM, 1942)
Stage Door Canteen (UA, 1943)
Seeds of Freedom (Potemkin Productions, 1943) [narrator]

Dragon Seed (MGM, 1944)
Guest in the House (UA, 1944)
The Mighty McGurk (MGM, 1946)
The Search (MGM, 1948)
Roseanna McCoy (MGM, 1949)
The Flame and the Arrow (WB, 1950)
The Eddie Cantor Story (WB, 1953)
The Man from Laramie (Col, 1955)
Cimarron (MGM, 1960)
The Young Doctors (UA, 1961)
Diamond Head (Col, 1963)
I Could Go On Singing (UA, 1963)
All the Way Home (Par, 1963)

GEORGE MACREADY

With Virginia Leith in A Kiss Before Dying *(1956).*

Born August 29, 1908, Providence, Rhode Island. Married Elizabeth Dana, children: Michael, Lisa, Marcia; divorced (1942). Died July 2, 1973, Los Angeles, California. Steel-eyed, Teutonic-looking screen hissable. Displayed his true cinema penchant—villains—as Ballin Mundson, Rita Hayworth's bisexual husband in *Gilda*. Often was the dastardly cad in costume pictures (Sir Daniel Bracley in *The Black Arrow*). Should have been Oscar-nominated for his General Mireau, the French World War I military man who court-martials innocent men for a costly battle maneuver he approved in *Paths of Glory*. Final film, a cameo appearance in *The Return of Count Yorga*, produced by his son. TV series: "Peyton Place" (as Martin Peyton).

> **George Macready** regarding his knife-concealing cane to
> Glenn Ford in *Gilda*: "It is silent when I wish it to be silent.
> It talks when I wish it to."

Films

The Commandos Strike at Dawn (Col, 1942)
The Seventh Cross (MGM, 1944)
Wilson (20th, 1944)
The Story of Dr. Wassell (Par, 1944)
The Conspirators (WB, 1944)
Follow the Boys (Univ, 1944)
Soul of a Monster (Col, 1944)
The Missing Juror (Col, 1945)
Counter-Attack (Col, 1945)
Don Juan Quilligan (20th, 1945)
The Fighting Guardsman (Col, 1945)
I Love a Mystery (Col, 1945)
The Monster and the Ape (Col serial, 1945)
A Song to Remember (Col, 1945)
My Name Is Julia Ross (Col, 1945)
Gilda (Col, 1946)

The Man Who Dared (Col, 1946)
The Walls Came Tumbling Down (Col, 1946)
The Return of Monte Cristo (Col, 1946)
The Bandit of Sherwood Forest (Col, 1946)
The Swordsman (Col, 1947)
Down to Earth (Col, 1947)
The Big Clock (Par, 1948)
The Black Arrow (Col, 1948)
Coroner Creek (Col, 1948)
Beyond Glory (Par, 1948)
The Gallant Blade (Col, 1948)
Alias Nick Beal (Par, 1949)
Knock on Any Door (Col, 1949)
Johnny Allegro (Col, 1949)
The Doolins of Oklahoma (Col, 1949)
The Nevadan (Col, 1950)
A Lady Without Passport (MGM, 1950)

The Desert Hawk (Univ, 1950)
Fortunes of Captain Blood (Col, 1950)
Rogues of Sherwood Forest (Col, 1950)
Tarzan's Peril (RKO, 1951)
The Golden Horde (Univ, 1951)
Detective Story (Par, 1951)
The Desert Fox (20th, 1951)
The Green Glove (UA, 1952)
Treasure of the Golden Condor (20th, 1953)
Julius Caesar (MGM, 1953)
The Stranger Wore a Gun (Col, 1953)
The Golden Blade (Univ, 1953)
Duffy of San Quentin (WB, 1954)
Vera Cruz (UA, 1954)
A Kiss Before Dying (UA, 1956)
Thunder over Arizona (Rep, 1956)
The Abductors (20th, 1957)

Gunfire at Indian Gap (Rep, 1957)
Paths of Glory (UA, 1957)
The Alligator People (20th, 1959)
Plunderers of Painted Flats (Rep, 1959)
Jet over the Atlantic (Intercontinent Releasing, 1959)

Two Weeks in Another Town (MGM, 1962)
Taras Bulba (UA, 1962)
Seven Days in May (Par, 1964)
Dead Ringer (WB, 1964)
Where Love Has Gone (Par, 1964)

The Great Race (WB, 1965)
The Human Duplicators (AA, 1965)
Tora! Tora! Tora! (20th, 1970)
The Return of Count Yorga (AIP, 1971)

ROBERT McWADE

Will Rogers and Robert McWade in The County Chairman *(1934).*

Born January 25, 18__, Buffalo, New York. Died January 20, 1938, Culver City, California. Stage actor (in the original *Ben-Hur*) who turned to films as a general utility player: *Grand Hotel* (Meierheim), *Operator 13* (Colonel Sharpe), *The Kennel Murder Case* and *The Dragon Murder Case* (both as District Attorney John F. X. Markham), *Frisco Kid* (judge), *Gold Is Where You Find It* (Crouch). Died on the set of *Of Human Hearts* in which he was Dr. Lupus Crumm. Brother was actor Edward McWade.

Robert McWade to James Stewart in *Of Human Hearts:*
"Come come, my lad—you can't study medicine and miss amputations. It can't be done."

Films

Second Youth (MG, 1924)
New Brooms (Par, 1925)
The Home Towners (WB, 1928)
Feet First (Par, 1930)
Good Intentions (Fox, 1930)
Night Work (Pathe, 1930)
The Pay-Off (RKO, 1930)
Sins of the Children [a.k.a. The Richest Man in the World] (MGM, 1930)
Cimarron (RKO, 1931)

It's a Wise Child (MGM, 1931)
Kept Husbands (RKO, 1931)
Too Many Cooks (RKO, 1931)
New Adventures of Get-Rich-Quick Wallingford (MGM, 1931)
Skyline (Fox, 1931)
Girls About Town (Par, 1931)
Ladies of the Jury (RKO, 1931)
Grand Hotel (MGM, 1932)
The First Year (Fox, 1932)

Madame Racketeer (Par, 1932)
Big City Blues (WB, 1932)
Two Seconds (FN, 1932)
Movie Crazy (Par, 1932)
The Phantom of Crestwood (RKO, 1932)
Once in a Lifetime (Univ, 1932)
The Match King (FN, 1932)
Back Street (Univ, 1932)
42nd Street (WB, 1933)
Employees' Entrance (FN, 1933)

357

Hard to Handle (WB, 1933)
Ladies They Talk About (WB, 1933)
Pick Up (Par, 1933)
The Big Cage (Univ, 1933)
Heroes for Sale (FN, 1933)
I Loved a Woman (FN, 1933)
Solitaire Man (MGM, 1933)
The Kennel Murder Case (WB, 1933)
The Prizefighter and the Lady (MGM, 1933)
Fog (Col, 1934)
Cross Country Cruise (Univ, 1934)
Hold That Girl (Fox, 1934)
Journal of a Crime (FN, 1934)
A Lost Lady (FN, 1934)
Operator 13 (MGM, 1934)
The Countess of Monte Cristo (Univ, 1934)
Let's Be Ritzy (Univ, 1934)

Thirty Day Princess (Par, 1934)
Midnight Alibi (FN, 1934)
The Dragon Murder Case (FN, 1934)
The Lemon Drop Kid (Par, 1934)
College Rhythm (Par, 1934)
The President Vanishes (Par, 1934)
The County Chairman (Fox, 1935)
No Ransom (Liberty, 1935)
Straight from the Heart (Univ, 1935)
Mary Jane's Pa (FN, 1935)
The Healer (Mon, 1935)
Diamond Jim (Univ, 1935)
Cappy Ricks Returns (Rep, 1935)
Here Comes the Band (MGM, 1935)
His Night Out (Univ, 1935)
Frisco Kid (WB, 1935)
Society Doctor [a.k.a. *Only Eight Hours*] (MGM, 1935)
Moonlight Murder (MGM, 1936)

Next Time We Love (Univ, 1936)
The Big Noise (WB, 1936)
Anything Goes (Par, 1936)
Early to Bed (Par, 1936)
Bunker Bean (RKO, 1936)
High Tension (20th, 1936)
Mister Cinderella (MGM, 1936)
Old Hutch (MGM, 1936)
15 Maiden Lane (20th, 1936)
We're on the Jury (RKO, 1937)
California Straight Ahead (Univ, 1937)
Under Cover of Night (MGM, 1937)
Good Old Soak (MGM, 1937)
Mountain Justice (WB, 1937)
This Is My Affair (20th, 1937)
On Such a Night (Par, 1937)
Gold Is Where You Find It (WB, 1938)
Of Human Hearts (MGM, 1938)

NOEL MADISON
(Noel Moscovitch)

In the 1930s.

Born New York City, New York. Married Joyce _____, child: Toby. Died January 6, 1975, Fort Lauderdale, Florida. Actor son of Maurice Moscovitch. Usually seen as the ominous gangster: *The Last Mile* (D'Amoro), etc. Could be a sinister Axis agent: Saito *(Secret Agent of Japan)*, etc.

Noel Madison to Dorothy Tree in *Charlie Chan in City of Darkness:* "You're not going to put me on the spot for murder! I'll tell the police everything!"

Films

Sinners' Holiday (WB, 1930)
Doorway to Hell (WB, 1930)
The Star Witness (WB, 1931)
The Hatchet Man (FN, 1932)
Play Girl (WB, 1932)
Symphony of Six Million (RKO, 1932)
Man About Town (Fox, 1932)
The Trial of Vivienne Ware (Fox, 1932)
The Last Mile (WW, 1932)
Hat Check Girl (Fox, 1932)
Me and My Gal (Fox, 1932)
Laughter in Hell (Univ, 1932)
Humanity (Fox, 1933)
West of Singapore (Mon, 1933)
Destination Unknown (Univ, 1933)
Important Witness (Tower, 1933)
The House of Rothschild (UA, 1934)
Journal of a Crime (FN, 1934)
I Like It That Way (Univ, 1934)
Manhattan Melodrama (MGM, 1934)
Four Hours to Kill (Par, 1935)

G-Men (WB, 1935)
What Price Crime? (Beacon, 1935)
Woman Wanted (MGM, 1935)
The Girl Who Came Back (Chesterfield, 1935)
Three Kids and a Queen (Univ, 1935)
My Marriage (Fox, 1935)
The Morals of Marcus (Br, 1935)
Murder at Glen Athol (Invincible, 1935)
Muss 'em Up (RKO, 1936)
Champagne Charlie (20th, 1936)
Straight from the Shoulder (Par, 1936)
Our Relations (MGM, 1936)
Easy Money (Invincible, 1936)
Missing Girls (Chesterfield, 1936)
House of Secrets (Chesterfield, 1937)
Man of the People (MGM, 1937)
Gangway (Br, 1937)
Nation Aflame (Br, 1937)
Sailing Along (Br, 1938)
Man with a Hundred Faces (Br, 1938)

Missing Evidence (Univ, 1938)
Charlie Chan in City in Darkness (20th, 1939)
Crackerjack (Br, 1939)
Climbing High (MGM Br, 1939)
The Great Plane Robbery (Col, 1940)
Ellery Queen's Penthouse Mystery (Col, 1941)
Footsteps in the Dark (WB, 1941)
A Shot in the Dark (WB, 1941)
Queen of Crime (Film Alliance, 1941)
Highway West (WB, 1941)
Secret Agent of Japan (20th, 1942)
Joe Smith, American (MGM, 1942)
Bombs over Burma (PRC, 1942)
Miss V from Moscow (PRC, 1943)
Shantytown (Rep, 1943)
Jitterbugs (20th, 1943)
Forever and a Day (RKO, 1943)
The Black Raven (PRC, 1943)
The Gentleman from Nowhere (Col, 1948)

MARJORIE MAIN

In Meet Me in St. Louis *(1944).*

Born February 24, 1890, Acton, Illinois. Married Stanley Krebs (1921); widowed (1935). Died April 10, 1975, Los Angeles, California. Former schoolteacher and performer on the Chautauqua circuit; later a Broadway player. Excelled as tenement mother type, especially in re-creating her stage role of Mrs. Martin, the disgusted mother of killer Baby Face in *Dead End*. Range of portrayals increased under MGM contract: Reverend Mrs. Varner *(Honky Tonk)*, housekeeper Emma *(A Woman's Face)*, etc. Big-boned, raucous woman. Frequently teamed with hammy Wallace Beery from *Wyoming* onward; a good attempt to revive the screen chemistry of gross Beery and crude Marie Dressler. In Universal's *The Egg and I* (she and Percy Kilbride as the hickish Ma and Pa Kettle), which spawned a long-running comedy series.

> **Majorie Main** to Donna Reed in *Gentle Annie:* "Why, you ain't much more than a yearling—and downright pretty too."

Films

A House Divided (Univ, 1932)
Hot Saturday (Par, 1932)
Take a Chance (Par, 1933)
Music in the Air (Fox, 1934)
Crime Without Passion (Par, 1934)
Love in a Bungalow (Univ, 1937)
The Man Who Cried Wolf (Univ, 1937)
City Girl (20th, 1937)
Stella Dallas (UA, 1937)
Dead End (UA, 1937)
The Wrong Road (Rep, 1937)
The Shadow (Col, 1937)

Boy of the Streets (Mon, 1937)
Penitentiary (Col, 1938)
Girls' School (Col, 1938)
Romance of the Limberlost (Mon, 1938)
Under the Big Top (Mon, 1938)
King of the Newsboys (Rep, 1938)
Test Pilot (MGM, 1938)
Too Hot to Handle (MGM, 1938)
Prison Farm (Par, 1938)
Little Tough Guy (Univ, 1938)
There Goes My Heart (UA, 1938)
Three Comrades (MGM, 1938)

They Shall Have Music (UA, 1939)
Angels Wash Their Faces (WB, 1939)
The Women (MGM, 1939)
Another Thin Man (MGM, 1939)
Two Thoroughbreds (RKO, 1939)
Lucky Night (MGM, 1939)
I Take This Woman (MGM, 1940)
Women Without Names (Par, 1940)
Dark Command (Rep, 1940)
Turnabout (UA, 1940)
Wyoming (MGM, 1940)
Susan and God (MGM, 1940)

The Captain Is a Lady (MGM, 1940)	*Murder, He Says* (Par, 1945)	*The Law and the Lady* (MGM, 1951)
The Trial of Mary Dugan (MGM, 1941)	*The Harvey Girls* (MGM, 1946)	*Mr. Imperium* (MGM, 1951)
A Woman's Face (MGM, 1941)	*Undercurrent* (MGM, 1946)	*It's a Big Country* (MGM, 1951)
Wild Man of Borneo (MGM, 1941)	*Bad Bascomb* (MGM, 1946)	*The Belle of New York* (MGM, 1952)
Barnacle Bill (MGM, 1941)	*The Show-Off* (MGM, 1946)	*Ma and Pa Kettle at the Fair* (Univ, 1952)
Honky Tonk (MGM, 1941)	*The Egg and I* (Univ, 1947)	*Ma and Pa Kettle on Vacation* (Univ, 1953)
Shepherd of the Hills (Par, 1941)	*The Wistful Widow of Wagon Gap* (Univ, 1947)	*Fast Company* (MGM, 1953)
The Bugle Sounds (MGM, 1941)	*Feudin', Fussin', and A-Fightin'* (Univ, 1948)	*The Long, Long Trailer* (MGM, 1954)
We Were Dancing (MGM, 1942)	*Ma and Pa Kettle* (Univ, 1949)	*Rose Marie* (MGM, 1954)
Jackass Mail (MGM, 1942)	*Big Jack* (MGM, 1949)	*Ma and Pa Kettle at Home* (Univ, 1954)
The Affairs of Martha [a.k.a. *Once upon a Thursday*] (MGM, 1942)	*Ma and Pa Kettle Go to Town* (Univ, 1950)	*Ricochet Romance* (Univ, 1954)
Tish (MGM, 1942)	*Summer Stock* (MGM, 1950)	*Ma and Pa Kettle at Waikiki* (Univ, 1955)
Tennessee Johnson (MGM, 1942)	*Mrs. O'Malley and Mr. Malone* (MGM, 1950)	*The Kettles in the Ozarks* (Univ, 1956)
Johnny Come Lately (UA, 1943)	*Ma and Pa Kettle Back on the Farm* (Univ, 1951)	*Friendly Persuasion* (AA, 1956)
Heaven Can Wait (20th, 1943)		*The Kettles on Old MacDonald's Farm* (Univ, 1957)
Rationing (MGM, 1944)		
Gentle Annie (MGM, 1944)		
Meet Me in St. Louis (MGM, 1944)		

MILES MANDER
(Lionel Mander)

Frank Wilcox, Miles Mander, Mitzi Mayfair, Martha Raye, and Carole Landis in Four Jills and a Jeep *(1944).*

Born May 14, 1888, Wolverhampton, England. Married Kathleen Bernadette French (1923). Died February 8, 1946, Hollywood, California. Embarked on moviemaking after turning from a playboy's career to a jack-of-all-trades in the theater. Wrote, directed, and acted in the British film *The First Born*; wrote and directed *Loose Ends*, *The Missing Rembrandt*, etc. On screen could be cunning: Richelieu (1935's *The Three Musketeers*—his Hollywood debut); or stately: Benjamin Disraeli (*Suez*). Occasionally took a departure: e.g., Homer, Ginger Rogers' drunken stepfather in *Primrose Path*. Superior as Lockwood in Merle Oberon's *Wuthering Heights*.

Miles Mander to Basil Rathbone in *The Pearl of Death:*
"You're still full of your 'little surprises,' Mr. Holmes."

Films

The Pleasure Garden (Br, 1926)
The First Born (Br, 1928)
The Physician (Tif, 1928)
Doctors' Women (Br, 1929)
Loose Ends (Br, 1930)
Murder (Br, 1930)
Jaws of Hell (WOW, 1930)
The Missing Rembrandt (FD, 1932)
That Night in London [a.k.a. *Overnight*] (Par Br, 1932)
Lilly Christine (Par Br, 1932)
Bittersweet (UA Br, 1933)
The Private Life of Henry VIII (UA Br, 1933)
The Four Masked Men (Univ Br, 1934)
Loyalties (Br, 1934)
The Battle (Br, 1934)
Don Quixote (UA Br, 1934)
The Three Musketeers (RKO, 1935)
Here's to Romance (20th, 1936)
Lloyds of London (20th, 1936)
Wake Up and Live (20th, 1937)
Slave Ship (20th, 1937)
Youth on Parole (Rep, 1937)
Kidnapped (20th, 1938)
Suez (20th, 1938)
The Mad Miss Manton (RKO, 1938)

Wuthering Heights (UA, 1939)
The Three Musketeers (20th, 1939)
The Little Princess (20th, 1939)
The Man in the Iron Mask (UA, 1939)
Stanley and Livingstone (20th, 1939)
Tower of London (Univ, 1939)
Daredevils of the Red Circle (Rep serial, 1939)
Road to Singapore (Par, 1940)
Primrose Path (RKO, 1940)
The House of Seven Gables (Univ, 1940)
Babies for Sale (Col, 1940)
Captain Caution (UA, 1940)
Laddie (RKO, 1940)
South of Suez (WB, 1940)
That Hamilton Woman (UA, 1941)
Shadows on the Stairs (WB, 1941)
They Met in Bombay (MGM, 1941)
Dr. Kildare's Wedding Day (MGM, 1941)
Fingers at the Window (MGM, 1942)
Fly by Night (Par, 1942)
A Tragedy at Midnight (Rep, 1942)
To Be or Not to Be (UA, 1942)
Tarzan's New York Adventure (MGM, 1942)
Journey for Margaret (MGM, 1942)

This Above All (20th, 1942)
Apache Trail (MGM, 1942)
The War Against Mrs. Hadley (MGM, 1942)
Assignment in Brittany (MGM, 1943)
The Return of the Vampire (Col, 1943)
The Phantom of the Opera (Univ, 1943)
Secrets of the Underground (Rep, 1943)
Five Graves to Cairo (Par, 1943)
Guadalcanal Diary (20th, 1943)
Enter Arsene Lupin (Univ, 1944)
Murder, My Sweet (RKO, 1944)
Four Jills in a Jeep (20th, 1944)
The White Cliffs of Dover (MGM, 1944)
The Pearl of Death (Univ, 1944)
The Scarlet Claw (Univ, 1944)
Captain Kidd (UA, 1945)
The Brighton Strangler (RKO, 1945)
Week-End at the Waldorf (MGM, 1945)
The Crime Doctor's Warning (Col, 1945)
Confidential Agent (WB, 1945)
The Picture of Dorian Gray (MGM, 1945)
The Walls Came Tumbling Down (Col, 1946)
The Imperfect Lady (Par, 1946)
The Bandit of Sherwood Forest (Col, 1946)

E. G. MARSHALL
(Everett G. Marshall)

With Angie Dickinson in The Poppy Is Also a Flower *(1966).*

Born June 18, 1910, Owatonna, Minnesota. Married 1) Helen Wolf (1931), children: Jill, Degan; divorced (1953); 2) Judith Coy, children, Sam, Sarah. Multimedia performer with a well-modulated voice and expressive eyebrows. Most effective in intense proletarian drama: *The Bachelor Party* (Walter), *Twelve Angry Men* (Juror #4), etc. Could be the annoyed wealthy gentleman (Val Rogers of *The Chase*) or the overworked military officer (Lt. Colonel Bratton of *Tora! Tora! Tora!*). TV series: "The Defenders" (as Lawrence Preston), "The Bold Ones: The Doctors," and "American Lifestyles" (narrator).

> **E. G. Marshall** to Voltaire Perkins in *Compulsion:* "Your Honor, defense counsel is making a mockery of procedure."

Films

The House on 92nd Street (20th, 1945)
13 Rue Madeleine (20th, 1946)
Untamed Fury (PRC, 1947)
Call Northside 777 (20th, 1948)
The Caine Mutiny (Col, 1954)
Pushover (Col, 1954)
The Bamboo Prison (Col, 1954)
Broken Lance (20th, 1954)
The Silver Chalice (WB, 1954)

The Left Hand of God (20th, 1955)
The Scarlet Hour (Par, 1956)
The Mountain (Par, 1956)
Twelve Angry Men (UA, 1957)
The Bachelor Party (UA, 1957)
Man on Fire (MGM, 1957)
The Buccaneer (Par, 1958)
The Journey (MGM, 1959)
Compulsion (20th, 1959)

Cash McCall (WB, 1959)
Town Without Pity (UA, 1961)
The Chase (Col, 1966)
Is Paris Burning? (Par, 1966)
The Poppy Is Also a Flower (Comet, 1966)
The Bridge at Remagen (UA, 1969)
Tora! Tora! Tora! (20th, 1970)
The Pursuit of Happiness (Col, 1971)

TULLY MARSHALL
(William Phillips)

Karl Dane, Tully Marshall, Dolores Del Rio, and Ralph Forbes *in* The Trail of '98 *(1928).*

Born April 13, 1864, Nevada City, California. Married Marion Neiswanger. Died March 9, 1943, Encino, California. A consummate silent screen interpreter, whether as Fagin (*Oliver Twist*), the high priest of Bel (*Intolerance*), Bridger, the Indian scout (*The Covered Wagon*), or King Louis XI (*The Hunchback of Notre Dame*). Equally resourceful in talkies: Muff Potter (*Tom Sawyer*), Gerstenkorn (*Grand Hotel*), woodcutter (1935's *A Tale of Two Cities*), Professor Robinson, one of the stodgy scholars taught by burlesque performer Barbara Stanwyck (*Ball of Fire*), etc. Notable as Alvin Brewster, the fifth columnist/manufacturer of *This Gun for Hire*.

Tully Marshall surveying candles on his birthday cake in *Stand-In*: "Looks like a forest fire."

Films

The Sable Lorcha (Tri, 1915)
Let Katie Do It (Tri, 1915)
A Child of the Paris Streets (Fine Arts-Tri, 1916)
The Devil's Needle (Fine Arts-Tri, 1916)
Oliver Twist (Par, 1916)
Intolerance (Griffith-Wark Distributing, 1916)
Joan the Woman (Par, 1917)
Romance of the Redwoods (Par, 1917)
The Golden Fetter (Par, 1917)
The Countess Charming (Par, 1917)
We Can't Have Everything (Par-Artcraft, 1917)
Unconquered (Par, 1917)
The Devil's Stone (Par-Artcraft, 1917)
A Modern Musketeer (Par-Artcraft, 1918)

The Whispering Chorus (Par, 1918)
The Things We Love (Par, 1918)
M'liss (Par, 1918)
Old Wives for New (Par, 1918)
Bound in Morocco (Par, 1918)
Too Many Millions (Par, 1918)
The Squaw Man (Par, 1918)
Arizona (Par, 1918)
The Man from Funeral Range (Hodkinson, 1918)
Maggie Pepper (Par, 1919)
The Girl Who Stayed Home (Par, 1919)
Cheating Cheaters (Selznick, 1919)
The Crimson Gardenia (G, 1919)
Her Kingdom of Dreams (FN, 1919)
The Life Line (Par, 1919)
The Lottery Man (Par, 1919)
Hawthorne of the USA (Par, 1919)

Everywoman (Par, 1919)
Daughter of Mine (G, 1919)
The Grim Game (Par, 1919)
Double Speed (Par, 1920)
The Dancin' Fool (Par, 1920)
Excuse My Dust (Par, 1920)
The Gift Supreme (Selznick, 1920)
Sick Abed (Par, 1920)
The Slim Princess (G, 1920)
Honest Hutch (G, 1920)
Her Beloved Villain (Realart, 1921)
Little 'Fraid Lady (Robertson-Cole, 1921)
What Happened to Rosa? (G, 1921)
The Cup of Life (Associated Exhibitors, 1921)
Hail the Woman (Associated FN, 1921)
Lotus Blossom (Associated FN, 1921)

Silent Years (FBO, 1921)
The Three Musketeers (UA, 1921)
Any Night (Amalgamated, 1922)
The Beautiful and the Damned (WB, 1922)
Deserted at the Altar (G, 1922)
Fools of Fortune (A. F. Films, 1922)
Good Men and True (FBO, 1922)
Is Matrimony a Failure? (Par, 1922)
The Ladder Jinx (Vit, 1922)
Without Compromise (Fox, 1922)
The Super Sex (American Releasing Company, 1922)
The Village Blacksmith (Fox, 1922)
Too Much Business (Vit, 1922)
The Lying Truth (American Releasing Company, 1923)
Only a Shop Girl (CBC, 1923)
Penrod (Associated FN, 1923)
The Marriage Chance (Selznick, 1923)
Defying Destiny (Selznick, 1923)
The Barefoot Boy (CBC, 1923)
Dangerous Trails (Ambassador, 1923)
The Brass Bottle (Associated FN, 1923)
The Dangerous Maid (Associated FN, 1923)
The Covered Wagon (Par, 1923)
Broken Hearts of Broadway (Cunnings, 1923)
Thundergate (Associated FN, 1923)
Fools and Riches (Univ, 1923)
Temporary Marriage (Principal, 1923)
Her Temporary Husband (Associated FN, 1923)
Richard the Lion-Hearted (Allied Producers, 1923)
His Last Race (G, 1923)
Ponjola (Associated FN, 1923)
The Hunchback of Notre Dame (Univ, 1923)
Let's Go (Truart, 1923)
The Law of the Lawless (Par, 1923)
The Ridin' Kid from Powder River (Univ, 1924)
Along Came Ruth (MG, 1924)
Reckless Romance (PDC, 1924)
For Sale (Associated FN, 1924)
Passion's Pathway (Lee-Bradford Company, 1924)
Hold Your Breath (PDC, 1924)
He Who Gets Slapped (MG, 1924)
Pagan Passions (Selznick, 1924)
The Stranger (Par, 1924)

The Right of the Strongest (Selznick, 1924)
Smouldering Fires (Univ, 1924)
The Talker (FN, 1925)
Anything Once (Aywon, 1925)
Clothes Make the Pirate (FN, 1925)
The Pace That Thrills (FN, 1925)
The Half-Way Girl (FN, 1925)
The Merry Widow (MGM, 1925)
Twinkletoes (FN, 1926)
Her Big Night (Univ, 1926)
Old Loves and New (FN, 1926)
The Torrent (MGM, 1926)
Jim, the Conqueror (PDC, 1927)
Beware of Widows (Univ, 1927)
The Cat and the Canary (Univ, 1927)
The Gorilla (FN, 1927)
Queen Kelly (UA, 1928)
Conquest (WB, 1928)
Drums of Love (UA, 1928)
Mad Hour (FN, 1928)
The Perfect Crime (FBO, 1928)
The Trail of '98 (MGM, 1928)
Redskin (Par, 1929)
The Bridge of San Luis Rey (MGM, 1929)
Thunderbolt (Par, 1929)
Skin Deep (WB, 1929)
Alias Jimmy Valentine (MGM, 1929)
Tiger Rose (WB, 1929)
The Show of Shows (WB, 1929)
The Mysterious Dr. Fu Manchu (Par, 1929)
She Couldn't Say No (WB, 1930)
Burning Up (Par, 1930)
Mammy (WB, 1930)
Redemption (MGM, 1930)
Murder Will Out (FN, 1930)
Numbered Men (FN, 1930)
Common Clay (Fox, 1930)
Dancing Sweeties (WB, 1930)
The Big Trail (Fox, 1930)
Tom Sawyer (Par, 1930)
One Night at Susie's (FN, 1930)
Under a Texas Moon (WB, 1930)
Virtuous Husband (Univ, 1931)
Fighting Caravans (Par, 1931)
The Millionaire (WB, 1931)
The Unholy Garden (UA, 1931)
Broken Lullaby [a.k.a. The Man I Killed] (Par, 1932)
The Hatchet Man (FN, 1932)
Arsene Lupin (MGM, 1932)

The Beast of the City (MGM, 1932)
Scarface: The Shame of a Nation (UA, 1932)
Grand Hotel (MGM, 1932)
Night Court (MGM, 1932)
Scandal for Sale (Univ, 1932)
Strangers of the Evening (Tif, 1932)
Two Fisted Law (Col, 1932)
Exposure (Capital, 1932)
Klondike (Mon, 1932)
Cabin in the Cotton (FN, 1932)
Red Dust (MGM, 1932)
Afraid to Talk (Univ, 1932)
The Hurricane Express (Mascot serial, 1932)
Night of Terror (Col, 1933)
Corruption (Imperial, 1933)
Laughing at Life (Mascot, 1933)
Fighting with Kit Carson (Mascot serial, 1933)
Massacre (FN, 1934)
Murder on the Blackboard (RKO, 1934)
Black Fury (FN, 1935)
Diamond Jim (Univ, 1935)
A Tale of Two Cities (MGM, 1935)
California Straight Ahead (Univ, 1937)
Mr. Boggs Steps Out (GN, 1937)
She Asked for It (Par, 1937)
Souls at Sea (Par, 1937)
Stand-In (UA, 1937)
Hold 'em Navy (Par, 1937)
House of Mystery (Col, 1938)
A Yank at Oxford (MGM, 1938)
Arsene Lupin Returns (MGM, 1938)
Making the Headlines (Col, 1938)
College Swing (Par, 1938)
The Kid from Texas (MGM, 1939)
Blue Montana Skies (Rep, 1939)
Invisible Stripes (WB, 1940)
Brigham Young—Frontiersman (20th, 1940)
Youth Will Be Served (20th, 1940)
Go West (MGM, 1940)
Chad Hanna (20th, 1940)
For Beauty's Sake (20th, 1941)
Ball of Fire (RKO, 1941)
This Gun for Hire (Par, 1942)
Moontide (20th, 1942)
Ten Gentlemen from West Point (20th, 1942)
Behind Prison Walls (PRC, 1943)
Hitler's Madman (MGM, 1943)

CHRIS-PIN MARTIN
(Ysabel Chris-Pin Martin Piaz)

Andy Clyde, Eva Puig, and Chris-Pin Martin in Undercover Man *(1942).*

Born 1893, Tucson, Arizona. Married Margaret Avella, children: four. Died June 27, 1953, Montebello, California. Roly-poly Yaqui Indian who provided comic moments in musicals and Westerns, usually with an exaggerated broken English gimmick. In the long-running *Cisco Kid* series as Gordito.

Chris-Pin Martin to Randolph Scott in *Frontier Marshal:*
"Doc, he drink whiskey like crazy man."

Films

In Old Arizona (Fox, 1929)
Safe In Hell (FN, 1931)
The Squaw Man (MGM, 1931)
The Cisco Kid (Fox, 1931)
South of Santa Fe (WW, 1932)
Girl Crazy (RKO, 1932)
The Stoker (Allied Pictures, 1932)
The Painted Woman (Fox, 1932)
Outlaw Justice (Majestic, 1933)
California Trail (Col, 1933)
Four Frightened People (Par, 1934)
Grand Canary (Fox, 1934)
Marie Galante (Fox, 1934)
Lazy River (MGM, 1934)
Captain Blood (FN, 1935)
Under the Pampas Moon (Fox, 1935)
Bordertown (FN, 1935)
Hi, Gaucho! (RKO, 1935)
In Caliente (WB, 1935)
The Gay Desperado (UA, 1936)
The Border Patrolman (20th, 1936)
The Bold Caballero (Rep, 1936)
Boots and Saddles (Rep, 1937)
A Star Is Born (UA, 1937)
Swing High, Swing Low (Par, 1937)
Too Hot to Handle (MGM, 1938)
Tropic Holiday (Par, 1938)

The Texans (Par, 1938)
Flirting with Fate (MGM, 1938)
The Girl and the Gambler (RKO, 1939)
I'm from the City (RKO, 1938)
Frontier Marshal (20th, 1939)
Stagecoach (UA, 1939)
The Return of the Cisco Kid (20th, 1939)
Espionage Agent (WB, 1939)
The Fighting Gringo (RKO, 1939)
Charlie Chan in Panama (20th, 1940)
The Cisco Kid and the Lady (20th, 1940)
The Llano Kid (Par, 1940)
Lucky Cisco Kid (20th, 1940)
Viva, Cisco Kid (20th, 1940)
Down Argentine Way (20th, 1940)
The Gay Caballero (20th, 1940)
The Mark of Zorro (20th, 1940)
Romance of the Rio Grande (20th, 1941)
The Bad Man (MGM, 1941)
Ride On, Vaquero (20th, 1941)
Week End in Havana (20th, 1941)
Undercover Man (UA, 1942)
Tombstone, the Town Too Tough to Die (Par, 1942)
American Empire (UA, 1942)
The Ox-Bow Incident (20th, 1943)
The Sultan's Daughter (Mon, 1943)

Ali Baba and the Forty Thieves (Univ, 1944)
Tampico (20th, 1944)
Along Came Jones (RKO, 1945)
San Antonio (WB, 1945)
Holiday in Mexico (MGM, 1946)
Suspense (Mon, 1946)
Gallant Journey (Col, 1946)
Robin Hood of Monterey (Mon, 1947)
The Fugitive (RKO, 1947)
King of the Bandits (Mon, 1947)
The Secret Life of Walter Mitty (RKO, 1947)
Blood on the Moon (RKO, 1948)
Belle Starr's Daughter (20th, 1948)
Mexican Hayride (Univ, 1948)
The Return of Wildfire (Screen Guild, 1948)
The Beautiful Blonde from Bashful Bend (20th, 1949)
Rimfire (Screen Guild, 1949)
The Arizona Cowboy (Rep, 1950)
A Millionaire for Christy (20th, 1951)
The Lady from Texas (Univ, 1951)
Ride the Man Down (Rep, 1952)

MIKE MAZURKI
(Michail Mazuruski)

With Anne Jeffreys in Dick Tracy *(1945).*

Born December 25, 1909, Tarnopol, Austria. Married 1) _____ ; 2) Jeanette Briggs (1943), children: two daughters; divorced (1950); 3) Sylvia Weinblatt (1968). Ex-wrestler who used his oversized, rugged presence to good effect as Moosey in Dick Powell's *Murder, My Sweet.* Typically cast as the faithful goon. Actually well educated. Some zesty roles: *Behind the Rising Sun* (Japanese wrestler), *Dick Tracy* (Splitface), etc. In later years became a wrestling referee; recently the character star (hero!) of the family-oriented *Challenge to Be Free.* TV series: "It's About Time" and "The Chicago Teddy Bears."

> **Mike Mazurki** to Dick Powell in *Murder, My Sweet:* "Moose
> . . . the name is *Moose* on account of I'm large. . . . *Moose
> Malloy.* You heard of me, maybe?"

Films

Black Fury (FN, 1935)
The Shanghai Gesture (UA, 1941)
Gentleman Jim (WB, 1942)
That Other Woman (20th, 1942)
Henry Aldrich Haunts a House (Par, 1943)
Taxi, Mister (UA, 1943)
Mission to Moscow (WB, 1943)
Bomber's Moon (20th, 1943)
Behind the Rising Sun (RKO, 1943)
Murder, My Sweet (RKO, 1944)
The Missing Juror (Col, 1944)

Summer Storm (UA, 1944)
The Canterville Ghost (MGM, 1944)
Abbott and Costello in Hollywood (MGM, 1945)
Dakota (Rep, 1945)
Dick Tracy (RKO, 1945)
The Horn Blows at Midnight (WB, 1945)
The Spanish Main (RKO, 1945)
The French Key (Rep, 1946)
Live Wires (Mon, 1946)
Mysterious Intruder (Col, 1946)
Killer Dill (Screen Guild, 1947)

Sinbad the Sailor (RKO, 1947)
I Walk Alone.(Par, 1947)
Nightmare Alley (20th, 1947)
Unconquered (Par, 1947)
Relentless (Col, 1948)
The Noose Hangs High (EL, 1948)
Come to the Stable (20th, 1949)
Neptune's Daughter (MGM, 1949)
Abandoned (Univ, 1949)
Rope of Sand (Par, 1949)
The Devil's Henchman (Col, 1949)
Samson and Delilah (Par, 1949)

Night and the City (20th, 1950)
Dark City (Par, 1950)
He's a Cockeyed Wonder (Col, 1950)
Pier 23 (Lip, 1951)
Criminal Lawyer (Col, 1951)
My Favorite Spy (Par, 1951)
Ten Tall Men (Col, 1951)
The Light Touch (MGM, 1951)
The Egyptian (20th, 1954)
New York Confidential (WB, 1955)
New Orleans Uncensored (Col, 1955)
Davy Crockett—King of the Wild Frontier
  (BV, 1955)
Blood Alley (WB, 1955)
Kismet (MGM, 1955)

Comanche (UA, 1956)
Man in the Vault (RKO, 1956)
Around the World in 80 Days (UA, 1956)
Hell Ship Mutiny (Rep, 1957)
The Buccaneer (Par, 1958)
The Man Who Died Twice (Rep, 1958)
Alias Jesse James (UA, 1959)
Some Like It Hot (UA, 1959)
The Facts of Life (UA, 1960)
The Errand Boy (Par, 1961)
Pocketful of Miracles (UA, 1961)
Five Weeks in a Balloon (20th, 1962)
Zotz! (Col, 1962)
Donovan's Reef (Par, 1963)
Four for Texas (WB, 1963)

It's a Mad, Mad, Mad, Mad World (UA,
  1963)
Cheyenne Autumn (WB, 1964)
Requiem for a Gunfighter (Emb, 1965)
Seven Women (MGM, 1966)
The Adventures of Bullwhip Griffin (BV,
  1967)
Which Way to the Front? (WB, 1970)
The Centerfold Girls (General Film,
  1974)
Challenge to Be Free (Pacific Inter-
  national Enterprises, 1975)
The Wild McCullochs (AIP, 1975)
Won Ton Ton, the Dog Who Saved Holly-
  wood (Par, 1976)

DONALD MEEK

Donald Meek and Wallace Beery in Rationing *(1944).*

Born July 14, 1880, Glasgow, Scotland. Married Belle Walken (1909). Died November 18, 1946, Woodland Hills, California. Short, bald-pated man. Lived up to his name on screen, cornering the market on Casper Milquetoast roles: the timid liquor salesman Samuel Peacock in John Ford's *Stagecoach* and later Hippenstahl, the inebriated food taster of Jeanne Crain's *State Fair*.

Donald Meek to Clark Gable in *Love on the Run:* "We must hurry. You see, at 12 o'clock I turn into a pumpkin."

Films

Six Cylinder Love (Fox, 1923)

The Hole in the Wall (Par, 1929)

The Love Kiss (Celebrity Pictures, 1930)

The Girl Habit (Par, 1931)

Personal Maid (Par, 1931)

Wayward (Par, 1932)

Love, Honor and Oh, Baby! (Univ, 1933)

College Coach (WB, 1933)

The Defense Rests (Col, 1934)

Hi, Nellie! (WB, 1934)

Bedside (FN, 1934)

Mrs. Wiggs of the Cabbage Patch (Par, 1934)

Murder at the Vanities (Par, 1934)

What Every Woman Knows (MGM, 1934)

The Merry Widow (MGM, 1934)

The Last Gentleman (UA, 1934)

The Captain Hates the Sea (Col, 1934)

Romance in Manhattan (RKO, 1934)

Biography of a Bachelor Girl (MGM, 1935)

The Whole Town's Talking (Col, 1935)

The Informer (RKO, 1935)

Village Tale (RKO, 1935)

The Return of Peter Grimm (RKO, 1935)

Old Man Rhythm (RKO, 1935)

The Gilded Lily (Par, 1935)

Accent on Youth (Par, 1935)

The Bride Comes Home (Par, 1935)

Society Doctor (MGM, 1935)

Mark of the Vampire (MGM, 1935)

Baby Face Harrington (MGM, 1935)

Kind Lady (MGM, 1935)

Barbary Coast (UA, 1935)

She Couldn't Take It (Col, 1935)

Captain Blood (FN, 1935)

China Seas (MGM, 1935)

Peter Ibbetson (Par, 1935)

Happiness C.O.D. (Chesterfield, 1935)

Top Hat (RKO, 1935)

Everybody's Old Man (20th, 1936)

And So They Were Married (Col, 1936)

Pennies from Heaven (Col, 1936)

One Rainy Afternoon (UA, 1936)

Three Wise Guys (MGM, 1936)

Old Hutch (MGM, 1936)

Love on the Run (MGM, 1936)

Three Married Men (Par, 1936)

Two in a Crowd (Univ, 1936)

Maid of Salem (Par, 1937)

Artists and Models (Par, 1937)

Parnell (MGM, 1937)

Double Wedding (MGM, 1937)

Three Legionnaires (General Films, 1937)

Behind the Headlines (RKO, 1937)

The Toast of New York (RKO, 1937)

Make a Wish (RKO, 1937)

Breakfast for Two (RKO, 1937)

You're a Sweetheart (Univ, 1937)

Double Danger (RKO, 1938)

Having Wonderful Time (RKO, 1938)

Adventures of Tom Sawyer (UA, 1938)

Goodbye Broadway (Univ, 1938)

Little Miss Broadway (20th, 1938)

Hold That Co-ed (20th, 1938)

You Can't Take It with You (Col, 1938)

Jesse James (20th, 1939)

Young Mr. Lincoln (20th, 1939)

Hollywood Cavalcade (20th, 1939)

Stagecoach (UA, 1939)

Blondie Takes a Vacation (Col, 1939)

The Housekeeper's Daughter (UA, 1939)

Nick Carter, Master Detective (MGM, 1939)

My Little Chickadee (Univ, 1940)

Dr. Ehrlich's Magic Bullet (WB, 1940)

Turnabout (UA, 1940)

The Man from Dakota (MGM, 1940)

The Ghost Comes Home (MGM, 1940)

Oh Johnny, How You Can Love (Univ, 1940)

Phantom Raiders (MGM, 1940)

Sky Murder (MGM, 1940)

Third Finger, Left Hand (MGM, 1940)

Hullabaloo (MGM, 1940)

Star Dust (20th, 1940)

The Return of Frank James (20th, 1940)

A Woman's Face (MGM, 1941)

Wild Man of Borneo (MGM, 1941)

Blonde Inspiration (MGM, 1941)

Come Live with Me (MGM, 1941)

Rise and Shine (20th, 1941)

Babes on Broadway (MGM, 1941)

The Feminine Touch (MGM, 1941)

Barnacle Bill (MGM, 1941)

Tortilla Flat (MGM, 1942)

Maisie Gets Her Man (MGM, 1942)

Seven Sweethearts (MGM, 1942)

The Omaha Trail (MGM, 1942)

Keeper of the Flame (MGM, 1942)

Air Raid Wardens (MGM, 1943)

They Got Me Covered (RKO, 1943)

Du Barry Was a Lady (MGM, 1943)

Lost Angel (MGM, 1943)

Rationing (MGM, 1944)

Two Girls and a Sailor (MGM, 1944)

Bathing Beauty (MGM, 1944)

Barbary Coast Gent (MGM, 1944)

Maisie Goes to Reno (MGM, 1944)

The Thin Man Goes Home (MGM, 1944)

Colonel Effingham's Raid (20th, 1945)

State Fair (20th, 1945)

Because of Him (Univ, 1946)

Janie Gets Married (WB, 1946)

Affairs of Geraldine (Rep, 1946)

The Hal Roach Comedy Carnival: The Fabulous Joe (UA, 1947)

Magic Town (RKO, 1947)

BERYL MERCER

Nora Cecil, Beryl Mercer, and Daisy Belmore in Seven Days' Leave *(1930).*

Born August 13, 1882, Seville, Spain. Married 1) Maitland Sabrina-Pasley; 2) Holmes Herbert, child: Joan. Died July 28, 1939, Santa Monica, California. Played very mature mothers to tear-provoking perfection from a relatively young age: *Seven Days' Leave* (Gary Cooper's adopted), *All Quiet on the Western Front* (Lew Ayres'), *The Public Enemy* (James Cagney's), etc. Later reduced to cameos: 1935's *Magnificent Obsession* (little woman), 1937's *Night Must Fall* (saleslady), *The Little Princess* (Queen Victoria).

Beryl Mercer to Lew Ayres in *All Quiet on the Western Front:*
"Be on your guard against the women out there. They're no good."

Films

Broken Chains (G, 1922)
The Christian (G, 1923)
We Americans (Univ, 1928)
Mother's Boy (Pathé, 1929)
Three Live Ghosts (UA, 1929)
Seven Days' Leave (Par, 1930)
In Gay Madrid (MGM, 1930)
All Quiet on the Western Front (Univ, 1930)
Dumbbells in Ermine (WB, 1930)
The Matrimonial Bed (WB, 1930)
Common Clay (Fox, 1930)
Outward Bound (WB, 1930)
East Lynne (Fox, 1931)
The Public Enemy (WB, 1931)
Inspiration (MGM, 1931)
Always Goodbye (Fox, 1931)
Merely Mary Ann (Fox, 1931)
The Miracle Woman (Col, 1931)

The Man in Possession (MGM, 1931)
Sky Spider (Action Pictures, 1931)
Are These Our Children? (RKO, 1931)
The Devil's Lottery (Fox, 1932)
Forgotten Women (Mon, 1932)
Lovers Courageous (MGM, 1932)
Lena Rivers (Tif, 1932)
Young America (Fox, 1932)
No Greater Love (Col, 1932)
Unholy Love (Allied, 1932)
Midnight Morals (Mayfair, 1932)
Smilin' Through (MGM, 1932)
Six Hours to Live (Fox, 1932)
Cavalcade (Fox, 1933)
Supernatural (Par, 1933)
Berkeley Square (Fox, 1933)
Her Splendid Folly (Progressive Pictures, 1933)
Blind Adventure (RKO, 1933)

Broken Dreams (Mon, 1933)
Change of Heart (Fox, 1934)
Jane Eyre (Mon, 1934)
The Little Minister (RKO, 1934)
The Richest Girl in the World (RKO, 1934)
Age of Indiscretion (MGM, 1935)
My Marriage (Fox, 1935)
Hitchhike Lady (Rep, 1935)
Three Live Ghosts (MGM, 1935)
Magnificent Obsession (Univ, 1935)
Forbidden Heaven (Rep, 1936)
Call It a Day (WB, 1937)
Night Must Fall (MGM, 1937)
The Hound of the Baskervilles (20th, 1939)
The Little Princess (20th, 1939)
A Woman Is the Judge (Col, 1939)

UNA MERKEL

Hans Conried, Una Merkel, Marcel Dalio, Vic Damone, Jame Powell, and Wendell Corey in Rich, Young and Pretty *(1951).*

Born December 10, 1903, Covington, Kentucky. Married Ronald Burla (1932); divorced (1945). Occasional leading lady (Ann Rutledge in D. W. Griffith's *Abraham Lincoln*), but better cast as the wisecracking chipper-voiced other woman (Robert Montgomery's unwanted bride in *Private Lives*) or pal of the heroine (Eleanor Powell's in *Born to Dance*). Well showcased during her MGM contract years in the 1930s. At Universal fought Marlene Dietrich in a lengthy barroom tussle in *Destry Rides Again;* dealt with daddy W. C. Fields in *The Bank Dick*. Thoughtful performance as Geraldine Page's mentally disturbed mama in *Summer and Smoke* (Oscar-nominated but lost BSAAA to Rita Moreno of *West Side Story*).

> **Una Merkel** to Eleanor Powell in *Born to Dance:* "Say, whoever gave *you* the gong ought to be hit over the head with it."

Films

Way Down East (UA, 1920)
The White Rose (UA, 1923)
The Fifth Horseman (E. M. MacMahon, 1924)
Abraham Lincoln (UA, 1930)
Eyes of the World (UA, 1930)
The Bat Whispers (UA, 1930)
Command Performance (Tif, 1931)
Don't Bet on Women (Fox, 1931)
The Maltese Falcon (WB, 1931)
The Bargain (WB, 1931)
Daddy Long Legs (Fox, 1931)
Six-Cylinder Love (Fox, 1931)
Terror by Night [a.k.a. *The Secret Witness*] (Family Attractions, 1931)

Wicked (Fox, 1931)
Private Lives (MGM, 1931)
Red-Headed Woman (MGM, 1932)
Men Are Such Fools (RKO, 1932)
She Wanted a Millionaire (Fox, 1932)
Man Wanted (WB, 1932)
Huddle (MGM, 1932)
They Call It Sin (WB, 1932)
Impatient Maiden (Univ, 1932)
Whistling in the Dark (MGM, 1933)
42nd Street (WB, 1933)
Reunion in Vienna (MGM, 1933)
Midnight Mary (MGM, 1933)
Beauty for Sale (MGM, 1933)
Broadway to Hollywood (MGM, 1933)

Bombshell (MGM, 1933)
Day of Reckoning (MGM, 1933)
Her First Mate (Univ, 1933)
Clear All Wires (MGM, 1933)
The Women in His Life (MGM, 1933)
Bulldog Drummond Strikes Back (UA, 1934)
The Secret of Madame Blanche (MGM, 1933)
This Side of Heaven (MGM, 1934)
Murder in the Private Car (MGM, 1934)
Have a Heart (MGM, 1934)
Paris Interlude (MGM, 1934)
The Merry Widow (MGM, 1934)
Evelyn Prentice (MGM, 1934)

The Cat's Paw (Fox, 1934)
The Night Is Young (MGM, 1935)
Biography of a Bachelor Girl (MGM, 1935)
One New York Night (MGM, 1935)
Baby Face Harrington (MGM, 1935)
Murder in the Fleet (MGM, 1935)
Broadway Melody of 1936 (MGM, 1935)
It's in the Air (MGM, 1935)
Riffraff (MGM, 1935)
Speed (MGM, 1936)
We Went to College (MGM, 1936)
Born to Dance (MGM, 1936)
Don't Tell the Wife (RKO, 1937)
The Good Old Soak (MGM, 1937)
Saratoga (MGM, 1937)
True Confession (Par, 1937)
Checkers (20th, 1937)
Test Pilot (MGM, 1938)
Some Like It Hot (Par, 1939)

Four Girls in White (MGM, 1939)
On Borrowed Time (MGM, 1939)
Destry Rides Again (Univ, 1939)
Saturday's Children (WB, 1940)
The Bank Dick (Univ, 1940)
Sandy Gets Her Man (Univ, 1940)
Comin' 'Round the Mountain (Par, 1940)
Road to Zanzibar (Par, 1941)
Double Date (Univ, 1941)
Cracked Nuts (Univ, 1941)
The Mad Doctor of Market Street (Univ, 1942)
Twin Beds (UA, 1942)
This Is the Army (WB, 1943)
Sweethearts of the U.S.A. (Mon, 1944)
It's a Joke, Son (EL, 1947)
The Bride Goes Wild (MGM, 1948)
The Man from Texas (EL, 1948)
Emergency Wedding (Col, 1950)
My Blue Heaven (20th, 1950)

Kill the Umpire (Col, 1950)
Rich, Young and Pretty (MGM, 1951)
Golden Girl (20th, 1951)
A Millionaire for Christy (20th, 1951)
With a Song in My Heart (20th, 1952)
The Merry Widow (MGM, 1952)
I Love Melvin (MGM, 1953)
The Kentuckian (UA, 1955)
The Kettles in the Ozarks (Univ, 1956)
Bundle of Joy (RKO, 1956)
The Girl Most Likely (Univ, 1957)
The Fuzzy Pink Nightgown (UA, 1957)
The Mating Game (MGM, 1959)
Summer and Smoke (Par, 1961)
The Parent Trap (BV, 1961)
Summer Magic (BV, 1963)
A Tiger Walks (BV, 1964)
Spinout (MGM, 1967)

CHARLES MIDDLETON

Robert Lowery, Lionel Atwill, Cora Witherspoon, Charles Middleton, Claire DuBrey, Victor Sen Yung, and Sidney Toler in Charlie Chan's Murder Cruise *(1940).*

Born October 3, 1878, Elizabethtown, Kentucky. Died April 23, 1949, Los Angeles, California. Challenged Buster Crabbe's *Flash Gordon* in three serials as the devious bald-domed (shaved for the part) archfiend Ming the Merciless. Made several other chapterplays. Especially good as the vengeful ex-convict in the serial *Daredevils of the Red Circle*. Some non-dastardly roles for the tall, angular player with the deep voice: doctor (*Jesse James*), Jefferson Davis (*Virginia City*), etc.

Charles Middleton to Priscilla Lawson in *Flash Gordon:*
"Perhaps you would care to see what happens to those
who dare to dispute my power."

Films

The Farmer's Daughter (Fox, 1928)
The Bellamy Trial (MGM, 1929)
The Far Call (Fox, 1929)
Welcome Danger (Par, 1929)
East Is West (Univ, 1930)
Beau Bandit (RKO, 1930)
Way Out West (MGM, 1930)
Framed (RKO, 1930)
An American Tragedy (Par, 1931)
Ship of Hate (Mon, 1931)
Safe in Hell (FN, 1931)
Caught Plastered (RKO, 1931)
The Miracle Woman (Col, 1931)
Palmy Days (UA, 1931)
Sob Sister (Fox, 1931)
Alexander Hamilton (WB, 1931)
A Dangerous Affair (Col, 1931)
High Pressure (WB, 1932)
The Hatchet Man (FN, 1932)
Manhattan Parade (WB, 1932)
Strange Love of Molly Louvain (FN, 1932)
Pack Up Your Troubles (MGM, 1932)
Hell's Highway (RKO, 1932)
Mystery Ranch (Fox, 1932)
Kongo (MGM, 1932)
The Sign of the Cross (Par, 1932)
The Phantom President (Par, 1932)
I Am a Fugitive from a Chain Gang (WB, 1932)
Silver Dollar (FN, 1932)
Breach of Promise (WW, 1932)
Rockabye (RKO, 1932)
Tomorrow at Seven (RKO, 1933)
Sunset Pass (Par, 1933)
Pickup (Par, 1933)
Destination Unknown (Univ, 1933)
Disgraced (Par, 1933)
This Day and Age (Par, 1933)
Big Executive (Par, 1933)
White Woman (Par, 1933)
Duck Soup (Par, 1933)
Lone Cowboy (Par, 1933)
The Last Roundup (Par, 1934)
Murder at the Vanities (Par, 1934)
Behold My Wife! (Par, 1934)
Whom the Gods Destroy (Col, 1934)
Massacre (FN, 1934)
David Harum (Fox, 1934)

Mrs. Wiggs of the Cabbage Patch (Par, 1934)
When Strangers Meet (Liberty, 1934)
Red Morning (RKO, 1934)
Special Agent (WB, 1935)
Steamboat 'Round the Bend (Fox, 1935)
Frisco Kid (WB, 1935)
The County Chairman (Fox, 1935)
Hopalong Cassidy (Par, 1935)
Square Shooter (Col, 1935)
In Spite of Danger (Col, 1935)
The Virginia Judge (Par, 1935)
The Texas Rangers (Par, 1936)
Road Gang (WB, 1936)
Trail of the Lonesome Pine (Par, 1936)
Flash Gordon (Univ serial, 1936)
 [feature versions: *Rocket Ship, Space-ship to the Unknown*]
Empty Saddles (Univ, 1936)
Sunset of Power (Univ, 1936)
Showboat (Univ, 1936)
Song of the Saddle (FN, 1936)
Jailbreak (WB, 1936)
A Son Comes Home (Par, 1936)
John Meade's Woman (Par, 1937)
Career Woman (20th, 1936)
We're on the Jury (RKO, 1937)
Two-Gun Law (Col, 1937)
Slave Ship (20th, 1937)
Hollywood Cowboy [a.k.a. *Wings over Wyoming*] (RKO, 1937)
Yodelin' Kid from Pine Ridge (Rep, 1937)
Dick Tracy Returns (Rep serial, 1938)
Flaming Frontiers (Univ serial, 1938)
Flash Gordon's Trip to Mars (Univ serial, 1938) [feature version: *Deadly Ray from Mars, Peril from the Planet Mongo*]
Outside the Law (Univ, 1938)
Kentucky (20th, 1938)
Jesse James (20th, 1939)
Captain Fury (UA, 1939)
The Oklahoma Kid (WB, 1939)
Blackmail (MGM, 1939)
Daredevils of the Red Circle (Rep serial, 1939)
Wyoming Outlaw (Rep, 1939)
Cowboys from Texas (Rep, 1939)
Juarez (WB, 1939)

Way Down South (RKO, 1939)
The Flying Deuces (RKO, 1939)
$1,000 a Touchdown (Par, 1939)
Thou Shalt Not Kill (Rep, 1940)
Abe Lincoln in Illinois (RKO, 1940)
Chad Hanna (20th, 1940)
The Grapes of Wrath (20th, 1940)
Rangers of Fortune (Par, 1940)
Shooting High (20th, 1940)
Charlie Chan's Murder Cruise (20th, 1940)
Virginia City (WB, 1940)
Santa Fe Trail (WB, 1940)
Island of Doomed Men (Col, 1940)
Flash Gordon Conquers the Universe (Univ serial, 1940) [feature version: *Purple Death from Outer Space*]
Jungle Man (PRC, 1941)
Western Union (20th, 1941)
Wild Geese Calling (20th, 1941)
Belle Starr (20th, 1941)
Wild Bill Hickok Rides (WB, 1941)
Mystery of Marie Roget (Univ, 1942)
Men of San Quentin (PRC, 1942)
Two Weeks to Live (RKO, 1943)
The Black Raven (Univ, 1943)
The Town Went Wild (PRC, 1944)
Kismet [TV title: *Oriental Dreams*] (MGM, 1944)
How Do You Do? (PRC, 1945)
Hollywood and Vine (PRC, 1945)
Captain Kidd (UA, 1945)
Our Vines Have Tender Grapes (MGM, 1945)
Strangler of the Swamp (PRC, 1945)
The Killers (Univ, 1946)
Spook Busters (Mon, 1946)
The Pretender (Rep, 1947)
Welcome Stranger (Par, 1947)
Road to Rio (Par, 1947)
Stations West (RKO, 1948)
Jiggs and Maggie in Court (Mon, 1948)
The Black Arrow (Col, 1948)
Mr. Blandings Builds His Dream House (Selznick Releasing Organization, 1948)
The Last Bandit (Rep, 1949)

JOHN MILJAN

With Mae West in Belle of the Nineties *(1934).*

Born November 9, 1892, Lead City, South Dakota. Married Victoria Lowe Hale; child: son. Died January 24, 1960, Los Angeles, California. Generally the suave villain (William Boyd's rival in *The Yankee Clipper*), who sometimes went berserk (Orchid Joe in *Sailor Izzy Murphy*). Consistently leading a heroine astray (Dorothy Sebastian in *Our Blushing Brides*). Infrequently turned to the side of the law: Inspector Burke (*Paid*), Inspector Tobin (*The Fallen Sparrow*). Very smooth operator.

John Miljan to Mae West in *Belle of the Nineties:* "I'll make you queen of the gambling salons; I'll clothe you with diamonds; I'll lay the world at your feet."

Films

Love Letters (Fox, 1923)
Lone Chance (Col, 1924)
The Painted Lady (Fox, 1924)
Romance Ranch (Fox, 1924)
On the Stroke of Three (FBO, 1924)
Empty Hearts (Banner, 1924)
Sackcloth and Scarlet (Par, 1925)
The Phantom of the Opera (Univ, 1925)
Wreckage (Banner, 1925)
The Unholy Three (MGM, 1925)
Overland Limited (Lumas-Gotham, 1925)
Silent Sanderson (PDC, 1925)
Flaming Waters (FBO, 1925)
The Unnamed Woman (Arrow, 1925)
Morals for Men (Tif, 1925)
The Unchastened Woman (Chadwick, 1925)
Sealed Lips (Col, 1925)
My Official Wife (WB, 1926)
Brooding Eyes (Kahn, 1926)
The Devil's Circus (MGM, 1926)

Unknown Treasures (Sterling, 1926)
Race Wild (Ellbee, 1926)
Footloose Widows (WB, 1926)
The Amateur Gentleman (FN, 1926)
Devil's Island (Chadwick, 1926)
Almost a Lady (PDC, 1926)
The Clown (Col, 1927)
Husbands for Rent (WB, 1927)
Sailor Izzy Murphy (WB, 1927)
Wolf's Clothing (WB, 1927)
Final Extra (Lumas, 1927)
What Happened to Father? (WB, 1927)
Quarantined Rivals (Lumas, 1927)
The Satin Woman (Gotham, 1927)
Paying the Price (Col, 1927)
Lovers? (MGM, 1927)
Rough House Rosie (Par, 1927)
The Ladybird (Chadwick, 1927)
Stranded (Sterling, 1927)
The Silver Slave (WB, 1927)
Desired Woman (WB, 1927)
A Sailor's Sweetheart (WB, 1927)

The Slaver (Anchor, 1927)
Ham and Eggs at the Front (WB, 1927)
The Yankee Clipper (PDC, 1927)
Framed (FN, 1927)
Old San Francisco (WB, 1927)
The Little Snob (WB, 1928)
The Crimson City (WB, 1928)
Tenderloin (WB, 1928)
Lady Be Good (FN, 1928)
Glorious Betsy (WB, 1928)
Women They Talk About (WB, 1928)
The Terror (WB, 1928)
Land of the Silver Fox (WB, 1928)
The Home Towners (WB, 1928)
Devil-May-Care (MGM, 1929)
Fashions in Love (Par, 1929)
Innocents of Paris (Par, 1929)
Queen of the Night Clubs (WB, 1929)
The Desert Song (WB, 1929)
Hard-Boiled Rose (WB, 1929)
Speedway (MGM, 1929)
The Voice of the City (MGM, 1929)

Stark Mad (WB, 1929)
Eternal Woman (Col, 1929)
Times Square (Lumas, 1929)
Untamed (MGM, 1929)
The Unholy Night (MGM, 1929)
The Sea Bat (MGM, 1930)
The Woman Racket (MGM, 1930)
Show Girl in Hollywood (FN, 1930)
His Night Out (Univ, 1930)
Our Blushing Brides (MGM, 1930)
The Unholy Three (MGM, 1930)
War Nurse (MGM, 1930)
Remote Control (MGM, 1930)
Not So Dumb (MGM, 1930)
Free and Easy (MGM, 1930)
Paid (MGM, 1930)
Inspiration (MGM, 1931)
Iron Man (Univ, 1931)
The Secret Six (MGM, 1931)
A Gentleman's Fate (MGM, 1931)
Son of India (MGM, 1931)
The Great Meadow (MGM, 1931)
Politics (MGM, 1931)
Hell Drivers (MGM, 1931)
Susan Lenox: Her Fall and Rise (MGM, 1931)
Possessed (MGM, 1931)
Emma (MGM, 1932)
Sky Devils (UA, 1932)
West of Broadway (MGM, 1932)
Beast of the City (MGM, 1932)
Arsene Lupin (MGM, 1932)
The Wet Parade (MGM, 1932)
Are You Listening? (MGM, 1932)
Grand Hotel (MGM, 1932)
The Rich Are Always with Us (FN, 1932)
Unashamed (MGM, 1932)
Flesh (MGM, 1932)
Night Court (MGM, 1932)
Prosperity (MGM, 1932)
The Kid from Spain (UA, 1932)
The Nuisance (MGM, 1932)
King for a Night (Univ, 1933)
Blind Adventure (RKO, 1933)
The Way to Love (Par, 1933)

What! No Beer? (MGM, 1933)
Whistling in the Dark (MGM, 1933)
The Mad Game (Fox, 1933)
The Sin of Nora Moran (Majestic, 1933)
The Poor Rich (Univ, 1934)
Madame Spy (Univ, 1934)
Whirlpool (Col, 1934)
The Line-Up (Col, 1934)
Belle of the Nineties (Par, 1934)
Young and Beautiful (Mascot, 1934)
Unknown Blonde (Majestic, 1934)
The Ghost Walks (Chesterfield, 1934)
Twin Husbands (Chesterfield, 1934)
Mississippi (Par, 1935)
Charlie Chan in Paris (Fox, 1935)
Under the Pampas Moon (Fox, 1935)
Tomorrow's Youth (Mon, 1935)
Murder at Glen Athol [a.k.a. *The Criminal Within*] (Invincible, 1935)
Three Kids and a Queen (Univ, 1935)
Sutter's Gold (Univ, 1936)
Private Number (20th, 1936)
The Gentleman from Louisiana (Rep, 1936)
North of Nome (Col, 1936)
The Plainsman (Par, 1936)
Arizona Mahoney (Par, 1936)
Man-Proof (MGM, 1938)
Pardon Our Nerve (20th, 1938)
Border G-Man (RKO, 1938)
Ride a Crooked Mile (Par, 1938)
If I Were King (Par, 1939)
Juarez (WB, 1939)
Torchy Runs for Mayor (WB, 1939)
Fast and Furious (MGM, 1939)
The Oklahoma Kid (WB, 1939)
Emergency Squad (Par, 1940)
Women Without Names (Par, 1940)
Queen of the Mob (Par, 1940)
New Moon (MGM, 1940)
Young Bill Hickok (Rep, 1940)
Texas Rangers Ride Again (Par, 1940)
The Cowboy and the Blonde (20th, 1941)
The Deadly Game (Mon, 1941)
Forced Landing (Par, 1941)

Riot Squad (Mon, 1941)
Double Cross (PRC, 1941)
True to the Army (Par, 1942)
The Big Street (RKO, 1942)
Scattergood Survives a Murder (RKO, 1942)
Boss of Big Town (PRC, 1942)
North of the Rockies (Col, 1942)
Criminal Investigator (Mon, 1942)
Bombardier (RKO, 1943)
The Iron Major (RKO, 1943)
Submarine Alert (Par, 1943)
The Fallen Sparrow (RKO, 1943)
Bride by Mistake (RKO, 1944)
I Accuse My Parents (PRC, 1944)
The Merry Monahans (Univ, 1944)
It's in the Bag (UA, 1945)
Wildfire (Screen Guild, 1945)
Back to Bataan (RKO, 1945)
The Last Crooked Mile (Rep, 1946)
The Killers (Univ, 1946)
White Tie and Tails (Univ, 1946)
Unconquered (Par, 1947)
Sinbad the Sailor (RKO, 1947)
Queen of the Amazons (Screen Guild, 1947)
That's My Man (Rep, 1947)
The Flame (Rep, 1947)
Perilous Waters (Mon, 1948)
Samson and Delilah (Par, 1949)
Stampede (AA, 1949)
Adventure in Baltimore (RKO, 1949)
Mrs. Mike (UA, 1949)
Mule Train (Col, 1950)
M (Col, 1951)
The Savage (Par, 1952)
Bonzo Goes to College (Univ, 1952)
Pirates of Tripoli (Col, 1955)
Run for Cover (Par, 1955)
The Wild Dakotas (Associated Films, 1956)
The Ten Commandments (Par, 1956)
Apache Warrior (20th, 1957)
The Lone Ranger and the Lost City of Gold (UA, 1958)

GRANT MITCHELL

Paul Ellis, Grant Mitchell, and Dorothy Mackaill in No Man of Her Own *(1932).*

Born June 17, 1874, Columbus, Ohio. Died May 1, 1957, Los Angeles, California. Ex-lawyer who found continual stage work, then transferred to the screen. Often pressured by a grasping wife, or could be besieged by a flighty spouse (Billie Burke in *The Man Who Came to Dinner*). Typical scope of roles: *The Life of Emile Zola* (Georges Clemenceau), *Arsenic and Old Lace* (Reverend Mr. Harper), *Laura* (Corey), etc.

Grant Mitchell to Pat O'Brien (regarding Dick Powell) in *Twenty Million Sweethearts:* "I wouldn't care if he sang baritone like Lawrence Tibbett and soprano like Lily Pons! I wouldn't care if he sang *duets!* Get out!"

Films

Radio-Mania [a.k.a. *M.A.R.S.*] (Tele-View-Hodkinson, 1922)
Man to Man (WB, 1930)
The Star Witness (WB, 1931)
A Successful Calamity (WB, 1932)
The Famous Ferguson Case (FN, 1932)
No Man of Her Own (Par, 1932)
Week End Marriage (FN, 1932)
Big City Blues (WB, 1932)
Three on a Match (FN, 1932)
He Learned About Women (Par, 1933)
20,000 Years in Sing Sing (FN, 1933)
Central Airport (WB, 1933)
Lilly Turner (FN, 1933)
Heroes for Sale (FN, 1933)
I Love That Man (Par, 1933)
Tomorrow at Seven (RKO, 1933)
Dinner at Eight (MGM, 1933)
The Stranger's Return (MGM, 1933)

Dancing Lady (MGM, 1933)
Saturday's Millions (Univ, 1933)
King for a Night (Univ, 1933)
Wild Boys of the Road (FN, 1933)
Convention City (FN, 1933)
Our Betters (RKO, 1933)
Shadows of Sing Sing (Col, 1933)
The Poor Rich (Univ, 1934)
The Show-Off (MGM, 1934)
We're Rich Again (RKO, 1934)
The Gridiron Flash (RKO, 1934)
Twenty Million Sweethearts (FN, 1934)
The Secret Bride (WB, 1934)
The Cat's Paw (Fox, 1934)
The Case of the Howling Dog (WB, 1934)
365 Nights in Hollywood (Fox, 1934)
One Exciting Adventure (Univ, 1934)
One More Spring (Fox, 1935)
Traveling Saleslady (FN, 1935)

Gold Diggers of 1935 (FN, 1935)
Straight from the Heart (Univ, 1935)
Men Without Names (Par, 1935)
Broadway Gondolier (WB, 1935)
A Midsummer Night's Dream (WB, 1935)
In Person (RKO, 1935)
It's in the Air (MGM, 1935)
Seven Keys to Baldpate (RKO, 1935)
Next Time We Love (Univ, 1936)
The Garden Murder Case (MGM, 1936)
Moonlight Murder (MGM, 1936)
Piccadilly Jim (MGM, 1936)
The Devil Is a Sissy (MGM, 1936)
Her Master's Voice (Par, 1936)
My American Wife (Par, 1936)
Parole! (Univ, 1936)
The Ex-Mrs. Bradford (RKO, 1936)
The Life of Emile Zola (WB, 1937)
First Lady (WB, 1937)

Hollywood Hotel (WB, 1937)
Music for Madame (RKO, 1937)
The Last Gangster (MGM, 1937)
Lady Behave (Rep, 1938)
The Headleys at Home (Standard, 1938)
Women Are Like That (WB, 1938)
Peck's Bad Boy with the Circus (RKO, 1938)
Reformatory (Col, 1938)
Youth Takes a Fling (Univ, 1938)
That Certain Age (Univ, 1938)
6,000 Enemies (MGM, 1939)
Juarez (WB, 1939)
On Borrowed Time (MGM, 1939)
The Secret of Dr. Kildare (MGM, 1939)
Hell's Kitchen (WB, 1939)
Mr. Smith Goes to Washington (Col, 1939)
The Grapes of Wrath (20th, 1940)
It All Came True (WB, 1940)
Castle on the Hudson (WB, 1940)
My Love Came Back (WB, 1940)
Edison the Man (MGM, 1940)
New Moon (MGM, 1940)

We Who Are Young (MGM, 1940)
Father Is a Prince (WB, 1940)
Tobacco Road (20th, 1941)
Footsteps in the Dark (WB, 1941)
The Bride Wore Crutches (20th, 1941)
Nothing but the Truth (Par, 1941)
Skylark (Par, 1941)
One Foot in Heaven (WB, 1941)
The Feminine Touch (MGM, 1941)
The Penalty (MGM, 1941)
The Great Lie (WB, 1941)
The Man Who Came to Dinner (WB, 1941)
Larceny, Inc. (WB, 1942)
Meet the Stewarts (Col, 1942)
My Sister Eileen (Col, 1942)
The Gay Sisters (WB, 1942)
Cairo (MGM, 1942)
Orchestra Wives (20th, 1942)
The Amazing Mrs. Holliday (Univ, 1943)
Dixie (Par, 1943)
All by Myself (Univ, 1943)
See Here, Private Hargrove (MGM, 1944)
Step Lively (RKO, 1944)

Arsenic and Old Lace (WB, 1944)
When the Lights Go On Again (PRC, 1944)
And Now Tomorrow (Par, 1944)
The Impatient Years (Col, 1944)
Laura (20th, 1944)
A Medal for Benny (Par, 1945)
Crime, Inc. (PRC, 1945)
Bring On the Girls (Par, 1945)
Bedside Manner (UA, 1945)
Conflict (WB, 1945)
Guest Wife (UA, 1945)
Colonel Effingham's Raid (20th, 1945)
Leave Her to Heaven (20th, 1945)
Easy to Wed (MGM, 1946)
Cinderella Jones (WB, 1946)
Blondie's Holiday (Col, 1947)
Honeymoon (RKO, 1947)
Blondie's Anniversary (Col, 1947)
It Happened on Fifth Avenue (AA, 1947)
The Corpse Came C.O.D. (Col, 1947)
Who Killed Doc Robin? (UA, 1948)

THOMAS MITCHELL

Joel McCrea, Maureen O'Hara, and Thomas Mitchell in Buffalo Bill *(1944).*

Born July 11, 1892, Elizabeth, New Jersey. Married 1) Anne Stuart Brewer, child: Anne; divorced; 2) Rachel Hartzell; divorced. Died December 17, 1962, Beverly Hills, California. Fleshy, curly haired, with staring eyes. Won BSAAA for his whiskey-soaked Dr. Boone in John Ford's *Stagecoach*. Previously Oscar-nominated for Dr. Kersaint in Ford's *The Hurricane* (but lost BSAAA to Joseph Schildkraut of *The Life of Emile Zola*). Played Gerald O'Hara, master of Tara in *Gone with the Wind*. Other noteworthy roles included: *Mr. Smith Goes to Washington* (Diz Moore), *The Outlaw* (Pat Garrett), *The Sullivans* (the father), *High Noon* (Judge Jonas Henderson). Frequent stage performer. TV series: "Mayor of the Town," "O. Henry Playhouse," and "Glencannon."

> **Thomas Mitchell** to George Barbier in *Song of the Islands*:
> "There are a lot of things on this island to take the place of them pills you've been takin'."

Films

Six-Cylinder Love (Fox, 1923)
Craig's Wife (Col, 1936)
Adventure in Manhattan (Col, 1936)
Theodora Goes Wild (Col, 1936)
Man of the People (MGM, 1937)
When You're in Love (Col, 1937)
Lost Horizon (Col, 1937)
The Hurricane (UA, 1937)
I Promise to Pay (Col, 1937)
Make Way for Tomorrow (Par, 1937)
Love, Honor and Behave (WB, 1938)
Trade Winds (UA, 1938)
Only Angels Have Wings (Col, 1939)
Stagecoach (UA, 1939)

Mr. Smith Goes to Washington (Col, 1939)
The Hunchback of Notre Dame (RKO, 1939)
Gone with the Wind (MGM, 1939)
Swiss Family Robinson (RKO, 1940)
Three Cheers for the Irish (WB, 1940)
Our Town (UA, 1940)
The Long Voyage Home (UA, 1940)
Angels over Broadway (Col, 1940)
Flight from Destiny (WB, 1941)
Out of the Fog (WB, 1941)
Joan of Paris (RKO, 1942)
Song of the Islands (20th, 1942)

This Above All (20th, 1942)
Moontide (20th, 1942)
Tales of Manhattan (20th, 1942)
The Black Swan (20th, 1942)
The Immortal Sergeant (20th, 1943)
The Outlaw (RKO, 1943)
Bataan (MGM, 1943)
Flesh and Fantasy (Univ, 1943)
The Sullivans (20th, 1944)
Wilson (20th, 1944)
Dark Waters (UA, 1944)
Buffalo Bill (20th, 1944)
The Keys of the Kingdom (20th, 1944)
Within These Walls (20th, 1945)

Captain Eddie (20th, 1945)
Adventure (MGM, 1945)
It's a Wonderful Life (RKO, 1946)
Three Wise Fools (MGM, 1946)
The Dark Mirror (Univ, 1946)
High Barbaree (MGM, 1947)
The Romance of Rosy Ridge (MGM, 1947)

Silver River (WB, 1948)
Alias Nick Beal (Par, 1949)
The Big Wheel (UA, 1949)
Journey into Light (20th, 1951)
High Noon (UA, 1952)
Tumbleweed (Univ, 1953)
Secret of the Incas (Par, 1954)

Destry (Univ, 1954)
While the City Sleeps (RKO, 1956)
Handle with Care (MGM, 1958)
By Love Possessed (UA, 1961)
Pocketful of Miracles (UA, 1961)

JUANITA MOORE

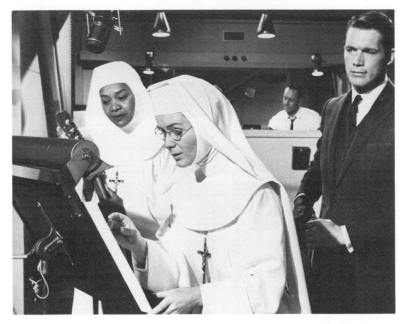

Juanita Moore, Debbie Reynolds, and Chad Everett (right) in The Singing Nun (1966).

Born October 18, 1922, Los Angeles, California. Quietly resourceful black actress, noted for interpretation of Louise Beavers' old role in revamped *Imitation of Life* starring Lana Turner.

Juanita Moore to Lana Turner in *Imitation of Life:* "Give her a real *bridey weddin'* with all the fixin's."

Films

Lydia Bailey (20th, 1952)
Affair in Trinidad (Col, 1952)
Witness to Murder (UA, 1954)
Women's Prison (Col, 1955)
Ransom (MGM, 1956)
The Girl Can't Help It (20th, 1956)
The Green-Eyed Blonde (WB, 1957)

Imitation of Life (Univ, 1959)
Tammy Tell Me True (Univ, 1961)
Raisin in the Sun (Col, 1961)
Walk on the Wild Side (Col, 1962)
Papa's Delicate Condition (Par, 1963)
The Singing Nun (MGM, 1966)
Rosie! (Univ, 1967)

Up Tight (Par, 1968)
The Mack (Cin, 1973)
Fox Style (Presidial, 1973)
Thomasine and Bushrod (Col, 1974)
Abby (AIP, 1974)

MANTAN MORELAND

Mantan Moreland, Benson Fong, and Marianne Quon in Charlie Chan in the Secret Service *(1944).*

Born September 3, 1901, Monroe, Louisiana. Married Hazel _____ , child: daughter. Died September 28, 1973, Hollywood, California. Chunky, round-faced black actor who in pre-racial-equality times was the prototype of the superstitious, eye-rolling, double-talking servant. (Trademark expression: "Feet . . . do your thing!") Played Birmingham, the chauffeur in many *Charlie Chan* entries.

Mantan Moreland to Benson Fong in *Dark Alibi:* "Why do you always have to *hurry* to a murder case? Why can't you just o-o-o-z-e on down to one?"

Films

Spirit of Youth (GN, 1937)
Next Time I Marry (RKO, 1938)
Frontier Scout (GN, 1938)
There's That Woman Again (Col, 1938)
Gang Smashers (Million Dollar Productions, 1938)
Harlem on the Prairie (Associated Features, 1938)
Two-Gun Man from Harlem (Hollywood Productions, 1938)
One Dark Night (Million Dollar Productions, 1939)
Irish Luck (Mon, 1939)
Tell No Tales (MGM, 1939)
Riders of the Frontier (Mon, 1939)
Millionaire Playboy (RKO, 1940)
Chasing Trouble (Mon, 1940)
Pier 13 (20th, 1940)
The City of Chance (20th, 1940)

The Girl in 313 (20th, 1940)
The Man Who Wouldn't Talk (20th, 1940)
Star Dust (20th, 1940)
Maryland (20th, 1940)
Viva Cisco Kid (20th, 1940)
On the Spot (Mon, 1940)
Laughing at Danger (Mon, 1940)
Drums of the Desert (Mon, 1940)
Four Shall Die (Million Dollar Productions, 1940)
Lady Luck (Dixie National Productions, 1940)
Professor Creeps (Dixie National Productions, 1940)
While Thousands Cheer (Million Dollar Productions, 1940)
Mr. Washington Goes to Town (Dixie National Productions, 1940)

Up Jumped the Devil (Dixie National Productions, 1941)
Ellery Queen's Penthouse Mystery (Col, 1941)
Cracked Nuts (Univ, 1941)
Bachelor Daddy (Univ, 1941)
It Started with Eve (Univ, 1941)
Accent on Love (20th, 1941)
Up in the Air (Mon, 1941)
King of the Zombies (Mon, 1941)
The Gang's All Here (Mon, 1941)
Hello, Sucker (Univ, 1941)
Dressed to Kill (20th, 1941)
Four Jacks and a Jill (RKO, 1941)
Footlight Fever (RKO, 1941)
You're out of Luck (Mon, 1941)
Sign of the Wolf (Mon, 1941)
Let's Go Collegiate (Mon, 1941)
Sleepers West (20th, 1941)

Marry the Boss's Daughter (20th, 1941)
World Premiere (Par, 1941)
Professor Creeps (Dixie National, 1942)
Freckles Comes Home (Mon, 1942)
A–Haunting We Will Go (20th, 1942)
Andy Hardy's Double Life (MGM, 1942)
The Strange Case of Dr. X (Univ, 1942)
Treat 'em Rough (Univ, 1942)
Mexican Spitfire Sees a Ghost (RKO, 1942)
The Palm Beach Story (Par, 1942)
Footlight Serenade (20th, 1942)
The Phantom Killer (Mon, 1942)
Eyes in the Night (MGM, 1942)
Girl Trouble (20th, 1942)
Tarzan's New York Adventure (MGM, 1942)
Hit the Ice (Univ, 1943)
Cosmo Jones, Crime Smasher (Mon, 1943)
Cabin in the Sky (MGM, 1943)
Sarong Girl (Mon, 1943)
Revenge of the Zombies (Mon, 1943)
Melody Parade (Mon, 1943)
She's for Me (Univ, 1943)
He Hired the Boss (20th, 1943)
It Comes Up Love (Univ, 1943)
My Kingdom for a Cook (Col, 1943)
Slightly Dangerous (MGM, 1943)
Swing Fever (MGM, 1943)

You're a Lucky Fellow, Mr. Smith (Univ, 1943)
We've Never Been Licked (Univ, 1943)
This Is the Life (Univ, 1944)
The Mystery of the River Boat (Univ serial, 1944)
The Chinese Cat (Mon, 1944)
Moon over Las Vegas (Univ, 1944)
Chip off the Old Block (Univ, 1944)
Pin-Up Girl (20th, 1944)
South of Dixie (Univ, 1944)
Black Magic (Mon, 1944)
Bowery to Broadway (Univ, 1944)
Charlie Chan in the Secret Service (Mon, 1944)
See Here, Private Hargrove (MGM, 1944)
She Wouldn't Say Yes (Col, 1945)
The Scarlet Clue (Mon, 1945)
The Jade Mask (Mon, 1945)
The Shanghai Cobra (Mon, 1945)
The Spider (20th, 1945)
Captain Tugboat Annie (Rep, 1945)
Mantan Messes Up (Toddy Pictures, 1946)
Mantan Runs for Mayor (Toddy Pictures, 1946)
Dark Alibi (Mon, 1946)
Shadows over Chinatown (Mon, 1946)
Riverboat Rhythm (RKO, 1946)

Tall, Tan and Terrific (Astor, 1946)
What a Guy (Lucky Star Productions, 1947)
Ebony Parade (Astor, 1947)
The Red Hornet (Mon, 1947)
The Trap (Mon, 1947)
The Chinese Ring (Mon, 1947)
Docks of New Orleans (Mon, 1948)
The Mystery of the Golden Eye (Mon, 1948)
The Feathered Serpent (Mon, 1948)
The Shanghai Chest (Mon, 1948)
Best Man Wins (Col, 1948)
Come On, Cowboy (Goldmax, 1948)
The Dreamer (Astor, 1948)
She's Too Mean to Me (Goldmax, 1948)
Return of Mandy's Husband (Lucky Star, 1948)
Sky Dragon (Mon, 1949)
Rockin' the Blues (Fritz Pollard Associates, 1956)
Rock 'n' Roll Revue (Studio Films, 1956)
Rock 'n' Roll Jamboree (Studio Films, 1957)
Enter Laughing (Col, 1967)
Watermelon Man (Col, 1970)
The Biscuit Eater (BV, 1972)
The Young Nurses (New World, 1973)

FRANK MORGAN
(Francis Wuppermann)

Ann Morriss, Frank Morgan, Eleanor Powell, and Ian Hunter in Broadway Melody of 1940 (1940).

Born June 1, 1890, New York City, New York. Married Alma Muller (1914), children: two. Died September 18, 1949, Beverly Hills, California. The woebegone ruler of Emerald City in *The Wizard of Oz.* Had numerous stage and film credits before tackling this pinnacle role as an MGM contractee. In free-lancing times was Oscar-nominated for Best Actor as the indecisive Duke of Florence in *The Affairs of Cellini* (but lost to Clark Gable of *It Happened One Night).* Sometimes played a good-natured cad (Una Merkel's lover in *Saratoga)* or a jealous merchant (*The Shop Around the Corner).* Could turn in a very serious interpretation: the persecuted Professor Roth of *The Mortal Storm.* Prototype was the befuddled tippler. Played it to perfection as Lana Turner's dad in *Honky Tonk.* Oscar-nominated for role of "The Pirate" in *Tortilla Flat* (but lost BSAAA to Van Heflin of *Johnny Eager).* Best as Uncle Sid (*Summer Holiday).* Literally died with his boots on—playing Buffalo Bill in *Annie Get Your Gun* (replaced by Louis Calhern).

Frank Morgan to Robert Montgomery in *Piccadilly Jim:* "We met in the lift. It was one of those push-button affairs."

Films

The Suspect (Vit, 1916)
The Daring of Diana (Vit, 1917)
Light in the Darkness (Vit, 1917)
A Modern Cinderella (Fox, 1917)
The Girl Philippa (Vit, 1917)
Who's Your Neighbor? (Vit, 1917)
A Child of the Wild (Fox, 1917)
Baby Mine (G, 1917)
Raffles—The Amateur Cracksman (Hiller & Wilk, 1917)
The Knife (Selig, 1918)
At the Mercy of Men (Selznick, 1918)

Gray Towers of Mystery (Vit, 1919)
The Golden Shower (Vit, 1919)
Manhandled (Par, 1924)
Born Rich (FN, 1924)
The Man Who Found Himself (Par, 1925)
The Crowded Hour (Par, 1925)
The Scarlet Saint (FN, 1925)
Love's Greatest Mistake (Par, 1927)
Queen High (Par, 1930)
Dangerous Nan McGrew (Par, 1930)
Fast and Loose (Par, 1930)
Laughter (Par, 1930)

The Half-Naked Truth (RKO, 1932)
Secrets of the French Police (RKO, 1932)
Luxury Liner (Par, 1933)
Hallelujah, I'm a Bum (UA, 1933)
Reunion in Vienna (MGM, 1933)
The Nuisance (MGM, 1933)
When Ladies Meet (MGM, 1933)
Broadway to Hollywood (MGM, 1933)
Bombshell (MGM, 1933)
The Best of Enemies (Fox, 1933)
The Billion Dollar Scandal (Par, 1933)
The Kiss Before the Mirror (Univ, 1933)

The Cat and the Fiddle (MGM, 1934)	*Beg, Borrow or Steal* (MGM, 1937)	*The Vanishing Virginian* (MGM, 1941)
The Affairs of Cellini (UA, 1934)	*Rosalie* (MGM, 1937)	*Night Monster* (Univ, 1942)
By Your Leave (RKO, 1934)	*Paradise for Three* (MGM, 1938)	*Tortilla Flat* (MGM, 1942)
There's Always Tomorrow (Univ, 1934)	*Port of Seven Seas* (MGM, 1938)	*White Cargo* (MGM, 1942)
Success at Any Price (RKO, 1934)	*The Crowd Roars* (MGM, 1938)	*A Stranger in Town* (MGM, 1943)
Sisters Under the Skin (Col, 1934)	*Sweethearts* (MGM, 1938)	*The Human Comedy* (MGM, 1943)
A Lost Lady (WB, 1934)	*Broadway Serenade* (MGM, 1939)	*Thousands Cheer* (MGM, 1943)
The Good Fairy (Univ, 1935)	*The Wizard of Oz* (MGM, 1939)	*The White Cliffs of Dover* (MGM, 1943)
Naughty Marietta (MGM, 1935)	*Balalaika* (MGM, 1939)	*Casanova Brown* (RKO, 1944)
Escapade (MGM, 1935)	*The Shop Around the Corner* (MGM, 1940)	*Yolanda and the Thief* (MGM, 1945)
I Live My Life (MGM, 1935)	*Henry Goes to Arizona* (MGM, 1940)	*Courage of Lassie* (MGM, 1945)
The Perfect Gentleman (MGM, 1935)	*Broadway Melody of 1940* (MGM, 1940)	*The Great Morgan* (MGM, 1946)
Enchanted April (RKO, 1935)	*The Ghost Comes Home* (MGM, 1940)	*The Cockeyed Miracle* (MGM, 1946)
The Dancing Pirate (RKO, 1936)	*The Mortal Storm* (MGM, 1940)	*Lady Luck* (RKO, 1946)
The Great Ziegfeld (MGM, 1936)	*Boom Town* (MGM, 1940)	*Green Dolphin Street* (MGM, 1947)
Trouble for Two (MGM, 1936)	*Hullabaloo* (MGM, 1940)	*Summer Holiday* (MGM, 1948)
Piccadilly Jim (MGM, 1936)	*Keeping Company* (MGM, 1941)	*The Three Musketeers* (MGM, 1948)
Dimples (20th, 1936)	*Washington Melodrama* (MGM, 1941)	*Any Number Can Play* (MGM, 1949)
The Last of Mrs. Cheyney (MGM, 1937)	*Wild Man of Borneo* (MGM, 1941)	*The Great Sinner* (MGM, 1949)
The Emperor's Candlesticks (MGM, 1937)	*Honky Tonk* (MGM, 1941)	*The Stratton Story* (MGM, 1949)
Saratoga (MGM, 1937)		*Key to the City* (MGM, 1950)

HENRY "HARRY" MORGAN
(Harry Bratsburg)

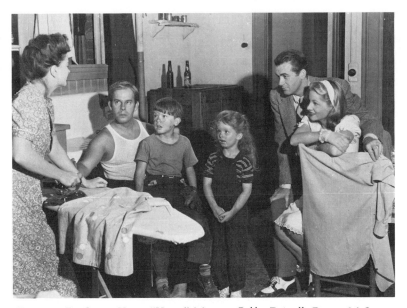

Rosemary De Camp, Henry "Harry" Morgan, Bobby Driscoll, Doreen McCann, Mark Stevens, and Joan Fontaine in From This Day Forward *(1946).*

Born April 10, 1915, Detroit, Michigan. Married Eileen Detchon (1940), children: Christopher, Timothy, David, Paul. Meek-looking proletarian performer who could become extremely perturbed; later a prime interpreter of the harassed (or harassing) loudmouth. TV series: "December Bride" (as Pete Porter); "Pete and Gladys"; "The Richard Boone Show"; "Kentucky Jones"; "Oh, Those Bells!"; "Dragnet" (as Officer Bill Gannon, 1967-70); "The D.A."; "Hec Ramsey"; and "M*A*S*H" (as Colonel Sherman Potter).

Henry "Harry" Morgan to James Stewart in *The Glenn Miller Story:* "Still got that crazy idea in your head . . . that 'sound'?"

Films

The Omaha Trail (MGM, 1942)
To the Shores of Tripoli (20th, 1942)
The Loves of Edgar Allan Poe (20th, 1942)
Orchestra Wives (20th, 1942)
Crash Dive (20th, 1943)
The Ox-Bow Incident (20th, 1943)
Happy Land (20th, 1943)
Roger Touhy—Gangster (20th, 1944)
The Eve of St. Mark (20th, 1944)
Wing and a Prayer (20th, 1944)
Gentle Annie (MGM, 1944)
A Bell for Adano (20th, 1945)
State Fair (20th, 1945)
Dragonwyck (20th, 1946)
Johnny Comes Flying Home (20th, 1946)
It Shouldn't Happen to a Dog (20th, 1946)
Somewhere in the Night (20th, 1946)
From This Day Forward (RKO, 1946)
The Gangster (AA, 1947)
The Big Clock (Par, 1948)
All My Sons (Univ, 1948)
Race Street (RKO, 1948)
Yellow Sky (20th, 1948)
The Saxon Charm (Univ, 1948)
Moonrise (Rep, 1948)
Down to the Sea in Ships (20th, 1949)
Madame Bovary (MGM, 1949)
The Red Light (UA, 1949)
Holiday Affair (RKO, 1949)

Strange Bargain (RKO, 1949)
Outside the Wall (Univ, 1950)
The Showdown (Rep, 1950)
Dark City (Par, 1950)
Belle le Grand (Rep, 1951)
Appointment with Danger (Par, 1951)
The Highwayman (AA, 1951)
When I Grow Up (EL, 1951)
The Well (UA, 1951)
The Blue Veil (RKO, 1951)
Bend of the River (Univ, 1952)
Scandal Sheet (Col, 1952)
My Six Convicts (Col, 1952)
Boots Malone (Col, 1952)
High Noon (UA, 1952)
Apache War Smoke (MGM, 1952)
The Toughest Man in Arizona (Rep, 1952)
What Price Glory? (20th, 1952)
Stop, You're Killing Me (WB, 1952)
Arena (MGM, 1953)
Torch Song (MGM, 1953)
Thunder Bay (Univ, 1953)
Champ for a Day (Rep, 1953)
The Glenn Miller Story (Univ, 1954)
About Mrs. Leslie (Par, 1954)
The Forty-Niners (AA, 1954)
Prisoner of War (MGM, 1954)
The Far Country (Univ, 1955)

Not as a Stranger (UA, 1955)
Strategic Air Command (Par, 1955)
Backlash (Univ, 1956)
The Bottom of the Bottle (20th, 1956)
The Teahouse of the August Moon (MGM, 1956)
Under Fire (20th, 1957)
It Started with a Kiss (MGM, 1959)
Inherit the Wind (UA, 1960)
Cimarron (MGM, 1960)
The Mountain Road (Col, 1960)
How the West Was Won (MGM, 1962)
John Goldfarb, Please Come Home (20th, 1964)
Frankie and Johnnie (UA, 1966)
What Did You Do in the War, Daddy? (UA, 1966)
The Flim Flam Man (20th, 1967)
Support Your Local Sheriff (UA, 1969)
Viva Max (CUE, 1969)
The Barefoot Executive (BV, 1971)
Support Your Local Gunfighter (UA, 1971)
Scandalous John (BV, 1971)
Jeremiah Johnson (WB, 1972)
Snowball Express (BV, 1972)
Charley and the Angel (BV, 1973)
The Apple Dumpling Gang (BV, 1975)
The Shootist (Par, 1976)

RALPH MORGAN
(Raphael Wuppermann)

Ralph Morgan and Bradley Metcalfe in Barefoot Boy *(1938)*.

Born July 6, 1883, New York City, New York. Married Georgiana Iversen, child: Claudia. Died June 11, 1956, New York City, New York. The older and less famous and flamboyant brother of Frank Morgan who was first of the family to go on stage, but who came to the cinema far later. Infrequently in costume drama: *Rasputin and the Empress* (Czar Nicholas II), *The Life of Emile Zola* (Paris commandant). More often the red herring who turned out to be the culprit in low-budget whodunit features and serials.

Ralph Morgan to William Henry in *Geronimo:* "I've tried to make a soldier out of you—a man to be proud of!"

Films

Penny Philanthropist (Webster Pictures, 1923)
The Man Who Found Himself (Par, 1925)
Honor Among Lovers (Par, 1931)
Charlie Chan's Chance (Fox, 1931)
Dance Team (Fox, 1932)
Strange Interlude (MGM, 1932)
Rasputin and the Empress (MGM, 1932)
Cheaters at Play (Fox, 1932)
Disorderly Conduct (Fox, 1932)
The Devil's Lottery (Fox, 1932)
The Son-Daughter (MGM, 1932)
Humanity (Fox, 1933)
Trick for Trick (Fox, 1933)
The Power and the Glory (Fox, 1933)
Shanghai Madness (Fox, 1933)
Walls of Gold (Fox, 1933)
Dr. Bull (Fox, 1933)
The Mad Game (Fox, 1933)
The Kennel Murder Case (WB, 1933)
Little Men (Mascot, 1934)

Orient Express (Fox, 1934)
Stand Up and Cheer (Fox, 1934)
She Was a Lady (Fox, 1934)
No Greater Glory (Col, 1934)
Transatlantic Merry-Go-Round (UA, 1934)
Girl of the Limberlost (Mon, 1934)
The Last Gentleman (UA, 1934)
Their Big Moment (RKO, 1934)
Hell in the Heavens (Fox, 1934)
Star of Midnight (RKO, 1935)
Unwelcome Stranger (Col, 1935)
Condemned to Live (Chesterfield, 1935)
Calm Yourself (MGM, 1935)
I've Been Around (Univ, 1935)
Magnificent Obsession (Univ, 1935)
Yellowstone (Univ, 1936)
Muss 'em Up (RKO, 1936)
The Ex-Mrs. Bradford (RKO, 1936)
Little Miss Nobody (20th, 1936)
Human Cargo (20th, 1936)

Speed (MGM, 1936)
General Spanky (MGM, 1936)
Anthony Adverse (WB, 1936)
Crack-Up (20th, 1937)
The Man in Blue (Univ, 1937)
The Life of Emile Zola (WB, 1937)
Exclusive (Par, 1937)
Wells Fargo (Par, 1937)
Behind Prison Bars (Mon, 1937)
Love Is a Headache (MGM, 1938)
Out West with the Hardys (MGM, 1938)
Army Girl (Rep, 1938)
Mannequin (MGM, 1938)
Wives Under Suspicion (Univ, 1938)
Orphans of the Street (Rep, 1937)
Mother Carey's Chickens (RKO, 1938)
Barefoot Boy (Mon, 1938)
Shadows over Shanghai (GN, 1938)
That's My Story (Univ, 1938)
Off the Record (WB, 1939)
Fast and Loose (MGM, 1939)

Man of Conquest (Rep, 1939)
Smuggled Cargo (Rep, 1939)
Way Down South (RKO, 1939)
Geronimo (Par, 1939)
Trapped in the Sky (Col, 1939)
The Lone Wolf Spy Hunt (Col, 1939)
Forty Little Mothers (MGM, 1940)
I'm Still Alive (RKO, 1940)
The Mad Doctor (Par, 1941)
Dick Tracy vs. Crime, Inc. (Rep serial, 1941)
Adventure in Washington (Col, 1941)
A Close Call for Ellery Queen (Col, 1942)
Klondike Fury (Mon, 1942)

The Traitor Within (Rep, 1942)
Gang Busters (Univ serial, 1942)
Night Monster (Univ, 1942)
Hitler's Madman (MGM, 1943)
Stage Door Canteen (UA, 1943)
Jack London (UA, 1943)
Trocadero (Rep, 1944)
Weird Woman (Univ, 1944)
The Imposter (Univ, 1944)
The Monster Maker (PRC, 1944)
The Great Alaskan Mystery (Univ serial, 1944)
I'll Be Seeing You (UA, 1944)
Enemy of Women (Mon, 1944)

Hollywood and Vine (PRC, 1945)
This Love of Ours (Univ, 1945)
Black Market Babies (Mon, 1945)
The Monster and the Ape (Col, 1945)
Mr. District Attorney (Col, 1947)
Song of the Thin Man (MGM, 1947)
The Last Roundup (Col, 1947)
Sleep My Love (UA, 1948)
The Creeper (20th, 1948)
Sword of the Avenger (EL, 1948)
Blue Grass of Kentucky (Mon, 1950)
Heart of the Rockies (Rep, 1951)
Gold Fever (Mon, 1952)

MAURICE MOSCOVITCH
(Morris Maaskoff)

In Lancer Spy *(1937).*

Born November 23, 1871, Odessa, Russia. Married Rosa Baumar, child: Noel. Died June 18, 1940, Los Angeles, California. Russian-born player who performed on the Yiddish stage in New York City. Enjoyed a versatile showcase during brief Hollywood tenure: *Winterset* (Esdras, father of Margo and Paul Guilfoyle), *Make Way for Tomorrow* (Max Rubens, the storekeeper), *Lancer Spy* (General von Meinhardt), *Suez* (Mohammad Ali), *Susannah of the Mounties* (Big Eagle), *The Great Dictator* (Mr. Jaeckel). Died on the set of Lucille Ball–Maureen O'Hara's *Dance, Girl, Dance.* Father of actor Noel Madison.

Maurice Moscovitch to customer in *Make Way for Tomorrow:*
"If you're honest by the week, I guess you can be honest by the month too. So we make it by the week."

Films

Winterset (RKO, 1936)
Make Way for Tomorrow (Par, 1937)
Lancer Spy (20th, 1937)
Gateway (20th, 1938)
Suez (20th, 1938)

Love Affair (RKO, 1939)
Susannah of the Mounties (20th, 1939)
In Name Only (RKO, 1939)
Rio (Univ, 1939)
The Great Commandment (20th, 1939)

Everything Happens at Night (20th, 1939)
South to Karanga (Univ, 1940)
The Great Dictator (UA, 1940)
Dance, Girl, Dance (RKO, 1940)

ALAN MOWBRAY

With Billie Burke in Where Sinners Meet *(1934).*

Born August 18, 1893, London, England. Married Lorraine Carpenter, children: two. Died March 25, 1969, Hollywood, California. Possessed of a pompous (sometimes imperious) manner. Ideally suited for lofty figures in his early (trim) movie days: *Alexander Hamilton* (George Washington—later played a comedy version of the President in *Where Do We Go from Here?*), *The House of Rothschild* (Metternick), *Mary of Scotland* (Trockmorton). Displayed a penchant for the archsnob: Captain Randon Crowley *(Becky Sharp)*, Sir William Hamilton *(Lady Hamilton)*, Ralph Layton *(Rainbow on the River)*, etc. Frequently a butler: *My Man Godfrey, Topper, His Butler's Sister.* TV series: "Colonel Flack," "Hey, Mulligan!," "Dante," and "The Best in Mystery."

> **Alan Mowbray** to Karen Morley in *On Such a Night:*
> "Madame, it pains me that life should force one of my knightly nature to be so mercenary."

Films

God's Gift to Women (WB, 1931)
The Man in Possession (MGM, 1931)
Leftover Ladies (Tif, 1931)
Alexander Hamilton (WB, 1931)
Guilty Hands (MGM, 1931)
Honor of the Family (FN, 1931)
The Silent Witness (Fox, 1932)
Nice Women (Univ, 1932)
Lovers Courageous (MGM, 1932)
The World and the Flesh (Par, 1932)
Man About Town (Fox, 1932)
Winner Take All (WB, 1932)
Jewel Robbery (WB, 1932)
Two Against the World (WB, 1932)
The Man Called Back (Tif, 1932)
Sherlock Holmes (Fox, 1932)
Hotel Continental (Tif, 1932)
The Phantom President (Par, 1932)

The Man from Yesterday (Par, 1932)
Peg o' My Heart (MGM, 1933)
A Study in Scarlet (WW, 1933)
Voltaire (WB, 1933)
Berkeley Square (Fox, 1933)
Midnight Club (Par, 1933)
The World Changes (FN, 1933)
Roman Scandals (UA, 1933)
Our Betters (RKO, 1933)
Her Secret (Ideal, 1933)
Long Lost Father (RKO, 1934)
Where Sinners Meet (RKO, 1934)
The Girl from Missouri (MGM, 1934)
Charlie Chan in London (Fox, 1934)
The House of Rothschild (UA, 1934)
Cheaters (Bert Lubin, 1934)
Little Man, What Now? (Univ, 1934)
One More River (Univ, 1934)

Embarrassing Moments (Univ, 1934)
Night Life of the Gods (Univ, 1935)
Lady Tubbs (Univ, 1935)
Becky Sharp (RKO, 1935)
The Gay Deception (Fox, 1935)
In Person (RKO, 1935)
She Couldn't Take It (Col, 1935)
Rose-Marie (MGM, 1936)
Rainbow on the·River (RKO, 1936)
Muss 'em Up (RKO, 1936)
Ladies in Love (20th, 1936)
Mary of Scotland (RKO, 1936)
Desire (Par, 1936)
Give Us This Night (Par, 1936)
The Case Against Mrs. Ames (Par, 1936)
Fatal Lady (Par, 1936)
My Man Godfrey (Univ, 1936)
Four Days' Wonder (Univ, 1937)

As Good as Married (Univ, 1937)
Topper (MGM, 1937)
Vogues of 1938 (UA, 1937)
Stand-In (UA, 1937)
On Such a Night (Par, 1937)
Music for Madame (RKO, 1937)
On the Avenue (20th, 1937)
The King and the Chorus Girl (WB, 1937)
Marry the Girl (WB, 1937)
Hollywood Hotel (WB, 1937)
Merrily We Live (MGM, 1938)
There Goes My Heart (MGM, 1938)
Topper Takes a Trip (UA, 1938)
Never Say Die (Par, 1939)
The Llano Kid (Par, 1939)
Way Down South (RKO, 1939)
Music in My Heart (Col, 1940)
Curtain Call (RKO, 1940)
The Villain Still Pursued Her (RKO, 1940)
Scatterbrain (RKO, 1940)
The Boys from Syracuse (Univ, 1940)
The Quarterback (Par, 1940)
That Hamilton Woman (UA, 1941)
That Uncertain Feeling (UA, 1941)
Footlight Fever (RKO, 1941)
The Cowboy and the Blonde (20th, 1941)
Moon over Her Shoulder (20th, 1941)
I Wake Up Screaming [a.k.a. *Hot Spot*] (20th, 1941)

Ice-Capades Revue (Rep, 1941)
The Perfect Snob (Rep, 1941)
The Mad Martindales (20th, 1942)
Panama Hattie (MGM, 1942)
A Yank at Eton (MGM, 1942)
We Were Dancing (MGM, 1942)
Isle of Missing Men (Mon, 1942)
Yokel Boy (Rep, 1942)
The Devil with Hitler (UA, 1942)
So This Is Washington (RKO, 1942)
The Powers Girl (UA, 1942)
Slightly Dangerous (MGM, 1943)
His Butler's Sister (Univ, 1943)
Holy Matrimony (20th, 1943)
Stage Door Canteen (UA, 1943)
The Doughgirls (WB, 1944)
My Gal Loves Music (Univ, 1944)
Ever Since Venus (Col, 1944)
The Phantom of 42nd Street (PRC, 1945)
Bring on the Girls (Par, 1945)
Men in Her Diary (Univ, 1945)
Sunbonnet Sue (Mon, 1945)
Earl Carroll's Vanities (Rep, 1945)
Tell It to a Star (Rep, 1945)
Where Do We Go from Here? (20th, 1945)
Terror by Night (Univ, 1946)
My Darling Clementine (20th, 1946)
Idea Girl (Univ, 1946)
Lured (UA, 1947)
Merton of the Movies (MGM, 1947)

The Pilgrim Lady (Rep, 1947)
Man About Town (RKO, 1947)
Captain from Castile (20th, 1947)
The Prince of Thieves (Col, 1948)
The Main Street Kid (Rep, 1948)
My Dear Secretary (UA, 1948)
Don't Trust Your Husband [a.k.a. *An Innocent Affair*] (UA, 1948)
Every Girl Should Be Married (RKO, 1948)
You're My Everything (20th, 1949)
Abbott and Costello Meet the Killer—Boris Karloff (Univ, 1949)
The Lovable Cheat (Film Classics, 1949)
The Lone Wolf and His Lady (Col, 1949)
The Jackpot (20th, 1950)
Wagonmaster (RKO, 1950)
The Lady and the Bandit (Col, 1951)
Crosswinds (Par, 1951)
Just Across the Street (Univ, 1952)
Androcles and the Lion (RKO, 1952)
Blackbeard the Pirate (RKO, 1952)
Ma and Pa Kettle at Home (Univ, 1954)
The Steel Cage (UA, 1954)
The King's Thief (MGM, 1955)
The King and I (20th, 1956)
The Man Who Knew Too Much (Par, 1956)
Around the World in 80 Days (UA, 1956)
A Majority of One (WB, 1961)

HERBERT MUNDIN

Herbert Mundin, Diana Wynyard, Clive Brook, and Una O'Connor in Cavalcade *(1933).*

Born August 21, 1898, Lancashire, England. Died March 5, 1939, Van Nuys, California. Short earnest-looking Britisher (former music-hall player) who was a starring character lead for Fox and on loanouts. Made a habit of the Cockney pubkeeper *(Sherlock Holmes, Cavalcade)* and the steward/mess boy *(One Way Passage, Mutiny on the Bounty)*. Comical as Much the Miller entranced with Una O'Connor in *The Adventures of Robin Hood*. Dramatically adept as Wilkins, the British soldier out to prove he is not a coward in *Another Dawn*.

> **Herbert Mundin** to Henrietta Crosman in *Charlie Chan's Secret:* "To be perfectly frank, madam . . . this sort of thing makes me quite creepy."

Films

Enter the Queen (Br, 1930)
Immediate Possession (Br, 1931)
We Dine at Seven (Br, 1931)
Peace and Quiet (Br, 1931)
East Lynne on the Western Front (Br, 1931)
The Devil's Lottery (Fox, 1932)
The Trial of Vivienne Ware (Fox, 1932)
The Silent Witness (Fox, 1932)
Love Me Tonight (Par, 1932)
Almost Married (Fox, 1932)
Life Begins (FN, 1932)
Bachelor's Affairs (Fox, 1932)
One Way Passage (FN, 1932)
Chandu the Magician (Fox, 1932)
Sherlock Holmes (Fox, 1932)
Dangerously Yours (Fox, 1933)
Pleasure Cruise (Fox, 1933)
Adorable (Fox, 1933)

Cavalcade (Fox, 1933)
It's Great to Be Alive (Fox, 1933)
Arizona to Broadway (Fox, 1933)
Shanghai Madness (Fox, 1933)
Hoopla (Fox, 1933)
The Devil's in Love (Fox, 1933)
Ever Since Eve (Fox, 1934)
Hell in the Heavens (Fox, 1934)
Orient Express (Fox, 1934)
Bottoms Up (Fox, 1934)
All Men Are Enemies (Fox, 1934)
Springtime for Henry (Fox, 1934)
Call It Luck (Fox, 1934)
Such Women Are Dangerous (Fox, 1934)
Love Time (Fox, 1934)
David Copperfield (MGM, 1935)
Mutiny on the Bounty (MGM, 1935)
The Widow from Monte Carlo (WB, 1935)

Ladies Love Danger (Fox, 1935)
Black Sheep (Fox, 1935)
The Perfect Gentleman (MGM, 1935)
King of Burlesque (20th, 1935)
Charlie Chan's Secret (20th, 1936)
A Message to Garcia (20th, 1936)
Under Two Flags (20th, 1936)
Champagne Charlie (20th, 1936)
Tarzan Escapes (MGM, 1936)
Another Dawn (WB, 1937)
You Can't Beat Love (RKO, 1937)
Angel (Par, 1937)
The Adventures of Robin Hood (WB, 1938)
Invisible Enemy (Rep, 1938)
Lord Jeff (MGM, 1938)
Exposed (Univ, 1938)
Society Lawyer (MGM, 1939)

CLARENCE MUSE

Coleen Gray, Clarence Muse, and Bing Crosby in Riding High *(1950).*

Born October 7, 1889, Baltimore, Maryland. Married 1) Willabelle Marshbanks, children: three; 2) Irene Kellman (1953). Onetime minstrel singer, vaudevillian, jack-of-all-trades in the theater, who abandoned a career in law for show business. Usually the shuffling, obliging black domestic. Appeared in a variety of genres: 1931's *Huckleberry Finn* (Jim), *White Zombie* (driver), 1934's *The Count of Monte Cristo* (Ali), 1936's *Daniel Boone* (Pompey), Irene Dunne's *Showboat* (Sam), *The Black Swan* (Daniel), *Jamaica Run* (Mose), etc. Wrote and starred in *Broken Strings*.

Clarence Muse to Donald MacBride in *Murder over New York:* "I don't know nothin' 'bout nothin', sir. I'se completely in the dark."

Films

Hearts in Dixie (Fox, 1929)
Guilty? (Col, 1930)
A Royal Romance (Col, 1930)
Rain or Shine (Col, 1930)
Dirigible (Col, 1931)
Safe in Hell (FN, 1931)
The Last Parade (Col, 1931)
The Fighting Sheriff (Col, 1931)
Huckleberry Finn (Par, 1931)
Secret Witness [a.k.a. Terror by Night] (Col, 1931)
The Woman from Monte Carlo (FN, 1932)
Prestige (RKO, 1932)
Lena Rivers (Tif, 1932)
Night World (Univ, 1932)
The Wet Parade (MGM, 1932)
Winner Take All (WB, 1932)
Attorney for the Defense (Col, 1932)
Is My Face Red? (RKO, 1932)

White Zombie (UA, 1932)
Hell's Highway (RKO, 1932)
Washington Merry-Go-Round (Col, 1932)
Cabin in the Cotton (FN, 1932)
Laughter in Hell (Col, 1932)
Man Against Woman (Col, 1932)
From Hell to Heaven (Par, 1933)
Flying Down to Rio (RKO, 1933)
The Mind Reader (FN, 1933)
The Wrecker (Col, 1933)
Massacre (FN, 1934)
Fury of the Jungle (Col, 1934)
Black Moon (Col, 1934)
The Personality Kid (WB, 1934)
The Count of Monte Cristo (UA, 1934)
Broadway Bill (Col, 1934)
Alias Mary Dow (Univ, 1935)
O'Shaughnessy's Boy (MGM, 1935)

So Red the Rose (Par, 1935)
East of Java (Univ, 1935)
Harmony Lane (Mascot, 1935)
Laughing Irish Eyes (Rep, 1936)
Muss 'em Up (RKO, 1936)
Showboat (Univ, 1936)
Follow Your Heart (Rep, 1936)
Daniel Boone (RKO, 1936)
Mysterious Crossing (Univ, 1937)
Spirit of Youth (GN, 1937)
The Toy Wife (MGM, 1938)
Prison Train (Malcolm-Browne, 1938)
Secrets of a Nurse (Univ, 1938)
Way Down South (RKO, 1939)
Broken Earth (_____, 194__)
Broken Strings (International Road-shows, 1940)
Zanzibar (Univ, 1940)
Maryland (20th, 1940)

Sporting Blood (MGM, 1940)	*Honeymoon Lodge* (Univ, 1943)	*Live Today for Tomorrow* [a.k.a. *An Act of*
That Gang of Mine (Mon, 1940)	*Heaven Can Wait* (20th, 1943)	*Murder*] (Univ, 1948)
Murder over New York (20th, 1940)	*Flesh and Fantasy* (Univ, 1943)	*The Great Dan Patch* (UA, 1949)
Adam Had Four Sons (Col, 1941)	*Johnny Come Lately* (UA, 1943)	*Riding High* (Par, 1950)
The Flame of New Orleans (Univ, 1941)	*Follow the Boys* (Univ, 1944)	*County Fair* (Mon, 1950)
The Invisible Ghost (Mon, 1941)	*In the Meantime, Darling* (20th, 1944)	*My Forbidden Past* (RKO, 1951)
Love Crazy (MGM, 1941)	*The Soul of a Monster* (Col, 1944)	*Apache Drums* (Univ, 1951)
Gentleman from Dixie (Mon, 1941)	*Jam Session* (Col, 1944)	*Caribbean* (Par, 1952)
Among the Living (Par, 1941)	*The Racket Man* (Col, 1944)	*Jamaica Run* (Par, 1953)
Belle Starr (20th, 1941)	*The Thin Man Goes Home* (MGM, 1944)	*She Couldn't Say No* (RKO, 1954)
Kisses for Breakfast (WB, 1941)	*Double Indemnity* (Par, 1944)	*Porgy and Bess* (Col, 1959)
Talk of the Town (Col, 1942)	*San Diego, I Love You* (Univ, 1944)	*Buck and the Preacher* (Col, 1972)
Tales of Manhattan (20th, 1942)	*The Lost Weekend* (Par, 1945)	*The World's Greatest Athlete* (BV, 1974)
Sin Town (Univ, 1942)	*Night and Day* (WB, 1946)	*Car Wash* (Univ, 1976)
The Black Swan (20th, 1942)	*Two Smart People* (MGM, 1946)	*Passing Through* (Larry Clark Films,
Watch on the Rhine (WB, 1943)	*She Wouldn't Say Yes* (Col, 1946)	1977)
Shadow of a Doubt (Univ, 1943)	*Joe Palooka in the Knock-Out* (Mon, 1947)	

J. CARROLL NAISH
(Joseph Carroll Naish)

J. Carroll Naish and Arturo de Cordova in A Medal for Benny *(1945).*

Born January 21, 1897, New York City, New York. Married Gladys Hearney (1928), child: Elaine. Died January 24, 1973, La Jolla, California. Swarthy-complexioned New Yorker who had an amazing facility for dialects and makeup. In disguise as: Sun Yat Ming (*The Hatchet Man*), Cahusac (*Captain Blood*), Subahdar Major Puran Singh (*The Charge of the Light Brigade*), Juan Can (*Ramona*), Adram (*Think Fast, Mr. Moto*), Garabato (*Blood and Sand*), the Japanese publisher (*Behind the Rising Sun*), etc. Was the dastardly Dr. Daka in the *Batman* serial. Oscar-nominated for his Giuseppe, the confused Italian prisoner of war in *Sahara* (but lost BSAAA to Charles Coburn of *The More the Merrier*). Also Oscar-nominated for his Mexican father in *A Medal for Benny* (but lost BSAAA to James Dunn of *A Tree Grows in Brooklyn*). TV series: "Life with Luigi," "The New Adventures of Charlie Chan," and "Guestward Ho" (as Chief Hawkeye).

J. Carroll Naish to George McKay in *Illegal Traffic:* "Our friend Martin turns out to be a copper."

Films

What Price Glory? (Fox, 1926)
Cheer Up and Smile (Fox, 1930)
Double Cross Roads (Fox, 1930)
Good Intentions (Fox, 1930)
Scotland Yard (Fox, 1930)
Homicide Squad (Univ, 1931)
Kick In (Par, 1931)
Tonight or Never (UA, 1931)
Ladies of the Big House (Par, 1931)
Gun Smoke (Par, 1931)
The Royal Bed (RKO, 1931)
The Conquerors (RKO, 1932)
Cabin in the Cotton (FN, 1932)
The Kid from Spain (UA, 1932)
The Beast of the City (MGM, 1932)
The Mouthpiece (FN, 1932)
Week End Marriage (FN, 1932)
Big City Blues (WB, 1932)
It's Tough to Be Famous (FN, 1932)
Two Seconds (FN, 1932)
The Famous Ferguson Case (FN, 1932)
Tiger Shark (FN, 1932)
Crooner (FN, 1932)
Washington Merry-Go-Round (Col, 1932)
No Living Witness (Mayfair, 1932)
The Hatchet Man (FN, 1932)
Elmer the Great (FN, 1933)
The Infernal Machine (Fox, 1933)
The Devil's in Love (Fox, 1933)
The Mad Game (Fox, 1933)
Mystery Squadron (Mascot serial, 1933)
Central Airport (FN, 1933)
Arizona to Broadway (Fox, 1933)
The World Gone Mad (Majestic, 1933)
The Whirlwind (Col, 1933)
The Past of Mary Holmes (RKO, 1933)
Captured (WB, 1933)
The Avenger (Mon, 1933)
Notorious but Nice (Chesterfield, 1933)
Silent Men (Col, 1933)
The Last Trail (Fox, 1933)
No Other Woman (RKO, 1933)
Frisco Jenny (FN, 1933)
The Big Chance (Arthur Greenblatt, 1933)
What's Your Racket? (Mayfair, 1934)
Upper World (WB, 1934)
Murder in Trinidad (Fox, 1934)
One Is Guilty (Col, 1934)
The Hell Cat (Col, 1934)
Sleepers East (Fox, 1934)
Return of the Terror (WB, 1934)
Bachelor of Arts (Fox, 1934)
British Agent (FN, 1934)
Girl in Danger (Col, 1934)
The Defense Rests (Col, 1934)
Hell in the Heavens (Fox, 1934)

The President Vanishes (Par, 1934)
Marie Galante (Fox, 1934)
The Lives of a Bengal Lancer (Par, 1935)
The Crusades (Par, 1935)
Behind Green Lights (Mascot, 1935)
Confidential (Mascot, 1935)
Black Fury (WB, 1935)
Captain Blood (WB, 1935)
Under the Pampas Moon (Fox, 1935)
Front Page Woman (WB, 1935)
Little Big Shot (WB, 1935)
Special Agent (WB, 1935)
Two in the Dark (RKO, 1936)
Special Investigator (RKO, 1936)
We Who Are About to Die (RKO, 1936)
Exclusive Story (MGM, 1936)
Return of Jimmy Valentine (Rep, 1936)
The Leathernecks Have Landed (Rep, 1936)
Robin Hood of El Dorado (MGM, 1936)
Moonlight Murder (MGM, 1936)
Absolute Quiet (MGM, 1936)
Charlie Chan at the Circus (20th, 1936)
Ramona (20th, 1936)
Anthony Adverse (WB, 1936)
The Charge of the Light Brigade (WB, 1936)
Crack-Up (20th, 1936)
Think Fast, Mr. Moto (20th, 1937)
Song of the City (MGM, 1937)
Border Cafe (RKO, 1937)
Hideaway (RKO, 1937)
Sea Racketeers (Rep, 1937)
Bulldog Drummond Comes Back (Par, 1937)
Thunder Trail (Par, 1937)
Night Club Scandal (Par, 1937)
Daughter of Shanghai (Par, 1937)
Tip-Off Girls (Par, 1938)
Her Jungle Love (Par, 1938)
Hunted Men (Par, 1938)
Prison Farm (Par, 1938)
Bulldog Drummond in Africa (Par, 1938)
King of Alcatraz (Par, 1938)
Illegal Traffic (Par, 1938)
Persons in Hiding (Par, 1939)
Hotel Imperial (Par, 1939)
Undercover Doctor (Par, 1939)
King of Chinatown (Par, 1939)
Beau Geste (Par, 1939)
Island of Lost Men (Par, 1939)
Typhoon (Par, 1940)
Queen of the Mob (Par, 1940)
Golden Gloves (Par, 1940)
A Night at Earl Carroll's (Par, 1940)
Down Argentine Way (20th, 1940)
That Night in Rio (20th, 1941)
Mr. Dynamite (Univ, 1941)
Blood and Sand (20th, 1941)

Accent on Love (20th, 1941)
Forced Landing (Par, 1941)
Birth of the Blues (Par, 1941)
The Corsican Brothers (UA, 1941)
A Gentleman at Heart (Fox, 1942)
Dr. Broadway (Par, 1942)
Jackass Mail (MGM, 1942)
The Pied Piper (20th, 1942)
Tales of Manhattan (20th, 1942)
The Man in the Trunk (20th, 1942)
Dr. Renault's Secret (20th, 1942)
Sunday Punch (MGM, 1942)
Harrigan's Kid (MGM, 1943)
Good Morning, Judge (Univ, 1943)
Sahara (Col, 1943)
Behind the Rising Sun (RKO, 1943)
Batman (Col serial, 1943)
Gung Ho! (Univ, 1943)
Calling Dr. Death (Univ, 1943)
The Monster Maker (PRC, 1944)
House of Frankenstein (Univ, 1944)
Waterfront (PRC, 1944)
The Whistler (Col, 1944)
Two-Man Submarine (Col, 1944)
Voice in the Wind (UA, 1944)
Jungle Woman (Univ, 1944)
Dragon Seed (MGM, 1944)
Enter Arsene Lupin (Univ, 1944)
Mark of the Whistler (Col, 1944)
A Medal for Benny (Par, 1945)
The Southerner (UA, 1945)
Strange Confession (Univ, 1945)
Getting Gertie's Garter (UA, 1945)
The Beast with Five Fingers (WB, 1946)
Humoresque (WB, 1946)
Bad Bascomb (MGM, 1946)
Carnival in Costa Rica (20th, 1947)
The Fugitive (RKO, 1947)
The Road to Rio (Par, 1947)
The Kissing Bandit (MGM, 1948)
Joan of Arc (RKO, 1948)
That Midnight Kiss (MGM, 1949)
Canadian Pacific (20th, 1949)
The Toast of New Orleans (MGM, 1950)
Annie Get Your Gun (MGM, 1950)
Rio Grande (Rep, 1950)
Please Believe Me (MGM, 1950)
The Black Hand (MGM, 1950)
Across the Wide Missouri (MGM, 1951)
Mark of the Renegade (Univ, 1951)
Bannerline (MGM, 1951)
The Denver and Rio Grande (Par, 1952)
Woman of the North Country (Rep, 1952)
Ride the Man Down (Rep, 1952)
Clash by Night (RKO, 1952)
Fighter Attack (AA, 1953)
Beneath the Twelve-Mile Reef (20th, 1953)

Saskatchewan (Univ, 1954)	*Violent Saturday* (20th, 1955)	*This Could Be the Night* (MGM, 1957)
Sitting Bull (Univ, 1954)	*The Last Command* (Rep, 1955)	*The Young Don't Cry* (Col, 1957)
Hit the Deck (MGM, 1955)	*Desert Sands* (UA, 1955)	*Force of Impulse* (Sutton Pictures, 1961)
New York Confidential (WB, 1955)	*Rebel in Town* (UA, 1956)	*Dracula vs. Frankenstein* (Independent-
Rage at Dawn (RKO, 1955)	*Yaqui Drums* (AA, 1956)	International, 1973)

MARY NASH
(Mary Ryan)

In the 1930s.

Born August 15, 1885, Troy, New York. Married Jose Rubens; divorced. Died December 3, 1976, Brentwood, California. Expert stage performer who came to films at a mature age. Twice abused Shirley Temple on screen (*Heidi, The Little Princess*) but then was well-behaved society mother of Katharine Hepburn in *The Philadelphia Story*. Sympathetic as the all-wise queen who is assassinated in *Cobra Woman*.

> **Mary Nash** to Shirley Temple in *The Little Princess*: "Sarah, from now on you're not to sit with us. Return to your room and smooth down those curls, and then go to the kitchen."

Films

Uncertain Lady (Univ, 1934)	*The Rains Came* (20th, 1939)	*In the Meantime, Darling* (20th, 1944)
College Scandal (Par, 1935)	*Charlie Chan in Panama* (20th, 1940)	*Cobra Woman* (Univ, 1944)
Come and Get It (UA, 1936)	*Sailor's Lady* (20th, 1940)	*The Lady and the Monster* (Rep, 1944)
The King and the Chorus Girl (WB, 1937)	*Gold Rush Maisie* (MGM, 1940)	*Yolanda and the Thief* (MGM, 1945)
Easy Living (Par, 1937)	*The Philadelphia Story* (MGM, 1940)	*Monsieur Beaucaire* (Par, 1946)
Heidi (20th, 1937)	*Men of Boys Town* (MGM, 1941)	*Swell Guy* (Univ, 1946)
Wells Fargo (Par, 1937)	*Calling Dr. Gillespie* (MGM, 1942)	*Till the Clouds Roll By* (MGM, 1946)
The Little Princess (20th, 1939)	*The Human Comedy* (MGM, 1943)	

MILDRED NATWICK

In Barefoot in the Park *(1967).*

Born June 19, 1908, Baltimore, Maryland. Polished sharp-nosed stage performer who made her screen bow in John Ford's *The Long Voyage Home* (Freda). Thereafter in Ford's *Three Godfathers* (mother), *She Wore a Yellow Ribbon* (Mrs. Allshard), and *The Quiet Man* (Mrs. Sarah Tillane). Oscar-nominated for playing Jane Fonda's fun-loving mother in *Barefoot in the Park* (but lost BSAAA to Estelle Parsons of *Bonnie and Clyde*).

Mildred Natwick to Ronald Colman in *The Late George Apley:* "I should have been the boy. Father always said so."

Films

The Long Voyage Home (UA, 1940)	*Cheaper by the Dozen* (20th, 1950)	*If It's Tuesday, This Must Be Belgium* (UA, 1970)
The Enchanted Cottage (RKO, 1945)	*The Quiet Man* (Rep, 1952)	*The Maltese Bippy* (MGM, 1970)
Yolanda and the Thief (MGM, 1945)	*Against All Flags* (Univ, 1952)	*Trilogy* (AA, 1970)
The Late George Apley (20th, 1947)	*The Trouble with Harry* (Par, 1955)	*Daisy Miller* (Par, 1974)
A Woman's Vengeance (Univ, 1947)	*The Court Jester* (Par, 1956)	*At Long Last Love* (20th, 1975)
Three Godfathers (MGM, 1948)	*Teenage Rebel* (20th, 1956)	
The Kissing Bandit (MGM, 1948)	*Tammy and the Bachelor* (Univ, 1957)	
She Wore a Yellow Ribbon (RKO, 1949)	*Barefoot in the Park* (Par, 1967)	

BARBARA NICHOLS
(Barbara Nickeraeur)

With Glenn Ford in Dear Heart *(1964).*

Born 1932, Long Island, New York. Died October 5, 1976, Hollywood, California. Excelled as the fleshy blonde floozie. Had a tart way with repartee, delivered in a raucous, nasal voice. Played inventive variations on the broad: *Pal Joey* (Gladys, the chorine outshone by Kim Novak), *The Naked and the Dead* (Mildred, the "mooing" wife of Aldo Ray), *Who Was That Lady?* (one of the sluttish Coogle sisters, along with Joi Lansing), *Where the Boys Are* (Lola, the aquatic nightclub performer), *The George Raft Story* (Texas Guinan), *Dear Heart* (June, the countergirl with an eye for Glenn Ford), etc. TV series: "The Jack Benny Show," "Love That Jill," and "The Beverly Hillbillies."

Barbara Nichols in *House of Women:* "It's just a question of finding the kind of jam a man goes for."

Films

River of No Return (20th, 1954)
Manfish (UA, 1956)
Miracle in the Rain (WB, 1956)
Beyond a Reasonable Doubt (RKO, 1956)
The King and Four Queens (UA, 1956)
Sweet Smell of Success (UA, 1957)
Pal Joey (Col, 1957)
The Pajama Game (WB, 1957)
Ten North Frederick (20th, 1958)
The Naked and the Dead (WB, 1958)

Woman Obsessed (20th, 1959)
That Kind of Woman (Par, 1959)
Who Was That Lady? (Col, 1959)
Where the Boys Are (MGM, 1960)
The George Raft Story (AA, 1961)
The Scarface Mob (Cari Pictures, 1962)
House of Women (WB, 1962)
Looking for Love (MGM, 1964)
The Disorderly Orderly (Par, 1964)
Dear Heart (WB, 1964)

The Loved One (MGM, 1965)
The Human Duplicators (AA, 1965)
The Swinger (Par, 1966)
The Power (MGM, 1968)
Charley and the Angel (BV, 1973)
The Photographer (Avco Emb, 1975)
Won Ton Ton, the Dog Who Saved Hollywood (Par, 1976)

JACK NORTON
(Mortimer J. Naughton)

Ernest Truex, Cecilia Callejo, and Jack Norton in It's a Wonderful World *(1939).*

Born 1889, Brooklyn, New York. Married Lucille Haley (191_). Died October 15, 1958, Saranac Lake, New York. The cinema's, vaudeville's, and TV's most recurrent professional drunk, who, ironically, was a teetotaler in real life. Usually well dressed, congenial, but incoherent; the nearest solid object was his favorite prop.

Jack Norton (on train) to the other inebriated members of the Ale and Quail Club in *The Palm Beach Story:* "Where's the dogs? You can't have a posse without the dogs."

Films

Cockeyed Cavaliers (RKO, 1934)
Sweet Music (WB, 1935)
Calling All Cars (Empire, 1935)
Stolen Harmony (Par, 1935)
Don't Bet on Blondes (WB, 1935)
His Night Out (Univ, 1935)
Bordertown (FN, 1935)
Ship Cafe (Par, 1935)
The Preview Murder Mystery (Par, 1936)
Too Many Parents (Par, 1936)
Marked Woman (WB, 1937)
Pick a Star (MGM, 1937)
A Day at the Races (MGM, 1937)
Meet the Missus (RKO, 1937)
Meet the Girls (20th, 1938)
Thanks for the Memory (Par, 1938)
Grand Jury Secrets (Par, 1939)
Joe and Ethel Turp Call on the President (MGM, 1939)

It's a Wonderful World (MGM, 1939)
The Villain Still Pursued Her (RKO, 1940)
The Farmer's Daughter (Par, 1940)
Opened by Mistake (Par, 1940)
A Night at Earl Carroll's (Par, 1940)
The Bank Dick (Univ, 1940)
No Greater Sin (University Pictures, 1941)
Road Show (UA, 1941)
Louisiana Purchase (Par, 1941)
The Spoilers (Univ, 1942)
Moonlight in Havana (Univ, 1942)
Dr. Renault's Secret (20th, 1942)
The Palm Beach Story (Par, 1942)
Tennessee Johnson (MGM, 1942)
The Fleet's In (Par, 1942)
Brooklyn Orchid (UA, 1942)
It Ain't Hay (Univ, 1943)

Lady Bodyguard (Par, 1943)
Taxi, Mister (UA, 1943)
Prairie Chickens (UA, 1943)
The Chinese Cat (Mon, 1944)
Ghost Catchers (Univ, 1944)
Cover Girl (Col, 1944)
Hail the Conquering Hero (Par, 1944)
The Big Noise (20th, 1944)
Wonder Man (RKO, 1945)
Fashion Model (Mon, 1945)
Hold That Blonde (Par, 1945)
The Naughty Nineties (Univ, 1945)
Her Highness and the Bellboy (MGM, 1945)
The Scarlet Clue (Mon, 1945)
A Guy, a Gal and a Pal (Col, 1945)
Flame of the Barbary Coast (Rep, 1945)
Man Alive (RKO, 1945)
Strange Confession (Univ, 1945)

Captain Tugboat Annie (Rep, 1945)
The Strange Mr. Gregory (Mon, 1946)
Blue Skies (Par, 1946)
No Leave, No Love (MGM, 1946)

The Kid from Brooklyn (RKO, 1946)
Rendezvous 24 (20th, 1946)
Shadows over Chinatown (Mon, 1946)
Linda Be Good (EL, 1947)

Mad Wednesday [a.k.a. The Sin of Harold Diddlebock] (UA, 1947)
Variety Girl (Par, 1947)
Variety Time (RKO, 1948)

UNA O'CONNOR

With Frank Morgan and Richard Waring in The Perfect Gentleman *(1935).*

Born October 23, 1880, Belfast, Ireland. Died February 4, 1959, New York City, New York. Birdlike crone with a shrill voice who began as an Abbey Player in Dublin; later acted in London and New York. Re-created her stage role of the mournful maid Ellen Bridges in Fox's *Cavalcade;* thereafter many snobbish domestics of various ethnic extractions. Unforgettable as the screamer in *The Invisible Man* and *Bride of Frankenstein.* Was the dramatic Mrs. McPhillips, Wallace Ford's mother in *The Informer* and excelled as the flirtatious Bess, the maid courting Herbert Mundin in *The Adventures of Robin Hood.* Memorable as Mrs. Emma Lory, the castrating mother of Charles Laughton in *This Land Is Mine.*

Una O'Connor to Lucien Prival in *Bride of Frankenstein:*
"Albert! It's alive! The monster! It's alive!"

Films

Dark Red Roses (Br, 1929)
To Oblige a Lady (Br, 1930)
Timbuctoo (Br, 1930)
Murder (Br, 1930)
Cavalcade (Fox, 1933)

Pleasure Cruise (Fox, 1933)
The Invisible Man (Univ, 1933)
Mary Stevens, M.D. (FN, 1933)
The Poor Rich (Univ, 1934)
The Barretts of Wimpole Street (MGM,

1934)
Orient Express (Fox, 1934)
All Men Are Enemies (Fox, 1934)
Stingaree (RKO, 1934)
Chained (MGM, 1934)

David Copperfield (MGM, 1935)
The Informer (RKO, 1935)
Father Brown, Detective (Par, 1935)
Bride of Frankenstein (Univ, 1935)
Thunder in the Night (Fox, 1935)
The Perfect Gentleman (MGM, 1935)
Rose-Marie (MGM, 1936)
Little Lord Fauntleroy (UA, 1936)
Lloyds of London (20th, 1936)
Suzy (MGM, 1936)
The Plough and the Stars (RKO, 1936)
Call It a Day (WB, 1937)
Personal Property (MGM, 1937)
The Return of the Frog (Br, 1938)
The Adventures of Robin Hood (WB, 1938)
We Are Not Alone (WB, 1939)
The Sea Hawk (WB, 1940)

Lillian Russell (20th, 1940)
He Stayed for Breakfast (Col, 1940)
It All Came True (WB, 1940)
All Women Have Secrets (Par, 1940)
Kisses for Breakfast (WB, 1941)
How Green Was My Valley (20th, 1941)
The Strawberry Blonde (WB, 1941)
Her First Beau (Col, 1941)
Three Girls About Town (Col, 1941)
Always in My Heart (WB, 1942)
My Favorite Spy (RKO, 1942)
Random Harvest (MGM, 1942)
This Land Is Mine (RKO, 1943)
Forever and a Day (RKO, 1943)
Holy Matrimony (20th, 1943)
Government Girl (RKO, 1943)
My Pal Wolf (RKO, 1944)

The Canterville Ghost (MGM, 1944)
The Bells of St. Mary's (RKO, 1945)
Christmas in Connecticut (WB, 1945)
The Return of Monte Cristo (Col, 1946)
Banjo (RKO, 1946)
Child of Divorce (RKO, 1946)
Cluny Brown (20th, 1946)
Of Human Bondage (WB, 1946)
Unexpected Guest (UA, 1946)
Lost Honeymoon (EL, 1947)
The Corpse Came C.O.D. (Col, 1947)
Ivy (Univ, 1947)
Fighting Father Dunne (RKO, 1948)
The Adventures of Don Juan (WB, 1948)
Witness for the Prosecution (UA, 1957)

EDNA MAY OLIVER
(Edna May Nutter)

Ann Harding and Edna May Oliver in The Conquerors *(1932).*

Born November 9, 1883, Boston, Massachusetts. Married David Pratt (1928); divorced (1931). Died November 9, 1942, Hollywood, California. Horse-faced stage and screen star with a trade-marked sniff and arched eyebrow. No scene was safe from her accomplished mugging. Pumped life into her array of hard-seeming spinsters who usually possessed some facet of kindness: **Katharine Hepburn's** *Little Women* **(Aunt March), Paramount's** *Alice in Wonderland* **(the Red Queen), Freddie Bartholomew's** *David Copperfield* **(Aunt Betsy), MGM's** *A Tale of Two Cities* **(Miss Pross), Norma Shearer's** *Romeo and Juliet* **(the nurse),** *Nurse Edith Cavell* **(Countess Maron),** *Pride and Prejudice* **(Lady Catherine de Bourgh). Oscar-nominated for her pioneer widow, Mrs. McKlennan, in** *Drums Along the Mohawk* **(but lost BSAAA to Hattie McDaniel of** *Gone with the Wind***). Played schoolteacher Hildegarde Withers, the amateur sleuth, three times:** *The Penguin Pool Murder, Murder on the Blackboard,* **and** *Murder on a Honeymoon.*

Edna May Oliver to Roger Imhof in *Drums Along the Mohawk:* "Well, General Herkimer, a fine mess you've gotten yourself into this time."

Films

Three O'Clock in the Morning (C. C. Burr, 1923)
Wife in Name Only (Selznick, 1923)
Restless Wives (C. C. Burr, 1923)
Icebound (Par, 1924)
Manhattan (Par, 1924)
The Lady Who Lied (FN, 1925)
The Lucky Devil (Par, 1925)
Lovers in Quarantine (Par, 1925)
Let's Get Married (Par, 1926)
The American Venus (Par, 1926)
The Saturday Night Kid (Par, 1929)
Hook, Line and Sinker (RKO, 1930)
Half Shot at Sunrise (RKO, 1930)
Laugh and Get Rich (RKO, 1931)
Fanny Foley Herself (RKO, 1931)
Cimarron (RKO, 1931)
Cracked Nuts (RKO, 1931)

Newly Rich [a.k.a. *Forbidden Adventure*] (Par, 1931)
Lost Squadron (RKO, 1932)
Ladies of the Jury (RKO, 1932)
Hold 'em Jail! (RKO, 1932)
The Penguin Pool Murder (RKO, 1932)
The Conquerors (RKO, 1932)
The Great Jasper (RKO, 1933)
Ann Vickers (RKO, 1933)
It's Great to Be Alive (Fox, 1933)
Strawberry Roan (Univ, 1933)
Only Yesterday (Univ, 1933)
Meet the Baron (MGM, 1933)
Little Women (RKO, 1933)
Alice in Wonderland (Par, 1933)
The Poor Rich (Univ, 1934)
The Last Gentleman (UA, 1934)
We're Rich Again (RKO, 1934)

Murder on the Blackboard (RKO, 1934)
Murder on a Honeymoon (RKO, 1935)
David Copperfield (MGM, 1935)
No More Ladies (MGM, 1935)
A Tale of Two Cities (MGM, 1935)
Romeo and Juliet (MGM, 1936)
My Dear Miss Aldrich (MGM, 1937)
Parnell (MGM, 1937)
Rosalie (MGM, 1937)
Paradise for Three (MGM, 1938)
Little Miss Broadway (20th, 1938)
The Story of Vernon and Irene Castle (RKO, 1939)
Nurse Edith Cavell (RKO, 1939)
Second Fiddle (20th, 1939)
Drums Along the Mohawk (20th, 1939)
Pride and Prejudice (MGM, 1940)
Lydia (UA, 1941)

MORONI OLSEN

Bing Crosby, Gloria Jean, and Moroni Olsen in If I Had My Way *(1940).*

Born July 27, 1889, Ogden, Utah. Died November 22, 1954, Los Angeles, California. Onetime Chautauqua circuit performer who later headed his own touring company. Directed and played in Pasadena Playhouse productions; also directed the annual Pilgrimage Play in Hollywood for several years. In 1935, his first screen year, played Buffalo Bill to Barbara Stanwyck's *Annie Oakley* and Porthos in Walter Abel's *The Three Musketeers* (in the 1939 Ritz Brothers' version, Olsen was the bailiff; in the sequel, *At Sword's Point,* starring Cornel Wilde, he was Old Porthos). Thick build. Made an imposing personage: Robert E. Lee in *Santa Fe Trail;* Ralph Henry, Brian Donlevy's gubernatorial rival in *The Glass Key;* Inspector Peterson in Joan Crawford's *Mildred Pierce;* Don Taylor's dad in *Father of the Bride* and *Father's Little Dividend.* One of his final assignments: Pope Leo (*Sign of the Pagan*).

> **Moroni Olsen** to Joan Crawford in *Mildred Pierce:* "You know, Mrs. Beragon, there are times when I regret being a policeman."

Films

The Three Musketeers (RKO, 1935)
Annie Oakley (RKO, 1935)
Seven Keys to Baldpate (RKO, 1935)
The Farmer in the Dell (RKO, 1936)
We're Only Human (RKO, 1936)
Yellow Dust (RKO, 1936)
Two in the Dark (RKO, 1936)
Two in Revolt (RKO, 1936)
Mary of Scotland (RKO, 1936)
The Witness Chair (RKO, 1936)
M'liss (RKO, 1936)
Grand Jury (RKO, 1936)
The Plough and the Stars (RKO, 1936)
Mummy's Boys (RKO, 1936)
Adventure's End (Univ, 1937)

Manhattan Merry-Go-Round (Rep, 1937)
Kentucky (20th, 1938)
Gold Is Where You Find It (WB, 1938)
Kidnapped (20th, 1938)
Submarine Patrol (20th, 1938)
Homicide Bureau (Col, 1939)
Rose of Washington Square (20th, 1939)
Code of the Secret Service (WB, 1939)
The Three Musketeers (20th, 1939)
Susannah of the Mounties (20th, 1939)
Allegheny Uprising (RKO, 1939)
Dust Be My Destiny (WB, 1939)
That's Right, You're Wrong (RKO, 1939)
Barricade (20th, 1939)

Virginia City (WB, 1940)
Invisible Stripes (WB, 1940)
Brother Rat and a Baby (WB, 1940)
If I Had My Way (Univ, 1940)
Brigham Young—Frontiersman (20th, 1940)
East of the River (WB, 1940)
Santa Fe Trail (WB, 1940)
Life with Henry (Par, 1941)
Dive Bomber (WB, 1941)
One Foot in Heaven (WB, 1941)
Three Sons o' Guns (WB, 1941)
Dangerously They Live (WB, 1941)
Sundown Jim (20th, 1942)
Nazi Agent (MGM, 1942)

My Favorite Spy (RKO, 1942)
Mrs. Wiggs of the Cabbage Patch (Par, 1942)
The Glass Key (Par, 1942)
Reunion in France (MGM, 1942)
Madame Curie (MGM, 1943)
Air Force (WB, 1943)
We've Never Been Licked (Univ, 1943)
Mission to Moscow (WB, 1943)
The Song of Bernadette (20th, 1943)
Ali Baba and the Forty Thieves (Univ, 1944)
Buffalo Bill (20th, 1944)
Roger Touhy—Gangster (20th, 1944)
Cobra Woman (Univ, 1944)
Pride of the Marines (WB, 1945)
Behind City Lights (Rep, 1945)

Mildred Pierce (WB, 1945)
Don't Fence Me In (Rep, 1945)
Week-End at the Waldorf (MGM, 1945)
A Night in Paradise (Univ, 1946)
Boys' Ranch (MGM, 1946)
The Walls Came Tumbling Down (Col, 1946)
Notorious (RKO, 1946)
The Strange Woman (UA, 1946)
Possessed (WB, 1947)
The Long Night (RKO, 1947)
Life with Father (WB, 1947)
Black Gold (AA, 1947)
The Beginning or the End? (MGM, 1947)
That Hagen Girl (WB, 1947)
The High Wall (MGM, 1947)
Call Northside 777 (20th, 1948)

Up in Central Park (Univ, 1948)
Command Decision (MGM, 1948)
The Fountainhead (WB, 1949)
Task Force (WB, 1949)
Samson and Delilah (Par, 1949)
Father of the Bride (MGM, 1950)
Father's Little Dividend (MGM, 1951)
No Questions Asked (MGM, 1951)
Payment on Demand (RKO, 1951)
Submarine Command (Par, 1951)
At Sword's Point (RKO, 1952)
Lone Star (MGM, 1952)
The Washington Story (MGM, 1952)
So This Is Love (WB, 1953)
Marry Me Again (RKO, 1953)
The Long, Long Trailer (MGM, 1954)
Sign of the Pagan (Univ, 1954)

BARBARA O'NEIL

With Kurt Kasznar in Flame of the Islands (1955).

Born July 10, 1911, St. Louis, Missouri. Married Joshua Logan (1940); divorced (1941). Apt stage actress who debuted on screen as Helen, for whom John Boles left Barbara Stanwyck in Stella Dallas. Was genteel as Edward G. Robinson's spouse in I Am the Law and a pillar of strength as Mrs. O'Hara in Gone with the Wind. In a turn of casting type, played the demented wife of Charles Boyer in Irene Dunne's When Tomorrow Comes and presented a sharper variation of the same role in All This, and Heaven Too. Played the shrewish Duchesse de Praslin in the latter, who suspected governess Bette Davis of wooing the Duc (Boyer). Oscar-nominated (but lost BSAAA to Jane Darwell of The Grapes of Wrath). Last screen role was as Mother Katherine (The Nun's Story). Has generally been overlooked in the hoopla every time Gone with the Wind has been revived.

Barbara O'Neil to Charles Boyer in *All This, and Heaven Too:*
"I'll not step one foot out of this house with *that* woman
you've chosen to replace me!"

Films

Stella Dallas (UA, 1937)
Love, Honor and Behave (WB, 1938)
The Toy Wife (MGM, 1938)
I Am the Law (Col, 1938)
The Sun Never Sets (Univ, 1939)
When Tomorrow Comes (Univ, 1939)

Tower of London (Univ, 1939)
Gone with the Wind (MGM, 1939)
All This, and Heaven Too (WB, 1940)
Shining Victory (WB, 1941)
The Secret Beyond the Door (Univ, 1948)
I Remember Mama (RKO, 1948)

Whirlpool (20th, 1949)
Angel Face (RKO, 1952)
Flame of the Islands (Rep, 1955)
The Nun's Story (WB, 1959)

HENRY O'NEILL

Henry O'Neill, Viveca Lindfors, and Glenn Ford in The Flying Missile *(1950).*

Born August 10, 1891, Orange, New Jersey. Married Anna Barry (1924), child: Patricia. Died May 18, 1961, Hollywood, California. Tall patrician player in several Eugene O'Neill Broadway plays. Ran the gamut of upper-class roles on screen, continually as a parent or professional man (especially doctors, district attorneys, military officers). Worked hard at Warner Bros—23 features in 1934 alone. In the 1940s transferred to MGM.

> **Henry O'Neill** to Mickey Rooney in *Girl Crazy:* "Son,
> you're living in a world of weekend whimsy, and growing
> up to be a 'rich man's son.'"

Films

I Loved a Woman (FN, 1933)
The Kennel Murder Case (FN, 1933)
The World Changes (WB, 1933)
From Headquarters (WB, 1933)
Lady Killer (WB, 1933)
The House on 56th Street (WB, 1933)
Ever in My Heart (WB, 1933)
Fog over Frisco (FN, 1934)
Fashions of 1934 (FN, 1934)
Side Streets (FN, 1934)
Flirtation Walk (FN, 1934)
Murder in the Clouds (FN, 1934)
Massacre (FN, 1934)
The Key (WB, 1934)
Bedside (FN, 1934)
Wonder Bar (FN, 1934)
I've Got Your Number (WB, 1934)
Journal of a Crime (FN, 1934)
The Big Shakedown (FN, 1934)
Twenty Million Sweethearts (FN, 1934)
Now I'll Tell (Fox, 1934)
Upper World (WB, 1934)
Madame Du Barry (WB, 1934)
The Personality Kid (WB, 1934)
Midnight Alibi (FN, 1934)
The Man with Two Faces (FN, 1934)
Big-Hearted Herbert (WB, 1934)
Gentlemen Are Born (FN, 1934)
Midnight (Univ, 1934)
The Secret Bride (WB, 1934)
Living on Velvet (FN, 1935)
Sweet Music (WB, 1935)
The Florentine Dagger (WB, 1935)
Bordertown (WB, 1935)
The Man Who Reclaimed His Head (Univ, 1935)
The Great Hotel Murder (Fox, 1935)
While the Patient Slept (FN, 1935)
Black Fury (FN, 1935)
Dinky (WB, 1935)
Bright Lights (FN, 1935)
Alias Mary Dow (Univ, 1935)
Stranded (WB, 1935)
Oil for the Lamps of China (WB, 1935)
We're in the Money (FN, 1935)
The Case of the Lucky Legs (WB, 1935)
Special Agent (WB, 1935)
Dr. Socrates (WB, 1935)
The Story of Louis Pasteur (WB, 1935)
Boulder Dam (WB, 1936)
Freshman Love (WB, 1936)
Road Gang (WB, 1936)
The Walking Dead (WB, 1936)
Bullets or Ballots (WB, 1936)

Two Against the World (FN, 1936)
The Big Noise (WB, 1936)
The Golden Arrow (FN, 1936)
Anthony Adverse (WB, 1936)
The White Angel (FN, 1936)
Rainbow on the River (RKO, 1936)
The Great O'Malley (WB, 1937)
Marked Woman (WB, 1937)
The Go-Getter (WB, 1937)
The Green Light (WB, 1937)
Draegerman Courage (WB, 1937)
The Life of Emile Zola (WB, 1937)
Mr. Dodd Takes the Air (WB, 1937)
The Singing Marine (WB, 1937)
First Lady (WB, 1937)
The Great Garrick (WB, 1937)
Submarine D-1 (WB, 1937)
Wells Fargo (Par, 1937)
The Amazing Dr. Clitterhouse (WB, 1938)
Racket Busters (WB, 1938)
Jezebel (WB, 1938)
Gold Is Where You Find It (WB, 1938)
Yellow Jack (MGM, 1938)
White Banners (WB, 1938)
The Chaser (MGM, 1938)
Girls on Probation (WB, 1938)
Brother Rat (WB, 1938)
Dodge City (WB, 1939)
Torchy Blane in Chinatown (WB, 1939)
Wings of the Navy (WB, 1939)
Confessions of a Nazi Spy (WB, 1939)
Juarez (WB, 1939)
Lucky Night (MGM, 1939)
The Man Who Dared (WB, 1939)
Angels Wash Their Faces (WB, 1939)
Everybody's Hobby (WB, 1939)
Four Wives (WB, 1939)
They Drive by Night (WB, 1940)
A Child Is Born (WB, 1940)
Invisible Stripes (WB, 1940)
Calling Philo Vance (WB, 1940)
The Story of Dr. Ehrlich's Magic Bullet (WB, 1940)
Castle on the Hudson (WB, 1940)
The Fighting 69th (WB, 1940)
'Til We Meet Again (WB, 1940)
Money and the Woman (WB, 1940)
Santa Fe Trail (WB, 1940)
Honky Tonk (MGM, 1941)
Johnny Eager (MGM, 1941)
The Bugle Sounds (MGM, 1941)
The Trial of Mary Dugan (MGM, 1941)
Men of Boys Town (MGM, 1941)

Billy the Kid (MGM, 1941)
Blossoms in the Dust (MGM, 1941)
The Get-Away (MGM, 1941)
Down in San Diego (MGM, 1941)
Whistling in the Dark (MGM, 1941)
Shadow of the Thin Man (MGM, 1941)
This Time for Keeps (MGM, 1942)
Born to Sing (MGM, 1942)
Tortilla Flat (MGM, 1942)
White Cargo (MGM, 1942)
Stand By for Action (MGM, 1942)
The Human Comedy (MGM, 1943)
Best Foot Forward (MGM, 1943)
Air Raid Wardens (MGM, 1943)
Dr. Gillespie's Criminal Case (MGM, 1943)
Whistling in Brooklyn (MGM, 1943)
A Guy Named Joe (MGM, 1943)
Girl Crazy (MGM, 1943)
Lost Angel (MGM, 1943)
The Heavenly Body (MGM, 1943)
Rationing (MGM, 1944)
Two Girls and a Sailor (MGM, 1944)
Barbary Coast Gent (MGM, 1944)
Nothing but Trouble (MGM, 1944)
Keep Your Powder Dry (MGM, 1945)
Anchors Aweigh (MGM, 1945)
This Man's Navy (MGM, 1945)
Dangerous Partners (MGM, 1945)
The Virginian (Par, 1946)
The Green Years (MGM, 1946)
Three Wise Fools (MGM, 1946)
The Hoodlum Saint (MGM, 1946)
Little Mr. Jim (MGM, 1946)
Bad Bascomb (MGM, 1946)
The Beginning or the End? (MGM, 1947)
The Return of October (Col, 1948)
Leather Gloves (Col, 1948)
You're My Everything (20th, 1949)
Alias Nick Beal (Par, 1949)
Holiday Affair (RKO, 1949)
The Reckless Moment (Col, 1949)
Strange Bargain (RKO, 1949)
Convicted (Col, 1950)
The Milkman (Univ, 1950)
The Flying Missile (Col, 1950)
No Man of Her Own (Par, 1950)
The Second Woman (UA, 1951)
The People Against O'Hara (MGM, 1951)
The Family Secret (Col, 1951)
Scandal Sheet (Col, 1952)
Scarlet Angel (Univ, 1952)
The Sun Shines Bright (Rep, 1953)
Untamed (20th, 1955)
The Wings of Eagles (MGM, 1957)

MARIA OUSPENSKAYA

In The Wolf Man *(1941)*.

Born July 29, 1867, Tula, Russia. Died December 3, 1949, Los Angeles, California. Russian-born actress (Moscow Art Theatre) who made films in Hollywood to support her New York acting school. Oscar-nominated for re-creating her stage role of the baroness in *Dodsworth*, the noble woman who refused to allow her son (Gregory Gaye) to wed capricious Ruth Chatterton (but lost BSAAA to Gale Sondergaard of *Anthony Adverse*). Engaged in a card game with Napoleon Bonaparte (Charles Boyer) as the Countess Pelagia in *Conquest*. In *Love Affair* played Boyer's all-wise grandmama. Again Oscar-nominated for the latter assignment (but lost BSAAA to Hattie McDaniel of *Gone with the Wind*). A tiny, very wrinkled actress, with a commanding presence. A game person who tried most any type of role: *The Rains Came* (Maharani), *Waterloo Bridge* (the demanding ballet teacher), *The Shanghai Gesture* (the mute Amah), *The Wolf Man* and *Frankenstein Meets the Wolf Man* (the all-knowing but superstitious gypsy), *Tarzan and the Amazons* (the Amazon queen), *Wyoming* (as Vera Ralston's chaperone in the Wild West). Well regarded as a painter.

Maria Ouspenskaya to Lon Chaney, Jr., in *The Wolf Man*:
"Whoever is bitten by a werewolf and *lives*, becomes a werewolf himself."

Films

Sverchok Na Pechi [a.k.a. *The Cricket on the Hearth*] (Rus, 1915)
Nichtozhniye [a.k.a. *Worthless*] (Rus, 1916)
Tsveti Zapozdaliye [a.k.a. *Belated Flowers/ Dr. Toporkov*] (Rus, 1917)
Zazhivo Pogrebenni [a.k.a. *Buried Alive*] (Rus, 1919)
Khveska [a.k.a. *Hospital Guard Khveska*] (Rus, 1923)
Tanka-Traktirschitsa/Protiv Otsa [a.k.a. *Tanka the Inn-Keeper/Against Her Father*] (Rus, 1929)

Dodsworth (UA, 1936)
Conquest (MGM, 1927)
Love Affair (RKO, 1939)
The Rains Came (20th, 1939)
Judge Hardy and Son (MGM, 1940)
Dr. Ehrlich's Magic Bullet (WB, 1940)
Beyond Tomorrow (RKO, 1940)
Dance, Girl, Dance (RKO, 1940)
Waterloo Bridge (MGM, 1940)
The Mortal Storm (MGM, 1940)
The Man I Married (20th, 1940)
The Shanghai Gesture (UA, 1941)
Kings Row (WB, 1941)

The Wolf Man (Univ, 1941)
Mystery of Marie Roget (Univ, 1942)
Frankenstein Meets the Wolf Man (Univ, 1943)
Tarzan and the Amazons (RKO, 1945)
I've Always Loved You (Rep, 1946)
Wyoming (Rep, 1947)
A Kiss in the Dark (WB, 1949)

LYNNE OVERMAN

Fred MacMurray, Lynne Overman, and Ray Milland in Star Spangled Rhythm (1942).

Born September 19, 1887, Maryville, Missouri. Married Emily _____. Died February 19, 1943, Santa Monica, California. Stage veteran who spiced many films with his dry wit and meandering voice. Could be a wisecracking Damon Runyonesque hood (*Little Miss Marker, Yours for the Asking***), or the hero/heroine's pal; always stole the limelight. A standout as Tod McDuff, the Scottish scout in ***North West Mounted Police***.**

> **Lynne Overman** to Joel McCrea in *Union Pacific:* "There's only one thing wrong with dyin' in the snow, Jefferson. A fella's liable to catch cold."

Films

Midnight (Univ, 1934)
Little Miss Marker (Par, 1934)
The Great Flirtation (Par, 1934)
She Loves Me Not (Par, 1934)
You Belong to Me (Par, 1934)
Broadway Bill (Col, 1934)
Enter Madame! (Par, 1934)
Rumba (Par, 1935)
Paris in Spring (Par, 1935)
Men Without Names (Par, 1935)
Two for Tonight (Par, 1935)
Collegiate (Par, 1935)
Poppy (Par, 1936)
Yours for the Asking (Par, 1936)
Three Married Men (Par, 1936)
The Jungle Princess (Par, 1936)
Blonde Trouble (Par, 1937)

Partners in Crime (Par, 1937)
Nobody's Baby (MGM, 1937)
Don't Tell the Wife (RKO, 1937)
Murder Goes to College (Par, 1937)
Wild Money (Par, 1937)
Hotel Haywire (Par, 1937)
Night Club Scandal (Par, 1937)
True Confession (Par, 1937)
The Big Broadcast of 1938 (Par, 1938)
Her Jungle Love (Par, 1938)
Hunted Men (Par, 1938)
Spawn of the North (Par, 1938)
Sons of the Legion (Par, 1938)
Men with Wings (Par, 1938)
Ride a Crooked Mile (Par, 1938)
Persons in Hiding (Par, 1939)
Death of a Champion (Par, 1939)

Union Pacific (Par, 1939)
Edison the Man (MGM, 1940)
Typhoon (Par, 1940)
Safari (Par, 1940)
North West Mounted Police (Par, 1940)
Aloma of the South Seas (Par, 1941)
Caught in the Draft (Par, 1941)
New York Town (Par, 1941)
The Hard Boiled Canary [a.k.a. *There's Magic in Music*] (Par, 1941)
Roxie Hart (20th, 1942)
Reap the Wild Wind (Par, 1942)
The Forest Rangers (Par, 1942)
The Silver Queen (UA, 1942)
Star Spangled Rhythm (Par, 1942)
Dixie (Par, 1943)
The Desert Song (WB, 1943)

REGINALD OWEN

Lee Bowman, Heather Thatcher, Reginald Owen, Norma Shearer, and Melvyn Douglas in We Were Dancing *(1942).*

Born August 5, 1887, Wheathampstead, England. Married 1) Lydia Bilbrooke (1908); divorced (1923); 2) Mrs. Harold Austin, children: two; widowed (1956); 3) Barbara Haveman (1956). Died November 5, 1972, Boise, Idaho. British stage actor who migrated to Broadway in 1923. Made American film debut in the New York-filmed *The Letter* as Jeanne Eagel's tormented husband. Had unique opportunity of playing Dr. Watson in Clive Brook's *Sherlock Holmes* and was the British sleuth himself in the next year's *A Study in Scarlet* (also wrote the dialogue). Often cast in the 1930s as a v-e-r-e-e British gentleman; could play other nationalities: King Louis XIV (*Voltaire*), Prince Charles of Sweden (*Queen Christina*). Utilized in vast quantity of quality productions once under contract (1935-53) to MGM. Played Scrooge in *A Christmas Carol*, Mr. Foley in both *Mrs. Miniver* and *The Miniver Story*. On loanout, played a bumbling Oxford don for Jack Benny's *Charley's Aunt*, the Duke of Malmunster in *Kitty*, and Judith Anderson's repressed spouse in *The Diary of a Chambermaid*. Last for Metro was Red Skelton's anemic *The Great Diamond Robbery*. Wrote plays, co-wrote the story for *Stablemates* (1938); was writing autobiography at time of death. Returned to Broadway in 1972 in the Phil Silvers' edition of *A Funny Thing Happened on the Way to the Forum*. TV series:"The Queen and I."

Reginald Owen to Edward Arnold in *The Earl of Chicago*:
"I've just been to Canada—Porcupine, Ontario. Sounds a
very uncomfortable place —and it jolly well is."

Films

Sally in Our Alley (Turner, 1916)	*The Man in Possession* (MGM, 1931)	*A Study in Scarlet* (WW, 1933)
A Place in the Sun (Br, 1919)	*A Woman Commands* (RKO, 1932)	*The Big Brain* (RKO, 1933)
The Grass Orphan (Ideal, 1923)	*Lovers Courageous* (MGM, 1932)	*Double Harness* (RKO, 1933)
Phroso (Fr, 1923)	*Downstairs* (MGM, 1932)	*Voltaire* (FN, 1933)
The Letter (Par, 1929)	*The Man Called Back* (Tif, 1932)	*The Narrow Corner* (FN, 1933)
Platinum Blonde (Col, 1931)	*Sherlock Holmes* (Fox, 1932)	*Queen Christina* (MGM, 1933)

406

Fashions of 1934 (FN, 1934)
Nana (UA, 1934)
The House of Rothschild (UA, 1934)
Madame Du Barry (FN, 1934)
Mandalay (FN, 1934)
The Countess of Monte Cristo (Univ, 1934)
Where Sinners Meet (RKO, 1934)
Of Human Bondage (RKO, 1934)
Here Is My Heart (Par, 1934)
The Human Side (Univ, 1934)
Stingaree (RKO, 1934)
Music in the Air (Fox, 1934)
The Good Fairy (Univ, 1935)
Call of the Wild (UA, 1935)
Anna Karenina (MGM, 1935)
Escapade (MGM, 1935)
A Tale of Two Cities (MGM, 1935)
The Bishop Misbehaves (MGM, 1935)
Enchanted April (RKO, 1935)
Rose-Marie (MGM, 1936)
Petticoat Fever (MGM, 1936)
Trouble for Two (MGM, 1936)
The Great Ziegfeld (MGM, 1936)
Love on the Run (MGM, 1936)
Girl on the Front Page (Univ, 1936)
Adventure in Manhattan (Col, 1936)
Yours for the Asking (Par, 1936)
Dangerous Number (MGM, 1937)
Personal Property (MGM, 1937)
Madame X (MGM, 1937)
The Bride Wore Red (MGM, 1937)
Conquest (MGM, 1937)
Rosalie (MGM, 1937)
Paradise for Three (MGM, 1938)
Everybody Sing (MGM, 1938)
Three Loves Has Nancy (MGM, 1938)
Vacation from Love (MGM, 1938)

A Christmas Carol (MGM, 1938)
The Girl Downstairs (MGM, 1938)
Kidnapped (20th, 1938)
Sweethearts (MGM, 1938)
Balalaika (MGM, 1939)
Fast and Loose (MGM, 1939)
Bridal Suite (MGM, 1939)
The Bad Little Angel (MGM, 1939)
Remember? (MGM, 1939)
Hotel Imperial (Par, 1939)
The Real Glory (UA, 1939)
The Earl of Chicago (MGM 1940)
Pride and Prejudice (MGM, 1940)
The Ghost Comes Home (MGM, 1940)
Florian (MGM, 1940)
Hullabaloo (MGM, 1940)
Blonde Inspiration (MGM, 1941)
Free and Easy (MGM, 1941)
They Met in Bombay (MGM, 1941)
Lady Be Good (MGM, 1941)
Tarzan's Secret Treasure (MGM, 1941)
A Woman's Face (MGM, 1941)
Charley's Aunt (20th, 1941)
Mrs. Miniver (MGM, 1942)
White Cargo (MGM, 1942)
We Were Dancing (MGM, 1942)
Woman of the Year (MGM, 1942)
I Married an Angel (MGM, 1942)
Pierre of the Plains (MGM, 1942)
Random Harvest (MGM, 1942)
Somewhere I'll Find You (MGM, 1942)
Cairo (MGM, 1942)
Reunion in France (MGM, 1942)
Above Suspicion (MGM, 1943)
Three Hearts for Julia (MGM, 1943)
Forever and a Day (RKO, 1943)
Salute to the Marines (MGM, 1943)
Madame Curie (MGM, 1943)

Assignment in Brittany (MGM, 1943)
National Velvet (MGM, 1944)
The Canterville Ghost (MGM, 1944)
She Went to the Races (MGM, 1945)
Valley of Decision (MGM, 1945)
The Sailor Takes a Wife (MGM, 1945)
Kitty (Par, 1945)
Captain Kidd (UA, 1945)
The Diary of a Chambermaid (UA, 1946)
Monsieur Beaucaire (Par, 1946)
Cluny Brown (20th, 1946)
Piccadilly Incident (MGM Br, 1946)
Thunder in the Valley (20th, 1947)
Green Dolphin Street (MGM, 1947)
If Winter Comes (MGM, 1947)
The Imperfect Lady (Par, 1947)
The Pirate (MGM, 1948)
Julia Misbehaves (MGM, 1948)
The Hills of Home (MGM, 1948)
The Three Musketeers (MGM, 1948)
Challenge to Lassie (MGM, 1949)
The Secret Garden (MGM, 1949)
Kim (MGM, 1950)
Grounds for Marriage (MGM, 1950)
The Miniver Story (MGM, 1950)
The Great Diamond Robbery (MGM, 1953)
Red Garters (Par, 1954)
Darby's Rangers (WB, 1958)
Five Weeks in a Balloon (20th, 1962)
The Thrill of It All (Univ, 1963)
Tammy and the Doctor (Univ, 1963)
Mary Poppins (BV, 1964)
Voice of the Hurricane (Selected Pictures, 1964)
Rosie! (Univ, 1967)
Bedknobs and Broomsticks (BV, 1971)

NESTOR PAIVA

Olin Howlin, Robert Clarke, Estelita Rodriguez, Rita Moreno, and Nestor Paiva in The Fabulous Senorita *(1952).*

Born June 30, 1905, Fresno, California. Married Maxine Kuntzman (1941), children: Joseph, Caetana. Died September 9, 1966, Sherman Oaks, California. Characterized by a big mouth, piercing eyes, a bald head, and a pigeon chest. Mostly a celluloid hood, but could interpret other roles, often in ethnic disguise: *North West Mounted Police* (halfbreed), *Road to Morocco* (Arab vendor), *The Crystal Ball* (Russian bad guy), *The Falcon in Mexico* (Mexican), etc. Also played the drunken club goer who tormented *Mighty Joe Young*.

Nestor Paiva to Broderick Crawford in *Broadway:* "No, Steve, we don't fight. She's a' too skinny to fight about."

Films

Prison Train (Malcolm-Browne, 1938)
Ride a Crooked Mile (Par, 1938)
The Magnificent Fraud (Par, 1939)
Midnight (Par, 1939)
Another Thin Man (MGM, 1939)
Beau Geste (Par, 39)
Bachelor Mother (RKO, 1939)
Union Pacific (Par, 1939)
The Sea Hawk (WB, 1940)
Phantom Raiders (MGM, 1940)
The Devil's Pipeline (Univ, 1940)
The Primrose Path (RKO, 1940)
North West Mounted Police (Par, 1940)
Arise, My Love (Par, 1940)
The Marines Fly High (RKO, 1940)
Dark Streets of Cairo (Univ, 1940)
Hold Back the Dawn (Par, 1941)
Tall, Dark and Handsome (20th, 1941)
Hold That Ghost (Univ, 1941)
Meet Boston Blackie (Col, 1941)
Pot o' Gold (UA, 1941)

The Kid fom Kansas (Univ, 1941)
Johnny Eager (MGM, 1941)
Reap the Wild Wind (Par, 1942)
The Road to Morocco (Par, 1942)
Fly-by-Night (Par, 1942)
Flying Tigers (Rep, 1942)
Jail House Blues (Univ, 1942)
The Girl from Alaska (Rep, 1942)
Broadway (Univ, 1942)
The Hard Way (WB, 1942)
Timber (Univ, 1942)
Pittsburgh (Univ, 1942)
The Crystal Ball (UA, 1943)
Rhythm of the Islands (Univ, 1943)
The Dancing Masters (20th, 1943)
The Desert Song (WB, 1943)
The Song of Bernadette (20th, 1943)
Tornado (Par, 1943)
Kismet [TV title: Oriental Dreams] (MGM, 1944)
The Purple Heart (20th, 1944)

Tampico (20th, 1944)
The Falcon in Mexico (RKO, 1944)
A Medal for Benny (Par, 1945)
The Southerner (UA, 1945)
Salome, Where She Danced (Univ, 1945)
Nob Hill (20th, 1945)
A Thousand and One Nights (Col, 1945)
Along the Navajo Trail (Rep, 1945)
Fear (Mon, 1945)
Road to Utopia (Par, 1945)
Humoresque (WB, 1946)
Sensation Hunters (Mon, 1946)
The Well-Groomed Bride (Par, 1946)
The Last Crooked Mile (Rep, 1946)
Badman's Territory (RKO, 1946)
The Lone Wolf in Mexico (Col, 1947)
Ramrod (UA, 1947)
Carnival in Costa Rica (20th, 1947)
Shoot to Kill (Screen Guild, 1947)
A Likely Story (RKO, 1947)
Robin Hood of Monterey (Mon, 1947)

Road to Rio (Par, 1947)
Mr. Reckless (Par, 1948)
Adventures of Casanova (EL, 1948)
Angels' Alley (Mon, 1948)
Joan of Arc (RKO, 1948)
Mr. Blandings Builds His Dream House (RKO, 1948)
The Paleface (Par, 1948)
Bride of Vengeance (Par, 1949)
Alias Nick Beal (Par, 1949)
Mighty Joe Young (RKO, 1949)
Follow Me Quietly (RKO, 1949)
Oh, You Beautiful Doll (20th, 1949)
The Inspector General (WB, 1949)
Young Man with a Horn (WB, 1950)
Flame of Stamboul (Col, 1951)
The Great Caruso (MGM, 1951)
Jim Thorpe—All-American (WB, 1951)
A Millionaire for Christy (20th, 1951)
The Lady Pays Off (Univ, 1951)
Double Dynamite (RKO, 1951)
On Dangerous Ground (RKO, 1951)
Phone Call from a Stranger (20th, 1952)
Five Fingers (20th, 1952)

Mara Maru (WB, 1952)
The Fabulous Senorita (Rep, 1952)
South Pacific Trail (Rep, 1952)
Call Me Madam (20th, 1953)
The Bandits of Corsica (UA, 1953)
Prisoners of the Casbah (Col, 1953)
The Killer Ape (Col, 1953)
Jivaro (Par, 1954)
Casanova's Big Night (Par, 1954)
Thunder Pass (Lip, 1954)
Four Guns to the Border (Univ, 1954)
The Creature from the Black Lagoon (Univ, 1954)
The Desperado (AA, 1954)
New York Confidential (WB, 1955)
Revenge of the Creature (Univ, 1955)
Tarantula (Univ, 1955)
Hell on Frisco Bay (WB, 1955)
Comanche (UA, 1956)
The Mole People (Univ, 1956)
Ride the High Iron (Col, 1956)
Scandal, Inc. (Rep, 1956)
Guns of Fort Petticoat (Col, 1957)
Les Girls (MGM, 1957)

10,000 Bedrooms (MGM, 1957)
The Deep Six (WB, 1958)
The Lady Takes a Flyer (Univ, 1958)
Outcasts of the City (Rep, 1958)
The Left-Handed Gun (WB, 1958)
The Case Against Brooklyn (Col, 1958)
Pier 5—Havana (UA, 1959)
Vice Raid (UA, 1959)
The Purple Gang (AA 60)
Can-Can (20th, 1960)
Frontier Uprising (UA, 1961)
The Three Stooges in Orbit (Col, 1962)
Girls! Girls! Girls! (Par, 1962)
The Four Horsemen of the Apocalypse (MGM, 1962)
The Wild Westerners (Col, 1962)
California (AIP, 1963)
Madman of Mandoras (Crown International, 1964)
Ballad of a Gunfighter (Parade, 1964)
Jesse James Meets Frankenstein's Daughter (Emb, 1966)
The Spirit Is Willing (Par, 1967)

EUGENE PALLETTE

Larry Steers, Henry Fonda, and Eugene Pallette in The Lady Eve *(1941).*

Born July 8, 1899, Winfield, Kansas. Married Marjorie Cagnacci (1932). Died September 3, 1954, Los Angeles, California. Respectably trim in his silent film days. In D. W. Griffith's *The Birth of a Nation* (Union soldier) and *Intolerance* (Prosper Latour); had some leading roles in the 1910s. By the 1920s had moved on to character parts: Aramis in Douglas Fairbanks' *The Three Musketeers;* played in several Westerns. By the talkies his girth had expanded tremendously. Proved his capable worth as gruff-voiced Sergeant Heath of the *Philo Vance* detective series at Paramount and Warner Bros.: *The Canary Murder Case,* etc. Adept at screwball comedy: *My Man Godfrey, Topper, There Goes My Heart.* Also shone in costume adventures: the very portly Friar Tuck in Errol Flynn's *The Adventures of Robin Hood,* Father Felipe in Tyrone Power's *The Mark of Zorro,* etc. Frequently the wealthy character in Deanna Durbin features: *One Hundred Men and a Girl, First Love,* etc.

> **Eugene Pallette** to Alice Brady in *My Man Godfrey:* "I've been a pretty patient man—but when people start riding horses up the front steps and parking them in the library— that's going a little bit too far!"

Films

The Birth of a Nation (Epoch, 1915)
Intolerance (Wark Producing Corp., 1916)
Going Straight (Tri, 1916)
Hell to Pay Austin (Tri, 1916)
Sunshine Dad (Tri, 1916)
Gretchen the Greenhorn (Tri, 1916)
His Guardian Angel (Tri, 1916)
Children in His House (Tri, 1916)
Whispering Smith (PDC, 1916)
Lonesome Chap (Par, 1917)
The Bond Between (Par, 1917)
The Purple Scar (Univ, 1917)

The Marcellini Millions (Par, 1917)
The Winning of Sally Temple (Par, 1917)
World Apart (Par, 1917)
The Victim (Par, 1917)
Each to His Kind (Par, 1917)
Heir of the Ages (Par, 1917)
A Man's Man (J. W. Kerrigan Films, 1917)
Ghost House (Par, 1917)
Madame Who (Peralta, 1918)
No Man's Land (M, 1918)
His Robe of Honor (Peralta-Hodkinson, 1918)

The Turn of a Card (Hodkinson, 1918)
Tarzan of the Apes (FN, 1918)
Breakers Ahead (M, 1918)
Vivette (Par, 1918)
The Amateur Adventuress (M, 1919)
Words and Music By (Fox, 1919)
Be a Little Sport (Fox, 1919)
Fair and Warmer (M, 1919)
Alias Jimmy Valentine (M, 1920)
Twin Beds (Associated FN, 1920)
Terror Island (Par, 1920)
Parlor, Bedroom and Bath (M, 1920)
Fine Feathers (M, 1921)

The Three Musketeers (UA, 1921)
Two Kinds of Women (FBO, 1922)
Without Compromise (Fox, 1922)
Hell's Hole (Fox, 1923)
A Man's Man (FBO, 1923)
The Ten Commandments (Par, 1923)
North of Hudson Bay (Fox, 1923)
To the Last Man (Par, 1923)
The Galloping Fish (FN, 1924)
The Cyclone Rider (Fox, 1924)
Wandering Husbands (Hodkinson, 1924)
The Wolf Man (Fox, 1924)
Ranger of the Big Pines (Vit, 1925)
Wild Horse Mesa (Par, 1925)
The Light of Western Stars (Par, 1925)
Without Mercy (PDC, 1925)
Desert Valley (Fox, 1926)
The Fighting Edge (WB, 1926)
Mantrap (Par, 1926)
Yankee Senor (Fox, 1926)
Rocking Moon (PDC, 1926)
Whispering Canyon (Sterling, 1926)
Whispering Smith (PDC, 1926)
Chicago (Pathé, 1927)
Moulders of Men (FBO, 1927)
The Good-Bye Kiss (FN, 1928)
His Private Life (Par, 1928)
Out of the Ruins (FN, 1928)
Lights of New York (WB, 1928)
The Red Mark (Pathé, 1928)
The Canary Murder Case (Par, 1929)
The Dummy (Par, 1929)
The Greene Murder Case (Par, 1929)
The Studio Murder Mystery (Par, 1929)
The Love Parade (Par, 1929)
Pointed Heels (Par, 1929)
The Virginian (Par, 1929)
The Kibitzer (Par, 1929)
The Benson Murder Case (Par, 1930)
Follow Through (Par, 1930)
The Sea God (Par, 1930)
Slightly Scarlet (Par, 1930)
Let's Go Native (Par, 1930)
The Border Legion (Par, 1930)
Men Are Like That (Par, 1930)
Sea Legs (Par, 1930)

Playboy of Paris (Par, 1930)
The Santa Fe Trail (Par, 1930)
Paramount on Parade (Par, 1930)
Fighting Caravans (Par, 1931)
It Pays to Advertise (Par, 1931)
Gun Smoke (Par, 1931)
Dude Ranch (Par, 1931)
The Adventures of Huckleberry Finn (Par, 1931)
Girls About Town (Par, 1931)
Shanghai Express (Par, 1932)
Dancers in the Dark (Par, 1932)
Tom Brown of Culver (Univ, 1932)
Thunder Below (Par, 1932)
Strangers of the Evening (Tif, 1932)
The Night Mayor (Col, 1932)
Wild Girl (Fox, 1932)
The Half-Naked Truth (RKO, 1932)
Made on Broadway (MGM, 1933)
Hell Below (MGM, 1933)
Storm at Daybreak (MGM, 1933)
Shanghai Madness (Par, 1933)
Mr. Skitch (Fox, 1933)
The Kennel Murder Case (WB, 1933)
From Headquarters (FN, 1933)
Caravan (Fox, 1934)
Cross Country Cruise (Univ, 1934)
Friends of Mr. Sweeney (WB, 1934)
I've Got Your Number (FN, 1934)
The Dragon Murder Case (WB, 1934)
Strictly Dynamite (RKO, 1934)
One Exciting Adventure (Univ, 1934)
Bordertown (WB, 1935)
All the King's Horses (Par, 1935)
Baby Face Harrington (MGM, 1935)
Black Sheep (Fox, 1935)
Steamboat 'Round the Bend (Fox, 1935)
The Ghost Goes West (UA, 1936)
Dishonour Bright (Br, 1936)
The Golden Arrow (WB, 1936)
Easy to Take (Par, 1936)
My Man Godfrey (Univ, 1936)
The Luckiest Girl in the World (Univ, 1936)
Stowaway (20th, 1936)
The Crime Nobody Saw (Par, 1937)
Clarence (Par, 1937)

Topper (MGM, 1937)
Song of the City (MGM, 1937)
She Had to Eat (20th, 1937)
One Hundred Men and a Girl (Univ, 1937)
The Adventures of Robin Hood (WB, 1938)
There Goes My Heart (UA, 1938)
Wife, Husband and Friend (20th, 1939)
Mr. Smith Goes to Washington (Col, 1939)
First Love (Univ, 1939)
Young Tom Edison (MGM, 1940)
It's a Date (Univ, 1940)
Sandy Is a Lady (Univ, 1940)
A Little Bit of Heaven (Univ, 1940)
He Stayed for Breakfast (Col, 1940)
The Mark of Zorro (20th, 1940)
Ride, Kelly, Ride (20th, 1941)
The Lady Eve (Par, 1941)
Unfinished Business (Univ, 1941)
Appointment for Love (Univ, 1941)
World Premiere (Par, 1941)
Swamp Water (20th, 1941)
The Bride Came C.O.D. (WB, 1941)
The Male Animal (WB, 1942)
The Big Street (RKO, 1942)
Almost Married (Univ, 1942)
Lady in a Jam (Univ, 1942)
Are Husbands Necessary? (Par, 1942)
The Forest Rangers (Par, 1942)
Tales of Manhattan (20th, 1942)
Silver Queen (UA, 1942)
Slightly Dangerous (MGM, 1943)
It Ain't Hay (Univ, 1943)
Heaven Can Wait (20th, 1943)
The Gang's All Here (20th, 1943)
The Kansan (UA, 1943)
Pin-Up Girl (20th, 1944)
Heavenly Days (RKO, 1944)
Sensations of 1945 (UA, 1944)
Step Lively (RKO, 1944)
In the Meantime, Darling (20th, 1944)
Lake Placid Serenade (Rep, 1945)
The Cheaters (Rep, 1945)
In Old Sacramento (Rep, 1946)
Suspense (Mon, 1946)
Silver River (WB, 1948)

FRANKLIN PANGBORN

Beatrice Lillie, Laura Hope Crews, and Franklin Pangborn in Doctor Rhythm *(1938).*

Born January 23, 1893, Newark, New Jersey. Died July 20, 1958, Santa Monica, California. The epitome of the prissy a-r-t-i-s-t, who became typecast after his appearance as the frantic score-keeper in Carole Lombard's *My Man Godfrey*. Usually won the part if the role called for a haughty hotel clerk, floorwalker, dress designer, or storekeeper. A whiz at creatively using a pince-nez. Final film: *Oh, Men! Oh, Women!* (bartender).

Franklin Pangborn to Ginger Rogers et al. in *Flying Down to Rio:* "I will dismiss, discharge, and disqualify any employee who gets familiar with the guests!"

Films

Exit Smiling (MGM, 1926)
The Cradle Snatchers (Fox, 1927)
Fingerprints (WB, 1927)
Getting Gertie's Garter (PDC, 1927)
The Girl in the Pullman (Pathé, 1927)
My Friend from India (Pathé, 1927)
The Night Bride (PDC, 1927)
The Rejuvenation of Aunt Mary (PDC, 1927)
Blonde for a Night (Pathé, 1928)
The Rush Hour (Pathé, 1928)
On Trial (WB, 1928)
The Sap (WB, 1929)
Lady of the Pavements (UA, 1929)
A Lady Surrenders (Univ, 1930)
Cheer Up and Smile (Fox, 1930)
Not So Dumb (MGM, 1930)
Her Man (Pathé, 1931)
A Woman of Experience (Pathé, 1931)
International House (Par, 1933)

Design for Living (Par, 1933)
Professional Sweetheart (RKO, 1933)
Headline Shooters (RKO, 1933)
The Important Witness (Tower, 1933)
Only Yesterday (Univ, 1933)
Flying Down to Rio (RKO, 1933)
Manhattan Love Song (Mon, 1934)
Young and Beautiful (Mascot, 1934)
Strictly Dynamite (RKO, 1934)
Unknown Blonde (Majestic, 1934)
Many Happy Returns (Par, 1934)
King Kelly of the U.S.A. (Mon, 1934)
Stand Up and Cheer (Fox, 1934)
Cockeyed Cavaliers (RKO, 1934)
Imitation of Life (Univ, 1934)
College Rhythm (Par, 1934)
That's Gratitude (Col, 1934)
Headline Woman (Mascot, 1935)
Flirtation (FD, 1935)
$1,000 a Minute (Rep, 1935)

Tomorrow's Youth (Mon, 1935)
Eight Bells (Col, 1935)
She Couldn't Take It (Col, 1935)
Mr. Deeds Goes to Town (Col, 1936)
Give Us This Night (Par, 1936)
Three Smart Girls (Univ, 1936)
The Luckiest Girl in the World (Univ, 1936)
Don't Gamble with Love (Col, 1936)
My Man Godfrey (Univ, 1936)
To Mary—With Love (20th, 1936)
The Mandarin Mystery (Rep, 1936)
Hats Off (GN, 1936)
Tango (Chesterfield-Invincible, 1936)
Doughnuts and Society (Mascot, 1936)
Step Lively, Jeeves (20th, 1937)
I'll Take Romance (Col, 1937)
They Wanted to Marry (RKO, 1937)
The Lady Escapes (20th, 1937)
She Had to Eat (20th, 1937)

Swing High, Swing Low (Par, 1937)
It Happened in Hollywood (Col, 1937)
Danger! Love at Work (20th, 1937)
High Hat (Imperial, 1937)
Turn Off the Moon (Par, 1937)
Easy Living (Par, 1937)
Thrill of a Lifetime (Par, 1937)
When Love Is Young (Univ, 1937)
A Star Is Born (UA, 1937)
Dangerous Number (MGM, 1937)
She's Dangerous (Univ, 1937)
Hotel Haywire (Par, 1937)
Dangerous Holiday (Rep, 1937)
All over Town (Rep, 1937)
The Life of the Party (RKO, 1937)
Stage Door (RKO, 1937)
Living on Love (RKO, 1937)
Vivacious Lady (RKO, 1938)
It's All Yours (Col, 1938)
She Married an Artist (Co, 1938)
Rebecca of Sunnybrook Farm (20th, 1938)
Three Blind Mice (20th, 1938)
Always Goodbye (20th, 1938)
Joy of Living (RKO, 1938)
Just Around the Corner (20th, 1938)
Carefree (RKO, 1938)
Bluebeard's Eighth Wife (Par, 1938)
Dr. Rhythm (Par, 1938)
Love on Toast (Par, 1938)
Mad About Music (Univ, 1938)
Meet the Mayor (Times Films, 1938) [made in 1932]

Topper Takes a Trip (UA, 1938)
Four's a Crowd (WB, 1938)
The Girl Downstairs (MGM, 1938)
Broadway Serenade (MGM, 1939)
Fifth Avenue Girl (RKO, 1939)
Turnabout (UA, 1940)
The Villain Still Pursued Her (RKO, 1940)
Public Deb No. 1 (20th, 1940)
Christmas in July (Par, 1940)
The Hit Parade of 1941 (Rep, 1940)
The Bank Dick (Univ, 1940)
Spring Parade (Univ, 1940)
Where Did You Get That Girl? (Univ, 1941)
A Girl, a Guy and a Gob (RKO, 1941)
Flame of New Orleans (Univ, 1941)
Sullivan's Travels (Par, 1941)
Bachelor Daddy (Univ, 1941)
Obliging Young Lady (RKO, 1941)
Tillie the Toiler (Col, 1941)
Never Give a Sucker an Even Break (Univ, 1941)
Week-End for Three (RKO, 1941)
Mr. District Attorney in the Carter Case (Rep, 1941)
George Washington Slept Here (WB, 1942)
Strictly in the Groove (Univ, 1942)
Moonlight Masquerade (Rep, 1942)
The Palm Beach Story (Par, 1942)
Now, Voyager (WB, 1942)
What's Cookin'? (Univ, 1942)

Call Out the Marines (RKO, 1942)
Two Weeks to Live (RKO, 1943)
Stage Door Canteen (UA, 1943)
Reveille with Beverly (Col, 1943)
Holy Matrimony (20th, 1943)
Crazy House (Univ, 1943)
Honeymoon Lodge (Univ, 1943)
His Butler's Sister (Univ, 1943)
Hail the Conquering Hero (Par, 1944)
My Best Gal (Rep, 1944)
The Great Moment (Par, 1944)
The Reckless Age (Univ, 1944)
Allergic to Love (Univ, 1944)
The Horn Blows at Midnight (WB, 1945)
Hollywood and Vine (PRC, 1945)
See My Lawyer (Univ, 1945)
You Came Along (Par, 1945)
Tell It To a Star (Rep, 1945)
Lover Come Back (Univ, 1946)
Two Guys from Milwaukee (WB, 1946)
Calendar Girl (Rep, 1947)
I'll Be Yours (Univ, 1947)
Mad Wednesday [a.k.a. *The Sin of Harold Diddlebock*] (UA, 1947)
Romance on the High Seas (WB, 1948)
My Dream Is Yours (WB, 1949)
Down Memory Lane (EL, 1949)
Her Wonderful Lie (Col, 1950)
The Story of Mankind (WB, 1957)
Oh, Men! Oh, Women! (20th, 1957)

LEE PATRICK

With Leo Carrillo in Larceny with Music *(1943).*

Born November 22, 1906, New York City, New York. Married Thomas Wood (1937). Stage work sharpened her skills as general utility player. Quite expert at life-toughened blondes. **Remembered as Effie Perine, Humphrey Bogart's aggressive secretary in** *The Maltese Falcon;* Maggie Binderhof, Bruce Bennett's consoler in *Mildred Pierce;* a mental-asylum inmate in *The Snake Pit;* and Mrs. Upson to Rosalind Russell's *Auntie Mame.* Returned to films to play Effie Perine in *The Black Bird*, the weak comedy follow-up to *The Maltese Falcon.* TV series: "Topper" (as Henrietta Topper) and "Mr. Adams and Eve."

> **Lee Patrick** to Humphrey Bogart in *The Maltese Falcon:* "The part about the bird is thrilling."

Films

Strange Cargo (Pathé, 1929)
Border Cafe (RKO, 1937)
Music for Madame (RKO, 1937)
Danger Patrol (RKO, 1937)
Crashing Hollywood (RKO, 1938)
Night Spot (RKO, 1938)
Maid's Night Out (RKO, 1938)
Condemned Women (RKO, 1938)
Law of the Underworld (RKO, 1938)
The Sisters (WB, 1938)
Fisherman's Wharf (RKO, 1939)
Invisible Stripes (WB, 1940)
Strange Cargo (MGM, 1940)
Saturday's Children (WB, 1940)
City for Conquest (WB, 1940)
Ladies Must Live (WB, 1940)
Money and the Woman (WB, 1940)

South of Suez (WB, 1940)
Father Is a Prince (WB, 1940)
The Maltese Falcon (WB, 1941)
Kisses for Breakfast (WB, 1941)
Footsteps in the Dark (WB, 1941)
Million Dollar Baby (WB, 1941)
Honeymoon for Three (WB, 1941)
The Nurse's Secret (WB, 1941)
The Smiling Ghost (WB, 1941)
Dangerously They Live (WB, 1941)
Now, Voyager (WB, 1942)
George Washington Slept Here (WB, 1942)
In This Our Life (WB, 1942)
Somewhere I'll Find You (MGM, 1942)
A Night to Remember (Col, 1943)
Jitterbugs (20th, 1943)
Nobody's Darling (Rep, 1943)

Larceny with Music (Univ, 1943)
Mrs. Parkington (MGM, 1944)
Faces in the Fog (Rep, 1944)
Gambler's Choice (Par, 1944)
Moon over Las Vegas (Univ, 1944)
Mildred Pierce (WB, 1945)
Over 21 (Col, 1945)
Keep Your Powder Dry (MGM, 1945)
See My Lawyer (Univ, 1945)
Strange Journey (20th, 1946)
Wake Up and Dream (20th, 1946)
The Walls Came Tumbling Down (Col, 1946)
Mother Wore Tights (20th, 1947)
Inner Sanctum (Film Classics, 1948)
Singing Spurs (Col, 1948)
The Snake Pit (20th, 1948)

The Doolins of Oklahoma (Col, 1949)
Caged (WB, 1950)
The Lawless (Par, 1950)
The Fuller Brush Girl (Col, 1950)
Tomorrow Is Another Day (WB, 1951)
Take Me to Town (Univ, 1953)
There's No Business Like Show Business
   (20th, 1954)

Vertigo (Par, 1958)
Auntie Mame (WB, 1958)
Pillow Talk (Univ, 1959)
A Visit to a Small Planet (Par, 1960)
Goodbye Again (UA, 1961)
Summer and Smoke (Par, 1961)
A Girl Named Tamiko (Par, 1962)
Wives and Lovers (Par, 1963)

The Seven Faces of Dr. Lao (MGM, 1964)
The New Interns (Col, 1964)
The Black Bird (Col, 1975)

ELIZABETH PATTERSON

With Marjorie Rambeau in Tobacco Road *(1941).*

Born November 22, 1874, Savannah, Tennessee. Died January 31, 1966, Los Angeles, California. Thin, fragile interpreter of maiden aunts. Occasionally left her spotless kitchens and immaculate gingham-dress-and-apron outfits for roles like Ada Lester (*Tobacco Road*). In the whodunit *Who Killed Aunt Maggie?* played the victim of the title. TV series: "I Love Lucy" (as Mrs. Trumbul, the neighbor).

Elizabeth Patterson to Lynne Overman in *Men Without Names: Frier-less cookers!* Seems like it's goin' against nature, somehow."

Films

The Boy Friend (MGM, 1926)
The Return of Peter Grimm (Fox, 1926)
Timothy's Quest (Gotham, 1929)
Words and Music (Fox, 1929)
South Sea Rose (Fox, 1929)

The Lone Star Ranger (Fox, 1930)
Harmony at Home (Fox, 1930)
The Big Party (Fox, 1930)
The Cat Creeps (Univ, 1930)
Tarnished Lady (Par, 1931)

The Smiling Lieutenant (Par, 1931)
Daddy Long Legs (Fox, 1931)
Penrod and Sam (WB, 1931)
Heaven on Earth (Univ, 1931)
Husband's Holiday (Par, 1931)

So Big (WB, 1932)
The Expert (WB, 1932)
Play Girl (WB, 1932)
Miss Pinkerton (WB, 1932)
Two Against the World (FN, 1932)
Love Me Tonight (Par, 1932)
New Morals for Old (MGM, 1932)
Guilty as Hell (Par, 1932)
Breach of Promise (WW, 1932)
The Conquerors (RKO, 1932)
A Bill of Divorcement (RKO, 1932)
No Man of Her Own (Par, 1932)
Life Begins (WB, 1932)
They Call It Sin (WB, 1932)
Doctor Bull (Fox, 1933)
They Just Had to Get Married (Univ, 1933)
Golden Harvest (Par, 1933)
Dinner at Eight (MGM, 1933)
The Story of Temple Drake (Par, 1933)
The Infernal Machine (Fox, 1933)
Hold Your Man (MGM, 1933)
The Secret of the Blue Room (Univ, 1933)
Hide-Out (MGM, 1934)
Chasing Yesterday (RKO, 1935)
Men Without Names (Par, 1935)
So Red the Rose (Par, 1935)
Mississippi (Par, 1935)
Timothy's Quest (Par, 1936)
Her Master's Voice (Par, 1936)
The Return of Sophie Lang (Par, 1936)

Three Cheers for Love (Par, 1936)
Go West, Young Man (Par, 1936)
Small Town Girl (MGM, 1936)
Old Hutch (MGM, 1936)
A Night of Mystery (Par, 1937)
High, Wide and Handsome (Par, 1937)
Hold 'em Navy (Par, 1937)
Night Club Scandal (Par, 1937)
Scandal Street (Par, 1938)
Bulldog Drummond's Peril (Par, 1938)
Bluebeard's Eighth Wife (Par, 1938)
The Adventures of Tom Sawyer (UA, 1938)
Sing, You Sinners (Par, 1938)
Sons of the Legion (Par, 1938)
The Story of Alexander Graham Bell (20th, 1939)
Bulldog Drummond's Bride (Par, 1939)
Our Leading Citizen (Par, 1939)
Bulldog Drummond's Secret Police (Par, 1939)
The Cat and the Canary (Par, 1939)
Bad Little Angel (MGM, 1939)
Anne of Windy Poplars (RKO, 1940)
Remember the Night (Par, 1940)
Earthbound (20th, 1940)
Who Killed Aunt Maggie? (Rep, 1940)
Michael Shayne, Private Detective (20th, 1940)
Adventure in Diamonds (Par, 1940)
Kiss the Boys Goodbye (Par, 1941)

Tobacco Road (20th, 1941)
Belle Starr (20th, 1941)
The Vanishing Virginian (MGM, 1941)
Almost Married (Univ, 1942)
Beyond the Blue Horizon (Par, 1942)
Her Cardboard Lover (MGM, 1942)
My Sister Eileen (Col, 1942)
I Married a Witch (UA, 1942)
Lucky Legs (Col, 1942)
The Sky's the Limit (RKO, 1943)
Follow the Boys (Univ, 1944)
Hail the Conquering Hero (Par, 1944)
Together Again (Col, 1944)
Colonel Effingham's Raid (20th, 1945)
Lady on a Train (Univ, 1945)
The Secret Heart (MGM, 1946)
I've Always Loved You (Rep, 1946)
The Shocking Miss Pilgrim (20th, 1947)
Out of the Blue (EL, 1947)
Welcome Stranger (Par, 1947)
Miss Tatlock's Millions (Par, 1948)
Little Women (MGM, 1949)
Intruder in the Dust (MGM, 1949)
Song of Surrender (Par, 1949)
Bright Leaf (WB, 1950)
Katie Did It (Univ, 1951)
The Washington Story (MGM, 1952)
Las Vegas Shakedown (AA, 1955)
Pal Joey (Col, 1957)
The Oregon Trail (20th, 1959)
Tall Story (WB, 1960)

NAT PENDLETON

With Pert Kelton in Sing and Like It *(1934).*

Born August 9, 1895, Davenport, Iowa. Married 1) _____ ; widowed; 2) _____ ; divorced; 3) Barbara _____ . Died October 11, 1967, San Diego, California. Olympic champion with a college degree; turned to films after a wrestling career. Generally seen as the dumb mug. Was Sandow the Strong Man to William Powell's *The Great Ziegfeld* and was Joe Wayman, the ambulance driver in several *Dr. Kildare* features. Matched "wits" with Abbott and Costello in *Buck Privates* and *Buck Privates Come Home* and was parrying clues as Lieutenant Guild with William Powell in *The Thin Man* and *Another Thin Man*. Wrote the story to *Deception* (1933), in which he appeared.

Nat Pendleton to Humphrey Bogart in *Swing Your Lady:*
"Aw gee, talk United States, will ya."

Films

The Hoosier Schoolmaster (PDC, 1924)
Let's Get Married (Par, 1926)
The Laughing Lady (Par, 1929)
The Big Pond (Par, 1930)
Last of the Duanes (Fox, 1930)
The Sea Wolf (Fox, 1930)
Liliom (Fox, 1930)
Fair Warning (Fox, 1931)
The Ruling Voice (FN, 1931)
Mr. Lemon of Orange (Fox, 1931)
The Star Witness (WB, 1931)
Blonde Crazy (WB, 1931)
The Spirit of Notre Dame (Univ, 1931)
The Seas Beneath (Fox, 1931)
Terror by Night [a.k.a. The Secret Witness]
   (Famous Attractions, 1931)
Play Girl (WB, 1932)
Taxi! (WB, 1932)
Attorney for the Defense (Col, 1932)
Hell Fire Austin (Tif, 1932)
Exposure (Capital, 1932)
You Said a Mouthful (FN, 1932)

Beast of the City (MGM, 1932)
State's Attorney (RKO, 1932)
By Whose Hand? (Col, 1932)
Night Club Lady (Col, 1932)
Horse Feathers (Par, 1932)
Manhattan Parade (WB, 1932)
The Sign of the Cross (Par, 1932)
Deception (Col, 1933)
Baby Face (WB, 1933)
Parachute Jumper (WB, 1933)
The White Sister (MGM, 1933)
Whistling in the Dark (MGM, 1933)
College Coach (WB, 1933)
Goldie Gets Along (RKO, 1933)
Lady for a Day (Col, 1933)
Penthouse (MGM, 1933)
The Chief (MGM, 1933)
I'm No Angel (Par, 1933)
Fugitive Lovers (MGM, 1934)
Lazy River (MGM, 1934)
Manhattan Melodrama (MGM, 1934)
Death on the Diamond (MGM, 1934)

The Thin Man (MGM, 1934)
The Gay Bride (MGM, 1934)
Sing and Like It (RKO, 1934)
The Defense Rests (Col, 1934)
The Cat's Paw (Fox, 1934)
The Girl from Missouri (MGM, 1934)
Straight Is the Way (MGM, 1934)
Times Square Lady (MGM, 1935)
Baby Face Harrington (MGM, 1935)
Reckless (MGM, 1935)
Murder in the Fleet (MGM, 1935)
Calm Yourself (MGM, 1935)
Here Comes the Band (MGM, 1935)
It's in the Air (MGM, 1935)
The Garden Murder Case (MGM, 1936)
The Great Ziegfeld (MGM, 1936)
Sworn Enemy (MGM, 1936)
Trapped by Television (Col, 1936)
Two in a Crowd (Univ, 1936)
The Luckiest Girl in the World (Univ, 1936)
Sing Me a Love Song (FN, 1936)

Under Cover of Night (MGM, 1937)
Song of the City (MGM, 1937)
Gangway (Br, 1937)
Life Begins in College (20th, 1937)
Swing Your Lady (WB, 1938)
Arsene Lupin Returns (MGM, 1938)
Fast Company (MGM, 1938)
Shopworn Angel (MGM, 1938)
The Chaser (MGM, 1938)
The Crowd Roars (MGM, 1938)
Meet the Mayor (Times Pictures, 1938)
  [made in 1932]
Young Dr. Kildare (MGM, 1938)
Burn 'em Up O'Connor (MGM, 1939)
Calling Dr. Kildare (MGM, 1939)

It's a Wonderful World (MGM, 1939)
6,000 Enemies (MGM, 1939)
On Borrowed Time (MGM, 1939)
At the Circus (MGM, 1939)
Another Thin Man (MGM, 1939)
The Secret of Dr. Kildare (MGM, 1939)
Northwest Passage (MGM, 1940)
The Ghost Comes Home (MGM, 1940)
Dr. Kildare's Strange Case (MGM, 1940)
Phantom Raiders (MGM, 1940)
The Golden Fleecing (MGM, 1940)
Dr. Kildare's Crisis (MGM, 1940)
Dr. Kildare Goes Home (MGM, 1940)
Flight Command (MGM, 1940)
Buck Privates (Univ, 1941)

Dr. Kildare's Wedding Day (MGM, 1941)
Top Sergeant Mulligan (Mon, 1941)
The Mad Doctor of Market Street (Univ, 1941)
Jail House Blues (Univ, 1942)
Calling Dr. Gillespie (MGM, 1942)
Dr. Gillespie's New Assistant (MGM, 1942)
Dr. Gillespie's Criminal Case (MGM, 1943)
Swing Fever (MGM, 1943)
Death Valley (Screen Guild, 1946)
Buck Privates Come Home (Univ, 1947)
Scared to Death (Screen Guild, 1947)

IRVING PICHEL

Cesar Romero and Irving Pichel in Armored Car *(1937).*

Born June 24, 1891, Pittsburgh, Pennsylvania. Died July 13, 1954, Hollywood, California. Efficient character performer: Yomadori (*Madame Butterfly*), Apollodorus (*Cleopatra*), Carbajal (*Juarez*). Also directed features: *The Most Dangerous Game* (with Ernest B. Schoedsack), *Hudson's Bay* (1941), *A Medal for Benny* (1945), *Quicksand* (1950). Sometimes acted in films he directed: Randolph Scott's *She, The Sheik Steps Out, Santa Fe,* and *Martin Luther* (which he also scripted).

Irving Pichel to Tallulah Bankhead in *The Cheat:* "If you're trying to appeal to my better nature, it's hopeless . . . because I haven't any."

418

Films

The Right to Love (Par, 1930)
An American Tragedy (Par, 1931)
Murder by the Clock (Par, 1931)
The Road to Reno (Par, 1931)
The Cheat (Par, 1931)
The Miracle Man (Par, 1932)
Madame Butterfly (Par, 1932)
Two Kinds of Women (Par, 1932)
Forgotten Commandments (Par, 1932)
Westward Passage (RKO, 1932)
The Painted Woman (Fox, 1932)
Strange Justice (RKO, 1932)
Wild Girl (Fox, 1932)
The Mysterious Rider (Par, 1933)
The Woman Accused (Par, 1933)
The Billion Dollar Scandal (Par, 1933)
King of the Jungle (Par, 1933)
Oliver Twist (Mon, 1933)
The Story of Temple Drake (Par, 1933)

I'm No Angel (Par, 1933)
The Right to Romance (RKO, 1933)
Fog over Frisco (FN, 1934)
Such Women Are Dangerous (Fox, 1934)
British Agent (FN, 1934)
Return of the Terror (FN, 1934)
I Am a Thief (WB, 1934)
Silver Streak (RKO, 1934)
She Was a Lady (Fox, 1934)
Cleopatra (Par, 1934)
Special Agent (WB, 1935)
She (RKO, 1935)
Three Kids and a Queen (Univ, 1935)
Don't Gamble with Love (Col, 1936)
The House of a Thousand Candles (Rep, 1936)
Hearts in Bondage (Rep, 1936)
Dracula's Daughter (Univ, 1936)
Down to the Sea (Rep, 1936)

General Spanky (MGM, 1936)
Join the Marines (Rep, 1937)
Armored Car (Univ, 1937)
The Sheik Steps Out (Rep, 1937)
High, Wide and Handsome (Par, 1937)
Jezebel (WB, 1938)
There Goes My Heart (UA, 1938)
Gambling Ship (Univ, 1938)
Topper Takes a Trip (UA, 1938)
Juarez (WB, 1939)
Newsboys' Home (Univ, 1939)
Torture Ship (Producers Pictures, 1939)
Dick Tracy's G-Men (Rep serial, 1939)
Exile Express (GN, 1939)
Rio (Univ, 1939)
The Moon Is Down (20th, 1943)
Santa Fe (Col, 1951)
Martin Luther (UA, 1953)

SLIM PICKENS
(Louis Bert Lindley)

In Rancho DeLuxe *(1975).*

Born June 29, 1919, Kingsburg, California. Married Margaret ————, children: Darryle Ann, Thom, Margaret Lou. Scraggly Western film player who had a prior career as a leading rodeo clown. Noted for his twangy drawl. Rode the death-dealing rocket missile in *Dr. Strangelove* as Major T. J. "King" Kong. A folksy fixture of Westerns, but can be a mean s.o.b. in contemporary drama (*White Line Fever*). TV series: "The Outlaws" and "The Legend of Custer."

Slim Pickens to John Payne in *Santa Fe Passage:* "You know, it seems like I can smell an Injun behind every rock. I've got that old crawly feelin' again."

Films

Rocky Mountain (WB, 1950)
Old Oklahoma Plains (Rep, 1952)
South Pacific Trail (Rep, 1952)
The Last Musketeer (Rep, 1952)
Colorado Sundown (Rep, 1952)
Border Saddlemates (Rep, 1952)
The Story of Will Rogers (WB, 1952)
Thunderbirds (Rep, 1952)
Iron Mountain Trail (Rep, 1952)
Down Laredo Way (Rep, 1952)
Old Overland Trail (Rep, 1952)
Shadows of Tombstone (Rep, 1952)
The Sun Shines Bright (Rep, 1953)
Red River Shore (Rep, 1954)
The Boy from Oklahoma (WB, 1954)
The Outcast (Rep, 1954)
Santa Fe Passage (Rep, 1955)
The Last Command (Rep, 1955)
The Great Locomotive Chase (BV, 1956)
Stranger at My Door (Rep, 1956)
When Gangland Strikes (Rep, 1956)
Gun Brothers (UA, 1956)

Gunsight Ridge (UA, 1957)
The Sheepman (MGM, 1958)
Tonka (BV, 1958)
Escort West (UA, 1959)
The Chartroose Caboose (Univ, 1960)
One-Eyed Jacks (Par, 1961)
A Thunder of Drums (MGM, 1961)
Savage Sam (BV, 1963)
Dr. Strangelove (Col, 1964)
Major Dundee (Col, 1965)
In Harm's Way (Par, 1965)
Up from the Beach (20th, 1965)
The Glory Guys (UA, 1965)
Stagecoach (20th, 1966)
An Eye for an Eye (Emb, 1966)
The Flim Flam Man (20th, 1967)
Rough Night in Jericho (Univ, 1967)
Will Penny (Par, 1968)
Never a Dull Moment (BV, 1968)
Skidoo (Par, 1968)
The Battle of Cable Hogue (WB, 1970)
80 Steps to Jonah (WB, 1970)

The Deserter (Par, 1971)
The Cowboys (WB, 1972)
The Honkers (UA, 1972)
The Getaway (National General, 1972)
J.C. (Avco Emb, 1972)
Outdoor Rambling (Dick Chamberlin, 1972) [documentary]
Pat Garrett & Billy the Kid (MGM, 1973)
Ginger in the Morning (National Films, 1973)
Blazing Saddles (WB, 1974)
Bootleggers (Howco International, 1974)
The Legend of Earl Durand (Howco International, 1974)
Poor Pretty Eddie (Westamerica, 1974)
White Line Fever (Col, 1975)
Rancho DeLuxe (UA, 1975)
The Apple Dumpling Gang (BV, 1975)
Hawmps! (Mulberry Square, 1976)
Mr. Billion (20th, 1977)
The White Buffalo (UA, 1977)

PAUL PORCASI

As "Nick the Greek" in Broadway *(1929).*

Born 1880, Palermo, Italy. Died August 8, 1946, Hollywood, California. Abandoned singing career in Italy to become Hollywood performer, often as unyielding official or boss. On display in a range of poses: *Devil and the Deep* (Hassain), *Footlight Parade* (Appolinaris, the belligerent stage producer), *Flying Down to Rio* (the mayor), *Charlie Chan in Egypt* (Soueida), *Maytime* (Trentini, the composer), *Dr. Kildare's Strange Case* (Antonio), etc.

Paul Porcasi to Marian Marsh in *Svengali:* "All Paris is waiting at your feet!"

Films

The Fall of the Romanoffs (A. H. Woods, 1917)
Say It Again (Par, 1926)
Broadway (Univ, 1929)
Born Reckless (Fox, 1930)
Derelict (Par, 1930)
A Lady's Morals [a.k.a. Jenny Lind] (MGM, 1930)
Men of the North (MGM, 1930) [Italian language version]
Morocco (Par, 1930)
Murder on the Roof (Col, 1930)
The Three Sisters (Fox, 1930)
Svengali (WB, 1931)
Children of Dreams (WB, 1931)
Doctors' Wives (Fox, 1931)
Smart Money (WB, 1931)
Gentleman's Fate (MGM, 1931)
I Like Your Nerve (FN, 1931)

The Criminal Code (Col, 1931)
Party Husband (FN, 1931)
Good Bad Girl (Col, 1931)
Bought (WB, 1931)
The Man Who Played God (WB, 1932)
A Woman Commands (RKO, 1932)
The Passionate Plumber (MGM, 1932)
Under 18 (WB, 1932)
While Paris Sleeps (Fox, 1932)
Stowaway (Univ, 1932)
Painted Woman (Fox, 1932)
Devil and the Deep (Par, 1932)
Red-Haired Alibi (Tower, 1932)
A Parisian Romance (Allied, 1932)
Men Are Such Fools (RKO, 1932)
The Kid from Spain (UA, 1932)
Undercover Man (Par, 1932)
Cynara (UA, 1932)
Grand Slam (FN, 1933)

Terror Aboard (Par, 1933)
When Strangers Marry (Col, 1933)
Gigolettes of Paris (Equitable, 1933)
The Devil's Mate (Mon, 1933)
Footlight Parade (FN, 1933)
I Loved a Woman (FN, 1933)
Saturday's Millions (Univ, 1933)
He Couldn't Take It (Mon, 1933)
Flying Down to Rio (RKO, 1933)
The Great Flirtation (Par, 1934)
Wake Up and Dream (Univ, 1934)
British Agent (FN, 1934)
Enter Madame! (Par, 1934)
Gay Divorcee (RKO, 1934)
Imitation of Life (Univ, 1934)
Million Dollar Baby (Mon, 1935)
Rumba (Par, 1935)
Stars over Broadway (WB, 1935)
A Night at the Ritz (WB, 1935)

The Florentine Dagger (WB, 1935)
Charlie Chan in Egypt (Fox, 1935)
Under the Pampas Moon (Fox, 1935)
Waterfront Lady (Rep, 1935)
I Dream Too Much (RKO, 1935)
Hi, Gaucho (RKO, 1935)
The Lady Consents (RKO, 1936)
The Leathernecks Have Landed (Rep, 1936)
Muss 'em Up (RKO, 1936)
Down to the Sea (Rep, 1936)
Crash Donovan (Univ, 1936)
Two in a Crowd (Univ, 1936)
Maytime (MGM, 1937)
Seventh Heaven (20th, 1937)

Cafe Metropole (20th, 1937)
The Emperor's Candlesticks (MGM, 1937)
The Bride Wore Red (MGM, 1937)
Vacation from Love (MGM, 1938)
Crime School (WB, 1938)
Everything Happens at Night (20th, 1939)
Lady of the Tropics (MGM, 1939)
Dr. Kildare's Strange Case (MGM, 1940)
Torrid Zone (WB, 1940)
I Was an Adventuress (20th, 1940)
Argentine Nights (Univ, 1940)
The Border Legion (Rep, 1940)
Rags to Riches (Rep, 1941)
It Started with Eve (Univ, 1941)

Doctors Don't Tell (Rep, 1941)
Two in a Taxi (Col, 1941)
The Trial of Mary Dugan (MGM, 1941)
We Were Dancing (MGM, 1942)
The Road to Happiness (Mon, 1942)
Star Spangled Rhythm (Par, 1942)
Quiet Please—Murder (20th, 1942)
Hi Diddle Diddle (UA, 1943)
Hot Rhythm (Mon, 1944)
Hail the Conquering Hero (Par, 1944)
Nothing but Trouble (MGM, 1944)
Swing Hostess (PRC, 1944)
I'll Remember April (Univ, 1945)

TOM POWERS

Tom Powers, Isabel Randolph, Fred MacMurray, Claudette Colbert, and Cecil Kellaway in Practically Yours (1944).

Born July 7, 1890, Owensboro, Kentucky. Died November 9, 1955, Hollywood, California. Esteemed stage performer who had made films in the 1910s, including some Vitagraph shorts. Returned to the cinema in Double Indemnity (as Barbara Stanwyck's husband and victim). Usually in popular contemporary drama as slightly harassed but loyal soul. Played Metellus Cimber to Louis Calhern's Julius Caesar.

Tom Powers to Dick Powell in Station West: "I've been in this territory for a number of years. I think you'll find it a little rougher here than a suburb of Washington, D.C."

422

Films

Be Sure of Your Sins (Br, 1915)
Barnaby Rudge (Br, 1915)
As Ye Repent [a.k.a. Redeemed] (Br, 1915)
The Painted Lady Betty (Br, 1915)
A Lancashire Lass (Br, 1915)
The Traitor [a.k.a. Court-Martialled] (Br, 1915)
The Passing of a Soul (Br, 1915)
The Auction Block (Rex Beach-G, 1917)
Double Indemnity (Par, 1944)
Practically Yours (Par, 1944)
The Phantom Speaks (Rep, 1945)
The Chicago Kid (Rep, 1945)
The Blue Dahlia (Par, 1946)
The Last Crooked Mile (Rep, 1946)
Two Years Before the Mast (Par, 1946)
Her Adventurous Night (Univ, 1946)
Angel and the Badman (Rep, 1947)
The Farmer's Daughter (RKO, 1947)
They Won't Believe Me (RKO, 1947)
Son of Rusty (Col, 1947)

The Time of Your Life (UA, 1948)
I Love Trouble (Col, 1948)
Up in Central Park (Univ, 1948)
Mexican Hayride (Univ, 1948)
Angel in Exile (Rep, 1948)
Station West (RKO, 1948)
Scene of the Crime (MGM, 1949)
Special Agent (Par, 1949)
Chicago Deadline (Par, 1949)
East Side, West Side (MGM, 1949)
Chinatown at Midnight (Col, 1950)
The Nevadan (Col, 1950)
Right Cross (MGM, 1950)
Destination Moon (EL, 1950)
Fighting Coast Guard (Rep, 1951)
The Well (UA, 1951)
The Tall Target (MGM, 1951)
The Strip (MGM, 1951)
Phone Call from a Stranger (20th, 1952)
The Fabulous Senorita (Rep, 1952)
The Denver and Rio Grande (Par, 1952)

Bal Tabarin (Rep, 1952)
Diplomatic Courier (20th, 1952)
Deadline—U.S.A. (20th, 1952)
We're Not Married (20th, 1952)
Jet Job (Mon, 1952)
The Steel Trap (20th, 1952)
Horizons West (Univ, 1952)
Scared Stiff (Par, 1953)
Devil's Canyon (RKO, 1953)
Julius Caesar (MGM, 1953)
Sea of Lost Ships (Rep, 1953)
The Marksman (AA, 1953)
Donovan's Brain (UA, 1953)
The Last Posse (Col, 1953)
Outaw Territory (Realart, 1953)
The Americano (RKO, 1955)
Ten Wanted Men (Col, 1955)
New York Confidential (WB, 1955)
The Eternal Sea (Rep, 1955)

JED PROUTY

With Shirley Deane (holding his arm) in Borrowing Trouble *(1937).*

Born April 6, 1879, Boston, Massachusetts. Married Marian Murray; widowed (1951). Died May 10, 1956, New York City, New York. Best noted as the bespectacled father of 20th Century–Fox's *The Jones Family* series, coping with flighty wife Spring Byington and their enterprising offspring. Played the stuttering Uncle Bernie of *The Broadway Melody* and supplied rural flavor for many pictures.

Jed Prouty to Stuart Erwin in *Small Town Boy:* "Son, if you're doing something wrong, I'll stick by you."

Films

The Conquest of Canaan (Par, 1921)
Experience (Par, 1921)
The Great Adventure (Associated FN, 1921)
Room and Board (Realart, 1921)
Kick In (Par, 1922)
The Girl of the Golden West (Associated FN, 1923)
The Gold Diggers (WB, 1923)
Souls for Sale (G, 1923)
The Coast of Folly (Par, 1925)
The Knockout (FN, 1925)
Scarlet Saint (FN, 1925)
The Unguarded Hour (FN, 1925)
Bred in Old Kentucky (FBO, 1926)
Don Juan's Three Nights (FN, 1926)
Ella Cinders (FN, 1926)
Everybody's Acting (Par, 1926)
Her Second Chance (FN, 1926)
Miss Nobody (Par, 1926)
The Mystery Club (Univ, 1926)
Unknown Treasures (Sterling, 1926)
The Gingham Girl (FBO, 1927)
No Place to Go (FN, 1927)
Orchids and Ermine (FN, 1927)
The Siren (Col, 1927)
Smile, Brother, Smile (FN, 1927)
Domestic Meddlers (Tif, 1928)
Name the Woman (Col, 1928)
Sonny Boy (WB, 1929)
Why Leave Home? (Fox, 1929)
The Fall of Eve (Col, 1929)
His Captive Woman (FN, 1929)
Two Weeks Off (FN, 1929)
The Broadway Melody (MGM, 1929)
It's a Great Life (MGM, 1929)
Girl in the Show (MGM, 1929)
The Devil's Holiday (Par, 1930)
True to the Navy (Par, 1930)
The Florodora Girl (MGM, 1930)
Strangers May Kiss (MGM, 1931)
Night Nurse (WB, 1931)

Annabelle's Affairs (Fox, 1931)
The Secret Call (Par, 1931)
Age for Love (UA, 1931)
Business and Pleasure (Fox, 1932)
Manhattan Tower (Remington Pictures, 1932)
Hold 'em Jail (RKO, 1932)
Skyway (Mon, 1933)
Jimmy and Sally (Fox, 1933)
The Big Bluff (Tower, 1933)
I Believed in You (Fox, 1934)
The Life of Vergie Winters (RKO, 1934)
Hollywood Party (MGM, 1934)
Music in the Air (Fox, 1934)
Private Scandal (Par, 1934)
One Hour Late (Par, 1934)
George White's 1935 Scandals (Fox, 1935)
Ah, Wilderness! (MGM, 1935)
Navy Wife [a.k.a. *Beauty's Daughter*] (Fox, 1935)
Alibi Ike (WB, 1935)
Black Sheep (Fox, 1935)
Every Saturday Night (20th, 1936)
Little Miss Nobody (20th, 1936)
Educating Father (20th, 1936)
Back to Nature (20th, 1936)
Can This Be Dixie? (20th, 1936)
Under Your Spell (20th, 1936)
Special Investigator (RKO, 1936)
His Brother's Wife (MGM, 1936)
The Texas Rangers (Par, 1936)
College Holiday (Par, 1936)
Happy-Go-Lucky (Rep, 1936)
Off to the Races (20th, 1937)
Big Business (20th, 1937)
Hot Water (20th, 1937)
Borrowing Trouble (20th, 1937)
Life Begins in College (20th, 1937)
The Crime Nobody Saw (Par, 1937)
Sophie Lang Goes West (Par, 1937)
Dangerous Holiday (Rep, 1937)
100 Men and a Girl (Univ, 1937)

Small Town Boy (GN, 1937)
You Can't Have Everything (20th, 1937)
Love on a Budget (20th, 1938)
Walking Down Broadway (20th, 1938)
A Trip to Paris (20th, 1938)
Keep Smiling (20th, 1938)
Safety in Numbers (20th, 1938)
Everybody's Baby (20th, 1938)
The Duke of West Point (UA, 1938)
Goodbye Broadway (Univ, 1938)
Danger on the Air (Univ, 1938)
Down on the Farm (20th, 1938)
The Gracie Allen Murder Case (Par, 1939)
The Jones Family in Hollywood (20th, 1939)
Quick Millions (20th, 1939)
Second Fiddle (20th, 1939)
Hollywood Cavalcade (20th, 1939)
Too Busy to Work (20th, 1939)
Exile Express (GN, 1939)
On Their Own (20th, 1940)
Young as You Feel (20th, 1940)
Remedy for Riches (RKO, 1940)
Barnyard Follies (Rep, 1940)
The Lone Wolf Keeps a Date (Col, 1940)
Pot o' Gold (UA, 1941)
Roar of the Press (Mon, 1941)
Father Steps Out (Mon, 1941)
Bachelor Daddy (Univ, 1941)
Unexpected Uncle (RKO, 1941)
City Limits (Mon, 1941)
Look Who's Laughing (RKO, 1941)
Go West, Young Lady (Col, 1941)
The Affairs of Jimmy Valentine [a.k.a. *Unforgotten Crime*] (Rep, 1942)
Scattergood Rides High (RKO, 1942)
It Happened in Flatbush (20th, 1942)
The Old Homestead (Rep, 1942)
Moonlight Masquerade (Rep, 1942)
Mug Town (Univ, 1943)
Guilty Bystander (Film Classics, 1950)

JOHN QUALEN

(John Oleson)

John Qualen, Maude Eburne, and Alan Dinehart in Reunion *(1936).*

Born December 8, 1899, Vancouver, British Columbia, Canada. Married Pearle Larson (1924), children: Meredith, Kathleen, Elizabeth. The son of a Norwegian pastor. Made a full career of interpreting low-keyed foreigners. Repeated Broadway assignment of Karl Olsen, the Swedish janitor in *Street Scene*. Shone as Papa Dionne in Fox's three features on the Dionne quintuplets: *The Country Doctor, Reunion,* and *Five of a Kind*. For John Ford was Muley (*The Grapes of Wrath*), the sea-weary sailor Axel Swanson (*The Long Voyage Home*), the doctor (*The Fugitive*), father of Harry Carey, Jr. (*The Searchers*), and Ole Knudsen (*Two Rode Together*). TV series: "Make Room for Daddy" and "The Real McCoys" (as Frank, the handyman).

John Qualen to Marjorie Main in *The Shepherd of the Hills:* "I ain't never been no good; the sorriest critter in the creek."

Films

Street Scene (UA, 1931)
Arrowsmith (UA, 1931)
Counsellor at Law (Univ, 1933)
Let's Fall in Love (Col, 1934)
Upper World (WB, 1934)
Hi, Nellie! (WB, 1934)
Sing and Like It (RKO, 1934)
Straight Is the Way (MGM, 1934)
Private Scandal (Par, 1934)
He Was Her Man (WB, 1934)
Our Daily Bread (UA, 1934)
Servants' Entrance (Fox, 1934)
365 Nights in Hollywood (Fox, 1934)
One More Spring (Fox, 1935)
The Great Hotel Murder (Fox, 1935)
Charlie Chan in Paris (Fox, 1935)
Doubting Thomas (Fox, 1935)
Orchids to You (Fox, 1935)
Thunder in the Night (Fox, 1935)

The Farmer Takes a Wife (Fox, 1935)
Silk Hat Kid (Fox, 1935)
Chasing Yesterday (RKO, 1935)
The Three Musketeers (RKO, 1935)
Black Fury (FN, 1935)
Man of Iron (WB, 1935)
Cheers of the Crowd (Rep, 1935)
Whipsaw (MGM, 1936)
The Country Doctor (20th, 1936)
The Road to Glory (20th, 1936)
Girls' Dormitory (20th, 1936)
Reunion (20th, 1936)
Ring Around the Moon (Chesterfield, 1936)
Meet Nero Wolfe (Col, 1936)
Nothing Sacred (UA, 1937)
Seventh Heaven (20th, 1937)
Fifty Roads to Town (20th, 1937)
Angel's Holiday (20th, 1937)

She Had to Eat (20th, 1937)
Fit for a King (RKO, 1937)
The Bad Man from Brimstone (MGM, 1937)
The Chaser (MGM, 1938)
Joy of Living (RKO, 1938)
Five of a Kind (20th, 1938)
The Mad Miss Manton (RKO, 1938)
Stand Up and Fight (MGM, 1939)
Honeymoon in Bali (Par, 1939)
Career (RKO, 1939)
Mickey the Kid (Rep, 1939)
Thunder Afloat (MGM, 1939)
Four Wives (WB, 1939)
His Girl Friday (Col, 1940)
Blondie on a Budget (Col, 1940)
Angels over Broadway (Col, 1940)
The Grapes of Wrath (20th, 1940)
On Their Own (20th, 1940)

The Long Voyage Home (UA, 1940)
Youth Will Be Served (20th, 1940)
Ski Patrol (Univ, 1940)
Knute Rockne—All-American (WB, 1940)
Million Dollar Baby (WB, 1941)
Out of the Fog (WB, 1941)
The Shepherd of the Hills (Par, 1941)
Model Wife (Univ, 1941)
All That Money Can Buy [a.k.a. The Devil and Daniel Webster] (RKO, 1941)
New Wine [TV title: Melody Master] (UA, 1941)
Larceny, Inc. (WB, 1942)
Jungle Book (UA, 1942)
Tortilla Flat (MGM, 1942)
Arabian Nights (Univ, 1942)
Casablanca (WB, 1942)
Swing Shift Maisie (MGM, 1943)
The Impostor (Univ, 1944)
An American Romance (MGM, 1944)
Dark Waters (UA, 1944)
Roughly Speaking (WB, 1945)
River Gang (Univ, 1945)
Captain Kidd (UA, 1945)
Adventure (MGM, 1945)

The Fugitive (RKO, 1947)
Song of Scheherazade (Univ, 1947)
High Conquest (Mon, 1947)
My Girl Tisa (WB, 1948)
Alias a Gentleman (MGM, 1948)
Sixteen Fathoms Deep (Mon, 1948)
Hollow Triumph [a.k.a. The Scar] (EL, 1948)
The Big Steal (RKO, 1949)
Captain China (Par, 1949)
Buccaneer's Girl (Univ, 1950)
The Jackpot (20th, 1950)
Woman on the Run (Univ, 1950)
The Flying Missile (Col, 1951)
Belle le Grand (Rep, 1951)
Goodbye, My Fancy (WB, 1951)
Hans Christian Andersen (RKO, 1952)
Ambush at Tomahawk Gap (Col, 1953)
I, the Jury (UA, 1953)
The Student Prince (MGM, 1954)
The High and the Mighty (WB, 1954)
Passion (RKO, 1954)
The Other Woman (20th, 1954)
Unchained (WB, 1955)
The Sea Chase (WB, 1955)
At Gunpoint (AA, 1955)

The Searchers (WB, 1956)
Johnny Concho (UA, 1956)
The Big Land (WB, 1957)
The Gun Runners (UA, 1958)
Revolt in the Big House (AA, 1958)
Anatomy of a Murder (Col, 1959)
Hell Bent for Leather (Univ, 1960)
Elmer Gantry (UA, 1960)
North to Alaska (20th, 1960)
Two Rode Together (Col, 1961)
The Comancheros (20th, 1961)
The Man Who Shot Liberty Valance (Par, 1962)
The Prize (MGM, 1963)
The Seven Faces of Dr. Lao (MGM, 1964)
Cheyenne Autumn (WB, 1964)
Those Calloways (BV, 1964)
A Patch of Blue (MGM, 1965)
I'll Take Sweden (UA, 1965)
The Sons of Katie Elder (Par, 1965)
A Big Hand for the Little Lady (WB, 1966)
P.J. (Univ, 1968)
Firecreek (WB-7 Arts, 1968)
Hail, Hero! (National General, 1969)
Frasier, the Sensuous Lion (LCS, 1973)

RAGS RAGLAND
(John Morgan Ragland)

June Allyson and Rags Ragland in Her Highness and the Bellboy *(1945).*

Born August 23, 1905, Louisville, Kentucky. Married _____ , child: John; divorced (1926). Died August 20, 1946, Los Angeles, California. From boxer to Minsky burlesque comedian to Broadway performer and on to filmmaking. Always the smiling, enthusiastic roughneck. The lovable mug was brought to Hollywood to re-create his stage role of the rollicking sailor in MGM's *Panama Hattie*. As Metro contractee was Red Skelton's sidekick (Sylvester) in *Whistling in the Dark* and the two follow-ups: *Whistling in Dixie* and *Whistling in Brooklyn*. At his best on camera when he demonstrated that beneath his battered face and fractured English there beat a warm heart—scene-stealing sympathizer of Judy Garland (*Girl Crazy*), June Allyson (*Her Highness and the Bellboy*), and proved to be a friendly cop in *Anchors Aweigh*. Inherited Nat Pendleton's role of the talkative ambulance driver in the *Dr. Gillespie* entry *Three Men in White*.

Rags Ragland to June Allyson in *Her Highness and the Bellboy*:
"I brought you some flowers. They're fornot-me-gets."

Films

Ringside Maisie (MGM, 1941)
Whistling in the Dark (MGM, 1941)
Born to Sing (MGM, 1942)
Sunday Punch (MGM, 1942)
Maisie Gets Her Man (MGM, 1942)
Panama Hattie (MGM, 1942)
The War Against Mrs. Hadley (MGM, 1942)

Somewhere I'll Find You (MGM, 1942)
Whistling in Dixie (MGM, 1942)
Du Barry Was a Lady (MGM, 1943)
Girl Crazy (MGM, 1943)
Whistling in Brooklyn (MGM, 1943)
Meet the People (MGM, 1944)
Three Men in White (MGM, 1944)
The Canterville Ghost (MGM, 1944)

Her Highness and the Bellboy (MGM, 1945)
Anchors Aweigh (MGM, 1945)
Abbott and Costello in Hollywood (MGM, 1945)
Ziegfeld Follies (MGM, 1946)
The Hoodlum Saint (MGM, 1946)

JESSIE RALPH
(Jessica Chambers)

In Camille *(1936).*

Born November 5, 1864, Gloucester, Massachusetts. Married William Patton; widowed. Died May 30, 1944, Gloucester, Massachusetts. Survived a long stage career (with some acting forays abroad) before embarking on her Hollywood years. Could steal any scene with a glance of her sparkling eyes or a well-timed gesticulation. Often on tap to serve and cheer up others: *David Copperfield* (elderly nurse Peggotty), *After the Thin Man* (Aunt Katherine Forrest), *Camille* (Nanine, the maid), *The Blue Bird* (Fairy Berylune). Had some eccentric roles: *The Good Earth* (Cuckoo), *The Bank Dick* (W. C. Fields' mother-in-law), *They Met in Bombay* (the gem-laden Duchess of Beltravers). Most recalled for her resolute Mrs. Talbot, the Nob Hill mother of Jack Holt in *San Francisco.*

Jessie Ralph in *They Met in Bombay:* "I *hate* caviar. It's like eating a lot of little golf balls."

Films

Such a Little Queen (Par, 1921)	*The Affairs of Cellini* (UA, 1934)	*Captain Blood* (FN, 1935)
Elmer the Great (FN, 1933)	*David Copperfield* (MGM, 1935)	*Bunker Bean* (RKO, 1936)
Cocktail Hour (Col, 1933)	*Enchanted April* (RKO, 1935)	*The Garden Murder Case* (MGM, 1936)
Child of Manhattan (Col, 1933)	*Les Miserables* (UA, 1935)	*The Unguarded Hour* (MGM, 1936)
Ann Carver's Profession (Col, 1933)	*Paris in Spring* (Par, 1935)	*San Francisco* (MGM, 1936)
Coming-Out Party (Fox, 1934)	*Vanessa: Her Love Story* (MGM, 1935)	*After the Thin Man* (MGM, 1936)
One Night of Love (Col, 1934)	*Mark of the Vampire* (MGM, 1935)	*Camille* (MGM, 1936)
Evelyn Prentice (MGM, 1934)	*I Live My Life* (MGM, 1935)	*Little Lord Fauntleroy* (UA, 1936)
Nana (UA, 1934)	*Jalna* (RKO, 1935)	*Yellow Dust* (RKO, 1936)
We Live Again (UA, 1934)	*Metropolitan* (Fox, 1935)	*Walking on Air* (RKO, 1936)
Murder at the Vanities (Par, 1934)	*I Found Stella Parish* (FN, 1935)	*The Good Earth* (MGM, 1937)

Double Wedding (MGM, 1937)
The Last of Mrs. Cheyney (MGM, 1937)
Love Is a Headache (MGM, 1938)
Port of Seven Seas (MGM, 1938)
Hold That Kiss (MGM, 1938)
St. Louis Blues (Par, 1939)
Cafe Society (Par, 1939)

Four Girls in White (MGM, 1939)
The Kid from Texas (MGM, 1939)
Mickey the Kid (Rep, 1939)
Drums Along the Mohawk (20th, 1939)
The Blue Bird (20th, 1940)
Star Dust (20th, 1940)
The Girl from Avenue A (20th, 1940)

I Can't Give You Anything but Love, Baby
   (Univ, 1940)
The Bank Dick (Univ, 1940)
I Want a Divorce (Par, 1940)
The Lady from Cheyenne (Univ, 1941)
They Met in Bombay (MGM, 1941)

MARJORIE RAMBEAU

With Eddie Dunn in Army Wives (1944).

Born July 15, 1889, San Francisco, California. Married 1) Willard Mack (1912); divorced (1917); 2) Hugh Dilman (1919); divorced (1923); 3) Francis Gudger (1931); widowed (1967). Died July 7, 1970, Palm Springs, California. Comely stage star who had leading roles in several silents. Returned to motion pictures in 1930, generally as the shopworn floozy. Played Bella, whom Marie Dressler killed in *Min and Bill*; Peaches, the discarded moll in Wallace Beery's *The Secret Six*, etc. Could be very touching: life-weary Flossie of the shanty huts in *A Man's Castle*; very gruff in *Tugboat Annie Sails Again* (an attempt to revive the Marie Dressler property). Her raucous performance in *Primrose Path* led to Oscar-nomination (but lost BSAAA to Jane Darwell of *The Grapes of Wrath*). Very touching as Joan Crawford's reminiscing mother in *Torch Song* (Oscar-nominated again, but lost to Donna Reed of *From Here to Eternity*). Last role was as Gert, the veteran actress in James Cagney's *The Man of a Thousand Faces*.

Marjorie Rambeau to Herbert Marshall in *Woman Against Woman:* "I promise *everybody* the first rumba. So pay no attention to it."

Films

The Dazzling Miss Davison (Mutual, 1916)
The Greater Woman (Powell Mutual, 1916)
Mary Moreland (Mutual, 1917)
The Debt (Mutual, 1917)
The Mirror (Mutual, 1917)
Motherhood (Mutual, 1917)
The Common Cause (Vit, 1918)
The Fortune Teller (Vit, 1920)
On Her Honor (Tri-Artclass, 1922)
Syncopating Sue (FN, 1926)
Her Man (Pathé, 1930)
Min and Bill (MGM, 1930)
Leftover Ladies (Tif, 1931)
Son of India (MGM, 1931)
Inspiration (MGM, 1931)
The Easiest Way (MGM, 1931)
Silence (Par, 1931)
A Tailor-Made Man (MGM, 1931)
Strangers May Kiss (MGM, 1931)
The Secret Six (MGM, 1931)
This Modern Age (MGM, 1931)
Laughing Sinners (MGM, 1931)

Hell Divers (MGM, 1931)
Strictly Personal (Par, 1933)
The Warrior's Husband (Fox, 1933)
A Man's Castle (Col, 1933)
Palooka (UA, 1934)
A Modern Hero (WB, 1934)
Ready for Love (Par, 1934)
Grand Canary (Fox, 1934)
Under Pressure (Fox, 1935)
Dizzy Dames (Liberty, 1935)
First Lady (WB, 1937)
Merrily We Live (MGM, 1938)
Woman Against Woman (MGM, 1938)
Sudden Money (Par, 1939)
The Rains Came (20th, 1939)
Laugh It Off (Univ, 1939)
Heaven with a Barbed Wire Fence (20th, 1939)
Santa Fe Marshal (Par, 1940)
Primrose Path (RKO, 1940)
Twenty-Mule Team (MGM, 1940)
Tugboat Annie Sails Again (WB, 1940)
East of the River (WB, 1940)
Tobacco Road (20th, 1941)

So Ends Our Night (UA, 1941)
Three Sons o' Guns (WB, 1941)
Broadway (Univ, 1942)
In Old Oklahoma [a.k.a. *War of the Wildcats*] (Rep, 1943)
Oh, What a Night! (Mon, 1944)
Army Wives (Mon, 1944)
Salome, Where She Danced (Univ, 1945)
The Walls of Jericho (20th, 1948)
Any Number Can Play (MGM, 1949)
The Lucky Stiff (UA, 1949)
Abandoned Woman (Univ, 1949)
Torch Song (MGM, 1953)
Forever Female (Par, 1953)
Bad for Each Other (Col, 1953)
A Man Called Peter (20th, 1955)
The View from Pompey's Head (20th, 1955)
Slander (MGM, 1956)
The Man of a Thousand Faces (Univ, 1957)

FRANK REICHER

With Polly Rowles in Westbound Limited *(1937).*

Born December 22, 1875, Munich, Germany. Died January 19, 1965, Playa del Rey, California. Recognizable in any makeup because of prominent nose and baggy eyes. Directed such features as *The Eternal Mother* (1917), *Behind Masks,* and *Wise Husbands* (played in last two). In sound era: *Mata Hari* (the spy-cook), *King Kong* (Captain Englehorn), *Under Two Flags* (French general), *The Story of Louis Pasteur* (Dr. Pfeiffer), *To Be or Not to Be* (Polish official), etc.

Surgeon **Frank Reicher** to Pat O'Brien in *The Great O'Malley:* "You let *me* worry about the money. You have that little girl here at two tomorrow."

Films

Behind Masks (Par, 1921)
Idle Hands (Pioneer, 1921)
Out of the Depths (Pioneer, 1921)
Wise Husbands (Pioneer, 1921)
Her Man o' War (PDC, 1926)
Beau Sabreur (Par, 1928)
The Blue Danube (Pathé, 1928)
Four Sons (Fox, 1928)
The Masks of the Devil (MGM, 1928)
Sins of the Fathers (Par, 1928)
Someone to Love (Par, 1928)
Big News (Pathé, 1929)
Her Private Affair (Pathé, 1929)
Strange Cargo (Pathé, 1929)
Black Waters (WW, 1929)
Paris Bound (Pathé, 1929)
Mr. Antonio (Tif, 1929)
His Captive Woman (FN, 1929)
Girl of the Port (RKO, 1930)
The Grand Parade (Pathé, 1930)
Die Sehnsucht Jeder Frau (Ger, 1930)
A Gentleman's Fate (MGM, 1931)

Mata Hari (MGM, 1931)
Beyond Victory (Pathé, 1931)
Suicide Fleet (Pathé, 1931)
A Woman Commands (RKO, 1932)
The Crooked Circle (WW, 1932)
Scarlet Dawn (WB, 1932)
Jennie Gerhardt (Par, 1933)
Captured (WB, 1933)
Ever in My Heart (WB, 1933)
Before Dawn (RKO, 1933)
King Kong (RKO, 1933)
Son of Kong (RKO, 1933)
Topaze (RKO, 1933)
Employees' Entrance (FN, 1933)
Hi, Nellie! (WB, 1934)
Journal of a Crime (FN, 1934)
Countess of Monte Cristo (Univ, 1934)
I Am a Thief (WB, 1934)
Little Man, What Now? (Univ, 1934)
Let's Talk It Over (Univ, 1934)
No Greater Glory (Col, 1934)
Return of the Terror (FN, 1934)

The Case of the Howling Dog (WB, 1934)
The Fountain (RKO, 1935)
A Dog of Flanders (RKO, 1935)
Mills of the Gods (Col, 1935)
The Florentine Dagger (WB, 1935)
Kind Lady (MGM, 1935)
Remember Last Night (Univ, 1935)
Rendezvous (MGM, 1935)
The Man Who Broke the Bank at Monte Carlo (Fox, 1935)
Life Returns (Univ, 1935)
The Story of Louis Pasteur (WB, 1935)
Star of Midnight (RKO, 1935)
The Great Impersonation (Univ, 1935)
Magnificent Obsession (Univ, 1935)
The Invisible Ray (Univ, 1936)
The Murder of Dr. Harrigan (FN, 1936)
Sutter's Gold (Univ, 1936)
Old Hutch (MGM, 1936)
The Country Doctor (20th, 1936)
Under Two Flags (20th, 1936)
Girls' Dormitory (20th, 1936)

Along Came Love (Par, 1936)
Star for a Night (20th, 1936)
'Til We Meet Again (WB, 1936)
Murder on a Bridle Path (RKO, 1936)
The Ex-Mrs. Bradford (RKO, 1936)
Second Wife (RKO, 1936)
Anthony Adverse (WB, 1936)
Stolen Holiday (WB, 1936)
The Great O'Malley (WB, 1937)
Westbound Limited (Univ, 1937)
Midnight Madonna (Par, 1937)
Under Cover of Night (MGM, 1937)
Espionage (MGM, 1937)
Stage Door (RKO, 1937)
The Emperor's Candlesticks (MGM, 1937)
The Road Back (Univ, 1937)
Prescription for Romance (Univ, 1937)
Fit for a King (RKO, 1937)
Lancer Spy (20th, 1937)
Laughing at Trouble (20th, 1937)
Night Key (Univ, 1937)
The Mighty Treve (Univ, 1937)
On Such a Night (Par, 1937)
Beg, Borrow or Steal (MGM, 1937)
Letter of Introduction (Univ, 1938)
Of Human Hearts (MGM, 1938)
Rascals (20th, 1938)
Prison Nurse (Rep, 1938)
City Streets (Col, 1938)
I'll Give a Million (20th, 1938)
The Storm (Univ, 1938)
Suez (20th, 1938)
Torchy Gets Her Man (WB, 1938)
Mystery of the White Room (Univ, 1939)
Woman Doctor (Rep, 1939)
Juarez (WB, 1939)
The Magnificent Fraud (Par, 1939)
Society Smugglers (Univ, 1939)

Ninotchka (MGM, 1939)
Our Neighbors, the Carters (Par, 1939)
Unexpected Father (Univ, 1939)
The Escape (20th, 1939)
South of the Border (Rep, 1939)
Everything Happens at Night (20th, 1939)
Never Say Die (Par, 1939)
All This, and Heaven Too (WB, 1940)
Dr. Cyclops (Par, 1940)
Typhoon (Par, 1940)
The Man I Married (20th, 1940)
Devil's Island (WB, 1940)
South to Karanga (Univ, 1940)
Sky Murder (MGM, 1940)
The Lady in Question (Col, 1940)
Flight from Destiny (WB, 1941)
They Dare Not Love (Col, 1941)
Shining Victory (WB, 1941)
Father Takes a Wife (RKO, 1941)
The Nurse's Secret (WB, 1941)
Underground (WB, 1941)
Dangerously They Live (WB, 1941)
Nazi Agent (MGM, 1942)
To Be or Not to Be (UA, 1942)
The Mystery of Marie Roget (Univ, 1942)
Beyond the Blue Horizon (Par, 1942)
Secret Enemies (WB, 1942)
The Gay Sisters (WB, 1942)
The Mummy's Tomb (Univ, 1942)
Scattergood Survives a Murder (RKO, 1942)
Night Monster (Univ, 1942)
The Song of Bernadette (20th, 1943)
Mission to Moscow (WB, 1943)
Yanks Ahoy (UA, 1943)
Tornado (Par, 1943)
Watch on the Rhine (WB, 1943)
In Our Time (WB, 1944)

The Adventures of Mark Twain (WB, 1944)
The Canterville Ghost (MGM, 1944)
Address Unknown (Col, 1944)
The Mummy's Ghost (Univ, 1944)
Gildersleeve's Ghost (RKO, 1944)
The Hitler Gang (Par, 1944)
The Conspirators (WB, 1944)
The House of Frankenstein (Univ, 1944)
The Big Bonanza (Rep, 1944)
A Medal for Benny (Par, 1945)
The Jade Mask (Mon, 1945)
Hotel Berlin (WB, 1945)
Voice of the Whistler (Col, 1945)
Rhapsody in Blue (WB, 1945)
Blonde Ransom (Univ, 1945)
The Tiger Woman (Rep, 1945)
The Shadow Returns (Mon, 1946)
The Strange Mr. Gregory (Mon, 1946)
My Pal Trigger (Rep, 1946)
Home in Oklahoma (Rep, 1946)
Sister Kenny (RKO, 1946)
Mr. District Attorney (Col, 1947)
Violence (Mon, 1947)
Yankee Fakir (Rep, 1947)
The Secret Life of Walter Mitty (RKO, 1947)
Escape Me Never (WB, 1947)
Carson City Raiders (Rep, 1948)
Fighting Mad (Mon, 1948)
Barbary Pirate (Col, 1949)
Samson and Delilah (Par, 1949)
Cargo to Capetown (Col, 1950)
The Happy Years (MGM, 1950)
Kiss Tomorrow Goodbye (WB, 1950)
The Lady and the Bandit (Col, 1951)

ANNE REVERE

With Robert Moore in Tell Me That You Love Me, Junie Moon *(1970).*

Born June 25, 1903, New York City, New York. Married Samuel Rosel (1935). Thin-faced Yankee who came to Hollywood to re-create her Broadway role from *The Double Door*. Oscar-nominated for playing Jennifer Jones' mother in *The Song of Bernadette* (but lost BSAAA to Katina Paxinou of *For Whom the Bell Tolls*). However won BSAAA as Elizabeth Taylor's mom in *National Velvet*. Nominated again, for being Gregory Peck's mother in *Gentleman's Agreement* (but lost BSAAA to Celeste Holm of *Gentleman's Agreement*). Out of films until the 1970s because of the 1950s blacklistings. TV series: "Search for Tomorrow" (as Agnes Lake), "The Edge of Night" (as Mrs. Stewart), and "The Secret Storm."

> **Anne Revere** to Gregory Peck in *Gentleman's Agreement:* "I just love waiting for people. I always say there's nothing as much fun as standing around waiting for people who are always late."

Films

The Double Door (Par, 1934)
One Crowded Night (RKO, 1940)
The Howards of Virginia (Col, 1940)
Men of Boys Town (MGM, 1941)
Remember the Day (20th, 1941)
The Devil Commands (Col, 1941)
Design for Scandal (MGM, 1941)
H. M. Pulham, Esq. (MGM, 1941)
The Flame of New Orleans (Univ, 1941)
The Gay Sisters (WB, 1942)
Are Husbands Necessary? (Par, 1942)
The Falcon Takes Over (RKO, 1942)
Meet the Stewarts (Col, 1942)
Star Spangled Rhythm (Par, 1942)
The Song of Bernadette (20th, 1943)

Shantytown (Rep, 1943)
Old Acquaintance (WB, 1943)
The Meanest Man in the World (20th, 1943)
Standing Room Only (Par, 1944)
Rainbow Island (Par, 1944)
The Keys of the Kingdom (20th, 1944)
Sunday Dinner for a Soldier (20th, 1944)
The Thin Man Goes Home (MGM, 1944)
National Velvet (MGM, 1944)
Don Juan Quilligan (20th, 1945)
Fallen Angel (20th, 1945)
Dragonwyck (20th, 1946)
The Shocking Miss Pilgrim (20th, 1947)
Forever Amber (20th, 1947)

Body and Soul (UA, 1947)
Gentleman's Agreement (20th, 1947)
Carnival in Costa Rica (20th, 1947)
Secret Beyond the Door (Univ, 1948)
Scudda Hoo! Scudda Hay! (20th, 1948)
Deep Waters (20th, 1948)
You're My Everything (20th, 1949)
The Great Missouri Raid (Par, 1950)
A Place in the Sun (Par, 1951)
Tell Me That You Love Me, Junie Moon (Par, 1970)
Macho Callahan (Avco Emb, 1970) [TV version only]
Birch Interval (Gamma III, 1976)

ERIK RHODES

Fred Astaire, Ginger Rogers, and Erik Rhodes in
The Gay Divorcee *(1934).*

Born February 10, 1906, El Reno, Oklahoma. Married Emmala _____ . Broadway comedy actor who made a lasting impression as the professional co-respondent in Fred Astaire-Ginger Rogers' *The Gay Divorcee*. He was the hyperactive Italian who brags, "Your wife is safe with Tonetti . . . he prefers spaghetti. . . ." He was Alberto Beddini, the excitable dress designer in the dance team's *Top Hat*. TV series: "The Secret Storm."

Erik Rhodes to Ginger Rogers in *Top Hat:* "All my life I have promised my dresses I'd take them to Italy . . . and you must be in them."

Films

The Gay Divorcee (RKO, 1934)
A Night at the Ritz (WB, 1935)
Charlie Chan in Paris (Fox, 1935)
The Nitwits (RKO, 1935)
Old Man Rhythm (RKO, 1935)
Top Hat (RKO, 1935)
Another Face (RKO, 1935)
Two in the Dark (RKO, 1936)

Chatterbox (RKO, 1936)
One Rainy Afternoon (UA, 1936)
Special Investigator (RKO, 1936)
Second Wife (RKO, 1936)
The Smartest Girl in Town (RKO, 1936)
Criminal Lawyer (RKO, 1937)
Woman Chases Man (UA, 1937)
Music for Madame (RKO, 1937)

Fight for Your Lady (RKO, 1937)
Beg, Borrow or Steal (MGM, 1937)
Dramatic School (MGM, 1938)
Say It in French (Par, 1938)
Meet the Girls (20th, 1938)
The Mysterious Mr. Moto (20th, 1938)
On Your Toes (WB, 1939)

ADDISON RICHARDS

Addison Richards and Don Terry in Mutiny in the Arctic *(1941).*

Born October 20, 1902, Zanesville, Ohio. Married Patricia _____ , child: Ann. Died March 22, 1964, Los Angeles, California. Former stage actor and later director at the Pasadena Playhouse; Warner Bros. contractee through the late 1930s. Almost always played a trustworthy professional; occasionally would be shockingly sinister (as his Mallison in *The Black Doll*). Played Polly Benedict's (Ann Rutherford's) dad in a few *Andy Hardy* entries. TV series: "Fibber McGee and Molly."

Addison Richards to John Wayne in *Flying Tigers:* "It's a job for a volunteer, of course."

Films

Riot Squad (Mayfair, 1933)
Lone Cowboy (Par, 1933)
Let's Be Ritzy (Univ, 1934)
A Lost Lady (FN, 1934)
Girl from Missouri (MGM, 1934)
Love Captive (Univ, 1934)
British Agent (FN, 1934)
Beyond the Law (Col, 1934)
Our Daily Bread UA, 1934)
The Case of the Howling Dog (WB, 1934)
Gentlemen Are Born (FN, 1934)
St. Louis Kid (WB, 1934)
Babbitt (FN, 1934)
Society Doctor (MGM, 1935)
The White Cockatoo (WB, 1935)
Home on the Range (Par, 1935)
Sweet Music (WB, 1935)
Dinky (WB, 1935)
G-Men (WB, 1935)
Alias Mary Dow (Univ, 1935)
A Dog of Flanders (RKO, 1935)
Front Page Woman (WB, 1935)

The Crusades (Par, 1935)
Here Comes the Band (MGM, 1935)
Little Big Shot (WB, 1935)
Freckles (RKO, 1935)
The Eagle's Brood (Par, 1935)
Frisco Kid (WB, 1935)
Ceiling Zero (WB, 1935)
Colleen (WB, 1936)
China Clipper (FN, 1936)
Man Hunt (WB, 1936)
Road Gang (WB, 1936)
Song of the Saddle (FN, 1936)
The Walking Dead (WB, 1936)
Sutter's Gold (Univ, 1936)
The Law in Her Hands (FN, 1936)
Jailbreak (WB, 1936)
Anthony Adverse (WB, 1936)
Public Enemy's Wife (WB, 1936)
The Case of the Velvet Claws (FN, 1936)
Hot Money (WB, 1936)
Trailin' West (FN, 1936)
The Black Legion (WB, 1936)

Smart Blonde (WB, 1936)
Ready, Willing and Able (WB, 1937)
Her Husband's Secretary (WB, 1937)
Draegerman Courage (WB, 1937)
God's Country and the Woman (WB, 1937)
Dance, Charlie, Dance (WB, 1937)
White Bondage (WB, 1937)
The Singing Marine (WB, 1937)
Love Is on the Air (FN, 1937)
The Barrier (Par, 1937)
Prison Nurse (Rep, 1938)
The Devil's Party (Univ, 1938)
Gateway (20th, 1938)
The Black Doll (Univ, 1938)
Alcatraz Island (WB, 1938)
Accidents Will Happen (WB, 1938)
Valley of the Giants (WB, 1938)
Boys Town (MGM, 1938)
The Last Express (Univ, 1938)
Flight to Fame (Col, 1938)
They Made Her a Spy (RKO, 1939)

Slightly Honorable (UA, 1939)
Exile Express (GN, 1939)
Twelve Crowded Hours (RKO, 1939)
The Mystery of the White Room (Univ, 1939)
I Was a Convict (Rep, 1939)
The Gracie Allen Murder Case (Par, 1939)
Whispering Enemies (Col, 1939)
Off the Record (WB, 1939)
Burn 'em Up O'Connor (MGM, 1939)
Inside Information (Univ, 1939)
Andy Hardy Gets Spring Fever (MGM, 1939)
They All Come Out (MGM, 1939)
Thunder Afloat (MGM, 1939)
Espionage Agent (WB, 1939)
Geronimo (Par, 1939)
Bad Lands (RKO, 1939)
Nick Carter, Master Detective (MGM, 1939)
Boom Town (MGM, 1940)
Northwest Passage (MGM, 1940)
The Man from Montreal (Univ, 1940)
The Man from Dakota (MGM, 1940)
Island of Doomed Men (Col, 1940)
Charlie Chan in Panama (20th, 1940)
The Lone Wolf Strikes (Col, 1940)
Edison the Man (MGM, 1940)
Gangs of Chicago (Rep, 1940)
Andy Hardy Meets Debutante (MGM, 1940)
South to Karanga (Univ, 1940)
The Girl from Havana (Rep, 1940)
Wyoming (MGM, 1940)
Black Diamonds (Univ, 1940)
Cherokee Strip (Par, 1940)
Moon over Burma (Par, 1940)
Arizona (Col, 1940)
Flight Command (MGM, 1940)
My Little Chickadee (Univ, 1940)
Flight Angels (WB, 1940)
Ball of Fire (RKO, 1941)
Western Union (20th, 1941)
Strawberry Blonde (WB, 1941)
The Trial of Mary Dugan (MGM, 1941)
Design for Scandal (MGM, 1941)
Tall, Dark and Handsome (20th, 1941)
Andy Hardy's Private Secretary (MGM, 1941)
Back in the Saddle (Rep, 1941)
Our Wife (Col, 1941)
I Wanted Wings (Par, 1941)
The Great Lie (WB, 1941)
Men of Boys Town (MGM, 1941)
Sheriff of Tombstone (Rep, 1941)

Mutiny in the Arctic (Univ, 1941)
Her First Beau (Col, 1941)
Badlands of Dakota (Univ, 1941)
International Squadron (WB, 1941)
Texas (Col, 1941)
They Died with Their Boots On (WB, 1941)
My Favorite Blonde (Par, 1942)
Secret Agent of Japan, (20th, 1942)
The Lady Has Plans (Par, 1942)
The Man with Two Lives (Mon, 1942)
Cowboy Serenade (Rep, 1942)
Pacific Rendezvous (MGM, 1942)
Friendly Enemies (UA, 1942)
A-Haunting We Will Go (20th, 1942)
Top Sergeant (Univ, 1942)
War Dogs (Mon, 1942)
Seven Days' Leave (RKO, 1942)
Men of Texas (Univ, 1942)
Underground Agent (Col, 1942)
The Pride of the Yankees (RKO, 1942)
Secret Enemies (WB, 1942)
The Flying Tigers (Rep, 1942)
Secrets of a Co-ed (PRC, 1942)
Air Force (WB, 1943)
Headin' for God's Country (Rep, 1943)
Always a Bridesmaid (Univ, 1943)
Corvette K-225 (Univ, 1943)
A Guy Named Joe (MGM, 1943)
Where Are Your Children? (Mon, 1943)
The Mystery of the Thirteenth Guest (Mon, 1943)
Mystery Broadcast (Rep, 1943)
Smart Guy (Mon, 1943)
The Deerslayer (Rep, 1943)
Salute to the Marines (MGM, 1943)
The Sullivans (20th, 1944)
The Fighting Seabees (Rep, 1944)
Follow the Boys (Univ, 1944)
Three Men in White (MGM, 1944)
Moon over Las Vegas (Univ, 1944)
A Night of Adventure (RKO, 1944)
Roger Touhy—Gangster (20th, 1944)
Are These Our Parents? (Mon, 1944)
Marriage Is a Private Affair (MGM, 1944)
Since You Went Away (UA, 1944)
Three Little Sisters (Rep, 1944)
Barbary Coast Gent (MGM, 1944)
Bordertown Trail (Rep, 1944)
The Mummy's Curse (Univ, 1944)
God Is My Co-Pilot (WB, 1945)
The Chicago Kid (Rep, 1945)
Bells of Rosarita (Rep, 1945)
Bewitched (MGM, 1945)
Lady on a Train (Univ, 1945)

Black Market Babies (Mon, 1945)
The Master Key (Univ serial, 1945)
The Adventures of Rusty (Col, 1945)
Spellbound (UA, 1945)
Strange Confession (Univ, 1945)
Leave Her to Heaven (20th, 1945)
Betrayal from the East (RKO, 1945)
Come Out Fighting (Mon, 1945)
Danger Signal (WB, 1945)
Grissly's Million (Rep, 1945)
I'll Remember April (Univ, 1945)
Men in Her Diary (Univ, 1945)
Rough, Tough and Ready (Col, 1945)
The Tiger Woman (Rep, 1945)
The Shanghai Cobra (Mon, 1945)
Anna and the King of Siam (20th, 1946)
Courage of Lassie (MGM, 1946)
Love Laughs at Andy Hardy (MGM, 1946)
Secrets of a Sorority Girl (PRC, 1946)
Angel on My Shoulder (UA, 1946)
Criminal Court (RKO, 1946)
The Hoodlum Saint (MGM, 1946)
Dragonwyck (20th, 1946)
Renegades (Col, 1946)
Step by Step (RKO, 1946)
Don't Gamble with Strangers (Mon, 1946)
The Millerson Case (Co, 1947)
Call Northside 777 (20th, 1948)
Lulu Belle (Col, 1948)
Rustlers (RKO, 1949)
Henry the Rainmaker (Mon, 1949)
Mighty Joe Young (RKO, 1949)
Davy Crockett—Indian Scout (UA, 1950)
High Society (AA, 1955)
Illegal (WB, 1955)
Fort Yuma (UA, 1955)
The Broken Star (UA, 1956)
Fury at Gunsight Pass (Col, 1956)
Walk the Proud Land (Univ, 1956)
When Gangland Strikes (Rep, 1956)
Reprisal! (Col, 1956)
Everything but the Truth (Univ, 1956)
Last of the Badmen (AA, 1957)
Gunsight Ridge (UA, 1957)
The Saga of Hemp Brown (Univ, 1958)
The Oregon Trail (20th, 1959)
Frontier Uprising (UA, 1961)
The Gambler Wore a Gun (UA, 1961)
The Flight That Disappeared (UA, 1961)
Saintly Sinners (UA, 1962)
The Raiders (Univ, 1963)
For Those Who Think Young (Univ, 1964)

STANLEY RIDGES
(Stanley Charles Ridges)

Stanley Ridges, Francis McDonald, and Joel McCrea in Union Pacific *(1939).*

Born July 17, 1891, Southampton, England. Married Dorothea Crawford, child: daughter. Died April 22, 1951, Westbrook, Connecticut. Familiar on screen as the ingratiating American physician, lawyer, etc., despite his English nationality. On the London and New York stage before making film bow in *Crime Without Passion*. Other roles: *Union Pacific* (Casement), *The Sea Wolf* (Johnson), *They Died with Their Boots On* (Major Romulus Taipe), *To Be or Not to Be* (Professor Siletsky), *Wilson* (Admiral Grayton), *Possessed* (attending psychiatrist), etc.

Stanley Ridges to Barbara Stanwyck in *Internes Can't Take Money:* "I've got a nice little place up in the country. Think it over."

Films

Success (MG, 1923)
Crime Without Passion (Par, 1934)
The Scoundrel (Par, 1935)
Winterset (RKO, 1936)
Sinner Take All (MGM, 1936)
Internes Can't Take Money (Par, 1937)
Yellow Jack (MGM, 1938)
The Mad Miss Manton (RKO, 1938)
If I Were King (Par, 1938)
There's That Woman Again (Col, 1938)
Let Us Live! (Col, 1939)
Confessions of a Nazi Spy (WB, 1939)
I Stole a Million (Univ, 1939)

Silver on the Sage (Par, 1939)
Union Pacific (Par, 1939)
Each Dawn I Die (WB, 1939)
Espionage Agent (WB, 1939)
Dust Be My Destiny (WB, 1939)
Nick Carter, Master Detective (MGM, 1939)
Black Friday (Univ, 1940)
The Sea Wolf (WB, 1941)
Mr. District Attorney (Rep, 1941)
Sergeant York (WB, 1941)
They Died with Their Boots On (WB, 1941)

The Lady Is Willing (Col, 1942)
The Big Shot (WB, 1942)
To Be or Not to Be (UA, 1942)
Eagle Squadron (Univ, 1942)
Eyes in the Night (MGM, 1942)
Tarzan Triumphs (RKO, 1943)
Air Force (WB, 1943)
This Is the Army (WB, 1943)
The Master Race (RKO, 1944)
The Sign of the Cross (Par, 1944) [prologue to reissue of 1932 feature]
The Story of Dr. Wassell (Par, 1944)

Wilson (20th, 1944)
The Suspect (Univ, 1945)
Captain Eddie (20th, 1945)
God Is My Co-Pilot (WB, 1945)
The Phantom Speaks (Rep, 1945)
Because of Him (Univ, 1946)
Mr. Ace (UA, 1946)

Canyon Passage (Univ, 1946)
Possessed (WB, 1947)
An Act of Murder [a.k.a. Live Today for Tomorrow] (Univ, 1948)
You're My Everything (20th, 1949)
Streets of Laredo (Par, 1949)
The File on Thelma Jordan (Par, 1949)

Task Force (WB, 1949)
There's a Girl in My Heart (AA, 1949)
Paid in Full (Par, 1950)
No Way Out (20th, 1950)
The Groom Wore Spurs (Univ, 1951)

ELISABETH RISDON
(Elisabeth Evans)

Elisabeth Risdon, Peter Holden, Brandon Tynan, and Virginia Weidler in The Great Man Votes (1939).

Born 1887, Wandsworth, London, England. Died December 2, 1958, Santa Monica, California. Broad-faced London stage and screen player who had a long sojourn on the Broadway stage before turning to Hollywood films. Adept at creating all types of screen mothers: *Dead End* (Joel McCrea's), *The Roaring Twenties* (Priscilla Lane's), *Reap the Wild Wind* (Paulette Goddard's); or countrified grandmoms: *High Sierra* (Joan Leslie's). Sometimes stuffy aunts: *Theodora Goes Wild* (Irene Dunne's). Occasionally played her own nationality: *Random Harvest* (Mrs. Lloyd).

Elisabeth Risdon to Lupe Velez in *Mexican Spitfire's Blessed Event:* "You've ruined Dennis' career. Why don't you get out of his life before you ruin it *completely?*"

Films

The Cup Final Mystery (Br, 1914)
The Finger of Destiny (Br, 1914)
Inquisitive Ike (Br, 1914)
The Suicide Club (Br, 1914)
The Loss of the Birkenhead (Br, 1914)

Beautiful Jim [a.k.a. The Price of Justice] (Br, 1914)
The Bells of Rheims (Br, 1914)
It's a Long, Long Way to Tipperary (Br, 1914)

Her Luck in London (Br, 1914)
The Courage of a Coward (Br, 1914)
The Sound of Her Voice (Br, 1914)
The Idol of Paris (Br, 1914)
There's Good in Everyone (Br, 1915)

438

A Honeymoon for Three (Br, 1915)
Gilbert Gets Tiger-itis (Br, 1915)
Midshipman Easy (Br, 1915)
London's Yellow Peril (Br, 1915)
Florence Nightingale (Br, 1915)
From Shopgirl to Duchess (Br, 1915)
Another Man's Wife (Br, 1915)
Her Nameless Child (Br, 1915)
Grip (Br, 1915)
Home (Br, 1915)
The Christian (Br, 1915)
A Will of Her Own (Br, 1915)
Charity Ann (Br, 1915)
Fine Feathers (Br, 1915)
Love in a Wood (Br, 1915)
Meg the Lady (Br, 1916)
Esther (Br, 1916)
Driven [a.k.a. Desperation] (Br, 1916)
The Hypocrites [a.k.a. The Morals of Wey-
     bury] (Br, 1916)
Motherly Love (Br, 1916)
The Princess of Happy Chance (Br, 1916)
The Mother of Dartmoor (Br, 1916)
The Manxman (Br, 1916)
A Mother's Influence (Br, 1916)
Smith (Br, 1917)
A Star Overnight (Br, 1919)
Guard That Girl (Col, 1935)
Crime and Punishment (Col, 1935)
Don't Gamble with Love (Col, 1936)
Lady of Secrets (Col, 1936)
The King Steps Out (Col, 1936)
The Final Hour (Col, 1936)
Craig's Wife (Col, 1936)
Theodora Goes Wild (Col, 1936)
The Woman I Love (RKO, 1937)
Make Way for Tomorrow (Par, 1937)
Mountain Justice (WB, 1937)
They Won't Forget (WB, 1937)
Dead End (UA, 1937)
Mannequin (MGM, 1938)
Mad About Music (Univ, 1938)
Tom Sawyer, Detective (Par, 1938)
Cowboy from Brooklyn (WB, 1938)
My Bill (WB, 1938)

Girls on Probation (WB, 1938)
The Affairs of Annabel (RKO, 1938)
The Great Man Votes (RKO, 1939)
Sorority House (RKO, 1939)
The Girl from Mexico (RKO, 1939)
Five Came Back (RKO, 1939)
Full Confession (RKO, 1939)
The Man Who Dared (WB, 1939)
Mexican Spitfire (RKO, 1939)
The Adventures of Huckleberry Finn
     (MGM, 1939)
The Roaring Twenties (WB, 1939)
The Forgotten Woman (Univ, 1939)
Disputed Passage (Par, 1939)
The Man Who Wouldn't Talk (20th,
     1940)
Abe Lincoln in Illinois (RKO, 1940)
Honeymoon Deferred (Univ, 1940)
Ma, He's Making Eyes at Me (Univ,
     1940)
Saturday's Children (WB, 1940)
Sing, Dance, Plenty Hot [a.k.a. Mania for
     Melody] (Rep, 1940)
The Howards of Virginia (Col, 1940)
Mexican Spitfire Out West (RKO, 1940)
Slightly Tempted (Univ, 1940)
Let's Make Music (RKO, 1940)
High Sierra (WB, 1941)
Footlight Fever (RKO, 1941)
Mr. Dynamite (Univ, 1941)
Nice Girl? (Univ, 1941)
Mexican Spitfire's Baby (RKO, 1941)
Jail House Blues (Univ, 1942)
Mexican Spitfire at Sea (RKO, 1942)
The Man Who Returned to Life (Col,
     1942)
The Lady Is Willing (Col, 1942)
Reap the Wild Wind (Par, 1942)
Paris Calling (Univ, 1942)
Mexican Spitfire Sees a Ghost (RKO,
     1942)
Are Husbands Necessary? (Par, 1942)
I Live on Danger (Par, 1942)
Journey for Margaret (MGM, 1942)
Mexican Spitfire's Elephant (RKO, 1942)

Random Harvest (MGM, 1942)
The Amazing Mrs. Holliday (Univ, 1943)
Higher and Higher (RKO, 1943)
Lost Angel (MGM, 1943)
Mexican Spitfire's Blessed Event (RKO,
     1943)
Never a Dull Moment (Univ, 1943)
The Canterville Ghost (MGM, 1944)
Cobra Woman (Univ, 1944)
Weird Woman (Univ, 1944)
In the Meantime, Darling (20th, 1944)
Tall in the Saddle (RKO, 1944)
Blonde Fever (MGM, 1944)
The Fighting Guardsman (Col, 1945)
Grissly's Millions (Rep, 1945)
Mama Loves Papa (RKO, 1945)
A Song for Miss Julie (Rep, 1945)
The Unseen (Par, 1945)
Lover Come Back (Univ, 1946)
Roll On, Texas Moon (Rep, 1946)
They Made Me a Killer (Par, 1946)
The Walls Came Tumbling Down (Col,
     1946)
The Egg and I (Univ, 1947)
The Romance of Rosy Ridge (MGM, 1947)
The Shocking Miss Pilgrim (20th, 1947)
High Wall (MGM, 1947)
Life with Father (WB, 1947)
Mourning Becomes Electra (RKO, 1947)
The Bride Goes Wild (MGM, 1948)
Every Girl Should Be Married (RKO,
     1948)
Sealed Verdict (Par, 1948)
Bodyguard (RKO, 1948)
Down Dakota Way (Rep, 1949)
Guilty of Treason (EL, 1949)
Sierra (Univ, 1950)
The Secret Fury (RKO, 1950)
Bunco Squad (RKO, 1950)
Hills of Oklahoma (Rep, 1950)
The Milkman (Univ, 1950)
In Old Amarillo (Rep, 1951)
My True Story (Col, 1951)
Bannerline (MGM, 1951)
Scaramouche (MGM, 1952)

WILLARD ROBERTSON

Willard Robertson, Larry Steers, John St. Polis, Fred Santley, Herbert Moulton, and Richard Bennett in If I Had a Million *(1932).*

Born January 1, 1886, Runnels, Texas. Died April 5, 1948. Texas-born attorney who abandoned politics to become an actor. Circulated on camera as physician, lawyer, policeman, military officer, etc.

Willard Robertson to James Cagney in *Each Dawn I Die:*
"Listen, Ross, you're going to talk if we have to bury you in the hole for 20 years!"

Films

Last of the Duanes (Fox, 1930)
Skippy (Par, 1931)
Murder by the Clock (Par, 1931)
Silence (Par, 1931)
The Cisco Kid (Fox, 1931)
The Ruling Voice (FN, 1931)
Sooky (Par, 1931)
The Gay Caballero (Fox, 1932)
The Broken Wing (Par, 1932)
Sky Devils (UA, 1932)
The Famous Ferguson Case (FN, 1932)
I Am a Fugitive from a Chain Gang (WB, 1932)
So Big (WB, 1932)
Behind the Mask (Col, 1932)
If I Had a Million (Par, 1932)
The Strange Love of Molly Louvain (FN, 1932)
Tom Brown of Culver (Univ, 1932)
Doctor X (FN, 1932)
Guilty as Hell (Par, 1932)
Call Her Savage (Fox, 1932)
Central Park (FN, 1932)

Central Airport (FN, 1933)
Trick for Trick (Fox, 1933)
Destination Unknown (Univ, 1933)
Another Language (MGM, 1933)
Tugboat Annie (MGM, 1933)
The World Changes (FN, 1933)
The Mad Game (Fox, 1933)
Lady Killer (WB, 1933)
Whirlpool (Col, 1934)
Let's Talk It Over (Univ, 1934)
Operator 13 (MGM, 1934)
Heat Lightning (WB, 1934)
Wild Gold (Fox, 1934)
Dark Hazard (FN, 1934)
Gambling Lady (WB, 1934)
One Is Guilty (Col, 1934)
Two Alone (RKO, 1934)
I'll Tell the World (Univ, 1934)
Upper World (WB, 1934)
Murder in the Private Car (MGM, 1934)
Death on the Diamond (MGM, 1934)
Housewife (WB, 1934)
Here Comes the Navy (WB, 1934)

Have a Heart (MGM, 1934)
The Secret Bride (WB, 1934)
Biography of a Bachelor Girl (MGM, 1935)
Million Dollar Baby (Mon, 1935)
Mills of the Gods (Col, 1935)
Laddie (RKO, 1935)
Straight from the Heart (Univ, 1935)
Black Fury (FN, 1935)
Oil for the Lamps of China (WB, 1935)
The Old Homestead (Liberty, 1935)
O'Shaughnessy's Boy (MGM, 1935)
Dante's Inferno (Fox, 1935)
The Virginia Judge (Par, 1935)
His Night Out (Univ, 1935)
Forced Landing (Rep, 1935)
The Three Godfathers (MGM, 1936)
Dangerous Waters (Univ, 1936)
I Married a Doctor (FN, 1936)
The First Baby (20th, 1936)
The Gorgeous Hussy (MGM, 1936)
The Last of Mohicans (UA, 1936)
The Man Who Lived Twice (Col, 1936)

Wanted: Jane Turner (RKO, 1936)
Winterset (RKO, 1936)
That Girl from Paris (RKO, 1936)
John Meade's Woman (Par, 1937)
Larceny on the Air (Rep, 1937)
Park Avenue Logger (RKO, 1937)
The Go-Getter (WB, 1937)
This Is My Affair (20th, 1937)
Roaring Timber (Col, 1937)
Exclusive (Par, 1937)
Hot Water (20th, 1937)
Of Human Hearts (MGM, 1938)
Gangs of New York (Rep, 1938)
Island in the Sky (20th, 1938)
You and Me (Par, 1938)
Men with Wings (Par, 1938)
Kentucky (20th, 1938)
Torchy Gets Her Man (WB, 1938)

Jesse James (20th, 1939)
Heritage of the Desert (Par, 1939)
My Son Is a Criminal (Col, 1939)
Main Street Lawyer (Rep, 1939)
Each Dawn I Die (WB, 1939)
Range War (Par, 1939)
The Cat and the Canary (Par, 1939)
Two Bright Boys (Univ, 1939)
My Little Chickadee (Univ, 1940)
Remember the Night (Par, 1940)
Castle on the Hudson (WB, 1940)
Lucky Cisco Kid (20th, 1940)
Brigham Young—Frontiersman (20th, 1940)
North West Mounted Police (Par, 1940)
The Monster and the Girl (Par, 1941)
I Wanted Wings (Par, 1941)
Men of the Timberland (Univ, 1941)

The Night of January 16th (Par, 1941)
Texas (Col, 1941)
Juke Girl (WB, 1942)
Air Force (WB, 1943)
The Ox-Bow Incident (20th, 1943)
Background to Danger (WB, 1943)
No Time for Love (Par, 1943)
Nine Girls (Col, 1944)
Along Came Jones (RKO, 1945)
The Virginian (Par, 1946)
Perilous Holiday (Col, 1946)
Renegades (Col, 1946)
Gallant Journey (Col, 1946)
To Each His Own (Par, 1946)
My Favorite Brunette (Par, 1947)
Deep Valley (WB, 1947)
Fury at Furnace Creek (20th, 1948)
Sitting Pretty (20th, 1948)

MAY ROBSON
(Mary Robison)

David Holt, May Robson, Harry Myers, and Marcia Mae Jones in The Adventures of Tom Sawyer *(1938).*

Born April 19, 1858, Melbourne, Australia. Married 1) Edward Gore (1880), children: Edward, two others died in childhood; widowed (1883); 2) A. H. Brown (1889); widowed (1922). Died October 20, 1942, Beverly Hills, California. Extensive stage appearances as character actress before dabbling in silent films: *A Harp in Hock* (landlady), *The King of Kings* (mother of Gestas), etc. Found her stride as the flinty, sharp-featured granny in talkies who could be incorrigible, self-sufficient, but basically kind. Oscar-nominated for Best Actress as Apple Annie in Frank Capra's *Lady for a Day* (but lost to Katharine Hepburn of *Morning Glory*). Was imperious and impish as Clark Gable's chic mother in *Wife vs. Secretary* but back to her proletarian self as Aunt Polly in *The Adventures of Tom Sawyer*. Crusty Aunt Etta in the *Four Daughters/Daughters Courageous* series and had her own starring vehicle (*Granny Get Your Gun*) at Warner Bros.

May Robson to Greta Garbo in *Anna Karenina*: "You, my dear, have the divine gift of silence."

Films

How Molly Made Good (Sterling, 1915)
Pals in Paris (PDC, 1926)
The Angel of Broadway (Pathé, 1927)
Chicago (Pathé, 1927)
A Harp in Hock (Pathé, 1927)
The King of Kings (Pathé, 1927)
The Rejuvenation of Aunt Mary (PDC, 1927)
Rubber Tires (PDC, 1927)
Turkish Delight (PDC, 1927)
The Blue Danube (Pathé, 1928)
Mother's Millions (Univ, 1931)
Letty Lynton (MGM, 1932)
Strange Interlude (MGM, 1932)

Two Against the World (WB, 1932)
Red-Headed Woman (MGM, 1932)
Little Orphan Annie (RKO, 1932)
If I Had a Million (Par, 1932)
Reunion in Vienna (MGM, 1933)
Dinner at Eight (MGM, 1933)
Beauty for Sale (MGM, 1933)
Broadway to Hollywood (MGM, 1933)
Solitaire Man (MGM, 1933)
Dancing Lady (MGM, 1933)
Lady for a Day (Col, 1933)
One Man's Journey (RKO, 1933)
Alice in Wonderland (Par, 1933)
The White Sister (MGM, 1933)

Men Must Fight (MGM, 1933)
You Can't Buy Everything (MGM, 1934)
Straight Is the Way (MGM, 1934)
Lady by Choice (Col, 1934)
Vanessa—Her Love Story (MGM, 1935)
Reckless (MGM, 1935)
Grand Old Girl (RKO, 1935)
Age of Indiscretion (MGM, 1935)
Anna Karenina (MGM, 1935)
Strangers All (RKO, 1935)
Mills of the Gods (Col, 1935)
Three Kids and a Queen (Univ, 1935)
Wife vs. Secretary (MGM, 1936)
The Captain's Kid (WB, 1936)

Rainbow on the River (RKO, 1936)
Woman in Distress (Col, 1937)
A Star Is Born (UA, 1937)
The Perfect Specimen (WB, 1937)
Top of the Town (Univ, 1937)
The Adventures of Tom Sawyer (UA, 1938)
Bringing Up Baby (RKO, 1938)
The Texans (Par, 1938)

Four Daughters (WB, 1938)
They Made Me a Criminal (WB, 1939)
Yes, My Darling Daughter (WB, 1939)
Daughters Courageous (WB, 1939)
Four Wives (WB, 1939)
The Kid from Kokomo (WB, 1939)
Nurse Edith Cavell (RKO, 1939)
That's Right, You're Wrong (RKO, 1939)
Irene (RKO, 1940)

The Texas Rangers Ride Again (Par, 1940)
Granny Get Your Gun (WB, 1940)
Four Mothers (WB, 1941)
Million Dollar Baby (WB, 1941)
Playmates (RKO, 1941)
Joan of Paris (RKO, 1942)

SIG RUMANN
(Siegfried Albon Rumann)

Edward Everett Horton, Donna Reed, and Sig Rumann in Faithful in My Fashion (1946).

Born October 11, 1884, Hamburg, Germany. Married Claire Tuttleman. Died February 14, 1967, Julian, California. Veteran of German and New York stage; came to films in mid-1930s as a Fox contractee. Stern demeanor and expressively bushy eyebrows and thick accent. Could play drama or farce—good or bad guys—with equal ease. A favorite foil of the Marx Brothers: *A Night at the Opera* (Herman Gottlieb), *A Day at the Races* (Dr. Leopold X. Steinberg), etc. Would later trade double-takes and insults with Jerry Lewis *(Living It Up, The Errand Boy*, etc.), the Bowery Boys *(The Spy Chasers)*, and even Judy Canova *(Carolina Cannonball)*. Well remembered for his Iranoff, one of the Russian trio trailing Greta Garbo to Paris in *Ninotchka* and as Colonel "Concentration Camp" Ehrhardt in Jack Benny and Carole Lombard's *To Be or Not to Be*. Often played Axis agents during World War II period: *Confessions of a Nazi Spy* (Krogman), *They Came to Blow Up America* (Dr. Baumer), etc.

Sig Rumann to Luis Alberni in *World Premiere:* "A grand piece of sabotage, and a splendid toll of human life. I shall never forget it."

Films

Royal Box (Ger, 1929)
The World Moves On (Fox, 1934)
Servants' Entrance (Fox, 1934)
Marie Galante (Fox, 1934)
The Wedding Night (UA, 1935)
East of Java (Univ, 1935)
Under Pressure (Fox, 1935)
Spring Tonic (Fox, 1935)
The Farmer Takes a Wife (Fox, 1935)
A Night at the Opera (MGM, 1935)
The Princess Comes Across (Par, 1936)
The Bold Caballero (Rep, 1936)
On the Avenue (20th, 1937)
Seventh Heaven (20th, 1937)
Midnight Taxi (20th, 1937)
Think Fast, Mr. Moto (20th, 1937)
This Is My Affair (20th, 1937)
Love Under Fire (20th, 1937)
Thin Ice (20th, 1937)
Lancer Spy (20th, 1937)
Heidi (20th, 1937)
Thank You, Mr. Moto (20th, 1937)
Maytime (MGM, 1937)
The Great Hospital Mystery (20th, 1937)
A Day at the Races (MGM, 1937)
Nothing Sacred (UA, 1937)
Paradise for Three (MGM, 1938)
The Great Waltz (MGM, 1938)
The Saint in New York (RKO, 1938)
I'll Give a Million (20th, 1938)
Suez (20th, 1938)
Girls on Probation (WB, 1938)
Never Say Die (Par, 1939)
Honolulu (MGM, 1939)
Ninotchka (MGM, 1939)

Remember? (MGM, 1939)
Confessions of a Nazi Spy (WB, 1939)
Only Angels Have Wings (Col, 1939)
Dr. Ehrlich's Magic Bullet (WB, 1940)
Outside the Three-Mile Limit (Col, 1940)
I Was an Adventuress (20th, 1940)
Comrade X (MGM, 1940)
Four Sons (20th, 1940)
Bitter Sweet (MGM, 1940)
Victory (Par, 1940)
So Ends Our Night (UA, 1941)
That Uncertain Feeling (UA, 1941)
The Man Who Lost Himself (Univ, 1941)
This Woman Is Mine (Univ, 1941)
Shining Victory (WB, 1941)
Love Crazy (MGM, 1941)
World Premiere (Par, 1941)
The Wagons Roll at Night (WB, 1941)
Remember Pearl Harbor (Rep, 1942)
Crossroads (MGM, 1942)
Enemy Agents Meet Ellery Queen (Col, 1942)
China Girl (20th, 1942)
Berlin Correspondent (20th, 1942)
To Be or Not to Be (UA, 1942)
Desperate Journey (WB, 1942)
They Came to Blow Up America (20th, 1943)
Sweet Rosie O'Grady (20th, 1943)
The Song of Bernadette (20th, 1943)
Tarzan Triumphs (RKO, 1943)
Government Girl (RKO, 1943)
The Hitler Gang (Par, 1944)
The House of Frankenstein (Univ, 1944)
It Happened Tomorrow (UA, 1944)

Summer Storm (UA, 1944)
A Royal Scandal (20th, 1945)
The Dolly Sisters (20th, 1945)
The Men in Her Diary (Univ, 1945)
She Went to the Races (MGM, 1945)
A Night in Casablanca (UA, 1946)
Faithful in My Fashion (MGM, 1946)
Night and Day (WB, 1946)
Mother Wore Tights (20th, 1947)
If You Knew Susie (RKO, 1948)
The Emperor Waltz (Par, 1948)
Give My Regards to Broadway (20th, 1948)
Border Incident (MGM, 1949)
Father Is a Bachelor (Col, 1950)
On the Riviera (20th, 1951)
The World in His Arms (Univ, 1952)
O. Henry's Full House (20th, 1952)
Houdini (Par, 1953)
Stalag 17 (Par, 1953)
Ma and Pa Kettle on Vacation (Univ, 1953)
The Glenn Miller Story (Univ, 1954)
White Christmas (Par, 1954)
Three-Ring Circus (Par, 1954)
Living It Up (Par, 1954)
Many Rivers to Cross (MGM, 1955)
Carolina Cannonball (Rep, 1955)
The Spy Chasers (AA, 1955)
The Wings of Eagles (MGM, 1957)
The Errand Boy (Par, 1961)
Robin and the Seven Hoods (WB, 1964)
36 Hours (MGM, 1965)
The Fortune Cookie (UA, 1966)
The Last of the Secret Agents? (Par, 1966)

JOE SAWYER
(Joseph Sauer)

Joe Sawyer and George J. Lewis in Gilda *(1946).*

Born 1901. The exasperated tough cop, tough top sergeant, tough anything. TV series: "The Adventures of Rin Tin Tin" (as Sergeant Biff O'Hara).

Joe Sawyer in *The Arizonian:* "A thousand dollars to anybody that'll plug another marshal!"

Films

As Joseph Sauer:
Forgotten Commandments (Par, 1932)
Huddle (MGM, 1932)
Saturday's Millions (Univ, 1933)
Ace of Aces (RKO, 1933)
College Humor (Par, 1933)
Son of a Sailor (FN, 1933)
The Stranger's Return (MGM, 1933)
Looking for Trouble (UA, 1934)
Stanboul Quest (MGM, 1934)
Death on the Diamond (MGM, 1934)
Jimmy the Gent (WB, 1934)
Behold My Wife! (Par, 1934)
The Notorious Sophie Lang (Par, 1934)
The Band Plays On (MGM, 1934)
The Westerner (Col, 1934)
Car 99 (Par, 1935)
The Informer (RKO, 1935)
Broadway Gondolier (WB, 1935)
The Arizonian (RKO, 1935)
The Whole Town's Talking (Col, 1935)

Special Agent (WB, 1935)

As Joe (Joseph) Sawyer:
Little Big Shot (WB, 1935)
Moonlight on the Prairie (WB, 1935)
I Found Stella Parish (FN, 1935)
Frisco Kid (WB, 1935)
Man of Iron (WB, 1935)
The Petrified Forest (WB, 1936)
Freshman Love (WB, 1936)
Big Brown Eyes (Par, 1936)
The Walking Dead (WB, 1936)
And Sudden Death (Par, 1936)
High Tension (20th, 1936)
Murder with Pictures (Par, 1936)
Special Investigator (RKO, 1936)
Crash Donovan (Univ, 1936)
Great Guy (GN, 1936)
The Leathernecks Have Landed (Rep, 1936)
Pride of the Marines (Col, 1936)
Two in a Crowd (Univ, 1936)

The Black Legion (WB, 1936)
San Quentin (FN, 1937)
Slim (WB, 1937)
Navy Blues (Rep, 1937)
Midnight Madonna (Par, 1937)
Reported Missing (Univ, 1937)
The Lady Fights Back (Univ, 1937)
Motor Madness (Col, 1937)
They Gave Him a Gun (MGM, 1937)
Tarzan's Revenge (MGM, 1938)
Passport Husband (20th, 1938)
Always in Trouble (20th, 1938)
Heart of the North (WB, 1938)
Stolen Heaven (Par, 1938)
The Storm (Univ, 1938)
Gambling Ship (Univ, 1938)
The Lady and the Mob (Col, 1939)
Union Pacific (Par, 1939)
You Can't Get Away with Murder (WB, 1939)
Inside Information (Univ, 1939)

I Stole a Million (Univ, 1939)
Frontier Marshal (20th, 1939)
Sabotage (Rep, 1939)
The Roaring Twenties (WB, 1939)
The Grapes of Wrath (20th, 1940)
The House Across the Bay (UA, 1940)
The Man from Montreal (Univ, 1940)
Dark Command (Rep, 1940)
King of the Lumberjacks (WB, 1940)
Lucky Cisco Kid (20th, 1940)
The Long Voyage Home (UA, 1940)
Melody Ranch (Rep, 1940)
The Border Legion (Rep, 1940)
Wildcat Bus (RKO, 1940)
Santa Fe Trail (WB, 1940)
The Lady from Cheyenne (Univ, 1941)
Sergeant York (WB, 1941)
Tanks a Million (UA, 1941)
Belle Starr (20th, 1941)
Last of the Duanes (20th, 1941)
Down Mexico Way (Rep, 1941)
Swamp Water (20th, 1941)
They Died with Their Boots On (WB, 1941)
You're in the Army Now (WB, 1941)
Sundown Jim (20th, 1942)
Hay Foot (UA, 1942)
Brooklyn Orchid (UA, 1942)
Wrecking Crew (Par, 1942)
Taxi, Mister (UA, 1943)
Cowboy in Manhattan (Univ, 1943)

Buckskin Frontier (UA, 1943)
The Outlaw (RKO, 1943)
Fall In (UA, 1943)
Hit the Ice (Univ, 1943)
Prairie Chickens (UA, 1943)
Tornado (Par, 1943)
Yanks Ahoy (UA, 1943)
Alaska Highway (Par, 1943)
Let's Face It (Par, 1943)
Sleepy Lagoon (Rep, 1943)
Tarzan's Desert Mystery (RKO, 1943)
Moon over Las Vegas (Univ, 1944)
South of Dixie (Univ, 1944)
Hey, Rookie (ol, 1944)
The Singing Sheriff (Univ, 1944)
High Powered (Par, 1945)
Brewster's Millions (Univ, 1945)
The Naughty Nineties (Univ, 1945)
Deadline at Dawn (RKO, 1946)
Gilda (Col, 1946)
Joe Palooka—Champ (Mon, 1946)
Inside Job (Univ, 1946)
G.I. War Brides (Rep, 1946)
The Runaround (Univ, 1946)
Roses Are Red (20th, 1947)
Christmas Eve [a.k.a. Sinners' Holiday] (UA, 1947)
Big Town After Dark (Par, 1947)
A Double Life (Univ, 1947)
If You Knew Susie (RKO, 1948)
Fighting Father Dunne (RKO, 1948)

Half Past Midnight (20th, 1948)
Here Comes Trouble (UA, 1948)
Coroner Creek (Col, 1948)
Fighting Back (20th, 1948)
The Untamed Breed (Col, 1948)
Deputy Marshal (Screen Guild, 1949)
The Stagecoach Kid (RKO, 1949)
The Gay Amigo (UA, 1949)
Kazan (Col, 1949)
And Baby Makes Three (Col, 1949)
The Lucky Stiff (UA, 1949)
Tucson (20th, 1949)
Curtain Call at Cactus Creek (Univ, 1950)
Traveling Saleswomen (Col, 1950)
Blondie's Hero (Col, 1950)
Operation Haylift (Lip, 1950)
The Flying Missile (Col, 1950)
The Pride of Maryland (Rep, 1951)
Comin' Round the Mountain (Univ, 1951)
As You Were (Lip, 1951)
Indian Uprising (Col, 1952)
Red Skies of Montana (20th, 1952)
It Came from Outer Space (Univ, 1953)
Taza, Son of Cochise (Univ, 1954)
Riding Shotgun (WB, 1954)
Johnny Dark (Univ, 1954)
The Kettles in the Ozarks (Univ, 1955)
The Killing (UA, 1956)
North to Alaska (20th, 1960)
How the West Was Won (MGM, 1962)

NATALIE SCHAFER

In Forever, Darling *(1956).*

Born November 5, 1912, Red Bank, New Jersey. Married Louis Calhern (1934); divorced (1942). Elegant dizzy society dame on screen, whose characters are usually concerned more with gossip and etiquette than with substance. Was the well-bred madam in *The Day of the Locust*. Extensive stage work. TV series: "Gilligan's Island" (as Lovey Howell) and "The New Adventures of Gilligan's Island" (as the voice of Lovey Howell).

Natalie Schafer to Hedy Lamarr in *Dishonored Lady:* "Darling, I'm just dying to hear what you've been up to . . . you must tell me *everything.*"

Films

The Body Disappears (WB, 1941)
Reunion in France (MGM, 1942)
Marriage Is a Private Affair (MGM, 1944)
Masquerade in Mexico (Par, 1945)
Molly and Me (20th, 1945)
Keep Your Powder Dry (MGM, 1945)
Wonder Man (RKO, 1945)
Dishonored Lady (UA, 1947)
The Other Love (UA, 1947)
Repeat Performance (EL, 1947)

Secret Beyond the Door (Univ, 1948)
The Snake Pit (20th, 1948)
The Time of Your Life (UA, 1948)
Caught (MGM, 1949)
Payment on Demand (RKO, 1951)
Take Care of My Little Girl (20th, 1951)
The Law and the Lady (MGM, 1951)
Callaway Went Thataway (MGM, 1951)
Has Anyone Seen My Gal? (Univ, 1952)
Just Across the Street (Univ, 1952)
The Girl Next Door (20th, 1953)

Female on the Beach (Univ, 1955)
Forever, Darling (MGM, 1956)
Anastasia (20th, 1956)
Oh, Men! Oh, Women! (20th, 1957)
Bernardine (20th, 1957)
Susan Slade (WB, 1961)
Back Street (Univ, 1961)
40 Carats (Col, 1973)
The Day of the Locust (Par, 1975)

JOSEPH SCHILDKRAUT

Sally Eilers, Neil Hamilton, Patricia Farr, and Joseph Schildkraut in Lady Behave! *(1937).*

Born March 22, 1895, Vienna, Austria. Married 1) Elise Bartlett; divorced; 2) Mary McKay; 3) Lenora Rogers (1963). Died January 21, 1964, New York City, New York. Admired Austrian theater star who made a solid reputation on the New York stage. Handsome leading man of the silents who played villains occasionally: *The King of Kings* (Judas Iscariot). Was Gaylord Ravenal to Laura La Plante's Magnolia in the part-talking *Show Boat*. From mid-1930s onward a sleak character lead, usually as sophisticated villains (e.g., Ferencz Vadas of *The Shop Around the Corner*). But won a BSAAA for his sympathetic portrait of Captain Dreyfus in *The Life of Emile Zola*. Later career highlighted by his sensitive portrayal of Otto Frank in *The Diary of Anne Frank*. TV series: "Joseph Schildkraut Presents" (as the host).

Joseph Schildkraut to Norma Shearer in *Marie Antoinette:* "I am a *power* in Paris. I have the confidence—yes, even the disgusting *affection*—of the mob."

Films

Schlemiehl (Ger, 1914)
The Life of Theodore Herzl (Aus, 1918)
Orphans of the Storm (UA, 1922)
The Song of Love (Associated FN, 1924)
The Road to Yesterday (Pathé, 1925)
Shipwrecked (PDC, 1926)
Young April (PDC, 1926)
Meet the Prince (PDC, 1926)
The King of Kings (Pathé, 1927)
The Heart Thief (PDC, 1927)
His Dog (Pathe, 1927)
The Forbidden Woman (Pathé, 1927)
The Blue Danube (Pathé, 1928)
Tenth Avenue (Pathé, 1928)
Show Boat (Univ, 1929)

The Mississippi Gambler (Univ, 1929)
Cock o' the Walk (Sono Art-World Wide, 1930)
Night Ride (Univ, 1930)
Die Sehnsucht Jeder Frau (MGM, 1930) [Ger-language version of *A Lady to Love*]
Carnival (Br, 1931)
Cleopatra (Par, 1934)
Viva Villa! (MGM, 1934)
Sisters Under the Skin (Col, 1934)
Blue Danube (Br, 1934)
The Crusades (Par, 1935)
The Garden of Allah (UA, 1936)
Slave Ship (20th, 1937)

The Life of Emile Zola (WB, 1937)
Souls at Sea (Par, 1937)
Lancer Spy (20th, 1937)
Lady Behave (Rep, 1937)
The Baroness and the Butler (20th, 1938)
Marie Antoinette (MGM, 1938)
Suez (20th, 1938)
Idiot's Delight (MGM, 1939)
The Three Musketeers (20th, 1939)
The Man in the Iron Mask (UA, 1939)
Mr. Moto Takes a Vacation (20th, 1939)
Lady of the Tropics (MGM, 1939)
The Rains Came (20th, 1939)
Barricade (20th, 1939)
Pack Up Your Troubles (20th, 1939)

The Shop Around the Corner (MGM, 1940)
Phantom Raiders (MGM, 1940)
Rangers of Fortune (Par, 1940)
Meet the Wildcat (Univ, 1940)
The Parson of Panamint (Par, 1941)

Flame of Barbary Coast (Rep, 1945)
The Cheaters (Rep, 1945)
Monsieur Beaucaire (Par, 1946)
Plainsman and the Lady (Rep, 1946)
Northwest Outpost (Rep, 1947)
Old Los Angeles (Rep, 1948)

Gallant Legion (Rep, 1948)
The Diary of Anne Frank (20th, 1959)
King of the Roaring Twenties—The Story of Arnold Rothstein (AA, 1961)
The Greatest Story Ever Told (UA, 1965)

ARTHUR SHIELDS

With Robert Mitchum in River of No Return *(1954).*

Born February 15, 1896, Dublin, Ireland. Married Aileen O'Connor (1950), children: two. Died April 27, 1970, Santa Barbara, California. Less famous Irish actor brother of Barry Fitzgerald. Member of Dublin's Abbey Players, where he also directed. Made silent shorts in England. In Hollywood often used by director John Ford: *The Plough and the Stars* (Padraic Pearse), *Drums Along the Mohawk* (Father Rosenkranz), *The Long Voyage Home* (Donkeyman), *How Green Was My Valley* (Mr. Parry), *She Wore a Yellow Ribbon* (Dr. O'Laughlin), and *The Quiet Man* (Reverend Cyril Playfair).

Arthur Shields to Ian Hunter in *The Long Voyage Home:* "Best thing to do with memories is *forget 'em.*"

Films

The Plough and the Stars (RKO, 1936)
Drums Along the Mohawk (20th, 1939)
The Long Voyage Home (UA, 1940)
Little Nellie Kelly (MGM, 1940)
Lady Scarface (RKO, 1941)
The Gay Falcon (RKO, 1941)
How Green Was My Valley (20th, 1941)
Confirm or Deny (20th, 1941)
Broadway (Univ, 1942)
This Above All (20th, 1942)

Pacific Rendezvous (MGM, 1942)
Gentleman Jim (WB, 1942)
Nightmare (Univ, 1942)
Random Harvest (MGM, 1942)
The Black Swan (20th, 1942)
Madame Curie (MGM, 1943)
Lassie Come Home (MGM, 1943)
The Man from Down Under (MGM, 1943)
The Keys of the Kingdom (20th, 1944)

The White Cliffs of Dover (MGM, 1944)
The Sign of the Cross (Par, 1944) [prologue to reissue of 1932 feature]
National Velvet (MGM, 1944)
Youth Runs Wild (RKO, 1944)
Roughly Speaking (WB, 1945)
The Corn Is Green (WB, 1945)
Too Young to Know (WB, 1945)
The Valley of Decision (MGM. 1945)
The Picture of Dorian Gray (MGM, 1945)

Three Strangers (WB, 1946)
Gallant Journey (Col, 1946)
The Verdict (WB, 1946)
Never Say Goodbye (WB, 1946)
The Shocking Miss Pilgrim (20th, 1947)
Easy Come, Easy Go (Par 1947)
The Fabulous Dorseys (UA, 1947)
Seven Keys to Baldpate (RKO, 1947)
Fighting Father Dunne (RKO, 1948)
Tap Roots (Univ, 1948)
My Own True Love (Par, 1948)
The Fighting O'Flynn [a.k.a. The O'Flynn] (Univ, 1949)
Challenge to Lassie (MGM, 1949)

Red Light (UA, 1949)
She Wore a Yellow Ribbon (RKO, 1949)
Tarzan and the Slave Girl (RKO, 1950)
The People Against O'Hara (MGM, 1951)
Apache Drums (Univ, 1951)
Sealed Cargo (RKO, 1951)
Blue Blood (Mon, 1951)
A Wonderful Life (Protestant Films, 1951)
The Barefoot Mailman (Col, 1951)
The Quiet Man (Rep, 1952)
Scandal at Scourie (MGM, 1953)
Main Street to Broadway (MGM, 1953)

South Sea Woman (WB, 1953)
Pride of Blue Grass (AA, 1953)
World for Ransom (AA, 1954)
River of No Return (20th, 1954)
The King and Four Queens (UA, 1956)
The Daughter of Dr. Jekyll (AA, 1957)
Enchanted Island (WB, 1958)
Night of the Quarter Moon (MGM, 1959)
For the Love of Mike (20th, 1960)
King of the Roaring Twenties—The Story of Arnold Rothstein (AA, 1961)
The Pigeon That Took Rome (Par, 1962)

IVAN SIMPSON

In Man of Two Worlds (1934).

Born February 4, 1875, Glasgow, Scotland. Died October 12, 1951, New York City, New York. A great favorite of star George Arliss, performing in Arliss' silent and sound versions of *The Green Goddess* (Watkins/Hawkins) and *The Man Who Played God* (Carter); also in his *Disraeli* (Hugh Myers), *Old English* (Joe Phillin), *The Millionaire* (Dr. Harvey), *The House of Rothschild* (Amschel Rothschild), etc.

Ivan Simpson to Henry Fonda in *The Male Animal*: "Such a Sunday I never hope to see again. You were the subject of every sermon in town."

Films

The Dictator (Independent, 1915)
Out of the Drifts (Par, 1916)
The Man Who Played God (UA, 1922)
The Green Goddess (G, 1923)
Twenty-One (Associated FN, 1924)

$20.00 a Week (Selznick, 1924)
Miss Bluebeard (Par, 1925)
Wild, Wild Susan (Par, 1925)
Lovers in Quarantine (Par, 1926)
A Kiss for Cinderella (Par, 1926)

Woman Handled (Par, 1926)
Disraeli (WB, 1929)
Evidence (WB, 1929)
The Green Goddess (WB, 1930)
Old English (WB, 1930)

Inside the Lines (RKO, 1930)
Isle of Escape (WB, 1930)
Manslaughter (Par, 1930)
The Sea God (Par, 1930)
The Way of All Men (FN, 1930)
The Millionaire (WB, 1931)
The Lady Who Dared (FN, 1931)
The Reckless Hour (FN, 1931)
I Like Your Nerve (FN, 1931)
Safe in Hell (FN, 1931)
The Man Who Played God (WB, 1932)
A Passport to Hell (Fox, 1932)
The Crash (FN, 1932)
The Phantom of Crestwood (RKO, 1932)
The Monkey's Paw (RKO, 1933)
The Past of Mary Holmes (RKO, 1933)
The Silk Express (WB, 1933)
Midnight Mary (MGM, 1933)
Voltaire (WB, 1933)
Charlie Chan's Greatest Case (20th, 1933)
Blind Adventure (RKO, 1933)
The Mystery of Mr. X (MGM, 1934)
Man of Two Worlds (RKO, 1934)
The House of Rothschild (UA, 1934)
The World Moves On (Fox, 1934)
British Agent (FN, 1934)

Among the Missing (Col, 1934)
Shadow of Doubt (MGM, 1935)
Mark of the Vampire (MGM, 1935)
David Copperfield (MGM, 1935)
The Bishop Misbehaves (MGM, 1935)
The Perfect Gentleman (MGM, 1935)
Mutiny on the Bounty (MGM, 1935)
East of Java (Univ, 1935)
Splendor (UA, 1935)
Captain Blood (FN, 1935)
Trouble for Two (MGM, 1936)
Small Town Girl (MGM, 1936)
Little Lord Fauntleroy (UA, 1936)
Mary of Scotland (RKO, 1936)
Lloyds of London (20th, 1936)
Maid of Salem (Par, 1937)
A Night of Mystery (Par, 1937)
The Prince and the Pauper (WB, 1937)
London by Night (MGM, 1937)
Invisible Enemy (Rep, 1938)
The Baroness and the Butler (20th, 1938)
The Adventures of Robin Hood (WB, 1938)
Marie Antoinette (MGM, 1938)
Booloo (Par, 1938)
The Sun Never Sets (Univ, 1939)

The Hound of the Baskervilles (20th, 1939)
The Adventures of Sherlock Holmes (20th, 1939)
Made for Each Other (UA, 1939)
Never Say Die (Par, 1939)
Rulers of the Sea (Par, 1939)
The Invisible Man Returns (Univ, 1940)
New Moon (MGM, 1940)
The Body Disappears (WB, 1941)
Nazi Agent (MGM, 1942)
Nightmare (Univ, 1942)
The Male Animal (WB, 1942)
They All Kissed the Bride (Col, 1942)
Youth on Parade (Rep, 1942)
Random Harvest (MGM, 1942)
Government Girl (RKO, 1943)
This Land Is Mine (RKO, 1943)
Two Weeks to Live (RKO, 1943)
Forever and a Day (RKO, 1943)
My Kingdom for a Cook (Col, 1943)
The Hour Before the Dawn (Par, 1944)
Jane Eyre (20th, 1944)
My Girl Tisa (WB, 1948)

RUSSELL SIMPSON

Johnny Mack Brown, George Shelley, and Russell Simpson in the serial Wild West Days *(1937).*

Born June 17, 1880, San Francisco, California. Married Gertrude _____, child: Roberta. Died December 12, 1959, Hollywood, California. Participated in the Alaskan gold rush; later on Broadway for producer David Belasco. Starred in several silent Westerns (a handsome leading man). Tall actor with penetrating eyes who had switched to character roles by the 1930s— efficient as the grizzly pioneer type. Often employed by John Ford: *Drums Along the Mohawk* (Dr. Petry), *The Grapes of Wrath* (Pa Joad), *Tobacco Road* (sheriff), *They Were Expendable* (Dad, the shipyard chief), *My Darling Clementine* (John Simpson), etc.

Russell Simpson to Walter Huston in *Abraham Lincoln:* "Abe, I ain't payin' you no forty cents a day to spark a pretty gal."

Films

The Girl of the Golden West (Par, 1915)
The Old Homestead (Par, 1916)
Lovely Mary (Col, 1916)
The Feud Girl (Par, 1916)
Fate's Boomerang (World, 1916)
The Barrier (Rex Beach Productions, 1917)
Blue Jeans (M, 1918)
Bill Apperson's Boy (FN, 1919)
The Brand (G, 1919)
Fighting Cressy (Pathé, 1919)
Our Teddy (FN, 1919)
The Branding Iron (G, 1920)
Bunty Pulls the Strings (G, 1921)
Godless Men (G, 1921)
Shadows of Conscience (Russell, 1921)
Snowblind (G, 1921)
Under the Lash (Par, 1921)

When Love Is Young (Arista, 1922)
Across the Deadline (Univ, 1922)
Rags to Riches (WB, 1922)
Fools of Fortune (Allied Pictures, 1922)
Peg o' My Heart (M, 1922)
The Kingdom Within (Hodkinson, 1922)
Human Hearts (Univ, 1922)
Circus Days (Associated FN, 1923)
The Virginian (Preferred, 1923)
Defying Destiny (Selznick, 1923)
The Rip-Tide (Arrow, 1923)
The Girl of the Golden West (Associated FN, 1923)
The Huntress (Associated FN, 1923)
Hflame (M, 1923)
Painted People (Associated FN, 1924)
The Narrow Street (WB, 1924)
Beauty and the Bad Man (PDC, 1925)

The Eagle (UA, 1925)
Why Women Love (FN, 1925)
Faint Perfume (B. P. Schulberg, 1925)
Thunder Mountain (Fox, 1925)
Old Shoes (Hollywood Pictures, 1925)
Paint and Powder (Chadwick, 1925)
The Splendid Road (FN, 1925)
The Re-Creation of Brian Kent (Principal, 1925)
Ship of Souls (Associated Exhibitors, 1925)
The Social Highwayman (WB, 1926)
The Earth Woman (Associated Exhibitors, 1926)
Rustling for Cupid (Fox, 1926)
Lovey Mary (MGM, 1926)
Annie Laurie (MGM, 1927)
The Frontiersman (MGM, 1927)

452

Wild Geese (Tif, 1927)
Now We're in the Air (Par, 1927)
The First Auto (WB, 1927)
The Heart of the Yukon (Pathé, 1927)
God's Great Wilderness (American Cinema, 1927)
Tropical Nights (Tif, 1928)
The Trail of '98 (MGM, 1928)
Life's Mockery (Chadwick, 1928)
The Bushranger (MGM, 1928)
After the Fog (Beacon, 1929)
Innocents of Paris (Par, 1929)
Noisy Neighbors (Pathé, 1929)
My Lady's Past (Tif, 1929)
The Kid's Clever (Tif, 1929)
The Sap (WB, 1929)
The Loan Star Ranger (Fox, 1930)
Abraham Lincoln (UA, 1930)
Billy the Kid [TV title: *The Highwayman Rides*] (MGM, 1930)
Man to Man (WB, 1930)
Alexander Hamilton (WB, 1931)
The Great Meadow (MGM, 1931)
Susan Lenox, Her Fall and Rise (MGM, 1931)
Law and Order (Univ, 1932)
Ridin' for Justice (Col, 1932)
Lena Rivers (Tif, 1932)
Honor of the Press (Mayfair, 1932)
Riding Tornado (Col, 1932)
Flames (Mon, 1932)
Cabin in the Cotton (FN, 1932)
Hello, Trouble (Col, 1932)
Silver Dollar (FN, 1932)
Call Her Savage (Fox, 1932)
Face in the Sky (Fox, 1933)
Hello, Everybody! (Par, 1933)
Three on a Honeymoon (Fox, 1934)
Carolina (Fox, 1934)
Frontier Marshal (Fox, 1934)
Ever Since Eve (Fox, 1934)
Sixteen Fathoms Deep (Mon, 1934)
The World Moves On (Fox, 1934)
West of the Pecos (RKO, 1935)
Motive for Revenge (Majestic, 1935)
The Hoosier Schoolmaster (Mon, 1935)
Way Down East (Fox, 1935)
Paddy O'Day (Fox, 1935)
The County Chairman (Fox, 1935)

Man Hunt (WB, 1936)
The Harvester (Rep, 1936)
Girl of the Ozarks (Par, 1936)
The Crime of Dr. Forbes (20th, 1936)
Ramona (20th, 1936)
San Francisco (MGM, 1936)
The Green Light (WB, 1937)
That I May Live (20th, 1937)
Mountain Justice (WB, 1937)
Maid of Salem (Par, 1937)
Yodelin' Kid from Pine Ridge (Rep, 1937)
Wild West Days (Univ serial, 1937)
Paradise Isle (Mon, 1937)
Gold Is Where You Find It (WB, 1938)
The Arizona Wildcat (20th, 1938)
The Girl of the Golden West (MGM, 1938)
Valley of the Giants (WB, 1938)
Heart of the North (WB, 1938)
Dodge City (WB, 1939)
Western Caravans (Col, 1939)
Mr. Smith Goes to Washington (Col, 1939)
Young Mr. Lincoln (20th, 1939)
Geronimo (Par, 1939)
Desperate Trails (Univ, 1939)
Drums Along the Mohawk (20th, 1939)
Wyoming (MGM, 1940)
The Grapes of Wrath (20th, 1940)
Virginia City (WB, 1940)
Three Faces West [a.k.a. *The Refugee*] (Rep, 1940)
Brigham Young—Frontiersman (20th, 1940)
Santa Fe Trail (WB, 1940)
Tobacco Road (20th, 1941)
Citadel of Crime (Rep, 1941)
Meet John Doe (WB, 1941)
Wild Geese Calling (20th, 1941)
The Last of the Duanes (20th, 1941)
Swamp Water (20th, 1941)
Bad Men of Missouri (WB, 1941)
Wild Bill Hickok Rides (WB, 1941)
The Lone Star Ranger (20th, 1942)
Shut My Big Mouth (Col, 1942)
The Spoilers (Univ, 1942)
Tennessee Johnson (MGM, 1942)
This Time for Keeps (MGM, 1942)
Border Patrol (UA, 1943)

Moonlight in Vermont (Univ, 1943)
Woman of the Town (UA, 1943)
Texas Masquerade (UA, 1944)
Man from Frisco (Rep, 1944)
The Big Bonanza (Rep, 1944)
Along Came Jones (RKO, 1945)
Incendiary Blonde (Par, 1945)
They Were Expendable (MGM, 1945)
Roughly Speaking (WB, 1945)
Lady Luck (RKO, 1946)
California Gold Rush (Rep, 1946)
Bad Bascomb (MGM, 1946)
My Darling Clementine (20th, 1946)
Death Valley (Screen Guild, 1946)
My Dog Shep (Screen Guild, 1946)
The Romance of Rosy Ridge (MGM, 1947)
The Millerson Case (Col, 1947)
Bowery Buckaroos (Mon, 1947)
The Fabulous Texan (Rep, 1947)
Albuquerque (Par, 1948)
Tap Roots (Univ, 1948)
Coroner Creek (Col, 1948)
Sundown in Santa Fe (Rep, 1948)
Tuna Clipper (Mon, 1949)
The Gal Who Took the West (Univ, 1949)
Free for All (Univ, 1949)
The Beautiful Blonde from Bashful Bend (20th, 1949)
Wagonmaster (RKO, 1950)
Saddle Tramp (Univ, 1950)
Call of the Klondike (Mon, 1950)
Comin' Round the Mountain (Univ, 1951)
Across the Wild Missouri (MGM, 1951)
Ma and Pa Kettle at the Fair (Univ, 1952)
Lone Star (MGM, 1952)
Meet Me at the Fair (Univ, 1952)
Feudin' Fools (Mon, 1952)
The Sun Shines Bright (Rep, 1953)
Broken Lance (20th, 1954)
Seven Brides for Seven Brothers (MGM, 1954)
The Last Command (Rep, 1955)
The Tall Men (20th, 1955)
The Brass Legend (UA, 1956)
Friendly Persuasion (AA, 1956)
These Wilder Years (MGM, 1956)
The Tin Star (Par, 1957)
The Lonely Man (Par, 1957)
The Horse Soldiers (UA, 1959)

ALISON SKIPWORTH
(Alison Groom)

In the 1930s.

Born July 25, 1863, London, England. Married Frank Markam Skipworth; widowed. Died December 20, 1948, New York City, New York. Plump British character actress who made her mark in Hollywood. As Paramount contractee, a frequent partner of W. C. Fields: *If I Had a Million, Tillie and Gus, Six of a Kind*. Was the foil of screen newcomer Mae West in *Night After Night*. In *Satan Met a Lady*, the second of three versions of *The Maltese Falcon*, she was the rotund villainess, Madame Barabbas, employing her double takes and arched eyebrows to good effect. Previously, in *Madame Racketeer*, she played a genteel crook. Near end of film career teamed with Polly Moran in several films (such as *Two Wise Maids*)—an unsuccessful bid to duplicate the joyous, raucous team of Moran and Marie Dressler in early 1930s.

Alison Skipworth to Claudette Colbert in *Tonight Is Ours*: "I followed my own heart *several times*—with the most devastating results."

Films

Handcuffs or Kisses (Selznick, 1921)
Du Barry, Woman of Passion (UA, 1930)
Oh, For a Man! (Fox, 1930)
Outward Bound (WB, 1930)
Raffles (UA, 1930)
Strictly Unconventional (MGM, 1930)
Devotion (Pathé, 1931)
Virtuous Husband (Univ, 1931)
Tonight or Never (UA, 1931)
Night Angel (Par, 1931)
The Road to Singapore (WB, 1931)
High Pressure (WB, 1932)
Sinners in the Sun (Par, 1932)
Madame Racketeer (Par, 1932)
Night After Night (Par, 1932)
The Unexpected Father (Univ, 1932)
If I Had a Million (Par, 1932)

He Learned About Women (Par, 1933)
A Lady's Profession (Par, 1933)
Tonight Is Ours (Par, 1933)
Song of Songs (Par, 1933)
Midnight Club (Par, 1933)
Tillie and Gus (Par, 1933)
Alice in Wonderland (Par, 1933)
Six of a Kind (Par, 1934)
Wharf Angel (Par, 1934)
The Notorious Sophie Lang (Par, 1934)
Here Is My Heart (Par, 1934)
Shoot the Works (Par, 1934)
The Captain Hates the Sea (Col, 1934)
Coming-Out Party (Fox, 1934)
The Casino Murder Case (MGM, 1935)
The Devil Is a Woman (Par, 1935)
Shanghai (Par, 1935)

Becky Sharp (RKO, 1935)
Doubting Thomas (Fox, 1935)
The Girl from Tenth Avenue (WB, 1935)
Dangerous (WB, 1935)
Hitch Hike Lady (Rep, 1935)
The Princess Comes Across (Par, 1936)
Satan Met a Lady (WB, 1936)
The Gorgeous Hussy (MGM, 1936)
Two in a Crowd (Univ, 1936)
White Hunter (20th, 1936)
Stolen Holiday (WB, 1936)
Two Wise Maids (Rep, 1937)
King of the Newsboys (Rep, 1938)
Ladies in Distress (Rep, 1938)
Wide Open Faces (Col, 1938)

EVERETT SLOANE

With Paul Newman in Somebody Up There Likes Me *(1956).*

Born October 1, 1909, New York City, New York. Married Luba Herman (1933), children: Nathaniel, Erika. Died August 6, 1965, Brentwood, California. Road-show player/stock-market runner/radio actor/Broadway player. Member of Orson Welles' Mercury Theatre who joined the Master in Hollywood for *Citizen Kane* (Bernstein, the lawyer), *The Lady from Shanghai* (Arthur Bannister—Rita Hayworth's scorned, revengeful husband), *Prince of Foxes* (Belli). Re-created his TV role of Walter Ramsey for the film version of *Patterns*. Was Dr. Gachet in *Lust for Life*, Natalie Wood's father in *Marjorie Morningstar*, and played straight man to Jerry Lewis in *The Patsy* and *The Disorderly Orderly*. Tremendously active TV performer. In 1965, worried about failing health, committed suicide.

Everett Sloane to William Alland in *Citizen Kane:* "It's no trick to make a lot of money—if all you want is to make a lot of money."

Films

Citizen Kane (RKO, 1941)
Journey into Fear (RKO, 1942)
We Accuse (Film Rights, 1945) [narrator]
The Lady from Shanghai (Col, 1948)
Prince of Foxes (20th, 1949)
The Men (UA, 1950)
Bird of Paradise (20th, 1951)
The Blue Veil (RKO, 1951)
The Enforcer (WB, 1951)

Sirocco (Col, 1951)
The Desert Fox (20th, 1951)
The Prince Who Was a Thief (Univ, 1951)
The Sellout (MGM, 1951)
Way of a Gaucho (20th, 1952)
The Big Knife (UA, 1955)
Patterns (UA, 1956)
Somebody Up There Likes Me (MGM, 1956)
Lust for Life (MGM, 1956)

Marjorie Morningstar (WB, 1958)
The Gun Runners (UA, 1958)
Home from the Hill (MGM, 1960)
By Love Possessed (UA, 1961)
Brushfire! (Par, 1962)
The Man from the Diners' Club (Col, 1963)
The Patsy (Par, 1964)
The Disorderly Orderly (Par, 1964)
Ready for the People (WB, 1964)

SIR C. AUBREY SMITH
(Charles Aubrey Smith)

With Mary Astor in The Hurricane *(1937).*

Born July 21, 1863, London, England. Married Isobel Wood (1896), child: Honor. Died December 20, 1948, Beverly Hills, California. Very seasoned London stage and film actor who came to Hollywood in the early 1930s. The grand old Britisher: tweedy suit, lit pipe, autocratic but sympathetic, extremely mobile, bushy eyebrows, and thick moustache just right for fussing with (and scene stealing). With a hulking frame, quite useful for costume pictures: *Queen Christina* (Aage), *Cleopatra* (Enobarbus), *Clive of India* (prime minister), Ronald Colman's *The Prisoner of Zenda* (Colonel Zapt), etc. Anglophilish Hollywood kept him professionally busy for two decades. In later years was quite deaf and had to read lips on the set.

> **Sir C. Aubrey Smith** to Leslie Howard in *Never the Twain Shall Meet:* "This girl's of a different race . . . of a different world. You've got your friends, your position."

Films

The Builder of Bridges (World, 1915)
The Witching Hour (Frohman, 1916)
Red Pottage (Br, 1918)
The Face at the Window (Br, 1920)
Castles in Spain (Br, 1920)
The Bump (Br, 1920)
The Shuttle of Life (Br, 1920)
Flames of Passion (Br, 1922)
The Bohemian Girl (Br, 1922)
The Temptations of Carlton Earlye (Br, 1923)
The Unwanted (Br, 1924)
The Rejected Woman (MG, 1924)
Birds of Prey (Br, 1930)
Such Is the Law (Br, 1930)
Contraband (Br, 1931)

Trader Horn (MGM, 1931)
The Bachelor Father (MGM, 1931)
Dancing Partner (Br, 1931)
Never the Twain Shall Meet (MGM, 1931)
The Perfect Alibi (RKO, 1931)
Just a Gigolo (MGM, 1931)
The Man in Possession (MGM, 1931)
Guilty Hands (MGM, 1931)
Daybreak (MGM, 1931)
Son of India (MGM, 1931)
Surrender (Fox, 1931)
Polly of the Circus (MGM, 1932)
Phantom of Paris (MGM, 1931)
Tarzan the Ape Man (MGM, 1932)
But the Flesh Is Weak (MGM, 1932)

Love Me Tonight (Par, 1932)
No More Orchids (Col, 1932)
Trouble in Paradise (Par, 1932)
They Just Had to Get Married (Univ, 1933)
The Barbarian (MGM, 1933)
Adorable (Fox, 1933)
Luxury Liner (Par, 1933)
Secrets (UA, 1933)
Morning Glory (RKO, 1933)
Bombshell (MGM, 1933)
Queen Christina (MGM, 1933)
The Monkey's Paw (RKO, 1933)
The House of Rothschild (UA, 1934)
Bulldog Drummond Strikes Back (UA, 1934)
One More River (Univ, 1934)

The Scarlet Empress (Par, 1934)
Cleopatra (Par, 1934)
Riptide (MGM, 1934)
We Live Again (UA, 1934)
Caravan (Fox, 1934)
Curtain at Eight (Majestic, 1934)
Madame Du Barry (WB, 1934)
The Firebird (WB, 1934)
Gambling Lady (WB, 1934)
The Gilded Lily (Par, 1935)
The Right to Live (WB, 1935)
Clive of India (UA, 1935)
The Crusades (Par, 1935)
The Lives of a Bengal Lancer (Par, 1935)
The Florentine Dagger (WB, 1935)
China Seas (MGM, 1935)
Jalna (RKO, 1935)
Transatlantic Tunnel (Br, 1935)
Little Lord Fauntleroy (UA, 1936)
The Garden of Allah (UA, 1936)
Romeo and Juliet (MGM, 1936)
Lloyds of London (20th, 1936)

Wee Willie Winkie (20th, 1937)
The Prisoner of Zenda (UA, 1937)
The Hurricane (UA, 1937)
Thoroughbreds Don't Cry (MGM, 1937)
Four Men and a Prayer (20th, 1938)
Sixty Glorious Years [a.k.a. *Queen of Destiny/Queen Victoria*] (Br, 1938)
Kidnapped (20th, 1939)
East Side of Heaven (Univ, 1939)
The Sun Never Sets (Univ, 1939)
The Under-Pup (Univ, 1939)
The Four Feathers (UA Br, 1939)
Five Came Back (RKO, 1939)
Eternally Yours (UA, 1939)
Another Thin Man (MGM, 1939)
Balalaika (MGM, 1939)
A Bill of Divorcement (RKO, 1940)
City of Chance (20th, 1940)
Beyond Tomorrow (RKO, 1940)
Rebecca (UA, 1940)
Waterloo Bridge (MGM, 1940)
A Little Bit of Heaven (Univ, 1940)

Maisie Was a Lady (MGM, 1941)
Free and Easy (MGM, 1941)
Dr. Jekyll and Mr. Hyde (MGM, 1941)
Forever and a Day (RKO, 1943)
Two Tickets to London (Univ, 1943)
Madame Curie (MGM, 1943)
Flesh and Fantasy (Univ, 1943)
The White Cliffs of Dover (MGM, 1944)
Secrets of Scotland Yard (Rep, 1944)
They Shall Have Faith [a.k.a. *Forever Yours*] (Rep, 1944)
Sensations of 1945 (UA, 1944)
The Adventures of Mark Twain (WB, 1944)
Scotland Yard Investigator (Rep, 1945)
And Then There Were None (20th, 1945)
Rendezvous with Annie (Rep, 1946)
Cluny Brown (20th, 1946)
High Conquest (Mon, 1947)
Unconquered (Par, 1947)
An Ideal Husband (20th, 1948)
Little Women (MGM, 1949)

VLADIMIR SOKOLOFF

Vladimir Sokoloff (third from left), Herbert Heywood, John Halliday, and Madeleine Carroll in Blockade *(1938).*

Born December 25, 1889, Moscow, Russia. Married Elizabeth _____ ; widowed (1948). Died February 14, 1962, West Hollywood, California. Small-sized Russian actor who worked in films on the Continent before reaching Hollywood. Wrinkle-faced dialectician who was exceedingly versatile in ethnic delineations: *Road to Morocco* (Hyder Khan), *Mission to Moscow* (President Kalinin), *For Whom the Bell Tolls* (Anselmo), *Passage to Marseille* (Grandpere), *The Conspirators* (Miguel), *Cloak and Dagger* (Dr. Polka), *Taras Bulba* (Old Stepan), etc.

Vladimir Sokoloff to Gary Cooper in *Cloak and Dagger:*
"Once a week I cry. The other nights I drink."

Films

Die Abenteuer Eins Zehnmarkscheines/K13 513 [a.k.a. *Adventures of a Ten Mark Note*] (Ger, 1926)
Die Liebe der Jeanne Ney [a.k.a. *The Loves of Jeanne Ney*] (Ger, 1927)
Der Sohn der Hogar [a.k.a. *Out of the Mist*] (Ger, 1927)
Die Weisse Sonate (Ger, 1928)
Katherina Knie (Ger, 1929)
Das Schiff der Verlorenen Menschem (Ger, 1929)
Sensation im Wintergarten (Ger, 1929)
Moral ilm Mitternacht (Ger, 1930)
Loebling der Gotter (Ger, 1930)
Abschied [a.k.a. *Adieu*] (Ger, 1930)
Das Flotenkonzert von Sansseuci [a.k.a. *The Flute Concert at San Souci*] (Ger, 1930)
Westfront (Ger, 1930)
Die heliige Flamme (Ger, 1930)
L'Opera de Quat-sous (Fr, 1930)

Kismet (Ger, 1931)
Der Grosse Tenor (Ger, 1931)
Niemandsland [a.k.a. *Hell on Earth*] (Ger, 1931)
Die Dreigroschenoper [a.k.a. *The Beggar's Opera*] (Ger, 1931)
Strafsache van Geldern (Ger, 1932)
Die Herren von Atlantis (Atlantide) (Ger-Fr, 1932)
Teilnehmer Antwortet nicht (Ger, 1932)
Gehetzte Menschen [*Steckbrief Z*] (Ger, 1932)
Don Quichotte (Fr, 1933)
Dans les Rues (Fr, 1933)
Due Haut en Bas (Fr, 1933)
Le Lac aux Dames (Fr, 1934)
Le Secret de Waronzeff (Fr, 1934)
Napoleon (Fr, 1934)
Mayerling (Fr, 1935)
Les Bas-fonds (Fr, 1936)

Mister Flow (Fr, 1936)
Sous les Jeux d'Accident (Fr, 1936)
La Vie est a Nous (Fr, 1936)
The Prisoner of Zenda (UA, 1937)
Tovarich (WB, 1937)
The Life of Emile Zola (WB, 1937)
Expensive Husbands (WB, 1937)
West of Shanghai (WB, 1937)
Conquest (MGM, 1937)
Beg, Borrow or Steal (MGM, 1937)
The Amazing Dr. Clitterhouse (WB, 1938)
Arsene Lupin Returns (MGM, 1938)
Alcatraz Island (WB, 1938)
Blockade (UA, 1938)
Spawn of the North (Par, 1938)
Ride a Crooked Mile (Par, 1938)
Song of the Street (Fr, 1939)
Juarez (WB, 1939)
The Real Glory (UA, 1939)

Comrade X (MGM, 1940)
Love Crazy (MGM, 1941)
Compliments of Mr. Flow (Fr, 1941)
Crossroads (MGM, 1942)
Road to Morocco (Par, 1942)
Mission to Moscow (WB, 1943)
For Whom the Bell Tolls (Par, 1943)
Song of Russia (MGM, 1943)
Mr. Lucky (RKO, 1943)
Passage to Marseille (WB, 1944)
Till We Meet Again (Par, 1944)
The Conspirators (WB, 1944)
Back to Bataan (RKO, 1945)

The Blonde from Brooklyn (Col, 1945)
Paris Underground (UA, 1945)
A Royal Scandal (20th, 1945)
Scarlet Street (Univ, 1945)
Cloak and Dagger (WB, 1946)
A Scandal in Paris [a.k.a. Thieves' Holiday] (UA, 1946)
Two Smart People (MGM, 1946)
To the Ends of the Earth (Col, 1948)
The Baron of Arizona (Lip, 1950)
Macao (RKO, 1952)
While the City Sleeps (RKO, 1956)
Istanbul (Univ, 1957)

I Was a Teenage Werewolf (AIP, 1957)
Sabu and the Magic Ring (AA, 1957)
The Monster from Green Hell (DCA, 1957)
Twilight for the Gods (Univ, 1958)
Man on a String (Col, 1960)
Beyond the Time Barrier (AIP, 1960)
The Magnificent Seven (UA, 1960)
Cimarron (MGM, 1960)
Mr. Sardonicus (Col, 1961)
Taras Bulba (UA, 1962)

GALE SONDERGAARD
(Edith Holm Sondergaard)

With Bob Hope in My Favorite Blonde *(1942).*

Born February 15, 1899, Litchfield, Minnesota. Married 1) Neill O'Malley (1922); divorced (1930); 2) Herbert Biberman (1930), children: Daniel, Joan; widowed (1971). Thin faced, dark, and exotic-looking. Actually a Danish-American Midwesterner. Worked with a traveling Shakespearean company, then with a Detroit stock troupe, and thereafter with the Theatre Guild. For her debut movie role—Faith in *Anthony Adverse*—she won a BSAAA. Occasionally had sympathetic roles: Lucie Dreyfus (*The Life of Emile Zola*), Lady Thiang (*Anna and the King of Siam*). Infrequent comic assignments: the flirtatious Inez Quintero, wife of J. Edward Bromberg in *The Mark of Zorro*; Mme. Stephanie Runick, one of the Nazis pursuing Madeleine Carroll and Bob Hope in *My Favorite Blonde*. Best remembered for: *The Letter* (Eurasian rival of Bette Davis), *The Spider Woman* (Sherlock Holmes-Basil Rathbone's deadly opponent). She and her film-director husband Herbert Biberman were blacklisted in the 1950s. She eventually returned to the screen. TV series: "The Best of Everything" (as Amanda Key).

Gale Sondergaard to Brenda Joyce in *The Spider Woman Strikes Back*: "You're going to die, Jean—like the others— but it won't be really dying, because you'll live on in this beautiful plant."

Films

Anthony Adverse (WB, 1936)
Maid of Salem (Par, 1937)
Seventh Heaven (20th, 1937)
The Life of Emile Zola (WB, 1937)
Lord Jeff (MGM, 1938)
Dramatic School (MGM, 1938)
Juarez (WB, 1939)
Never Say Die (Par, 1939)
The Cat and the Canary (Par, 1939)
The Llano Kid (Par, 1940)
The Blue Bird (20th, 1940)
The Mark of Zorro (20th, 1940)
The Letter (WB, 1940)
The Black Cat (Univ, 1941)
Paris Calling (Univ, 1941)

My Favorite Blonde (Par, 1942)
Enemy Agents Meet Ellery Queen (Col, 1942)
Appointment in Berlin (Col, 1943)
A Night to Remember (Col, 1943)
Isle of Forgotten Sins (PRC, 1943)
The Strange Death of Adolf Hitler (Univ, 1943)
The Spider Woman (Univ, 1944)
The Climax (Univ, 1944)
The Invisible Man's Revenge (Univ, 1944)
Follow the Boys (Univ, 1944)
Gypsy Wildcat (Univ, 1944)
Enter Arsene Lupin (Univ, 1944)
Christmas Holiday (Univ, 1944)

A Night in Paradise (Univ, 1945)
Anna and the King of Siam (20th, 1946)
The Spider Woman Strikes Back (Univ, 1946)
The Time of Their Lives (Univ, 1946)
Road to Rio (Par, 1947)
The Pirates of Monterey (Univ, 1947)
East Side, West Side (MGM, 1949)
Slaves (Continental, 1969)
Hollywood Horror House [a.k.a. *A Maniac Is Loose*] (Avco Emb–New Line Cinema, 1975)
The Return of a Man Called Horse (UA, 1976)

NED SPARKS
(Edward A. Sparkman)

Ned Sparks and Jed Prouty in Private Scandal *(1934).*

Born 1884, Ontario, Canada. Married _____ , child: Laura. Died April 3, 1957, Victorville, California. Cigar-smoking sourpuss of numerous features. Nasal twang accentuated his dour press agents, reporters, etc. Onetime participant in Alaskan gold rush. Had been carnival, medicine-show, and Broadway performer.

Ned Sparks to Bring Crosby in *The Star Maker:* "I hate kids. Hated them ever since I saw myself in the family album draped over a polar-bear rug."

Films

A Virtuous Vamp (FN, 1919)
The Bond Boy (Associated FN, 1922)
A Wide Open Town (Selznick, 1922)
His Supreme Moment (FN, 1925)
Faint Perfume (B.P. Schulberg, 1925)
The Boomerang (B.P. Schulberg, 1925)
Seven Keys to Baldpate (Par, 1925)
Bright Lights (MG, 1925)
The Only Thing (MG, 1925)
Soul Mates (MGM, 1926)
The Hidden Way (Associated Exhibitors, 1926)
Mike (MGM, 1926)
Love's Blindness (MGM, 1926)
The Auction Block (MGM, 1926)
Oh, What a Night (Sterling, 1926)
Money Talks (MGM, 1926)
When the Wife's Away (Col, 1926)
Alias the Lone Wolf (Col, 1927)
The Secret Studio (Fox, 1927)
Alias the Deacon (Univ, 1927)
The Small Bachelor (Univ, 1927)
The Magnificent Flirt (Par, 1928)
On to Reno (Pathé, 1928)

The Big Noise (FN, 1928)
Nothing but the Truth (Par, 1929)
The Canary Murder Case (Par, 1929)
Strange Cargo (Pathé, 1929)
Street Girl (RKO, 1929)
Love Comes Along (RKO, 1930)
Fall Guy (RKO, 1930)
Double Cross Roads (Fox, 1930)
The Devil's Holiday (Par, 1930)
Conspiracy (RKO, 1930)
Leathernecking (RKO, 1930)
Iron Man (Univ, 1931)
The Secret Call (Par, 1931)
Corsair (UA, 1931)
Kept Husbands (RKO, 1931)
The Miracle Man (Par, 1932)
Big City Blues (WB, 1932)
Blessed Event (WB, 1932)
The Crusader (Majestic, 1932)
Gold Diggers of 1933 (WB, 1933)
Lady for a Day (Col, 1933)
Too Much Harmony (Par, 1933)
Alice in Wonderland (Par, 1933)
Going Hollywood (MGM, 1933)

42nd Street (WB, 1933)
Secrets (UA, 1933)
Hi, Nellie! (WB, 1934)
Servants' Entrance (Fox, 1934)
Private Scandal (Par, 1934)
Marie Galante (Fox, 1934)
Imitation of Life (Univ, 1934)
Sing and Like It (RKO, 1934)
Down to Their Last Yacht (RKO, 1934)
Sweet Adeline (WB, 1935)
Sweet Music (WB, 1935)
George White's Scandals of 1935 (Fox, 1935)
Collegiate (Par, 1935)
The Bride Walks Out (RKO, 1936)
One in a Million (20th, 1936)
Two's Company (Br, 1936)
Wake Up and Live (20th, 1937)
This Way, Please (Par, 1937)
Hawaii Calls (RKO, 1938)
The Star Maker (Par, 1939)
For Beauty's Sake (20th, 1941)
Stage Door Canteen (UA, 1943)
Magic Town (RKO, 1947)

LIONEL STANDER

In Pulp *(1972)*.

Born January 11, 1908, New York City, New York. Married 1) Lucy Dietz (1928), child: Mikele; divorced (1936); 2) Alice Twitchell (1938); divorced (1942); 3) Vehanne Havens Monteagle (1945), children: two daughters; divorced (1950); 4) Diana Radbec (1953), child: daughter; divorced (1963); 5) Maria Penn (1963), child: daughter; divorced; 6) Stephanie Van Hennick (1971), child: Jennifer. Curly-haired player of offbeat thugs. Active stage and radio actor before starting cinema career. Made many short subjects before first features. Played in *Mr. Deeds Goes to Town* (Cornelius Cobb), Janet Gaynor's *A Star Is Born* (Casey Burke), *The Last Gangster* (Curly), *St. Benny the Dip* (Monk), *The Gang That Couldn't Shoot Straight* (Baccala), etc. Blacklisted in Hollywood in late 1940s and thereafter moved to Rome.

Lionel Stander to steer in cattle car in *Professor Beware:* "Get off my foot! Get off my foot or I'll cut a steak out of you."

Films

The Scoundrel (Par, 1935)
Page Miss Glory (WB, 1935)
The Gay Deception (Col, 1935)
We're in the Money (WB, 1935)
Hooray for Love (RKO, 1935)
I Live My Life (MGM, 1935)
If You Could Only Cook (Col, 1935)
The Music Goes Round (Col, 1936)
Mr. Deeds Goes to Town (Col, 1936)
Meet Nero Wolfe (Col, 1936)

More Than a Secretary (Col, 1936)
The Milky Way (Par, 1936)
Soak the Rich (Par, 1936)
They Met in a Taxi (Col, 1936)
The League of Frightened Men (Col, 1937)
A Star Is Born (UA, 1937)
The Last Gangster (MGM, 1937)
No Time to Marry (Col, 1938)
Professor Beware (Par, 1938)
The Crowd Roars (MGM, 1938)

Ice Follies of 1939 (MGM, 1939)
What a Life (Par, 1939)
The Bride Wore Crutches (20th, 1941)
Guadalcanal Diary (20th, 1943)
Tahiti Honey (Rep, 1943)
Hangmen Also Die (UA, 1943)
The Big Show-Off (Rep, 1945)
Specter of the Rose (Rep, 1946)
In Old Sacramento (Rep, 1946)
The Kid from Brooklyn (RKO, 1946)

Gentleman Joe Palooka (Mon, 1946)
Mad Wednesday [a.k.a. The Sin of Harold Diddlebock] (UA, 1947)
Texas, Brooklyn and Heaven (UA, 1948)
Call Northside 777 (20th, 1948)
Unfaithfully Yours (20th, 1948)
Trouble Makers (Mon, 1948)
Two Gals and a Guy (UA, 1951)
St. Benny the Dip (UA, 1951)
Blast of Silence (Univ, 1961) [voice only]
The Moving Finger (Moyer, 1963)
The Loved One (MGM, 1965)
Promise Her Anything (Par, 1966)
Cul de Sac (Sigma III, 1966)
A Dandy in Aspic (Col, 1967)
Gates to Paradise (Br, 1967)
Sette Volte Sette (It-Fr, 1968)
Al Di la Della Legge (It, 1968)
C'era una Volta il West [a.k.a. Once upon a Time in the West] (It, 1968)
H2S (It, 1969)

Zenabel (It, 1969)
La Collina Degli Stivali (It, 1969)
Infanzia, Vocazione Prime Esperienze di Giacomo Casanova, Veneziano (It, 1969)
Mir Hat Es Immer Spass Gemacht (Ger, 1970)
Le Avventure di Pinocchi [a.k.a. Les Aventures de Pinocchio] (It-Fr-West German, 1971)
Stanze 17-17, Palazzo Delle Tasse, Ufficio Imposte (It, 1971)
Per Grazia Ricevuta (It, 1971)
The Gang That Couldn't Shoot Straight (MGM, 1971)
Pulp (UA, 1972)
Treasure Island (NG, 1972)
Te Deum (It, 1972)
All onorevole piaccione le donne [a.k.a. Mon depute plait aux femmes] (It-Fr, 1972)
Don Camillo e I Giovani D'Oggi (It, 1972)

Tutti Fratelli Nel West . . . Per Parte di Padre (It, 1972)
Siamo Tutti in Liberta Provvisoria (It, 1972)
Milano Calibro 9 (It, 1972)
La "Mano Nera," Prima della Mafia, Più della Mafia (It, 1973)
L'Isola del Tesoro L'Ile au Tresor (It-Fr-Sp-Ger, 1973)
Crescete e Moltiplicatevi (It, 1973)
Mordi e Fuggi [a.k.a. Rapt a L'Italienne] (It-Fr, 1973)
Paolo il Caldo (It, 1973)
Partirono Preti, Tornarono Curati (It, 1973)
Giubbe Rosse (It, 1975)
The Black Bird (Col, 1975)
Cassandra's Crossing (Avco Emb, 1976)
The Sensual Man (It, 1977)
Matilda (AIP, 1978)
Cyclone (Mex, 1978)

SIR GUY STANDING

Sir Guy Standing and Richard Cromwell in Annapolis Farewell *(1935).*

Born September 1, 1873, London, England. Married Dorothy Hammond, children: Guy, Dorothy Katherine. Died February 24, 1937, Apple Valley, California. Respected British stage actor who buoyed many Paramount pictures with his cultivated, low-keyed presence: *The Story of Temple Drake* (the judge—father of Miriam Hopkins), *Death Takes a Holiday* (Duke Lambert—at whose villa the tale unfolds), *The Lives of a Bengal Lancer* (Colonel Stone—father of Richard Cromwell), *Lloyds of London* (Angerstein), etc. Offscreen father of actress Kay Hammond.

Sir Guy Standing to Fredric March in *The Eagle and the Hawk*: "That's a tough sector, Jerry. Wouldn't you rather have Crocker with you than that youngster?"

Films

The Story of Temple Drake (Par, 1933)
Midnight Club (Par, 1933)
Hell and High Water (Par, 1933)
The Cradle Song (Par, 1933)
A Bedtime Story (Par, 1933)
The Eagle and the Hawk (Par, 1933)
Death Takes a Holiday (Par, 1934)

Now and Forever (Par, 1934)
The Witching Hour (Par, 1934)
Double Door (Par, 1934)
The Lives of a Bengal Lancer (Par, 1935)
Car 99 (Par, 1935)
Annapolis Farewell (Par, 1935)
The Big Broadcast of 1936 (Par, 1935)

The Return of Sophie Lang (Par, 1936)
Palm Springs (Par, 1936)
I'd Give My Life (Par, 1936)
Lloyds of London (20th, 1936)
Bulldog Drummond Escapes (Par, 1937)

HENRY STEPHENSON
(Henry S. Garroway)

Henry Stephenson and William Gargan in The Animal Kingdom *(1932).*

Born April 16, 1871, Granada, British West Indies. Married Ann Shoemaker. Died April 24, 1956, San Francisco, California. Firm chin, telling eyes, and a capacity for understatement. Generally the worldly but unhaughty individual: *Little Women* (Mr. Laurence), *Mutiny on the Bounty* (Sir Joseph Banks), etc. Supported Errol Flynn in several swashbuckling vehicles: *Captain Blood* (Lord Willoughby), *The Charge of the Light Brigade* (Sir Charles Macefield), *The Prince and the Pauper* (Duke of Norfolk), and *The Private Lives of Elizabeth and Essex* (Lord Burghley).

Henry Stephenson to Cary Grant in *Night and Day*: "I'm leaving a large estate to my heirs; but I don't propose there should be one drop of sherry in it. . . . Heh—heh—heh."

Films

The Spreading Dawn (G, 1917)
The Black Panther's Cub (Equity, 1921)
Men and Women (Par, 1925)
Wild, Wild Susan (Par, 1925)
Cynara (UA, 1932)
Red-Headed Woman (MGM, 1932)
Guilty as Hell (Par, 1932)
Bill of Divorcement (RKO, 1932)
The Animal Kingdom (RKO, 1932)
Little Women (RKO, 1933)
Queen Christina (MGM, 1933)
Tomorrow at Seven (RKO, 1933)
Double Harness (RKO, 1933)
My Lips Betray (Fox, 1933)
If I Were Free (RKO, 1933)
Blind Adventure (RKO, 1933)
Man of Two Worlds (RKO, 1934)
The Richest Girl in the World (RKO, 1934)
Thirty Day Princess (Par, 1934)
Stingaree (RKO, 1934)
The Mystery of Mr. X (MGM, 1934)
What Every Woman Knows (MGM, 1934)
One More River (Univ, 1934)
Outcast Lady (MGM, 1934)
She Loves Me Not (Par, 1934)
All Men Are Enemies (Fox, 1934)
Mutiny on the Bounty (MGM, 1935)
Vanessa: Her Love Story (MGM, 1935)
Reckless (MGM, 1935)

The Flame Within (MGM, 1935)
O'Shaughnessy's Boy (MGM, 1935)
The Night Is Young (MGM, 1935)
Rendezvous (MGM, 1935)
The Perfect Gentleman (MGM, 1935)
Captain Blood (WB, 1935)
Beloved Enemy (UA, 1936)
Half Angel (Fox, 1936)
Hearts Divided (WB, 1936)
Give Me Your Heart (WB, 1936)
Walking on Air (RKO, 1936)
Little Lord Fauntleroy (UA, 1936)
The Charge of the Light Brigade (WB, 1936)
When You're in Love (Col, 1937)
The Prince and the Pauper (WB, 1937)
The Emperor's Candlesticks (MGM, 1937)
Conquest (MGM, 1937)
Wise Girl (RKO, 1937)
The Young in Heart (UA, 1938)
The Baroness and the Butler (20th, 1938)
Suez (20th, 1938)
Marie Antoinette (MGM, 1938)
Dramatic School (MGM, 1938)
Tarzan Finds a Son! (MGM, 1939)
The Private Lives of Elizabeth and Essex (WB, 1939)
The Adventures of Sherlock Holmes (20th, 1939)
It's a Date (Univ, 1940)
Little Old New York (20th, 1940)

Spring Parade (Univ, 1940)
Down Argentine Way (20th, 1940)
The Man Who Lost Himself (Univ, 1941)
The Lady from Louisiana (Rep, 1941)
This Above All (20th, 1942)
Rings on Her Fingers (20th, 1942)
Half Way to Shanghai (Univ, 1942)
Mr. Lucky (RKO, 1943)
The Man Trap (Rep, 1943)
The Hour Before the Dawn (Par, 1944)
Secrets of Scotland Yard (Rep, 1944)
The Reckless Age (Univ, 1944)
Two Girls and a Sailor (MGM, 1944)
Tarzan and the Amazons (RKO, 1945)
The Green Years (MGM, 1946)
Her Sister's Secret (PRC, 1946)
The Locket (RKO, 1946)
Heartbeat (RKO, 1946)
Night and Day (WB, 1946)
Of Human Bondage (WB, 1946)
The Return of Monte Cristo (Col, 1946)
Dark Delusion (MGM, 1947)
The Homestretch (20th, 1947)
Time out of Mind (Univ, 1947)
Ivy (Univ, 1947)
Song of Love (MGM, 1947)
Julia Misbehaves (MGM, 1948)
Enchantment (RKO, 1948)
Challenge to Lassie (MGM, 1949)
Oliver Twist (UA, 1951)

PAUL STEWART

With Edward G. Robinson in Hell on Frisco Bay *(1955).*

Born March 13, 1908, New York City, New York. Married Peg La Centra (1939). Determined (or hard-boiled) looking ex-stage actor who came to Hollywood with Orson Welles' Mercury Theatre. Played Raymond in *Citizen Kane*. Often in underworld melodramas: *Johnny Eager* (Julio), *Mr. Lucky* (Zepp), *Kiss Me Deadly* (Carl Evello), etc. Was Syd Murphy in *The Bad and the Beautiful*, Questor in *The Greatest Story Ever Told*, and the reporter in *In Cold Blood*. TV series: "Top Secret U.S.A."

Paul Stewart to Ralph Meeker in *Kiss Me Deadly*: "What's it worth to you to turn your considerable talents back to the gutter you crawled out of?"

Films

Johnny Eager (MGM, 1941)
Citizen Kane (RKO, 1941)
The World at War (War Activities Committee, 1942) [narrator]
Government Girl (RKO, 1943)
Mr. Lucky (RKO, 1943)
The Window (RKO, 1949)
Easy Living (RKO, 1949)
Illegal Entry (Univ, 1949)
Champion (UA, 1949)
Twelve O'Clock High (20th, 1949)
Walk Softly, Stranger (RKO, 1950)
Edge of Doom (RKO, 1950)
Appointment with Danger (Par, 1951)

Loan Shark (Lip, 1952)
Deadline, U.S.A. (20th, 1952)
The Bad and the Beautiful (MGM, 1952)
We're Not Married (20th, 1952)
Carbine Williams (MGM, 1952)
The Juggler (Col, 1953)
The Joe Louis Story (UA, 1953)
Prisoner of War (MGM, 1954)
Deep in My Heart (MGM, 1954)
The Cobweb (MGM, 1955)
Chicago Syndicate (Col, 1955)
Hell on Frisco Bay (WB, 1955)
Kiss Me Deadly (UA, 1955)
The Wild Party (UA, 1956)

Top Secret Affair (WB, 1957)
King Creole (Par, 1958)
A Child Is Waiting (UA, 1963)
The Greatest Story Ever Told (UA, 1965)
In Cold Blood (Col, 1967)
How to Commit Marriage (Cin, 1969)
Jigsaw (Univ, 1969)
Murph the Surf (AIP, 1974)
Bite the Bullet (Col, 1975)
The Day of the Locust (Par, 1975)
F for Fake (Filmex, 1975)
Opening Night (Faces Distributing Corp, 1978)

GEORGE E. STONE
(George Stein)

George E. Stone, George "Gabby" Hayes, Barbara Britton, and Sonny Tufts in The Untamed Breed *(1948).*

Born May 23, 1903, Lodz, Poland. Married Marjorie Ramey (1946). Died May 26, 1967, Woodland Hills, California. Pint-sized stage player who was the Sewer Rat in Janet Gaynor's *Seventh Heaven*. In talkies gained repute as a tough little thug: *Little Caesar* (Otero, Edward G. Robinson's righthand man), *The Front Page* (escaped convict Williams—also had a bit in the remake, *His Girl Friday*), Preston Foster's *The Last Mile* (Berg, the death-row convict who goes to the electric chair). Later was Chester Morris' pleasant but dull-witted cohort, the Runt, in *11 Boston Blackie* episodes. The long-time friend of Damon Runyon played Society Max in the Runyon-derived *Guys and Dolls* and Shimkey in *Pocketful of Miracles*, etc.

> **George E. Stone** to Billy Halop in *You Can't Get Away with Murder*: "I laid bets that 21 guys would go to the chair, and every one of them *went*."

Films

Children of the Feud (Fine Arts–Tri, 1916)
Going Straight (Fine Arts–Tri, 1916)
Gretchen the Greenhorn (Fine Arts–Tri, 1916)
The Little School Ma'am (Fine Arts, 1916)
Sudden Jim (Tri, 1917)
'Til I Come Back to You (Artcraft, 1918)
Jackie (Fox, 1921)
Penny of Top Hill Trail (Federated, 1921)
The Whistle (Par, 1921)
Desperate Trails (Univ, 1921)
White and Unmarried (Par, 1921)

The Fourth Musketeer (FBO, 1923)
Brass Knuckles (WB, 1927)
Seventh Heaven (Fox, 1927)
The Racket (Par, 1928)
San Francisco Nights (Gotham, 1928)
Turn Back the Hours (Gotham, 1928)
Walking Back (Pathé, 1928)
Beautiful but Dumb (Tif, 1928)
Clothes Make the Woman (Tif, 1928)
State Street Sadie (WB, 1928)
Tenderloin (WB, 1928)
Redeeming Sin (WB, 1929)
Naughty Baby (FN, 1929)
Weary River (FN, 1929)
The Girl in the Glass Cage (FN, 1929)

Two Men and a Maid (Tif, 1929)
Skin Deep (WB, 1929)
Melody Lane (Univ, 1929)
Under a Texas Moon (WB, 1930)
The Medicine Man (Tif, 1930)
Little Caesar (FN, 1930)
The Front Page (UA, 1931)
Cimarron (RKO, 1931)
Five Star Final (FN, 1931)
The Spider (Fox, 1931)
Sob Sister (Fox, 1931)
Taxi! (WB, 1932)
File No. 113 (Hollywood Films, 1932)
The Woman from Monte Carlo (FN, 1932)
The World and the Flesh (Par, 1932)

467

The Last Mile (WW, 1932)
The Phantom of Crestwood (RKO, 1932)
Vampire Bat (Majestic, 1933)
42nd Street (WB, 1933)
Sailor Be Good (RKO, 1933)
Song of the Eagle (Par, 1933)
Emergency Call (RKO, 1933)
The Wrecker (Col, 1933)
The Big Brain (RKO, 1933)
Sing, Sinner, Sing (Majestic, 1933)
Penthouse (MGM, 1933)
Ladies Must Love (Univ, 1933)
King for a Night (Univ, 1933)
He Couldn't Take It (Mon, 1933)
Frontier Marshal (Fox, 1934)
Viva Villa! (MGM, 1934)
The Return of the Terror (FN, 1934)
The Dragon Murder Case (FN, 1934)
Embarrassing Moments (Univ, 1934)
One Hour Late (Par, 1934)
Secret of the Chateau (Univ, 1934)
Million Dollar Baby (Mon, 1935)
Public Hero No. 1 (MGM, 1935)
Hold 'em Yale (Par, 1935)
Make a Million (Mon, 1935)
Moonlight on the Prairie (WB, 1935)
Frisco Kid (WB, 1935)
Bullets or Ballots (FN, 1936)
Freshman Love (WB, 1936)
Man Hunt (WB, 1936)
Anthony Adverse (WB, 1936)
King of Hockey (WB, 1936)
Jailbreak (WB, 1936)
Rhythm on the Range (Par, 1936)
Polo Joe (WB, 1936)
The Captain's Kid (FN, 1936)
Here Comes Carter (FN, 1936)

Back in Circulation (WB, 1937)
The Adventurous Blonde (WB, 1937)
Mr. Moto's Gamble (20th, 1938)
A Slight Case of Murder (WB, 1938)
Over the Wall (WB, 1938)
Alcatraz Island (WB, 1938)
You and Me (Par, 1938)
The Long Shot (GN, 1938)
Submarine Patrol (20th, 1938)
You Can't Get Away With Murder (WB, 1939)
The Housekeeper's Daughter (UA, 1939)
The Night of Nights (Par, 1939)
I Take This Woman (MGM, 1940)
Island of Doomed Men (Col, 1940)
North West Mounted Police (Par, 1940)
Slightly Tempted (Univ, 1940)
Cherokee Strip (Par, 1940)
Road Show (UA, 1941)
The Face Behind the Mask (Col, 1941)
Broadway Limited (UA, 1941)
Last of the Duanes (Fox, 1941)
Confessions of Boston Blackie (Col, 1941)
The Affairs of Jimmy Valentine (Rep, 1942)
The Lone Star Ranger (20th, 1942)
Boston Blackie Goes Hollywood (Col, 1942)
Little Tokyo, U.S.A. (20th, 1942)
The Devil with Hitler (UA, 1942)
After Midnight with Boston Blackie (Col, 1943)
The Chance of a Lifetime (Col, 1943)
Strangers in the Night (Rep, 1944)
Timber Queen (Par, 1944)
My Buddy (Rep, 1944)
One Mysterious Night (Col, 1944)

Roger Touhy—Gangster (20th, 1944)
Nob Hill (20th, 1945)
Scared Stiff (Par, 1945)
Boston Blackie Booked on Suspicion (Col, 1945)
Boston Blackie's Rendezvous (Col, 1945)
Doll Face (20th, 1945)
Boston Blackie and the Law (Col, 1946)
A Close Call for Boston Blackie (Col, 1946)
The Phantom Thief (Col, 1946)
Sentimental Journey (20th, 1946)
Suspense (Mon, 1946)
Abie's Irish Rose (UA, 1946)
Trapped by Boston Blackie (Col, 1948)
The Untamed Breed (Col, 1948)
Dancing in the Dark (20th, 1949)
A Girl in Every Port (RKO, 1952)
Bloodhounds of Broadway (20th, 1952)
Pickup on South Street (20th, 1953)
The Robe (20th, 1953)
Combat Squad (Col, 1953)
The Miami Story (Col, 1954)
The Steel Cage (UA, 1954)
Broken Lance (20th, 1954)
Three-Ring Circus (Par, 1954)
Guys and Dolls (MGM, 1955)
The Man with the Golden Arm (UA, 1955)
Slightly Scarlet (RKO, 1956)
The Story of Mankind (WB, 1957)
Sierra Stranger (Col, 1957)
Some Like It Hot (UA, 1959)
The Tijuana Story (Col, 1959)
Baby Face Nelson (UA, 1959)
Calypso Heat Wave (Col, 1959)
Pocketful of Miracles (UA, 1961)

LEWIS STONE

In Andy Hardy Gets Spring Fever *(1939)*.

Born November 15, 1879, Worcester, Massachusetts. Married 1) Margaret Langham; widowed; 2) Florence Oakley, children: Virginia, Barbara; divorced; 3) Hazel Wolf (1930). Died September 12, 1953, Los Angeles, California. Tall, lean, handsome leading man of the stage who had equal success in silent films. Had the swashbuckling role in the 1920s' *The Prisoner of Zenda;* joined with Alice Terry and Ramon Novarro in *Scaramouche.* Perhaps best recalled in silents for playing Sir John Roxton, a member of Wallace Beery's expedition in *The Lost World.* Was Oscar-nominated for his Count Phalen, adviser to Czar Paul I (Emil Jannings) in *The Patriot* (but lost Best Actor Award to Warner Baxter of *In Old Arizona*). Contracted with MGM in 1928, where he remained till the end of his career. Was the resonant-voiced elder in assorted offerings: *The Big House* (the warden), *The Secret Six* (Newton, the amoral lawyer), *Grand Hotel* (Dr. Otternschlag, the scarred, cynical observer), *Queen Christina* (Oxenstierna, adviser to Greta Garbo), *David Copperfield* (Mr. Wickfield), *China Seas* (Tom Davids, the alleged coward who redeems himself), etc. Most famous for interpreting Judge Hardy in the *Andy Hardy* series, conducting fireside chats with Mickey Rooney, and keeping life in Carvel, U.S.A., running smoothly. Final film: *All the Brothers Were Valiant* (Captain Holt).

Lewis Stone to Cecilia Parker in *The Courtship of Andy Hardy:* "I think a newspaper article should be about as long as a lady's skirt—long enough to cover the subject, but short enough to be interesting."

Films

The Man Who Found Out (Essanay, 1915)

The Havoc (Essanay, 1916)

Honor's Altar (Tri, 1916)

According to the Code (Essanay, 1916)

Inside of the Lines (Pyramid-World, 1918)

Man's Desire (Robertson-Cole, 1919)

Man of Bronze (World, 1919)

Two Brides (Par, 1919)

Johnny Get Your Gun (Artcraft, 1919)

Milestones (G, 1920)

Nomads of the North (Associated FN, 1920)

Held by the Enemy (Par, 1920)

The River's End (Associated FN, 1920)

The Child Thou Gavest Me (Associated FN, 1921)

The Concert (G, 1921)

The Golden Snare (FN, 1921)

Beau Revel (Par, 1921)

Don't Neglect Your Wife (G, 1921)

Pilgrims of the Night (Associated Producers, 1921)

The Dangerous Age (Associated FN, 1922)

The Rosary (Associated FN, 1922)

A Fool There Was (Fox, 1922)

The Prisoner of Zenda (M, 1922)

Trifling Women (M, 1922)

The World's Applause (Par, 1923)

You Can't Fool Your Wife (Par, 1923)

Scaramouche (M, 1923)

The Stranger (Par, 1924)

Why Men Leave Home (Associated FN, 1924)

Cytherea (Associated FN, 1924)

Husbands and Lovers (Rimax, 1924)

Inez from Hollywood (Associated FN, 1924)

Cheaper to Marry (MG, 1925)

The Talker (FN, 1925)

Confessions of a Queen (MG, 1925)

Fine Clothes (FN, 1925)

The Lady Who Lied (FN, 1925)

The Lost World (FN, 1925)

What Fools Men (FN, 1925)

The Girl from Montmartre (FN, 1926)

Midnight Lovers (FN, 1926)

Old Loves and New (FN, 1926)

Too Much Money (FN, 1926)

Don Juan's Three Nights (FN, 1926)

The Blonde Saint (FN, 1926)

An Affair of the Follies (FN, 1927)

Lonesome Ladies (FN, 1927)

The Notorious Lady (FN, 1927)

The Private Life of Helen of Troy (FN, 1927)

The Prince of Headwaiters (FN, 1927)

The Foreign Legion (Univ, 1928)

The Patriot (Par, 1928)

Freedom of the Press (Univ, 1928)

A Woman of Affairs (MGM, 1928)

Madame X (MGM, 1928)

The Trial of Mary Dugan (MGM, 1929)

Wild Orchids (MGM, 1929)

Wonder of Women (MGM, 1929)

Their Own Desire (MGM, 1930)

Strictly Unconventional (MGM, 1930)

The Big House (MGM, 1930)

Romance (MGM, 1930)

The Office Wife (WB, 1930)

Passion Flower (MGM, 1930)

Father's Son (WB, 1930)

Strictly Dishonorable (Univ, 1931)

The Bargain (WB, 1931)

The Phantom of Paris (MGM, 1931)

My Past (WB, 1931)

The Sin of Madelon Claudet (MGM, 1931)

Always Goodbye (Fox, 1931)

The Secret Six (MGM, 1931)

Inspiration (MGM, 1931)

Mata Hari (MGM, 1931)

Letty Lynton (MGM, 1932)

Grand Hotel (MGM, 1932)

New Morals for Old (MGM, 1932)

The Wet Parade (MGM, 1932)

Unashamed (MGM, 1932)

Red-Headed Woman (MGM, 1932)

Night Court (MGM, 1932)

Divorce in the Family (MGM, 1932)

The Mask of Fu Manchu (MGM, 1932)

The Son-Daughter (MGM, 1932)

Looking Forward (MGM, 1933)

Men Must Fight (MGM, 1933)

Queen Christina (MGM, 1933)

The Bureau of Missing Persons (WB, 1933)

The White Sister (MGM, 1933)

You Can't Buy Everything (MGM, 1934)

The Girl from Missouri (MGM, 1934)

Treasure Island (MGM, 1934)

The Mystery of Mr. X (MGM, 1934)

David Copperfield (MGM, 1935)

Vanessa: Her Love Story (MGM, 1935)

West Point of the Air (MGM, 1935)

Public Hero No. 1 (MGM, 1935)

Woman Wanted (MGM, 1935)

China Seas (MGM, 1935)

Shipmates Forever (WB, 1935)

Three Godfathers (MGM, 1936)

The Unguarded Hour (MGM, 1936)

Small Town Girl (MGM, 1936)

Sworn Enemy (MGM, 1936)

Suzy (MGM, 1936)

Don't Turn 'em Loose (RKO, 1936)

Outcast (Par, 1937)

The Thirteenth Chair (MGM, 1937)

The Man Who Cried Wolf (Univ, 1937)

You're Only Young Once (MGM, 1937)

Bad Man of Brimstone (MGM, 1937)

Judge Hardy's Children (MGM, 1938)

Love Finds Andy Hardy (MGM, 1938)

Yellow Jack (MGM, 1938)

The Chaser (MGM, 1938)

Out West with the Hardys (MGM, 1938)

Stolen Heaven (Par, 1938)

Ice Follies of 1939 (MGM, 1939)

The Hardys Ride High (MGM, 1939)

Andy Hardy Gets Spring Fever (MGM, 1939)

Joe and Ethel Turp Call on the President (MGM, 1939)

Judge Hardy and Son (MGM, 1939)

Sporting Blood (MGM, 1940)

Andy Hardy Meets Debutante (MGM, 1940)

Andy Hardy's Private Secretary (MGM, 1941)

Life Begins for Andy Hardy (MGM, 1941)

The Bugle Sounds (MGM, 1941)

The Courtship of Andy Hardy (MGM, 1942)

Andy Hardy's Double Life (MGM, 1942)

Andy Hardy's Blonde Trouble (MGM, 1944)

The Hoodlum Saint (MGM, 1946)

Love Laughs at Andy Hardy (MGM, 1946)

Three Wise Fools (MGM, 1946)

State of the Union (MGM, 1948)

The Sun Comes Up (MGM, 1949)

Any Number Can Play (MGM, 1949)

Stars in My Crown (MGM, 1950)

The Key to the City (MGM, 1950)

Grounds for Marriage (MGM, 1950)

Night into Morning (MGM, 1951)

Angels in the Outfield (MGM, 1951)

Bannerline (MGM, 1951)

The Unknown Man (MGM, 1951)

It's a Big Country (MGM, 1951)

Just This Once (MGM, 1952)

Talk About a Stranger (MGM, 1952)

Scaramouche (MGM, 1952)

The Prisoner of Zenda (MGM, 1952)

All the Brothers Were Valiant (MGM, 1953)

MILBURN STONE

Al "Lash" LaRue, Jan Wiley, Dennis Moore, and Milburn Stone in the serial The Master Key *(1945).*

Born July 5, 1904, Burrton, Kansas. Married 1) _____ , child: _____ ; 2) Jane _____ . Physically solid individual of action and Western films and an occasional serial (*The Great Alaskan Mystery*). TV series: "Gunsmoke" (as Doc Galen Adams).

Milburn Stone to Lloyd Corrigan in *Captive Wild Woman:* "I tell you that girl's power over animals is uncanny."

Films

Ladies Crave Excitement (Mascot, 1935)
The Three Musketeers (RKO, 1935)
The Milky Way (Par, 1936)
China Clipper (FN, 1936)
The Princess Comes Across (Par, 1936)
Two in a Crowd (Univ, 1936)
A Doctor's Diary (Par, 1937)
Atlantic Flight (Mon, 1937)
Federal Bullets (Mon, 1937)
Blazing Barriers (Mon, 1937)
Music for Madame (RKO, 1937)
Swing It, Professor (Conn Pictures, 1937)
Youth on Parole (Rep, 1937)
The Thirteenth Man (Mon, 1937)
The Man in Blue (Univ, 1937)
Port of Missing Girls (Mon, 1937)
Mr. Boggs Steps Out (GN, 1937)
Wives Under Suspicion (Univ, 1938)
Sinners in Paradise (Univ, 1938)
Crime School (WB, 1938)
Paroled from the Big House (Syndicate, 1938)
California Frontier (Col, 1938)
Mystery Plane (Mon, 1939)
King of the Turf (UA, 1939)

Society Smugglers (Univ, 1939)
Blind Alley (Col, 1939)
Young Mr. Lincoln (20th, 1939)
Tail Spin (20th, 1939)
Stunt Pilot (Mon, 1939)
Tropic Fury (Univ, 1939)
Sky Patrol (Mon, 1939)
Danger Flight (Mon, 1939)
Nick Carter, Master Detective (MGM, 1939)
Charlie McCarthy, Detective (Univ, 1939)
Crashing Through (Mon, 1939)
Chasing Trouble (Mon, 1940)
Enemy Agent (Univ, 1940)
An Angel from Texas (WB, 1940)
Framed (Univ, 1940)
Colorado (Rep, 1940)
Lillian Russell (20th, 1940)
Give Us Wings (Univ, 1940)
The Great Plane Robbery (Col, 1940)
The Phantom Cowboy (Rep, 1941)
The Great Train Robbery (Rep, 1941)
Death Valley Outlaws (Rep, 1941)
Reap the Wild Wind (Par, 1942)
Rubber Racketeers (Mon, 1942)
Frisco Lil (Univ, 1942)

Police Bullets (Mon, 1942)
Keep 'em Slugging (Univ, 1943)
You Can't Beat the Law (Mon, 1943)
Sherlock Holmes Faces Death (Univ, 1943)
Captive Wild Woman (Univ, 1943)
Get Going (Univ, 1943)
Corvette K-225 (Univ, 1943)
Gung Ho! (Univ, 1943)
The Mad Ghoul (Univ, 1943)
The Impostor (Univ, 1944)
Hi, Good Lookin' (Univ, 1944)
Hat Check Honey (Univ, 1944)
Moon over Las Vegas (Univ, 1944)
Jungle Woman (Univ, 1944)
Phantom Lady (Univ, 1944)
Twilight on the Prairie (Univ, 1944)
The Great Alaskan Mystery (Univ serial, 1944)
The Master Key (Univ serial, 1945)
The Beautiful Cheat (Univ, 1945)
The Daltons Ride Again (Univ, 1945)
The Frozen Ghost (Univ, 1945)
I'll Remember April (Univ, 1945)
On Stage, Everybody (Univ, 1945)
She Gets Her Man (Univ, 1945)
Strange Confession (Univ, 1945)

Swing Out, Sister (Univ, 1945)
Danger Woman (Univ, 1946)
Inside Job (Univ, 1946)
Little Miss Big (Univ, 1946)
The Spider Woman Strikes Back (Univ, 1946)
Strange Conquest (Univ, 1946)
Her Adventurous Night (Univ, 1946)
Cass Timberlane (MGM, 1947)
Killer Dill (Screen Guild, 1947)
The Michigan Kid (Univ, 1947)
Headin' for Heaven (El, 1947)
Train to Alcatraz (Rep, 1948)

The Green Promise (RKO, 1949)
Calamity Jane and Sam Bass (Univ, 1949)
Sky Dragon (Mon, 1949)
The Judge (Film Classics, 1949)
No Man of Her Own (Par, 1950)
The Fireball (20th, 1950)
Snow Dog (Mon, 1950)
Branded (Par, 1950)
Road Block (RKO, 1951)
The Atomic City (Par, 1952)
The Savage (Par, 1952)
The Sun Shines Bright (Rep, 1953)
Second Chance (RKO, 1953)

Arrowhead (Par, 1953)
Pickup on South Street (20th, 1953)
The Siege at Red River (20th, 1954)
Black Tuesday (UA, 1954)
The Long Gray Line (Col, 1955)
White Feather (20th, 1955)
Smoke Signal (Univ, 1955)
The Private War of Major Benson (Univ, 1955)
Drango (UA, 1957)
The World of Sport Fishing (AA, 1972) [documentary]

ROBERT STRAUSS

Robert Strauss, William Holden, and Richard Erdman in Stalag 17 (1953).

Born November 8, 1913, New York City, New York. Married 1) _____ , children: three; 2) Audrey Bratty (1951). Died February 20, 1975, New York City, New York. Thickset stage and screen actor (former salesman) who excelled at slow-witted stooges: *Stalag 17* (Animal), *The Man with the Golden Arm* (Schwiefka), *Li'l Abner* (Romeo Scragg), etc. TV series: "Mona McCluskey."

Robert Strauss to Dean Martin in *Money from Home:* "You are headin' yourself for a mess of funeral."

Films

Native Land (Frontier Films, 1942)
Sailor Beware (Par, 1951)
Jumping Jacks (Par, 1952)
The Redhead from Wyoming (Univ, 1952)
Stalag 17 (Par, 1953)
Here Come the Girls (Par, 1953)
Money from Home (Par, 1953)
Act of Love (UA, 1953)
The Atomic Kid (Rep, 1954)
The Bridges at Toko-Ri (Par, 1954)
The Seven Year Itch (20th, 1955)
The Man with the Golden Arm (UA, 1955)

Attack! (UA, 1956)
Frontier Gun (20th, 1958)
I, Mobster (20th, 1958)
The 4-D Man (Univ, 1959)
Li'l Abner (Par, 1959)
Inside the Mafia (UA, 1959)
September Storm (20th, 1960)
Wake Me When It's Over (20th, 1960)
Dondi (AA, 1961)
The Last Time I Saw Archie (UA, 1961)
The George Raft Story (AA, 1961)
Twenty Plus Two (AA, 1961)

Girls! Girls! Girls! (Par, 1962)
The Wheeler Dealers (MGM, 1963)
The Thrill of It All (Univ, 1963)
Stage to Thunder Rock (Par, 1964)
The Family Jewels (Par, 1965)
Harlow (Magna, 1965)
That Funny Feeling (Univ, 1965)
Frankie and Johnny (UA, 1966)
Fort Utah (Par, 1967)
Dagmar's Hot Pants (Trans American, 1971)

SLIM SUMMERVILLE
(George J. Summerville)

With ZaSu Pitts in Out All Night *(1933).*

Born July 10, 1892, Albuquerque, New Mexico. Married Eleanor _____ , child: Elliot. Died January 5, 1946, Laguna Beach, California. Gagman, director, and actor for Mack Sennett. Noted as the mournful, lanky hick with the vacant stare, curling upper lip, and slow drawl. The comedy relief in serious films (*All Quiet on the Western Front, The Bad Sister,* etc.). Frequently teamed with ZaSu Pitts: *Her First Mate; Love, Honor and Oh, Baby!* etc.

Slim Summerville to Lee Bowman in *Gold Rush Maisie:*
"*She's* people, ain't she? The worst kind—*female.*"

Films

Tillie's Punctured Romance (Keystone, 1914)
Cinders of Love (Tri, 1916)
The Winning Punch (Tri, 1917)
Villa of the Movies (Tri, 1917)
Are Witnesses Safe? (Tri, 1917)
Skirts (Fox, 1921)
The Texas Steer (FN, 1926)
The Denver Dude (Univ, 1927)
The Beloved Rogue (UA, 1927)
The Chinese Parrot (Univ, 1927)
Hey Hey Cowboy (Univ, 1927)
Painted Ponies (Univ, 1927)
Riding for Fame (Univ, 1928)
The Shannons of Broadway (Univ, 1929)
Strong Boy (Fox, 1929)
King of the Rodeo (Univ, 1929)
Tiger Rose (WB, 1929)
The Last Warning (Univ, 1929)
One Hysterical Night (Univ, 1930)
Troopers Three (Tif, 1930)
Under Montana Skies (Tif, 1930)

All Quiet on the Western Front (Univ, 1930)
King of Jazz (Univ, 1930)
Little Accident (Univ, 1930)
Her Man (Pathé, 1930)
The Spoilers (Par, 1930)
See America Thirst (Univ, 1930)
Free Love (Univ, 1930)
Heaven on Earth (Univ, 1931)
The Front Page (UA, 1931)
Reckless Living (Univ, 1931)
The Bad Sister (Univ, 1931)
Many a Slip (Univ, 1931)
Lasca of the Rio Grande (Univ, 1931)
The Unexpected Father (Univ, 1932)
Racing Youth (Univ, 1932)
Tom Brown of Culver (Univ, 1932)
Airmail (Univ, 1932)
They Just Had to Get Married (Univ, 1932)
Her First Mate (Univ, 1933)
Out All Night (Univ, 1933)

Love, Honor and Oh, Baby! (Univ, 1933)
The Love Birds (Univ, 1934)
Their Big Moment (RKO, 1934)
Life Begins at 40 (Fox, 1935)
The Farmer Takes a Wife (Fox, 1935)
Way Down East (Fox, 1935)
Captain January (20th, 1936)
Can This Be Dixie? (20th, 1936)
The Country Doctor (20th, 1936)
Pepper (20th, 1936)
White Fang (20th, 1936)
Reunion (20th, 1936)
Off to the Races (20th, 1937)
Love Is News (20th, 1937)
The Road Back (Univ, 1937)
Fifty Roads to Town (20th, 1937)
Kentucky Moonshine (20th, 1938)
Submarine Patrol (20th, 1938)
Up the River (20th, 1938)
Rebecca of Sunnybrook Farm (20th, 1938)
Five of a Kind (20th, 1938)
Jesse James (20th, 1939)

Winner Take All (20th, 1939)	*Western Union* (20th, 1941)	*Miss Polly* (UA, 1941)
Charlie Chan in Reno (20th, 1939)	*Tobacco Road* (20th, 1941)	*Bride by Mistake* (RKO, 1944)
Henry Goes to Arizona (MGM, 1940)	*Puddin'head* (Rep, 1941)	*Swing in the Saddle* (Col, 1944)
Anne of Windy Poplars (RKO, 1940)	*Highway West* (WB, 1941)	*I'm from Arkansas* (PRC, 1944)
Gold Rush Maisie (MGM, 1940)	*Niagara Falls* (UA, 1941)	*The Hoodlum Saint* (MGM, 1946)

GRADY SUTTON

C. Aubrey Smith, Lynn Bari, and Grady Sutton in City of Chance (1940).

Born April 5, 1908, Chattanooga, Tennessee. Nearly everyone's favorite prissy bungler. Played the pudgy dunce who asked wallflower Katharine Hepburn to dance in *Alice Adams*, was Von Ronkel in William Powell's *My Man Godfrey*. Many times in W. C. Fields' comedies: *The Man on the Flying Trapeze*, *You Can't Cheat an Honest Man*, and *The Bank Dick* (in the latter as Og Oggilby, Una Merkel's fiance). TV series: "The Egg and I" and "The Pruitts of Southampton."

Grady Sutton to Helen Parrish in *Three Smart Girls Grow Up:*
"Would you mind terribly if we had this dance?"

Films

Skinner's Dress Suit (Univ, 1925)	*Pack Up Your Troubles* (MGM, 1932)	*Stone of Silver Creek* (Univ, 1935)
The Mad Whirl (Univ, 1925)	*This Reckless Age* (Par, 1932)	*Alice Adams* (RKO, 1935)
The Freshman (Pathé, 1925)	*Hot Saturday* (Par, 1932)	*The Man on the Flying Trapeze* (Par, 1935)
The Boy Friend (MGM, 1926)	*The Story of Temple Drake* (Par, 1933)	
The Sophomore (Pathé, 1928)	*College Humor* (Par, 1933)	*Dr. Socrates* (WB, 1935)
Tanned Legs (RKO, 1929)	*The Sweetheart of Sigma Chi* (Mon, 1933)	*Palm Springs* (Par, 1936)
Hit the Deck (RKO, 1930)	*Only Yesterday* (Univ, 1933)	*The Singing Kid* (FN, 1936)
Let's Go Native (Par, 1930)	*Bachelor Bait* (RKO, 1934)	*Valiant Is the Word for Carrie* (Par, 1936)
Wild Company (Fox, 1930)	*Gridiron Flash* (RKO, 1934)	*My Man Godfrey* (Univ, 1936)
Movie Crazy (Par, 1932)	*Laddie* (RKO, 1935)	*King of the Royal Mounted* (20th, 1936)

Pigskin Parade (20th, 1936)
We Have Our Moments (Univ, 1937)
Dangerous Holiday (Rep, 1937)
Stage Door (RKO, 1937)
Love Takes Flight (GN, 1937)
Waikiki Wedding (Par, 1937)
Turn Off the Moon (Par, 1937)
Two Minutes to Play (Victory, 1937)
Behind the Mike (Univ, 1937)
Vivacious Lady (RKO, 1938)
Having Wonderful Time (RKO, 1938)
Alexander's Ragtime Band (20th, 1938)
Hard to Get (WB, 1938)
Three Loves Has Nancy (MGM, 1938)
The Mad Miss Manton (RKO, 1938)
In Name Only (RKO, 1939)
Naughty but Nice (WB, 1939)
You Can't Cheat an Honest Man (Univ, 1939)
It's a Wonderful World (MGM, 1939)
The Flying Irishman (RKO, 1939)
Three Smart Girls Grow Up (Univ, 1939)
Three Sons (RKO, 1939)
Angels Wash Their Faces (WB, 1939)
Anne of Windy Poplars (RKO, 1940)
Torrid Zone (WB, 1940)
Lucky Partners (RKO, 1940)
The Bank Dick (Univ, 1940)
City of Chance (20th, 1940)
She Knew All the Answers (Col, 1941)
Father Takes a Wife (RKO, 1941)

Flying Blind (Par, 1941)
Doctors Don't Tell (Rep, 1941)
The Bashful Bachelor (RKO, 1942)
Somewhere I'll Find You (MGM, 1942)
Dudes Are Pretty People (UA, 1942)
Whispering Ghosts (20th, 1942)
The More the Merrier (Col, 1943)
A Lady Takes a Chance (RKO, 1943)
What a Woman! (Col, 1943)
Johnny Doesn't Live Here Anymore [a.k.a. *And So They Were Married*] (Mon, 1944)
Nine Girls (Col, 1944)
Allergic to Love (Univ, 1944)
The Great Moment (Par, 1944)
Dragonwyck (20th, 1944)
Since You Went Away (UA, 1944)
Goin' to Town (RKO, 1944)
Grissly's Millions (Rep, 1945)
Hi, Beautiful (Univ, 1945)
A Royal Scandal (20th, 1945)
Three's a Crowd (Rep, 1945)
Her Lucky Night (Univ, 1945)
Captain Eddie (20th, 1945)
A Bell for Adano (20th, 1945)
Anchors Aweigh (MGM, 1945)
The Fabulous Suzanne (Rep, 1946)
My Dog Shep (Screen Guild, 1946)
Hit the Hay (Col, 1946)
Ziegfeld Follies (MGM, 1946)
It's Great to Be Young (Col, 1946)

The Magnificent Rogue (Rep, 1946)
Nobody Lives Forever (WB, 1946)
Partners in Time (RKO, 1946)
Susie Steps Out (UA, 1946)
Beat the Band (RKO, 1947)
Dead Reckoning (Col, 1947)
My Wild Irish Rose (WB, 1947)
Philo Vance's Gamble (PRC, 1947)
My Dear Secretary (UA, 1948)
Jiggs and Maggie in Court (Mon, 1948)
Last of the Wild Horses (Screen Guild, 1948)
Grand Canyon (Screen Guild, 1949)
Air Hostess (Col, 1949)
A Star Is Born (WB, 1954)
White Christmas (Par, 1954)
Living It Up (Par, 1954)
Madison Avenue (20th, 1962)
The Chapman Report (WB, 1962)
Billy Rose's Jumbo (MGM, 1962)
Come Blow Your Horn (Par, 1963)
My Fair Lady (WB, 1964)
Tickle Men (AA, 1965)
Paradise Hawaiian Style (Par, 1966)
I Love You, Alice B. Toklas (WB, 1968)
Myra Breckinridge (20th, 1970)
Dirty Dingus Magee (MGM, 1970)
Suppose They Gave a War and Nobody Came? (Cin, 1970)
Support Your Local Gunfighter (UA, 1971)

LYLE TALBOT
(Lysle Henderson)

Michael Vallon, Jack Haley, William Edmunds, Lyle Talbot, and Lucien Littlefield in One Body Too Many *(1944).*

Born February 8, 1902, Pittsburgh, Pennsylvania. Married 1) Marjorie Cramer (1937); divorced; 2) Kevin McClure (1946); divorced (1947); 3) Margaret _____ (1948), children: Stephen, David, Cynthia, Margaret Ann. Square-built, hard-working stage, screen, radio, and TV player. In early Warner Bros. years concentrated on slick, man-about-town parts, often charming the leading lady astray: *Three on a Match* (Ann Dvorak), *Mandalay* (Kay Francis); sometimes *he* was led astray: *Fog over Frisco* (by Bette Davis). Played hero to Ginger Rogers' heroine in two poverty-row quickies: *The Thirteenth Guest* (Phil Winston) and *A Shriek in the Night* (Ted Rand). Ground out many other double-bill items in the 1930s-40s. Was the baldplated villain Luthor in *Atom Man vs. Superman* serial. TV series: "The Adventures of Ozzie and Harriet" (as Joe Randolph), "Love That Bob" (as Paul Fonda, Rosemary De Camp's boyfriend), and "Ben Jerrod."

Lyle Talbot to Patricia Ellis in *The Case of the Lucky Legs:* "Do you think you've made possible our marriage by winning a leg show? You've made it impossible!"

Films

Three on a Match (FN, 1932)
Love Is a Racket (FN, 1932)
Big City Blues (FN, 1932)
No More Orchids (Col, 1932)
The Purchase Price (WB, 1932)
Unholy Love (Allied, 1932)
Stranger in Town (WB, 1932)
The Thirteenth Guest (Mon, 1932)
Klondike (Mon, 1932)
Ladies They Talk About (WB, 1933)
A Shriek in the Night (Allied, 1933)
20,000 Years in Sing Sing (FN, 1933)
Girl Missing (WB, 1933)

Mary Stevens, M.D. (WB, 1933)
College Coach (WB, 1933)
She Had to Say Yes (FN, 1933)
The Life of Jimmy Dolan (WB, 1933)
Havana Widows (FN, 1933)
Parachute Jumper (WB, 1933)
Mandalay (FN, 1934)
Registered Nurse (FN, 1934)
The Dragon Murder Case (FN, 1934)
Return of the Terror (FN, 1934)
A Lost Lady (FN, 1934)
Murder in the Clouds (FN, 1934)
Fog over Frisco (FN, 1934)

Heat Lightening (WB, 1934)
One Night of Love (Col, 1934)
Party Wire (Col, 1935)
Red Hot Tires (WB, 1935)
While the Patient Slept (FN, 1935)
Oil for the Lamps of China (WB, 1935)
Page Miss Glory (WB, 1935)
It Happened in New York (Univ, 1935)
Chinatown Squad (Univ, 1935)
Our Little Girl (Fox, 1935)
The Case of the Lucky Legs (WB, 1935)
Broadway Hostess (FN, 1935)
Trapped by Television (Col, 1936)

476

The Singing Kid (FN, 1936)
Murder by an Aristocrat (FN, 1936)
Boulder Dam (WB, 1936)
The Law in Her Hands (FN, 1936)
Go West, Young Man (Par, 1936)
Mind Your Own Business (Par, 1936)
Three Legionnaires (General Films, 1937)
The Affairs of Cappy Ricks (Rep, 1937)
Second Honeymoon (20th, 1937)
What Price Vengeance? (Rialto, 1937)
Change of Heart (20th, 1938)
One Wild Night (20th, 1938)
Getaway (20th, 1938)
Call of the Yukon (Rep, 1938)
I Stand Accused (Rep, 1938)
The Arkansas Traveler (Par, 1938)
Forged Passport (Rep, 1939)
Second Fiddle (20th, 1939)
They Asked for It (Univ, 1939)
Torture Ship (Producers Pictures Corporation, 1939)
He Married His Wife (20th, 1940)
Parole Fixer (Par, 1940)
A Miracle on Main Street (Col, 1940)
Mexican Spitfire's Elephant (RKO, 1942)
She's in the Army (Mon, 1942)
A Night for Crime (PRC, 1942)
They Raid by Night (PRC, 1942)
Man of Courage (PRC, 1943)
Are These Our Parents? (Mon, 1944)
Up in Arms (RKO, 1944)
Sensations of 1945 (UA, 1944)
One Body Too Many (Par, 1944)
Dixie Jamboree (PRC, 1944)
The Falcon Out West (RKO, 1944)
Mystery of the River Boat (Univ serial, 1944)
Gambler's Choice (Par, 1944)
Trail to Gunsight (Univ, 1945)

Strange Impersonation (Rep, 1946)
Song of Arizona (Rep, 1946)
Murder Is My Business (PRC, 1946)
Chick Carter, Detective (Col serial, 1946)
Gun Town (Univ, 1946)
Shep Comes Home (Screen Guild, 1946)
The Vigilante (Col serial, 1947)
Danger Street (Par, 1947)
The Vicious Circle (AA, 1948)
Joe Palooka in Winner Take All (Mon, 1948)
Appointment with Murder (Film Classics, 1948)
The Devil's Cargo (Film Classics, 1948)
Parole, Inc. (El, 1948)
Highway 13 (Screen Guild, 1948)
Fighting Fools (Mon, 1949)
The Mutineers (Col, 1949)
Sky Dragon (Mon, 1949)
Ringside (Screen Guild, 1949)
Mississippi Rhythm (Col, 1949)
Joe Palooka in the Big Fight (Mon, 1949)
Batman and Robin (Col serial, 1949)
Atom Man vs. Superman (Col serial, 1950)
The Jackpot (20th, 1950)
Champagne for Caesar (Univ, 1950)
Border Rangers (Lip, 1950)
Revenue Agent (Col, 1950)
Cherokee Uprising (Mon, 1950)
Tall Timber (Mon, 1950)
Blue Blood (Mon, 1951)
The Man from Sonora (Mon, 1951)
Fingerprints Don't Lie (Lip, 1951)
Abilene Trail (Mon, 1951)
Hurricane Island (Col, 1951)
Jungle Manhunt (Col, 1951)
Gold Raiders (UA, 1951)
Purple Heart Diary (Col, 1951)
Varieties on Parade (Lip, 1951)

Fury of the Congo (Col, 1951)
Sea Tiger (Mon, 1952)
Untamed Woman (UA, 1952)
The Old West (Col, 1952)
Outlaw Women (Lip, 1952)
With a Song in My Heart (20th, 1952)
Desperadoes' Outpost (Rep, 1952)
Son of Geronimo (Col serial, 1952)
Feudin' Fools (Mon, 1952)
Kansas Territory (Mon, 1952)
African Treasure (Mon, 1952)
Montana Incident (Mon, 1952)
Texas City (Mon, 1952)
Trail Blazers (AA, 1953)
Down Among the Sheltering Palms (20th, 1953)
Star of Texas (AA, 1953)
White Lightning (AA, 1953)
Captain Kidd and the Slave Girl (UA, 1954)
Gunfighters of the Northwest (Col serial, 1954)
Tobor the Great (Rep, 1954)
The Steel Cage (UA, 1954)
There's No Business Like Show Business (20th, 1954)
Trader Tom of the China Seas (Rep serial, 1954)
Jail Busters (AA, 1955)
Sudden Danger (AA, 1955)
The Great Man (Univ, 1956)
Calling Homicide (AA, 1956)
She Shoulda Said No (Hallmark, 1957)
The Notorious Mr. Monks (Rep, 1958)
High School Confidential (MGM, 1958)
The Hot Angel (Par, 1958)
City of Fear (Col, 1959)
Plan 9 from Outer Space (DCA, 1959)
Sunrise at Campobello (WB, 1960)

AKIM TAMIROFF

Peter Ustinov and Akim Tamiroff in Topkapi *(1964).*

Born October 29, 1898, Tiflis, Russia. Married Tamara Shayne. Died September 17, 1972, Palm Springs, California. Squat, swarthy, hairy; graduate of the Moscow Art Theatre, Broadway productions, Chicago nightclubs. Supplied zest and imagination to his gallery of cinema portrayals. Oscar-nominated for his Chinese bandit, General Yang, in *The General Died at Dawn* (but lost BSAAA to Walter Brennan of *Come and Get It*). Had some leads in Paramount programmers: *The Great Gambini* (flamboyant magician), *King of Gamblers* (gangland boss), *Ride a Crooked Mile* (Cossack on the Western range), etc. Won another BSAAA nomination for his Pablo, the Spanish Civil War guerrilla leader in *For Whom the Bell Tolls* (but lost to Charles Coburn of *The More the Merrier*). Was a whiz at ethnic delineations: *Anthony Adverse* (Carlo Cibo, the Cuban), *The Lives of a Bengal Lancer* (the sympathetic emir), *The Soldier and the Lady* (the Tartar upstart), *North West Mounted Police* (the French Canadian Dan Duroc), *Dragon Seed* (Wu Lien, the Chinese spying for the Japanese), etc. Effective as the frightened Grandi in *Touch of Evil* and the bewildered elder citizen of *Alphaville*.

Akim Tamiroff to Gary Cooper in *The General Died at Dawn:*
"You eat fresh fish tonight. When we arrive in Shanghai tomorrow, maybe fresh fish eat you."

Films

Okay, America (Univ, 1932)
Gabriel over the White House (MGM, 1933)
The Devil's in Love (Fox, 1933)
Queen Christina (MGM, 1933)
Storm at Daybreak (MGM, 1933)
Fugitive Lovers (MGM, 1933)
The Scarlet Empress (Par, 1934)
Now and Forever (Par, 1934)
The Merry Widow (MGM, 1934)
Murder in the Private Car (MGM, 1934)

La Veueve Joyeuse (MGM, 1934) [Fr version of The Merry Widow]
Chained (MGM, 1934)
Here Is My Heart (Par, 1934)
The Captain Hates the Sea (Col, 1934)
Sadie McKee (MGM, 1934)
The Great Flirtation (Par, 1934)
Whom the Gods Destroy (Col, 1934)
The Lives of a Bengal Lancer (Par, 1935)
Naughty Marietta (MGM, 1935)
The Winning Ticket (MGM, 1935)

China Seas (MGM, 1935)
Rumba (Par, 1935)
Reckless (MGM, 1935)
The Last Outpost (Par, 1935)
Black Sheep (Fox, 1935)
The Big Broadcast of 1936 (Par, 1935)
Paris in Spring (Par, 1935)
Two Fisted (Par, 1935)
Go into Your Dance (WB, 1935)
Black Fury (WB, 1935)
The Gay Deception (Fox, 1935)

The Story of Louis Pasteur (WB, 1935)
Desire (Par, 1936)
Woman Trap (Par, 1936)
The General Died at Dawn (Par, 1936)
The Jungle Princess (Par, 1936)
Anthony Adverse (WB, 1936)
The Solider and the Lady [a.k.a. *Michael Strogoff*] (RKO, 1937)
Her Husband Lies (Par, 1937)
This Way Please (Par, 1937)
King of Gamblers (Par, 1937)
High, Wide and Handsome (Par, 1937)
The Great Gambini (Par, 1937)
The Buccaneer (Par, 1938)
Spawn of the North (Par, 1938)
Dangerous to Know (Par, 1938)
Ride a Crooked Mile (Par, 1938)
Paris Honeymoon (Par, 1939)
Union Pacific (Par, 1939)
The Magnificent Fraud (Par, 1939)
King of Chinatown (Par, 1939)
Honeymoon in Bali (Par, 1939)
Disputed Passage (Par, 1939)
Geronimo (Par, 1939)
The Way of All Flesh (Par, 1940)
Untamed (Par, 1940)
The Great McGinty (Par, 1940)
North West Mounted Police (Par, 1940)
Texas Rangers Ride Again (Par, 1940)
New York Town (Par, 1941)

The Corsican Brothers (UA, 1941)
Tortilla Flat (MGM, 1942)
Are Husbands Necessary? (Par, 1942)
Five Graves to Cairo (Par, 1943)
For Whom the Bell Tolls (Par, 1943)
His Butler's Sister (Univ, 1943)
The Bridge of San Luis Rey (UA, 1944)
Dragon Seed (MGM, 1944)
The Miracle of Morgan's Creek (Par, 1944)
Can't Help Singing (Univ, 1944)
Pardon My Past (Col, 1946)
A Scandal in Paris [a.k.a. *Thieves Holiday*] (UA, 1946)
Fiesta (MGM, 1947)
The Gangster (AA, 1947)
My Girl Tisa (WB, 1948)
Tenth Avenue Angel (MGM, 1948)
Relentless (Col, 1948)
Black Magic (UA, 1949)
Outpost in Morocco (UA, 1949)
Desert Legion (Univ, 1953)
You Know What Sailors Are (UA, 1954)
They Who Dare (Br, 1955)
Mr. Arkadin [a.k.a. *Confidential Report*] (WB, 1955)
The Black Sleep (UA, 1956)
Anastasia (20th, 1956)
Battle Hell [a.k.a. *The Yangtse Incident*] (DCA, 1957)

Cartouche (RKO It, 1957)
Touch of Evil (Univ, 1958)
Me and the Colonel (Col, 1958)
Desert Desperadoes (RKO, 1959)
Ocean's Eleven (WB, 1960)
Romanoff and Juliet (Univ, 1961)
The Reluctant Saint (Davis Royal, 1962)
The Trial (Fr, 1962)
Panic Button (Gorton Associates, 1964)
Topkapi (UA, 1964)
Bambole (It, 1965)
Alphaville (Fr, 1965)
Lord Jim (Col, 1965)
Chimes at Midnight (Sp, 1965)
The Happening (Col, 1965)
Lieutenant Robin Crusoe, USN (BV, 1966)
Marco the Magnificent (MGM, 1966)
The Liquidator (MGM, 1966)
Hotel Paradiso (MGM, 1966)
After the Fox (UA, 1966)
Every Man's Woman [a.k.a. *A Rose for Everyone*] (It, 1966)
The Great Catherine (WB-7 Arts, 1967)
The Vulture (Par, 1967)
The Great Bank Robbery (WB-7 Arts, 1969)
The Girl Who Couldn't Say No (20th, 1970)
Death of a Jew (Cine Globe, 1972)

RAY TEAL

In the 1940s.

Born January 12, 1902, Grand Rapids, Michigan. Former band (saxophone) player and musical conductor who became typed as a screen sheriff—honest or corrupt. TV series: "Bonanza" (as Sheriff Roy Coffee).

Ray Teal in *Utah Blaine*: "Well, boys, that makes one man less to share the land with."

Films

Western Jamboree (Rep, 1938)
Cherokee Strip (Par, 1940)
The Trail Blazers (Rep, 1940)
Kitty Foyle (RKO, 1940)
I Love You Again (MGM, 1940)
Pony Post (Univ, 1940)
Prairie Schooners (Col, 1940)
The Adventures of Red Ryder (Rep serial, 1940)
Northwest Passage (MGM, 1940)
Florian (MGM, 1940)
Bad Men of Missouri (WB, 1941)
They Met in Bombay (MGM, 1940)
They Died with Their Boots On (WB, 1941)
Honky Tonk (MGM, 1941)
Wild Bill Hickok Rides (WB, 1941)
Juke Girl (WB, 1942)
Apache Trail (MGM, 1942)

Tennessee Johnson (MGM, 1942)
Madame Curie (MGM, 1943)
The Youngest Profession (MGM, 1943)
The Lost Angel (MGM, 1943)
The North Star [a.k.a. *Armored Attack*] (RKO, 1943)
The Princess and the Pirate (RKO, 1944)
Maisie Goes to Reno (MGM, 1944)
Wing and a Prayer (20th, 1944)
Strange Affair (Col, 1944)
None Shall Escape (Col, 1944)
Hollywood Canteen (WB, 1944)
The Thin Man Goes Home (MGM, 1944)
Anchors Aweigh (MGM, 1945)
Circumstantial Evidence (20th, 1945)
Captain Kidd (UA, 1945)
Adventure (MGM, 1945)
Along Came Jones (RKO, 1945)
Sudan (Univ, 1945)

The Fighting Guardsman (Col, 1945)
Strange Voyage (Mon, 1945)
The Best Years of Our Lives (RKO, 1946)
The Bandit of Sherwood Forest (Col, 1946)
Blondie Knows Best (Col, 1946)
Canyon Passage (Univ, 1946)
Deadline for Murder (20th, 1946)
The Missing Lady (Mon, 1946)
Till the Clouds Roll By (MGM, 1946)
Road to Rio (Par, 1947)
Unconquered (Par, 1947)
Michigan Kid (Univ, 1947)
Brute Force (Univ, 1947)
Ramrod (UA, 1947)
Driftwood (Rep, 1947)
Cheyenne (WB, 1947)
Deep Valley (WB, 1947)
Road House (20th, 1948)
The Man from Colorado (Col, 1948)

Raw Deal (EL, 1948)
I Wouldn't Be in Your Shoes (Mon, 1948)
The Black Arrow (Col, 1948)
Daredevils of the Clouds (Rep, 1948)
The Countess of Monte Cristo (Univ, 1948)
Whispering Smith (Par, 1948)
Joan of Arc (RKO, 1948)
The Miracle of the Bells (RKO, 1948)
Once More, My Darling (Univ, 1949)
Kazan (Col, 1949)
It Happens Every Spring (20th, 1949)
Ambush (MGM, 1949)
The Streets of Laredo (Par, 1949)
Blondie Hits the Jackpot (Col, 1949)
Rusty's Birthday (Col, 1949)
Where Danger Lives (RKO, 1950)
The Kid from Texas (Univ, 1950)
No Way Out (20th, 1950)
The Men (Col, 1950)
Our Very Own (RKO, 1950)
The Redhead and the Cowboy (Par, 1950)
Davy Crockett—Indian Scout (UA, 1950)
Harbor of Missing Men (Rep, 1950)
Edge of Doom (RKO, 1950)
When You're Smiling (Col, 1950)

Winchester 73 (Univ, 1950)
Fort Worth (WB, 1951)
Tomorrow Is Another Day (WB, 1951)
Ace in the Hole [a.k.a. The Big Carnival] (Par, 1951)
Along the Great Divide (WB, 1951)
Lorna Doone (Col, 1951)
The Secret of Convict Lake (20th, 1951)
Distant Drums (WB, 1951)
The Flaming Feather (Par, 1951)
The Lion and the Horse (WB, 1952)
Captive City (UA, 1952)
Montana Belle (RKO, 1952)
The Turning Point (Par, 1952)
The Wild North (MGM, 1952)
Jumping Jacks (Par, 1952)
Carrie (Par, 1952)
Hangman's Knot (Col, 1952)
Cattle Town (WB, 1952)
Ambush at Tomahawk Gap (Col, 1953)
The Wild One (Col, 1954)
About Mrs. Leslie (Par, 1954)
The Command (WB, 1954)
Rogue Cop (MGM, 1954)
Rage at Dawn (RKO, 1955)
The Indian Fighter (UA, 1955)

Run for Cover (Par, 1955)
The Desperate Hours (Par, 1955)
The Man from Bitter Ridge (Univ, 1955)
Apache Ambush (Col, 1955)
The Young Guns (AA, 1956)
Canyon River (AA, 1956)
The Burning Hills (WB, 1956)
Band of Angels (WB, 1957)
Utah Blaine (Col, 1957)
The Phantom Stagecoach (Col, 1957)
The Oklahoman (AA, 1957)
The Wayward Girl (Rep, 1957)
The Tall Stranger (AA, 1957)
Decision at Sundown (Col, 1957)
The Guns of Fort Petticoat (Col, 1957)
Saddle the Wind (MGM, 1958)
Gunman's Walk (Col, 1958)
Inherit the Wind (UA, 1960)
Home from the Hill (MGM, 1960)
One-Eyed Jacks (Par, 1961)
Posse from Hell (Univ, 1961)
Judgment at Nuremberg (UA, 1961)
Cattle King (MGM, 1963)
Taggart (Univ, 1964)
The Liberation of L. B. Jones (Col, 1970)
Chisum (WB, 1970)

VERREE TEASDALE

George Brent, Jean Muir, and Verree Teasdale in Desirable *(1934).*

Born March 15, 1906, Spokane, Washington. Married 1) William J. O'Neal (1927); divorced (1933); 2) Adolphe Menjou (1934), child: Peter, widowed (1963). The chic best friend or "other woman" who had a deft way with an elegant comic delivery.

Verree Teasdale to Rafael Storm in *I Take This Woman*: "Raoul, you have your qualities, but intelligence is not one of them."

Films

Syncopation (RKO, 1929)
The Sap from Syracuse (Par, 1930)
Skyscraper Souls (MGM, 1932)
Payment Deferred (MGM, 1932)
Luxury Liner (Par, 1933)
They Just Had to Get Married (Univ, 1933)
Terror Aboard (Par, 1933)
Love, Honor and Oh, Baby! (Univ, 1933)

Roman Scandals (UA, 1933)
Fashions of 1934 (FN, 1934)
Goodbye Love (RKO, 1934)
A Modern Hero (WB, 1934)
Madame Du Barry (WB, 1934)
Desirable (WB, 1934)
The Firebird (WB, 1934)
Dr. Monica (WB, 1934)
A Midsummer Night's Dream (WB, 1935)

The Milky Way (Par, 1936)
First Lady (WB, 1937)
Topper Takes a Trip (UA, 1938)
Fifth Avenue Girl (RKO, 1939)
Turnabout (UA, 1940)
I Take This Woman (MGM, 1940)
Love Thy Neighbor (Par, 1940)
Come Live with Me (MGM, 1941)

MAX TERHUNE

In the late 1930s.

Born February 12, 1891, Franklin, Indiana. Married _____ , children: Robert, daughter; widowed. Died June 5, 1973, Cottonwood, Texas. Accomplished vaudevillian (ventriloquist, impressionist, juggler, imitator, etc.) who joined the "National Barn Dance" radio program (with Gene Autry) in 1933. Introduced by Autry to Republic Pictures where he soon became part of *The Three Mesquiteers* series (with Robert Livingston and Ray Corrigan) for 21 entries. Played comedy relief in these—Lullaby Joslin with his ever-present dummy Elmer. At Monogram made 24 of *The Range Busters* episodes with Corrigan and John King. Still later was Johnny Mack Brown's sidekick on the celluloid trail.

Max Terhune to Doreen McKay in *Pals of the Saddle*: "Our pardner don't usually go around murderin' strangers."

Films

The Big Show (Rep, 1936)	*Heroes of the Hills* (Rep, 1938)	*Trail Riders* (Mon, 1942)
Ghost Town Gold (Rep, 1936)	*Santa Fe Stampede* (Rep, 1938)	*Boot Hill Bandits* (Mon, 1942)
The Hit Parade (Rep, 1937)	*Pals of the Saddle* (Rep, 1938)	*Texas Trouble Shooters* (Mon, 1942)
Roarin' Lead (Rep, 1937)	*Overland Stage Raiders* (Rep, 1938)	*Two-Fisted Justice* (Mon, 1943)
Come On, Cowboys (Rep, 1937)	*The Night Riders* (Rep, 1939)	*Cowboy Commandos* (Mon, 1943)
Riders of the Whistling Skull (Rep, 1937)	*Man of Conquest* (Rep, 1939)	*Black Market Rustlers* (Mon, 1943)
Range Defenders (Rep, 1937)	*Three Texas Steers* (Rep, 1939)	*Cowboy Canteen* (Col, 1943)
Gunsmoke Ranch (Rep, 1937)	*The Range Busters* (Mon, 1940)	*Sheriff of Sundown* (Rep, 1944)
Mama Runs Wild (Rep, 1937)	*Trailing Double Trouble* (Mon, 1940)	*Along the Oregon Trail* (Rep, 1947)
Manhattan Merry-Go-Round (Rep, 1937)	*West of Pinto Basin* (Mon, 1940)	*The White Stallion* (Astor, 1947)
The Trigger Trio (Rep, 1937)	*Trail of the Silver Spurs* (Mon, 1941)	*Sheriff of Medicine Bow* (Mon, 1948)
Wild Horse Rodeo (Rep, 1938)	*Tumbledown Ranch in Arizona* (Mon, 1941)	*Law of the West* (Mon, 1949)
Call of the Mesquiteers (Rep, 1938)	*Wranglers' Roost* (Mon, 1941)	*Trail's End* (Mon, 1949)
The Purple Vigilantes (Rep, 1938)	*The Kid's Last Ride* (Mon, 1941)	*Gunning for Justice* (Mon, 1949)
Outlaws of Sonora (Rep, 1938)	*Fugitive Valley* (Mon, 1941)	*Square Dance Jubilee* (Lip, 1949)
Riders of the Black Hills (Rep, 1938)	*Rock River Renegades* (Mon, 1942)	*Range Justice* (Mon, 1949)
Ladies in Distress (Rep, 1938)	*Texas to Bataan* (Mon, 1942)	*West of El Dorado* (Mon, 1949)
		Western Renegades (Mon, 1949)

TORIN THATCHER

Torin Thatcher, Judi Meredith, and Walter Burke in Jack the Giant Killer *(1962).*

Born January 15, 1905, Bombay, India. Married 1) Rita Daniel, child: Phillip; 2) Ann Le Bourne (1952). Rugged-looking stage and film actor with crisp voice. Often in costume dramas: *The Black Rose* (Harry), *Blackbeard the Pirate* (Sir Henry Morgan), *The Robe* (Senator Gallio), *The Seventh Voyage of Sinbad* (Sokurah), *Hawaii* (Reverend Mr. Thorn), etc.

Torin Thatcher to Burt Lancaster in *The Crimson Pirate*: "If you'll forgive my pointing it out, Skipper, you can't leave a pretty woman unmolested aboard ship. It'll give piracy a bad name."

Films

But the Flesh Is Weak (MGM, 1932)
General John Regan (Br, 1934)
Irish Hearts [a.k.a. *Norah O'Neal*] (Br, 1934)
Drake of England (Br, 1935)
School for Stars (Br, 1935)
The Red Wagon (Br, 1935)
Sabotage [a.k.a. *The Woman Alone*] (Br, 1936)
The Man Who Could Work Miracles (UA Br, 1936)
Climbing High (MGM Br, 1938)
Young and Innocent (Br, 1938)
Let George Do It (Br, 1940)
Last Train to Munich (Br, 1941)
Law and Disorder (RKO Br, 1941)
The Case of the Frightened Lady (Br, 1941)
Barabbas (Br, 1941)
Old Mother Riley, M.P. (Br, 1941)
Major Barbara (UA Br, 1941)

Next of Kin (Br, 1942)
The Captive Heart (Br, 1947)
Great Expectations (Br, 1947)
The Man Within [a.k.a. *The Smugglers*] (Br, 1947)
When the Bough Breaks (Br, 1948)
Jassy (Br, 1948)
The End of the River (Br, 1948)
Bonnie Prince Charlie (Br, 1948)
Lost Illusion (Br, 1948)
The Fallen Idol (Br, 1949)
The Black Rose (20th, 1950)
The Crimson Pirate (WB, 1952)
Affair in Trinidad (Col, 1952)
The Snows of Kilimanjaro (20th, 1952)
Blackbeard the Pirate (RKO, 1952)
The Desert Fox (20th, 1953)
Houdini (Par, 1953)
The Robe (20th, 1953)
Knock on Wood (Par, 1954)

The Black Shield of Falworth (Univ, 1954)
Bengal Brigade (Univ, 1954)
Helen of Troy (WB, 1955)
Lady Godiva (Univ, 1955)
Diane (MGM, 1955)
Love Is a Many-Splendored Thing (20th, 1955)
Istanbul (Univ, 1957)
Band of Angels (WB, 1957)
Witness for the Prosecution (UA, 1957)
The Seventh Voyage of Sinbad (Col, 1958)
Darby's Rangers (WB, 1958)
The Miracle (WB, 1959)
The Canadians (20th, 1961)
Jack the Giant Killer (UA, 1962)
Mutiny on the Bounty (MGM, 1962)
Drums of Africa (MGM, 1963)
The Sandpiper (MGM, 1965)
Hawaii (UA, 1966)
The King's Pirate (Univ, 1967)

CHIEF THUNDER CLOUD
(Victor Daniels)

In Geronimo (1939).

Born April 12, 1889, Muskogee, Oklahoma. Married Frances Delmar, children: two sons, two daughters. Died November 30, 1955, Ventura, California. Onetime miner, boxer, and rodeo performer who became a movie stuntman and an extra in the late 1920s. Played Tonto in two **serials:** *The Lone Ranger* and *The Lone Ranger Rides Again*. Had title role in 1939's *Geronimo*.

Chief Thunder Cloud to Randolph Scott in *Western Union:*
"You give whiskey."

Films

Fighting Pioneers (Resolute, 1935)
Rustler's Paradise (Ajax, 1935)
The Farmer Takes a Wife (20th, 1935)
Custer's Last Stand (Stage & Screen
  serial, 1936)
Ramona (20th, 1936)
Silly Billies (RKO, 1936)
The Plainsman (Par, 1936)
Renfrew of the Royal Mounted (GN, 1937)
The Lone Ranger (Rep serial, 1938) [fea-
  ture version: Hi Yo, Silver (Rep,
  1940)]
The Great Adventures of Wild Bill Hickok
  (Col serial, 1938)
Flaming Frontiers (Univ serial, 1938)
The Lone Ranger Rides Again (Rep serial,
  1939)
Union Pacific (Par, 1939)
Geronimo (Par, 1939)

Typhoon (Par, 1940)
Murder on the Yukon (Mon, 1940)
Wyoming (MGM, 1940)
Young Buffalo Bill (Rep, 1940)
North West Mounted Police (Par, 1940)
Hudson's Bay (20th, 1940)
Western Union (20th, 1941)
Law and Disorder (RKO Br, 1941)
The Silver Stallion (Mon, 1941)
My Gal Sal (Mon, 1942)
Shut My Big Mouth (Col, 1942)
King of the Stallions (Mon, 1942)
Black Arrow (Col serial, 1944)
Fighting Seabees (Rep, 1944)
The Falcon Out West (RKO, 1944)
Buffalo Bill (20th, 1944)
Outlaw Trail (Mon, 1944)
Sonora Stagecoach (Mon, 1944)
Badman's Territory (RKO, 1946)

Romance of the West (PRC, 1946)
Renegade Girl (Screen Guild, 1946)
The Senator Was Indiscreet (Univ, 1947)
Unconquered (Par, 1947)
Blazing Across the Pecos (Col, 1948)
Call of the Forest (Lip, 1949)
Ambush (MGM, 1949)
Colt .45 (WB, 1950)
Davy Crockett—Indian Scout (UA, 1950)
A Ticket to Tomahawk (20th, 1950)
I Killed Geronimo (UA, 1950)
The Traveling Saleswoman (Col, 1950)
Santa Fe (Col, 1951)
Buffalo Bill in Tomahawk Territory (UA,
  1952)
The Half-Breed (RKO, 1952)
The Snows of Kilimanjaro (20th, 1952)

GEORGE TOBIAS

Stanley Ridges (colonel), George Tobias, Alan Hale, George Murphy, and Charles Butterworth in This Is the Army *(1943).*

Born July 14, 1901, New York City, New York. Congenial Warner Bros. contract player with prior stage work. Generally the hero's down-to-earth, loyal New Yorker pal, frequently with bemused look: *Sergeant York* (Pusher), *Yankee Doodle Dandy* (Dietz), *Objective, Burma!* (Gabby Gordon), *The Glenn Miller Story* (Si Schribman). TV series: "Hudson's Bay," "Adventures in Paradise," and "Bewitched" (as Abner Kravitz).

George Tobias to Ann Sheridan in *Torrid Zone:* "Confidentially, as a lover, I have not had a complaint in all this territory."

Films

Maisie (MGM, 1939)
Ninotchka (MGM, 1939)
They All Came Out (MGM, 1939)
The Hunchback of Notre Dame (RKO, 1939)
Balalaika (MGM, 1939)
Music in My Heart (Col, 1940)
East of the River (WB, 1940)
The Man Who Talked Too Much (WB, 1940)
River's End (WB, 1940)
Saturday's Children (WB, 1940)
Torrid Zone (WB, 1940)
City for Conquest (WB, 1940)
They Drive by Night (WB, 1940)
Calling All Husbands (WB, 1940)

South of Suez (WB, 1940)
The Bride Came C.O.D. (WB, 1941)
You're in the Army Now (WB, 1941)
The Strawberry Blonde (WB, 1941)
Sergeant York (WB, 1941)
Affectionately Yours (WB, 1941)
Out of the Fog (WB, 1941)
My Sister Eileen (Col, 1942)
Juke Girl (WB, 1942)
Wings for the Eagle (WB, 1942)
Captains of the Clouds (WB, 1942)
Yankee Doodle Dandy (WB, 1942)
Thank Your Lucky Stars (WB, 1943)
This Is the Army (WB, 1943)
Mission to Moscow (WB, 1943)
Air Force (WB, 1943)

The Mask of Dimitrios (WB, 1944)
Between Two Worlds (WB, 1944)
Make Your Own Bed (WB, 1944)
Passage to Marseille (WB, 1944)
Mildred Pierce (WB, 1945)
Objective, Burma! (WB, 1945)
Nobody Lives Forever (WB, 1946)
Her Kind of Man (WB, 1946)
Gallant Bess (MGM, 1946)
My Wild Irish Rose (WB, 1947)
Sinbad the Sailor (RKO, 1947)
The Adventures of Casanova (EL, 1948)
The Set-Up (RKO, 1949)
Everybody Does It (20th, 1949)
The Judge Steps Out (RKO, 1949)
Southside 1-1000 (AA, 1950)

The Tanks Are Coming (WB, 1951)	*The Glenn Miller Story* (Univ, 1954)	*Bullet for a Badman* (Univ, 1964)
Mark of the Renegade (Univ, 1951)	*The Seven Little Foys* (Par, 1955)	*Nightmare in the Sun* (Zodiac, 1964)
Rawhide (20th, 1951)	*The Tattered Dress* (Univ, 1957)	*The Glass Bottom Boat* (MGM, 1966)
Ten Tall Men (Col, 1951)	*Silk Stockings* (MGM, 1957)	*The Phynx* (WB, 1970)
The Magic Carpet (Col, 1951)	*Marjorie Morningstar* (WB, 1958)	
Desert Pursuit (Mon, 1952)	*A New Kind of Love* (Par, 1963)	

SIDNEY TOLER

Kane Richmond, Ricardo Cortez, and Sidney Toler in Charlie Chan in Reno *(1939).*

Born April 28, 1874, Warrensburg, Missouri. Married Viva Tattersal. Died February 12, 1947, Beverly Hills, California. Southerner who gained cinema prominence replacing Warner Oland as Charlie Chan. Was the Oriental sleuth 22 times before Roland Winters took over the post. Screen debut as the British Mr. Merivel in Ruth Chatterton's *Madam X*. Some others: *Blonde Venus* (Wilson, the detective), *Operator 13* (Major Allen), *The Gorgeous Hussy* (Daniel Webster), etc. During Chan tenure had occasional other roles: Maria Montez's *White Savage* (Wong), Loretta Young's *A Night to Remember* (Inspector Hankins).

> **Sidney Toler** to C. Henry Gordon in *Charlie Chan at the Wax Museum*: "Most odd that owner of museum cannot explain wedding of electricity with chair reserved for humble self."

Films

Madame X (MGM, 1920)	*Is My Face Red?* (RKO, 1932)	*The World Changes* (FN, 1933)
Strictly Dishonorable (Univ, 1930)	*Radio Patrol* (Univ, 1932)	*Billion Dollar Scandal* (Par, 1933)
White Shoulders (RKO, 1931)	*Blondie of the Follies* (MGM, 1932)	*The Narrow Corner* (WB, 1933)
Strangers in Love (Par, 1932)	*Tom Brown of Culver* (Univ, 1932)	*Dark Hazard* (WB, 1934)
The Phantom President (Par, 1932)	*He Learned About Women* (Par, 1933)	*Massacre* (WB, 1934)
Speak Easily (MGM, 1932)	*King of the Jungle* (Par, 1933)	*Registered Nurse* (WB, 1934)
Blonde Venus (Par, 1932)	*The Way to Love* (Par, 1933)	*Spitfire* (RKO, 1934)

Romance in Manhattan (RKO, 1934)
The Trumpet Blows (Par, 1934)
Upper World (WB, 1934)
Operator 13 (MGM, 1934)
Call of the Wild (UA, 1935)
Daring Young Man (Fox, 1935)
Orchids to You (Fox, 1935)
Champagne for Breakfast (Col, 1935)
This Is the Life (Fox, 1935)
Three Godfathers (MGM, 1936)
The Gorgeous Hussy (MGM, 1936)
The Longest Night (MGM, 1936)
Our Relations (MGM, 1936)
Give Us This Night (Par, 1936)
That Certain Woman (WB, 1937)
Quality Street (RKO, 1937)
Double Wedding (MGM, 1937)
Gold Is Where You Find It (WB, 1938)
One Wild Night (20th, 1938)
Up the River (20th, 1938)
Charlie Chan in Honolulu (20th, 1938)

If I Were King (Par, 1938)
The Mysterious Rider (Par, 1938)
Three Comrades (MGM, 1938)
Wide Open Faces (Col, 1938)
Disbarred (Par, 1939)
Law of the Pampas (Par, 1939)
The Kid from Kokomo (WB, 1939)
Charlie Chan in Reno (20th, 1939)
Charlie Chan at Treasure Island (20th, 1939)
Charlie Chan in City in Darkness (20th, 1939)
King of Chinatown (Par, 1939)
Heritage of the Desert (Par, 1939)
Charlie Chan in Panama (20th, 1940)
Charlie Chan's Murder Cruise (20th, 1940)
Charlie Chan at the Wax Museum (20th, 1940)
Murder over New York (20th, 1940)
Charlie Chan in Rio (20th, 1941)

Dead Men Tell (20th, 1941)
Castle in the Desert (20th, 1942)
A Night to Remember (Col, 1943)
Adventures of Smilin' Jack (Univ serial, 1943)
White Savage (Univ, 1943)
Isle of Forgotten Sins (PRC, 1943)
Charlie Chan in the Secret Service (Mon, 1944)
The Chinese Cat (Mon, 1944)
Black Magic (Mon, 1944)
The Secret Clue (Mon, 1944)
The Jade Mask (Mon, 1945)
It's in the Bag (UA, 1945)
The Shanghai Cobra (Mon, 1945)
The Red Dragon (Mon, 1945)
Dark Alibi (Mon, 1946)
Shadows over Chinatown (Mon, 1946)
Dangerous Money (Mon, 1946)
The Trap (Mon, 1947)

REGIS TOOMEY

With Maude Turner Gordon and Clara Blandick (right) in Shopworn (1932).

Born August 13, 1902, Pittsburgh, Pennsylvania. Married Kathryn Scott (1925), children: two. Clean-cut and wholesome; had some leads: Clara Bow's vis-a-vis Chick Hewes in *Kick In*. Rarely a crook (Tony Breezzi in *24 Hours*). Frequently on the side of the law, often the hero's faithful subordinate: *Submarine D-1* (Tom Callam), *North West Mounted Police* (Constable Jerry Moore), *Dive Bomber* (Tim Griffin), *The Big Sleep* (Detective Bernie Ohls), etc. Later the elderly do-gooder (Arvid Abernathy in *Guys and Dolls*). TV series: "The Best in Mystery"; "Hey Mulligan"; "Richard Diamond, Private Detective"; "Burke's Law"; "Petticoat Junction"; and "Shannon."

Regis Toomey to other reporters in *His Girl Friday*: "I still say anybody who can write like that isn't going to give it up to sew socks for a guy in the insurance business."

Films

Wheel of Life (Par, 1929)
Illusion (Par, 1929)
Rich People (Par, 1929)
Alibi (UA, 1929)
Crazy That Way (Fox, 1930)
Good Intentions (Fox, 1930)
The Light of Western Stars (Par, 1930)
Street of Chance (Par, 1930)
Framed (RKO, 1930)
Shadow of the Law (Par, 1930)
A Man from Wyoming (Par, 1930)
Perfect Alibi (RKO, 1931)
Murder by the Clock (Par, 1931)
Finn and Hattie (Par, 1931)
The Finger Points (FN, 1931)
Graft (Univ, 1931)
Kick In (Par, 1931)
Scandal Sheet (Par, 1931)
Other Men's Women (WB, 1931)
24 Hours (Par, 1931)
Touchdown (Par, 1931)
Under 18 (WB, 1922)
The Crowd Roars (WB, 1932)
Sky Bride (Par, 1932)
Shopworn (Col, 1932)
Midnight Patrol (Mon, 1932)
They Never Come Back (Artclass Pictures, 1932)
The Penal Code (Freuler Film Associates, 1932)
A Strange Adventure (Mon, 1932)
State Trooper (Col, 1933)
Soldiers of the Storm (Col, 1933)
Laughing at Life (Mascot, 1933)
She Had to Say Yes (FN, 1933)
Picture Brides (Allied, 1933)
What's Your Racket? (Mayfair, 1934)
Big Time or Bust (Tower, 1934)
Red Morning (RKO, 1934)
Murder on the Blackboard (RKO, 1934)
Redhead (Mon, 1934)
She Had to Choose (Majestic, 1934)
Shadow of Doubt (MGM, 1935)
G-Men (WB, 1935)
Skull and Crown (Reliable, 1935)
One Frightened Night (Mascot, 1935)
Manhattan Moon (Univ, 1935)
Reckless Roads (Majestic, 1935)
The Great God Gold (Mon, 1935)
Bulldog Edition (Rep, 1936)
Shadows of the Orient (Mon, 1937)
Midnight Taxi (20th, 1937)
Back in Circulation (WB, 1937)
The Big City (MGM, 1937)
Submarine D-1 (WB, 1937)
Hunted Men (Par, 1938)
Illegal Traffic (Par, 1938)

His Exciting Night (Univ, 1938)
The Invisible Menace (WB, 1938)
Street of Missing Men (Rep, 1939)
Society Smugglers (Univ, 1939)
Smashing the Spy Ring (Col, 1939)
The Mysterious Miss X (Rep, 1939)
Wings of the Navy (WB, 1939)
Confessions of a Nazi Spy (WB, 1939)
Indianapolis Speedway (WB, 1939)
Trapped in the Sky (Col, 1939)
Hidden Power (Col, 1939)
Union Pacific (Par, 1939)
The Phantom Creeps (Univ serial, 1939)
Thunder Afloat (MGM, 1939)
His Girl Friday (Col, 1940)
Arizona (Col, 1940)
Northwest Passage (MGM, 1940)
Till We Meet Again (WB, 1940)
North West Mounted Police (Par, 1940)
Meet John Doe (WB, 1941)
Reaching for the Sun (Par, 1941)
A Shot in the Dark (WB, 1941)
The Nurse's Secret (WB, 1941)
Law of the Tropics (WB, 1941)
Dive Bomber (WB, 1941)
They Died with Their Boots On (WB, 1941)
You're in the Army Now (WB, 1941)
Bullet Scars (WB, 1942)
I Was Framed (WB, 1942)
Forest Rangers (Par, 1942)
Tennessee Johnson (MGM, 1942)
Jack London (UA, 1943)
Destroyer (Col, 1943)
Adventures of the Flying Cadets (Univ serial, 1943)
Follow the Boys (Univ, 1944)
Phantom Lady (Univ, 1944)
Song of the Open Road (UA, 1944)
Dark Mountain (Par, 1944)
Murder in the Blue Room (Univ, 1944)
The Doughgirls (WB, 1944)
When the Lights Go On Again (PRC, 1944)
Raiders of Ghost City (Univ serial, 1944)
Spellbound (UA, 1945)
Betrayal from the East (RKO, 1945)
Follow That Woman (Par, 1945)
Strange Illusion (PRC, 1945)
The Big Sleep (WB, 1946)
Her Sister's Secret (PRC, 1946)
Child of Divorce (RKO, 1946)
Mysterious Intruder (Col, 1946)
The Thirteenth Hour (Col, 1947)
The Guilty (Mon, 1947)
The Big Fix (PRC, 1947)
High Tide (Mon, 1947)

Magic Town (RKO, 1947)
I Wouldn't Be in Your Shoes (Mon, 1948)
Raw Deal (EL, 1948)
Station West (RKO, 1948)
The Bishop's Wife (RKO, 1948)
The Boy with Green Hair (RKO, 1948)
Mighty Joe Young (RKO, 1949)
Come to the Stable (20th, 1949)
Beyond the Forest (WB, 1949)
The Devil's Henchmen (Col, 1949)
Dynamite Pass (RKO, 1950)
Undercover Girl (Univ, 1950)
Frenchie (Univ, 1950)
Navy Bound (Mon, 1951)
Cry Danger (RKO, 1951)
The Tall Target (MGM, 1951)
The People Against O'Hara (MGM, 1951)
Show Boat (MGM, 1951)
My Six Convicts (Col, 1952)
The Battle at Apache Pass (Univ, 1952)
Just for You (Par, 1952)
My Pal Gus (20th, 1952)
Never Wave at a WAC (RKO, 1952)
It Happens Every Thursday (Univ, 1953)
Island in the Sky (WB, 1953)
The Nebraskan (Col, 1953)
The High and the Mighty (WB, 1954)
Human Jungle (AA, 1954)
Drums Across the River (Univ, 1954)
Guys and Dolls (MGM, 1955)
Top Gun (UA, 1955)
Great Day in the Morning (RKO, 1956)
Three for Jamie Dawn (AA, 1956)
Dakota Incident (Rep, 1956)
Sing, Boy, Sing (20th, 1958)
Joy Ride (AA, 1958)
Warlock (20th, 1959)
Guns of the Timberland (WB, 1960)
The Last Sunerland (WB, 1960)
The Last Sunset (Univ, 1961)
Voyage to the Bottom of the Sea (20th, 1961)
King of the Roaring '20s: The Story of Arnold Rothstein (AA, 1961)
Man's Favorite Sport? (Univ, 1964)
The Night of the Grizzly (Par, 1966)
Gunn (Par, 1967)
Change of Habit (Univ, 1969)
Cover Me Babe (20th, 1970)
The Carey Treatment (MGM, 1972)
God Damn Dr. Shagetz (L-T Films, 1974)
Won Ton Ton, the Dog Who Saved Hollywood (Par, 1976)

ERNEST TORRENCE

In the mid-1920s.

Born June 26, 1878, Edinburgh, Scotland. Married Elsie Reamer. Died May 15, 1933, New York City, New York. Extremely resourceful player. Ex-stage singer (Europe and New York) who made a solid impression in his feature film debut: the dastardly Luke Hatburn of Richard Barthelmess' *Tol'able David*. Thereafter: *The Covered Wagon* (inebriated, grizzled trail scout Jackson), *The Hunchback of Notre Dame* (beggar king, Clopin), Betty Bronson's *Peter Pan* (Captain Hook), Cecil B. DeMille's *The King of Kings* (Peter), *Steamboat Bill, Jr.* (riverboat captain—Buster Keaton's dad), Lily Damita's *The Bridge of San Luis Rey* (Uncle Pio), etc. Final role: Kirk, the smuggler-fisherman father of Claudette Colbert in *I Cover the Waterfront*. Brother of actor David Torrence.

Ernest Torrence to Claudette Colbert in *I Cover the Waterfront*: "If *you* love him, he's worth it. It's more than *I* ever was."

Films

Tol'able David (Associated FN, 1921)
Broken Chains (G, 1922)
The Kingdom Within (Hodkinson, 1922)
The Prodigal Judge (Vit, 1922)
Singed Wings (Par, 1922)
The Brass Bottle (Associated FN, 1923)
The Covered Wagon (Par, 1923)
The Hunchback of Notre Dame (Univ, 1923)

Ruggles of Red Gap (Par, 1923)
The Trail of the Lonesome Pine (Par, 1923)
The Fighting Coward (Par, 1924)
The Heritage of the Desert (Par, 1924)
North of '36 (Par, 1924)
Peter Pan (Par, 1924)
The Side Show of Life (Par, 1924)
West of the Water Tower (Par, 1924)
The Dressmaker from Paris (Par, 1925)

Night Life for New York (Par, 1925)
The Pony Express (Par, 1925)
The American Venus (Par, 1926)
The Blind Goddess (Par, 1926)
The Lady of the Harem (Par, 1926)
Mantrap (Par, 1926)
The Rainmaker (Par, 1926)
The Wanderer (Par, 1926)
Captain Salvation (MGM, 1927)

The King of Kings (Pathé, 1927)
Twelve Miles Out (MGM, 1927)
Across to Singapore ((MGM, 1928)
The Cossacks (MGM, 1928)
Steamboat Bill, Jr. (UA, 1928)
Desert Nights (MGM, 1929)
The Bridge of San Luis Rey (MGM, 1929)
Speedway (MGM, 1929)
The Unholy Night (MGM, 1929)

Untamed (MGM, 1929)
Officer O'Brien (Pathé, 1930)
Strictly Unconventional (MGM, 1930)
Call of the Flesh (MGM, 1930)
Sweet Kitty Bellaire (WB, 1930)
Shipmates (MGM, 1931)
Fighting Caravans (Par, 1931)
The Great Lover (MGM, 1931)
Sporting Blood (MGM, 1931)

The Cuban Love Song (MGM, 1931)
New Adventures of Get-Rich-Quick Wallingford (MGM, 1931)
Sherlock Holmes (Fox, 1932)
Hypnotized (WW, 1932)
The Masquerader (UA, 1933)
I Cover the Waterfront (UA, 1933)

HENRY TRAVERS
(Travers Heagerty)

In It's a Wonderful Life *(1946).*

Born March 5, 1874, Herwick-on-Tweed, England. Married Amy Forrest-Rhodes. Died October 18, 1965, Hollywood, California. Well-tutored British and American stage player who left his mark as Mr. Ballard, the rose-growing stationmaster in *Mrs. Miniver.* (Oscar-nominated but lost BSAAA to Van Heflin of *Johnny Eager.*) Bushy-browed and gentle, but occasionally played an unpleasant sort—the grouchy landlord Mr. Bogardus in Bing Crosby's *The Bells of St. Mary's.* Back in form the next year—the angel Clarence in Jimmy Stewart's *It's a Wonderful Life.*

Henry Travers to Rita Johnson and Joe Sawyer in *The Naughty Nineties*: "I can't let you run your crooked gambling on my showboat. I've operated honestly."

Films

Reunion in Vienna (MGM, 1933)
Another Language (MGM, 1933)
My Weakness (Fox, 1933)
The Invisible Man (Univ, 1933)
The Party's Over (Col, 1934)
Death Takes a Holiday (Par, 1934)
Ready for Love (Par, 1934)
Born to Be Bad (UA, 1934)
Maybe It's Love (FN, 1935)
After Office Hours (MGM, 1935)
Escapade (MGM, 1935)
Pursuit (MGM, 1935)
Captain Hurricane (RKO, 1935)
Seven Keys to Baldpate (RKO, 1935)
Four Hours to Kill (Par, 1935)
Too Many Parents (Par, 1936)
The Sisters (WB, 1938)
Dark Victory (WB, 1939)

You Can't Get Away with Murder (WB, 1939)
Dodge City (WB, 1939)
On Borrowed Time (MGM, 1939)
Remember? (MGM, 1939)
Stanley and Livingstone (20th, 1939)
The Rains Came (20th, 1939)
The Primrose Path (RKO, 1940)
Anne of Windy Poplars (RKO, 1940)
Edison the Man (MGM, 1940)
Wyoming (MGM, 1940)
Ball of Fire (RKO, 1941)
High Sierra (WB, 1941)
A Girl, a Guy and a Gob (RKO, 1941)
The Bad Man (MGM, 1941)
I'll Wait for You (MGM, 1941)
Mrs. Miniver (MGM, 1942)
Pierre of the Plains (MGM, 1942)

Random Harvest (MGM, 1942)
Shadow of a Doubt (Univ, 1943)
The Moon Is Down (20th, 1943)
Madame Curie (MGM, 1943)
Dragon Seed (MGM, 1944)
None Shall Escape (Col, 1944)
The Very Thought of You (WB, 1944)
Thrill of a Romance (MGM, 1945)
The Naughty Nineties (Univ, 1945)
The Bells of St. Mary's (RKO, 1945)
Gallant Journey (Col, 1946)
It's a Wonderful Life (RKO, 1946)
The Yearling (MGM, 1946)
The Flame (Rep, 1947)
Beyond Glory (Par, 1948)
The Girl from Jones Beach (WB, 1949)

ARTHUR TREACHER
(Arthur Veary)

In Splendor *(1935).*

Born July 23, 1894, Brighton, England. Married Virginia Taylor (1940). Died December 16, 1975, Manhasset, Long Island, New York. Settled into a rut as the screen's perfect butler, which led to his brief *Jeeves* series at 20th Century-Fox. Occasionally played other types of roles: *David Copperfield* (Donkeyman), *A Midsummer Night's Dream* (Ninny's Tomb), etc. Final film: *Mary Poppins* (Constable Jones). On television: sidekick on Merv Griffin's talk show. Left as a legacy a chain of fast-food restaurants (Arthur Treacher's Fish & Chips).

Arthur Treacher to John Harrington in *Step Lively, Jeeves:*
"One's tie is to one's suit what one's wine is to one's dinner."

Films

The Battle of Paris (Par, 1929)
Fashions of 1934 (WB, 1934)
Desirable (WB, 1934)
Gambling Lady (WB, 1934)
The Key (WB, 1934)
Riptide (MGM, 1934)
Viva Villa! (MGM, 1934)
Madame Du Barry (WB, 1934)
The Captain Hates the Sea (Col, 1934)
Here Comes the Groom (Par, 1934)
Hollywood Party (MGM, 1934)
Forsaking All Others (MGM, 1934)
Bordertown (WB, 1935)
The Woman in Red (FN, 1935)
Orchids to You (Fox, 1935)
Magnificent Obsession (Univ, 1935)

The Nitwits (RKO, 1935)
No More Ladies (MGM, 1935)
David Copperfield (MGM, 1935)
Cardinal Richelieu (UA, 1935)
I Live My Life (MGM, 1935)
Personal Maid's Secret (WB, 1935)
Bright Lights (WB, 1935)
Curly Top (Fox, 1935)
Remember Last Night? (Univ, 1935)
Let's Live Tonight (Col, 1935)
The Daring Young Man (Fox, 1935)
Splendor (UA, 1935)
Hitch-Hike Lady (Rep, 1935)
A Midsummer Night's Dream (WB, 1935)
Go into Your Dance (WB, 1935)
Mister Cinderella (MGM, 1936)

The Winning Ticket (MGM, 1935)
Stowaway (20th, 1936)
The Case Against Mrs. Ames (Par, 1936)
Hearts Divided (FN, 1936)
Satan Met a Lady (WB, 1936)
Under Your Spell (20th, 1936)
Anything Goes (Par, 1936)
Thank You, Jeeves (20th, 1936)
Heidi (20th, 1937)
Step Lively, Jeeves (20th, 1937)
You Can't Have Everything (20th, 1937)
Thin Ice (20th, 1937)
She Had to Eat (20th, 1937)
Mad About Music (Univ, 1938)
My Lucky Star (20th, 1938)
Always in Trouble (20th, 1938)

Up the River (20th, 1938)
Bridal Suite (MGM, 1939)
Barricade (20th, 1939)
The Little Princess (20th, 1939)
Irene (RKO, 1940)
Brother Rat and a Baby (WB, 1940)
Star Spangled Rhythm (Par, 1942)

The Amazing Mrs. Holliday (Univ, 1943)
Forever and a Day (RKO, 1943)
Chip off the Old Block (Univ, 1944)
In Society (Univ, 1944)
National Velvet (MGM, 1944)
Delightfully Dangerous (UA, 1945)
That's the Spirit (Univ, 1945)

Slave Girl (Univ, 1947)
The Countess of Monte Cristo (Univ, 1948)
That Midnight Kiss (MGM, 1949)
Love That Brute (20th, 1950)
Mary Poppins (BV, 1964)

CHARLES TROWBRIDGE

With Myrna Dell in The Bushwhackers *(1952).*

Born January 10, 1882, Vera Cruz, Mexico. Died October 30, 1967. Abandoned architecture for Broadway showcasing. Played opposite Mary Garden on screen in *Thais*, and with Corinne Griffith in *Island Wives*. With his distinguished looks and piercing eyes, many times cast as ranking executive: *Rendezvous* (Secretary of War Baker), *Sergeant York* and *Mission to Moscow* (both as Cordell Hull). Played intelligence officers: e.g., *Confessions of a Nazi Spy;* even a President in *The Gorgeous Hussy* (Martin Van Buren).

Charles Trowbridge to Humphrey Bogart in *Racket Busters:*
"Rackets and racketeering can and must be abolished."

Films

Thais (G, 1916)
Island Wives (Vit, 1922)
Damaged Love (WW, 1931)
I Take This Woman (Par, 1931)
Silence (Par, 1931)
24 Hours (Par, 1931)
The Secret Call (Par, 1931)
Calm Yourself (MGM, 1935)
Murder Man (MGM, 1935)
Mad Love (MGM, 1935)
Rendezous (MGM, 1935)
It's in the Air (MGM, 1935)
Exclusive Story (MGM, 1936)
The Garden Murder Case (MGM, 1936)
We Went to College (MGM, 1936)
Born to Dance (MGM, 1936)
Man of the People (MGM, 1936)
The Gorgeous Hussy (MGM, 1936)
Libeled lady (MGM, 1936)
The Devil Is a Sissy (MGM, 1936)
Robin Hood of El Dorado (MGM, 1936)
Moonlight Murder (MGM, 1936)
Love on the Run (MGM, 1936)
Dangerous Number (MGM, 1937)
Reported Missing (Univ, 1937)
Espionage (MGM, 1937)
A Day at the Races (MGM, 1937)
Captains Courageous (MGM, 1937)
They Gave Him a Gun (MGM, 1937)
Sea Racketeers (Rep, 1937)
Exiled to Shanghai (Rep, 1937)
That Certain Woman (WB, 1937)
Fit for a King (RKO, 1937)
Saturday's Heroes (RKO, 1937)
The Thirteenth Chair (MGM, 1937)
Alcatraz Island (WB, 1938)
The Buccaneer (Par, 1938)
Submarine Patrol (20th, 1938)
Thanks for Everything (20th, 1938)
Holiday (Col, 1938)
Kentucky (20th, 1938)
Crime School (WB, 1938)
Gang Bullets (Mon, 1938)
The Last Express (Univ, 1938)
Gangs of New York (Rep, 1938)
Racket Busters (WB, 1938)
Crime Ring (RKO, 1938)
Men with Wings (Par, 1938)
The Invisible Menace (WB, 1938)
The Patient in Room 18 (WB, 1938)
College Swing (Par, 1938)
Nancy Drew, Detective (WB, 1938)
Undercover Doctor (Par, 1939)
Risky Business (Univ, 1939)

Sergeant Madden (MGM, 1939)
King of Chinatown (Par, 1939)
Tropic Fury (Univ, 1939)
King of the Underworld (WB, 1939)
Pride of the Navy (Rep, 1939)
On Trial (WB, 1939)
The Story of Alexander Graham Bell (20th, 1939)
Elsa Maxwell's Hotel for Woman (20th, 1939)
Swanee River (20th, 1939)
Each Dawn I Die (WB, 1939)
Let us Live (Col, 1939)
Confessions of a Nazi Spy (WB, 1939)
Lady of the Tropics (MGM, 1939)
Joe and Ethel Turp Call on the President (MGM, 1939)
Mutiny on the Blackhawk (Univ, 1939)
The Man They Could Not Hang (Col, 1939)
Johnny Apollo (20th, 1940)
Dr. Kildare Goes Home (MGM, 1940)
The Man with Nine Lives (Col, 1940)
Sailor's Lady (20th, 1940)
Before I Hang (Col, 1940)
Andy Hardy Meets Debutante (MGM, 1940)
Virginia City (WB, 1940)
Edison the Man (MGM, 1940)
I Take This Woman (MGM, 1940)
Knute Rockne—All-American (WB, 1940)
The Mummy's Hand (Univ, 1940)
Cherokee Strip (Par, 1940)
Trail of the Vigilantes (Univ, 1940)
The Fighting 69th (WB, 1940)
The Fatal Hour (Mon, 1940)
The Man Who Wouldn't Talk (20th, 1940)
The House of Seven Gables (Univ, 1940)
My Love Came Back (WB, 1940)
The Great Lie (WB, 1941)
Design for Scandal (MGM, 1941)
Strange Alibi (WB, 1941)
The Nurse's Secret (WB, 1941)
Dressed to Kill (20th, 1941)
Rags to Riches (Rep, 1941)
Hurricane Smith (Rep, 1941)
Sergeant York (WB, 1941)
Great Guns (20th, 1941)
We Go Fast (20th, 1941)
The Great Mr. Nobody (WB, 1941)
Belle Starr (20th, 1941)
Blue, White and Perfect (20th, 1941)

Who Is Hope Schuyler? (20th, 1942)
Ten Gentlemen from West Point (20th, 1942)
Sweetheart of the Fleet (Col, 1942)
That Other Woman (20th, 1942)
Tennessee Johnson (MGM, 1942)
Over My Dead Body (20th, 1942)
Action in the North Atlantic (WB, 1943)
The Amazing Mrs. Holliday (Univ, 1943)
She's for Me (Univ, 1943)
Madame Curie (MGM, 1943)
Mission to Moscow (WB, 1943)
Wintertime (20th, 1943)
Sweet Rosie O'Grady (20th, 1943)
Salute to the Marines (MGM, 1943)
Faces in the Fog (Rep, 1944)
The Fighting Seabees (Rep, 1944)
Summer Storm (UA, 1944)
Wing and a Prayer (20th, 1944)
Heavenly Days (RKO, 1944)
Hey, Rookie (Col, 1944)
Colonel Effingham's Raid (20th, 1945)
The Red Dragon (Mon, 1945)
Mildred Pierce (WB, 1945)
They Were Expendable (MGM, 1945)
The Hoodlum Saint (MGM, 1946)
Shock (20th, 1946)
Smooth as Silk (Univ, 1946)
Undercurrent (MGM, 1946)
Valley of the Zombies (Rep, 1946)
Don't Gamble with Strangers (Mon, 1946)
Secret of the Whistler (Col, 1946)
The Beginning or the End? (MGM, 1947)
Shoot to Kill (Screen Guild, 1947)
Mr. District Attorney (Col, 1947)
The Private Affairs of Bel Ami (UA, 1947)
The Sea of Grass (MGM, 1947)
Michigan Kid (Univ, 1947)
Tarzan and the Huntress (RKO, 1947)
Black Gold (AA, 1947)
Her Husband's Affairs (Col, 1947)
Key Witness (Col, 1947)
Song of My Heart (AA, 1947)
Tycoon (RKO, 1947)
Stage Struck (Mon, 1948)
Paleface (Par, 1948)
Hollow Triumph (EL, 1948)
Bad Boy (AA, 1949)
Mr. Soft Touch (Col, 1949)
Unmasked (Rep, 1950)
Peggy (Univ, 1950)
The Bushwackers (Realart, 1952)
The Wings of Eagles (MGM, 1957)

ERNEST TRUEX

Joyce Reynolds and Ernest Truex in Always Together *(1948).*

Born September 19, 1889, Kansas City, Missouri. Married 1) Julia Mills; widowed; 2) Mary Jane Barrett, child: one; divorced; 3) Sylvia Field. Died June 27, 1973, Fallbrook, California. Twinkling eyes, a sly smile, and a somewhat nasal voice. Once billed as "The youngest *Hamlet* on stage." Joined with Mary Pickford in *A Good Little Devil;* made several other silents. Hit his peak as a timorous—often henpecked—individual. With little effort could add puckish humor to a film—e.g., his Binguccio the bookkeeper—companion of Gary Cooper in *The Adventures of Marco Polo.* TV series: "The Truex Family" (with actress wife Sylvia Fields), "Jamie," "Mr. Peepers," "The Ann Sothern Show," and "Pete and Gladys."

Ernest Truex to Helen Westley in *Lillian Russell:* "It's *got* to be a boy. This one's *got* to be a boy."

Films

A Good Little Devil (Par, 1914)
Come On In (Par, 1918)
Goodbye, Bill (Par, 1918)
Oh, You Women! (Par, 1919)
Six Cylinder Love (Fox, 1923)
Whistling in the Dark (MGM, 1933)
Get that Venus (Regent, 1933)
The Warrior's Husband (Fox, 1933)
Everybody Dance (Br, 1936)
Mama Runs Wild (Rep, 1937)
Freshman Year (Univ, 1938)
Swing That Cheer (Univ, 1938)
Swing, Sister, Swing (Univ, 1938)
Start Cheering (Col, 1938)
The Adventures of Marco Polo (UA, 1938)
Ambush (Par, 1939)
Slightly Honorable (UA, 1939)
Island of Lost Men (Par, 1939)

These Glamour Girls (MGM, 1939)
Bachelor Mother (RKO, 1939)
The Under-Pup (Univ, 1939)
Little Accident (Univ, 1939)
His Girl Friday (Col, 1940)
Little Orvie (RKO, 1940)
Lillian Russell (20th, 1940)
Dance, Girl, Dance (RKO, 1940)
Calling All Husbands (WB, 1940)
Christmas in July (Par, 1940)
The Gay Vagabond (Rep, 1941)
Tillie the Toiler (Col, 1941)
We Go Fast (20th, 1941)
Unexpected Uncle (RKO, 1941)
Twin Beds (UA, 1942)
Private Buckaroo (Univ, 1942)
Star-Spangled Rhythm (Par, 1942)
True to Life (Par, 1943)

This Is the Army (WB, 1943)
Sleepy Lagoon (Rep, 1943)
Rhythm of the Islands (Univ, 1943)
Fired Wife (Univ, 1943)
The Crystal Ball (UA, 1943)
Chip off the Old Block (Univ, 1944)
Her Primitive Man (Univ, 1944)
Club Havana (PRC, 1945)
Men in Her Diary (Univ, 1945)
Pan-American (RKO, 1945)
Life with Blondie (Col, 1946)
A Night in Paradise (Univ, 1946)
Always Together (WB, 1948)
The Girl from Manhattan (UA, 1948)
The Leather Saint (Par, 1956)
All Mine to Give (Univ, 1957)
Twilight for the Gods (Univ, 1958)
Fluffy, (Univ, 1965)

TOM TULLY

With *Sylvia Sidney in* Behind the High Wall *(1956)*.

Born August 21, 1908 Durango, Colorado. Married 1) _____ ; 2) Frances McHugh (1938); widowed (1953); 3) Ida Johnson (1954). Pugnacious of face, but soft of heart. Former newspaper reporter, and radio and Broadway actor. Played Shirley Temple's dad in *I'll Be Seeing You* and *A Kiss for Corliss,* but later was the corrupt warden of *Behind the High Wall.* Oscar-nominated for his Captain De Vriess in *The Caine Mutiny* (but lost BSAAA to Edmond O'Brien of *The Barefoot Contessa*). TV series: "The Line-up" (as Inspector Matt Grebb), "Shane," "The Dick Van Dyke Show" (as Sam Petrie, Rob's father), and "Hey, Landlord!"

Tom Tully to Thomas Mitchell in *Adventure:* "A guy that won't drink a lost ship down, reflects on his bos'n."

Films

Mission to Moscow (WB, 1943)
Northern Pursuit (WB, 1943)
Destination Tokyo (WB, 1943)
The Sign of the Cross (Par, 1944) [prologue to reissue of 1932 feature]
Secret Command (Col, 1944)
I'll Be Seeing You (UA, 1944)
The Town Went Wild (PRC, 1944)
Kiss and Tell (Col, 1945)
The Unseen (Par, 1945)
Adventure (MGM, 1945)
Lady in the Lake (MGM, 1946)
Til the End of Time (RKO, 1946)
The Virginian (Par, 1946)
Intrigue (UA, 1947)
Killer McCoy (MGM, 1947)
Scudda Hoo! Scudda Hay! (20th, 1948)

Blood on the Moon (RKO, 1948)
June Bride (WB, 1948)
Rachel and the Stranger (RKO, 1948)
A Kiss for Corliss [a.k.a. Almost a Bride] (UA, 1949)
The Lady Takes a Sailor (WB, 1949)
Illegal Entry (Univ, 1949)
Branded (Par, 1950)
Where the Sidewalk Ends (20th, 1950)
Tomahawk (Univ, 1951)
The Lady and the Bandit (Col, 1951)
Texas Carnival (MGM, 1951)
Love Is Better Than Ever (MGM, 1952)
Return of the Texan (20th, 1952)
Lure of the Wilderness (20th, 1952)
The Turning Point (Par, 1952)
Ruby Gentry (20th, 1952)

Trouble Along the Way (WB, 1953)
The Jazz Singer (WB, 1953)
The Moon Is Blue (UA, 1953)
The Sea of Lost Ships (Rep, 1953)
The Caine Mutiny (Col, 1954)
Arrow in the Dust (AA, 1954)
Love Me or Leave Me (MGM, 1955)
Solidier of Fortune (20th, 1955)
Behind the High Wall (Univ, 1956)
Ten North Frederick (20th, 1958)
The Wackiest Ship in the Army (Col, 1960)
The Carpetbaggers (Par, 1964)
McHale's Navy Joins the Air Force (Univ, 1965)
Coogan's Bluff (Univ, 1968)
Charley Varrick (Univ, 1973)

497

JO VAN FLEET

With Peter Sellers in I Love You, Alice B. Toklas! *(1968).*

Born December 30, 1919, Oakland, California. Married William Bales (1946), child: Michael. Resilient stage actress who concentrated on playing old(er) women. Won a BSAAA as James Dean's mother and operator of a Salinas brothel in *East of Eden*. On screen that same year in a shouting match with Anna Magnani in *The Rose Tattoo* and nearly stole the limelight from Susan Hayward (as Lillian Roth), playing her show-business mother. Definitive performance as the crusty 80-year-old Ella Garth, who in *Wild River* fights the Tennessee Valley Authority to protect her land. As Big Momma she headed *The Gang That Couldn't Shoot Straight*.

Jo Van Fleet to Silvana Mangano in *This Angry Age:* "I always done the best I could for you and your brother."

Films

East of Eden (WB, 1955)
The Rose Tattoo (Par, 1955)
I'll Cry Tomorrow (MGM, 1955)
The King and Four Queens (UA, 1956)
Gunfight at the O.K. Corral (Par, 1957)

This Angry Age (Col, 1958)
Wild River (20th, 1960)
Cool Hand Luke (WB, 1967)
I Love You, Alice B. Toklas! (WB–7 Arts, 1968)

80 Steps to Jonah (WB, 1969)
The Gang That Couldn't Shoot Straight (MGM,1971)

EDWARD VAN SLOAN

With Bela Lugosi in a stage production of Dracula.

Born November 1, 1881, San Francisco, California. Died March 6, 1964, San Francisco, California. Characterized by a prominent nose and intense stare. Consistently populated horror films, often as the aged occult specialist: *Dracula* (Professor Van Lesing), *Frankenstein* (Dr. Waldman), *The Mummy* (Dr. Muller), *Dracula's Daughter* (Dr. Von Helsing). Played Chief Jarvis in the serial *The Phantom Creeps*, combating mad scientist Bela Lugosi. Last film was *Betty Co-ed*, an inexpensive campus musical with Jean Porter.

Edward Van Sloan to Gilbert Emery in *Dracula's Daughter*:
"The strength of the vampire, Sir Basil, lies in the fact that he *is* unbelievable"

Films

Dracula (Univ, 1931)
Frankenstein (Univ, 1931)
The Infernal Machine (Fox, 1932)
Manhattan Parade (WB, 1932)
Play Girl (WB, 1932)
The Death Kiss (WW, 1932)
Man Wanted (WB, 1932)
Behind the Mask (Col, 1932)
The Mummy (Univ, 1932)
Thunder Below (Par, 1932)
Forgotten Commandments (Par, 1932)
The Last Mile (WW, 1932)

Silk Express (WB, 1933)
The World Gone Mad (Majestic, 1933)
Murder on the Campus (Chesterfield, 1933)
The Working Man (WB, 1933)
Trick for Trick (Fox, 1933)
It's Great to Be Alive (Fox, 1933)
The Deluge (RKO, 1933)
Billion Dollar Scandal (Par, 1933)
Death Takes a Holiday (Par, 1934)
The Crosby Case (Univ, 1934)
The Scarlet Empress (Par, 1934)

The Life of Vergie Winters (RKO, 1934)
Manhattan Melodrama (MGM, 1934)
I'll Fix It (Col, 1934)
Grand Old Girl (RKO, 1935)
Mills of the Gods (Col, 1935)
Woman in Red (FN, 1935)
A Shot in the Dark (Chesterfield, 1935)
The Last Days of Pompeii (RKO, 1935)
Air Hawks (Col, 1935)
The Black Room (Col, 1935)
Grand Exit (Col, 1935)
The Story of Louis Pasteur (WB, 1935)

Road Gang (WB, 1936)
Dracula's daughter (Univ, 1936)
Sins of Man (20th, 1936)
The Man Who Found Himself (RKO, 1937)
Penitentiary (Col, 1938)
Storm over Bengal (Rep, 1938)
Danger on the Air (Univ, 1938)

The Phantom Creeps (Univ serial, 1939)
Abe Lincoln in Illinois (RKO, 1940)
The Doctor Takes a Wife (Col, 1940)
The Secret Seven (Col, 1940)
Before I Hang (Col, 1940)
A Man's World (Col, 1942)
Valley of Hunted Men (Rep, 1943)
Mission to Moscow (WB, 1943)

Riders of the Rio Grande (Rep, 1943)
Submarine Alert (Par, 1943)
End of the Road (Rep, 1943)
The Conspirators (WB, 1944)
The Mask of Dijon (PRC, 1946)
Betty Co-ed (Col, 1947)

HELEN VINSON
(Helen Rulfs)

With George Raft in Midnight Club (1933).

Born September 17, 1907, Beaumont, Texas. Married 1) Harry Vickerman; divorced; 2) Fred Perry divorced (1935); 3) Donald Hardenbrook (1946). Sophisticated actress who was superior at delineating the cool "other woman." Occasionally she could become steamy, as when trading insults with Ann Sheridan in *Torrid Zone*. At times very sympathetic: *I Am a Fugitive from a Chain Gang* (Paul Muni's upper-class girlfriend Helen).

Helen Vinson to Charles Boyer in *Private Worlds*: "Go on living with your turtle! He's a good companion for you!"

Films

Jewel Robbery (WB, 1932)
Two Against the World (WB, 1932)
The Crash (FN, 1932)
They Call It Sin (FN, 1932)
I Am a Fugitive from a Chain Gang (WB, 1932)
Lawyer Man (WB, 1932)
Second Hand Wife (Fox, 1933)
Midnight Club (Par, 1933)
The Power and the Glory (Fox, 1933)
As Husbands Go (Fox, 1933)
The Kennel Murder Case (WB, 1933)
Little Giant (FN, 1933)
Grand Slam (WB, 1933)

The Gift of Gab (Univ, 1934)
The Life of Vergie Winters (RKO, 1934)
Let's Try Again (RKO, 1934)
Broadway Bill (Col, 1934)
The Captain Hates the Sea (Col, 1934)
A Notorious Gentleman (Univ, 1935)
The Wedding Night (UA, 1935)
Private Worlds (Par, 1935)
Age of Indiscretion (MGM, 1935)
Transatlantic Tunnel (Br, 1935)
Love in Exile (Br, 1936)
King of the Damned (Br, 1936)
Reunion (20th, 1936)
Vogues of 1938 (UA, 1937)

Live, Love and Learn (MGM, 1937)
In Name Only (RKO, 1939)
Married and in Love (RKO, 1940)
Curtain Call (RKO, 1940)
Enemy Agent (Univ, 1940)
Torrid Zone (WB, 1940)
Beyond Tomorrow (RKO, 1940)
The Bowery Boy (Rep, 1940)
Nothing but the Truth (Par, 1941)
Chip off the Old Block (Univ, 1944)
The Lady and the Monster (Rep, 1944)
Are These Our Parents? (Mon, 1944)
The Thin Man Goes Home (MGM, 1944)

RAYMOND WALBURN

In Confirm or Deny *(1941).*

Born September 9, 1887, Plymouth, Indiana. Married 1) Gertrude Steinman; widowed; 2) Jane Davis (1955). Died July 26, 1969, New York City, New York. Bug-eyed rotund bumbler with a haughty manner. Endeared himself to decades of stage and moviegoers. Made his feature film bow as the philandering husband of Ruth Chatterton in *Laughing Lady.* Set his stride as the phony Dixie Colonel Pettigrew in Frank Capra's *Broadway Bill,* a part he repeated in the musical remake (*Riding high*). In *Mr. Deeds Goes to Town,* played Gary Cooper's pretentious butler Walter. Began his *Henry the Rainmaker* series in 1949 as pompous and cheeky as ever. On Broadway in the 1960s: *A Funny Thing Happened on the Way to the Forum* and with Ruth Gordon in *A Very Rich Woman.*

Raymond Walburn to Ralph Bellamy in *It Can't Last Forever:*
"Ahem! My vocal cords are dry. Perhaps some liquid refreshment . . ."

Films

The Laughing Lady (Par, 1929)
The Great Flirtation (Par, 1934)
The Defense Rests (Col, 1934)
Lady by Choice (Col, 1934)
Jealousy (Col, 1934)
Broadway Bill (Col, 1934)
The Count of Monte Cristo (UA, 1934)
Thanks a Million (Fox, 1935)
Death Flies East (Col, 1935)
Mills of the Gods (Col, 1935)

I'll Love You Always (Col, 1935)
It's a Small World (Fox, 1935)
Welcome Home (Fox, 1935)
She Married Her Boss (Col, 1935)
Redheads on Parade (Fox, 1935)
Society Doctor (MGM, 1935)
The Great Ziegfeld (MGM, 1936)
Mr. Deeds Goes to Town (Col, 1936)
The Lone Wolf Returns (Col, 1936)
Absolute Quiet (MGM, 1936)

They Met in a Taxi (Col, 1936)
Three Wise guys (MGM, 1936)
The King Steps Out (Col, 1936)
Mr. Cinderella (MGM, 1936)
Craig's Wife (Col, 1936)
Born to Dance (MGM, 1936)
Breezing Home (Univ, 1937)
Let's Get Married (Col, 1937)
High, Wide and Handsome (Par, 1937)
It Can't Last Forever (Col, 1937)

Broadway Melody of 1938 (MGM, 1937)
Thin Ice (20th, 1937)
Murder in Greenwich Village (Col, 1937)
Professor Beware (Par, 1938)
Start Cheering (Col, 1938)
Battle of Broadway (20th, 1938)
Gateway (20th, 1938)
Sweethearts (MGM, 1938)
Let Freedom Ring (MGM, 1939)
It Could Happen to You (20th, 1939)
Eternally Yours (UA, 1939)
The Under-Pup (Univ, 1939)
Heaven with a Barbed Wire Fence (20th, 1939)
Dark Command (Rep, 1940)
Millionaires in Prison (RKO, 1940)
Flowing Gold (WB, 1940)
Third Finger, Left Hand (MGM, 1940)
Christmas in July (Par, 1940)
San Francisco Docks (Univ, 1940)

Kiss the Boys Goodbye (Par, 1941)
Puddin'head (Rep, 1941)
Bachelor Daddy (Univ, 1941)
Confirm or Deny (20th, 1941)
Rise and Shine (20th, 1941)
Louisiana Purchase (Par, 1941)
The Man in the Trunk (20th, 1942)
Lady Bodyguard (Par, 1943)
Dixie Dugan (20th, 1943)
The Desperadoes (Col, 1943)
Let's Face It (Par, 1943)
Dixie (Par, 1943)
And the Angels Sing (Par, 1944)
Hail the Conquering Hero (Par, 1944)
Heavenly Days (RKO, 1944)
Music in Manhattan (RKO, 1944)
The Cheaters (Rep, 1945)
Honeymoon Ahead (Univ, 1945)
I'll Tell the World (Univ, 1945)
The Affairs of Geraldine (Rep, 1946)

Breakfast in Hollywood (UA, 1946)
Lover Come Back (Univ, 1946)
The Plainsman and the Lady (Rep, 1946)
Rendezvous with Annie (Rep, 1946)
Mad Wednesday [a.k.a. The Sin of Harold Diddlebock] (UA, 1947)
State of the Union (MGM, 1948)
Red, Hot and Blue (Par, 1949)
Riding High (Par, 1949)
Leave It to Henry (Mon, 1949)
Henry the Rainmaker (Mon, 1949)
The Key to the City (MGM, 1950)
Father Makes Good (Mon, 1950)
Short Grass (AA, 1950)
Father's Wild Game (Mon, 1950)
Excuse My Dust (MGM, 1951)
Golden Girl (20th, 1951)
Father Takes the Air (Mon, 1951)
She Couldn't Say No (RKO, 1954)
The Spoilers (Univ, 1955)

NELLA WALKER

Charles Boyer, Irene Dunne, Barbara O'Neil, and Nella Walker in When Tomorrow Comes (1939).

Born March 6, 1886, Chicago, Illinois. Married William Mack; divorced. Died March 22, 1971, Los Angeles, California. Crisp actress who could be high-toned (Mrs. Van Tyle of Fashions of 1934) or wifely (spouse of warden Arthur Byron of 20,000 Years in Sing Sing). Married to Inspector Fernack (Jonathan Hale) in The Saint Takes Over.

Nella Walker (regarding son Lee Bowman) in *Buck Privates*:
"How can they make a Yale man a *private?*"

Films

Seven Keys to Baldpate (RKO, 1929)
The Vagabond Lover (RKO, 1929)
Tanned Legs (RKO, 1929)
Extravagance (Tif, 1930)
Rain or Shine (Col, 1930)
What a Widow (UA, 1930)
The Hot Heiress (FN, 1931)
Indiscreet (UA, 1931)
Daughter of the Dragon (Par, 1931)
Hush Money (Fox, 1931)
Their Mad Moment (Fox, 1931)
The Bargain (FN, 1931)
The Public Defender (RKO, 1931)
Lady with a Past (RKO, 1932)
Trouble in Paradise (Par, 1932)
They Call It Sin (FN, 1932)
20,000 Years in Sing Sing (FN, 1933)
Dangerously Yours (Fox, 1933)
Second Hand Wife (Fox, 1933)
Humanity (Fox, 1933)
Reunion in Vienna (MGM, 1933)
This Day and Age (Par, 1933)
Ever in My Heart (WB, 1933)
Sensation Hunters (Mon, 1933)
The House on 56th Street (WB, 1933)
Four Frightened People (Par, 1934)
Big-Hearted Herbert (WB, 1934)
All of Me (Par, 1934)
The Ninth Guest (Col, 1934)
Fashions of 1934 (FN, 1934)

Change of Heart (Fox, 1934)
Madame Du Barry (WB, 1934)
Elmer and Elsie (Par, 1934)
Fugitive Lady (Col, 1934)
Behold My Wife! (Par, 1934)
Under Pressure (Fox, 1935)
Coronado (Par, 1935)
The Woman in Red (FN, 1935)
McFadden's Flats (Par, 1935)
Going Highbrow (WB, 1935)
A Dog of Flanders (RKO, 1935)
Red Salute (UA, 1935)
Small Town Girl (MGM, 1936)
Captain January (20th, 1936)
Don't Turn 'em Loose (RKO, 1936)
Three Smart Girls (Univ, 1936)
Stella Dallas (UA, 1937)
45 Fathers (20th, 1937)
The Crime of Dr. Hallet (Univ, 1938)
The Rage of Paris (Univ, 1938)
Hard to Get (WB, 1938)
Professor Beware (Par, 1938)
Young Dr. Kildare (MGM, 1938)
Three Smart Girls Grow Up (Univ, 1939)
Espionage Agent (WB, 1939)
When Tomorrow Comes (Univ, 1939)
In Name Only (RKO, 1939)
Swanee River (20th, 1939)
No Time for Comedy (WB, 1940)

The Saint Takes Over (RKO, 1940)
I Love You Again (MGM, 1940)
Kitty Foyle (RKO, 1940)
Buck Privates (Univ, 1941)
Back Street (Univ, 1941)
A Girl, a Guy and a Gob (RKO, 1941)
Repent at Leisure (RKO, 1941)
Kathleen (MGM, 1941)
Hellzapoppin (Univ, 1941)
Kid Glove Killer (MGM, 1942)
We Were Dancing (MGM, 1942)
Air Raid Wardens (MGM, 1943)
What a Woman! (Col, 1943)
Wintertime (20th, 1943)
Hers to Hold (Univ, 1943)
In Society (Univ, 1944)
Ladies of Washington (20th, 1944)
Murder in the Blue Room (Univ, 1944)
Take It or Leave It (20th, 1944)
Follow That Woman (Par, 1945)
A Guy, a Gal and a Pal (Col, 1945)
Two Sisters from Boston (MGM, 1946)
The Locket (RKO, 1946)
This Time for Keeps (MGM, 1947)
The Beginning or the End? (MGM, 1947)
Undercover Maisie (MGM, 1947)
Variety Girl (Par, 1947)
That Hagen Girl (WB, 1947)
Nancy Goes to Rio (MGM, 1950)
Sabrina (Par, 1954)

RAY WALSTON

Ray Walston (second from left), Clint Eastwood, Jean Seberg, Lee Marvin, and Harve Presnell (second from right) in Paint Your Wagon *(1969).*

Born November 2, 1917, New Orleans, Louisiana. Married Ruth Calvert (1943), child: one daughter. Comic stage actor with a penchant for flippancy: the devilish Applegate (*Damn Yankees*), the woman-hungry Luther Billis (*South Pacific*); recently as Patrick McGoohan's murdering stooge (*Silver Streak*). TV series: "My Favorite Martian."

Ray Walston to Felicia Farr in *Kiss Me, Stupid!*: "You *trust* me.
That's a *lousy thing* to say about your husband!"

Films

Kiss Them for Me (20th, 1957)
South Pacific (20th, 1958)
Damn Yankees (WB, 1958)
Say One for Me (20th, 1959)
The Apartment (UA, 1960)
Tall Story (WB, 1960)

Potrait in Black (Univ, 1960)
Convicts Four (AA, 1962)
Wives and Lovers (Par, 1963)
Who's Minding the Store? (Par, 1963)
Kiss Me, Stupid! (Lopert, 1964)
Caprice (20th, 1967)

Paint Your Wagon (Par, 1969)
Viva Max! (CUE, 1969)
The Sting (Univ, 1973)
Silver Streak (20th, 1976)
The Happy Hooker Goes to Washington
    (Cannon Releasing, 1977)

HENRY B. WALTHALL

With Dorothy Revier in Anybody's Blonde *(1931).*

Born March 16, 1878, Shelby City, Alabama. Married 1) Isabel Fenton; divorced; 2) Mary Charleston, child: one. Died June 17, 1936, Monrovia, California. One of D. W. Griffith's ablest stars. Most noted for sensitive interpretation of the Little Colonel in *The Birth of a Nation*. Short of stature but possessed of an expressive visage. A forceful film performer from 1909 onward. Griffith assignments included *The Battle of Elderberry Gulch* and such features as *Judith of Bethulia* (Holofernes, the Assyrian general), *Home Sweet Home* (composer John Howard Payne), *The Avenging Conscience* (the nephew), and *Abraham Lincoln* (Colonel Marshall). By the mid-1920s, was alternating between leads (*The Face on the Barroom Floor, Kentucky Pride*) and supporting roles (*The Road to Mandalay* as Father James). Was a character player in all varieties of talkie features and serials: *42nd Street* (the old actor), *Judge Priest* (Reverend Ashby Brand), *Viva Villa!* (Madero), *A Tale of Two Cities* (Dr. Manette), etc.

Henry B. Walthall to Spencer Tracy in *Dante's Inferno:* "Dante, in giving us a terrifying picture of the tormented souls of those who live ruthlessly, tried to make us realize that by our own actions and thoughts towards our fellow man we make our own heaven or hell on earth."

Films

Judith of Bethulia (American Biograph, 1913)
Home Sweet Home (Mutual, 1914)
The Avenging Conscience (Mutual, 1914)
The Floor Above (Mutual, 1914)
The Birth of a Nation (Epoch, 1915)
Ghosts (Reliance, 1915)
The Misleading Lady (Essanay, 1915)
The Circular Path (Essanay, 1915)
The Raven (Essanay, 1915)

The Spider and the Fly (Fox, 1916)
The Sting of Victory (Essanay, 1916)
The Pillars of Society (Tri–Fine Arts, 1916)
The Truant Soul (Essanay, 1916)
The Little Shoes (Essanay, 1917)
The Saint's Adventure (Essanay, 1917)
Burning the Candle (Essanay, 1917)
His Robe of Honor (Peralta-Hodkinson, 1918)

The False Faces (Par-Artcraft, 1918)
Humdrum Brown (Peralta-Hodkinson, 1918)
With Hoops of Steel (Peralta-Hodkinson, 1919)
The Great Love (Par-Artcraft, 1919)
And a Still Small Voice (National-Robertson-Cole, 1919)
The Boomerang (National-Pioneer, 1919)

The Long Lane's Turning (Exhibitors Mutual, 1919)

Modern Husbands (Robertson-Cole, 1919)

The Long Arm of Mannister (National-Pioneer, 1919)

A Splendid Hazard (Mayflower Photoplay Company, 1920)

The Confession (Associated FN, 1920)

The Flower of the North (Vit, 1921)

The Parted Curtains (WB, 1921)

The Ableminded Lady (Pacific Film Company, 1922)

One Clear Call (Associated FN, 1922)

The Kick Back (FBO, 1922)

The Long Chance (Univ, 1922)

The Marriage Chance (America, 1922)

The Face on the Barroom Floor (Fox, 1923)

Gimme (G, 1923)

The Unknown Purple (Truart Film Corp, 1923)

Boy of Mine (Associated FN, 1923)

The Woman on the Jury (Associated FN, 1924)

Single Wives (Associated FN, 1924)

The Bowery Bishop (Selznick, 1924)

The Golden Bed (Par, 1925)

On the Threshold (PDC, 1925)

The Girl Who Wouldn't Work (B. P. Schulberg, 1925)

Kit Carson over the Great Divide (Sunset-Aywon Film Corp., 1925)

Kentucky Pride (Fox, 1925)

Dollar Down (Truart Film Corp., 1925)

Simon the Jester (PDC-Metropolitan, 1925)

The Plastic Age (B. P. Schulberg, 1925)

Three Faces East (PDC, 1926)

The Barrier (MGM, 1926)

The Unknown Soldier (Renaud Hoffman, 1926)

The Road to Mandalay (MGM, 1926)

Everybody's Acting (Par, 1926)

The Scarlet Letter (MGM, 1927)

The Ice Flood (Univ, 1927)

Fighting Love (De Mille Picture Corp., 1927)

The Enchanted Island (Tif, 1927)

Wings (Par, 1927)

The Rose of Kildare (Lumas Film Corp., 1927)

A Light in the Window (Rayart, 1927)

London After Midnight (MGM, 1927)

Love Me and the World Is Mine (Univ, 1928)

Freedom of the Press (Univ, 1928)

Stark Mad (WB, 1929)

Speakeasy (Fox, 1929)

The Bridge of San Luis Rey (MGM, 1929)

The Jazz Age (FBO, 1929)

Black Magic (Fox, 1929)

The Man from Headquarters (WB, 1929)

River of Romance (Par, 1929)

The Trespasser (UA, 1929)

In Old California (Audible Pictures, 1929)

Phantom in the House (Continental, 1929)

Blaze o' Glory (Sono Art-World Wide, 1929)

Tol'able David (Col, 1930)

Temple Tower (Fox, 1930)

Abraham Lincoln (UA, 1930)

The Love Trader (Tif, 1930)

Is There Justice? (Sono Art-World Wide, 1931)

Anybody's Blonde (Action, 1931)

Hotel Continental (Tif, 1932)

Police Court (Mon, 1932)

Strange Interlude (MGM, 1932)

Alias Mary Smith (Mayfair, 1932)

Chandu the Magician (Fox, 1932)

Klondike (Mon, 1932)

Cabin in the Cotton (FN, 1932)

Ride Him, Cowboy (WB, 1932)

Central Park (FN, 1932)

Me and My Gal (Fox, 1932)

Wolf Dog (Mascot serial, 1933)

42nd Street (WB, 1933)

Self Defense (Mon, 1933)

Flaming Signal (Invincible, 1933)

The Whispering Shadow (Mascot serial, 1933)

Somewhere in Sonora (WB, 1933)

Laughing at Life (Mascot, 1933)

Headline Shooter (RKO, 1933)

Her Forgotten Past (Mayfair, 1933)

The Sin of Nora Moran (Majestic, 1933)

Viva Villa! (MGM, 1934)

Men in White (MGM, 1934)

Dark Hazard (FN, 1934)

Beggars in Ermine (Mon, 1934)

Operator 13 (MGM, 1934)

Murder in the Museum (Progressive, 1934)

City Park (Chesterfield, 1934)

Judge Priest (Fox, 1934)

The Girl of the Limberlost (Mon, 1934)

The Lemon Drop Kid (Par, 1934)

The Scarlet Letter (Majestic, 1934)

Love Time (Fox, 1934)

Bachelor of Arts (Fox, 1934)

Helldorado (Fox, 1935)

Dante's Inferno (Fox, 1935)

A Tale of Two Cities (MGM, 1935)

The Garden Murder Case (MGM, 1936)

The Mine with the Iron Door (Col, 1936)

Hearts in Bondage (Rep, 1936)

The Last Outlaw (RKO, 1936)

The Devil Doll (MGM, 1936)

China Clipper (FN, 1936)

JACK WARDEN

Jack Warden, Edward Binns, E. G. Marshall, John Fiedler, Henry Fonda, Ed Begley, Robert Webber, Jack Klugman, George Voskovec, Martin Balsam, and Joseph Sweeney in Twelve Angry Men *(1957).*

Born September 18, 1920, Newark, New Jersey. Married Wanda De Pre (1958), child: son. Burly stage, screen, and television performer. At his best in proletarian drama: *Twelve Angry Men* (Juror No. 7), *Bachelor Party* (Eddie), *Bye, Bye Braverman* (Barnet Weiner). Sometimes cast as military officer: *Blindfold* (General Pratt), *Welcome to the Club* (General Strapp). Recently displayed a strong screen presence as the braggart father of Richard Dreyfuss in *The Apprenticeship of Duddy Kravitz* and was Oscar-nominated for his wealthy financier Lester Karpf—husband of Lee Grant and dabbler with Julie Christie—of *Shampoo* (but lost BSAAA to George Burns of *The Sunshine Boys*). TV series: "The Wackiest Ship in the Army."

Jack Warden to Elisabeth Allen in *Donovan's Reef:* "Amelia, I couldn't care *less* about the Dedham Shipping Company."

Films

The Asphalt Jungle (MGM, 1950)
The Man with My Face (UA, 1951)
The Frogmen (20th, 1951)
You're in the Navy Now [a.k.a. U.S.S. Teakettle] (20th, 1951)
Red Ball Express (Univ, 1952)
From Here to Eternity (Col, 1953)
Twelve Angry Men (UA, 1957)
Edge of the City (MGM, 1957)
Bachelor Party (UA, 1957)
Darby's Rangers (WB, 1958)

Run Silent, Run Deep (UA, 1958)
The Sound and the Fury (20th, 1959)
That Kind of Woman (Par, 1959)
Wake Me When It's Over (20th, 1960)
Escape from Zahrain (Par, 1962)
Donovan's Reef (Par, 1963)
The Thin Red Line (AA, 1964)
Blindfold (Univ, 1966)
Bye, Bye Braverman (WB-7 Arts, 1968)
Summertree (Col, 1971)
The Sporting Club (Avco Emb, 1971)

Welcome to the Club (Col, 1971)
Who Is Harvey Kellerman and Why Is He Saying Those Terrible Things About Me? (National General, 1971)
The Man Who Loved Cat Dancing (MGM, 1973)
Billy Two Hats (UA, 1974)
The Apprenticeship of Duddy Kravitz (Par, 1974)
Shampoo (Col, 1975)
All the President's Men (WB, 1976)

H. B. WARNER
(Henry Byron Warner)

With Maria Ouspenskaya in The Rains Came *(1939).*

Born October 26, 1876, London, England. Married 1) Mrs. F. R. Hamlin; divorced; 2) Marguerite Stanwood; divorced (1933). Died December 21, 1958, Los Angeles, California. Tall, stately British stage actor whose well-chiseled features made him an asset for motion pictures. Joined with Dorothy Dalton in *The Vagabond Prince*, with Gloria Swanson in *Zaza*, and Anna Q. Nilsson in (among other projects) *Sorrell and Son* (would replay the role in a 1934 British release). The peak of his acting career was Jesus the Christ in Cecil B. DeMille's *The King of Kings*. Respected character player in talkies: *Liliom* (chief magistrate), *Charlie Chan's Chance* (Inspector Fife), *A Tale of Two Cities* (Gabelle), *Mr. Deeds Goes to Town* (Judge Walker), *The Adventures of Marco Polo* (Chen Tsu), etc. Oscar-nominated for his role of Chang in *Lost Horizon* (but lost BSAAA to Joseph Schildkraut of *The Life of Emile Zola*). One of Miss Swanson's "waxworks," along with Anna Q. Nilsson, in *Sunset Boulevard*; played Amminadab in DeMille's last film, *The Ten Commandments*.

> **H. B. Warner** to Gary Cooper in *Mr. Deeds Goes to Town:* "In the opinion of this court, you are not only sane, you're the sanest man who ever walked into this courtroom."

Films

Your Ghost and Mine (Selig, 1914)
The Ghost Breaker (Jesse L. Lasky Feature Play Co, 1914)
The Raiders (Tri, 1915)
A Wife's Sacrifice (Fox, 1916)
The Market of Vain Desire (Tri, 1916)
The Beggar of Cawnpore (Tri, 1916)

The House of a 1,000 Candles (Selig, 1916)
Shell 43 (Tri, 1916)
The Vagabond Prince (Tri, 1916)
The Seven Deadly Sins (McClure, 1917)
God's Man (Frohman–States Rights, 1917)

Danger Trail (Selig, 1917)
The Man Who Turned White (Exhibitor, 1919)
For a Woman's Honor (Exhibitor-Mutual, 1919)
A Fugitive from Matrimony (Robertson-Cole, 1919)

508

The Pagan God (Robertson-Cole, 1919)

Uncharted Channels (Robertson-Cole, 1919)

Haunting Shadows (Robertson-Cole, 1920)

The White Dove (Hampton, 1920)

Grey Wolf's Ghost (Exhibitor, 1920)

One Hour Before Dawn (Pathé, 1920)

Once a Plumber (Univ, 1920)

Felix O'Day (Pathé, 1920)

Dice of Destiny (Pathé, 1920)

Below the Deadline (Asher, 1920)

When We Were Twenty-One (Pathe, 1921)

Zaza (Par, 1923)

Is Love Everything? (Associated Exhibitors, 1924)

Silence (PDC, 1926)

Whispering Smith (PDC, 1926)

The King of Kings (Pathe, 1927)

French Dressing (FN, 1927)

Sorrell and Son (UA, 1927)

Man-Made Woman (Pathé, 1928)

The Romance of a Rogue (Quality, 1928)

The Naughty Duchess (Tif-Stahl, 1928)

Conquest (WB, 1928)

The Divine Lady (FN, 1929)

The Trial of Mary Dugan (MGM, 1929)

The Doctor's Secret (Par, 1929)

Stark Mad (WB, 1929)

The Gamblers (WB, 1929)

The Argyle Case (WB, 1929)

The Show of Shows (WB, 1929)

Tiger Rose (WB, 1929)

The Green Goddess (WB, 1929)

Wedding Rings (FN, 1930)

The Furies (FN, 1930)

Second Floor Mystery (WB, 1930)

Wild Company (Fox, 1930)

On Your Back (Fox, 1930)

Liliom (Fox, 1930)

The Princess and the Plumber (Fox, 1930)

Expensive Women (WB, 1931)

Five Star Final (FN, 1931)

Woman of Experience (RKO, 1931)

The Reckless Hour (FN, 1931)

The Menace (Col, 1932)

Tom Brown of Culver (Univ, 1932)

A Woman Commands (RKO, 1932)

Cross-Examination (Artclass, 1932)

Charlie Chan's Chance (Fox, 1932)

Unholy Love (Allied, 1932)

The Crusader (Majestic, 1932)

The Phantom of Crestwood (RKO, 1932)

The Son-Daughter (MGM, 1932)

Jennie Gerhardt (Par, 1933)

Justice Takes a Holiday (Mayfair, 1933)

Supernatural (Par, 1933)

Christopher Bean (MGM, 1933)

Grand Canary (Fox, 1934)

In Old Santa Fe (Mascot, 1934)

Night Alarm (Majestic, 1934)

Behold My Wife! (Par, 1934)

Sorrell and Son (Br, 1934)

Born to Gamble (Liberty, 1935)

A Tale of Two Cities (MGM, 1935)

The Garden Murder Case (MGM, 1936)

Rose of the Rancho (Par, 1936)

Moonlight Murder (MGM, 1936)

Mr. Deeds Goes to Town (Col, 1936)

Blackmailer (Col, 1936)

Along Came Love (Par, 1936)

Lost Horizon (Col, 1937)

Our Fighting Navy [a.k.a. *Torpedoed*] (Br, 1937)

Victoria the Great (Br, 1937)

The Adventures of Marco Polo (UA, 1938)

Girl of the Golden West (MGM, 1938)

Toy Wife (MGM, 1938)

Kidnapped (20th, 1938)

Bulldog Drummond in Africa (Par, 1938)

Army Girl (Rep, 1938)

You Can't Take It with You (Col, 1938)

Arrest Bulldog Drummond (Par, 1939)

Let Freedom Ring (MGM, 1939)

Bulldog Drummond's Secret (Par, 1939)

Bulldog Drummond's Bride (Par, 1939)

The Gracie Allen Murder Case (Par, 1939)

Mr. Smith Goes to Washington (Col, 1939)

Nurse Edith Cavell (RKO, 1939)

The Rains Came (20th, 1939)

New Moon (MGM, 1940)

Topper Returns (UA, 1941)

The City of Missing Girls (Select, 1941)

All That Money Can Buy [a.k.a. *The Devil and Daniel Webster*] (RKO, 1941)

Ellery Queen and the Perfect Crime (Col, 1941)

South of Tahiti (Univ, 1941)

The Corsican Brothers (UA, 1941)

A Yank in Libya (PRC, 1942)

Boss of Big Town (PRC, 1942)

Crossroads (MGM, 1942)

Hitler's Children (RKO, 1942)

Women in Bondage (Mon, 1943)

Action in Arabia (RKO, 1944)

Enemy of Women (Mon, 1944)

Faces in the Fog (Rep, 1944)

Rogues' Gallery (PRC, 1945)

Captain Tugboat Annie (Rep, 1945)

Strange Impersonation (Rep, 1946)

It's a Wonderful Life (RKO, 1946)

Gentleman Joe Palooka (Mon, 1946)

Driftwood (Rep, 1947)

The High Wall (MGM, 1947)

The Prince of Thieves (Col, 1948)

Hellfire (Rep, 1949)

The Judge Steps Out (RKO, 1949)

El Paso (Par, 1949)

Sunset Boulevard (Par, 1950)

The First Legion (UA, 1951)

Journey into Light (20th, 1951)

Savage Drums (Lip, 1951)

Here Comes the Groom (Par, 1951)

The Ten Commandments (Par, 1956)

Darby's Rangers (WB, 1958)

ROBERT WARWICK
(Robert Taylor Bien)

Piper Laurie, Tyrone Power, and Robert Warwick (right) in Mississippi Gambler *(1953).*

Born October 9, 1878, Sacramento, California. Married 1) Stella Lattimore; divorced; 2) Josephine Whittell; divorced. Died June 6, 1964, West Los Angeles, California. Strikingly handsome leading man of road shows and Broadway. Made career strides in such silent features as *The Argyle Case, A Modern Othello,* and *Secret Service.* Was Detective Craig Kennedy in his first sound feature, the low-budget *Unmasked.* A much-in-demand character actor, usually offering vignettes as stentorian aristocrats, judges, noblemen, military officers: *A Tale of Two Cities* (tribunal judge), *Mary of Scotland* (Sir Francis Knellys), *Romeo and Juliet* (Lord Montague), *The Adventures of Robin Hood* (Sir Geoffrey), *Sullivan's Travels* (Lebrand, the studio executive), *Salome* (courier), 1958's *The Buccaneer* (Captain Lockyer), *It Started with a Kiss* (Congressman Muir), etc.

> **Robert Warwick** to Veronica Lake in *Sullivan's Travels:* "You were his last discovery, his last gift to the world. We'll take care of you always."

Films

The Dollar Mark (World, 1914)
Man of the Hour (World, 1914)
The Face in the Moonlight (World, 1915)
Human Driftwood (Equitable-World, 1916)
The Mad Lover (Pathé, 1917)
The Argyle Case (Rapf, 1917)
The Silent Master (Selznick, 1917)
An Accidental Honeymoon (Rapf, 1918)
Told in the Hills (Par, 1919)
The Secret Service (Par, 1919)
In Mizzoura (Par, 1919)
The City of Masks (Par, 1920)
Thou Art the Man (Par, 1920)
Fourteenth Man (Par, 1920)
The Spitfire (Par, 1924)

Unmasked (Artclass, 1930)
A Holy Terror (Fox, 1931)
Three Rogues (Fox, 1931)
The Royal Bed (RKO, 1931)
Not Exactly Gentlemen (Fox, 1931)
So Big (WB, 1932)
The Dark Horse (FN, 1932)
The Woman from Monte Carlo (FN, 1932)
Unashamed (MGM, 1932)
Dr. X (FN, 1932)
The Rich Are Always with Us (FN, 1932)
I Am a Fugitive from a Chain Gang (WB, 1932)
Silver Dollar (FN, 1932)
The Girl from Calgary (Mon, 1932)
Afraid to Talk (Univ, 1932)

Secrets of Wu Sin (Chesterfield, 1932)
Charlie Chan's Greatest Case (Fox, 1933)
Fighting with Kit Carson (Mascot serial, 1933)
Frisco Jenny (FN, 1933)
Ladies They Talk About (WB, 1933)
Pilgrimage (Fox, 1933)
Female (FN, 1933)
The Dragon Murder Case (FN, 1934)
Jimmy the Gent (WB, 1934)
Cleopatra (Par, 1934)
School for Girls (Liberty, 1934)
Night Life of the Gods (Univ, 1935)
A Shot in the Dark (Chesterfield, 1935)
Murder Man (MGM, 1935)
A Tale of Two Cities (MGM, 1935)

Code of the Mounted (Ambassador, 1935)
Hopalong Cassidy (Par, 1935)
Whipsaw (MGM, 1936)
Tough Guy (MGM, 1936)
Return of Jimmy Valentine (Rep, 1936)
Bulldog Edition (Rep, 1936)
In His Steps [a.k.a. Sins of the Children] (GN, 1936)
The Bold Caballero (Rep, 1936)
Sutter's Gold (Univ, 1936)
The Bride Walks Out (RKO, 1936)
Ace Drummond (Univ serial, 1936)
Can This Be Dixie? (20th, 1936)
Timber War (Ambassador, 1936)
Mary of Scotland (RKO, 1936)
Romeo and Juliet (MGM, 1936)
White Legion (GN, 1936)
Adventure in Manhattan (Col, 1936)
The Prince and the Pauper (WB, 1937)
The Life of Emile Zola (WB, 1937)
Let Them Live (Univ, 1937)
The Road Back (Univ, 1937)
The Awful Truth (Col, 1937)
Counsel for Crime (Col, 1937)
The Trigger Trio (Rep, 1937)
Conquest (MGM, 1937)
The Spy Ring (Univ, 1938)
Going Places (WB, 1938)
The Adventures of Robin Hood (WB, 1938)
Gangster's Boy (Mon, 1938)
Blockade (UA, 1938)
Army Girl (Rep, 1938)

Law of the Plains (Col, 1938)
Come On, Leathernecks (Rep, 1938)
Squadron of Honor (Col, 1938)
The Private Lives of Elizabeth and Essex (WB, 1939)
Almost a Gentleman (RKO, 1939)
The Magnificent Fraud (Par, 1939)
In Old Monterey (Rep, 1939)
Devil's Island (WB, 1940)
On the Spot (Mon, 1940)
New Moon (MGM, 1940)
Konga—The Wild Stallion (Col, 1940)
Murder in the Air (WB, 1940)
The Sea Hawk (WB, 1940)
A Woman's Face (MGM, 1941)
I Was a Prisoner on Devil's Island (Col, 1941)
Louisiana Purchase (Par, 1941)
Sullivan's Travels (Par, 1941)
The Palm Beach Story (Par, 1942)
Secret Enemies (WB, 1942)
Tennessee Johnson (MGM, 1942)
Cadets on Parade (Col, 1942)
Eagle Squadron (Univ, 1942)
I Married a Witch (UA, 1942)
Two Tickets to London (Univ, 1943)
Dixie (Par, 1943)
Petticoat Larceny (RKO, 1943)
The Deerslayer (Rep, 1943)
The Princess and the Pirate (RKO, 1944)
Bowery to Broadway (Univ, 1944)
Kismet [TV title: Oriental Dreams] (MGM, 1944)

Secret Command (Col, 1944)
The Man from Frisco (Rep, 1944)
Sudan (Univ, 1945)
Criminal Court (RKO, 1946)
The Falcon's Adventure (RKO, 1946)
Gentleman's Agreement (20th, 1947)
The Pirates of Monterey (Univ, 1947)
Fury at Furnace Creek (20th, 1948)
Adventures of Don Juan (WB, 1948)
Million Dollar Weekend (EL, 1948)
Gun Smugglers (RKO, 1948)
A Woman's Secret (RKO, 1949)
Impact (UA, 1949)
Francis (Univ, 1949)
In a Lonely Place (Col, 1950)
Vendetta (RKO, 1950)
Tarzan and the Slave Girl (RKO, 1950)
The Sword of Monte Cristo (20th, 1951)
Sugarfoot (WB, 1951)
Mark of the Renegade (Univ, 1951)
Mississippi Gambler (Univ, 1953)
Jamaica Run (Par, 1953)
Salome (Col, 1953)
Silver Lode (RKO, 1954)
Passion (RKO, 1954)
Chief Crazy Horse (Univ, 1955)
Escape to Burma (RKO, 1955)
Lady Godiva (Univ, 1955)
Walk the Proud Land (Univ, 1956)
Shoot-Out at Medicine Bend (WB, 1957)
The Buccaneer (Par, 1958)
Night of the Quarter Moon (MGM, 1959)
It Started with a Kiss (MGM, 1959)

BRYANT WASHBURN

With Hedda Hopper in Mystery Train *(1931).*

Born April 28, 1889, Chicago, Illinois. Married Mabel Forest, children: Bryant, another child. Died April 30, 1963, Hollywood, California. With a dimpled chin, dark eyes, and dark wavy hair, this stage actor soon switched from bad- to good-guy roles in Essanay short subjects: *Little Straw Wife, One Wonderful Night,* etc. Made the *Skinner* feature series at Essanay (with one for FBO in 1928); by 1918 was starring at Paramount. In mid-1920s wavered between playing secondary roles—*Rupert of Hentzau* (Count Fritz), *The Wizard of Oz* (Prince Kynde)—or leads in low-budget entries—*Black Tears.* Was heavier (and dissipated) by the talkies, and was reduced to small roles: one of the has-been silent stars used for *Hollywood Boulevard.* Cavalry Captain Simmons in *Stagecoach,* Dr. Howard in Robert Mitchum's *West of the Pecos.* Had larger roles in serials: *The Return of Chandu* (Prince Andre), *King of the Royal Mounted* (villain Crandall), etc. Father of actor Bryant Washburn, Jr.

Bryant Washburn to George Meeker in *Night of Terror:* "Do you realize that if anything was to happen to us, if we should mysteriously die, our share would go to these servants?"

Films

The Blindness of Virtue (Essanay, 1915)
Marriage a la Carte (World, 1916)
The Prince of Graustark (Essanay, 1916)
Destiny (Essanay, 1916)
Havoc (Essanay, 1916)
The Spider's Web (Essanay, 1916)
The Golden Idiot (Essanay, 1916)
The Man Who Was Afraid (Essanay, 1917)
Filling his Own Shoes (Essanay, 1917)
Skinner's Baby (Essanay, 1917)
The Breaker (Essanay, 1917)

The Girl God Made for Jones (Essanay, 1917)
Skinner's Dress Suit (Essanay, 1917)
A Four Cent Courtship (Essanay, 1917)
Skinner's Bubble (Essanay, 1917)
The Fibbers (Essanay, 1917)
The Final Fraud (Essanay, 1917)
Voice of Conscience (M, 1917)
The Gypsy Trail (Par, 1918)
Twenty-One (Pathé, 1918)
Kidder and Ko (Pathé, 1918)
Ghost of the Rancho (Pathé, 1918)

'Til I Come Back to You (Par, 1918)
Putting It Over (Par, 1919)
Venus in the East (Par, 1919)
The Way of a Man with a Maid (Par, 1919)
The Poor Boob (Par, 1919)
Something to Do (Par, 1919)
Why Smith Left Home (Par, 1919)
It Pays to Advertise (Par, 1919)
Love Insurance (Par, 1919)
A Full House (Par, 1920)
Burglar Proof (Par, 1920)

What Happened to Jones? (Par, 1920)
Amateur Devil (Par, 1920)
The Road to London (Pathé, 1921)
Night Life in Hollywood (Arrow, 1922)
Hungry Hearts (G, 1922)
June Madness (M, 1922)
White Shoulders (Associated FN, 1922)
The Woman Conquers (Associated FN, 1922)
The Commonn Law (Selznick, 1923)
Hollywood (Par, 1923)
The Love Trap (Asher, 1923)
Mary of the Movies (FBO, 1923)
The Meanest Man in the World (Associated FN, 1923)
Mine to Keep (Asher, 1923)
Other Men's Daughters (Asher, 23)
Rupert of Hentzau (Selznick, 1923)
Temptation (CBC, 1923)
My Husband's Wives (Fox, 1924)
The Star Dust Trail (Fox, 1924)
Try and Get It (PDC, 1924)
The Parasite (B. P. Schulberg, 1925)
Passionate Youth (Truart, 1925)
Wandering Footsteps (CBC, 1925)
The Wizard of Oz (Chadwick, 1925)
Flames (Associated Exhibitors, 1926)
Her Sacrifice (Sanford, 1926)
Meet the Prince (PDC, 1926)
The Sky Pirate (Aywon, 1926)
That Girl from Oklahoma (Pathe, 1926)
Wet Paint (Par, 1926)
Sitting Bull at the Spirit Lake Massacre (Sunset Productions, 1926)
Young April (PDC, 1926)
Beware of Widows (Univ, 1927)
Black Tears (Hollywood Pictures, 1927)
Breakfast at Sunrise (FN, 1927)
In the First Degree (Sterling, 1927)
The Love Thrill (Univ, 1927)
Modern Daughters (Rayart, 1927)
The King of Kings (Pathé, 1927)
A Bit of Heaven (Excellent Pictures, 1928)

The Chorus Kid (Gotham, 1928)
Honeymoon Flats (Univ, 1928)
Jazzland (Quality, 1928)
Nothing to Wear (Col, 1928)
Skinner's Big Idea (FBO, 1928)
Undressed (Sterling, 1928)
Swing High (Pathé, 1930)
Kept Husbands (RKO, 1931)
Mystery Train (Continental Pictures, 1931)
The Reckoning (Peerless, 1932)
Arm of the Law (Mon, 1932)
Drifting Souls (Toer, 1932)
Exposure (Capital, 1932)
What Price Hollywood? (RKO, 1932)
Forbidden Company (Invincible, 1932)
A Parisian Romance (Allied, 1932)
Thrill of Youth (Invincible, 1932)
What Price Innocence? (Col, 1933)
Night of Terror (Col, 1933)
The Devil's Mate (Mon, 1933)
Public Stenographer (Marcy Exchange, 1934)
The Return of Chandu (Principal serial, 1934)
The Curtain Fall (Chesterfield, 1934)
The Back Page (General Pictures, 1934)
The Woman Who Dared (Imperial, 1934)
When Strangers Meet (Liberty, 1934)
The World Accuses (Chesterfield, 1935)
$20.00 a Week (Ajax, 1935)
The Call of the Savage (Univ serial, 1935)
Swell Head (Col, 1935)
Danger Ahead (Victory, 1935)
The Throwback (Univ, 1935)
Tailspin Tommy in the Great Air Mystery (Univ serial, 1935)
The Millionaire Kid (Reliable, 1936)
Bridge of Sighs (Invincible, 1936)
. . . And Sudden Death (Par, 1936)
Gambling with Souls (Jay Dee Kay Productions, 1936)
The Preview Murder Mystery (Par, 1936)
Hollywood Boulevard (Par, 1936)
Sutter's Gold (Univ, 1936)

Conflict (Univ, 1936)
Three of a Kind (Invincible, 1936)
It Couldn't Have Happened (Invincible, 1936)
The Black Coin (Stage & Screen, 1936)
We Who Are About to Die (RKO, 1936)
Jungle Jim (Univ serial, 1937)
Sea Racketeers (Rep, 1937)
The Westland Case (Univ, 1937)
Million Dollar Racket (Victory 1937)
I Demand Payment (Imperial, 1938)
Stagecoach (UA, 1939)
Ambush (Par, 1939)
Midnight (Par, 1939)
Sky Patrol (Mon, 1939)
King of the Royal Mounted (Rep serial, 1940) [feature version: *Yukon Patrol*]
The Adventures of Captain Marvel (Rep serial, 1941)
The Spider Returns (Col serial, 1941)
Paper Bullets (PRC, 1941)
Gangs Inc. (PRC, 1941)
The Yukon Patrol (Rep, 1942)
War Dogs (Mon, 1942)
Maisie Gets Her Man (MGM, 1942)
Sin Town (Univ, 1942)
Captain Midnight (Col serial, 1942)
Carson City Cyclone (Rep, 1943)
The Girl from Monterey (PRC, 1943)
Shadows on the Sage (Rep, 1943)
You Can't Beat the Law (Mon, 1943)
The Law Rides Again (Mon, 1943)
The Falcon in Mexico (RKO, 1944)
My Pal, Wolf (RKO, 1944)
Nabonga (PRC, 1944)
Two O'Clock Courage (RKO, 1945)
West of the Pecos (RKO, 1945)
Sweet Genevieve (Col, 1947)

PIERRE WATKIN

Noel Neill, Kirk Alyn, Lyle Talbot, and Pierre Watkin in the serial Atom Man vs. Superman *(1950).*

Born December 29, 1889, Sioux City, Iowa. Died February 3, 1960, Hollywood, California. Prosperous-looking individual usually assigned to being the physician, attorney, military officer, or father: *It Had to Happen* (district attorney), *Green Light* (Dr. Booth), *Stage Door* (wealthy Mr. Carmichael), *King of the Underworld* (district attorney), *Mr. Smith Goes to Washington* (Senator Barnes), *The Pride of the Yankees* (father of Teresa Wright), *Over 21* (filmmaker Joel I. Nixon), etc.

> **Pierre Watkin** to Robert Sterling in *Yesterday's Heroes:* "Of course, I plan to make it very profitable for you if you don't oppose the annulment proceedings."

Films

Dangerous (WB, 1935)
Forgotten Faces (Par, 1936)
It Had to Happen (20th, 1936)
Counterfeit (Col, 1936)
The Gentleman from Louisiana (Rep, 1936)
Sitting on the Moon (Rep, 1936)
The Country Gentlemen (Rep, 1936)
Nobody's Fool (Univ, 1936)
Swing Time (RKO, 1936)
Bunker Bean (RKO, 1936)
Love Letters of a Star (Univ, 1936)
Daughter of Shanghai (Par, 1937)
Green Light (WB, 1937)
The Go-Getter (WB, 1937)
Ever Since Eve (WB, 1937)
The Singing Marine (WB, 1937)
She's Dangerous (Univ, 1937)
Reported Missing (Univ, 1937)
The Devil's Playground (Col, 1937)
Larceny on the Air (Rep, 1937)

Bill Cracks Down (Rep, 1937)
The Hit Parade (Rep, 1937)
Sea Devils (RKO, 1937)
Stage Door (RKO, 1937)
The Last Gangster (MGM, 1937)
Mountain Justice (WB, 1937)
Breakfast for Two (RKO, 1937)
Paradise Isle (Mon, 1937)
Michael O'Halloran (Rep, 1937)
Internes Can't Take Money (Par, 1937)
The Californian (20th, 1937)
Marked Woman (WB, 1937)
Midnight Intruder (Univ, 1938)
Valley of the Giants (WB, 1938)
State Police (Univ, 1938)
Mr. Moto's Gamble (20th, 1938)
Dangerous to Know (Par, 1938)
Tip-Off Girls (Par, 1938)
Illegal Traffic (Par, 1938)
There's Always a Woman (Col, 1938)
Girls' School (Col, 1938)

There's That Woman Again (Col, 1938)
The Chaser (MGM, 1938)
Mr. Doodle Kicks Off (RKO, 1938)
Young Dr. Kildare (MGM, 1938)
The Lady Objects (Col, 1938)
Risky Business (Univ, 1939)
The Spirit of Culver (Univ, 1939)
King of the Underworld (WB, 1939)
Wings of the Navy (WB, 1939)
Off the Record (WB, 1939)
Adventures of Jane Arden (WB, 1939)
The Jones Family in Hollywood (20th, 1939)
The Mysterious Miss X (Rep, 1939)
Covered Trailer (Rep, 1939)
Wall Street Cowboy (Rep, 1939)
They Made Her a Spy (RKO, 1939)
Society Lawyer (MGM, 1939)
Mr. Smith Goes to Washington (Col, 1939)
Geronimo (Par, 1939)

Mr. Smith Goes to Washington (Col, 1939)

Everything's on Ice (RKO, 1939)

Death of a Champion (Par, 1939)

The Great Victor Herbert (Par, 1939)

Mystery Sea Raider (Par, 1940)

The Road to Singapore (Par, 1940)

The Saint Takes Over (RKO, 1940)

Street of Memories (20th, 1940)

Captain Caution (UA, 1940)

I Love You Again (MGM, 1940)

Rhythm on the River (Par, 1940)

Golden Gloves (Par, 1940)

Out West with the Peppers (Col, 1940)

Five Little Peppers in Trouble (Col, 1940)

The Bank Dick (Univ, 1940)

Yesterday's Heroes (20th, 1940)

Knute Rockne—All-American (WB, 1940)

Father Is a Prince (WB, 1940)

Life with Henry (Par, 1941)

For Beauty's Sake (20th, 1941)

Cheers for Miss Bishop (UA, 1941)

Father Takes a Wife (RKO, 1941)

Lady for a Night (Rep, 1941)

Petticoat Politics (Rep, 1941)

A Man Betrayed (Rep, 1941)

The Trial of Mary Dugan (MGM, 1941)

Meet John Doe (WB, 1941)

She Knew All the Answers (Col, 1941)

Adventures in Washington (Col, 1941)

Naval Academy (Col, 1941)

Nevada City (Rep, 1941)

Buy Me That Town (Par, 1941)

Ellery Queen and the Murder Ring (Col, 1941)

Ice-Capades Revue (Rep, 1941)

Jesse James at Bay (Rep, 1941)

The Adventures of Martin Eden (Col, 1942)

Heart of the Rio Grande (Rep, 1942)

Yokel Boy (Rep, 1942)

The Magnificent Dope (20th, 1942)

The Pride of the Yankees (RKO, 1942)

Whistling in Dixie (MGM, 1942)

We Were Dancing (MGM, 1942)

What a Woman! (Col, 1943)

This Is the Army (WB, 1943)

Cinderella Swings It (RKO, 1943)

DuBarry Was a Lady (MGM, 1943)

They Came to Blow Up America (20th, 1943)

Mission to Moscow (WB, 1943)

Old Acquaintance (WB, 1943)

Jack London (UA, 1943)

Swing Shift Maisie (MGM, 1943)

Riding High (Par, 1943)

Week-End Pass (Univ, 1944)

Wing and a Prayer (20th, 1944)

Bermuda Mystery (20th, 1944)

Ladies of Washington (20th, 1944)

South of Dixie (Univ, 1944)

Jungle Woman (Univ, 1944)

Oh, What a Night (Mon, 1944)

Atlantic City (Rep, 1944)

The Great Mike (PRC, 1944)

Dead Men's Eyes (Univ, 1944)

Shadow of Suspicion (Mon, 1944)

End of the Road (Rep, 1944)

Song of the Range (Rep, 1944)

Meet Miss Bobby-Socks (Col, 1944)

Strange Illusion (PRC, 1945)

Honeymoon Ahead (Univ, 1945)

Miss Susie Slagle's (Par, 1945)

Roughly Speaking (WB, 1945)

She Gets Her Man (Univ, 1945)

Adventure (MGM, 1945)

The Phantom Speaks (Rep, 1945)

Docks of New York (Mon, 1945)

I'll Remember April (Univ, 1945)

Mr. Muggs Rides Again (Mon, 1945)

Over 21 (Col, 1945)

Follow That Woman (Par, 1945)

Keep Your Powder Dry (MGM, 1945)

Three's a Crowd (Rep, 1945)

Allotment Wives (Mon, 1945)

Dakota (Rep, 1945)

Captain Tugboat Annie (Rep, 1945)

I'll Tell the World (Univ, 1945)

I Love a Bandleader (Col, 1945)

I Ring Doorbells (PRC, 1946)

Little Giant (Univ, 1946)

The Madonna's Secret (Rep, 1946)

So Goes My Love (Univ, 1946)

The Shadow Returns (Mon, 1946)

Murder Is My Business (PRC, 1946)

Swamp Fire (Par, 1946)

Behind the Mask (Mon, 1946)

High School Hero (Mon, 1946)

The Missing Lady (Mon, 1946)

Claudia and David (20th, 1946)

Secrets of a Sorority Girl (PRC, 1946)

Sioux City Sue (Rep, 1946)

G. I. War Brides (Rep, 1946)

Shock (20th, 1946)

The Kid from Brooklyn (RKO, 1946)

Her Sister's Secret (PRC, 1946)

Violence (Mon, 1947)

Song of Love (MGM, 1947)

Hard-Boiled Mahoney (Mon, 1947)

The Red Stallion (EL, 1947)

Her Husband's Affair (Col, 1947)

The Wild Frontier (Rep, 1947)

The Shocking Miss Pilgrim (20th, 1947)

The Secret Life of Walter Mitty (RKO, 1947)

The Hunted (AA, 1948)

Don't Trust Your Husband [a.k.a. An Innocent Affair] (UA, 1948)

The Gentleman from Nowhere (Col, 1948)

Mary Lou (Col, 1948)

Glamour Girl (Col, 1948)

State of the Union (MGM, 1948)

Trapped by Boston Blackie (Col, 1948)

Daredevils of the Clouds (Rep, 1948)

The Counterfeiters (20th, 1948)

The Strange Mrs. Crane (EL, 1948)

Incident (Mon, 1948)

Fighting Back (20th, 1948)

The Shanghai Chest (Mon, 1948)

Knock on Any Door (Col, 1949)

Tulsa (EL, 1949)

The Story of Seabiscuit (WB, 1949)

Frontier Outpost (Col, 1949)

Miss Mink of 1949 (20th, 1949)

Hold That Baby (Mon, 1949)

Alaska Patrol (Film Classics, 1949)

Zamba (EL, 1949)

The Big Hangover (MGM, 1950)

Rock Island Trail (Rep, 1950)

Blue Grass of Kentucky (Mon, 1950)

Over the Border (Mon, 1950)

Atom Man vs. Superman (Col serial, 1950)

Radar Secret Service (Lip, 1950)

Sunset in the West (Rep, 1950)

Redwood Forest Trail (Rep, 1950)

Last of the Buccaneers (Col, 1950)

The Second Face (EL, 1950)

Two Lost Worlds (EL, 1950)

In Old Amarillo (Rep, 1951)

A Yank in Indo-China (Col, 1952)

Scandal Sheet (Col, 1952)

Lovely to Look At (MGM, 1952)

Thundering Caravans (Rep, 1952)

Hold That Line (Mon, 1952)

The Stranger Wore a Gun (Col, 1953)

Count the Hours (RKO, 1953)

Johnny Dark (Univ, 1954)

About Mrs. Leslie (Par, 1954)

The Creature with the Atom Brain (Col, 1955)

The Eternal Sea (Rep, 1955)

The Big Bluff (UA, 1955)

Sudden Danger (AA, 1955)

The Maverick Queen (Rep, 1956)

Thunder over Arizona (Rep, 1956)

Don't Knock the Rock (Col, 1956)

Spook Chasers (AA, 1957)

Beginning or the End (Rep, 1957)

Pal Joey (Col, 1957)

Marjorie Morningstar (WB, 1958)

The Flying Fontaines (Col, 1959)

LUCILE WATSON

In 1945.

Born May 27, 1879, Quebec, Canada. Married 1) Rockcliffe Fellowes; divorced; 2) Louis Ship-man; widowed (1933). Died June 24, 1962, New York City, New York. Patrician stage, screen, and TV performer who gave dimension to regal dowagers: *Made for Each Other* (James Stewart's mother), *The Women* (Norma Shearer's mater), *My Reputation* (Barbara Stanwyck's mother), etc. Was at her best as the politician's widow and the mother of Bette Davis in *Watch on the Rhine* (Oscar-nominated but lost BSAAA to Katina Paxinou of *For Whom the Bell Tolls*).

> **Lucile Watson** to Carole Lombard in *Made for Each Other:* "I wasn't always a bitter old woman....I wasn't always a pest and a nuisance."

Films

What Every Woman Knows (MGM, 1934)
The Bishop Misbehaves (MGM, 1935)
A Woman Rebels (RKO, 1936)
The Garden of Allah (UA, 1936)
Three Smart Girls (Univ, 1937)
The Young in Heart (UA, 1938)
Sweethearts (MGM, 1938)
Made for Each Other (UA, 1939)
The Women (MGM, 1939)
Florian (MGM, 1940)
Waterloo Bridge (MGM, 1940)

Mr. and Mrs. Smith (RKO, 1941)
Rage in Heaven (MGM, 1941)
Footsteps in the Dark (WB, 1941)
The Great Lie (WB, 1941)
Model Wife (Univ, 1941)
Watch on the Rhine (WB, 1943)
Till We Meet Again (Par, 1944)
The Thin Man Goes Home (MGM, 1944)
Uncertain Glory (WB, 1944)
My Reputation (WB, 1946)
Tomorrow Is Forever (RKO, 1946)
Never Say Goodbye (WB, 1946)

The Razor's Edge (20th, 1946)
Song of the South (RKO, 1946)
Ivy (Univ, 1947)
The Emperor Waltz (Par, 1948)
Julia Misbehaves (MGM, 1948)
That Wonderful Urge (20th, 1948)
Little Women (MGM, 1949)
Everybody Does It (20th, 1949)
Harriet Craig (Col, 1950)
Let's Dance (Par, 1950)
My Forbidden Past (RKO, 1951)

MINOR WATSON

Raymond Massey, Warren Douglas, Craig Stevens, John Ridgely, Minor Watson, and Dennis Morgan in God Is My Co-Pilot (1945).

Born December 22, 1889, Marianna, Arkansas. Married Elinor Hewitt. Died July 28, 1965, Alton, Illinois. Abandoned a sagging theatrical career for screen employment; remained tremendously active in the medium for nearly three decades. With his solid build and determined gaze, usually cast in authoritarian parts: *Boys Town* (bishop), *Huckleberry Finn* (Captain Brandy), *Maisie* (prosecuting attorney), Charlie Ruggles' *The Parson of Panamint* (Sheriff Nickerson), *They Died with Their Boots On* (Senator Smith), *Woman of the Year* (William J. Harding—Katharine Hepburn's father), etc. Played the caretaker Moose whom Bette Davis murders in the "campy" *Beyond the Forest;* was the film producer in Davis' *The Star.* Final roles included General Harvey in *The Ambassador's Daughter.*

Minor Watson to Katherine Emery in *Untamed Frontier:*
"Until my son regains his senses, I forbid his name being mentioned in this house."

Films

No. 28 Diplomat (Essanay, 1914)
24 Hours (Par, 1931)
Our Betters (RKO, 1933)
Another Language (MGM, 1933)
Babbitt (FN, 1934)
Pursuit of Happiness (Par, 1934)
Charlie Chan in Paris (Fox, 1935)
Mr. Dynamite (Univ, 1935)
Lady Tubbs (Univ, 1935)
Mary Jane's Pa (FN, 1935)
Age of Indiscretion (MGM, 1935)
Pursuit (MGM, 1935)
Annapolis Farewell (Par, 1935)
Rose of the Rancho (Par, 1936)
The Longest Night (MGM, 1936)

When's Your Birthday? (RKO, 1937)
The Woman I Love (RKO, 1937)
Saturday's Heroes (RKO, 1937)
Dead End (UA, 1937)
That Certain Woman (WB, 1937)
Navy Blue and Gold (MGM, 1937)
Checkers (20th, 1937)
Of Human Hearts (MGM, 1938)
Fast Company (MGM, 1938)
Boys Town (MGM, 1938)
Stablemates (MGM, 1938)
Touchdown, Army! (Par, 1938)
While New York Sleeps (20th, 1938)
Love, Honor and Behave (WB, 1938)
Huckleberry Finn (MGM, 1939)

The Hardys Ride High (MGM, 1939)
Maisie (MGM, 1939)
The Boy Friend (20th, 1939)
News Is Made at Night (20th, 1939)
Here I Am a Stranger (20th, 1939)
Angels Wash Their Faces (WB, 1939)
The Flying Irishman (RKO, 1939)
Television Spy (Par, 1939)
The Llano Kid (Par, 1940)
Twenty-Mule Team (MGM, 1940)
Hidden Gold (Par, 1940)
Abe Lincoln in Illinois (RKO, 1940)
Young People (20th, 1940)
Rangers of Fortune (Par, 1940)
Viva Cisco Kid! (20th, 1940)

Gallant Sons (MGM, 1940)
The Monster and the Girl (Par, 1941)
Mr. District Attorney (Rep, 1941)
Western Union (20th, 1941)
The Parson of Panamint (Par, 1941)
Moon over Miami (20th, 1941)
Kiss the Boys Goodbye (Par, 1941)
Birth of the Blues (Par, 1941)
They Died with Their Boots On (WB, 1941)
To the Shores of Tripoli (20th, 1942)
The Remarkable Andrew (Par, 1942)
Woman of the Year (MGM, 1942)
Yankee Doodle Dandy (WB, 1942)
The Big Shot (WB, 1942)
Flight Lieutenant (Col, 1942)
Enemy Agents Meet Ellery Queen (Col, 1942)
Gentleman Jim (WB, 1942)

Frisco Lil (Univ, 1942)
Action in the North Atlantic (WB, 1943)
Guadalcanal Diary (20th, 1943)
Yanks Ahoy (UA, 1943)
Crash Dive (20th, 1943)
Mission to Moscow (WB, 1943)
Princess O'Rourke (WB, 1943)
Happy Land (20th, 1943)
The Falcon Out West (RKO, 1944)
Shadows in the Night (Col, 1944)
Henry Aldrich, Boy Scout (Par, 1944)
That's My Baby (Rep, 1944)
Here Come the Waves (Par, 1944)
The Story of Dr. Wassell (Par, 1944)
The Thin Man Goes Home (MGM, 1944)
God Is My Co-Pilot (WB, 1945)
Bewitched (MGM, 1945)
A Bell for Adano (20th, 1945)
You Came Along (Par, 1945)

Boys' Ranch (MGM, 1946)
The Courage of Lassie (MGM, 1946)
A Southern Yankee (MGM, 1948)
The File on Thelma Jordan (Par, 1949)
Beyond the Forest (WB, 1949)
Mr. 880 (20th, 1950)
The Jackie Robinson Story (EL, 1950)
Bright Victory (Univ, 1951)
As Young as You Feel (20th, 1951)
Little Egypt (Univ, 1951)
Untamed Frontier (Univ, 1952)
My Son John (Par, 1952)
Face to Face (RKO, 1952)
The Star (20th, 1953)
The Roar of the Crowd (AA, 1953)
Ten Wanted Men (Col, 1955)
The Rawhide Years (Univ, 1956)
Trapeze (UA, 1956)
The Ambassador's Daughter (UA, 1956)

GORDON WESTCOTT

In the 1930s.

Born November 6, 1903, St. George, Utah. Died October 30, 1935, Hollywood, California. Good-looking support player, mostly in Warner Bros.–First National offerings: *Enemies of the Law* (Blackie), *Voltaire* (the captain), *Fashions of 1934* (Harry Brent), *Fog over Frisco* (Joe Bellow), etc.

Gordon Westcott to Grace Bradley in *Two Fisted:* "I could make things a lot easier for you."

Films

Enemies of the Law (Regal, 1931)
Guilty as Hell (Par, 1932)
Devil and the Deep (Par, 1932)
Love Me Tonight (Par, 1932)
Heritage of the Desert (Par, 1932)
Crime of the Century (Par, 1933)
He Learned About Women (Par, 1933)
The Working Man (WB, 1933)
Lilly Turner (FN, 1933)
Private Detective 62 (WB, 1933)
Heroes for Sale (FN, 1933)
Voltaire (WB, 1933)

Heritage of the Desert (Par, 1933)
Footlight Parade (WB, 1933)
Convention City (FN, 1933)
The World Changes (FN, 1933)
Fashions of 1934 (FN, 1934)
Fog over Frisco (FN, 1934)
I've Got Your Number (WB, 1934)
Dark Hazard (FN, 1934)
Call It Luck (Fox, 1934)
Circus Clown (FN, 1934)
Registered Nurse (FN, 1934)
Six Day Bike Rider (FN, 1934)

The Case of the Howling Dog (WB, 1934)
Kansas City Princess (WB, 1934)
Murder in the Clouds (FN, 1934)
White Cockatoo (WB, 1935)
A Night at the Ritz (WB, 1935)
Go into Your Dance (FN, 1935)
Going Highbrow (WB, 1935)
Bright Lights (FN, 1935)
Front Page Woman (WB, 1935)
This Is the Life (Fox, 1935)
Two Fisted (Par, 1935)

HELEN WESTLEY
(Henrietta Manney)

Helen Westley and Constance Bennett in Moulin Rouge *(1934).*

Born March 28, 1875, Brooklyn, New York. Married John Westley (1900), child: one; separated (1912). Died December 12, 1942, Franklin, New Jersey. Stage and screen player who favored playing acidy matrons with a quick eye for "propriety": *Anne of Green Gables* (sharp-tongued Marilla Cuthbert), *Roberta* (Aunt Minnie, who owns the Parisian fashion-design business), *Show Boat* (henpecking Parthy Hawks), *Lillian Russell* (Grandma Leonard), Kay Kyser's *My Favorite Spy* (Aunt Jessie). Frequently on screen with Shirley Temple: *Dimples* (Mrs. Drew), *Stowaway* (Mrs. Hope), *Heidi* (Blind Anna), and *Rebecca of Sunnybrook Farm* (Aunt Mirande Wilkins).

> **Helen Westley** to Robert Kent in *Dimples:* "If you leave this house, you need never expect to come back to it, as long as I live."

Films

Moulin Rouge (UA, 1934)
The House of Rothschild (UA, 1934)
Death Takes a Holiday (Par, 1934)
Age of Innocence (RKO, 1934)
Anne of Green Gables (RKO, 1934)
Captain Hurricane (RKO, 1935)
Chasing Yesterday (RKO, 1935)
Roberta (RKO, 1935)
Splendor (UA, 1935)
The Melody Lingers On (UA, 1935)
Show Boat (Univ, 1936)
Half Angel (20th, 1936)
Dimples (20th, 1936)

Banjo on My Knee (20th, 1936)
Stowaway (20th, 1936)
Cafe Metropole (20th, 1937)
Heidi (20th, 1937)
Sing and Be Happy (20th, 1937)
I'll Take Romance (Col, 1937)
The Baroness and the Butler (20th, 1938)
Rebecca of Sunnybrook Farm (20th, 1938)
Alexander's Ragtime Band (20th, 1938)
Keep Smiling (20th, 1938)
She Married an Artist (Col, 1938)
Zaza (Par, 1939)
Wife, Husband and Friend (20th, 1939)

Lillian Russell (20th, 1940)
All This, and Heaven Too (WB, 1940)
The Captain Is a Lady (MGM, 1940)
Lady with Red Hair (WB, 1940)
Henry Aldrich for President (Par, 1941)
Adam Had Four Sons (Col, 1941)
Lady from Louisiana (Rep, 1941)
Sunny (RKO, 1941)
Million Dollar Baby (WB, 1941)
The Smiling Ghost (WB, 1941)
Bedtime Story (Col, 1941)
My Favorite Spy (RKO, 1942)

JESSE WHITE
(Jesse Wiedenfeld)

Jesse White and Ernie Kovacs in Sail a Crooked Ship *(1961).*

Born January 3, 1918, Buffalo, New York. Married Simmy Cohn (1942), children: two daughters. Pudgy cigar-chewing mug with a whiny voice. Often cast as a thug or pushy agent. TV series: "Private Secretary" and "The Ann Sothern Show."

> **Jesse White** to Joan O'Brien in *It's Only Money:* "Listen, Lester's my buddy. I don't want him killed . . . until I claim the reward."

Films

Kiss of Death (20th, 1947)
Texas, Brooklyn and Heaven (UA, 1948)
Harvey (Univ, 1950)
Death of a Salesman (Col, 1951)
Callaway Went Thataway (MGM, 1951)
Katie Did It (Univ, 1951)
Bedtime for Bonzo (Univ, 1951)
Francis Goes to the Races (Univ, 1951)
Million Dollar Mermaid (MGM, 1952)
The Girl in White (MGM, 1952)
Forever Female (Par, 1953)
Gunsmoke (Univ, 1953)
Champ for a Day (Rep, 1953)
Witness to Murder (UA, 1954)
Hell's Half Acre (Rep, 1954)
Not as a Stranger (UA, 1955)
The Girl Rush (Par, 1955)
The Bad Seed (WB, 1956)
Back from Eternity (RKO, 1956)
The Come On (AA, 1956)

He Laughed Last (Col, 1956)
Designing Woman (MGM, 1957)
God Is My Partner (20th, 1957)
Johnny Trouble (WB, 1957)
Marjorie Morningstar (WB, 1958)
County Music Holiday (Par, 1958)
The Rise and Fall of Legs Diamond (WB, 1960)
The Big Night (Par, 1960)
A Fever in the Blood (WB, 1961)
The Right Approach (20th, 1961)
The Tomboy and the Champ (Univ, 1961)
On the Double (Par, 1961)
Three Blondes in His Life (Cinema Associates, 1961)
Sail a Crooked Ship (Col, 1961)
It's Only Money (Par, 1962)
It's a Mad, Mad, Mad, Mad World (UA, 1963)
The Yellow Canary (20th, 1963)

Looking for Love (MGM, 1964)
A House Is Not a Home (Emb, 1964)
Pajama Party (AIP, 1964)
Dear Brigitte (20th, 1965)
The Ghost in the Invisible Bikini (AIP, 1966)
The Spirit Is Willing (Par, 1967)
The Reluctant Astronaut (Univ, 1967)
Bless the Beasts and the Children (Col, 1971)
The Brothers O'Toole (CVD, 1973)
Return to Campus (Harold Cornsweet, 1975)
Las Vegas Lady (Crown International, 1976)
New Girl in Town (New World, 1977)

DAME MAY WHITTY

With Lassie in Lassie Come Home *(1943).*

Born June 19, 1865, Liverpool, England. Married Ben Webster (1891), child: Margaret; widowed (1946). Died May 29, 1948, Beverly Hills, California. Consummate British and Broadway stage star who settled into a vital Hollywood career, mostly at MGM. Oscar-nominated for repeating her stage role of the wheelchair-bound Mrs. Bramson in *Night Must Fall* (but lost BSAAA to Alice Brady of *In Old Chicago*). Again Oscar-nominated for her lofty Lady Beldon in *Mrs. Miniver* (but lost BSAAA to Teresa Wright of *Mrs. Miniver*). Played the marvelous Miss Fray, the title figure of Alfred Hitchcock's *The Lady Vanishes*, and the loving elderly governess in *The White Cliffs of Dover*. *Gaslight* found her as the talkative rich neighbor of Ingrid Bergman. Was to play Walter Pidgeon's mother in *Julia Misbehaves* (1948) but became ill and died; replaced by Lucile Watson.

Dame May Whitty to John Sutton in *Thunder Birds:* "You're the last in your line, Peter—the last Stackhouse."

Films

Enoch Arden (Br, 1914)
The Little Minister (Br, 1915)
Colonel Newcome, the Perfect Gentleman (Br, 1920)
Night Must Fall (MGM, 1937)
Conquest (MGM, 1937)
The Thirteenth Chair (MGM, 1937)
I Met My Love Again (UA, 1938)
The Lady Vanishes (Br, 1938)
Raffles (UA, 1939)
A Bill of Divorcement (RKO, 1940)

Return to Yesterday (Br, 1940)
One Night in Lisbon (Par, 1941)
Suspicion (RKO, 1941)
Mrs. Miniver (MGM, 1942)
Thunder Birds (20th, 1942)
The Constant Nymph (WB, 1943)
Flesh and Fantasy (Univ, 1943)
Lassie Come Home (MGM, 1943)
Madame Curie (MGM, 1943)
Stage Door Canteen (UA, 1943)
Forever and a Day (RKO, 1943)

Slightly Dangerous (MGM, 1943)
Crash Dive (20th, 1943)
The White Cliffs of Dover (MGM, 1944)
Gaslight (MGM, 1944)
My Name Is Julia Ross (Col, 1945)
Devotion (WB, 1946)
This Time for Keeps (MGM, 1947)
Green Dolphin Street (MGM, 1947)
If Winter Comes (MGM, 1947)
Sign of the Ram (Col, 1948)
The Return of October (Col, 1948)

MARY WICKES
(Mary Isabelle Wickenhauser)

In the 1960s.

Born June 13, 1912, St. Louis, Missouri, Hawk-nosed, gangling actress who made a mini-career (Broadway, films, TV) of her sprinting Nurse Preen in *The Man Who Came to Dinner*. Again nursing—this time tyrannical matriarch Gladys Cooper—in *Now, Voyager* as astute Nurse Pickford. Gave full dimension to the flippant celluloid domestic: *June Bride, On Moonlight Bay, White Christmas*, etc. Was gossipy conventioneer Miss Fox in *Dear Heart* and rambunctious Sister Clarissa in both *The Trouble with Angels* and *Where Angels Go . . . Trouble Follows*. Has performed in a good deal of summer and winter stock. Played lead in *Mary Poppins* on "Studio One" TV in 1949; many commercials. TV series: "Make Room for Daddy," "Bonino," "Dennis the Menace" (as Miss Cathcart), "Mrs. G Goes to College," "Sigmund and the Sea Monsters," and "Doc" (as Nurse Beatrice Tully).

Mary Wickes to Betty Davis in *Now, Voyager:* "Pickford's my name—Dora, *not* Mary. I'm the nurse."

Films

The Man Who Came to Dinner (WB, 1941)
The Mayor of 44th Street (RKO, 1942)
Private Buckaroo (Univ, 1942)
Now, Voyager (WB, 1942)
Who Done It? (Univ, 1942)
Rhythm of the Islands (Univ, 1943)
Happy Land (20th, 1943)

My Kingdom for a Cook (Col, 1943)
How's About It? (Univ, 1943)
Higher and Higher (RKO, 1943)
The Decision of Christopher Blake (WB, 1944)
June Bride (WB, 1944)
Anna Lucasta (Col, 1949)
The Petty Girl (Col, 1950)

On Moonlight Bay (WB, 1951)
I'll See You in My Dreams (WB, 1951)
The Will Rogers Story (WB, 1952)
Young Man with Ideas (MGM, 1952)
By the Light of the Silvery Moon (WB, 1953)
The Actress (MGM, 1953)
Half a Hero (MGM, 1953)

Destry (Univ, 1954)
White Christmas (Par, 1954)
Good Morning, Miss Dove (20th, 1955)
Dance with Me, Henry (UA, 1956)
Don't Go Near the Water (MGM, 1957)
It Happened to Jane (Col, 1959)
Cimarron (MGM, 1960)

101 Dalmatians (BV, 1961) [voice only]
Sins of Rachel Cade (WB, 1961)
The Music Man (WB, 1962)
Fate Is the Hunter (20th, 1964)
Dear Heart (WB, 1964)
How to Murder Your Wife (UA, 1965)
The Trouble with Angels (Col, 1966)

Where Angels Go . . . Trouble Follows (Col, 1967)
The Spirit Is Willing (Par, 1967)
Napoleon and Samantha (BV, 1972)
Snowball Express (BV, 1972)

JEAN WILLES
(Jean Donahue)

With Ernest Borgnine in McHale's Navy *(1964).*

Usually the big and brassy prostitute: *The Revolt of Mamie Stover* (Gladys) and *These Thousand Hills* (Jen). Out to win Clark Gable in *The King and Four Queens* along with Barbara Nichols, Eleanor Parker, and Sara Shane.

Jean Willes to Lana Turner in *By Love Possessed:* "I'm here to get my rights."

Films

The Winner's Circle (20th, 1948)
Chinatown at Midnight (Col, 1949)
A Woman of Distinction (Col, 1950)
Revenue Agent (Col, 1950)
A Yank in Indo-China (Col, 1952)
Gobs and Gals (Rep, 1952)
Jungle Jim and the Forbidden Land (Col, 1952)
All Ashore (Col, 1953)
From Here to Eternity (Col, 1953)
Abbott and Costello Go to Mars (Univ, 1953)
Masterson of Kansas (Col, 1954)

Bowery to Bagdad (AA, 1954)
Five Against the House (Col, 1955)
Count Three and Pray (Col, 1955)
Bobby Ware Is Missing (AA, 1955)
Invasion of the Body Snatchers (AA, 1956)
The Lieutenant Wore Skirts (20th, 1956)
The Revolt of Mamie Stover (20th, 1956)
The King and Four Queens (UA, 1956)
The Man Who Turned to Stone (Col, 1957)
Hear Me Good (Par, 1957)
The Tijuana Story (Col, 1957)
Desire Under the Elms (Par, 1958)

No Time for Sergeants (WB, 1958)
These Thousand Hills (20th, 1959)
The FBI Story (WB, 1959)
Ocean's 11 (WB, 1960)
The Crowded Sky (WB, 1960)
By Love Possessed (UA, 1961)
Gun Street (UA, 1962)
Gypsy (WB, 1962)
McHale's Navy (Univ, 1964)
Cheyenne Social Club (National General, 1970)
Bite the Bullet (Col, 1975)

GUINN "BIG BOY" WILLIAMS

Guinn "Big Boy" Williams and David Landau in a publicity pose for Heritage of the Desert *(1932).*

Born April 26, 1899, Decatur, Texas. Married Dorothy _____ , child: Tyler. Died June 6, 1962, Hollywood, California. Sunny disposition, cloudy thought patterns. Big-boned actor (a would-be professional baseball player). Smiled his way through six decades of films. Made a long string of low-budget Westerns for Aywon distribution in the 1920s. Often a good-natured thug (*You and Me*) or serviceman (*The Marines Are Here*). Participated in some big-budgeted Westerns: *Dodge City* (Tex Baird), *Santa Fe Trail* (Tex Bell), Robert Taylor's *Billy the Kid* (Ed Bronson), *The Alamo* (Lieutenant Finn), etc. TV series: "Circus Boy."

> **Guinn "Big Boy" Williams** to John Garfield in *Castle on the Hudson:* "I knew a guy who spent six months diggin' his way out of here, and came up in the warden's office."

Films

Almost a Husband (G, 1919)
Jubilo (G, 1919)
The Jack Rider (Aywon, 1921)
The Vengeance Trail (Aywon, 1921)
Western Firebrands (Aywon, 1921)
Blaze Away (Aywon, 1922)
The Freshie (Frederick Herbst Productions, 1922)
Trail of Hate (Frederick Herbst Productions, 1922)
Across the Border (Aywon, 1922)
The Cowboy King (Aywon, 1922)
Rounding Up the Law (Aywon, 1922)
Cyclone Jones (Aywon, 1923)
End of the Rope (Aywon, 1923)
$1,000 Reward (Aywon, 1923)
Riders at Night (Aywon, 1923)

The Avenger (Aywon, 1924)
The Eagle's Claw (Aywon, 1924)
Black Cyclone (Pathé, 1925)
Bad Man from Bodie (Aywon, 1925)
Big Stunt (Aywon, 1925)
Courage of Wolfheart (Aywon, 1925)
Fangs of Wolfheart (Aywon, 1925)
Red Blood and Blue (Aywon, 1925)
Riders of the Sand Storm (Aywon, 1925)
Rose of the Desert (Aywon, 1925)
Sporting West (Aywon, 1925)
Whistling Jim (Aywon, 1925)
Wolfheart's Revenge (Aywon, 1925)
Brown of Harvard (MGM, 1926)
The Desert's Toll (MGM, 1926)
Babe Comes Home (FN, 1927)
The College Widow (WB, 1927)

The Down Grade (Lumas, 1927)
Quarantined Rivals (Lumas, 1927)
Backstage (Tif, 1927)
Lightning (Tif, 1927)
Slide, Kelly, Slide (MGM, 1927)
Snowbound (Tif, 1927)
The Woman Who Did Not Care (Lumas, 1927)
Burning Daylight (FN, 1928)
Vamping Venus (FN, 1928)
Ladies' Night in a Turkish Bath (FN, 1928)
My Man (WB, 1928)
Lucky Star (Fox, 1928)
Noah's Ark (WB, 1929)
Forward Pass (FN, 1929)
From Headquarters (WB, 1929)

The Big Fight (WW, 1930)
The Bad Man (FN, 1930)
College Lovers (FN, 1930)
Liliom (Fox, 1930)
City Girl (Fox, 1930)
The Great Meadow (MGM, 1931)
The Phantom (Artclass, 1931)
Bachelor Father (MGM, 1931)
Ladies of the Jury (RKO, 1932)
Polly of the Circus (MGM, 1932)
Drifting Souls (Tower, 1932)
70,000 Witnesses (Par, 1932)
You Said a Mouthful (FN, 1932)
The Devil Is Driving (Par, 1932)
Heritage of the Desert (Par, 1932)
The Phantom Broadcast (Mon, 1933)
Man of the Forest (Par, 1933)
Mystery Squadron (Mascot serial, 1933)
College Coach (WB, 1933)
Laughing at Life (Mascot, 1933)
Rafter Romance (RKO, 1934)
Palooka (UA, 1934)
Half a Sinner (Univ, 1934)
Our Daily Bread (UA, 1934)
Flirtation Walk (WB, 1934)
Romance in the Rain (Univ, 1934)
Thunder over Texas (Beacon, 1934)
Here Comes the Navy (WB, 1934)
The Cheaters (Bert Lubin, 1934)
Silver Streak (RKO, 1934)
One in a Million (Invincible, 1935)
Cowboy Holiday (Beacon, 1935)
Private Worlds (Par, 1935)
The Glass Key (Par, 1935)
Village Tale (RKO, 1935)
Society Fever (Chesterfield, 1935)
Gun Play (FD, 1935)
Powdersmoke Range (RKO, 1935)
Danger Trail (FD, 1935)
Big Boy Rides Again (FD, 1935)
The Law of .45s (FD, 1935)
The Littlest Rebel (Fox, 1935)
Miss Pacific Fleet (WB, 1935)
Muss 'em Up (RKO, 1936)
Grand Jury (RKO, 1936)
The Big Game (RKO, 1936)
Kelly the Second (MGM, 1936)
End of the Trail (Col, 1936)

North of Nome (Col, 1936)
Career Woman (20th, 1936)
The Vigilantes Are Coming (Rep serial, 1936)
You Only Live Once (UA, 1937)
Girls Can Play (Col, 1937)
A Star Is Born (UA, 1937)
Don't Tell the Wife (RKO, 1937)
The Singing Marine (WB, 1937)
Dangerous Holiday (Rep, 1937)
She's No Lady (Par, 1937)
Big City (MGM, 1937)
My Dear Miss Aldrich (MGM, 1937)
Wise Girl (RKO, 1937)
Bad Man from Brimstone (MGM, 1937)
Everybody's Doing It (RKO, 1938)
Army Girl (Rep, 1938)
Down in Arkansaw (Rep, 1938)
You and Me (Par, 1938)
Professor Beware (Par, 1938)
Hold That Co-ed (20th, 1938)
I Demand Payment (Imperial, 1938)
The Marines Are Here (Mon, 1938)
Flying Fists (PRC, 1938)
Crashin' Through Danger (Excelsior, 1938)
Pardon Our Nerve (20th, 1939)
Dodge City (WB, 1939)
6,000 Enemies (MGM, 1939)
Blackmail (MGM, 1939)
Fugitive at Large (Col, 1939)
Street of Missing Men (Rep, 1939)
Mutiny on the Blackhawk (Univ, 1939)
Legion of Lost Flyers (Univ, 1939)
Bad Lands (RKO, 1939)
The Fighting 69th, (WB, 1940)
Castle on the Hudson (WB, 1940)
Virginia City (WB, 1940)
Money and the Woman (WB, 1940)
Santa Fe Trail (WB, 1940)
Alias the Deacon (Univ, 1940)
Dulcy (MGM, 1940)
Wagons Westward (Rep, 1940)
Six Lessons from Madame La Zonga (Univ, 1941)
Country Fair (Rep, 1941)
Billy the Kid (MGM, 1941)
You'll Never Get Rich (Col, 1941)

Swamp Water (20th, 1941)
The Bugle Sounds (MGM, 1941)
Riders of Death Valley (Univ serial, 1941)
Mr. Wise Guy (Mon, 1942)
Silver Queen (UA, 1942)
American Empire (UA, 1942)
Between Us Girls (Univ, 1942)
Lure of the Islands (Mon, 1942)
The Desperadoes (Col, 1943)
Minesweeper (Par, 1943)
Buckskin Frontier (UA, 1943)
Hands Across the Border (Rep, 1943)
Belle of the Yukon (RKO, 1944)
Thirty Seconds over Tokyo (WB, 1944)
Swing in the Saddle (Col, 1944)
Nevada (RKO, 1944)
The Cowboy and the Senorita (Rep, 1944)
The Cowboy Canteen (Col, 1944)
The Man Who Walked Alone (PRC, 1945)
Cowboy Blues (Col, 1946)
Singing on the Trail (Col, 1946)
Throw a Saddle on a Star (Col, 1946)
That Texas Jamboree (Col, 1946)
King of the Wild Horses (Col, 1947)
Over the Santa Fe Trail (Col, 1947)
Singin' in the Corn (Col, 1947)
Road to the Big House (Screen Guild, 1947)
Station West (RKO, 1948)
Bad Men of Tombstone (AA, 1948)
Brimstone (Rep, 1949)
Hoedown (Col, 1950)
Rocky Mountain (WB, 1950)
Al Jennings of Oklahoma (Col, 1951)
Man in the Saddle (Col, 1951)
Springfield Rifle (WB, 1952)
Hangman's Knot (Col, 1952)
Southwest Passage (UA, 1954)
Outlaw's Daughter (20th, 1954)
Hidden Guns (Rep, 1956)
The Man from Del Rio (UA, 1956)
The Hired Gun (MGM, 1957)
The Alamo (UA, 1960)
The Comancheros (20th, 1961)

CHILL WILLS

Chill Wills, Charles Watts, Phil Harris, and James Garner in The Wheeler Dealers *(1963).*

Born July 18, 1903, Seagoville, Texas. Married 1) Betty Chappelle, children: Jill, Will; widowed (1971); 2) Novadeen Googe (1973); divorced (1974). Tent show, vaudeville, and stage performer from early childhood. Made screen debut with his singing group (Chill Wills & His Avalon Boys) in *Hopalong Cassidy* entry: *Bar 20 Rides Again*. Mostly in Westerns, but has been in period pictures: Mr. Neely, the wagon driver (*Meet Me in St. Louis*); domestic comedies: Fred (*Family Honeymoon*); drama: Captain Chatham (*The Saxon Charm*). Deep, rough-sounding voice—was most exploited in the *Francis the Talking Mule* series. Appeared in the first entry as General Kaye and supplied the animal's off-camera voice. Heard in five of the six remaining segments (Paul Frees became the voice for the final one). Lately has taken to recording LP albums. Oscar-nominated for his beekeeper in *The Alamo* (but lost BSAAA to Peter Ustinov of *Spartacus*). TV series: "Frontier Circus."

Chill Wills in *Honky Tonk:* "Always wondered what they drew in a drawing room—pictures or guns?"

Films

Bar 20 Rides Again (Par, 1935)
The Call of the Prairie (Par, 1936)
Way Out West (MGM, 1936)
Lawless Valley (RKO, 1938)
Arizona Legion (RKO, 1939)
Sorority House (RKO, 1939)
Racketeers of the Range (RKO, 1939)
Timber Stampede (RKO, 1939)
Allegheny Uprising (RKO, 1939)
Trouble in Sundown (RKO, 1939)
Boom Town (MGM, 1940)
Sky Murder (MGM, 1940)
The Westerner (UA, 1940)

Tugboat Annie Sails Again (WB, 1940)
Western Union (20th, 1941)
The Bad Man (MGM, 1941)
Billy the Kid (MGM, 1941)
Belle Starr (20th, 1941)
Honky Tonk (MGM, 1941)
The Bugle Sounds (MGM, 1941)
Tarzan's New York Adventure (MGM, 1942)
Her Cardboard Lover (MGM, 1942)
Apache Trail (MGM, 1942)
The Omaha Trail (MGM, 1942)
Stand By for Action (MGM, 1942)

Best Foot Forward (MGM, 1943)
A Stranger in Town (MGM, 1943)
See Here, Private Hargrove (MGM, 1944)
Barbary Coast Gent (MGM, 1944)
Meet Me in St. Louis (MGM, 1944)
Sunday Dinner for a Soldier (20th, 1944)
I'll Be Seeing You (UA, 1944)
Leave Her to Heaven (20th, 1945)
What Next, Corporal Hargrove? (MGM, 1945)
Gallant Bess (MGM, 1946)
The Harvey Girls (MGM, 1946)
The Yearling (MGM, 1946)

Heartaches (PRC, 1947)
That Wonderful Urge (20th, 1948)
The Sainted Sisters (Par, 1948)
Family Honeymoon (Univ, 1948)
The Saxon Charm (Univ, 1948)
Raw Deal (EL, 1948)
Northwest Stampede (EL, 1948)
Loaded Pistols (Col, 1949)
Tulsa (EL, 1949)
Red Canyon (Univ, 1949)
Francis (Univ, 1949) [animal's voice also]
Rio Grande (Rep, 1950)
Rock Island Trail (Rep, 1950)
High Lonesome (EL, 1950)
The Sundowners (EL, 1950)
Oh! Susannah (Rep, 1951)
Cattle Drive (Univ, 1951)
The Sea Hornet (Rep, 1951)
Francis Goes to the Races (Univ, 1951) [voice only]
Bronco Buster (Univ, 1952)

Ride the Man Down (Rep, 1952)
Francis Goes to West Point (Univ, 1952) [voice only]
Small Town Girl (MGM, 1953)
The City That Never Sleeps (Rep, 1953)
The Man from the Alamo (Univ, 1953)
Francis Covers the Big Town (Univ, 1953) [voice only]
Tumbleweed (Univ, 1954)
Francis Joins the WACS (Univ, 1954) [voice only]
Ricochet Romance (Univ, 1954)
Hell's Outpost (Rep, 1955)
Timberjack (Rep, 1955)
Francis in the Navy (Univ, 1955) [voice only]
Giant (WB, 1956)
Santiago (WB, 1956)
Francis in the Haunted House (Univ, 1956) [voice only]
Gun for a Coward (Univ, 1957)
Gun Glory (MGM, 1957)

From Hell to Texas (20th, 1958)
The Sad Horse (20th, 1959)
The Alamo (UA, 1960)
Gold of the Seven Saints (WB, 1961)
Where the Boys Are (MGM, 1961)
The Deadly Companions (Pathe-American, 1961)
The Little Shepherd of Kingdom Come (20th, 1961)
Young Guns of Texas (20th, 1962)
The Wheeler Dealers (MGM, 1963)
McLintock! (UA, 1963)
The Cardinal (Col, 1963)
The Rounders (MGM, 1965)
Fireball 500 (AIP, 1966)
The Liberation of L. B. Jones (Col, 1970)
The Steagle (Avco Emb, 1971)
Pat Garrett & Billy the Kid (MGM, 1973)
Guns of a Stranger (Univ, 1973)
Mr. Billion (20th, 1977)
Poco (Cinema Shares, 1977)

CHARLES WINNINGER

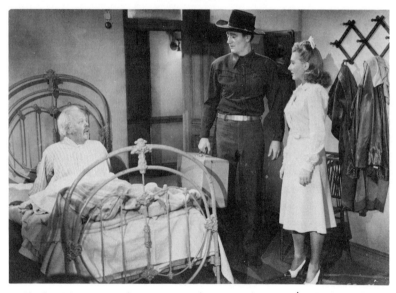

Charles Winninger, John Wayne, and Jean Arthur in A Lady Takes a Chance (1943).

Born May 26, 1884, Athens, Wisconsin. Married Blanche Ring; divorced. Died January 27, 1969, Palm Springs, California. Chubby, convivial, round-faced ex-vaudevillian and stage star who did two-reeler slapstick comedies in the mid-1910s. Had a few character roles in mid-1920s films, but gave his finest performance in talkies as Captain Andy in Irene Dunne's *Show Boat*. Played the errant but lovable dad in Deanna Durbin's *Three Smart Girls* and *Three Smart Girls Grow Up*, the drunken Wash Dimsdale in Jimmy Stewart's *Destry Rides Again*, and Mickey Rooney's vaudevillian dad in *Babes in Arms* (a draw as to which actor spread more blarney). Reinterpreted Will Rogers' old role of Judge William Priest in John Ford's *The Sun Shines Bright*. TV series: "The Charles Farrell Show."

Charles Winninger to Loretta Young in *Cafe Metropole:*
"Yes, I'm an American 'Babbitt' who loves his daughter,
and doesn't want to see you get hurt."

Films

Pied Piper Malone (Par, 1924)
The Canadian (Par, 1926)
Summer Bachelors (Fox, 1926)
Soups to Nuts (Fox, 1930)
Bad Sister (Univ, 1931)
Night Nurse (WB, 1931)
Flying High (MGM, 1931)
God's Gift to Women (WB, 1931)
Fighting Caravans (Par, 1931)
Gun Smoke (Par, 1931)
Children of Dreams (WB, 1931)
The Sin of Madelon Claudet (MGM, 1931)
Husband's Holiday (Par, 1931)
Social Register (Col, 1934)
Show Boat (Univ, 1936)
White Fang (Fox, 1936)
Three Smart Girls (Univ, 1937)
You're a Sweetheart (Univ, 1937)
Woman Chases Man (UA, 1937)
Nothing Sacred (UA, 1937)

Cafe Metropole (20th, 1937)
You Can't Have Everything (20th, 1937)
The Go-Getter (WB, 1937)
Every Day's a Holiday (Par, 1937)
Goodbye Broadway (Univ, 1938)
Hard to Get (WB, 1938)
Three Smart Girls Grow Up (Univ, 1939)
Destry Rides Again (Univ, 1939)
Babes in Arms (MGM, 1939)
Barricade (20th, 1939)
If I Had My Way (Univ, 1940)
My Love Came Back (WB, 1940)
Beyond Tomorrow (RKO, 1940)
Little Nellie Kelly (MGM, 1940)
When Ladies Meet (MGM, 1941)
Ziegfeld Girl (MGM, 1941)
The Get-Away (MGM, 1941)
My Life with Caroline (RKO, 1941)
Pot o' Gold (UA, 1941)
Friendly Enemies (UA, 1942)
Coney Island (20th, 1943)

A Lady Takes a Chance (RKO, 1943)
Flesh and Fantasy (Univ, 1943)
Hers to Hold (Univ, 1943)
Broadway Rhythm (MGM, 1944)
Belle of the Yukon (RKO, 1944)
Sunday Dinner for a Soldier (20th, 1944)
She Wouldn't Say Yes (Col, 1945)
State Fair (20th, 1945)
Lover Come Back (Univ, 1946)
Living in a Big Way (MGM, 1947)
Something in the Wind (Univ, 1947)
The Inside Story (Rep, 1948)
Give My Regards to Broadway (20th, 1948)
Father Is a Bachelor (Col, 1950)
The Sun Shines Bright (Rep, 1953)
Torpedo Alley (AA, 1953)
A Perilous Journey (Rep, 1953)
Champ for a Day (Rep, 1953)
Las Vegas Shakedown (AA, 1955)
Raymie (AA, 1960)

ROLAND WINTERS

Roland Winters and James Garner in Cash McCall *(1960).*

Born November 22, 1904, Boston, Massachusetts. Married Ada Rowe (1930). Stocky stage, radio, and TV performer who was the last actor to play Charlie Chan in feature films (from *The Chinese Ring* to *Sky Dragon*). Very efficient as the authoritarian (*Blue Hawaii*—keeping wife Angela Lansbury and son Elvis Presley under "control"). TV series: "Doorway to Danger," "Meet Millie," and "The Smothers Brothers Show."

Roland Winters to Nils Asther in *The Feathered Serpent:* "Very difficult to estimate size of the well by size of the bucket."

Films

13 Rue Madeleine (20th, 1946)
The Chinese Ring (Mon, 1947)
The Red Hornet (Mon, 1947)
The Return of October (Col, 1948)
Mystery of the Golden Eye (Mon, 1948)
Cry of the City (20th, 1948)
The Feathered Serpent (Mon, 1948)
Kidnapped (Mon, 1948)
Docks of New Orleans (Mon, 1948)
The Shanghai Chest (Mon, 1948)
Once More, My Darling (Univ, 1949)
Abbott and Costello Meet the Killer, Boris Karloff (Univ, 1949)
Tuna Clipper (Mon, 1949)

Sky Dragon (Mon, 1949)
A Dangerous Profession (RKO, 1949)
Guilty of Treason (EL, 1949)
Malaya (MGM, 1949)
The West Point Story (WB, 1950)
Captain Carey, U.S.A. (Par, 1950)
Convicted (Col, 1950)
Killer Shark (Mon, 1950)
To Please a Lady (MGM, 1950)
Between Midnight and Dawn (Col, 1950)
Follow the Sun (20th, 1951)
Inside Straight (MGM, 1951)
Raton Pass (WB, 1951)
Sierra Passage (Mon, 1951)

She's Working Her Way Through College (WB, 1952)
So Big (WB, 1953)
Bigger Than Life (20th, 1956)
Jet Pilot (Univ, 1957)
Top Secret Affair (WB, 1957)
Never Steal Anything Small (Univ, 1959)
Cash McCall (WB, 1960)
Everything's Ducky (Col, 1961)
Blue Hawaii (Par, 1961)
Follow That Dream (UA, 1962)
Loving (Col, 1970)

JOSEPH WISEMAN

In Dr. No (1963) (at right).

Born May 15, 1919, Montreal, Quebec, Canada. Married Nell Kinard (1943), children: son, daughter. Lean, mannered actor: *Detective Story* (arrested crook Charles Gennini), *Viva Zapata!* (Fernando), *The Silver Chalice* (Mijamin), *Dr. No* (the title role, combating Sean Connery's James Bond), *The Valachi Papers* (gangland figure Salvatore Maranzano), *The Apprenticeship of Duddy Kravitz* (Uncle Benjy), etc.

Joseph Wiseman to Denholm Elliott and Harry Andrews
in *The Night They Raided Minsky's:* "You speak with *the fist of authority,* gentlemen. But you don't know your *fingers.*"

Films

With These Hands (Classic Pictures, 1950)
Detective Story (Par, 1951)
Viva Zapata! (20th, 1952)
Les Miserables (20th, 1952)
Champ for a Day (Rep, 1953)
The Silver Chalice (WB, 1954)
The Prodigal (MGM, 1955)
Mella (documentary, 1955) [narrator]
Three Brave Men (20th, 1957)

The Garment Jungle (Col, 1957)
Eliahu (documentary, 1957) [narrator]
The Unforgiven (UA, 1960)
The Happy Thieves (UA, 1962)
Dr. No (UA, 1963)
Bye, Bye Braverman (WB–7 Arts, 1968)
The Night They Raided Minsky's (UA, 1968)
The Counterfeit Killer (Univ, 1968)

Stiletto (Avco Emb, 1969)
Lawman (UA, 1971)
The Valachi Papers (Col, 1972)
The Apprenticeship of Duddy Kravitz (Par, 1974)
Journey into Fear [a.k.a. Burn-Out] (A. Stirling Gold, 1975)
The Betsy (AA, 1978)
Homage to Chagall (Canadian, 1978) [documentary narrator]

GRANT WITHERS

In the 1950s.

Born January 17, 1904, Pueblo, Colorado. Married 1) Inez _____; divorced; 2) Loretta Young (1930); divorced (1931); 3) Gladys Joyce Walsh (1933); divorced; 4) Shirley Paschal; divorced; 5) Estelita Rodriguez (1953). Died March 27, 1959, Hollywood, California. Ex-newspaper reporter who used his handsomeness to advantage on camera: W. C. Fields' *Tillie's Punctured Romance* (the boy trapezist), *Sinner's Holiday* (the barker), *Too Young to Marry* (with ex-wife Loretta Young). Did best in serials of mid-1930s: *The Red Rider* (Buck Jones' pal Silent Slade), *Jungle Jim* (the lead), etc. When looks went, accepted small roles—mostly Westerns. Later committed suicide.

Grant Withers to Randolph Scott in *Gunfighters:* "Start driftin'."

Films

The Gentle Cyclone (Fox, 1926)
College (UA, 1927)
In a Moment of Temptation (FBO, 1927)
The Final Extra (Lumas, 1927)
Upstream (Fox, 1927)
Bringing Up Father (MGM, 1928)
Golden Shackles (Peerless, 1928)
Tillie's Punctured Romance (Par, 1928)
The Road to Ruin (True Life Photoplays, 1928)
Greyhound Limited (WB, 1929)
Tiger Rose (WB, 1929)
Madonna of Avenue A (WB, 1929)
The Show of Shows (WB, 1929)
Saturday's Children (FN, 1929)
The Time, the Place and the Girl (WB, 1929)
In the Headlines (WB, 1929)
Hearts in Exile (WB, 1929)
So Long Letty (WB, 1929)
Sinner's Holiday (WB, 1930)
Soldiers and Women (Col, 1930)
Back Pay (FN, 1930)

Scarlet Pages (FN, 1930)
The Other Tomorrow (FN, 1930)
The Second Floor Mystery (WB, 1930)
Dancing Sweeties (WB, 1930)
Other Men's Women (WB, 1931)
Too Young to Marry (WB, 1931)
Swanee River (WW, 1931)
First Aid (WW, 1931)
Red-Haired Alibi (Tower, 1932)
Gambling Sex (Freuler Films, 1932)
Secrets of Wu Sin (Chesterfield, 1932)
The Red River (Univ serial, 1934)
Tailspin Tommy (Univ serial, 1934)
Waterfront Lady (Rep, 1935)
Storm over the Andes (Univ, 1935)
Rip Roaring Riley (Puritan, 1935)
Fighting Marines (Mascot serial, 1935)
Hold 'em Yale (Par, 1935)
Goin' to Town (Par, 1935)
Ship Cafe (Par, 1935)
Vally of Wanted Men (Conn Pictures, 1935)
Society Fever (Chesterfield, 1935)

Skybound (Puritan, 1935)
Border Flight (Par, 1936)
The Sky Parade (Par, 1936)
Lady Be Careful (Par, 1936)
Arizona Raiders (Par, 1936)
Let's Sing Again (RKO, 1936)
Jungle Jim (Univ serial, 1937)
Paradise Express (Rep, 1937)
Bill Cracks Down (Rep, 1937)
Radio Patrol (Univ serial, 1937)
Hollywood Roundup (Col, 1937)
Secret of Treasure Island (Col serial, 1938)
Three Loves Has Nancy (MGM, 1938)
Touchdown, Army! (Par, 1938)
Mr. Wong, Detective (Mon, 1938)
Telephone Operator (Mon, 1938)
Held for Ransom (GN, 1938)
Irish Luck (Mon, 1939)
Navy Secrets (Mon, 1939)
Boys' Reformatory (Mon, 1939)
Mr. Wong in Chinatown (Mon, 1939)
Mutiny in the Big House (Mon, 1939)

Mystery of Mr. Wong (Mon, 1939)
Daughter of the Tong (Times Pictures, 1939)
The Fatal Hour (Mon, 1940)
Son of the Navy (Mon, 1940)
On the Spot (Mon, 1940)
Tomboy (Mon, 1940)
Doomed to Die (Mon, 1940)
Phantom of Chinatown (Mon, 1940)
Men Against the Sky (RKO, 1940)
Mexican Spitfire Out West (RKO, 1940)
Let's Make Music (RKO, 1941)
Country Fair (Rep, 1941)
Billy the Kid (MGM, 1941)
You'll Never Get Rich (Col, 1941)
Swamp Water (20th, 1941)
The Bugle Sounds (MGM, 1941)
The Get-Away (MGM, 1941)
Parachute Battalion (RKO, 1941)
The Masked Rider (Univ, 1941)
Northwest Rangers (MGM, 1942)
Apache Trail (MGM, 1942)
Between Us Girls (Univ, 1942)
Woman of the Year (MGM, 1942)
Lure of the Islands (Mon, 1942)
Butch Minds the Baby (Univ, 1942)
Tennessee Johnson (MGM, 1942)
In Old Oklahoma [a.k.a. *War of the Wildcats*] (Rep, 1943)
A Lady Takes a Chance (RKO, 1943)
Gildersleeve's Bad Day (RKO, 1943)
Petticoat Larceny (RKO, 1943)
No Time for Love (Par, 1943)
Silent Partner (Rep, 1944)
The Yellow Rose of Texas (Rep, 1944)
The Girl Who Dared (Rep, 1944)
Goodnight Sweetheart (Rep, 1944)
The Cowboy and the Senorita (Rep, 1944)
Cowboy Canteen (Col, 1944)
The Fighting Seabees (Rep, 1944)

Road to Alcatraz (Rep, 1945)
China's Little Devils (Mon, 1945)
Dakota (Rep, 1945)
Bells of Rosarita (Rep, 1945)
The Vampire's Ghost (Rep, 1945)
Utah (Rep, 1945)
Bring On the Girls (Par, 1945)
Dangerous Partners (MGM, 1945)
In Old Sacramento (Rep, 1946)
My Darling Clementine (20th, 1946)
Affairs of Geraldine (Rep, 1946)
Throw a Saddle on a Star (Col, 1946)
Singing on the Trail (Col, 1946)
Cowboy Blues (Col, 1946)
Singin' in the Corn (Col, 1946)
The Ghost Goes Wild (Rep, 1947)
Gunfighters (Col, 1947)
The Trespasser (Rep, 1947)
Wyoming (Rep, 1947)
Blackmail (Rep, 1947)
Tycoon (RKO, 1947)
King of the Wild Horses (Col, 1947)
Over the Santa Fe Trail (Col, 1947)
Bad Men of Tombstone (Mon, 1948)
Station West (RKO, 1948)
Wake of the Red Witch (Rep, 1948)
Fort Apache (RKO, 1948)
Old Los Angeles (Rep, 1948)
The Fighting Kentuckian (Rep, 1948)
Gallant Legion (Rep, 1948)
Daredevils of the Clouds (Rep, 1948)
Sons of Adventures (Rep, 1948)
Angel in Exile (Rep, 1948)
Night Time in Nevada (Rep, 1948)
The Plunderers (Rep, 1948)
Homicide for Three (Rep, 1948)
Brimstone (Rep, 1949)
The Last Bandit (Rep, 1949)
Duke of Chicago (Rep, 1949)
Hellfire (Rep, 1949)

Tripoli (Par, 1950)
Rock Island Trail (Rep, 1950)
Bells of Coronado (Rep, 1950)
Trigger, Jr. (Rep, 1950)
The Savage Horde (Rep, 1950)
Rio Grande (Rep, 1950)
Hit Parade of 1951 (Rep, 1950)
Hoedown (Col, 1950)
Spoilers of the Plains (Rep, 1951)
The Sea Hornet (Rep, 1951)
Million Dollar Pursuit (Rep, 1951)
Utah Wagon Train (Rep, 1951)
Man in the Saddle (Col, 1951)
Al Jennings of Oklahoma (Col, 1951)
Hoodlum Empire (Rep, 1952)
Captive of Billy the Kid (Rep, 1952)
Woman of the North Country (Rep, 1952)
Oklahoma Annie (Rep, 1952)
Leadville Gunslinger (Rep, 1952)
Tropical Heat Wave (Rep, 1952)
Springfield Rifle (WB, 1952)
Hangman's Knot (Col, 1952)
Fair Wind to Java (Rep, 1953)
Champ for a Day (Rep, 1953)
The Sun Shines Bright (Rep, 1953)
Iron Mountain Trail (Rep, 1953)
Massacre Canyon (Col, 1954)
Southwest Passage (UA, 1954)
The Outlaw's Daughter (20th, 1954)
Run for Cover (Par, 1955)
Lady Godiva (Univ, 1955)
The White Squaw (Col, 1956)
Hidden Guns (Rep, 1956)
The Man from Del Rio (UA, 1956)
Hell's Crossroads (Rep, 1957)
The Last Stagecoach West (Rep, 1957)
The Hired Gun (MGM, 1957)
I, Mobster (20th, 1958)

JOHN WRAY
(John Malloy)

Edward G. Robinson and John Wray in Blackmail *(1939).*

Born February 13, 1888, Philadelphia, Pennsylvania. Married Florence Miller. Died June 5, 1940, Los Angeles, California. Dressed up gangster melodramas during his screen decade: *Quick Millions* (Marguerite Churchill's brother), *I Am a Fugitive from a Chain Gang* (Nordine), *The Whole Town's Talking* (one of Edward G. Robinson's henchmen, along with Joe Sawyer), *You Only Live Once* (warden), *Blackmail* (Diggs), etc.

John Wray to Edward G. Robinson in *The Whole Town's Talking:* "I tell you, boss, this town's gettin' too hot for us."

Films

The Czar of Broadway (Univ, 1930)
New York Nights (UA, 1930)
All Quiet on the Western Front (Univ, 1930)
Quick Millions (Fox, 1931)
Silence (Par, 1931)
Safe in Hell (FN, 1931)
I Am a Fugitive from a Chain Gang (WB, 1932)
High Pressure (WB, 1932)
The Death Kiss (WB, 1932)
The Woman from Monte Carlo (FN, 1932)
The Miracle Man (Par, 1932)
The Mouthpiece (WB, 1932)
The Rich Are Always with Us (FN, 1932)
Miss Pinkerton (FN, 1932)
Doctor X (FN, 1932)
Central Park (FN, 1932)
The Match King (FN, 1932)
After Tonight (RKO, 1933)
Lone Cowboy (Par, 1934)
The Captain Hates the Sea (Col, 1934)
Bombay Mail (Univ, 1934)
The Big Shakedown (FN, 1934)
The Crosby Case (Univ, 1934)

Most Precious Thing in Life (Col, 1934)
The Love Captive (Univ, 1934)
The Defense Rests (Col, 1934)
Fifteen Wives (Invincible, 1934)
Embarrassing Moments (Univ, 1934)
I'll Fix It (Col, 1934)
Green Eyes (Chesterfield, 1934)
I Am a Thief (WB, 1934)
The Great Hotel Murder (Fox, 1935)
The Whole Town's Talking (Col, 1935)
Ladies Love Danger (Fox, 1935)
Stranded (WB, 1935)
Men Without Names (Par, 1935)
Atlantic Adventure (Col, 1935)
Bad Boy (Fox, 1935)
Frisco Kid (WB, 1935)
Mr. Deeds Goes to Town (Col, 1936)
Poor Little Rich Girl (20th, 1936)
A Son Comes Home (Par, 1936)
Sworn Enemy (MGM, 1936)
We Who Are About to Die (RKO, 1936)
The President's Mystery (Rep, 1936)
Valiant Is the Word for Carrie (Par, 1936)
You Only Live Once (UA, 1937)
Circus Girl (Rep, 1937)

A Man Betrayed (Rep, 1937)
Outcast (Par, 1937)
The Devil Is Driving (Col, 1937)
On Such a Night (Par, 1937)
House of Mystery (Col, 1938)
Making the Headlines (Col, 1938)
The Black Doll (Univ, 1938)
Gangs of New York (Rep, 1938)
Crime Takes a Holiday (Col, 1938)
The Tenth Avenue Kid (Rep, 1938)
Spawn of the North (Par, 1938)
Professor Beware (Par, 1938)
A Man to Remember (RKO, 1938)
Risky Business (Univ, 1939)
Pacific Liner (RKO, 1939)
Golden Boy (Col, 1939)
Each Dawn I Die (WB, 1939)
The Amazing Mr. Williams (Col, 1939)
The Cat and the Canary (Par, 1939)
Smuggled Cargo (Rep, 1939)
Blackmail (MGM, 1939)
Swiss Family Robinson (RKO, 1940)
The Man from Dakota (MGM, 1940)
Remember the Night (Par, 1940)

WILL WRIGHT

Robert Walker and Will Wright in Vengeance Valley *(1951).*

Born March 26, 1891, San Francisco, California. Died June 19, 1962, Hollywood, California. Tall, with pointed features and a mournful look—frequently the rural type. Quite effective as Dad Newell, the apartment-house detective in *The Blue Dahlia*.

Will Wright to Hugh Beaumont in *The Blue Dahlia:* "I ain't the wristwatch type, y' know."

Films

China Clipper (FN, 1936)
Silver on the Sage (Par, 1939)
Blondie Plays Cupid (Col, 1940)
Honky Tonk (MGM, 1941)
The Richest Man in Town (Col, 1941)
Rookies on Parade (Rep, 1941)
World Premiere (20th, 1941)
True to the Army (Par, 1942)
Parachute Nurse (Col, 1942)
The Postman Didn't Ring (20th, 1942)
Wildcat (Par, 1942)
Shut My Big Mouth (Col, 1942)
Tennessee Johnson (MGM, 1942)
Lucky Legs (Col, 1942)
In Old Oklahoma [a.k.a. War of the Wildcats] (Rep, 1943)
Reveille with Beverly (Col, 1943)
Murder in Times Square (Col, 1943)
A Night to Remember (Col, 1943)
Cowboy in Manhattan (Univ, 1943)
Saddles and Sagebrush (Col, 1943)
Sleepy Lagoon (Rep, 1943)
One Mysterious Night (Col, 1944)
Practically Yours (Par, 1944)
State Fair (20th, 1945)

Salome, Where She Danced (Univ, 1945)
Eve Knew Her Apples (Col, 1945)
Road to Utopia (Par, 1945)
Gun Smoke (Mon, 1945)
Rhapsody in Blue (WB, 1945)
Grissly's Millions (Rep, 1945)
The Strange Affair of Uncle Harry (Univ, 1945)
You Came Along (Par, 1945)
Bewitched (MGM, 1945)
The Blue Dahlia (Par, 1946)
Hot Cargo (Par, 1946)
Lover Come Back (Univ, 1946)
The Inner Circle (Rep, 1946)
Johnny Comes Flying Home (20th, 1946)
The Madonna's Secret (Rep, 1946)
One Exciting Week (Rep, 1946)
Rendezvous with Annie (Rep, 1946)
Blaze of Noon (Par, 1947)
Cynthia (MGM, 1947)
Along the Oregon Trail (Rep, 1947)
Keeper of the Bees (Col, 1947)
Mother Wore Tights (20th, 1947)
Mr. Blandings Builds His Dream House (RKO, 1948)

Act of Violence (MGM, 1948)
An Act of Murder [a.k.a. Live Today for Tomorrow] (Univ, 1948)
Relentless (Col, 1948)
The Inside Story (Rep, 1948)
Green Grass of Wyoming (20th, 1948)
They Live by Night (RKO, 1948)
The Walls of Jericho (20th, 1948)
Disaster (Par, 1948)
Whispering Smith (Par, 1948)
Black Eagle (Col, 1948)
Little Women (MGM, 1949)
Mrs. Mike (UA, 1949)
Lust for Gold (Col, 1949)
Impact (UA, 1949)
Big Jack (MGM, 1949)
Brimstone (Rep, 1949)
Adam's Rib (MGM, 1949)
Miss Grant Takes Richmond (Col, 1949)
No Way Out (20th, 1950)
A Ticket to Tomahawk (20th, 1950)
All the King's Men (Col, 1950)
Dallas (WB, 1950)
The House by the River (Rep, 1950)
The Savage Horde (Rep, 1950)

No Way Out (20th, 1950)
Sunset in the West (Rep, 1950)
My Forbidden Past (RKO, 1951)
Vengeance Valley (MGM, 1951)
Excuse My Dust (MGM, 1951)
The Tall Target (MGM, 1951)
People Will Talk (20th, 1951)
The Las Vegas Story (RKO, 1952)
Holiday for Sinners (MGM, 1952)
Lydia Bailey (20th, 1952)
The Happy Time (20th, 1952)
Paula (Col, 1952)
Lure of the Wilderness (20th, 1952)
O. Henry's Full House (20th, 1952)

Niagara (20th, 1953)
The Last Posse (Col, 1953)
The Wild One (Col, 1954)
Johnny Guitar (Rep, 1954)
River of No Return (20th, 1954)
The Raid (20th, 1954)
The Man with the Golden Arm (UA, 1955)
The Tall Men (20th, 1955)
The Court-Martial of Billy Mitchell (WB, 1955)
These Wilder Years (MGM, 1956)
The Iron Sheriff (UA, 1957)
Johnny Tremaine (BV, 1957)

The Wayward Bus (20th, 1957)
The Missouri Traveler (BV, 1958)
Quantrill's Raiders (AA, 1958)
Gunman's Walk (Col, 1958)
Alias Jesse James (UA, 1959)
The 30-Foot Bride of Candy Rock (Col, 1959)
The Deadly Companions (Pathé-American, 1961)
Twenty Plus Two (AA, 1961)
Cape Fear (Univ, 1962)
Fail-Safe (Col, 1964)

ROLAND YOUNG

George E. Stone, Olympe Bradna, and Roland Young in Night of Nights (1939).

Born November 11, 1887, London, England. Married 1) Marjorie Kummer (1921); divorced (1940); 2) Patience DuCroz (1948). Died June 5, 1953, New York City, New York. Forever pursing his lips, crinkling his face to avoid chuckling, jamming his hands into his tuxedo coat pocket, or stammering. The screen's perennial king of whimsy. A past master at screwball comedy. Oscar-nominated for his ghost-pestered Topper (lost BSAAA to Joseph Schildkraut of The Life of Emile Zola). Played well-heeled Cosmo Topper in two sequels. Starred in a version of H. G. Wells' The Man Who Worked Miracles in his native England. Played the irrepressible Uncle Willie (The Philadelphia Story). Could also go against type: villainous Uriah Heap (David Copperfield), the strangler C. J. Dabney (Bob Hope's The Great Lover).

Roland Young to Cary Grant in Topper: "Would you mind if I just sat here and sort of sneaked a little dance with my feet?"

536

Films

Sherlock Holmes (G, 1922)
Grit (PDC, 1924)
The Unholy Night (MGM, 1929)
Her Private Life (FN, 1929)
The Bishop Murder Case (MGM, 1930)
Wise Girl (MGM, 1930)
Madam Satan (MGM, 1930)
New Moon (MGM, 1930)
The Prodigal (MGM, 1931)
Don't Bet on Women (Fox, 1931)
Annabelle's Affairs (Fox, 1931)
The Guardsman (MGM, 1931)
The Pagan Lady (Col, 1931)
The Squaw Man (MGM, 1931)
One Hour With You (Par, 1932)
A Woman Commands (RKO, 1932)
Wedding Rehearsal (Br, 1932)
Lovers Courageous (MGM, 1932)
This Is the Night (Par, 1932)
Street of Women (WB, 1932)
Pleasure Cruise (Fox, 1933)
A Lady's Profession (Par, 1933)
Blind Adventure (RKO, 1933)

They Just Had to Get Married (Univ, 1933)
His Double Life (Par, 1933)
Here Is My Heart (Par, 1934)
David Copperfield (MGM, 1935)
Ruggles of Red Gap (Par, 1935)
The Unguarded Hour (MGM, 1936)
One Rainy Afternoon (UA, 1936)
Give Me Your Heart (WB, 1936)
The Man Who Could Work Miracles (UA Br, 1936)
Gypsy (FN Br, 1937)
Call It a Day (WB, 1937)
King Solomon's Mines (Br, 1937)
Ali Baba Goes to Town (20th, 1937)
Topper (MGM, 1937)
Sailing Along (Br, 1938)
The Young in Heart (UA, 1938)
Topper Takes a Trip (UA, 1938)
Yes, My Darling Daughter (WB, 1939)
Here I Am a Stranger (20th, 1939)
Night of Nights (Par, 1939)
He Married His Wife (20th, 1940)

Private Affairs (Univ, 1940)
Star Dust (20th, 1940)
Irene (RKO, 1940)
No, No, Nanette (RKO, 1940)
Dulcy (MGM, 1940)
The Philadelphia Story (MGM, 1940)
Topper Returns (UA, 1941)
Flame of New Orleans (Univ, 1941)
Two-Faced Woman (MGM, 1941)
They All Kissed the Bride (Col, 1942)
Tales of Manhattan (20th, 1942)
The Lady Has Plans (Par, 1942)
Forever and a Day (RKO, 1943)
Standing Room Only (Par, 1944)
And Then There Were None (20th, 1945)
Bond Street (Br, 1948)
You Gotta Stay Happy (Univ, 1948)
The Great Lover (Par, 1949)
Let's Dance (Par, 1950)
St. Benny, the Dip (UA, 1951)
That Man from Tangier (UA, 1953)

BLANCHE YURKA

In the mid-1940s.

Born June 18, 1887, St. Paul, Minnesota. Married Ian Keith; divorced. Died May 30, 1974, New York City, New York. Classical stage actress with very dramatic, taut-faced presence: *A Tale of Two Cities* (Madame DeFarge), *Queen of the Mob* (the Ma Barker-ish title role), *The Southerner* (Ma Tucker), etc.

Blanche Yurka in *A Tale of Two Cities:* "I am that *sister*! And I demand the death of the last of the Evremondes! I *demand* it!"

Films

A Tale of Two Cities (MGM, 1935)
Queen of the Mob (Par, 1940)
City for Conquest (WB, 1940)
Escape (MGM, 1940)
Ellery Queen and the Murder Ring (Col, 1941)
Lady for a Night (Rep, 1941)
Pacific Rendezvous (MGM, 1942)

The Song of Bernadette (20th, 1943)
Tonight We Raid Calais (20th, 1943)
A Night to Remember (Col, 1943)
Hitler's Madman (MGM, 1943)
The Cry of the Werewolf (Col, 1944)
The Bridge of San Luis Rey (UA, 1944)
One Body Too Many (Par, 1944)
The Southerner (UA, 1945)

13 Rue Madeleine (20th, 1946)
The Flame (Rep, 1947)
The Furies (Par, 1950)
At Sword's Point (RKO, 1952)
Taxi! (20th, 1953)
Thunder in the Sun (Par, 1959)

GEORGE ZUCCO

George Zucco, Harry Worth, and Allan Jones in The Firefly *(1937).*

Born January 11, 1886, Manchester, England. Married Frances Hawke. Died May 28, 1960, New York City, New York. Efficient vaudeville and stage player who exuded suave villainy with elan: Charles Laughton's *The Hunchback of Notre Dame* (procurator), *The Adventures of Sherlock Holmes* (Moriarty), etc. Adept at portraying hateful Nazis on screen: *International Lady* (Webster), *My Favorite Blonde* (Dr. Hugo Streger), etc. Found himself cast frequently in Universal's *The Mummy* series, offering high priestly advice; performed in many other of the Grand Guignol genre. Played the Egyptian ambassador in *David and Bathsheba*, one of his last films.

> **George Zucco** to Richard Lane in *Charlie Chan in Honolulu:*
> "The surgeon's knife rather than a prison cell is *my* solution to crime. Some day I shall build a magnificent laboratory and call it 'The Crime Clinic,' and then . . . "

Films

There Goes the Bride (Br, 1931)
The Man from Toronto (Br, 1931)
The Dreyfus Case (Col Br, 1931)
The Midshipmaid (Br, 1932)
The Good Companions (Fox Br, 1933)
The Roof (Br, 1933)
What Happened Then? (Br, 1934)
What's in a Name? (Br, 1934)
Autumn Crocus (Br, 1934)
It's a Bet (Br, 1935)
Abdul the Damned (Br, 1935)
After the Thin Man (MGM, 1936)
Sinner Take All (MGM, 1936)
The Man Who Could Work Miracles (UA Br, 1936)
Parnell (MGM, 1937)
The Firefly (MGM, 1937)
Saratoga (MGM, 1937)

London by Night (MGM, 1937)
Madame X (MGM, 1937)
The Bride Wore Red (MGM, 1937)
Conquest (MGM, 1937)
Rosalie (MGM, 1937)
Souls at Sea (Par, 1937)
Arsene Lupin Returns (MGM, 1938)
Marie Antoinette (MGM, 1938)
Lord Jeff (MGM, 1938)
Fast Company (MGM, 1938)
Vacation from Love (MGM, 1938)
Three Comrades (MGM, 1938)
Suez (20th, 1938)
Charlie Chan in Honolulu (20th, 1938)
Arrest Bulldog Drummond! (Par, 1939)
The Magnificent Fraud (Par, 1939)
The Cat and the Canary (Par, 1939)
Captain Fury (UA, 1939)

The Adventures of Sherlock Holmes (20th, 1939)
Here I Am a Stranger (20th, 1939)
The Hunchback of Notre Dame (RKO, 1939)
New Moon (MGM, 1940)
The Mummy's Hand (Univ, 1940)
Dark Streets of Cairo (Univ, 1940)
Arise, My Love (Par, 1940)
The Monster and the Girl (Par, 1941)
Topper Returns (UA, 1941)
International Lady (UA, 1941)
A Woman's Face (MGM, 1941)
Ellery Queen and the Murder Ring (Col, 1941)
My Favorite Blonde (Par, 1942)
Half-Way to Shanghai (Univ, 1942)
The Black Swan (20th, 1942)

Dr. Renault's Secret (20th, 1942)
The Mummy's Tomb (Univ, 1942)
The Mad Ghoul (Univ, 1943)
The Black Raven (PRC, 1943)
Dead Men Walk (PRC, 1943)
Sherlock Holmes in Washington (Univ, 1943)
Song of Russia (MGM, 1943)
Holy Matrimony (20th, 1943)
Never a Dull Moment (Univ, 1943)
One Body Too Many (Par, 1944)
The House of Frankenstein (Univ, 1944)
The Seventh Cross (MGM, 1944)
Shadows in the Night (Col, 1944)
The Mummy's Ghost (Univ, 1944)

The Voodoo Man (Mon, 1944)
Hold That Blonde (Par, 1945)
Midnight Manhunt (Par, 1945)
Sudan (Univ, 1945)
Having Wonderful Crime (RKO, 1945)
Confidential Agent (WB, 1945)
Fog Island (PRC, 1945)
Week-End at the Waldorf (MGM, 1945)
One Exciting Night (Par, 1945)
The Flying Serpent (PRC, 1946)
Scared to Death (Screen Guild, 1947)
Desire Me (MGM, 1947)
The Captain from Castile (20th, 1947)
Moss Rose (20th, 1947)
Where There's Life (Par, 1947)

The Imperfect Lady (Par, 1947)
Lured (UA, 1947)
Tarzan and the Mermaids (Univ, 1948)
Who Killed "Doc" Robbins? (UA, 1948)
Secret Service Investigator (Rep, 1948)
Joan of Arc (RKO, 1948)
The Pirate (MGM, 1948)
Madame Bovary (MGM, 1949)
The Secret Garden (MGM, 1949)
The Barkleys of Broadsway (MGM, 1949)
Let's Dance (Par, 1950)
Harbor of Missing Men (Rep, 1950)
David and Bathsheba (20th, 1951)
Flame of Stamboul (Col, 1951)
The First Legion (UA, 1951)

Staff

JAMES ROBERT PARISH, New York-based biographer, was born in Cambridge, Massachusetts. He attended the University of Pennsylvania and graduated as a Phi Beta Kappa with a degree in English. A graduate of the University of Pennsylvania Law School, he is a member of the New York Bar. As president of Entertainment Copyright Research Co., Inc., he headed a major researching facility for the media industries. Later he was a film interviewer and reviewer for *Motion Picture Daily* and *Variety*. He is the author of many books including *The Fox Girls, The RKO Gals, Actors TV Credits (1952–72 and Supplement), The Tough Guys, The Jeanette MacDonald Story,* and *The Elvis Presley Scrapbook*. Among those he has co-authored are *The MGM Stock Company, The Debonairs, Liza!, The Leading Ladies,* and *The Great Science Fiction Pictures*. Mr. Parish is also a film commentator for national magazines.

EARL ANDERSON, a native of San Francisco, was educated at San Francisco State College (B.A.) and the University of Washington (M.A.). Over the years he has contributed career articles on Marion Davies, Wallace Berry, Gladys Cooper, and others to *Films in Review*. Since 1960 he has been the assistant to the director of the California Palace of the Legion of Honor, where he has written museum bulletins devoted to aspects of the collection and has organized film series devoted to Irene Dunne, Mary Pickford, and the Western film. He has contributed to such books as *The Debonairs* and *The Swashbucklers*.

RICHARD E. BRAFF was born in Los Angeles and was raised in Hollywood where he was an extra in several films. After his discharge from the Air Force, he moved to San Francisco where he currently resides. He is an ardent movie buff, having amassed an enormous collection of reference material, especially on the silent era. He has co-written several articles for *Films in Review* and has contributed numerous filmographies for cinema history books.

JOHN ROBERT COCCHI has been viewing and collecting data on motion pictures since childhood and is now regarded as one of the most thorough film researchers in the world. He is the New York editor of *Boxoffice* magazine. He was research associate on *The American Movie Reference Book, The Fox Girls,* and many others. He has written cinema history articles for such journals as *Film Fan Monthly, Screen Facts,* and *Films in Review*. He recently wrote *The Westerns: A Picture Quiz Book* and is the co-founder of one of Manhattan's leading film societies.

HARRY PURVIS, a free-lance writer, was born in Hamilton, Ontario, Canada, where he still resides. His many articles on motion pictures (mostly humorous) have appeared in such publications as *TV Guide, Motion Picture, Films in Review, Playboy, Mad, Help, Humbug,* and *Variety*.

ROBERT A. EVANS of Piermont, New Hampshire, is internationally known as a movie historian. His "Evans' Chronicle," published annually in *Films in Review*, is the result of a lifetime hobby of collecting show business data. He is a correspondent for several area newspapers in New Hampshire and Vermont.

WILLIAM T. LEONARD, currently research director for the Free Library of the Philadelphia Theatre Collection, has spent many years in theatrical and cinema research, contributing articles to several publications including *Films in Review* and *Classic Film Collector*. During World War II he wrote and appeared in his play *Hurry Up and Wait*. He has written reports for proposed culture centers, including Lincoln Center for the Performing Arts, and was one of the principal contributors of data for the American Film Institute's catalog volume, *Feature Films: 1921–30*. Books he has co-written include *Hollywood Players: The Forties*, *Hollywood Players: The Thirties*, and *The Funsters* (to be published by Arlington House in early 1979).

New York–born FLORENCE SOLOMON attended Hunter College and then joined Ligon Johnson's copyright research office. Later she was director of research at Entertainment Copyright Research Co., Inc. She is currently a reference supervisor at ASCAP's Index Division in Manhattan. Ms. Solomon has collaborated on such works as *The American Movies Reference Book*, *TV Movies*, *Vincent Price Unmasked*, *Film Actors Guide: Western Europe*, and *The Great Science Fiction Pictures*. She is the niece of the noted sculptor, the late Sir Jacob Epstein.